Selected Data for the United States

Year	Population (thousands)	Civilian Unemployment Rate (%)	Civilian Employment Rate (%)	Median Family Income (1987 dollars)	Consumer Price Index (...)	...	Change in M2 Money Supply (%)
1929	121,767	3.2					
1933	125,579	24.9					
1939	130,880	17.2					
1940	132,122	14.6	47.6				
1941	133,402	9.9	50.4				
1942	134,860	4.7	54.5				
1943	136,739	1.9	57.6				
1944	138,397	1.2	57.9				
1945	139,928	1.9	56.1				
1946	141,389	3.9	53.6		19.5		
1947	144,126	3.9	56.0		22.3	14.4	
1948	146,631	3.8	56.6		24.1	8.1	
1949	149,188	5.9	55.4		23.8	−1.2	
1950	152,271	5.3	56.1		24.1	1.3	
1951	154,878	3.3	57.3		26.0	7.9	
1952	157,553	3.0	57.3		26.5	1.9	
1953	160,184	2.9	57.1		26.7	0.9	
1954	163,026	5.5	55.5		26.9	0.7	
1955	165,931	4.4	56.7		26.8	−0.4	
1956	168,903	4.1	57.5		27.2	1.5	
1957	171,984	4.3	57.1		28.1	3.3	
1958	174,882	6.8	55.4		28.9	2.8	
1959	177,830	5.5	56.0		29.1	0.7	
1960	180,671	5.5	56.1		29.6	1.7	4.9
1961	183,691	6.7	55.4		29.9	1.0	7.4
1962	186,538	5.5	55.5		30.2	1.0	8.1
1963	189,242	5.7	55.4		30.6	1.3	8.4
1964	191,889	5.2	55.7		31.0	1.3	8.0
1965	194,303	4.5	56.2	25,060	31.5	1.6	8.1
1966	196,560	3.8	56.9	26,377	32.4	2.9	4.5
1967	198,712	3.8	57.3	27,004	33.4	3.1	9.2
1968	200,706	3.6	57.5	28,199	34.8	4.2	8.0
1969	202,677	3.5	58.0	29,244	36.7	5.5	4.1
1970	205,052	4.9	57.4	28,880	38.8	5.7	6.5
1971	207,661	5.9	56.6	28,862	40.5	4.4	13.5
1972	209,896	5.6	57.0	30,199	41.8	3.2	13.0
1973	211,909	4.9	57.8	30,820	44.4	6.2	6.9
1974	213,854	5.6	57.8	29,735	49.3	11.0	5.5
1975	215,973	8.5	56.1	28,970	53.8	9.1	12.6
1976	218,035	7.7	56.8	29,863	56.9	5.8	13.7
1977	220,239	7.1	57.9	30,025	60.6	6.5	10.6
1978	222,585	6.1	59.3	30,730	65.2	7.6	8.0
1979	225,055	5.8	59.9	30,669	72.6	11.3	8.0
1980	227,757	7.1	59.2	28,996	82.4	13.5	8.9
1981	230,138	7.6	59.0	27,977	90.9	10.3	9.9
1982	232,520	9.7	57.8	27,591	96.5	6.2	8.8
1983	234,799	9.6	57.9	28,147	99.6	3.2	11.8
1984	237,001	7.5	59.5	28,923	103.9	4.3	8.2
1985	239,279	7.2	60.1	29,302	107.6	3.6	8.4
1986	241,613	7.0	60.7	30,534	109.6	1.9	9.6
1987	243,915	6.2	61.5	30,853	113.6	3.6	3.3
1988	246,113	5.5	62.3		118.3	4.1	5.1

Source: *Economic Report of the President,* 1989, Tables B-30, B-31, B-32, B-33, B-58, B-61, B-67; and *Survey of Current Business,* May 1989, pp. S-5, S-9, S-10, S-15.

MACROECONOMICS

MACROECONOMICS

Third Edition

Martin Bronfenbrenner

Aoyama Gakuin University, Japan
Professor Emeritus, Duke University

Werner Sichel

Western Michigan University

Wayland Gardner

Western Michigan University

HOUGHTON MIFFLIN COMPANY   BOSTON
Dallas   Geneva, Illinois   Palo Alto   Princeton, New Jersey

Library of Congress Catalog Card Number: 89-80922

ISBN: 0-395-472660

BCDEFGHIJ-VHP-96543210

CREDITS

Cover painting by Glenn R. Bradshaw.
Photograph by David Caras.

We gratefully acknowledge the following sources for providing photographs used in this book: Part I essay—Brown Brothers; Culver Pictures. Part II essay—Wide World. Part III essay—Bettmann Archive. Part IV essay—Bettmann Archive; Photo Researchers. Part V essay—UPI/Bettmann Newsphotos; Patricia Evans/University of Chicago; The Hoover Institution/Stanford University. Part VI essay—Wide World. Part VII essay—Brown Brothers; Bettmann Archive; Wide World.

We dedicate our efforts on this third edition to our colleagues who prescribe our text and ancillary package to their students as the most efficacious and painless remedy for the common ailment of economic ignorance.

MB   WS   WG

Preface

As in the first two editions, our goal in this third edition was to write a textbook that will fulfill the needs of students and instructors concerned with the well-established as well as the controversial topics in economics. We believe that a beginning text should (1) be open-minded and strive to present the best in all schools of thought especially where there is disagreement, (2) be thorough and realistic in the presentation of material that is generally accepted, (3) be flexible and be oriented to a broad view in matters such as international trade, economic development, and comparative economic systems, and (4) above all, be as accessible to introductory economics students as possible.

We believe that the characteristics of our book are as appropriate in the 1990s as they were in the 1980s. We also believe that they form the foundation for the type of "economic literacy" that will allow students to understand the *applicability* of economic principles beyond the specific applications in any one topic or any one period of time.

We feel this edition is a substantial enhancement of the previous edition. The changes are not minor, cosmetic, tune-ups of a few parts. In some key areas—particularly in macroeconomics—the changes amount to a significant overhaul. Some of the more important improvements are noted as follows.

MACROECONOMICS

We have made major improvements in our sections on macroeconomics. There is a significant amount of new material and much of the old material has been revised. The new material includes a substantially expanded treatment of rational expectations, new classical economics, neo-Keynesian economics, and post-Keynesian economics, as well as several up-to-date applications of monetary economics. Here is a list of some of the new macro features of our third edition, in the order of their appearance.

1. The first chapter of the macro section now contains the circular-flow model which previously we introduced in a later chapter. Our experience with the first and second editions shows that students find our circular-flow illustration—which includes both government and international trade—to be an extremely useful overview of macroeconomics. In the third edition, we use this illustration to introduce the subject and to provide students with a way to maintain their perspective as they work through specific macro models.

2. The basic aggregate-demand and aggregate-supply format for macroeconomics is also

introduced in the first chapter of the macro section. Our introductory explanation of the *AD-AS* model includes effective illustrations of macroeconomic equilibrium and disequilibrium, but is nevertheless simple enough for presentation at the start of the macro course. This thoroughly reliable but no-frills approach to the *AD-AS* system is repeated in the chapter on economic fluctuations and in introducing both the Keynesian and the monetarist models when they appear. In this way, the *AD-AS* system provides continuity throughout the macro section and the Keynesian and monetarist models are developed according to their roles in a full modern macro system.

3. The subject of economic fluctuations (cast in the aggregate-demand and aggregate-supply framework) is now the fourth chapter in the initial macro part, following chapters on the *AD-AS* model, national income accounting, and inflation and unemployment. This substantially revised fluctuations chapter provides a lead-in for the Keynesian and monetarist models of income determination. Fluctuations are explained as movements along and shifts of aggregate-demand and aggregate-supply curves, thus providing useful practice in the *AD-AS* way of thinking.

4. We have streamlined our presentation of the basic Keynesian model. It now requires only two, easily teachable chapters. This has been accomplished by moving the fluctuations material forward to the earlier section (as noted) and by placing our discussion of deficits and the national debt in an appendix.

5. In our chapter on the Federal Reserve System, we have added new material on interest-rate and borrowed-reserves targeting in the operation of monetary policy and a discussion of the problems of deposit insurance, nonbank banks, and interstate banking, all topics that receive a great deal of attention in the media.

6. Our chapter on monetary economics has been substantially revised and strengthened. It now includes an aggregate-demand and aggregate-supply illustration of the quantity-of-money theory. We also have added emphasis on anticipated, as contrasted with unanticipated, inflation and have strengthened (with graphic illustration) our explanation of inflationary expectations.

7. The first chapter of the final part in the macro section uses the Keynesian and monetarist models that have just been covered to develop the aggregate-demand and aggregate-supply model in greater detail than was possible earlier in the course. The *AD-AS* model is then applied (in the following chapter) to the subject of inflation, starting with the Phillips curve and proceeding through the adaptive-expectations (Friedman-Phelps) model. This chapter focuses on policy alternatives for an economy in which inflationary expectations are a problem.

8. An integrated treatment of rational expectations, new classical economics, neo-Keynesian economics, post-Keynesian economics, and supply-side economics is presented in the next-to-last chapter in the macro section. This chapter, most of which is new to this edition, provides students with a way to further recognize, analyze, and synthesize modern schools of macroeconomic thought. It includes an explanation of the Lucas supply curve as well as an elementary *IS-LM* model which may be omitted without loss of continuity.

9. The final macro chapter, ''Macroeconomics as a Branch of Knowledge,'' is a brand new chapter. It begins with the question: ''Is macroeconomics a science?'' We suggest that the answer to this question is ''yes,'' but that macroeconomics is a relatively immature science, likely to experience significant revision in its future development. It is, however, a science worthy of serious study. By recognizing the scientific aspects of macroeconomics, students can begin to understand the economist's role, albeit a difficult one, in forecasting future trends in the economy. This chapter also considers public choice viewpoints on the federal government's deficit and poses questions concerning debt policy in the event of a serious recession.

Two additional points should be noted about improvements in the macro section of our third edition. First, we have used appendices to chapters more than in the previous editions—one for the leakages-and-injections presentation of the basic Keynesian system, one for the national debt, and one for the history of monetary policy. We have learned from colleagues around the country that they appreciate the flexibility that this system offers. Second, and most important, though this edition contains considerably more material than the second edition, we are confident in saying—and our many reviewers agree—that the reorganization and revisions add so much to clarify and apply the content that students will find the material considerably *easier* to comprehend and enjoy.

INTERNATIONAL ECONOMICS

We have received much praise for our innovative international coverage and, if emulation is a form of flattery, we have been amply flattered. Our treatment of international economics is even stronger in our third edition. Perhaps the most important feature of our treatment of international economics is that it is an integral part of our chapters on basic macroeconomics. Since international trade and finance are part of the macro model from the very beginning, students do not have to "unlearn" later the model that they were taught earlier.

We have added new material on both the macro and the micro dimensions of international economics. We present a set of macroeconomic identities that show the inherent relationships between the U.S. trade deficit, government budget deficits, and the relatively low saving rate in the U.S. economy. In the microeconomics context, we show that the U.S. trade deficit extends to most of our trading partners and cannot be blamed solely on Japanese "dirty tricks." Our chapter on "Free Trade versus Protection" now includes material on administrative protection ("dirty tricks") and market-opening strategies that countries use to combat such actions. These market-opening strategies are called "protection against protection."

ECONOMIC GROWTH AND DEVELOPMENT

In our third edition, economic growth and economic development each has its own chapter, rather than sharing a single chapter as in our earlier editions. Both chapters include significant amounts of new material. The growth chapter explores the consequences of aging populations and examines, more deeply than before, the impact of growth on the environment. In the development chapter, we have added a section on the history and problems of Third-World debt.

COMPARATIVE-SYSTEMS COVERAGE

Gorbachev and *perestroika* provide new material for our chapter on comparative economic systems. We also have new material on "Taking Japan Seriously," showing the Japanese economic system as a modern version of a *corporate society* described as "in the neighborhood of capitalism." In our chapter on radical economics, we have added new material on the present status and future prospects of the New Left.

TOPICAL ESSAYS

We continue to offer thought-provoking essays at the close of each of the seven parts of the book. Four (*) of the seven are new or substantially revised for the third edition:

- Classical Economics: The Dismal Science?
- *• The Gross Anatomy of Gross Unemployment
- John Maynard Keynes and the Great Depression
- *• Economics of Inflation
- *• Macroeconomic Policy: The New Frontier and After
- *• Japanese-American Economic Warfare?
- From Karl Marx to the New Left

These essays lead the student beyond the regular text material and show a broader perspective to the subject covered.

"ECONOMICS IN FOCUS" APPLICATIONS OF ECONOMIC PRINCIPLES

As an entirely new feature of our third edition, we close each chapter with a brief, real-world application of some topic covered in the chapter. For example, at the close of our chapter on the Federal Reserve System, our *Economics in Focus* application is called "The FED Divided" and describes differences of opinion concerning monetary policy among members of the Board of Governors and other members of the Federal Open Market Committee. Following our initial chapter on "What Economics Is" the *Economics in Focus* application compares contrasting contemporary reports on the question "Is Socialism Dying?" These new additions to our text put economics "in focus." They are designed to help the student bridge the gap between textbook explanations and real-world applications of economic models.

INSTRUCTIONAL USE OF COLOR

With a virtually unlimited array of colors available for our third edition, we have carefully developed a consistent color-coding system for our art program. Rather than using color, as do most economics books, as a decorative or highlighting tool, our color system promotes the understanding of economic concepts and relationships. This is true for both our graphs and tables.

First, the consistent color-coding system helps students recognize economic relationships in the graphs and follow the logic of the analysis. For example, a particular curve—such as supply, demand, aggregate demand, aggregate supply, and so on—is printed in the same color every time it appears. When a curve is shifted, it retains its original color, but with less intensity.

Second, to further clarify the underlying economic meaning, tables are consistently color-coded to appropriate graphs. For example, in the total planned expenditure and macroeconomic equilibrium table, the numerical values below the equilibrium level are shaded to correspond to the same shading of values in the macroeconomic equilibrium graph. Values above the equilibrium level in the table are shaded in a different color; the shading is repeated appropriately in the graph. The equilibrium values are not shaded.

We believe that our efforts result in a dramatic improvement over the art in other texts because our colors are purposeful. Color mobilizes an additional dimension of the human senses and puts it to work in the learning process.

INNOVATIVE LEARNING AIDS

We, and the people at Houghton Mifflin, have made concerted efforts to make our text material ultimately accessible to students. We have retained the well-received glossary, index, end-of-chapter summaries, and end-of-chapter discussion questions (some of them new) from the earlier editions. We have added two innovative learning aids—easy reference text notes and key terms at chapter ends. Therefore, we now offer:

1. **Glossary** A very thorough glossary that is both conceptual and descriptive. These definitions are useful reference tools in that they are more comprehensively written than the key terms.

2. **Index** Our index is considered the most comprehensive listing in the market. As with previous editions, we have included both conceptual and descriptive entries with much cross-referencing.

3. **Discussion Questions at Chapter Ends** Each chapter concludes with a list of questions that are useful for classroom discussion or a student's individual study. We have purposefully chosen questions that will generate interesting analysis and commentary.

4. **Summary at Chapter Ends** Summary statements are listed at the end of each chapter and are page-referenced to the body of the text. These statements allow students to quickly review the most important topics and concepts in each chapter.

5. **Easy Reference Text Notes** Throughout the text, bold-faced "text notes" concisely state the fundamental ideas of the material just covered. They provide instant reinforcement for the student as he or she studies the text. The text notes assure that the preceding material is well understood before the student goes on to the next topic.

6. **Key Terms at Chapter Ends** Key terms, carefully defined in the context of the material of the particular chapter, are listed alphabetically at the end of each chapter so that the student can build his or her economics vocabulary as he or she proceeds through the course. Each key term is page-referenced to where the topic is defined and discussed in the body of the text. For reference purposes, the key terms are repeated with more general definitions in the glossary at the back of the book.

COMPLETE ANCILLARY PACKAGE

Our ancillaries are better than ever. They were developed to make the myriad of economic concepts more accessible to both instructors and students. Our computer-assisted interactive learning system is new. We have multicolor transparencies (some with overlays) and many new questions in our revised test bank, plus an altogether new test bank. Here is a list of the ancillaries.

1. **Instructor's Manual** Prepared by the text authors, the instructor's manual provides, for each chapter, a schematic outline, teaching tips about especially important or difficult points, and condensed answers to the end-of-chapter discussion questions. The manual also includes transparency masters for all the figures and all the tables in the text.

2. **Study Guide** Prepared by Dr. Rose Pfefferbaum, Mesa Community College, our study guide is recognized as one of the best in the industry. For each chapter, it contains a summary, a list of learning objectives, review terms, new terms, completion exercises, problems and applications, sample true-false ques-

tions, sample multiple-choice questions, and discussion questions.

3. **Test Banks** With this edition we publish two complete test banks: SERIES 1 (Chapters 1–40) and SERIES II (Chapters 1–40). In total, our test banks offer over 5,000 multiple-choice questions with a significant percentage of items requiring graphical analysis. Questions are coded for level of difficulty and type.

4. **Overhead Transparencies** We provide our adopters with over 150 multicolored overhead transparencies. Fifteen percent of these overheads are produced as overlays, allowing instructors to visually demonstrate the dynamic nature of economics.

For the Computer

5. **PC Test Bank Plus** All of our test questions are available free of charge to our adopters, on computer disk in IBM PC, PS/2 and compatibles, and Apple Macintosh format. PC Test Bank Plus is an innovative test assembly program that saves time and assures accuracy. The program renders precise, pre-programmed graphs on the computer which eliminates the need to draw graphs or paste them in place.

   In addition to this offering, adopters can use Houghton Mifflin's Call-in Test Service for test generation.

6. **Computerized Tutorial Package** New to this edition is an exciting tutorial program consisting of over 15 modules. Providing students with a highly interactive environment that fully utilizes the dynamic capabilities of the computer, each module reviews the major concepts in a single chapter and then asks questions that allow students to change variables to interact with appropriate graphs. Students are scored at the end of each module. For questions that they did not answer correctly, students are referred back to the text discussion via actual page numbers. Available to adopters for IBM PC, PS/2, and compatible computers.

7. **Computerized Simulation** New to this edition is a highly dynamic simulation program consisting of over 15 modules. Each

module asks students to apply their chapter knowledge to a real-world situation. By assuming various jobs that require economic understanding, students must make economic decisions and evaluate the consequences. Unlike most simulation packages, ours is highly graphical, thereby furthering analytical education. In addition, when a student has problems with a particular decision, they are referred back to both the text and appropriate tutorial module. Available to adopters for IBM PC, PS/2, and compatible computers.

8. **Computerized Study Guide** With this edition we offer a brand new computerized version of the printed Study Guide. When questions are answered incorrectly, explanations are offered to guide the students to the correct answer. Available to adopters for IBM PC, PS/2, and compatible computers.

9. **Computerized Instructor's Handbook** This ancillary includes lecture outlines for each chapter. Instructors can modify these lecture files using any commercial word processor to produce personalized lecture notes, course syllabi, or handouts for use in the classroom. Available to adopters for IBM PC, PS/2, and Apple Macintosh computers.

THE AUTHORS

Each of us has instructed thousands of students in elementary economics. We have used many different texts, and each of us has taught many parts of the subject—micro, macro, international, comparative systems, and points between and beyond. Each of us has his areas of special interest. Also, we have learned a lot from each other and from the experience of writing and revising our first two editions. Therefore, the final product is far less the work of three individuals than it is the combined efforts of a team. Each chapter is the result of the cooperative efforts of all the authors. The result, we believe, is far superior to what any one of us could have accomplished alone.

ACKNOWLEDGMENTS

It is a pleasure to acknowledge the help we have received in writing this book and preparing it for publication. Since Martin Bronfenbrenner was a visiting professor at Western Michigan University in 1989, all three of us are able to express our gratitude to our colleagues who shared generously their knowledge of economics and their teaching insights. Especially helpful were Sisay Asefa, Phillip Caruso, Kevin Collins, Bassam Harik, Salim Harik, Wei Chiao Huang, William Kern, Jon Neill, Susan Pozo, Theo Sypris, and Raymond Zelder. Also, we benefited from conversations with a former colleague, Barry Krissoff, now with the United States Department of Agriculture, and with a long-time friend, Harry Trebing, professor of economics at Michigan State University. All three of us are grateful for the typing services of Bonnie Guminski and Becky Ryder.

Especially helpful reviews were provided by Professor David Colander of Wesleyan University and by Professor Nancy Jianakoplos of Michigan State University; also Ira Gang of Rutgers University, Harry Holzer of Michigan State University, Pradeep Kotamraju of the University of Minnesota, Harry Landreth of Centre College, Lester Manderschied of Michigan State University, Emlyn Norman of Texas Southern University, Susan Pozo of Western Michigan University, Gerald Sazama of the University of Connecticut, Robert Stuart of Rutgers University, and Jay Sultan of Arizona State University. Rose Pfefferbaum provided especially thoughtful comments as she studied the manuscript in preparing the Study Guide. Insights and inspiration were received from six Nobel Laureate economists (Kenneth Arrow, James Buchanan, Lawrence Klein, Herbert Simon, Robert Solow, and James Tobin) who lectured on "The State of Economic Science" at Western Michigan University during the 1988–1989 academic year.

In the previous two editions, we received expert advice from many reviewers. We are very grateful for their comments which resulted in two very successful editions and the foundation for what promises to be the best edition yet.

David Abel
Mankato State University

Jack Adams
University of Arkansas

Richard Agnello
University of Delaware

J. Barry
Fordham University

Philip Bartholomew
University of Michigan

Paul T. Bechtol
Ohio State University

Klaus Becker
University of Kansas

Carolyn Shaw Bell
Wellesley College

Robert E. Berry
Miami University, Ohio

Calvin Blair
Wilson College

Paul Blume
Hanover College

Joe Brum
Fayetteville Technical Institute

E. Buchholz
Santa Monica College

J. Alvin Carter
Catawba College

Phillip Caruso
Western Michigan University

J. Cavallo
College of Mt. St. Vincent

Ming Chow
Kansas State University

K. Chu
California State University

Charles Cole
California State University

Robert Collier
Western Washington University

Michael T. Cook
William Jewell College

Eleanor Craig
University of Delaware

James M. Cypher
California State University, Fresno

Michael T. Doyle
University of Nebraska, Omaha

Peter Eelkema
University of Kansas

William Field
Depauw University

Max E. Fletcher
University of Idaho

Carroll Foster
University of Michigan

R. Freed
California State University, Dominguez Hills

Mark Gardner
Emory & Henry College

Ann Garrison
University of Northern Colorado

Kathie Gilbert
Mississippi State University

Otis W. Gilley
University of Texas, Austin

Constantine Glezakos
California State University, Long Beach

Douglas Gordon
Arapahoe Community College

A. Grow
Mesa Community College

Nicholas D. Grunt
Tarrant County Junior College

George Hartley
Northwestern State University

Curtis Harvey
University of Kentucky

Frank Hefner
Washburn University

Ali Hekmat
Western Washington University

Robert E. Herman
Nassau Community College

C. A. Hofmann
Idaho State University

Donald Holley
Boise State University

Estelle Horowitz
Pratt Institute

Brooks Hull
University of Michigan

Paul C. Huszar
Colorado State University

Harry Hutchinson
University of Delaware

Eric Jacobson
University of Delaware

Jack L. Jeppesen
Cerritos College

Stanley R. Keil
Ball State University

Larry Kendra
Cuyahoga Community College

Dan Knighton
Moorhead State University

A. Kohen
James Madison University

R. Kolinski
University of Michigan

B. Lanciaux
Hobart & William Smith College

John Larson
University of Oregon

Soyen Lee
Illinois Benedictine College

E. Liebhafsky
University of Houston, Clear Lake

M. London
Butte College

Alan B. Mandelstamm
Virginia Polytechnic Institute & State University

Gabriel Manrique
Quincy College

Wolfgang Mayer
University of Cincinnati

Michelle McAlpin
Tufts University

Roger McCain
*City University of New York,
Brooklyn College*

Norris McClain
Old Dominion University

Joan M. McCrea
University of Texas, Arlington

Jesse Mercer
College of the Albemarle

Ellen Miller
University of North Carolina

Jack Minkoff
Pratt Institute

Eric Mitchell
University of New Hampshire

Gary Mongiovi
St. John's University

R. B. Moore
U.S. Naval Academy

W. Morrison
Mesa Community College

Joseph Murray
Community College of Philadelphia

P. J. Nickless
University of North Carolina

T. Lee Norman
Idaho State University

James O'Neill
University of Delaware

Carl D. Parker
Ft. Hayes State University

Peter Penndorf
Quinsigamond Community College

R. D. Peterson
Colorado State University

Rose Pfefferbaum
Mesa Community College

John Pisciotta
University of Southern Colorado

Dean Popp
San Diego State University

John A. Powers
University of Cincinnati

Myron Re
Gogebic Community College

Mike Reed
University of Nevada

Terry Riddle
*Central Virginia Community
College*

Richard Roehl
University of Michigan

G. Roth
Hofstra University

Lars G. Sandberg
Ohio State University

Paul J. Schmitt
*St. Clair County Community
College*

Carole Scott
West Georgia College

William Shingleton
Ball State University

Arlene Silvers
Drexel University

Nat Simons
Ohio State University

Gordon Skinner
University of Cincinnati

Charles Skoro
Boise State University

Russell E. Smith
Washburn University

J. Ronald Stanfield
Colorado State University

M. Dudley Stewart, Jr.
Stephen F. Austin State University

Barry Stregeusky
Ball State University

Emily Sun
Manhattan College

Gilbert Suzawa
University of Rhode Island

W. Swift
Hofstra University

K. Taylor
University of Southern California

Tom Till
St. Andrew's Presbyterian College

Ralph Townsend
University of Maine

John F. Walker
Portland State University

Harold L. Wattel
Hofstra University

Charles Weber
University of Michigan

James Wible
University of New Hampshire

Jeffrey J. Wright
Bryant College

William Wood
University of Virginia

Werner Sichel wishes especially to thank Peter Eckstein, his co-author of a previous book, *Basic Economic Concepts,* for his efforts on that volume, which have surely carried over and benefited this one. While Werner Sichel was very careful to use only examples and other material that he had initially contributed, he is indebted to Peter Eckstein for helping him to develop his ideas and materials for the earlier book.

All three of us acknowledge the help of students who, over the years, have plied us with questions that remained in our minds long after the answer was given. And, most importantly, each of us wants to acknowledge the help and support from family members who did without our company, sacrificed vacations, and in many ways were essential to the completion of the project. We trust that they understand the depth of our appreciation.

We also want to thank the many people at Houghton Mifflin who worked hard and well to create an attractive finished product.

M.B.   W.S.   W.G.

The Complete Teaching/Learning System

- *Economics*, the hardcover text
- *Macroeconomics* and *Microeconomics*, paperbacks. International trade, comparative economic systems, and radical economics chapters included in both volumes.
- *Instructor's Manual*, prepared by the text authors. Provides for each chapter:

  Schematic Outline

  Teaching Notes

  Suggested answers to all discussion questions in the text

  The Instructor's Manual also provides transparency masters for all figures and tables in the text; and instructions for using the computerized Test Bank.

- *Study Guide*, by Rose Pfefferbaum, Mesa Community College. Provides for each chapter:

  Summary

  List of Objectives

  Review Terms

  New Terms

  Completion Exercises

  Problems and Applications

  True-False Questions

  Multiple-Choice Questions

  Discussion Questions

- *Test Banks*, Series I: Chapters 1–40, prepared by the text authors with Rose Pfefferbaum, Mesa Community College; Series II: Chapters 1–40, prepared by the text authors and Ronald Cipcic of Kalamazoo Community College and Western Michigan University.
- *Overhead Transparencies*, over 150 including overlays.

For the Computer

- *PC Test Bank Plus*, computerized Test Bank in IBM PC, PS/2 and compatibles, and Apple Macintosh formats.
- *Computerized Macro and Micro Tutorial Package*, over 15 modules available for IBM PC, PS/2, and compatible computers.
- *Computerized Study Guide*, available for IBM PC, PS/2, and compatible computers.
- *Computerized Instructor's Handbook*, available for IBM PC, PS/2, and Apple Macintosh computers.

Contents

MACROECONOMICS

PART I
INTRODUCTION TO ECONOMICS

1
What Economics Is

Preview Surely you have heard at least one of the following opinions: "Economists know the price of everything and the value of nothing." "Economists have an irrational passion for dispassionate rationality." "Supply and demand—that's all there is to economics. The rest is nonsense." "If economics were a science, the economists would have all the money, and the rest of us would be broke." "Economics is about what everyone knows in language nobody understands." "Economists are a bunch of do-gooders who want to create a welfare state." "Economists are stooges and mouthpieces of Wall Street; they are for sale to the highest bidder." "If you stretched all the economists end to end, it would be a good thing, but they would reach no conclusion." Notice that some of these criticisms are inconsistent with others. Any of them may be true of one or more particular economists, but they cannot *all* be true of *all* economists (or of economics) at the same time.

This chapter gives an overview of what economics is. After some formal definitions of the subject, we consider its two main divisions, microeconomics and macroeconomics. Microeconomics focuses on individual decision makers, like consumers and business firms, whereas macroeconomics deals with the overall performance of the economy. We also examine economic growth and development, which consider how economies may change over time.

After surveying the basic content of economics, we explore how economic systems are organized to deal with economic problems. Some are organized around systems of markets; others are based on planning. Similarly, some are based on private property ownership and others have collectivist agencies that own the tools of production.

We close by listing a set of criteria that might be used to decide which type of economic system works best. We stress, however, that each person must use his or her own values in answering that sort of question. Our list can only start you thinking about this subject.

WHAT IS ECONOMICS?

Many definitions have been offered for **economics**. Most focus on either (a) the problems that economists usually deal with or (b) the methods that economists use in dealing with these problems. An example of the "problem" type of definition is the following, taken from a widely used textbook:

> Economics can be defined as the social science concerned with the problem of using or administering scarce resources (the means of producing) so as to attain the greatest or maximum fulfillment of society's unlimited wants (the goal of producing).[1]

An example of the "methods" type of definition comes from the famous economist John Maynard Keynes (1883–1946), who said,

> It [economics] is a method rather than a doctrine, an apparatus of the mind, a technique of thinking which helps its possessor to draw correct conclusions.[2]

Most definitions of economics focus on either the problems that economists deal with or the methods that economists use in dealing with these problems.

Most of the "problems" definitions, such as the first one given above, focus on situations that arise as a result of **scarcity**—defined as a situation in which the amount of something actually available would not be sufficient to satisfy the desire for it if it were provided "free of charge." Because of

1. Campbell McConnell, *Economics*, 10th ed. (New York: McGraw-Hill, 1987), p. 21.
2. J. M. Keynes, in introducing each of a series of *Cambridge Economic Handbooks* in the 1920s.

scarcity, people find it necessary to give up some things they enjoy so they can obtain other things they want more urgently. In other words, they have to make choices.

Scarcity is a situation in which the amount of something actually available would not be sufficient to satisfy the desire for it if it were provided free.

The "methods" definitions focus on how economists deal with problems rather than on the problems themselves. They see economics as a tool kit or "apparatus of the mind" that enables the economist to draw correct conclusions not only about subjects ordinarily considered economic but about human actions quite generally. For example, the "new home economics" of Professor Gary Becker and his disciples applies the technical apparatus of economics to the analysis of such problems as whether or not to marry, to have children, to engage in criminal activity, or to make a contribution to a charitable organization.

By combining both approaches, we offer the following definition: **Economics** is (a) the study of how individuals and societies deal with scarcity and (b) the development of methodologies for analyzing such problems.

Now it is time for you to make an economic decision—that is, whether or not to memorize one or more definitions of economics. Memorizing a definition will take some time, and that time could be used by you to do other things. The "problems" approach focuses on the fact that you do not have enough time to do everything that you would like to do. The "methods" approach suggests comparing the benefits of memorizing a definition with the benefits that would come from the best alternative use of your time. Memorizing can be a useful method of learning. But understanding that economics is about scarcity and practicing the processes of economic reasoning will probably do you more good than memorizing a definition. You must make your own evaluation of benefits when comparing one alternative with another. Economic training can sharpen the ability to do this, but each person's own values must be used in actual decisions.

MICROECONOMICS AND MACROECONOMICS

The study of economics is generally divided into two main parts, one called microeconomics and the other called macroeconomics. These two divisions make up the main body of economic analysis. However, there are many special areas of application, such as international trade, government finance, industrial organization, and labor economics, that are important extensions of both parts of this main body.

Microeconomics: Three Basic Choices

Microeconomics focuses on the behavior of decision makers in the economy. A person in his or her role as a consumer or a worker is a decision maker. Business firms and governments are decision makers too. Microeconomics centers on how these decision makers choose among alternatives and what the results of these choices are.

Microeconomics is built around three basic types of choice that must be made in any economy: (1) What goods and services shall be produced, and how much of each per time period? (2) How shall they be produced, with what proportions of labor to machinery (including robots), or of machinery to natural resources, or of natural resources to labor—and within the work force, with what proportions of more-skilled to less-skilled workers? (3) To whom shall the final products be distributed? How much should go to the suppliers of labor, how much to the suppliers of natural resources, and how much to the suppliers of machinery and equipment? Or if we look at the distribution question through personal glasses, how much should go to the poor, how much to the middle classes, and how much to the rich? All these problems are interrelated.

What to Produce Every economic system must establish some way of deciding what to produce. Each must make this decision because of scarcity. Consider, for example, the question of what to produce with certain land resources available to an economy. Shall dairy cattle be grazed so that milk can be produced? Shall beef cattle be grazed so that meat can be produced? Shall corn be grown so that breakfast cereal (or bacon) can be produced? Shall the land be used for a baseball playing field so that recreational services can be produced? Shall a factory be built on it so that manufactured goods can be produced? Shall residential houses be built on it? The possibilities are almost unlimited, but some decision must be made.

How to Produce The question of how to produce is quite different from the question of what to produce. Ice cream can be made in a small shop with a hand-cranked or motor-driven ice cream maker, or it can be produced in a large automated factory in quantities large enough to serve all the people in a great city or a large region. Corn can be grown intensively, with much fertilizer and irrigation, or it can be grown extensively, with more land and less fertilizer or irrigation. Roads can be built with thousands of pick-and-shovel laborers moving soil in woven baskets, or they can be built with huge earth-moving machines and fewer workers. Every economic system must provide some method of choosing among the different available technologies of production.

For Whom to Produce Microeconomic decisions must also be made about which individuals or groups of people will enjoy the goods and services that are produced. Should all persons who are part of the economy share equally in the results of its productive undertakings? Should inequality be permitted in the distribution of the finished goods and services? How much inequality can be justified? If some are to receive more than others, how shall the lucky ones be chosen? This is the "for whom" aspect of microeconomics. It often is called "distribution of income," although income should be understood as goods and services rather than money. Every economic system must establish ways of answering this question.

Microeconomics focuses on the behavior of decision makers in the economy. Every economic system must answer the microeconomic questions of what to produce, how to produce, and for whom to produce.

Macroeconomics: Analysis of Aggregate Economic Activity

Macroeconomics is the part of economic analysis that deals with aggregate, or grand total, economic activity. The actions of the separate decision makers that are analyzed in microeconomics are added together in macroeconomics in order to focus on things that affect the economy as a whole. The two main topics of macroeconomics are inflation and unemployment, although there are important macroeconomics aspects to international trade and economic growth as well.

Macroeconomics deals with aggregate, or grand total, economic activity. Its two

---

main topics of analysis are inflation and unemployment.

Inflation is a sustained increase in the general level of prices. Figure 1 illustrates inflation in the United States since 1969. The price level today is more than three times as high as it was in 1969, which means that a dollar today buys less than one-third as much as one did in 1969. Inflation can put great strains on an economy and on the social arrangements supporting it.

Inflation is a sustained increase in the general level of prices.

FIGURE 1
Inflation in the United States

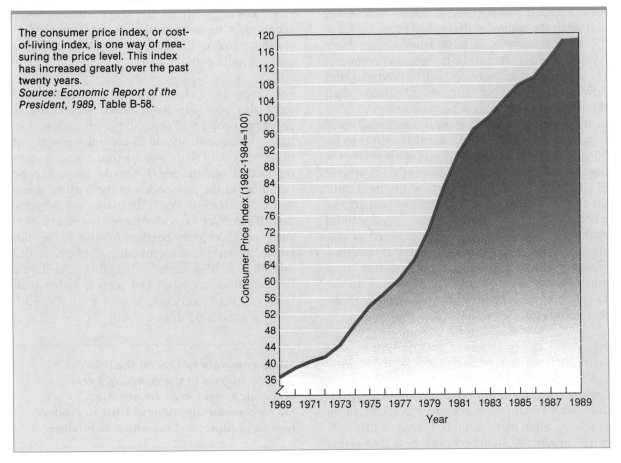

The consumer price index, or cost-of-living index, is one way of measuring the price level. This index has increased greatly over the past twenty years.
Source: Economic Report of the President, 1989, Table B-58.

Unemployment, the second main topic of macroeconomics, means that some people who are qualified and would like to work at the going wage rates are not able to find a job. Unemployment in the United States over the past twenty years, as measured by official statistics, is shown in Figure 2.

Unemployment means that some people who are qualified and willing to work at the going wage rates are not able to find a job.

Unemployment actually is a topic that fits into both macroeconomics and microeconomics—in other words, there are two general types of unemployment as far as economic analysis is concerned.

Unemployment is a microeconomic matter if a person's failure to find a job can be traced to decisions about what to produce or how to produce. For example, if people decide to stop playing golf and start playing tennis, there is likely to be unemployment among people who are trained to work as golf pros and are trying to find such jobs. This would be **microeconomic unemployment** because the reason can be traced to decisions about what to produce. Similarly, if banks switch to electronic teller machines operated by bank customers, people who are trained as bank tellers may fail to find jobs in that line of work. This kind of unemployment can be traced to a decision about how to produce, so it also can be called microeconomic unemployment. In most economies, changes are taking place almost continually in matters of what

FIGURE 2
Unemployment in the United States

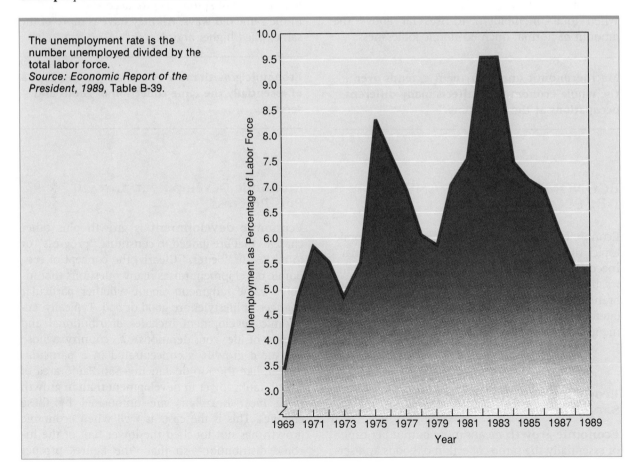

The unemployment rate is the number unemployed divided by the total labor force.
Source: Economic Report of the President, 1989, Table B-39.

and how to produce. Therefore, some amount of microeconomic unemployment usually exists. But this unemployment will be concentrated in certain industries or areas and will be more or less short-term.

Microeconomic unemployment occurs because of changes in the types of goods and services produced or in the ways of producing them.

Macroeconomic unemployment is the kind that exists throughout the whole economy (or at least affects many parts of the economy at the same time) and that is not related to particular decisions about what or how to produce. Golf pros, bank tellers, tennis pros, and many others are out of work at the same time, and their job searches are all unsuccessful. Macroeconomic unemployment sometimes is called "cyclical" unemployment because it comes during bad times or recessions, when total unemployment rises far above the amount of normal microeconomic joblessness.

Macroeconomic unemployment extends over the whole economy and affects many different occupations at the same time.

ECONOMIC GROWTH AND DEVELOPMENT

Economic growth and development are economic topics that are considered sometimes part of macroeconomics and sometimes part of microeconomics, but they could, perhaps, be considered separate branches of economics in themselves. Though related, economic growth and economic development are not the same thing.

Economic Growth: More of the Same Output

Economic growth means more output per capita of essentially the same collection of goods and ser-

vices. Development, on the other hand, means "progress," usually represented by some different and presumably "better" lifestyle or collection of goods. We can illustrate the difference between them with the aid of the well-known story of Robinson Crusoe and his Man Friday, catching fish and raising vegetables on their Pacific island. Imagine a female Crusoe and a female Friday somehow added to the party, so that the Crusoes and Fridays increase and multiply. Imagine too that every Crusoe, as well as every Friday, becomes a successful practitioner of fishing, farming, boat making, or net making by the original Crusoe-Friday methods. The amount of boats and nets, total and per capita, increases steadily, along with the income to the island population. Does this fanciful tale represent economic growth? Yes, it does. After a generation or two the Crusoes and the Fridays are economically better off than before. Is it economic development? Probably not. The islanders are still consuming the same old products produced and distributed in the same old ways. All they have is more of the same, piled higher and deeper.

Economic growth means more output per capita of essentially the same collection of goods and services.

Economic Development: Growth Plus Progress

Economic development is growth plus other changes that are judged to constitute "progress" or to make life "better." Clearly, the concept of economic development raises many questions that involve value judgments about whether particular changes or lifestyles are good or bad. Typically, economic development includes distributional and quality-of-life considerations. A country whose measured growth is concentrated in a particular region, like the Rio de Janeiro–São Paulo area of Brazil, ranks lower in development than in growth since most Brazilians are untouched by these changes. This is the case as well when economic growth has not touched the lower half of the income distribution—so that "the figures prosper while the people suffer," to quote Premier George Papandreou of Greece.

What are some of the indexes used to measure economic development? Some that have to do with health, education, and welfare are a rising life expectancy at birth, a rising literacy rate, equalizing trends in the distributions of income and wealth, rising numbers of educational and health service personnel per thousand people, falling death and illness rates from contagious and deficiency diseases, and falling dependence on subsistence agriculture. Other kinds of indexes are the rising consumption of steel and electricity per capita, rising ratios of saving and investment to total income,

and rising proportions of the representative family budget available for purchases other than food. Each measure has its bias, and no one index tells the whole story. Even so, it is fairly clear what all these indexes are driving at. Figure 3 below and Figure 4 (on page 8) show how some countries compare according to two indexes of development, infant mortality and illiteracy.

Economic development means economic growth plus improvements in the quality of life and distribution of goods and services.

FIGURE 3
Infant Mortality (Selected Countries), 1988

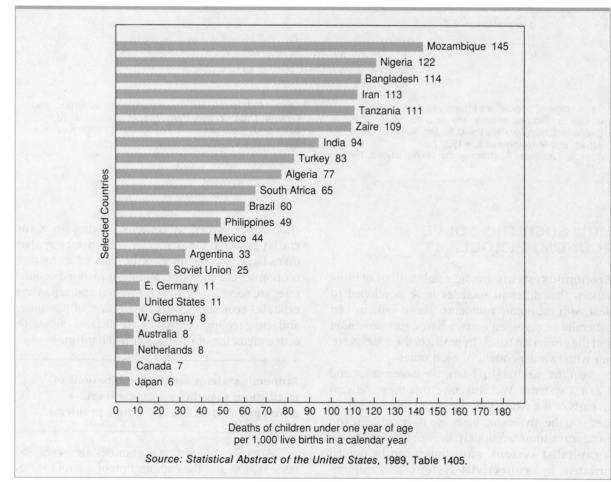

Source: *Statistical Abstract of the United States*, 1989, Table 1405.

FIGURE 4
Illiteracy (Selected Countries), Recent Years

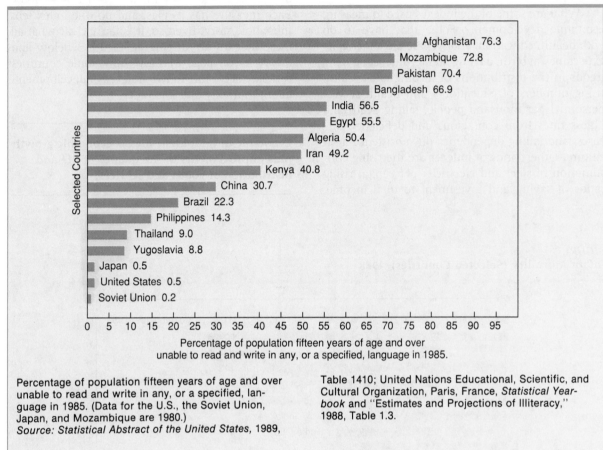

Percentage of population fifteen years of age and over
unable to read and write in any, or a specified, language in 1985.

Percentage of population fifteen years of age and over unable to read and write in any, or a specified, language in 1985. (Data for the U.S., the Soviet Union, Japan, and Mozambique are 1980.)
Source: Statistical Abstract of the United States, 1989,

Table 1410; United Nations Educational, Scientific, and Cultural Organization, Paris, France, *Statistical Yearbook* and "Estimates and Projections of Illiteracy," 1988, Table 1.3.

HOW SOCIETIES SOLVE ECONOMIC PROBLEMS

Economic systems are the combinations of institutions that different societies have developed to deal with economic problems. These systems can generally be classified on two bases, the *mechanism* and the *ownership* bases. In practice, these bases are not wholly independent of each other.

On the mechanism basis, we have *market* and *planned* systems. We also have *traditional* systems in parts of the world that are not highly industrialized. On the ownership basis, we have *capitalist* and *socialist* (or more accurately, *collectivist*) systems. In a **capitalist system,** most things can be owned privately. In a **collectivist system,** land and ma-

chinery are owned by collective bodies. In a **socialist system,** the particular collective body that owns land and machinery is the state. Most market economies are capitalist, and most planned economies are socialist. However, Sweden and Japan are capitalist economies with a great deal of planning, and Hungary and Yugoslavia are socialist ones with active elements of the market mechanism.

Economic systems are the combinations of institutions that different societies have developed to deal with economic problems.

Actually, all existing economies are *mixed* and none is *pure*. But the composition of the mix varies so greatly that they can be treated as different in kind. We shall call the United States a *market capitalist economy,* despite important elements of planning and/or socialism, ranging from the defense establishment to your city's water-purification plant. And we shall call the Soviet Union a *planned socialist economy,* despite important elements of capitalism and the market mechanism, such as peasants growing and selling products from their private plots within the collective farms. We do not call the Soviet Union a communist economic system, however. A **communist** is a socialist who believes that, after a few generations of near-worldwide socialism, socialist economies will reach a state of communism where most or all important goods will become free, scarcity will have been eliminated, and economics will have no excuse for existence. The Soviet leaders profess to believe that someday the U.S.S.R. will approach a communist economy, but that this utopia has not yet been attained.

Economic systems can be classified on a mechanism basis—market, planned, or traditional—or on an ownership basis—capitalist or collectivist (socialist).

Which Mechanism— Market or Planned?

Every economic system devises, or more often inherits, *mechanisms* that it uses to make the three basic microeconomic decisions of *what* goods and services (and how much of each) to produce, *how* to combine inputs to produce these things, and *for whom* among the population these goods and services are being produced. In modern economies, these decisions are made more or less impersonally and automatically by market mechanisms, or more or less deliberately and personally by planning mechanisms, or by some combination of the two.

Market Economies Figure 5 presents a simple picture of how these decisions are organized in a **market economy**—an economy in which the interaction of buyers and sellers is the main mechanism for making choices. In this figure, each of the cir-

FIGURE 5
Microeconomic Decisions in a Market Economy

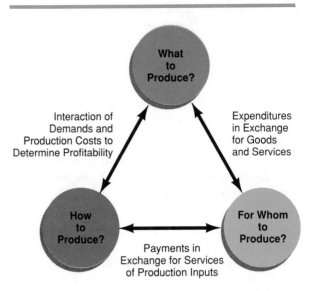

The three circles identify the three microeconomic questions that must be answered in any economic system. The double-headed arrows suggest that, in market systems, the answer to each question both requires information from and provides information for the answer to each of the other questions.

cles stands for one of the basic decisions that must be made in an economic system. Each of these circles is connected to each of the other circles. If we put ourselves inside the "for whom" circle, we are members of households that (under the capitalist system) own productive inputs such as labor, machinery, and natural resources and buy goods and services to consume. We are connected to the "how" circle because we provide inputs for and receive income from the production of goods and services. We are connected to the "what" circle because we spend our income and receive goods and services in exchange.

Business firms occupy both the "what" and the "how" circles. In the "what" circle, they are deciding what goods and services (and how much of each) to produce. They do this by interpreting the dollar votes that come from the "for whom" circle when households purchase goods and services and by combining this with information from the "how" circle about the costs of using alternative technologies for producing goods and services.

In the "how" circle, firms are deciding what mixtures of productive inputs to use in producing goods and services. Information is received from the "what" circle about which goods and services are demanded and from the "for whom" circle about the costs of the different productive inputs that can be used to produce them.

Our tour of the connected circles shows that the market mechanism is actually an integrated process, not just pure chance or "jungle law."

A market economy is an economy in which the interaction of buyers and sellers is the main mechanism for making choices.

Planned Economies The planning mechanism answers the same three microeconomic questions, but does so in a different way. The Soviet revolutionary leader Vladimir Ilich Lenin (1870–1924) thought this way was so simple that it could be explained in adequate detail to any semiliterate Russian worker or peasant. However, he seems to have been too optimistic.

The three microeconomic decisions for a **planned economy** are again shown by three circles in Figure 6. In addition, there is a fourth circle, representing the government in its planning function; in the U.S.S.R., it is an institution called Gosplan. The government (Gosplan) coordinates decisions in the three areas of microeconomics. In a pure planned system, there are no direct links between "what," "how," and "for whom." Each of the three microeconomic decisions depends upon the priorities set by government in the central circle.

Not being fools and having lived through failures, the bureaucrats of Gosplan (as well as the party politicians and military people looking over their shoulders) realize that a plan is not a magic wand. They know that the three types of decisions must be consistent with each other. Writing numbers down on paper will not produce the "shoes and ships and sealing wax" represented by these quantities. So the planners use elaborate statistical techniques to replace the market in integrating their several decisions. Not only is the detail of these techniques beyond the understanding of the Soviet worker or peasant whom Lenin hoped to draw into the planning process, but it is beyond the

FIGURE 6
Microeconomic Decisions in a Planned Economy

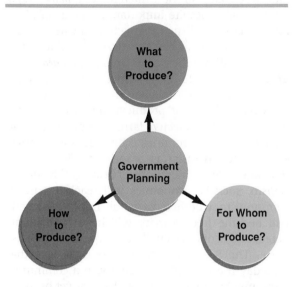

The three circles identify the three microeconomic questions that must be answered in any economic system. The single-headed arrows suggest that, in a planned economy, the answers to the three questions are worked out and coordinated through government planning in the central circle.

level of this book. The plans seldom work out perfectly. Neither, however, does "the obvious and simple system of natural liberty" of the market mechanism as described by Adam Smith, the eighteenth-century scholar who wrote the *Wealth of Nations* and who is credited with launching the modern study of how markets operate.

A planned economy is one in which the government coordinates decisions in the three microeconomic areas of what to produce, how to produce, and for whom to produce.

Traditional Economies It is, of course, much harder to generalize about **traditional economies,** but certain features are common to a good many of them. A great deal of property, particularly in land, is often held by a clan or tribe in common; Karl Marx spoke of this as "primitive communism." At the same time, there is much barter trade (exchanging goods for goods without the use of money) both within tribes and across tribal lines; the anthropologist Sol Tax calls this "penny capitalism." As for the major economic decisions, they are generally made by rulers (priests, kings and queens, chiefs, feudal barons, medicine men) either singly or in conference. They tend to be made on the basis of ethical ideas like "just" prices for goods and "fair" wages for labor, or the "duty" of at least the eldest child to follow the family's occupation of farming or fishing or pottery making. Rather than attempting economic planning or trusting any abstract market mechanism, primitive economies count on divine help, achieved through magic, prayers, and sacrifices, to solve any problems that may result from droughts or floods or earthquakes. The Islamic Republic of Iran under the late Ayatollah Khomeini can be regarded as a revival of a traditional kind of economy. The guiding principles are religious or ethical in nature, with little concern for efficiency or progress in the modern sense.

A traditional economy is characterized by common ownership of property, bartering, centralization of decision-making authority in the rulers, and reliance on divine help.

Ownership—Capitalism or Socialism?

Let us now turn to the *ownership* basis for classifying economic systems. In a *capitalist economy*, which usually relies upon the market mechanism, natural resources and machinery may be privately owned just like food, clothing, or other consumption goods. Not only is private ownership legal, either by individuals or by those "legal persons" called corporations, but it is the dominant form of ownership. In capitalist countries, people engage in the economic game routinely and automatically. They do so as decision makers, as property owners, as workers, and as consumers. The most important motives for engaging in economic activities are, of course, the increase in income and wealth and the satisfaction derived from income and wealth.

In a capitalist economy, natural resources and machinery may be privately owned, just like consumption goods. Private ownership is the dominant form of ownership.

In a *collectivist economy*, natural resources and machinery are owned only by collective groups. Individuals, however, may own consumption goods privately. The main appeal of socialism and all other collectivist systems is greater equality. These systems strive for a higher standard of living for the poor and an end to poverty, at the expense of the rich rather than of the people in general. Socialists believe that property in productive inputs should belong predominantly to the political state as trustee for the community as a whole.

In a collectivist economy, natural resources and machinery are owned only by collective groups, although individuals may own consumption goods. In a socialist system, the collective body that owns the natural resources and machines is the state.

EVALUATING ECONOMIC SYSTEMS

When Nikita Khrushchev banged his shoe on a United Nations table in the early 1960s and roared, "We shall bury you!" we can only guess what the head of the Soviet state may have meant. The meaning for some is that Khrushchev expected a few more years of competitive coexistence—the period 1960–1980 was often mentioned—to prove the superiority of planned socialism over market capitalism. Other leaders, who favored capitalism, were making exactly the opposite forecasts for the same period, without (to our knowledge) emphasizing their arguments with their shoes.

Six Criteria

What do we mean, anyhow, when we say that one economic system outperforms another? This is basically a subjective value judgment. It may be based on a great many criteria weighted in a great many different ways, not all of them conscious. We suggest here six criteria, or bases of judgment, with no weighting system at all. (Other economists use somewhat different criteria, and some try to rank them by importance.) On some of our criteria, some would say that the United States performs better than the Soviet Union; on others, they would argue that the Soviet Union comes out on top.

1. *Current Standard of Living*   Nearly all of us believe that, other things being equal, a high standard of living here and now is better than a lower one. As the famous singer Sophie Tucker put it, "I been rich and I been poor, but believe me, rich is better." It can be said, however, that even our present living standard may be too high for our own good, because some of us "dig our graves with our teeth," not to mention our lack of exercise. To quote Oliver Goldsmith's *The Deserted Village,*

> Ill fares the land, to hast'ning ills a prey,
> Where wealth accumulates, and men decay.

The **standard of living** is a measure of the material well-being of a person or a community. It is usually expressed in terms of current income or consumption per person, but the results differ when other measures are used. Not enough attention is paid to per capita *wealth*. Also, this criterion allows an economic system to claim credit for what may be due to a favorable location, rich natural resources, or a large population of working age.

The standard of living is a measure of the material well-being of a person or a community.

---

2. *Economic Growth—Future Standard of Living*   Nearly all of us believe that living standards, at least for "the poor," should improve over time, and also that overall economic growth will make this more likely to happen. People are generally happier when they expect progress than when "Tomorrow, and tomorrow, and tomorrow,/ Creeps in this petty pace from day to day." The prospect of progress is also an incentive for people to put forth the extra effort to make it a reality. At the same time, there may be limits to growth set by food, energy, raw materials, pollution, and sheer physical entropy, so that the same growth that

raises economic prospects for our children may only make things worse for our grandchildren.

3. *Equity of Distribution*   Everyone is in favor of "equity" and "fairness," but nobody knows what they consist of, or how important they are. **Equity** may, but need not, mean "equality" in consumption, income, or wealth. Without economic incentives for risk taking and the development of their economic potentials, the gifted and talented may complain of unfair treatment. Some balance— called by economists a tradeoff—must be achieved between what socialists call the "freedom to exploit" and the ethical judgments of ordinary people who feel that some limits should be placed on inequality. Different economies have consciously or unconsciously hit upon different compromises. Socialist distributions, incidentally, are *not* automatically closer to being equal than capitalist ones. Peter J.D. Wiles, in *Distribution of Income: East and West*, for example, argues that the capitalist United Kingdom is more egalitarian in practice than either the capitalist United States or the socialist Soviet Union. The same argument might be made for capitalist Holland or the Scandinavian countries. On the other hand, he finds socialist Poland more egalitarian than Britain.[3]

Intergroup income distributions within a society are also important. Japanese critics, among others, fault the income position of blacks, Hispanics, and American Indians in the United States, charging quite reasonably that it is due to racial discrimination. But if Japan's own minorities were as large as the American ones, Japanese discrimination and racism problems would probably be about as serious as those in the United States.

Equity may, but need not, mean equality in consumption, income, or wealth. True equity may not be attainable in either a socialist or a capitalist system.

---

4. *Security of the Living Standard*   People want to be sure that they will not wake up tomorrow morning to find that their jobs have disappeared

3. Peter J.D. Wiles, *Distribution of Income: East and West* (Amsterdam: North Holland Publishing Co., 1974).

without warning in a business cycle downturn, and that they have no other way to maintain their standard of living. Neither do they want to lose their living standards more gradually but just as hopelessly because of technological changes, such as when railroad trains are replaced by trucks and airplanes, or unskilled labor is made idle by robots. This goal suggests an advantage of the large country over the small one, given the difficulties of international migration. It also suggests that an economy, particularly a small one, should not be tied to a single industry. Finally, it suggests the desirability of defenses against these cyclical and technological changes.

5. Compatibility with Human Rights Without going into detail as to precisely what human rights are or by what actions they should be protected, we may safely say that an economy that depends on conscripts and prisoners for a major part of its labor force can be faulted on these grounds. This is what Solzhenitsyn says about the Soviet Union in *The Gulag Archipelago*. So, obviously, may be faulted a slave economy like the American South for about two hundred years before the Civil War—and in some states for several generations afterward. Both China under Mao Zedong and the Soviet Union ever since the Russian Revolution have been accused of working people to death in and out of prison camps to speed up their economic development. In the nineteenth century, similar accusations were made against the Central Pacific Railroad in the United States, where the workers concerned were Chinese contract laborers.

6. Compatibility with Physical and Mental Health A high "standard of living" is not synonymous with a high "quality of life." A particular economic system may enhance one while making the other more difficult to achieve. In the United States today, some argue that the competitive "rat race" of the capitalist struggle to get ahead drives people to mental hospitals in large numbers.[4] Ac-

cording to some psychologists and psychiatrists, any economy that encourages "keeping up with the Joneses" and conspicuous consumption, while making inadequate provision for the poor, is incompatible with physical and mental health. In such an economy, there are many sources of harmful stress: too heavy a workload, impossible deadlines, the loss of a job, and all sorts of financial worries. It should not be inferred, however, that similar problems are unknown in collectivist societies. Unrealistic expectations and work quotas, the possible loss of a job, and other economic ills are part of the worker's lot in the Soviet Union too.

Six criteria can be used for evaluating the performance of different economic systems: (1) current standard of living; (2) economic growth; (3) equity of distribution; (4) security of the living standard; (5) compatibility with human rights; and (6) compatibility with physical and mental health.

Policy Tradeoffs

Conflicts often arise among accepted social goals, so that choices and tradeoffs are necessary at the most general policy levels. We have noted already what the late economist Arthur Okun called "the big tradeoff" between the common desire to maintain incentives for work and risk taking and the common desire to limit inequality in income and wealth. Another example is the experience of the United Nations in promoting economic growth and development between 1950 and 1970. Measured *economic growth,* our second criterion, appeared to be going quite well. In fact, the less-developed countries grew more rapidly as a group than did the more-developed (industrialized) countries, narrowing the measured gap between them. But *economic development,* which is generally defined to include most or all of our last four criteria, was disappointing. Conditions in rural areas and for the urban poor remained largely unaffected and unimproved in many countries with the highest growth rates. So development specialists, including economists, rejected as "growthmanship" the focus on measured national income and its rate of change per capita. They offered instead a plan based on

---

4. It cannot be doubted that the statistical probability of spending part of one's life in a mental institution is unusually high in the United States; it has been estimated as high as one out of eight. But this figure reflects greater availability of such institutions in the United States and also the greater life expectancy of the adult American, which increases the likelihood of senility.

providing every family in every developing country, rural as well as urban, with **basic human needs.** These needs were defined as minimal amounts of food, clothing, shelter, education, health care, and sometimes also ''access'' to public decision making. Only after these needs are met, runs the argument, should attention be paid to attaining economic growth. The conflict continues in the developing countries, in the aid-giving industrial countries, and in the international agencies, with no solution or compromise presently in sight.

Conflicts often arise among accepted social goals; mere economic growth without an accompanying improvement in the delivery of such basic human needs as food, clothing, shelter, education, and health care may be a hollow victory.

WHY SO HARD?

Why is economics supposed to be so hard—harder for many students than history or the other social sciences? There are three reasons; if you are prepared, you will have less to worry about.

The first reason is that economics and economists are likely to challenge some of your previous half-formed ideas. You may temporarily find yourself unlearning more than you learn, or operating in a fog of confusion.

The second reason is that economics, like Switzerland, talks three languages at once. There is the language of words, which for us is English. There is the language of diagrams and graphs. And there is also the language of mathematics, which is used more and more extensively as the student goes on to advanced work. Just as the educated Swiss is translator and interpreter between and among the three languages of his or her country, the good economist should be a translator and interpreter among the three languages of this discipline. This is not, for many people, an easy task to accomplish.

A third reason is that economics makes extensive use of theories and models involving more assumptions and higher levels of abstraction than many students have yet encountered. These theories and models are a fundamental part of the ''methods,'' or ''way of thinking,'' view of economics. Since one theory often builds on another, it is important to get a solid grasp of each one before going on to the next. So careful learning, step by step, is important in economics.

Economics in Focus

Is Socialism Dying?

As recently as the 1960s, many observers thought that socialism or communism was the wave of the future. Dozens of new countries in Africa and Asia, freed from their former colonial masters, adopted systems that combined centralized economic planning with state ownership of crucial industries. Socialist parties of one brand or another played leading roles throughout Europe and Latin America. Old American allies such as Britain—not to mention close neighbors like Cuba—were governed by parties at least loosely committed to socialism. In the United States itself, supposedly the bastion of capitalism, the federal government with its social and economic planners increasingly dominated the economy.

But in the 1980s the pattern began to change. In Britain, West Germany, Belgium, the Netherlands, France, and a number of other European countries, conservative, capitalist-oriented governments pushed aside the socialists. Even Eastern Bloc nations such as Poland and Hungary began to experiment with capitalism. In the United States the Reagan administration, with an old-fashioned appeal to the self-help ethic, tried to reduce the federal role in citizens' everyday lives and liberate the free-market economy.

Most important, the twin giants of socialism, the U.S.S.R. and China, began to adopt capitalist reforms. In the Soviet Union, under the banner of *perestroika* (restructuring), Mikhail Gorbachev struggled to introduce competition and decentralization to the stagnant socialist system. In China similar reforms allowed a flourishing of entrepreneurial centers in the coastal provinces. By the end of the 1980s Gorbachev faced strong opposition, and China was in political turmoil.

From 1980 to 1987 more than 56 state-owned corporations around the world were sold to private shareholders. Small and emerging countries now had a new model to look to. Tanzania, for example, described by *U.S. News & World Report* as "an economic basket case" in the 1970s, abandoned its collective-farm system and introduced free-market capitalism. The result was a startling resurgence for Tanzania's economy.

All in all, the transition toward capitalism has been dramatic enough for magazine headlines to trumpet "the death of socialism." Some observers say that socialism simply cannot compete in an increasingly diverse and high-tech world economy, because central bureaucracies do not adapt as quickly as free-wheeling entrepreneurs. But if socialism is indeed dying, its death rattles will continue for some time, and no one is suggesting that its legacy will disappear. The economies of the twenty-first century will evolve new forms that we cannot yet predict, and capitalism and socialism as we know them will both be important influences.

Sources: Richard I. Kirkland, Jr., "The Death of Socialism," *Fortune,* January 4, 1988, pp. 64–72; "Communism in Turmoil," Special Report, *Business Week,* June 5, 1989, pp. 34–87; John Barnes, "Africa Makes a Hard Choice," *U.S. News & World Report,* June 27, 1988, pp. 28–32 (quotation at p. 28); Louise Lief, "The West's Recipe: Try Again," *U.S. News & World Report,* June 27, 1988, pp. 30–31; Zbigniew Brzezinski, "Will the Soviet Empire Self-Destruct?" *New York Times Magazine,* February 26, 1989, pp. 38–41; Ronald Bailey, "The World Turns," *Forbes,* May 15, 1989, pp. 43–44; Timothy Garton Ash, "Revolution: The Springtime of Two Nations," *New York Review of Books,* June 15, 1989, pp. 3–10.

SUMMARY

1. Some definitions of economics stress subject matter—how scarcity is dealt with and how people's wants are satisfied. Another type of definition stresses the methods and techniques used by economists. (See page 2.)

2. The two main branches of economics are microeconomics and macroeconomics. Microeconomics is the part that focuses on the behavior of decision makers who are inside or part of a larger economic system. Every economic system must provide ways of answering the microeconomic questions of what to produce, how to produce, and for whom to produce. (See page 3.)

3. Macroeconomics is the branch of economics that deals with aggregate, or "grand total," economic activity. It examines how the whole economic system operates and focuses mainly on the topics of inflation and unemployment. (See page 4.)

4. Inflation is a sustained increase in the general price level. Unemployment may be either microeconomic or macroeconomic, depending on the reason why a person is unable to find work. Microeconomic unemployment arises because of changes in the types of goods and services produced or in the ways of producing them—the what and how decisions in microeconomics. Macroeconomic unemployment extends over the whole economy and affects many different occupations at the same time. (See pages 4–6 and Figures 1 and 2, pages 4 and 5.)

5. Economic growth and development are two other important economic subjects. Economic growth is a measured percentage rise each year or each decade in production, either total or per capita. Economic development means economic growth as well as some improvements in the "quality of life" and in the distribution of income. (See pages 6–7.)

6. Economic systems are the combinations of institutions that societies have set up to deal with economic problems. On a mechanism basis, they can be classified as market economies or planned economies. Market economies integrate the various economic questions through the institutions of free exchange in markets. Planned economies use governments and other agencies to accomplish this integration. All existing economies are mixed, with elements of both market and planning systems. (See pages 8–10.)

7. Economic systems can also be classified on the basis of ownership. In capitalist systems, private property rights extend from ordinary consumption goods to productive inputs. In collectivist systems, productive inputs (except for labor) are collectively owned. If the agency owning these goods is the political state or an agency of the state, we have socialism, which is the most important form of collectivism. (See page 11.)

8. In traditional economies, custom and religion play major parts. Much property is usually held in common, and occupations tend to remain in families. There is much stress on "justice" in price and wage fixing, and often we find resort to prayer, magic, and the supernatural. In these economies, the important decisions are made by kings and queens, chiefs, priests, or feudal lords. (See pages 10–11.)

9. A capitalist economy is more apt to rely on the market mechanism than is a collectivist one. Collectivist (including socialist) economies are more likely to be planned than are capitalist ones. Conversely, a market economy is apt to be capitalistic, and a planned economy socialistic, but there are important exceptions to this generalization. (See page 11.)

10. Six criteria are suggested for evaluating economic systems: (a) a high current living standard; (b) economic growth, pointing to a high future living standard; (c) "equitable" distributions of income and wealth; (d) security of the living standard against downward shocks; (e) compatibility with human rights; and (f) compatibility with physical and mental health. (See pages 11–13.)

KEY TERMS

basic human needs: minimal amounts of food, clothing, shelter, education, health care, and access to public decision making (page 14)

capitalist system: an economic system in which natural resources and machinery can be privately owned (page 8).

collectivist system: an economic system in which natural resources and machinery are owned by collective bodies (page 8).

communist: a socialist who believes that socialist economies will eventually reach a state of communism, in which most or all important goods will be free, scarcity will no longer exist, and there will be no need for economics (page 9).

economic development: economic growth plus improvements in the quality of life and distribution of goods and services (page 16).

economic growth: more output per capita of essentially the same collection of goods and services (page 6).

economics: the study of how individuals and societies deal with the problems of scarcity and the methodologies that have been developed for analyzing such problems (page 2).

economic systems: the combinations of institutions that different societies have developed to deal with economic problems (page 8).

equity: fairness in the distribution of consumption, income, or wealth (page 12).

inflation: a sustained increase in the general level of prices (page 4).

macroeconomics: the part of economic analysis that deals with aggregate economic activity; its two main topics are inflation and unemployment (page 4).

macroeconomic unemployment: unemployment that exists throughout the whole economy and that is not related to particular decisions about what or how to produce (page 6).

market economy: an economy in which the interaction of buyers and sellers is the main mechanism for making choices (page 9).

microeconomics: the part of economic analysis that deals with the behavior of decision makers in the economy (page 3).

microeconomic unemployment: unemployment that is due to decisions about what or how to produce (page 5).

planned economy: an economy in which the government coordinates decisions in the three microeconomic areas of what to produce, how to produce, and for whom to produce (page 10).

scarcity: a situation in which the amount of something actually available would not be sufficient to satisfy the desire for it if it were provided free (page 2).

socialist system: an economic system in which the state owns the natural resources and machinery (page 8).

standard of living: a measure of the material wellbeing of a person or a community (page 12).

traditional economy: an economic system characterized by common ownership of property, bartering, centralization of decision making authority in the rulers, and reliance on divine help (page 10).

unemployment: when some people who are qualified and willing to work at going wage rates are not able to find a job (page 5).

DISCUSSION QUESTIONS

1. The famous economist Alfred Marshall defined economics as "a study of mankind in the ordinary business of life; it examines that part of individual and social action which is most closely connected to the attainment and with the use of the material requisites of wellbeing."[5] Is this closer to the problems type of definition or the methodology type of definition? Explain your answer.

2. In market economies, the what, how, and for whom decisions are linked to one another. In fact, many events have roots in all three of these economic decisions. Consider the increase in the quantity of computers produced in our society. Explain how the what, how, and for whom decisions each played a part in this outcome.

3. Market economies use profits and losses to stimulate the search for better production methods. What nonmoney rewards for success exist in capitalist market systems? Is the money or the honor more important for Nobel Prize winners? Is a gold watch better than money for a retirement gift?

4. Do you believe the present distribution of income in the United States is unfair or unjust in any way? If so, how should it be different? What changes would you expect in the way the economy operates if your desired reforms were actually to take place?

5. Alfred Marshall, *Principles of Economics,* 8th ed. (London: Macmillan, 1920), p. 1.

5. The figures in this chapter showing the relations of what, how, and for whom in market and planned economies are great simplifications of reality. Most actual systems are mixed. Explain how the U.S. economy would be better illustrated by putting a government planning circle in the center of Figure 5. Explain how the Soviet Union's economy would be better illustrated by adding arrows between the three outer circles in Figure 6.

6. The distinction between microeconomic and macroeconomic unemployment is helpful in theorizing about the economy. But the unemployed worker may not know (or really care) which has put him or her out of work. Consider an unemployed auto worker in Flint, Michigan, in the early 1980s. Remember that car sales are especially sensitive to general economic conditions and that the economy was in recession during those years. Also, the U.S. auto firms faced severe competition from imported Japanese and German automobiles. Discuss the unemployment in Flint in terms of microeconomic and macroeconomic determinants.

7. As you learned in this chapter, economic development means economic growth plus some qualitative changes in the conditions of life. Growth is a part of development. What arguments can you think of against growth itself? In your opinion, is the United States experiencing economic development today? Explain your answer.

8. Our list of ways to evaluate economic systems may not be the same as a list you would make. If you could add one item to the list, what would it be? Do you believe that people in China or the Soviet Union would want a different set of goals? Explain your answers.

9. President Warren Harding once said, "There is more happiness in the American small town than anywhere else on earth." Do you think he was correct then—in the 1920s? Do you think his statement is true today? Explain.

10. Do you think that human happiness has the best chance of being realized under capitalism, socialism, or a traditional economy? Explain your answer to this question.

2

The Actors on the Economic Stage

Preview Understanding how an economic system works requires economists to identify the major actors on the economic stage and the roles they play in the operation of the system. We introduce them in this chapter.

We shall look first at households. In a capitalist economic system, households actually contain *two* decision-making entities—consumers and resource owners.[1] Imagine that each member of the household wears two hats, one marked "consumer" and the other marked "resource owner." As consumers, household members help to make the "what to produce" decisions in the economy. As resource owners, they are involved with both the "how" and the "for whom" decisions.

Next we will look at business firms, which are the economic units concerned with production. In the capitalist system, business firms help make all three microeconomic decisions. Business firms obtain resources from households and combine them to produce goods and services. Household members place their resources in the hands of business firms because they expect to be rewarded with income. The firm, if successful, is able to make a profit from its operations.

The third major element in the economy is government. We will describe the major functions and responsibilities that economists say properly fall upon government in a market-capitalist system. These responsibilities involve (1) financing certain goods and services (which contributes to the "what to produce" decision), (2) redistributing income (which influences the "for whom" decision), and (3) moderating business cycles (which is a macroeconomic activity).

1. See pages 44–46 for a discussion of rational economic decision makers.

Households, business firms, and governments in foreign countries are the fourth major element influencing an economy. Foreigners buy goods and services produced in the United States, thus adding to the demand for products from U.S. firms and the demand for U.S. resources. But foreigners also are producers of goods and services bought by Americans, thus competing with U.S. resource owners and firms.

The interactions among the actors on the economic stage—households, business firms, government, and foreigners—will be examined in detail in later chapters.

HOUSEHOLDS

For statistical purposes, a **household** may be defined either as a family group living together or as one or more persons living together in the same dwelling unit. There are about 92 million households in the United States today. Households are made up of individuals who, in capitalist-market economic systems, are the owners of resources as well as consumers of goods and services. Each individual, of course, is the owner of his or her own labor resource. But in capitalist economic systems, nonhuman resources, too, are owned by individuals, either directly or indirectly. Land and buildings can be owned directly by individuals. Indirect ownership, on the other hand, occurs when corporations hold title to resources. This is indirect ownership by individuals, since corporations themselves are owned by shareholders, who are individuals. As resource owners, individuals receive the income generated in the production activities of the economy.

When household members spend the income they have earned as resource owners, they are functioning in their economic capacity as consumers. They are casting "dollar votes" for the goods and services that they want. In this way, they help make the "what to produce" decisions.

A household is a family group (or one or more unrelated persons) living together in the same dwelling unit.

Households are made up of individuals who are the owners of resources as well as consumers of goods and services.

As resource owners, individuals receive the income generated in the production activities of the economy. When they spend the income as consumers, they help determine what goods and services get produced.

Population and Age Groups

The size and age distribution of the population are facts of great importance to economics because they affect production and spending. Will people, or households, demand baby food, rock concerts and sports cars, or retirement homes? What proportion of the population will be of working age, and how many nonworkers will there be for every worker? Will the typical person make decisions with the aggressiveness and flexibility of youth or with the caution and stability of older age?

Figure 1 shows the age distribution of the United States population from 1960 to 2000, based on both actual data and estimates. The total population is expected to increase by almost 50 percent over this forty-year span. The numbers in this figure show the effects of the "baby boom" of the 1950s and 1960s and of the sharp drop in the birthrate during the 1970s. Though the percentage of the population 17 years and under declined greatly during the 1970s, it is expected to decline only moderately through the end of the century as the people born in the 1950s and 1960s produce their own children. The younger working-age group, from age 18 through 44, continued to increase during the 1980s but will decline in the 1990s. The older working-age group, from 45 through 64 years, is expected to begin its growth spurt in the decade of the 1990s. The over-65 age group probably will grow moderately through the end of the century but then experience a major expansion.

This population "ripple" may be one of the most significant economic events in the lives of college students today. Students graduating during the mid-1990s will be entering a labor force that will include a much larger percentage of the popu-

FIGURE 1
Population Size and Age Distribution in the United States, 1960–2000

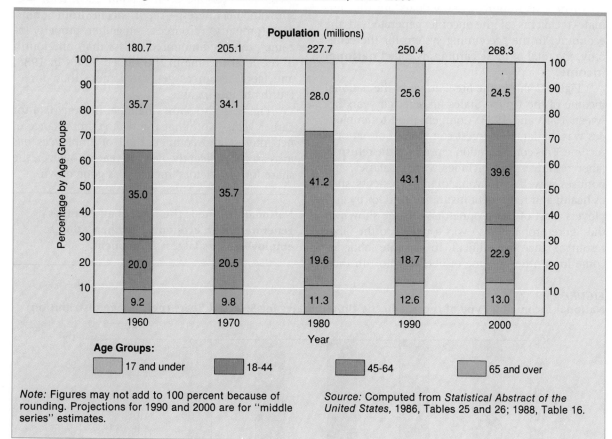

Population (millions)

| | 180.7 | 205.1 | 227.7 | 250.4 | 268.3 |

Age Groups:
- ☐ 17 and under
- ☐ 18-44
- ☐ 45-64
- ☐ 65 and over

Note: Figures may not add to 100 percent because of rounding. Projections for 1990 and 2000 are for "middle series" estimates.

Source: Computed from *Statistical Abstract of the United States*, 1986, Tables 25 and 26; 1988, Table 16.

lation than was the case for students graduating in the 1960s and early 1970s. Competition for jobs will probably be vigorous, but living standards may be high because the percentage of nonworkers will be relatively low. These graduates will face different challenges when they will be entering the 45–64 "older-worker" category. The expanding proportion of people over age 65 then will place increasing pressures on those still working, who will be expected to support a larger and larger nonworking population.

The political effect of the "ripple" may also be important. Many believe that people tend to be "liberal" when they are young and "conservative" when they are old. In fact, there is persuasive economic logic behind this observation, since older people have more at stake in the status quo than do younger people. The young people of the 1960s

and 1970s were influential in bringing about many changes in the United States through their political activity. Civil rights, women's liberation, antiwar, and antinuclear movements relied heavily on the support of young people. As these same people grow older, they will continue to leave their mark on political history—this time as an older generation.

The size and age distribution of the population are facts of great importance to economics because they affect production and spending. The U.S. population is characterized by the "baby boom" of the 1950s and 1960s, followed by a sharp drop in the birthrate in the 1970s.

Sources of Income

As owners of resources, individuals are the ultimate recipients of the income generated in the economy. In the accounting system for the economy, the total of these earnings is called **national income.**

Figure 2 shows the breakdown of the national income of the United States for selected years between 1940 and 1988. Compensation to employees was, by far, the largest component of national income. This compensation represents the return to labor resources and includes wages, salaries, and bonuses as well as the value of fringe benefits, such as health and retirement insurance paid for by employers. Part of the proprietors' income shown in the figure probably also was a return to the labor resource, since it is difficult to separate labor income from other income of people who run their own businesses. The other components of national income—corporate profits, rental income of persons, and net interest—report income from nonhuman (property) resources. Altogether, property income probably amounted to less than one-fourth of the total income in the United States in 1988, and labor resources generated more than three-fourths of this income.

Figure 2 also shows national income data for earlier years. Note that the relative importance of net interest and compensation of employees has increased significantly over the years. However, the share for proprietors' income has gone down.

National income is the total of all earnings generated in an economy. Compensation to employees is its largest component.

FIGURE 2
National Income by Type of Income in the United States for Selected Years (percentage distribution)

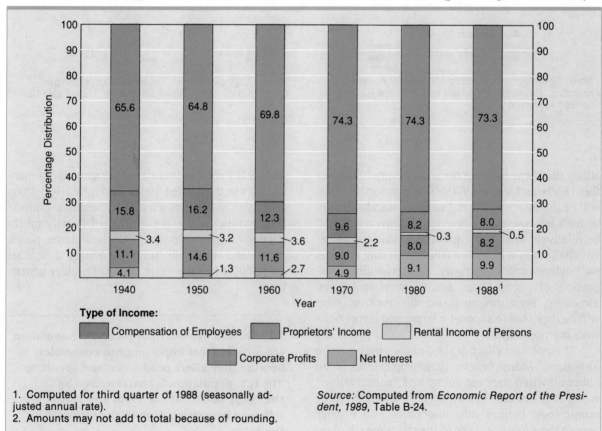

1. Computed for third quarter of 1988 (seasonally adjusted annual rate).
2. Amounts may not add to total because of rounding.

Source: Computed from *Economic Report of the President, 1989*, Table B-24.

FIGURE 3
Median Money Income of U.S. Families in Constant (1986) Dollars, 1960–1986

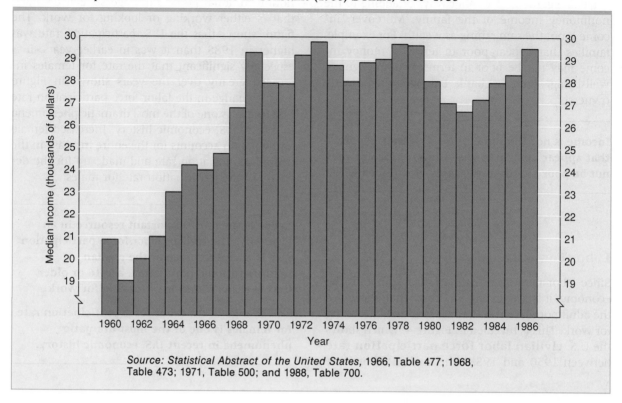

Source: *Statistical Abstract of the United States*, 1966, Table 477; 1968, Table 473; 1971, Table 500; and 1988, Table 700.

Median Family Income

Figure 3 shows the median family income in the United States from 1960 through 1986. The "median" means that half the families in the country had incomes higher than the one shown for each year and that half had incomes lower than this amount. Also, the income figures have been adjusted so as to remove changes in the cost of living that arose from changes in the price level. All the figures are in dollars of the purchasing power that prevailed in 1986. Therefore, they are useful in showing what has happened to the standard of living of U.S. families over this twenty-seven-year period.

At first you may notice that the median family income was much higher in 1986 than it was in 1960—41.6 percent higher, in fact. A closer examination, however, shows that the highest median family income shown in Figure 3 is for 1973. In the thirteen years from 1960 to 1973, the median family income in the United States increased by almost 43 percent, but the median family income fell in 1974 and 1975 and in the years from 1978 through 1982. Although the median family income increased after 1982, as of 1986 it had not yet regained the level of 1973.

Economists are, of course, very interested in the forces that may cause changes in the levels of family income. Even a casual reflection on the numbers in Figure 3 suggest that the shocks to the economy that were caused by large changes in the price of crude oil in 1973 and 1978 may have been at least partly responsible for the lack of growth in U.S. median family income in the late 1970s and early 1980s.

Several words of caution are appropriate even at this early stage in our exploration of economics. Money income tells only part of the story about the economic well-being of a family. Nonmoney incomes, such as subsidized food, housing, and health care, also are important. "Do-it-yourself" home building and repair, as well as back-yard vegetable gardens, are other ways of adding to the nonmoney income of the family. Moreover, income is not the same thing as wealth. For example, families that appear poor in terms of money income may not be poor in terms of other signs of well-being, such as bank balances or property ownership.

Income is not the same as wealth. Households that appear poor in terms of money income may not be poor by other measures of well-being.

Labor Force Participation

Since labor is the most important resource in the economy, it is interesting to know what portion of the adult population actually is working or looking for work. This is revealed in Figure 4, which shows the U.S. **civilian labor force participation rate** between 1950 and 1988. The civilian labor force

participation rate is the percentage of the civilian noninstitutional population, age sixteen or older, that is either working or looking for work. The figure shows that the U.S. participation rate was higher in 1988 than it was in earlier years. It is especially significant that the rate for females increased greatly over the years shown in Figure 4. This change in the labor force participation rate for females is one of the most dramatic phenomena in recent U.S. economic history. Increased female participation accounts for the entire increase in the overall participation rate and made up for the decrease in the participation rate for males.

Labor is the most important resource in an economy. The civilian labor force participation rate is the percentage of the civilian noninstitutional population, age 16 or older, that is either working or looking for work.

The change in the labor force participation rate for females is one of the most dramatic phenomena in recent U.S. economic history.

FIGURE 4
Civilian Labor Force Participation Rate (percent)

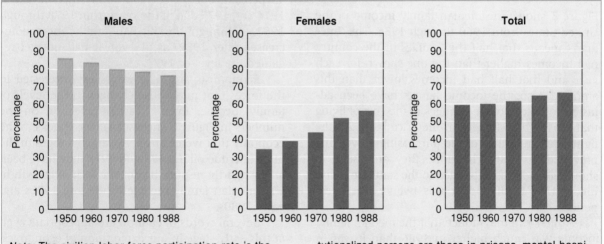

Note: The civilian labor force participation rate is the percentage of the civilian noninstitutional population in the group specified. Data relate to persons sixteen years of age or over. A person is in the labor force if he or she is either working or looking for work. Insti-

tutionalized persons are those in prisons, mental hospitals, and so on.
Source: Economic Report of the President, 1989, Table B-36.

FIGURE 5
Disposition of Personal Income in the United States for Selected Years (percentage distribution)

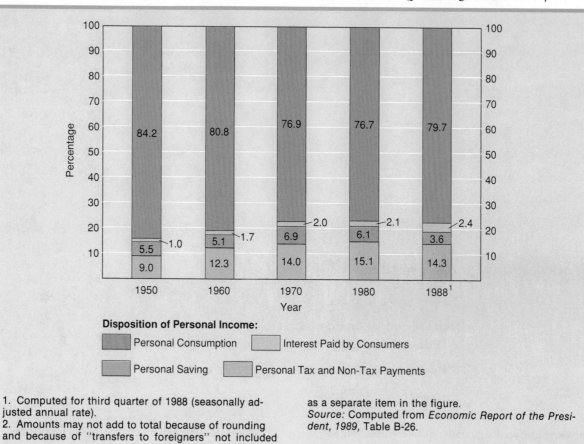

1. Computed for third quarter of 1988 (seasonally adjusted annual rate).
2. Amounts may not add to total because of rounding and because of "transfers to foreigners" not included as a separate item in the figure.
Source: Computed from *Economic Report of the President, 1989,* Table B-26.

Uses of Income

As we have said, household members are helping make the "what to produce" decision when they purchase goods and services. Figure 5 shows how households disposed of their income. In 1988, 79.7 percent went for consumption goods and services, 14.3 percent for taxes, 2.4 percent for interest payments, and 3.6 percent was saved. As you continue to study economics, you will see that each of these dispositions of household income is carefully analyzed by economists in their efforts to understand the economy. The figure shows that the percentage of income used for consumption goods and services has dropped since 1950, while the percentage paid in taxes and interest has increased. Even the

money that is saved plays a role in the "what to produce" decision. This happens when savings are placed in banks or other financial institutions and then borrowed by a person or a business firm that wants to buy something.

The percentage of income used for consumption goods and services has dropped since 1950, while the percentage paid in taxes and interest has increased.

Figure 6 gives a breakdown of the consumption expenditures of households. As you can see, housing and household operation now account for

FIGURE 6
Personal Consumption Expenditures in the United States for Selected Years (percentage distribution)

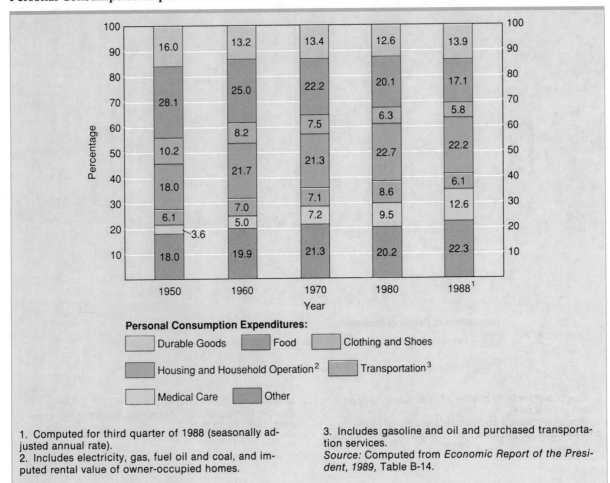

1. Computed for third quarter of 1988 (seasonally adjusted annual rate).
2. Includes electricity, gas, fuel oil and coal, and imputed rental value of owner-occupied homes.

3. Includes gasoline and oil and purchased transportation services.
Source: Computed from *Economic Report of the President, 1989*, Table B-14.

almost one-fourth of consumption expenditure, while food claims less than 20 percent. The famous trio of "food, clothing, and shelter" add up to considerably less than half of all consumption. The percentages spent for food and clothing decreased significantly while the percentage spent for medical care showed a spectacular increase.

In this sense, business brings resource owners and consumers together.

Business firms purchase resources from households and combine them to produce goods and services.

BUSINESS FIRMS

The business firm is the second actor on the economic stage to be examined in this chapter. Business firms purchase resources or resource services and combine them to produce goods and services.

Forms of Business Organization

The three basic forms of business organization are the proprietorship, the partnership, and the corporation. Each form has special features, which we shall describe briefly.

The Proprietorship A **proprietorship** exists simply because some person decides to start his or her own business. No legal papers have to be filled out, and no formal declaration about being in business is necessary unless there are laws that relate to the particular work to be done, such as the necessity of obtaining a license to practice medicine or permission from a health department to operate a restaurant. The owner, or proprietor, is responsible for financing and managing the business. Assuming the risks of possible losses, the proprietor has the right to whatever profits may come after all outside debts have been paid. A large percentage of small retail stores, small farms, and very small manufacturing companies in the United States are proprietorships.

Proprietorships are businesses owned by one person.

The Partnership A **partnership** exists when two or more people agree to share the financial and managerial responsibilities of a business firm as well as its profits and losses. A partnership agreement is necessary because partners must set the terms and conditions of their participation in the business. The agreement does not have to be in writing, but experience suggests that written agreements will cause much less trouble than oral agreements. In the agreement, the partners can set up almost any methods of financing, managing, and profit sharing that they choose.

A partnership exists when two or more people agree to share the financial and managerial responsibilities of a business firm as well as its profits and losses.

There are two very important legal requirements that apply to *both* proprietorships and partnerships but pose special problems for partnerships. These are unlimited liability and limited life.

Each partner must accept **unlimited liability** (complete responsibility) for all the debts of the business. The partnership agreement may specify how debts are to be paid in most cases, but if any partners fail to meet their obligations, the other partners must make sure that the partnership meets all its commitments to outsiders. Because each partner is liable for the obligations of the whole business, outsiders have extra assurance that any promises made by the partnership will be kept. Of course, before joining a partnership, individuals must be sure that they trust and share the business goals of other members of the partnership.

Unlimited liability means that partners and proprietors bear complete responsibility for all the debts of the business.

Proprietorships and partnerships have **limited life.** A partnership lasts only as long as the partnership agreement is in force. Many events can put an end to the agreement and thus to the life of the partnership. If a partner dies or leaves the business, the other partners must make a new agreement in order to continue together in business. To add a new partner also means making a new agreement. The limited life of the partnership gives the partners the necessary flexibility to deal with changes but at the same time makes it a very fragile form of business organization.

Proprietorships and partnerships have limited life. A proprietorship lasts only as long as the proprietor is in business; a partnership lasts only as long as the partnership agreement is in force.

Creating partnerships and adding partners with special talents or training can give financial power and technical specialization to a business such as a law firm or a medical practice. However, the problems connected with limited life and unlimited liability make many people hesitate to join a partnership.

The Corporation A **corporation** comes into being when the government issues a charter. In the United States, corporate charters are issued by state governments. Obtaining a charter is simple and inexpensive, and the charter itself places very few restrictions on the operations of corporations. The charter authorizes the corporation to issue and sell shares of stock. The people who own these shares, the stockholders, are the owners of the corporation. Also, the charter establishes the corporation as a "legal person," separate from the "real persons" who are the owners and the managers of the corporation.

A corporation is a "legal person" separate from the "real persons" who own and manage it. Corporations are authorized by government charter. They have the right to issue and sell shares of stock that confer ownership rights on those who buy them.

As a legal person, the corporation can enter into contracts and make commitments in its own name. Under the law, the corporation itself is responsible for these obligations. Neither the owners nor the managers are individually liable for its debts and obligations. If the corporation does well, the stockholders reap the profits, but if corporate operations are not successful, a stockholder's loss is limited to the value of the shares owned. This **limited liability** feature of corporations greatly increases their ability to accumulate large sums of money for the enterprise. Because stockholders can share the profits and face only limited liability for losses, they are generally willing to let other people carry out the day-to-day management of the corporation.

The legal person created by the corporate charter has perpetual or **unlimited life,** which means that the corporation itself does not have to be reorganized every time individual persons enter or leave the ownership or management of the corporation. This stability is attractive to shareholders, who need not fear that their wealth will be tied up in endless legal battles, as may happen in partnerships. Also, customers, banks, and other firms can enter into long-term contracts with the corporation, knowing that its existence does not hinge on the lives of mortal human beings.

Thus the corporate form of business overcomes the problems of unlimited liability and limited life to which both proprietorships and partnerships are subject. The corporate form opens up vast possibilities for business firms to bring together financial power and technical expertise. Even though U.S.

proprietorships far outnumber U.S. corporations, it is no wonder that the great majority of business assets in the United States are held by corporations. The corporate share of manufacturing output in the United States is about 98 percent.

Corporations have limited liability— stockholders are not liable for their debts— and unlimited life—their existence is not dependent on a single person or a partnership agreement.

The great majority of business assets in the United States are held by corporations.

The chief disadvantage of the corporate form of business is that the net income of corporations is subject to taxation by the U.S. federal government and also by many state governments. These taxes are in addition to the individual income tax paid by stockholders on the profits they receive from corporations as dividends. Thus, corporation dividends are taxed twice, once when the money is earned by the corporation and again when it is received by the stockholder. From the point of view of the individual decision maker, taxation cancels some of the advantages of the corporate form of business.

The chief disadvantage of the corporate form of business organization is that corporation dividends are taxed twice, once when the money is earned by the corporation and again when it is received by the stockholder.

The Stock Market

The outstanding feature of the corporate form of business is that corporations obtain funds by selling securities that convey ownership rights to the buyers of the securities. These securities are called **shares**, or **stock**, in the corporation. Those who purchase shares or stock obtain, among other things, specified rights to vote on certain matters of corporate policy and in elections for the corporation's board of directors, which is the overall policy-making body. Stockholders also have specified rights to receive **dividends**, which are distributions of money (or additional stock) from the corporation. However, stockholders do not necessarily receive dividends equal to all the profits of the corporation in any particular period of time. The corporation's board of directors decides how much of the profit will be paid out as dividends and how much retained to finance future corporate operations.

Stockholders obtain specified rights to vote on matters of corporate policy and in elections for the corporation's board of directors; they also may receive dividends.

One of the reasons why corporations are able to obtain huge amounts of money to finance their operations is that stockholders can sell some or all of their stock whenever they want to reduce or terminate their association with the corporation. Most buying and selling of shares or stock in corporations is carried out in a stock exchange, where those who want to sell stock carry out transactions with those who want to buy it. There are stock exchanges in major cities all over the world and they are linked by a very effective communication network. Only those individuals or firms that are members of a stock exchange— that is, who own a "seat" on the exchange—are allowed to do business on the "floor" of the exchange. Therefore, a person who wants to buy or sell stock usually works through a **stockbroker**, who can have the transaction carried out on behalf of the buyer or seller. The broker, or brokerage firm, either owns a seat on an exchange or works through someone who does own one. The broker has the transaction carried out on a stock exchange and charges a fee, or **commission**, for the service. Stock exchange memberships are limited in number and are themselves bought and sold.

A person who wants to buy or sell stock in a stock exchange usually works through a stockbroker, who earns a commission for his or her service.

Figure 7 reproduces a portion of a newspaper report of stock market transactions on Tuesday, March 7, 1989.[2] To learn how to read the stock exchange report, look at the line reporting that day's transactions in the common stock of American Express (abbreviated AmExpress and with the symbol of AXP). The numbers in the first two columns report the highest and lowest prices per share paid for this stock over the past 52 weeks; in this example, the highest price was $31.875 a share (31⅞) and the lowest price was $22.875 a share (22⅞). The first number following the symbol of the stock shows that the annual amount of dividend paid per share is 84¢, which is a yield of 2.8 percent (shown in the next column) on its current price. The next number, which is 13, shows the price/earnings (P-E) ratio. This means that the current price of the stock is 13 times the amount of the annual profits per share of the corporation. The last five numbers report this particular day's transactions for this stock. On that day, 16,722 "blocks" (of 100 shares each) were traded. The highest-priced block traded at $30.75 per share (30¾), the lowest-priced block at $30.00 per share (30), and the last block sold that day went at $30.375 per share (30⅜). The price in this "closing" transaction was the same as the price of the closing transaction on the preceding business day.

As you can see, a huge amount of information is contained in the stock exchange reports. Investors and brokerage firms study this information carefully in deciding whether and what to buy or sell. Since stock market prices reflect expectations about future profitability, they provide useful information for guiding resources among alternative uses in capitalist-market economies.

Business Accounting

Keeping records is extremely important in business operations. Thus it is not surprising that some of the earliest known writing and calculating techniques were developed to keep business records. Information provided through business records can improve management's ability to make wise decisions. It also helps others, such as stockholders, banks, and investors, to judge the profitability of the business. Economists study these records to

2. *The Wall Street Journal,* March 8, 1989, p. C3.

FIGURE 7
Newspaper Report of Stock Exchange Transactions

NEW YORK STOCK EXCHANGE COMPOSITE TRANSACTIONS

WEDNESDAY, MARCH 8, 1989

Quotations as of 4:30 p.m. Eastern Time
Tuesday, March 7, 1989

	52 Weeks Hi	52 Weeks Lo	Stock	Sym	Div	Yld %	PE	Vol 100s	Hi	Lo	Close	Net Chg
	38¼	28	AlbertoCl	ACV	.36	1.0	18	78	35⅝	35⅛	35⅛	− ½
	29¾	21	AlbertoCl A	ACVA	.36	1.3	15	236	28¼	28¼	28¼	− ¼
	43	28	Albertsons	ABS	.80	2.0	18	1657	41¾	40¾	41	− ½
s	36⅛	26¼	Alcan	AL	1.68	5.3	6	7512	32½	32	32	− ⅜
	28	22	AlcoStd	ASN	.76	2.9	11	769	26¼	25¾	26	...
	28⅛	21¼	Alex&Alex	AAL	1.00	4.1	14	581	24⅜	24⅛	24⅛	...
	77	49¾	Alexanders	ALX		...	88	8	63½	63¼	63¼	− ⅜
	85½	69⅛	AlleghanyCp	Y		...	11	18	82½	82	82⅜	+1
	4½	**1¼**	**vjAllegInt**	**AG**		...	...	**122**	**1⅝**	**1½**	**1⅝**	**+ ⅛**
	27⅛	7½	vjAllegInt pf			...	...	2	12⅜	12⅜	12⅜	− ¼
↑	38	21⅝	AllegLud	ALS	1.00a	2.6	8	558	38½	37¾	38½	+ ⅝
x	40⅜	35⅞	AllegPwr	AYP	3.08	8.4	9	x692	36⅞	36⅝	36⅞	+ ¼
	15¾	9¼	AllenGp	ALN		...	77	88	15½	15	15⅜	+ ⅜
	18⅞	13	AllenGp pf		1.75	9.6	...	41	18⅜	18⅛	18¼	+ ⅛
n	12½	9⅝	AllncCapMgt	AC	1.33	11.0	24	103	12¼	12	12⅛	− ⅛
	21	13¾	AlliedPdts	ADP		...	...	18	16¾	16½	16¾	+ ⅛
	36⅞	30¾	AlliedSgnl	ALD	1.80	5.3	11	1924	34⅜	34	34	− ¼
	10¾	9⅝	AllstMuniTr	ALM	.78a	7.5	...	199	10⅜	10¼	10⅜	+ ⅛
n	10	9⅜	AllstMunPrem	ALI	.04e	.4	...	133	9⅝	9½	9½	− ⅛
n	10¼	9¼	AllstMunInll	ALT	.50e	5.1	...	418	9⅞	9¾	9¾	...
n	10½	9⅞	AllstMunInTr	AMO	.24e	2.4	...	284	10⅛	10	10	...
↑	41	29⅞	ALLTEL	AT	1.72	4.3	14	2312	41¾	39⅜	40	+ ⅝
	65⅝	41½	Alcoa	AA	1.60a	2.6	6	5046	61¼	60⅝	61⅛	+ ¼
	15¼	10	AmcastInd	AIZ	.48	4.0	9	83	11⅞	11¾	11⅞	...
	14⅝	7½	Amdura	ADU		...	22	797	14½	13⅞	14¼	+ ¼
	25¼	19½	Amdura pf		1.95	7.7	...	262	25¼	25	25¼	+ ¼
↑x	36	25¾	AmerHess	AHC	.60	1.7	24	x9669	36⅜	36	36	+ ¼
	23	14¾	AmBarrick	ABX	.10e	.4	...	1716	22⅞	22⅜	22⅜	− ¼
	71¾	42¼	AmBrand	AMB	2.44	3.8	11	3817	65½	63⅞	64½	+ ¼
	30⅝	26⅝	AmBrand pf		2.75	10.1	...	27	27⅛	26⅞	27⅛	+ ⅜
	134½	85½	AmBrand pf		2.67	2.0	...	3	131	129½	131	+2½
	29⅞	20⅝	AmBldgMaint	ABM	.92	3.2	16	12	29⅛	29	29	− ⅛
	29	23¼	AmBusnPdts	ABP	.96	3.3	13	22	28¾	28⅜	28¾	+ ⅜
↓	22¼	19¾	AmCapBdFd	ACB	2.20e	11.1	...	96	19⅞	19⅝	19¾	...
	24⅝	19¼	AmCapCvSec	ACS	3.03e	14.2	...	21	21¾	21⅜	21⅜	− ⅛
n	10⅛	8⅞	AmCapIncTr	ACD	1.10a	12.1	...	121	9¼	9	9⅛	...
	14	8¼	AmCapMgt	ACA	1.00	9.2	11	23	10⅞	10¾	10⅞	...
	55⅛	44	AmCyanmd	ACY	1.20	2.4	14	3574	49⅝	49	49¼	− ⅝
	29¼	25⅞	AmElecPwr	AEP	2.32a	8.7	8	1537	26⅝	26⅜	26⅝	− ⅛
	31⅞	22⅞	AmExpress	AXP	.84	2.8	13	16722	30¾	30	30⅜	...
	17	11½	AmFamily	AFL	.28	1.8	12	1215	16	15¾	15¾	...
	36⅞	27⅜	AmGenerl	AGC	1.50	4.4	10	2059	34	33½	33¾	− ½
n	8½	7½	AmGvIncFd	AGF	.84a	10.8	...	146	7¾	7½	7¾	...
n	10⅛	9⅛	AmGvIncoP	AAF	1.06a	11.6	...	111	9⅜	9⅛	9⅛	− ¼
	19½	17	AmHlthProp	AHE	2.16	11.4	12	261	19⅛	19	19	...
x	27	24¼	AmHeritgLf	AHL	1.08	4.1	11	x1	26½	26½	26½	+ ⅛
	88¾	70⅜	AmHomePdts	AHP	3.90	4.6	13	1278	86	85¼	85⅝	− ⅛
s	52¾	42¼	Ameritech	AIT	2.92	5.7	11	2520	51⅞	51¼	51¼	− ¾
↑	75½	49	AmIntGroup	AIG	.40	.5	10	3803	75⅞	75	75⅛	+ ⅛
	18¾	13⅞	AMI	AMI	.72	3.9	19	2854	18¾	18½	18½	...
	36¾	26¼	AmPresidnt	APS	.50	1.4	10	178	35⅝	35	35⅝	+ ⅜
	62⅜	53½	AmPresidnt pf		3.50	5.9	...	6	59½	59½	59½	+ ½
	16⅞	14¾	AmRE Ptnrs	ACP	2.00	12.8	8	80	15⅞	15⅝	15⅝	...
	5⅛	3⅞	AmRltyTr	ARB	.72	16.9	3	403	4⅜	4¼	4¼	− ⅛
	18⅝	11¾	AmSvgBk	ASB	.80	4.8	4	242	16⅞	16¾	16¾	...

	52 Weeks Hi	52 Weeks Lo	Stock	Sym	Div	Yld %	PE	Vol 100s	Hi	Lo	Close	Net Chg
s	20⅛	9⅝	BannerInd	BNR		...	13	167	19⅞	19⅝	19⅝	+ ⅛
x	33⅜	21	Barclays	BCS	1.85e	6.0	16	x125	30⅞	30¾	30¾	+ ¾
s	24⅝	18⅛	Bard CR	BCR	.32	1.5	15	2074	21½	20¾	21	− ½
	37¼	32⅛	BarnesGp	B	1.40	4.1	11	15	34¼	34	34	...
	37⅜	29⅛	BarnettBks	BBI	1.04	3.2	9	606	33⅜	32½	32⅞	− ⅜
n	6½	4⅜	BaroidCp	BRC	.05e	.8	38	2202	6⅜	6⅛	6⅜	+ ¼
	9	4¼	BarryWrgt	BAR		...	34	83	4¾	4⅝	4¾	+ ⅛
	1¼	⅛	vjBasix	BAS		...	...	4	13/32	13/32	13/32	...
	19⅛	13⅛	BattleMtn	BMG	.10	.6	17	1706	15⅝	15¼	15⅝	+ ⅜
x	48	39⅞	BauschLomb	BOL	1.16	2.5	14	x864	46⅜	45⅛	46¼	+ ⅝
	26⅛	16¼	BaxterInt	BAX	.56	2.8	15	18564	20⅛	19⅜	20	+ ½
	47¾	37⅛	BaxterInt pf		3.65e	9.2	...	58	39⅞	39¾	39⅞	...
	83	56¾	BaxterInt pf		3.50	5.3	...	225	66	64¾	66	+1⅜
	19¾	9⅞	BayFnl	BAY		...	...	100	10⅜	10¼	10⅜	− ⅛
	27	21	BayStGas	BGC	1.68	6.3	10	29	26⅞	26½	26⅝	− ⅛
	15½	11⅛	BearStearns	BSC	.56	3.7	10	3634	15¼	15	15¼	+ ⅛
	41⅞	30⅝	BearingsInc	BER	.80a	2.1	12	65	38⅜	38	38⅛	+ ⅛
	15⅜	10¾	Beazer	BZR	.52e	3.4	9	3	15⅛	15⅛	15⅛	+ ¼
n	19½	17⅛	BeckmanInstr	BEC	.07e	.4	13	12	18⅞	18⅞	18⅞	+ ⅛
	62⅛	46½	BectonDksn	BDX	1.00	1.9	13	953	52⅞	52	52	− ⅞
	40	24	BeldenHem	BHY	.52	1.9	11	52	27¼	26⅞	27¼	+ ⅜
	75¾	64⅛	BellAtlantic	BEL	4.08	5.5	11	3224	74½	73¼	74⅛	+ ¼
	16⅛	13½	BellIndus	BI	.28	1.8	15	3	15⅜	15⅜	15⅜	...
	53¾	41⅝	Beneficial	BNL	2.20	4.9	11	523	44¾	44⅜	44½	− ⅜
	26½	23¼	Beneficial pf		2.50	10.0	...	z30	25	25	25	− ⅜
	4⅝	3⅛	Benguet B	BE	.19r	4.8	6	125	4	3⅞	4	+ ⅛
↓	4¼	11/64	vjBerkey	BKY		...	...	210	11/64	5/32	11/64	...
	5050	3075	BerkHathwy	BRK		...	17	z10	4825	4825	4825	+25
	15⅜	6⅞	BestBuy	BBY		...	21	60	10⅛	9⅞	9⅞	− ⅛
	28½	18	BethSteel	BS		...	5	2085	25⅞	25½	25⅝	− ¼
	56¼	46¼	BethSteel pf		5.00	9.5	...	106	52⅞	52¾	52⅞	− ⅜
	27⅝	22½	BethSteel pf		2.50	9.6	...	106	26	25⅞	26	− ⅛
	9¼	3¾	BeverlyEnt	BEV		...	...	3839	9	8⅝	9	+ ¼
	20¼	9¾	BeverlyInv	BIP	1.79e	14.2	10	99	12⅞	12½	12⅝	...
	21⅜	7½	BiocraftLabs	BCL		...	18	69	10⅛	9⅞	9⅞	− ¼
s	29⅞	16⅝	BirmghamStl	BIR	.50	1.9	8	126	27	26⅜	26⅜	− ½
	25¼	17⅛	BlackDeck	BDK	.40	1.7	13	911	23⅞	23½	23¾	+ ⅛
	28¼	24½	BlackHills	BKH	1.52	5.8	11	51	26½	26⅜	26⅜	...
n	10⅛	9⅛	BlackstnIncTr	BKT	1.10	12.1	...	733	9¼	9⅛	9⅛	− ⅛
n	10⅛	9⅜	BlackstnTgt	BTT	1.00	10.3	...	1369	9¾	9⅝	9¾	...
x	33	22¾	BlockHR	HRB	1.04	3.7	16	x1425	28⅜	27⅝	28	+ ⅜
n	22¾	14⅝	BlueArrow	BAW	.39e	2.5	...	1259	16⅛	15⅞	15⅞	− ¼
	6⅝	5½	BlueChipFd	BLU	.34e	5.3	...	135	6½	6¼	6⅜	− ⅛
	67⅝	44½	Boeing	BA	1.60	2.4	16	5323	65¾	65	65⅜	...
	50	39¼	BoiseCasc	BCC	1.40	3.3	7	2767	42⅛	41¾	42	+ ¼
	19⅜	9	BoltBerNew	BBN	.06	.6	31	142	9⅞	9¾	9¾	...
n	11¾	6¾	BondIntGold	BIG		...	...	594	7⅜	7¼	7¼	...
	4⅛	**1⅛**	**BondIntGold wt**			...	...	**12**	**1½**	**1½**	**1½**	**+ ⅛**
	23½	13⅛	BordChm un	BCP	3.02e	13.1	7	1462	23	22¾	23	...
n	23	17	BordChm	BCU	3.02e	13.4	7	814	22⅝	22⅜	22½	− ⅛
	61⅛	48⅜	BordenInc	BN	1.56	2.7	14	1060	58	57¼	57⅜	−1
	15¾	12¼	BostCelts	BOS	1.60e	11.3	8	22	14¼	14	14⅛	...
	17¼	12½	BostEdsn	BSE	1.82	11.4	10	337	16⅛	15⅞	16	...
	91¼	82	BostEdsn pf		8.88	10.6	...	z1090	84	84	84	+1
	36⅞	25¼	Bowater	BOW	1.12	4.1	6	2590	27½	27¼	27⅜	+ ⅛

Source: *The Wall Street Journal*, March 8, 1989, p. C3. Reprinted by permission of *The Wall Street Journal*,

TABLE 1
Precision Printing Company, Balance Sheet, December 31, 1990

Assets		Liabilities	
Current Assets		**Current Liabilities**	
Cash	$ 30,000	Accounts Payable	$ 40,000
Inventory	210,000	Notes Payable	70,000
Fixed Assets		**Long-Term Liabilities**	
Equipment	420,000	Bonds	380,000
Buildings	160,000	Total Liabilities	$490,000
		Net Worth	
		Preferred Stock	$ 30,000
		Common Stock	220,000
		Retained Earnings	80,000
		Total Net Worth	$330,000
		Total Liabilities and	
Total Assets	$820,000	Net Worth	$820,000

discover trends and changes in the economy. The two basic financial statements of a firm are the balance sheet and the income statement.

The Balance Sheet   The **balance sheet** is an accountant's report on the condition of a business firm as of the close of business on a particular date. It is like a snapshot or still photograph that shows the firm's financial condition at some instant in time. The balance sheet has three elements, called assets, liabilities, and net worth (or owners' equity). **Assets** represent all the things that the firm owns. **Liabilities** are the claims that outsiders have for payments from the firm. The amount that is left over for the owners of the firm is called **net worth**. These three elements make up the balance-sheet equation:

$$\text{assets} = \text{liabilities} + \text{net worth}$$

Accountants make the best estimates they can of the actual values for assets and liabilities. Then, to satisfy the balance-sheet equation, the net worth of the business (the value that belongs to the owners) must be adjusted upward or downward until the equality is established. But first the accountant will need to evaluate both assets and liabilities as objectively as possible. Because legitimate accounting must stick to the facts in evaluating assets and liabilities, the value of the owners' equity (net worth) is the only item that can be adjusted to achieve the necessary balance.

The balance sheet shows assets (all the things the firm owns), liabilities (all the claims outsiders have for payments from the firm), and net worth (the amount left over for the owners of the firm) as of the close of business on a particular date.

A hypothetical balance sheet is illustrated in Table 1. Assets are listed on the left side of the account, and liabilities and net worth are listed on the right side. The total on one side must equal the total on the other side; that is, the balance sheet must "balance." Though the specific items that will be listed on a balance sheet depend on the nature of the business itself, there are some general rules or guidelines that accountants follow in presenting balance sheets. On the asset side, items are listed according to how quickly they can be converted into cash. In the illustrated balance sheet, cash itself comes first, of course, followed by inventory (goods on hand), equipment, and buildings. The assets that ordinarily would be converted to cash in the course of a normal year's business are called current assets. Items that would not be converted to cash during a normal year's operation are called fixed, or long-term, assets. The order of the liabilities (on the right side of the balance sheet) follows a similar pattern. Current liabilities are obligations that normally are payable during a year's business operations. Long-term liabilities are obligations that will be payable at some more distant time.

On the asset side of the balance sheet, items are listed according to how quickly they can be converted into cash. Items that would not be converted to cash in the course of a normal year's business are called fixed assets.

Current liabilities are obligations that normally are payable during a year's business operations. Long-term liabilities are obligations that will be payable at some more distant time.

Of special interest to the owners or potential owners of a company, of course, is the net worth section of the balance sheet. The entries in this section will vary depending on whether the firm is organized as a proprietorship, a partnership, or a corporation. The net worth section for a partnership will show the ownership interests of the different partners, and the net worth section for a corporation will show the interests of the various classes of stockholders. Also, a distinction is usually made between amounts paid in by owners and amounts of earnings that have been retained by the firm.

The Income Statement   The **income statement,** or **profit and loss statement,** is an accountant's report of the operations of a business firm over some specified period of time. In a sense, it is like a movie, or part of one, because it reports the firm's activities over a finite period. It is different from the balance sheet, which, as we said, is like a still picture or snapshot and describes the condition of the firm at some fixed point in time.

The income (profit and loss) statement is an accountant's report of the operations of a business firm over some specified period of time.

Table 2 illustrates a hypothetical income statement. There is no balancing feature in this statement. Instead, it starts at the top with a report of the net amount of money received from sales during the time period. Then it shows how various items are subtracted from these receipts. At the bottom is the amount left over or remaining with the business. The specific items that appear on the income statement will differ greatly among firms, but certain general categories appear in almost all statements. For example, businesses usually want to separate manufacturing costs, selling and administrative costs, interest costs, and taxes. Cost-accounting and tax-accounting techniques are used to determine these various amounts. After costs and taxes have been subtracted, the statement shows the amount of income left. This is the amount available to be paid to the owners (as dividends in the corporate form of business) or to be retained for use by the company. The income statement will report the disposition that was made of these earnings.

Balance sheets and income statements can be fitted together to give a full and continuous account of the financial life of a firm. Balance sheets report the condition of a business firm at specific points in time, and income statements report its operations over periods of time. The difference between the balance sheet picture on one date and the balance sheet picture on another date is "explained" by the income statements that cover the period of time between the balance sheets.

Balance sheets report the condition of a business firm at specific points in time, and income statements report its operation over periods of time. Income statements and balance sheets can be fitted together to give a full and continuous account of the financial life of a firm.

GOVERNMENTS

Government is the third actor on the economic stage. The economic role of government depends a great deal upon the type of economic system in a

TABLE 2
Income Statement for Precision Printing Company
for the Year Ended December 31, 1990

Net Sales		$380,000
Manufacturing Cost		
Materials	$ 40,000	
Labor	90,000	
Depreciation	75,000	
Subtotal		$205,000
Plus Beginning Inventory	$245,000	
Less Closing Inventory	−210,000	
Subtotal		35,000
Total Manufacturing Cost		240,000
Gross Profit from Sales		$140,000
Selling and Administrative Costs		40,000
Fixed Interest Charges and State and Local Taxes		15,000
Net Income Before Income Taxes		$ 85,000
Corporation Income Taxes		35,000
Net Income After Taxes		$ 50,000
Dividends Paid on Preferred Stock		2,000
Net Income After Preferred Stock Dividends		$ 48,000
Dividends Paid on Common Stock		26,000
Addition to Retained Earnings		$ 22,000

country. For example, you learned in Chapter 1 that socialist governments own many natural and capital resources and may develop detailed plans for the economy. On the other hand, government typically plays a much smaller role in capitalist-market economies. In this chapter, we shall limit our discussion to the main functions of government in capitalist-market economies. In these economic systems, there are three basic economic responsibilities or functions of government—the allocation function, the distribution function, and the stabilization function.

The Allocation Function

The **allocation function** refers to the allocation of resources among alternative uses. Specifically, the allocation responsibility of government is to take appropriate corrective action in circumstances where private markets fail to provide the combination of goods and services desired by the people. Such **market failures** occur when the markets, left to themselves, produce too much of certain goods and services and not enough of others. In other words, without government action, resources would be misallocated.

The allocation responsibility of government is to take appropriate corrective action in circumstances where private markets fail to provide the combination of goods and services desired by the people.

There are several reasons why markets may give wrong answers to the "what to produce" question and thus misallocate resources. One is that monopolistic firms (*inadequate competition*) may restrict output, thereby causing the prices of their products to rise and distorting the choices available to consumers. A second source of allocational market failure lies with **externalities,** which arise when the production or consumption of a good or service affects people who have no way, through the markets, to influence the decision about how much of the good or service should be produced. Pollution is a common example of a harmful ("negative") externality. Smoke in the air can damage the lungs of people who have no way, through markets, to cause factories to install filters on their smokestacks. In this case, there may be overproduction of the good manufactured in the smoke-producing factory. Beneficial ("positive") externalities also can arise, as when people other than parents, students, and teachers benefit from the education of children in the community. In this situation, the market system might provide too small a quantity of education service.

Third, markets typically fail to provide efficient quantities of **collective goods**. Collective goods are those which, by their nature, must be consumed in common by all the people in an area, that is, all must consume the same quality and quantity of the good or service. Examples of collective goods include national defense, police, and judicial services.

Collective goods are those which, by their nature, must be consumed in common by all the people in an area.

The Distribution Function

Under the **distribution function**, government has the responsibility to adjust the distribution of income among individuals. This responsibility relates directly to the "for whom" decision that must be made in every economic system. The distribution responsibility arises because the normal operation of the market system results in some amount of inequality in the distribution of income among individuals. If the markets fail to generate the degree of inequality that is considered desirable, the government may redistribute incomes to achieve a better distribution.

Government has the responsibility to adjust the distribution of income among individuals to achieve an appropriate degree of equality.

There are many causes of inequality in a market-capitalist system. If the system is operating effectively, people who have great talent, are skillful, work hard, and are lucky will be rewarded with high incomes. Others can gain income if they have rich parents or obtain monopoly power. But the market system generates very little income for people who lack these advantages. Therefore, market-capitalist (as well as most collectivist-planned) economic systems are likely to generate more inequality than the people, speaking through the political system, say ought to exist. Of course, people do not agree on exactly what is a "fair" or "just" or "equitable" distribution of income, and there is no scientific way to prove that one distribution is necessarily better than another. Nevertheless, voters do let their governments know what kind of distribution they want. Their instructions may be vague, since they are filtered through political candidates who may campaign on confusing and complicated sets of promises. They may often be self-serving too, since most people apparently feel that fairness means more income for themselves. But the fact is that citizens do expect their government to take steps to ensure that the distribution of income is not unreasonable. Government programs aimed, in part at least, at income redistribution include progressive income taxes, welfare programs, and a complicated set of taxes and subsidies for particular goods and services that are intended to improve the income position of certain groups. Minimum wage laws and farm subsidies illustrate this last redistributive approach.

One aspect of income distribution must be emphasized now, before you go further in your study of economics. The demand curves that you will study in this book reflect both the willingness and the ability of people to purchase products. The ability to purchase goods and services reflects the income distribution. How much caviar and how much corn flakes we produce depends in part on the distribution of income. Demand-and-supply analysis will work equally well under any income distribution, but whether the choice of goods and services that comes out of the market process fits what you believe is right depends in part on whether you approve of the income distribution influencing demand throughout the economy.

The Stabilization Function

The **stabilization function**, or responsibility, of government is to achieve price stability, a high level of employment, and a reasonable rate of economic growth for the economy. It is a function that focuses heavily on macroeconomics, although microeconomic instruments also are involved. The stabilization responsibility arises because the market system of economic organization has a record of business cycles, or fluctuations, bringing unemployment, inflation, or both. Before the 1930s, most economists (Karl Marx and his followers excepted) believed that fluctuations in the capitalist system were fairly minor and self-correcting so that there was no need for government to step in. But the experience of the Great Depression and the economic theories of the famous British economist John Maynard Keynes (1883–1946) brought a great change in economic thought about this aspect of government activity. Since Keynes, macroeconomics has been important in influencing government policy.

You probably have heard about the major instruments of government stabilization policy, since they often make headlines in newspapers and television news reports. For example, government may try to control the size of the nation's money supply in the belief that the amount of money in the economy has a lot to do with inflation or other changes in the price level. Similarly, a lot of attention is paid to whether or not the government's budget is balanced because deficits are thought to stimulate the economy, whereas surpluses are thought to slow down economic activity.

THE REST OF THE WORLD

The fourth actor on the economic stage for any particular economy is "the rest of the world"—that is, the exporting, importing, and financial transactions that take place with households, business firms, and governments in other countries. In 1988, U.S. business firms sold $536.1 billion of goods and services to foreigners, which amounted to 10.9 percent of the total production in the U.S. economy. In that same year, Americans bought $616 billion of goods and services from foreigners, so that the United States had a trade deficit of some $79.9 billion.[3] Clearly, these transactions are important in the operation of the U.S. economy. Many American workers have jobs producing goods for export, and American consumers enjoy the products that they buy from foreigners. But other American workers feel that their jobs are threatened by foreign competitors.

Figure 8 shows that the dollar value of U.S. exports as a percent of gross national product (the value of total production) has increased substantially since World War II. This means that "the rest of the world" is much more important to the U.S. economy today than it was in earlier times. Important as "the rest of the world" is for the United States, it is much more important for many other countries in the world. A country that allows relatively unrestricted trade across its borders is called an **open economy**; if such an economy is small, it is likely that transactions with foreigners will be extremely important. On the other hand, large countries that have a great variety of resources have to depend less on obtaining goods from foreigners, and for them "the rest of the world" is less important. Of course, **closed economies**, which severely restrict trade across their borders, are more insulated from outside forces. China and the Soviet

3. *Economic Report of the President, 1989*, Table B-1. The import and export numbers that we reported as 1988 are actually third quarter of 1988 data that have been seasonally adjusted and annualized.

FIGURE 8
U.S. Exports as a Percentage of Gross National Product for Selected Years

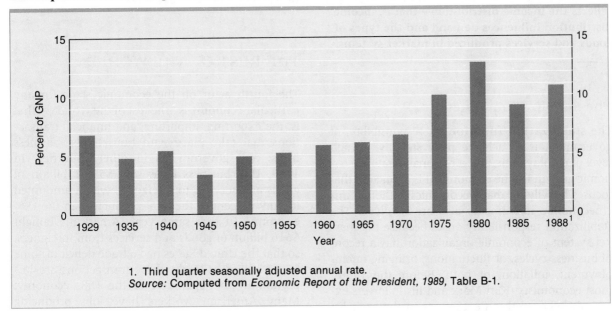

1. Third quarter seasonally adjusted annual rate.
Source: Computed from *Economic Report of the President, 1989,* Table B-1.

Union are relatively closed economies, although China is becoming more and more involved in international transactions.

The dollar value of U.S. exports as a percent of gross national product has increased substantially since World War II.

The importing, exporting, and financial transactions that take place with households, business firms, and governments in other countries are much more important to the U.S. economy today than in earlier times.

A country that allows relatively unrestricted trade across its borders is called an open economy. Closed economies severely restrict trade across their borders.

Exports and imports are not the only reasons why "the rest of the world" is an important actor on a country's economic stage. Money also flows from country to country in search of the best returns in interest on bonds and bank accounts or dividends from corporate stocks. These financial, or "capital account," transactions have important effects on economic conditions in the countries involved, since they influence economic growth by affecting the funds available to finance new capital goods. Business firms, governments, the United Nations, and major banking houses are active in international lending and finance.

THE ACTORS IN ACTION

The economic actors that you have met in this chapter—households, business firms, governments, and "the rest of the world"—will appear again and again in your study of economics. In microeconomics, you will learn about decision-making criteria and processes and how the actors interact with each other. In macroeconomics, you will find that the four actors provide the organizing scheme for the model of how the macroeconomy works and how the national income accounting system keeps track of total income and production in the economy.

Economics in Focus

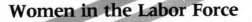

Women in the Labor Force

The change has been so rapid and fundamental that economists have called it a revolution in the U.S. labor force. A generation ago the "typical" American woman, with or without children, was not employed outside the household. By the late 1980s, however, well over 50 percent of all American women worked outside the home; in the key age group of 25 to 44, the labor-force participation rate was over 70 percent.

Not only do more women have jobs, but they work longer hours, and motherhood is not as much of a deterrent as it used to be. Sixty percent of school-age children have mothers in the labor force, compared to 39 percent in 1970. Moreover, the fastest-growing segment of the labor force consists of women with children under six years old.

The revolution is expected to continue. Now that the baby-boom generation has begun to reach middle age, the pool of young workers is shrinking. As companies cast their nets ever wider to find qualified new employees, the proportion of jobs held by women will continue rising, so that by the year 2000 the total number of working women will nearly equal the number of working men.

This revolution has had—and will continue to have—profound social and economic consequences. Day care, for example, has become a burning issue. Some women are dissuaded from working because of a lack of acceptable day care for their children; others lose valuable productivity when they have to deal with such problems as the babysitter quitting or Johnny catching the flu. Although both the federal and state governments are getting involved, businesses themselves will provide part of the solution. More and more, large companies are realizing that one way to attract and keep women workers is to offer help with day care. As late as 1988 only about 300 corporations sponsored their own day-care facilities, but the number should grow rapidly as companies compete for female employees. Flexible schedules, family leaves, alternative work styles—these are other corporate accommodations that allow women to balance the demands of home and work.

Overall, the feminization of the work force has proceeded smoothly—perhaps surprisingly so for a "revolution." But many sensitive issues remain to be dealt with in the 1990s and beyond. Should companies have a "mommy track," and is this an aid for female employees or a new form of discrimination? Is sexual harassment on the job increasing, and are companies doing enough to prevent it? Should special executive-training or mentoring programs be established to offer women a better chance of advancement?

Sources: Sharon Nelton, "Meet Your New Work Force," *Nation's Business,* July 1988, pp. 14–21; Thomas W. Merrick and Stephen J. Tordella, "Demographics: People and Markets," *Population Bulletin,* vol. 43 (February 1988), pp. 17–19; Elizabeth Ehrlich with Susan B. Garland, "For American Business, a New World of Workers," *Business Week,* September 19, 1988, pp. 112–120; Susan E. Shank, "Women and the Labor Market: The Link Grows Stronger," *Monthly Labor Review,* March 1988, pp. 3–8; Elizabeth Ehrlich, "Is the Mommy Track a Blessing—or a Betrayal?" *Business Week,* May 15, 1989, pp. 98–99; Gretchen Morgenson, "Watch That Leer, Stifle That Joke," *Forbes,* May 15, 1989, pp. 69–72.

SUMMARY

1. To understand how economic systems operate, economists consider four actors on the economic stage—households, business firms, governments, and "the rest of the world." (See pages 19–21.)

2. Households are made up of individuals, who, in capitalist economic systems, are the owners of resources. As the owners of resources in capitalist systems, individuals are the ultimate recipients of the income generated by production. (See page 20.)

3. Household members also are the ultimate consumers of the goods and services produced in an economy. When individuals spend the income earned as owners of resources, that is, when they function in their role as consumers, they are helping to make the "what to produce" decision. (See page 20.)

4. Business firms are the decision-making units concerned with production. They purchase resources and resource services from households and combine them to produce goods and services. Thus, their role is to make the "how to produce" decisions in the economy. (See page 26.)

5. Proprietorships, partnerships, and corporations are the three major kinds of business organizations. Corporations have become large and powerful because their charters grant limited liability and unlimited life, which allow them to accumulate large quantities of money and technical expertise. (See pages 27–29.)

6. Corporations obtain funds by selling shares, or stock, which convey to the buyer certain ownership rights in the corporation. The shareholders may receive dividends and normally may vote in electing the board of directors and in deciding corporate policy. (See page 28.)

7. The sale and purchase of corporate stock usually is carried out in stock exchanges located in major cities. An individual wishing to buy or sell stock works through a stockbroker, who carries out the transaction and charges a commission for the service. Reports of stock exchange transactions are published regularly in major newspapers. (See pages 28–29 and Figure 7, page 30.)

8. Balance sheets and income statements are accounting reports about the condition and the operation, respectively, of firms. Together these two reports give a continuing record of a company's financial life. (See pages 31–32.)

9. Most economists recognize three basic responsibilities, or "functions," of government in capitalist-market economic systems—the allocation function, the distribution function, and the stabilization function. In its allocation function, government is viewed as correcting for market failures in deciding "what to produce." In its distribution function, government is expected to promote a desirable distribution of income among individuals. The stabilization function involves moderating business cycles while maintaining high-level employment and stability in the general price level. (See pages 32–35.)

10. Households, business firms, and governments in "the rest of the world" make up the fourth actor on the economic stage of any given country. This actor has become increasingly important for the U.S. economy. (See pages 35–36.)

KEY TERMS

allocation function: the responsibility of government to take appropriate corrective action in circumstances where private markets fail to provide the combination of goods and services desired by the people (page 33).

assets: the value of all the things a business firm owns (page 31).

balance sheet: an accountant's report on the condition of a business firm as of the close of business on a particular date (page 31).

civilian labor force participation rate: the percentage of the civilian noninstitutional population, age sixteen or older, that is either working or looking for work (page 24).

closed economy: a country that severely restricts trade across its borders (page 35).

collective goods: goods that must be consumed in common by all the people in an area (page 34).

commission: the fee earned by a stockbroker for carrying out a transaction for a buyer or seller on a stock exchange (page 29).

corporation: a business firm that is granted "legal person" status by government charter; it has limited liability, unlimited life, and the ability to issue and sell shares of stock (page 27).

distribution function: the responsibility of government to adjust the distribution of income among individuals (page 34).

dividends: distributions of money (or additional stock) from a corporation to its owners (page 29).

externalities: a source of allocational market failure that arises when the production or consumption of a good or service affects people who have no way, through markets, to influence decisions about how much of the good or service should be produced (page 33).

household: a family group (or one or more persons) living together in the same dwelling unit (page 20).

income (profit and loss) statement: an accountant's report of the operations of a business firm over some specified period of time (page 32).

liabilities: the claims that outsiders have for payments from a business firm (page 31).

limited liability: a feature of corporations whereby stockholders are not responsible for the corporation's debts (page 28).

limited life: a characteristic of proprietorships and partnerships; a proprietorship lasts only as long as the proprietor is in business, and a partnership lasts only as long as the partnership agreement is in force (page 27).

market failure: when markets, left to themselves, produce too much of certain goods and services and not enough of others (page 33).

national income: the total of all earnings generated in an economy (page 24).

net worth: the amount that is left over for the owners of a business firm after total liabilities have been subtracted from total assets (page 31).

open economy: a country that allows relatively unrestricted trade across its borders (page 35).

partnership: a business that is formed when two or more people agree to share the financial and managerial responsibilities of a firm as well as its profits and losses (page 27).

profit and loss statement: *see* **income statement.**

proprietorship: a business owned by one person (page 27).

shares (stock): securities sold by a corporation that convey ownership rights to the buyers (page 28).

stabilization function: the responsibility of government to achieve price stability, a high level of employment, and a reasonable rate of economic growth for the economy (page 35).

stock: *see* **shares.**

stockbroker: a person who buys or sells stock on a stock exchange on behalf of another (page 29).

unlimited liability: a characteristic of proprietorships and partnerships whereby the proprietor or each partner must accept complete responsibility for all the debts of the business (page 27).

unlimited life: a characteristic of a corporation whereby the corporation does not have to be reorganized every time individual persons enter or leave the ownership or management of the firm (page 28).

DISCUSSION QUESTIONS

1. It is often observed that, in political action dealing with legislation, consumer-interest lobbies are unable to prevail against lobbies promoting the interests of producers and resource owners. But each individual involved is a consumer as well as an owner of resources. Why, in your opinion, do people tend to place their interests as resource owners ahead of their interests as consumers?

2. The population ripple is one of the causes of problems in financing the Social Security retirement program. In view of these population changes, some experts estimate that Social Security taxes as high as 25 percent may be necessary to support the large retired population. You may be asked to pay this tax to help those ten or fifteen years older than yourself. Will you vote for such a tax on your paycheck? What effects might such a tax have on the economy?

3. Adding together the percentages in Figure 2 for compensation of employees and proprietors' income yields a sum that is fairly constant over a forty-five-year period. But compensation has increased significantly while proprietors' income has decreased as a percentage of national income. What trends in the society might, in your opinion, tend to produce this result?

4. Although the distribution of income receives a great deal of attention in the media and in government debate, many economists believe that the distribution of wealth is equally (or perhaps more) important. Describe a set of circumstances in which a person would have low income but a significant quantity of wealth. Describe the circumstances in which a person would have high income but little wealth.

5. Many forces have combined to increase the percentage of the female population in the labor force. Identify two such forces and explain how you believe they have led to greater female labor force participation. What changes do you expect in the future?

6. Explain how both unlimited liability and limited life can cause problems for firms organized under the proprietorship or the partnership form. Explain how the corporate form of business organization resolves these problems.

7. Suppose that you believe that the future profitability of corporation A will be better than the future profitability of corporation B, in which you now own some stock. Therefore, you sell your shares of B and purchase shares of A. How would the prices of these stocks be affected if many people behave the same as you?

8. Using the following information, construct a simple balance sheet for a business firm: accounts payable, $15,000; equipment owned, $120,000; stock outstanding, $70,000; notes payable, $40,000; cash on hand, $10,000; retained earnings, $15,000; inventory, $50,000; bonds outstanding, $100,000; buildings, $60,000. Explain how a balance sheet is different from an income statement.

9. Name the three functions of government that are described in this chapter. Which do you believe will be the most important to voters in the next election? Under which function would you place a responsibility to promote economic growth? Why?

10. The increasing importance of "the rest of the world" in the economy of the United States has been accompanied, lately, by great political pressure for laws that would restrict entry of foreign goods into the United States. Discuss how this is related to the differing interests of individuals as consumers and as resource owners.

3

How Economists Approach Problems

Preview We human beings are curious creatures who want to know what makes things "tick." More important, we have problems to be solved. Very often we do not have enough of the things we would like to have, yet sometimes we may even have too much. These are the problems that economists try to solve, or at least try to describe clearly, using economic theories and mathematical models of functional relationships.

In this chapter we look at the methods used in economics—how economists deal with economic problems. Most of what will be described and explained applies to all fields that use scientific analysis. A few terms and concepts may be unique to economics.

We begin with a discussion of economic theory and the difficulties inherent in testing these theories. We describe how the analysis of economic theories rests on assumptions, and the role played by the central assumption of economic rationality. Then we explain how economists show the relationships among variables in terms of functions, and we give a short review of how functions are shown in graphs. Next we introduce marginal analysis and equilibrium, two very important ideas often used in economics.

The rest of the chapter points out some difficulties that often beset beginning students of economics (and sometimes careless veterans as well). One such problem is that fairly common terms may take on entirely different meanings in economics. Other difficulties lie in assuming that when one event follows another in time, there is necessarily a cause-and-effect relationship, and in assuming that what is true for a part is also going to be true for the whole. Two final problems result from not paying enough attention to time lags and to expectations.

ECONOMIC THEORY

The discipline of economics consists of a large number of theories. A reasonable, if not precise, definition of an economist is one who knows the major economic theories and is engaged in testing and modifying some of them.

A **theory** is a systematically organized body of knowledge that can be applied in a fairly wide range of circumstances. It provides a set of rules or assumptions for analyzing information, for studying cause-and-effect relationships, and for solving real-life problems by enabling us to better explain economic happenings and/or to improve our ability to predict future events. In fact, theory guides research.

Economic theories are often called models. A **model** is a formal statement of a theory—a simplified view of how some part of the economy is assumed to operate. For example, a simple model of total consumption might describe it as dependent only on current income, whereas a more sophisticated model might describe other influences, like wealth or expected future income. Economic models are often expressed mathematically, but we shall minimize our dependence on mathematics in this elementary textbook.

A theory is a systematically organized body of knowledge that provides a set of rules for analyzing information, studying cause-and-effect relationships, and predicting future events. A model is a formal statement of a theory.

The study of economics is a search for relationships that occur between different economic variables. A **variable** is a quantity that can assume any of a set of values. For example, the price of a good is a variable, and the quantity of this good that is demanded is another variable. We may be interested in the relationship between them. That is, we want to know how a change in the price will affect the amount people will buy. Theory, however, is more than just a description of particular relationships. It is an effort to generalize about relationships that occur regularly, not about coincidental happenings. The observation that a certain rela-tionship between two variables occurs very often leads to the prediction that it will occur again in the future.

A variable is a quantity that can assume any of a set of values.

The most important requirement of a theory is that it be useful. Most economists are not interested in theorizing for its own sake. They want to learn how to solve economic problems, and the answers lie in the use of present theories or of theories not yet devised.

Testing Economic Theory

Economics is a social science. In general, the social sciences are less exact than the natural or physical sciences. For this reason the social scientist must often be satisfied with predicting the direction of change rather than the amount. The natural scientist deals with molecules and cells and is concerned with people in an anatomical or physiological sense; the social scientist is interested in people's behavior. Therefore, the social scientist is usually not able to use the "laboratory method," or the controlled experiment, as effectively as can the natural scientist. If a chemist wants to discover the color reaction of chemical A with chemical B, he or she can place in two identical and sterile test tubes the same measured amount of chemical B and then add a certain amount of chemical A to one of the two test tubes. If the chemist now sees a color change in the test tube to which chemical A was added but observes no color change in the other test tube, the color change may clearly be attributed to the reaction between chemicals A and B. If this experiment were performed hundreds of times, we would expect the same results to occur each time.

Economics is a social science and, as such, is concerned with people's behavior. The controlled experiments that characterize the natural and physical sciences are usually not feasible in economics.

How would a simple experiment in economics be performed? Suppose that we want to find out by means of a controlled experiment what effect a one-shot $1,000 increase in income will have on people's spending and saving patterns. We choose 100 people for group A and another 100 people for group B. These people are not chosen at random. They are selected because they have certain similar characteristics: all have annual incomes of $25,000, all have about the same wealth, all are thirty years of age, all have three dependents, and all live in the same section of the same city. After giving $1,000 to each person in group A but nothing to the people in group B, we note the difference in spending patterns of the two groups. Let us assume we find that group A spends more than group B; specifically, that group A members spend an average of $738.50 more per person than do members of group B. How much faith do you have in this experiment? Would you expect that if the $1,000 had been given to the people in group B instead of group A, they, too, would have spent $738.50 more per person than those of group A? The chances are that the figure would be at least slightly different—perhaps quite different. Why? The reason is that we are dealing with people, who do not all behave in the same way. Though this experiment may allow us to predict that a one-shot increase in income will cause people to spend more, it does not allow us to predict confidently that they will spend 73.85 percent of their additional income.

From this example it is clear that the social scientist must make use of "experiments" that come from everyday experiences. Irrelevant variables must be filtered out by using statistical methods. How do we do this? First, we develop a theory predicting that, if one event occurs, another event will follow. Next, we devise a way of measuring exactly when and where the two events actually took place. Then we use statistical techniques to find out whether the time and place of the first event are associated, or correlated, with the time and place of the second event, as predicted by the theory. This correlation procedure can measure the probability, or likelihood, that the relationship between the two events could nave arisen purely by chance. If we find the relationship too strong to be attributed to chance, the statistical technique has

given us some evidence that the theory being tested has a foundation in fact or in the real world. Of course, many more tests would have to be run to convince social scientists that a theory is valid and useful. Perhaps the two events were really the common outcome of some third event. This possibility would have to be tested through the development of another theory, which, in turn, would be tested against actual experience.

Social scientists must make use of data that come from everyday experience. They use statistical techniques to find out whether events are related to one another as predicted by theory.

Clearly, the approach to truth and understanding in economics and the other social sciences is a continuing process. New evidence may arise that casts doubt on long-established theories, and new theories can offer fresh approaches to understanding that may make older theories obsolete. But knowledge builds on knowledge, and new theories, when tested and supported by evidence, should be better than the old knowledge that is displaced. Economics is an optimistic science.

The Role of Assumptions

A theory need not fit all the facts. This statement often bothers beginning students of economics. It should not. Nor does ignoring certain real-world happenings mean that the theory is naive. Reality is often too complex to be grasped all at once. Sometimes we must simplify and isolate facts in order to see and understand relationships between particular variables. This is the role of **assumptions**—to set forth the limits of the variables in a theory and to state which of the variables are to be omitted.

An especially useful assumption in economics is expressed by the Latin phrase **ceteris paribus**, which means "other things being equal," that is, all other variables are held constant. For example, in order to analyze the effect of a change in the price of fuel oil on the quantity of fuel oil that is consumed, it may be helpful, at least initially, to disregard such other relevant variables as consumer incomes, the prices of competitive energy sources, and the severity of the weather. Thus, we might say, "When the price of a good such as fuel oil changes in one direction, the amount consumed changes in the opposite direction, *ceteris paribus*." This may be a valid and useful theory that can yield reliable and meaningful predictions about things or events that we may not yet have observed.

Assumptions set the limits of the variables in a theory and state which of the variables are to be omitted. The assumption of *ceteris paribus* means that all other variables are held constant.

However, this simple theory may not be sufficient for predicting events in the real world. During a very mild winter or just after a big price change in a substitute fuel, we would certainly not want to predict on the assumption that these variables had not changed. Theories that take into account these important variables must be brought into the total analysis before any predictions are made and real-world policy conclusions are drawn.

Ceteris paribus is, of course, an example of only one simplifying assumption. Countless others may be made. For example, we shall next discuss "economic rationality," which assumes that people behave in a particular way. Some other frequently used assumptions are those about the degree of certainty of a particular outcome, about the level of information that people have, about the degree of competition that exists, and about the role that government does or does not play.

Economic Rationality

How would you describe human behavior in a word? Puzzling? Unpredictable? Because it is so complex, economists must make certain assumptions about the way people are likely to act. Thus, most economic theories contain a key assumption—that people act rationally. Economically rational behavior, or **economic rationality**, is any action that people take to make them better off or to prevent them from becoming worse off. The assumption of economic rationality allows economists to predict on the basis that people are motivated by self-interest. It is assumed that individuals

appraise alternative courses of action and then choose that one that promises the greatest net gains.

The assumption of economic rationality means that economic predictions are based on the belief that people are motivated by self-interest.

Rational behavior need not be totally selfish. "Good things" come in many different packages. Though it is rational for Sally to prefer two new pairs of jeans to only one new pair, it may also be rational for her to prefer to buy her brother a shirt for his birthday rather than buy herself the second pair of jeans. If a rich old uncle wishes to be well remembered after he leaves this world and feels a sense of responsibility to his relatives, it is rational for him to leave $500,000 to his favorite niece. Furthermore, it is rational to give to one's favorite charity. Self-interest, then, has a broader meaning in economics than it does in common usage. People not only consider themselves better off when they add to their stock of material goods but also feel better off when they believe that they have done the right thing.

Actually, most individuals base decisions on social, political, and ethical considerations as well as on personal gain. Also, what people do may be strongly affected by habit, custom, and tradition. Every society weaves a fabric of institutions that guide economic behavior. Whether self-interest is institutionally determined or whether it is just part of human nature is a question that few economists feel qualified to explore. Instead, they merely recognize that theories using this assumption have been tested time and again and found to be good predictors. Self-interest is a powerful economic insight.

In studying economic rationality, we shall examine four decision-making groups: (1) consumers; (2) business decision makers; (3) owners of capital, natural resources, and labor; and (4) government. Let us see what economic rationality means for each of these groups.

The Rational Consumer   The rational consumer is one who seeks to gain the greatest possible satisfaction from purchases. To get the best value from income, the consumer chooses to buy a set of goods and services that is more attractive than any other set that he or she can afford. This means that the rational consumer is consistent and can calculate. If this person prefers corn to beans and beans to peas, then he or she must prefer corn to peas. The consumer need not be maximizing satisfaction under perfect conditions, but doing so in an uncertain environment and with the limited information available at the time. Therefore the consumer who is disappointed after a purchase will buy different things on the next shopping trip because he or she now has more or better information.

The rational consumer is one who seeks to gain the greatest possible satisfaction from purchases.

The Rational Business Decision Maker The rational *entrepreneur*—the business decision maker—is defined as one who seeks maximum profits. Therefore, an entrepreneur will be willing to produce more goods only as long as expected additional revenue (income) is greater than expected additional cost. Likewise, he or she will be willing to limit output if such action is expected to result in lowering cost more than revenue. In this way profits can be increased—or losses reduced.

The rational entrepreneur seeks maximum profits.

The Rational Owner of Capital, Natural Resources, and Labor The rational owner of capital, natural resources, and labor tries to get the greatest possible return. In much the same way as the rational entrepreneur, the rational owner of capital (such as machines and factory buildings) seeks the maximum interest payment, the rational owner of natural resources (such as land and minerals) seeks maximum rent payment, and the rational owner of labor (the laborer) seeks the maximum wage. Suppose, for example, that someone is offered a job as a nurse at the XYZ hospital at a wage of $11.00 per hour. This person would not be a rational laborer if he or she would accept what appears to that person to be the same job for the same number of hours

and under similar working conditions at the ABC hospital at a wage rate of only $10.00 per hour.

The rational owner of capital seeks maximum interest payment, the rational owner of natural resources seeks maximum rent payment, and the rational owner of labor seeks maximum wage payment.

Rational Government The groups discussed so far are all concerned primarily with maximizing their own incomes or satisfactions. Clearly, however, this is not the function that governments are supposed to perform. We shall briefly describe several approaches to the concept of rational government.

One approach is for the economist to recognize that government is made up of individuals who have their own personal motives. Here the economist tries to predict government behavior on the assumption that government workers, just like other workers, will direct their behavior toward ends that will serve their self-interest. Specifically, government workers are expected to try to maximize their own job security, income, and glory. In the case of elected officials, job security—or being re-elected—is of major importance. This goal may lead them to advocate "popular" policies or at least to offer whatever they believe the majority of their constituents favor. But all government workers, including those whose jobs do not depend on the voting public, are concerned with keeping their jobs, being promoted, and enjoying good working conditions. In this view, rational government action is that which brings government workers closer to these goals, however useless it may be to the public.[1]

Quite a different approach is to define rational government in terms of the functions and services that government should perform, such as the allocation, distribution, and stabilization responsibilities outlined in Chapter 2. Economists might define a rational government as one that can most accurately reflect what its citizens want government to do in these areas. Other economists define a rational government as one that will maximize social

1. In terms of maximization, it has been suggested that each government bureau or department tries to maximize its own appropriation, or budget, year in and year out.

welfare (if they can define social welfare), even if the policies to be followed are not always popular. For example, suppose that a policymaker decides on the basis of a value judgment that the elderly widows of World War I veterans are more deserving of additional income than are wheat growers. Then it is rational to cut price supports for wheat and use the money to increase pensions for the widows, even though the wheat growers may represent many more votes than the widows. In this view, rational government is judged in the light of its own goals, rather than those of the majority of its citizens.

According to one view, rational government action is driven by government workers acting in a manner that maximizes their personal goals such as high income, keeping their jobs, being promoted, and enjoying good working conditions. Rational government can also be defined in terms of the functions and services that government should perform, as a government that accurately reflects what its citizens want, or as a government that maximizes social welfare.

Positive and Normative Economics

Economics plays an important role in our lives. It is therefore not surprising that people have strong feelings concerning many economic issues, such as inflation, unemployment, nationalization of industry, unionization, minimum wages, energy, and environmental pollution. So that we are not misled by those who hope to have us side with them, a distinction is made between positive and normative approaches in economics.

Positive economics deals with what is. It tries to be objective and to stay away from value judgments or opinions. **Normative economics** concerns itself with what ought to be. It is subjective and expresses a person's or a group's opinion. One example of positive economics would be a front-page newspaper article on the facts and figures of inflation. Another would be an article presenting various economic theories that try to explain inflation. By contrast, the same newspa-

per's editorial stating that inflation is the country's most serious problem and calling for certain courses of action is an example of normative economics.

Positive economics deals with what is; normative economics concerns itself with what ought to be.

One approach is not necessarily better than the other—as long as it is clear to the reader which is being employed. People can easily be fooled, however, when normative economics is disguised in positive clothes.

Of course, the positive-normative separation can become quite fuzzy when normative ideas enter the choice of subjects to be studied positively. Some suggest that for a long time black-white and male-female wage differences were not approved subjects for detailed study, because the results might provide ammunition to "radicals."

FUNCTIONAL RELATIONSHIPS

In discussing economic theory, we pointed out that economists look for relationships that occur between different economic variables. Such a relationship is often expressed in terms of a **function**—a statement of how one variable depends on one or more other variables. For example, one variable—the weekly earnings of coal miners in West Virginia—may be a function of such variables as the number of hours worked per week and the wage rate per hour. This relationship may be written as

$$E = f(H, W)$$

where E is the weekly earnings of the coal miners, f is a symbol for function and can be read as "depends on," H is the number of hours worked per week, and W is the hourly wage rate.

A function is a statement of how one variable depends on one or more other variables.

Dependent and Independent Variables

When one variable is being described as a function of other variables, it is called the **dependent variable**, and the variables upon which it depends are called the **independent variables**. Thus, in our example, the dependent variable is the weekly earnings of West Virginia coal miners, and the independent variables are the number of hours that they work per week and the hourly wage rate that they receive. If we were considering another functional relationship, however, the classification of variables might change. For example, the hourly wage rate of the miners might be treated as a function of such variables as the desirability of the particular task performed on the job (that is, how clean, safe, and pleasurable it is), the number of years worked on the job, and the level of skill that the job requires. If these were the independent variables, the hourly wage rate of the miners would then be the dependent variable in this functional relationship.

The dependent variable is a function of one or more other variables. An independent variable is one upon which another variable depends.

Direct and Inverse Relationships

The relationship between the dependent and independent variables in a function may be either direct or inverse. A **direct relationship** is one where the dependent and the independent variables change in the same direction. The relationship $E = f(H, W)$ is a direct one between earnings and hours worked and between earnings and the wage rate. Coal miners' earnings go up when they work more hours or when their hourly wages are higher, *ceteris paribus*. Likewise, their earnings go down when they work fewer hours or when their wage rates are lower, *ceteris paribus*. An **inverse relationship** is one in which the dependent and independent variables change in opposite directions. An example is the case where we related the hourly wage rate of miners to the desirability of the task per-

formed. This relationship may be expressed as

$$W = f(T)$$

where the symbols W and f are as before and T is the degree of desirability of the task. The more desirable the task is for the miners, the lower the wage rate would be; the less desirable they find the task, the higher the wage rate would be, other things being equal.

In a direct relationship, the dependent and the independent variables change in the same direction. In an inverse relationship, the dependent and independent variables change in opposite directions.

Graphs

Functional relationships are often expressed algebraically or geometrically. The geometrical expression, by means of graphs, is usually simpler for most students than the algebraic one. There is an old saying that ''a picture is worth a thousand words.'' In economics that is often the case. The ''thousand words,'' or even a hundred words, are not as easy to grasp as a simple ''picture''—a graph. Learning to read graphs will help you to understand a functional relationship at a glance.

Quadrants and Scales   A review of the basics of graphing will be helpful. Figure 1 shows the four sections, or **quadrants**, that are formed when a horizontal axis is placed on a vertical axis. The point of intersection is at zero and is called the **origin**. Each axis is marked off with numbers, or **scaled**, to show the different values for the variable being measured along that axis. In the upper right part of the graph is quadrant I, showing values that are positive on both axes. To the left, quadrant II is for values that are negative on the horizontal axis and positive on the vertical axis. Just below, quadrant III provides for values that are negative on both axes. In the lower right, quadrant IV takes care of values that are positive on the horizontal axis and negative on the vertical axis. Most graphs in this book will be in quadrant I, where both axes show positive values.

FIGURE 1
Axes and Quadrants for Graphing

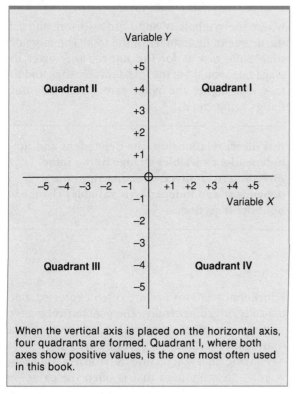

When the vertical axis is placed on the horizontal axis, four quadrants are formed. Quadrant I, where both axes show positive values, is the one most often used in this book.

TABLE 1
Relation of Coal Miners' Earnings to Hours Worked (Hypothetical Numbers)

Coal Miners' Weekly Earnings (in dollars)	Number of Hours Worked per Week
50	5
100	10
200	20
350	35

establishes the other three points (B, C, and D in Figure 2). The plotted points may then be joined by drawing a line through them, and additional information can be obtained from this line. Though Table 1 did not contain information about coal miners' earnings when they work 15 hours or when they work 23½ hours a week, the line or curve provides good estimates of such intermediate values. Just draw a perpendicular from the horizontal axis at 23½ hours to the curve and then read off the earnings ($235) for that point on the vertical axis. The graph, then, is a quick way of summarizing information about the relationship between coal miners' earnings and the number of hours they work.

The intersection of the horizontal axis and the vertical axis is called the origin. Four quadrants are formed by the intersection.

Plotting Recall the functional relationship $E = f(H, W)$, where coal miners' earnings are a function of the number of hours they work and of their hourly wage rate. Table 1 shows a hypothetical relationship between the weekly earnings of coal miners and the number of hours they work per week. The wage rate is held constant at $10 per hour.

In Figure 2 the information from Table 1 has been plotted on a graph. Each point is located by drawing two straight lines, called **perpendiculars**, from the values along the axes. For example, the perpendicular drawn at $100 of earnings meets the perpendicular drawn at 10 hours to determine point A. The information in Table 1 also

---

Data are plotted on a graph through the use of perpendiculars drawn to the appropriate values on the axes of the graph.

Slope When dealing with functional relationships, economists are often very much interested in knowing the size of the change in one variable that is associated with a one-unit change in the size of the other variable. The term used to express this relation is **slope**.

Slope is stated in the following form:

$$\text{slope} = \frac{\text{change in variable on vertical axis}}{\text{change in variable on horizontal axis}}$$

Slope may be positive, negative, zero, or undefined. A direct relationship between the variables indicates a **positive slope**, and an inverse relationship a **negative slope.** The slope of a horizontal straight line is zero. The slope of a vertical

FIGURE 2
Relation of Coal Miners' Earnings to Hours Worked

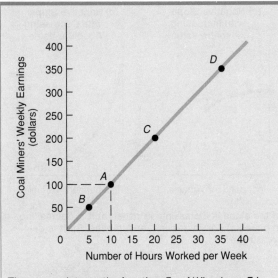

The curve pictures the function $E = f(H)$, where E is the weekly earnings of coal miners and H is the number of hours per week that they work. Their hourly wage rate is fixed at $10.

The numbers plotted from Table 1 establish the points B, A, C, and D. The line or curve that is drawn to join these points gives you good estimates of intermediate values.

straight line is undefined since we can not divide by zero.

Slope is the magnitude of the change in the variable on the vertical axis that is associated with a one unit change in the magnitude of the variable on the horizontal axis. A direct relationship between the variables indicates a positive slope; an inverse relationship indicates a negative slope.

The example that was pictured in Figure 2 illustrated positive slope, since when a coal miner works an additional hour, earnings increase by $10, and when the miner works an hour less, earnings decrease by $10. The slope in this example is therefore 10/1, or 10. Clearly, the slope of a line depends on the scaling values that were used in constructing the graph. If earnings were scaled in pennies, the slope would be 1,000/1, or 1,000.

The case of the inverse relationship between hourly wage rates received by coal miners and the desirability of the task performed offers an example of a negative slope. This is graphed in Figure 3, where the curve goes down from left to right, indicating that the slope is negative. (This is in contrast to the curve in Figure 2, which goes up from left to right, showing that the slope is positive.)

The curves drawn in Figures 2 and 3 are straight lines and represent **linear relationships**. This means that for the range of values shown, the dependent variable is uniformly responsive to changes in the independent variable. In other words, the slope is constant throughout the length of the curve.

Many relationships between economic variables are **nonlinear**, which means that equal changes in the independent variable do not always bring about the same response in the dependent variable. Simple nonlinear curves fall into four

FIGURE 3
Relation of Coal Miners' Wage Rates to Desirability of Tasks

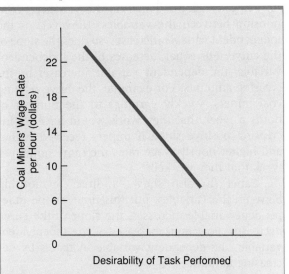

The curve pictures the function $W = f(T)$, where W is the hourly wage rate received by coal miners for performing different tasks and T is the desirability of the task performed (how clean, safe, and pleasurable it is). It shows an inverse relationship between these variables and therefore has a negative slope.

FIGURE 4
Nonlinear Curves

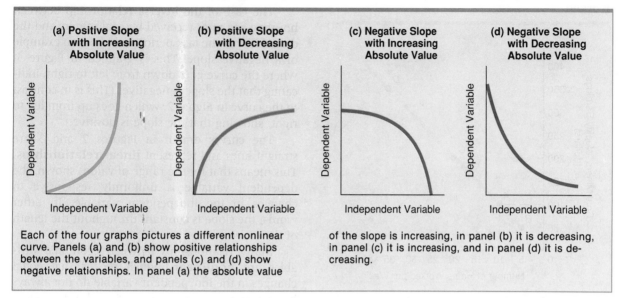

(a) Positive Slope with Increasing Absolute Value

Dependent Variable | Independent Variable

(b) Positive Slope with Decreasing Absolute Value

Dependent Variable | Independent Variable

(c) Negative Slope with Increasing Absolute Value

Dependent Variable | Independent Variable

(d) Negative Slope with Decreasing Absolute Value

Dependent Variable | Independent Variable

Each of the four graphs pictures a different nonlinear curve. Panels (a) and (b) show positive relationships between the variables, and panels (c) and (d) show negative relationships. In panel (a) the absolute value of the slope is increasing, in panel (b) it is decreasing, in panel (c) it is increasing, and in panel (d) it is decreasing.

categories, which are graphed in Figure 4. In describing slopes as increasing or decreasing, we use *absolute values* (values without reference to sign) to avoid confusion when dealing with curves that have negative slopes. Panel (a) shows a direct relationship between the variables. However, as the independent variable increases, so does the slope of the curve. For equal increases of the independent variable, the dependent variable increases by increasing amounts. For example, the curve relating coal miners' weekly earnings to the number of hours a week that they work would have an increasing positive slope if miners received higher and higher hourly wage rates the more hours per week that they worked.

Panel (b) also shows a direct relationship between the variables, but this time, as the independent variable increases, the slope of the curve decreases. For equal increases of the independent variable, the dependent variable increases by decreasing amounts.

Panels (c) and (d) illustrate nonlinear inverse relationships. In (c), as the independent variable increases, the dependent variable decreases at an increasing rate—the curve becomes steeper, showing that the absolute value of the slope becomes greater. In (d), as the independent variable in-

creases, the dependent variable decreases at a decreasing rate—the curve becomes flatter, showing that the absolute value of the slope becomes smaller.[2]

Linear relationships (shown on graphs by a straight line) have a constant slope. Nonlinear relationships have increasing or decreasing slopes.

In Figure 4, the dependent variable appears on the vertical axes and the independent variable appears on the horizontal axes of the graphs. This is convenient for our explanation of slope. In illustrating actual economic theories, the dependent variable is *not* always on the vertical axis and the independent variable is *not* always on the horizontal axis. In each economic graph, the theory itself

2. *Percentage* changes present us with special problems in graphing. For example, a quantity rising at a constant percentage rate is rising by increasing amounts. Therefore, it would be shown in our diagrams as a curve that is concave upward. If you have studied logarithms, you will remember that a linear *logarithmic* function represents a constant *percentage* rise or fall. Curvature on a logarithmic function represents rising or falling percentage changes. The slope of a logarithmic function is therefore a percentage change.

must be consulted to determine which variable is dependent and which is independent. However, slope is always measured as the change on the vertical axis divided by the change on the horizontal axis.

MARGINAL ANALYSIS

Economists often use **marginal analysis** to predict or evaluate the outcome of economic decisions. **Marginal** means "extra" or "additional." It refers to either the last unit that has been added or the next unit that may be added. For an individual thinking about how much of a product to buy, the marginal unit is the last one bought, or the next one that might be bought. Being "on the margin" means being in the process of deciding between alternatives. The child standing in front of a candy counter with 40¢ in hand is on the margin for various kinds of candy. The youngster may buy one more Hershey bar, one more roll of Lifesavers, or one more Milky Way.

Marginal **means "extra" or "additional"—either the last unit that has been added or the next unit that may be added.**

Marginal analysis recognizes that economic decisions are only rarely of an all-or-nothing nature. Business firms are not usually trying to decide whether to produce or not to produce. Rather, they are more often concerned with how much of certain goods to produce this week or this year. Individuals, likewise, rarely ask whether they should purchase food, clothing, or shelter, but instead ask what combination of these things they should purchase. Should they buy a little more food and a little less clothing, or more of both at the expense of renting a somewhat less attractive apartment? Individuals also face marginal decisions in regard to the amount of work they wish to do. Students typically do not think in terms of studying versus not studying at all. Rather they decide how much time to devote to study and therefore how much to leisure activities or to outside jobs. Should a third hour be devoted to studying for an exam, or should that hour be spent resting?

Marginal Analysis in Functional Relationships

Marginal analysis can be joined with the earlier discussion of functional relationships. Economists are often concerned with how much one variable changes as another variable changes. How much will an individual miner's weekly earnings increase if the hourly wage rate increases by a certain amount? The miner may receive an increase in hourly wage rate from $10 to $12, so that the marginal change in the hourly wage rate is $2. If the miner works 40 hours a week, then the weekly earnings will increase from $400 to $480, or a marginal increase of $80.

Relationship Between Marginal, Average, and Total Amount

Many theories in economics make use of marginal, average, and total measures. Thus, it is important to recognize how they differ and how they are related. The *total* is the whole of whatever variable is being measured. What is added to the total or subtracted from it in any one step is the *marginal* amount. The *average* is the total divided by the number of units. For example, a student may have gone to the movies 25 times this year and paid $4 each time. The total amount spent on movies is $100, the average expense is $4 ($100/25), and the marginal expense is also $4 (the price of the last movie). The total amount is always the sum of all the marginal amounts—25 movies at $4 per movie add up to $100. Suppose that the student were to go once more to the movies and find that the price had suddenly increased to $5. In this case, the marginal expense (on the 26th movie) is $5, the new total expense is $105, and the new average expense is about $4.04 ($105/26 = $4.04). Note that the increased marginal expenditure caused an increase in the average expense. Whenever a marginal amount is higher than an average amount, the average amount must be increasing over that range of values. Likewise, whenever a marginal amount is below an average amount, the average amount must be decreasing. Therefore, only when the marginal amount is equal to the average amount— as in our case before the price of movies increased—is the average amount neither increasing nor decreasing. This relationship will always hold because the marginal amount causes the average amount to rise or fall or remain the same.

The total is the whole of whatever variable is being measured. What is added to the total or subtracted from it in any one step is the marginal amount. The total amount is always the sum of all the marginal amounts.

The average is the total divided by the number of units.

Marginal Cost and Marginal Benefit

Many economic theories predict by comparing **marginal cost** with **marginal benefit.**[3] People are expected to act so as to maximize their well-being, and they will normally do so by equating their marginal cost with their marginal benefit.

Many important economic theories predict by assuming that people generally maximize their well-being by equating their marginal cost with their marginal benefit.

The idea of equating marginal cost and marginal benefit is best explained in terms of an example. Suppose you are out hiking in the woods and come across an area where wild blueberries are growing. You reach down and pick a handful growing at your feet. Since you were hungry, the blueberries give you a good deal of benefit in return for very little cost in terms of effort. You see more berries growing nearby and walk over and pick those as well. The satisfaction of eating fresh blueberries is still well worth a little bit of extra effort. After you have spent twenty minutes or so eating blueberries, you are no longer as hungry as you were, but still you derive some satisfaction from eating additional blueberries. The longer you pick

and eat, however, the harder it is to find berries that are conveniently located. Some of them are up on a hill, others are guarded by thistles, and still others are perilously close to what looks like poison ivy. So as you continue picking blueberries, the cost of picking them becomes greater, since it is harder to get to them. At the same time, the longer you continue eating blueberries, the less enjoyment the next handful provides. After half an hour or so, you reach the point where the benefit to you from eating another handful of blueberries is just equal to the cost (in inconvenience) of picking another handful. At this point, you stop picking blueberries and continue with your hike. Any additional berries you might pick at this time would be more trouble than they would be worth. Thus, consciously or not, you used marginal analysis to reach an optimal—best—level of blueberry picking and eating. You continued up to the point at which the marginal benefit of eating blueberries was equal to

FIGURE 5
The Marginal Benefit and Marginal Cost of Picking and Eating Blueberries

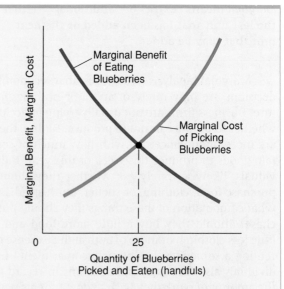

Well-being is maximized by picking and eating 25 handfuls of blueberries. If you eat any less than that amount, the marginal benefit of eating blueberries is greater than the marginal cost of picking them, and so you have not taken full advantage. Any more than 25 handfuls finds the marginal cost greater than the marginal benefit, so that well-being has been reduced.

---

3. This is an important example of an "apparatus of the mind" and why we introduced a methods definition of economics at the beginning of Chapter 1.

the marginal cost of picking blueberries, and after that you stopped.

This example is clearly illustrated through the use of a diagram. Figure 5 includes a positively sloped curve, showing the marginal cost of picking blueberries, and a negatively sloped curve, showing the marginal benefit from eating blueberries. On the far left part of the diagram, the marginal benefit is far greater than the marginal cost (you're very hungry and the blueberries are very easy to reach). On the far right part, the marginal cost is much greater than the marginal benefit (your hunger is pretty well satisfied and the blueberries are quite hard to reach). Anywhere to the left of the intersection of the two curves (less than 25 handfuls of blueberries), the marginal benefit exceeds the marginal cost, and it pays to continue picking. Anywhere to the right of the intersection of the two curves (more than 25 handfuls of blueberries), the marginal cost exceeds the marginal benefit, and it is not economically rational to pick and eat blueberries. Therefore, during this particular stop on your hike you pick and eat exactly 25 handfuls of blueberries, your optimal level of picking and eating.

This simple story illustrates a technique that can be applied to a great many economic problems. When marginal benefits are high but declining and marginal costs are low but rising, it generally is true that an individual or an organization will reach an optimum point by equating marginal cost and marginal benefit. A worker may use this technique in deciding how many hours of overtime to put in. Sometimes a family uses it in deciding how big a car to buy. It can also be used by a company in deciding how much of a good to produce or how many workers to hire. And a government may use it in deciding how many tax dodgers to prosecute. Equating marginal benefit and marginal cost, then, is the basis upon which economists predict the outcomes of decisions made by individuals and organizations.

When marginal benefits are declining and marginal costs are rising, it generally is true that an individual or organization will reach an optimum point by equating marginal cost and marginal benefit.

Criticism of Marginal Analysis

The marginal technique is not every economist's "cup of tea." The institutionalist school of American economists argues that economic choice can be understood only in the framework of history and contemporary economic laws, customs, and attitudes. Radical political economists take particular issue with marginalism. They argue that marginalism deliberately ignores history and present institutions and is too narrowly concerned with the mechanics of choice. Furthermore, they believe that marginalism diverts the economist's attention from other issues, such as income distribution, freedom of consumer choice, economic growth and the environment, that are of greater importance. The question is whether the usefulness of marginal analysis as a tool can be separated from normative questions about the issues themselves. The majority of American economists believe that it can, and therefore that marginalism is equally consistent with both changing institutions and constant ones.

EQUILIBRIUM

Equilibrium is a state of balance. In a state of equilibrium, forces for change within a system offset each other so that there is no net tendency for the system to change.

Equilibrium is a state of balance—forces for change offset each other, so there is no net tendency for the system to change.

An example will help to make the meaning of equilibrium clearer. Imagine a line of three adjoining rooms, connected by two doors. These doors are closed. The room on the right is heated to, say, 90°. The room on the left is air-conditioned, say, at 30°. There is neither heating nor air-conditioning in the middle room. If the doors are opened, both hot air and cold air will rush into the middle room. After a while the temperature in the middle room will reach an equilibrium position—that is, a state of balance.

Stable and Unstable Equilibrium

Equilibrium may be stable or unstable. In our example it is likely that the temperature of the middle room will go to about 60° and stay there. This would be a **stable equilibrium**—one that tends to restore itself following disturbances. For example, if a large cake of ice were placed in the middle room, it would cause the temperature to drop, say, to 50°. However, after a while the ice will melt and the temperature in the room will return to 60°—the stable equilibrium.

Unstable equilibrium may also be observed. Suppose that you are attempting to balance an egg on its end. Small shifts in direction that you make with your hand allow you to bring it to an equilibrium position and leave it there. However, one small gust of wind or a gentle push will cause it to fall over. There will be no tendency for it to bounce back up and regain its unstable (upright) equilibrium position.

Stable equilibrium tends to restore itself following disturbances. Unstable equilibrium, once disturbed, does not tend to return to its state of equilibrium.

Equilibrium is an important idea in economic analysis because it is a basic tool that economists use to predict future situations. Knowing the requirements for an equilibrium enables economists to identify events that might cause a change, the direction of that change, and what the new equilibrium will be. If an event upsets an existing equilibrium, economists try to find out whether a new equilibrium has been established or whether the initial equilibrium will tend to be restored. If the initial equilibrium is considered to be a stable one, economists can predict on that basis. If a new equilibrium has been established, a different set of predictions will be needed. Disturbances to equilibrium happen almost continuously, so that most of the time situations are moving from one equilibrium to another. In our earlier example involving the three adjoining rooms, the thermostats controlling the temperature in the heated room and in the air-conditioned room may be changed from time to time, altering the equilibrium temperature in the

middle room. But disturbances do not make the equilibrium concept any less useful as a tool for predicting what will happen as a result of disturbances. In fact, the idea of economics as a useful guide for carrying out economic policy is based on this ability to predict consequences of disturbances. If the consequences of a certain disturbance are judged to be desirable by policymakers, the disturbance itself may be created as an instrument of policy.

Equilibrium is a basic tool that economists use to predict future situations.

Partial Equilibrium versus General Equilibrium

Equilibrium analysis may be partial or general. **Partial equilibrium analysis** deals with the effects of a disturbance on one set of economic variables, assuming that all other variables are unaffected. **General equilibrium analysis** takes into account the disturbance's effects on all variables.

Widely used in economics, partial equilibrium analysis can be justified by the need to simplify and handle as few variables as possible at one time. This approach is proper for a wide range of economic problems. For example, in the automobile industry—one of the largest and most influential industries in the United States—partial equilibrium analysis is appropriate in some cases, but in other cases general equilibrium analysis is necessary. A rise in the hourly wage rate for auto workers will raise the cost of producing cars. Partial equilibrium analysis would examine this immediate effect, which may be all that is of concern. However, several other effects could be examined if a general equilibrium framework were used. The increase in the income of auto workers will increase their ability to buy automobiles. But if the increase in the cost of producing automobiles leads to higher prices of automobiles, it may change the percentage of consumers' incomes spent on automobiles and therefore affect how much they buy of other goods and services. These effects could, in turn, feed back on the automobile market and thus influence the price and quantity of automobiles sold as well. Partial equilibrium analysis does not take all these factors into account, but general equilibrium analysis tries to take account of them. In the automobile industry, where a wage hike may have a great impact on the demand for both automobiles and other goods, the use of partial equilibrium will sometimes be insufficient. However, in smaller and less economically important industries, such as those producing watchbands or golf carts, a wage hike would have fairly mild effects, and the use of partial equilibrium would usually be sufficient.

Partial equilibrium analysis deals with the effects of a disturbance on one set of economic variables. General equilibrium analysis takes into account the disturbance's effects on all variables.

Statics, Comparative Statics, and Dynamics

The description of an equilibrium state is called **static analysis.** No element of time is introduced. Since there is no action or change in static analysis, it is of limited usefulness in analyzing the impact of events or in developing policies designed to bring about new situations. When chance is brought into the picture, some variable in the initial static equilibrium situation is altered and a new equilibrium situation arises. The procedure of comparing the initial static equilibrium situation with the new static equilibrium situation is called the method of **comparative statics.** Comparative statics analysis is used widely by practicing economists and is the method most often relied upon in this book.

Another economic methodology is called **dynamic analysis,** which deals with time as a variable. It concerns itself with the process of adjustment that takes place between equilibrium situations. Dynamic analysis usually is reserved for relatively advanced courses in economics.

Comparative statics compares different equilibrium situations. It is the most widely used method of economic analysis.

A WORD TO THE WISE . . .

So far we have described some essential tools for understanding and using economics. A few warnings are needed now to identify some of the problems that can lead to wrong conclusions.

Terms

When students enter a new field, they usually expect to encounter some unfamiliar terms. What they may not expect, however, is that familiar words can take on quite different meanings. An important example is **capital.** In everyday language, particularly in a business context, the word refers to money. A person who is thinking of starting a neighborhood restaurant may wonder how much "capital" is required to make a go of it— $150,000 or $200,000? In economics, however, *capital* refers to real goods, such as machinery and factory buildings, which are used in a production process.

A related term, **investment**, is another good example of a word that has a particular meaning in economics. In everyday language, a person is said to "invest" when he or she buys financial securities such as stocks and bonds, or real estate, or works of art. In economics, investment refers to the creation of capital. Business people invest when they purchase goods that enable them to produce yet other goods.

In economics, *capital* refers to real goods, such as machinery and factory buildings, which are used in a production process. *Investment* refers to the creation of capital.

Cause and Effect

Mistaken causation is another danger in economic reasoning. The fact that one event precedes another does not necessarily mean that the first causes the second to occur. Just after more and more college students began to wear jeans to school, they got higher and higher grades in their courses. Would the rise in grades have occurred if jeans had not become so popular? It probably would have. There is no apparent cause-and-effect logic showing that the increased wearing of jeans led to students' higher course grades.

It has been suggested that union-imposed wage increases cause inflation and that the massive stock market crash of 1929 caused the Great Depression of the 1930s. More careful analysis leads us to regard these ideas with great skepticism. Though facts are important, they cannot be relied upon alone to explain relationships. Theory based on logical analysis must serve as the real foundation of the search for truth.

The fact that one event precedes another does not necessarily mean that the first caused the second. Facts alone cannot be relied upon to explain relationships.

Fallacy of Composition

The **fallacy of composition** is another pitfall to watch out for in economics. We can avoid the difficulty by understanding that what is true for one part is not necessarily true for the whole. A person watching a soccer match in a crowded stadium may be better able to see an exciting play when she stands up. But if the whole crowd stands up to see the play, no one will be able to see any better than when all were seated. Similarly in economics, what is advantageous behavior for a single individual may be quite harmful if engaged in by many individuals or an entire economy. Consider a wheat farmer who produces more wheat in order to increase his income. If he were the only one, or one of a few, to do so, he might achieve his objective. But if all or most of the wheat farmers in the country increased output, the much greater amount of wheat produced would lower the price of wheat so much that each individual farmer's income might actually be reduced.

The fallacy of composition is another pitfall to watch out for in economics. We can avoid the difficulty by understanding that what is true for one part is not necessarily true for the whole.

Time Lags

Yet another difficulty often faced in economics is the matter of **time lags**—the amount of time it takes for a change in an economic variable to have an effect. For example, consider the effect that a tuition increase will have on enrollment at a certain college or university. The immediate effect may be very minor, since most students will already have paid tuition for the present semester or term and are not affected until the next one begins. In the new term some students will drop out or transfer to other schools, but probably most will grudgingly pay the higher tuition rather than leave their friends, lose credits in transfer, and go through the hassle of making a move. Just the same, the effect of the tuition hike may still be substantial on new enrollment. Students who would have enrolled for the next and subsequent terms may decide that the higher tuition is too much. There are a number of time lags in this example, and the more time that passes, the greater the effect. In order to make a useful prediction about the effect on enrollment of the tuition increase, valid information about the length of the time lags must be examined.

A time lag refers to the amount of time it takes for a change in an economic variable to take effect. Time lags should not be ignored in economic analysis.

Uncertainty and Expectations

We live in a world of **uncertainty;** that is, we can never predict with absolute accuracy what will happen next. We have to rely on the past as a guide to the future. We usually react to events according to our past experience, tempered by any additional information that we might have. In other words, we form certain *expectations* and react to what we expect will happen rather than to what actually is happening. The more sure we are of a particular outcome, the more willing we are to react to our expectations. For example, a large increase in the price of a good usually discourages people from buying it. However, there are cases where we find the opposite result. The price rise may make people think that the price will go up even more—in other words, it changes their expectations concerning future prices. If the good is storable, purchasers hurry to buy it in order to avoid the still higher price yet to come.

What is the explanation for the fact that at one time the price of General Motors stock goes up after the company reports higher earnings and at another time the stock price goes down after just as glowing a report? The answer may be expectations. In the first instance, the earnings increase may have been a pleasant surprise since people had expected poorer earnings. The second time, it may have been a disappointment because people expected even higher earnings. Likewise, a government action such as a tax cut may at one time cause people to spend the extra money, but at another time have no such effect. The explanation may be that in the second case the tax cut had been anticipated for months so that people were spending according to the amount of money they expected to receive long before the tax cut actually took place.

It is important to be aware of the effect that a change in a variable has on expectations. Changes in expectations depend upon a great many different variables, which extend well beyond the realm of economics and are very difficult to predict.

Often people react to what they expect will happen rather than to what actually is happening.

Pervasive Errors

The major problems of amateur economic thinking lie, we think, not so much in errors of logic as in *nonrational ways of knowing* and in *temporal limitations.*

The main nonrational ways of knowing are intuition, faith, and slogan thinking. Do you believe an economic argument or policy is right or wrong simply because it is "radical" or "progressive" or "conservative" or "reactionary" or "hard-headed" or "compassionate" or "probusiness" or "prolabor" or "socialistic" or "fascistic" or "old-fashioned" or "un-American"? (The list is endless.) If you do, you are indulging in some combination of these nonrational ways of knowing, as indeed everyone does some of the time.

One temporal limitation—a most common one among politicians—is a refusal to consider ideas or policies that are not likely to win votes in the next election—for example, the possibility that problems can ever be caused by any wage rate being too high. Another mistake—more common among professional economists—is to consider only policies that will work too slowly to help in emergencies—like doing nothing in a depression while waiting for wages and prices to fall.

In addition to errors of logic, students should be wary of nonrational forms of knowing, such as intuition, faith, and slogan thinking, and of temporal limitations.

Economics in Focus

Economic Experiments

Traditionally economics has not been a laboratory science. For the most part economists study patterns created by actual economies, not simulations in a lab. But during the last three decades a number of economists have changed the traditional approach, turning to experimentation in order to test prevailing economic theories.

In a typical experiment a group of volunteers (usually students) will create a miniature version of a particular kind of market. Students assigned to be "sellers" might receive a list of possible sale prices for an imaginary commodity. Other students, playing the role of "buyers," would work from a separate list of possible purchase prices. Then a trading session would start; the buyers would try to buy at the lowest prices, the sellers to sell at the highest prices. Of course the students would need some motivation to play their roles with enthusiasm; normally the students earn cash or other rewards based on their success in the game.

Experiments have been especially useful in analyzing auctions—sales in which the goods are sold to the highest bidder. In some auction experiments economists were surprised at how well the results matched theoretical expectations. For instance, in double oral auctions (auctions in which buyers are free to announce their offers and sellers to announce their prices) the participants tend to reach an equilibrium level of prices, and that level is just what supply and demand curves might have predicted. Because auctions of one type or another can be found in many real-life situations (the stock market being an obvious example), the insights gained from auction experiments help researchers extend and refine their theories.

Experiments can shed light on the *why* of economic behavior as well as the *how*. Why do people buy at certain prices or at certain times? What reasoning or impulses are they following? In a carefully designed experiment the participants can indicate their motives and thoughts much more clearly than people in a real-life situation would do. According to Vernon L. Smith, one of the pioneers of experimental economics, people start out with "homegrown beliefs" about economic markets—beliefs that often reflect a notion of "fairness." Their original behavior reflects these beliefs, but they adjust that behavior over time as they see how a certain market actually functions.

Critics of the experimental approach say that studies of a few people in controlled conditions have little bearing on the real world. Experimentalists retort that theories need to be tested, and experiments offer the most direct testing method available to economists. Gradually the experimental approach has won more converts, and its best contributions probably still lie ahead.

Sources: Vernon L. Smith, "Theory, Experiment and Economics," *Journal of Economic Perspectives,* vol. 3 (Winter 1989), pp. 151–168; Edgar K. Browning and Jacquelene M. Browning, *Microeconomic Theory and Applications,* third edition (Glenview, Ill.: Scott, Foresman, 1989), pp. 422–425.

SUMMARY

1. Economic theory is used for logically analyzing information, studying cause and effect, and solving real problems in economics. (See page 42.)

2. Because economics is a social science, it must often be satisfied with predicting the direction of change instead of the exact amount of change. (See pages 42–43.)

3. In order to keep theories as simple as possible and to isolate extraneous, or less important, variables, economists often use assumptions such as *ceteris paribus* and economic rationality. (See pages 43–44.)

4. Economically rational behavior is any action that people take to make them better off or to keep them from becoming worse off. Economists predict on the basis that all economic units—consumers; businesses; owners of natural resources, capital, and labor; and government—act in a rational way. (See pages 44–45.)

5. Positive economics deals with what is— with facts. Normative economics concerns itself with what ought to be—with opinions. It is important to be aware of this difference. (See page 46.)

6. Functional relationships between dependent and independent variables may be direct or inverse. Economists find it useful to present these functions by means of graphs or diagrams. On these graphs, direct relationships are shown as a positive slope, and inverse relationships are shown as a negative slope. If the slope of a curve is constant throughout its length, it will be linear (appear as a straight line), and if the slope increases or decreases, the curve will be nonlinear. (See pages 46–51.)

7. Marginal means extra or additional—one more or one less. Marginal analysis recognizes that most economic decisions are made "on the margin" and are not of an all-or-nothing type. (See page 51.)

8. When the marginal cost of an activity is increasing and marginal benefit from the same activity is decreasing, a person will maximize his or her well-being gained from the activity by equating marginal cost and marginal benefit. (See pages 52–53.)

9. Equilibrium is a state of balance. Though the economy may only rarely be at equilibrium, this is an important concept. It allows economists to focus on the effects of particular disturbances and to predict future events. (See pages 53–55.)

10. It is important to watch out for several problems in the study of economics:

- *a.* Some familiar terms, such as *capital* and *investment,* take on quite different meanings in economics from those in common usage.
- *b.* The fact that one event precedes another does not necessarily indicate a cause-and-effect relationship between them.
- *c.* What is true for a part is not necessarily true for the whole.
- *d.* It is important to consider time lags—how long it takes for a change in an economic variable to have an effect.
- *e.* Living in a world of uncertainty, people often react to what they expect will happen, rather than to what is actually occurring. (See pages 55–57.)

KEY TERMS

assumptions: statements that set forth the limits of the variables in a theory and identify which of the variables are to be omitted (page 43).

capital: real goods, such as machines and factory buildings, which are used in a production process (page 55).

ceteris paribus: Latin for "other things being equal"; it is an assumption that states that all other variables are held constant (page 43).

comparative statics: the technique of studying variations in equilibrium positions that result from changes in the underlying variables (page 55).

dependent variable: a variable that is a function of one or more other variables (page 47).

direct relationship: one where the dependent and the independent variables change in the same direction (page 47).

dynamic analysis: the description of the process of adjustment between equilibrium positions (page 55).

economic rationality: the assumption that people act to make themselves better off or to prevent themselves from becoming worse off (page 44).

equilibrium: a state of balance wherein forces for change within a system offset each other so that there is no net tendency for the system to change (page 53).

fallacy of composition: a type of faulty reasoning that assumes that what is true for one part is true for the whole (page 56).

function: a statement of how one variable depends on one or more other variables (page 46).

general equilibrium analysis: analysis of a state of equilibrium that takes into account all the effects related to the specific economic disturbance that is being studied (page 54).

independent variable: a variable upon which one or more other variables depend (page 47).

inverse relationship: one in which the dependent and independent variables change in opposite directions (page 47).

investment: the creation of goods that are used to produce other goods (page 55).

linear relationship: a relationship that has a constant slope (page 49).

marginal: extra; additional; incremental (page 51).

marginal analysis: a type of analysis that predicts or evaluates the outcome by comparing incremental values (page 51).

marginal benefit: the additional advantage gained when one more unit of a good is consumed or produced (page 52).

marginal cost: the addition to total cost when one more unit of output is produced (page 52).

model: a formal statement of a theory (page 42).

negative slope: an inverse relationship between variables as shown in a graph (page 48).

nonlinear relationship: a relationship between variables in which equal changes in the independent variable do not always bring about the same response in the dependent variable (page 49).

normative economics: an economic approach that concerns itself with what ought to be (page 46).

origin: the intersection of the horizontal and vertical axes of a graph (page 47).

partial equilibrium analysis: analysis of a state of equilibrium that deals with the effects of a disturbance on one set of economic variables, assuming that all other variables are unaffected (page 54).

perpendiculars: straight lines drawn from values along the horizontal or vertical axes of a graph (page 48).

positive economics: an economic approach that deals with what is. It tries to be objective and avoid value judgments (page 46).

positive slope: a direct relationship between variables, as shown in a graph (page 48).

quadrants: the four sections that are formed when a horizontal axis is placed on a vertical axis (page 47).

scale: to mark value-intervals on the axes of a graph (page 47).

slope: the change in the variable read on the vertical axis of a graph divided by the associated change in the variable read on the horizontal axis of that graph (page 48).

stable equilibrium: an equilibrium that tends to restore itself following disturbances (page 55).

static analysis: the description of an equilibrium state (page 55).

theory: a systematically organized body of knowledge that can be applied in a fairly wide range of circumstances (page 42).

time lags: the amount of time it takes for an economic variable to have an effect (page 56).

uncertainty: the condition of not knowing the probability of the outcome of an event (page 56).

unstable equilibrium: an equilibrium that does not tend to restore itself following a disturbance (page 54).

variable: a quantity that can assume any of a set of values (page 42).

DISCUSSION QUESTIONS

1. Marcia and Jim are having a discussion concerning a certain theory of inflation. Jim explains the theory, including the variables involved, the relationships among the variables, and the assumptions that the theory sets forth. Marcia responds that she considers the theory to be quite meaningless because it seems to be based on several quite unrealistic assumptions. Putting yourself in the place of Jim, how would you defend yourself?

2. Experimentation ought to be left to physical scientists. Since economics is a social science, economists should stick to describing human behavior. Do you agree? Explain.

3. Using the economist's assumption that human beings act rationally in their economic decision making, describe how:

a. a consumer will shop

b. an entrepreneur will decide what and how many inputs to use and outputs to produce

c. a worker will choose among job alternatives

4. Why is it so much more difficult to describe rational government than to describe rational consumers, entrepreneurs, and the owners of capital, natural resources, and labor?

5. Differentiate between positive and normative economics. Give three examples of positive statements and three examples of normative statements in the field of economics. Would a positively or a normatively oriented economist be of greater value to a politician?

6. How is the demand for public transportation related to the price of gasoline? Tell what type of variable each is and how they interact.

7. The Greasy Spoon is open daily from 4 P.M. to 4 A.M.. The employees (primarily college students) may choose the number of hours they wish to work. Their daily earnings, then, depend on the number of hours worked and the hourly wage, which is $5.00. On weekends they choose to work fewer hours than on weekdays. Write the function for this relationship. Using the following information, graph the relationship and show the slope:

Daily Earnings	Hours Worked
$15.00	3 (Friday)
15.00	3 (Saturday)
20.00	4 (Sunday)

Daily Earnings	Hours Worked
25.00	5 (Monday)
30.00	6 (Tuesday)
35.00	7 (Wednesday)
40.00	8 (Thursday)

8. The Miller Brewing Company buys barley from a group of farmers in Iowa. The more Miller buys, the greater is its total expenditure on barley. However, the more Miller buys, the lower is the price per bushel that it has to pay. What is the sign of the relationship between the amount of barley purchased and the total expenditure on barley? Is this a linear relationship? Draw a graph that shows the relationship between the amount of barley purchased and the total amount paid for barley.

9. During a certain month John buys a pound of hamburger every third day (ten pounds in all). He pays $1.50 for each of the first five pounds, $1.60 for each of the next four pounds, and $1.70 for the tenth pound. Calculate John's total cost, average cost, and marginal cost for hamburger for that month.

10. Suppose that you have an economics exam tomorrow and decide to study for it tonight. Suppose further that your negatively sloped marginal-benefit curve for studying intersects your positively sloped marginal-cost curve for studying at four hours of studying. (You may now want to draw these two curves on a set of axes, scaling marginal benefit and marginal cost along the vertical axis and the number of study hours along the horizontal axis.)

Using marginal benefit–marginal cost analysis, explain why you would not want to stop studying after only three hours.

Using marginal benefit–marginal cost analysis, explain why you would not want to study as much as five hours.

11. Why are economists so concerned with equilibrium when, in fact, it is very seldom reached?

12. Under what conditions might an economist prefer to use partial rather than general equilibrium analysis?

4

Scarcity: The Economic Problem

Preview This chapter returns to the concept of *scarcity*, which you briefly met at the beginning of Chapter 1. Most economists assume, despite the doubts of the communists, that scarcity is unavoidable and that there is no such thing as an economy of abundance.

Scarcity is the central problem of economics. All our everyday economic problems can be traced back to it. Furthermore, goods and services are scarce because they are produced by combining resources, which are themselves scarce. These resources are divided into labor, natural resources, and capital (further divided into physical and human capital), and we shall discuss each in turn. The special function of combining these resources—particularly in the production of new goods or services and in the application of new ways to produce standard goods and services, all under conditions of uncertainty—we call enterprise or entrepreneurship, an important form of the labor resource.

A major theme running through this chapter is that the existence of scarcity necessitates choice. In other words, we must answer the basic questions raised in Chapter 1: what to produce, how to produce it, and to whom it should go. Also because of scarcity we must consider opportunity cost, the idea that the real cost of something is what is given up to obtain it. Opportunity cost applies to both consumption and production decisions. The chapter is thus an introduction to the important topics of consumer choice, to the production decisions of firms, and to the concepts of supply and demand.

SCARCITY

There are many economic problems. We have them, our neighbors have them, business firms have them, and government agencies have them—not just in this country, but around the whole world. You would like to have a new car but cannot afford it. You want to go to a party on Thursday night; however, there is an economics exam Friday morning and you need time to study for it. Your family wants to live in a better house, but it costs too much. The farmer wants a new tractor, but the bank is unwilling to provide a loan. Though the Pentagon desires a new-generation bomber, Congress refuses to pass the enabling legislation. The family in rural Bangladesh wishes to have enough to eat but does not have the means to grow or buy the food. These and trillions of other economic problems are common. Though they vary greatly in type and in urgency, they are all just examples of a single problem—scarcity, *the* economic problem.

Scarcity means that the amount of something actually available is not sufficient to meet some requirement. The critical word in this definition is *requirement*, since a given amount of something may or may not constitute scarcity, depending on how this amount compares with the requirement. In the illustrations given in the preceding paragraph, the requirement appeared in such terms as "would like to have," "wishes," "wants," or "desires." The things discussed were scarce because the amount actually available was less than the amount wanted or desired. Thus, economics specifies a very distinctive meaning for the term *scarcity*. It is an important term to remember.

Scarcity means that the amount of something actually available is not sufficient to meet some requirement. Scarcity is the central problem of economics.

Scarce Goods and Services

We warned you in the previous chapter that economists use some words in ways that differ from ordinary usage. *Scarcity* is such a word. In everyday language a good or a service is "scarce" when the demand for it is greater than the supply available.

Economists agree *only* if the terms *demand* and *supply* are understood to refer to amounts demanded and supplied at a price of zero. (Price also does not have to take the form of money. So the "price of zero" can mean that a demander does not have to give up goods or time and that a supplier does not receive goods or anything else in the exchange.) Whenever people want more of a good or service than is available free of charge, economists refer to that good or service as scarce. Suppose that a clothing manufacturer decides to introduce a new line of designer socks and after doing some market research offers 1,000 pairs per day for sale at a price of $8 per pair. If only 400 pairs are sold per day, these socks would not be considered scarce in everyday language. However, economists would want to withhold judgment until they had information about the quantity demanded at prices below $8. If, indeed, 1,000 pairs per day are sold at $3 per pair and if consumers would buy more than 1,000 pairs at some even lower price, then economists would consider these socks to be scarce. At a price of zero, the quantity of pairs of socks demanded would far exceed the quantity offered by suppliers. Economists reason that the good (in this case, socks) is the same whether sold for $8, $3, or 10¢. No matter what the price is, scarce resources are used to produce them, and some other goods are not produced with those resources. Indeed, if these socks are defined as scarce at a price of 10¢, they are also scarce at a price of $8.

Whenever people want more of a good or service than is available free of charge, economists refer to that good or service as scarce.

A good or service becomes scarce over time if the difference between the quantities demanded and supplied at a price of zero increases. Similarly, a good or service becomes less scarce over time if the difference between the quantities demanded and supplied at a price of zero decreases.

A good or service becomes more scarce over time if the difference between the quantities demanded and supplied at a price of zero increases.

Scarce Resources

Why do most goods and services command a positive price? Why are most goods and services scarce? The answer can be found by examining how goods and services are produced.

Production involves bringing together certain inputs—called **factors of production** or **resources**—to create goods and services, that is, the output. Resources are the ingredients necessary for producing goods and services. Just as you cannot bake a cake without the ingredients of flour, eggs, sugar, and so on, you cannot produce goods and services without resources. It is these resources that are scarce and, in turn, cause goods and services that are produced with them to be scarce.

Goods and services are scarce because the resources, or factors of production, needed to create them are scarce.

It is useful to separate resources into three broad classes:

1. **Labor resources** are all kinds of human work efforts that are or can be directed at production or at enterprise, which is the organizing of production.
2. **Natural resources** are all things provided by nature that can be used in production, such as land and minerals.
3. **Capital resources** are goods or tools or skills that are produced for use in further production.

These three kinds of resources—labor, natural, and capital—are defined broadly enough to cover everything that goes into production.

There are three kinds of resources: labor, natural, and capital.

Labor Resources   Labor includes all forms of human work, blue-collar and white-collar alike, from the most menial and routine to the most intellectual and managerial.

It is easy to recognize the labor of the machine operator, the ditch digger, the assembly-line worker, and the fruit picker. But other types of labor are included in the concept of the labor resource. The accountant, the secretary, and the company president are all examples here. Also classified as labor are **enterprisers**, or **entrepreneurs**—those who seek the best opportunities for production and take risks when making such decisions.

Labor resources include all kinds of human work, from manual laborers to office laborers to entrepreneurial labor.

Enterprise differs from administrative and managerial labor in that it is less routine. The labor done by the entrepreneur is to make the basic choices and decisions within a company, particularly those decisions that involve taking chances. The entrepreneur must judge the merits of past and present ways of producing goods or services and must decide how to apply new production methods or how to produce new goods. Thus an enterpriser, or entrepreneur, is often an innovator, but only rarely an inventor.

The distinction between innovator and inventor is worth clarifying. It is the **inventor** who discovers or devises a new or improved process or product. The **innovator** is the one who brings the invention out of the laboratory, makes it practical, and applies it to actual production. The physicist Enrico Fermi was an inventor of the fission process of releasing atomic energy, but he was not an important innovator in either the civilian or the military applications of atomic energy. Henry Ford was the innovator who applied assembly-line techniques to automobile production, and Alfred Sloan, Jr., was the innovator who introduced the annual model change in automobile marketing. So far as we know, neither invented anything of importance. Many of us are surprised that the innovators of new products and processes so often make higher incomes and amass greater wealth than the inventors do. Both Ford and Sloan made more money from their innovations than Fermi did from his invention. (Of course, Fermi won a Nobel Prize—something that Ford and Sloan never did.)

Quantity and Quality of Labor   The quantity of labor available to a society is determined by the size of its population, the age distribution, and the prevailing attitudes about who should work, over what periods of their lives, and for how long each year. Countries with large populations and with small percentages of very young (below working age) and very old (above working age) people have large amounts of labor. Societies that deny work to certain groups of people or support a leisure class possess less labor. Those that offer many years of schooling to young people and provide retirement income to older people have less labor. Finally, the amount of labor that a country has will depend on the length of the workday and the workweek, and the amount of holiday and vacation time that workers receive.

The quantity of labor available to a society is determined by the size of its population, the age distribution, and prevailing institutions.

There is also a qualitative aspect of the labor resource. Certainly, production is more than simply expending energy. The workers' attitude toward the job, for example, is important to production. When that attitude is wholesome and constructive and when the workers enjoy what they are doing and take pride in the results, there will be more production from the work effort than when the attitude is negative.

Combination with Other Resources Because the labor resource is usually employed in combination with other resources, it is sometimes difficult in practice to recognize these resources separately. For example, the skills that people use in combination with their labor effort are a kind of capital, called **human capital**. These skills are the results of production efforts (education or training) carried out sometime in the past and used for future production. A long period of schooling, then, lowers the society's quantity of labor resource, but the lost working time is offset by the greater amount of human capital that results from the knowledge and skill gained from the education. Even the strength, health, and vigor that are displayed along with the work effort can be distinguished from the work effort itself, but it is hard to decide whether these should be considered natural resources or capital. Does health come from the "natural resource" of

being born healthy or from capital that previously provided health care?

Human capital consists of the skills that people use in combination with their labor effort.

Actually, none of the resource categories can be fully understood if examined in a vacuum. The quantity and quality of natural resources and capital will affect labor's ability to produce, just as the productivity of capital depends on the quantity and quality of the labor and natural resources that can be combined with it. A worker with a bulldozer can produce more than the same worker with a shovel. Should the whole difference be attributed to the bulldozer? A bulldozer with a worker can produce a lot, but the bulldozer could produce nothing without the worker. Should the entire difference be attributed to the worker?

Natural Resources Natural resources are things that are provided by nature and that are used or usable in production. These "gifts of nature" include the land in its natural state, the sea, the minerals in the ground, the vegetation that grows without anyone planting it, and all the living creatures that are found in the wild.

To be usable, natural resources must often be combined with labor resources and capital resources. Crude oil in a pool deep under the surface of the earth is a natural resource, but bringing it to the surface requires labor and machines (capital). So when the crude oil becomes available for use in production, it has already been mixed with labor and capital. Land in its natural state is a pure natural resource, but land with an irrigation system or with contour plowing is more than a natural resource, since it has been combined with labor and capital.

The idea that a natural resource is something that is "usable" in production brings up still another interesting aspect of the relationships among the resources of labor, natural resources, and capital. For many hundreds of years, crude oil seeped to the surface of the earth. However, it had no value as a natural resource until knowledge and skills were developed to allow this crude oil to be used in production. Future advances in knowledge may bring to light some natural resources that exist today but are as yet unrecognized. Are natural resources being used up in production, or is the development of knowledge expanding the quantity of recognized natural resources?

Natural resources are things provided by nature that are usable in production. To be usable, natural resources must often be combined with labor resources and capital resources.

Capital Resources Capital resources are goods, tools, and skills that are meant for use in further production. Factory buildings as well as many machines and tools are produced, not for consumers or households to enjoy, but for the entrepreneur to combine with labor and natural resources to produce consumer goods.

Capital goods are "derived" rather than "original" resources because they are produced from other resources. They are made by people and/or other capital goods. An old-fashioned textbook definition was "Capital is wealth used to produce other wealth," and economists spoke of production that makes use of capital as a "roundabout" way of using labor and natural resources in production. Karl Marx wrote that capital was "dead labor that, vampire-like, lives by sucking living labor." Most modern economists do not resent capital, but instead give it credit for providing billions of people with a much higher standard of living than would otherwise be possible. Public and private capital resources are used to educate and train labor. In the form of tools and human skills, capital is also used to explore for coal, iron, or oil, which increases the amount of known natural resources. Various combinations of capital resources are used to raise or maintain the fertility of farmland, as well as to produce the land in Boston's Back Bay, Tokyo's Marunouchi, or half of Holland by filling in and desalinating sea bottoms, river bottoms, or swamps.

Capital resources are goods, tools, and skills that are meant for use in further production. They are made from other resources including other capital goods.

Capital is a very important resource for production. The quantity and quality of capital in a country depend upon decisions made concerning the use of its scarce resources. The more a nation chooses to employ its resources in the production of consumer goods and services, the less will be available for the production of capital (and vice versa). Consider the case of a poor nation that is endowed with few and low-grade natural and labor resources. Its people are probably living near the subsistence level, with barely enough consumption goods and services to sustain their lives. It is unlikely that much capital would be produced under such conditions, since almost all of this country's resources would be used to produce consumer goods.

The quantity and quality of capital in a country depend upon decisions made concerning the use of its scarce resources. The more a nation uses its resources in the production of consumer goods and services, the less is available for the production of capital.

The definition of capital offered at the beginning of this section included human skills. Skill, or **technological know-how**, is the ability to combine resources in producing the goods and services that a society wants. It is a kind of capital because skills are developed through experience, that is, through the use of resources in some sort of an educational process.

Technological know-how is an especially important kind of capital because it helps to determine how much a society will be able to produce with its limited amounts of other resources. A society with a substantial stock of technological know-how will be able to produce a great many more goods and services with its other resources than it could produce if it had less. No level of technological excellence will "solve" the economic problem of scarcity, but gains in "know-how" can go a long way toward easing the burden of scarcity.

One form of capital resources is skill or technological know-how—the ability to combine resources to produce the goods and services a society wants.

Choice

The economic problem—the existence of scarcity—necessitates choice. Since we cannot all have as much of everything as we would like, choices, or economic decisions, have to be made. Chapter 1 introduced the three major decisions that face all societies: what to produce, how to produce, and who shall receive the finished goods and services. It also explored some of the economic arrangements that societies have made to answer these questions. Now, these three questions can be applied directly to the problems of scarcity and choice.

The question of what to produce is based on the realization that choices have to be made between alternative uses of scarce resources. How many telephones shall be produced? How much toothpaste? How many factories? How many machines? How much conservation? How much research? Clearly, the "what to produce" question not only divides resources among alternative consumer goods but also allocates resources to the creation of capital, which will open the way for more and better consumer goods in the future.

In deciding what to produce, choices have to be made between alternative uses of scarce resources.

The question of how to produce involves the choice of which resources to use in production. It is almost always possible to substitute one resource for another, such as a machine (capital) for some labor, or a more elaborate machine for two less elaborate ones. Certainly, in the case of an economy that finds itself with a large amount of labor and a small amount of capital, this question would be answered differently than it would be in an economy in the opposite situation.

In deciding how to produce, choices also have to be made about which resources to use.

The question of for whom to produce also shows the existence of scarcity in the real world. If there were enough resources for us all to have as much of everything as we wanted, there would be little need to make the hard choices of providing more to some people and less to other people. The fact that societies have to make this choice is the "bottom line" of the economic problem. Because receiving goods and services is a powerful incentive, the way goods and services are distributed has a lot to do with the labor, natural resources, and capital resources that will be available in the future.

In deciding for whom to produce, choices have to be made about the distribution of goods and services.

OPPORTUNITY COST

Since resources are scarce, the decision to use them for one thing means that something else will be given up. Suppose that a company could manufacture either 100 chairs or 30 tables using the same resources. The opportunity cost of using its resources to produce 100 chairs is the benefit that could have been obtained from producing 30 tables (the best alternative) with the same resources. Thus, **opportunity cost** is the true cost of choosing one alternative over another. With limited resources, people cannot "have their cake and eat it too." Opportunity cost recognizes the fact that when resources are employed in a certain way, there is a simultaneous choice made not to use those resources in some other way. That which is given up, then, is the opportunity cost of what is actually chosen. If, instead of producing one case of beer, we might have produced three dresses or five taxi rides or seven hours of leisure, the opportunity cost of one case of beer is whichever of these would yield the most benefit. It is certainly *not* the sum of all three.

Opportunity cost is the true cost of choosing one alternative over another. That which is given up is the opportunity cost of what is actually chosen.

Opportunity Cost in Consumption

Opportunity cost applies to both consumption and production. In discussing consumption, we consider how consumers spend their income, wealth, and time and how governments spend the resources that they have at their disposal.

The Individual Since people have only so much income and hold a limited amount of wealth, they are continually faced with buying decisions. When consumers decide to spend their dollars for one item, those dollars are not available to them for some other item. The opportunity cost of buying a blue sweater may be the green sweater that was therefore not bought. Taking a trip to the Caribbean might mean forgoing, or giving up, a new car.

To get a better understanding of the opportunity cost involved in consumer choice, consider the following example. Suppose that you are having dinner in a seafood restaurant and that you select the combination shrimp and scallop plate shown on the menu for $10. This restaurant allows you to choose the particular mix of shrimps and scallops that you want. Shrimps, however, are twice as expensive ($1 each) as scallops (50¢ each). Thus, the opportunity cost of each shrimp is two scallops, and the opportunity cost of each scallop is one-half shrimp.

Your eleven possible combinations are listed in Table 1 and are plotted graphically in Figure 1. Since shrimps are on one axis and scallops on the other, any point on the diagram represents some combination of shrimps and scallops. Your $10 plate will not allow you, however, to choose a point in the blue area (like X with 8 shrimps plus 10 scallops). You would not want to order a combination in the purple area (like Z with 4 shrimps plus 4 scallops), since you can have more shrimps and/or scallops for your $10. Depending upon your

TABLE 1
Alternative Combinations of Shrimps and Scallops (Hypothetical Example))

Combination	Number of Shrimps	Number of Scallops
1	10	0
2	9	2
3	8	4
4	7	6
5	6	8
6	5	10
7	4	12
8	3	14
9	2	16
10	1	18
11	0	20

taste, your order might be all shrimps (point A) or all scallops (point B), but most likely it will be some combination like C (6 shrimps plus 8 scallops) because it offers some variety.

The graph in Figure 1 helps you to visualize opportunity cost. The slope of the line (ignoring the sign) measures opportunity cost of scallops because it shows how many shrimp must be sacrificed to obtain one more scallop. In this illustration, the curve is actually a straight line, which means that the slope is the same all along the line, because opportunity cost neither increases nor decreases from one combination on the line to another.

People also face opportunity costs in allocating their time and their effort. This choice may be between work and leisure, between one kind of work and another kind of work, or between one leisure activity and another leisure activity. If a particular Saturday night offers a college student both a movie show and a basketball game, and if these are the best alternatives available, the event that the student doesn't attend is the opportunity cost of the one that he or she does decide to attend. A student who decides to attend a summer session may experience three kinds of opportunity costs. The first cost is the goods and services that the student forgoes so that he or she can pay for tuition and books. A second includes the goods and services that the student could have bought with the money he or she would have earned on a summer job. The

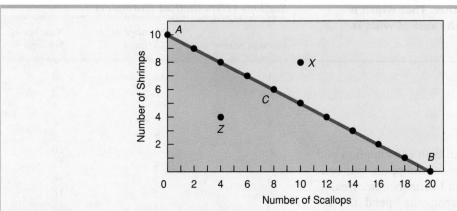

The numbers plotted from Table 1 establish the points along the curve *AB*. These eleven possible combinations of shrimps and scallops are available to a person ordering the $10 shrimp and scallop plate in the restaurant. The opportunity cost of each shrimp is two scallops, and the opportunity cost of each scallop is one-half shrimp.

Any combination that lies in the blue area above *AB* (such as *X*) is not available on the $10 plate. Any combination that lies in the purple area below *AB* (such as *Z*) is available but offers fewer shrimps and/or scallops than the restaurant is willing to provide on the $10 plate.

third is the extra leisure time that the student would have enjoyed, since school is more time-consuming than a job would have been.

People continually face opportunity-cost decisions when allocating their income, time, and effort.

The Government   Government also is faced with opportunity costs. At first, it may seem that government is exempted because it can tax people, borrow money, or even print money if it wishes to undertake more programs. On closer examination, however, we discover that when government draws additional resources from private individuals or businesses, private goods must be forgone. This is the opportunity cost of the expanded government operation. For example, if a country became fearful of its neighbors, it might raise taxes to buy more military equipment. The opportunity cost of the defense buildup would be the private goods, such as clothing and vacations, that the taxpayers could no longer afford to buy.

If a total dollar budget has already been set, the opportunity cost of one government program is an-

other program that must be given up. A state legislature may have to decide between funding mass transportation or the prison system. If you are told the amount of the total budget and the prices of mass transportation and prison facilities, this opportunity-cost calculation can be illustrated just like the consumer-choice case involving shrimps and scallops.

Government is also faced with opportunity costs. If government operations expand, some private goods must be forgone. If only one government program can be funded, the opportunity cost is another government program that must be given up.

Opportunity Cost in Production

The concept of opportunity cost can be applied to production choices in a way similar to consumption choices. Opportunity cost in production is also a **tradeoff**—how much of one good or service must be given up to gain a certain quantity of another good or service. Extending opportunity cost further leads us to the concept of **production possibility**, which describes the limits to the quantities of goods and services that can be produced with a given supply of resources including technological knowledge during any given time period. We shall consider production possibilities both for an individual firm and for an entire nation.

Production choices made by firms involve opportunity costs—how much of one good or service must be given up to gain a certain quantity of another good or service.

Production possibilities are the limits to the quantities of goods and services that can be produced during any given time period with a given supply of resources including technological knowledge.

The Firm   Suppose that a firm is set up to manufacture only two products: ice cream and sherbet. Suppose further that its factory building contains machinery that can be used equally well to produce ice cream or sherbet and that its workers can produce either product equally well. The capacity of the factory building and the machinery is 500,000 gallons of ice cream and/or sherbet per month.

Figure 2 illustrates this case. The amount of ice cream is on one axis and the amount of sherbet is on the other. Any point on the diagram represents some combination of the production of ice cream and sherbet. If the company chooses to produce all the ice cream that it can (and therefore no sherbet), it can produce 500,000 gallons (point *A*). Alternatively, if it chooses to produce all the sherbet that it can (and therefore no ice cream), it can produce 500,000 gallons of sherbet (point *B*). All the remaining maximum production possibilities are combinations of positive amounts of both ice cream and sherbet and fall along the curve drawn between *A* and *B*. (It is actually a straight line because all the resources in this example are able to produce either good equally well.) We call *AB* a **production possibilities boundary**—a curve that represents all the alternative maximum combinations that can be produced during a given time period with a given supply of resources including technological knowledge.

FIGURE 2
Production Possibilities for an Ice Cream–Sherbet Firm (Hypothetical Example)

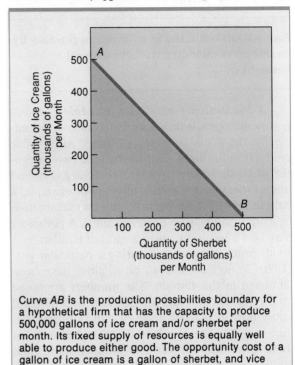

Curve *AB* is the production possibilities boundary for a hypothetical firm that has the capacity to produce 500,000 gallons of ice cream and/or sherbet per month. Its fixed supply of resources is equally well able to produce either good. The opportunity cost of a gallon of ice cream is a gallon of sherbet, and vice versa.

A production possibilities boundary is a curve that represents all the alternative maximum combinations that can be produced during a given time period with a given supply of resources including technological knowledge.

The Whole Economy   Let's see how opportunity cost in production may now be applied to an entire economy. No matter what economic system prevails—whether private business firms like the ice cream–sherbet company exist or not—each nation is limited in what it can produce by its resources, including its technological know-how. Of course, the actual production possibilities of a nation are too diverse to be expressed in tabular form or to be represented in a diagram. But for illustrative purposes all the different goods and services that a nation produces can be lumped together in two categories, such as "consumption goods" and "capital goods," or "guns" and "butter," or "goods" and "services."

Each nation is limited in what it can produce by its resources including its technological know-how.

A Production Possibilities Schedule Table 2 represents a production possibilities table or schedule for the fictitious nation of Yano. All possible production has been divided into the two categories of goods and services, and there is a common unit of measure for each category. For example, a haircut may be 1 service unit, and an examination by a physician may be 10 service units. A potholder may be 1 goods unit, and a pound of hamburger 3 goods units. Imagine that during a particular year (1990) Yano's production possibilities have been tabulated in this fashion. The numbers are based on the amount of resources including technological know-how available for use in Yano's production during 1990. The numbers in Table 2 show that there is no way for Yano to produce more than 10,000 billion units of goods or to produce more than 4,000 billion units of services. In fact, the only way to produce such a high level of either category is to produce none of the other.

Between these all-of-one-and-none-of-the-other choices are many possible combinations of goods and services for Yano to produce. The schedule gives seven examples (such as 9,800 billion units of goods plus 500 billion units of services, or 7,000 billion units of goods plus 2,500 billion units of services), but there are countless others. It follows from the data that if Yano decides, for example, to produce 2,000 billion units of services in 1990, then no more than 8,000 billion units of goods can be produced. Alternatively, if Yano decides to produce 9,400 billion units of goods, it can produce no more than 1,000 billion units of services.

Increasing Marginal Opportunity Costs The tradeoff between goods and services is different in different parts of the table. At the top is the combination of 10,000 billion units of goods and no services. By giving up 200 billion units of these goods, Yano can gain 500 billion units of services.

TABLE 2
Production Possibilities for the Nation of Yano in 1990

Goods (in billions of units)	Services (in billions of units)
10,000	0
9,800	500
9,400	1,000
8,800	1,500
8,000	2,000
7,000	2,500
5,800	3,000
4,400	3,500
0	4,000

This table, or schedule, shows nine of the countless alternative combinations of goods and services that the fictitious nation of Yano is able to produce in 1990. The alternatives range from 10,000 billion units of goods plus no services to no goods plus 4,000 billion units of services. It is most likely that the people of Yano will want a mix of goods and services, and so they might choose a combination such as 8,000 billion units of goods plus 2,000 billion units of services.

Thus the opportunity cost of 500 billion units of services is 200 billion units of goods. However, Yano must give up 400 billion units of goods to get the next 500 billion units of services. The marginal opportunity cost of 500 billion units of services has increased from 200 billion units of goods to 400 billion units of goods. Note that this pattern continues. As you move down Table 2, larger and larger amounts of goods must be given up in order to gain additional blocks of 500 billion units of services. If you compare the last two lines in the table, you will see that the opportunity cost of the last 500 billion units of services is 4,400 billion units of goods.

Likewise, the marginal opportunity cost of goods in terms of services increases as you move up Table 2. Going from the combination of no goods and 4,000 billion units of services to the next higher combination, you will see that the opportunity cost of 4,400 billion units of goods is only 500 billion units of services. Finally, when you compare the top two lines in the table, you will observe that the opportunity cost of only 200 billion units of goods is 500 billion units of services.

Why should increasing marginal opportunity costs be expected? Why is it that the more goods or the more services that Yano has, the higher the opportunity cost of gaining even more units? The answer is that not all of Yano's resources are equally suited to producing both goods and services. Some are much more capable of producing goods, and others are much better at producing services. Workers skilled in performing appendectomies may be unsuited for producing cars. Land that is just right for growing wheat may be a poor location for a barbershop. And a factory building designed for manufacturing steel may be poorly suited as a dental clinic.

It is reasonable to expect that, at some combination around the middle of Table 2, most resources are being used in the way that suits them reasonably well. Perhaps this combination would be 8,000 billion units of goods plus 2,000 billion units of services. At other combinations—either up or down the table—resources are shifted to tasks for which they are less well suited. Toward the very top of the table, only the resources best fitted to the production of services will be producing services. At the same time, it is necessary to use less-suitable resources for producing goods, making it very expensive to produce any more goods by giving up more services. Likewise, toward the very bottom of the table, only the resources best suited to the production of goods will be producing goods and those resources less capable of producing services will be doing so, making it very expensive in terms of goods forgone to produce any more services.

A Production Possibilities Boundary Just as a production possibilities boundary was drawn for the ice cream–sherbet firm in Figure 2, a production possibilities boundary may be drawn for the nation of Yano. Figure 3 (page 74) plots the data from Table 2 on a set of axes and joins the points to obtain a production possibilities boundary. The curve is bowed out, reflecting increasing marginal opportunity costs because Yano's resources are not all equally good at producing both goods and services. In contrast, the straight-line production possibilities boundary for the ice cream–sherbet firm reflected a constant marginal opportunity cost, since all its resources were equally good at producing ice cream and sherbet.

The production possibilities boundary in Figure 3 represents the maximum amounts that Yano can produce in 1990. Production levels in the blue area (such as X, a combination of 9,500 billion units of goods plus 3,000 billion units of services, or Z, a combination of 8,500 billion units of goods plus 3,500 billion units of services) are impossible for Yano to achieve. However, the entire purple area is made up of combinations of goods and services that are attainable. For example, point A (a combination of 6,500 billion units of goods plus 1,500 billion units of services) is an attainable combination for Yano. But, given its resources including technological know-how, Yano can do better than point A by producing more goods, or more services, or more of both. Instead of 6,500 billion units of goods, it could produce 8,800 billion (which would place it at point B), with no reduction in the services produced. Or, instead of 1,500 billion units of services, it could produce 2,700 billion (which would place it at point C), with no reduction in the amount of goods produced. Finally, it could produce more of both and move to a point such as D (7,500 billion units of goods plus 2,250 billion units of services).

Suppose that Yano is producing at point A in the purple area of Figure 3. What does this fact tell us about the Yano economy? One possible cause of the relatively low production indicated by point A may be that some resources are idle—that is, unemployed. For example, certain workers may not be able to find jobs, some mineral deposits may not be mined, or machines to stamp out automobile bodies may not be in operation. The other possibility that gives rise to producing below the production possibilities boundary is the inefficient use of resources. This could be due to outright waste, for example, not allowing qualified and healthy people over the age of sixty-five to hold jobs. Or it could be due to combining resources in a less than optimal way. For instance, if each individual Chevrolet fender were cut out by hand instead of stamped out by a press, the cost of production would be greatly increased. Whenever goods or services are produced at higher cost than could be achieved by using another combination of resources, production is not efficient.

Whenever goods and services are produced at higher cost than could be achieved by using another combination of resources, production is not efficient.

FIGURE 3
Production Possibilities for the Nation of Yano, 1990

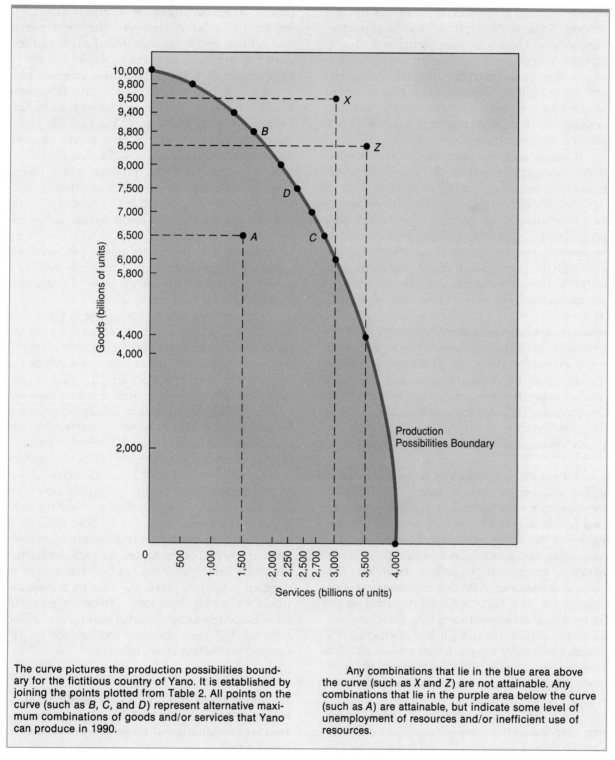

The curve pictures the production possibilities boundary for the fictitious country of Yano. It is established by joining the points plotted from Table 2. All points on the curve (such as B, C, and D) represent alternative maximum combinations of goods and/or services that Yano can produce in 1990.

Any combinations that lie in the blue area above the curve (such as X and Z) are not attainable. Any combinations that lie in the purple area below the curve (such as A) are attainable, but indicate some level of unemployment of resources and/or inefficient use of resources.

Point *A* production, or some other point in the purple area below the production possibilities boundary, is a very likely combination for Yano. In fact, Yano would be a very rare nation if it did not experience some unemployment of resources and some production inefficiencies. It is important to understand, however, that a country producing below its production possibilities boundary can increase output without an expansion of its resource base which takes time to achieve. In Yano's case, the nation could produce more goods or more services, or more of both, with its present resources.[1] But if Yano were producing on its production possibilities boundary, it could increase its production of goods at this time only by decreasing its production of services. Alternatively, Yano could increase its production of services only by decreasing its production of goods.

A country producing below its production possibilities boundary can increase output without an expansion of its resource base. A country producing on its production possibilities boundary can increase its production of something only by decreasing its production of something else.

Shifts in Production Possibilities Boundaries

What might the production possibilities boundary for Yano be expected to look like in 1995? Since the 1990 boundary was limited by Yano's resource base including technological knowledge, it would be very surprising if the boundary had not shifted by 1995. Figure 4 illustrates an outward shift. The 1995 production possibilities boundary is everywhere above the 1990 boundary because Yano has increased its resources related to both goods and services during those five years. Resources may have increased because the population has grown (more working-age people), the amount of physical capital has increased, or more new natural resources have been discovered than have been used up. Probably the technological knowledge, or the

---

1. Such improvement may be made through better management by Yano's private businesses and through more enlightened policy by the government of Yano.

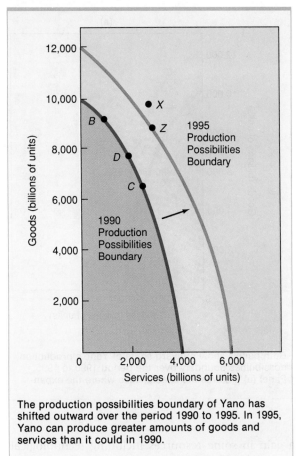

FIGURE 4
Shift of Production Possibilities Boundary for the Nation of Yano, 1990 to 1995

The production possibilities boundary of Yano has shifted outward over the period 1990 to 1995. In 1995, Yano can produce greater amounts of goods and services than it could in 1990.

"state of the art," in many industries has also improved, so that by 1995 more goods and services could be produced even with no additional physical resources.

Figure 4 shows the output points *B*, *D*, and *C*—maximum output combinations in 1990—to be less than maximum output combinations in 1995. Point *Z*, which was impossible to reach in 1990, is on the new production possibilities boundary and therefore attainable in 1995. But point *X*, which was impossible to reach in 1990, is still unattainable, though not by nearly so much.

Alternative shifts are shown in Figure 5. Panel (a) shows a situation in which the 1995 production possibilities boundary has expanded for goods, but not for services. This might have been the result of

FIGURE 5
Alternative Production Possibilities Shifts for the Nation of Yano, 1990 to 1995

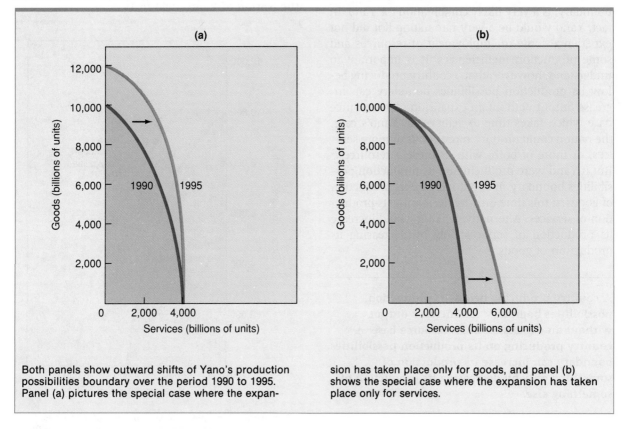

Both panels show outward shifts of Yano's production possibilities boundary over the period 1990 to 1995. Panel (a) pictures the special case where the expan-sion has taken place only for goods, and panel (b) shows the special case where the expansion has taken place only for services.

a gain in some resources including technological knowledge that can only produce goods. In 1995, Yano can produce as much as 2,000 billion additional units of goods, but still no more than 4,000 billion units of services. Note, however, that in 1995 compared with 1990, with the exception of the "all-services" output choice, Yano is able to produce combinations of output with more goods and the same amount of services, with more services and the same amount of goods, or with more goods and more services.

Panel (b) shows an alternative situation—the production possibilities boundary has expanded for services, but not for goods. This might have occurred because of a gain in resources including technological knowledge that can only produce services.

Production possibilities boundaries are expected to shift outward over time, but there is no guarantee that they will. They could remain the same or actually shift inward. Population—especially of working age—could drop. A decrease in capital goods could take place if saving and investment do not keep up with the replacement of capital goods as they wear out. And natural resources may be used up faster than new discoveries are made.

Production possibilities boundaries are expected to shift outward over time, but they could remain the same or even shift inward.

Economics in Focus

Opportunity Costs in Health Care

Sometimes opportunity-cost decisions can be difficult to make. This is particularly true in the health care field where choices can literally involve life and death. In 1987 the Oregon legislature voted to cut off Medicaid funds for expensive transplants that benefited only a few patients and use the money instead to expand health care for poor women who were pregnant. On the face of it, this seemed a reasonable decision, but soon the media reported the case of Coby Howard, seven years old and suffering from leukemia, whose family could not pay for the bone-marrow transplant he needed. Without Medicaid funds for the transplant, Coby died. With Medicaid support, he might have lived. Thus his life was one small fraction of the opportunity cost problem in the legislature's decision.

Cases like Coby Howard's are receiving increased attention because of a recent move to "ration" health care. Costs for health care services have been spiraling out of control—reaching nearly 12 percent of U.S. GNP by 1988—and many experts argue that the nation does not have the resources to offer the best medical care to everyone who may want it. Therefore, the critics say, we ought to make sensible decisions about the ways in which health care is allocated. To determine whether a particular kind of procedure should be offered or withheld (or funded or not funded), we should consider its life-saving potential, its effect on quality of life, and its relative cost. Some analysts have even suggested that very elderly people should not be given expensive life-prolonging treatments, such as open-heart surgery and liver transplants, because the resources could be better used for other patients.

Arguments such as these often bring an angry response. *Omni* magazine envisioned the following scary scenario: Two Medicare patients, both having severe heart attacks, appear in an emergency room. One is 79, the other 80. The 79-year-old is given an expensive drug that saves his life. But the 80-year-old is past the maximum age for Medicare sponsorship of such treatments. Because there are no family members on hand to promise to pay for the drug, the doctors let the patient die.

If the decisions in a rationing plan are made intelligently, the overall benefits should be greater than the opportunity costs. But many people believe it is unethical to deny medical care for any reason related to economics or budgets. They point out that each human life is priceless, at least to the person who owns it, and often to others as well. Could we tell an aged Picasso that he was too old for government-funded surgery?

In practice, of course, the health care system rations scarce resources every day. Nurses run to the patient who needs them most; hospitals choose whether to spend money on a new dialysis unit or a larger staff; states decide who qualifies for Medicaid and who does not. But the debate on rationing has raised public awareness of the opportunity costs involved in all health care decisions.

Sources: Susan B. Garland with Barbara Buell, "Health Care for All or an Excuse for Cutbacks?" *Business Week,* July 26, 1989, p. 68; Michael D. Reagan, "Health Care Rationing: What Does It Mean?" *New England Journal of Medicine,* vol. 319 (October 27, 1988), pp. 1149–1151; Bill Lawren, "We're Sorry, Your Time Is Up," *Omni,* May 1988, p. 31; Eli Ginzberg, "US Health Policy—Expectations and Realities," *Journal of the American Medical Association,* vol. 260 (December 23, 1988), pp. 3647–3650.

SUMMARY

1. Scarcity refers to the limitations on obtaining all the goods and services that people want. Scarcity is considered *the* economic problem since it gives rise to the trillions of economic problems experienced by people everywhere. Most economists believe that scarcity of the goods and services that people want is unavoidable. (See page 64.)

2. Goods and services are considered scarce whenever people want more of a good or service than is available to them at a price of zero. They are scarce because the ingredients necessary to produce them, called resources, or factors of production, are scarce. (See page 64.)

3. Resources, or factors of production, are divided into three broad categories: (a) labor resources, (b) natural resources, and (c) capital resources. On closer examination, it becomes clear that the productive ability of any one of these resources depends very much on the quantity and quality of the other resources. (See pages 65–68.)

4. Whenever resources are scarce, the decision to produce or consume something involves an opportunity cost. Opportunity cost—that which is given up—can be seen as the true cost of choosing a particular alternative. (See pages 68–69.)

5. People face an opportunity cost in allocating their limited incomes as well as their time and effort. Government, too, must make choices; the opportunity cost of certain programs may be other programs, or it may be private sector spending. (See pages 69–70.)

6. Opportunity cost in production may be applied to a single firm or to an entire economy. In both cases it can be incorporated into a production possibilities boundary—a curve that shows all the alternative maximum combinations that can be produced with a given supply of resources including technological knowledge. (See pages 70–72.)

7. Production possibilities are expected to reflect increasing marginal opportunity costs. This means that the more units of a good or service that are produced, the higher the opportunity cost of producing even more units. The reason is that resources are generally not equally well suited for producing all kinds of goods or services. (See pages 72–73.)

8. A business firm or a country cannot produce amounts that are beyond its production possibilities boundary. It may, however, produce below the boundary. When it does so, it is either not using all of its resources or using them in an inefficient way. (See pages 73–75.)

9. Over time, production possibilities boundaries may shift outward or inward. It is more likely that the shift will be outward, reflecting an increase in resources including technological know-how. There will be an inward shift when fewer resources are available for production. (See pages 75–76.)

KEY TERMS

capital resources: goods, tools, or skills that are produced for use in further production (page 65).

enterpriser (entrepreneur):   one who seeks the best opportunities for production and takes risks when making such decisions (page 65).

entrepreneur: see **enterpriser.**

factors of production: see **resources.**

human capital: the skills that people use in combination with their labor effort (page 66).

innovator: one who brings an invention out of the laboratory, makes it practical, and applies it to actual production (page 65).

inventor: one who discovers or devises a new or improved process or product (page 65).

labor resources: all kinds of human work efforts that are or can be directed at production or enterprise (page 65).

natural resources: all things provided by nature that can be used in production (page 65).

opportunity cost: the true cost of choosing one alternative over another; the best alternative forgone when a choice is made (page 68).

production possibility: the limits to the quantities of goods and services that can be produced during any given time period with a given supply of resources including technological knowledge (page 71).

production possibilities boundary: a curve that represents all the alternative maximum combinations that can be produced during a given time period with a given supply of resources including technological knowledge (page 71).

resources (factors of production): input; the ingredients necessary for producing goods and services (output) (page 65).

scarcity: a condition that exists when the amount of something actually available and free of charge would not be sufficient to meet some requirement (page 64).

technological know-how: the ability to combine resources in producing the goods and services that a society wants (page 67).

tradeoff: when one good or service must be given up to gain a certain quantity of another good or service (page 70).

DISCUSSION QUESTIONS

1. Alex, who has just studied this chapter, tells his friend Beth that new cars are scarce in this country even though there are many unsold cars sitting around in new-car dealer show rooms and lots. Beth disagrees. She argues that these cars are not scarce goods, since there are plenty around waiting to be sold. Putting yourself in Alex's place, convince Beth that these cars are indeed scarce goods according to the definition of scarcity in economics.

2. Explain the relationship between the scarcity of goods and services and the factors of production, or resources, available in an economy.

3. The three classes of resources—labor, natural resources, and capital—are defined so broadly that all ingredients of production can be included. Classify each of the following and justify your answer:

    a. an automatic fruit picker
    b. a brain surgeon
    c. a wild horse
    d. an inventor
    e. an irrigated piece of land

4. Suppose you were the ruler of the country of Tava. Because you would like to increase the productive output of Tava, you decide to do whatever you can to increase the quantity of labor available for production. List ten different actions that you might take.

5. Joe says to Mary, "I just bought a beautiful blue cardigan sweater. It cost me $29.95." Mary responds, "It did? I thought it cost you those $29.95 slacks that you also wanted but now can't afford to buy." Who is right? Explain.

6. Government has the power to tax, borrow money, and even print money if it wishes to provide more goods and services. Therefore, government is *not* subject to opportunity cost. True or false? Explain.

7. Suppose that the nation of Doodag can produce only doods and dags and that its production possibilities schedule is the following:

Doods	Dags
0	1,000
200	800
350	600
425	400
500	200
550	0

    a. Construct a graph showing Doodag's production possibilities curve.
    b. Pick a point on the diagram that shows a combination of doods and dags that Doodag cannot now produce.
    c. Pick another point on the diagram that shows a combination of doods and dags consistent with some idle resources.
    d. Pick a third point at which no more doods can be produced, no matter how many or how few dags are being produced.

8. The production possibilities curve that you drew in the previous question was bowed out.

    a. What does that tell you about the marginal opportunity cost of doods in terms of dags and dags in terms of doods?
    b. Set up a new production possibilities schedule for Doodag, using output levels of doods and dags that result in a straight-line production possibilities curve.
    c. What does that tell you about the marginal opportunity cost of doods in terms of dags and dags in terms of doods?
    d. Set up yet another production possibilities schedule for Doodag, using output levels of doods and dags that result in a bowed-in production possibilities curve.

e. What does that tell you about the marginal opportunity cost of doods in terms of dags and dags in terms of doods?

9. What are the public policy implications for a nation that is producing on its production possibilities curve compared with those for one that is producing below (to the left of) its production possibilities curve?

10. Suppose that you know the production possibilities curve for a particular nation. What would you expect this nation's production possibilities curve to look like ten years later? Why?

11. Describe a set of specific circumstances that you believe would result in an inward (to the left) shift of a nation's production possibilities boundary.

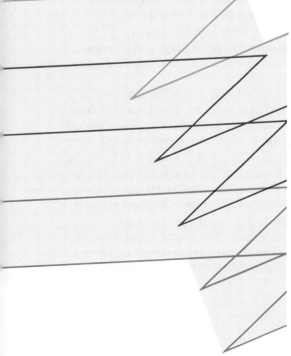

5

Demand and Supply— or Supply and Demand

Preview Ask the man or woman on the street what economics is about. The answer is apt to be either "supply and demand" or "demand and supply." If you ask a few more questions, you may hear about an "economic law" of supply and demand, which says that demand and supply determine prices and employment and the standard of living. You may also hear about the dangers that come from tampering with this "law." But if you go still further and inquire how we can tell what demand or supply *is* without already knowing the price, you can expect a blank stare, or hostility, or some less-than-flattering comment about economics and economists.

There is a problem here, which we must face at once. *Demand* and *supply* are used in two meanings. The person on the street uses them in the sense of *quantity*—amounts actually demanded or supplied, usually per week, month, or year. In this sense, the "economic law" of demand and supply means nothing more than that the amount bought must also be the amount sold. But most economists most of the time use *demand* and *supply* in the sense of a *schedule*, involving planned amounts demanded or supplied over a range of different prices. As will become clear in this chapter, no more than one point on a demand schedule, or on a demand curve graphed from a demand schedule, represents demand in the quantity sense. The same is true for supply.

This chapter introduces demand and supply in a schedule sense on two levels: (1) the individual consumer and individual firm, and (2) consumers and firms in markets. Let us take a quick look at these.

Individual consumer demand stems from each consumer's decisions. A consumer who has the money to spend will decide just what and how much to buy. Likewise, individual firm supply stems from decisions made by each business firm. A company that can attract labor resources, natural resources, and capital will decide what and how much to offer for sale.

Market demand is the sum of all the individual consumers' demands for a particular good or service in a certain location. Market supply is the sum of all the individual firms' supplies of that good or service in that same location. The interaction of market demand and market supply determines the market price used in buying and selling and the amount that is bought and sold in the quantity sense.

INDIVIDUAL CONSUMER DEMAND DECISIONS

Individual consumer demand refers to the quantity of a good or service that an individual consumer is willing and able to purchase at a particular moment at each possible price that might be charged for that good or service.

The term *demand* should not be confused with words such as *want, desire,* or *need.* A college student may very much want or desire to purchase an expensive sports car, but that does not constitute demand unless he or she is also able to buy it. The same college student may even be convinced that he or she really needs that sports car. But, once again, if the student cannot afford to buy the car, it is not considered demand. On the other hand, a very wealthy person may be able to afford to buy five such sports cars, but if that person decides to keep the money in the bank, there is also no demand. Demand requires both willingness and ability to buy a product.

The definition at the start of this section indicated that economists view demand "at a particular moment at each possible price." How is it possible for a consumer actually to be faced with different prices for the same good at the same time? It isn't, of course. The point is that the economist conceives of the individual's demand as his or her *plan* about how much to buy at different possible prices. The "at a particular moment" part of the definition simply means that we do not have to consider at the same time any variables other than the price and the quantity demanded of the good being

studied. It is thus a simplifying assumption—a somewhat disguised use of the *ceteris paribus* assumption, which was introduced in Chapter 3.

Individual consumer demand is the quantity of a good or service that an individual consumer is willing and able to purchase at a particular moment at each possible price that might be charged for that good or service.

To illustrate the relationship between price and quantity demanded by an individual consumer, let's take the case of Alex, who buys and wears jeans. Economists might express his demand function for jeans as follows:

$$QD_j^A = f(P_j), \textit{ceteris paribus}$$

In this functional relationship, QD_j^A is the quantity demanded of good j (jeans) by person A (Alex), f is the symbol for function (which may be read "depends on"), P_j is the price of jeans, and *ceteris paribus* means that all other variables are held constant. That is, we assume that there are no changes in such influential variables as Alex's tastes, his income, and the prices of other goods that he could or does buy. (Later in this chapter we shall discuss the effects of changes in these other variables.)

The relationship between price and quantity demanded of a good or service may be expressed in the form of a functional relationship such as: $QD_j = f(P_j)$, *ceteris paribus*.

Think of Alex being interviewed as part of a market survey that seeks to discover consumers' demand for jeans at various prices. During a period of a minute or so, the interviewer may ask Alex how many pairs of jeans he would buy over the next twelve months at five different prices. The interview is not long enough for Alex's tastes to have changed, nor does Alex receive any new information about his income or the prices of other goods that he could or does buy. Thus the interview setting comes close to meeting economists' requirements for defining demand: at alternative prices, different quantities of a good are demanded, provided other influential variables are held constant.

The Demand Schedule and Curve

Information such as that obtained from interviewing Alex may be recorded in a **demand schedule**—a table showing different prices for a good and the quantity of that good demanded at each of these prices.

Table 1 illustrates a demand schedule that is based on the interview with Alex. His answers are not surprising, since he said that he would demand fewer pairs of jeans at higher prices and more pairs at lower prices.

The information given in the demand schedule may be plotted on a graph. It is customary in eco-

TABLE 1
Alex's Demand Schedule for Jeans,
September 24, 1990

Price per Pair of Jeans (in dollars)	Quantity of Jeans Demanded (over next 12 months)
50	0
40	1
30	2
20	4
10	7

nomics to put the price on the vertical axis and quantity demanded on the horizontal axis. Price is the independent variable, and the quantity demanded is the dependent variable. Panel (a) of Figure 1 includes exactly the same information as is

FIGURE 1
Alex's Demand for Jeans, September 24, 1990

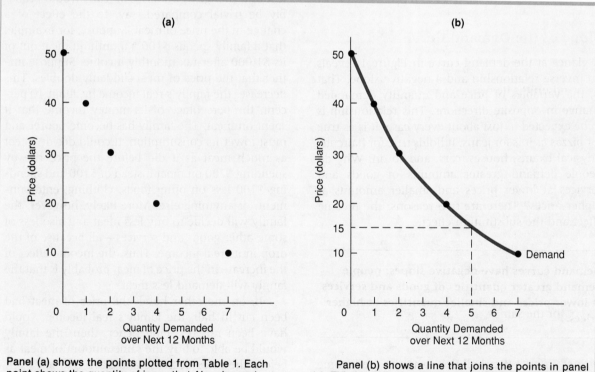

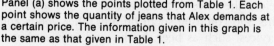

Panel (a) shows the points plotted from Table 1. Each point shows the quantity of jeans that Alex demands at a certain price. The information given in this graph is the same as that given in Table 1.

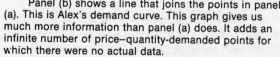

Panel (b) shows a line that joins the points in panel (a). This is Alex's demand curve. This graph gives us much more information than panel (a) does. It adds an infinite number of price–quantity-demanded points for which there were no actual data.

given in the demand schedule in Table 1. In panel (b) of Figure 1, a line has been drawn through these five plotted points to join them. This line adds an infinite number of price–quantity-demanded points. For example, you can read from the graph that, at a price of $15, Alex will demand five pairs of jeans. However, since the interviewer did not ask Alex how many jeans he would demand at $15, it is only an assumption that his answer would have been five pairs. All the points along the demand curve, except those few that come from actual data, are based on the assumption that the connecting line accurately describes the consumer's demand.

A demand schedule is a table that shows different prices for a good and the quantity of that good demanded at each of these prices. A demand curve is a graphic representation of the relation of quantity demanded and price.

Slope of the Demand Curve

A glance at the demand curve in Figure 1 reveals an inverse relationship and a negative slope. That is, the variables of price and quantity demanded change in opposite directions. This relationship is to be expected in just about every case. It is as true for pizzas as it is for jeans. It holds true for haircuts, physical exams, houses, cars, and so on. Why do people demand greater amounts of goods and services at lower prices and smaller amounts at higher prices? There are two reasons: the income effect and the substitution effect.

Demand curves have negative slopes: people demand greater quantities of goods and services at lower prices and smaller quantities at higher prices.

Income Effect   We shall first examine the income effect. Whenever a good or a service that a person buys goes up or down in price, it will affect that person's **real income**, that is, it will affect the purchasing power of that person's money (dollar) income. If the good or service goes up in price, the

person's real income will go down (other things being equal). Alternatively, if it goes down in price, the person's real income will go up. Alex is somewhat "richer" when jeans are $10 per pair than when they are $30 per pair because he can buy more with his money income. The **income effect** is the influence that a change in a person's real income (resulting from a change in the price of a good or service that this person buys) has on the quantity that this person demands of that good or service.

Whenever a good or service that a person buys goes up or down in price, it affects the purchasing power of that person's money income and therefore changes his or her real income.

For a typical American family, the income effect of a change in the price of jeans would probably be trivial compared, say, to the effect of a change in the price of meat. Suppose, for example, that a family spends $100 a month on meat out of its $1,000 after-tax monthly income. Suppose further that the price of meat suddenly doubles. This decreases the family's real income by about 10 percent, the percentage of its money income that it spent on meat. The family has become poorer and must lower its consumption. It could decide to eat as much meat as it did before the price rise by spending $200 on meat instead of $100 and spending $100 less on other foods, clothing, entertainment, or anything else. More likely, however, the family will decide to buy less meat and also less of some other goods and services—all because of the drop in its real income. Thus, the income effect of the increase in the price of meat probably is that the family will demand less meat.

If, on the other hand, the price of meat had been cut in half, the family's real income would have been raised. Being richer, then, the family would be able to buy the same amount of meat as before the price decrease and have $50 left over. This $50 could be spent on any other goods and services, such as beer, books, and movies, but it could also be spent on meat. The drop in the price of meat raises the family's real income and probably increases the quantity of meat it will demand.

The income effect is the influence that a change in a person's real income has on the quantity of a specific good or service this person demands.

Substitution Effect The second reason why the demand curve is expected to be negatively sloped is the **substitution effect**. This is the effect that a change in *relative* prices of substitute goods or services (resulting from a change in the price of a good or service) has on the quantity that a person demands of that good or service. Whenever the price of any one good or service changes while other prices stay constant, relative prices are altered. People will wish to substitute goods that became relatively cheaper for those that became relatively higher priced. At higher prices for jeans, Alex will find that other types of pants, such as cotton casuals, will be relatively cheaper. He will probably substitute some cotton casuals for some jeans. On the other hand, at lower prices for jeans, cotton casuals are relatively higher priced, and Alex will most likely buy more jeans and fewer cotton casuals. Thus, because of the substitution effect, the quantity demanded of a good will be higher at lower prices of that good and lower at higher prices of that good.

The substitution effect is the effect that a change in relative prices of substitute goods or services has on the quantity that a person demands of a good or service.

The preceding discussion has treated the income effect and the substitution effect separately; in fact, they occur together. Alex is quite typical in that he finds that at higher prices of jeans his real income is lower *and* he will substitute other types of pants for jeans. Thus the income effect and the substitution effect work together to explain the negative slope of the demand curve.

The income effect and the substitution effect occur together; higher prices cause lower real incomes and lead people to substitute other goods and services.

Changes in the Quantity Demanded and Changes in Demand

Economists usually mean something different when they talk about a "change in the quantity demanded" than when they talk about a "change in demand." The quantity demanded of a good is expected to be different at different prices of that good. A *change in the quantity demanded* is reflected in a **movement along a demand curve**. It is important to keep in mind that while this movement along the demand curve is taking place, tastes, income, and prices of other goods are being held constant through the *ceteris paribus* assumption. As you will recall, Alex said that he would demand four pairs of jeans at a price of $20 per pair, but only two pairs at a price of $30 per pair. A glance back at panel (b) of Figure 1 reveals several such changes in the quantity demanded—movements from one plotted point to another along Alex's demand curve for jeans.

A "change in demand," on the other hand, is not caused by a change in the price of that good. A *change in demand* is reflected in a **shift of the demand curve**—a displacement of the entire curve to the right or to the left. But this can happen only when the *ceteris paribus* assumption is relaxed or removed. If time is allowed to enter the model (another interview takes place at a different time), tastes, income, and prices of other goods may change. This means that at any given price of the good, either more or less may be demanded. Figure 2 illustrates two alternative demand shifts. Curve D_1—the original demand curve—is the same demand curve as that derived for Alex in Figure 1. Curve D_2 is the result of a demand shift to the right, which shows that Alex will demand more jeans at any given price. Curve D_3 is the result of a demand shift to the left, which shows that Alex will demand fewer jeans at any given price. For example, Figure 2 shows that Alex originally demanded four pairs of jeans at $20 a pair. When Alex demands seven pairs at $20 a pair, it shows that the demand curve has shifted to the right (to D_2). When he demands only two pairs of jeans at the same $20 price, the demand curve has shifted to the left (to D_3).

A change in quantity demanded is reflected in a movement along a demand curve. A change in

FIGURE 2
Alex's Demand for Jeans: Two Alternative Demand Shifts

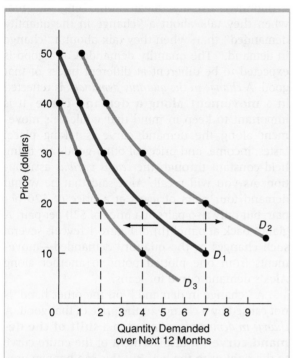

Curve D_1 is the original demand curve that was derived for Alex in Figure 1. When time is allowed to enter the model so that Alex's taste, his income, or the prices that he pays for other goods may change, his demand curve may shift to D_2 or D_3. A shift to D_2 shows that Alex will demand more jeans at any given price. A shift to D_3 shows that Alex will demand fewer jeans at any given price.

demand is reflected in a shift of the whole demand curve.

Shift Variables Economists use the term *shift variables* to refer to variables that cause a curve to be relocated—to "shift"—on a graph. Clearly, there can be a great many shift variables for any function or curve, since there is no limit to the number of variables that are covered by the *ceteris paribus* assumption. There are three especially important shift variables for an individual's demand curve.

An increase in a consumer's *taste* for a good or service will cause the demand curve to shift to the

right, and a decrease in taste will bring about a shift to the left, other things being equal. If Alex, who has been wearing dress pants to work, suddenly decides that jeans are more comfortable and just as appropriate, his demand curve for jeans will shift to the right. On the other hand, if Alex has been wearing jeans to work and his boss "suggests" that dress pants are more correct, his demand curve for jeans will probably shift to the left.

An increase in a consumer's *income* will usually cause his or her demand curve to shift to the right, and a decrease in income usually brings about a shift to the left. Alex can afford to buy more jeans when his income is higher and fewer when it is lower. Only in rare cases will higher income cause people to demand less and lower income cause them to demand more. It is possible, however, that at very much higher income levels some people will demand fewer hamburgers since they will have switched to steak.[1]

Shifts in demand for a good also result from *price changes of other goods*, especially closely related goods. Such "other" goods may be grouped into two categories: substitutes and complements.

Shift variables, related to demand, are variables, such as taste, income, and price changes of other goods, that may cause an individual's demand curve to shift (be relocated on a graph).

Substitutes **Substitutes** are goods that may be used instead of one another. Examples of good substitutes are beer and ale, Coca-Cola and Pepsi-Cola, and vinyl kitchen flooring and kitchen carpeting. An increase in the price of a substitute will cause the demand curve for the other good to shift to the right, and a decrease in the price of a substitute brings about a shift to the left. If Alex finds that jeans and cotton casuals are fairly good substitutes, and if cotton casuals go up in price, he will buy more jeans and fewer cotton casuals. In this case, Alex's *quantity demanded* for cotton casuals goes down and his *demand* for jeans goes up. Similarly, a decrease in the price of cotton casuals will cause Alex to demand fewer jeans and more cotton casuals. This time Alex's *quantity demanded* for cotton

1. When the demand for a product is negatively related to a person's income (such as the hamburgers in our example), economists refer to that product as *inferior*.

casuals goes up and his *demand* for jeans goes down.

Complements   **Complements** are goods that are used with each other. Examples are automobiles and gasoline, ski boots and ski poles, and kites and string. Alex will demand fewer jeans if the type of belt that he wears with jeans, but not with other pants, goes up in price. That is, if the package, made up of a pair of jeans and one of these belts, has gone up in price, he will demand fewer jeans. Also, if the price of these belts decreases, Alex may demand more jeans.

Substitutes are goods that may be used instead of one another; complements are goods that are used with each other.

When goods have several uses, they may be complementary in some cases and substitutable in others. It is then a complicated problem in economic statistics (econometrics) to discover which relation dominates at any particular time or place. And, of course, the answer may vary from time to time or from place to place. At a time or place where soft drinks like Coca-Cola or Seven-Up are never used as mixers for alcoholic drinks, soft drinks will be substitutes for alcoholic ones. At a time or place where soft drinks are used almost entirely as mixers and almost never consumed by themselves, the dominant relation will be complementary.

This discussion of complementary and substitute goods has been limited to the demand side of the market. As you will see, there are similar relationships on the supply side, and it will be useful to distinguish between the effects of complementarity and substitutability in demand (as here) and the effects of complementarity and substitutability in supply.

INDIVIDUAL FIRM SUPPLY DECISIONS

Individual firm supply refers to the amount of a good or service that an individual business firm is willing and able to sell at a particular moment at

each possible price. Notice that this definition is quite similar to the one offered for demand on page 82. The only real difference is that the word *sell* is substituted for the word *purchase*.

More than just the willingness to supply a good is needed in order to supply it. A firm must be able to attract the resources, or factors of production, that are necessary to produce the good or service. A company that manufactures jeans may wish to produce 10,000 pairs per week, but it will not supply that many if it lacks the right machinery or enough employees to do the work.

As was true of demand, economists use the *ceteris paribus* assumption when viewing supply. Thus they avoid having to consider at the same time any variables other than the price and the quantity supplied of the good being studied.

Individual firm supply is the quantity of a good or service that an individual business firm is willing and able to sell at a particular moment at each possible price.

To illustrate the functional relationship between price and quantity supplied by an individual firm, we shall use the hypothetical Cohen Clothing Corporation, which manufactures jeans, as an example. In economics, we might express the relationship as follows:

$$QS_j^C = f(P_j), \text{ ceteris paribus}$$

Here QS_j^C is the quantity supplied of good j (jeans) by firm C (Cohen Clothing Corporation), f is the symbol for function (and may be read as "depends on"), P_j is the price of jeans, and *ceteris paribus* means that all other variables are held constant.

Specifically, *ceteris paribus* holds constant a number of influential variables. Most important among them are the prices of inputs needed for production, the state of the technology, the company's expectations about the prices of other goods that it does or could produce, and its goals. (As you will see, these are *shift variables* in respect to the firm's supply curve.)

Imagine that Mr. Cohen, the president of Cohen Clothing Corporation, is being interviewed as part of a survey trying to discover the quantity of jeans supplied by companies at various prices. During a very short interview, the interviewer may ask Mr. Cohen how many pairs of jeans his firm would supply over the next twelve months at each of five alternative prices. The interview is not long enough for Mr. Cohen's goals to change, nor does he receive any new information on the prices of inputs, the state of jean technology, or the prices of other goods that his firm is or could be producing. Thus, this interview setting, like that used in defining demand, closely meets economists' needs for defining supply: at alternative prices, different quantities of a good are supplied, as long as other influential variables are held constant.

The Supply Schedule and Curve

Information such as that obtained from interviewing Mr. Cohen may be placed on a **supply schedule**—a table showing different prices for a good and the quantity of that good supplied at each of these prices.

Table 2 illustrates the supply schedule based on the interview with Mr. Cohen. Economists are not surprised to learn that his firm would supply more jeans at higher prices and fewer jeans at lower prices.

A supply schedule is a table showing different prices for a good and the quantity of that good supplied at each of these prices.

The information in the supply schedule is plotted on the graphs in Figure 3. As we pointed out earlier, the economist customarily places price on

TABLE 2
Cohen Clothing Corporation's Supply Schedule for Jeans, September 24, 1990

Price per Pair of Jeans (in dollars)	Quantity of Jeans Supplied (over next 12 months)
50	80,000
40	70,000
30	50,000
20	30,000
10	0

the vertical axis and the quantity variable—quantity supplied in this case—on the horizontal axis. Price is the independent variable, and quantity supplied is the dependent variable. Panel (a) of Figure 3 shows the plotted points from Table 2. Panel (b) of Figure 3 has a line drawn through the plotted points to show all the price–quantity-supplied points, whether plotted from actual interview data or only assumed, which make up the supply curve.

Slope of the Supply Curve

The supply curve in Figure 3 shows a direct relationship and a positive slope—the variables of price and quantity supplied change in the same direction. This relationship can be expected in just about every instance as long as we stick to the conditions existing for the interview with Mr. Cohen. Under these conditions, which hold other influential variables constant, what is true for jeans will be true for almost any good or service that a firm might produce. Why, under these circumstances, do firms supply greater amounts at higher prices and smaller amounts at lower prices? In a word, the reason is *profit*. The supply curve for an individual firm is expected to be positively sloped because profits are an important goal for businesses. Under the *ceteris paribus* assumption used in deriving the supply curve, supplying jeans will be more profitable when their price is $30 than when their price is $20. Therefore, the company will naturally want to put more resources into the production of jeans when their price is $30 than it would when the price is only $20.

The company might find that it pays to use some of its older equipment (despite a higher production cost) to produce more jeans when their price reaches a certain higher level. It is likely that the Cohen Clothing Corporation produces other clothing besides jeans—that it is a multiproduct firm. It may also produce shirts, skirts, and socks. If, indeed, the Cohen Clothing Corporation is a multiproduct firm, it will probably find that, at a high price of jeans, it pays to alter its product mix. Thus it will commit more of its production facilities and its employees to the production of jeans and less to the production of shirts, skirts, and socks. Taken together, these various explanations make it quite clear why firms find it profitable to supply

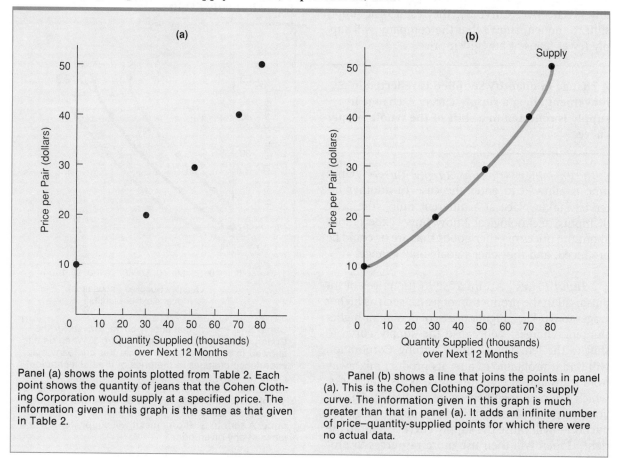

Panel (a) shows the points plotted from Table 2. Each point shows the quantity of jeans that the Cohen Clothing Corporation would supply at a specified price. The information given in this graph is the same as that given in Table 2.

Panel (b) shows a line that joins the points in panel (a). This is the Cohen Clothing Corporation's supply curve. The information given in this graph is much greater than that in panel (a). It adds an infinite number of price–quantity-supplied points for which there were no actual data.

more of a good when they can sell it at a higher price and less of a good when its price is lower.

Supply curves have positive slopes; firms find it profitable to commit more resources to the production of a good or service when its price is higher and less when its price is lower, *ceteris paribus.*

Changes in the Quantity Supplied and Changes in Supply

Now it is time to make a distinction between a "change in the quantity supplied" and a "change in supply," which is similar to the distinction made between a "change in the quantity demanded" and

a "change in demand." The *quantity supplied* of a good is expected to be different at different prices of that good (shown as a **movement along a supply curve**). A *change in supply* is expected to take place when the variables held constant by the *ceteris paribus* assumption, which we can call "shift variables," are allowed to change (shown as a **shift of the supply curve**).

Panel (b) of Figure 3 showed several changes in the quantity supplied—movements from one plotted point to another—along the Cohen Clothing Corporation's supply curve for jeans. Figure 4 shows changes in supply—two possible shifts of Cohen's supply curve that result from relaxing or removing the *ceteris paribus* assumption. Curve S_1, the original supply curve, is the same as that derived for the Cohen Clothing Corporation in Figure

3. Curve S_2, the result of a supply shift to the right, shows that the company will supply more jeans at any given price. Curve S_3, the result of a supply shift to the left, shows that the company will supply fewer jeans at any given price.

A change in quantity supplied is reflected in a movement along a supply curve. A change in supply is reflected in a shift of the whole supply curve.

Shift Variables Affecting Supply Curves Once time is allowed to enter the case (if another interview takes place at a different time), the price of inputs, technological know-how, expectations about the prices of other goods that are or could be produced, and the seller's goals may change.

Input Prices An increase in the prices of inputs used in the production of jeans, such as higher wages to workers, higher prices of denim, or higher shipping charges, will cause the supply curve to shift to the left. The Cohen Clothing Corporation will find it profitable to alter its product mix away from jeans and in favor or shirts, skirts, and socks, which are now relatively more profitable. The reverse case—decreasing prices of inputs used in production—will cause the supply curve to shift to the right. Cohen will then use more resources to produce more jeans at each price.

Technological Know-How An advance in technological know-how related to producing jeans, such as new and more efficient sewing machines or a better managerial technique, results in decreased costs. The Cohen Clothing Corporation would not be expected to adopt a new method of producing jeans unless it lowered costs and increased profits. In such cases, the supply curve shifts to the right.

Expected Prices of Other Goods The supply curve may also shift because of a change in the expected prices of other goods that the supplying firm does or can produce. At any given price of jeans, the Cohen Clothing Corporation will alter its product mix in favor of more jeans if it expects

FIGURE 4
Cohen Clothing Corporation's Supply of Jeans: Two Alternative Shifts

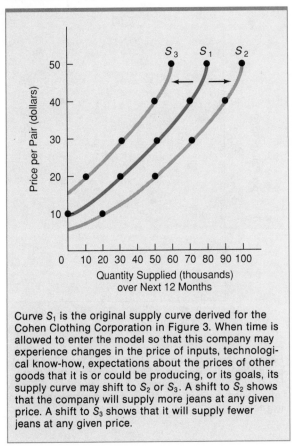

Curve S_1 is the original supply curve derived for the Cohen Clothing Corporation in Figure 3. When time is allowed to enter the model so that this company may experience changes in the price of inputs, technological know-how, expectations about the prices of other goods that it is or could be producing, or its goals, its supply curve may shift to S_2 or S_3. A shift to S_2 shows that the company will supply more jeans at any given price. A shift to S_3 shows that it will supply fewer jeans at any given price.

lower prices for shirts, skirts, and socks. Likewise, it will produce fewer jeans and more shirts, skirts, and socks if its price expectations for these other goods are raised. Hence, a firm's supply curve for one product tends to shift to the right when expected prices of its other products fall and to shift to the left when expected prices of its other products rise.

Goals of Sellers Finally, supply curves shift because of changes in the goals or motives of sellers. Throughout this discussion it has been assumed that the sellers were in business to make profits. If firms did not care about profits, the theory of supply would break down, since they would just as soon sell more as less when the price is low.

However, the assumption that firms prefer more rather than less profit does not mean that no other motives can play a role.

The desire to *do good* may be a strong motive. Part of Cohen's desire to sell more jeans may be that they last well and give people good value for their money. *Security*, or a concern about survival, may be another motive for firms. Perhaps the Cohen Clothing Corporation wants to sell more jeans because it expects *"bigness"* will give greater long-term security, and not because it expects larger profits. Firms may wish to avoid large risks—even if there is a chance that they will pay off handsomely—and decide not to commit themselves to produce certain goods whose prices have temporarily gone up.

Individual managers' goals—as distinct from the firm's goals—may also affect supply. The president of the Cohen Clothing Corporation may seek the *prestige* and *salary* that go with being the head of a very large firm. Thus the supply curve would shift to the right, as he would be willing to supply more at any given price. Of course, another firm's president may be motivated to act in exactly the opposite way. That president may wish to decrease the size of the firm so that he or she can have a hand in every part of the business. In that case, the supply curve would shift to the left, as the firm would supply less at any given price.

Shift variables that affect supply curves include changes in input prices, advances in technological know-how, changes in the expected price of other goods the firm can or does produce, and changes in the goals or motives of sellers.

"Increases" and "Decreases" in Supply   When is a supply shift an increase in supply, and when is it a decrease? Because supply curves usually slope upward, there sometimes is confusion on this important point. (Because demand curves normally slope downward, there is no similar problem on the demand side.) To illustrate the problem, we shall return to Figure 4. The shift from S_1 to S_2 is an increase in supply, since for any given price, quantity supplied is greater on curve S_2 than on curve

S_1. The shift from S_1 to S_3 is a decrease in supply, since for any given price, quantity supplied is less on curve S_3 than on curve S_1. The direction of the arrows tells us which is which, but notice that S_3 lies vertically *above* S_1, which lies vertically above S_2. When reading supply and demand curves, then, we should remember to concentrate on horizontal rather than vertical comparisons.

MARKET DEMAND AND SUPPLY

A **market** is the organized action between potential buyers (market demand) and potential sellers (market supply) that enables them to carry on exchange or trade. In a free market, demand and supply determine the terms of trade, or the price at which a purchase or sale is made.

A market is the organized action between potential buyers and potential sellers that enables them to carry on exchange or trade.

Market demand is the sum of all of the individual consumers' demands (the information found in their demand schedules) for a particular good or service in a certain place over some period of time. Recall Alex, whose demand schedule for jeans was shown in Table 1. Suppose that Alex lives in Chicago and that everyone in that city also gives us his or her demand schedule for jeans. All the quantities demanded at each possible price can then be added together to determine the market demand for jeans in Chicago over the same twelve-month period. Table 3 presents some hypothetical numbers, and Figure 5 illustrates that market-demand curve.

Market supply is the sum of all of the individual firms' supplies (the information found in their supply schedules) of a particular good or service in a certain place over some period of time. One such schedule, the Cohen Clothing Corporation's supply schedule for jeans, was given in Table 2. Suppose that the Cohen Clothing Corporation supplies jeans only to the Chicago area and that all the other clothing firms that also serve Chicago

TABLE 3
Market-Demand Schedule for Jeans in Chicago,
September 24, 1990

Price per Pair of Jeans (in dollars)	Quantity of Jeans Demanded (over next 12 months)
50	50,000
40	500,000
30	2,000,000
20	5,000,000
10	9,000,000

provide us with their Chicago supply schedules for jeans as well. The quantities supplied at each possible price can then be added up to determine the market supply for jeans in Chicago over the same twelve-month period. Table 4 provides some hypothetical numbers, and Figure 6 pictures that market-supply curve.

FIGURE 5
Market Demand for Jeans in Chicago, September 24, 1990

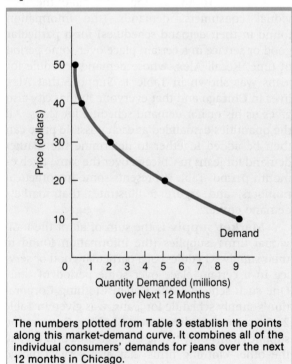

The numbers plotted from Table 3 establish the points along this market-demand curve. It combines all of the individual consumers' demands for jeans over the next 12 months in Chicago.

Market demand is the sum of all the individual consumers' demands for a particular good or service in a certain place over some period of time. Market supply is the sum of all the individual firms' supplies of a particular good or service in a certain place over some time period.

Equilibrium Price and Quantity

Up to this point, demand and supply have been treated separately but in a similar way. In real life, of course, demand and supply actions take place at the same time. Only when they are examined together, therefore, can it be seen how market demand and market supply determine the price of a product and the quantity that is bought and sold.

Both market demand and market supply limit the quantity of a product that is traded. The amount of a product that is sold at a certain price cannot exceed the demand for it at that price. Nor can more of a product be bought at a particular price than firms are willing to supply at that price. Therefore, the price tends to change whenever it does not equate the quantities of market demand and market supply.

Market demand and market supply determine the price of a product and the quantity that is bought and sold.

The price that does equate quantity demanded with quantity supplied in the market is called the **equilibrium price**, and the accompanying quantity is called the **equilibrium quantity**. As you will recall, equilibrium means that a state of balance has been achieved and that there is no longer a tendency for change.

The price that equates quantity demanded with quantity supplied in the market is called the equilibrium price; the accompanying quantity is called the equilibrium quantity.

TABLE 4
**Market-Supply Schedule for Jeans in Chicago,
September 24, 1990**

Price per Pair of Jeans (in dollars)	Quantity of Jeans Supplied (over next 12 months)
50	8,000,000
40	7,000,000
30	5,000,000
20	3,000,000
10	0

To illustrate equilibrium price and quantity, let us return to our example involving the market demand and market supply of jeans in Chicago. Figure 7 combines the market-demand curve shown in Figure 5 and the market-supply curve shown in Figure 6 in a single diagram. At any price above $23.50, more jeans will be supplied than are demanded. For example, Figure 7 shows that at a

FIGURE 6
**Market Supply of Jeans in Chicago,
September 24, 1990**

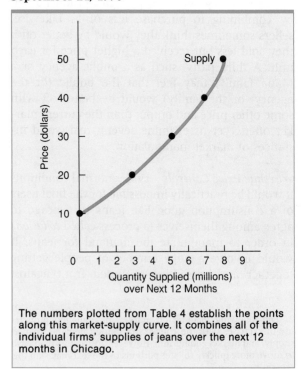

The numbers plotted from Table 4 establish the points along this market-supply curve. It combines all of the individual firms' supplies of jeans over the next 12 months in Chicago.

FIGURE 7
Market Demand and Market Supply for Jeans in Chicago, September 24, 1990

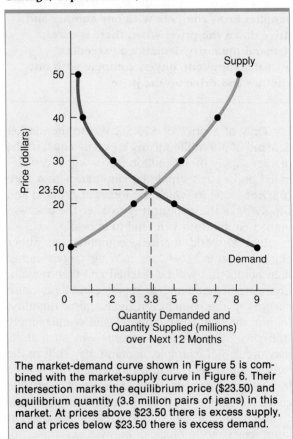

The market-demand curve shown in Figure 5 is combined with the market-supply curve in Figure 6. Their intersection marks the equilibrium price ($23.50) and equilibrium quantity (3.8 million pairs of jeans) in this market. At prices above $23.50 there is excess supply, and at prices below $23.50 there is excess demand.

price of $30 a pair, only 2 million would be demanded but 5 million would be offered by suppliers. (These numbers can also be taken from the market-demand and market-supply schedules shown in Tables 3 and 4.) Such **excess supply**—quantity supplied exceeding quantity demanded—will cause supplier firms to compete with one another in an attempt to sell their jeans, thereby driving down the price. Alternatively, at any price below $23.50, more jeans will be demanded than firms are willing to supply. Figure 7 shows, for example, that at a price of $20 per pair of jeans, 3 million would be supplied, but 5 million would be demanded. Such **excess demand**—quantity demanded exceeding quantity supplied—will cause buyers to compete with one another in an attempt to buy jeans, thereby driving up the price.

When there is excess supply (the quantity supplied exceeding the quantity demanded), supplier firms compete with one another and drive down the price. When there is excess demand (quantity demanded exceeding quantity supplied), buyers compete with one another and drive up the price.

Only at a price of $23.50, where the market demand of 3.8 million jeans is exactly equal to the market supply of 3.8 million jeans, will excess demand and excess supply be eliminated. In a **free market**—one in which the forces of demand and supply have the opportunity to alter the price—a market equilibrium will tend to appear.

In real-world markets, equilibria are rather elusive—that is, they are moving targets rather than points that will be reached and then remain. Changing demand and/or supply conditions cause changes in the equilibrium price and/or quantity. In our discussion of demand shifts and supply shifts, we offered several reasons why such shifts may occur. For example, demand may shift to the right if consumers' incomes increase, if their taste for the good gets stronger, if prices of substitute goods increase, or if prices of complementary goods go down. Supply may shift as a result of changes in input costs, technological knowledge, prices of other goods that firms are or could be producing, or the motives to which sellers respond. We expect fairly frequent changes in some of these variables. Every such change will bring about a shift, except for the coincidental case in which changes exactly offset each other—as, for example, where income goes up at the same time as there is a compensating decrease in the price of a substitute good. Every shift will bring with it a new equilibrium price and/or quantity. But supply and demand curves usually shift so often that there is not enough time to adjust to any one equilibrium before a new one appears. Thus, market equilibria are seen as moving targets that may never be reached.

In a free market—one in which the forces of demand and supply have the opportunity to

alter the price—a market equilibrium tends to appear, although shifts in demand and/or supply cause the equilibrium state to be a moving target.

Market Manipulation[2]

Markets can be manipulated, or controlled, by buyers, sellers, or outsiders (regulators). These manipulators can try either to change the equilibrium position or to preserve a disequilibrium position. Equilibrium and disequilibrium cases should be distinguished carefully. As you know, equilibrium in a market is a state of balance between quantity demanded and quantity supplied. When the two are unequal, there is **disequilibrium**.

When quantity demanded and quantity supplied do not balance in a market, disequilibrium exists.

Buyers sometimes think that they would be better off if they forced the price of a product down by combining to purchase less of it. Likewise, sellers sometimes think they would be better off if they sold less but received a higher price for each unit. A third party, such as a public agency or a Mafia family, may feel that the public (or the agency, or the family) would be better off with some other price and output than the current market offers. Let us examine several real-world instances of market manipulation.

Wartime Price Controls   Under normal conditions it would be practically impossible for the final users of a consumption good like jeans in Chicago to agree among themselves (a process called *collusion*) in order to manipulate the demand for jeans. It would involve a huge number of people getting together and presenting a united front against

---

2. The following material on market manipulation provides useful exercises with the concepts of market demand, market supply, and market equilibrium. However, instructors who wish to move more quickly to later portions of the text may skip this section.

those who broke their agreement, often called "chiselers." But consider the market for a civilian good—jeans will do—in a war economy, after productive capacity has been diverted to the production of a military good—uniforms. Look at Figure 8, which again shows the supply (S_1) and demand (D_1) curves found in Figure 7. Think of these curves as describing the prewar situation—the equilibrium quantity is 3.8 million pairs of jeans, and the equilibrium price is $23.50. Next, consider how diverting production from jeans to military uniforms will affect the supply of jeans. Because of the war, supply has fallen (shifted to the left) from S_1 to S_2 and the free-market price has risen from $23.50 to $30.

Now suppose that the government proposes to hold the price at $23.50 without restraining civilian demand in general by some means such as higher taxes. Government can try to hold the price of jeans at $23.50 by either an equilibrium or a disequilibrium method. Since the disequilibrium method is simpler, at least on the diagram, we will examine it first. The government may establish a **ceiling price**—a maximum price at which a product may legally be sold—at $23.50. This is called a *disequilibrium method* because, since the new supply curve (S_2) shows that only 1.1 million pairs of jeans will be supplied at $23.50, an excess demand, or a **shortage**, of 2.7 million pairs is created (3.8 million demanded minus 1.1 million supplied equals the 2.7 million shortage). The legal price can be enforced reasonably well for a time, especially if the war is a popular one like World War II in the United States between 1942 and 1945. (No such method was tried during the unpopular Vietnam War between 1963 and 1973.)

The disequilibrium method of market manipulation involves creating shortages or surpluses of goods and services.

The *equilibrium method* of market manipulation involves shifting the demand curve or the supply curve for a good or service. For example, the demand curve may be shifted through "formal" rationing. (Shortages usually also give rise to "informal rationing," through individual merchants reserving supplies for their best customers, and so

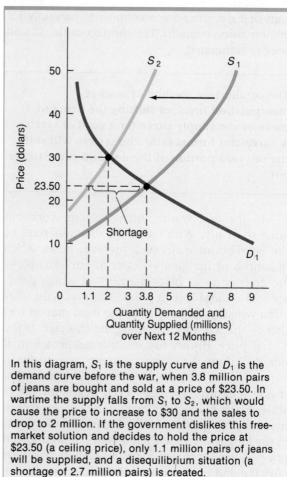

FIGURE 8
Market Manipulation: Disequilibrium Method with a Ceiling (Maximum) Price in the Market for Jeans

In this diagram, S_1 is the supply curve and D_1 is the demand curve before the war, when 3.8 million pairs of jeans are bought and sold at a price of $23.50. In wartime the supply falls from S_1 to S_2, which would cause the price to increase to $30 and the sales to drop to 2 million. If the government dislikes this free-market solution and decides to hold the price at $23.50 (a ceiling price), only 1.1 million pairs of jeans will be supplied, and a disequilibrium situation (a shortage of 2.7 million pairs) is created.

on.) Formal **rationing** calls for a detailed and often complicated plan involving the issuance by government of special coupons, or tokens, that act as a second form of money.[3] For example, it might take $23.50 plus a special ration coupon to buy a pair of jeans. If successful, a formal rationing sys-

---

3. Consider gasoline rationing. The plan would need to take into account many different factors. For example, some families have more cars and some more drivers than others. Some people live much closer to work than others. Access to public transportation and to car pooling also varies greatly. Some people use automobiles in their jobs more than others, especially in emergencies. And a few also use gasoline for tractors, trucks, and other vehicles.

tem will cut demand. This is shown in Figure 9, which is identical to Figure 8 except that it shows a shift of the demand curve from D_1 to D_2. The new demand curve is shown to be vertical at 1.1 million pairs of jeans, since the government issues only 1.1 million ration coupons. The shortage at the $23.50 price is eliminated.

The equilibrium method of market manipulation involves shifting the demand curve or the supply curve for a good or service. A successful formal rationing system will shift the relevant portion of the demand curve to the left.

In the real world, things seldom work out quite so neatly. With either the disequilibrium or the equilibrium method, a problem arises when quantities of the goods—jeans in our example—are diverted to a "black market," in which goods are sold at illegally high prices. This makes the situation worse by shifting S_2 in the legal market further to the left and increasing the shortage at the $23.50 price. History suggests that neither a formal nor an informal rationing system can satisfy all consumers as "equitable." It also suggests that strong measures (perhaps even death for large-scale black-marketing) would be necessary to maintain an equilibrium or a disequilibrium system in the long run. In the United States, rationing and price controls practically collapsed within a year after the end of World War II.

Both the disequilibrium and the equilibrium methods of market manipulation can be stymied by the development of black markets, in which goods are sold at illegally high prices.

Farm Price Supports and OPEC Manipulations that set minimum prices, or floor prices, for certain products can also be analyzed and explained with our supply and demand curves. We shall describe the American farm price supports as a case of disequilibrium and the OPEC (Organization of Petro-

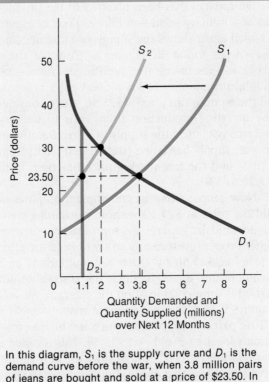

FIGURE 9
Market Manipulation: Equilibrium Method with Rationing in the Market for Jeans

In this diagram, S_1 is the supply curve and D_1 is the demand curve before the war, when 3.8 million pairs of jeans are bought and sold at a price of $23.50. In wartime the supply falls from S_1 to S_2, which would cause the price to increase to $30 and the sales to drop to 2 million. If the government dislikes this free-market solution, it may wish to hold the $23.50 price through rationing, shown as lowering the demand to D_2. A new equilibrium situation is created as 1.1 million pairs of jeans are bought and sold at $23.50.

leum Exporting Countries) system as a case of equilibrium.

Agricultural price supports have been in use in the United States for over fifty years. They are applied on a product-by-product basis. Figure 10 illustrates a hypothetical case involving wheat. Let's say that if a free market were allowed to determine equilibrium price and quantity, the price would settle at $4.50 a bushel, and the quantity bought and sold would be 1.2 billion bushels. If, instead, a **floor price**, or **support price**—a minimum price that is legally set for a product—of $5.25 were established by the government, a surplus would be

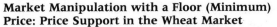
FIGURE 10
Market Manipulation with a Floor (Minimum) Price: Price Support in the Wheat Market

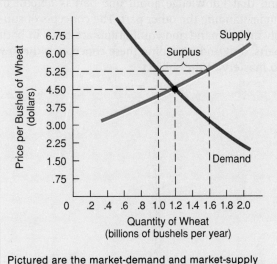

Pictured are the market-demand and market-supply curves for wheat. The equilibrium price is $4.50 per bushel of wheat, and the equilibrium quantity is 1.2 billion bushels per year. The government decides to impose a support price of $5.25. At this disequilibrium price, the quantity supplied is 1.6 billion bushels per year, and the quantity demanded is only 1.0 billion bushels. The result is a surplus of 0.6 billion bushels per year.

The OPEC experience illustrates an equilibrium variety of market manipulation aimed at achieving a higher price. Formed in 1960, OPEC became an effective international petroleum force in the early 1970s. Through market manipulation it was successful in raising the price of crude oil about forty-fold in less than a decade. Figure 11 is a simplified illustration of how this system operates. The market-supply and market-demand curves are labeled S_1 and D, respectively. If a free market were allowed to determine equilibrium price and quantity, the price would be $13 per barrel, and the quantity bought and sold would be 39 million barrels per day. But OPEC has the authority to reduce supply to 17 million barrels per day, as shown by the vertical line labeled S_2. The new price of $28 per barrel of crude oil is an equilibrium one that leaves no surplus.

FIGURE 11
Market Manipulation with a Floor (Minimum) Price: OPEC Price in the Crude Petroleum Market

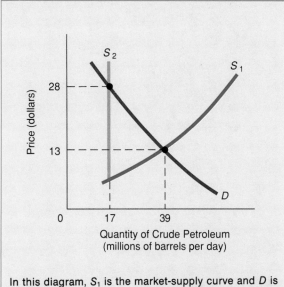

In this diagram, S_1 is the market-supply curve and D is the market-demand curve. In a free market, 39 million barrels of crude oil per day are bought and sold at $13 per barrel. When OPEC reduces the supply to 17 million barrels, as shown by the new vertical supply segment S_2, the resulting equilibrium price increases to $28 per barrel.

created. A **surplus** is the amount of excess supply that stems from a disequilibrium situation. The amount of the surplus in this example is 0.6 billion bushels. At the support price of $5.25, consumers would demand 0.2 billion bushels less and farmers would supply 0.4 billion bushels more than they would have at the free-market price of $4.50. Government can maintain the floor price by purchasing the surplus.[4]

A floor price (support price) is a minimum price that is legally set for a product. Government can maintain a floor price by purchasing the surplus, or excess supply, of a product.

---

4. In practice, a system of production controls is used along with government purchase of the surplus.

WHICH SEQUENCE: MACRO-MICRO OR MICRO-MACRO?

You may study macroeconomics before you study microeconomics, or you may study microeconomics first and then study macroeconomics. The sequence depends in part on the plans made by your own college or university. Whichever sequence you use, it is important to remember that each is simply a portion of the total subject of economics and that knowledge about one part is helpful in understanding the other part. The concepts of supply and demand and equilibrium are basic in both parts, and understanding these concepts is the key to mastery of the subject.

Economics in Focus

Drought and Food Prices *or* No Rain—A Lot of Pain

The price of eggs jumped 9.6 percent in one month. Fruit and vegetable prices rose 4.7 percent, poultry prices 7.4 percent. The month was July 1988, and shoppers across the nation felt the pinch. A severe drought was damaging U.S. farm crops, causing food prices to surge upward. Newspapers, magazines, and TV news programs offered pictures of dying corn stalks and dry, cracked earth.

The drought of 1988 provides a dramatic illustration of how changes in supply affect everyday life. As dry weather continued throughout the summer, grain crops withered in the field. The reduction in crops shifted the grain supply curve to the left; this meant that for any given price of grain, the quantity reaching the market would be less than before. By August corn prices stood at $2.89 per bushel, up from $1.60 in July 1987—an increase of over 80 percent. In the same period the price of wheat rose 49 percent.

The rise in grain prices soon affected others foods as well. Since farmers fed grain to their livestock, their costs shot up, and these higher costs reached the consumer as increased prices for eggs and milk products. Meat supplies increased temporarily as many farmers slaughtered their stock to avoid large feed bills; but after a while meat prices tended to follow the general upward trend.

The U.S. market was also influenced by foreign supply and demand. By late 1988 farmers in Argentina, attracted by the high price of soybeans in the United States, were planting more of that crop. This might have been good news for consumers of soybean products, but the situation was complicated by several other factors: (1) In planting more soybeans, the Argentinians reduced their acreage devoted to corn; (2) Argentina was a major supplier of corn to the Soviet Union, which also bought corn from the United States; and (3) Argentina too was suffering from a drought. The overall outcome, some analysts feared, would be a tiny corn crop in Argentina and a resulting increase in Soviet purchases from the United States; then the price of U.S. corn would be forced up even further.

The 1988 rise in grain prices did not cause any substantial drop in the quantity demanded. As prices start up, buyers do not curtail their buying by very much. One paradoxical effect is that many U.S. farmers do well in drought years such as 1988. Although harvests are reduced, prices rise so quickly that farmers often make a greater profit on their small crop than they would in a normal year on a large crop. This is not true, of course, for farmers whose fields are entirely devastated by the lack of rain. They can only hope that the next year will bring better weather for themselves and bad weather for other farmers who grow the same crops.

Sources: "Heatstroke," *Time*, September 5, 1988, p. 51; Timothy Tregarthen, "Drought Sends Farm Prices Soaring," *The Margin*, January–February 1989, pp. 22–23; Theodore Young, "The Drought Will Boost Food Prices—and Farmers' Incomes," *Fortune*, September 12, 1988, pp. 19–22.

SUMMARY

1. The economic meaning of *demand* is that a consumer is both willing and able to purchase a good or a service, and not that he or she merely wants, desires, or needs that good or service. Likewise, the term *supply* means that a firm is both willing and able to produce a good or a service. (See pages 81–82.)

2. Individual consumer demand and individual firm supply are defined at a particular moment in time. This method of definition holds all variables constant except for the quantity and price of the good or service being studied. The functional relationships of demand and supply relate the respective quantities to the respective prices, while all other variables are held constant. (See pages 82–83.)

3. Demand curves have negative slopes, which means that the variables of price and quantity demanded change in opposite directions. The first reason for this relationship is the income effect, or the effect that a change in a person's real income (brought on by a change in the price of a good) has on the quantity that he or she demands of that good. The second is the substitution effect, or the effect that a change in relative prices of substitute goods (brought on by a change in the price of a good) has on the quantity demanded of that good. (See pages 84–87.)

4. Supply curves have positive slopes, which means that the variables of price and quantity supplied change in the same direction. The reason is that firms find it profitable to commit more resources to the production of a good or a service when its price is higher and less when its price is lower, other things being equal. (See pages 88–89.)

5. Changes in the quantity demanded and in the quantity supplied are reflected as movements along their respective curves, whereas changes in demand and supply are reflected as shifts of the curves. A movement along a curve is caused by a change in the price of the good or service being studied. A shift of a curve occurs when the *ceteris paribus* assumption is relaxed. Demand curves shift when tastes, income, or prices of other goods change. Supply curves shift when input prices, technological know-how, expectations about the prices of other goods that the firm is or could be producing, or a seller's goals change. (See pages 89–91.)

6. Market demand and market supply are derived by adding up, at each possible price, individual consumer demands and individual firm supplies of a particular good or service in a certain place over some period of time. (See pages 91–92.)

7. When market supply is greater than market demand, there is excess supply, causing supplier firms to compete with one another and thereby driving down the price. When market demand is greater than market supply, there is excess demand, causing buyers to compete with one another and thus driving up the price. In a market, when quantity demanded is equal to quantity supplied, there is a state of balance—the equilibrium price and the equilibrium quantity have been reached. (See pages 92–94.)

8. Markets are sometimes manipulated by buyers or by sellers. This manipulation may result from a collusive agreement. Buyers may shift the market-demand curve to the left, thereby achieving a lower equilibrium price. Sellers may shift the market-supply curve to the left, thereby achieving a higher equilibrium price. (See pages 94–96.)

9. Disequilibrium in a market is the condition in which quantity demanded is not equal to quantity supplied. It may arise as a temporary situation, or it may be maintained by government action. Government may impose a higher-than-equilibrium price, which will be marked by excess supply, or a surplus. Or the government may impose a lower-than-equilibrium price, which will be marked by excess demand, or a shortage. (See pages 96–97.)

KEY TERMS

ceiling price: a maximum price at which a product may legally be sold (page 95).

complements: goods that are used with each other (page 87).

demand schedule: a table showing different prices for a good and the quantity of that good demanded at each of these prices (page 83).

disequilibrium: a market state in which the

quantity demanded does not equal the quantity supplied (page 94).

equilibrium price: the price that equates quantity demanded with quantity supplied in a market (page 92).

equilibrium quantity: a quantity of a good or service that equates the quantity supplied and the quantity demanded at a particular price in a market (page 92).

excess demand: the extent to which the quantity demanded exceeds the quantity supplied (page 93).

excess supply: the extent to which the quantity supplied exceeds the quantity demanded (page 93).

floor price (support price): a minimum price that is legally set for a product (page 96).

free market: a market in which the forces of demand and supply determine the price (page 94).

income effect: the influence that a change in a person's real income (resulting from a change in the price of a good or service that this person buys) has on the quantity that this person demands of that good or service (page 84).

individual consumer demand: the quantity of a good or service that an individual consumer is willing and able to purchase at a particular moment at each possible price that might be charged for that good or service (page 82).

individual firm supply: the quantity of a good or service that an individual business firm is willing and able to sell at a particular moment at each possible price that might be charged for that good or service (page 87).

market: the organized action between potential buyers and potential sellers that enables them to carry on exchange or trade (page 91).

market demand: the sum of all of the individual consumers' demands for a particular good or service in a certain place over some period of time (page 91).

market supply: the sum of all the individual firms' supplies of a particular good or service in a certain place over some period of time (page 91).

movement along a demand curve: a change from one point on a demand curve to another point on the same curve due to a change in the price of the product (page 85).

movement along a supply curve: a change from one point on a supply curve to another point on the same curve due to a change in the price of the product (page 88).

rationing: any method of restricting the demand for a good or service. Government may formally invoke a system of rationing in order to deal "fairly" with what would otherwise be an excess demand situation (page 95).

real income: the purchasing power of a person's money income (page 84).

shift of the demand curve: a displacement of an entire demand curve to the right or left showing a change in demand (page 85).

shift of the supply curve: a displacement of an entire supply curve to the right or left showing a change in supply (page 88).

shortage: the extent to which the quantity supplied of a good or service is less than the quantity demanded for it (page 95).

substitutes: goods that may be used instead of one another (page 86).

substitution effect: the effect that a change in relative prices of substitute goods or services (resulting from a change in the price of a good or service) has on the quantity that a person demands of that good or service (page 85).

supply schedule: a table showing different prices for a good and the quantity of that good supplied at each of these prices (page 88).

support price: see **floor price.**

surplus: the amount of excess supply that stems from a disequilibrium situation (page 96).

DISCUSSION QUESTIONS

1. Dave says, "I need three pairs of shoes this year." Will this information help you in constructing Dave's demand curve for shoes? Explain your answer.

2. Carefully describe what is meant by an income effect and a substitution effect. Then explain how the income effect and the substitution effect of a price change normally cause the demand curve for a good or service to be negatively sloped.

3. Construct a graph showing a demand curve for automobiles as you would expect it to look. On this diagram show a "change in the quantity demanded" and a "change in demand" that exactly compensate for each other. (The quantity of automobiles shown on the horizontal axis should be the same before and after these two changes occur.) What do you suppose happened to bring about these two changes?

4. Give five examples of pairs of goods and/or services that are viewed as substitutes by some consumers and as complements by others. For each pair, tell what conditions cause them to be both substitutes and complements.

5. A company's supply curve for micro-computers has shifted to the right. Give four reasons why this may have occurred.

6. Becky Ryder buys one pound of Jarlsberg cheese for $5.60, but when the price rises to $6.00, she buys only three-fourths of a pound. Draw a demand curve that shows her purchases. Is this a shift or a movement along a curve? Becky's favorite cheese is Brie, the price of which has just

dropped to $4.00 a pound. Show the effect of this change on her demand curve for Jarlsberg. Is this a shift or a movement along a curve?

7. If faced with a serious excess supply in a particular market, what would you advise the government to do? Explain the basis for your recommendation.

8. During an emergency period a government may impose a ceiling price on a certain good in order to slow down the flow of an important resource into the production of that good. This ceiling price may go along with either an equilibrium or a disequilibrium situation. How might the government bring about each of these situations? Why might it choose one over the other?

9. In New York City certain apartments have been "rent controlled" for the last several decades. (Rent control is a form of ceiling price.) How does this help you to explain each of the following?

a. Poor maintenance of these apartment houses

b. Apartment shortages

c. Well-to-do rental agents (often superintendents)

Classical Economics: The Dismal Science?

Two unflattering terms, "dismal science" and "pig philosophy," were attached to political economy, as economics was called, in mid-Victorian Britain. They both come from the pen of the great Scottish historian and social critic Thomas Carlyle (1795–1881). The term "dismal science" has survived, though "pig philosophy" has not. Which economic doctrines of Carlyle's day inspired the term "dismal science"?

Adam Smith, who died before Carlyle was born, could hardly be called a dismal scientist, for his doctrine was quite upbeat. In an essay on development, written in 1755, Smith said,

> Little else is requisite, to carry a state to the highest level of opulence from the lowest barbarism, but peace, easy taxes, and a tolerable administration of justice, all the rest being brought about by the natural course of things.

FIVE DISMAL IDEAS

It was with the two following generations of economists, writing under the influence of the French Revolution, the Napoleonic Wars, and the Industrial Revolution, that the "dismal" ideas—some indeed implied by other passages in Smith's work—achieved their prominence. We stress five of these doctrines:

1. The Malthusian principle of population
2. The subsistence theory of wages
3. The principle of diminishing returns (to both labor and capital)
4. The tendency of profits to a minimum
5. Economic stagnation in the stationary state

Adam Smith (1723–1790)

The first of these ideas is due primarily to Thomas Robert Malthus (1766–1834) and the others mainly to David Ricardo (1772–1823). These doctrines are all related to each other in what is called "the English classical system." Even though they refer only to a pure market economy, their proponents are sure that no other economic organization can do better than what Adam Smith described as "the obvious and simple system of natural liberty."

The first two doctrines (of the above five) are dismal in their implication that the ordinary worker gains little or nothing from economic progress. The

David Ricardo (1772–1823)

Thomas Robert Malthus (1766–1834)

second pair imply that the ordinary capitalist may also lose as capital is accumulated in a growing economy, so that the major beneficiary of economic growth is a passive and unproductive class of land-owners. The fifth and last of these ideas predicts that economic progress itself will be short lived, and will eventually peter out in a dull and gloomy stagnation.

It is interesting to note, however, that the most popular ''classical'' economics textbook, John Stuart Mill's *Principles of Political Economy* (1848), was far from dismal as to either the future of the working class or the nature of the stationary state. Mill thought wages might rise gradually to meet the basic needs of the workers. And he imagined the stationary state as a pleasant period of economic inactivity, when people might turn their attention from money grubbing and materialism to plain living, high thinking, and the higher culture generally.

But let us return to the five dismal ideas themselves.

Malthusian Principle of Population Malthus believed he observed, mainly from what happened in the American colonies, a natural tendency for population to grow faster than the means of subsistence (the food supply). As the population grew at a geometric rate (2, 4, 8, . . .), the food supply would rise only at an arithmetical one (1, 2, 3, 4, . . .). Only the ''positive checks'' of famine, war, and disease would hold the population within bounds, unless of course human nature could be changed to accept such ''preventive checks'' as later marriage and sexual continence within marriage.[1]

Subsistence Theory of Wages From Malthusian demography to a subsistence theory of wages is only a short step. If wage rates, set by supply and demand, remain higher than the workers' customary level of subsistence, workers will marry earlier and more of their children will live, until the rising supply of workers pushes wage rates down again. On the

1. Malthus, an ordained clergyman of the Church of England, regarded contraception, abortion, infanticide, and homosexuality as forms of ''vice,'' and did not include them in his ''preventive checks.''

other hand, if wage rates fall below the subsistence level, later marriage, infant mortality, and emigration will after a time lower the supply of workers and raise wages again. There is a complication, however, because the classical economists all knew that English wages and subsistence levels were higher than those of Ireland or of Continental Europe. They reasoned that this could happen if wages remained high or low for long enough to improve or lower workers' levels of living in general—raising the staple diet from potatoes to wheat, or lowering it from wheat to potatoes. But this important complication was often overlooked in the simpler statements of classical wage theory.

Principle of Diminishing Returns "With every mouth," said Benjamin Franklin, "God sends a pair of hands." And so, especially if more machinery is accumulated along with the extra hands, why should food ever run short? Because, according to the dismal scientists, the principle of diminishing returns is operating. The extra hands, even with extra equipment, yield lesser amounts of additional output from a constant stock of agricultural land and other natural resources. It follows, then, that a doubling of the population, even if accompanied by a doubling of the capital supply, does not double the total output. For this reason, output per person falls off. (This argument ignores any qualitative improvements in either physical or human capital—as when a tractor replaces a team of oxen or a literate peasant steps into the shoes of his or her illiterate parent.)

Tendency of Profits to a Minimum Classical economists used the term "profits" to refer to the returns to capital. As physical capital in particular is accumulated and becomes subject to diminishing returns, new investment will only be demanded at a real rate of interest that tends to fall over time.[2] And as the return on their savings falls, capitalists will save less. These processes of falling real interest rates and falling saving rates will continue until the rate of return to capital is so low, and capitalists'

savings are so small, that there is no longer any net increase in the capital stock. In other words, capitalists' savings will just balance the depreciation and obsolescence of the existing stock.

Economic Stagnation With wages approximately constant and return on capital falling to a minimum, which some economists suspect is near zero, the principal gainer from economic progress becomes the landlord. Landlords win out because both increasing population and increasing capital raise the demand for land, both good and bad. Much land that is infertile or remote and that commands no rent in "the early and rude state of society" comes to earn substantial rent as society grows—in the American case as the frontier moved west. The gain comes with minimum effort on the part of the landowning family, which may be descended from a successful capitalist of a few generations back.

ARE THE IDEAS STILL ALIVE TODAY?

Some combination of the five gloomy ideas that gave economics the name of "the dismal science" has outlived the English classical school itself. The depressing ideas live on today in such statements as "American agriculture is a losing proposition, subsidized by returns from land speculation," and in assurances that no other system could do better than the free market.[3] Perhaps the name itself persists also because so many students are required to take economics when they would rather study an easier or more immediately appealing subject.

Strange as it may seem, there are more than a few economists today who, calling themselves "new-classicals" or "neo-Ricardians," propose to bring back these ideas about the working of a market economy. However, they would substitute the gloomy ideas for the pleasanter "neoclassical" ideas that succeeded them and to some extent de-dismalized the subject!

---

2. A real rate of interest is one that has been adjusted to correct for inflation.

3. The argument here is that every individual is a better judge of his or her own interest than is any government bureau, and that every individual will work harder in his or her own interest than in carrying out the orders of superiors.

The Circular Flow, Aggregate Demand, and Aggregate Supply

National Income Accounting

Inflation and Unemployment

Economic Fluctuations

PART II
THE
MACROECONOMY

6

The Circular Flow, Aggregate Demand, and Aggregate Supply

Preview You cannot see, touch, hear, smell, or taste a macroeconomy. You are not likely to meet one on the street or be introduced to one at a party. What *is* a macroeconomy, then? This chapter answers that question by providing a way of visualizing a macroeconomy as a *circular flow* of economic activity. It emphasizes interactions among the various actors on the economic stage and shows that one person's expenditures or expenses become another person's income. In a sense, we support ourselves by "taking in each other's laundry." This circular flow of income and expenditures through the economy shows how the different actors depend on each other and how they experience together the ups and downs of the macroeconomy.

The circular flow also provides an introductory explanation of the concepts of equilibrium and disequilibrium in the macroeconomy. It illustrates how business firms make production plans based on forecasts of future sales receipts. It shows how the macroeconomy changes when actual sales receipts turn out to be different than planned.

The last part of the chapter introduces the concepts of aggregate demand and aggregate supply—the macroeconomic counterparts of the microeconomic demand and supply concepts presented in Chapter 5. The aggregate demand and aggregate supply concepts not only illustrate macroeconomic equilibrium but they also provide the analytical framework that will integrate the various theories examined in later chapters.

THE CIRCULAR FLOW OF ECONOMIC ACTIVITY

Macroeconomics is the part of economics that is concerned with aggregate, or *grand total,* economic activity.[1] In contrast to **microeconomics,** which studies the activities of individuals and business firms, macroeconomics examines the functioning of the entire economy—the aggregate supply of goods and services and the aggregate demand for them.

Macroeconomics examines the functioning of the entire economy—the aggregate supply of goods and services and the aggregate demand for them.

In order to provide a visual representation of the macroeconomy, economists have developed various illustrations of the **circular flow** of aggregate economic activity. Like satellite pictures on television weather shows, these illustrations help viewers see patterns that are too vast to be recognized easily from ground level. From the perspective of the circular-flow model, it is easier to understand relationships among the various parts of the macroeconomy and to appreciate the internal consistencies needed for its continued operation. The circular flow provides an introduction to the macroeconomy.

A circular-flow representation of the macroeconomy is shown in Figure 1. All the households in the economy are represented by the red box on the left side of the figure. Inside this box, the functions of households as consumers and resource owners are noted. All the firms in the economy are represented by the purple box on the right side of the figure. The functions of firms as buyers of resources and producers of final goods and services are noted inside this box. The circular flow itself is shown by the arrows going in a clockwise direction around the circle. These arrows represent flows of income and expenditures. Although they are not shown in Figure 1, you may imagine another set of arrows, running opposite to those shown. These imagined arrows would represent flows of goods and services moving counterclockwise around the

1. See Chapter 1, page 6.

circle. The flows represented by the arrows are payments made in exchange for goods and services. We will first give a quick survey of these flows, without interruption for definitions and discussion. Then we will follow each path in detail.

A circular-flow diagram can be used to represent the working of the macroeconomy. The arrows show the flow of income and expenditures.

The flow across the bottom of the figure represents payments by firms to households in exchange for the use of resources that, in a capitalist economy, are owned by household members. These payments consist of wages (and benefits), rents, interest, and profits. These payments are the income of the factors of production—labor, natural resources, capital, and entrepreneurship. Because entrepreneurs are members of households, profits are included in this flow. We assume that this income amounts to $1,000 billion per year.

In the upper half of the circle, the flow of expenditures is divided into four streams.

1. Consumption purchases, where expenditures are made directly to firms. This is the largest use of funds by households. In our illustration, we assume that $700 billion is spent for consumption purchases.

2. Saving, which flows to financial markets and then, if borrowed to finance purchases of capital goods, goes on to the firms as investment purchases. We assume that saving amounts to $50 billion, which is 5 percent of income.

3. Net taxes, which flow to the government and then, if spent for government purchases, go on to the firms. We assume net taxes of $150 billion, or 15 percent of income.

4. Purchases of imports, which flow through international markets and, if spent by foreigners to buy products from the country whose flows are illustrated, go on to the firms as purchases by foreigners (exports). We assume $100 billion spent for imports.

The arrow across the bottom of the circular-flow diagram represents income to

FIGURE 1
The Circular Flow of Economic Activity

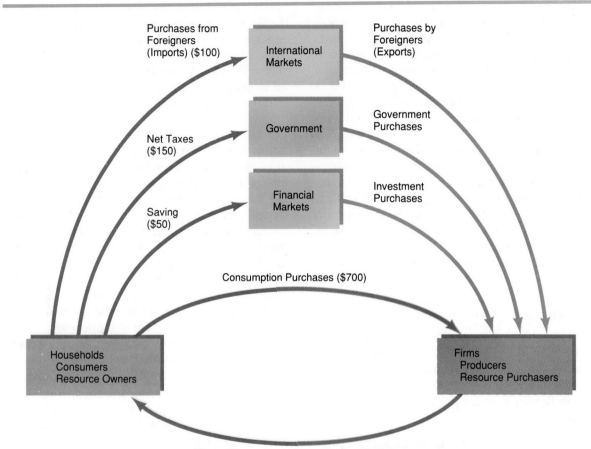

Wages, Rents, Interest, and Profits ($1,000)

Firms are producers of goods and services and also purchasers of resource services. They pay wages, rents, and interest to owners of resources and expect to earn profits for entrepreneurs. These payments flow through the stream at the bottom of the circle. Households, which are consumers and resource owners, receive payments from firms and divide this income among consumption purchases, saving, net taxes, and purchases from foreigners (imports), as shown by arrows on the top left part of the circle. Saving, net taxes, and import payments pass through financial markets, governments, and international markets, respectively, and flow on to firms as investment purchases, government purchases, and purchases by foreigners (exports). Circular-flow equilibrium exists if the amount received by firms through the top streams of the circle matches the amount paid out in the lower stream, including expected profits. (The illustrative amounts in parentheses are in billions of dollars.)

households. The arrows across the top represent expenditures.

To get a taste of how a macroeconomy operates, we will now follow the flow of income and expenditure around the circle, from the payments of income by firms to hire resources until the money returns to the firms in receipts from the sale of goods and services.

Payments for Resources

As you know, firms are the "actors on the economic stage" responsible for production.[2] In the

2. See Chapter 2, page 28.

circular flow, this means that, inside the purple box representing firms, entrepreneurs make forecasts about the prices and quantities of goods and services they expect to sell in the coming time period. If we think of the circle as representing the flows that take place in a year, entrepreneurs are planning production for the year ahead. We assume that the firms forecast a grand total sales volume of $1,000 billion for the coming year. To obtain the resources needed to produce these goods and services, firms expect to pay $1,000 billion for labor compensation, rent, interest, and profits. Except for profits, these payments are assumed to be contractual obligations during the period. As we will see, profits may turn out to be larger or smaller than expected but, if actual sales match the forecast, $1,000 billion will flow through the lower part of the circle. As noted earlier, entrepreneurs are members of households and expect to receive the planned amount of profit.

Household Uses of Funds

In the circular flow, households (in the red box at the left side of Figure 1) receive, or expect to receive, $1,000 billion from firms. Let us examine alternative uses for these funds and how they flow back to the firms across the upper portion of the diagram.

Consumption Purchases **Consumption purchases (C)** are expenditures by households to acquire the goods and services used during the period. If Figure 1 is for the United States economy, the arrow labeled "consumption purchases" shows income spent by U.S. households to buy goods and services produced by U.S. domestic firms during that accounting period. These expenditures flow directly to the firms and are used to finance labor, natural resources, capital, and profits in the production plans of the firms. We assume that $700 billion flows in this stream during the accounting period.

Saving and Investment Purchases **Saving (S)** means setting aside current income in order to increase wealth. Households may wish to prepare for consumption purchases or other expenditures they plan to make in the future, or they may wish to transfer wealth to others, through gifts or bequests,

at some future time. In the circular flow, the arrow labeled "saving" represents the income that households save during the year. The funds flow to banks, credit unions, savings and loan associations, stock and bond brokers, etc., which are located in the blue financial markets box in the diagram. These **financial intermediaries** accept deposits of income saved and offer to loan these funds, in return for interest payments, to those who wish to borrow.

Our simple circular flow does not contain an arrow to represent saving carried out by firms. But firms do set aside funds for future use and therefore do contribute to the aggregate flow of saving. They do this when some or all of their profits are not actually paid as dividends to stockholders and when funds are put into depreciation reserves to prepare for the eventual replacement of capital goods. Instead of drawing another arrow on the diagram and making it more complicated, imagine that household saving includes saving from firms and that the firms are saving on behalf of the stockholders, who are members of households.

In the circular-flow diagram, the **investment purchases (I)** arrow that emerges from the financial markets box represents expenditures on domestically produced **capital goods** (buildings, machines, and human capital) during the period. We assume that those who want to acquire capital goods borrow the needed funds in the financial markets. Firms do this explicitly when they borrow from financial institutions or sell stocks or bonds in financial markets. Even funds from "in-house" saving such as undistributed profits and funds put into depreciation reserves (which we include in household saving) usually are placed in financial institutions until the firms actually acquire the capital goods.

Does the amount of domestic investment (I) exactly match the amount of saving (S)—$50 billion a year in our illustration? Not necessarily. As we will see, some of the $50 billion saved may be diverted to government or to international markets so that domestic investment could be less than the amount saved. On the other hand, it is possible for the financial markets to draw funds *from* government or international markets so that domestic investment could exceed the amount saved. We will examine these possibilities later.

FIGURE 2
Government Borrowing in Financial Markets

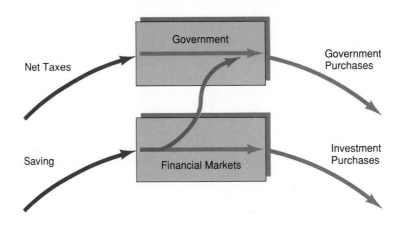

The green arrow represents funds borrowed by governments to finance deficits in their income and product budgets. In this way, funds that have been saved may pay for government purchases rather than for investment purchases. Investment purchases are *crowded out* by the government purchases financed with the borrowed funds.

Net Taxes and Government Purchases The money that flows from the household box to the government as **net taxes (Tn)** consists of the total amount of tax paid by households and firms minus **transfer payments,** such as checks sent from the government to welfare recipients, veterans, unemployed workers, and social security retirees. Transfer payments do not arise from any service rendered or product sold during the accounting period. Instead they are negative taxes—payments that are the opposite of taxes and go *from* government *to* households. In our illustration, we assume net taxes (taxes minus transfer payments) of $150 billion.

Inside the blue government box, net taxes constitute receipts for federal, state, and local governments, calculated to match the macroeconomist's treatment of transfer payments as negative taxes. Subtracting these transfer payments from total government expenditures leaves **government purchases (G)** of currently produced goods and services from domestic firms. These purchases provide a way for income paid in taxes to find its way back to the firms that hire resources to produce goods and services. Government budgets that treat transfer payments as negative taxes rather than as expenditures are called **income and product budgets.**

Does the amount received by firms through government purchases exactly equal the amount of net taxes? If the government income and product budgets are balanced, the answer is "yes." But if these budgets show a **deficit** (government purchases greater than net taxes), expenditures from governments to firms are greater than the amount of net taxes. Where do governments get the funds to cover their deficits? They borrow in the financial markets. This is illustrated in Figure 2, which focuses on the portion of the circular flow showing the government box and the financial markets box. The green arrow from the financial markets box to the government box represents funds borrowed by governments when their budgets are in deficit. In the United States, it is the responsibility of the U.S. Treasury to finance federal government purchases. So the arrow between the boxes in Figure 2 includes funds used to purchase U.S. Treasury securities. The securities become part of the national debt of the United States. This means that some of the saving flowing through the financial markets is used to pay for government purchases rather than to finance investment purchases. It is said that the

FIGURE 3
Government Budget Surplus Funds Flowing into Financial Markets

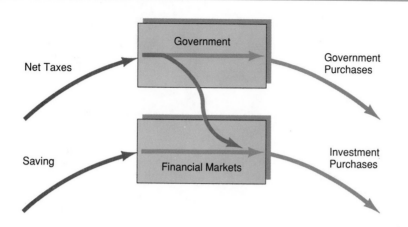

The green arrow represents funds from a government income and product budget surplus flowing into financial markets to retire government securities. In this way, income paid in taxes may finance private purchases of capital goods (investment).

government deficit is **crowding out** potential private uses of these funds.

In a *deficit* budget, government purchases are greater than net taxes. Government borrowing from financial markets in response to a deficit budget tends to *crowd out* private investment purchases.

If government purchases are less than net taxes paid, budgets are in **surplus.** In this situation, some tax receipts can be used to retire some of the securities that make up the national debt. Figure 3 shows funds flowing from the government into the financial markets. This is the reverse of crowding out, because some tax receipts are used to retire government debt securities and then may go on to firms to be used to finance private investment purchases.

If government purchases are less than net taxes paid, budgets are in surplus. In the case of a budget surplus, government can channel funds into financial markets. In this way, some tax receipts can be used to retire government debt securities and then become available to finance private investment purchases.

Imports and Exports The top stream of the circular-flow diagram in Figure 1 shows income flowing to international markets as households use some of their income to purchase goods and services produced abroad—to pay for **imports (Im).** We may imagine that this channel also includes payments for foreign-made capital goods, semifinished goods, and raw materials purchased by government or firms acting on behalf of those members of households who are stockholders. We assume that $100 billion is used to pay for imports.

Income that reaches international markets through payments for imports may emerge from those markets as purchases by foreigners, that is, as payments for **exports (X)** from the country whose circular flow is illustrated. The exports arrow represents payments by foreigners for goods and services produced by domestic firms. If the value of exports exactly equals the value of imports, the amount received by firms from export sales exactly matches the amount paid for imports. The country's **balance of trade** is in balance.

Imports **are purchases of goods and services produced abroad.** *Exports* **are domestically produced items purchased by foreigners.**

Although exports and imports the world over must balance, individual nations rarely achieve a perfect balance of trade. If a country has a deficit in its trade with the rest of the world, the amount of income flowing into the international markets box is greater than the expenditures flowing from that box to firms in that country. Foreigners have received more income from the importing country than they wish to spend on goods and services produced in that country. What do they do with this extra income? The answer is that they probably use it to earn interest and dividends by purchasing securities in the financial markets of the importing country. This is illustrated in Figure 4, which focuses on relationships between international markets and financial markets. The green arrow represents funds that flow from the international markets to the financial markets and become available to finance capital goods purchases (invest-

ment) or, if the government budget is in deficit, securities purchases by foreigners may help finance this deficit. A substantial amount of funds actually did follow this route in the U.S. macroeconomy in the 1980s, when the country had sizable deficits both in international trade and in its government budget. The United States went heavily into debt to foreigners.

If a country has a deficit in international trade, foreigners are receiving more income from the importing country than they wish to spend on goods and services produced in that country. In this instance, international markets may channel funds into domestic financial markets.

When a country has a surplus in international trade, the value of goods and services that foreigners are buying (exports of the country whose circular flow is illustrated) exceeds the value of goods and services that foreigners are selling to households and firms in that country (imports of

FIGURE 4
Inflow of Funds from International Markets

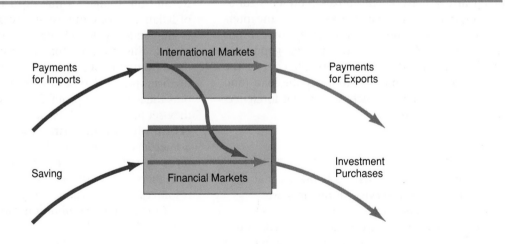

The green arrow represents funds flowing into domestic financial markets from international markets. This may happen when a country has a deficit in its trade with foreigners and the foreigners find attractive investment opportunities in the importing coun-

try. In this situation, purchases from foreigners (imports) are financed by going into debt to or selling assets to foreigners. The income paid for imports returns to the circular flow as foreigners finance investment in the importing country.

FIGURE 5
Outflow of Funds Due to an International Trade Surplus

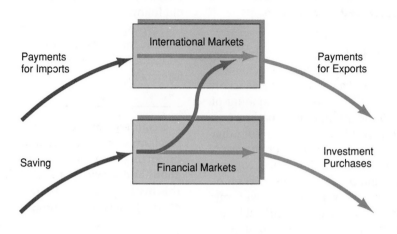

The green arrow represents funds flowing from domestic financial markets into international markets as foreigners borrow to help pay for goods and serv-ices they have purchased. In this way, some domestic saving returns to firms through the payments-for-exports channel.

that country). In this situation, foreigners may finance their extra purchases by borrowing in the financial markets of the country that has the trade surplus. This is illustrated in Figure 5, where the green arrow between the boxes represents funds flowing from the financial markets box to the international markets box. In this case, some funds saved by households and firms pay for goods and services purchased by foreigners. Of course, the foreigners have to promise to repay the loan (and also to pay interest), which means that foreigners are going into debt.

A surplus in international trade means that the value of goods and services foreigners are buying from a country exceeds the value of goods and services that foreigners are selling to that country. In this case, household savings and government budget surplus funds may flow into international markets.

MACROECONOMIC EQUILIBRIUM AND DISEQUILIBRIUM

Recall from Chapter 3 that **equilibrium** is a state of balance among opposing forces such that there is no tendency for change. In the circular-flow model, this requires that payments received by firms from sales of their products equal the amount the firms planned to pay out to purchase resources, plus the amount of profit that they expected when they set production plans. In other words, **macroeconomic equilibrium** exists when the sum of domestic consumption, investment and government purchases, plus exports (purchases by foreigners) equals the amount paid out by firms for resources used in production plus expected profits.

Circular-flow equilibrium can be expressed in the equation

$$C + I + G + (X - Im) = Y$$

where Y is income (the total earnings of resources, including expected profits), C is total purchases (including imports) of consumption goods by households, I is total purchases (including imports) of investment (capital) goods, G is total purchases (including imports) by governments, X is exports (total purchases by foreigners), and Im is imports (total purchases from foreigners). We have placed $X - Im$ in parentheses because it sometimes is convenient to refer to the terms together as *net exports*. The letter Y represents the amount of income flowing through the bottom stream of the circular flow in Figure 1, while the streams in the upper-right part of the circle represent total expenditures: consumption purchases, investment purchases, government purchases, and exports.[3]

When equilibrium exists, the plans firms made when they undertook production are fulfilled, so there is no reason (*ceteris paribus*) for them to plan any different level of production in the next round of the circle. In other words, given the level of prices expected when the plans were made, the output demanded by consumers, investors, governments, and foreigners equals the output supplied by firms. The firms find that inventories at the end of the process are exactly as they had planned.

Macroeconomic equilibrium exists (*ceteris paribus*) when payments received by firms from sales of their products equal the amount they planned to pay out to purchase resources, plus the amount of profit they expected when they set production plans.

Disequilibrium means that there is an imbalance among opposing forces such that there is some tendency for change. In the circular-flow model, disequilibrium exists when the total of purchases by consumers, investors, governments, and foreigners does not equal payments firms have made to employ resources plus their planned profit. Disequilibrium may be either *expansionary* or *contractionary*.

Expansionary Disequilibrium

Expansionary disequilibrium exists when the value of purchases by consumers, investors, governments, and foreigners is *greater than* the amount firms have paid for resources used in production plus their planned profits. That is,

$$C + I + G + (X - Im) > Y$$

Disequilibrium often originates in one of the three blue boxes at the top of the circular-flow diagram in Figure 1. Money may be created by financial institutions or by government or may flow into an economy from abroad. If the new money finances added investment purchases, added government purchases, or exports, it may cause expansionary disequilibrium.

Because profits are greater than planned, firms usually are delighted with this situation. However, the total quantity of output supplied according to the firms' plans has not been sufficient to meet the greater demand. Inventories have been depleted to satisfy the greater than expected demand for output. At the close of the path around the circle, the firms' inventories are smaller than desired.

Economists predict that, when inventories are smaller than desired, firms will increase production and/or prices for the coming round of the circle.[4] The increase in planned output may arise because estimates for the previous round had been too low. But even if the entrepreneurs stick with the sales estimates of the previous round, restoring inventories to desired levels will require a production increase. Prices will be increased in order to increase profits and slow the depletion of inventories.

Expansionary disequilibrium **exists when the value of purchases by consumers, investors, governments, and foreigners is** *greater than* **the amount firms have paid for resources used in production plus their planned profits.**

---

3. The letter Y is the symbol customarily used by economists to represent total production or total income in an economy.

4. Actually, firms may increase prices *during* the round of the circular flow. To simplify the description, we assume that prices do not change until the next round of the circular flow.

Contractionary Disequilibrium

Contractionary disequilibrium exists when the value of purchases by consumers, investors, governments, and foreigners is *less than* the amount paid for resources used in production plus the firms' expected profits. That is,

$$C + I + G + (X - Im) < Y$$

Again, the cause of the disequilibrium often lies in the blue boxes at the top of the circular-flow diagram. It may be that the supply of money has been reduced by the banking system, by the government, or by international transactions, so that investment purchases, government purchases, or exports are reduced, causing payments received by firms to decrease. Firms are unhappy with this situation because profits are less than expected. At the prices expected when the plans were made, the quantity of output demanded is less than the quantity supplied. The output that is not sold is added to business inventories. At the close of the round, inventories are greater than desired.

Economists predict that, when inventories are larger than desired, firms will reduce production and/or prices for the coming round of the circle.[5] Planned output may be reduced because estimates in the previous round proved to be too high. But even if firms make the same estimate of sales for the next round, some reduction in output will be needed to bring inventories down to desired levels. Firms also may reduce the prices of their products

in order to help reduce inventories, especially if there is vigorous competition for customers.

Contractionary disequilibrium **exists when the value of purchases by consumers, investors, governments, and foreigners is** *less than* **the amount paid for resources used in production plus the firms' expected profits.**

When inventories are smaller than desired, firms tend to increase production and/or prices; when inventories are larger than desired, firms tend to reduce production and/or prices.

---

5. Again, for simplicity, we assume that prices are not changed *during* the round of the circular flow.

AGGREGATE DEMAND AND AGGREGATE SUPPLY

The circular flow and the idea of equilibrium that you have just studied can now be used to introduce the macroeconomic concepts of aggregate demand and aggregate supply—concepts that provide the basic organizing scheme for modern macroeconomics. We will introduce these concepts now, in an elementary way. As we develop specific macroeconomic models, we will refer back to these basic organizing concepts to show how the specific models fit into the full picture. In Chapter 15, we will return to the aggregate demand and aggregate supply concepts and develop them in greater analytical and theoretical detail.

Aggregate Demand

The concept of demand was introduced in Chapter 5. In that chapter, the concept was applied to a specific good—jeans. At any specified price, consumers would be willing and able to purchase a given quantity of jeans per week or per year. This is the concept of *quantity demanded*. At different possible prices, different quantities of jeans would be demanded, *ceteris paribus*. The entire set of possible prices along with the quantity demanded at each price made up a *demand schedule*. The demand schedule, in turn, was represented on a graph as a *demand curve*. Applying the demand concept to jeans (or to any specified good or service) is an exercise in microeconomics. Let us now see how the concept of demand can be applied at the macroeconomic level of analysis.

Aggregate Quantity Demanded In macroeconomics, the quantity demanded cannot relate to a specific good or service, but must relate, instead, to the total of all goods and services that consumers (households), investors (business firms), governments, and foreigners are willing and able to buy during some time period (such as a year) and at some specified price level (average of all prices). In our circular-flow diagram, the sum of total purchases, $C + I + G + X - Im$ (the flows across the top half of the circle), constitute the **aggregate quantity demanded** at the prices prevailing at the time. If the economy illustrated in Figure 1 were at equilibrium so that all of the $1,000 billion of household income actually completed the route across the top of the circle and was received by the firms, the aggregate quantity demanded would be $1,000 billion of goods and services, valued at prevailing prices. Thus, the concept of aggregate quantity demanded is a simple extension of the demand concept introduced in Chapter 5.

The aggregate quantity demanded in an economy is the sum of total purchases made, $C + I + G + X - Im$, during a specified time period at a certain price level.

The Aggregate-Demand Curve In macroeconomics, other things remaining unchanged, a change in the price level (the average of all prices) leads to a change in the aggregate quantity demanded—that is, it leads to a change in the quantities purchased by households (C), business firms (I), governments (G), and foreigners ($X - Im$). If prices rise, smaller quantities of goods and services will be demanded and if prices go down, larger quantities will be demanded. This negative (inverse) relationship between the price level and the aggregate quantity demanded is the same pattern that is expected for microeconomic demand schedules and curves. But we must note, even in this introductory explanation, that the logic behind the aggregate-demand relationship is different from the logic behind the price to quantity-demanded relationship in microeconomics.[6] The logic of the aggregate-demand relationship requires knowledge about interest rates and about how people respond to changes in wealth. Since you have not yet studied these matters, the theoretical derivation of aggregate demand

---

6. Recall from Chapter 5 that the microeconomic price to quantity-demanded relationship depends on changes in relative prices (*substitution effects*) and on changes in real incomes (*income effects*).

FIGURE 6
An Aggregate-Demand Curve

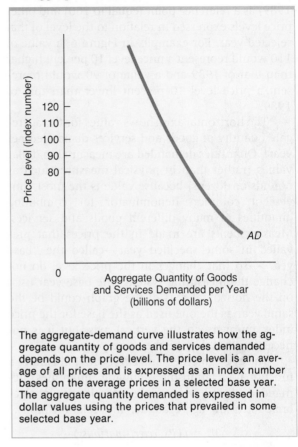

The aggregate-demand curve illustrates how the aggregate quantity of goods and services demanded depends on the price level. The price level is an average of all prices and is expressed as an index number based on the average prices in a selected base year. The aggregate quantity demanded is expressed in dollar values using the prices that prevailed in some selected base year.

schedules and curves must come later in your study of macroeconomics (see Chapter 15).

An **aggregate-demand curve** is the graphic representation of the relationship between changes in the price level and the resulting changes in the aggregate quantity demanded, *ceteris paribus*. Since several leading theories of macroeconomics direct special attention to aggregate demand, it will be useful to know what an aggregate-demand curve looks like. An aggregate-demand curve is illustrated in Figure 6. As with any new graph, we first must examine the labels on the axes. They identify the variables whose relationship is represented by the curve.

The variable on the vertical axis is the **price level,** showing averages for the prices of all goods and services in the economy. The numbers on this axis are **index numbers,** computed with the prices that prevailed in a selected base year (such as 1989) as a reference point (equal to 100) and other price levels expressed in relation to the level of that selected year. For example, in Figure 6, a value of 110 would represent a price level 10 percent higher than that of 1989 and a value of 90 would represent a price level 10 percent lower than that of 1989.[7]

The horizontal axis shows values for the aggregate quantity of goods and services demanded per year.[8] Quantities demanded are measured in dollar values (rather than in physical measures such as pounds or dozens) because value is the most convenient common denominator for combining quantities of many different goods and services. Measurements are made in the prices that prevailed in some specified year—called the "base year"—so that changes in the price level do not change the measuring system. The base year used on the horizontal axis of the graph could be the same year as the one used as the base for the price index numbers on the vertical axis, but it is not necessary that they be the same year.

The aggregate-demand curve (*AD*) illustrates a functional relationship showing quantities demanded at various possible price levels. In algebraic form, the aggregate demand relationship is

$$QD = f(P), ceteris paribus,$$

which states that the aggregate quantity demanded (*QD*) depends on or "is a function of" the price level (*P*), assuming that other variables remain unchanged. The price level is the independent variable that causes changes in the quantity of goods and services demanded, which is the dependent variable. As you see in Figure 6, the aggregate-demand curve shows a negative relationship between changes in the price level and the resulting changes in quantity demanded. Increases in the price level lead to reductions in aggregate quantities demanded and decreases in the price level lead

to increases in aggregate quantities demanded (*ceteris paribus*).

An aggregate-demand curve shows the negative relationship between the price level (the independent variable) and the aggregate quantity of goods and services demanded (the dependent variable) for an economy.

Shifts of the Aggregate-Demand Curve In Chapter 5 you learned that the demand curve for jeans may shift—change its location—due to changes in variables *other than* the price of jeans. Similarly, in macroeconomics, the aggregate-demand curve may shift due to changes in variables other than the price level. The blue boxes in the upper half of the circular flow diagram in Figure 1 suggest some of the variables that may shift the aggregate-demand curve. For example, changed economic conditions in foreign countries can easily increase or decrease the willingness and ability of people and governments of those countries to purchase goods and services from the United States. If foreigners buy more from the U.S., net exports (*X − Im*) would increase and the aggregate-demand curve would shift to the right, *ceteris paribus*. If they buy less from the U.S., net exports (*X − Im*) would decrease and the aggregate-demand curve would shift to the left, *ceteris paribus*. Shifts in aggregate demand can also come from changes that take place in the government box of the circular-flow diagram. For example, a national emergency may arise or policies may change and lead to increases in government purchases (*G*) which, *ceteris paribus*, would shift the curve to the right. Conversely, decreases in government purchases would shift aggregate demand to the left, *ceteris paribus*.

Shifts of the aggregate-demand curve are especially likely to come from changes that take place in the financial markets box of the circular-flow diagram. As we will learn in Chapter 13, financial institutions and the country's central bank are able to increase or decrease the quantity of money in the economy. Providing additional money can easily increase investment purchases (*I*) if the new money is loaned to firms which desire to purchase more capital goods. The new money also may

---

7. Index numbers and the calculation of other price level measures are explained on pages 142–145.

8. Gross National Product (GNP) is a familiar measure of total production in an economy in a year and could be the variable on this axis. The measurement of Gross National Product is explained on pages 126–130.

come into the hands of governments, or consumers, or even of foreigners and lead these groups to increase the quantity of goods and services they would be willing and able to buy at any given price level. So the aggregate-demand curve would shift to the right, *ceteris paribus*. Of course, if financial institutions reduce the money supply, the quantities of goods and services demanded may fall and the aggregate-demand curve shift to the left.

Shifts of the aggregate-demand curve are very important in macroeconomics. Sometimes such shifts are the intended results of official policies and sometimes they arise from random events. In your study of economics, you will find that the "action" often starts with a shift of the aggregate-demand curve.

The aggregate-demand curve for an economy may shift due to changes in variables other than the price level.

Aggregate Supply

You studied the microeconomic concept of supply in Chapter 5. As you recall, the Cohen Clothing Corporation had to make a decision about the quantity of jeans it would be willing and able to offer for sale at various possible prices. In order to maximize profit, the quantity supplied by the Cohen Corporation would be greater at higher prices for jeans than at lower prices for jeans, *ceteris paribus*. The entire set of possible prices along with the quantity supplied at each price made up a supply schedule, which, when represented on a graph was the Cohen Company's supply curve for jeans. With the help of the circular-flow model, we can now offer an introductory explanation of aggregate supply.

Aggregate Quantity Supplied At the macroeconomic level of analysis, the Cohen Corporation is just one of the many firms in the purple box on the right-hand side of the circular-flow diagram in Figure 1. Each of these firms must select the quantities of its particular products or services to produce and offer for sale in the forthcoming round of the circular flow. The price that a firm expects to receive for its product is one of the variables it must consider

in making the production decision. However, since macroeconomic analysis deals with many firms and many different goods and services, the aggregate supply concept uses the price level (the average of all prices) as the variable on which the **aggregate quantity supplied** depends. In the circular-flow diagram in Figure 1, the $1,000 billion amount shown as wages, interest, rents, and expected profit flowing through the bottom half of the circle indicates that, on the basis of the prices that firms expect will prevail, they have decided to supply $1,000 billion worth of goods and services.

The aggregate quantity supplied in an economy is the value of the sum of all the goods and services that firms will produce and offer for sale in that economy during a specified time period at a certain price level.

The Aggregate-Supply Curve The **aggregate-supply curve** is the graphic representation of the relationship between changes in the price level and the resulting changes in the aggregate quantity of goods and services supplied in an economy during some specified period of time and assuming that no other variables change. In algebraic terms, this can be expressed as

$$QS = f(P), \text{ ceteris paribus}$$

where QS is the aggregate quantity supplied, f means "depends on" or "is a function of," P stands for the price level, and *ceteris paribus* states the assumption that no other variables change.

In Chapter 5, you learned that supply curves for specific goods or services typically slope upward and to the right, that is, that changes in quantities supplied are directly related to changes in price. The Cohen Corporation, for example, was expected to supply a greater quantity of jeans at higher prices than at lower prices, *ceteris paribus*. In macroeconomics, most economists agree that, at least in most circumstances, changes in the aggregate quantity supplied also have a direct or positive relationship with changes in the price level. However, we must offer a word of caution: *the slope of the aggregate-supply curve is hotly debated among macro-economists.* In some circumstances, they see the curve as horizontal, with quantities supplied determined by variables other than the price level. In other circumstances, they see the curve as vertical so that changes in the price level have no effect on quantities supplied. Between these two extremes are circumstances in which changes in the aggregate quantity supplied vary directly with changes in the price level—a relationship similar to the typical microeconomic supply curve.[9]

An aggregate-supply curve with a middle-range positive slope is illustrated in Figure 7. As in Figure 6, where the aggregate-demand curve was illustrated, the label on the vertical axis is the price level. The horizontal axis shows the aggregate value of goods and services supplied in the economy in a year.

The aggregate-supply curve (*AS*) shown in Figure 7 states that an increase in the price level leads to an increase in the aggregate quantity of goods and services supplied. In terms of the circular-flow diagram in Figure 1, it suggests that the firms in the purple box on the right-hand side of the diagram will decide to supply larger quantities of goods and services when the price level goes up and smaller quantities when it goes down.

An aggregate-supply curve shows the relationship between the price level (the independent variable) and the aggregate quantity of goods and services supplied (the dependent variable) for an economy.

Shifts of the Aggregate-Supply Curve Shifts of the aggregate-supply curve are the result of changes in variables other than the price level. It is too early in your study of macroeconomics to go into much detail about the causes of such shifts. Basically, these shifts come from changes (other than price-level changes) that alter the profitability of producing goods and services. For example, if

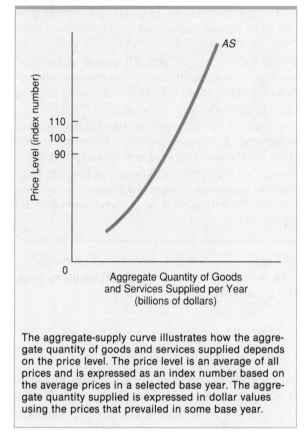

FIGURE 7
An Aggregate-Supply Curve

The aggregate-supply curve illustrates how the aggregate quantity of goods and services supplied depends on the price level. The price level is an average of all prices and is expressed as an index number based on the average prices in a selected base year. The aggregate quantity supplied is expressed in dollar values using the prices that prevailed in some base year.

the relationship between production costs and final-product prices changes so that profit margins are squeezed, firms may react by reducing quantities supplied, thereby shifting the curve to the left. In the reverse situation, if the relationship between final product prices and production costs changes to offer opportunities for larger profit margins, firms may increase quantities supplied in order to obtain more profits. This shifts the aggregate-supply curve to the right.

Shifts of the *AS* curve are important in macroeconomics. Sometimes shifts come from official policies, such as those designed to strengthen profitability and work incentives. Sometimes shifts come from random events that increase or decrease available resources. Sometimes shifts come from subtle changes in attitudes of workers or business firms and their expectations about the future course of the economy.

---

9. Lest you conclude that macroeconomics is unreasonably complicated about the aggregate-supply curve, we must note that microeconomic analysis more advanced than that in Chapter 5 recognizes all the supply-curve possibilities noted above and, in addition, finds circumstances in which microeconomic supply curves can have *negative* slopes!

The aggregate-supply curve for an economy may shift due to changes in variables other than the price level. When such variables affect firms' profit margins, they may shift an economy's aggregate-supply curve.

Macroeconomic Equilibrium

In the circular-flow model, macroeconomic equilibrium exists when the amount received by firms from sales of their products (the total of the spending flows through the top half of the circle) equals the amount that they had planned to receive from these sales. In the equilibrium situation, firms can pay the planned amounts for wages, rents, and interest and enjoy the level of profits they had built into these plans. The total flow through the top half of the circle represents aggregate quantity demanded and the flow through the bottom half represents aggregate quantity supplied, including planned profits.

In the aggregate-demand and aggregate-supply model, the macroeconomic equilibrium situation is illustrated by the intersection of the aggregate-demand curve and the aggregate-supply curve. In Figure 8, the aggregate-demand curve from Figure 6 is combined with the aggregate-supply curve from Figure 7. At one particular price level, shown as the price index value of 100, the aggregate quantity demanded of $1,000 billion equals the aggregate quantity supplied, also $1,000 billion. The plans of business firms are fulfilled and there is no reason to expect, *ceteris paribus*, that firms will make different plans for the next round of the circle.

Macroeconomic equilibrium exists when an economy's aggregate quantity demanded is equal to its aggregate quantity supplied.

Macroeconomic Disequilibrium

Macroeconomic disequilibrium exists when the aggregate quantity supplied at a given price level does *not* equal the aggregate quantity demanded at that price level. In terms of the circular-flow model, a contractionary disequilibrium arises when receipts from sales (aggregate quantity demanded as shown in the top half of the circle) are less than the firms had planned. After paying wages, interest, and rents, the firms' profits are lower than planned and the firms have undesirably large inventories of unsold merchandise. Economists expect that they will reduce output and lower prices in the next round of the circle.

In the aggregate demand and aggregate supply graph of Figure 8, the contractionary disequilibrium situation suggests a price level such as 110, that is, one higher than the one that would balance aggregate quantities demanded and supplied. There is excess aggregate supply. As firms cut back production and lower prices, the economy moves toward the equilibrium illustrated by the intersection of the curves in Figure 8.

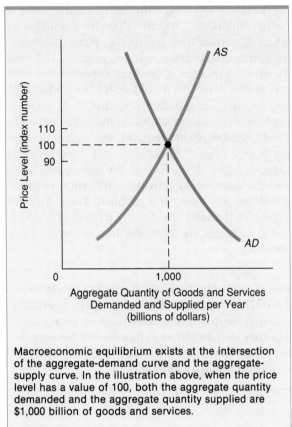

FIGURE 8
Macroeconomic Equilibrium

Macroeconomic equilibrium exists at the intersection of the aggregate-demand curve and the aggregate-supply curve. In the illustration above, when the price level has a value of 100, both the aggregate quantity demanded and the aggregate quantity supplied are $1,000 billion of goods and services.

Expansionary disequilibrium exists when aggregate quantities demanded (the upper flows in the circular-flow diagram) bring to the firms a greater amount of income than they anticipated when they made their production plans. After paying planned amounts for wages, interest, and rent, the firms' profits are larger than expected and their inventories have been sold down to undesirably low levels. The expected response is to increase production and to raise prices, that is, to expand.

In the aggregate-demand and aggregate-supply graph of Figure 8, expansionary disequilibrium suggests a price level such as 90, that is, one *below* the one that would provide equilibrium between quantities demanded and supplied. There is excess aggregate demand. As firms increase production and raise prices, the economy moves toward equilibrium.

Macroeconomic disequilibrium may be either contractionary because the economy's aggregate quantity supplied is greater than its aggregate quantity demanded or expansionary because its aggregate quantity demanded is greater than its aggregate quantity supplied.

A LOOK AHEAD

This chapter has explained the concept of macroeconomic equilibrium. But it is only a first step in macroeconomic analysis. It merely opens the door to many questions that economists try to answer. What events or behavior changes are most likely to shift aggregate-demand or aggregate-supply curves and thereby affect the economy? Can these events or behavior changes be anticipated, controlled, or counteracted? What can be done to help reestablish equilibrium once disequilibrium has set in? Does equilibrium represent the best the economy can do? Let us look briefly at some examples of the types of questions examined in macroeconomics.

Changes in Buying Behavior

Many economists believe that the Great Depression of the 1930s was brought on by events that caused households, investors, governments, and foreigners to greatly reduce their purchases of currently produced goods and services. The stock market crash of 1929 was said to have weakened the confidence investors needed to justify purchases of new capital goods. International trade restrictions reduced purchases by foreigners. Consumers, fearful of unemployment, reduced purchases and hoarded cash. Bank failures reduced the money supply and governments, determined to balance their budgets in the face of falling tax receipts, reduced purchases of public goods. Each of these changes tended to shift the aggregate-demand curve to the left, leaving firms with unsold inventories and leading to reductions in employment and output. Economists desperately looked for ways to bring about the economy's recovery. But, because of the unprecedented seriousness of the depression and because of uncertainty about how to deal with it, the economy did not recover until purchases associated with World War II shifted the aggregate-demand curve to the right.

The Great Depression in the United States may be seen as a period of time during which circumstances caused a significant leftward shift of the economy's aggregate demand curve.

Oil Shocks and the Great Stagflation

Twice during the 1970s, many industrialized economies in the world experienced leftward shifts of aggregate supply caused by cuts in the production of crude oil by members of the Organization of Petroleum Exporting Countries (OPEC). These supply shocks caused unemployment, higher price levels, and reductions in production and living standards in economies not benefiting from the higher prices of crude oil. This combination of faltering production and increasing prices is called **stagflation,** a word created by combining the words *stagnation* and *inflation*.

Once again, economists desperately tried to find ways to ease the burdens of inflation and unemployment but no comfortable solutions could be found. Compromise policies attempted to divide the hardships more or less equitably among different groups in the society and to help workers and other resources transfer their activities into occupations less dependent on low priced petroleum. Both unemployment rates and inflation rates remained high for extended periods of time while these adjustments were made. As oil consuming countries accomplished the transitions and as crude oil sources were found in countries not members of OPEC, the scarcity of petroleum diminished and its price stabilized. Eventually, OPEC countries themselves increased oil production, shifting aggregate-supply curves to the right in most industrialized economies and bringing production increases, higher living standards, and a slackening of inflation in many economies.

The stagflation period in the United States during the 1970s may be seen as a time during which two major oil shocks caused a significant leftward shift of the economy's aggregate-supply curve.

Government Monetary and Fiscal Policy

Shifting the aggregate demand curve is one of the key elements in government macroeconomic policy. Suppose, for example, that the economy is suffering from a recession caused by a leftward shift in aggregate demand—the situation described above in connection with the Great Depression of the 1930s. Government policy makers undoubtedly want to shift the aggregate-demand curve to the right to recover from the recession. **Monetary policy** offers one method of increasing aggregate

demand. In the context of the *AD-AS* model, increasing the money supply increases purchases of currently produced goods and services. The aggregate-demand curve shifts to the right and a greater quantity of output is demanded at any given price level. The rightward shift of the *AD* curve reverses the process that caused the recession or depression, returning prices and output to their original levels.

Government policy makers also may use **fiscal policy** to shift the aggregate-demand curve. In fiscal policy, government purchases are increased in order to increase aggregate demand or taxes are reduced so that households and business firms will increase purchases.

Government monetary and fiscal policies also can be used to shift the aggregate-demand curve to the left. This may be done if policy makers want to "cool off" the economy and reduce inflationary pressures. The money supply can be reduced, or its rate of growth slowed, leading to a reduction in the demand for goods and services. Or government purchases can be reduced and/or taxes increased, if policy makers choose to use fiscal instruments to shift the aggregate-demand curve.

An economy's aggregate demand curve may be shifted by its government's use of fiscal policy (changes in the amount that it taxes or spends) and monetary policy (changes in the amount of money that it supplies).

We will have much more to say about government fiscal policies in Part IV and about government monetary policies in Part V.

Economics in Focus

Econometric Models

The circular flow is an elementary, intuitive model of the operation of the macroeconomy. In recent years, aided by the computer, economists have produced many new and powerful econometric models. *Econometrics* is the area of economics that uses a combination of theory, mathematics, and statistics to analyze economic questions. Econometric models are especially useful in forecasting what the economy is likely to do.

When Federal Reserve officials responsible for the nation's money supply contemplate a change in monetary policy, econometric models help them predict the new policy's effect on interest rates and money reserves. Researchers have used econometric models to analyze patterns in tax receipts, government expenditures, wage-price relationships, unemployment, and so on. But perhaps the most widespread use of econometrics is in forecasting for business firms.

One of the early leaders in the business-forecasting field was Wharton Econometric Associates, now The WEFA Group. Founded by Nobel Prize-winner Lawrence Klein, the firm has based its forecasts on a variety of econometric models: for example, a quarterly model for short-term cycles, a long-term model with a heavier emphasis on industrial trends and demographics, and specialized models for predicting prices, wages, and productivity for specific industries. To keep such models useful, economists must continually reevaluate not only the input data and assumptions but also the performance of the basic equations.

Many firms use their own computer programs to help them predict business trends. Even small firms can do econometric modeling with the aid of software packages for microcomputers. Packages already on the market can simulate macroeconomic forces, perform fairly complex statistical manipulations, and print out the results in an easy-to-read format. Economists themselves often find such ready-made packages helpful for research purposes. Recently a number of scholars have also used econometric modeling to investigate some very untraditional approaches to economics. For instance, some economists have questioned the basic notion of equilibrium, arguing that economic fluctuations are more irregular than equilibrium theories suggest. Along with computer scientists and experts from such remote disciplines as physics, these untraditional economists have developed computer models of nonlinear systems that produce variable patterns much like the ones of a real economy.

As software continues to grow better and more sophisticated, econometric modeling should increase in vigor and usefulness. Of course, no model, no matter how fine-tuned, can predict all the changes in our world, but computerized econometric modeling is a powerful tool that has already changed the discipline and will continue to change it in years to come.

Sources: John R. Connelly, "Econometric Modeling," *PC Magazine,* March 14, 1989, pp. 203–220; Howard J. Howe and Gene D. Guill, "The Wharton Model," in A. Migliaro and C. L. Jain, *An Executive's Guide to Econometric Forecasting* (Flushing, N.Y.: Graceway, 1983), pp. 44–49; Elizabeth Corcoran, "Disequilibrium," *Scientific American,* December 1988, pp. 108–110; Everette S. Gardner, Jr., "How to Monitor Your Forecasts," *Lotus,* April 1989, pp. 54–57.

SUMMARY

1. The circular-flow model provides a visual representation of the macroeconomy and illustrates how income flows from firms to households as resources are hired to engage in production. It also illustrates household uses of income for consumption purchases, saving, net taxes, and purchases from foreigners. Finally, the circular flow illustrates how income dispensed by households flows to firms, through purchases of consumption goods, investment purchases of capital goods, government purchases of public goods, and foreign purchases of exported goods. (See pages 104–110 and Figure 1, page 105.)

2. Governments borrow from financial markets when their budgets are in deficit. Therefore, governments obtain funds that came to financial markets either from household saving or from foreigners who had sold goods to domestic households (imports) and did not care to use these funds to purchase exports from the domestic economy. In this manner, government borrowing can crowd out private investment purchases. (See pages 107–108 and Figure 2, page 107.)

3. Governments can channel funds into financial markets if they have budget surpluses, and use the extra net tax collections to retire debt securities. In this way, income paid in net taxes becomes available for lending to investors to finance capital goods purchases or to foreigners to finance their purchases of exports from the domestic economy. (See page 108 and Figure 3, page 108.)

4. International markets may channel funds into domestic financial markets. If the economy represented by the circle has a deficit in its international trade, leaving more income in the hands of foreigners than they wish to use to pay for goods and services purchases from that country, these funds may flow into domestic financial markets. In this situation, the domestic economy goes into debt or sells assets to foreigners, and funds from foreigners become available for lending to investors to finance capital goods purchases. (See page 109 and Figure 4, page 109.)

5. Household saving or government income and product budget surpluses may flow from financial markets into international markets when the economy has a surplus in its international trade.

Foreigners borrow funds to help finance their purchases of goods and services exported by firms of the domestic economy. (See pages 109–110 and Figure 5, page 110.)

6. Circular-flow equilibrium exists when the total of consumption purchases, investment purchases, government purchases, and purchases by foreigners (exports) *equals* income, the total earnings of resource owners plus expected profits—that is, when $C + I + G + (X - Im) = Y$. (See page 110.)

7. Expansionary disequilibrium exists when the total of consumption purchases, investment purchases, government purchases, and purchases by foreigners (exports) is *greater than* the total earnings of resource owners plus expected profits—when $C + I + G + (X - Im) > Y$. (See page 111.)

8. Contractionary disequilibrium exists when the total of consumption purchases, investment purchases, government purchases, and purchases by foreigners (exports) is *less than* the total earnings of resource owners plus expected profits—that is, when $C + I + G + (X - Im) < Y$. (See page 112.)

9. Aggregate quantity demanded is represented by the spending streams in the top half of the circular-flow diagram. In the aggregate-demand and aggregate-supply model, aggregate demand is represented by the equation $QD = f(P)$, *ceteris paribus*, where QD is the value of goods and services demanded in an economy and P is the price level. The relationship is negative (inverse), showing that increases in the price level result in reductions in aggregate quantity demanded and vice versa, *ceteris paribus*. The aggregate-demand curve illustrates this function graphically. (See pages 112–115.)

10. Aggregate quantity supplied is decided by business firms represented by the purple box at the right-hand side of the circular-flow diagram. In the aggregate-demand and aggregate-supply model, aggregate supply is represented by the equation $QS = f(P)$, *ceteris paribus*, where QS is the value of goods and services supplied in an economy and P is the price level. Although economists disagree about the magnitude of the slope of the AS curve, a positive relationship suggests that increases in the price level result in increases in aggregate quantity supplied and vice versa, *ceteris paribus*. The aggre-

gate-supply curve illustrates this function graphically. (See pages 115–117.)

11. Macroeconomic equilibrium exists at the price level that equates aggregate quantity demanded with aggregate quantity supplied, that is, at the intersection of the aggregate-demand curve and the aggregate-supply curve. (See page 117.)

12. Expansionary disequilibrium exists when, at the existing price level, aggregate quantity demanded exceeds aggregate quantity supplied. In the circular-flow model, firms have sold more goods and services than they planned. Inventories are depleted below desired levels and production and/or prices will be increased in the next round of the circle, *ceteris paribus.* (See page 118.)

13. Contractionary disequilibrium exists when, at the existing price level, aggregate quantity demanded is less than aggregate quantity supplied. In the circular-flow model, firms have sold less goods and services than they planned. Inventories are above desired levels and production and/or prices will be decreased in the next round of the circle, *ceteris paribus.* (See page 117.)

14. Macroeconomists devote a great amount of time and energy to forecasting events or behavior changes that will shift aggregate-demand or aggregate-supply curves. They also attempt to find ways to restore macroeconomic equilibrium after disequilibrium conditions have set in. The Great Depression of the 1930s illustrates problems associated with disequilibrium caused by shifts in aggregate demand. The Great Stagflation of the 1970s illustrates problems associated with disequilibrium caused by shifts in aggregate supply. (See pages 118–119.)

15. Monetary policies and fiscal policies are government actions commonly used in dealing with macroeconomic disequilibrium situations. Monetary policy emphasizes changes in the money supply. Fiscal policy emphasizes changes in government spending and taxation. (See page 119.)

KEY TERMS

aggregate-demand curve: the graphic representation of the relationship between changes in the price level prevailing in an economy and the resulting changes in the aggregate quantity demanded in that economy, *ceteris paribus* (page 113).

aggregate quantity demanded: the sum of total purchases, $C + I + G + X - Im,$ of an economy during a specified time period at a certain price level (page 113).

aggregate quantity supplied: the sum of all the goods and services that firms will produce and offer for sale in an economy during a specified time period at a certain price level (page 115).

aggregate-supply curve: the graphic representation of the relationship between changes in the price level prevailing in an economy and the resulting changes in the aggregate quantity of goods and services supplied in that economy, *ceteris paribus* (page 115).

balance of trade: when the value of exports equals the value of imports (page 108).

capital goods: buildings, machines, and human capital (page 106).

circular-flow equilibrium: when the sum of consumption purchases, investment purchases, government purchases, and net exports equals the amount paid out by firms for resources used in production plus expected profits: $C + I + G + (X - Im) = Y$ (page 104).

consumption purchases (C): expenditures by households to acquire goods and services for use during the accounting period (page 106).

contractionary disequilibrium: when the aggregate quantity supplied is greater than the aggregate quantity demanded so that output will be reduced and/or prices lowered (page 112).

crowding out: when some of the saving flowing through the financial markets is used to pay for government purchases rather than to finance investment purchases (page 108).

deficit: the extent to which government purchases are greater than net taxes (page 107).

disequilibrium: an imbalance among opposing forces such that there is some tendency for change (page 111).

equilibrium: a state of balance among opposing forces such that there is no tendency for change (page 110).

expansionary disequilibrium: when the aggregate quantity demanded is greater than the aggregate quantity supplied so that output will be increased and/or prices raised (page 111).

exports: goods and services produced by domestic firms and purchased by foreigners (page 108).

financial intermediaries: banks, credit unions, saving and loan associations, stock and bond brokers and other institutions that accept deposits of income saved and offer to loan these funds, in return for interest payments, to those who wish to borrow (page 106).

fiscal policy: a government's attempt to influence macroeconomic variables by changing the amount that it taxes or spends (page 119).

government purchases (G): purchases by government of currently produced goods and services (page 107).

imports: goods and services, produced abroad and purchased for use by domestic firms, governments and households (page 108).

income and product budgets: budgets that treat government transfer payments as negative taxes rather than as expenditures (page 107).

index number: a number that expresses a particular value in relation to some other value that has been specified as a base or reference value (page 114).

investment purchases (I): expenditures for newly produced capital goods (page 106).

macroeconomic equilibrium: when the aggregate quantity demanded is equal to the aggregate quantity supplied in an economy. The intersection of an economy's aggregate demand and aggregate supply curves (page 110).

macroeconomics: the part of economics concerned with aggregate economic activity—the functioning of the entire economy (page 104).

microeconomics: the part of economics that studies the activities of individual persons and business firms (page 104).

monetary policy: a government's attempt to influence macroeconomic variables by changing the economy's money supply (page 119).

net taxes (Tn): the total amount of tax paid by households and firms minus transfer payments received (page 107).

price level: an average of all prices prevailing in an economy that is expressed as an index number based on the average prices that prevailed in a selected base year (page 113).

saving (S): setting aside current income in order to increase wealth (page 106).

stagflation: the prolonged combination of inflation, substantial unemployment, and sluggish growth (page 106).

surplus: the extent to which government purchases are less than net taxes received (page 118).

transfer payments: funds paid by government to welfare recipients, veterans, unemployed workers, social security retirees, etc.; considered to be negative taxes (page 117).

DISCUSSION QUESTIONS

1. Without looking at Figure 1, construct the circular-flow diagram showing the four streams of household uses of funds. Compare your drawing with Figure 1 to be sure you have it right. Assuming that financial institutions can expand or reduce the quantity of money in the economy, discuss how disequilibrium can arise in the circular flow.

2. Net taxes differ from total tax collections by government. Explain why. Government purchases differ from the total budget expenditure of government. Explain why. How do transfer payments provide the key to the differences? How does income conveyed through transfer payments enter into the circular flow?

3. Since government has the power to control both its inflows and its outflows, why should a disequilibrium condition ever arise in the net taxes-government purchases flow? Is government's control complete? Explain. Is disequilibrium undesirable? Explain.

4. Carefully explain the connections between the government box and the financial-markets box in the circular flow. Explain the concept of crowding out and discuss when it may be desirable and when it may be undesirable.

5. Explain how dollars spent by U.S. households to purchase foreign goods and services can be used by foreigners to purchase investment goods in the United States or U.S. national debt securities. The "twin deficits" (international trade and governmental budget) problem experienced by the U.S. economy in the middle 1980s was said to set the stage for lower U.S. living standards in the future. Discuss why that could happen.

6. Draw a graph illustrating an aggregate-demand curve, taking special care to label the axes correctly. Compare your drawing with Figure 6. Write the algebraic expression for the aggregate-demand curve and discuss the roles played by dependent and independent variables in this equation. Also discuss why it is essential to add the *ceteris paribus* condition to the equation.

7. On the graph that you have drawn for question 6, add an aggregate-supply curve. Then shift *one* of the curves to illustrate the effect of an increase in quantity of money circulating in the economy. As a result of the increased spending, will firms have inventories that are too large or too small? Illustrate the inventory imbalance on the graph.

7

National Income Accounting

Preview Since macroeconomics is concerned with aggregate, or "grand total," economic activity, it is essential to have a way to measure total production and income in the economy.[1]

In this chapter, we explore the system of national income and product accounting that is used to measure the overall performance of the U.S. economy. This system is made up of five different measures of economic activity, each used for its own purpose. The best known is called the gross national product, which measures the market value of all the goods and services produced in the economy in a given year. The other measures break down this grand total to focus on particular parts that are useful in understanding how the economy works.

We also describe some of the shortcomings of the American national accounting system. For example, it does not count the work that people do at home, such as caring for their children and keeping house. Nor does it take into account the damage done to the environment that is an undesired by-product of certain kinds of production. In some areas, it may overstate income by counting intermediate products as final products.

Of course, no accounting system can be perfect in the sense that it provides all the information that anyone might want about the economy. What matters is that there is a consistent set of definitions and measures to help economists in their efforts to understand how the economy operates and what it is likely to do in the future.

1. See Chapter 1, page 6.

NATIONAL INCOME AND PRODUCT ACCOUNTS

The **national income and product accounts** are a set of reports on the volume and composition of economic activity in the United States over a specified time period. This accounting system was developed during the 1920s at a private research agency, the National Bureau of Economic Research. One of its principal developers, Simon Kuznets, later received a Nobel Prize in Economics for his work. Today, the tasks of collecting data and preparing the accounts are carried on by the Department of Commerce. The major components of the accounts are published regularly in *The Survey of Current Business*. Macroeconomic forecasts usually are made in terms of these accounts. Also, one of the best-known parts of the accounts—the gross national product—is the measure usually presented on the horizontal axis of the aggregate-demand and aggregate-supply graph.

The national income and product accounts are a set of reports of the volume and composition of economic activity in the United States over a specified time period. Macroeconomics forecasts are usually made in terms of these accounts.

Table 1 presents the essentials of the U.S. national income and product accounts for the calendar year 1988. This table shows the three major sections of the system: the national product section, the national income section, and the personal income section. The *national product* section, on the upper left in the table, shows the value of total production in the economy, as measured by the market value of all goods and services produced in the economy during the year. The best-known entry in this section is for the gross national product, which we shall discuss in detail later. The classification of gross national product as consumer spending, investment spending, government spending on goods and services, and net exports corresponds with the spending paths illustrated in the upper half of the circular-flow diagram in Chapter 6.

The national income and product accounting system has three major sections: the national product section, the national income section, and the personal income section.

The *national income* section, on the upper right in Table 1, shows the total amount earned by owners of resources used in producing goods and services during the year.[2] Note that the bottom-line entry in the national income section equals the bottom-line entry in the national product section. This relationship shows the kind of double-entry bookkeeping used in the national accounts. The idea behind this double-entry system is that the amount spent for goods and services (national product) should equal the amount earned by owners of the resources used in producing these goods and services (national income). The national income section contains amounts for the flows of income represented by the lower half of the circular-flow diagram in Chapter 6.

There are some complications in making the double-entry system actually work in the national accounting system. These are resolved through the specific entries in the lower portion of the national product section in Table 1. These adjustments (capital consumption allowance, indirect business taxes and subsidies, and statistical discrepancy) will be explained later.

The third major part of the national accounting system is the *personal income* section, at the bottom in Table 1. This section breaks down the total national income into special categories that are useful in economic forecasting. The most useful entry in this section is for disposable personal income. This figure shows the amount that people can divide between consumption spending and saving. It is widely used in forecasting.

---

2. It is interesting to note that the United States includes all services performed by lawyers, doctors, barbers, civil servants, etc., as part of its national income and product. Marxist countries, particularly the Soviet Union and the People's Republic of China, include services only insofar as they contribute directly to the production of *physical* goods.

TABLE 1
National Income and Product in the United States, 1988 (billions of dollars)

National Product Section		National Income Section	
Consumption spending	$3,227.5	Compensation of employees	$2,904.7
Investment spending	766.5		
Government spending on goods and services	964.9	Proprietor's income	324.5
Net exports	− 94.6		
Gross national product	$4,864.3	Rental income of persons	19.3
Capital consumption allowance (subtract)	− 506.4	Corporate profits	328.1
Net national product	$4,357.9		
Indirect business taxes and subsidies	− 375.6	Net interest	391.5
Statistical discrepancy	− 14.1		
National income	$3,968.2	**National income**	$3,968.2

Personal Income Section

National income (from above)	$3,968.2
Earnings not received (subtract)	−492.1
Receipts not earned (add)	586.0
Personal income	$4,062.1
Personal tax and nontax payments (subtract)	−590.3
Disposable personal income	$3,471.8
Disposition:	
Personal consumption	$3,227.5
Personal saving	144.3
Interest paid to business	98.9
Transfers to foreigners	1.0
	$3,471.8

The national product section records the value of goods and services produced during the year. The national income section records amounts earned by owners of resources used in producing goods and services. This is a double-entry bookkeeping system, and the same total appears at the bottom of each section. The personal income section records certain additions and subtractions that are necessary to show amounts actually received by people and available to use for consumption and saving.

Note: Items may not add to total because of rounding.

Source: U.S. Department of Commerce, Bureau of Economic Analysis, *Survey of Current Business,* Vol. 69, No. 3 (March 1989). Tables 1.1, 1.9, and 2.1.

The national product section of the national income and product accounts records the market value of goods and services produced during the year. The national income section records amounts earned by owners of resources used in producing goods and services. The personal income section breaks down the total national income into special categories used to make economic forecasts.

The National Product Section

The national product section shows the market value of goods and services produced during the year. In other words, it records the "value" of the year's production.

Two basic requirements govern the Commerce Department's system for estimating national production. First, it must include only current-year production and must not include transactions that merely transfer title to goods produced in earlier years. Thus, exchanges of old houses or used cars are not recorded, although the services of the realtor and the used-car salesperson—that is, their salaries and commissions—are included as currently produced services.

The second requirement is that the values assigned are those applicable to the final sale of the good or service during the accounting period. In most instances, this is a sale of a final good or service to a consumer, a firm, a government, or a foreigner. However, at the close of the year, some of the year's production is in inventory, either as a semifinished good or as a good not yet sold to its final purchaser. In the accounts, the value of the year's beginning inventory is subtracted from the value of the year's closing inventory and the difference is included as an investment purchase (positive or negative) during the year.

It is not possible, of course, actually to record each of the billions of final-sales transactions that occur in the economy each year. Instead, the calculation of GNP and its components is done by the Department of Commerce with information from tax returns, surveys, and other data sources. Their results are estimates based on statistical samples rather than exact figures.

The procedure used estimates the value of the goods and services sold by firms and then subtracts an estimate of the value of the inputs, or "intermediate goods," that firms purchase from each other. What remains is an estimate of the **value added** by firms and reflects the production from resources employed directly by them. The value-added method estimates the value of current production, avoids multiple-counting, and gives the same results as a summation of final sales.

The market value of a firm's final sales minus the amounts paid by the firm to purchase intermediate goods from other firms equals the value added by the resources employed by the firm.

Table 2 illustrates how the value-added calculation accounts for the full final-sale value of a good or service. As shown in the sales-value column, a loaf of bread sells for 70 cents at retail. In the value-added column, the contributions from all the resource owners who helped to produce the bread also add up to 70 cents. For simplicity, we have assumed that the farmer does not purchase any intermediate goods, such as seed or fertilizer. We avoid double-counting because we do not count any of the payments made for intermediate goods. As you will see, the U.S. system is not entirely successful in excluding payments for intermediate goods. However, many countries, including the Soviet Union, use a measure called **value of output**, which makes no attempt to avoid double-counting.

Gross National Product In the national product section, spending is divided into four categories: consumption, investment, government, and net exports. In general, *consumption spending* refers to goods and services purchased by households, including durable goods such as autos and appliances. *Investment spending* includes purchases of buildings and equipment for use in future production and net additions to inventories of raw materials, goods in process, and unsold final products. (It does not refer to purchases of stocks and bonds, which are titles to goods already in existence or claims against future goods and services. Such pur-

TABLE 2
Value Added and Final Sales

	Sales Value	Cost of Intermediate Goods	Value Added
Farmer sells wheat	.15	− .00	= .15
Miller sells flour	.35	→ .15	= .20
Baker sells bread (wholesale)	.60	→ .35	= .25
Grocer sells bread (retail)	.70	→ .60	= .10
Totals	$1.80	− 1.10	= $.70

The sales value of the final product (bread at retail) is equal to the sum of the values added by the firms that have processed raw materials and intermediate goods into this final product.

chases, of course, are what the person in the street means by "investment.") The investment category also includes new residential structures. Included in *government spending* are purchases of goods and services by federal, state, and local governments, as well as by public companies like the postal service.[3] It does not include cash **transfer payments**, which is money paid to people even though these people did not provide a good or service to earn this money during the accounting period. Welfare, Social Security, and veterans' benefit checks are examples of cash transfer payments. They are not counted in the government purchases category of the national product section but are counted (in the consumption section) when the recipients spend the money received from the government. Governments also can transfer actual goods and services, such as food or hospital care, directly to individual recipients. Since the government must purchase these goods and services, their value is counted in the government entry in the accounts.

The consumption spending category of the GNP refers to goods and services purchased by households.

3. The United States treats all government purchases as public consumption; there is no separate "public investment" account. In the United Nations system, however, this distinction is made and investment has a public component. An example of public investment would be highway construction.

The investment spending category of the GNP includes purchases of buildings and equipment for use in future production and net additions to inventories of raw materials, goods in process, and unsold final products.

The government spending part of the GNP includes purchases of goods and services by federal, state, and local governments.

Net exports represent the value of American goods and services purchased by foreigners less the value of foreign goods and services purchased by Americans. Often it is a negative quantity. That is, the value of U.S. exports may be less than the value of imports from other countries. The **gross national product (GNP)**, perhaps the most familiar measure of aggregate economic activity, is the total of all purchases—by consumers, by investors, by governments, and (net) by foreigners—of currently produced goods and services.

The net exports part of the GNP represents the value of American goods and services purchased by foreigners minus the value of foreign goods and services purchased by Americans.

The gross national product (GNP) is the total of all purchases—by consumers, by investors, by

governments, and by foreigners—of currently produced goods and services.

Net National Product The only difference between the gross and the net national product is the treatment of depreciation and obsolescence. Some of the new buildings and equipment included as investment in GNP were needed to replace buildings and equipment that had worn out, become obsolete, or suffered accidental damage during the year. We say that some capital goods (production equipment) were "consumed" in the process of producing other goods. Therefore, a **capital consumption allowance** is estimated and subtracted from the gross national product to obtain a figure for the **net national product (NNP)**. In other words, GNP is gross of capital consumption allowances, whereas NNP is net of them. (It is a good idea, when using the terms *gross* and *net* in economics, to be able to answer the question "gross (or net) of *what*?")

Net national product (NNP) is GNP minus a capital consumption allowance (replacement costs for worn-out or obsolete buildings and equipment).

Since the capital consumption allowance relates to buildings and equipment, it is really an adjustment to the investment component of GNP. This means that the only difference between GNP and NNP is the difference between investment before the subtraction of the capital consumption allowance ("gross" investment) and investment after this subtraction ("net" investment). So we may write

$$GNP = C + I_g + G + X - Im$$

and

$$NNP = C + I_n + G + X - Im$$

where C is consumption, I_g is gross investment, I_n is net investment, G is government purchases, X is exports, Im is imports, GNP is gross national product, and NNP is net national product. Expressing net exports as $X - Im$ will be useful later when we explain what determines these amounts. Also, it

will be helpful to remember these equations. As we will see, many macroeconomic theories are built around the summation of consumption, investment, government purchases, and net exports.

National Product Section Adjustments Net national product is a figure that estimates the actual (net) gain from all production during the year. It would equal the total income earned by all persons and companies engaged in production, except for two problems that arise in our double-entry accounting system.

The first problem arises because taxes and government subsidies drive a wedge between amounts paid by purchasers of goods and services and amounts received by the resources used in producing them. In the double-entry system, the national product section is computed at market prices, which are higher because of taxes on these products and lower because of subsidies given to them. But the national income section is computed according to the earnings of the factors of production and adds up to an estimate of what the market prices would have been without any sales taxes, excise taxes, property taxes, or subsidies. Therefore, a major adjustment is needed in the national product section to adjust for the tax and subsidy components of market prices. This is the **indirect business taxes and subsidies** entry in Table 1.

A handy way to understand the necessity of this adjustment for indirect taxes and subsidies is as follows. Think about the federal tax on gasoline, which increases the price that you pay for gasoline at the pump. The tax part of this price is counted (along with your purchase of gasoline) as a consumption purchase (C) in estimating gross and net national product. The tax revenue is used by the government to pay for construction and repair of the highway system, and this spending is counted as part of the government purchases (G) component of GNP and NNP. In other words, the tax revenue is counted twice in the national product calculations of the accounting system. But in the national income section of the accounts, it is counted only once—as the payment to the resources (labor, capital, natural) used in the highway work. Therefore, the indirect tax must be subtracted to remove the double-counting and to secure a balance with the earnings reported in the national income section of the accounts. Government subsidies to business work the other way—they reduce the prices paid for final goods, but do finance the earnings of factors of production. Therefore, these subsidies are an added item in the adjustments section.

The indirect business taxes and subsidies entry in the national product section is an adjustment that adjusts for the tax and subsidy component of market prices.

The second problem in securing a balance between net national product and national income arises because, in figuring both national product and national income, estimating procedures are used rather than full and complete tabulations of all production and all incomes. Also, national product is estimated separately from national income. The **statistical discrepancy** entry in the national product section in Table 1 simply reports the extent to which the two estimates were not equal to each other, or the difference between them. Because the national income estimates are usually more accurate than the national product estimates, the statistical discrepancy entry is placed in the national product section.

The statistical discrepancy entry in the national product section reflects the fact that the Department of Commerce makes separate estimates for the national product and the national income sections of the accounts.

The National Income Section

National income (NI) is the total amount that is earned in producing the national product. The five parts of national income are listed in Table 1. They are compensation of employees, proprietors' income, rental income of persons, corporate profits, and net interest. *Compensation of employees* covers both money wages and the amounts that are spent by employers for such things as Social Security and fringe benefits (paid vacation, sick and holiday pay, and so on). *Proprietors' income* records the incomes

of all unincorporated businesses and in fact combines profits, rental income, and the labor income of the partners and proprietors in these businesses. The rents received on properties owned by businesses are included in the income or profit for these businesses, so that only the *rental income of persons* is stated as a separate item in the accounts. Capital consumption allowances are subtracted in calculating the rental income of persons and the incomes of proprietorships, partnerships, and corporations. Inventory-value adjustments are made for price-level changes that occur during the year. *Corporate profits* are recorded before the payment of dividends. *Net interest* is the total interest income of persons, minus interest paid by consumers to businesses and net interest paid by government, which are considered transfer payments (and not production) in the accounting system. Adding these five components together gives the amount of national income, which is equal to the net national product after the adjustments noted earlier (indirect business taxes and subsidies, statistical discrepancy) have been made.

National income (NI) is the total amount that is earned in producing the national product. National income is equal to net national product after certain adjustments are made.

A half-whimsical illustration of all this is as follows. Consider a super-stereo sound system selling for $4,864—an amount about one-billionth of the 1988 GNP. You buy it. Where does your money go? Part ($506) goes into a fund to replace machines that were worn out in producing this glorious stereo system, and part ($376) goes for sales, excise, and property taxes (net of subsidies) and a $14 statistical discrepancy in adding up the sales slip! The remainder ($3,968) is the total earned by the people who worked to produce the stereo or who owned other resources that were used in its production. Most ($2,905) goes to workers, salaried managers, etc. Smaller amounts go to others in the production process—$325 as profits to proprietors or partners (perhaps subcontractors for component parts of the stereo), $19 to pay rent for land under some factory building, $328 as profits to the corporation that was the prime producer of the stereo, and $391 as interest to people who loaned money to the prime producing company or to the subcontractors. You enjoy listening to the stereo. Other people enjoy having the money you spent. The next step is to see what they do with it.

The Personal Income Section

The personal income section of the accounting system starts with the amount of national income. It then shows amounts that must be added or subtracted in order to arrive at the amount of income that was actually available to people for spending and saving decisions.[4] Two steps are used in this process. The first reports personal income and the second reports disposable personal income.

Personal Income The adjustment process begins by recognizing that some of the income that was earned in a given year was not actually received by the people who earned it. In Table 1, this is called *earnings not received*. The biggest part of the earnings not received is contributions for social insurance, or Social Security taxes. This category also includes corporate profits that were not paid out in dividends. The gap between profits and dividends includes both corporate income taxes paid to the government and earnings retained for reinvestment by the corporation. All these items are subtracted from national income as "earnings not received."

Receipts not earned is a companion item to earnings not received. In other words, some income that people received during a year was not earned by them in that year. The largest item under this heading is government transfer payments, which include Social Security benefits and welfare checks. It also includes interest that the government pays to people (as for savings bonds). Adjusting national income by adding receipts not earned and by subtracting earnings not received, we derive the amount of **personal income (PI)**.

Personal income (PI) is calculated by adjusting national income by adding receipts not earned and by subtracting earnings not received.

---

4. *People* refers primarily to households, but nonprofit institutions are also included.

Disposable Personal Income The last step in the adjustment process recognizes that people have certain obligations that must be subtracted from personal income to discover how much income is left for spending or saving. We subtract payments of *personal taxes* (individual income, estate, and inheritance taxes) and then certain other small *non-tax items*, such as traffic fines, penalties, and charges for government services. The amount that remains after these obligations are subtracted is called **disposable personal income (DPI)**.

Disposable personal income is that amount of personal income actually available to people for spending or saving.

Finally, the accounting system reports on the disposition of DPI—how disposable personal income was actually used in a given year. It comes as no surprise that *personal consumption* spending claims most of disposable personal income. *Personal saving* is another very important item here. Finally, personal transfer payments, including *interest paid to businesses* and *transfers to foreigners*, must also be recorded in accounting for disposable personal income.

Why Five Series?

The accounting system gives us five data series to estimate the volume of economic activity. In their usual order of size, these are GNP, NNP, NI, PI, and DPI. Just what, you may ask, *is* the national income or product anyway? Why bother with five separate series? What kind of dodge-ball game are the statisticians playing with us?

Economists believe that the five series, even though they are correlated closely with one another, have different meanings and can be used for different purposes. Of the five series, gross national product is the most closely related to measured *employment* and *unemployment*. Net national product, which is GNP minus capital consumption allowances, comes close to defining the economist's all-purpose symbol *Y* as a measure of national income and product. When stated on a per capita basis, national income is a rough but useful measure of *long-run economic welfare*, though the whole welfare idea is really much more complicated than this estimate. Personal income, on the other hand, is often used as a rough measure of *short-run economic welfare*. In the short run, it is a gain for persons to have their incomes raised when transfer payments increase or business maintains dividend rates even when profits fall. However, the long-run effects may be unfavorable if savings are neglected or debts pile up. Finally, disposable personal income is closely connected to *consumption expenditures*, which play an important part in macroeconomic theories.

The public has not objected to the duplication and "mystification" involved in having five national series to deal with all at once. On the contrary, private bodies have gone beyond the government and have come up with estimates of their own. Some private economic and statistical consulting firms deduct "necessary consumption" (defined in different ways) from DPI to obtain what they call "discretionary" or "supernumerary" income, which they say is correlated closely with consumption spending for durable goods such as stoves, radios, and washing machines. Another innovation is "final buying income," which eliminates rises and falls in inventories—stocks of unsold goods either finished or in the process of production. Because "final buying income" smooths out a good part of the short-term fluctuations in economic activity, administration politicians are especially fond of it when recessions seem to be getting under way.

SHORTCOMINGS OF THE SYSTEM

No social accounting system is perfect for all purposes. It may omit production and income that some people think should be counted. To this extent, it understates actual income and production. For example, Americans criticize the Soviet system for omitting services, except those directly related to the production of goods. Or the system may include certain items that some people think should not be counted at all. To this extent, the system overstates national income and product. The Soviets criticize the American system for including

meaningless and artificial consumer frills as items of national income. We shall mention some of the more controversial points in the American system.

"Do-It-Yourself" Production

"Do-it-yourself" production is not counted in the national income accounting system, except for estimates of farmers' home-produced food and the imputed rent on owner-occupied housing (what the cost would be to a nonowner). The problem is that it is impossible to estimate the value of most "do-it-yourself" production with much accuracy.

Housekeeping and child rearing illustrate the importance of do-it-yourself production and the seriousness of its omission from the national accounts. If both husband and wife are employed in wage-paying jobs, both of their earnings will be recorded as part of the national income. If they hire help with housekeeping and child rearing (domestic servants, baby sitters, nursery schools, TV dinners), the earnings of those who produce these goods and services will also be counted. If one spouse chooses to be a housewife or househusband, the value of these services is not included. The national income declines not only by the wages of the one who keeps house but also by those of the housekeeper or baby sitter who is not hired. There is an old saw in national income statistics: "When you marry your cook, you lower the national income of the country."

Important as do-it-yourself production is in the United States, it is much more important in less-developed countries (LDCs). Thus, the comparison between income per head in the United States, or in any other more-developed country (MDC), and income per head in the typical LDC is apt to be biased and misleading. The MDC standard of living is not as much higher than the LDC standard of living as the national income figures would suggest. And by the same token, the present U.S. standard of living is probably not so much higher than the standard of living in pioneer days, when women made the family's clothes and families built their own cabins. Their replacement by frame houses built by specialized building contractors and hired labor represented a smaller rise in the true national income than in the recorded one.

The Underground Economy

Allied to the do-it-yourself economy is the **underground economy**. Much income and production is not included in the national accounts because no records are kept of transactions that take place in terms of **barter** (direct exchange of one good or service for another), or even in terms of cash transfers between unlicensed business units. Rough estimates can be made of the volume of such unrecorded transactions if conditions are stable. But in periods of rapid change, serious errors in the estimate are likely. Some have estimated that the underground economy amounts to over 20 percent of the measured American GNP.

In the United States as well as in many other countries, both capitalist and socialist, there seems to be a movement away from recorded market transactions toward unrecorded barter deals and other nonmarket and off-the-books transactions. Thus we have come to speak of an "underground," "parallel," "second," or "black" economy.

Services are generally better fitted to the underground economy than is the production of physical goods. A house painter may paint a house for his garage proprietor neighbor in exchange for an engine overhaul, an auto paint job, and body work done by the neighbor. A lawyer may draw up a will or a contract in exchange for carpentry or cabinet work in her home. The tax laws are quite clear: all such earnings should be reported at their money values. But when they are not in fact reported, the national accounts may underestimate the national income at the same time that taxes are evaded.

Other motives besides tax evasion inspire the underground economy. Sometimes people wish to evade certification and licensing rules, as when bureaucrats or law clerks sell advice on legal matters without a license to practice law. Others want to get around certain trade-union rules, as when union plumbers work on their own below the union scale, or do the electrical or painting or carpentry work associated with a plumbing job. At times the motive is to evade labor and welfare laws. So an "unemployed" worker will operate his or her own business while continuing to receive unemployment benefits and/or welfare payments. (In Italy, the term *lavoro nero*, or "black labor," refers not to the labor of blacks but to work done below the minimum wage and without deductions for Social Security.) Also, workers who use their employers' tools, truck, or premises for work on their own during or after working hours will, of course, not report income received from the job. Nor will those involved in criminal activities like prostitution, gambling, and the narcotics trade report their profits.

Intermediate Products

An **intermediate product**, such as a ton of steel girders, is something that is produced as an input to further production. The national accounts, by using the "value-added" system, try to avoid the double-counting that would result if they included both the intermediate products used in producing a good or service *and* the final good or service as well. (If the accounts were to include a gross "value of output" series, as the Soviet ones do, there would be no problem.)

An intermediate product is one that is produced as an input to further production.

The distinction between intermediate products and final products, however, is often hard to apply in practice. Consider gasoline that a suburbanite buys and uses mainly for commuting to and from a job in the city. Is this gasoline a final product (a consumption good) or an intermediate product (an input to the production generated at the city job)? Or should it be an intermediate good on the morning trip to the job but a final good on the way from the job to home "consumption"? Would the problem be different if the commuter took a train or bus instead of his or her own car? What if the employer were to provide a special bus?

The problem is that many goods and services are used both for consumption and for further production. The two sorts of uses are separated in the accounts by a set of rules of thumb, which probably lead on balance to an overestimate of the national income.

Relations with the Environment

The relations between people and their environment give rise to more problems in social accounting. To understand the problem, consider the following illustration.

To control or modify my immediate small environment, I purchase a furnace, fuel, insulation, sweaters, and gloves in the winter. In the summer, I buy air-conditioning equipment, fuel, fans, and sunglasses. Producing these things generates income, which is recorded in the national income and product accounts, even though we may think they are overcoming "bads" rather than providing "goods" in themselves.

Complications for the accounting system arise when we recognize that millions of other people also are doing the same things that I am doing. On this large scale, human behavior burdens the ecosystem, making the air around us less pure than it once was. So I equip my heating and cooling systems with filters to keep out the polluted air, after doing my share to cause the pollution. Should the production of these filters be counted as part of the GNP, without offsetting (or negative) entries somewhere in the accounts to record the environmental damage that made the filters necessary? The accounts do record the filters, but they use no negative entry to record the harm done. For this reason, the accounting system may overstate the actual amount of income and production, if we mean by "income and production" truly positive contributions to welfare and living standards.

The problem has many illustrations in the U.S. economy. In addition to air purification filters, there are devices to lessen automobile emissions, to dispose of radioactive wastes, and to purify drinking water. Should the treatment of lung cancer be a positive entry in the accounts if the air pollution that helps to cause the cancer is not a negative entry?

The problem of environmental degradation has applications in the economies of many LDCs as well, since primitive farming methods can harm the environment. The "slash-and-burn" technique, which calls for cutting and burning trees to clear land, leads to air pollution, soil erosion, floods, and fouled water supplies. There is no negative entry in the accounts to record the reduced value of the environment.

Consider the opposite case, too, when nature destroys the works of human beings. The capital consumption allowance, with which you are familiar, includes certain estimates of the results of nature's violent side. But the capital consumption allowance for nature's violence is spread evenly over the years, while the violence itself is not. How, then, would national income be affected if we suffered a major disaster like the destruction of Pompeii and Herculaneum by volcanic eruption, or of Tokyo and Yokohama by earthquake and fire? Such a disaster would result in an increase in national income, as people would earn incomes repairing the damage caused by nature and replacing what was beyond repair.

War and Violence

Preparing for war and waging war are recorded as parts of national income and production. People earn incomes for producing weapons of destruction and for serving in the armed forces. In fact, durable military goods like tanks are treated as consumption goods like loaves of bread rather than as investment goods like farm tractors. So total tank production is included in NNP as well as in GNP, even when the new tanks simply replace older ones, which wear out or become obsolete. (Loaves of bread are treated in this way for obvious reasons, but tractors are subject to capital consumption allowances.)

The issues involved in national accounting for war goods are both subtle and controversial. Does production of nuclear weapons deter war in the same way that riot police on duty at sports events deter rioting? If so, nuclear weapons production and riot-police training are legitimate entries in the social accounts, like the production of dikes as insurance against flood damage. But if weapons invite wars and police incite riots,[5] a case can be made to exclude these activities from production and income. (Criminal activity is not counted as

---

5. Consider the remark by the late Richard J. Daley, long-time mayor of Chicago: "The police are not there to create disorder. They are there to preserve disorder."

part of national income, though crime prevention is counted.)

The U.S. national income accounting system is not perfect; its flaws include its inability to take into account "do-it-yourself" production and the underground economy, the difficulty of distinguishing between intermediate and final products, and serious problems in measuring the effects of environmental damage and war.

Usefulness of the Accounts

As you can see, no accounting system provides completely acceptable measures of production or income in terms of welfare and living standards. Over the years, many ideas have been offered for making the system a better measure of "genuine" production in the sense of contributions to the standard of living. In the early 1970s, experimental systems called the measure of economic welfare (MEW) and net national welfare (NNW) were worked out for the United States and Japan, respectively. They attempted to subtract estimated environmental damage and wartime destruction.

Though they have been compared and criticized, they have not been continued on a permanent basis by any government.

The faults in our own and other national accounting systems, however, should not dim their usefulness. As a tool for the study of macroeconomics, the system offers information on changes in the volume of economic activity over time.

Changes over time are very important to the understanding of how an economy operates in the aggregate (macro) sense. Macroeconomics studies both the short-term changes and the long-term growth trends in the aggregate performance of an economy. When we focus on movements of uniformly defined measures over time, many of the problems concerning the absolute values used in the accounting system disappear. For example, the difference between one year and the next may be measured with reasonable accuracy even by questionable methods when the same rules for measurement have been used for each year.

Although the national income accounting system has flaws, it still serves a valuable purpose as a means of understanding the macroeconomy.

Economics in Focus

Legalizing the Underground Economy: A Boon for Third World Nations?

Food retailing in Lima, Peru, is dominated by 90,000 street vendors who sell their goods illegally. Most of the taxis and buses also are unlicensed. But none of this "informal" or "black market" activity seems unusual to the city residents, almost half of whom, according to one estimate, live in housing that was built illegally.

Lima offers a good example of the kind of underground economy that flourishes in many less-developed countries. Legalize the underground, some economists argue, and less-developed nations can reduce their debts, raise their standards of living, and compete on more equal terms with developed countries. The idea has been forcefully advanced in *The Other Path: The Invisible Revolution in the Third World*, a book by Peruvian Hernando de Soto.

But why are ordinary citizens like food vendors "underground" in the first place? The answer, in many countries in Latin America and Africa, lies in government regulations and bureaucratic tangles that make it impossible for a small entrepreneur to get legal approval. Those who apply for the proper permit or license may wait years while the bureaucracy fiddles; worse, bribes are often necessary. Wealthy business owners may use their political influence to keep out the small-time competition.

In Peru de Soto estimates that the underground economy adds an extra 29 percent to the nation's official GNP. In Argentina, where most of the managers and professionals participate in the underground economy, the unofficial GNP has been calculated at almost three-quarters the size of the official GNP. In the view of de Soto and his allies, legalizing underground economies would greatly increase their contribution to national welfare. Freed of the need to evade official scrutiny, small entrepreneurs could expand their businesses. They would have the security of legal title to their property, and access to the courts would help them enforce their contracts. They could borrow money more easily and at better rates.

Some economists disagree with these predictions, contending that underground businesses are less important than de Soto thinks. Nevertheless, a number of steps have been taken in the direction de Soto and his supporters advocate. The U.S. Agency for International Development (AID) helped to sponsor a 1988 conference on underground economies. AID and other international agencies have also assisted "microbanks" such as Ademi, an organization that supplies small-scale loans to unofficial businesses in the Dominican Republic. Research institutes in several Third World countries have begun to study underground economies and pressure governments for reform. Endorsing some of the new ideas, Malcolm Forbes declared that less-developed nations have "entrepreneurial energy of almost volcanic proportions waiting for release"—if they can be freed from the strangleholds their governments impose.

Sources: Jeremy Main, "How to Make Poor Countries Rich," *Fortune*, January 16, 1989, pp. 101–106; Robert McGough, "Let a Thousand Flowers Bloom," *Forbes*, April 28, 1986, pp. 57–60; Ronald Bailey, "The Right Path," *Forbes*, January 23, 1989, pp. 80–81; quotation from Malcolm S. Forbes, Jr., "Self-Made Crisis," *Forbes*, February 20, 1989, p. 27. See also Hernando de Soto, *The Other Path: The Invisible Revolution in the Third World* (New York: Harper & Row, 1989).

SUMMARY

1. Measuring the amount of economic activity is an important first step in understanding short- and long-term changes in the economy. (See page 125.)

2. The national income and product system has three main parts, one for measuring current production, one for measuring current income earned, and one for measuring amounts received as personal income. (See page 126 and Table 1, page 127.)

3. Gross national product is broken down into different kinds of spending: consumption, investment, government purchases, and net exports. The spending classification parallels the spending streams illustrated in the top half of the circular-flow diagram in Chapter 6. GNP records only currently produced goods and services. (See page 128.)

4. Net national product is smaller than gross national product by the amount of the capital consumption allowance, which takes into account the depreciation of capital goods. After certain adjustments are made, NNP becomes equal to national income. (See page 130.)

5. National income records the total earnings of factors of production during the accounting year. It corresponds with the income flows represented by the bottom half of the circular-flow diagram in Chapter 6. It is broken down into compensation of employees, proprietors' income, rental income of persons, corporate profits, and net interest. National income is equal to net national product after adjustments have been made for indirect business taxes, subsidies, and the statistical discrepancy. (See page 131.)

6. Personal income is the sum that remains after "earnings not received" have been subtracted and "receipts not earned" have been added to national income. When personal tax and nontax payments have been subtracted from personal income, the amount left is called disposable personal income. (See page 132.)

7. Attempts to explain national income and product in terms of human welfare face difficulties because of such matters as "do-it-yourself" production, the underground economy, intermediate goods and services, cleaning up the environ-

ment, and producing goods for war. (See page 133.)

8. Even though there is disagreement about how the national income and product accounting system should record certain activities, the system still is very useful for understanding the economy and making predictions. This is because changes in national production may be reliably reported if the same accounting methods are used consistently throughout the period. (See page 136.)

KEY TERMS

barter: the direct exchange of one good or service for another (page 134).

capital consumption allowance: estimated replacement costs for buildings and equipment that wear out or become obsolete during the accounting period (page 130).

disposable personal income (DPI): the amount of personal income actually available to people for spending or saving (page 132).

gross national product (GNP): the total market value of all currently produced goods and services (page 129).

indirect business taxes and subsidies: an entry in the national product section that removes the tax and subsidy components of market prices (page 130).

intermediate product: something that is produced as an input to further production (page 134).

national income (NI): the total amount that is earned in producing the national product (page 131).

national income and product accounts: a set of reports on the volume and composition of economic activity in the United States over a specified time period; it consists of three major parts: the national product section, the national income section, and the personal income section (page 126).

net national product (NNP): GNP minus the capital consumption allowance (page 130).

personal income (PI): an amount calculated by adjusting national income by adding receipts not earned and subtracting earnings not received (page 132).

statistical discrepancy: an entry in the national product section that reports the extent to which the estimate of net national product differs from the estimate of national income (page 131).

transfer payments: money paid to people even though they did not provide a good or service to earn this money during the accounting period (page 129).

underground economy: unrecorded barter or cash transactions (page 134).

value added: the market value of a firm's final sales minus the amounts paid by the firm to purchase intermediate goods from other firms (page 128).

DISCUSSION QUESTIONS

1. Name the three major parts of the national income and product accounting system. Which two are related through a double-entry bookkeeping system? Explain the adjustments that must be made to assure that these two sections balance with each other.

2. Suppose that the values added in producing a pair of shoes are $14 by the cattle raiser, $7 by the processing plant and tannery, $12 by the shoe manufacturer, $2 by the truck lines, and $11 by the retailer. Assuming no intermediate goods were purchased by the cattle raiser, what would the shoes sell for as a final product? How much double-counting would arise if intermediate goods were not excluded in evaluating this product?

3. List the five major components in the national income section of the U.S. income and product accounts. In which entry would you record fringe benefits received by workers? Where would you put the rent payment for land owned by a corporation? Where would you record interest on the national debt?

4. Suppose that national income is $100 billion. Calculate the amount of personal income if Social Security taxes are $10 billion, undistributed corporate profits are $1 billion, Social Security benefit checks are $11 billion, corporation profits taxes are $2 billion, government transfer payments are $2 billion, and interest on government bonds and consumer credit is $1 billion. (Assume that these are all the entries that are needed in this section.)

5. A good way to summarize the national income and product accounting system is to list the "big five" data entries in the system and to explain how each differs from those closest to it. Try this exercise. Then note for each entry the particular use that economists make of it.

6. The national income and product accounting system uses estimates of the rental value of owner-occupied homes but does not use estimates of the wage value of do-it-yourself housekeeping services. Why are estimates used in the one case and not in the other? List three other types of do-it-yourself income that are not included in the national income and product statistics.

7. The chapter discusses how gasoline cannot be easily classified as either a final good or an intermediate good. Identify two other products that in some uses are intermediate products and in other uses are final products. How do you believe these items should be treated in the accounting system?

8. Many states have bottle-deposit laws that encourage people to return empty beer and soft-drink containers to the store to recover their deposit. The store must hire people to handle this transaction and to return the empties to the bottler. Should the wages of these workers be counted as part of national income? What difference, if any, do you see between producing a "good" and preventing a "bad"?

8

Inflation and Unemployment

Preview   In this chapter, we examine the two problems that are of greatest concern to macroeconomists—inflation and unemployment. The economists' concern with inflation is two-fold. First, inflation upsets social relationships and adds uncertainty to economic decision making. Second, since the price level is the independent variable in aggregate-demand and aggregate-supply analyses, inflation (an increase in the price level) plays a key role in explaining the causes of economic fluctuations. Economists are concerned about employment because of the personal hardship of unemployed persons and because of the lost production that results from it.

The first part of the chapter discusses inflation, explaining the economists' concept of inflation and the index numbers used to measure it. The choices made by all the actors on the economic stage are affected by inflation and by expectations of future inflation. Also, unanticipated inflation redistributes income and wealth in ways that many people believe to be unfair. The effects of inflation on economic, social, and political life are profound.

The second part of the chapter deals with unemployment. Economists have a well-defined concept of unemployment, but measuring the actual amount of unemployment in the economy is difficult. After examining the economists' concept of unemployment and the methods used for measuring the amount of unemployment, we note how unemployment affects different groups in the society. If allowed to go too far, either inflation or unemployment can disrupt an economy and a society.

INFLATION AND THE PRICE LEVEL

Inflation is a significant and sustained increase in the general price level. We start our study of inflation by learning about index numbers and how they are used to compare different prices. Then we examine two methods of applying the index-number technique to the average of all prices in the economy. These will give us actual measurements of the changes in the general price level that occur with inflation and deflation. We will look at the record of price-level changes in the United States. Finally, we will consider some of the economic and social consequences of inflation.

Inflation is a significant and sustained increase in the general price level.

Price-Index Numbers

Statisticians, economists, and others use index numbers as a method of comparing one value with another. We can define an **index number** as a way of stating a value by expressing it in terms of some other reference, or "base" value. For example, if the number 25 were the base value, the number 20 would have an index-number value of 0.80, because 20/25 equals 0.80.

An index number is a way of stating a value by expressing it in terms of some other reference value. Price-index numbers provide a standardized system for measuring price-level changes.

Since an index number expresses values in terms of some reference point, the first step is to select this reference point. To apply the index-number method to prices, the prices that prevailed in some specified year are chosen as the base, or reference point, for constructing the index. Then the prices prevailing in other years are expressed in relation to these base-year prices. For example, if the price of apples increases from 50 cents a pound

in year 1 to 60 cents a pound in year 2 and then to $1.00 a pound in year 3, and if we select year 1 as the base, we can construct price-index numbers for apples by dividing each year's apple price by the base-year apple price, as follows.

Year	Apple Price ($)	Base-Period Apple Price ($)	Index Number
1	0.50	0.50	1.00
2	0.60	0.50	1.20
3	1.00	0.50	2.00

As you can see, the index numbers provide a standardized system for measuring the change that has taken place in apple prices. In our illustration, in year 2, the price of apples was 20 percent above the base-period price, as shown by the 1.20 value of the index number. In year 3, the apple price was twice what it was in the base period, and the index number was 2.0.

Price-index numbers are useful because they provide a way to adjust for changes in prices. In order to find the base-year equivalent of any price in the series, all we have to do is divide by its index number. For example, the price of a pound of apples in year 2 was 60 cents. If we divide 60 by 1.2 (the index number for year 2), the answer is 50. So 60 cents worth of apples in year 2 is equivalent to 50 cents worth of apples in year 1, assuming that apple quality is the same in both years. In year 3, the price of a pound of apples is $1.00. If we divide $1.00 by 2.0 (the index number for year 3), the answer is $0.50. So one dollar's worth of apples in year 3 is equivalent to $0.50 worth of apples in year 1, again assuming the quality of apples has not changed. Price-index numbers also can be used to compare any pair of prices in the series. This is done by dividing one index number by the other. For example, by dividing the index number for year 3 (2.00) by the index number for year 2 (1.20), we obtain a value of 1.67, which indicates that the price of a pound of apples had risen by 67 percent between the two years. In this way, index numbers can be used to measure price changes.

TABLE 1
Computing a Consumer Price Index

Item	Market-Basket Quantity	Base-Year Price	Base-Year Cost	Current-Year Price	Current-Year Cost
Hamburger	100 lbs.	$0.80	$ 80.00	$1.80	$ 180.00
Gasoline	500 gals.	0.40	200.00	1.60	800.00
Movies	40 shows	3.00	120.00	3.50	140.00
Total			$400.00		$1,120.00

$$\text{consumer price index} = \frac{\text{current-year cost}}{\text{base-year cost}} \times 100 = \frac{\$1,120}{\$400} \times 100 = 280$$

The index number is based on the cost of a specified collection of goods and services in the base year. The cost of purchasing this "market basket" of goods is calculated both in base-year prices and in current-year prices. The index number is the ratio of current-year cost to base-year cost, multiplied by 100.

Sometimes it is desirable to change the base period in a series of index numbers. To accomplish this, all we have to do is divide each index number in the series by the index number for the year we want to establish as the base period. With year 3 as the base period, the index number for year 1 becomes 0.50 (1.00/2.00) and the index number for year 2 becomes 0.60 (1.20/2.00). It often is convenient to adjust the base period of a series of index numbers to the most recent time possible, since it is easier for most people to relate to recent prices.

It is common practice to move the decimal point two places to the right in published price-index numbers so that the index number for the base period is 100. Thus, our basic formula for a price-index number becomes

$$\frac{\text{current price}}{\text{base-period price}} \times 100 = \text{index number}$$

With this system, the published index number for year 3 in our illustration would be calculated as

$$\frac{1.00}{0.50} \times 100 = 200$$

Now that you know what a price-index number is and how it can be used, we proceed to the next step, which is computing a measure of the general price level—an average of all the prices in the economy. Two different systems are widely used to compute these averages. One is used with the gross national product (GNP), and the other is used in estimating the cost of living with the consumer price index.

The Consumer Price Index

The **consumer price index (CPI),** often called the "cost-of-living index," is an index number used to measure changes in the cost of purchasing a specific group, or "market basket," of consumer goods and services. This collection of consumer goods and services is determined from studying actual purchases by families chosen because they represent important types of spending units in the economy.

Table 1 shows how to calculate a consumer price-index number. We assume that the selected market basket consists of 100 pounds of hamburger, 500 gallons of gasoline, and 40 movie tickets a year. In the prices of the base year, this market basket of goods and services cost $400.00. In the current year, the prices of these goods and services are higher, and the cost of purchasing the market basket is $1,120.00. To calculate the index number, divide the current-year cost of the market basket by its base-year cost and multiply the result by 100, as follows: ($1,120/$400) × 100 = 280. In this case, the index number is 280, meaning that the cost of the market basket in the current year is 2.8 times its cost in the base year. Thus, the "cost of living" increased by 180 percent.

Table 2 shows the consumer price index for the United States for the years 1960 to 1988. The base period for these data is the average of prices for the three years 1982, 1983, and 1984. By dividing the index number for 1988 (118.3) by the index number for 1960 (29.6), we find that the "cost of living" measured by this method had increased by 300 percent. In other words, by this measure, the price level was four times higher in 1988 than in 1960. The table also shows the **purchasing power of the dollar**, which is the reciprocal of the consumer price-index number, that is, it is 1 divided by the index number. Compared to the base period of 1982 to 1984 the dollar's purchasing power had fallen to 85.0 cents by 1988. By dividing the index number for 1960 (29.6) by the index number for 1988 (118.3), we find that the dollar's purchasing power had fallen from $1.00 in 1960 to 25.0 cents in 1988.

The consumer price index (CPI), also called the cost-of-living index, is an index number used to measure changes in the cost of purchasing a specific group of consumer goods and services. It is calculated by dividing the current-year cost of the goods and services by the base-year cost and multiplying the result by 100.

The purchasing power of the dollar is the value of goods and services that can be bought with a dollar compared with the value of goods and services that could have been bought with a dollar in a selected reference (base) period. It can be computed as the reciprocal of the consumer price-index number.

The consumer price index is the most widely publicized price-index number in the United States. It often is used in **cost-of-living adjustment (COLA)** clauses in contracts between labor and management. When agreed to in a contract, a COLA clause specifically connects changes in wage rates to changes in the consumer price index. For example, a COLA clause may state that the wage rate will be increased by a specified amount an hour as a result of some specified increase in the CPI. COLA clauses offer a way to build future price-level changes into a contract.

A cost-of-living adjustment (COLA) clause in a contract connects changes in wage rates to changes in the CPI.

The Weighting Bias of the CPI As a measure of the cost of living, the consumer price index suffers from several biases. One of the most serious of these involves the weighting system used to establish the relative importance of the different goods and services in the market basket. In computing the CPI, the relative importance, or "weight," of each good or service in the market basket is set according to the quantity purchased by representative households in some past year. The **weighting bias of the CPI** arises because this system fails to recognize that consumer buying patterns—and therefore the relative importance of the different goods and services in the market basket—their "weights"—tend to change when the price level changes. For example, consider the index number calculated in Table 1. The price of gasoline increased very substantially relative to the prices of the other goods and services. In the base year, a gallon of gasoline cost half as much as a pound of hamburger and less than one-seventh as much as a movie ticket. But in the "current" year, a gallon of gasoline cost almost as much as a whole pound of hamburger and was almost half the cost of a movie ticket. The CPI implies that people buy the same quantities of gasoline, hamburger, and movie tickets after the change in relative prices as they did before. Actually, when gasoline becomes more expensive in relation to other goods and services, it is likely that some consumers will switch some of their buying from gasoline to other things. People will go to the movies instead of driving to the Rockies. The CPI does not recognize these switches. Since consumers do change their buying habits to escape the higher prices, the CPI tends to overstate the rise in the cost of living. We may say that the CPI shows the change in the cost of the base-year "way of living" but that most families probably don't live that way any more.

TABLE 2
The Consumer Price Index and the Purchasing Power of the Consumer Dollar (1982–1984 = 100)

Year	Consumer Price Index	Purchasing Power of the Dollar	Year	Consumer Price Index	Purchasing Power of the Dollar
1960	29.6	3.38	1975	53.8	1.86
1961	29.9	3.34	1976	56.9	1.76
1962	30.2	3.31	1977	60.6	1.65
1963	30.6	3.27	1978	65.2	1.53
1964	31.0	3.23	1979	72.6	1.38
1965	31.5	3.17	1980	82.4	1.21
1966	32.4	3.09	1981	90.9	1.10
1967	33.4	2.99	1982	96.5	1.04
1968	34.8	2.87	1983	99.6	1.01
1969	36.7	2.72	1984	103.9	0.96
1970	38.8	2.57	1985	107.6	0.93
1971	40.5	2.47	1986	109.6	0.91
1972	41.8	2.39	1987	113.6	0.88
1973	44.4	2.25	1988[a]	118.3	0.85
1974	49.3	2.03			

The consumer price index shows the cost of purchasing a "market basket" of goods, which represents actual purchases by families. The base year for this series is 1982–1984. The purchasing power of the consumer dollar is computed as the reciprocal of the CPI—that is, 1/CPI.

[a] Estimated.

Source: Economic Report of the President, 1989, Table B-58, p. 373.

One weakness of the CPI as a measure of changes in the cost of living is its weighting bias: this system fails to recognize that consumer buying patterns tend to change when the price level changes.

The Quality Bias of the CPI The consumer price index implies that the quality of goods and services stays the same over the years. However, this is surely not the case. In fact, there is a **quality bias**. Because new products are invented and improvements are made in existing products, the goods produced in the current year are generally of higher quality, per dollar of constant value, than were their counterparts in the base year. If quality is generally improving, the "cost of living" has not risen as much as the CPI implies. People are living "better" because products have improved.

Students sometimes find it hard to believe that quality is generally improving, when we all know of cases where it seems to be getting worse. Ask yourself, however, what would happen if someone invented a new type of television set that was inferior in picture quality to those already on the market. Would anyone buy it? That would depend on its relative price. If its price were equal to (or higher than) the price of the earlier model, the new set would not survive in a competitive market. The market would "weed out" such products and would assure that product quality, adjusted for price changes, would not go down. To test whether quality has actually gone up, you might think about exchanging today's television set for the equivalent model of several years ago, assuming, of course, that the old-style set was new and unused. If the exchange were even, with no money changing hands, would you be willing to make the exchange? If your answer is "no," then quality has gone up.

The hypothetical exchange of today's product for the product of past times illustrates an inescapable problem in comparing quality over time. Often it is not possible to find a truly equivalent product. For example, videocassette recorders (VCRs) were not on the market twenty years ago but are popular products today. Also, one kind of quality sometimes is exchanged for another kind of quality. Automobiles today offer poorer "performance" (that is, acceleration) than those of twenty years ago, but they also create less air pollution. It is still technically possible to produce the old-style cars. The fact that we choose (in this case through various government regulations) not to produce them is some indication that we prefer the new type of quality to the old type of quality in automobiles. In this sense, quality is higher and the cost of living has not increased as much as implied by the consumer price index. The CPI has overstated the increase in the cost of living.

Another weakness of the CPI is its quality bias: it assumes that the quality of goods and services stays the same, whereas in reality, the quality of goods and services generally improves over time.

Biases That Understate Inflation   In some cases, the CPI fails to reveal the full impact of price increases on the actual cost of living. For example, if official price controls are in effect, along with their predictable shortages, consumers may buy products at higher (illegal) prices in **black markets**—markets that operate outside the law and sell at illegal prices. In this case, the CPI reported at official prices understates the actual cost of living. Moreover, the quality of goods and services may decline in these circumstances.

The CPI also may fail to reflect accurately changes in the cost of living for specific groups in the population when there are large changes in relative prices of important goods or services. For example, during the 1970s and early 1980s, the prices of certain necessities—food, housing, medical care, and fuel—increased more than did the CPI as a whole. Large families and low-income families, including retirees, tend to spend much of their incomes on these goods and services. For them, the official consumer price index understated the actual increase in the cost of living.[1]

---

1. For further information on how inflation affects different groups in the society, see Robert T. Michael, "Variations Across Households in the Rate of Inflation," *Journal of Money, Credit and Banking* (February 1979): 32–46.

The CPI may also fail to reveal the full impact of price increases on the actual cost of living or may fail to reflect changes in the cost of living for specific groups in the population.

The GNP Implicit Price Deflator

As you learned in Chapter 7, the **gross national product** is a measure of the value of a year's total production in the economy. In estimating GNP for the United States, the U.S. Department of Commerce evaluates production at the prices that actually prevail during the year in question. The result is gross national product measured in **current dollars** or **nominal values**. But the use of current dollars or nominal values leads to a problem in comparing one year's GNP with another year's GNP when the price level changes. What part of the change in nominal or current-dollar GNP is due to changes in production and what part is due to the change in the price level? When the current-dollar GNP has been adjusted to remove the influence of price level changes it is called the **constant-dollar GNP** or the GNP in **real values**. Separating these components is the job of a special type of index number, called the **GNP implicit price deflator**.

Table 3 illustrates how the GNP implicit price deflator is determined. In this very simple illustration, we assume that the entire GNP consists of the stated quantities of apples, oranges, and bananas, valued at the prices indicated for the current year. As you can see, the nominal, or current-dollar, value of the GNP is $250.00. But when these quantities are valued in the prices that prevailed in the year chosen as the base year, the GNP is only $167.50. With this information, we can calculate an index number to compare the average of prices in these two years. We simply apply the basic index-number formula to these two GNP values as follows:

$$\frac{\text{current-year value GNP}}{\text{base-year value GNP}} \times 100 = \text{index number}$$

which is equal to

$$\frac{\$250.00}{\$167.50} \times 100 = 149.25$$

TABLE 3
Computing a Price Deflator

Item	Current-Year Quantity	Current-Year Price	Current-Year Value	Base-Year Price	Base-Year Equivalent Value
Apples	100 lbs.	$1.00	$100.00	$0.60	$ 60.00
Oranges	75	1.50	112.50	0.90	67.50
Bananas	50	0.75	37.50	0.80	40.00
GNP			$250.00		$167.50

$$\text{implicit GNP deflator} = \frac{\text{current-year-value GNP}}{\text{base-year-equivalent-value GNP}} \times 100$$

$$= \frac{\$250.00}{\$167.50} \times 100 = 149.25$$

Values for goods in the current year are compared with the amounts that would have been needed to purchase the same goods at the base-year prices. The deflator index number is equal to 100 times current-year GNP divided by base-year equivalent GNP.

By dividing the current, or nominal value, GNP by the implicit GNP deflator, we find the amount of money that would have been needed to purchase the same goods and services at the prices that prevailed in the base year. Table 4 shows the results of applying this deflation procedure to the U.S. GNP from 1960 through 1988. In this table, 1982 is the base year (that is, the 1982 prices are the common denominator). So current-dollar GNP for 1982 is exactly the same as the constant-dollar (1982) GNP, and the implicit price deflator for 1982 is 100.0. The current-dollar columns show nominal values and the constant-dollar (1982) columns show real values, that is, values adjusted for changes in the price level. Note how much the real economic growth rates (measured as the percentage change in GNP from the preceding year) differ from the growth rates measured in nominal values. In real terms, economic growth was negative in five years (1970, 1974, 1975, 1980, and 1982) and reached a high point of 6.8 percent in 1984.

Special-Purpose Index Numbers

Index numbers can be used for many purposes other than measuring changes in the cost of living or in real GNP. Dozens of special-purpose index

numbers are published monthly in the *Survey of Current Business*.[2] Indexes of producer prices for farm products, chemicals, fuels, and so forth, are computed regularly. These are widely used to predict future changes in consumer prices, since price changes at the producer's level will probably be passed on soon to the consumer. Price-index numbers and deflators also are regularly published for many specific producer goods, such as agricultural chemicals, lumber, iron, and steel. These data are useful in anticipating changes in relative prices for food, housing, automobiles, and so forth. Still another special-purpose index number is maintained for purchases by governments. This index can be used to translate government budget figures from nominal to real values in order to compare real budget amounts for different time periods. Over the past decade, the prices for goods and services purchased by governments have risen more rapidly than the general price level.

Index numbers and deflators must be used carefully. The prices of goods that some consumers

2. Price indexes and deflators for many components of national income and product and for many different industrial inputs and outputs are published regularly in the *Survey of Current Business*. Cost-of-living index numbers for different cities and countries are published every year in almanacs and in *The Statistical Abstract of the United States*.

TABLE 4
U.S. GNP in Current and Constant (1982) Dollars, 1960–1988

	Current Dollars		Constant (1982) Dollars		
Year	GNP ($ Billions)	% Change	Implicit GNP Deflator	GNP ($ Billions)	% Change
1960	515.3	3.9	30.9	1,665.3	2.2
1961	533.8	3.6	31.2	1,708.7	2.6
1962	574.6	7.6	31.9	1,799.4	5.3
1963	606.9	5.6	32.4	1,873.3	4.1
1964ᵃ	649.8	7.1	32.9	1,973.3	5.3
1965	705.1	8.5	33.8	2,087.6	5.8
1966	772.0	9.5	35.0	2,208.3	5.8
1967	816.4	5.8	35.9	2,271.4	2.9
1968	892.7	9.3	37.7	2,365.6	4.1
1969	963.9	8.0	39.8	2,423.3	2.4
1970	1,015.5	5.4	42.0	2,416.2	−.3
1971	1,102.7	8.6	44.4	2,484.8	2.8
1972	1,212.8	10.0	46.5	2,608.5	5.0
1973	1,359.3	12.1	49.5	2,744.1	5.2
1974	1,472.8	8.3	54.0	2,729.3	−.5
1975	1,598.4	8.5	59.3	2,695.0	−1.3
1976	1,782.8	11.5	63.1	2,826.7	4.9
1977	1,990.5	11.7	67.3	2,958.6	4.7
1978	2,249.7	13.0	72.2	3,115.2	5.3
1979	2,508.2	11.5	78.6	3,192.4	2.5
1980	2,732.0	8.9	85.7	3,187.1	−.2
1981	3,052.6	11.7	94.0	3,248.8	1.9
1982	3,166.0	3.7	100.0	3,166.0	−2.5
1983	3,405.7	7.6	103.9	3,279.1	3.6
1984	3,772.2	10.8	107.7	3,501.4	6.8
1985	4,014.9	6.4	110.9	3,618.7	3.4
1986	4,240.3	5.6	113.9	3,721.7	2.8
1987	4,526.7	6.8	117.7	3,847.0	3.4
1988ᵃ	4,866.4	7.5	121.7	3,997.3	3.9

Current values have been adjusted to their equivalent in prices that prevailed in 1982. Growth rates are shown as the percentage change from the preceding year.

ᵃ Estimated.

Source: Economic Report of the President, 1989, Tables B-1, B-2, and B-3.

buy may not change in the same way as prices for goods that other consumers buy. There are at least two reasons for this difference. First, prices themselves are not the same at all locations. For example, prices may be higher in urban areas than in rural areas. Second, different people (old and young, rich and poor) buy different goods and so face different situations when prices change. There-

fore, those who use price indexes should be sure that both the price data and their choice of goods are suited to the way in which they are using the index.

Price-index numbers and deflators are useful but they must be used carefully, since the prices

---

of goods that some consumers buy may not change in the same way as prices for goods that other consumers buy.

Inflation in the United States

Figure 1 shows recent U.S. price-level history. Panel (a) shows the GNP implicit price deflator for 1960 through 1988, plotted from the values in Table 4. As you can see, the price level, as measured by the GNP deflator, rose gradually during the 1960s, climbed rapidly during the 1970s, and resumed a more gradual rate of increase during the 1980s.

Panel (b) in Figure 1 plots the percentage change in the GNP implicit price deflator from one year to the next, calculated by dividing the GNP deflator value for each year by the GNP deflator value for the previous year, subtracting 1.0, and multiplying the result by 100. The resulting figure is the annual **inflation rate**. For example, the GNP deflator (1982 = 100) was 121.7 for 1988 and 117.7 for 1987, which means that the price level in the United States increased by 3.4 percent during 1988 (121.7/117.7 = 1.034). The rate of inflation was 3.4 percent.

Panel (b) in Figure 1 provides a picture of inflation in the United States over those years. In the first half of the 1960s, the inflation rate hovered around 1½ percent a year. This was called inflation at the time, since it was a sustained increase in the general price level, but might not now be called inflation as compared with other periods. Price-level increases in this modest range can quite possibly be offset against normal increases in the quality of the goods and services that make up the GNP.

Inflation clearly existed after 1965. If we accept the early 1960s as a benchmark, or point of reference, the years after 1965 brought the longest period of sustained significant price-level increases in the nation's history. The rate of increase in the price level remained above the benchmark throughout the entire period, and the 1988 price level was 3.6 times the 1965 price level (121.7/33.8 = 3.6). Prices had more than tripled. For comparison, the inflationary period in the United States

from 1940 through 1948, during and after World War II, lasted for nine years, and the price level did not even double (52.98/29.06 = 1.82).

The annual inflation rate is calculated by dividing the GNP deflator value for each year by the GNP deflator value for the previous year, subtracting 1.0, and multiplying by 100.

Figure 1(b) also shows that the rate of inflation decreased greatly after 1981. Economists use the term **disinflation** to refer to a falling inflation rate. During periods of disinflation, the price level is still rising and inflation is taking place, but the rate of increase in the price level is becoming less and less.

Disinflation means that the inflation rate is falling—the rate of increase in the price level is becoming less and less.

Economic Consequences of Inflation

As you learned in Chapter 6, changes in the general price level—inflation, disinflation, and deflation—play a key role in aggregate-demand and aggregate-supply analyses. Changes in the price level are expected to cause changes in the aggregate quantity demanded and in the aggregate quantity supplied. This is why an index number representing the price level (usually the GNP implicit price deflator) is used on the vertical axes of aggregate-demand and aggregate-supply graphs. Therefore, your understanding of price index numbers is a useful preparation for your study of modern macroeconomic theories in later chapters.

It is important to understand, however, that there is nothing sacred about any particular price level. The price level in 1990 is no better or worse than the price level in 1980 or 1970. An economy can function satisfactorily at any price level. Even changes in the price level can take place without seriously upsetting economic systems, if these changes are small and reasonably predictable. But fairly substantial and unanticipated inflation can cause serious problems. The consequences of infla-

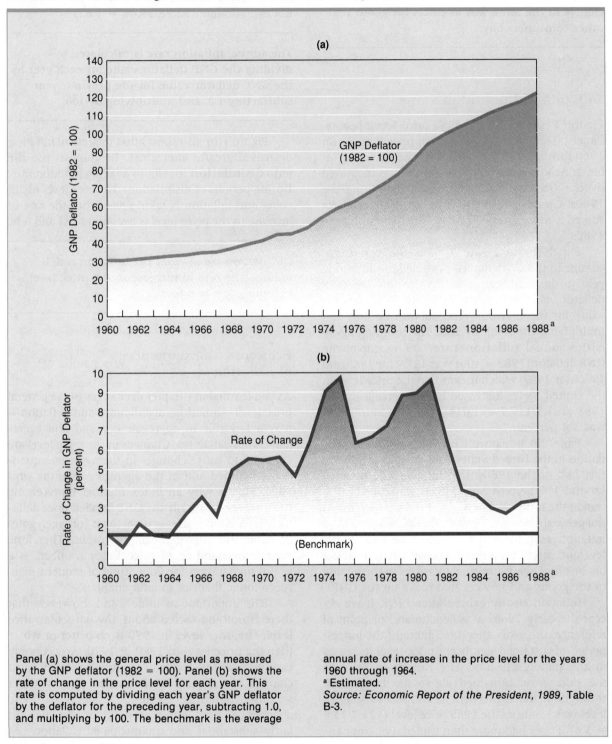

Panel (a) shows the general price level as measured by the GNP deflator (1982 = 100). Panel (b) shows the rate of change in the price level for each year. This rate is computed by dividing each year's GNP deflator by the deflator for the preceding year, subtracting 1.0, and multiplying by 100. The benchmark is the average annual rate of increase in the price level for the years 1960 through 1964.
[a] Estimated.
Source: Economic Report of the President, 1989, Table B-3.

tion differ importantly depending on how well people have been able to forecast or anticipate the change in the price level.

Imperfectly Anticipated Inflation   The most serious consequences of inflation arise because a price-level-change factor must be included in the day-to-day decisions that guide the operation of the economy. Labor must predict the price-level change when it bargains for wages. Firms must predict price-level changes when they plan new investments and estimate depreciation allowances. Individuals must consider price-level changes when deciding about consumption spending and saving. To estimate the costs of services, governments must take account of price-level changes. If price-level changes are not correctly anticipated, it will lead to mistakes concerning all of these important decisions. Of course, mistakes are made even when the price level does not change, but more mistakes are likely to be made in periods of unanticipated inflation. Unanticipated inflation can change aggregate quantities demanded and supplied and distort the operation of the macroeconomy.

American farmers are painfully aware of the hardships that arise from failure to correctly forecast the rate of inflation. During the 1970s, many farmers borrowed large sums to expand production. Because the rate of inflation was high and was expected to continue at a high rate, lenders insisted on relatively high interest rates on loans. Farmers also expected rapid inflation to continue, so they agreed to these relatively high rates and pledged their farmlands as security for the loans. There seemed little cause for concern, since the price of farmland was rising even more rapidly than the general price level. Hardship came because farmers failed to correctly foresee the great disinflation of the early 1980s. The inflation rate fell to approximately half its earlier rate. As a result, interest rates and the prices of farmland went down, and the prices of farm crops were not as high as expected. Many farmers could not earn enough to meet the interest payments required on their loans. Because of the unexpected low prices for farmland, many farmers lost their farms when lenders foreclosed on mortgages. Had the disinflation been accurately

forecast, farmers would have been more cautious about borrowing, interest rates would have been lower, and there would have been fewer farms lost as a result of mortgage foreclosures.

Imperfectly anticipated inflation also can cause changes in the distribution of wealth among groups in a society. Imperfectly anticipated changes in the price level redistribute wealth by changing the real purchasing power of the monetary unit—the dollar in the United States, the yen in Japan, the mark in Germany. Wealth that is held in cash, savings accounts, bonds, insurance policies, and other forms of "paper wealth" specified in dollar amounts, drops in *real* value when the price level rises and rises in *real* value when the price level falls. If their holders did not expect the inflation and insist on adjustments such as a lower purchase price or a higher interest rate, they will be victims of inflation. Their wealth will be redistributed to those who transferred the cash or who sold the paper wealth to them or who made better decisions about inflation. The winners from inflation may have been wiser and anticipated that inflation was coming. Perhaps they borrowed money to purchase land, "collectibles" such as art, stamps or coins, precious metals such as gold or silver, or precious gems such as diamonds or emeralds—all goods whose nominal values would increase along with the inflation. As often as not, however, their gains may have been "just luck."

Luck may be randomly distributed, but this cannot be said for knowledge or for the possession of the kinds of wealth that are most vulnerable to inflation. Inflation tends to be especially damaging to those people in a society who have a large portion of their wealth in savings accounts and insurance policies, which are most vulnerable to inflation. Unexpected inflation drains wealth from this group. Since these people generally have a moderating and stabilizing effect on the social and political system, their loss of wealth can lead to radical shifts in political positions, either to the left or to the right. After World War I, groups hurt by inflation showed a greater tendency to move to the right than to the left.

Even though redistribution of wealth due to past inflation is "water over the dam," it may leave its mark on the society's future.

Perfectly Anticipated Inflation   The problems of wealth redistribution and decision errors would not arise if everyone in the economy made accurate forecasts of the future price level, that is, if inflation were perfectly anticipated. It is, of course, virtually impossible that price-level changes could be perfectly anticipated by all economic decision makers, but it is equally true that inflation is seldom entirely unexpected. It is not likely to come as a complete surprise to everyone in the economy. Since the real world includes some accurate inflation forecasting and since experience with inflation may lead to still better forecasts, it is useful to ask whether price-level changes would cause any difficulty if they were perfectly anticipated.

Even if it were perfectly anticipated, inflation would cause some problems. For example, firms would have to update price lists frequently or else work out ways to communicate prices without using published price lists. These are called **menu costs** of inflation, because the costs are illustrated by restaurants having the expense of printing new menus oftener than in noninflationary times. Another drain on resources would arise because people would have to go to the trouble of transferring assets from one form to another whenever they anticipated a change in the inflation rate. For example, real estate may be a good wealth form when prices are rising, while bonds may be better when prices are falling or when the rate of inflation is decreasing, that is, in times of disinflation. The costs of switching ownership rights back and forth are called **shoe-leather costs** of inflation. Finally, even if perfectly anticipated, inflation imposes losses on firms and individuals who must use currency in their day-to-day activities. This is because the purchasing power of a unit of currency (one dollar, for example) goes down when the price level goes up. So economic activities that must use currency, such as fast-food restaurants and vending machine operations, would be hurt by inflation because the currency they must hold loses value while in their possession. Making currency less useful and desirable reduces the efficiency of the economy.

The menu costs of inflation are those costs entailed by frequent updating of price lists.

Shoe-leather costs of inflation are those costs incurred when assets are transferred from one form to another.

Political Consequences of Inflation

History offers many examples of political changes both from sustained periods of rising prices (inflations) and from sustained periods of falling prices (deflations). In Europe, price levels rose in the 1500s and 1600s after the Spanish discovered the gold and silver mines of Mexico and South America and began taking their riches back home. Feudal lords who had converted the obligations of their serfs from services to fixed money rents grew poorer as prices rose. For support they turned to the rising group of national monarchs who could collect money from growing trade and business activities. These events hastened the decline of feudalism and the rise of nation-states in Europe.

In the United States, price levels dropped greatly from the end of the Civil War until the close of the 1800s. Farmers and small business people who depended on debt financing were hurt as prices fell and they had to repay loans in money of a higher value than the money they had borrowed. The resulting political agitation led to reform movements that had lasting effects on government in the United States.[3] Resentment against big business and banking, believed to be gainers from the falling price level, was widespread around the turn of the century and still colors political and economic thought in the United States.

In Germany after World-War I, inflation wiped out the savings of many middle-income people. The resulting frustrations provided a fertile seedbed for the rise of Hitler's National Socialist (actually fascist) party. The following is quoted from the reminiscences of a German woman about her experiences in 1923:

> ". . . workers had discovered the 'trick of inflation,' which was to figure the value of money in gold. Time and again the workers struck for the

---

3. Douglass C. North, *Structure and Change in Economic History* (New York: W. W. Norton & Co., 1982).

'adjustment of their wages.' After their strikes, their wages had been adjusted—to the actual price increases. But the price increases went on and so the workers had to strike again for new adjustments. What they asked for now was wages paid daily.

"While this struggle went on, chaos increased. The Middle Ages came back. Communities printed their own money, based on goods, on a certain amount of potatoes, of rye, for instance. Shoe factories paid their workers in bonds for shoes which they could exchange at the bakery for bread or the meat market for meat.

"At this stage, the Communists believed that their time had come. They attempted an uprising. . . ."[4]

In the United States, the inflation of the 1970s played a prominent role in political affairs. Taxpayer revolts flared because citizens blamed the government for the inflation and because both property-tax and income-tax bills were pushed upward by inflation. Popular reaction against inflation contributed to the defeat of President Ford in 1976 and to the defeat of his successor, President Carter, in 1980.

EMPLOYMENT

Along with inflation, employment and unemployment are major concerns in macroeconomics. Both employment and unemployment are closely related to the standard of living and to the volume of real GNP in the economy. Therefore, policy makers and macroeconomists pay close attention to changes in employment and unemployment and have developed detailed theories about the causes of these changes. Real GNP—the total output of the economy adjusted for price-level changes— varies directly with the level of employment and inversely with the level of unemployment. Therefore, understanding changes in employment and unemployment help economists understand changes in the level of real GNP.

The horizontal axis on the aggregate-demand and aggregate-supply graph shows real GNP.

4. Pearl S. Buck, *How It Happens*, as cited in Fritz K. Ringer (ed.), *The German Inflation of 1923* (New York: Oxford University Press, 1969), pp. 144–145.

Movements to the right along that axis indicate increases in production, and movements to the left indicate decreases in production. Such changes in the volume of production come from changes in quantities of resources (labor, natural resources, and capital) used in production and from changes in technology—the application of science to the production process. If we assume that technology is fixed (a not-too-unreasonable assumption for short intervals of time), we can say that movements to the right along the horizontal axis of an aggregate-demand and aggregate-supply graph correspond with increases in the quantities of resources employed and that movements to the left correspond with decreases in the quantity of resources employed.

Macroeconomists are concerned about the employment of all resources, but they are particularly interested in the labor resource because it receives such a large portion (about three-fourths) of total income and because it affects human beings so directly. Therefore, in economics, the term **employment** usually is used in reference to the labor resource and is defined as "labor engaged in regular work for pay." Movements to the right on the horizontal axis of the aggregate-demand and aggregate-supply graph reflect increasing employment of labor, and movements to the left reflect decreasing labor employment. As you can imagine, measuring the precise connection between changes in real GNP and changes in the number of workers employed is an important focus of research by statisticians and economists.

In economics, the term *employment* means "labor engaged in regular work for pay."

The Civilian Employment Rate

The **civilian employment rate** is the percentage of the civilian noninstitutional population, age 16 and over, that is regularly working for pay. To estimate this rate, the Bureau of Labor Statistics of the United States Department of Labor conducts surveys of representative samples of the U.S. population, excluding those in active military service and in institutions such as mental hospitals and prisons. One of the questions on the survey asks whether the individual is currently working for pay or has been employed during the past month. Part-time work on a regular basis is counted—a person who works regularly as little as one hour a week for pay is classified as employed. Using this method, the Department of Labor reported that there were 115,976,000 people employed in the United States in November 1988. To compute the civilian employment rate, this figure is divided by the total U.S. civilian noninstitutional population, age 16 and over, which, on that date, was 185,244,000. Thus, the civilian employment rate for November 1988 was 62.6 percent.

Figure 2 shows the civilian employment rate for the United States from 1970 to 1988. Low points were reported for 1971, 1975, and 1982. High points for the civilian employment rate were reported for 1973 and 1974, 1979, and 1988.

The civilian employment rate is the percentage of the civilian noninstitutional population, age 16 and over, that is regularly working for pay.

The Civilian Labor Force Participation Rate

Figure 2 shows not only fluctuations in the employment rate but also a general upward trend. Successive high points and low points tend to be somewhat higher than their predecessors, and a line fitted to represent the long-term trend of the employment rate would slope upward from left to right. Why might this happen? Is an increasingly larger percentage of the civilian noninstitutional population interested in regular employment for pay?

It is true that a larger percentage of the civilian noninstitutional population is either working or actively looking for work now than in 1970. This fact is illustrated in Figure 4 (on page 24 in Chapter 2), which displays the **civilian labor force participation rate**—the percent of the civilian non-institutional population that is sixteen years of age or older and either working or actively looking for work. The latter conditions—sixteen years of age or older and either working or looking for work—are the official requirements for a person to be counted in the **civilian labor force**. Therefore, the civilian labor force participation rate is equal to the number of people in the civilian labor force divided by the number in the civilian noninstitutional population, age 16 and over. In November 1988, there were 122,572,000 persons in the civilian labor force in the United States and 185,244,000 persons in the comparable civilian noninstitutional population. Therefore, the civilian labor force participation rate was 66.2 percent.

Between 1960 and 1988 the civilian labor force participation rate increased partly because a much larger percentage of the female population held paying jobs or was looking for paid employment. Another reason was that, as a result of the "baby boom" of the 1950s, an especially large portion of the population was between ages sixteen and sixty-five. Many economists believe that the U.S. economy did well in providing jobs for this large increase in the civilian labor force, especially in view of the problems often encountered by people entering the labor force for the first time.

The civilian labor force consists of those members of the civilian noninstitutional population who are sixteen years of age or older who are either working or looking for work. The civilian labor force participation rate is the percentage of the noninstitutional civilian population, sixteen years of age or older, that is either working or looking for work.

UNEMPLOYMENT

To understand economic theories about unemployment, it is important to distinguish between the economic concept of unemployment and the definition of unemployment used in official statistics. We shall examine the economic concept first and then look at the statistical definition.

The Economic Concept of Unemployment

The economic concept of **unemployment** is that a person is spending more time for leisure and less

FIGURE 2
Civilian Employment Rate, United States, 1970–1988

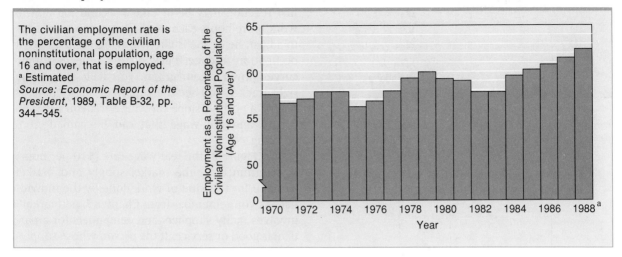

The civilian employment rate is the percentage of the civilian noninstitutional population, age 16 and over, that is employed.
^a Estimated
Source: Economic Report of the President, 1989, Table B-32, pp. 344–345.

time for wage earning than he or she desires at the going wage rate for his or her occupation. To understand this concept of unemployment, we use the demand and supply concepts you learned in Chapter 5 and examine the supply of labor from the point of view of an individual worker. Then we broaden this concept and look at labor demand and supply for the entire economy.

In economics, the term *unemployment* means that a person is spending more time for leisure and less time for wage earning than he or she desires at the going wage rate for his or her occupation.

An Individual's Supply-of-Labor Curve Figure 3 shows an individual's supply-of-labor curve. On the vertical axis are different possible wage rates, which we specify to be **real wage rates**—that is, wage rates adjusted for expected price-level changes so that they represent the goods and services the individual expects to be able to purchase with the earnings. We use real wage rates because we believe workers and employers use the real wage rate, or what they believe is the real wage rate, in making work decisions.

Real wage rates are wage rates adjusted for expected price-level changes so that they

represent the goods and services the individual expects to be able to purchase.

The horizontal axis shows quantities of work the individual will supply. The curve on the graph shows the number of hours of work per week that the individual is willing and able to supply at various possible real wage rates. To understand this curve, remember that when a person is working, he or she is exchanging leisure-time activities for wage income. The supply-of-labor curve shows his or her willingness to make this exchange. The curve slopes upward, suggesting that a person is willing to give up more leisure activity when real wage rates are high than when they are low, *ceteris paribus.*

A useful way to view an individual's supply-of-labor curve is to think of the wage rate as the opportunity cost of leisure-time activities. In other words, when a person takes time off to enjoy leisure activities, he or she is giving up the wage income that otherwise would have been earned during that time. At low wage rates, leisure activities are inexpensive and people use more of their time for them. But at higher wage rates, the trade-off is more favorable for wage income and less favorable for leisure. This is another way of saying that the quantity of labor an individual supplies is

FIGURE 3
An Individual's Supply-of-Labor Curve and the Concept of Unemployment

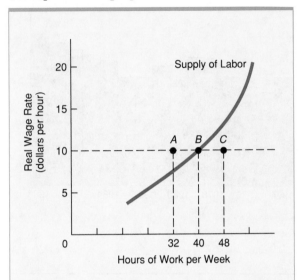

The supply-of-labor curve shows the number of hours per week that a person would like to work at various possible wage rates. When the wage rate is $10.00 per hour, a person is underemployed if he or she is working 32 hours per week (point A), fully employed if working 40 hours per week (point B), and overemployed if working 48 hours per week (point C).

positively related to the wage rate.[5]

An individual's supply-of-labor curve shows a person's willingness to exchange leisure for wage income.

Before you go on, take a moment to think through this concept of the individual's supply-of-labor curve. Be sure you understand the reasoning behind the idea that people want to work more hours when the real wage rate is high than when it is low. Of course, we realize that low-wage earners sometimes work more hours per week than high-wage earners, but since that proposition compares different people, it does not match the specifica-

5. In microeconomics you learn that some part of the individual's supply-of-labor curve may have a negative slope—the so-called backward bending supply curve of labor. In dealing with macroeconomics and aggregate data, this possibility can be ignored.

tions of our graph in Figure 3. Also, we realize that, when a worker experiences a wage cut, his or her first reaction may be to take a second job and to work more hours each week. But, given more time to adjust, he or she is likely to switch to a different occupation and get back on the type of supply curve shown in our graph. You will stay on the right track if you see the supply-of-labor curve as having a positive slope showing a tradeoff between leisure and the wage that can be gained from working.

In Figure 3, the real wage rate ($10 per hour) is determined by the market supply and market demand for the kind of work done by the individual. As you remember from Chapter 5, a "market" involves many suppliers and demanders for a particular good or service. If the person whose supply-of-labor curve is shown is working forty hours per week at this wage rate (point B), he or she is fully employed—working exactly the desired number of hours per week. But if that person is working only thirty-two hours per week (point A), he or she is underemployed—working fewer hours per week than desired at $10.00 per hour. At point C, the person is overemployed, since, at forty-eight hours of work per week, he or she is giving up more hours of leisure than desired at that wage rate. Neither point A nor point C is an equilibrium situation for this individual.

A person who is working exactly the desired number of hours at the going real wage rate for a particular occupation is considered to be fully employed. If that person is working fewer hours per week than desired at that wage rate, he or she is underemployed. If the person is giving up more hours of leisure than desired at that wage rate, he or she is overemployed.

Macroeconomic Unemployment Figure 3 illustrated overemployment, full employment, and underemployment from the perspective of an individual worker. We now broaden the scope to consider all workers in an economy. Figure 4 represents the labor market for the entire economy. The vertical axis shows average real wage rates, and the horizontal axis records the aggregate quantities of labor supplied by individuals at various possible

FIGURE 4
The Labor Market for an Entire Economy

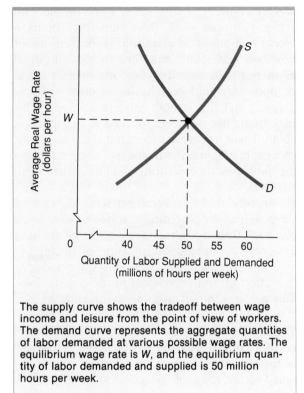

The supply curve shows the tradeoff between wage income and leisure from the point of view of workers. The demand curve represents the aggregate quantities of labor demanded at various possible wage rates. The equilibrium wage rate is *W*, and the equilibrium quantity of labor demanded and supplied is 50 million hours per week.

real wage rates, *ceteris paribus*. The supply curve shows the tradeoff between wage income and leisure from the point of view of workers, and the demand curve represents the aggregate quantities of labor demanded by firms in the economy at various possible average real wage rates.[6] The intersection of the demand curve, *D*, and the supply curve, *S*, identifies the equilibrium average real wage rate—the rate at which the quantity of labor supplied equals the quantity demanded. In Figure 4, the equilibrium average real wage rate is *W*. At *W* the equilibrium quantity of labor demanded and supplied is 50 million hours per week.

Figure 5 illustrates how unemployment may arise in the macroeconomy. In this graph, point *A*

6. The demand for labor is derived from the demand for the goods and services that labor produces. When other inputs are held constant, the marginal product of labor declines as more labor is used so employers are willing to pay less for successive units of labor input. This accounts for the downward slope of the labor-demand curve.

represents the equilibrium illustrated in Figure 4. To illustrate how unemployment can arise, suppose that the labor-demand curve shifts unexpectedly to the left, from D_1 to D_2. The equilibrium real wage rate falls from $10.00 to $9.50, and the equilibrium quantity of labor falls from 50 million hours per week to 45 million hours per week. However, actual wage rates usually are slow in moving to the new equilibrium. Some wages are set by contracts that last for a year or more and even when they are not set by contract they have a tendency to be quite sticky. They lag behind changes in other prices. As long as the *actual* wage rate stays above the new *equilibrium* rate ($9.50 an hour in Figure 5), the quantity of labor demanded will be less than the new equilibrium quantity. This is because, in nonequilibrium situations, actual employment is determined by the *lesser* of the

FIGURE 5
Macroeconomic Unemployment as Disequilibrium in the Labor Market

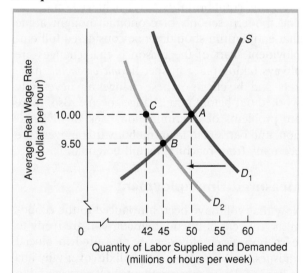

The initial equilibrium is at point *A* with a real wage rate of $10.00 an hour and 50 million hours of work per week demanded and supplied. If the demand curve shifts from D_1 to D_2, the new equilibrium is at point *B*, with a real wage rate of $9.50 an hour and 45 million hours of work demanded and supplied per week. Point *C* illustrates a case of disequilibrium with 42 million hours of work per week demanded, 3 million hours per week of macroeconomic unemployment, and 8 million hours a week of measured unemployment.

Chapter 8   Inflation and Unemployment **157**

quantity demanded and the quantity supplied. When the actual wage rate is above the equilibrium wage rate, **macroeconomic unemployment** exists. In Figure 5, if the actual wage rate were to remain at $10.00 an hour, actual employment would be 42 million hours per week and macroeconomic unemployment would amount to 8 million hours per week.

Macroeconomic unemployment exists when the actual wage rate is above the equilibrium wage rate.

Does the Labor Market "Clear" at Equilibrium? Is the economy at full employment when equilibrium is achieved in the labor market? According to the logic of the aggregate-demand and aggregate-supply model, if the demand curve and the supply curve have been stable long enough for workers and firms to adjust fully to the equilibrium real wage rate, the answer is "yes." Realistically, however, this equilibrium is never achieved, and several modern schools of economic thought argue that equilibrium should *not* be considered full employment. Part of the reason is that changes are always taking place in specific *microeconomic* markets, and the effects of these changes are never fully worked out before new changes occur. Also, there are problems of discrimination, lack of information, and barriers to labor mobility that prevent the economy from reaching its full potential.[7]

Measured Unemployment

Now that you have been introduced to the economists' concept of unemployment, you are ready to learn how unemployment is measured in official statistics. In this section, you will discover why it is so hard to devise measurements that correspond to the economists' concept of unemployment.

Economists define unemployment by comparing actual work time with a person's desired work time. Many difficulties arise in finding a measuring system consistent with the theory. Take, for example, the forty-hour workweek, which is more or less standard in the United States today. At the

7. These views are discussed further in Chapter 17.

current wage rate, do you feel that this workweek provides the best combination of leisure time and wage income? You may know some people who prefer part-time work (less than forty hours a week) and others who want to work overtime or hold two jobs at the same time (moonlighters). If all these people actually work forty hours a week, economists would call the first group "overemployed" and the second "underemployed." This may sound like a strange conclusion, but thinking about it will help you understand the economists' concept of unemployment and will suggest some of the problems in measuring unemployment with statistics.

In official U.S. government statistics, each of the people in the preceding example is called "employed." Thus it is clear that the official statistics are only an approximate measure of unemployment, in the economists' view. But since decisions that affect all of us are based on official statistics, they are very important in policy making.

The Civilian Unemployment Rate The published **civilian unemployment rate** is the percentage of the civilian labor force that is unemployed. As noted earlier, the civilian labor force consists of the civilian noninstitutional population, age sixteen and over, who are working or looking for work. The civilian unemployment rate is calculated by dividing the number of unemployed people by the number of people in the civilian labor force. In other words,

$$\frac{\text{civilian}}{\text{unemployment rate}} = \frac{\text{unemployed persons}}{\text{civilian labor force}}$$

In November 1988 there were 6,595,000 people unemployed and the civilian labor force totaled 122,572,000 people. Therefore the civilian unemployment rate was .054. It is customary, however, to move the decimal point two places to the right by multiplying by 100, so as to give the rate as a percentage. The published civilian unemployment rate in our illustration was 5.4 percent.

The civilian unemployment rate is the percentage of the civilian labor force that is unemployed. It is calculated by dividing the

---

number of unemployed people by the number of people in the civilian labor force.

The civilian unemployment rate is computed monthly by the Bureau of Labor Statistics of the Department of Labor. As stated earlier in the chapter, a representative sample of people is selected for interview. If a person is not working, the interviewer asks whether he or she is searching for work. If the answer is "yes," the person is classified as unemployed.

The question about the job search is important because it helps establish the size of the civilian labor force, which is the denominator of the fraction used in computing the civilian unemployment rate. A person who is neither holding a job nor searching for one is not part of the civilian labor force according to the official statistics. In this group are retired people as well as students, homemakers, and others who have chosen nonmarket activities. Some may be **discouraged workers**—labor force dropouts who have stopped searching for work because they believe there is little chance of ever finding a job. Others may claim to be looking for work but really are not because they prefer unemployment compensation to the best job they expect to find.

Drawing the line at the sixteenth birthday may be somewhat arbitrary, but you will agree that some cutoff is needed for a meaningful definition of the civilian labor force. There are proposals to raise the cutoff line to seventeen or eighteen. If these changes were made, they would lead to important changes in the civilian unemployment rate because sixteen- and seventeen-year-old job seekers, who are often high school dropouts, have great difficulty in finding work. Not counting people in this age group would lower the official civilian unemployment rate. On the other hand, including the "discouraged worker" would raise the rate.

The Unemployment Record Figure 6 shows the official civilian unemployment rate for the United States from 1970 through 1988. The lowest rate during this period was 4.9 percent. This point was reached in 1970 and again in 1973. The highest rate for any full year during the period was 9.7

percent, reached in 1982. Compared with the 1950s and 1960s, unemployment was relatively high all through the 1970s and 1980s. In the 1950s, annual civilian unemployment rates averaged 4.5 percent and never exceeded 6.8 percent. In the 1960s, civilian unemployment rates averaged 4.8 percent and never exceeded 6.7 percent. For 1933, during the Great Depression, measured civilian unemployment was 24.9 percent. For 1944, during World War II, it was 1.2 percent.

Types of Unemployment

In Chapter 1 you learned to classify unemployment as either microeconomic or macroeconomic. Now it is time to refine the classification still further. In common usage, economists generally classify unemployment as seasonal, frictional, structural, or cyclical.

Seasonal Unemployment **Seasonal unemployment** arises because some occupations require workers during only part of each year. Many seasonal occupations, such as picking and processing fruits and vegetables, depend on the growing seasons for various crops. Some, like tourism and resorts, depend on annual climatic conditions. Some, like the post office or retail sales, arise from the Christmas rush or other special annual events. People who work in occupations such as these often are unemployed part of the time each year.

Seasonal unemployment explains why some people have low money incomes, but for others it is an opportunity to earn extra income. Because this type of unemployment follows a pattern that is more or less regular each year, it can be predicted with reasonable accuracy. To avoid misleading numbers, most published statistics on unemployment are "seasonally adjusted," meaning that the seasonal component has been smoothed out or averaged so that direct month-to-month and year-to-year comparisons can be made for other types of unemployment.

Seasonal unemployment occurs because some occupations require workers during only part of each year.

FIGURE 6
Unemployment in the United States, 1970 through 1988

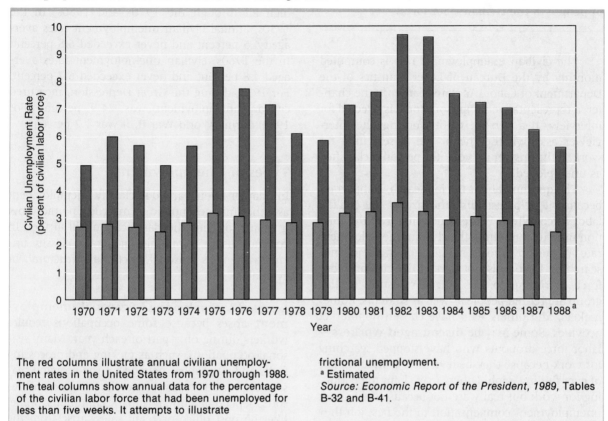

The red columns illustrate annual civilian unemployment rates in the United States from 1970 through 1988. The teal columns show annual data for the percentage of the civilian labor force that had been unemployed for less than five weeks. It attempts to illustrate frictional unemployment.
^a Estimated
Source: Economic Report of the President, 1989, Tables B-32 and B-41.

Frictional Unemployment **Frictional unemployment** arises because it takes time to move from one job to another. Because people do not have perfect information about alternative jobs, they must take time to search and to make decisions among jobs. They may need to learn a new skill as they move from their old jobs to ones that pay better or that they expect to like better. Delays arise, too, in gaining entry to a new line of work. All of these facts of life suggest that some frictional unemployment will always exist in a society in which people are free to move from place to place and job to job.

Barriers to the freedom of movement that increase frictional unemployment are of course not desirable. Some barriers are particularly unfair to groups or individuals, such as discrimination based on age, race, or sex, unnecessary apprenticeship requirements, or union membership limitations. However, frictional unemployment is not considered a serious problem in itself. Continuous movement among jobs and locations is the way in which an economy refines and tunes its operations to the preferences of people.

Actual measurements of frictional unemployment are not exact. One way to estimate its size is to look at very short-term unemployment. Looking back to Figure 6, we see the percentage of the civilian labor force for whom the current spell of unemployment had lasted less than five weeks. This percentage changed only a little each year (though it increased slightly over this period). It is like a "background noise" regularly picked up by government unemployment statistics.[8]

8. Many labor economists prefer to estimate frictional unemployment by using the percentage unemployed for up to fourteen weeks. For this reason, Figure 6 may understate the amount of frictional unemployment, but it illustrates the idea that frictional unemployment almost always exists in the economy.

Figure 7 shows another way to distinguish frictional from other kinds of unemployment. This chart shows not only the civilian unemployment rate but also the unemployment rate for people who left their last job voluntarily or who were entering the civilian labor force either for the first time or after being out of the civilian labor force for a while. The unemployment rate for this group is quite similar to that in Figure 6 for people out of work for less than five weeks.

Frictional unemployment arises because it takes time to move from one job to another. Some frictional unemployment will always exist in a society in which people are free to move from job to job.

Even though these illustrations of frictional unemployment are helpful, a precise measure of this kind of joblessness is impossible. The barriers to movement between jobs that lead to frictional unemployment are hard to separate from the more serious problems that define structural unemployment.

Structural Unemployment **Structural unemployment** involves a mismatch between worker qualifications and job requirements. It often arises when changes take place in production methods (how to produce) and in the types of goods and services produced (what to produce). It corresponds to our definition of microeconomic unemployment. As we noted in Chapter 1, new automatic banking machines may mean unemployment for bank tellers and bookkeepers, and a switch in consumer preference from golf to tennis might mean unemployment for golf pros and golf-ball makers. Structural unemployment also comes

FIGURE 7
Reasons for Unemployment in the United States, 1970 through 1988

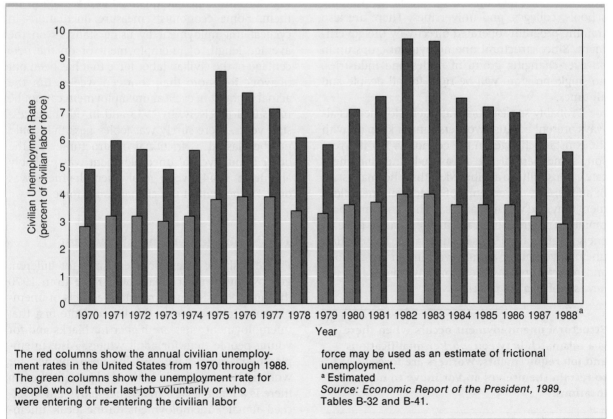

The red columns show the annual civilian unemployment rates in the United States from 1970 through 1988. The green columns show the unemployment rate for people who left their last job voluntarily or who were entering or re-entering the civilian labor force may be used as an estimate of frictional unemployment.
[a] Estimated
Source: Economic Report of the President, 1989, Tables B-32 and B-41.

from job discrimination and other barriers in the job market.

Structural unemployment is more serious than frictional unemployment because workers are not leaving their old jobs voluntarily in order to search for better ones. Their old jobs have disappeared owing to circumstances beyond their control, so they are forced to retrain themselves and move their families to wherever new jobs are opening up. Moreover, the new job often will not pay as well as the old one, and some time may pass before the worker recognizes the reality of his or her lower real wage and living standard. This can cause delay in accepting the new job.

Dealing with structural unemployment requires programs that not only retrain people but also help them discover and move to where new jobs are available. However, it is hard to design and operate these retraining and relocation programs. An approach that sometimes succeeds is on-the-job training, in which employers receive government subsidies to help pay the workers who are being trained for new jobs. Another program provides tuition aid to persons who enroll in training schools, colleges, and universities. There are also training programs operated directly by the government. Since structural unemployment crops up in an ever-changing group of trades and industries, no single program will be right for all people and all times.

Probably some structural unemployment is always present because workers cannot keep up with the constant changes in the economy. For this reason, some part of the measured unemployment rate can usually be attributed to this "normal" state of affairs. But the amount of structural unemployment may rise when changes in the economy come rapidly. The great increase in the relative price of energy during the 1970s brought a rise in structural unemployment for people working in gas stations and resort hotels as the economy adapted to the new set of relative prices.

Structural unemployment occurs when there is a mismatch between worker qualifications and job requirements. Workers are forced to retrain themselves and/or move to new locations.

The rate of unemployment that combines seasonal, frictional, and structural unemployment is sometimes called the **natural rate of unemployment** for an economy. This is the unemployment rate measured by official statistics when the economy's labor market is at equilibrium (as illustrated in Figure 3). Many economists contend that the economy has reached full employment when the official unemployment rate equals this natural rate of unemployment. If measured unemployment falls below the natural rate, they fear that inflation pressures will arise in the economy.

The rate of unemployment that combines seasonal, frictional, and structural unemployment is called the natural rate of unemployment.

Cyclical Unemployment **Cyclical unemployment** shows alternating ups and downs, and affects the whole economy rather than particular industries. There are simply not enough job openings for all the people qualified and willing to fill them. Some economists measure fluctuations in cyclical unemployment by using statistics on the average length of unemployment or on the percentage of the civilian labor force that has been out of work for more than fourteen weeks. But the actual amount of cyclical unemployment cannot be measured precisely. In 1933 and in other depression years, there surely was joblessness that could not be classed as frictional or structural. On the other hand, cyclical unemployment was probably absent in 1944, when total unemployment was only 1.2 percent of the civilian labor force.

The Incidence of Unemployment

Figure 8 shows unemployment rates for different groups within the civilian labor force from 1970 through 1988. Several important aspects of unemployment are shown in this figure. Note first that unemployment rates are higher for blacks and for young people than for adult whites. Also, unemployment rates have usually been higher for women than for men in both racial groups, though there is a tendency for male unemployment to exceed female unemployment during peak unem-

FIGURE 8
The Incidence of Unemployment in the United States, 1970 through 1988

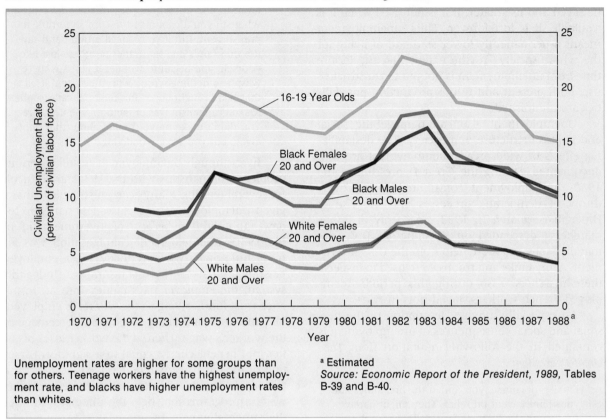

Unemployment rates are higher for some groups than for others. Teenage workers have the highest unemployment rate, and blacks have higher unemployment rates than whites.

ᵃ Estimated
Source: Economic Report of the President, 1989, Tables B-39 and B-40.

ployment periods. Unemployment rates for young people, age sixteen through nineteen, are much higher than for any of the other groups shown in the chart. The figure does not show male–female or racial distinctions within the sixteen- to nineteen-year-old group, but important differences do exist. Unemployment rates are much higher for black teenagers than for whites in this age group. These facts show that unemployment does not affect different groups in the society equally. Some are much more vulnerable to unemployment than others.

There is also another message in the data shown in Figure 8. All the unemployment rates move up and down together. This fact suggests that all groups share a common experience of fluctuating good and bad times. The range between peaks and troughs is greater for sixteen- to nineteen-year-olds and for black males than it is for others, so these people gain more from prosperity and lose

more from recession than others do. But effective policies on unemployment are important to all segments of the labor force.

Some groups in society, such as blacks and young people, are more vulnerable to unemployment than others.

The Social Consequences of Unemployment

Unemployment is more than a statistic and more than just a topic in economic theory. Anyone who has lost his or her job or has been laid off recognizes the shock, the frustrations, and the fears of unemployment. Few events in life are more devastating both to individuals and to families. For the society as a whole, unemployment is a loss of production that can never be replaced. No factor of production is more perishable than labor. It cannot be saved and used later. If it is not used when it is available, it is lost forever. Thus, unemployment means a permanently lower standard of living for the whole society. To the extent that the leisure time from unemployment is not put to constructive use, both present and future production possibilities are diminished.

Unemployment also can damage the social and political structure of a society. The destabilizing effects of widespread unemployment are well documented. During the Great Depression of the 1930s, unemployment contributed to the overthrow of democratic processes and the rise of Hitler in Germany. In 1932, an "army of bonus marchers" descended on Washington, D.C., demanding jobs and more help from the U.S. government. Army tanks and troops were used to disperse these marchers. Also during this period, unemployed French workers staged riots in Paris.

An especially moving description of the personal and social consequences of unemployment is contained in the following quotation from *The Great Depression*:

> Finally, of course, you joined the breadlines and your family went on relief. They might barely survive on the three or four dollars a week that local relief agencies could afford. Or they might break up. You might go to the local poorhouse, your children to an orphanage. Or the family might scatter to stay with more fortunate relatives in the country, where food, at least, could be grown for consumption. If your children were over the age of eight or nine, they might start wandering over the countryside, looking for handouts at farmhouse doors. In the end, it would seem to you that you had never known any other life than that of a beggar. Even humiliation would be too exhausting an emotion for you; only numb hopelessness and sick despair could

find room in your emaciated body. And you wondered what you'd done wrong. You wracked your brain to find out where you'd made a false turn, what sin you'd committed to earn so terrible a punishment. But if you looked around and saw the thousands and thousands of others just like yourself, you began to wonder if perhaps there wasn't something wrong with the system itself that had brought about this national catastrophe. Maybe capitalism was at fault, maybe democracy. You didn't make up your mind about that right away, but you were wondering.[9]

Even though unemployment is still a serious problem, comparisons with the 1930s are difficult for several reasons. Many economists believe that a given unemployment rate causes less hardship today than it did then because of government aid. In the 1930s unemployment compensation was almost unknown, whereas today most employed persons are covered by this insurance. Under this system, the employer pays money into an insurance trust fund as long as the worker is employed. The amounts paid in are based on a percentage of the worker's wage. Then, if the worker loses his or her job, benefit checks equal to a significant fraction of the old wage will be received, at least for a period of time. In addition, today there are many welfare programs that help the unemployed after their unemployment insurance benefits run out. To a large extent, it was the suffering of the 1930s that brought the introduction of many of these programs.

Another important difference between now and the Great Depression years is the increase in the number of women in the labor force. During the 1930s, few women worked outside the home, so when a man lost his job, there were usually devastating economic effects on the family and psychological effects on the family "breadwinner." Today, with a second income often available to the family, unemployment is less damaging.

9. Robert Goldston, *The Great Depression* (New York: Bobbs-Merrill, 1968), pp. 48–49.

Economics in Focus

Can the Unemployment Rate Fall Too Low?

Can the unemployment rate fall too low? Is it possible for too few people to be jobless? According to many economists, it is indeed possible. They believe that whenever unemployment drops below the natural unemployment rate, there is a strong tendency for inflation to accelerate. Since inflation is generally undesirable, an unemployment rate lower than the natural rate is considered too low.

When the natural rate of unemployment prevails, the only members of the labor force who are out of work are those between jobs or those who require retraining or relocation to qualify for jobs. When unemployment dips below this level, employers often struggle to fill their job vacancies. They have to entice applicants and they may be forced to raise wage rates. Most analysts believe that under these conditions wage rates do in fact go up, forcing an upward trend in prices.

This theory prompted a good deal of discussion in late 1988 and 1989, after monthly figures for the unemployment rate actually fell to 5 percent, the lowest point in fourteen years. Many economists, believing that the natural rate was about 6 percent, worried that the drop in unemployment heralded a surge in inflation. They urged the government (Federal Reserve Board) to pursue anti-inflationary policies. Other economists disagreed. Some thought the natural unemployment rate might be lower than 6 percent. Others feared that excessive economic restraint would plunge the nation into recession. Some unconventional economists even dismissed the entire theory, arguing that low unemployment rates would not affect inflation.

It was also suggested that changing demographics may have altered the way the system works. Largely because of the baby boom from the late 1940s to the early 1960s, the percentage of persons in their prime working years (ages 25 to 54) increased from the late 1960s to the early 1980s. The baby boom also caused changes in the ranks of the unemployed. In the late 1960s and 1970s, only 40 to 45 percent of the jobless were in their prime years; by the late 1980s that figure exceeded 55 percent. Consequently, some economists reason, the unemployed are more likely to have families to support and more likely to accept job offers quickly; hence, they exert less pressure on employers to boost wage rates.

According to this analysis, a very low unemployment rate no longer means that inflation must accelerate—or, at least, the link is weaker than it used to be. As the 1990s unfold, economists will continue to debate the complex association between the natural rate of unemployment and inflation.

Sources: Alan S. Blinder, "Right Now, an Ounce of Prevention Is All Inflation Needs," *Business Week,* March 20, 1989, p. 22; Gene Koretz, "Age vs. Wage: How Baby Boomers May Cool Inflation," *Business Week,* February 6, 1989, p. 26; Randall W. Forsyth, "Jobs Jump Brings Market Back to Earth," *Barron's,* November 7, 1988, pp. 120–121; Henry F. Myers "Talk of Stagflation: Hot Issue or Hot Air?" *Wall Street Journal,* April 24, 1989, p. A1; James C. Cooper and Kathleen Madigan, "A Feast of Jobs Is Setting the Table for Inflation," *Business Week,* November 21, 1988, pp. 29–30.

SUMMARY

1. Inflation is a sustained and significant increase in the general price level. The rate of inflation is the percentage change, from one year to the next, in whatever index number is chosen to measure the price level. (See page 142.)

2. A price-index number is calculated by dividing the price existing in a given year by the price for the equivalent item (or items) in the year selected as the base year. The price in a given year can be converted to its base-year equivalent by dividing it by the index number for that given year. (See page 142.)

3. The consumer price index is used to compare the cost of a selected "market basket" of goods and services in the current year with the cost of the same market basket of goods in the base year. It is often called the "cost-of-living" index. However, it may overstate the increase in the cost of living because it fails to recognize quality improvements and changes in the composition of family purchases. Similarly, it may understate inflation in the cost of living if prices of necessities increase more than the cost of other goods and services. (See pages 143–144.)

4. The implicit price deflator for the gross national product (GNP) shows the ratio between GNP measured at current prices and the amount that would have been required to purchase the same goods in a base year. It is used to convert GNP in "nominal" values to GNP in "real" values. (See page 146.)

5. Index numbers are used for many purposes in economic statistics. For example, index numbers for producers' goods help to predict future changes in the prices of goods and services to consumers. (See page 147.)

6. Inflation has serious economic effects because a price-level-change factor must be included in decisions that guide the operation of the economy. To many of these decisions, inflation adds uncertainty and can cause the economy to operate less efficiently. (See pages 149–150.)

7. History suggests that the social and political consequences of inflation can be serious. Some of these problems arise because unanticipated inflation redistributes wealth and tends to impoverish the groups in society that contribute stability and moderation to the social and political order. (See pages 152–153.)

8. Employment is related directly and unemployment is related inversely to changes in real GNP, which is the variable on the horizontal axis of the aggregate-demand and aggregate-supply graph. (See page 153.)

9. A commonly used measure of employment is the civilian employment rate, which is the percentage of the civilian noninstitutional population, age 16 and over, that is actually working. This rate has increased significantly in the United States over the past 50 years. (See page 153.)

10. The civilian labor force participation rate is the percentage of the civilian noninstitutional population, age 16 and over, that is in the civilian labor force. In order to be counted in the civilian labor force a person must be sixteen years of age or older, working or looking for work, and neither institutionalized nor in military service. (See page 154.)

11. The economic concept of unemployment is that people are consuming unwanted quantities of leisure time and devoting less time to wage earning than desired at the going wage rate. The individual's supply-of-labor curve, which shows a person's willingness to exchange leisure for money, is a key to understanding this concept of unemployment. A person is unemployed or underemployed if he or she is operating under a wage and hour combination to the left of his or her supply-of-labor curve. (See pages 154–155.)

12. The measured civilian unemployment rate is the percentage of the civilian labor force that is out of work. Included in the civilian labor force are only those noninstitutionalized civilians who are either working or looking for work and who are over sixteen years of age. Not included are retirees, persons in institutions or active military service, and people under age sixteen. A person is counted as employed even if working only part time if the work is on a regular basis. (See page 158.)

13. Seasonal unemployment is joblessness that arises because the person is engaged in an occupation that does not require workers all year round. For some, this is a cause of low income. For others, it is a source of extra income. In most published statistics, adjustments are made for seasonal unemployment to avoid confusion in comparing

month-to-month or year-to-year changes in unemployment. (See page 159.)

14. Frictional unemployment is joblessness that arises because of the time needed to move from one job to another. Some amount of this kind of unemployment is always present in an economy where people are free to move from one job to another. It is not considered a serious problem for an economy. (See page 160.)

15. Structural unemployment arises when changes take place in production methods and in the kinds of goods and services produced in the economy. People must be retrained and relocated to match the requirements of different jobs. Training programs are helpful in dealing with structural unemployment. (See pages 161–162.)

16. The rate that combines seasonal, frictional, and structural unemployment is sometimes called the natural rate of unemployment. (See page 162.)

17. Measured cyclical unemployment affects most parts of the economy at the same time and arises because jobs are not available for all who want to work at the going wage rate. Though the actual amount of cyclical unemployment cannot be measured exactly, it can clearly cause serious problems for an economy. (See page 162.)

18. Unemployment rates are higher for some groups in the civilian labor force than for others. Blacks experience a higher unemployment rate than whites, and teenagers have especially high unemployment rates. (See pages 162–163.)

19. Serious consequences follow from widespread cyclical unemployment. Potential production is irretrievably lost. Moreover, an economic system is flawed if it fails to provide employment for persons willing and able to work at prevailing wage rates. Unemployed persons suffer economic and emotional hardships. (See pages 163–164.)

KEY TERMS

black market: a market that operates outside the law and sells goods at illegal prices (page 146).

civilian employment rate: the percentage of the civilian noninstitutional population, age 16 or over, that is regularly working for pay (page 153).

civilian labor force: noninstitutional civilians who are age 16 or over and either working or actively looking for work (page 154).

civilian labor force participation rate: the percent of the civilian noninstitutional population that is age 16 or over and either working or actively looking for work (page 154).

civilian unemployment rate: the percentage of the civilian labor force that is unemployed (page 158).

constant-dollar GNP: GNP measured in dollars that have been adjusted for price level changes (page 146).

consumer price index (CPI): an index number used to measure changes in the cost of purchasing a specific group of consumer goods and services; also called the cost-of-living index (page 143).

cost-of-living adjustment (COLA): a clause in a labor contract that connects changes in wage rates to changes in the consumer price index (page 144).

current dollars: the purchasing power of the dollar reflecting the price level prevailing at the time of a transaction (page 146).

cyclical unemployment: unemployment that occurs when there are not enough job openings in the economy for all the people qualified and willing to fill them at the prevailing wage rate (page 162).

discouraged workers: labor force dropouts who have stopped searching for work (page 159).

disinflation: a period when the rate of increase in the price level is becoming less and less (page 149).

employment: labor engaged in regular work for pay (page 153).

frictional unemployment: the unemployment that occurs as workers move from one job to another (page 160).

GNP implicit price deflator: an index number that shows the ratio between GNP measured at current prices and the amount that would have been required to purchase the same goods and services in a base year (page 146).

gross national product (GNP): a measure of the value of a year's total production in the economy (page 146).

index number: a way of stating a value by expressing it in terms of some other reference value (page 142).

inflation: a significant and sustained increase in the general price level (page 142).

inflation rate: a measurement of the change in the price level calculated by dividing the GNP deflator value for each year by the GNP deflator value for the previous year, subtracting 1.0, and multiplying the result by 100 (page 149).

macroeconomic unemployment: unemployment that exists throughout the whole economy or affects many parts of the economy at the same time and is not related to particular decisions about what or how to produce (see page 158).

menu costs: costs entailed during a period of inflation by the need for frequent updating of price lists (page 152).

natural rate of unemployment: the rate of unemployment that combines seasonal, frictional, and structural unemployment; believed by many economists to approximate full employment (page 162).

nominal values: values expressed in current dollars; values not adjusted for changes in the price level (page 146).

purchasing power of the dollar: a measure of the value of the dollar in terms of its purchasing power of goods and services. It can be computed as the reciprocal of the consumer price-index number (page 144).

quality bias: a flaw of the consumer price index arising from its implication that the quality of goods and services stays the same over time (page 145).

real values: values adjusted for changes in the price level (page 146).

real wage rates: wage rates adjusted for price-level changes so that they represent the goods and services the individual expects to be able to purchase with his or her earnings (page 155).

seasonal unemployment: unemployment that occurs because some occupations require workers for only part of each year (page 159).

shoe-leather costs: costs entailed during a period of inflation by the switching of assets from one form to another (page 162).

structural unemployment: unemployment that occurs when there is a mismatch between worker qualifications and job requirements; it often arises when changes occur in production methods and in the types of goods and services produced (page 161).

unemployment: the economic concept of unemployment refers to a person who is spending more time for leisure and less time for wage earning than he or she desires at the going wage rate for his or her occupation (page 154).

weighting bias: the failure of the CPI to recognize that consumer buying patterns tend to change when the price level changes (page 144).

DISCUSSION QUESTIONS

1. Index numbers are illustrated in this chapter with a set of prices for apples. But the index-number principle appears in many places, such as the use of IQ values for comparing intellectual capabilities. Describe three other examples of the use of the index-number principle of stating one value by reference to some other ''standard'' value. (Hint: consider baseball players.)

2. The CPI is based on a selection of commodities purchased by urban households and the prices paid by them. If you live in a nonurban area, discuss how your selection of commodities and the prices you pay may differ from those used in the CPI. Would you gain or lose if the CPI were used to adjust your wage rate for inflation? Explain.

3. Try this exercise about the quality bias in index numbers. Think of a product that you believe has gone down in quality over the past ten years. Use the CPI (or some other) index number to find out whether the product has increased or decreased in price after the inflation effect has been removed. If its real price has fallen, lower quality may have been exchanged for lower price. If its real price has risen, you may have a genuine case of falling quality. Try to explain why this has happened.

4. In Table 4, the base year is 1982, and all the numbers in the constant-dollar column are expressed in terms of 1982 dollars. How could we adjust the numbers in this column to express them in dollars valued for some other base year, say, 1977? There is a simple method for doing this.

5. From the *Survey of Current Business* or the *Economic Report of the President* or from recent issues of news magazines, look up the GNP deflator or the consumer price index for last year and for the year before. From these data, calculate the rate of inflation for that year. How does this rate compare with those shown in Figure 1? How can it be that the price level itself may not matter but that changes in the price level can cause problems in the economy? Discuss.

6. Construct an individual's supply-of-labor curve using the real wage rate on the vertical axis and the hours of work supplied per week on the horizontal axis. With reference to this graph, explain the economic concepts of underemployment and overemployment. Why can unemployment not be measured (to the economist's satisfaction) unless the wage rate is specified?

7. Suppose you are working a forty-hour week and receiving the going wage rate for that kind of work. Are you "employed" in terms of official statistics? If you would prefer to work only thirty-two hours at this wage rate, are you, in the economist's theoretical view, overemployed, underemployed, or fully employed? Explain your reasoning.

8. From memory, write down the formulas for computing the civilian unemployment rate, the civilian employment rate, and the civilian labor force participation rate. Check to be sure you have them right. Explain how both the unemployment rate and the employment rate can increase at the same time. Explain how the participation rate is involved in this situation. Do you believe that the civilian labor force participation rate will grow or decrease over your lifetime? Does it matter?

9. Explain how each of the following is counted in computing the official civilian unemployment rate: a full-time student who has no paying job, a person working regularly but only part time, a retired person, a fifteen-year-old with a paper route, a person in military service, a person who is out of a job and has given up looking for another because no jobs appear to be available.

10. Explain the difference between seasonal and frictional unemployment. Discuss whether seasonal unemployment is a problem in the economy. Why is seasonal unemployment usually removed (by a statistical adjustment) from most published unemployment statistics? Why is frictional unemployment usually not considered to be a serious problem in the United States? Describe two causes of frictional unemployment that you believe *are* damaging to the economy. Explain your reasons for finding them damaging.

11. Why is structural unemployment likely to be higher during periods when rapid technological change is taking place in the economy? Do you believe that government help should be given to people who are unemployed because of structural changes in the economy? If so, what type of help should be given? Explain the basis for your answer.

12. "Although unemployment still is a serious economic problem, the human and social consequences of unemployment are less today than they were in the Great Depression." Do you believe that this is a correct statement? Explain your answer. What are some changes since the Great Depression that have affected the human and social aspects of unemployment?

9

Economic Fluctuations

Preview   Fluctuations in the level of economic activity are familiar aspects of capitalist-market economies. Periods of rising production are followed by periods of falling production in a seemingly endless sequence of economic ups and downs. Price levels also have risen and fallen over the years. Even if these fluctuations were harmless to human welfare, curiosity undoubtedly would lead economists to try to understand them. But the fact is that economic fluctuations are not harmless. Declines in output mean declines also in employment, causing workers to lose their jobs and forcing lower living standards upon them and their families. Even periods of rising production can generate harmful consequences. Economies that expand too far or too fast may suffer inflationary price-level increases. Changes in price levels, either upward or downward, redistribute income and wealth among individuals and families in ways that may be quite unjust.

     This chapter uses the aggregate-demand and aggregate-supply model introduced in Chapter 6 to provide an explanation of what happens during economic fluctuations. After a brief review of this model and a short summary of the history of economic fluctuations, we describe two types of fluctuations—one brought on by an increase in aggregate demand and one brought on by a decrease. These illustrations show the workings of the aggregate-demand and aggregate-supply model and explain why one phase of a fluctuation leads to later phases. They also provide an introduction to one of the most important questions debated by macroeconomists: "What is the best way to help the economy recover from recession and severe unemployment?" Most of the remaining chapters on macroeconomics are devoted to explaining alternative answers to this question.

Finally we offer a brief description of how shocks from the supply side can cause an economy either to enjoy prosperity or to be plunged into recession. This is followed by a look ahead at the specific theories and models that economists use to prescribe policies for moderating economic fluctuations.

FLUCTUATION THEORIES AND PATTERNS

Economic fluctuations are alternating expansions and contractions in the volume of real GNP in an economy. These alternating expansions and contractions suggest that the equilibrium level of GNP changes through time with periods of increasing equilibrium GNP followed by periods of decreasing equilibrium GNP, and so on. It makes sense, therefore, to begin our analysis of economic fluctuations by reviewing the aggregate-demand and aggregate-supply (*AD-AS*) model.

To refresh your understanding of the *AD-AS* model, look at Figure 1, which illustrates an aggregate-demand curve (*AD*) and an aggregate-supply curve (*AS*). In this graph, equilibrium is at *A*, with price level 100 and real GNP demanded and supplied of $1,000 billion per year.[1]

As explained in Chapter 6, the aggregate-demand curve can shift either to the left or to the right as a result of the events that increase or decrease, at any given price level, the total spending by consumers, investors, governments, or foreigners—that is, by events that increase or decrease $C + I + G + X - Im$. At any given price level, the aggregate quantity demanded in the economy can increase or decrease. Look at Figure 1 and imagine the *AD* curve shifting either to the right or to the left. If the *AS* curve remains unchanged, a shift to the right of the *AD* curve causes the equilibrium point (the intersection of the curves) to move upward and to the right along the *AS* curve. The equi-

1. In the aggregate-demand and aggregate-supply graphs in Chapter 6, the horizontal-axis label was "Value of Goods and Services Demanded and Supplied Per Year (in billions of dollars)." Now that you have studied the national income accounts, we can simplify this to "Real GNP (billions of dollars per year)."

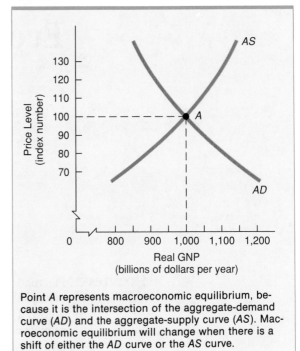

FIGURE 1
Aggregate Demand and Aggregate Supply

Point *A* represents macroeconomic equilibrium, because it is the intersection of the aggregate-demand curve (*AD*) and the aggregate-supply curve (*AS*). Macroeconomic equilibrium will change when there is a shift of either the *AD* curve or the *AS* curve.

librium real GNP increases, meaning that the economy expands while the equilibrium price level increases. If the *AD* curve shifts to the left, the equilibrium point (the intersection of the curves) moves downward and to the left along the *AS* curve. The equilibrium real GNP decreases, meaning that the economy contracts while the equilibrium price level falls.

If you now look again at Figure 1 and imagine shifts of the aggregate-supply curve to the left or to the right, it is evident that aggregate-supply shifts also can cause expansions and contractions in equilibrium real GNP. A shift of the *AS* curve to the right, *ceteris paribus,* causes an economic expansion and a shift of the *AS* curve to the left, *ceteris paribus*, causes an economic contraction.

As we proceed in our analysis, we will find that alternating expansions and contractions in real GNP (economic fluctuations) can be understood as sequences or patterns through time of shifts in aggregate-demand and aggregate-supply curves. For example, an increase in equilibrium real GNP (an expansion) followed by a decrease in equilibrium real GNP (a contraction) can result from a rightward shift of the *AD* curve followed by a leftward shift of the *AS* curve. Or, the fluctuation may be seen in the alternative sequence, with the contraction coming first, probably from a leftward shift of the *AD* curve, followed by the expansion as the *AS* curve shifts to the right.

Essentially, modern macroeconomic theory suggests that a fluctuation begins with a shift of one of the curves (usually the *AD* curve) and that the fluctuation is completed when the other curve (usually the *AS* curve) shifts in the opposite direction—an *AD* shift to the right followed by an *AS* shift to the left or an *AD* shift to the left followed by an *AS* shift to the right. Although demand shifts are most likely to start fluctuations, a supply shift sometimes is the initiating event.

Shifts of the aggregate-demand curve or the aggregate-supply curve result in changes in employment and real GNP.

The Historical Record

Figure 2 gives a picture of economic fluctuations in the United States from 1881 to 1987. The vertical axis is scaled with an index number for some measure of aggregate economic performance. Real GNP could be used for this axis. Both positive and negative values appear on the vertical axis because the index measures deviations above and below the growth trend of the economy. In unadjusted data, the trend line would slope upward toward the right because the economy tends to grow larger year by year. However, in order to make it easier to see the fluctuations of the economy, the trend line has been made horizontal by statistical manipulations that remove the growth component from the data. As you can see, the economy has fluctuated both above and below this line. Sometimes the economy has been above the line and enjoyed "prosperity," and sometimes it has been below the line and suffered "panics" and "depressions." Closer examination reveals that fluctuations, up and down, also have occurred *during* prosperity or depression periods. It appears that the economy changes direction from downward to upward and vice versa every

few years—sometimes entirely above the line, sometimes entirely below it, and sometimes pushing across the line and moving all the way from prosperity to depression or from depression to prosperity.

Several points should be made regarding Figure 2. The first is a matter of terminology. Should we refer to *fluctuations* or should we use the word *cycles* to characterize the experience of the economy? **Cycle theories** imply that a regular pattern exists, that the causes for an upswing lie in the preceding downswing and that the causes for a downswing lie in the preceding upswing. Cycle theories have long-standing prominence in economic and business literature. However, some economists argue that the word *cycle* implies more regularity than actually exists. They contend that cycle theories are too mechanical, that they divert attention from events outside the economy, and that they leave too little room for policy initiatives to direct the course of the economy. In this chapter, we will examine some theories that follow the cycle idea, but our main focus will be on happenings and policies that cause fluctuations—movements in real GNP that may be unique to particular policies or events.

Cycle theories imply that a regular, predictable pattern exists to explain changes in the economy. The term *fluctuations* is preferred by those who find the cycle concept too narrow and too mechanical.

A second point to note from Figure 2 is the enormous magnitude and length of the depression during the 1930s and the large size of the World War II prosperity. This helps explain the great interest in macroeconomics around the world since those times. Also, note the relatively minor magnitude of fluctuations since 1945. Does this mean that macroeconomic policy has been successful in smoothing the course of the economy? Periods of prosperity have been longer than periods of depression. Some economists are concerned, however, because recessions were sharper and deeper in the 1970s and 1980s than at any time since the immediate post–World War II period. Does this suggest

FIGURE 2
Historical Record of U.S. Economic Fluctuations, 1881–1987

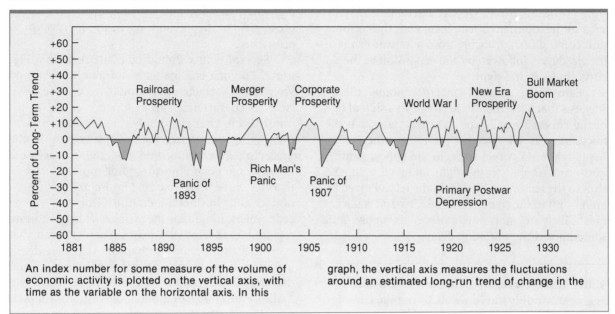

An index number for some measure of the volume of economic activity is plotted on the vertical axis, with time as the variable on the horizontal axis. In this graph, the vertical axis measures the fluctuations around an estimated long-run trend of change in the

that there will be more serious depressions in the future?

The U.S. economy fluctuates both above and below its long-run trend of economic growth. Major fluctuations occurred during the Great Depression and World War II.

Measuring Fluctuations

The first step in analyzing economic fluctuations is to identify and name their recurring features. These features and names are shown in Figure 3. Note first the upward-sloping black line called the **trend line**. It represents growth that is taking place in the economy because of increases in the size and quality of the labor force (labor), the quantity of machinery, equipment, and human skills (capital), and better technology. This trend expresses essentially the same concept as the horizontal line in the historical record chart of Figure 2. Deviations from this trend line provide the statistical measures of fluctuations.

The trend line represents growth that is taking place in the economy because of increases in labor and capital and improvements in technology.

Next note the sequence of terms describing the fluctuations themselves—lower turning point, expansion, upper turning point, and contraction. Expansions and contractions sometimes are called *cumulative* phases of the fluctuation because they describe periods or intervals during which the economy's course proceeds in a given direction—either upward or downward. The **upper turning points** sometimes are called *peaks,* representing high points in the volume of economic activity. Similarly, **lower turning points** sometimes are called *troughs* because they represent low points of economic activity.

Expansion and contraction are called *cumulative phases* of the fluctuations because they describe periods during which the economy's course

---

Figure 2 (cont.)

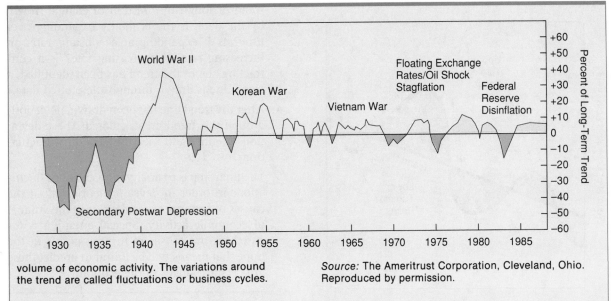

volume of economic activity. The variations around
the trend are called fluctuations or business cycles.

Source: The Ameritrust Corporation, Cleveland, Ohio.
Reproduced by permission.

proceeds in a given direction—either upward or
downward.

Upper turning points are called *peaks;* **lower
turning points are called** *troughs.*

The length, or period, of a complete fluctuation or cycle is the time between either a pair of
upper turning points or a pair of lower turning
points. The length of an expansion is the time between a lower turning point and the next upper
turning point. Similarly, the length of a contraction
is the time from an upper turning point to the next
lower turning point. Since fluctuations often are
not symmetrical, different measuring systems may
give different answers even using the same data.
The amplitude of an expansion or a contraction is
measured by the change in the volume of economic activity between one turning point and the
next. Here also there are great differences among
fluctuations. Some expansions are weak and peaks
occur *below* the trend line, and some contractions
are minor and troughs occur *above* the trend line.
Each fluctuation is, to some extent, unique.

**The length, or period, of a complete fluctuation
or cycle is the time between either a pair of
upper turning points or a pair of lower turning
points.**

Statistical measurements of economic fluctuations use index numbers. You have already learned
how index numbers can be developed for prices,
production, and many other series of data. The following five steps describe how index-number data
are used to measure economic fluctuations.

1. A series of index numbers (or a composite of
   several series) is selected to show GNP, industrial production, or some other measure of
   economic activity. This is an important step
   because different data series perform differently in relation to the economy as a whole.
   Some, like stock market prices or the average
   hours worked per week, are **leading indicators** and tend to anticipate or "lead" changes
   in the total economy. Others, like wage rates,
   are **lagging indicators** and tend to change
   direction after changes in the volume of total

FIGURE 3
Characteristics of Economic Fluctuations

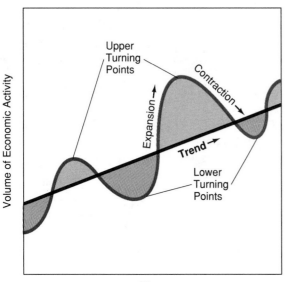

The vertical axis records some measure of the volume of economic activity. Time is recorded on the horizontal axis. Each fluctuation consists of an expansion phase and a contraction phase, an upper turning point and a lower turning point. The period, or length, of a fluctuation is measured from one upper turning point to the next or from one lower turning point to the next.

economic activity. **Coincident indicators** that move along with the total economy should be chosen to measure fluctuations.

Fluctuations should be measured by *coincident indicators*—**index numbers that move along with the total economy—rather than by** *leading indicators* **(which tend to anticipate changes) or by** *lagging indicators* **(which tend to change direction after changes in total economic activity).**

---

2. Statistical adjustments are made to remove seasonal variations from the selected data series. Seasonal variations arise due to growing seasons, holiday shopping patterns, the school year, and so on. Removing seasonal variations simplifies the data and makes it easier to spot actual fluctuations.

3. Next, the adjusted data series is plotted on a time-series chart, and the analyst looks for any trend or long-run direction of change shown by the data. Is the economy expanding over time? Is it expanding at a constant rate, an increasing rate, or decreasing rate? Is it contracting? Once the trend has been identified, a trend line is drawn through the plotted data.

4. After the trend line has been drawn, deviations around this trend are calculated. These deviations identify and measure economic fluctuations.

5. The final step is to analyze the cycles or fluctuations in order to develop theories about the causes of patterns or regularities in the volume of economic activity. Special attention is focused on the causes of turning points in the hope that means will be found to predict these important changes in the economy.

Statistical measurement of fluctuations involves selecting index numbers, adjusting them to remove seasonal variations, plotting them on a time-series chart, calculating deviations from the trend, and analyzing the fluctuations in the hope of learning how to predict them in the future.

Cycle Patterns

Analysts believe that they have identified several clear cyclical patterns for the U.S. economy. These are distinguished from one another by their length, by their causes, and by their names—since each has been named for the economist who is credited with discovering and explaining the particular pattern.

The shortest one, named the **Kitchin cycle**, has a length of some three to five years between turning points. Because it is believed to be connected with the alternate buildup and depletion of business inventories, it is sometimes called the **inventory cycle**. You may recall from the circular-flow model introduced in Chapter 6 that the build-up of excess inventory leads to a subsequent reduction in output and employment.

Next in length is the **Juglar cycle**, which has a period of some seven to ten years. Though this is a major pattern in U.S. economic history, economists have not agreed on specific causes for it. The Great Depression of the 1930s came between the upper turning points on either side of one of these cycles.

The statistical record reveals a cycle that appears to last between fifteen and twenty-five years and to run from the construction of buildings and transportation facilities until the time when they wear out and must be replaced. This is called the **building** (or **Kuznets**) **cycle**. Since its length corresponds roughly to the length of a generation, one theory is that it may be related to population waves set in motion by birthrate changes following wars.

Finally, some theories assume a long wave, or **Kondratieff cycle**, of economic activity with a length of thirty to fifty years. Reliable records have not been kept over a long enough time for economists to agree on these very long cycles. Some theories suggest that they may be associated with major technological innovations, such as railroads and automobiles.

All of these cycles (Kitchin, Juglar, Kuznets, and Kondratieff) are occurring at the same time and interact with one another. The shorter cycles that come during the expansion phases of the long cycles display long and vigorous expansion phases of their own with short and mild contraction phases. The short cycles that occur during the contraction phases of long cycles show the opposite pattern.

Some common cyclical patterns in the U.S. economy are the Kitchin cycle (three to five years), the Juglar cycle (seven to ten years), the Kuznets cycle (fifteen to twenty-five years), and the Kondratieff cycle (thirty to fifty years).

Cycles and Capitalism

Over the years, the persistence of cyclical patterns in the volume of economic activity in capitalist-market economies has prompted scholars, reformers, and revolutionaries to see these fluctuations as fundamental characteristics of these systems. Some have prophesied far-reaching consequences from

cycles. We shall describe two theories that, we think, deserve attention.

Karl Marx on Cycles Cycle theory plays an important part in the teachings of Karl Marx (1818–1883), who believed in the inevitable collapse of capitalism and rise of socialism. According to Marx, capitalists have an insatiable drive to earn profits and to invest in machinery and equipment to expand production capacity. Indeed, the capitalist is a necessary part of the evolution from an agricultural economy to an industrial economy. The capitalist's profits, which, according to Marx, come from the exploitation of workers, pay for these machines. The "contradiction" in capitalism is that these machines reduce the chances to exploit current labor and so lower the rate of profit—driving the capitalist to more frantic efforts at exploitation and capital accumulation.

The falling rate of profit that comes from the capitalist's drive to accumulate is very important to Marx's theory. Capitalists use machines to gain the capacity to produce more goods and services than the workers, with their low incomes, are able to buy. Because there is not enough demand to buy the output of the added capital capacity, the economy contracts and a depression follows. The depression does not end until the excess capacity has been worn out. Then the process starts all over again. Marx believed that depressions would become worse and worse and would in time cause the overthrow of the capitalist system by the ever-growing and ever more exploited working class. In the 1930s, many people saw the Great Depression as the fulfillment of Marx's prophecies.

Marx believed that economic depression would be the occasion for the overthrow of capitalism.

Joseph Schumpeter and Innovations Joseph Schumpeter (1883–1950) offered an explanation of business cycles based on the timing of major innovations in a capitalist system. Under this system, great, though temporary, rewards often come to the successful innovator. Major breakthroughs, such as railroads, automobiles, and electricity, bring bursts of expanding economic activity. Eventually these booms run their course and give way to relative declines in business activity as the economy waits for the next burst of innovation. "Long waves," or cycles, of economic activity may be traced (after the fact) to major innovations. Shorter cycles, such as those described earlier in this chapter, may occur along with these longer waves.

Schumpeter also predicted that capitalism would someday be replaced by a different economic system. In Schumpeter's model, business cycles were simply part of the capitalist system and could not be eliminated, but cycles themselves would not be the reason or occasion (as in Marx) for replacing that system. Instead, the very success of capitalist innovation in raising living standards and in generating wealth would help to draw attention away from production itself and toward matters of distribution of income and welfare and toward less purely "economic" values. So, in Schumpeter's view, capitalism's success in solving economic problems would someday lead to its replacement by planning, by socialism, and, he feared, by a dictatorship. He did not want to live under such a regime.

Schumpeter believed that business cycles were related to major technological innovations.

EXPANSIONARY DEMAND-SHOCK FLUCTUATIONS

Let us see how the aggregate-demand and aggregate-supply model of the economy describes a fluctuation that starts with an increase in aggregate demand, such as might arise from preparation for war.

The Expansion Phase

In Figure 4 point *A* represents the equilibrium situation at the start of the fluctuation. The expansionary demand shock is represented by a shift of the aggregate-demand curve to the right, from AD_1 to AD_2 (shown by arrow number 1), causing real GNP to expand to $1,100 billion as equilibrium moves

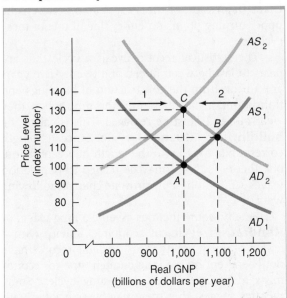

FIGURE 4
An Expansionary Demand-Shock Fluctuation

An expansionary demand-shock fluctuation is started by an increase in aggregate demand, which shifts AD_1 to the right to AD_2, shown by arrow number 1. During the expansion phase, macroeconomic equilibrium moves from its initial position at point *A* up and to the right along the AS_1 curve to point *B*. As wage rates and other resource costs eventually start to rise, the aggregate-supply curve shifts from AS_1 to AS_2, shown by arrow number 2. Thus, the upper turning point of the fluctuation occurs at point *B* and the contraction phase occurs while equilibrium moves from point *B* to point *C*.

up and to the right along the AS_1 curve to point *B*. Before the end of the expansion is reached, it is likely that the economy will be operating with unemployment below the natural rate.

An expansionary demand shock is an increase in aggregate demand.

As the economy expands, production and employment increase month by month. Times are "good," and both households and firms are optimistic about the future. In terms of the circular flow, higher incomes earned in each round of the circle provide funds to finance increased purchases in the next round so that each round builds on the previous one. Thus the expansion has a cumulative character.[2]

During the expansion, the rate of increase in production is greater than the rate of increase in production capacity—the economy is expanding faster than its long-run trend in production capacity. The price level is driven upward. As the expansion proceeds, purchases through the consumption, saving-investment, and net tax-government purchases channels increase, fueling continuation of the expansion. The import-export channel, however, is likely to play a moderating or dampening role in the expansion. Higher household income increases import purchases, sending some of the expansion's force into foreign economies. The rising price level is expected to reduce exports so that a deficit in the economy's international trade will develop.

During the expansion, the rate of increase in production is greater than the rate of increase in production capacity; the price level is driven upward.

The Upper Turning Point

Why can't the expansion continue? The main reason is that expansion in the fluctuation means a rate of increase in output and employment that is greater than the long-run trend of growth of the economy itself. In other words, an upper turning point may be reached simply because the expansion has bumped into "capacity," or resource limits. During the expansion, the use of natural resources, labor, and capital has been rising. New capital goods can still be produced, but labor and natural resources are limited. At some point, shortages or bottlenecks in these inputs will bring a slowdown in the expansion of total output.

Eventually the expansion reaches the upper turning point as the limits of labor and natural resources are reached.

---

2. The Keynesian concept of the multiplier, discussed in Chapter 11, pages 223–231, deals further with this cumulative effect.

The Accelerator The slowing down in the *rate* of economic expansion can lead to an *absolute* contraction in production and employment in industries that produce machines and other capital goods. This is called an **accelerator effect**. In capital goods industries, production schedules have been geared to provide equipment for the expanding economy and to replace machines that wear out. The slackening of the expansion brings an absolute drop in demand for new capital goods. So capital goods producers cut down production schedules and lay off some workers. This decline is a key factor in turning the expansion into a contraction. Lower earnings by labor and other resources in the capital goods industries lead to decreases in consumption, which bring reductions elsewhere in the economy and further cuts in spending. The economy will turn around and move into the contraction phase.

The slowing down in the rate of economic expansion can lead to an absolute contraction in production and employment in industries that produce machines and other capital goods. This is called the accelerator effect. This decline is a key factor in turning the expansion into a contraction.

Smaller Profit Margins In the aggregate-demand and aggregate-supply model, the upper turning point comes as tighter labor and resource markets cause wage rates and other input prices to rise, squeezing business firm profit margins. Layoffs occur and some businesses fail. In Figure 4, the upper turning point comes at point *B*, when the AS_1 curve starts to shift to AS_2 (shown by arrow number 2). Thus, after expansions have gone on for some time, analysts fear that an upper turning point is near and are on the watch for signs of tightness in labor and other resource markets. When prices in these markets start to rise, they predict that the turning point will arrive soon.

The upper turning point comes as wage rates and other input prices start to rise and reduce profit margins.

Circumstances and Events Nearly all expansions *top out*, or reach their upper turning points, long before actual capacity has been reached. Why? Part of the answer is that bottlenecks may arise in some sectors of the economy while idle capacity still exists in other sectors. Resources are not fully interchangeable. For this reason, the pattern of the fluctuation may depend on which industries or parts of the economy are leading the expansion. Sometimes external events, such as the "oil shock" following the embargo by OPEC (Organization of Petroleum Exporting Countries) in 1973, can bring an end to expansion. At other times, the ending of a war may put a stop to spending on war-related items. Upper turning points also may be triggered by subtle changes in business psychology, by decreases in demand from foreign customers, or by disappointing outcomes from business ventures that were begun in the enthusiasm of the expansion.

One of the aims of economic policy is to moderate the economy's expansion rate to bring it into line with the rate of growth of the economy's capacity. If the two rates could be brought together, expansion might continue as long as no external shocks occurred. Unfortunately, bringing the two expansion rates together is even harder than linking up two spacecraft in flight. In short, the idea that the economy might be sustained for very long at a high rate of economic activity implies a delicate balancing of many forces.

One of the aims of economic policy is to moderate the economy's expansion rate to bring it into line with the rate of growth of the economy's capacity.

Those who favor planning contend that planned economies can control business fluctuations because decision making is more highly concentrated in a central planning agency, and also because they can cut themselves off from changes elsewhere in the world. Even if these claims could be proved, there may be a tradeoff between the slope of the trend line and fluctuations around it. Planned economies may sacrifice some growth in favor of greater stability.

The Contraction Phase

In fluctuations initiated by increases in aggregate demand, the contraction phase takes place as wage rates and resource prices rise and reduce profit margins, causing the aggregate-supply curve to shift to the left. In Figure 4, the contraction takes place as equilibrium moves along the AD_2 curve from B to C. Profit margins are squeezed, and production and employment decrease month by month. Times are "bad," and firms and households are likely to be pessimistic. Falling average real income leads to reductions in consumption purchases by households and investment purchases by firms. Unsold inventories bring declines in output, which reduce real income and production in each successive round of the circular flow so that the contraction feeds upon itself and has a cumulative character. The contraction continues as long as wage rates and other costs continue to force smaller profit margins on firms. Since layoffs are taking place and new jobs are not being created, unemployment increases. The combination of a rising price level along with increasing unemployment is called **stagflation**.

The contraction phase takes place as rising wage rates and resource prices reduce profit margins.

The combination of a rising price level and increasing unemployment is called stagflation.

The Lower Turning Point

What about the bottoming out of the economy after a contraction? Why doesn't the contraction in the flow of income and production continue indefinitely? Part of the explanation is that there is a *floor*, which at some point will end the decline in expenditure and production. Some consumption spending is needed simply for survival. Households will borrow money, sell assets, or dip into savings to pay for this minimum. Even though net investment may be negative in severe contractions, gross investment (except for inventory) cannot be negative. Government purchases will not fall to zero and, in fact, may be made specifically to reverse the direction of the economy. As we shall see later in the book, a major thrust of macroeconomics is that the worst-case scenario need not be played out in the contraction. In other words, the experience of the 1930s Great Depression need not be repeated.

At some point in a contraction phase, a floor will be reached that will end the decline in expenditure and production.

The Accelerator, Again The **lower turning point** of a fluctuation requires not only the leveling off of a contraction but also the upturn into a new expansion. Once again, the accelerator concept can help us understand how the economy operates. As the economy experiences the contraction of business activity, idle capacity has been increasing. Labor, capital, and natural resources are not being fully used. According to the accelerator concept, capital equipment producers help to bring the upturn, just as they helped to bring the downturn earlier in the fluctuation. Some machines and equipment will wear out even at the relatively low rates of use that characterize the economy during the contraction. At first, idle machines can be put into service when other machines wear out. But at some point, the reserves of idle machinery will be gone, and some expansion of capital equipment production will be needed to meet the demand for replacement. This rise in capital equipment production starts a new expansion of the economy. Rising output, employment, and income in these industries will lead to increases in expenditure, and the economy will be back on the expansion path of economic activity.

Random Events Must the timing of the upturn wait until all reserves of capital equipment have been used up? Not necessarily. The upturn may come from a particularly successful innovation, which can create investor optimism in some important line of business. Foreign demand may rise, or government spending may stimulate the economy. With the start of World War II in 1939, increases in spending helped the country recover from the Great Depression. The point is that the exact timing of the upturn may depend on particu-

lar events. But reliable forecasting of such events is almost impossible.

The upturn into a new expansion can be caused by the accelerator effect, random events, or government policy.

Wage Rate and Input Price Adjustments The aggregate-demand and aggregate-supply model in Figure 4 suggests that the fluctuation ends at point *C*, when wage rates and other production costs have ceased to rise and price-level increases have brought profit margins back to normal. However, a more complex version of this model (which will be explained in Chapter 15) suggests that the leftward-shifting *AS* curve could overshoot the long-run equilibrium point at *C* and push the economy into further contraction. The model says that since the price level has been rising more or less continuously since the expansion started (at point *A*), labor and other resource owners may believe that it will continue to rise. If they build these **inflationary expectations** into their contract demands from firms, profit margins may be squeezed even further, and the contraction could continue to an output level of less than $1,000 billion—until rising unemployment and increasing resistance from firms force reductions in costs. The contraction could continue until wage rates and other costs were forced down or until some event or government policy shifted aggregate demand to the right thereby launching another demand-driven expansion.

CONTRACTIONARY DEMAND-SHOCK FLUCTUATIONS

A contractionary demand shock is some event that causes a drop in purchases by consumers or investors or governments or foreigners or by several or all of these groups. For example, the stock market crash of 1929 was an event that many analysts believe cast a cloud of fear and uncertainty over consumers and investors, causing them to cut back on purchasing. This demand shock led, they say, to the Great Depression of the 1930s.[3] Contractionary demand shocks often come at the end of major wars, when government purchases drop abruptly. For economies that depend heavily on international trade, a drop in purchases by foreigners can be a demand shock.

The theory for contractionary demand-shock fluctuations is generally similar to the one just explained for expansionary demand shocks, but there are some important differences. For one thing, the story of the cycle starts with its contractionary phase. More important, the price level tends to fall. This deflationary aspect is important because of its consequences for international trade and for financial institutions, and because it opens the way for government to play a more active role in bringing about the lower turning point.

The Contraction Phase

Figure 5 is an aggregate-demand and aggregate-supply graph illustrating a contractionary demand-shock fluctuation. When the aggregate-demand curve shifts to the left, from AD_1 to AD_2 (shown by arrow number 1), equilibrium moves downward and to the left along the aggregate-supply curve, AS_1, from point A to point B. The drop in production from $1,000 billion to $900 billion shows the magnitude of the contraction of output and employment. The contraction feeds on itself as lower production and income (the lower half of the circular flow) lead to lower purchases (the upper half of the circular flow) and still lower production and income in each successive round of the circle. According to the theory of the aggregate-supply curve, wage rates and input prices do not decline as quickly as prices of final goods so that the declining price level reduces profit margins, causing some firms to go out of business and others to cut production.

A contractionary demand shock is some event that causes a drop in purchases by consumers, investors, governments, and/or foreigners—that is, there is a decrease in aggregate demand.

---

3. When the stock market suffered a severe drop in October 1987, analysts kept careful track of the reactions of consumers and investors to see if history would repeat itself.

FIGURE 5
A Contractionary Demand-Shock Fluctuation

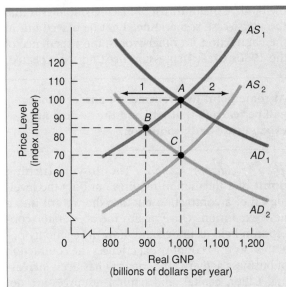

A contractionary demand-shock fluctuation is started by a decrease in aggregate demand, which shifts AD_1 to the left to AD_2, shown by arrow number 1. During the contraction phase, macroeconomic equilibrium moves from its initial position at point A down and to the left along the AS_1 curve to point B. As wage rates and other resource costs begin to fall, the aggregate-supply curve shifts from AS_1 to AS_2, shown by arrow number 2. The lower turning point of the fluctuation occurs at point B and the expansion phase occurs while equilibrium moves from point B to point C or returns from point B to point A if government policy shifts AD_2 back to AD_1.

The declining price level is the major difference between the contractionary demand-shock model and the expansionary demand-shock model presented earlier. Two consequences of the declining price level merit special attention. They relate to breakdowns in international trade and in financial markets.

The difference between the contractionary demand-shock model and the expansionary demand-shock model is the declining price level.

Restriction of International Trade For an economy experiencing a demand-shock contraction, declining prices for goods it produces reduce household and business purchases from foreigners (imports) and increase purchases by foreigners (exports), thereby moderating the severity of the contraction. However, this moderating effect comes at the expense of the foreign economies, which experience the opposite set of effects—increasing imports and decreasing exports. Their economies are then in danger of suffering a contractionary demand shock. Rather than allowing this to happen, they are likely to impose tariffs, quotas, and other restrictions on international trade to reduce their imports. During the Great Depression of the 1930s, international trade was severely restricted.

Collapse of Financial Institutions   A second important consequence of a declining price level is the danger that it will bring collapse and bankruptcy for firms in the financial sector of the economy—firms that carry out transactions in the financial markets box of the circular-flow diagram. This is because a substantial portion of the assets of banks, insurance companies, and other financial institutions consists of loans made to business firms. A falling price level makes it very difficult for business firms and other borrowers to repay loans, since the real value of the repayment is going up at the very time that business profits are falling. When business firms fail, banks and other financial institutions suffer declines in the value of their assets and may themselves be forced into bankruptcy. When financial institutions fail, depositors—including many financially sound households and firms—may lose the savings and reserves they had on deposit and may themselves be forced into bankruptcy.[4] Moreover, when financial institutions have failed, firms that want to borrow to finance continued or expanded production may be unable to obtain credit. Thus, falling prices can greatly increase the severity of the contraction.

There are two major consequences of a declining price level: the breakdown of international trade and the danger of bankruptcy for firms in the financial sector.

The Lower Turning Point

It is generally agreed that some of the causes of lower turning points, such as floors on economic activity and the accelerator effect, apply as well to contractionary demand-shock fluctuations as to expansionary demand-shock fluctuations. But, for reasons that will become clear as we trace the lower-turning-point logic of the aggregate-demand and aggregate-supply model, debate among economists and government policymakers goes far beyond these generally accepted phenomena.

In contractionary demand-shock fluctuations, as illustrated in Figure 5, the lower turning point comes at point B, when wage rates and other resource prices begin to fall fast enough to ease the pressures on profit margins, that is, when the aggregate-supply curve starts to shift to the right, from AS_1 to AS_2 (shown by arrow number 2). This shift comes when contracts for labor and other inputs are renegotiated and when the pressures of unemployment have become great enough so that lower wage rates and resource prices are accepted. According to the aggregate-demand and aggregate-supply model, when the AS_1 curve starts to shift toward AS_2, profit margins improve, leading to increased production.

How severe must the contraction be and how long must it last before the AS curve will start to shift to the right? This is a crucial question for economic policymakers. If prices—especially wage rates—respond quickly (are "flexible"), the contraction may be brief and only a modest amount of unemployment need arise. But if prices—especially wage rates—do not respond quickly (are "inflexible"), the contraction may go on for a long time, and unemployment may become so severe that the society's political and social structure are threatened. In such cases the government may step in and bring about the lower turning point by boosting aggregate demand back toward its original level of AD_1. On the other hand, wages could prove flexible enough so that government intervention would not be necessary. These views, and their supporting theories and arguments, will be examined at length in later chapters.[5]

---

4. Since the financial disaster of the Great Depression, government-sponsored insurance systems such as the Federal Deposit Insurance Corporation and the Federal Savings and Loan Insurance Corporation have been set up to protect deposits in financial institutions.

5. The original Keynesian versus classical debate arose during the Great Depression of the 1930s. Today, there are modern versions of these positions, called "Neo Keynesian" and "new classical." These are examined in Chapter 17, pages 373–383.

The Expansion Phase

In contractionary demand-shock fluctuations, the character of the expansion, or recovery, phase depends on whether or not the government intervention has been responsible for the lower turning point. If the government has been able to shift the aggregate-demand curve to the right, the expansion is essentially the same as the expansion phase of the expansionary demand-shock fluctuation described earlier. The profit margins of firms improve because the added demand boosts final-product prices ahead of wage rates and other resource costs. Equilibrium moves upward and to the right along the AS_1 curve from point B to point A. Unemployment decreases, and workers are not required to accept the wage-rate cuts that appeared imminent at point B.

If the aggregate-demand curve has not been shifted to the right, the expansion phase of the fluctuation is characterized by declines in the wage rates and other resource prices. If wage rates and resource prices are flexible downward, the adjustment occurs quickly. Unemployment is reduced dramatically and real GNP increases.

Extremely divisive social pressures are expected to develop if the recovery from the demand-shock contraction is accomplished through deflation—the route from B to C in Figure 5. For one thing, the declining price level means an increase in the real (purchasing power) value of bonds and other fixed-dollar denominated assets. Many of these are held by the wealthy segment of the population. Therefore, the wealth of the wealthy increases at the same time that nominal and real wage rates are falling. It is easy to charge that the wealthy are using the recovery and the hardships of workers to increase their already comfortable economic situation. The retired segment of the population, together with those who own insurance policies, also gain from the declining price level, since the real value of their insurance policies and pension checks increases. Thus, the older and relatively better-off segments of the population benefit relative to younger and less well-off segments, where unemployment has been widespread and where real and nominal wage rates are falling. Finally, there is a rift between workers who are employed and those who are unemployed. Falling

real wage rates may be resented by those fortunate enough and skilled enough to have held their jobs during the preceding contraction. The re-employment of workers who had lost jobs earlier may offer little consolation.

In the absence of increases in aggregate demand, the recovery phase of a contractionary demand-shock fluctuation is characterized by divisive social pressures.

The Upper Turning Point

The aggregate-demand and aggregate-supply graph (Figure 5) implies that the upper turning point of the contractionary demand-shock fluctuation comes either at point A or point C, depending on whether the recovery from point B has come through a shift of aggregate demand or a shift in aggregate supply. It is conceivable, however, that the economy could overshoot this level of output ($1,000 billion of real GNP in Figure 5) if both labor and business firms develop expectations that the expansion will continue. As we will see, political pressures may build for still further rightward shifts of either the aggregate-demand curve or the aggregate-supply curve.

SUPPLY SHOCKS

In 1973 and again in 1978, the Organization of Petroleum Exporting Countries (OPEC) abruptly reduced supplies of crude petroleum available to the world markets. In each instance, in international crude-petroleum markets, equilibrium prices increased and equilibrium quantities demanded and supplied decreased. The economies of industrialized countries around the world experienced contractionary supply shocks, that is, their aggregate-supply curves shifted to the left, as illustrated in Figure 6. At any given price level, the aggregate quantity of output supplied was less than before the shock. The shift of the AS curve forced equilibrium up and to the left along the aggregate-demand curve, from point A to point B. Output and

FIGURE 6
A Contractionary Supply Shock

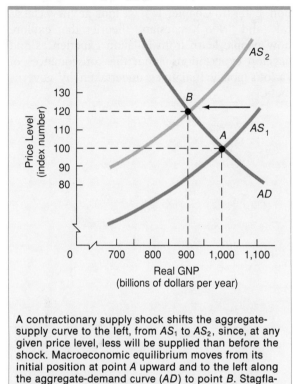

A contractionary supply shock shifts the aggregate-supply curve to the left, from AS_1 to AS_2, since, at any given price level, less will be supplied than before the shock. Macroeconomic equilibrium moves from its initial position at point A upward and to the left along the aggregate-demand curve (AD) to point B. Stagflation occurs as unemployment increases, real GNP decreases, and the price level rises.

employment decreased. These economies suffered stagflation, since their price levels rose at the same time that employment and production decreased.

Twice during the 1970s, the economies of industrialized countries experienced contractionary supply shocks when OPEC suddenly reduced supplies of crude petroleum available to world markets.

As equilibrium moved toward point B, economic policymakers confronted a dilemma. Shifting aggregate demand to the right in order to restore employment to its earlier level would push the price level still higher.[6] But shifting aggregate

6. OPEC leaders complained of such inflationist policies and threatened further supply cuts.

demand to the left to fight inflation would increase the severity of the contraction, cutting output and employment still more. Thus, demand-side policies had little to offer beyond allocating the hardships of the supply shock among different segments of population.

Since demand-side remedies were unattractive, policy focused on attempts to shift aggregate-supply curves back to the right. Crude-oil production from non-OPEC countries was encouraged, as were new technologies designed to use less energy from petroleum. Considerable time was required for these efforts to bear fruit. By the mid 1980s, however, the world had become less dependent on OPEC petroleum, partly because of new supplies from non-OPEC countries and partly from success in developing new, petroleum-conserving technologies. OPEC failed in its efforts to continue restrictions on crude-petroleum output. The collapse of OPEC's output restrictions increased supplies of petroleum, lowered its price, and shifted aggregate-supply curves to the right in countries around the world. This expansionary supply shock increased output and employment in industrialized countries and helped stamp out inflationary expectations that had become established during the 1970s. Although price levels did not fall in absolute terms, there was substantial **disinflation**. In the United States, the political careers of Presidents Ford and Carter suffered from the contractionary supply shocks of the 1970s, while that of President Reagan benefited from the expansionary shock of the 1980s.

A LOOK AHEAD

Economic fluctuations impose hardships. During contractions, output is lost that can never be regained, and workers, especially the unskilled, suffer unemployment. Hardships also are imposed by price-level changes, which usually accompany economic fluctuations. Unanticipated price-level changes redistribute income and wealth, and those least skilled in financial management are likely to suffer most. Large changes in either employment or the price level can destabilize the social and political order.

The chapters ahead explore theories about how economic fluctuations can be moderated. We start (in Chapters 10 and 11) with Keynesian theories, which grew out of the experience of the Great Depression of the 1930s and proposed government policies to speed recovery after a contractionary demand-shock. Next (in Chapters 12, 13, and 14), we examine money, banks, and monetarist economic theories, which focus on control of the money supply and place special emphasis on preventing inflation. Later (in Chapter 17), we look at "new classical" and "Neo-Keynesian" theories that explore how people learn from inflation experiences and develop expectations about the consequences of various policy initiatives undertaken by government.

Economics in Focus

Baby Booms and Economic Cycles

Much has been written about the baby boom following World War II and its effect on American society and culture. But economist Richard Easterlin has taken the analysis one step further, contending that population changes are responsible for fluctuations in our degree of social and economic contentment. He identifies what he calls a "new Kuznets cycle," a fluctuation caused not by changes in demand for goods or labor but rather by shifts in the supply of one basic commodity: babies.

Simplified, Easterlin's argument goes like this: In the economic boom following World War II, there were plenty of new jobs available. Because of low birth rates in the late 1920s and 1930s and federal laws restricting immigration, young American workers faced little competition in the postwar job market, and prospects for advancement looked good. With no fear of hard times to come, young people were quick to marry and produce offspring, causing the famous baby boom that lasted into the early 1960s. But as these children began to enter the labor force, their sheer numbers changed the economic outlook. There was much more competition for the available jobs. The average young worker had more difficulty finding appropriate work, advanced more slowly, saw fewer golden prospects ahead. In order to maintain a standard of living similar to their parents', the baby boomers had to marry later, find jobs for both spouses, and ultimately have fewer children.

In this way Easterlin uses population data to account for some well-known changes in American social behavior. He also argues that many disturbing trends of the 1960s and 1970s—increasing alienation among the young, as well as violence, crime, divorce, illegitimacy, and suicide—can be linked to the mass of young baby boomers and the stress caused by their difficulty in realizing their economic expectations.

Turning this analysis on its head, Easterlin then supposes that the generation now maturing will reverse the pattern. The children of the baby boomers are a relatively small group. Finding less competition for jobs and status, they will be less alienated, more willing and able to resume traditional husband-wife roles, and more prolific. Thus there may be a recurring cycle of roughly two generations in length, with baby booms producing economic tribulations and baby busts, which in turn produce times of greater opportunity and baby booms.

Because Easterlin's argument is extrapolated from a single instance of the supposed cycle, it is too early to judge its accuracy. Moreover, as he himself recognizes, many other factors may intervene; surges in immigration, for example, may disrupt the pattern. Clearly, too, demographic fluctuations by themselves cannot explain changes in marriage age, childbearing, and women's participation in the labor force. Still, economists and policymakers may want to ponder the means of interrupting the cycle or softening its effect on the unfortunate "boom" generations.

Source: Richard A. Easterlin, *Birth and Fortune: The Impact of Numbers on Personal Welfare,* 2nd edition (Chicago: University of Chicago Press, 1987).

SUMMARY

1. In the aggregate-demand and aggregate-supply model, shifts of either the aggregate-demand curve or the aggregate-supply curve result in changes in employment and real GNP. Fluctuations begin as the shift of one of these curves relocates the equilibrium intersection of the aggregate-demand curve and the aggregate-supply curve. (See pages 172–173 and Figure 1, page 172.)

2. The historical record shows that the U.S. economy fluctuates considerably around its long-run trend rate of growth. This historical picture is dominated by the Great Depression of the 1930s and the World War II economic boom. Since 1945, fluctuations have been relatively moderate. (See pages 174–175 and Figure 2, page 173.)

3. The period of a cycle or fluctuation is the time between a successive pair of upper turning points or a successive pair of lower turning points. The cumulative phases of fluctuations—the expansion phase and the contraction phase—occur between successive turning points. (See page 175 and Figure 3, page 176.)

4. Statistical identification and measurement of fluctuations involves selecting relevant data series, removing seasonal variations, plotting the trend, and calculating deviations from this trend. Identification and measurement is followed by theorizing about causes. (See page 176.)

5. Four cyclical patterns have been identified: the Kitchin (inventory) cycle of three to five years, the Juglar cycle of seven to ten years, the Kuznets (building) cycle of fifteen to twenty-five years, and the Kondratieff cycle of thirty to fifty years. (See pages 176–177.)

6. Both Karl Marx and Joseph Schumpeter believed that economic fluctuations reveal fundamental characteristics of capitalism. Marx argued that depressions would become worse and worse and would finally occasion the overthrow of capitalism. Schumpeter contended that fluctuations accompany economic growth, which would eventually shift attention from production to income redistribution and lead to a welfare state. (See pages 177–178.)

7. Expansionary demand-shock fluctuations are caused by shifts to the right of the aggregate-demand curve. The resulting expansion reaches its limit through the accelerator effect, increases of wage rates and other input prices, and/or from outside events. The contraction phase takes place while wage rates and other resource prices continue to squeeze profit margins. The lower turning point is reached through a floor to economic activity, the accelerator effect, random events, or government policy. (See pages 178–179 and Figure 4, page 178.)

8. Contractionary demand-shock fluctuations are caused by shifts to the left of the aggregate-demand curve. The model for these fluctuations parallels that for expansionary demand-shock fluctuations except that prices tend to fall rather than rise. Falling prices may make the contraction worse by leading to restrictions on international trade and causing collapse of financial institutions. (See pages 181–182 and Figure 5, page 182.)

9. Economic policy debates focus on how quickly wage rates and other resource prices adjust during contractions in the economy. If resource prices are flexible and can adjust rapidly, little or no government intervention is needed. If resource prices are inflexible, government intervention may be needed to speed recovery. (See page 183.)

10. The deflation remedy for a contraction caused by a demand shock exposes the social order to severe stress. Real values of bonds and insurance policies rise at the same time that real and nominal wage rates are falling. (See page 184.)

11. Contractionary supply shocks cause the aggregate-supply curve to shift to the left, leading to stagflation, that is, to increases in the price level and reductions in employment and output. Policies using shifts of the aggregate-demand curve face unattractive alternatives. Policies attempting to shift aggregate-supply curves to the right usually require a long time to be effective. (See pages 184–185 and Figure 6, page 185.)

KEY TERMS

accelerator effect: increases or decreases of capital goods production that tend to cause lower and upper turning points of economic fluctuations (page 179).

coincident indicators: index numbers that move along with the total economy; they should be used to measure fluctuations (page 176).

cycle theories: theories that imply that a regular, predictable pattern exists to explain changes in the economy (page 173).

disinflation: a period of decreasing inflation rates (page 185).

economic fluctuations: alternating expansions and contractions in the volume of real GNP in an economy (see page 172).

inflationary expectations: a belief that the price level will continue to rise (page 181).

Juglar cycle: a business cycle of seven to ten years (page 176).

Kitchin (inventory) cycle: a business cycle of three to five years that is believed to be connected to the alternate buildup and depletion of business inventories (page 176).

Kondratieff cycle: a business cycle of thirty to fifty years (page 177).

Kuznets (building) cycle: a business cycle of fifteen to twenty-five years that runs from the construction of buildings and transportation facilities until the time when they wear out and must be replaced (page 177).

lagging indicators: index numbers that tend to change direction after changes in the volume of total economic activity (page 175).

leading indicators: index numbers that tend to anticipate changes in the total economy (page 175).

lower turning points: also called *troughs*, they represent low points of economic activity (page 174).

stagflation: a period of a rising price level and increasing unemployment (page 180).

trend line of economic activity: a pattern of growth taking place in the economy because of increases in the size and quality of labor, the quantity of capital, and better technology (page 174).

upper turning points: also called *peaks*, they represent high points in the volume of economic activity (page 174).

DISCUSSION QUESTIONS

1. Draw a graph including a trend line and a complete economic cycle. Identify the parts of the cycle. How is the trend line related to the growth rate of the economy?

2. Explain the difference between the term *cycles* and the term *fluctuations* as applied to periodic changes in the volume of economic activity. Why is there some validity to each term? Why does neither tell the whole story?

3. Write down the names that have been given to the four major cycle patterns described in this chapter. After each, note its usual length and some of the causes that have been suggested for it. At what stage of each of these cycles do you believe the economy is operating at the present time? Discuss.

4. Both Karl Marx and Joseph Schumpeter placed great emphasis on business fluctuations. However, one saw them as signs of health and the other saw them as signs of sickness in capitalist economies. Explain their points of view. Both saw capitalism giving way to socialism, but for different reasons and by different processes. Explain.

5. Draw an aggregate-demand and aggregate-supply graph and explain the axis labels carefully. Then explain and illustrate on the graph how an event that increases aggregate demand launches a chain of responses that constitute an economic fluctuation. Which groups in a society are most likely to benefit from this process? Which are most likely to suffer?

6. Explain the concept of bottlenecks and how it helps in understanding the upper turning points of fluctuations. How does the accelerator effect operate when the rate of expansion in the economy slackens?

7. How might a sharp fall in prices on the stock market lead to a contraction of the economy? Illustrate such a contraction with an aggregate-demand and aggregate-supply graph. Discuss how falling prices may bring international trade restrictions and the collapse of financial institutions.

8. What are some of the factors that place a floor or lower limit on downswings of economic activity? Does the economy have to go all the way to the floor before it can start to recover? How may the accelerator process contribute to a lower turning point?

9. How is the flexibility or inflexibility of wage rates and other resource prices related to the length of a demand-shock contraction? Discuss the arguments for and against government intervention to bring about the lower turning point and recovery from a demand-shock contraction.

10. Think of some happening (other than another OPEC petroleum supply cut) that could bring a contractionary supply shock to an economy. Discuss whether shifts in aggregate demand could help resolve the stagflation problem. What other things might be done?

The Gross Anatomy of Gross Unemployment

Some are so immunized to numbers, especially to statistics, that unemployment rates of 50 percent in "Faroffistan" mean absolutely nothing. "Figures," it is said, "do not bleed." But most of us wonder, at least momentarily, how a society can survive with such rates and what these rates mean in human terms. Will these unemployed masses die of starvation next week or next month? Will they emigrate or revolt? Does Faroffistan have unemployment compensation or poor relief? Are employed family members obligated by Faroffistani custom to support their jobless relatives, even those cousins "whom they number by the dozens"? Are the numbers perhaps artifacts of some special Faroffistani form of statistical malpractice? Do these people really want to work, or are they waiting for venison on gold spoons, as Messrs. Gradgrind and Bounderby described their "hands" as doing in Charles Dickens's *Hard Times*?

The present discussion, however, concentrates on "the figures" rather than "the facts." At first glance, unemployment statistics seem simple enough for comparability over time and between countries. A community, which may be an entire country or a smaller unit, has a *labor force*, most of whose members are usually *employed*, while a minority are *unemployed*. The unemployed are subdivided further into the *involuntarily* unemployed, who are actively seeking work at going wages in occupations for which they are qualified, and the *voluntarily* unemployed, who insist on lower qualifications or rate their qualifications higher than the market seems to do.[1] Economic analysis and social criticism are concerned only with the involuntarily unemployed, but published statistics cannot in practice distinguish between them.[2]

Many countries also classify the unemployed by the length of time they have been unemployed and by whether or not they have ever been employed. The long-term unemployed are usually the more serious social problem. Together with the long-term "never worked," they comprise a large part of the economic underclass. If there is a waiting period between the loss of a job, or from entry into the labor force, and eligibility for unemployment benefits, some countries register jobless workers as unemployed only after this period ends. Much frictional unemployment is thus not reported at all, and the published unemployment rates are low by comparison with those of other countries.

Only after a quick look at the "bugs" and "gremlins" of the published figures can we be sure that Country A has a more or less serious unemployment problem than Country B, or that Country A's unemployment problem is more or less serious now than it was when the present administration came to power.

---

1. People who need not work, cannot work, or refuse to work are not included in the labor force, and therefore are not considered voluntarily unemployed—a statistical paradox.

2. Another statistical breakdown of unemployment is into the categories introduced in Chapter 8—*frictional, seasonal, cyclical,* and *structural* unemployment. A person briefly unemployed between jobs as a free-lance actor or carpenter is frictionally unemployed. A teacher with a nine-month contract may be seasonally unemployed during the summer vacation. A steelworker laid off because "business is bad" is ordinarily cyclically unemployed. But if his plant is closed for good, or his employer has moved his operations to another town (or out of the country), the steelworker is structurally unemployed, especially if there is no other steel mill in that particular metropolitan area. Here again, the statistician cannot keep pace with the analyst, except that employment and unemployment series can be adjusted more or less accurately for normal seasonal fluctuations associated with Christmas, Easter, or the crops. In our voluntary-involuntary classification system, the structurally unemployed fall in the involuntary category, since they are actively seeking work at the going wage. During the off-season, seasonally employed people are not in the labor force because they either need not work, they cannot work, or they refuse work.

Let us therefore sample a few of the bugs—a dozen or so—as an exercise in statistical entomology. (Almost nobody is proposing that the figures be thrown out, or that we should stop collecting them.)

UNEMPLOYMENT AND POVERTY

In the first place, we should remember to distinguish unemployment from poverty, and poverty from unemployment. Other things being equal—many other things—the unemployed are poorer than the employed. But many of the unemployed, especially the voluntarily unemployed, are far from poverty, even though the "wealthy playboys" hold no-work jobs or drop out of the labor force. Also, many if not most of the poor are employed at least part time, or are members of large families whose breadwinners are in low-paid jobs. Nor should it be forgotten that the representative unemployed person in a rich country—Canada or the United States, Sweden or Switzerland—is better off than the typical employed person in a poor country—Bangladesh or Haiti, Ethiopia or Somaliland.

TEMPORARILY NOT WORKING

A worker who is sick or injured, who is on strike, on vacation, or on leave of absence is not considered unemployed as long as he or she believes that there is a job to return to and intends to return to it. This is in most cases nothing more than common sense, but problems arise even here. A striker may have every intention to return to work after the strike is settled, but his or her employer may propose instead to replace the striker with a strikebreaker, or possibly with a machine. A woman on extended maternity leave may intend to resume work on the assumption that she can have her old job back, while her employer has vacancies only in inferior jobs. A worker on vacation, having quarreled with the boss or the supervisor, may spend this vacation job hunting and have no intention of ever going back—may even be reported as unemployed while still on the payroll, whether or not the former employer expects him or her back.

GROSS OR NET UNEMPLOYMENT?

Suppose a full-employment economy. For all sorts of jobs in such an economy, some people are seeking work and there are some job vacancies. The numbers are in balance, and so there is no *net* unemployment (net of job vacancies). There is, however, *gross* unemployment, which is reported as "unemployment" in all countries. (Job-vacancy statistics are less complete than unemployment statistics.) The differential between gross and net unemployment is estimated under American conditions as between 3 and 4 percent of the labor force. The reported unemployment statistics therefore have an upward bias when used as indicators of shortfalls from full employment.

THE MILITARY LABOR FORCE

A country's labor force excludes persons not seeking work, children below the school-leaving age, and the institutional population of prisoners, hospital patients, etc., some of whom may actually be at hard labor. The *civilian* labor force also excludes the uniformed military, naval, and air forces.[3] A country with large defense forces, whether volunteer or conscript, can sweeten its published unemployment statistics and exaggerate its statistical prosperity by relating unemployment to the total rather than to the civilian labor force, which is the more common procedure.[4]

MADE WORK

This term is chiefly used for public projects undertaken primarily as unemployment relief. Workers on such projects are an important part of the so-called *disguised unemployed*—persons who appear to be employed *only* because work was "made" for them. Also, no statistical account is taken of featherbedding, or excessive workers on other projects, either public or private. During the New Deal—the first two administrations of President Franklin Roosevelt (1933–1941)—employees of Civilian Conservation Corps (CCC) and Works Progress Administration (WPA) projects were counted as unemployed. In later periods, and in most other countries, such workers are counted as employed. Because of this change in American statistical practice, contemporary writers using contemporary concepts may unknowingly exaggerate the magnitude of unemployment during the Great Depression and also the magnitude of subsequent improvement.

3. Civilian employees of defense departments are not excluded from the civilian labor force. Neither are policemen, firemen, or members of such "private armies" as the Nazis' Storm Troopers or Peru's Shining Path guerrillas.

4. A hypothetical example: a country has a total labor force of 2 million, including 100 thousand members of the armed forces and 150 thousand unemployed. Its unemployment rates are 7.5 percent of the total labor force and 7.9 percent of the civilian labor force.

EXCESS WORKERS AND DISCOURAGED WORKERS

If a family breadwinner loses his or her job, other family members—housewives, househusbands, students, retirees—may join him or her in looking for work. In doing so, they enter or re-enter the labor force. Until they find jobs, their (temporary) presence in the labor markets exaggerates the extent of genuine unemployment. When one or more family members find jobs, and especially if the principal breadwinner does so, the others leave the labor market. Statistical "unemployment" is reduced unduly, and the statistical "recovery" is exaggerated.

A larger and therefore more important category is composed of the *discouraged unemployed*. This is another important component of disguised unemployment. A discouraged worker is one who is sure that no jobs fitting his or her skills are open in the community and who is unable or unwilling to move, to acquire new skills, or to seek unskilled work. This worker therefore stops looking for work in any regular or systematic way. Such behavior removes this worker from the statistical labor force. When prosperity returns, or when new firms enter the community, previously discouraged workers become an important source of new hires. For example, during World War II, the availability of discouraged workers seems to have been important in the acceleration of American war production in the critical period from 1940 to 1943.

HOUSEWIVES, STUDENTS, PENSIONERS

When not actively seeking work, people such as housewives, househusbands, students, and pensioners are not included in the labor force, although many of them swell the ranks of the discouraged workers and disguised unemployed. When they are employed, either full or part time, they are employed members of the labor force, even when they are part-timers actively seeking full-time jobs.

When these so-called *secondary workers* are seeking work but cannot find it, their statistical treatment varies across countries. American practice classifies them as unemployed. In Japan, however, they are not included in the labor force unless they are employed.[5] This is another reason why Japanese unemployment ratios are so low.

5. In Japanese practice, a person is first classified as working or not working. If he or she is not working, his or her

THE SELF-EMPLOYED

A physician, attorney, or accountant in independent professional practice is of course treated as employed, even without a formal employer. Problems arise when such a worker's income is insufficient for self-support or for the support of the worker's family. In an extreme case the worker is not a street vendor, musician, or artist but a beggar or panhandler, or the worker's earnings are supplemented by relatives, private charity, public relief, or criminal activities. In these gray areas, the worker's own classification of his or her status is usually accepted by the busy statistician or survey researcher. When street people,[6] for example, claim to be unemployed and seeking work, or to be discouraged unemployed, they are so classified, but if instead they claim to be self-employed, they are included in the employed population. This statistical liberalism also reduces comparability of employment statistics across countries. The Japanese word for an unemployed person, translated literally, is "a person who has lost a job," with undesirable connotations of dishonesty, incompetence, or laziness. A Japanese, then, is apt to call himself or herself self-employed in circumstances where an American would admit himself or herself to be unemployed. In the immediate postwar demobilization crisis of 1945–46, official Japanese unemployment remained low. Unemployment benefits were almost nonexistent, and people could not "afford" to be unemployed.

UNDEREMPLOYMENT AND SUBEMPLOYMENT

The underemployed and the subemployed are also included at times in the broad category of disguised unemployment. They are sometimes pointed to by critics who argue that a nation is really not doing as well as its low unemployment figures may suggest. Many of the underemployed are also subemployed, so that separate estimates of these two categories should not be added together.

The *underemployed* are of two sorts, quantitative and qualitative. The quantitatively underemployed work part time, but would prefer full-time jobs and may be actively seeking them. (A full-time worker seeking a moonlighting second job should not be included under this head.) The qualitatively underemployed are, by ordinary standards, overqualified for their present jobs. They would prefer, and may be actively seeking, jobs that use their skills at a higher level. Examples include the electrical engineer working as an electrician or TV repair person and the immigrant doctor or surgeon working as a hospital orderly because his or her foreign degree is not recognized in the United States.

The term *subemployment* refers to the level of the worker's pay. The subemployed are the lower levels of the so-called *working poor*. Their compensation falls below some standard, which most commonly is a poverty line but may be considerably higher. For example, for a construction worker, it may be anything below the union scale for the worker's trade in the worker's community. Or a feminist may consider secretarial work as subemployment until secretaries, mostly female, earn as much as workers in primarily male jobs of comparable worth, such as truck driving. A standard wage in a poor country in Black Africa or Central America may, of course, be a subemployment one in North America or Western Europe.

SEARCH UNEMPLOYMENT

In distinguishing between voluntary and involuntary unemployment, we tacitly assume that for each type of labor there are in each community well-known and recognized standards of wages, working conditions, and the qualifications required for employment. This is seldom if ever completely true. The actual situation is an imperfect market with considerable ranges of difference and ignorance about all these matters. Sometimes a single employer may use a tiering system with wages and working conditions better for the tier of workers hired in periods of labor shortage than for the tier hired in periods of unemployment.

Suppose a worker gets a job offer fairly close to his specialty in his home labor market area of Houston, Texas. He rejects this offer, thinking, rightly or wrongly, that he can do better, either in the Houston labor market or by broadening his search to other areas. He may have friends or relatives in Los Angeles. Is his continued unemployment, after his

---

dependency status is next ascertained. If he or she is found to be a dependent of a family, or of the state, the question whether or not he or she is seeking work is generally left unasked, since such dependents are usually ineligible for unemployment compensation.

6. Street people live or work on the public streets. They may but need not also be homeless; they may or may not also be unemployed.

rejection of the Houston offer, voluntary or involuntary?

Such consequences of labor-market imperfection are generally put in an intermediate category called *search unemployment*; neither strictly voluntary nor strictly involuntary. Some economists who prefer to deny the importance of involuntary unemployment do not consider search unemployment to be unemployment at all.[7] They describe job search rather as a form of employment, whose "wage" is the worker's unemployment compensation plus any assistance in cash or in kind that he or she may get from family, friends, or private charity.

NATURAL RATE AND NAIRU

We have noted that unemployment is recorded gross of unfilled vacancies. This implies that if there are more unfilled vacancies in most branches of labor than there are workers seeking jobs, there will be upward pressure on wages even in the presence of considerable gross unemployment as statistically recorded.

At what level of reported unemployment does such pressure begin? Is there, perhaps, a level of reported unemployment below which we cannot in practice lower the unemployment rate, because increased labor demand only accelerates wage inflation?

The belief that some such rate exists, and that it can be estimated with reasonable accuracy at any point in time, is more common among conservative labor economists and employment statisticians than among their reformist or radical colleagues. In the United States, such a rate (when presumed to exist) is called a *natural rate* of unemployment and used as an indicator of full employment. In Great Britain such a rate is called NAIRU, an acronym for the mouth-filling "nonaccelerating-inflation-rate-of-unemployment." Such a rate may of course vary over time. More generous unemployment compensation will increase it by subsidizing job search, and so will a higher velocity of circulation between jobs. The heterogeneity of both workers and jobs detracts from the usefulness of such estimates, as does the size or the openness of the labor market one has in mind. A shortage of computer programmers in California's Silicon Valley cannot be filled by a surplus of migrant labor in Florida's citrus groves. And free immigration from cheap-labor countries overseas or across a political border can lower natural rates and NAIRUs for jobs that immigrants can fill.

FINAL NOTE

Financial pages and financial journals may tell us that the published unemployment rate, adjusted or unadjusted for seasonal variation, has risen or fallen by one- or two-tenths of 1 percent, and they may go on to forecast what this change may imply for the economy as a whole. All that may have happened is statistical sampling error, and the forecasting may be entirely off base. It is often a mistake to put too much weight on minor changes, and likewise to ignore the failures of statistical comparability over time and space.

7. This is an aspect of *rational expectations* macroeconomics, which we will take up in Chapter 17. One can get the same results by considering search unemployment to be entirely voluntary.

The Keynesian Model of Income Determination

Fiscal Policy

PART III

KEYNESIAN ECONOMICS AND FISCAL POLICY

10
The Keynesian Model of Income Determination

Preview This chapter presents the basic Keynesian model of the macroeconomy. It begins with a brief description of how Keynes disagreed with the macroeconomic model of his time. It explains that Keynes was skeptical of models that suggest that market-capitalist economies necessarily and automatically generate "ideal" outcomes, such as full employment. Instead, Keynes argued that government may be able to improve macroeconomic outcomes.

The chapter explains the basic Keynesian model by referring to the four expenditure pathways (consumption, saving and investment, net taxes and government purchases, and imports and exports) of the circular-flow model. It shows how the Keynesian approach adds these expenditure flows together to develop the concept of total planned expenditure and to predict the equilibrium level of national income and product. The concept of macroeconomic equilibrium generated by the Keynesian model differs sharply from that held by mainstream economists and business people prior to Keynes's time. Most important, in the Keynesian model equilibrium need not correspond with full employment in the economy.

The appendix to this chapter explains how the Keynesian model can identify macroeconomic equilibrium by focusing on funds that are injected into the circular flow and on funds that leak out of that system. The leakage-and-injection procedure results in the same equilibrium conclusions as found through the total-planned-expenditure procedure.

KEYNESIAN ECONOMICS

Keynesian economics is a body of knowledge and a set of principles and procedures that have their roots in the work of the British economist John Maynard Keynes (pronounced "cains"), whose most famous work, *The General Theory of Employment, Interest, and Money,* appeared in 1936.[1] The theory presented in his book explained how government initiatives could bring recovery from the Great Depression that gripped industrialized capitalist countries at that time. Keynesian theory dominated macroeconomic thinking in the 1950s and 1960s, but encountered strong criticism for its inability to deal effectively with the simultaneous problems of inflation and rising unemployment that occurred during the 1970s. Today, the Keynesian school of economic thought faces several competing schools, most notably the monetarist, the new classical, and the supply-side schools. The competing schools, along with the modern Neo-Keynesian school, are explained in later chapters.[2] In this chapter, we explore the original and still basic Keynesian model of the macroeconomy.

Keynesian economics, developed in the 1930s by British economist John Maynard Keynes, has its roots in the inability of the then prevailing theories to adequately explain long periods of serious unemployment in market economies.

Two aspects of the basic Keynesian model are important at this stage of learning macroeconomics. First is the criticism that Keynes directed at the macroeconomic theories that prevailed before the Great Depression. Second is the macroeconomic model that Keynes offered as an alternative explanation of the determination of macroeconomic equilibrium. Keynesians believe that their model is more realistic and therefore more effective than the

1. John M. Keynes, *The General Theory of Employment, Interest, and Money* (New York: Harcourt, Brace and Co., Inc., 1936).

2. The monetarist model is examined in Chapters 12, 13, and 14. New classical, the supply-side, and Neo-Keynesian economics are explained in Chapter 17.

models offered by the competing schools of macroeconomic thought.

Rejection of Say's Identity

At the time Keynes wrote the *General Theory,* most non-Marxist economists were of the neoclassical school of economic thought. **Neoclassical** economists placed great emphasis on the role of suppliers in determining macroeconomic equilibrium and made special use of a proposition known as **Say's Identity,** named after Jean Baptiste Say (1767–1832), a French economist whose *Treatise on Political Economy* appeared in 1803.

The idea behind Say's Identity is that "supply creates its own demand." To understand this proposition, think back to the lower half of the circular-flow diagram—the flow made up of all wages, salaries, rents, interest, and profits in the economy. According to Say's Identity, the sum of all these payments must, by definition, provide enough purchasing power to allow the households to pay for all the goods and services produced at whatever price level was in effect when they were produced. This balance would be true at any given price level.

Of course, neoclassical economists recognized that households would use some of their income for purposes other than consumption and that the proportion so diverted might change from time to time. But they argued that prices, wage rates, and interest rates would move up or down in accordance with market forces so that all funds would complete the circle. For example, if households spent less on consumption, the prices of consumption goods would fall, so that unsold goods would not accumulate. At the same time, the additional funds flowing through the saving, net tax, or import stream would automatically lead to responses that would ensure that they also would complete the circle. Greater saving would lower interest rates in the financial markets, so that businesses would plan to spend more on investment and households would plan to save less. Increased funds in the foreign markets would drive up the relative price of foreign goods, so that there would be fewer imports and more exports. Government budgets, which were expected to balance, would not keep funds from completing the circle. Of course, because of time lags in price changes and in responding to them, there could be temporary changes in economic activity. However, these time lags would be relatively short, so that problems would soon disappear.

According to Say's Identity, the sum of all the wages, salaries, rents, interest, and profits in the economy must provide enough purchasing power to allow households to pay for all the goods and services produced at whatever price level was in effect when they were produced.

Say's Identity led to the conclusion that full employment would be the equilibrium condition in an economy. Flexible wage rates were the basis for this conclusion. If people lost their jobs, they would offer to work for wages a little below the rate currently being paid. They would surely find work, since the wages paid would (by Say's Identity) be just enough to ensure demand for their goods or services at the lower price level that would result. The only people who could remain unemployed would be those refusing to work for a wage that matched the value of the goods or services that they could produce.[3]

Say's Identity led to the conclusion that full employment is the equilibrium condition in an economy.

Keynes rejected the argument that changes in product prices, wage rates, and interest rates will accomplish the tasks assigned to them by Say's identity and the neoclassical economists. There were two dimensions to Keynes's criticism of the neoclassical model. First, he argued that consumer goods prices, interest rates, wage rates, and foreign exchange rates are not flexible enough to assure that all the money received by households will find its way across the top of the circular flow and be

3. This wage theory led to several doctrines with powerful social and political overtones. The so-called ''iron law of wages'' suggested that if population growth followed its ''natural'' course, wages would move toward subsistence levels. From ideas such as this, economics earned the ''dismal science'' label.

received by firms. This position is based on the view that modern economies do not follow competitive pricing practices. Business firms are not strongly pushed by rivals to lower prices when sales volume drops, preferring to lay off workers while unplanned inventories are used up. Also, powerful labor unions are unwilling to lower wage rates even when unemployment is widespread. Without flexibility of prices and wage rates, there is no assurance that ''supply will create its own demand'' and that full employment will exist at equilibrium.

Keynes also argued that changes in prices and wage rates, when and if they do come, may not bring economic recovery from a serious recession. This is because a drastic lowering of the price level will impoverish firms and individuals who incurred debt when the price level was high. If debts cannot be repaid, financial institutions may become bankrupt or unwilling to provide the financing needed to restore production and return the economy to prosperity. Firms that want to launch new products may not be able to borrow the funds needed to get started.

Keynes rejected Say's Identity and neoclassical economics because he believed that prices, interest rates, wage rates, and foreign exchange rates were not flexible enough to maintain the economy at full employment and that even if prices and wage rates were to change, they would not be able to effect economic recovery from a recession.

Aggregate Demand Is Crucial

Although Keynes raised important questions about competing models, his greatest influence came from the theory that aggregate-demand is the crucial determinant of GNP. Figure 1 shows how the aggregate-demand and aggregate-supply graph might be modified to illustrate the Keynesian view that aggregate demand is crucial in determining macroeconomic equilibrium. In this graph, the aggregate-demand curve appears the same as that illustrated in previous chapters, but the aggregate-supply curve is a horizontal line. Making the aggregate-supply curve horizontal is an exaggeration of the Keynesian view, since Keynesians do recognize that the supply side of the economy matters and that increases in aggregate-demand can result in inflation. The horizontal aggregate-supply curve simply reflects the view that an increase in aggregate demand *can*, in an economy with widespread unemployment, result in an increase in the aggregate quantity supplied without a *significant* increase in the price level.

What might explain a horizontal (or near-horizontal) aggregate-supply curve? Part of the Keynesian argument is that business firms choose to let demand changes have their first impact on the volume of sales rather than on prices. Prices, Keynesians say, are "sticky." Another reason for a horizontal (or almost horizontal) aggregate-supply curve is that the Keynesian model focuses on an economy in which there is a significant pool of unemployed resources, as typically is the case in a recession. In a situation with widespread unemployment, output can increase without bidding up input prices and forcing firms to increase product prices.

Keynes believed that aggregate demand is the crucial determinant of macroeconomic equilibrium: in an economy with widespread unemployment, an increase in aggregate demand can result in an increase in aggregate quantity supplied without a significant change in price level.

Focusing on the demand side of the economy, the Keynesian theory provides a detailed explanation of aggregate demand. It provides a system for estimating the flows in each of the four pathways in the upper portion of the circular flow—planned consumption, planned saving and investment, net taxes and government purchases, and imports and exports. According to the Keynesian model, the sum of the planned spending components of these pathways, called **total planned expenditure**, determines equilibrium GNP. Since the price level is not expected to change significantly, the change in equilibrium GNP is both nominal and real.

FIGURE 1
A Keynesian View of Aggregate Supply

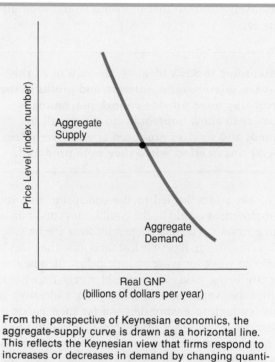

From the perspective of Keynesian economics, the aggregate-supply curve is drawn as a horizontal line. This reflects the Keynesian view that firms respond to increases or decreases in demand by changing quantities supplied rather than by changing prices. Also, the Keynesian approach focuses on situations where significant amounts of unemployed resources are available so that production can be increased without driving resource prices upward.

In the Keynesian model of the macroeconomy, the sum of planned consumption, planned saving and investment, government purchases, and net exports (total planned expenditure) determines equilibrium GNP.

PLANNED CONSUMPTION EXPENDITURE

The planned or intended behavior of consumers is at the heart of the Keynesian model. Consumption expenditure amounts to a large part of national product. It is clear, therefore, that relatively small changes in consumer spending can cause large proportional changes in the funds flowing through the other pathways of the circular flow. If households decide to spend a larger part of their income for consumption goods and services, the proportional impact of this change on the other pathways can be great. It is no surprise that Keynes focused great attention on consumption spending.

The key to the Keynesian model of the macroeconomy is the behavior of consumers. Relatively small changes in consumer spending can cause large proportional changes in the funds flowing through the other pathways of the circular flow.

The Consumption Function

The key idea in the theory of consumer behavior is the **consumption function,** which is the relationship between the amount that households plan to spend to buy consumption goods and services and the level of disposable personal income. More specifically, economists say that the amount of planned consumption purchases (C) *depends on* the amount of disposable personal income (DPI), *ceteris paribus*. Thus, the consumption function can be written

$$C = f(\text{DPI}), ceteris\ paribus$$

For economists using the Keynesian system, the task is to determine precisely the nature of this relationship.

To illustrate how the Keynesian model works, let us specify some values for the consumption function equation and trace through the model. For example, suppose that the consumption function is

$$C = \$100 \text{ billion} + 0.75(\text{DPI})$$

where C is the annual dollar flow for planned consumption purchases and DPI is disposable personal income. We will assume that there is no inflation either taking place or expected, so that the consumption behavior of households is not distorted by misunderstandings (illusions) about real in-

comes or about the real prices of the things they buy. With these assumptions, we can state that the values for planned consumption expenditure and disposable personal income are *real* values. The importance of these assumptions will be clear later in the book, when we study the theory of inflationary expectations.

Table 1 illustrates how the consumption function in our example provides a set of planned consumption and disposable personal income combinations for an economy. Reading the table, we see that if disposable personal income is zero, planned consumption expenditure is $100 billion. Households are obtaining the funds for their consumption purchases by reducing their savings accounts or by going into debt. These sources of funds are negative saving. So, when disposable personal income is zero, planned saving is −$100 billion.

If disposable personal income rises to $100 billion, the second term in our consumption function shows that planned consumption expenditure will rise by $75 billion to a total of $175 billion. But even at this higher level of income, households must fund part ($75 billion) of their planned consumption spending from past saving. According to our consumption function, planned consumption expenditure will equal disposable personal income when DPI has reached $400 billion a year. If DPI is higher than $400 billion, planned consumption can be funded entirely from current income and there will be positive amounts of planned saving.

The consumption function is the relationship between the amount that households plan to spend to buy consumption goods and services and the level of disposable personal income: $C = f(\text{DPI})$.

Marginal Propensities to Consume and Save

Keynesian theory has special names for the two numerical values that appear in the consumption function equation. The first value (the 100 in our illustration) is called **autonomous consumption**

TABLE 1

The Marginal Propensity to Consume (MPC) and the Marginal Propensity to Save (MPS) Based on Disposable Personal Income (DPI)

Disposable Personal Income (DPI) [in billions of dollars]	Planned Consumption Expenditure (C) [in billions of dollars]	Change in Planned Consumption (ΔC) [in billions of dollars]	MPC	Planned Saving (S) [in billions of dollars]	Change in Planned Saving (ΔS) [in billions of dollars]	MPS
$ 0	$100			$−100		
100	175	$75	0.75	− 75	$25	0.25
200	250	$75	0.75	− 50	$25	0.25
300	325	$75	0.75	− 25	$25	0.25
400	400	$75	0.75	0	$25	0.25
500	475	$75	0.75	25	$25	0.25
600	550	$75	0.75	50	$25	0.25
700	625	$75	0.75	75	$25	0.25
800	700	$75	0.75	100	$25	0.25
900	775	$75	0.75	125	$25	0.25
1,000	850			150		

These hypothetical schedules show planned consumption spending and planned savings at different levels of disposable personal income. The illustrated intervals of DPI are $100 billion. Over each interval, planned consumption spending increases by $75 billion and planned saving increases by $25 billion. Therefore, *MPC* = 0.75 and *MPS* = 0.25.

expenditure, meaning that this amount of planned consumption expenditure (C) is independent of the level of disposable personal income (DPI). In Table 1, autonomous consumption expenditure amounts to $100 billion—the amount that would be spent if disposable personal income (DPI) were zero. The amount of autonomous consumption expenditure is determined by variables not included in the equation.

Autonomous consumption expenditure is the amount of planned consumption spending that would take place if disposable personal income were zero; that is, this amount of planned consumption expenditure is independent of the level of DPI.

The second value in the equation (the 0.75 in our illustration) is called the **marginal propensity to consume (MPC)** because it shows how much planned consumption expenditure will be induced by a change in disposable personal in-

come. The *MPC* is expressed as a percentage of any change in the level of disposable personal income. In our equation, when disposable personal income increases by $100 billion, planned consumption expenditure increases by $75 billion, that is, by 75 percent of the change in DPI. Of course, the marginal propensity to consume (*MPC*) works in the opposite direction as well—when disposable personal income falls by $100 billion, planned consumption expenditure falls by $75 billion. Thus, on the basis of the consumption function in our example, the marginal propensity to consume value in Table 1 is calculated as follows:

$$MPC = \frac{\text{change in planned consumption}}{\text{change in disposable personal income}}$$

$$= \frac{\$75 \text{ billion}}{\$100 \text{ billion}} = 0.75$$

The marginal propensity to consume (MPC) expresses a relationship between changes in disposable personal income and changes in

---

planned consumption expenditure. The *MPC* is equal to the change in planned consumption spending divided by the change in disposable personal income that induced it.

In Keynesian theory, the companion to the marginal propensity to consume is the **marginal propensity to save (MPS),** which is the change in planned saving induced by a change in disposable personal income expressed as a percentage of the accompanying change in disposable personal income. If we assume that consumption and saving are the only uses for disposable personal income, $MPC + MPS = 1.0$. The marginal propensity to save value in Table 1 is calculated as follows:

$$MPS = \frac{\text{change in planned saving}}{\text{change in disposable personal income}}$$

$$= \frac{\$25 \text{ billion}}{\$100 \text{ billion}} = 0.25$$

The marginal propensity to save (MPS) is the change in planned saving expressed as a percentage of the change in disposable personal income that induced it.

We have set up the illustration in Table 1 so that *MPC* is 0.75 and *MPS* is 0.25 throughout the whole range of incomes shown. It is not essential to the theory that these values be constant over the whole range of incomes. It is a simplifying assumption for an introductory explanation of the Keynesian model.

Average Propensities to Consume and Save

Average propensities to consume and save should be clearly distinguished from the marginal propensities discussed above. The **average propensity to consume (APC)** is simply the amount of planned consumption expenditure (*C*) divided by the amount of disposable personal income (DPI). Similarly, the **average propensity to save (APS)**

is the amount of planned saving (*S*) divided by the amount of disposable personal income (DPI).

Table 2 illustrates the calculation of *APC* and *APS*, using the data from the same hypothetical consumption function used to illustrate the marginal propensities. Note that the average propensity to consume decreases as disposable personal income increases while the average propensity to save follows the opposite course, increasing as disposable personal income increases. These patterns in the data in Table 2 conform with the widely held belief that consumption absorbs a larger portion of lower incomes than it does of higher incomes. The point here, however, is not whether this widely held belief is true or false. There are, in fact, certain concepts of income—discussed later—where it may be false. At this stage in the explanation of the Keynesian model, the point is to underline the distinction between marginal values and average values in the consumption function. Marginal values, such as *MPC* and *MPS*, focus on what happens at the "growing edge" of changing levels of income. This is the focus that is basic in the Keynesian model. Average propensities also are important but are less critical to an initial understanding of the model. The important thing is to remember the difference between the marginal values and average values.

The average propensity to consume (APC) is the amount of planned consumption expenditure (C) divided by the amount of disposable personal income (DPI). The average propensity to save (APS) is the amount of planned saving (S) divided by the amount of disposable personal income (DPI).

The Keynesian-Cross Graph

Figure 2(a) illustrates the consumption function as the red line on a Keynesian-cross graph.[4] Instead of

4. The term *cross* in the name of this graph comes from the technique of showing equilibrium as the intersection of lines plotted on the graph. The technique is best known from the supply-and-demand graph of Chapter 5. That graph is often called a Marshallian cross, after the great English neoclassical economist Alfred Marshall (1842–1924).

TABLE 2
The Average Propensity to Consume (APC) and the Average Propensity to Save (APS) Based on Disposable Personal Income (DPI)

Disposable Personal Income (DPI) [in billions of dollars]	Planned Consumption Expenditure (C) [in billions of dollars]	Average Propensity to Consume (APC)	Planned Saving (S) [in billions of dollars]	Average Propensity to Save (APS)
0	100	———	−100	———
100	175	1.75	− 75	− .75
200	250	1.25	− 50	− .25
300	325	1.08	− 25	− .08
400	400	1.00	0	.0
500	475	.95	25	.05
600	550	.92	50	.08
700	625	.89	75	.11
800	700	.88	100	.12
900	775	.86	125	.14
1000	850	.85	150	.15

These hypothetical schedules show planned consumption spending and planned saving at different levels of disposable personal income. The average propensity to consume is the amount of planned consumption expenditure divided by the amount of disposable personal income. The average propensity to save is the amount of planned saving divided by the amount of disposable personal income.

price and quantity on the axes, the **Keynesian cross** measures dollar quantities on each of its axes. In Figure 2(a) the vertical axis measures dollars of planned consumption spending, and the horizontal axis measures dollars of disposable personal income. When disposable personal income is zero (at the origin of the graph), planned consumption spending is $100 billion (on the vertical axis). This shows the amount of autonomous consumption expenditure. When disposable personal income rises to $100 billion, planned consumption rises to $175 billion, and so on. The slope of the consumption line shows the marginal propensity to consume. (See Chapter 3 for measuring slope.) The marginal propensity to consume (*MPC*) here is 0.75 over the whole range of disposable personal income (DPI). For this reason, a straight line describes the functional relationship. Thus, our consumption function uses the algebraic equation $C = a + b$ (DPI) where *a* is autonomous consumption and *b* is the marginal propensity to consume.

The Keynesian-cross graph displays some measure of income on its horizontal axis and some measure of expenditure on its vertical axis.

On this graph, we also have drawn a straight line from the origin at a 45-degree angle. This **45-degree line** is very helpful because if the units of measure are the same on both axes (as is true here), the line will connect all points at which the value on one axis is equal to the value on the other axis. The 45-degree line is helpful in another way as well. The vertical distance to the 45-degree line from any specified point on the horizontal axis is equal to the horizontal distance from the origin of the graph to that same point on the horizontal axis. So values measured horizontally from the origin can also be measured vertically by referring to the 45-degree line. In effect, both variables can be compared in the vertical dimension on the graph. The geometry of isosceles right triangles explains why this is so.

In Figure 2(a) the red consumption line crosses this 45-degree line at a DPI of $400 billion. This is the **breakeven point**, since there is neither planned saving nor planned **dissaving** (negative saving, or financing current consumption by drawing on past savings) at this income level. With the 45-degree line, we can show planned saving and dissaving on the same graph with the consumption function. The red wedge-shaped gap between the consumption line and the 45-degree line, to the left of the intersection point, shows planned dissaving. The red wedge-shaped gap to the right of the intersection shows positive planned saving.

FIGURE 2
Consumption Function and Saving Function Based on Disposable Personal Income

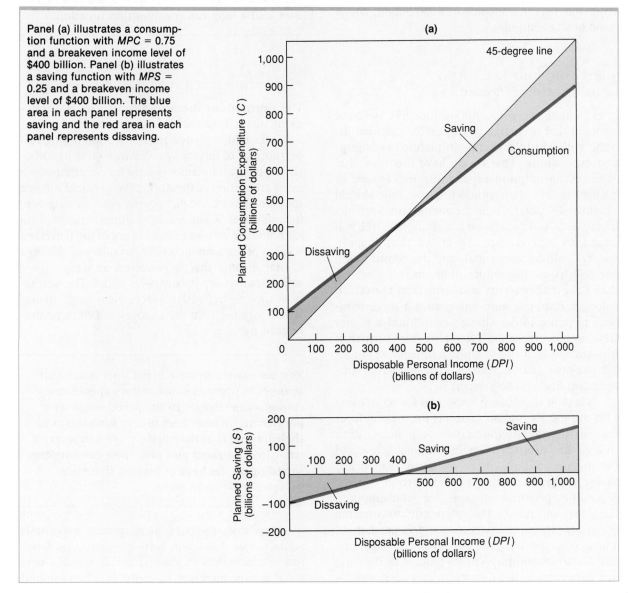

Panel (a) illustrates a consumption function with *MPC* = 0.75 and a breakeven income level of $400 billion. Panel (b) illustrates a saving function with *MPS* = 0.25 and a breakeven income level of $400 billion. The blue area in each panel represents saving and the red area in each panel represents dissaving.

> **Dissaving is negative saving: Financing current consumption by drawing on past savings.**

Figure 2(b) illustrates the saving function, drawn from the same hypothetical data. It is the blue line on this graph. When disposable personal income is zero, planned saving is −$100 billion (dissaving). The slope of the saving line shows the marginal propensity to save (equal to 0.25 in this figure), and the planned amount saved is zero at disposable personal income of $400 billion, which is the breakeven point.

Short-Run and Long-Run Consumption Functions

In explaining the consumption function, we have assumed that a change in disposable personal income will lead to a change in planned consumption expenditure. That is, we have theorized that planned consumption expenditure will *respond* to changes in DPI. How much response time should be allowed? Clearly, time is an important variable. If very little time is allowed, a change in DPI will bring very little change in planned consumption, the *MPC* will be very small, and the consumption line will have only a little slope. In this case, we shall have a **short-run consumption function**. A longer response time will permit a more complete response to the change in DPI and a higher *MPC* until we reach a **long-run consumption function**, which allows enough time for all potential responses to be realized. The long-run consumption line will be steeper.

It is clear that time is important for economists who use the Keynesian concepts for making forecasts or for prescribing economic policies. With enough time to adapt lifestyles to changing levels of DPI, it appears that, in the aggregate, Americans choose to spend about 90 to 95 percent of their disposable personal income for consumption. Thus, the long-run average propensity to consume (*APC*) appears to be between 90 and 95 percent. As it happens, the *marginal* propensity to consume (*MPC*) also is around 90 or 95 percent in the long run. However, in the Keynesian approach, unemployment and inflation are seen as problems that must be treated with short-run remedies. Therefore we shall, in our exposition of the basic Keynesian theory, use *MPC* values much lower than 90 or 95 percent.

> **Time is an important variable in the consumption function. If little response time is allowed, a change in DPI will bring about very little change in planned consumption. The result is a low *MPC* and a short-run consumption function. Longer response time leads to a higher *MPC* and a long-run consumption function.**

The Permanent Income Hypothesis

The **permanent income hypothesis** is a statement about household consumption and saving behavior that is related to short-run and long-run perceptions of income. According to this hypothesis, a household plans to spend for consumption a fixed proportion of the disposable personal income that it believes to be its "permanent," or long-run, income level. Changes in planned consumption spending are responses to changes in the perceived level of permanent income. A corollary of this idea is that income that is perceived as temporary—called **transitory income**—is saved. The permanent income hypothesis places great emphasis on whether households see changes in DPI as permanent or transitory.

> **The permanent income hypothesis states that changes in planned consumption spending are responses to changes in the perceived level of permanent income. People save increments to their income that they believe are temporary (transitory income) and plan their consumption spending on the basis of income that they perceive to be permanent.**

How does the permanent income hypothesis relate to our distinction between short- and long-run consumption functions? As disposable personal income increases, households at first respond as if they believe that the increase in the flow of income is transitory. So, in the short run, the *MPC* is low and the *MPS* is high. However, as time passes, a greater part of the increased income flow is perceived to be permanent. The *MPC* rises and the *MPS* falls. In the long run, the consumption function reflects basic attitudes about spending and thrift that are deeply embedded in the society itself.

In the short run, after a change in DPI the *MPC* is low and the *MPS* is high; in the long run, the *MPC* rises and the *MPS* falls.

Even though we shall be using short-run perspectives in explaining the Keynesian model for equilibrium national income, the permanent income hypothesis is a useful reminder that "perceptions" and "consumer psychology" are important in economics. For example, the question of whether a reduction in taxes would significantly increase consumer spending may depend on whether consumers expect that the reduction will continue year after year or whether they expect that it will be only temporary. So changes in the basic tax structure would be more likely to affect the economy than a one-year cut or hike in taxes.

Taxes and the Consumption Function

The consumption and saving functions illustrated in Table 1 and Figure 2 were calculated on the basis of disposable personal income. However, the problems of inflation and unemployment are more directly related to the concepts of net national product (NNP) and national income (NI) than to disposable personal income (DPI). Therefore, it will be helpful to adjust our consumption function so that it is based on national income and product rather than on disposable personal income. To make this adjustment, recall two points from the explanation of the national income and product accounts discussed in Chapter 7. First, national income and net national product are equal to each other conceptually, even though the accounting system shows a difference due to indirect business taxes and subsidies and the statistical discrepancy. In explaining the Keynesian theory, we will ignore these differences and treat NNP and NI as identical.

We will refer simply to national income or to national income and product and use the symbol Y to denote this value. Second, taxes and transfer payments account for the difference between national income (Y) and disposable personal income (DPI). If we lump taxes and transfer payments together in the concept of "net taxes" (as the term was used in the circular-flow model), we can simply add a value for net taxes to our assumed values for disposable personal income to arrive at values for national income and product.

In the United States, many different types of taxes are used—payroll taxes, individual income taxes, corporation income taxes, sales taxes, and property taxes. The combined effect of all these taxes may be roughly equivalent to a flat-rate tax on all income. However, calculating net tax as a percentage of income adds complications that are not necessary in an elementary explanation of the Keynesian model. Therefore, in adjusting our consumption function from a disposable personal income base to a national income and product base, we will assume that the government collects a "lump-sum tax" of $100 billion, regardless of the level of national income and product.

Table 3 illustrates how the assumed $100 billion lump-sum tax enables us to change the consumption function shown in Table 1 from a disposable personal income base to a national income and product base. All the columns in Table 3, except those in the box on the left side, are the same as in Table 1. The numbers in the box show that national income and product (Y) is higher than disposable personal income (DPI) by the amount of net tax, which we have assumed to be $100 billion at every level of national income and product.

To adjust the consumption function so that it is based on national income and product rather than on disposable personal income, a value for net taxes is added to the value for disposable personal income.

Figure 3 illustrates these consumption and saving functions based on national income and product. Because we have assumed that the amount of net tax is unchanged by changes in the level of

TABLE 3
Marginal Propensity to Consume (MPC) and Marginal Propensity to Save (MPS) Based on National Income and Product (Y)

National Income and Product (Y) [in billions of dollars]	Net Tax [in billions of dollars]	Disposable Personal Income (DPI) [in billions of dollars]	Planned Consumption Expenditure (C) [in billions of dollars]	Change in Planned Consumption (ΔC) [in billions of dollars]	MPC	Planned Saving (S) [in billions of dollars]	Change in Planned Saving (ΔS) [in billions of dollars]	MPS
$ 100	$100	$ 0	$100			$−100		
				$75	0.75		$25	0.25
200	100	100	175			− 75		
				$75	0.75		$25	0.25
300	100	200	250			− 50		
				$75	0.75		$25	0.25
400	100	300	325			− 25		
				$75	0.75		$25	0.25
500	100	400	400			0		
				$75	0.75		$25	0.25
600	100	500	475			25		
				$75	0.75		$25	0.25
700	100	600	550			50		
				$75	0.75		$25	0.25
800	100	700	625			75		
				$75	0.75		$25	0.25
900	100	800	700			100		
				$75	0.75		$25	0.25
1,000	100	900	775			125		
				$75	0.75		$25	0.25
1,100	100	1,000	850			150		

All of the columns except those in the box at the left side are the same as in Table 1. The box at the left shows an amount of net tax ($100 billion) that does not change as a result of changes in the level of national income and product. Therefore, national income and product is uniformly $100 billion larger than disposable personal income.

national income and product, the consumption line in panel (a) and the saving line in panel (b) have the same slopes as they did in Figure 2. Any given amount of planned consumption expenditure and any given amount of planned saving correspond with a level of national income and product that is $100 billion greater than the equivalent level of disposable personal income. In panel (a) of Figure 3, the wedge-shaped gap between the 45-degree line and the consumption line includes both savings and net taxes. The saving line, illustrated in panel (b) intersects the horizontal axis—indicating zero net saving—at $500 billion of national income and product which is made up of $400 billion of consumption expenditure and $100 billion of net taxes.

Shifting the Consumption Function

On the Keynesian-cross graph, planned consumption expenditure (C) is the *dependent* variable and national income and product (Y) is the *inde-*

pendent variable. Changes in the national income and product will cause *movements along* the consumption function line. But the consequences of changes in any other variable will be represented by a relocation, or *shift*, of the line itself. Thus, all nonincome variables are shift variables in the Keynesian-cross graph. Changes in these variables change the *average* propensity to consume, but they need not change the *marginal* propensity to consume.

Clearly, there are many variables that influence consumption and saving—variables that are held unchanged by the *ceteris paribus* assumption attached to the formal statement of the consumption function. For example, if households are stocking up on durable goods (cars, appliances, and the like) after a period of shortages or hard times, planned consumption may be an especially large fraction of income. Also, when financial wealth increases because of a rise in stock market prices, planned consumption may claim a higher fraction of income simply because households feel that they need not set aside as much of their current income as insurance against future financial problems. Expectations play an important role, too. When the outlook is promising, households may spend their incomes more freely than when they are fearful of bad times to come.

The list of nonincome variables that may influence planned consumption expenditure is very long. In the next chapter, we shall consider these matters in greater detail. For the moment, however, it is helpful to note that changes in these variables, indeed changes in *any* variable other than national income and product, may cause *shifts* in the consumption function as illustrated in the Keynesian-cross graph.

FIGURE 3

The Consumption Function and the Saving Function Based on National Income and Product

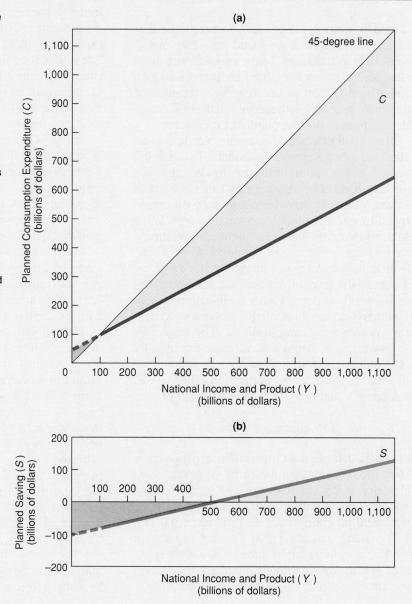

These graphs plot the data in Table 3 relating planned consumption expenditure and planned saving to national income and product. The red consumption line, in panel (a), and the blue saving line, in panel (b), have the same slopes as in Figure 2, when they were plotted in relation to disposable personal income, because the difference between disposable personal income and national income is the amount of net tax, which is assumed to be $100 billion regardless of the level of national income and product. (The dashed segments of these plotted functions extend them to values not shown in Table 3.) In panel (a), the blue area includes both saving and net taxes. In panel (b), the blue area includes only saving. The red area in panel (b) is dissaving. In panel (a), the red area is dissaving minus net taxes.

PLANNED INVESTMENT EXPENDITURE

Planned investment expenditure is the amount that business firms intend to spend on new capital goods, such as machines, tools, and buildings, and to finance the inventories that they plan to have on hand. The historical record suggests that planned investment probably is the most volatile or changeable component of total planned expenditure.

How shall planned investment expenditure be built into the Keynesian model? In building planned consumption into the model, the key proposition was the consumption function, which showed a relation between planned consumption expenditure and disposable personal income. What relationship exists between planned investment and national income and product? Most likely, planned investment expenditure also has a positive relation to the level of national income and product. However, building such a relationship into an elementary explanation of the Keynesian system adds unnecessary complications. Therefore, we will assume that planned investment expenditure is $35 billion regardless of the level of national income and product, *ceteris paribus*. In other words, we assume a planned investment function of

$$I = \$35 \text{ billion}, \textit{ceteris paribus}$$

This states that planned investment expenditure is determined entirely by nonincome, or "shift," variables, that is, by variables other than the level of national income and product. We could state the investment function as $I = \$35$ billion $+ 0.0\ (Y)$, *ceteris paribus*, indicating that planned investment spending is entirely autonomous. On a Keynesian-cross graph, this assumed planned investment function would plot as a straight, horizontal line.

Planned Investment and the Rate of Interest

In the Keynesian model, one of the most important determinants of the amount of planned investment expenditure in an economy is the rate of interest. The rate of interest is one of the variables held unchanged by the *ceteris paribus* assumption attached to the investment function just described. As long as the rate of interest and other variables are unchanged, the amount of planned investment expenditure is, according to the assumed investment function, $35 billion. But if the rate of interest falls, Keynesians predict that planned investment expenditure will increase, and vice versa. To understand the crucial role of the rate of interest, let us review how investment decisions are made in market-capitalist economies.

In a market-capitalist system, investment is made by firms for the purpose of earning profits. For each potential investment project, a business firm makes an estimate of the funds needed to obtain the capital good and the amount of income that it will generate. For example, suppose that a machine can be acquired for $1,000, and that the firm's production cost will be $100 less per year using this machine than using the existing method of production. That is, it will reduce the firm's cost by $100 each year. If we assume, for simplicity, that the machine does not wear out and does not need repairs or maintenance, we can say that the expected rate of return on this investment is 10 percent a year. Should this investment project be carried out? Is it profitable for the firm to use its resources to acquire this machine? The answer will depend on the rate of return that this firm can realize from alternative uses of its resources.

The rate of interest prevailing in the financial markets is a measure of the rate of return that can be realized from alternative uses of the firm's funds.

Therefore, the rate of interest plays a key role in the decision about whether the new machine should be acquired. If the rate of interest is, say, 8 percent, the company in the example just given could borrow $1,000 to acquire the machine and would pay $80 each year in interest to the lender. After the interest is paid, the firm would have $20 more profit each year because of the $100 cut in production cost. If the firm feels sure of this estimate, it will make the investment. If the interest rate had been 12 percent, so that annual interest payments would have been $120, the firm would not make the investment. Profits would be $20 less with the machine than without it.

Let us see how this illustration can be expanded to show a demand curve for planned investment for the whole economy. Instead of just one project with a rate of return of 10 percent, suppose that there are thousands of investment projects, some with rates of return greater than 10 percent and some with rates below 10 percent. Table 4 and Figure 4 show how these thousands of possible investment projects can be displayed as a planned-investment-demand curve. In this hypothetical illustration, $10 billion of possible investments are expected to yield rates of return of more than 14 percent. If the interest rate were 14 per-

FIGURE 4
Demand Curve for Planned Investment

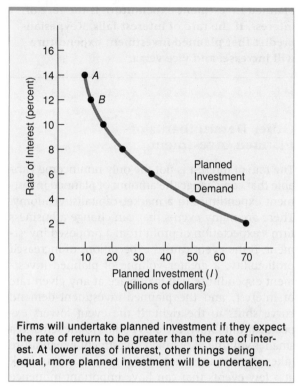

Firms will undertake planned investment if they expect the rate of return to be greater than the rate of interest. At lower rates of interest, other things being equal, more planned investment will be undertaken.

TABLE 4
Demand Schedule for Planned Investment

Rate of Interest (percent)	Planned Investment (in billions of dollars)
14	$10
12	12
10	17
8	25
6	35
4	48
2	70

Planned investment will be undertaken when the rate of return from the investment is expected to be greater than the rate of interest. In this hypothetical illustration, the planned-investment column shows the amount of investment that is expected to have a rate of return greater than the interest rate shown.

cent, all of these projects could be carried out profitably, and the amount of planned investment would be $10 billion (point A in Figure 4). An additional $2 billion of potential investment has an expected rate of return between 12 and 14 percent. If the interest rate were 12 percent, all of these projects, plus the $10 billion of investment yielding more than 14 percent, would be undertaken, so that total planned investment expenditure would be $12 billion. (See point B in Figure 4.) The demand curve for planned investment suggests that the rate of interest is one of the determinants of the volume of planned investment.

In the planned-investment-demand graph, the rate of interest is the *independent* variable that causes changes in the amount of planned investment expenditure—the *dependent* variable. The curve has a negative slope, meaning that falling interest rates bring increased planned investment expenditure and vice versa, *ceteris paribus*.

One of the key determinants of the amount of planned investment expenditure is the rate of interest. If the rate of interest falls, Keynesians predict that planned investment expenditure will increase, and vice versa.

Other nonincome variables that can affect the amount of planned investment expenditure include expected business conditions, changes in operating costs, government policies, and technological changes.

Other Determinants of Planned Investment

The rate of interest is not the only nonincome variable that can change the amount of planned investment expenditure in a market-capitalist economy. There are many events that can change a business firm's expectation of profit from a proposed investment. If the event causes expectations of increased profitability, a greater volume of planned investment expenditure will take place at any given rate of interest, and the planned-investment-demand curve shifts to the right. If the event lowers expected profitability, the curve shifts to the left and a smaller volume of planned investment expenditure takes place at any given rate of interest. Let us look at a few events that can have important influence on the planned-investment-demand curve.

Expected business conditions can be very important. If firms expect sales to increase, the expected rate of return on investments will probably be higher than if they expect sales to drop. The curve will shift to the right as optimism rises and to the left as pessimism grows. When a firm expects changes in the *cost of operating* some of its machines or equipment, the expected rates of return for different investment projects will be rearranged and may cause the curve to shift. *Government policies* relating to taxation or regulation also are important. For example, if Congress enacts a major tax cut, the demand curve for planned investment may shift to the right. On the other hand, laws calling for strict regulation of a major industry may shift the curve to the left. Also of great importance to the location of the planned-investment-demand curve are *technological changes*. A fast rate of technological change may offer substantial profit possibilities and shift the curve to the right, whereas a slowing rate of technological change may move the curve to the left.

GOVERNMENT PURCHASES

Fitting government purchases into the Keynesian model raises many of the same questions considered in our explanation of planned investment expenditure. Once again it is customary and convenient to assume a government-purchases function in which the amount of these purchases is independent of the level of national income and product. We will assume a government-purchases function of

$$G = \$100 \text{ billion, } ceteris \ paribus$$

In other words, we assume a government purchases function $G = \$100$ billion $+ 0.0(Y)$, *ceteris paribus*.

As with our assumed investment function, it probably is unrealistic to assume that the annual volume of government purchases is unrelated to the level of national income and product. In practice, government purchases probably are positively related to the level of national income and product. Nevertheless, in this introduction to the Keynesian system, we will assume that government purchases do not vary as a direct result of changes in the level of national income and product.

There are, of course, many nonincome variables that can influence the volume of government purchases and that are very important in the Keynesian system. These include government policies, domestic and world conditions, the attitudes of voters and taxpayers, and so on. In the Keynesian approach, the policy position taken by the government to deal with macroeconomic unemployment is especially important. As you recall, the neoclassical approach argued against active government intervention in the economy. Keynesians, on the other hand, suggest that government should take forceful action to bring the economy out of recession.

Many nonincome variables, such as government policies, domestic and world conditions, the attitude of voters, etc., can influence the volume of government purchases. Keynesians believe that government should intervene actively in the economy to combat recession.

IMPORTS AND EXPORTS

The import-export path in the circular flow remains to be studied. Again, building this pathway into the Keynesian model raises the question of how the volume of imports and exports (or "net exports") will respond to changes in the level of national income and product.

American purchases from foreigners (imports), like purchases of domestic goods, can be expected to increase as income rises. The reasoning is the same as that offered for planned consumption, planned investment, and for government purchases. Imported goods are probably "normal" in their relation to income, that is, increases in income bring increases in quantities demanded. However, purchases by foreigners from Americans (exports) are less likely to show a predictable response to changes in the U.S. national income and product. Instead, they respond to income changes in the foreign countries themselves, or to changes in foreign exchange rates (which we cover in Chapter 19).

When we combine imports and exports and then seek to find the relationship between "net exports" and national income and product, the normal goods assumption suggests that net exports are a declining function of national income and product. That is, net exports grow smaller as national income and product rises, because *gross* exports will remain the same while *gross* imports grow larger as U.S. national income rises. Americans *will* be buying more from foreign countries, but foreigners will *not* necessarily be buying more from the United States.

In our explanation of the Keynesian model, we assume a net export function of

$$X - Im = \$15 \text{ billion, } ceteris\ paribus$$

meaning that the volume of net exports is unrelated to the level of U.S. national income and product and that changes in net exports are determined by nonincome variables. This is a net export function of $X - Im = \$15$ billion $+ 0.0(Y)$, *ceteris paribus*. This is the same approach used for incorporating planned investment and government purchases into the Keynesian system. Although reality suggests a more complicated functional relationship, these complications can be left to more advanced courses in economics.

We assume that net exports do not change when national income and product changes, although in fact net exports grow smaller as national income and product rises because gross exports remain the same while gross imports grow larger.

EQUILIBRIUM NATIONAL INCOME

We now have studied the four spending streams that make up total planned expenditure. We have given them numerical values so that we can show a functional relationship between national income and product and total planned expenditure. In doing so, we shall, in turn, discover the equilibrium level for national income and product according to the Keynesian model.

Table 5 brings together all four components of planned expenditure. The columns for national income and product and for planned consumption expenditure are the same as those in Table 3. The next three columns—planned investment, government purchases, and net exports—illustrate our assumptions that these spending streams are not altered by changes in national income and product. We assume $35 billion of planned investment, $100 billion of government purchases, and $15 billion of net exports regardless of the level of national income and product. The last column shows

TABLE 5
Total Planned Expenditure and Macroeconomic Equilibrium (in billions of dollars)

(1) National Income and Product (Y)	(2) Planned Consumption Expenditure (C)	(3) Planned Investment Expenditure (I)	(4) Government Purchases (G)	(5) Net Exports (X − Im)	(6) Total Planned Expenditure (C + I + G + X − Im)
$ 100	$100	$35	$100	$15	$ 250
200	175	35	100	15	325
300	250	35	100	15	400
400	325	35	100	15	475
500	400	35	100	15	550
600	475	35	100	15	625
700	550	35	100	15	700
800	625	35	100	15	775
900	700	35	100	15	850
1,000	775	35	100	15	925
1,100	850	35	100	15	1,000

Columns 1 and 2 repeat data from Table 3. Columns 3, 4, and 5 illustrate our assumptions that the planned investment, government purchases, and net export spending streams are not altered by changes in national income and product. Column 6 shows the total of columns 2 through 5. Equilibrium exists when total planned expenditure equals national income and product ($700 billion).

the total planned expenditure corresponding to each level of national income and product, that is, $C + I + G + X − Im$. Macroeconomists devote a great deal of effort to finding accurate values for the components of total planned expenditure. However, for the purpose of introducing you to the theory, these hypothetical numbers are convenient.

The values in Table 5 indicate that the conditions for equilibrium exist when national income and product is $700 billion. This is shown by the row of numbers with the white background. For income levels of *less* than $700 billion, total planned expenditure is greater than production, so that inventories go down. As you learned from the circular flow, this is a case in which pressures arise for greater production and/or higher prices in the next production period. On the other hand, for all income levels *greater* than $700 billion, total planned expenditure is less than production. So unplanned inventory piles up, and there are pressures to lower production and/or prices in the next period. Only at a national income and product level of $700 billion are production and total planned expenditure equal. Here we have the condition for equilibrium national income and product. If we let the symbol

$Y*$ represent the equilibrium level of national income and product, we can state this equilibrium condition as

$$Y* = C + I + G + X − Im$$

This equation states that the equilibrium level of national income and product is determined by total planned expenditure.

Figure 5 shows this relationship on a Keynesian-cross graph. National income and product appears on the horizontal axis and planned expenditure on the vertical axis. The red consumption-function line (C) is the same as in Figure 3. Total planned expenditure is represented by the purple line labeled $C + I + G + X − Im$. This line lies above the consumption-function line by the amount of the other expenditure streams—planned investment (I), government purchases (G), and net exports (X − Im). The total-planned-expenditure line ($C + I + G + X − Im$) is parallel with the consumption-function line because we have assumed that each expenditure stream other than planned consumption is independent of the level of national income and product.

FIGURE 5
Macroeconomic Equilibrium Illustrated on a Keynesian-Cross Graph

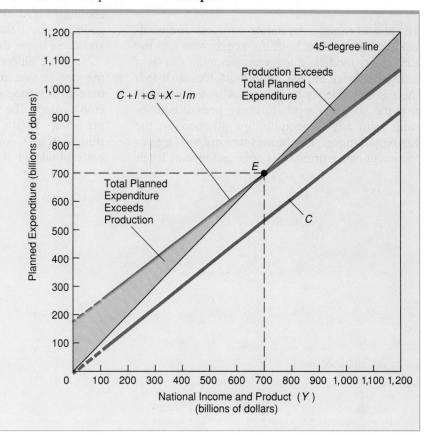

Planned consumption expenditure (C) is the same as in Figure 3. Planned investment expenditure (I), government purchases (G), and net exports (X − Im) are added on top of the red planned-consumption-expenditure line to show the purple total-planned-expenditure line C + I + G + X − Im. Macroeconomic equilibrium is at E, where total planned expenditure of $700 billion equals national income and product of $700 billion. At lower levels of national income and product, total planned expenditure exceeds production (as shown by the red area) so that inventories are drawn down, generating pressures for expansion. At national income and product levels above $700 billion, production exceeds total planned expenditure (as shown by the purple area) so that excess inventories accumulate, generating pressures for contraction of the economy. (The dashed lines extend to include data not shown in tables.)

The total-planned-expenditure line (C + I + G + X − Im) crosses the 45-degree line at the $700 billion level of national income and product. This intersection point identifies the equilibrium condition (E). To the left of this intersection, total planned expenditure is greater than production, as shown by the red space between the C + I + G + X − Im line and the 45-degree line. So inventories are driven down, and pressures for expansion are generated. To the right of the intersection point, total planned expenditure is less than production by amounts shown by the purple space. Unplanned inventory begins to pile up, and there are pressures to lower production and/or prices in the next period. Only at a national income and product level of $700 billion is there a balance among the opposing forces such that there is no tendency for change—that is, equilibrium.

It is important to remember that, in the Keynesian model, equilibrium is not necessarily a desirable situation for the economy. Serious unemployment may exist, or the economy may be plagued by inflation. All the model shows is that the economy will tend to move toward its equilibrium situation. Whether that situation is good or bad and whether something should be done to change the equilibrium point are matters of public policy.

Macroeconomic equilibrium exists when total planned expenditure equals national income and product: Y* = C + I + G + X − Im. In the Keynesian model, equilibrium can exist despite serious unemployment.

KEYNESIAN VERSUS NEOCLASSICAL EQUILIBRIUM

The idea of equilibrium national income and product is at the heart of both the neoclassical and the Keynesian models. Each views equilibrium as a state of balance among opposing forces such that there is no tendency for change. Also, both suggest that the economy tends to move toward equilibrium from any nonequilibrium situation. In the Keynesian model, inventories that are too large or too small cause firms to change production levels and thereby move the economy toward equilibrium. In the neoclassical model, disequilibrium conditions lead to changes in wage rates, prices of goods, interest rates, and foreign-exchange rates, and these move the economy toward equilibrium.

A basic difference between the Keynesian and the neoclassical models is the latter's prediction that, in the long run, equilibrium will bring full employment. The Keynesian model offers no such prediction. In the Keynesian model, the equilibrium level of national income and product need *not* correspond to full employment.

Economics in Focus

Consumer Psychology: Exploring the Mysteries of the Consumption Function

In late 1988, while economists and financial analysts worried about inflation, American consumers continued to spend freely. Although the Federal Reserve had acted to raise interest rates and cool the economy, consumers seemed to be paying little attention. In fact, the Index of Consumer Confidence, a measure of the optimism with which consumers view the economic future, jumped to its highest point in twenty years.

How could consumers remain so confident, and so free with their dollars, while economists were issuing dire warnings and short-term interest rates had risen 2.5 to 3 percentage points in the previous twelve months? First, the short-term interest rates did not greatly affect most consumers; their VISA and MasterCard rates might go up, but only after a fairly substantial lag. Also, if they paid off their balances quickly, the total interest costs increased only a small amount. Even for a relatively large purchase, such as a new car, the monthly payments did not rise enough to discourage most people. Second, and probably more important, disposable personal income (DPI) had continued to grow, partly because of the rise in employment. Consumers simply had more money available than they had the year before. According to some estimates, the percentage jump in consumer spending from the fourth quarter of 1987 to the fourth quarter of 1988 almost exactly matched the percentage growth in DPI. This parallel illustrates the close connection between DPI and consumer spending predicted by the Keynesian model.

But the continual shifts in consumer psychology are difficult to anticipate. A few months after the 1988 buying binge, car sales slowed, as did house sales and general retail sales. The growth in consumer spending eroded considerably in the first quarter of 1989. Consumer confidence had dropped. But—and this was the puzzling part—personal-income growth continued to accelerate, and disposable income was increasing much faster than spending. Thus the money was still available, but now it was being used to swell savings accounts and other financial assets.

Why did consumers, after speeding through the early stop signs, become suddenly cautious? The rise in interest rates must finally have produced its predicted effect. But this was a delayed reaction at best, and no one knew whether the downturn in consumer spending would continue or reverse itself. Although most economists believe in certain general principles of consumer psychology, accurately predicting which way the public will turn at a given moment can be difficult or impossible. Many factors, such as political news, overseas events, even the weather can have unforeseen impacts. Some say that such unpredictability makes economics an inexact science; but it also makes the field continually surprising and challenging.

Sources: Gene Koretz, "Why the Fed Can't Seem to Brake the Buying Binge," *Business Week*, January 23, 1989, p. 26; James C. Cooper and Kathleen Madigan, "Slower Growth? The Jury Still Can't Reach a Verdict," *Business Week*, May 15, 1989, pp. 27–28; Henry F. Myers, "Talk of Stagflation: Hot Issue or Hot Air?" *Wall Street Journal*, April, 24, 1989, p. A1; "The Fed Can't Lick Inflation Single-Handed," *Business Week*, April 10, 1989, p. 104; Jeffrey M. Laderman, "Is It Inflation? Recession? Or Just Spring Fever?" *Business Week*, April 10, 1989, pp. 70–71.

SUMMARY

1. The Keynesian approach to macroeconomic equilibrium was presented by the British economist John Maynard Keynes in his book, *The General Theory of Employment, Interest, and Money,* which appeared in 1936. (See page 192.)

2. Keynesian economists reject models, such as the neoclassical model and Say's Identity, that rely on flexible prices, wage rates, interest rates, and foreign-exchange rates to maintain the economy at equilibrium and to assure that full employment is the normal equilibrium situation. They believe that prices are not in fact flexible enough to assure this and that, even if prices were to fall drastically in a recession, the resulting distress among debtors and financial institutions would prevent the economy from recovering promptly. (See pages 192–193.)

3. An aggregate-supply curve representing the Keynesian approach in macroeconomics would be almost horizontal. This is because Keynesian economists believe that firms prefer to permit the initial impact of demand changes to fall on output rather than on prices and because Keynesians often concentrate on situations in which significant quantities of unemployed resources are available. For these reasons, prices are "sticky." In the Keynesian model, aggregate demand is the primary determinant of real GNP. (See pages 193–194 and Figure 1, page 194.)

4. The Keynesian theory uses the concept of the consumption function, which is a relationship between the level of disposable personal income and the amount of planned consumption expenditure in the economy. The marginal propensity to consume (*MPC*) expresses a relationship between changes in disposable personal income and changes in planned consumption expenditure. Autonomous consumption expenditure is the amount of planned consumption spending that would take place if disposable personal income were zero. (See pages 195–196.)

5. Saving is also a function of disposable personal income. The marginal propensity to save (*MPS*) is the relation between changes in disposable personal income and changes in planned saving. (See page 197.)

6. The value of the marginal propensity to consume is smaller when only a little time is allowed for households to respond to income changes than when more time is allowed to respond. The permanent income hypothesis states that people save increments to their income that they believe to be temporary or "transitory." As more time passes after a change in level of income, a larger part of the change is seen as "permanent" and available for expenditure on consumption. (See page 197.)

7. The Keynesian cross is a graph that displays national income and product on its horizontal axis and planned expenditure on its vertical axis. A 45-degree reference line is drawn from the origin of the Keynesian-cross graph. (See pages 197–200 and Figure 2, page 199.)

8. Adjustments for taxes allow consumption and saving functions to be calculated on a basis of national income and product rather than on a basis of disposable personal income. (See pages 201–202 and Table 3, page 202.)

9. Planned investment expenditure is an important component of the Keynesian theory. The rate of interest is a determinant of planned investment expenditure, as are also other considerations that affect business expectations about the profitability of investments. Government purchases and net exports also are important components of the Keynesian theory. (See pages 204–207.)

10. Total planned expenditure combines all streams of planned spending. In the Keynesian model, macroeconomic equilibrium exists when total planned expenditure equals national income and product, as indicated by the equation $Y^* = C + I + G + X - Im$. According to the Keynesian theory, this equilibrium need not correspond with full employment. (See pages 207–209 and Table 5, page 208.)

11. If national income and product is greater than total planned expenditure, inventories become larger than desired by business firms, leading them to reduce prices and/or output, thus lowering the level of national income and product. If national income and product is less than total planned expenditure, inventories will fall below the levels desired by business firms, leading them to increase prices and/or output, thus causing national income and product to rise. (See pages 207–209 and Figure 5, page 209.)

KEY TERMS

autonomous consumption expenditure: in the consumption function equation, it is the amount of planned consumption expenditure (C) that is independent of the level of disposable personal income (DPI) (page 195).

average propensity to consume (APC): the amount of planned consumption expenditure (C) divided by the amount of disposable personal income (DPI) (page 197).

average propensity to save (APS): the amount of planned saving (S) divided by the amount of disposable personal income (DPI) (page 197).

breakeven point: the income level at which there is neither net planned saving nor net planned dissaving (page 199).

consumption function: the relationship between the amount that households plan to spend to buy consumption goods and services and the level of disposable personal income (page 195).

dissaving: negative saving, or financing current consumption by drawing on past savings (page 199).

45-degree line: a straight line drawn at a 45-degree angle from the origin of a diagram, such as the Keynesian cross. If the units of measure are the same on both axes, the line will connect all points at which the value on one axis is equal to the value on the other axis (page 198).

injections: planned expenditures other than consumption purchases, that is, planned investment (I), government purchases (G), and exports (X) (page 215).

Keynesian cross: a graph that measures dollar amounts of spending on the vertical axis and dollar amounts of income on the horizontal axis (page 198).

Keynesian economics: an approach to macroeconomics developed by John Maynard Keynes in the 1930s that emphasizes the importance of demand in determining the equilibrium level of national income and product (page 192).

leakages: household uses of funds for other than consumption purchases, that is, saving (S), net taxes (T_n), and imports (Im) (page 215).

long-run consumption function: the relationship between a change in disposable personal income and the resulting change in planned consumption expenditure after enough time has elapsed for all potential responses to occur (page 200).

marginal propensity to consume (MPC): the value in the consumption function equation that shows how much planned consumption expenditure will change as a percentage of the associated change in the level of disposable personal income (page 196).

marginal propensity to save (MPS): the change in planned saving expressed as a percentage of the associated change in disposable personal income (page 197).

neoclassical: a school of economic thought that concludes that the macroeconomy tends toward equilibrium at full employment (page 192).

permanent income hypothesis: a hypothesis that states that a household plans to spend for consumption a fixed proportion of the disposable personal income that it believes to be its permanent, or long-run, income level (page 200).

Say's Identity: a proposition that states that the sum of all the wages, salaries, rents, interest, and profits in the economy must provide enough purchasing power to allow households to pay for all the goods and services produced at whatever price level was in effect when they were produced (page 192).

short-run consumption function: the relationship between a change in disposable personal income and the resulting change in planned consumption expenditure before enough time has elapsed for all the potential responses to be achieved (page 200).

total planned expenditure: the sum of planned consumption, planned investment, government purchases, and net exports (page 194).

transitory income: income that is perceived as temporary as distinguished from income that is perceived as permanent (page 200).

DISCUSSION QUESTIONS

1. Explain how Say's Identity provides a basis for arguing that an economy will tend to operate at full employment. If planned saving temporarily exceeds planned investment, how, according to this theory, would interest rates change? What would be the effect of this change?

2. Keynes challenged neoclassical macroeconomic theory by claiming that prices, wage rates, and interest rates actually do not change as quickly as the neoclassical economists believed. Describe one current government policy or program that relates to these adjustments. Does this policy or program strengthen or weaken the neoclassical adjustment mechanism?

3. If planned consumption spending increases by $80 billion whenever disposable personal income increases by $100 billion, what is the value of the marginal propensity to consume? What is the value of the marginal propensity to save? Given these values, what will be the breakeven level of disposable personal income if planned consumption spending is $50 billion when disposable personal income is zero?

4. If real disposable personal income in the United States goes up by $100 billion and enough time passes so that the long-run consumption function can be effective, by about how much would planned consumption spending increase? How would this increase differ if a shorter time period were being used? Give reasons for your answer.

5. According to the permanent income hypothesis, what do people do with an increase in income that they view as only temporary? If you were to win a large amount of money in a lottery, how much of your winnings would go to a higher day-to-day level of living and how much would go

into your savings account or to purchase something special that you had wanted for a long time? How much of that something special would be used up during the first year?

6. Without looking at Figure 4, draw the demand curve for planned investment, carefully labeling the variables shown on each axis. Now compare your graph with Figure 4 to be sure you have it right. How does the rate of return on a particular investment project determine its position along this demand curve? Name one change that would shift this curve to the left and one that would shift it to the right.

7. The assumption that in the short run government purchases do not change in response to changes in national income and product is useful to simplify the presentation of the Keynesian theory. The assumption *does* allow government purchases to change in response to policy actions. Explain whether this change should be shown as a shift or as a movement along a government-purchases curve graphed on a Keynesian-cross diagram.

8. In this chapter, total planned expenditure was $175 billion when national income and product was zero and the marginal propensity to consume was 0.75. Under these conditions, equilibrium national income and product was $700 billion. If equilibrium national income and product is Y^*, we can say that $Y^* = 175 + 0.75Y^*$. Solve this equation for Y^* to assure yourself that it works. Then test your understanding by assuming that the marginal propensity to consume is 0.80. What would the equilibrium national income and product be in that case?

9. The Keynesian equilibrium described at the end of this chapter differs sharply from the neoclassical theory on the matter of unemployment. Explain the nature of this difference.

Appendix:
The Leakage-and-Injection
Version of
the Keynesian Model

As an alternative to the concept of total planned expenditure, the Keynesian model can explain the equilibrium level of national income and product by using the concepts of **leakages** and **injections.** Leakages are household uses of funds for other than consumption purchases. That is, leakages consist of saving (S), net taxes (T_n), and imports (Im). Injections are planned expenditures other than consumption purchases, that is, planned investment (I), government purchases (G), and exports (X). Because imports are separated from exports in this analysis, investment and government purchases include only purchases of domestic (home) outputs. Thus, our notation for injections is that government purchases are G_d and planned investment expenditure is I_d, where the subscript stands for "domestic." With these definitions, macroeconomic equilibrium exists when planned injections equal planned leakages, that is, when

$$I_d + G_d + X = S + T_n + Im$$

Table 6 provides hypothetical values for injections and leakages related to various levels of national income and product. The values are the same as those used to explain the total-planned-expenditure method. This means that we assume that the investment and government purchases discussed there were all from domestic producers and that all imports were household purchases of consumption goods and services.

In Table 6, the injections columns for planned domestic investment (I_d) and for government domestic purchases (G_d) are taken directly from Table 5. For the other injection, exports (X), we use a constant value of $25 billion. In the leakages section, the numbers for planned saving and net taxes

are taken directly from Table 3, which showed the saving function and net taxes equal to $100. For imports (Im), we use a constant $10 billion in our example. We realize that it is unrealistic to assume that changes in national income and product do not change imports, but we make this assumption to simplify our explanation of the Keynesian system. Of course, exports of $25 billion minus imports of $10 billion equal the net export figure of $15 billion used in the explanation of total planned expenditure.

Leakages are household uses of funds for other than consumption purposes. Injections are planned expenditures other than consumption purchases.

Macroeconomic equilibrium exists when total leakages equal total injections, so that they offset each other. This occurs when they are both equal to $160 billion, when national income and product is $700 billion (the row of numbers with the white background in Table 6). This equilibrium point is shown at E in Figure 6, where the purple line for injections $(I_d + G_d + X)$ and the blue line for leakages $(S + T_n + Im)$ cross. At national income and product levels of less than $700 billion, total injections are greater than total leakages. So inventories are driven down below the desired levels, and there are pressures to raise production and/or prices in the next period. But when national income and product levels are higher than $700 billion, total leakages are greater than total injections, inventories become larger than desired, and pressures grow to lower production and/or prices. Note

TABLE 6
Injections and Leakages (in billions of dollars)

National Income and Product (Y)	Injections				Leakages			
	I_d +	G_d +	X =	Total	S +	T_n +	Im =	Total
$ 100	$35	$100	$25	$160	$-100	$100	$10	$ 10
200	35	100	25	160	$-$ 75	100	10	35
300	35	100	25	160	$-$ 50	100	10	60
400	35	100	25	160	$-$ 25	100	10	85
500	35	100	25	160	0	100	10	110
600	35	100	25	160	25	100	10	135
700	35	100	25	160	50	100	10	160
800	35	100	25	160	75	100	10	185
900	35	100	25	160	100	100	10	210
1,000	35	100	25	160	125	100	10	235
1,100	35	100	25	160	150	100	10	260

The hypothetical values for planned domestic investment (I_d) and government domestic purchases (G_d) are taken from Table 5. Exports (X) are assumed to be constant at $25 billion. Values for planned saving (S) and net taxes (T_n) are taken directly from Table 3. Imports (Im) are assumed to be constant at $10 billion. Equilibrium exists when total injections equal total leakages so that they offset each other. Equilibrium is illustrated by the row of numbers with a white background. Notice that equilibrium does not require a balance in each separate stream of the circular flow. In this illustration, planned saving exceeds planned domestic investment at equilibrium, but there is an excess of exports over imports.

that it is *not* necessary to have a balance in each separate stream of the circular flow. In our illustration of equilibrium, saving exceeds domestic investment, but exports exceed imports.

Macroeconomic equilibrium exists when planned injections equal planned leakages: $I_d + G_d + X = S + T_n + Im$.

You should be warned of possible confusion in comparing the injection–leakage approach with the planned-expenditure approach. The problem arises because of the different ways of treating imports. Using the injection–leakage approach, we record imports as a leakage and exports as an injection. However, when we use the planned-expenditure approach, we combine the two as "net exports." Therefore, in terms of our graphs, the wedges shown for total planned expenditure in Figure 5 are *not* the same as the wedges for injec-

tions and leakages in Figure 6. Since we believe it is easier to understand and more directly related to policy making, we shall depend on the total-planned-expenditure method rather than on injections and leakages.

DISCUSSION QUESTIONS

1. Write an algebraic statement showing that leakages are equal to injections when the economy is at equilibrium. Explain what would be wrong with this statement if investment and government purchases were not limited to domestic purchases.

2. Without looking at Figure 6, draw the graphic illustration of the leakages and injections model of equilibrium. Check to be sure you have it right. Why does the leakages line slope upward? Does each leakage component contribute to this slope? Discuss whether it is realistic to draw the injections line as horizontal.

FIGURE 6
Macroeconomic Equilibrium Illustrated on a Leakages-and-Injections Graph

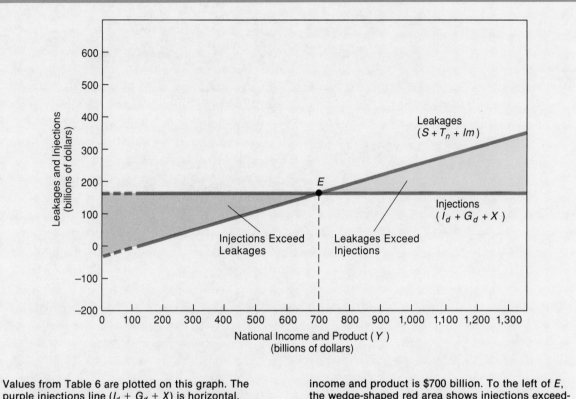

Values from Table 6 are plotted on this graph. The purple injections line ($I_d + G_d + X$) is horizontal, reflecting the assumption that none of these values changes because of a change in national income and product. The blue leakage line ($S + T_n + Im$) has a positive slope equal to the marginal propensity to save, since net taxes (T_n) and imports (Im) are assumed to be unchanged by changes in the level of national income and product. Equilibrium is at E, where injections are equal to leakages, and national income and product is $700 billion. To the left of E, the wedge-shaped red area shows injections exceeding leakages, reducing inventories below desired levels and generating pressures for expansion of the economy. To the right of E, the wedge-shaped blue area shows leakages exceeding injections so that inventories become larger than desired, generating pressures for contraction of the economy. (The dashed lines extend to include data not shown in Table 6.)

11
Fiscal Policy

Preview   What good is all this analysis? Can it tell us anything about what caused the Great Depression of the 1930s or about the possibility of it happening again? According to the Keynesian system, what tools can the government use to deal with inflation and unemployment? What can it do to prevent or to control these problems?

In this chapter we begin our study of the instruments or tools that a government can use to influence the aggregate performance of the economy. Here we consider the fiscal instruments, which make use of the taxing and spending powers of the government and which affect the government's budget.

We begin by discussing the target levels of national income and product. These are the levels that are thought to have the most desirable effects on employment, prices, and growth rates, as well as on other elements of the national economy. Congress, the president, and officials in various government agencies all take part in setting these targets.

Next we describe gaps between the target level of national income and product and the level that will prevail if the government takes no special action. An expansionary gap means that, if left to itself, the economy will expand beyond the target. A contractionary gap means that, if the economy is left to itself, national income and product will be less than the target.

The third part of the chapter explains the *multiplier* relationship that connects a change in total planned expenditure with the resulting change in equilibrium national income and product.

In the final part of the chapter, we describe the fiscal instruments that the government can use to alter total planned expenditure and move the economy to the target level of national income and product. These instruments include changes in planned government purchases, changes in planned tax collections, and changes in both at the same time. We show how the multiplier process operates in response to the use of the different fiscal instruments. We also describe how certain government programs work automatically to stabilize the economy.

The appendix to the chapter describes how the national debt is created and discusses the impact of the debt on the economy.

TARGET LEVELS OF NATIONAL INCOME AND PRODUCT

As noted in Chapter 10, Keynesians argue that the economy, left to its own adjustment mechanisms, may operate for long periods of time at levels of national income and product far lower than the level seen as desirable. During such lengthy recessions, a great amount of potential production can be lost and living standards can be depressed for large segments of the society. According to Keynesians, appropriate policy initiatives can shorten periods of recession, reduce the amount of lost production, and stabilize living standards.

According to the Keynesian model, public policies can influence the volume of total planned expenditure ($C + I + G + X - Im$) and thereby change the equilibrium level of national income and product in the economy. Therefore, the first step in putting the Keynesian model into practical operation is to identify a desired **target level of national income and product.** This is the level chosen through political processes as a goal for macroeconomic policy. It may include a target for real production and for the inflation rate as well.

Keynesian economists believe that public policies can influence the volume of total planned expenditure and thereby change the equilibrium level of national income and product. Before government policies can be put in place, government officials must identify a desired target level of national income and product.

Setting appropriate targets requires forecasts of the production capability of the economy. Several

agencies of the United States government are engaged in this task. In the executive branch of the government, the **Council of Economic Advisers (CEA),** which was established by the **Employment Act of 1946,** is particularly involved in this forecasting, since the council is responsible for advising the president on economic policy. For the legislative branch, similar work is done by the staff of the **Joint Economic Committee (JEC)** of Congress. Both use data provided by other agencies, such as the departments of commerce, labor, agriculture, and treasury. The CEA and the JEC receive reports on the amount of production in recent years and the labor, capital, and natural resource inputs used. Productivity data are calculated, showing output per hour of labor and per unit of capital. To make the forecast of production capability for a future time period, these agencies estimate the amounts of labor, capital and natural resources that will be available and multiply by their estimates of productivity.

There are many crucial judgments that must be made in setting the target level for national income and product the nation should try to achieve. The basic judgment is about the level of employment to seek. There is no iron-clad number that represents full employment as there is divided opinion as to the magnitude of the natural rate of unemployment. If the target is set too high—at an output and employment level that cannot be reached—attempts to reach the target may result in inflation. On the other hand, setting the target too low can result in failure to make full use of the nation's resources and impose hardships on the unemployed.

Choosing a target level involves making many crucial judgments, especially about the level of employment to seek.

In the United States, targets for national income and product usually are not formally spelled out in legislation.[1] Instead, they are considered when taxing and spending proposals are drafted

---

1. An exception is the **Humphrey-Hawkins Act of 1978,** which set specific goals for both price stability and employment but provided no enforcement mechanism to assure that these goals would be achieved.

and presented to Congress. The targets and the desirability of achieving them are used in arguments seeking legislative and citizen support. Different interest groups and political parties are likely to promote different targets as desirable and achievable. For our purpose of explaining government fiscal policies and instruments, it is the concept of a target level of national income and product that is important.

CONTRACTIONARY AND EXPANSIONARY GAPS

Contractionary or expansionary gaps exist when forecasts indicate that the performance of the economy will not match the target, or desired level, of national income and product. In other words, economists with the Council of Economic Advisers and the Joint Economic Committee forecast the volume of total planned expenditure and the corresponding equilibrium level of national income and product for some coming time period on the assumption that present economic programs remain in effect. Then they compare their forecasts with the target levels that have been set by policymakers to find out whether the economy will hit the target or whether a contractionary or an expansionary gap will exist. A **contractionary gap** exists if the predicted equilibrium level of national income and product is less than the target. An **expansionary gap** exists if the predicted equilibrium level of national income and product exceeds the target.

A contractionary gap exists if the predicted equilibrium level of national income and product is less than the target. An expansionary gap exists if the predicted equilibrium level of national income and product exceeds the target.

Contractionary Gaps

When a contractionary gap exists, Keynesian economists expect macroeconomic unemployment and idle production capacity in the economy. Figure 1 pictures such a gap. The $C + I + G + X - Im$ curve

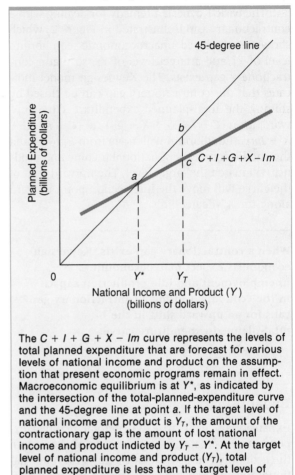

FIGURE 1
A Contractionary Gap

The $C + I + G + X - Im$ curve represents the levels of total planned expenditure that are forecast for various levels of national income and product on the assumption that present economic programs remain in effect. Macroeconomic equilibrium is at Y^*, as indicated by the intersection of the total-planned-expenditure curve and the 45-degree line at point a. If the target level of national income and product is Y_T, the amount of the contractionary gap is the amount of lost national income and product indicted by $Y_T - Y^*$. At the target level of national income and product (Y_T), total planned expenditure is less than the target level of national income and product by the distance from point b to point c.

represents the volume of total planned expenditure that is expected at various levels of national income and product if there are no changes in existing programs. So the equilibrium condition will be at point a, where this curve crosses the 45-degree line. The equilibrium level of national income and product is Y^*, but the target level is Y_T. Because the equilibrium is less than the target, there is a contractionary gap. The implication is that, if left alone, the economy will operate below the desired level, Y_T, that macroeconomic unemployment will exist, and that production of some goods and services will be lost. The size of the contractionary gap is equal to $Y_T - Y^*$. Total planned expenditure is too small to enable the economy to reach the target level of national income and product.

The basic Keynesian remedy for dealing with a contractionary gap is illustrated in Figure 2, which shows a predicted macroeconomic equilibrium level of Y^* and a target level of Y_T, so that a contractionary gap exists. The Keynesian model indicates that this contractionary gap can be closed by shifting the total-planned-expenditure curve upward, from $(C + I + G + X - Im)_1$ to $(C + I + G + X - Im)_2$. Equilibrium will move from E_1 to E_2 and the equilibrium level of national income and product will match the target level. The upward shift of the curve will move the intersection point upward along the 45-degree line.

When a contractionary gap exists, Keynesian economists expect macroeconomic unemployment and idle production capacity in the economy. Closing a contractionary gap calls for an upward shift in the total-planned-expenditure curve.

Expansionary Gaps

Expansionary gaps arise when total planned expenditure is greater than the value of the output the economy can provide at the target level of national income and product. These gaps are generally associated with shortages and inflationary pressures on the economy. Figure 3 pictures this situation. Here the forecast equilibrium level of economic activity, Y^*, is greater than the target, Y_T. If the target has been set at full employment or capacity production, the expansionary gap means that planned spending will be greater than production as measured at the existing price level.

In the Keynesian approach, closing an expansionary gap calls for a downward shift in the total-planned-expenditure curve. This is illustrated in Figure 4. The inflationary pressures being generated at equilibrium E_1 can be relieved by shifting the total-planned-expenditure curve downward, from $(C + I + G + X - Im)_1$ to $(C + I + G + X - Im)_2$. This will move the equilibrium from point E_1 to point E_2, so that macroeconomic equilibrium

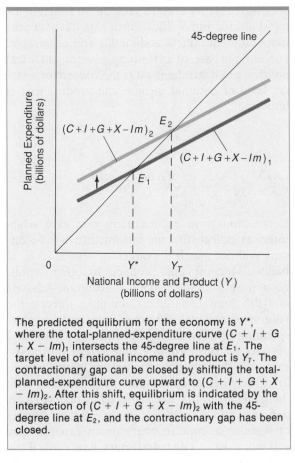

FIGURE 2
Closing a Contractionary Gap

The predicted equilibrium for the economy is Y^*, where the total-planned-expenditure curve $(C + I + G + X - Im)_1$ intersects the 45-degree line at E_1. The target level of national income and product is Y_T. The contractionary gap can be closed by shifting the total-planned-expenditure curve upward to $(C + I + G + X - Im)_2$. After this shift, equilibrium is indicated by the intersection of $(C + I + G + X - Im)_2$ with the 45-degree line at E_2, and the contractionary gap has been closed.

will correspond with the target level of national income and product.

When an expansionary gap exists, Keynesian economists expect shortages and pressure for inflation. Closing an expansionary gap calls for a downward shift in the total-planned-expenditure curve.

Although the Keynesian prescription for dealing with an expansionary gap is clear, the Keynesian system was designed for recession situations—not for situations in which the equilibrium GNP (Y^*) exceeds the target GNP (Y_T). For real GNP levels greater than the target level, Keynesians do not see the aggregate-supply curve as horizontal, that is, they do *not* see the *AS* curve as in the illustration of the Keynesian view in Figure 1 of Chapter 10. Instead, they expect the *AS* curve to slope upward so that an expansionary gap generates pressure for inflation. In this connection, it is important to note that many of the causes of the inflationary pressures of the 1970s can be traced to expansionary gaps arising from forces at work on the supply side of the economy. Problems arose owing to restrictions on the supply of petroleum imposed by the Organization of Petroleum Exporting Countries (OPEC). Also, supply-side effects arose as delayed reactions to price-level increases that had taken place during the 1960s. Difficulty in dealing with expansionary gaps caused by supply-side

FIGURE 3
An Expansionary Gap

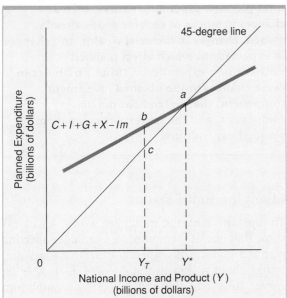

The $C + I + G + X - Im$ curve represents the levels of total planned expenditure that are forecast for various levels of national income and product on the assumption that present economic programs remain in effect. Macroeconomic equilibrium is at Y^*, as indicated by the intersection of the total-planned-expenditure curve and the 45-degree line at point *a*. At the target level of national income and product of Y_T, there is an excessive amount of planned expenditure, indicated by the distance from *b* to *c*. This extra expenditure may generate inflationary pressures.

FIGURE 4
Closing an Expansionary Gap

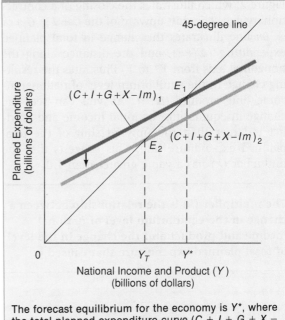

The forecast equilibrium for the economy is Y^*, where the total-planned-expenditure curve $(C + I + G + X - Im)_1$ intersects the 45-degree line at E_1. The target level of national income and product is Y_T. The expansionary gap can be closed by shifting the total-planned-expenditure curve downward to $(C + I + G + X - Im)_2$. After this shift, equilibrium is indicated by the intersection of $(C + I + G + X - Im)_2$ with the 45-degree line at E_2, and the expansionary gap has been closed.

events is one of the reasons the Keynesian model did not fare well during the Great Stagflation of the 1970s.

THE MULTIPLIER

The **multiplier** is the relationship between a change in the equilibrium level of national income and product and the change in the level of total planned expenditure that caused it. If we let the triangle "delta" (Δ) stand for "the change in," the multiplier is $\Delta Y^*/\Delta TPE$, where *TPE* stands for the volume of total planned expenditure. Expressed as a functional relationship,

$$\Delta Y^* = k(\Delta TPE), \textit{ ceteris paribus}$$

where k represents the multiplier. The multiplier relationship can be visualized by looking back to Figure 2, which illustrates the closing of a contractionary gap. The shift upward of the $C + I + G + X - Im$ line illustrates the change in total planned expenditure (ΔTPE), and the distance along the horizontal axis from Y^* to Y_T illustrates the resulting change in the equilibrium level of national income and product (ΔY^*). As you can see, the change in equilibrium national income and product is larger than the upward shift of the total planned expenditure line. This suggests that the multiplier (k) has a value greater than 1.0.

The multiplier (k) is the relationship between a change in the equilibrium level of national income and product and the change in the level of total planned expenditure that caused it.

Shifting the Total-Planned-Expenditure Curve

Since the multiplier and the resulting change in equilibrium national income and product start from a shift of the total-planned-expenditure line, it is helpful to examine some of the variables that can cause such a shift. Because we are dealing with a *shift* (and not a *movement along*) the total-planned-expenditure line, the only variable *not* eligible for consideration is a change in national income and product itself, since the effects of changes in this variable are already accounted for in the slope of the total-planned-expenditure line. But there are many variables that can cause a shift in this curve. For example, planned consumption expenditure can be affected by changes in stocks of durable goods already owned, by changes in financial wealth (stocks, bonds, savings accounts, etc.), and by changes in expectations about whether good times or bad times are in store. If any of these variables change, planned consumption expenditure at any specified level of national income and product may change and thus shift the total-planned-expenditure line.

Variables that can change the planned investment expenditure component of total planned expenditure include changes in the rate of interest

and all forces that bear upon estimates of the rate of return that will come from investment projects. Among these are anticipated business conditions, expected operating costs (especially wages), taxes and government regulations, new technologies, and a host of other matters.

The government purchases component can change when government policies change, when a national emergency arises, or when there is a change in voter attitudes toward government spending.

Finally, the net-export component of planned expenditure may change because of changes in the relative prices of foreign goods and in foreign exchange rates. It may also be affected by changes in economic conditions in the foreign countries themselves.

Many variables can cause a shift in the total-planned-expenditure curve, such as changes in stocks of durable goods already owned, changes in financial wealth, and changes in expectations which affect planned consumption expenditure. Other variables can cause changes in the planned investment component, the government purchases component, and the net-export component of planned expenditure.

Changing Equilibrium

To illustrate how the multiplier works, let us assume that one of the nonincome variables affecting planned investment expenditure (I) changes and brings about a shift in the $C + I + G + X - Im$ curve. How will this shift affect the equilibrium level of national income and product?

The multiplier process is started by a change in some nonincome determinant of planned spending, which alters the amount of planned spending and changes the equilibrium level of national income and product.

Suppose that someone discovers a new process to lower the cost of extracting fuel from a type of

TABLE 1
Increased Planned Expenditure and Equilibrium National Income and Product (in billions of dollars)

(1) National Income and Product (Y)	(2) Planned Consumption Expenditure (C)	(3) Planned Investment Expenditure (I)		(4) Government Purchases (G)	(5) Net Exports (X − Im)	(6) Total Planned Expenditure (C + I + G + X − Im)		
		Original	New			Original		New
$ 100	$100	$35	→ $85	$100	$15	$ 250	→	$ 300
200	175	35	→ 85	100	15	325	→	375
300	250	35	→ 85	100	15	400	→	450
400	325	35	→ 85	100	15	475	→	525
500	400	35	→ 85	100	15	550	→	600
600	475	35	→ 85	100	15	625	→	675
700	550	35	→ 85	100	15	700	→	750
800	625	35	→ 85	100	15	775	→	825
900	700	35	→ 85	100	15	850	→	900
1,000	775	35	→ 85	100	15	925	→	975
1,100	850	35	→ 85	100	15	1,000	→	1,050

At the original level of total planned expenditure, equilibrium occurs when both total planned expenditure and national income and product are $700 billion as shown by the row of red numbers. A $50 billion increase in planned investment increases total planned expenditure by $50 billion at all levels of national income and product. The new equilibrium is at a national income and product of $900 billion as shown by the row of blue numbers. Thus, a $50 billion increase in planned expenditure increases equilibrium national income and product by $200 billion in this illustration.

rock called oil shale. Let us imagine that this discovery convinces business firms to increase the flow of planned investment expenditure by $50 billion each year at all levels of national income and product. (We realize that this is an extremely large increase compared with the other values in our hypothetical illustration but the large size will make it easier to show changes in graphic form.) Because the discovery gives business people great hopes for profits, the demand curve for planned investment spending, such as the curve in Figure 4 on page 205, shifts to the right by $50 billion. At any specified rate of interest, planned investment is $50 billion greater than it was before the change in business outlook brought about by the discovery. To keep things simple, assume that this is the only change that takes place.[2] Let us see how this

2. Of course, we realize that a rise in the demand for investments may change the rate of interest and that many other related changes will take place. If we were presenting a *general equilibrium* model, we could not allow ourselves the simplifying assumption that planned investment is the only thing that changes. However, at this stage, we shall use *partial* analysis for simplicity.

change alters the equilibrium level of national income and product according to the Keynesian model.

In Table 1, we reproduce Table 5 of Chapter 10 (page 208) but increase every entry in the planned-investment-expenditure column by $50 billion, since we assume that, for every level of national income and product, every year, planned investment will be $50 billion greater than before the new production process began. Of course, we must also increase every entry for total planned expenditure by $50 billion. From this table we note that the conditions for macroeconomic equilibrium, which require an equality between total planned expenditure and national income and product, now exist when national income and product is $900 billion as shown by the row of numbers printed in blue. The equilibrium level of national income and product has increased from $700 billion to $900 billion.

The same information is presented in Figure 5, which illustrates the upward shift of the C + I + G + X − Im curve on a Keynesian-cross diagram. The $C + I_1 + G + X − Im$ line shows total planned

FIGURE 5

Shifting the Total-Planned-Expenditure Curve Produces a Change in the Equilibrium Level of National Income and Product

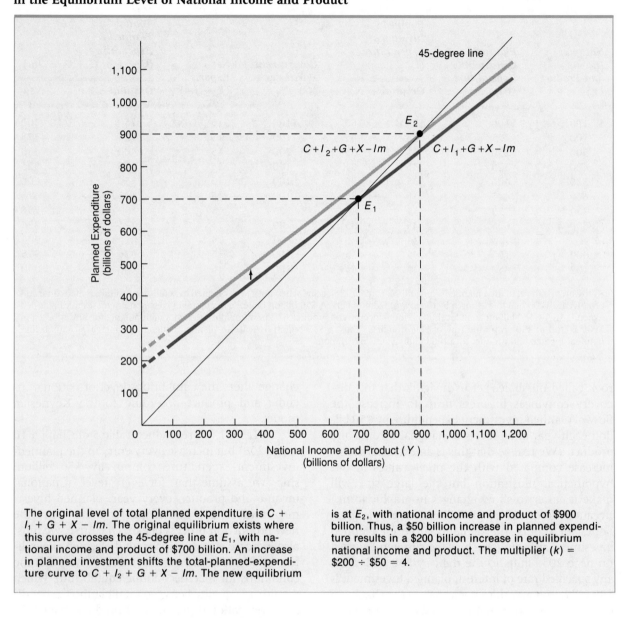

The original level of total planned expenditure is $C + I_1 + G + X - Im$. The original equilibrium exists where this curve crosses the 45-degree line at E_1, with national income and product of $700 billion. An increase in planned investment shifts the total-planned-expenditure curve to $C + I_2 + G + X - Im$. The new equilibrium is at E_2, with national income and product of $900 billion. Thus, a $50 billion increase in planned expenditure results in a $200 billion increase in equilibrium national income and product. The multiplier (k) = $200 ÷ $50 = 4.

expenditure before the assumed increase in planned investment, and the $C + I_2 + G + X - Im$ line shows total planned expenditure after this increase. The conditions for equilibrium exist where the total-planned-expenditure curve crosses the 45-degree line. Before the rise in planned expenditure, this happened at a national income and product of $700 billion. After the rise, the inter-

section is at national income and product of $900 billion.

The multiplier shows the size of the change in the equilibrium level of national income and product as a multiple of the shift in total planned expenditure that began the process.

TABLE 2
The Multiplier (in billions of dollars)

Time Period ("round")	This Period's Addition to Flow of National Income and Product	Additional Planned Expenditure Induced in This Period	Total Addition to National Income and Product Flow
1	$ 50	$ 37.5	$ 50
2	37.5	28.1	87.5
3	28.1	21.1	115.6
4	21.1	15.8	136.7
5	15.8	11.9	152.5
.	↓	↓	
.	(total of $47.5)	(total of $35.6)	(total of $47.5)
.	↓	↓	
nth	————	————	200.0
Sum total	$200.0	$150.0	—

We assume a $50 billion increase in planned expenditure caused by a change in some nonincome variable. This results in a $50 billion increase in the flow of national income and product in round 1. This added income *induces*, or brings about, a $37.5 billion increase in planned expenditure, which in round 2 generates a further increase in the flow of income and product. The process repeats itself. When induced planned spending is 0.75 of the national income and product change that caused it, the multiplier value will be 4. In the nth round (or limit), the income and product flows will have expanded by $200 billion as a result of an initial shift of $50 billion. This is shown in the right-hand column, which shows the total addition to the flow of national income and product.

The Multiplier Process

In this illustration, an increase in the annual volume of planned investment expenditure has resulted in an increase in equilibrium national income and product that shows the multiplier effect. The upward shift of the $C + I + G + X - Im$ curve in Figure 5 was $50 billion, but the equilibrium level of national income and product rose by $200 billion—four times as much as the increase in planned spending that brought it about. The multiplier implies that the average dollar of the initiating change in planned spending is multiplied several times (in this case, four times) in the process of reaching the new equilibrium level. In our illustration, dividing $200 billion by $50 billion, we get a multiplier of 4. Measuring the size of the multiplier in this way, however, is "after the fact" and of little use in forecasting changes in equilibrium national income and product. Let us see, then, how the multiplier comes about and what determines its size.

The multiplier process is illustrated in Table 2.

The initiating increase in planned investment expenditure takes place in round 1. At that time, income is paid to workers and the owners of other resources that are employed in producing the machinery and equipment involved in the new shale investment.[3] A $50 billion per year addition to the flow of income starts during this time period as shown in the right-hand column of the table. But this is not the final result of the increased rate of planned expenditure. The people who receive the additional $50 billion of income will spend some of it to buy things they want and save some of it. Our assumption about marginal propensities (see Chapter 10) was that 75 cents of each additional national income dollar would move around the circular flow as planned expenditure *induced*, or caused, by the increase in income. The planned

3. We shall assume that money to finance this new investment is available to companies without taking funds away from other planned expenditure. We shall have more to say about this assumption when we describe how the banking system operates and how the stock of money in the economy changes.

expenditure induced in round 1 is $37.5 billion ($50 billion × 0.75). This induced expenditure brings about new production and income in round 2, that is, the expenditure of $37.5 billion provides income for the resources used in producing these goods and services. During round 2, the flow of income and production includes both the $50 billion flow per period that started in round 1 and the $37.5 billion flow that started in round 2. So income and production flow at the rate of $87.5 billion more than before the multiplier process started, as shown in the "total addition" column. But the expansion has not ended. Equilibrium has not yet been reached.

The multiplier process continues in round after round. Each time, the flow of income and production increases (in our illustration) by an amount equal to 75 percent of the increase experienced in the preceding round—$37.5 billion in round 2, $28.1 billion in round 3, $21.1 billion in round 4, and so on. The total flow of national income and product is larger than its premultiplier level by $50 billion in round 1, $87.5 billion in round 2, $115.6 billion in round 3, $136.7 billion in round 4, and so on.

With each round of the multiplier process, the addition to national income and product becomes smaller. Mathematically, a progression of this kind approaches a limit. In this case, the total additions to the flow of income and production (the sum of the numbers in the second column in Table 2) will approach $200 billion. This total is made up of the initiating $50 billion increase in planned expenditure plus $150 billion in planned-expenditure increases induced by the expanded production and income (the sum of the numbers in the third column of the table). In the right-hand column, the entry for the total addition to the flow of national income and product in the nth round (the limit) is $200 billion. Equilibrium is reached when the flow of national income and product is $200 billion a year greater than it was before the upward shift in planned expenditure. At that point, the multiplier process has run its course.

The multiplier process operates through successive rounds of the circular flow.

Time Lags in the Multiplier Process   There is a time dimension in the operation of the multiplier. First of all, a certain amount of time will pass before the increased rate of spending brings about increases in incomes. Second, it will take time for these increases in incomes to induce still further increases in spending. It may be roughly accurate to assume that about three months are needed for each round of the multiplier process. In one year, then, about four rounds might be completed. In our example, these first four rounds expand the total flow of national income and product by $136.7 billion—from $700 billion to $836.7 billion. Though the whole multiplier effect is never fully realized, a great part of it comes fairly early in the process.

About three months are needed for each round of the multiplier process—for increases (or decreases) in incomes to induce further increases (or decreases) in spending.

The multiplier may operate in either an upward or a downward direction. The preceding example showed how an increase in planned expenditure would increase equilibrium national income and product. But, in a similar way, when total planned expenditure falls, the multiplier will have a downward effect on the economy.

An Algebraic Calculation of the Multiplier   The values shown in Table 2 involve a numerical process that is familiar to mathematicians. It is a geometric progression in which each number in a series is a constant proportion of the number before it. In this case, each addition to national income and product is 75 percent of the preceding one. If we let 1 represent the first value in the series, we can write a generalized description of the process as follows:

$$1 + (0.75) + (0.75)(0.75) + (0.75)(0.75)(0.75)$$
$$+ (0.75)(0.75)(0.75)(0.75) \text{ plus on and on}$$

Or we can write it in a more usual way:

$$1 + (0.75) + (0.75)^2 + (0.75)^3 + \cdots + (0.75)^n$$

where n is the final round of the process. Mathematicians demonstrate that the sum of this series will approach a predictable limit. In our illustration, this sum approaches a value of

$$\frac{1}{1 - 0.75} \quad \text{or} \quad \frac{1}{0.25} \quad \text{or} \quad 4$$

In Table 2, we started with a $50 billion increase in planned expenditure and ended with a $200 billion increase in the equilibrium level of national income and product. The multiplier had a value of 4.

The Multiplier Formula

We may now give a formula for the multiplier by recognizing that the value (0.75) in the case just given was the value of the slope of the $C + I + G + X - Im$ lines in Figure 5. The numerical value of this slope is equal to the amount of total planned expenditure induced by a change in national income and product divided by the size of that change in national income and product. The same idea appeared in Chapter 10, when we discussed the marginal propensity to consume. In that discussion, it was easy to understand how an increase in income could induce households to raise planned consumption expenditure. Now we simply apply this concept to total planned expenditure for the whole economy. If we assume that net taxes and all the other expenditure streams (planned investment, government purchases, and net exports) are not altered by changes in national income and product, we can put MPC into our multiplier calculation in place of the 0.75 value used in Table 2.[4] We can then say that the value of the multiplier is

$$\frac{1}{1 - MPC}$$

If the MPC is 0.75 (as in our case), the multiplier

will have a value of 4. So a $50 billion initial rise in total planned expenditure leads eventually to a $200 billion rise in national income and product. If the MPC were 0.60, the multiplier would have a value of 2½. In this case, a $50 billion initial increase in planned expenditure would result in a $125 billion change in the level of equilibrium national income and product. If the MPC were 0.8, the multiplier would have a value of 5, and so forth.

The equation given above for the multiplier can also be expressed by using the marginal propensity to save (MPS) rather than the marginal propensity to consume (MPC). If we assume that consumption and saving account for all disposable personal income, it follows that $MPS = 1 - MPC$. By substituting in the multiplier formula given above, we find that it also can be stated as

$$\frac{1}{MPS}$$

With our value for MPS of 0.25, this formula also gives a multiplier value of 4, since $1/0.25 = 4$.

If we assume that net taxes and all expenditure streams other than consumption are not altered by changes in national income and product, the formulas for the multiplier are

$$\frac{1}{1 - MPC} \quad \text{and} \quad \frac{1}{MPS}$$

A Summary of the Multiplier

The multiplier is not a complicated concept, but is an important one for understanding the application of the Keynesian model to achieve a target level of national income and product. In this process, a basic distinction is made between events that *initiate* the process (shifts the $C + I + G + X - Im$ curve) and responses that are *induced* by the resulting income changes (movements along the relocated curve). The multiplier process is launched by some externally caused change in planned expenditure. Feeding upon itself, it then generates changes in income and product until it finally dwindles to insignificance.

---

4. A more realistic model of equilibrium and of the multiplier could not make the assumption that the marginal propensities for net taxes, planned investment, government purchases, and net exports all are zero. Instead, it would have to recognize that changes in national income and product induce changes in each of these streams, just as our model has recognized that planned consumption spending is induced by income changes. The marginal propensities for planned investment and for government purchases probably would be positive, but the marginal propensity for net exports probably would be negative. In the more realistic model, the multiplier would be based on the increase in total planned expenditure that is induced by changes in national income and product.

FIGURE 6
The Multiplier Process

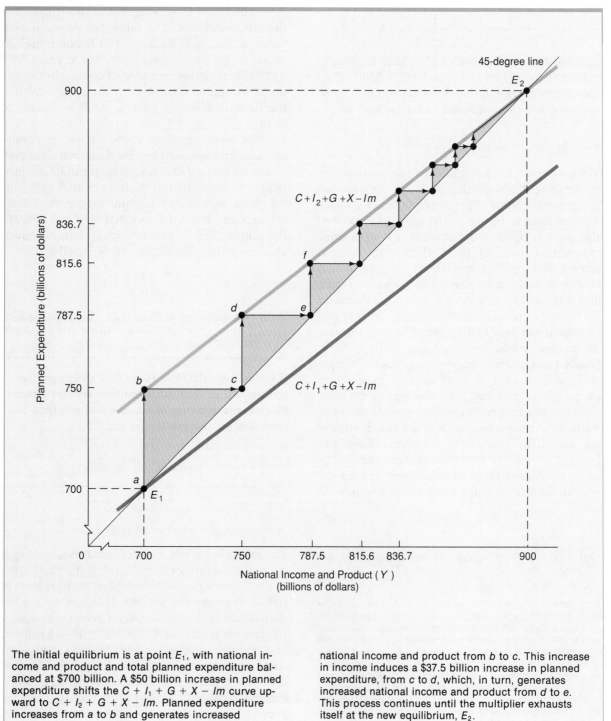

The initial equilibrium is at point E_1, with national income and product and total planned expenditure balanced at $700 billion. A $50 billion increase in planned expenditure shifts the $C + I_1 + G + X - Im$ curve upward to $C + I_2 + G + X - Im$. Planned expenditure increases from a to b and generates increased national income and product from b to c. This increase in income induces a $37.5 billion increase in planned expenditure, from c to d, which, in turn, generates increased national income and product from d to e. This process continues until the multiplier exhausts itself at the new equilibrium, E_2.

Figure 6 is a graphic illustration of the multiplier process. It is an enlargement of the part of Figure 5 that showed the area between the original equilibrium of $700 billion ($E_1$) and the new equilibrium of $900 billion ($E_2$). The process begins with an upward shift of the total-planned-expenditure curve, which we assumed to be $50 billion. In the figure, this is the distance from a to b. This spending generates an equal amount of national income and product ($50 billion), shown by the distance from b to c. The increase in national income and product *induces* a $37.5 billion increase in planned expenditure, shown by the distance from c to d. Then this increase generates additional income and product of $37.5 billion, shown as the distance from d to e. The multiplier process repeats itself in smaller and smaller steps, which dwindle to insignificance as the new equilibrium national income and product of $900 billion ($E_2$) is approached.

FISCAL INSTRUMENTS

The Keynesian model suggests that macroeconomic equilibrium need not correspond with full employment in the economy. Equally important, it suggests that government is able to alter the level of total planned expenditure and thus change the equilibrium level of national income and product. The actions that government can take to change total planned expenditure by altering its budget (revenues and expenditures) are called **fiscal instruments.**[5] Specifically, fiscal instruments include changes in government purchases, changes in net tax collections, and features of taxing and spending legislation that encourage households and firms to change their consumption, saving, and investing behaviors.

In the Keynesian model, government can change the equilibrium level of national income and

---

5. Other instruments also are available. Chief among these are **monetary instruments,** which change the amount of money in the economy.

---

product by using fiscal instruments—changes in government purchases, net tax collections, and taxing and spending legislation.

Changing Government Purchases

Change in the annual flow of government purchases of goods and services is a basic Keynesian fiscal instrument. As you remember from the circular-flow diagram in Chapter 6 and the model in Chapter 10, government purchases (G) consist of currently produced goods and services. They do not include transfer payments, such as veterans', welfare, or Social Security benefits, which are treated as negative taxes in calculating net taxes.

To begin our study of the government-purchases instrument, we assume that other things remain unchanged. Thus, in describing the effects of changes in the yearly volume of government purchases, we assume that no changes are made in the tax laws and that interest rates and the availability of money for private investment are not affected by the change in government purchases.

In the Keynesian approach, the purpose of changing the amount of government purchases is to shift the total-planned-expenditure curve and thereby to close contractionary or expansionary gaps. Increases in the volume of government purchases (G) will, other things being equal, shift the $C + I + G + X - Im$ curve upward and help to close a contractionary gap, as was illustrated in Figure 2. Conversely, decreases in the volume of government purchases will, other things being equal, shift the $C + I + G + X - Im$ curve downward, helping to close an expansionary gap, as was illustrated in Figure 4.

In each of these changes, the multiplier operates just as described previously. For example, if the *MPC* is 0.75, a $50 billion increase in the annual volume of government purchases will lead eventually to a $200 billion increase in the equilibrium level of national income and product. The multiplier will have a value of 4. Similarly, a $50 billion decrease will lead to a $200 billion decrease in this equilibrium level. The change in government purchases shifts the $C + I + G + X - Im$ curve, which then intersects the 45-degree line on a Keynesian-cross graph at a different equilibrium level of national income and product.

In the Keynesian model, increasing the volume of government purchases will shift the total-planned-expenditure curve upward; decreases in the volume of government purchases will shift the curve downward.

In real life, the government-purchases instrument does not always operate as smoothly as in our hypothetical cases. For one thing the multiplier is not as sure and precise as our illustration suggests. Much depends on the mood of the economy at the time. Also, sometimes a **displacement effect** will arise, that is, a change in one component of total planned expenditure causes an opposite change in some other component. For example, suppose that the expanded flow of goods and services provided by greater government purchases is a substitute for things that households ordinarily buy with their own income. What would happen if government expanded its purchases of medical services and delivered these services free to the public? Wouldn't household spending on health care go down as the government's spending on these services went up? Then wouldn't the decrease in household spending offset, to some degree, the increase in government purchases? If the goods and services involved in the increased government purchases are substitutes for things that consumers are already buying, then a downward shift in the consumption function (consumer purchases) may partly or fully offset the increase in government purchases. In such a case, the $C + I + G + X - Im$ curve does not shift by the full amount of the change in government purchases.

What happens when government decreases its purchases in order to close an expansionary gap? If consumers purchase more to make up for the things that are no longer provided by government, the shift in the $C + I + G + X - Im$ curve will again be less than the change in government purchases, and the government-purchases instrument will be less effective in closing the gap.

A displacement effect occurs when a change in one component of total planned expenditure causes an opposite change in some other component.

Changes in Taxes

Changing the amount of taxes collected is another fiscal instrument in government's macroeconomic tool kit. Changing tax collections, like changing the amount of government purchases, can shift the total-planned-expenditure curve and change the equilibrium level of national income and product. Let us examine how these changes operate in the Keynesian model.

Tax Increases   What happens when the government increases the amount of net tax that it collects, while keeping government purchases unchanged? In terms of the circular-flow model, an increase in net tax forces households to reduce the amounts that they use for other purposes. Let us first consider two extremes of possible household reaction to a tax increase and then look at a more realistic response.

If *all* of the added tax payments were obtained from reductions in planned saving, there would be no shift of the $C + I + G + X - Im$ curve, if we assume that planned investment (I), government purchases (G), and net exports ($X - Im$) are unchanged. The tax increase would be completely ineffective in changing the equilibrium level of national income and product.

If, on the other hand, *all* of the increase in net tax were taken from planned consumption expenditure, the $C + I + G + X - Im$ curve would shift downward by the full amount of the added tax, again assuming that the other spending streams remain unchanged. Since the total-planned-expenditure curve would shift by the full amount of the tax change, the multiplier effect of the tax change would be just as large as the multiplier effect of changes in government purchases, as explained earlier.

But neither of these cases is likely to fit the real world. In practice, the money for the additional tax bill is likely to be paid partly from consumption and partly from saving, so that the outcome of a change in net tax is likely to lie somewhere between the extremes just outlined. In the Keynesian model, the marginal propensities to consume and to save indicate how households will respond to changes in net taxes. For example, if the *MPC* is 0.75 and the *MPS* is 0.25, an application of the Keynesian model suggests that a $50 billion tax increase will cut planned consumption expenditure by $37.5 billion and planned saving by $12.5 billion. If the other spending streams continue as before, the total-planned-expenditure curve will shift downward by $37.5 billion. Since the multiplier [$1/(1 - MPC)$ or $1/MPS$] would have a value of 4, this shift would lower the equilibrium level of national income and product by $150 billion ($37.5 \times 4$).

Tax Decreases In the Keynesian model, a tax decrease is a fiscal instrument that can shift the total-planned-expenditure curve upward, raising the equilibrium level of national income and product and helping to close a contractionary gap. In other words, tax decreases operate in the same manner, but in the opposite direction, as tax increases.

When net taxes are cut, households have additional income that can be used to increase planned consumption expenditure and planned saving. The power or multiplier effect of a tax cut depends on how taxpayers use the income retained from the tax cut. In the Keynesian model, the marginal propensity to consume (*MPC*) gives an answer to this question. If the marginal propensity to consume is 0.75, a $50 billion cut in net taxes will lead to a $37.5 billion increase in planned consumption expenditure, *ceteris paribus*. The total-planned-expenditure curve will shift upward by this amount. Since the multiplier would again have a value of 4, the equilibrium level of national income and product would rise by $150 billion ($37.5 \times 4$). The logic is simply that some of the expansionary power of the tax cut is lost because households use some of the income to increase planned saving. The total-planned-expenditure curve does not shift by the total amount of the net tax change.

In the Keynesian model, a tax increase can shift the total-planned-expenditure curve downward;

a tax decrease can shift the curve upward. Changing the net tax causes changes in consumption expenditure.

The Tax-Change Multiplier In the Keynesian system, the power of changes in net taxes to alter the equilibrium level of national income and product is summarized in the concept of a **tax-change multiplier,** which is equal to the change in equilibrium national income and product divided by the change in net taxes that causes it. If we use a triangle (Δ) to mean "the change in," the tax-change multiplier is $\Delta Y^*/\Delta T_n$. In the illustrations given previously, the tax-change multiplier had a value of -3, since equilibrium national income and product changed by $150 billion (in the opposite direction) as a result of a change in net taxes of $50 billion.

The tax-change multiplier is smaller, by one unit in absolute terms, than the multiplier for investment changes or changes in government purchases. This relationship arises from the assumption that the *MPS* shows the percentage of a change in tax liability that comes out of saving in the case of a tax increase or goes into saving in the case of a tax reduction. This means that the change in total planned expenditure that arises is in the opposite direction from the tax change, and is smaller than the tax change by the percentage indicated by the *MPS*. When the regular multiplier process comes into play, it starts with only the part of the tax change that actually appears as a change in planned expenditure. For example, if the *MPS* is 0.25, the multiplier starts with a change in planned expenditure 25 percent smaller (and in the opposite direction) than the change in net tax. This shrinkage of the initial change in planned expenditure is itself multiplied as the multiplier process proceeds to the ultimate change in equilibrium national income and product. The multiplier values work in such a way that the shrinkage of the ultimate change in equilibrium national income and product equals (with the opposite sign) the initial change in net tax. For example, if the *MPS* is 0.25, the initial change in planned expenditure is 25 percent smaller than the amount of the tax change, but, since the multiplier value is 4 when the MPS is

0.25, the 25 percent shrinkage at the start leads to a reduction of the end result equal to 100 percent of the initial tax change. If the MPS were 0.20, an initial 20 percent shrinkage would be multiplied five times, and again equal 100 percent of the initial tax change, and so on.[6]

The tax-change multiplier is equal to the change in equilibrium national income and product divided by the change in net taxes that causes it. Tax changes have a smaller multiplier value than changes in planned investment expenditure.

The Balanced-Budget Multiplier

In practice, it is not necessary that either the government-purchases or the tax-change instrument be used by itself in closing a contractionary or expansionary gap. Usually, these instruments are combined (along with other instruments) so that several policy goals can be pursued at the same time. For example, contractionary gaps might be closed primarily with increases in government purchases if policy goals called for more public services, or with tax cuts if the goals called for more private services. The choice or the mixture of the two instruments would depend on how policymakers wanted to divide the hoped-for expansion of the economy.

6. The proposition that the tax-change multiplier value is (in absolute terms) smaller by one than the investment or government-purchases multiplier can be illustrated by a series of equations. We start with the multiplier that applies to changes in planned consumption expenditure, with ΔY^* representing a change in the equilibrium level of national income and product and ΔC representing a change in planned consumption expenditure. The regular multiplier calculation gives us

$$\Delta Y^* = \Delta C(1/MPS)$$

Next, we assume that a change in net tax affects planned consumption as follows:

$$\Delta C = -\Delta T_n(MPC)$$

where ΔT_n represents a tax change. By substituting the second equation into the first equation, we have

$$\Delta Y^* = -\Delta T_n(MPC)(1/MPS)$$

In this equation, we see that the tax-change multiplier is represented by $(MPC)(1/MPS)$. If we let $-K_{T_n}$ represent the tax-change multiplier, it can be written as

Government purchases and tax changes can be used together to alter the equilibrium level of national income and product.

Could the government-purchases and the tax-change instruments be used together to alter the equilibrium level of national income and product while also keeping the government's budget in balance? Yes. For example, a contractionary gap could be closed with just the right combination of increases in both government purchases and tax collections to maintain a balanced budget. The combination would be expansionary. This is because the upward shift of the $C + I + G + X - Im$ curve that comes from $50 billion of added government purchases, for example, is greater than the downward shift that comes from a $50 billion addition to tax collections each year. With an MPC of 0.75, this downward shift would be only $37.5 billion (75 percent of $50 billion), leaving a $12.5 billion net upward shift in the curve. Since the multiplier factor is 4, this $12.5 billion shift would bring a $50 billion rise in the equilibrium level of national income and product. This gives us what is sometimes called the **balanced-budget multiplier,** with a value of 1, or unity (the change in equilibrium national income and product is the same as the change in the size of the budget). Balanced changes in government purchases and tax collections could also close an expansionary gap. In this case, both

$$-K_{T_n} = (MPC)(1/MPS) = MPC/MPS$$

But we know that $MPS = 1 - MPC$. Therefore, we can express the tax-change multiplier as

$$-K_{T_n} = MPC/(1 - MPC)$$

which reduces to

$$-K_{T_n} = [1/(1 - MPC)] - 1$$

Since the term in the brackets $[1/(1 - MPC)]$ is the regular multiplier, the -1 in the equation indicates that the tax-change multiplier in absolute value is smaller, by one, than the regular multiplier.

A demonstration of the last step is as follows:

$$-K_{T_n} = MPC/(1 - MPC)$$
$$= [1 - (1 - MPC)]/(1 - MPC)$$
$$= [1/(1 - MPC)] - (1 - MPC)/(1 - MPC)$$
$$= [1/(1 - MPC)] - 1$$

government purchases and tax collections would be cut.

Combining the government-purchases multiplier with the tax-change multiplier gives a numerical value for the balanced-budget multiplier that is equal to the arithmetic difference between the two. If the government-purchases multiplier is 4 and the tax-change multiplier is −3, then the balanced-budget multiplier is 1. If the *MPC* were 0.80, so that the government-purchases multiplier would be 5, the tax-change multiplier would be −4, so that the balanced-budget multiplier would still be 1. In this way, the balanced-budget multiplier is 1, regardless of the size of the *MPC*.

The balanced budget multiplier is 1: the change in equilibrium national income and product is the same as the change in the size of the budget.

As a tool for closing expansionary or contractionary gaps, balanced changes in government purchases and tax collections make the balanced budget the determining consideration in the choice of fiscal instruments. However, other goals may be more important. Also, the great changes in the size of government required by the balanced-budget system could easily make the package less attractive.

Automatic or Built-in Stabilizers

Automatic or **built-in stabilizers** are specific provisions in the tax and spending laws that work automatically—without the need to take any action—to moderate economic fluctuations. Progressive income taxes are one of these stabilizers. When national income rises, taxpayers on the average move into a higher tax-rate bracket and pay more taxes in proportion to their income. Other things being equal, the increase in taxes leaves less of the households' additional income to use for consumption spending and puts a downward pressure on the $C + I + G + X - Im$ curve, limiting the expansion of national income and product. In times of inflation, this same "tax-bracket push" would put some people into a higher bracket even though they are no better off in real terms. "Index-ing" income taxes by automatically lowering tax rates or widening tax brackets in step with inflation reduces the automatic stabilization effect of progressive taxes in inflationary times. Of course, the stabilizing effect of automatic tax changes assumes that the government does not spend the extra tax revenues collected during economic expansions or cut its purchases when taxes fall automatically during economic contractions.

The built-in stabilizing effect of progressive tax rates can also be explained as a change in the power of the multiplier factor. In Chapter 10, our discussion of taxes and the marginal propensity to consume used a lump-sum tax. This tax produced a constant marginal propensity to consume based on national income and product. With progressive income tax rates, the total-planned-expenditure curve would become flatter and flatter as national income and product rose—and the multiplier effect would become smaller as well.

The progressive individual income tax is not the only built-in stabilizer that operates from the tax side of the budget. Corporation profits fluctuate disproportionately with the total economy so that tax collections based on these profits are unusually high in good times and unusually low in bad times. For this reason, they have an automatic stabilizing effect. Social Security taxes and unemployment taxes also behave in this way.

Automatic stabilizers can also be built into the expenditure side of the government budget. But since most of these government expenditures are for transfer payments, rather than for goods and services, we would call them changes in net taxes. Welfare, unemployment, and Social Security expenditures all tend to rise during a recession at the same time that payments into these funds become less. This combination of more benefit checks and fewer tax payments helps support consumer spending and moderates the contractionary gap. We have the opposite pattern during inflationary times, when expansionary gaps are moderated.

The existence of automatic stabilizers has led some economists to propose a policy called the **full-employment balanced budget.** Under this plan, the amount of government purchases and transfer payments would be based on how much the voters would want, and could afford, when the economy was operating at full employment. Tax rates would be set to balance this amount of spending when there was full employment. During economic contractions, the automatic stabilizers would lower net taxes. During expansions, the automatic stabilizers would raise net taxes. No legislative action is needed under this plan, since economic fluctuations are automatically moderated.

Automatic stabilizers have not been powerful enough to stop all fluctuations in the economy. Other policy matters put a limit on how progressive the tax rates can be, as well as on the level of corporation profit taxes and the size of transfer payments. So there is a ceiling on the amount of automatic stabilization that can be built into the fiscal system.

Automatic or built-in stabilizers are provisions in the tax and spending laws that work automatically to moderate economic fluctuations.

In a growing economy, the moderating effect of automatic stabilizers is sometimes called **fiscal drag**, since the automatic increase in net tax collections dampens the rate of growth of the economy. Of course, under the full-employment-balanced-budget policy, economic growth calls for a reevaluation of spending and tax legislation—meaning that the voters and their representatives must decide whether the benefits of growth are to be taken through more public goods and services or through tax reductions which allow more private goods and services. Thus, fiscal drag need not happen.

The operation of automatic stabilizers in the context of economic growth is called fiscal drag.

Influencing Economic Behavior Through Fiscal Instruments

So far we have looked only at the financial aspect of fiscal instruments. But the tax and expenditure system is also one of the most powerful instruments available to influence the economic behavior of important actors on the economic stage. Changing these behaviors may change planned expenditure and the performance of the economy. To illustrate the importance of these fiscal instruments, we shall briefly note how depreciation allowances and capital gains taxes can affect planned investment expenditure.

Depreciation is defined as the decline in the market value of a capital good as it wears out or becomes obsolete. On income tax returns, it is a deductible cost of doing business. The tax laws specify how quickly or how early in the life of a machine these deductions can be taken. Deductions that are taken earlier mean less tax payment and encourage businesses to invest in machines and equipment. Therefore, changing the schedules or timetables for depreciation is one of the favorite fiscal instruments for changing planned investment expenditure.

Depreciation is the decline in the market value of a capital good as it wears out or becomes obsolete. Changing depreciation schedules in income tax returns is a fiscal instrument for changing planned investment expenditure.

A **capital gain (or loss)** is the change in the market value of an asset that takes place while it is owned by the taxpayer. Many people buy stocks, hoping that the company will prosper and that the market value of the stock will rise, providing a capital gain. In a capitalist system, this is an important means of channeling resources into promising growth industries. In the United States, capital gains are taxable as income, but tax laws have changed over the years in specifying the fraction of such gains that must be listed for taxation. The 1986 law required full taxation of capital gains, but controversy continues about how heavily they should be taxed. Lowering tax rates on capital gains could increase the flow of funds into growth industries. So changing the capital gains tax rates is another fiscal instrument for influencing planned investment expenditure.

The list of the regulatory features of tax and expenditure laws could go on and on. There have even been proposals for using taxes to reward or punish people and companies for cooperating or not cooperating with nonfiscal regulations.

A capital gain (or loss) is the change in the market value of an asset that takes place while it is owned by a taxpayer. Changing the capital gains tax rate is a fiscal instrument for influencing planned investment expenditure.

Economics in Focus

Hard Choices: Austerity, Economic Expansion, and the National Debt Crisis

During the Reagan administration the national debt more than doubled, reaching a staggering $2.6 trillion by the end of 1988. Everyone agreed that something should be done or the massive burden would be passed on to future generations. William Simon, a former secretary of the treasury, stated the peril bluntly and dramatically: "If the next Administration does not mount an immediate, decisive and effective attack against those twin towers of debt—our budget deficit and our trade deficit—the United States cannot continue as leader of the free world."

Two basic choices emerged, loosely labeled "austerity" and "growth." Those who believed in austerity said that the budget deficit should be reduced at once, even if many Americans suffered. Simon, for example, favored strong cuts in government spending. "Nothing is sacrosanct," he declared, even Social Security. Others focused in particular on entitlement programs—Social Security being a prime example. These government outlays amounted to 11 percent of GNP, and some benefited the wealthy as well as the poor; thus many economists urged policymakers to bite the political bullet and cut entitlements—an action that, in the Keynesian model, would be an increase in net taxes.

Advocates of austerity often presumed that the consequence would be an economic slowdown, at least in the short term. This was an ill they were willing to accept. The alternative, they warned, would be spiraling inflation, instability, and an economy so out of control that the next downswing could be a disaster. The advocates of economic expansion, in contrast, argued that the austerity program would itself court a disaster—a severe recession or, at worst, complete financial collapse. They argued that the economy should be allowed to expand in a modest fashion, with a small continuing deficit, controlled inflation, intelligent investment, and a concentration on overcoming trade deficits. The supporters of these policies seemed less fearful of debt than their opponents; they pointed out that the current national debt actually represented no greater a proportion of GNP than the debt during the Kennedy administration—and a far smaller proportion than in the years following World War II.

For many champions of expansion, however, the key issue in austerity programs was the question of *whose* belt would be tightened. According to some statistical analyses, the Reagan years had increased the disparity between the rich and the poor, and the talk of austerity often implied a willingness to let the poor bear the brunt of the cutbacks. A short, sharp recession might cure the ills of the economy, but at what price?

Clearly this is a political debate which will be decided in the political arena. Debt-reduction policies established by the president, the Congress, and other economic policymakers will affect the lives of Americans throughout the 1990s and for many decades to come.

Sources: William Greider and William E. Simon, "Which Way Out of Debt: Growth or Austerity?" *New Perspectives Quarterly,* Spring 1988, pp. 8–15 (Simon quotations at pp. 12, 14); Robert Kuttner, "Against Austerity," *The New Republic,* December 28, 1987, pp. 16–18; "Get the Rich Off the Dole," an interview with Peter Peterson, *Time,* October 31, 1988, pp. 66–68; Peter Brimelow with Lisa Scheer, "Is the Reagan Prosperity for Real?" *Forbes,* October 31, 1988, pp. 85–90.

SUMMARY

1. Target levels of national income and product are chosen as goals of macroeconomic policy. Choosing a target for national income and product involves value judgments and tradeoffs among different goals. (See page 220.)

2. A contractionary or an expansionary gap is the difference between the chosen target and the equilibrium level of national income and product that is expected if no new initiatives are taken. A contractionary gap means that equilibrium will be below the target, and an expansionary gap means that equilibrium will be above the target. (See pages 221–223.)

3. The multiplier process is started by a shift in the $C + I + G + X - Im$ curve, that is, by a change in some nonincome determinant of planned spending. This change alters the amount of planned spending and changes the equilibrium level of national income and product. (See page 224.)

4. The multiplier shows the size of the change in the equilibrium level of national income and product as a multiple of the shift in total planned expenditure that launched the process. Equilibrium national income and product changes by several times as much as the initial spending change because further expenditure changes are induced by the income changes themselves. (See pages 225–226.)

5. The multiplier operates through successive "rounds" of the circular flow. Time is needed for these rounds of activity to take place. The full multiplier effect is never realized, but most of its potential will be felt within a year following the shift in total planned expenditure. (See pages 227–229.)

6. The value of the multiplier is determined by the propensity of income changes to induce changes in planned expenditure. If we assume zero marginal propensities for planned investment, government purchases, and net exports, the value of the multiplier is $1/(1 - MPC)$ or $1/MPS$, with MPC and MPS based on national income and product. (See page 229.)

7. Changing the yearly flow of government purchases of goods and services is a fiscal instrument that can shift the total-planned-expenditure curve up or down and so change the equilibrium level of national income and product. This tool be-

comes less effective if other components of total planned expenditure, such as household purchases, are displaced by a change in government purchases. (See pages 231–232.)

8. Changing the yearly flow of tax collections is another fiscal tool that can shift the total-planned-expenditure curve. Part of the change in net tax results in a change in consumption expenditure. (See pages 232–234.)

9. In the elementary Keynesian model, changes in government purchases have the same multiplier value as changes in planned investment expenditure. But, tax changes have a multiplier value that is smaller because some of the tax change goes into or comes out of planned saving. Combining changes in government purchases with changes in net tax results in a balanced-budget multiplier with a value of 1. (See page 234.)

10. Automatic, or built-in, stabilizers are provisions in the tax and spending laws, such as progressive income taxes, corporation profit taxes, and transfer payment systems, that work automatically to moderate economic fluctuations. The full-employment balanced budget is a policy that relies on built-in stabilizers. In the context of economic growth, automatic stabilizers are sometimes said to cause fiscal drag. (See page 235.)

11. Fiscal instruments can be used to regulate the economy by changing specific rules in the tax law. The tax treatment of capital gains and the allowances for depreciation are examples of the regulatory aspects of fiscal tools. (See page 236.)

KEY TERMS

automatic (built-in) stabilizers: provisions in the tax and spending laws that work automatically to moderate economic fluctuations (page 235).

balanced-budget multiplier: the change in equilibrium national income and product divided by the change in the size of the budget that caused it. It's value is 1 (page 234).

bankruptcy: a state of insolvency; the inability to repay creditors (page 236).

capital gain (or loss): the change in the market value of an asset that takes place while it is owned by the taxpayer (page 236).

contractionary gap: a gap between the equilibrium level and the target level of the national income and product that exists when the equilibrium level is less than the target level (page 221).

Council of Economic Advisers (CEA): part of the executive branch of the government; its main purpose is to advise the president on economic policy (page 220).

crowding out: the replacement of private investment expenditure by government purchases in a budget deficit situation (page 243).

cyclical deficit: the amount of government budget deficit that arises because the economy is operating below its target level of national income and product (page 242).

depreciation: the decline in the market value of a capital good as it wears out or becomes obsolete (page 236).

displacement effect: a change in one component of planned expenditure that causes an opposite change in some other component (page 232).

Employment Act of 1946: the law that established the Council of Economic Advisers and stated the responsibility of the United States government to promote high level employment, price stability, and economic growth (page 220).

expansionary gap: a gap between the equilibrium and the target level of national income and product that exists when the equilibrium level is higher than the target level (page 221).

fiscal instruments: the actions that government can take to change total planned expenditure by altering its laws relating to taxation and expenditure (page 231).

full-employment balanced budget: a plan to moderate economic fluctuations by basing the amount of government purchases and transfer payments on how much the citizens desire and are willing to pay for when the economy is operating at full employment and by setting tax rates to balance this budget when the economy is operating at full employment (page 235).

Humphrey-Hawkins Act of 1978: a law that set specific goals for both price stability and employment (page 220).

Joint Economic Committee (JEC): a con-gressional committee that is responsible for advising the legislative branch on economic policy (page 220).

monetary instruments: actions that the government can take to change the amount of money in the economy (page 231).

multiplier (k): the relationship between a change in the equilibrium level of national income and product and the change in the level of total planned expenditure that caused it (page 223).

structural deficit: the total government budget deficit minus that portion arising because the economy is operating below its target level of national income and product (page 242).

target level of national income and product: the level chosen through political processes as a goal for macroeconomic policy (page 218).

tax-change multiplier: a value that is equal to the change in equilibrium national income and product divided by the change in net taxes that causes it (page 233).

DISCUSSION QUESTIONS

1. Why was the setting of target levels for national income and product considered unnecessary and inappropriate in the neoclassical theory but important and necessary in the Keynesian theory?

2. Without looking at Figures 1 and 3, draw the Keynesian-cross diagrams that illustrate a contractionary gap and an expansionary gap. Then check to make sure you have them right. What is the standard Keynesian strategy for dealing with a contractionary gap?

3. Suppose that a new and much better type of home computer is developed. Would this development shift the planned-investment curve on a Keynesian-cross diagram? If so, in which direction? Explain. Might the development of this product shift any of the other components of total planned expenditure? Which one(s)? Why?

4. This chapter illustrated a multiplier started by a change in planned investment. Could the process be started by a change in some other component of total planned expenditure? Why or why not? What would the value of the multiplier be if the *MPC* were 0.9, based on national income and product? Would stable economic conditions exist if the *MPC* were greater than 1.0? Explain.

5. Without looking at Figure 6, draw an illustration of the multiplier process on a Keynesian-cross diagram. Be sure to label all axes and lines. Check your illustration with Figure 6 to be sure you have it right. How would your illustration be different if the *MPC* were smaller? If it were larger?

6. The multiplier illustration in this chapter is based on the assumption of a permanent increase in the annual flow of some spending stream. How would the multiplier be different if the initiating change were only a one-shot expenditure, which was not repeated in the next time period? Explain.

7. How large a contractionary gap would be closed by a $100 billion change in the annual amount of government purchases if the *MPC* is 0.80 and if other variables are held constant? Explain how you got your answer. If displacement effects are present, should your answer be larger or smaller? Explain.

8. If the *MPC* is 0.80, you know that the multiplier for government purchases is 5. What would the numerical value of the multiplier be for a tax cut, given this *MPC*? Why would it be different?

9. The choice between changes in government purchases and changes in tax collections involves microeconomic questions about the mix between public and private goods in the economy. How does this factor influence your preference between them as macroeconomic instruments? Do you have a different preference between purchases changes and tax changes when promoting economic expansion than when promoting economic restraint? Explain.

10. By combining the purchases multiplier and the tax-change multiplier, explain why the balanced-budget multiplier always has a value of 1. Compare the advantages and disadvantages of making the balanced budget a basic guideline for macroeconomic policy.

11. Explain why progressive taxes, corporation taxes, and transfer payments automatically tend to stabilize the economy. Under a progressive tax system, would a 10 percent change in national income and product bring about a change in tax collections of 10 percent, or more, or less? How does the answer to this question help you to understand the automatic stabilizers in the government budget? Explain. How would the full-employment balanced-budget policy operate?

Appendix:
Deficits and
The National Debt

In the Keynesian system for using fiscal instruments, deficits or surpluses in the government budget are almost inevitable. For example, in explaining the government-purchases instrument, we assumed no change in tax laws. Given the lump-sum tax that was assumed in that explanation, the government would continue to collect the same amount of net tax. If the government increased its purchases in order to close a contractionary gap, the increase in government purchases would move the government budget toward a deficit. Similarly, if government purchases were reduced in an effort to close an expansionary gap, the government's budget would move toward surplus.

These same conclusions hold even under more realistic assumptions about tax rates. For example, if the government uses a percentage income tax of 20 percent, a $50 billion increase in government purchases adds only $10 billion to government tax collections in the first round of the circular flow. Of course, annual tax collections would grow in future time periods, but, since the government would also continue its higher level of purchases, it would be a long time before a budget balance could be restored.[7]

It is even more apparent that the government's budget would move toward deficit or surplus with the use of the tax-change instrument. If government purchases remain unchanged while net taxes are reduced, the budget will move toward deficit. If net taxes are increased in an effort to close an expansionary gap, the budget will move toward surplus.

STRUCTURAL AND CYCLICAL DEFICITS

Government budget deficits are not always—and probably not usually—the result of purposeful attempts to engage in fiscal policy. Since the federal budget usually is in deficit, how can we estimate the part that can be related to fiscal policy? The answer is found by estimating how much more net-tax revenue would be collected under existing tax laws if the economy were operating at the target (or full employment) level of national income and product. A deficit equal to this amount—the revenue lost because the economy is operating below its target—is the **cyclical deficit.** In a sense, it is caused by the below-target level of economic activity.

If the actual deficit exceeds the revenue shortfall caused by the failure of the economy to reach the target level of national income and product, the additional part of the deficit is called the **structural deficit.** The structural deficit reflects an inability or unwillingness of the government to impose taxes sufficient to balance its budget in the context of a fully employed economy. Many observers believe that most of the federal budget deficits in the late 1980s were structural rather than cyclical, since, in those times, the economy was operating with approximately its natural rate of unemployment, that is, it was close to full employment. These observers concluded that the deficits in those years reflected not fiscal policy but an unwillingness of Congress to reduce expenditures and/or increase taxes.

The *cyclical deficit* **is the tax revenue shortfall due to the economy operating below the target level of national income and product. The remainder of any actual deficit is the** *structural deficit.*

---

7. You may wish to use the "Total Addition to National Income and Product Flow" column in Table 2 to estimate when the government budget would regain a balance if a percentage income tax were used.

DEFICITS AND CROWDING OUT

As you remember from the circular-flow model introduced in Chapter 6, budget deficits and surpluses activate connections between the government box and the financial-markets box. A government deficit takes funds out of the financial markets—funds that might otherwise flow on as planned investment in the circular flow. This is called **crowding out**. It means that some private investment expenditure is replaced ("crowded out") by government purchases. The reverse situation exists when the government's budget moves to surplus. Surplus funds are channeled to the financial markets and flow onward as increases in planned investment expenditure.

The process by which crowding out takes place is quite simple. The government sells bonds to finance its budget deficit. These bond sales increase the demand for funds available for borrowing in the financial markets. Other things being equal, this increase in demand for loans drives interest rates upward. These higher rates, in turn, mean that some private investment projects, which would have appeared profitable at the lower interest rates, will no longer appear to be so. These private investments are crowded out by the budget deficit.

In our explanation of the Keynesian use of fiscal instruments, we assumed that interest rates were unaffected by government deficits and surpluses. Although this may be the case in periods of extreme depression (as when Keynes wrote in the 1930s), it is not likely to be true in more normal times. If crowding out takes place, fiscal instruments that move the government budget toward a deficit will not be as effective in closing a contractionary gap as our simple model indicates. Similarly, fiscal instruments that move the budget toward a surplus will be less effective in closing an expansionary gap than the simple model indicates. Fiscal instruments may still have significant effects, but the connection between the government budget and the financial markets suggests that we must not make any final judgment about them until we have studied financial markets and government's monetary instruments. Also, it is important to remember that funds may enter the financial-markets box from the foreign-markets box. Inflows of funds from abroad can reduce the crowding-out effects of government budget deficits.

In a deficit situation, some private investment expenditure is replaced ("crowded out") by government purchases. In a surplus situation, there may be an increase in private planned investment.

HOW PUBLIC DEBT IS CREATED

When a deficit arises in the U.S. government budget, the Treasury Department, which is responsible for financing government operations, issues bonds and other securities and offers them for sale in securities markets. Private persons, depository institutions, insurance companies, business firms, and others purchase these securities just as they might buy other kinds of securities.[8] The Treasury uses the funds received from sales to finance the deficit in the government budget. These funds flow between the financial markets and the government as pictured in the circular flow.

When a deficit occurs in the U.S. government budget, the Treasury Department issues bonds and other securities and offers them for sale in securities markets.

It is not true that the government literally "prints money" to cover its deficits as is sometimes alleged. In the past, as during the "Greenback Era" of the Civil War, currency was issued directly by the Treasury Department, but this is not the case today. The currency now in circulation is issued by the Federal Reserve Banks. In Chapters 12 and 13, we shall explain how money is created.

HOW LARGE IS THE NATIONAL DEBT?

The national debt has not always been very large in the United States. In the 1830s, the debt had been completely eliminated, and excess federal revenues

8. Some national debt securities are issued to agencies of the federal government itself. These are "special issues" and are not bought and sold in the open market.

were turned over to the states. In 1917, before the United States entered World War I, the debt was $12.36 per capita. Today the debt is over $3 trillion, around $12,400 for every man, woman, and child in the country. Even when inflation and the vast growth in the economy are allowed for, it is evident that the national debt has increased significantly.

Table 3 shows the dollar amount of the gross federal debt from 1970 through 1990. In dollar amount, the debt grew continuously during these years. The dollar amount of public debt is a simple (and simplistic) way of stating the size of the debt. It is simply a monument to net budget deficits accumulated over the years.

A more interesting picture appears, however, when the debt is expressed as a percentage of GNP. As shown in Table 3, this percentage went down between 1970 and 1981, and then increased significantly. Expressing the debt as a percentage of GNP is better than focusing on the dollar amount because a large economy probably can support a larger debt than a small economy, other things being equal. But recording debt as a percentage of GNP also brings price-level changes into the calculation, since GNP is expressed in current dollars. When we bring price-level changes into our measurement of the debt, we run into great controversy. When inflation occurs, the GNP (in current dollars) goes up. But the face value of bonds that were bought before the inflation does not increase in dollar value along with the price level, unless they have been indexed to change in face value automatically with changes in the price level. Since U.S. bonds are not indexed, inflation automatically reduces the national debt as a percentage of GNP. In fact, some people believe that inflation amounts to partial default on the debt. The inflation rate was much higher during the 1970s than during the 1980s. The high inflation rate of the 1970s helped to hold down the debt-to-GNP percentage. The lower inflation rate of the 1980s contributed to the more rapid rise in this percentage.

Debt as a percentage of GNP has increased significantly since 1981.

TABLE 3
The Gross Federal Debt, 1970–1990

End of Year	Gross Federal Debt (billions of dollars)	Percentage of GNP	End of Year	Gross Federal Debt (billions of dollars)	Percentage of GNP
1970	380.9	38.5	1981	994.3	33.3
1971	408.2	38.7	1982	1,136.8	36.2
1972	435.9	37.8	1983	1,371.2	41.3
1973	466.3	36.4	1984	1,564.1	42.4
1974	483.9	34.2	1985	1,817.0	46.0
1975	541.9	35.6	1986	2,120.1	50.6
1976	629.0	37.0	1987	2,345.6	52.9
1977	706.4	36.5	1988	2,600.8	54.4
1978	776.6	35.8	1989[a]	2,868.8	56.0
1979	828.9	33.9	1990[a]	3,107.2	56.7
1980	908.5	34.0			

The gross federal debt grew continually between 1970 and 1990. When these amounts are expressed as a percentage of GNP, the percentage declined through 1974, fluctuated within fairly narrow bounds through 1981, and then increased significantly.

[a] Estimated
Source: Economic Report of the President, 1989, Table B-76.

CAN DEBT LEAD TO NATIONAL BANKRUPTCY?

Bankruptcy is a legal concept used to indicate a state of insolvency—of being unable to repay creditors. Could the national debt ever become so large that the federal government would become bankrupt? The standard answer to this question is that it depends on the taxing power of the government, the strength of the economy, and the wealth of the citizens. If the government is firmly established, if the economy is strong, and if valuable properties exist in the country, bankruptcy is unlikely. Certainly, the U.S. government is not likely to become bankrupt.

But governments that have borrowed heavily sometimes repudiate their debts or try to renegotiate their obligations. Also, when one government is replaced by another (as by revolution), the debts of the fallen government may or may not be assumed by the new government. Even the assumption of colonial debts by the new United States government was a controversial action. Several states refused to pay their debts for construction of canals and roadways in the 1830s, and the U.S. government repudiated the Confederate debt after the Civil War. After the 1917 revolution, the Soviets refused to pay the czarist debts. What about deliberate inflation as a means of eliminating the debt in real terms? In a sense, this would be another kind of repudiation, since debts would be paid back in money that was less valuable than the money originally borrowed.

DO DEFICITS BURDEN FUTURE GENERATIONS?

In private finance, debt financing is a way to postpone final payment for a good or service. Funds are borrowed and used to purchase something. The borrower uses the funds to acquire an asset and also has a liability—the obligation to pay off the loan. The burden of payment is put off while funds are "rented" and interest is paid. A future generation becomes involved because the heirs of a debtor inherit whatever remains of the assets purchased with the borrowed funds, and they inherit less of something else, since the debt will have to be paid off when the estate is settled. The debt itself (the "less of something else") is a burden. In this illustration, it is not obvious that the future generation is, on balance, worse off or better off, since this depends on the value of the assets bought with the borrowed funds.

What about the debt of the national government? Reasoning by analogy is, we agree, a dangerous procedure. However, analogy may point to some important issues. For example, if we consider only the debt and ignore whatever benefits may have been gained in exchange, it is easy to conclude that debt is a burden to future generations. The government of the future generation must pay interest on a debt that would not exist if the transaction had not been carried out or if the government expenditure had been financed by taxes. But this just introduces the main question.

If we consider both sides of the matter and penetrate the "money veil" to examine real goods and services and real resources, the question becomes very complex. U.S. government debt is not incurred on a project-by-project basis. For this reason, it is not possible to point to any specific government goods and services as being debt financed. Nor can the opportunity cost (the private goods and services that were given up in exchange) be clearly identified. In our circular-flow figure, the connections between the government box and the financial-markets box suggest that government debt financing may be at the expense of private capital goods investments (machines and equipment) that could have raised both productivity and the living standard of future generations. This may be as close as we can come to finding the opportunity cost to the future generation.

But we must record some reservations even here. A depression-period argument points out that the resources used by the debt-financed government operations might otherwise have been idle, so that there might have been no real burden to the future. When there is no depression, debt financing may be at the expense of private investment. But tax financing can also impinge on investment spending, though perhaps not quite so much.

Thus we cannot accept a strict "yes" or "no"

answer to the question of whether debt financing is a burden to future generations. Much depends on the wisdom of political decision makers and on the time horizons and incentive systems operating in the political processes. If political decisions are dominated by short-run considerations and if public funds are spent foolishly, debt financing may, on balance, result in a net burden on future generations.

SUMMARY

1. Movements toward deficit or surplus in the government budget typically arise from the use of fiscal instruments in the Keynesian model. Deficits extract funds from financial markets, and surpluses put funds into these markets. Thus, deficit financing may "crowd out" private investments and budget surpluses may lead to increases in private planned investment.

2. The U.S. national debt has grown continually in dollar amount. Debt as a percentage of GNP has increased significantly in recent years. The debt comes into being when the Treasury sells bonds to finance a budget deficit.

3. Bankruptcy is a state of insolvency—of not being able to repay creditors. The strength of the

government, its taxing power, the size of the economy, and the wealth of the citizens suggest that debt is not likely to mean bankruptcy for the U.S. government.

4. The effect of deficit financing on future generations depends on decisions made at the time when the debt is incurred. In some cases, deficit financing will be a burden on future generations, but in other cases, it will not be a real burden.

DISCUSSION QUESTIONS

1. Why is it overly simple to express the size of the national debt in total dollar figures? Why is it better to express its size as a percentage of GNP? But why does the latter method run into trouble when the economy has experienced inflation?

2. If the government borrowed a million dollars, used the funds to construct a highway, and paid off the debt (with interest) through taxes on people using the highway, would the debt have been a burden on the future generation? Explain your answer. Some of the U.S. debt arose in World War II. Do you suppose that the war would have been lost if taxation had been use instead of borrowing? If so, is today's generation burdened in net effect by this debt? Explain.

John Maynard Keynes and the Great Depression

The Great Depression of the 1930s, which began much earlier in Great Britain than in the United States, was no ordinary business-cycle downturn. It was the worst such depression of at least the preceding half century. In most countries complete recovery came only after the start of World War II. The depression itself confounded many mainstream economists, particularly in the United States, who believed or hoped in 1929 that they had entered a depression-proof "New Era."[1]

CAUSES AND CURES

When the Wall Street stock market crash of October 1929 was followed by depression, and when the depression showed signs of hanging on, many suggestions were made to bring about recovery. These suggestions ranged from doing nothing at all to what would later be called "voodoo economics." They also included business-dominated "economic plans." It is certainly not true that nobody had any ideas about the causes and cure of the Great Depression. The problem was rather that so few of the would-be saviors were able to convince anyone else that they knew what they were talking about.

Some of the more or less seriously considered ideas about depression control, dating from the early 1930s, are listed below. Their order is largely arbitrary:

1. Most cyclical booms had been accompanied by substantial price inflation. What was different about the 1920s boom was precisely its accompaniment by price-level stability, which led most economists to assume that prosperity might continue indefinitely.

1. Prosperity was "just around the corner," since the country's physical plant had not been damaged. Nothing need be done but wait patiently for prosperity to return.

2. The depression was the punishment by the Almighty for the sins of "flaming youth" during the "jazz age." The remedies were moral reform and prayers to the Almighty for forgiveness.

3. The depression had been foisted on the people by certain other wicked people, such as "the international bankers" or "the elders of Zion." The economic power of such groups should be broken, and all would be well.

4. Capitalism should be scrapped in favor of a system close to Soviet communism, since the U.S.S.R. had been able to maintain full employment.

5. A national plan should be devised primarily by the leaders of big business, with the government in a secondary role, to eliminate overproduction and assure profitable prices for output.

6. The supply of money and credit should be increased by going off the gold standard, raising the price of gold, or printing inconvertible paper money. This action would "reflate" the levels of prices, wages, and profits. A more extreme form of this proposal would introduce an entirely new monetary system based on an hour of labor or an erg (small unit) of physical energy.

7. Unemployment should be exported abroad, primarily by raising tariffs and otherwise decreasing imports, and secondarily by subsidizing exports of goods and services.

8. Unemployment should be reduced by keeping the young, the elderly, and married women out of the labor force and reserving jobs for heads of families.

9. Idle plants should be taken over and run by unemployed workers at minimum cost, with the products distributed as far as possible to the poor and the unemployed.

10. Income and wealth should be redistributed by taxation or confiscation from the rich to the poor (or from property to labor income) so as to increase purchasing power.

11. The government budget should be balanced as an aid to business confidence, preferably by cutting public expenditures but if necessary also by raising taxes.

12. The cause of the depression was that prices and wages had not yet fallen to their "natural" (pre-1914) levels. Therefore the cure was to force them down by drastic deflation, or "liquidation."

13. The government budget should be unbalanced deliberately to increase spending for public projects to employ the unemployed. These projects should be mainly in public works and construction, civil or military. The resulting deficit should be financed either by selling public securities or by expanding the money supply as in 6 above.

KEYNES AND HIS *GENERAL THEORY*

The contribution of John Maynard Keynes, later Lord Keynes (1883–1946), was to formalize, more fully and effectively than anyone else, the approach we

have numbered 13. Indeed, this was the method that was used a decade later to ward off any renewed depression after World War II. However, many of the individual building blocks of Keynes's *General Theory*—particularly the consumption function and the multiplier—had already been devised by less well-known members of the "economic underworld" years before the *General Theory* itself appeared in 1936. Also, some policies now called "Keynesian" had already been advocated and even enacted before 1936 in Britain, in Sweden, and in the United States under the New Deal.[2] On a larger scale and for military purposes, they had also been adopted by Nazi Germany and expansionist Japan as the "economics of rearmament."

AN ECONOMIC HERETIC

Who was this man, and how did he become so influential? The son of a well-known Cambridge University economist, Keynes received the best conventional education of his day. However, he was to become best known as an economic heretic.

As a young man, he wrote widely on both economic theory and policy for the intelligent general reader as well as for the scholarly professional. He

Depression soup kitchen

also taught at Cambridge University and achieved early prominence in the British Civil Service. In the world of economics he was noted for changing or at least modifying his views to suit changing conditions, and for placing small value on consistency over time. His most famous early work was *The Economic Consequences of the Peace* (1920), in which he concluded that the excessive burden of German monetary reparations would, if enforced, prevent the recovery of Germany and all of Europe after World War I. Many of Keynes's writings after 1920 were on monetary policy. In a period of low gold production, he was a leader among those economists who felt that the traditional gold standard (with circulating currency convertible to a fixed amount of gold) was a deflationary drag on the domestic economy.

The *General Theory* broke even more sharply with generally accepted ideas, as you know from reading Chapter 10, by attacking Say's Identity and calling for budgetary deficits to counter depression conditions.

KEYNESIAN AND POST-KEYNESIAN ECONOMICS

Keynes viewed his doctrines as a general theory, which is to say, as something more than "depression economics." He applied the same system to check inflation, when it threatened to become a problem during World War II, mainly by raising taxes.[3]

After the war, organized labor, business, and agriculture in Britain and elsewhere used the Keynesian doctrine as a means of guaranteeing "full employment and full production at whatever cost" despite inflationary wage, price, and profit increases. Keynes responded by turning his back on his own disciples, speaking of "modern stuff gone silly and sour." Not long afterward, in April 1946, he died.

Today the self-styled "post-Keynesians" are still important at Cambridge University and elsewhere. They go beyond Keynes and "generalize the *General*

John Maynard Keynes

Theory" in ways that Keynes himself might not have welcomed. They support wage controls, price controls, and capital rationing as necessary features of the peacetime high-employment economy, in the interests of inflation control, income redistribution, and accelerated economic growth. Occasionally they even claim that Keynes "never really understood the *General Theory*." What they mean is that in his haste to publish a tract for his time, he never developed what the post-Keynesians consider to be its full implications in a world of imperfect competition, simultaneous inflation and unemployment, and maldistribution that aims at high growth as well as full employment.[4] What Keynes would himself have said of all these ideas we cannot guess.

2. Keynes came to the United States, met President Franklin Roosevelt, and tried unsuccessfully to persuade Roosevelt to increase sharply the volume of New Deal spending and the size of the government budget deficits. Roosevelt apparently distrusted Keynes, believing him to be "more mathematician than economist."

3. Foreseeing postwar depression, however, Keynes proposed to "sweeten" wartime taxes by making them compulsory loans, to be repaid when depression conditions returned.

4. Post-Keynesian views are explained further in Chapter 17.

Money and Depository Institutions

The Federal Reserve System and Monetary Instruments

Monetary Economics

PART IV

MONEY, BANKING, AND MONETARY POLICY

12
Money and Depository Institutions

Preview   You may have some coins and some currency in your pocket or wallet at this moment. Perhaps you examined this money and discovered the year that the coin was minted (manufactured) and even the location of the mint itself. Did you notice that the currency is a Federal Reserve Note? Was it issued by a bank in Boston, Chicago, San Francisco, Dallas, or somewhere else? These bits of information may satisfy your curiosity, as long as you are sure that the coins and currency will buy your lunch or a ticket to the movie this evening. But economists want to know a lot more about what money is and what it does in the economy.

With this chapter we begin the study of the role of money in the economy and in the determination of equilibrium national income and product. We devote three chapters to this important topic. This chapter examines the nature of money itself and how depository institutions are able to expand and contract the amount of money in an economy. Chapter 13 explains how the Federal Reserve System (the "central" bank in the United States) controls the money supply. The final chapter in the trio, Chapter 14, develops the economic theory of how money may affect the equilibrium level of national income and product, both in real terms and in terms of inflation or deflation of the price level. Just as you learned about fiscal instruments and theory in Part III, you will come to understand monetary instruments and theory in Chapters 13 and 14.

This chapter, on money and depository institutions, starts with a brief discussion of the importance of money in the economy and why economists must understand money. After explaining the functions of money, we describe the things that actually serve as money in the United States.

In order to understand money, you will need to have some

information about depository institutions and how they operate. The second half of the chapter describes how depository institutions are organized as profit-seeking business enterprises that are usually able to operate successfully on partial reserves. That is, their obligations to depositors can be greatly in excess of their cash and readily available assets. Finally, you will learn how depository institutions influence the money supply in the economy as a by-product of their partial reserve operation.

MONEY

The economics that you have already learned will give you some clues about the importance of money. Business firms and governments keep track of their economic activities with accounts recorded in money amounts. In a similar way, the national income accounting system measures the volume of economic activity in money terms.

What would happen if the quantity of money itself were expanded or contracted? Could such expansions and contractions in the quantity of money affect the volume of economic activity in the economy? Could such changes make any real difference in production, jobs, and living standards? Or would they simply change the price level and bring inflation or deflation but leave real production unchanged? Can changes in the money supply be controlled so that money can be used as an instrument of policy?

Economists find that the answer to each of these questions is "yes." The speed, or velocity, of the circulation of money through the economy does change from time to time. It is also true that the amount of money itself changes. The resulting changes in the quantity and velocity of money can bring further changes, not only in the real volume of production and jobs but also in the general price level. We shall consider these questions in detail in Chapter 14. However, before we can do that, it is important to understand what money is and what determines the amount of money in the economy.

Changes in the amount of money in the economy and in the speed of its circulation

through the economy can affect the real volume of production and jobs and also the general price level.

The Functions of Money

Before you can understand what money is in terms of economics, you need to know the functions of money. The reason for this "function first" approach is that, in various times and places, many different things have served as money. For certain people, seashells or distinctively colored or shaped stones have been money. For others, cigarettes or the bark from particular trees have served as money. Livestock or even human slaves have been "money." Today, specially printed pieces of paper or specially minted pieces of metal (and other things as well, as you will see) serve as money. So it is clear that economists cannot define money in terms of its composition. Instead, they first specify certain "functions of money" and then define money itself as that which is generally used in carrying out these functions. If this way of defining money seems a little backwards at first, remember that you cannot define a "split end" or a "defensive linebacker" without first specifying their functions in the game of football. The position itself is defined by the functions it performs. In economics, we usually list four functions of money: medium of exchange, unit of account, store of purchasing power, and standard for deferred payment.

Medium of Exchange   The easiest way to understand the **medium of exchange** function of money is to compare a direct, or **barter,** exchange in which one item is traded directly for another with an exchange that takes place through an intermediate transaction, that is, through the "medium" of money. Consider the teacher-student exchange, for example. The famous painter and recorder of birds and animals, John James Audubon, agreed to tutor the children of a Mississippi family in exchange for room and board and half days free to roam the plantation and paint. This was a barter exchange. As you can see, there was no "medium," or intermediate step. It was a unique transaction because it required a specific combination of wants: Audubon wanted to be supported while painting, and the family wanted instruction for its children. These special conditions lasted for only one year. Then Audubon moved on. Today, the typical teacher-student exchange takes place through the medium of money. Instead of providing the teacher with room and board, students pay tuition in money. The teacher receives money, which he or she can use to pay for room and board, among other things.

Using money as a medium of exchange greatly extends the range of feasible exchanges. No longer do people need to match their specific wants with those of other people. The medium of exchange lubricates the economic machinery. Whenever the medium of exchange is eliminated, as has sometimes happened because of war or runaway inflation, the living standard falls rapidly as the system reverts to barter exchange. We can now see part of the definition of money: money must be generally accepted as a medium of exchange, that is, it must be used for the intermediate step in exchange.

The medium of exchange function is basic to the economist's definition of money. The other functions that we shall explain are closely related to this one, but they are to some degree subsidiary to it. That is, if something is not customarily used as a medium of exchange, it is not likely to be accepted for the other functions.

Unit of Account   The **unit of account** function of money is the "common denominator" function—a way of comparing the values of different items. It is simply easier to remember, for example, that the price of a loaf of bread is $0.80 or that the price of a gallon of milk is $2.40 than it is to remember that one gallon equals three loaves. Without the unit of account function of money, people would have to remember millions of continually changing exchange ratios, one for each pair of commodities. A common denominator, or unit of account, simplifies things by selecting one item, *money*, and expressing all other values in terms of that one item.

It is almost inevitable that the item that has been accepted as the medium of exchange will also be selected as the unit of account. The unit of account function is virtually a by-product of the medium of exchange function.

What happens when the two functions are different? If you travel in France, you expect price tags to be in francs. If you are carrying francs and

have gotten used to them, there is no problem. But if you are accustomed to thinking in dollars, the mental gymnastics of converting from one unit to the other can be troublesome, especially if prices are subject to bargaining. You may have the same type of problem in converting from yards to meters, or from gallons to liters, or from semesters to quarters. Conversion itself is the problem. When the same money is used for both a unit of account and a medium of exchange, no conversion is needed.

Store of Purchasing Power   The third commonly listed function of money is the **store of purchasing power** function. This simply means that people who have units of the medium of exchange want to have the option of saving some for use at some later time. Surely a medium of exchange that was good "today only" would be less than ideal for most people. Each day people who wished to save would want to exchange some of today's money for money stamped with tomorrow's (or some later) date. Even though we could expect special moneychangers to set up shop soon to help people manage their money over time, the whole process of dated money would be quite a waste of time and talent. Up to a point at least, what is used as the medium of exchange and the unit of account will probably be used as a store of purchasing power as well.

The store of purchasing power function adds a time dimension to the unit of account function of money. No longer is money comparable to yards and meters or to liters and gallons. In these physical measures, we expect tomorrow's liter to contain as much liquid as today's liter and tomorrow's meter to be the same as today's. Inflation and deflation don't affect these measures. Printing more meter sticks does not threaten the size of the meter. But money is different. Price levels do change (as we noted in discussing index numbers), and when this happens, we move part way back to having dated money—"today's money" can be different from "tomorrow's money." In inflationary times, holding money until tomorrow means converting it automatically into "tomorrow's money," which is less valuable. Thus, inflation threatens the store of purchasing power function of money. Because people become less and less willing to hold it for this purpose, moneychangers, banks, and dealers in money substitutes (such as securities, gold, and precious gems) do big business. Also, as you will see, interest rates may be pushed up as people insist on extra compensation for holding notes, bonds, and other IOUs that have fixed dollar amounts.

Standard for Deferred Payment The fourth function that people expect of their money is that it should serve as a **standard for deferred payment.** When people make an agreement that involves payments to be made at some time in the future, it is convenient to have some standard way to specify the amount of such payment. Of course, whatever is used as a medium of exchange and a unit of account is most likely to be used as the standard of deferred payment as well. A substantial portion of the transactions that take place in a modern economy involve contracts that extend over a period of time.

Changing price levels bring up some of the same problems for money as a standard for deferred payment as they did for money as a store of purchasing power. Inflation means that the money value of the deferred payment will overstate its future purchasing power equivalent measured at today's prices. Conversely, deflation means that the money value of the deferred payment will understate its future purchasing power equivalent in terms of today's prices. Of course, if the parties to the contract expect prices to change during the term of the agreement, their expectations can be built into the deferred payment amounts that are written into the contract.

Money has four functions: as a medium of exchange (used as the intermediate step in exchange), as a unit of account (a way of comparing the values of different items), as a store of purchasing power (can be saved for use at a later time), and as a standard for deferred payment (for payments due at some time in the future.)

Forms of Money in the United States

Having described the basic functions that money is expected to perform, we can now define **money.**

Money is anything generally accepted in an economy as a medium of exchange, a unit of account, a store of purchasing power, and a standard for deferred payment. A careful look at this definition, however, reveals that we still have to deal with some obscure concepts. The word *anything* places no limit on the composition of money. As you will see, money may be metal, paper, entries in an account book, or even electronic impulses on magnetic tape. Also, the term *generally accepted* is difficult to pin down. *Accepted* means that people routinely use the substance in exchanges, but, as we shall explain shortly, acceptance must sometimes be enforced by law. How general must acceptance be in order for something to be money? Again, the definition is loose. In the United States today, coins, currency, and checkable account balances (account balances against which checks can be written) are the basic forms of money. Let us take a brief look at each of these forms.

In the United States, coins, currency, and checkable account balances are the basic forms of money.

Coins The medium of exchange function goes a long way toward helping us understand why coins are a component of most money systems. People want a form of money that is durable, portable, and uniform because they want to carry money with them to make "convenience transactions," such as operating automatic vending machines. The absence of many of these characteristics helps explain why livestock, slaves, wampum, and tree bark did not fare well as money. But because cigarettes came quite close to having these qualities, they served reasonably well as money in prisoner-of-war camps during World War II. Of course, convenience, durability, portability, and uniformity do not guarantee success as money. The Susan B. Anthony dollar coin still does not circulate well in the United States, perhaps because people fear it will be mistaken for a twenty-five-cent piece.

Coins have the advantage of durability, portability, uniformity, and convenience.

The uniformity feature is especially important in making coins generally accepted. Long ago, gold dust or nuggets in a pouch had to be weighed when a transaction was made. But by minting the gold into a coin, it was possible to achieve uniformity. Sometimes, in an effort to gain a certain edge in the transaction, people would rub or chip away some of the coin. Though even kings and princes did this, they soon found that the official mint itself was the best place to cheat on the money system. To make more money with a given amount of gold, they could add *base* (less-valuable) metal before the coins were minted. This practice led to one of the earliest economic theories about money, called **Gresham's Law,** which states that base money always drives the *dear* (more-valuable) money out of circulation. Of two coins with the same face value, the one containing base metal circulates, while the one containing dear metal is hoarded or perhaps melted down to recover the metal. This law still operates today, it seems. The real silver coins in the United States are almost all in hoards or have been melted down.

Gresham's Law states that base money always drives more valuable or dear money out of circulation.

Currency Printed paper money is easy to carry, reasonably durable, and can be printed in whatever denominations are wanted and even in different colors to aid in recognition. Clipping and rubbing won't erode the value of the paper money. For larger transactions, paper money clearly has advantages over coin. In fact, paper currency evolved from coins and precious metal partly because of its extra convenience. Coins or, more likely, gold would be deposited with a bank or other institution of recognized reliability in exchange for deposit receipts, that is, for promises to return the coins or the gold when the receipt was presented. The certificate might read "Pay to the bearer on demand the sum of _____." This warehouse receipt payable to the bearer was, in fact, paper currency and was called a **bank note** when it was issued by a bank. Its acceptability depended on the integrity of the issuing bank or commercial establishment since it was backed by a promise to exchange coin or precious metal for the certificate.

Paper currency, which originated as bank notes, is more convenient than coins for large transactions.

The early days of paper money were confusing times because many different institutions would issue these notes, and some were more reliable than others. People could never be sure that their notes were really worth the amount printed on them. The reason for this confusion was that banks and others who issued notes had discovered that, in normal times, new deposits of gold or coins would just about balance withdrawals of these precious metals. So why not issue a few extra notes and lend them, charging interest, to people who want to borrow? As you will see, this was the beginning of modern partial reserve banking. However, our immediate point is that some banks would push their luck in issuing bank notes, and a bank failure would occur, shaking confidence in all bank notes, even those from banks that were not overextended. U.S. history is filled with accounts of bank panics triggered by the inability of some banks to redeem their notes. In an attempt to reduce this danger, a system of national banks was set up in 1863 to issue paper currency, and a tax was imposed on the circulation of bank notes issued by banks chartered by states. The tax drove the bank notes out of existence, but, as we shall see, the banks responded with something even better—the checkable account.

The history of government-sponsored currency is at least as fascinating as that of private bank notes. Governments also can yield to the temptation to issue too much currency. Government currency has often been issued without any (or very much) "backing" with precious metal. The official U.S. currency today, called the Federal Reserve Note, is not backed by any promise to exchange it for gold or silver or anything else. However, the particular advantage of government-issued currency is that an official government decree, or "fiat," usually states that the currency is **legal tender.** Your Federal Reserve Note, for example, bears the statement "This note is legal tender for all debts, public and private." This means that a person who is offered this currency but refuses to accept it in settling a debt cannot continue to collect interest on the debt or go to court to claim that the debtor had refused to pay. This goes a long way toward making the official currency generally acceptable, but it does not guarantee this result. In times of actual or prospective inflation, private contractors may try to force payment in real goods or precious metal rather than legal tender money. So even legal tender money can become worthless if people refuse to exchange goods and services for it. During the American Revolution, General Washington's troops at Valley Forge often went cold and hungry because of the difficulties the Continental Army had in buying supplies with continental currency. Similarly, during the Civil War, foreign money and gold became the most valuable part of the Confederacy's treasury. One of the last acts of the Confederacy was the attempt to get its gold and foreign money to Cuba for safe-keeping.

The official U.S. currency today is the Federal Reserve Note, which is backed by a government decree, or fiat, stating that it is legal tender.

Checkable Account Balances   In the United States today, balances in accounts against which checks can be written also serve as money. Although personal checks are not always accepted, a huge volume of obligations regularly are paid by check. Note that our description of this money refers to the balances in **checkable accounts**, not to the checks themselves. Under this definition, checks that are not backed by sufficient balances are not money.

Checkable account balances come into being partly as a result of deposits of coins or currency but mostly as a result of loans made by **depository institutions**—organizations such as banks, savings and loan associations, and credit unions that accept deposits of funds and offer checking services. When a person negotiates a loan, he or she may ask for and receive currency and coin, but most likely both the borrower and the lending institution will prefer the simple procedure of adding the borrowed sum to the balance in the borrower's checkable account. Through this simple operation, the borrower's promise to repay the loan (the borrower's debt) is "monetized." That is, it becomes

actual money. For this reason, many people say that most of our money supply is simply **monetized debt**. In the context of U.S. history, it is interesting that checkable account money expanded as bank note currency was eliminated. When taxes were imposed on the bank notes, bank lending switched to checkable account balances. Checks replaced the bank notes and had the extra convenience of being written for the exact amount needed to discharge an obligation. Instead of promises to pay issued by the bank, a check is a payment order to a depository institution signed by the person or business with rights to the checkable account. Bad checks are written, but they do not compromise the institution itself or invite a panic.

Depository institutions are profit-seeking business enterprises such as banks, savings and loan associations, and credit unions that accept deposits of funds and offer checking services on these accounts.

Balances in accounts against which checks can be written also serve as money. Most of the U.S. money supply today is monetized debt—loans by depository institutions that borrowers promise to repay.

The U.S. Money Supply

As you might expect from the phrase "anything that is generally accepted" in our definition of money, the actual measurement of the money supply can be somewhat complicated. Moreover, the things that are money may change from time to time as new technologies bring better ways to carry out exchanges. Four different measures of the U.S. money supply are illustrated in Figure 1. These are alternative definitions that are used in measuring the actual U.S. money supply. The definitions have been established by the Federal Reserve System, which we describe in Chapter 13. In Figure 1, we encounter broader and broader definitions of money as we move down the column.

M1   Coins and currency are listed at the very top of the money column in Figure 1 because these

FIGURE 1
Official Measures of the U.S. Money Supply, October 1988 (in billions of dollars)

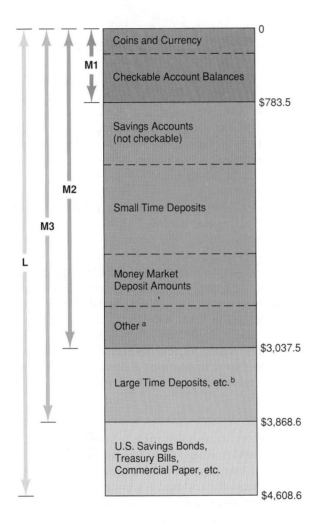

At the top of the money column are the most liquid, or spendable, types of money. The most widely used measure of the money supply (M1)—in the darkest shade of green—includes coins, currency, and checkable account balances. More inclusive measures of the money supply extend—in lighter shades of green—further down the column. Cumulative totals at the right show the larger and larger size of the money supply as more inclusive definitions are used.

a. Overnight repurchase agreements, Eurodollars, money market mutual fund shares.

b. Term repurchase agreements, term Eurodollars, institution-only money market mutual fund balances.

Source: Economic Report of the President, 1989, Table B-67.

items are extremely liquid—that is, they are easily used as a medium of exchange. Next in line come checkable account balances, which are also very liquid. Checkable account balances include not only the traditional demand deposits (on which the depository institution pays no interest) but also interest-bearing accounts such as NOW (negotiable orders of withdrawal) accounts, ATS (automatic transfer service) accounts, share-draft accounts in credit unions, and other accounts that offer check-writing services. Such interest-bearing checkable accounts expanded rapidly during the 1970s and have remained very popular ever since. Their advantage is that interest is earned during the period before checks are written against the account. The **M1 money supply concept**—shown in the darkest shade of green in Figure 1—is the one that is used most by economists and is the one we refer to when we discuss the money supply in later chapters.

The M1 measure of money includes coins, currency, and checkable account balances (including interest-bearing NOW, ATS, and share-draft accounts as well as the non-interest-bearing demand deposit accounts).

M2, M3, and L   As we proceed down the money supply column in Figure 1, we encounter assets that are less and less liquid. Small time deposits (such as certificates of deposit), money market deposit accounts, and (noncheckable) savings accounts are not spendable in their present form, but can usually be exchanged for directly spendable forms without delay or cost. These deposit balances generally are accessible on demand. A bit less liquid are "other" types of assets such as repurchase agreements (RPs)—arrangements with banks or with securities dealers that give the owner the chance to convert back to spendable money without great delay or cost. Also included in this "other" category are Eurodollars, which are dollar-denominated accounts outside the United States. Even though they appear in the accounts of American banks, the lending business on these accounts is done mainly in Europe. The **M2 money supply concept** consists of M1—the darker green area in

Figure 1—plus these less liquid accounts, which have a slightly lighter green background in the figure.

The **M3 money supply concept** includes, in addition to M2, large time deposits, fairly long-term repurchase agreements, and certain other assets, shown with a still lighter green background in Figure 1. All of these are somewhat harder to convert into spendable money. Finally, money watchers also keep track of U.S. Savings Bonds, several relatively liquid kinds of U.S. government securities, payment promises by large corporations, and other items that are potentially convertible into spendable money. The **L money supply** is M3 plus these forms of wealth, which are sometimes called **near money.**

M1, M2, M3, and L are definitions of the money supply established by the Federal Reserve System. They are used to measure the actual U.S. money supply. Their liquidity becomes less and less as we move from M1 to M2 to M3 and to L.

M2, M3, and L include assets that are less liquid than M1 assets.

Some observers contend that economists, bankers, government officials, and other money watchers have gone too far in developing so many different measures of the money supply. They argue that confusion results from such a variety of money measures. The problem is that there are many ways of holding wealth and that very gradual changes in liquidity occur as assets are moved from one form to another. Usually there is a trade-off between liquidity, which has its advantages, and interest earnings, which are desired for obvious reasons. The many asset forms simply give people a large number of options. In fact, the liquidity column could be extended still farther into such other less liquid assets as jewelry, stamp collections, and works of art. Even credit cards have some moneylike features, though they simply give a person an easy way to borrow money.

Sometimes the rate of change in the money supply according to one measure is different from its rate of change according to another measure.

Therefore, when economists use money supply changes to make predictions about the economy, it may make a difference which measure they use.

DEPOSITORY INSTITUTIONS

From the economist's definition of money, we know that balances in checkable accounts are money. Also, we know that these checkable account balances are part of the official M1, M2, M3, and L measures of the U.S. money supply. Our next step in understanding money is to examine the institutions in which these checkable account balances are kept.

In a modern economy, there are many types of firms that provide financial services. In studying the money supply, we concentrate on *depository institutions*, which include both commercial banks and thrift institutions. **Commercial banks** accept deposits and make all kinds of loans, including loans to business firms. **Thrift institutions**, such as savings and loan associations, mutual savings banks, and credit unions, accept deposits and make primarily consumer and mortgage loans. As we shall see, these institutions play an important role in determining the actual quantity of money in the economy.

Depository institutions include commercial banks, which accept deposits and make all kinds of loans, and thrift institutions, which accept deposits and make primarily consumer and mortgage loans.

Depository Institutions and Partial Reserves

Depository institutions are profit-seeking business enterprises. With money from depositors and shareholders, they earn income by lending money and by purchasing and holding interest-bearing securities. Some of the income that they obtain is used to pay interest to depositors. Some is used for other expenses, such as wages for employees. What is left are earnings that may be paid to shareholders if the firm is organized as a private corporation, or may be credited to the accounts of shareholder-depositor members of credit unions, mutual savings banks, or some savings and loan associations.

Depository institutions earn income by lending money and by purchasing and holding interest-bearing securities.

In many ways, starting a depository institution is similar to starting any new business. But what makes it somewhat different is that state and federal laws require that a charter must be obtained before the depository institution can do business. The **charter** is the legal authority to accept deposits and make loans, much as the corporate charter is the legal authority to do business as a corporation or a medical license is the legal authority to practice medicine.

In the United States, charters are issued both by the federal government and by state governments. Often, the institution's name will tell where its charter came from. The First National Bank has a federal charter, and the Home Town State Bank has a state charter, for example. Although federal and state charters have similar provisions specifying permissible operations, state charters are frequently more generous. Along with general legislation, the charter sets the rules that must be followed in doing business. Violating these rules may mean the withdrawal of the charter and the end of business. Once the charter is in hand, the depository institution can sell stock and/or otherwise gather the money needed to launch its operations.

Depository institutions must obtain charters (the legal authority to accept deposits and make loans) from either the federal government or a state government.

A key idea in understanding the operation of depository institutions is the concept of partial, or fractional, reserves. In their simplest form, **partial, or fractional, reserves** mean that the amount of cash or immediately available funds on hand is less than the total of the obligations to the people who have deposited money in the institution. If all depositors appeared at the same time and wanted their money, the institution would not be able to keep its promise of repayment. This would be a "run" on the institution and could be disastrous for the depositors, for the depository institution, and for those planning to borrow from it.

The partial reserve system under which depository institutions operate means that the amount of cash immediately available is less than the total of the institution's obligations to all who have deposited money in it.

Why do depository institutions operate on a partial reserve basis and run some risk of this disaster? Why are depositors willing to place their money in these institutions? The answers to these questions are not as difficult as you might imagine. Depository institutions engage in partial reserve operations because it is profitable to do so. Depositors place their funds in these institutions because they can receive checking and other services and can earn interest on their deposits. To understand how this system works, let's view it through the eyes of the management of the depository institution. If a wide variety of depositors can be persuaded to deposit their money, it will soon become apparent that day-after-day new deposits will just about equal withdrawals from these accounts. Some customers will be writing checks to others who hold deposits in the same institution. No change in net deposits will occur. Also, checks written to outsiders will approximately match checks from outsiders. Suppose that over a long period of time, the difference between withdrawals and new deposits fluctuates within a range of, say, 5 percent of the average amount on deposit. With this knowledge, the management recognizes that 95 percent of the deposited money (or perhaps only 90 percent, to leave a margin for safety) could be loaned out at interest. The interest earned from the loans enables the institution to pay interest to the depositors, and the spread between the interest charged to borrowers and the interest paid to depositors leaves money for expenses and for dividends to the owners and members.

There are also advantages from the point of view of the depositors. These people have wealth and can choose among many alternative ways to hold it. To obtain quick spendability (liquidity), they might hold cash but will earn no interest. To obtain dividend or interest earnings, they might purchase stocks or bonds, but their risk will be greater, and their wealth will have less liquidity. However, the depositor today can have both liquidity and interest earnings by placing funds in a depository institution.[1] As long as the danger of loss of deposits is minimal, there is little reason to forgo the advantages of earning interest. In a well-run depository institution, the stockholders and members, the depositors, and also those who borrow can all find the arrangement beneficial.

Depository institutions use the partial reserve system because it is profitable to do so. Depositors are willing to place their funds in these institutions because they receive checking and other services and can earn interest on their deposits.

The partial reserve feature clearly implies that money put into a depository institution, either by shareholders or by depositors, can be used as a reserve for a considerably greater quantity of money circulating in the economy. In times past, this money took the form of bank notes. Today, it takes the form of checkable account balances. We shall carefully explain this process of monetary expansion later in the chapter. But first it is important to understand how partial reserve banking can also be safe banking.

Regulation and Deposit Insurance

Government regulation of depository institutions has its roots in the attractiveness of the fractional,

or partial, reserve system and in the temptations that go along with it. For example, if operating with a 50 percent reserve is profitable, operating with only a 25 percent reserve is more profitable. Why not only 10 percent reserve, or even 5 percent, if depositors can be persuaded that their funds are safe? At various times in U.S. history, the virtual absence of effective regulation gave rise to the devious and unscrupulous practices generally referred to as **wildcat banking.** Institutions were started with the barest minimum amounts of initial funding from investors. Depositors were persuaded to entrust their savings to these institutions. Loans were made and bank notes were issued until obligations far exceeded readily available assets. In this precarious situation, uncollectible loans or the least hint of a business downturn could force the institution into bankruptcy. Then, one failure would follow another as depositors scrambled to withdraw deposits from surviving institutions. Runs on financial institutions would spread like wildfire until an entire region, or even the whole economy, was engulfed in a financial panic.

There are essentially two lines of defense against the panics and financial disasters that can come from fractional reserve systems. One is regulation of the operations of depository institutions and the other is insurance for deposits in them.

The partial reserve system can lead to financial panic if depositors lose trust and all try to withdraw their money at once. Runs on depository institutions can be averted by regulation and insurance.

Regulatory Agencies Each depository institution is subject to regulation by the government that issued its charter. Since charters are issued by the federal government and by each of the fifty state governments, there are many regulatory agencies. At the federal level, the chief regulatory agencies are the Federal Reserve System for member banks and bank holding companies, the Comptroller of the Currency for nationally chartered banks, the Federal Home Loan Bank Board for federal savings and loan associations, and the National Credit Union Administration for credit unions with federal charters.

---

1. Interest is not paid on demand deposit balances. But NOW accounts, ATS accounts, credit union share drafts, and the like, in effect offer both checking services and interest earnings for depositors. Before the introduction of these accounts, checking service was usually offered without charge—an arrangement that offered a valuable service in place of cash interest earnings.

The primary function of regulatory agencies is to examine the books of the institutions for which they are responsible and to determine whether they should be allowed to continue operation. Examiners from the regulatory agencies come unannounced to depository institutions and examine the records of deposits and withdrawals and of loans that these institutions have made. If the examiners conclude that a particular institution has many outstanding loans that will not be repaid and that it is in danger of bankruptcy, the regulatory agency has the authority to require the closing of the institution, the sale of its assets, and the distribution of the proceeds to satisfy the claims of depositors and other creditors. If the sale of the insolvent institution does not yield enough money to cover obligations to depositors, the deposit insurance system (described next) is called upon to make payments to the depositors to the extent of insurance obligations.

Each depository institution is regulated by an agency of the government that issued its charter. The regulatory agencies examine the records of deposits, withdrawals, and loans at depository institutions to make sure that they are financially sound.

Deposit Insurance The second line of defense against the problems of partial reserve operation is deposit insurance. Deposit insurance guarantees that, should an institution fail, depositors will recover their deposits up to the (current) limit of $100,000 per account. To purchase this insurance, depository institutions pay premiums to the insuring agency. Deposit insurance protects depository institutions against runs by depositors fearful that they might lose their deposits if the institution were to fail. If deposits are protected by insurance, there is no need for depositors to withdraw their funds.

As in the case of regulatory agencies, both federal and state agencies provide deposit insurance. At the federal level, the Federal Deposit Insurance Corporation (FDIC) insures deposits in banks, the Federal Savings and Loan Insurance Corporation (FSLIC) insures deposits in savings and loan associations, and the National Credit Union Share Insurance Funds (NCUSIF) insures accounts in credit unions.

Deposit insurance guarantees that depositors will recover their deposits (up to $100,000 per account) should the institution fail. Deposit insurance is designed to forestall runs on depository institutions.

Deregulation and the Crisis of Thrift Institutions

Despite the protection offered by regulatory agencies and deposit insurance, depository institutions can still face the threat of bankruptcy. Insolvency became a major concern in the 1970s and 1980s, when technological advances brought enormous changes to financial institutions. The combination of telecommunications and computers made it possible to transfer balances instantaneously between types of accounts and between one institution and another around the world. It became easy for depositors to move their balances between accounts and between institutions in their search for high rates of return. Competition among institutions to attract deposits became fierce.

Interest on Checkable Accounts One of the first results of the new technology was the inability of regulatory agencies to prevent the payment of interest on balances in checkable accounts. In their competition to attract deposits, institutions developed various procedures to allow interest to be paid on checkable balances. Basically, these procedures allow balances in interest-bearing accounts to be transferred automatically and instantaneously to a checkable account whenever a check is presented for payment. The various names for these procedures include **automatic transfer service (ATS) accounts** in banks, **negotiable order of withdrawal (NOW) accounts** in savings and loan associations, and **share-draft accounts** in credit unions. These procedures first became widespread in the early 1970s.

Technological advances led to fierce competition among financial institutions in the 1970s and 1980s. Interest payments on checkable balances became widespread as a means of attracting depositors.

Elimination of Interest-Rate Ceilings Record high nominal interest rates existed during the inflationary years of the late 1970s and early 1980s. These high nominal rates greatly increased competitive pressures among financial institutions and caused large losses of deposits from those depository institutions prevented, by government regulation, from paying more than a stated maximum rate of interest to their depositors. Especially hard hit by losses of deposits were savings and loan associations, for which interest-rate ceilings had been set at low levels in order to provide low-priced financing for residential mortgages. Funds were drained away from regulated depository institutions in favor of the more generous returns offered by money-market accounts maintained by stock brokerage firms. In an effort to help threatened savings and loan associations and other depository institutions, the Depository Institutions Deregulation and Monetary Control Act of 1980 mandated a gradual elimination of the interest rate ceiling that was allowed to be paid on deposits.

High nominal interest rates in the 1970s and 1980s greatly increased competitive pressures among financial institutions and led to large losses of deposits from those depository institutions that had to conform to government-set interest-rate ceilings.

Thrift Institution Bankruptcies Allowing thrift institutions to pay higher interest rates to their depositors opened the way for another threat of bankruptcy for these institutions. Although they could attract deposits with the higher interest rates, their earnings on already outstanding loans and mortgages continued at the low interest rates carried over from the era of regulation. Profit margins were squeezed, and an increasing number of thrift institutions faced bankruptcy. Further deregulation attempted to deal with this problem. The Thrift Institutions Restructuring Act of 1982 (Garn-St. Germain) relaxed regulations limiting the types of loans that these institutions might make. The purpose of this legislation was to enable thrift institutions to gain higher rates of return by extending loans in areas of greater yield (and greater risk) than offered by their previous home mortgage and consumer credit lending.

Although the federal government eased its restrictions on interest rates in 1980, depository institutions still faced financial difficulty because their earnings on already outstanding loans and mortgages continued at the low interest rates carried over from the era of regulation.

For most thrift institutions, the opportunity to move into higher-risk lending was not sufficient to overcome their difficulties. Problems were especially common in agricultural areas and in petroleum-producing regions of the southwestern United States. Falling land values and crude oil prices and the collapse of the oil drilling market added to the bad debt problems of thrifts and other financial institutions. Depository institution bankruptcies reached record high levels.

In 1982, the federal government relaxed regulations limiting the types of loans depository institutions may make in a further attempt to prevent widespread bankruptcies, but depository institution bankruptcies reached record high levels in the early and mid-1980s.

The Crisis in Deposit Insurance

What happens when a depository institution faces bankruptcy? First, examiners from regulatory agencies find that the institution is in danger of being unable to meet its obligations to depositors. Then, the regulatory agency must decide whether the institution should be closed, its assets sold, and its deposits returned to their owners. If the sale proceeds do not generate enough money to cover obligations to depositors, the deposit insurance agency is called upon to make good on its insurance commitment to these institutions.

In 1986, the Federal Savings and Loan Insurance Corporation did not have enough reserves to meet its insurance obligations to all the thrift institutions that were, at that time, believed to be insolvent. In other words, the crisis in the thrift industry had become so serious that it was a crisis for the insurance system as well. Since the FSLIC did not have enough reserve funds to close the insolvent institutions, "creative accounting" devices, including certificates provided by the FSLIC that could be counted as assets, were used so that the institutions could appear solvent and could continue to operate while the FSLIC looked for funds and strategies to bolster its ability to meet its insurance obligations. Nevertheless, by 1989, five hundred U.S. savings and loan associations were insolvent.

What were the FSLIC's options at this point? Should it raise insurance premiums on still-solvent thrifts and risk pushing them into bankruptcy also? Should it scale back its coverage to less than the promised $100,000 per account? Should it adjust its insurance premium schedules so that thrifts taking greater risks would have to pay more for their insurance? Should it deny insurance to thrifts that fail to follow prudent lending strategies?

The two strategies mentioned last—risk-based insurance premiums and denial of insurance to imprudent thrift institutions—point specifically to additional problems connected with the deposit insurance system. From the viewpoint of some thrift institution managers, the availability of deposit insurance and the relaxation of limitations on deposit interest payments opened up "heads I win, tails you lose" opportunities. Loans could be made at terms favorable to the borrower and at high risk to the lending institution. If the venture succeeded, the loan would be repaid and the lender would prosper. If the venture failed, the loans would default, the thrift institution would become insolvent, and the insurance system would be called upon to pay off the depositors. As more and more thrift managers, in desperation or for personal gain, took this path, more and more thrift institutions failed, and the insurance system fell further and further behind in its ability to fulfill its obligations to depositors.

In 1986, bankruptcies in the thrift industry reached such proportions that the FSLIC did not have enough reserves to meet its obligations to all the depository institutions that were insolvent. By 1989 five hundred savings and loan associations were insolvent.

Where will it end? At the time of this writing, it appears increasingly likely that U.S. taxpayers will eventually be required to make good the deficit in the deposit insurance system.

Interstate Banking and Nonbank Banks

The revolution in computer technology and telecommunications has made financial institutions more competitive and has broken through barriers that previously separated financial institutions from other business firms. Two areas of particular interest are interstate banking and nonbank banks.

Interstate Banking   In the United States, the business of **banking**—accepting deposits and making commercial (business) loans—has, for the most part, been confined within the boundaries of the separate states. Federal charters for banks were authorized by the National Banking Act of 1863, and a few of these national banks were allowed to open branches in states other than the one in which their head offices were located, but the McFadden Act of 1927 put a stop to this as it specifically prohibited bank extension across state lines.

During the past two decades, as the rapid transfer of account balances became more and more feasible through advancing technology, there arose new interest in permitting banks to extend branches across state lines. Part of the pressure for these extensions came from possible economies of scale in banking—a larger bank might experience lower unit cost and therefore offer more and better services. Another part came from the desire of financial interests in one state to take advantage of profit opportunities in other states.

The Douglas Amendment of 1970 to the Bank Holding Company Act of 1956 permitted bank holding companies (corporations that own one or more banks) to engage in **interstate banking**— to own banks in several states. However, holding companies could purchase banks only in those states passing laws permitting this type of activity. Starting with Maine in 1975, state after state changed its laws to allow interstate banking. By now interstate banking has become widespread, and many banks are owned by bank holding companies headquartered in other states.

Nonbank Banks The legal definition of a bank, according to the Bank Holding Company Act, is that it is an institution that accepts deposits and makes commercial loans. But what is the status of an institution that provides one of these services but not the other—for example, one that accepts deposits but does not make commercial loans? Is it a bank or isn't it? The answer is that it is a "nonbank bank"!

Nonbank banking began after 1970 when bank holding companies were authorized to acquire nonbanking subsidiaries. The question that arises with respect to mixing banking and nonbanking operations is whether firms that are not primarily in the banking business should be allowed to provide banking services. Should firms such as General Motors, Sears, American Express, or Merrill Lynch be allowed to mix banking with their other lines of business? Can it lead to undesirable financial practices or excessive concentrations of economic power? Or will it just be healthy competition in the financial industry? These questions have arisen time and again in recent discussions concerning bank legislation and regulation.

Interstate banking and nonbank banking (allowing firms not primarily in the banking business to provide banking services) became widespread in the 1980s.

DEPOSIT EXPANSION AND CONTRACTION

The fractional, or partial, reserve system described earlier in the chapter opens the way for depository institutions to expand or contract the money supply. This capability is a by-product of the fractional reserve system. There is nothing illegal or magical about financial institutions "creating" or "destroying" money. The process is not difficult to understand.

The partial reserve system allows depository institutions to expand or contract the money supply.

The Balance Sheet of a Depository Institution

In order to understand the deposit expansion process, it is necessary to have some acquaintance with the balance sheet of a depository institution. In Table 1, we present a simplified balance sheet for commercial banking institutions in the United States. The types of assets and liabilities on this balance sheet are representative of those for depository institutions in general. Assets are listed on the left side, and liabilities and net worth on the right.

Assets Let us briefly explain each entry on the left side first.

Reserves and Cash Items. **Reserves** consist mainly of deposits that depository institutions are required by law to maintain with the Federal Reserve System. In the next chapter, we shall describe the Federal Reserve System and how reserve requirements are set. This item on the balance sheet is very important in the deposit expansion process. Cash items consist of all cash in the vault and in the tellers' cages, along with other miscellaneous items.

A depository institution's reserves consist primarily of the deposits that it is required by law to maintain with the Federal Reserve System.

Loans. These are the IOUs from individuals and/or businesses who have borrowed from the institution. They are the main source of interest earnings for the depository institution. Interest earnings from these loans and from securities provide funds to pay interest to depositors, to cover operating expenses, and to pay dividends to shareholders or members.

Loans are the main source of interest earnings for depository institutions.

Securities. These are mainly government bonds that depository institutions buy and hold in order to generate interest income while at the same time retaining fairly quick access to funds.

Other Assets. These consist of buildings, furni-

TABLE 1
Balance Sheet of Commercial Banking Institutions in the United States, February 28, 1989 (in billions of dollars)

Assets		Liabilities and Net Worth	
Reserves and cash items	226.0	Checkable deposits	601.4
Loans	2,057.9	Savings deposits	528.7
Securities	535.5	Time deposits	991.7
Other assets	211.4	Borrowings	500.9
		Other liabilities	212.3
		Total liabilities	2,835.0
		Net worth	195.8
	3,030.8		3,030.8

Source: *Federal Reserve Bulletin,* May 1989, Table 1.25.

ture, and equipment needed to carry on the institution's operations. This category also includes minor items not conveniently listed elsewhere.

Liabilities and Net Worth   Now let's take a look at the entries on the right side of the balance sheet.

Checkable Deposits. These are amounts owed to holders of accounts against which checks can be written. When a depositor writes a check, he or she is placing a demand on the institution to transfer money to someone. These accounts are payable on demand and therefore sometimes called **demand deposits,** or **transaction deposits.**

Savings Deposits. These are amounts owed to holders of savings accounts. Checks cannot be written against these balances. Technically, they are not payable on demand. Some waiting period or advance notice may be required.

Checkable deposit (sometimes called demand or transaction deposit) accounts are payable upon demand—that is, whenever a depositor writes a check. Savings deposits are technically not payable upon demand, since checks cannot be written against them.

Time Deposits: Time deposits are obligations to the holders of accounts that have stated dates when they will have to be paid—that is, they have fixed maturity dates. Certificates of deposit are examples of this type of account. Depository institutions can

pay somewhat higher rates of interest on these deposits since they are committed to remain in the institution for a longer period of time. This kind of account gives greater flexibility in lending out this money.

Borrowings: These are IOUs given by depository institutions when they borrow from other financial institutions. If an institution can borrow at a low rate of interest and lend the money out at a higher rate, there is every reason to expect that it will do so.

Other Liabilities: These are obligations that depository institutions, like any other business, have but which do not fit into other categories.

Net Worth: Assets minus liabilities equal net worth—that is, the book value of the business to its owners. The net worth of a business includes the money that was paid in by original stockholders minus losses that have been suffered plus profits that have been earned but not paid out as dividends.

The Reserve Ratio

The **reserve ratio** is a key term in understanding how depository institutions expand and contract the money supply. This ratio is the institution's total of cash and official (government-approved) reserves divided by the amount of its checkable account liabilities. Suppose that a depository institution has $20 in cash and official reserves and $100 in checkable deposit liabilities. Its reserve ratio would be 20 percent. Official reserves must be held in the form of deposits with the Federal Reserve System or vault cash, except that sometimes institutions can arrange to hold these reserves with other financial institutions, which, in turn, maintain reserve deposits with the Federal Reserve System.

Another term that is important to understand is the **reserve requirement**—the amount of official reserves that depository institutions must maintain in order to avoid penalties. The reserve requirement is generally expressed as a minimum required reserve ratio. In our example, if the reserve requirement were 20 percent, the institution in our illustration would be exactly in conformity with the law. It would not have too few reserves, and it would have no **excess reserves.** This is another key idea in the expansion process. Excess reserves are official reserves over and above the reserve requirements.

A depository institution's reserve ratio is the total of cash and official reserves divided by the amount of its checkable account liabilities. The reserve requirement is the amount of official reserves that depository institutions must maintain in order to avoid penalties.

Excess reserves are those over and above the official reserve requirements.

The Deposit-Expansion Process

Depository institutions are able to expand and contract the nation's money supply because they operate with partial reserves. This means that, when a new deposit is received, only part must be held as reserve for the deposit itself and the rest can be loaned out. The money loaned out is, in effect, new money, because the original depositor still has full command over the whole amount of the initial deposit.

When a new deposit is received in a depository institution, only part must be held as reserve for the deposit itself, and the rest can be loaned

---

out. This process expands the money supply because the money loaned out is, in effect, new money.

We will illustrate the deposit-expansion process with a series of balance sheets starting with those in Table 2. These balance sheets are simplified to show only the entries needed to explain the expansion process and by showing zero balances initially (top panel) for each account. We shall assume that the reserve requirement for checkable accounts is 20 percent. We shall ignore the fact that depository institutions must also maintain reserves for other types of accounts.

The **deposit-expansion process** starts when a new deposit is made in a depository institution. This is shown in the middle panel of Table 2. To use the simplest illustration, we assume that Bill Brown deposits $100 of currency that previously had been circulating as hand-to-hand money.[2] He deposits the $100 in his checkable account, which is a liability entered on the right side of the balance sheet for Depository Institution A. On the asset side, the $100 is recorded in the "reserves and cash" category. In parentheses below this entry, you will note that these reserves consist of $20 that is required and $80 of excess reserves. No expansion of the money supply has yet taken place. Even though Bill Brown's checkable account balance is counted as money, only coins and currency *outside* depository institutions are included in the official definition of the money supply. Therefore, Bill's checkable account balance simply replaces the currency that he deposited.

The stage is set, however, for an expansion of the money supply. Depository Institution A has excess reserves in the amount of $80, given our assumed 20 percent reserve requirement for checkable accounts. If Ron Black wants to borrow $80 and if the institution is willing to lend it to him, an expansion of the money supply will take place. This step is shown in the bottom panel in Table 2. Mr. Black signs a note to the depository institution, which it lists as an asset in the loans category, and

---

2. You will learn in the next chapter that the central bank is the most likely originating source of new deposits into the banking system.

TABLE 2
Deposit-Expansion Process: Depository Institution A (amounts in dollars)

Start			
Assets		**Liabilities**	
Reserves and cash	0	Checkable deposits	0
(Required: __0__)			
(Excess: __0__)			
Loans	0		
Securities	0		
	0		0

New Deposit Step			
Assets		**Liabilities**	
Reserves and cash	100	Checkable deposits	
(Required: 20)		Bill Brown	100
(Excess: 80)			
Loans	0		
Securities	0		
	100		100

Loan Step			
Assets		**Liabilities**	
Reserves and cash	20	Checkable deposits	
(Required: 20)		Bill Brown	100
(Excess: __0__)			
Loans			
Ron Black	80		
Securities	0		
	100		100

The process begins in the "new-deposit step" when Bill Brown deposits $100 in his checkable account. The depository institution then has excess reserves of $80, which are loaned to Ron Black in the "loan step."

Mr. Black takes the proceeds of his loan in currency. The reserves and cash account is reduced to $20, all of which is required, and both Ron Black and Bill Brown have money to spend.

Since Mr. Black did not borrow the money for the sheer pleasure of paying interest, we assume that he soon spends it to buy something, say, electronic equipment from the Green Radio Company. Green Radio deposits the currency in its checkable account in Depository Institution B (top panel in Table 3). After this institution places the money in its reserves and cash account, it is ready (even eager) to lend out the $64, which is in excess of the prevailing 20 percent reserve requirement. The story continues. Sue Blue, who keeps her checkable account with Depository Institution B, has a good credit rating and wants to borrow $64 to pay for a repair on her car. So she signs a note to Depository Institution B, which lists it as an asset in the loans category (bottom panel in Table 3). For

TABLE 3
Deposit-Expansion Process: Depository Institution B (amounts in dollars)

New Deposit Step			
Assets		**Liabilities**	
Reserves and cash (Required: <u>16</u>)	80	Checkable deposits Green Radio Co.	80
(Excess: <u>64</u>)			
Loans	0		
Securities	<u>0</u>		—
	80		80

Loan Step			
Assets		**Liabilities**	
Reserves and cash (Required: <u>16</u>)	16	Checkable deposits Green Radio Co.	80
(Excess: <u>0</u>)			
Loans			
Sue Blue	64		
Securities	<u>0</u>		—
	80		80

When cash loaned by a depository institution returns to the system as a new deposit, the stage is set for a second round of deposit expansion. In this stage, Green Radio Company deposits the $80 spent by Ron Black. Depository Institution B now has excess reserves of $64, which it loans to Sue Blue.

convenience, Ms. Blue takes her loan in the form of a $64 addition to the balance in her checkable account and writes a check for $64 to the White Motor Company to pay for the auto repair. Since we expect borrowers (Ron Black and Sue Blue) to spend their money promptly, it does not matter whether they accept the loan in cash or as an entry in their checkable accounts. The depository institution expects the prompt departure of the borrowed money, either in cash or as soon as the White Motor Company or someone else presents Sue's check for payment.

As you probably expect, the deposit-expansion process is far from over. As soon as White Motor deposits the $64 in Depository Institution C (see top panel in Table 4), that institution finds that it has excess reserves in the amount of $51.20—the $64 deposit minus the $12.80 of required reserves. Depository Institution C decides to put these excess reserves to work by purchasing bonds in the bond market. Bonds of the Yellow Cab Company appear to be a good buy, and on that day Grace Gray happens to be selling her holdings of these bonds. The institution buys the bonds, which it lists as an asset in the securities category on its balance sheet (see the bottom panel of Table 4), and, through the system of markets and brokers, Grace Gray receives a check for $51.20. She deposits the check in her checking account in Depository Institution D, and the expansion process continues.

The deposit-expansion process is summarized in Table 5. It started in our example when Bill Brown put $100 of currency into a checkable account. Once this money was in the system of depository institutions, the expansion process went into operation as new checkable account balances were created for the Green Radio Company, the White Motor Company, Grace Gray, and others. The cumulative-totals column in Table 5 emphasizes that all of these balances exist at the same

TABLE 4
Deposit-Expansion Process: Depository Institution C (amounts in dollars)

New Deposit Step			
Assets		**Liabilities**	
Reserves and cash	64	Checkable deposits	
(Required: 12.80)		White Motor Co.	64
(Excess: 51.20)			
Loans	0		
Securities	0		
	64		64

Loan Step			
Assets		**Liabilities**	
Reserves and cash	12.80	Checkable deposits	
(Required: 12.80)		White Motor Co.	64
(Excess: 0)			
Loans	0		
Securities			
Yellow Cab Co.	51.20		
	64.00		64

In the third round of the deposit-expansion process, White Motor Company deposits the check written by Sue Blue, and Depository Institution C has excess reserves of $51.20. The institution purchases $51.20 of Yellow Cab Company securities from Grace Gray.

time and that all of them are money according to the prevailing definition. Our example assumed that money loaned out was then deposited in a different depository institution. However, the process would work in the same way if the money came back to the same institution that made the loan.

The **deposit-contraction process** follows the same sequence, except that it starts with a withdrawal instead of a deposit. If the depository institutions are in exact conformity with the reserve requirement when the withdrawal occurs, securities will be sold, and loans will be called in or not renewed. As a result, checkable deposits will shrink.

The deposit-contraction process follows the same sequence as the deposit-expansion process, except it begins with a withdrawal instead of a deposit.

The Deposit-Expansion Factor

You undoubtedly recognize that the arithmetic in Table 5 is like that used in the Keynesian model to explain the multiplier effect of changes in total planned expenditure on equilibrium national income and product. In other words, we have a geometric progression, in which each successive round generates new deposits equal to a fixed percentage of those created in the preceding round. The reserve ratio operates in the same way that $(1 - MPC)$ did in the formula for the multiplier. In terms of the reserve ratio actually operating in the depository institutions, the **deposit-expansion factor**

TABLE 5
Summary of Deposit-Expansion Process

	Checkable Deposit Balances	
	Individual Accounts	Cumulative Totals
Bill Brown (Depository Institution A)	$100.00	$100.00
Green Radio (Depository Institution B)	80.00	180.00
White Motor (Depository Institution C)	64.00	244.00
Grace Gray (Depository Institution D)	51.20	295.20
etc. (Depository Institution E)	40.96	336.16
etc. (Depository Institution F)	32.76	368.92
etc. (Depository Institution G)	26.21	395.13
.	.	.
.	.	.
.	.	.
(nth Depository Institution)	.	$500.00
	$500.00	

Bill Brown's initial deposit is expanded by deposits for Green Radio, White Motor, Grace Gray, and others. All of these demand deposits exist at the same time, and all count as money. With a 20 percent reserve ratio, total deposits may be five times the initial deposit.

is

$$\frac{1}{\text{reserve ratio}}$$

In our example, we assumed that the depository institutions were always in exact conformity with the legal reserve requirement, so that the reserve ratio was 20 percent at all times. In this case, the deposit-expansion factor was 1/0.2, which works out to a value of 5.[3] The first deposit of $100 was expanded to support an added $400 in checkable deposits, so that the total of checkable deposits was $500. If the reserve ratio had been kept at 25 percent, the expansion factor would have been 4. If the reserve ratio had been kept at 10 percent, the expansion factor would have been 10, and so on.

The deposit-expansion effect, like the multiplier effect, is a geometric progression, in which each

---

3. We arrive at the answer in the following way:

$$1 + (0.8) + (0.8)^2 + (0.8)^3 + \cdots$$
$$+ (0.8)^n = \frac{1}{1 - 0.8} = \frac{1}{0.2} = 5$$

successive round generates new deposits equal to a fixed percentage of those created in the preceding round.

Controlling the Expansion Factor

The reserve ratio, and therefore the expansion factor, is controlled through the Federal Reserve System's authority to set the official minimum reserve requirement. This is stated as a percentage of the amount on deposit in accounts that offer check-writing services. As of May 1989, the required reserve was 12 percent of such balances. We shall explain in the next chapter just how this official minimum ratio is set. The profit motive will encourage depository institutions to keep the actual reserve ratio fairly close to the official ratio, since excess reserves earn no interest and a deficiency in reserves will force the institution to borrow and pay interest. So the Federal Reserve System can control the deposit-expansion factor by setting the official reserve ratio.

Depository institutions may not always remain in exact conformity with the official reserve requirement, and therefore the Federal Reserve System's control of the expansion factor is less than perfect. Institutions may keep some excess reserves on hand to avoid problems from unexpected withdrawals or so that they will be ready to accommodate especially good customers when they ask for loans. These are called **desired excess reserves.** There also is a second reason why the control of the expansion factor is not exact. Our expansion process assumed that borrowers (Ron Black and Sue Blue) quickly spent every cent that they borrowed. However, if some of the funds borrowed are kept as pocket money or simply allowed to circulate from hand to hand in the economy, the deposit expansion will stop short of its full potential. The actual expansion, therefore, is not as exact as the deposit-expansion factor and our example imply.

The Federal Reserve System controls the expansion factor through its ability to set the

---

official minimum reserve requirement. However, its control is not perfect, because depository institutions may not always remain in exact conformity with the official reserve requirement and also because not all borrowed funds are quickly spent.

Controlling the Money Supply

In the United States, the money supply is regulated by (a) controlling the deposit-expansion factor and (b) by controlling the actual amount of reserves in the depository institution system, as will be described in the next chapter. You will learn about the Federal Reserve System, which is the "central bank" in the United States and is responsible, under legislation from Congress, for administering both of these steps in controlling the money supply.

Economics in Focus

The S&L Crisis

The 1980s brought a heady expansion in the savings and loan industry, then a resounding crash. By 1989 five hundred savings and loan institutions, commonly called S&Ls, were insolvent. Losses throughout the industry were climbing at a rate of a billion dollars a month. The Federal Savings and Loan Insurance Corporation (FSLIC), the agency that insures customers' deposits, was itself essentially bankrupt.

How did this happen? Before 1980 the S&L industry was a staid, conservative one. The federal government limited the interest rates that S&Ls could pay, and industry analysts joked about the 3-6-3 rule: pay 3 percent on deposits, make home mortgage loans at 6 percent, and leave for the golf course at 3 o'clock. But because S&Ls had trouble competing in the inflationary period of the late 1970s, Congress began to deregulate the industry. Soon S&LS were allowed to pay whatever interest they liked, compete with each other recklessly for "brokered" deposits (money deposited by such large money-management companies as Merrill Lynch), and enter such risky fields as development and construction.

The new rules attracted some unscrupulous players, especially in states such as Texas where real estate boomed in the early 1980s. Potential profits were huge, and the FSLIC was there to back up large mistakes. The situation was summed up "Heads I win, tails FSLIC loses."

But the mid-1980s brought a collapse in real estate values in the large oil cities of Texas. S&Ls began to slide, and some spectacular failures occurred. A too-late attempt by government regulators to curb the industry's excesses only made matters worse, and soon it became clear that the FSLIC could not possibly support all the failing institutions. The Federal Home Loan Bank Board, the FSLIC's parent agency, tried to bypass the problem by arranging mergers of weak S&Ls into stronger ones, but a massive government bailout program was still required.

Critics have charged that the federal government itself is responsible for much of the disaster. Government regulators, the critics say, had too cozy a relationship with S&L executives, lobbyists, and politicians. Lenient practices allowed S&Ls to conceal their losses and overstate their profits. Some aggressive S&Ls even made single loans greater than their net worth, with no objection from examiners. A few regulators who issued warnings were ignored. In the hastily arranged mergers certain rules were bent; takeover artists seemed to profit unduly; and some of the new "superthrifts" looked hardly less shaky than their predecessors.

In the end the public will foot the bill, and estimates of the long-run cost range as high as $230 billion. One lesson seems clear: However many safeguards are established by law, the banking system needs sensible and trustworthy supervision by the appropriate government agencies.

Sources: Thomas Moore, "The Bust of '89," *U.S. News & World Report,* January 23, 1989, pp. 36–43; Kathleen Day, "When Hell Sleazes Over," *The New Republic,* March 20, 1989, pp. 26–30; Catherine Yang and Frederic A. Miller, "Can Bush's Thrift Doctors Find a Treatment That Will Take?" *Business Week,* February 13, 1989, pp. 80–81; Robert E. Norton, "When You're in a Hole, Stop Digging," *U.S. News & World Report,* January 23, 1989, p. 46; Terry Bivens and Richard Burke, "A Look Inside Perelman's S&L Deal," *Philadelphia Inquirer,* May 7, 1989, pp. 1-A, 19-A; Rich Thomas, "How Taxpayers Lost the S&L Numbers Game," *Newsweek,* February 20, 1989, pp. 32–33.

SUMMARY

1. Most economists believe that changes in the amount of money in the economy and in the speed of its circulation can cause changes in the general price level and can also cause changes in real levels of production and employment. (See page 248.)

2. Economists define money as anything that is generally accepted as a medium of exchange, a unit of account, a store of purchasing power, and a standard for deferred payment. At various times and places, many different things have served as money. (See pages 250–251.)

3. According to the definition most widely used in the United States—called M1—the money supply consists of coins, currency, and checkable account balances. Checkable account balances are the largest component. The currency is "fiat money"; that is, the government specifies it to be legal tender. (See pages 252–253.)

4. Broader definitions of the money supply— M2, M3, and L—include forms of wealth that are somewhat less liquid than coins, currency, and checkable account balances. (See pages 253–254 and Figure 1, page 253.)

5. Depository institutions include banks, savings and loan associations, credit unions, and mutual savings banks. They earn their incomes by obtaining money from investors and depositors and lending money to individuals and businesses. The difference between interest charged and interest paid provides money to cover expenses and to pay dividends to shareholders. (See pages 254–255.)

6. Depository institutions operate with partial, or fractional, reserves, which means that money deposited can be used to support new checkable account balances that are created when the institution makes loans to customers. (See page 255.)

7. The partial reserve system involves risks of bank failure. These risks are reduced by officially designated examiners and by deposit insurance. Nevertheless, many thrift institutions became insolvent in the mid-1980s when interest rate ceilings were eliminated. In 1986, the Federal Savings and Loan Insurance Corporation did not have enough money to meet its insurance obligations to thrift institutions that were insolvent and by 1989 about five hundred were considered to be insolvent. (See pages 255–259.)

8. A depository institution's reserve ratio is its total of official reserves divided by its total checkable account liabilities. The reserve requirement is the official reserve ratio that must be kept in order to avoid penalties. Excess reserves are those over and above the official reserve requirement. (See pages 260–262.)

9. Because depository institutions operate with partial, or fractional, reserves, a new deposit gives rise to excess reserves. There is a deposit expansion when these excess reserves are loaned out or used to buy stocks and bonds. When the new loan or the payment for the securities is itself deposited in a depository institution, the expansion can be repeated. The deposit-expansion factor is 1 divided by the reserve ratio actually in use. (See pages 262–266 and Tables 2–5, pages 263–266.)

10. The Federal Reserve System's authority to set minimum reserve requirements allows it to regulate the size of the deposit-expansion factor. This regulation is not precise, however, because some depository institutions may not be in exact conformity with the official reserve requirement and because some of the money brought about through new loans may not be returned to the system. (See pages 266–267.)

11. The deposit-contraction factor operates to reduce the money supply. Deposit contraction is begun when deposits are withdrawn and not deposited again. In this case, depository institutions must sell some of their securities, call in loans, or refuse to renew loans when they fall due. (See page 265.)

12. The Federal Reserve System's control of the money supply is carried out in two ways: it can control both the deposit-expansion factor and the amount of reserves in depository institutions. (See page 267.)

KEY TERMS

automatic transfer service (ATS) account: a checkable account that permits the payment of interest (page 257).

banking: the business of accepting deposits and making loans including commercial loans (page 259).

bank note: a certificate issued by a bank which promises to pay a specified sum to the bearer of the certificate (page 251).

barter: a direct exchange of one good or service for another (page 248).

charter: the legal authority, issued by either the federal government or a state government, to operate a depository institution, that is, to accept deposits and accept loans (page 255).

checkable accounts: accounts in depository institutions against which checks can be written. Balances in these accounts are sometimes called demand deposits or transaction deposits (page 252).

commercial banks: banks that accept deposits and make all kinds of loans, including loans to business firms (page 254).

demand deposits: *see* **checkable accounts.**

deposit-contraction process: the process by which depository institutions are able to contract the nation's money supply (page 265).

deposit-expansion factor: 1 divided by the reserve ratio maintained by depository institutions (page 265).

deposit-expansion process: the process by which depository institutions are able to expand the nation's money supply by holding only part of a new deposit as reserve for the deposit and loaning the rest out (page 262).

depository institution: an organization such as a bank, a savings and loan association, or a credit union that accepts deposits of funds and offers checking services (page 252).

desired excess reserves: reserves held by depository institutions that are over and above those required by law so that they can avoid problems from unexpected withdrawals or be ready to accommodate customers who ask for loans (page 267).

excess reserves: reserves held by depository institutions that are over and above those required by law (page 262).

fractional reserves: *see* **partial reserves.**

Gresham's Law: the proposition that coins made with base (less-valuable) metal drives the more-valuable money out of circulation (page 251).

interstate banking: when holding companies own banks in more than one state (page 259).

L money supply: M3 money supply plus near money (U.S. Savings Bonds, certain kinds of U.S. government securities, payment promises by large corporations, and other items that are potentially convertible into spendable money) (page 254).

legal tender: government-issued currency that legally must be recognized as a valid offer of payment for a debt (page 251).

M1 money supply concept: coins, currency, and checkable account balances (page 252).

M2 money supply concept: M1 plus such less liquid assets as small time deposits, money market mutual fund balances, noncheckable savings balances, repurchase agreements, and Eurodollars (page 254).

M3 money supply concept: M1 and M2 plus large time deposit balances, long-term repurchase agreements, and certain other assets that are somewhat harder to convert into spendable money (page 254).

medium of exchange: something used for the intermediate step in exchange (page 248).

monetized debt: money created on the basis of debt obligations (page 253).

money: anything generally accepted in an economy as a medium of exchange, a unit of account, a store of purchasing power, and a standard for deferred payment (page 250).

near money: items such as U.S. Savings Bonds and several relatively liquid kinds of U.S. government securities, and payment promises by large corporations that are potentially convertible into spendable money (page 254).

negotiable order of withdrawal (NOW) account: a checkable account in a savings and loan association that permits the payment of interest (page 257).

partial (fractional) reserves: the situation in which cash or immediately available funds kept on hand by depository institutions are less than the total of the obligations to the people who have deposited money in the institutions (page 255).

reserve ratio: a depository institution's total of cash and official (government-approved) reserves divided by the amount of its checkable account liabilities (page 261).

reserve requirement: the amount of official reserves that depository institutions must maintain to avoid penalties (page 262).

reserves: cash on hand plus deposits that depository institutions maintain with the Federal Reserve System (page 260).

share-draft account: a checkable account in a credit union that permits the payment of interest (page 257).

standard for deferred payment: a standard way to specify the amount of a payment that is to be made some time in the future (page 250).

store of purchasing power: the ability to save some of the medium of exchange for use at a later date (page 249).

transactions deposits: *see* **checkable accounts.**

thrift institutions: depository institutions such as savings and loan associations, mutual savings banks, and credit unions that accept deposits and make primarily consumer and mortgage loans (page 254).

unit of account: a function of money that allows it to be used to compare the values of different items (page 249).

wildcat banking: banking practices in which depositors were persuaded to entrust their savings to institutions that then made loans and issued bank notes until their obligations far exceeded their readily available assets (page 256).

DISCUSSION QUESTIONS

1. Why is it not possible to define money in terms of its composition? Identify the four functions of money that are specified in economics. Which of them is the most basic? Why? Which is (are) most affected by inflation?

2. Write down the definition of money given in this chapter. Then explain why the words "generally accepted" are basic to this definition. What is Gresham's Law? Explain why it still works.

3. Explain how a bank note is an ancestor of modern paper currency. Does today's U.S. currency have more or less backing than did the early bank notes? Explain your answer. What does *legal tender* mean?

4. Describe two different ways in which you can add to the balance in your checkable account. Why is much of our money actually "monetized debt"? Explain.

5. Explain the term *liquidity*. Why do slight differences among assets in their liquidity create problems in measuring the money supply? Briefly summarize the types of assets included in the M1 category of the U.S. money supply.

6. What is a "run" on a depository institution? Since runs are always possible under the partial reserve system, why are depositors willing to expose their money to this risk? Explain how the partial reserve system operates to the advantage of all people involved.

7. Discuss the roles of examiners and deposit insurance in improving the safety of deposits under the partial reserve system. Why does a reserve requirement not guarantee safety? What is the reason for the legal reserve requirement in the U.S. depository institution system?

8. How did ceilings on interest rates payable by thrift institutions cause problems for these institutions during the 1970s? Why is it important to have premium payments on deposit insurance bear reasonably close relationships to the risks taken when deposited money is loaned out?

9. Without looking at Table 1, prepare a simplified balance sheet for a depository institution and record its major entries. Then check to make sure you have it right. Explain how electronic technology led regulators to allow interest to be paid on checkable account balances.

10. Carefully distinguish between the actual reserve ratio and the official required reserve ratio. What happens if the actual ratio is less than the requirement? What happens if the actual ratio is more than the requirement? Explain what is meant by "excess" reserves and why they are important in the economy.

11. Trace the process by which the depository institution system expands the amount of money when excess reserves appear. How does the official reserve requirement control the amount of this expansion? Write the formula for the deposit-expansion factor. Describe two situations that may cause the actual expansion not to follow exactly the formula for money expansion.

13

The Federal Reserve System and Monetary Instruments

Preview   As you have learned, depository institutions operate on partial reserves and are able to expand and contract the money supply. This chapter will explain how the Federal Reserve System, the central bank of the United States, regulates the money supply. Regulating the money supply is a key ingredient in the *monetarist* approach to macroeconomic policy, just as regulating taxes and government purchases are key ingredients in the *fiscalist* approach. In this chapter, we examine monetary instruments for macroeconomic policy.

We start by describing the beginnings of the Federal Reserve System—how it was set up after many years of dissatisfaction with an earlier system. Then we explain how the Federal Reserve System is organized through twelve district banks and describe the services that it offers. The Board of Governors of the system meets in Washington, D.C., to set policy. Many people believe these seven governors to be the most powerful nonelected officials in the country. The Federal Open Market Committee, which includes the seven members of the Board of Governors, buys and sells government securities to affect the money supply.

The second part of this chapter describes **monetary instruments,** or the tools used to regulate the money supply. Among the monetary tools are the setting of reserve requirements for depository institutions, the buying and selling of government securities (open market operations), the setting of interest rates on loans to depository institutions (called discount rates), and attempts to persuade them to cooperate with central bank policy. We explain the money multiplier concept to show how difficult it is to maintain exact control of the money supply.

We review the various guidelines or target variables that have been used in the operation of monetary policy. These discussions set the stage for the following chapter, which will explain the relation of the money supply to inflation and to the level of equilibrium real national income and product. Finally, in an appendix, we review the record of actions taken by the Federal Reserve in its job of controlling the money supply.

THE FEDERAL RESERVE SYSTEM

Most industrial countries have a centralized monetary authority, generally called a central bank, which is an arm of the Treasury or the finance ministry. The central bank of the United States, called the **Federal Reserve System,** is different from most central banks because of its relative independence from the Treasury and the other offices of the administration.

The Federal Reserve System is the central bank of the United States. Created in 1913, it is relatively independent of the Treasury Department and White House.

The Federal Reserve System, often called the "Fed," was begun by an Act of Congress in 1913 because Americans had come to dislike the earlier system. The National Banking System, which dated from the Civil War, operated without a central bank. It had developed two major problems. These were the seasonal "money shortages" in farming areas when crops had to be financed and a susceptibility to nationwide panics because of the "pyramiding" of reserves. The seasonal money shortages arose because the amount of currency that could be issued did not respond to seasonal changes in the demand for cash.

The system's susceptibility to nationwide panics was a more serious problem. This happened because a large part of the reserves of small banks could be held as deposits in banks in larger cities and because these banks, in turn, could hold a large part of their reserves as deposits in banks in a

few major cities. So, as small banks called for funds from the larger city banks and as these larger banks called for funds from the major city banks, cash demands and reserve problems arising in isolated areas would build up and create a panic. This **pyramiding of reserves** set the stage for repeated nationwide bank panics. One such panic in 1907 led to the passage of the Federal Reserve Act in 1913.

Many Americans favored a strong European type of central bank, but those in the agricultural parts of the country were suspicious of the East and "Wall Street" and wanted as much control as possible over regional monetary conditions. Because they did not really trust bankers, they wanted farmers and business people to share control of the system. Under the Federal Reserve Act, the country was divided into twelve districts, a Federal Reserve Bank was set up in each district, and a Board of Governors was charged with supervising the operation of the whole system. The new system was designed to control the money supply, to provide a more flexible currency (the Federal Reserve Note), and to be a lender of last resort that could prevent bank failures by making loans to banks when trouble arose, thus forestalling panics. Though modified by experience and additional legislation, the structure set up in 1913 is much the same today.

To ensure regional rather than central control over monetary conditions, the country was divided into twelve districts under the supervision of a Board of Governors. The Federal Reserve System was designed to control the money supply, to provide a more flexible currency, and to prevent bank failures.

The Board of Governors

On the **Board of Governors** of the Federal Reserve System are seven people appointed by the president of the United States and confirmed by the Senate. No two members can come from the same Federal Reserve District, and none can hold other jobs while they are a member of the board. Their terms are for fourteen years, with one member's term expiring every second year. Part of the reason for this long term of office is to protect the Board from short-run political pressures and so to give the Federal Reserve a degree of independence from the executive and legislative branches of the government.

The Board is responsible for directing the nation's monetary policy, which can be used either to counteract or to reinforce the fiscal policy undertaken by the president and Congress. Thus, the independence of the Board is one of the checks and balances that have been built into the U.S. system of government.

As a practical matter, however, we should not overstate the independence of the Board of Governors. Members sometimes resign before the end of their fourteen-year terms, so that appointments must usually be made oftener than every two years. Also, every four years the president can choose a member of the Board to serve as chairperson.

Over the years, the monetary policy followed by the Board has generally been consistent with the fiscal policy of the president and the Congress, but on important occasions conflict has arisen.

The seven members of the Board of Governors are appointed by the president to fourteen-year terms. These long terms are intended to give the Federal Reserve a degree of independence from political pressure.

The Federal Open Market Committee

The **Federal Open Market Committee (FOMC)** has twelve members, seven of whom are the members of the Board of Governors. The other five members come, one each, from five of the Federal Reserve District Banks. The Federal Reserve Bank of New York always provides one of these five committee members, and the other four positions are filled, on a rotating basis, from the other Federal Reserve Banks.

The Federal Open Market Committee was not a part of the original (1913) structure of the Federal Reserve System, but experience during the 1920s showed that the purchase and sale of securities by the Federal Reserve Banks could have important effects on the economy. When the FOMC became an official agency of the Federal Reserve System in the 1930s, informal cooperation among the banks was replaced by direct control by the Board of Governors. Buying and selling government securities in the open market is one of the most powerful tools of monetary policy, and most of the major decisions for the system are made at the regular meetings of the FOMC.

The Federal Open Market Committee has twelve members, the seven members of the Board of Governors plus five members from the Federal Reserve District Banks. The FOMC controls the buying and selling of government securities on the open market.

The Thrift Institutions Advisory Council

The Depository Institutions Deregulation and Monetary Control Act of 1980 extended the authority of the Federal Reserve System to all depository institutions, including savings and loan associations, mutual savings banks, and credit unions. The **Thrift Institutions Advisory Council** was set up in 1983 to provide a channel through which these newly covered institutions could present their views. The council has ten members, seven from savings and loan associations, two from mutual savings banks, and one from credit unions. Although it has no voting power, the council meets with the Board of Governors four times each year to present the views of thrift institutions.

Federal Reserve District Banks

The map in Figure 1 shows the locations of the twelve **Federal Reserve Banks** and the boundaries of their districts. This geographic distribution recognized the diverse interests of the various parts of the country and countered the fears of centralized banking and eastern domination that had plagued the earlier attempts to set up a central bank. Each district bank is expected to serve the banking and commercial interests of its district

FIGURE 1
The Federal Reserve System

Note: Alaska is in the Seattle Branch Territory and Hawaii in that served by the Head Office of the Federal Reserve Bank of San Francisco. Both are in the Twelfth District.
Source: Federal Reserve Bulletin, May 1989.

with appropriate expertise, such as ranching in Kansas City, oil and gas in Dallas, agriculture in Chicago, and trade and finance in New York. Each Federal Reserve Bank is owned by the banks in its district which become members of the system by purchasing stock in their district bank. All **national banks** (those chartered by the federal government) must be members of the system. If state banks choose to join, they may do so. The Federal Reserve Banks generate profits from interest on the securities they own and pay dividends to their shareholding member banks. However, federal law limits the amount of dividends that can be paid. Any "excess" profits must be turned over to the U.S. Treasury.

There are twelve Federal Reserve Banks; each district bank is owned by banks in its district and is expected to serve the banking and commercial interests of its district.

Each Federal Reserve Bank receives deposits and handles checks for the federal government and provides many services to depository institutions. Among their main services are check clearing and making loans. A detailed description of most of these services is best left to specialized courses in money and banking. However, their service of making loans is directly related to the Federal Reserve's regulation of the money supply, which is our focus in this chapter.

The Depository Institutions Deregulation and Monetary Control Act of 1980, which extended Federal Reserve authority to cover thrift institutions as well as banks, specified that Federal Reserve District banks could make loans to savings and loan associations, mutual savings banks, and credit unions in their districts. Making loans to depository institutions is a way to meet one of the major goals in setting up the Federal Reserve System in 1913—assuring the soundness of the financial system and preventing panics. To achieve this goal, each Federal Reserve Bank is expected to understand the economic needs of its district. If a depository institution has temporary difficulty, a loan from the Federal Reserve Bank can be arranged. This **lender of last resort** service ranked high among the objectives in setting up the system. Loans are carried out through a process called **discounting,** because originally securities or promises from a borrower were purchased by a Federal Reserve Bank at less than their value at maturity. Today, direct loans are made instead of the more complicated procedure of discounting. The **discount rate** is the rate of interest charged on these loans. Discounting not only can help depository institutions but also can be an instrument for controlling the money supply.

The Federal Reserve Banks clear checks for and make loans to depository institutions. The Federal Reserve System is able to influence the country's money supply by means of this loan-making service.

Federal Reserve Bank Balance Sheet

A simplified balance sheet for the twelve district banks of the Federal Reserve System is presented in Table 1. On the asset side, the most important item is U.S. government securities. These are debt instruments that have been issued by the U.S. Treasury. They make up part of the national debt. Even though most of the national debt is held by private

TABLE 1
*Balance Sheet for Federal Reserve Banks, February 28, 1989
(in billions of dollars)*

Assets		Liabilities	
U.S. Government securities	229.5	Federal Reserve Notes	222.8
Other securities	8.4	Deposits	
Other assets	46.7	Reserve accounts[a]	37.0
		U.S. Treasury	6.3
		Other	0.8
		Other liabilities	12.6
			279.5
		Capital Account	
		Paid in	2.1
		Other	3.0
Total	284.6	Total	284.6

a. These are deposits from depository institutions.
Source: Federal Reserve Bulletin, May 1989, Table 1.18.

citizens and firms (including depository institutions), the part held by the Federal Reserve Banks is very important. Most of this part consists of short-term securities (ninety-day Treasury bills) that have been acquired by the Federal Reserve Banks in carrying out open market operations, which are described later in this chapter.

On the liability side of the balance sheet, the major item is the Federal Reserve Notes circulating in the economy. These notes are the legal tender currency of the United States. Two other entries on the liabilities side also are important. One of these is the reserve accounts. In describing reserve requirements in Chapter 12, we noted that official reserves must be held as vault cash or as deposits in the Federal Reserve Banks. This is the balance sheet entry that records these reserve deposits. The other important entry on the liability side of the balance sheet is the deposit of the U.S. Treasury. One of the tasks of the Federal Reserve System is to handle the checking account of the federal government.

INSTRUMENTS OF MONETARY POLICY

Now that you know the structure of the Federal Reserve System and the services it provides, we can examine how it seeks to control the U.S. money supply. As you learned in the last chapter, checkable account balances are the major component of the money supply. You also know that the ability of banks to create checkable account balances depends on the amount of reserves in these banks and on their reserve ratios. Federal Reserve influences on the reserve ratio and the amount of reserves are the main elements of monetary policy in the United States.

Reserve Requirements

Cash and regular required reserves deposited with Federal Reserve District Banks earn no interest. Therefore, depository institutions try to keep the lowest possible reserve ratio that is safe and in keeping with the official reserve requirements. By setting minimum required reserve ratios, the Fed-

eral Reserve Board can strongly influence actual reserve ratios.

Federal Reserve influences on the reserve ratio and the amount of reserves are the main instruments of monetary policy in the United States. By setting minimum required reserve ratios, the Board can strongly influence actual reserve ratios and thus affect the deposit-expansion factor.

The deposit-expansion process described in Chapter 12 shows the importance of the Federal Reserve Board's power to raise or lower official reserve requirements. Raising the official reserve requirement will most likely raise the actual reserve ratio maintained by depository institutions and so will lower the deposit-expansion factor. Suppose that the actual reserve ratio is 12 percent. In this case, the depository institution system can support $833.33 of checkable deposits when the amount of reserves in the system is $100 ($100/0.12 = $833.33). But if the Board raises the reserve requirement so that the actual reserve ratio becomes 14 percent, this same $100 of reserves will support only $714.29 in checkable deposits ($100/0.14 = $714.29). The Board's action could force a great reduction in the money supply. On the other hand, lowering the reserve requirement so that the actual reserve ratio becomes 10 percent would allow these reserves to support $1,000 of checkable deposits ($100/0.10 = $1,000). The Board would have invited a large expansion in the money supply.

Raising the reserve requirement forces a reduction in the money supply. Lowering the reserve requirement invites an expansion in the money supply.

The Depository Institutions Deregulation and Monetary Control Act of 1980, which broadened the Federal Reserve System's authority to include all checkable and time accounts in all depository institutions, also specified ranges within which the Board of Governors could set official reserve requirements. For the first $31.7 million of checkable accounts in each institution, the law requires only a 3 percent reserve.[1] Above $31.7 million, the Board can set the reserve requirement anywhere it chooses between 8 percent and 14 percent. As of this writing, this required reserve ratio is 12 percent. For time deposits, the required reserve is 3 percent.

Before the 1980 law, the Federal Reserve System had had difficulty in regulating the money supply. There were different reserve requirements for different kinds of financial institutions. For this reason, the amount of required reserves would change when money was moved from one institution to another. These problems caused great trouble during the 1970s with the combination of very high interest rates and the vast changes taking place in the banking industry as computers and electronic bookkeeping systems were introduced. Operational distinctions between different types of accounts faded, as did the difference between banks and other kinds of depository institutions. In this atmosphere, the Depository Institutions Deregulation and Monetary Control Act of 1980 was seen as a necessary step to help the Federal Reserve System keep up with changing times.

Raising or lowering the official reserve requirement is a powerful instrument, but it is quite sparingly used. The main problem with the reserve-requirement instrument is that changes in reserve requirements can cause embarrassing problems for depository institutions as they try to serve their customers. Increases can cause the most trouble. If an institution is operating close to the official ratio in order to serve its stockholders or members, it may find that an increase in this ratio forces it to deny loans to customers or to borrow funds from a Federal Reserve Bank. For this reason, changing the reserve requirement is a heavy-handed and somewhat crude tool for adjusting the money supply. As you will see, there is another instrument that can perform more smoothly.

Open Market Operations

Open market operations consist of the buying and selling of government securities by the Federal Reserve Banks. These operations allow the Federal

1. This "break point" is determined by a formula. It stood at $31.7 million in 1988.

Reserve System to control the *quantity* of reserves in depository institutions, just as control of the reserve ratio makes it possible to control the deposit-expansion factor. Together, these two tools give the Federal Reserve System great power over the money supply in the United States.

Open market operations consist of the buying and selling of government securities by the Federal Reserve Banks. They enable the Fed to control the quantity of reserves in depository institutions.

Open market operations are directed by the Federal Open Market Committee (FOMC), which was described earlier. These operations are called "open market" because they are carried out in the same securities markets as those open to ordinary citizens and businesses. When the FOMC decides to buy securities, it pays the existing market price, and when it sells, it accepts the existing market price. The securities bought by the FOMC come from the holdings of private persons, depository institutions, or business firms, and those that are sold move into these private holdings. Even though the FOMC deals only in short-term government securities, the effects of its buying and selling are quickly felt in the prices of other securities in the open market.

Open market operations are directed by the FOMC.

Open Market Purchases A good way of illustrating open market operations is to describe the effects of a $100 purchase of government securities by the Federal Reserve System. The person, business, or depository institution that sells the securities receives a check from a Federal Reserve Bank in payment for the securities. When this check is deposited in a depository institution and cleared through the check-clearing system, the reserve account of the depository institution will be larger by $100. The Federal Reserve System has *created* $100 of reserves where nothing existed before. If the reserve ratio is 20 percent, only $20 of these new reserves will be required for the new deposit. The

TABLE 2
Open Market Purchase (amounts in dollars)

Federal Reserve Banks				The Depository Institution System			
Securities	+100	Reserve deposits	+100	Reserves	+100	Demand deposits	
						Seller of security	+100
				New loans	+400	New loans	+400
					+500		+500

When the Federal Reserve System purchases $100 of securities, its securities assets account expands by $100. When the check in payment for these securities is cleared, reserve deposits of depository institutions increase by $100. These accounts are liabilities to the Federal Reserve System and assets to individual depository institutions. If the reserve ratio is 20 percent, new loans can be made, so that the money supply may increase by as much as $500. The entries in the area with the white background represent new money created by the open market purchase.

remaining $80 is excess reserve, which the depository institution can use for lending. Because of the deposit-expansion process, which you studied earlier, the $100 open market purchase can expand the money supply by as much as $500.

Our hypothetical open market transaction is summarized in Table 2. On the balance sheet of the Federal Reserve Banks, the $100 expansion of the securities assets account is balanced by the $100 expansion of the liabilities account for reserve deposits. On the balance sheet for the depository institutions, the area with the white background shows that the $100 of new reserves supports $500 of new demand deposits, $100 of which came from the initial deposit and $400 from new loans made by the depository institutions. The effect on the money supply would have been the same if the security had been sold by a depository institution itself. New reserves would at first have come from a reduction in securities holdings, and all of these new reserves would have been "excess." The system could then generate up to $500 of new loans and demand deposits from these new reserves.

Open Market Sales Open market sales by the Federal Reserve System have the opposite effects from open market purchases; that is, sales contract the money supply. When the Federal Reserve sells a security, its asset account for securities shrinks. Then, when the purchaser sends his or her check to pay for it, clearing the check reduces the balance in the reserve accounts of the depository institution system. The $100 of reserves has been destroyed

and ceases to exist. If a 20 percent reserve ratio is being maintained, a $100 sale of securities by the Federal Reserve will bring as much as a $500 reduction in checkable account balances.

The Importance of Open Market Operations The great advantage of the open market instrument is its flexibility. Since the Federal Reserve Banks are trading most of the time in the open market, they can carry out policy in a subtle and gradual way. The net purchases or net sales position of the Federal Reserve can be adjusted day by day to meet seasonal or short-run needs for money and, at the same time, can lean in either an expansionary or a contractionary direction as long-term policy may require. Changes in policy need not subject individual depository institutions to untimely pressures, as is the case with changing reserve requirements. Through open market operations, changes in the money supply can be brought about without upsetting the routine operations of depository institutions.

The important part that could be played by open market operations was not recognized when the Federal Reserve System was set up in 1913. However, coordination of securities buying and selling among the Federal Reserve Banks began during the financially active 1920s. Then, in the 1930s, the FOMC was established, providing an orderly procedure for open market operations. Since that time, open market operations have become the most important instrument of monetary policy.

> **Since the creation of the FOMC in the 1930s, open market operations have become the most important instrument of monetary policy.**

The Discount Rate

The third basic instrument of monetary policy is the **discount rate,** which is the rate of interest that Federal Reserve Banks charge on loans to depository institutions. Loans to member banks and the discount rate were expected to be major monetary control tools when the Federal Reserve was set up in 1913. The loans would supplement reserves and allow the needed expansion of the money supply during prosperous times. Then, during recessions, the Federal Reserve Banks would be lenders of last resort to prevent bank failures and forestall bank panics. History was unkind to both of these expectations. As a money-supply regulator, the discount rate was largely displaced by open market operations. As a lender of last resort, the Federal Reserve System failed miserably to prevent bank failures in 1932 and 1933.

Changes in the discount rate have little *direct* impact on depository institutions unless they need to borrow from the Federal Reserve System. If a depository institution has excess reserves, it will not need to borrow, nor will borrowing be necessary if it holds government securities that can be sold on the open market to obtain reserves. For these reasons, most depository institutions are not directly affected by changes in the discount rate. However, these changes can have important *indirect* effects on lending and the money supply. A decision by the Board of Governors to raise the discount rate, for example, may be a signal that the Board plans to restrict the money supply, perhaps through future open market sales. Such action most likely will raise interest rates. In this case, the discount rate signal may suggest that depository institutions can earn a higher rate of interest by putting off lending until the higher rates really appear in the market. This can be a self-fulfilling prophecy, since lending restraint by depository institutions may, in fact, bring the higher interest rates that were expected. Of course, the signal can also operate in the other direction. Lowering the discount rate may lead to more aggressive lending operations in anticipation of expansionary open market policies from the Federal Reserve.

> **The discount rate is the rate of interest that Federal Reserve Banks charge on loans to depository institutions. Most depository institutions are not directly affected by changes in the discount rate, but these changes can have important indirect effects on lending and the money supply.**

The Federal Funds Rate

Borrowing by depository institutions through the discounting procedure is, according to Federal Reserve policy, a privilege rather than a right. Federal Reserve policy is that these loans should be made only when the institution's shortage of reserves is temporary and due to circumstances that could not reasonably have been anticipated by the borrowing institution. Thus, depository institutions are encouraged to look elsewhere for money before asking for a loan from the Federal Reserve. The logical place to look, of course, is to institutions that have excess reserves in their accounts in the Federal Reserve Bank. Balances in these accounts are called **federal funds.**

In the United States, there is a well-developed federal funds market. In this market, funds that are excess reserves for some depository institutions are loaned to others that need more reserves. The rate of interest charged on these loans is called the **federal funds rate.** This rate will generally rise when economic activity and lending are expanding rapidly.

> **Federal funds are reserve deposits in Federal Reserve Banks. Depository institutions can borrow these federal funds from one another. The federal funds rate is the interest rate charged on these loans.**

If the federal funds rate is lower than the discount rate set by the Federal Reserve System, depository institutions will clearly prefer to borrow in the federal funds market and will not come to their district Federal Reserve Bank for loans. But when the money supply is tightening, the federal funds rate may rise above the discount rate, and loans from the Federal Reserve Bank can ease the problems of individual depository institutions in adjusting to the tighter money situation. Thus, the "discount window" is a safety valve for individual depository institutions during a time when open market operations are restrictive. In these times, of course, the Federal Reserve Banks must carefully examine requests for loans and must ration this bank credit to prevent lending operations from canceling the effects of restrictive open market operations. The federal funds rate has also served as a guide for the implementation of Federal Reserve monetary policy. As will be described shortly, monetary policy has, at times, been "targeted" on the federal funds rate.

Other Instruments

Several other instruments are available to the Board of Governors besides the three that we have already mentioned. Even though reserve requirements, open market operations, and discounting are by far the most important, the other instruments do have their special uses.

Margin Requirements The Board may set **margin requirements** for stock market trading. In the language of the stock market, trading "on margin" means that money from the purchaser of a stock covers only a fraction of the price of the stock being bought, while the rest of the cost is borrowed from the stockbroker. The money put in by the purchaser is called the *margin*. The broker collects interest on the money loaned to the purchaser and is also protected by receiving the power to sell the stock to recover the amount loaned if the price of the stock falls far enough to wipe out the buyer's margin. The experience in 1929 showed that this arrangement could turn a stock market decline into a stock market disaster, since sales by brokers would force stock prices still farther down. Since the 1930s, the Board has had the power to set margin requirements in a range between 25 and 100 percent of the value of the stock. In the late 1960s, for example, the margin requirement was set at 80

percent, but since 1974 the margin requirement has been 50 percent.

Moral Suasion The Federal Reserve System can publicize the actions that it wants depository institutions to take. Using what is often called **moral suasion,** the Fed urges "cooperation" in promoting certain policy goals. Sometimes this approach is called jaw-boning. When there is danger of inflation, for example, the Fed may urge "restraint" in granting new loans. Moral suasion, like the other minor instruments of monetary control, may have some limited effect on the money supply and the behavior of depository institutions. However, the most important of the monetary instruments are the reserve requirements, open market buying and selling, and the discount rate for loans to depository institutions.

The three most important instruments of monetary policy used by the Federal Reserve System to control the money supply are reserve requirements, open market operations, and discounting. There are other instruments in addition to these, however, such as margin requirements on the purchase of stocks and moral suasion.

MONETARY POLICY

So far, we know that the Federal Reserve System is responsible for determining and implementing monetary policy. We also have examined the instruments available for implementing this policy. We now look at the goals that have been established for monetary policy and at the specific targets that are used in pursuit of these goals.

The Goals of Monetary Policy

Full employment, price stability, and economic growth are the accepted goals of national economic policy and therefore also of the monetary policy set by the Federal Reserve System. There is no generally agreed priority order among these goals. In times of slack economic activity, full employment is the top goal. When inflation threatens, priority is given to price stability. In the late 1970s and early 1980s, when the U.S. dollar rose and then fell greatly in relation to the monies of other countries and the U.S. trade deficit widened, "a reasonable balance in transactions with other nations" was included among the stated goals of monetary policy. Essentially, the Federal Reserve System examines the current economic scene, determines what it believes to be the most pressing problem facing the macroeconomy, and sets monetary policy to meet this problem.

Conflicts can arise among the goals of monetary policy. For example, in 1987 the U.S. dollar had fallen to low levels relative to major foreign monies. As a result, foreign goods sold in U.S. markets or used in U.S. factories had risen in price in terms of the dollar, raising fears of inflationary increases in the U.S. price level. Tightening the money supply and raising interest rates would strengthen the dollar and reduce the danger of inflation but could also slow economic growth, dampen economic activity, and cause unemployment. In early 1987, the Federal Reserve System saw inflation as the immediate threat and restricted money-supply growth.

The situation changed abruptly in October 1987, when the stock market experienced its most severe decline since the historic "crash" of 1929. Now, the Federal Reserve feared that economic uncertainty might stifle consumption and investment spending and plunge the economy into recession. A conflict existed between the price-stability goal and the goal of avoiding recession and unemployment. Stability in financial markets and in the economy became the priority goals of monetary policy. Fear of recession replaced fear of inflation, and money supply increases were permitted in spite of the effect they might have on the exchange value of the dollar and on the prices of imported goods.

The monetary policy goals set by the Federal Reserve System are full employment, price stability, and economic growth. The Fed sets monetary policy to solve what it feels are the most pressing economic problems at any given time.

Operating "Targets" for Monetary Policy

Once the "ultimate" goal has been selected, the Federal Reserve System must develop an effective procedure to carry out its policy. To do this, some variable that is important in the economy and readily available to money managers is selected and those who actually implement monetary policy—typically those in the New York Federal Reserve Bank who buy and sell on the open market—are directed to keep this **monetary-policy-target variable** within some range of values.

To carry out a monetary policy, the Federal Reserve System selects some variable that is important to the economy and directs those who actually implement monetary policy to keep this target variable within some range of values.

Interest-Rate Targeting A specific interest rate, such as the federal funds rate, may be selected as an operating target used for monetary policy. If the FOMC wanted to fight inflation by restricting growth of the money supply, it could raise the target level of the federal funds rate. In order to bring the federal funds rate to this target level, open market purchases would be scaled back, causing depository institutions to experience less than their usual growth in reserves. Some institutions would then be forced to borrow federal funds and, at the same time, the supply of these funds would be diminished, causing the federal funds rate to rise to the target level. Conversely, an easier, more expansionary monetary policy could be indicated by lowering the target for the federal funds rate. In this case, increased open market purchases would provide depository institutions with more reserves, reducing demand and increasing supply in the federal funds market and bringing the rate down to the target level.

Interest-rate targeting, such as stabilizing the federal funds rate, is called a policy of **accommodation.** It can be illustrated as follows. First, suppose an increase in demand for loans by businesses or consumers results in increased lending by depository institutions. This puts pressure on reserves and brings an increase in the federal funds rate as demand increases and supply decreases in that market. However, if the monetary target is to stabilize the federal funds rate, open market purchases would be increased, providing additional reserves and reducing the need for depository institutions to borrow in the federal funds market. In this way, the increased demand for loans (money) would be "accommodated" by an increase in the money supply.

Money Supply (*Nonborrowed Reserves*) *Targeting* Inflation rates reached unprecedented levels during the 1970s, and fighting inflation was an important goal of macroeconomic policy. Although inflationary pressures came from several directions, including government deficits and petroleum price increases orchestrated by the Organization of Petroleum Exporting Countries, the Federal Reserve System was criticized for not being more effective in stopping it. Some of the blame fell on interest-rate targeting and the policy of accommodation. In 1975, Congress mandated that the Federal Reserve System establish targets expressed as rates of increase in standard (M1, M2, and M3) measures of the money supply itself. In its annual reports to Congress and after its regular meetings every two months, the FOMC was to announce ranges for the percentage growth rates of M1, M2, and M3. Ranges rather than specific percentage rates were used partly because the FOMC recognized that its control of the money supply was not perfect and partly because the ranges left room for the exercise of judgment during the intervals between meetings of the FOMC.

In the 1970s, fighting inflation became an important goal of macroeconomic policy. In 1975, Congress directed the Federal Reserve System to establish target ranges for the percentage growth rates of the money supply.

Under the money-supply targeting system, those directly carrying out open market operations were instructed to base their actions on changes in the amount of **nonborrowed reserves** on hand in depository institutions—that is, on total reserves minus amounts borrowed through discounting

from Federal Reserve Banks. This was different from the federal-funds-rate target and the accommodation system used earlier. Specifically, increased demand for loans from depository institutions would not automatically be accommodated by open market purchases to increase the reserves of these institutions. Instead, when the FOMC specified stability or some limited rate of increase in nonborrowed reserves, institutions that wanted to expand lending would have to seek reserves either in the federal funds market or through loans from the discount window of their district Federal Reserve Bank. If the Federal Reserve System held firm against expanded lending through the discount window, expanded lending by depository institutions would cause higher interest rates and impose a moderating pressure on the economic expansion. Interest rates fluctuate more when money-supply targets are used than they do under an accommodation monetary policy regime.

To control money supply growth, the target ranges for percentage growth rates were based on the amount of nonborrowed reserves in depository institutions, that is, on total reserves minus amounts borrowed through discounting from Federal Reserve Banks.

Borrowed-Reserves Targeting In 1982, the operational guideline was changed from nonborrowed reserves to **borrowed reserves**—reserves borrowed at the discount window from district Federal Reserve Banks. Open market operations continued as the basic instrument of monetary policy, but day-to-day operations focused on borrowed reserves. Under the borrowed-reserves-targeting system, those in charge of open market operations are guided by the volume of borrowing through the discount windows of the Federal Reserve Banks. Low borrowed-reserve targets are used for expansionary monetary policy and high borrowed-reserve targets are used for restrictive monetary policy. This is because an expansionary monetary policy of open market purchases gives depository institutions more *nonborrowed* reserves and reduces their need to borrow at the discount window. A restrictive policy, on the other hand, reduces the *nonborrowed* reserves of depository institutions and increases borrowing at the discount windows.

In effect, borrowed-reserves targeting parallels interest-rate targeting, since lower levels of borrowed reserves typically are reflected in lower federal funds rates and higher levels of borrowed reserves typically involve higher federal funds rates. Thus, the use of borrowed-reserves targeting in the 1980s suggested an emphasis on stabilizing interest rates—a move part-way in the direction of accommodation.

In 1982, the Federal Reserve changed the operational guidelines for monetary policy from nonborrowed reserves to borrowed reserves—reserves borrowed at the discount window from district Federal Reserve Banks.

Problems in Targeting Monetary Aggregates

Three problems arise for monetary policy targeted on money supply aggregates such as M1, M2, and M3. They involve the monetary base, the money multiplier, and the velocity of circulation of money.

The Monetary Base   The **monetary base** is made up of reserves in depository institutions along with the coins and currency circulating in the economy. The Federal Reserve System can influence the size of the monetary base through open market operations and lending to depository institutions. But there are forces outside the Federal Reserve System that can also change the monetary base. For example, many U.S. dollars are held in foreign countries and are used in overseas operations. Changes in interest rates or in investment opportunities can bring funds into the U.S. economy or drain them out and so affect the U.S. monetary base. Similarly, U.S. Treasury operations influence the monetary base when there are changes in the flows of tax collections and transfer payments and when national debt securities are issued or retired. Therefore, when the Federal Reserve System uses its open market and lending ("discounting") instruments to regulate reserves, it must anticipate changes that may come from these outside influences.

The monetary base consists of reserves in depository institutions plus the coins and currency circulating in the economy. Several forces can influence the size of the monetary base, including flows of funds to and from foreign economies, and changes in the flows of tax collections and transfer payments.

The Money Multiplier   The **money multiplier** is the ratio between the amount of money (such as M1) in the economy and the size of the monetary base. For the money managers of the Federal Reserve System, the money multiplier is another variable that must be taken into account in doing their job of controlling the money supply. If the money multiplier is stable, their job is easier because they can be reasonably sure that a given change in the monetary base—achieved perhaps through open market operations—will result in a predictable change in the money supply. But if the money multiplier is not stable, it is difficult to predict accurately the effects of changes in the monetary base.

The money multiplier is the ratio between the amount of money in the economy and the size of the monetary base. If the money multiplier is not stable, it is difficult to predict accurately the effects of changes in the monetary base.

At least two forces can cause the money multiplier ratio to move up or down. One is that the reserve ratio actually maintained by depository institutions can fluctuate somewhat above the legal minimum reserve ratio set by the Board if these institutions maintain "desired" excess reserves. Therefore, the deposit-expansion factor may fluctuate. A second reason is that there is an ebb and flow of currency and coin between depository institution reserves and hand-to-hand circulation in the economy. When currency and coin are in hand-to-hand circulation, they count as money, but they are not official reserves. When they are deposited in depository institutions, they are not counted as money, but they become official reserves that can support several times their own worth in checkable account money. In other words, reserves themselves move up and down as currency and coin flow into and out of depository institutions.

Since the money multiplier equals the money supply divided by the monetary base, a different money multiplier is calculated for each of the three money supply concepts—M1, M2, and M3. When deposit holders shift their balances among different types of accounts, changes take place in the totals for the different money supply concepts and therefore also in the values of these different money multipliers. During the 1970s, when interest rates rose, depositors transferred funds out of M1-type (checkable) accounts, M1 became smaller relative to other asset categories, and the M1 multiplier fell. The trend reversed in the 1980s. Interest rates fell, depositors returned funds to M1-type accounts, and the M1 multiplier rose. Although their patterns were not so dramatic, the M2 and M3 multipliers also changed considerably over this period. Federal Reserve instruments influence the monetary base, but if the linkage to the money supply—the money multiplier—is unreliable, it is difficult to predict the ultimate effect on the money supply. Money supply management was difficult during the 1970s and 1980s.

Velocity of Money   The velocity of money is the third problem in carrying out monetary policy targeted on measures of the money supply. **Velocity** is the speed with which the average dollar circulates through the economy. For example, if the average dollar of the M1 money supply is used four times a year in purchasing currently produced goods and services, M1 velocity has a value of 4. In other words, M1 velocity is gross national product (GNP) divided by M1, M2 velocity is GNP divided by M2, and M3 velocity is GNP divided by M3. Velocity tells how hard the average dollar of the measured money supply works in the operation of the economy. Since the ultimate goals of monetary policy deal with the operation of the aggregate economy, velocity is important. Stable or reliably predictable velocity would greatly simplify the task of regulating macroeconomic activity through changes in the money supply. A given change in

the money supply would be expected to have a given effect on the economy, other things equal. But if velocity is not stable or reliably predictable, it is difficult to predict the effect of money-supply changes.

Velocity is the speed with which the average dollar circulates through the economy. If velocity is not stable, it is difficult to predict the effect of money-supply changes.

Computer technology and deregulation have led to great fluctuations in the velocity of money. Because of these innovations, account balances can be moved swiftly in response to changes in interest rates. If interest rates rise, balances are quickly withdrawn from M1 accounts, which offer relatively low interest rates, and redeposited in M2 or M3 accounts or used to purchase assets not included in the array of official measures of the money supply. The measured money supply shrinks and the measured velocity of money goes up. Conversely, when interest rates fall, the opposite movements take place. The measured money supply grows and measured velocity decreases. Obvious problems arise for monetary policy targeted on money supply data alone. For example, increased economic activity could cause higher interest rates and a consequent reduction in the measured M1 money supply. But a policy target of stable growth in M1 would lead Federal Reserve monetary operations to expand open market purchases, thus in effect accommodating the expansion of economic activity. In this way, a policy of stable growth in the measured money supply would have destabilizing effects on the macroeconomy.[2]

When interest rates rise, the measured money supply shrinks and the measured velocity of money goes up. When interest rates fall, the measured money supply grows and measured velocity decreases.

---

2. In October 1982, the Federal Reserve suspended the targeting of M1 because it believed that this measure of the money supply had become too volatile and was not a useful guide for implementing monetary policy.

Economics in Focus

The Fed Divided

Since its founding in 1913, there have been some dramatic disagreements between the Federal Reserve and the incumbent administration. Although the Fed does not have to follow administration dictates, the board usually trys to reach common ground on basic strategy with the White House. But what happens when the Fed cannot agree with itself?

Lately a strong division has developed between the seven-member Board of Governors and the presidents of the twelve regional banks. As of 1989, all seven governors were appointees of the Reagan administration; all, in fact, had joined the board between 1984 and 1988. As Reagan appointees, they tended to share the supply-side outlook that dominated the Reagan years. For example, Manuel H. Johnson, vice chairman of the board, was a former economics professor and Treasury official who had backed the Reagan tax cut of 1981. Martha Seger, the first woman appointed to serve a full term on the board, was a Michigan economist and professor who clearly remembered the damage done to Michigan's economy by the 1982 recession. Given their backgrounds and opinions, most of the board would be wary of continually forcing up interest rates to cool inflation; instead, they would tend to favor a somewhat looser monetary policy with more stimulus to the economy and less risk of recession.

Some of the twelve regional bank presidents, on the other hand, were holdovers from another era. By 1989 the Richmond bank's president, Robert P. Black, had been in his post for fifteen years; at the Philadelphia bank Edward G. Boehne had served for eight years. As a group, the regional presidents took a harder line against inflation.

A few years earlier, the differences of opinion would have had little impact because the Board of Governors, led by the chairman, dominated central policymaking. But by the end of the 1980s the balance of power had shifted somewhat, and the regional presidents—"the most articulate, most analytic group in modern history," according to one ex-board member—began to make their voices heard. Since the Fed's actions on the open market are determined by the Federal Open Market Committee (FOMC), on which regional presidents hold five of the twelve positions, the presidents do at least have a strong minority position. Moreover, their personal and intellectual clout has been greater than their number of votes would suggest.

Federal Reserve Chairman Alan Greenspan, appointed as the Fed's leader in 1987, seems to hold an intermediate view about the relative dangers of inflation and recession, and his general strategy has been to hammer out a compromise between the "hawks" (strongly anti-inflation) and the "doves" (afraid of recession). The approach appears to have worked well, at least in the short run. However, some veteran analysts have suggested that Greenspan's balancing act will not succeed indefinitely and there may at some point be a decisive showdown.

Sources: Mike McNamee, "Now the Inflation Battle Is Inside the Fed," *Business Week,* March 13, 1989, pp. 124–126 (quotation at p. 126); Louis Uchitelle, "Alan Greenspan: Caution at the Fed," *New York Times Magazine,* January 15, 1989, p. 18ff.; Mike McNamee, "The Group of Seven Is Acting More Like the Seven Dwarfs," *Business Week,* June 5, 1989, p. 90.

SUMMARY

1. The Federal Reserve System was established by an act of Congress in 1913 to provide a means for controlling the money supply, to assure a flexible national currency, and to be a lender of last resort to forestall financial panics. (See page 274.)

2. The Board of Governors of the Federal Reserve System is made up of seven persons appointed by the president and confirmed by the Senate. The Board sets policy for the Federal Reserve System. The independence of the Federal Reserve System from the elected officials of the government is an important issue, since the Fed wields great power in the economy. (See pages 274–275.)

3. The Federal Open Market Committee consists of the seven members of the Board of Governors plus five members from the Federal Reserve Banks. This committee directs and coordinates the purchase and sale of securities by the Federal Reserve System in the open market. (See page 275.)

4. There are twelve Federal Reserve Districts, and a Federal Reserve Bank is located in each district. These banks, which are owned by member banks in the district, provide services to the depository institutions and commercial interests of the district. Federal Reserve banks provide bank examiners, make loans to depository institutions, operate a check-clearing system, and serve as fiscal agent for the federal government. (See pages 275–276.)

5. From the beginnings of the Federal Reserve System, the Board had the power to set minimum required reserve ratios for banks that were members of the system. The Depository Institutions Deregulation and Monetary Control Act of 1980 broadened this power by giving the Board authority to set minimum reserve requirements for all checkable accounts in all depository institutions. By setting minimum required reserve ratios, the Board can strongly influence the deposit-expansion factor that relates depository institution reserves to the money supply. (See pages 275–279.)

6. Open market operations consist of the buying and selling of government securities by the Federal Reserve Banks in the general, or open, market. When securities are purchased by the system, reserves held by depository institutions are increased, inviting an expansion of the money supply. When securities are sold by the system, reserves held by depository institutions are reduced, and the money supply is restricted. Open market operations are the most actively used of all the monetary instruments of the Federal Reserve System. (See pages 279–280.)

7. The discount rate is the rate of interest charged by a Federal Reserve Bank on a loan to a depository institution. Since these loans are intended only as temporary aid to institutions that face unexpected reserve problems, the discount rate does not directly affect most depository institutions. However, the discount rate may be read as a signal of upcoming Federal Reserve policy. A higher discount rate may suggest a tightening of the money supply, and a lower discount rate may suggest an easing of the money supply. (See page 281.)

8. Federal funds are depository institution reserve deposits in Federal Reserve Banks. Depository institutions may borrow federal funds from one another as an alternative to borrowing through the discounting procedure with the Federal Reserve System. The federal funds rate is the rate of interest charged on these loans. A rising federal funds rate indicates a tightening of the money markets, and a falling federal funds rate indicates an easing of the money markets. (See pages 281–282.)

9. The Board of Governors has the authority to set margin requirements for stock market trading. These requirements specify the minimum percentage of the purchase price of stock that must be paid in by the purchaser himself or herself—the remainder of the purchase price being borrowed from the broker. Experience in 1929 showed that stocks owned on small margins could be "dumped" on the market, turning a modest decline into a stock market disaster. (See page 282.)

10. The goals of monetary policy are full employment, price stability, and economic growth in the economy. Conflicts can arise among these goals. Based on its evaluation of current situations, the Federal Reserve System determines which has top priority at any given time. (See pages 282–283.)

11. In order to achieve the goals of monetary policy, the Federal Reserve establishes operating targets, such as a selected interest rate, nonborrowed reserves, or borrowed reserves. Efforts to

target monetary aggregates such as M1, M2, and M3 have encountered problems, including (a) inability to fully control the monetary base, (b) instability of the money multiplier, and (c) changes in the velocity of circulation of money. (See pages 283–284.)

12. The monetary base consists of reserves in depository institutions plus coins and currency circulating from hand to hand in the economy. The Federal Reserve System can influence the monetary base by open market operations and by loans to depository institutions (discounting). The money multiplier is the relationship between the monetary base and a specified monetary aggregate, such as M1, M2, or M3. (See pages 285–286.)

13. The velocity of circulation of money is the number of times per year the average dollar of the money supply is used to purchase newly produced goods and services. It is equal to GNP divided by the chosen measure of the money supply. Changes in the velocity of circulation of money increase the difficulty of estimating the relationship between the money supply and the level of aggregate economic activity in the economy. (See page 286).

KEY TERMS

accommodation: the practice of increasing or decreasing the money supply as the demand for loans increases or decreases, thus tending to stabilize interest rates (page 283).

Board of Governors: a group of seven people who supervise the Federal Reserve System and thus direct the nation's monetary policy (page 274).

borrowed reserves: reserves borrowed by depository institutions at the discount window from district Federal Reserve Banks (page 284).

discounting: a loan process through which securities or promises from a borrower were purchased by a Federal Reserve Bank at less than their value at maturity (page 277).

discount rate: the rate of interest that Federal Reserve Banks charge on loans to depository institutions (page 281).

disintermediation: when people take funds out of financial institutions in order to get higher interest elsewhere (page 293).

federal funds: depository institution reserve deposits in Federal Reserve Banks (page 281).

federal funds rate: the rate of interest charged on loans of federal funds (page 281).

Federal Open Market Committee (FOMC): a twelve-member committee that controls Federal Reserve buying and selling of government securities on the open market (page 275).

Federal Reserve Banks: the twelve banks of the Federal Reserve System that control the money supply, provide a flexible currency (the Federal Reserve Note), and serve as lenders of last resort to prevent bank failures (page 275).

Federal Reserve System: the central bank of the United States (page 274).

gold standard: a promise by a government to exchange a fixed amount of gold for its currency (page 292).

lender of last resort: a function of the Federal Reserve System: if depository institutions have temporary difficulty, a loan from a Federal Reserve Bank can be arranged (page 277).

margin requirement: the percentage of the value of a stock which the purchaser must finance from his or her own resources (page 282).

monetary base: the reserves in depository institutions along with the coins and currency circulating in the economy (page 285).

monetary instruments: the tools used to regulate the money supply (page 273).

monetary-policy-target variable: a variable used by the Federal Reserve System as a guide in implementing monetary policy (page 283).

money multiplier: the ratio between the amount of money in the economy and the size of the monetary base (page 285).

moral suasion: the approach used by the Federal Reserve System when it urges cooperation in promoting certain policy goals (page 282).

national banks: banks chartered by the federal government (page 276).

nonborrowed reserves: total reserves in depository institutions minus amounts borrowed through discounting from Federal Reserve Banks (page 284).

open market operations: the buying and selling of government securities by the Federal

Reserve Banks (page 279).

pyramiding of reserves: when small banks keep their reserves on deposit in banks in larger cities, which, in turn, keep a large part of their reserves as deposits in banks in a few major cities (page 274).

stagflation: a combination of inflation, rising unemployment, and sluggish economic growth (page 294).

Thrift Institutions Advisory Council: a council set up in 1983 to provide a channel through which savings and loan associations, mutual savings banks, and credit unions can present their views to the Federal Reserve Board of Governors (page 275).

velocity of money: the speed with which the average dollar circulates through the economy (page 286).

DISCUSSION QUESTIONS

1. How are Federal Reserve Board members selected? What systems have been set up to insulate, to some degree, the Board of Governors of the Federal Reserve System from control by the president or the Congress? Do you believe that the Federal Reserve Board should be more closely or less closely tied to the president and the Congress? Explain your position.

2. How are members of the Federal Open Market Committee selected? Describe the operations carried out by this committee. Explain how these operations affect the money supply.

3. Explain how, under the pyramiding of reserves system, a relatively minor problem of a few banks not having enough reserves to cover withdrawal requests might build up to a nationwide crisis. How does the system today provide help for a depository institution that is short on reserves?

4. How is the help that a Federal Reserve Bank gives to depository institutions in its district related to the discount rate? Explain the conflict that sometimes arises between contracting the money supply in the economy and helping out troubled depository institutions.

5. Construct a balance sheet for the Federal Reserve Banks, showing the main entries on both the assets and the liabilities sides. Then compare your work with Table 1. Explain how the U.S. Government securities entry is related to the national debt. Explain how the reserve accounts entry is related to the laws that control individual depository institutions.

6. Explain how the profit motivation of depository institutions helps to assure that actual reserve ratios will stay close to legal reserve ratio requirements. If the Federal Reserve lowers the legal reserve requirement, how is the amount of checkable account money likely to be affected? Explain the process that leads to this result.

7. The Depository Institutions Deregulation and Monetary Control Act of 1980 broadened the Federal Reserve's authority over checkable accounts in two ways. What were they? How did technological changes create the need for these broader Federal Reserve powers?

8. By drawing a pair of balance sheets, one for the Federal Reserve Banks and one for the entire system of depository institutions, show how a Federal Open Market Committee purchase of securities can expand the money supply. Compare your balance sheets with Table 2. Select a different legal reserve requirement and rework your balance sheets to show a different change in the money supply.

9. What are federal funds? If an individual depository institution needs to borrow money, why might it wish to borrow federal funds rather than to borrow from its Federal Reserve Bank? In terms of the money supply and the demand for loans, what is usually happening in the economy when the federal funds rate is rising?

10. Two minor powers of the Federal Reserve are margin requirements and moral suasion. Briefly describe how they may have some influence on economic activity.

11. What did the Depository Institutions Deregulation and Monetary Control Act of 1980 do with respect to interest rate limits? Do you believe that deregulation will increase or decrease competition in financial markets? Explain.

12. What happens to the U.S. monetary base when dollars move to other countries to take advantage of investment opportunities? How does the money multiplier show the effect of a change such as this on the money supply in the United States? If you were trying to manage the U.S. money supply, would you want the money multiplier to be high, or low, or just stable? Explain.

Appendix:
A Brief History of
Federal Reserve Policies

Over the years that the Federal Reserve System has operated, there have been quiet intervals of "normalcy," but there also have been times when conditions changed quickly and the System faced choices that were controversial, important, and shrouded in uncertainty. We shall begin by describing the first real test of the System's ability to stabilize the economy.

THE RECESSION OF 1921

The Federal Reserve System was launched, in 1913, onto financial waters that soon would be stirred to great turbulence by World War I. As people tried to find a safe haven for their wealth, gold, which then was part of the money supply and could be used as reserves for loans, flowed into the United States and added to bank reserves.[3] Businesses borrowed large sums to build factories for war production, and the government sold Liberty Bonds to finance the war effort. When the war ended, some gold flowed back to Europe, foreign demand for U.S. products slackened, and the U.S. economy slipped into a severe, though short, recession in 1921. Somewhat belatedly, the Federal Reserve lowered the discount rate, which of course was an expansionary move, but otherwise did very little to stop the economic decline. Supporters of the Federal Reserve contend that its members were worried that expansionary policies might speed the outflow of gold. Critics say that the Federal Reserve was too timid and failed to ease the shock of the postwar recession.

THE STOCK MARKET CRASH: 1929

Rapid expansion in the automobile and other markets made the decade of the 1920s a period of prosperity for the United States, except for farmers, who had not recovered from the loss of wartime markets. In Europe, the aftermath of the war and the Versailles peace treaty were causing problems.[4] As people again began to seek safety and profitable investment, gold flowed back into the United States, bolstering the money supply. At the same time, the national debt, which had grown during the war, provided bonds and other securities that were well suited to bank holdings and open market dealings. The Federal Reserve Banks learned that open market operations could affect the economy. Even though the economy appeared to be running smoothly, the Federal Reserve worried about increased speculation in the stock market. Since it did not yet have the authority to regulate margin requirements, the Federal Reserve tried in early 1929 to reduce stock market speculation by putting modest restraints on the growth of the money supply. Economists do not agree about the causes of the crash. However, when the stock market crashed later that year, the Federal Reserve quickly reversed itself, lowering discount rates and buying government securities in the open market. The blow from the stock market crash in the United States was soon followed by further problems, as conditions kept growing worse in world financial markets. In Europe, declining economic conditions led, in 1931, to the failure of the leading banking house in Austria, the Credit Anstalt. Runs on European banks began as people withdrew gold and

---

3. Legislation in effect at this time and on through the 1970s authorized only banks to provide checking account services. Therefore, the term *bank* can be used rather than the term *depository institution*.

4. In one of the more remarkable exhibitions of economic forecasting, the British economist John Maynard Keynes in 1919 predicted that the Versailles peace treaty would mean economic misfortune for Europe. See Keynes, *The Economic Consequences of the Peace* (1920).

currencies in fear of further bank failures. First Austria, then Germany, and then Great Britain had to go back on their promises to exchange a fixed amount of gold for their paper currencies (in other words, they went off the **gold standard**). Fear spread that the United States might soon follow suit. As gold and currency started flowing out of U.S. banks, the stage was set for one of the most controversial and critical decisions yet faced by the Federal Reserve System.

The gold standard is a promise by the government to exchange a fixed amount of gold for its paper currency.

At this time (1931), the quantity of Federal Reserve Notes that could be issued was limited by the amount of gold and commercial paper (business IOUs obtained by the Federal Reserve Banks when loans were made to commercial banks) held by the Federal Reserve. The Federal Reserve Banks' holdings of both gold and commercial paper (the IOUs) were declining in 1931, and this decline threatened to force a drop in the Federal Reserve Note money supply. The Fed decided not to use open market purchases to expand the money supply because that would reduce the need for local banks to borrow from the Federal Reserve, thus further reducing the central bank's holding of business IOU backing for Federal Reserve Notes. Instead, the Federal Reserve Banks *raised* discount rates and allowed further tightening of the money supply, an act that would be unthinkable to today's understanding of appropriate monetary policy.

When a major bank in Detroit failed in early 1933, the governor of Michigan closed all the banks in the state to prevent runs on other banks. Soon all the other states followed with bank closings. One of the first acts of incoming President Franklin D. Roosevelt was to declare a nationwide "bank holiday." The money supply had fallen drastically, and the Federal Reserve System had again failed to stabilize the economy.

REPAIRING THE MONETARY SYSTEM

Repair of the monetary system started even before the collapse in 1933, though too late to prevent it.

In 1932, new legislation (the Glass–Steagall Act) allowed the Federal Reserve System to use government bonds for backing Federal Reserve Notes, thus clearing away the obstacle that had kept it from using open market operations vigorously. Under the Banking Act of 1935, the Federal Open Market Committee was officially established, further improving the ability to use open market operations.

In 1933, as panic spread and gold was withdrawn from the banks, the United States went off the gold standard, as Great Britain and others had done earlier. Thus, the government was no longer obligated to give up its gold holdings in exchange for currency. The United States remained off the gold standard for almost two years. In 1934, when conditions were more stable, a modified gold standard was established and a higher price for gold was offered. Gold flowed back into the U.S. banking system, strengthening the reserve position of the Federal Reserve System. Excess reserves in banks climbed to high levels. Strangely enough, the stage was now set for another Federal Reserve act that history has called a mistake.

In 1936, the large and growing excess reserves in the banking system led the Federal Reserve to fear the coming of inflation, which might get out of control. For this reason, it doubled reserve requirements over a short period of time and used open market sales to counteract the effect of gold imports. Within a year, the economy plunged into even deeper recession. Criticism was heaped on the Federal Reserve for once again having made the wrong move.

In fairness, however, it must be added that certain fiscal events were taking place at about the same time. The Social Security system had started collecting taxes but few could yet collect benefits. Also, through a legislative mistake, taxes on corporations were increased significantly.

MONEY GOES TO WAR: 1941–1945

After the disastrous experience of the 1937–1938 recession, the chastened Federal Reserve reversed itself and began to follow an expansionary, or easy-money, policy. In 1939, World War II started in Europe, and the U.S. economy expanded to produce war goods. After the attack on Pearl Harbor in December 1941, the U.S. economy went all out for war production. The Federal Reserve promised that open market operations would support the bond market to make sure that the massive sales of war bonds would not force interest rates upward. This meant huge and continuing open market purchases and a great expansion of the money supply. The money supply grew and grew during the war, while civilian production was cut back. To hold down inflation, the government used price and wage controls as well as rationing. Congress authorized and the Federal Reserve applied controls over lending and borrowing. Banks were permitted to play favorites among customers to favor war production and essential civilian needs. Money and prices had gone to war.

When the war ended, price controls were removed. Even though inflation was beginning in earnest, fear was widespread that the economy soon would fall back into recession, since this had happened in the past when wartime pressures subsided. At this time, the Federal Reserve again faced important and controversial questions. If open market purchases stopped supporting bond prices, would the bond market collapse and trigger financial chaos and bank failures? The Fed had been criticized for its restrictive policies in 1931 and in 1936. Should it risk another recession? The Treasury, wanting interest costs to stay low on the greatly expanded national debt, put strong pressures on the Federal Reserve to follow an easy-money policy. Under all this pressure, the Federal Reserve decided to continue open market purchasing to support the bond market and to limit its inflation fight to maintaining higher discount rates and reserve requirements. Inflation spread, reaching a peak in 1948.

THE "ACCORD" OF 1951

War-related problems and inflationary conditions arose again in 1950 as the United States became involved in the Korean War. Again the Treasury wanted more open market purchases to support the bond market, but this time the Federal Reserve chose to fight for its independence. After a great political struggle, open market operations were freed from the commitment to support the bond

market. The "accord" was announced on March 4, 1951. The Federal Reserve was again independent of the Treasury.

In the period after the accord of 1951, the Federal Reserve System generally followed a policy of "leaning against the wind." This meant using open market purchases and sales, as well as small adjustments in reserve requirements and discount rates, to moderate expansions and contractions of the economy. The Fed was neither swept along by the winds of war nor overcome by forces it wished to oppose.

DISINTERMEDIATION

The economy's performance was sluggish in the last half of the 1950s, but picked up speed in the early 1960s. Taxes were reduced in 1964 in a clear application of fiscal instruments and Keynesian economic theory. By 1966, the Federal Reserve detected inflationary dangers. As the "war on poverty" was waged and as hostilities increased in Vietnam, the federal budget moved deeper and deeper into deficit. Restrictive open market operations were applied, and almost no increase in the money supply was permitted. But because the demand for loans kept on growing while the money supply was stabilized, interest rates climbed. When market interest rates rose above the legal ceiling rates that banks and other regulated financial institutions were allowed to pay, many people took their deposits out of these institutions in order to get higher interest on their savings elsewhere. This process is called **disintermediation.** Thrift institutions and the home-building industry, which depends heavily on loans from them, suffered greatly from a shortage of available funds in 1967. Unfortunately, the inflationary danger that the Fed was trying to combat was only partly defused.

Disintermediation occurred in the 1960s when market interest rates rose above the legal ceiling rates that banks and other regulated financial institutions were permitted to pay, and people took their money out of these institutions to get higher interest on their savings elsewhere.

In 1968, the Federal Reserve System started using monetary tools in an expansionary direction. The reason was that the economy was beginning to contract. Gold and financial capital were flowing out of the country as the United States' competitive position in world trade grew weaker. Also, Congress raised taxes by 10 percent. To counter the economic overkill that it thought would come from the combined effect of these events, the Fed expanded open market buying. By this time, the U.S. economy was starting to show signs that were contradictory according to the prevailing economic theories. Growth was lagging, unemployment was increasing, and inflation continued. In other words, the economy was beginning to suffer from *stagflation*. At the end of the 1960s, the Federal Reserve tightened the money supply in an effort to slow the inflation. Interest rates rose, and disintermediation took place once again.

THE GREAT STAGFLATION

The combination of inflation, rising unemployment, and sluggish economic growth is called **stagflation.** As the stagflation problem grew in the early 1970s, the Nixon administration decided to use both fiscal and monetary tools to aid production and reduce unemployment. Taxes were cut, government spending was increased, the FOMC bought securities, and discount rates were lowered. To hold down inflation, President Nixon announced a freeze on prices and wage rates and a suspension of U.S. gold payments in international transactions. However, during the control period, the money supply was expanded. When the controls were lifted, inflation burst forth with new vigor. President Ford, who replaced President Nixon after the Watergate scandal, undertook a program called "Whip Inflation Now" (abbreviated "WIN"). Money supply growth was restricted and unemployment increased.

Stagflation is a combination of inflation, rising unemployment, and sluggish economic growth.

The election victory of President Carter in 1976 brought confrontation between the Federal Reserve on the one hand and the president and the Congress on the other. Armed with the election mandate to expand the economy, President Carter refused to name Board member Arthur Burns (who was associated with a "tight" money policy) to another term as chairman. Burns retired, and the Federal Reserve, under new leadership, expanded the money supply. Over the four years of the Carter administration, the M1 money supply grew at a yearly rate of 7.7 percent, and the inflation rate rose to around 9 percent a year, sometimes reaching a double-digit figure. Alarmed by these high inflation rates, President Carter installed a new Federal Reserve Board Chairman, Paul Volcker, and backed a tighter monetary policy.

The election of President Reagan in 1980 gave a further mandate for a strong anti-inflation policy. Restrictive monetary measures continued throughout 1981 and into 1982. Interest rates and unemployment remained high, but the inflation rate came down dramatically. Monetary instruments can claim some, but not all, of the credit for the very significant slackening of the inflation rate in the first half of the 1980s. The sluggish economy weakened the demand for funds. In addition, restrictive monetary policy was powerfully assisted by decreases in petroleum prices, as the Organization of Petroleum Exporting Countries (OPEC) encountered increased difficulty in limiting petroleum output. Although money supply increases were allowed, real interest rates—interest rates adjusted for the now much lower inflation rate—were very high by historical standards. Some argued that fear of future inflation prevented a sufficient downward movement of real interest rates. Whatever the cause, high interest rates caused great trouble for some financial institutions and for farmers, who faced the problem of lower prices for their crops along with extremely high interest costs on their indebtedness.

Through the middle and later 1980s, the economy enjoyed a long period of economic expansion. Following the stock market crash in late 1987, the Federal Reserve sharply increased the money supply in order to prevent the crash from pushing the economy into recession. No recession occurred and, by 1989, the economy was operating near to what many economists believed was the natural rate of unemployment. Price-level increases in 1989 led the Federal Reserve to adopt moderately restrictive monetary policies, hoping to prevent inflation while not leading the economy into recession.

AN OVERVIEW

As our brief history has suggested, the monetary policies of the Federal Reserve System have often been controversial. With 20–20 hindsight, it is clear that mistakes were made in 1921, 1931, and 1936, though it would be unfair to place all the blame for these hard times on monetary policy. The Fed's support for the war effort during World War II can hardly be faulted, and its fight for independence from the Treasury and its noninflationary financing of the Korean War merit praise. During the 1950s and the early 1960s, monetary policies operated smoothly most of the time.

Monetary policies, like most other demand-side approaches, were not able to solve the complicated riddle of stagflation in the 1970s, and, as in the Great Depression of the 1930s, the Federal Reserve was often blamed for unemployment. However, in 1980 and 1981, monetary instruments proved their power to bring down the inflation rate.

The relative independence of the Federal Reserve from control by the elected officials of the government continues to be a focus of debate. When monetary policies are unpopular, calls are heard to place monetary policy under the control of the Treasury or, by some other means, to give the president or Congress greater power over the Federal Reserve. So far, independent monetary policy has survived these attempts, providing another aspect of our checks-and-balances system.

DISCUSSION QUESTIONS

1. The Glass–Steagall Act of 1932 allowed the Federal Reserve System to use government bonds for backing the Federal Reserve Notes. What had the system been required to use before this law was passed? How could higher discount rates bring in more of the pre-1932 legal backing to the Federal Reserve?

2. Federal Reserve policy during and after World War II was to support the price of government bonds and to keep interest rates low. Explain how the Federal Open Market Committee was involved in these operations. How did these operations affect the money supply? What was the "accord" reached in 1951?

3. What is disintermediation? Why did disintermediation happen in 1967 when the Federal Reserve engaged in restrictive monetary policy? Would disintermediation have happened then if the Depository Institutions Deregulation and Monetary Control Act had been in effect? Explain.

14
Monetary Economics

Preview In the last chapter you learned how the Federal Reserve System (the central bank) uses various monetary instruments to influence the supply of money in the economy. Now it is time to see how changes in the money supply affect the equilibrium level of national income and product.

We start our study by examining the quantity-of-money theory, a model based on what is called the equation of exchange. We illustrate this theory in terms of aggregate demand and aggregate supply and discuss the long-run monetary policy implications of that theory.

We next examine how monetary policy is able to exert a short-run effect on interest rates and the equilibrium level of national income and product. This involves a study of the money market in which monetary actions are carried out. Our analysis is based on a model of how interest rates affect investment. We discuss the factors that make monetary instruments more or less able to influence employment and output. We include a discussion of the importance of the velocity of money and of alternative approaches to the day-to-day direction of monetary policy.

Price-level (inflation) effects are important in all theories relating to monetary policy. In the final portion of the chapter, we examine what happens if increases in the money supply lead people to expect the price level to increase. In a context of inflationary expectations, money supply increases are less able to promote expansion in real national income and product.

THE QUANTITY-OF-MONEY THEORY

The quantity-of-money theory has been famous in economics for a long time. It is based on a simple relationship called the **equation of exchange.** The equation is $MV = PQ$, where M stands for the quantity of money in the economy, V stands for its **velocity of circulation** (the average number of times each dollar is used per year to buy newly produced goods and services), P stands for the price level, and Q stands for the quantity of real output for the year.[1]

The equation of exchange states that the quantity of money in the economy multiplied by the number of times the average dollar is used each year to purchase newly produced final products must be equal to the quantity of these final products multiplied by their average price. It is called the equation of exchange because the left side, MV, represents total money spent by purchasers, and the right side, PQ, represents total money received by sellers. Because the two sides of the equation must be equal by definition, the equation is more properly called an *identity*.

Since a relationship that is true by definition cannot be used to prove a cause-and-effect relation, the equation of exchange does not establish any necessary connection between the quantity of money, as a cause, and the equilibrium level of national income and product, as an effect. But it does provide a framework for a great deal of debate about the importance of money in the economy.

The equation of exchange, $MV = PQ$, states that the quantity of money in the economy multiplied by the number of times the average dollar is used each year to purchase newly produced final goods and services must be equal to the quantity of these final goods and services multiplied by their average price.

---

1. In its original form, developed in 1911 by the American economist Irving Fisher, the equation was $MV = PT$, where T represented all transactions in the economy and V was defined as the number of times a year the average dollar was used in any type of transaction.

The equation of exchange is used in the **quantity-of-money theory,** which asserts that the velocity of money circulation is constant in the long run, so that changes in the quantity of money provide a good way to predict changes in gross national product (GNP), since the PQ part of the equation corresponds with the definition of GNP. In other words, if the V in the equation of exchange is constant, a 10 percent increase in the quantity of money (M) would mean a 10 percent increase in gross national product (PQ).

The quantity-of-money theory states that the velocity of money circulation is constant in the long run, so changes in the quantity of money provide a good way to predict changes in GNP.

An "Aggregate-Demand" View of the Quantity Theory

The equation of exchange can be rearranged to become a statement about the aggregate quantity of goods and services demanded in an economy. If we let Q in the equation represent the aggregate quantity of goods and services demanded, the equation of exchange says that $Q = MV/P$. In this arrangement, Q and P are inversely related, that is, a decrease in P (the price level) is associated with an increase in Q (real national income and product demanded) provided that there is no change in either M (the money supply) or V (the velocity of circulation of money). This inverse relationship is illustrated in Figure 1. In this figure, we have put quotation marks around the references to aggregate demand in the title and in the label on the curve because the line on the graph is merely a derivation from the equation of exchange and is not a true aggregate-demand curve. As you remember from Chapter 6, a true aggregate-demand curve is a statement of cause and effect—that the aggregate quantity or real GNP demanded *depends on* the price level, *ceteris paribus*, or $QD = f(P)$, *ceteris paribus*. Since the equation of exchange is an identity, it cannot be used to establish a cause-and-effect relationship.

FIGURE 1
An "Aggregate-Demand" Relationship Derived from the Equation of Exchange

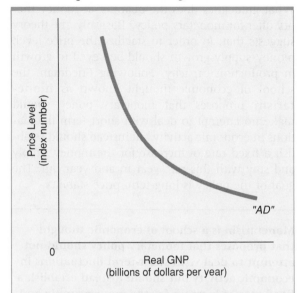

The curve "AD" is derived from the equation of exchange ($MV = PQ$), assuming that M and V are constant and therefore that the product of M and V also is constant. The curve is a rectangular hyperbola because each point on it represents a product of P and Q (price level times real GNP) that is constant. If the variable on the horizontal axis (real GNP) is understood to be the aggregate quantity of goods and services demanded, the curve illustrates the concept of "aggregate demand" implicit in the quantity theory.

The equation of exchange can be rearranged to become a statement about the aggregate quantity of goods and services demanded in an economy: $Q = MV/P$.

Although the "AD" curve in Figure 1 is not a true aggregate-demand curve, it is helpful in understanding the economics of the quantity-of-money theory. In drawing the curve in Figure 1, the money supply (M) and the velocity of money (V) are held constant. Changes in either of these variables, therefore, will shift the curve. Increasing the value of these variables shifts the curve to the right and decreasing their values shifts it to the left.

The Classical Aggregate-Supply Curve

According to the quantity-of-money theory, the velocity of money circulation is constant and there is a one-to-one relationship between percentage changes in the money supply and percentage changes in the price level—a 10 percent increase in M causes a 10 percent increase in the price level, and so on. What does this say about the aggregate quantity supplied? It says that the aggregate quantity supplied does not change when the price level changes. This is illustrated in Figure 2, where the "AD" curve is reproduced from Figure 1 and labeled "AD$_1$" and an "AD$_2$" curve is added to illustrate a 10 percent increase in the quantity of

FIGURE 2
"Aggregate Demand" and "Aggregate Supply" Derived from the Quantity-of-Money Theory

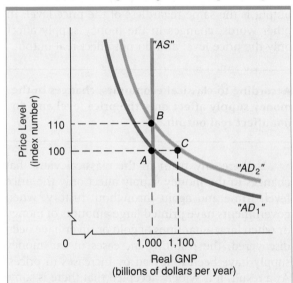

The "AD_1" curve shows the relationship between aggregate quantity or real GNP demanded and the price level according to the equation of exchange, assuming the money supply and the velocity of its circulation are constant. The "AD_2" curve illustrates a 10 percent increase in the money supply, with velocity remaining constant. Since the quantity-of-money theory states that a 10 percent increase in the money supply is associated with a 10 percent increase in the price level, the implicit aggregate supply curve is a vertical line, labeled "AS."

money. The original macroeconomic equilibrium is at *A*, with real GNP of $1,000 billion and a price level index of 100. The 10 percent increase in the money supply (illustrated by the distance from *A* to *C*) results in a 10 percent price level increase from *A* to *B*. The vertical line labeled "*AS*" is the aggregate supply curve implicit in the quantity theory argument.

According to the quantity-of-money theory, the velocity of money circulation is constant, and there is a one-to-one relationship between percentage changes in the money supply and percentage changes in the price level.

According to the quantity-of-money theory, the vertical "aggregate-supply" curve represents the full employment level of output for the economy and incorporates the view that this level of output is the same regardless of the price level. In other words, changes in the money supply affect only the price level and do not affect real output.

According to classical economics, changes in the money supply affect only the price level and do not affect real output.

Is there any truth in the classical view that changes in the money supply affect only the price level? Time and again throughout history, when governments have printed large amounts of money or when large quantities of gold or silver have been discovered, the resulting increases in the money supply have been followed by increases in prices. As a result, it is widely accepted that there is some truth in the quantity theory, although many believe that money-supply increases affect more than just the price level. Milton Friedman, the economist recognized as intellectual spokesman for monetarism, states that although there are significant and variable time lags between a change in the money supply and a resulting change in the price level, inflation "always and everywhere" is a monetary phenomenon.

The Steady-Money-Growth Policy

What guidelines does the quantity-of-money theory offer for monetary policy? Basically, the theory suggests that, in order to stabilize the price level, money-supply growth should be keyed to growth in production capacity. Following Friedman, the school of economic thought known as **monetarism** proposes that monetary policy should make no attempt to deal with short-term fluctuations in economic activity but instead should establish a fixed rate of increase for the money supply and stay with this rate year in and year out. The goal of the policy is long-term price stability.

Monetarism is a school of economic thought that proposes that monetary policy should not attempt to deal with short-term fluctuations in economic activity but should instead establish a fixed rate of increase for the money supply and stay with this rate.

The stable-money-growth policy suggests that the first task of the Federal Reserve is to estimate the growth rate in production capacity for the economy due to improvements in technology and increases in the labor force and the stock of physical and human capital. If the real growth in production capacity is expected to be 2½ percent a year, for example, and if the velocity of money is expected to be constant, monetary policy should aim at a steady 2½ percent a year increase in the money supply. In Figure 3 the rate of increase in the money supply shifts the aggregate-demand curve to the right each year by the same distance as that year's shift in the aggregate-supply curve, and the price level remains unchanged. Real GNP increases 2½ percent, from $1,000 billion to $1,025 billion, and the price level remains stable at an index number of 100.

The stable-money-growth policy suggests that the Federal Reserve should estimate the growth

FIGURE 3
The Steady-Money-Growth Policy

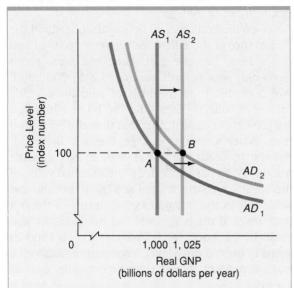

Initial macroeconomic equilibrium is at point *A*, with real GNP of $1,000 billion and a price level of 100. Growth in the production capacity of the economy shifts aggregate supply from AS_1 to AS_2, an increase of 2½ percent. The policy of steady money growth calls for a 2½ percent increase in aggregate demand, illustrated by the shift of the AD_1 curve to AD_2. If velocity is constant, this increase in aggregate demand is accomplished through a 2½ percent increase in the money supply. Macroeconomic equilibrium moves from point *A* to point *B*.

rate in production capacity for the economy and increase the money supply at the same rate.

The word *steady* is the key feature of the steady-money-growth policy. In other words, the rate of growth of the money supply should be the same, year in and year out, regardless of temporary fluctuations in actual output or the actual price level. According to its supporters, stabilizing the rate of money growth removes one source of uncertainty faced by participants in the economy's credit markets. In their view, the economy will operate more smoothly with the steady-money-

growth policy than with a monetary policy subject to change from day to day or month to month. They say that adjustments to temporary changes in real output and/or prices would take place quickly so that monetary changes would not be necessary.

According to its supporters, the economy operates more smoothly with a steady-money-growth policy than with a monetary policy subject to change from day to day or month to month.

The steady-money-growth policy does not require the rate of increase in the money supply to exactly match the rate of growth of real production capacity. In fact, the rate of money growth might be set slightly higher than the expected rate of growth of production capacity so that the measured price level would rise gradually. Advocates of the policy assert that this would cause no serious problems. All sectors of the economy soon would adapt to a steady and modest upward drift of the price level. Moreover, if price index numbers contain biases that ignore quality improvements, a modest upward drift of the measured price level might not be an actual increase in the quality-adjusted cost of living.

THE ROLE OF INTEREST RATES

The equation of exchange ($MV = PQ$) does not offer any guideline about what determines changes in the volume of production (Q) in the economy. It simply states that changes in MV must involve also changes in PQ. It is clear, therefore, that the quantity-of-money theory cannot tell us all we want to know about the relation of money to equilibrium national income and product. To gain an understanding of how the quantity of money affects real production, we must explore the **interest rate**— the annual payment for the use of funds, expressed as a percentage of the funds used. We must examine how interest rates are determined and how they affect production.

The interest rate is the annual payment for the use of funds, expressed as a percentage of the funds used.

You already have some understanding of how the rate of interest affects production. In Chapter 10, in the Keynesian model of income determination, the real interest rate appeared as a variable influencing the quantity of planned-investment purchases in the economy. As you recall, at lower real interest rates, the volume of planned-investment purchases was greater than at higher interest rates, *ceteris paribus*. So monetary policy can affect production in the economy (the Q in the equation of exchange) if it can change real interest rates.

Real and Nominal Values

In studying the relation between money, interest rates, and national income and product, it is essential to distinguish between real and nominal values. The distinction is especially important in connection with interest rates, since they are used in contracts that extend over considerable periods of time. With the passage of time, the price level may change so that, dollar for dollar, funds repaid may have a different purchasing power than the funds originally borrowed. Both lenders and borrowers are very concerned about such changes in the purchasing power of funds. They will surely want to distinguish between nominal values and real values. Therefore, in studying money and interest rates, we must also be clear about this distinction.

Nominal values are values that are stated or measured in terms of some monetary unit. In the United States, the monetary unit is the dollar. Thus, the nominal value of an item is the number of dollars that would be exchanged for it. Nominal values have *not* been adjusted for price-level changes by dividing them by an index number or deflator.

Real values are values that are stated or measured in terms of goods and services. The real value of an item is the quantity of goods and services that

would be exchanged for it. A real value *has* been adjusted for price-level changes by applying an index number or deflator.

Two illustrations will help you understand the importance of the difference between nominal and real values. Suppose that when you were seven years old, your parents purchased a $1,000 bond, which at that time would have paid for a year's tuition at college. They hold the bond while you are growing up, and during that time the price level rises. When you go to college, they sell the bond, but the proceeds are not enough to pay a year's tuition. What has happened? The nominal value of the bond stayed unchanged at $1,000, but the real value fell to less than $1,000 in terms of the old price level. If the price level had doubled, the real value of the bond would have fallen to $500 in terms of the old price level. Your parents suffered a *real* loss of $500, though they did not suffer a *nominal* loss.

As another illustration, suppose you borrow $1,000 and promise to pay it back on some future date. The nominal value of the promise is clearly stated in terms of money. But the real (goods and services) value of the promise depends on the price level that will exist when you must pay the money. Since that time has not come yet, neither you nor the person to whom you make the promise can be entirely sure about its real value. If the price level rises, the real value will fall, and vice versa.

Nominal values are values that are stated or measured in terms of some monetary unit. Real values are values that are stated or measured in terms of goods and services; they are always adjusted for price-level changes.

Real and Nominal Interest Rates

There is a simple rule about the relation between real and nominal interest rates. This rule states that the difference is equal to the rate of change in the price level.[2] Here is an illustration. If the price level

---

2. When both inflation rates and interest rates are extremely high, some modification of this simple rule is needed. This refinement will be left for more advanced courses.

is *rising* by 5 percent annually, a nominal 12 percent interest rate is a real 7 percent interest rate and a nominal 9 percent interest rate is a real 4 percent interest rate. We simply subtract the inflation rate from the nominal interest rate to determine the real interest rate. Conversely, if the price level is *falling,* the real interest rate will be above the nominal interest rate. If the price level is falling by 2 percent a year, a nominal interest rate of 5 percent is a real interest rate of 7 percent. The logic behind these adjustments is that the dollars used to pay back a loan will have a different purchasing power from the dollars that were borrowed. If the price level is rising, the loan will be paid back in dollars that are worth less than those initially borrowed, thus reducing the real cost of borrowing and the real return to the lender. The real interest rate is below the nominal interest rate. If the price level is falling, the loan will be paid back in dollars that are worth more than those that were borrowed, thus increasing the real cost of borrowing and the real return to the lender. Here, the real interest rate is higher than the nominal interest rate.

When the lender-borrower agreement is negotiated, neither side can be certain about the price-level change that may actually take place during the term of the loan. Each must make a best guess. In other words, it is the *expected* rate of price-level change (inflation) that each party uses to determine the difference between the nominal and the real interest rate. Of course, the two parties may not, in their own minds, be using the same expected rate of price-level change. One or the other, or both, may prove to have been mistaken, with consequent unexpected gains or losses.

As we proceed now to examine how interest rates are determined, we will use the *real rate of interest* in explaining the demand and the supply of money. It is important to remember that this is not necessarily the same as the *nominal* rate of interest that would get written into contracts and reported in the press.

The difference between real and nominal interest rates is equal to the rate of change in the price level.

Loanable-Funds Markets

In the quantity-of-money approach to monetary policy, changes in the money supply are not used to influence interest rates in the economy. Instead, interest rates are determined solely by the interaction of borrowers and lenders in **loanable-funds markets,** which bring together those who wish to lend and those who wish to borrow funds. If monetary policy follows the steady-growth rule and money-supply changes keep pace with changes in production capacity of the economy, the interest rates determined in these markets are **real interest rates**—rates that reflect actual purchasing-power values.

Real interest rates are determined by the interaction of borrowers and lenders in loanable-funds markets.

Figure 4 illustrates a loanable-funds market. The horizontal axis shows the real (adjusted for price-level change) quantities of money demanded and supplied for loans. The vertical axis shows the real rate of interest. The supply curve represents the behavior of people who are willing to let others use part of their wealth in exchange for the payment of interest. It comes from both households and financial institutions. It reflects **time preferences** between using wealth for current consumption or saving it for future uses. The supply curve has a positive slope because, other things being equal, suppliers are willing to loan more money when real interest rates are high than when they are low.

The demand curve in the loanable-funds market illustrates the behavior of borrowers, including households, governments, and business firms. It shows the amounts that they are willing to borrow at various possible real interest rates, *ceteris paribus.* In the loanable-funds model, one of the main reasons for borrowing is to finance capital, such as plant and equipment to be used in production. The quantity of funds that firms are willing to borrow, at any given interest rate, depends on the expected profitability of using capital in production. The location of the demand curve is determined by forces that influence the expected profitability of capital

FIGURE 4
The Loanable-Funds Market

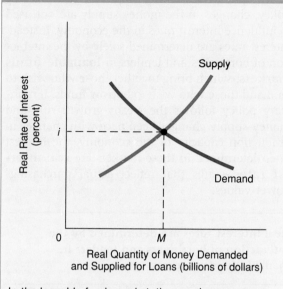

In the loanable-funds market, the supply curve represents the relationship between the real rate of interest and the amounts of money that households and financial institutions are willing to lend. Its location reflects the money supply and preferences between present use and future use of these funds. The demand curve represents the relationship between the real rate of interest and the amounts that borrowers are willing and able to borrow. Its location depends, among other things, on the expected profitability of capital goods. Governments, households, and business firms participate in the demand for loanable funds. At equilibrium, the real rate of interest balances the amount that lenders are willing to lend with the amount that borrowers are willing to borrow.

itself. Inventions, favorable government policies, and promising economic conditions shift this curve to the right. Conversely, forces that reduce expected profitability shift the curve to the left. The demand curve also reflects borrowing by consumers and governments that wish to purchase goods and services today but want to postpone payment until some future time.

The supply curve of the loanable-funds market has a positive slope because suppliers are willing to loan more money when real interest rates are high than when they are low. The demand

---

curve shows the amounts borrowers are willing to borrow at various real interest rates.

Most economists agree that, in the long run, real interest rates are determined in the loanable-funds markets and that monetary policies have little long-term impact on these rates. The policies that do affect real interest rates in the long run are those that shift the demand or the supply curves in these markets. For example, policies that encourage saving and a preference for future consumption rather than present consumption shift the supply curve of loanable funds to the right, and, other things unchanged, lower real interest rates and increase the volume of saving and investment. Policies that increase the profitability of capital goods shift the demand curve for loanable funds to the right and, *ceteris paribus,* raise real interest rates and the volume of saving and investment.[3]

THE MONEY MARKET

The loanable-funds market just described presents a great amount of important information about lending and borrowing and the determination of real interest rates. It illustrates, for example, how the time preferences of wealth holders and the profit expectations of investors affect real interest rates and the quantity of borrowing and lending. Monetary variables, such as changes in the money supply, are among the factors affecting the supply curve in that market. Increases in the money supply may, at least for a time, shift the loanable-funds supply curve to the right, and decreases may shift it, at least for a time, to the left. However, to provide a clearer and more direct illustration of the interest-rate effects of monetary policy, it is useful to examine another market—the **money market.** The money market illustrates the concepts of demand and supply for money itself.

The economic concept of the money market is illustrated in Figure 5. The vertical axis shows the

---

3. A more complete explanation of the loanable-funds market is presented in microeconomics.

---

real rate of interest—the rate after adjustments for expected changes in the price level. The horizontal axis shows the real quantity of money demanded or supplied *as of any given point in time*. Thus, this axis is different from the horizontal axes on graphs showing demand and supply for ordinary goods and services, where the values reflect flows *over a period of time*. The horizontal axis shows the real quantity of money according to some accepted measure such as the quantity of M1 dollars divided by a price-level index number, such as the GNP deflator. Amounts on this axis represent the real quantities of money that are demanded as an asset to be held as a form of wealth. The notion of money as an asset is important in understanding the money market.

The money market treats money itself as a commodity subject to the concepts of supply and demand.

The Demand-for-Money Curve

The demand-for-money curve is the graphic representation of the statement that the quantity of money demanded as an asset *depends on* the rate of interest, that is $QD = f(i)$, *ceteris paribus,* where QD is the quantity of money demanded as an asset and i is the rate of interest. In explaining the demand-for-money curve, economists consider the speculative demand, the transactions demand, and the precautionary demand for holding money. We shall describe each of these and explain how they help in understanding the slope and the location of the demand-for-money curve.

The quantity of money demanded as an asset depends on the rate of interest: $QD = f(i)$.

Speculative Demand Speculative demand is mainly responsible for the slope of the demand-for-money curve. To understand this point, you must understand what speculation is and how money can be used for this purpose.

FIGURE 5
The Money Market

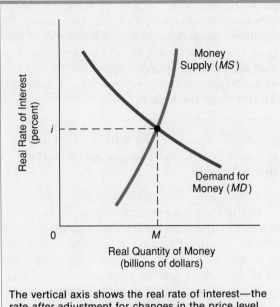

The vertical axis shows the real rate of interest—the rate *after* adjustment for changes in the price level. The horizontal axis shows the *real* quantity of money—the nominal quantity of money divided by a price-index number such as the GNP deflator. This axis shows quantities of money demanded and supplied at a given time as an asset, or form of wealth. The money-supply curve (*MS*) has a positive slope and its location may be influenced by monetary policy. The demand-for-money curve (*MD*) has a negative slope and its location may be shifted by changes in the level of income and wealth in the economy.

Most people think of speculation as the holding of risky assets like oil wells or uranium mines. Actually, **speculation** means taking actions based on expectations of *future changes* in the market values of assets. Imagine that you are wealthy (not an unpleasant thought) and that you want to manage your wealth to make it grow as much as you can. Managing your wealth means that you are placing it in money, stocks, bonds, real estate, and so on, depending on which forms promise you the best return.

For speculative purposes, the most important type of return on your wealth is not the rate of interest you can obtain but the gain that you can make from changes in the market value of whatever types of assets you have chosen as wealth forms. For example, if you expect the market value of bonds, stocks, or real estate to rise in the future, you will place your wealth in these promising forms and demand very little, if any, money for speculative purposes. On the other hand, if you expect the market value of bonds, stocks, or real estate to fall in the future, you will sell these assets and hold cash. In this case, you have a **speculative demand for money.**

Speculation means taking actions based on expectations of future changes in the market values of assets.

The next step in understanding the demand-for-money curve is to see how anticipated gains or losses on nonmoney assets are related to the real rate of interest, which is the variable on the vertical axis of the money-market graph. An inverse relationship exists between the rate of interest prevailing at a given time and the likelihood that the values of stocks, bonds, and other nonmoney assets will rise or fall in the future. This relationship is derived from the formula that converts a stream of expected future income into a present value. The standard formula for calculating the *present value* (*PV*) of income to be received in some future year is

$$PV = \frac{\text{expected income}_t}{(1 + i)^t}$$

where *i* is the rate of interest, and *t* is the number of years before the income is received. If we assume that the same amount of income is expected each year and that the stream of income will continue indefinitely, the present value formula reduces to

$$\text{present value} = \frac{\text{expected annual income flow}}{\text{rate of interest}}$$

Consider, for example, a nonmoney asset that will pay net income of $100 a year indefinitely. If the rate of interest that can be earned on similar wealth forms is 10 percent a year, the present value of this nonmoney asset will be $1,000—that is, $100/0.10. A person would not pay more than $1,000 because he or she would then earn a rate of return of less than the going rate of 10 percent. Some other form of wealth would be more attrac-

tive. Similarly, the seller would not accept less than $1,000.

According to the present value formula, when interest rates are low, the present value of any given expected annual income flow is high.

Let us apply this idea to our demand-for-money curve. The real quantity of money demanded for speculation will be large when real interest rates are considered "low." According to the present value formula, when interest rates are low, the present value of any given expected annual income flow is high, other things being equal. For example, if the interest rate were 3 percent, our hypothetical nonmoney asset earning $100 per year would have a present value of $3,333, that is $100/0.03. When the interest rate is "low" and the present value of nonmoney assets therefore are "high," speculators will sell the nonmoney assets because they expect their prices (present values) to fall as interest rates return to higher levels. In other words, speculators will hold money, speculating on the coming price decrease of nonmoney assets. On the other hand, the quantity of money demanded as a speculative asset will be small when interest rates are considered high because the present value of nonmoney assets then will be considered low. At an interest rate of 15 percent, for example, the asset bringing a net $100 a year will have a present value of only $667, that is $100/0.15. Speculators will hold nonmoney assets, expecting to profit when interest rates fall and the present values of these assets rise. In this way, the speculative demand for money assets provides a strong reason for the demand-for-money curve having a negative slope.

There is an inverse relationship between the real rate of interest prevailing at a given time and the likelihood that the real values of stocks, bonds, and other nonmoney assets will rise or fall in the future.

The speculative demand for money is sometimes called the **liquidity** demand for money. It is the "spendability" of an asset—that is, the ease with which it can be used in exchange or converted into a form that can be used in exchange. Cash and checkable accounts are fully liquid. They can be used directly in exchange for anything a person wants to buy. The liquidity demand for money simply means that people want to hold it so that they will be in a position to take advantage of opportunities to purchase other assets when favorable terms arise. When people hold money because they expect the prices of nonmoney assets to be lower in the future, their demand for liquidity is speculative.

The speculative demand for money is sometimes called the liquidity demand for money.
Liquidity is the ease with which an asset can be used in exchange or converted into a form that can be used in exchange.

Transactions and Precautionary Demands The **transactions demand for money** arises because people want to hold some of their wealth in a form that is convenient for day-to-day buying and selling of goods and services. The **precautionary demand for money** arises because people want to be prepared for unexpected changes in the pattern of their receipts and expenditures.

The transactions demand for money arises because people want to hold some of their wealth in a form that is convenient for day-to-day buying and selling of goods and services.

The precautionary demand for money arises because people want to be prepared for unexpected changes in the pattern of their receipts and expenditures.

The role of the interest rate in determining the quantity of money demanded for these purposes can be understood by using the concept of *opportunity cost.* The basic point is that people who hold money receive relatively little interest return on this portion of their wealth. Cash earns no interest at all and checkable accounts earn relatively low rates of interest. The amount of interest earning that is given up is the opportunity cost of holding money instead of nonmoney assets. It follows that the opportunity cost of holding money is greater when the rate of interest is high than when the rate of interest is low.

Economists expect that less money will be demanded for transactions and precautionary purposes when real interest rates are high and that more money will be demanded when real interest rates are low, other things being equal. In other words, the transactions and the precautionary demands for money impart a negative slope to the demand-for-money curve, just as the speculative motive did. In fact, opportunity cost reasoning also applies to the speculative demand for money, giving further support for the negative slope of the demand-for-money curve.

The opportunity cost of holding money is greater when the real rate of interest is high than when it is low. Less money will be demanded for transactions and precautionary purposes when real interest rates are high; more money will be demanded when real interest rates are low.

Shifting the Demand-for-Money Curve The demand-for-money curve may shift when there is a change in some variable other than the real rate of interest. There are many variables that might do this. Changes in the amount of wealth, for example, are expected to affect all three of the demands for money assets. When wealth increases, these demands for money are expected to increase, and when wealth decreases, these demands are expected to decrease. In macroeconomic analysis, one of the most important shift variables for the demand-for-money curve is the level of national income and product itself. When national income and product increases, the curve is expected to shift to the right and when it decreases, the curve is expected to shift to the left.

Changes in national income and product affect all of the demands for money, but their effects on the transactions demand is especially apparent. For most people, the transactions demand for money arises because receipts and expenditures are not perfectly timed with each other. For example, suppose that you receive $700 every two weeks and that you spend $50 every day. When you receive your pay, you have $700 in money. At the end of the first day you have $650, at the end of the next day you have $600, and at the end of the fourteenth day you have no money. On the average, your money holding is equal to half of your pay, that is, $350. Now suppose that your productivity improves and you get a 10 percent raise to $770 every two weeks and that you increase your spending also by 10 percent to $55 per day. At the end of the first day after you receive your pay, you have $715 ($770 − $55 = $715) and at the end of the fourteenth day you again have no money. In this case, your average money holding is $385 (half of $770), which is 10 percent greater than in the previous case. The 10 percent change in income has led to a 10 percent change in the transactions demand for money. In Figure 5, this change would appear as a shift (change in the location) of the demand-for-money curve because it was not the result of a change in the real rate of interest but was due to a change in some other variable—in this case, income. We conclude that income changes will shift the demand-for-money curve in the same direction as the change in income—that is, to the right when income increases and to the left when income decreases.

This example of the transactions demand shows no precautionary demand for money because we assume that you allow your money holding to fall all the way to nothing just before the next payday. It is more reasonable to expect that you would keep some "back-up" money on hand just in case the paycheck was late or some unusual expense, such as an illness, or buying opportunity, such as a sale, should come along. In our illustration, if you keep a $100 backup, your average money holding would have been $450 when your income was $700, and $485 when your income was $770. In each case, you would have had a $100 cash balance on hand just before you received your next pay. However, it seems reasonable that an increase in your income and in the volume of your routine transactions would also lead you to keep a larger backup of money. In this

way, changing the level of income is a shift variable for the precautionary demand for money as well.

Variables other than the real rate of interest, such as changes in the amount of wealth and changes in national income and product, can shift the demand-for-money curve.

The Money-Supply Curve

The money-supply curve (*MS*) in Figure 5 shows the relationship between the real rate of interest and the real quantity of M1 money in the economy. The curve is drawn with a positive slope because, in the deposit-expansion process, banks will work more eagerly to expand the money supply when real interest rates are high than when they are low. This is because the profitability of loaning money will be greater when real interest rates are high, other things being equal, and banks will hold smaller amounts of "desired" excess reserves. Therefore, with a given monetary base and reserve requirement, the amount of money that is supplied will be greater when real interest rates are high.

Banks will work more eagerly to expand the money supply when real interest rates are high because the profitability of loaning money will be greater.

The location of the money-supply curve is very important to the theory of interest-rate determination. The monetary instruments of the Federal Reserve (open market buying and selling, reserve requirements, and discount rates) shift this curve either to the left by restrictive policies or to the right by expansionary policies.

Equilibrium in the Money Market

In Figure 5, the point where the *MD* curve crosses the *MS* curve identifies the equilibrium condition. At the equilibrium real interest rate, *i*, the amount of money actually supplied is equal to the amount demanded. Given the location of these curves, no other real interest rate could bring about that balance.

At the equilibrium real interest rate (i in Figure 5) the quantity of money actually supplied equals the quantity demanded.

The equilibrating action of the interest rate becomes clear when we examine what would happen at interest rates above or below the equilibrium rate. Let us assume that i in Figure 5 represents a real interest rate of 5 percent. Consider a nonmoney asset that pays $100 a year to its owner. At the 5 percent rate of interest, the present value of this asset is $2,000 (that is, $100/0.05). Now think about what would happen at a real interest rate of 7 percent. At this higher interest rate, the quantity of money supplied is greater than the quantity demanded. Speculators use the extra money to bid for

the nonmoney asset, which has a value of $1,428.57 (that is, $100/0.07) when the interest rate is 7 percent. These bids push the price of the nonmoney asset upward. But when the price rises above $1,428.57, the yield, or rate of return, on the asset falls to less than 7 percent, since the asset still promises to pay only $100 per year to its owner. What this means is that no interest rate other than i (5 percent in our numerical illustration) can be sustained, given the locations of the *MS* and *MD* curves in the money market assumed for this illustration. In order for equilibrium to exist, the rate of interest in the money market must correspond with the yield, or rate of return, of the nonmoney assets that are alternative assets for holding wealth.

In order for equilibrium to exist, the rate of interest in the money market must correspond with the yield, or rate of return, of the nonmoney assets that are alternative assets for holding wealth.

FIGURE 6
Expansionary Monetary Policy (a No-Inflation Scenario)

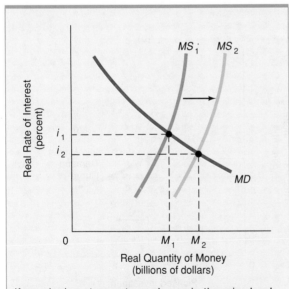

If people do not expect any change in the price level, expansionary Federal Reserve action can shift the *MS* curve to the right from MS_1 to MS_2 as illustrated by the arrow. This will cause real interest rates to fall from i_1 to i_2. Contractionary action would shift the *MS* curve to the left and raise real interest rates.

MONETARY INSTRUMENTS IN ACTION: A NO-INFLATION SCENARIO

We will now examine how the Federal Reserve System can influence real interest rates by shifting the *MS* curve in the money market. Figure 6 illustrates an expansionary central bank action. We begin with equilibrium at the intersection of the *MD* curve with the MS_1 curve, with real interest rate i_1 and the real quantity of money M_1. Next, we assume that the central bank takes some expansionary action, such as might be carried out through open market purchases, lower reserve requirements, and/or lower discount rates. If this leads to no expectation of any change in the price level, the money-supply curve will shift to the right (from MS_1 to MS_2). *The assumption that no price-level change is expected is critical in shifting this curve.* If no price-level rise is expected, each dollar of the M1 money recorded on the horizontal axis keeps its original purchasing power. So an increase in the number of these dollars is an increase in the real money supply. As a result, the real interest rate falls from i_1 to i_2. If, instead, the Federal Reserve Board wanted to raise real interest rates, the money supply would be reduced, shifting the MS curve to the left.

The Federal Reserve System can influence real interest rates by shifting the MS curve in the money market. The curve can be shifted to the right by expansionary actions (assuming no price-level changes are anticipated) and to the left by contractionary actions.

The process of moving to the new equilibrium is as follows. When the money supply is increased, people find that they have more money assets (and less nonmoney assets) than they want at the i_1 rate of interest. To adjust to this new situation, people

bid on such nonmoney assets as stocks, bonds, or real estate. Their bids push up the market prices of these assets, and, according to the present value formula, the rise in their prices leads to a drop in the rate of interest. On the other hand, if the money supply is reduced, shifting the MS curve to the left, wealth holders will find themselves with less money than they desire at the initial interest rate. In order to hold more wealth in the form of money, they will offer to sell stocks, bonds, real estate, and so forth. These sale offers will lower market prices for these assets and cause interest rates to rise.

Indirect Transmission

When monetary instruments shift the real money-supply curve and lower the real interest rate, as shown in Figure 6, how are the effects transmitted to the equilibrium level of real national income and product?

FIGURE 7
Transmission from Change in Real Money Supply to Change in Equilibrium Real National Income and Product

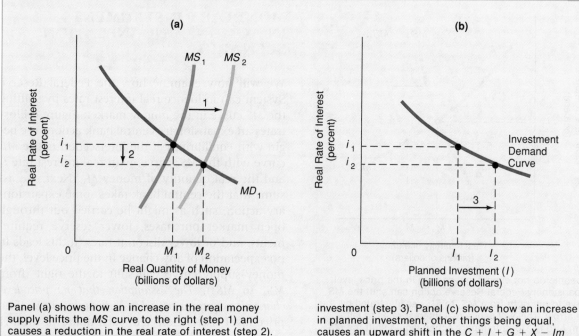

Panel (a) shows how an increase in the real money supply shifts the MS curve to the right (step 1) and causes a reduction in the real rate of interest (step 2). Panel (b) shows how this decrease in the real interest rate causes an increase in the volume of planned

investment (step 3). Panel (c) shows how an increase in planned investment, other things being equal, causes an upward shift in the $C + I + G + X - Im$ curve (step 4). This shift in planned expenditure brings an increase in equilibrium real national income and

The **indirect transmission mechanism** uses the Keynesian model and stresses the importance of planned investment. It is illustrated in Figure 7, which combines the interest-rate-determination model (which you have just studied) with the planned-investment and the Keynesian-cross models. Here is how the connections work. The Federal Reserve undertakes expansionary action by buying bonds in the open market, by reducing reserve requirements, or by reducing discount rates. This, according to the "no-inflation scenario," shifts the real money-supply curve in panel (a) from MS_1 to MS_2 (step 1). The real rate of interest falls from i_1 to i_2 (step 2). These lower real interest rates affect the volume of planned investment, as shown in panel (b). The original volume of planned investment was I_1, corresponding to the original rate of interest of i_1. When interest rates fall to i_2, the volume of planned investment rises to I_2 (step 3). Planned investment is part of total planned expenditure ($C + I + G + X - Im$). Panel (c) shows the effect of the change in planned investment on the equilibrium level of real national income and product. When the volume of planned investment rises, other things being equal, the total planned-expenditure curve shifts from $C + I_1 + G + X - Im$ to $C + I_2 + G + X - Im$ (step 4), and the equilibrium level of real national income and product rises from Y_1 to Y_2 through the operation of the multiplier process (step 5).

In the indirect transmission mechanism, an increase in the real money supply leads to lower real interest rates and a larger flow of planned investment which raises the equilibrium level of real national income and product.

The "no inflation" assumption is very important in the transmission displayed in Figure 7. This is because the variable displayed on the horizontal axis of the money-market graph, panel (a), is the *real* quantity of money, that is, the *nominal* quantity divided by a price-level index number. If the price-level rises, this index number becomes larger with the result that the *real* quantity of money shrinks. Therefore, if inflation takes place, the real money-supply curve shifts to the left. In panel (a), the MS_2 curve would shift back toward the MS_1 curve. Real interest rates would not fall as much as shown in panel (a), and all of the subsequent effects on planned investment and on the equilibrium level of real national income and product would be correspondingly reduced. The effectiveness of the expansionary monetary policy would be reduced. In an extreme case, inflation could cancel the entire impact of the expansionary monetary policy on real interest rates and real national income and product. Its only effect would be on the price level. If expansionary monetary policy triggers an *expectation* that the price level will rise, nominal interest rates will rise immediately, and little or no reduction in real interest rates will take place.

If expansionary monetary policy triggers an expectation that the price level will rise,

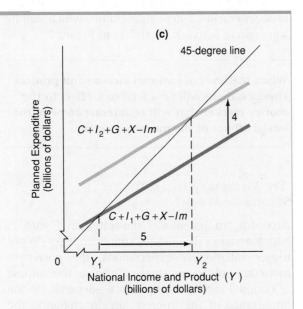

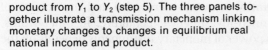

product from Y_1 to Y_2 (step 5). The three panels together illustrate a transmission mechanism linking monetary changes to changes in equilibrium real national income and product.

nominal interest rates will rise immediately, and little or no reduction in real interest rates will take place.

Direct Transmission

Many economists say that monetary instruments do not have to work through the complicated process of interest-rate changes, followed by planned-investment changes, and finally by changes in national income and product. They contend that changes in the money supply also work directly through household budgets and consumption expenditure. For example, if Federal Reserve Banks purchase securities in the open market, the households that sell the securities receive money, which they spend directly for consumption goods and services. The economy can expand without going through the step of an interest-rate change. This is called the **direct transmission mechanism.**

Monetary instruments can also work through the direct transmission mechanism: money-supply changes can directly affect household spending without going through the complicated process of interest-rate changes followed by planned-investment changes, followed by changes in national income and product.

Feedback to the Demand for Money

The transmission mechanism shown in Figure 7 does not tell the complete story of the effects of monetary actions. When the level of national income and product changes, as it did in step 5, there will be a feedback effect in the money market. This feedback will counteract some of the initial effects of the monetary action. It operates through *shifts* in the demand-for-money curve.

When you studied the speculative, transactions, and precautionary demands for money, you learned that changes in income and wealth shift the demand-for-money curve. Therefore the rise in national income and product from Y_1 to Y_2 (step 5 in Figure 7) leads to a shift in the demand-for-money curve. With higher incomes, people want more money because they are engaging in more transactions. This feedback shifts the demand-for-money curve to the right and increases the rate of interest to some level higher than i_2 in Figure 7. This rise partly offsets the drop in interest rates from the original policy action of the Federal Reserve. The rise in the interest rate carries over to panel (b) and partly offsets the rise in planned investment from the first round of the process. Finally, in panel (c), the reduction in the volume of planned investment caused by the feedback effect brings a downward shift in the total-planned-expenditure curve, from $C + I_2 + G + X - Im$, and a drop in the equilibrium level of national income and product. What happens is that some of the new money that pushed interest rates down initially is now being used in hand-to-hand circulation and is no longer being used in bidding for securities and other assets.

The feedback process repeats itself, in ever-weakening rounds, until the national income and product reaches a new equilibrium, which will lie somewhere between Y_1 and Y_2 in Figure 7.

When the level of national income and product changes, there will be a feedback effect in the money market that will counteract some of the initial effects of the monetary action.

Are Monetary Instruments Strong or Weak?

According to the model illustrated in Figure 7, which assumes that money supply changes do not trigger inflationary expectations, the power of monetary policy—its ability to change the volume of national income and product—depends on the importance of the interest rate in changing the quantity of money demanded and the volume of planned-investment expenditure. In other words, the power of monetary instruments depends on the responsiveness of the quantity of money demanded and the quantity of planned investment demanded to changes in the rate of interest.[4]

The power of monetary instruments depends on the responsiveness of the quantity of money demanded and of the quantity of planned investment demanded to changes in the rate of interest.

The Responsiveness of the Quantity of Money Demanded   Figure 8 illustrates a shift of the money-supply curve from MS_1 to MS_2. It has two demand-for-money curves, one called "more responsive" and the other called "less responsive." To understand the issue, start at point A, where equilibrium would exist between money-supply curve MS_1 and either of the two demand-for-money curves. Next, shift the money-supply curve to the right, from MS_1 to MS_2, to represent an expansionary application of monetary instruments. How great a change will take place in the rate of interest? The "less responsive" demand-for-money curve suggests a substantial drop in the interest rate, from i_1 to i_3, as shown at point B. But the "more responsive" demand-for-money curve suggests a smaller interest-rate decrease, from i_1 to only i_2, as shown at point C.

The lower the degree of responsiveness of the quantity of money demanded to changes in the interest rate, the more powerful is monetary policy, *ceteris paribus*. Shifts in the money-supply curve bring great changes in interest rates. But if the quantity of money demanded is highly responsive to changes in interest rates, shifts in the money-supply curve will have less influence on interest rates. Increases in the quantity of money are simply absorbed into greater money holdings. A flat demand-for-money curve illustrates what is called a **liquidity trap.** This is a problem mainly at very low interest rates (and very high asset prices) when people hold large amounts of money waiting for these asset prices to fall (and for interest rates to

4. Students who have studied microeconomics will recognize that the responsiveness of the quantity demanded to a change in price is the economic concept of *elasticity*. We use the term "responsiveness" here because many students study macroeconomics before they study microeconomics.

FIGURE 8
The Responsiveness of the Quantity of Money Demanded to Changes in the Rate of Interest

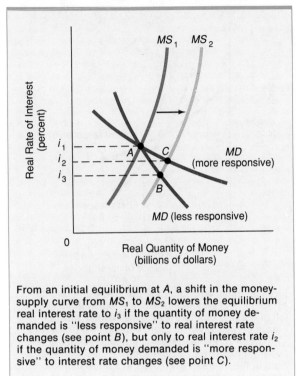

From an initial equilibrium at A, a shift in the money-supply curve from MS_1 to MS_2 lowers the equilibrium real interest rate to i_3 if the quantity of money demanded is "less responsive" to real interest rate changes (see point B), but only to real interest rate i_2 if the quantity of money demanded is "more responsive" to interest rate changes (see point C).

rise). Economists disagree about how important it has been in the past or may be in the future.

The less responsive the quantity of money demanded to changes in the rate of interest, the more effective monetary instruments will be.

The Responsiveness of Planned Investment Expenditure   The second issue about the strength or weakness of monetary instruments relates to the planned-investment-demand curve. To understand this question, look at Figure 9. This figure shows two planned-investment-demand curves, one labeled "more responsive" and the other labeled "less responsive." Consider what happens as a result of a fall in the rate of interest from i_1 to i_2. According to the more responsive demand curve, many potential investments become profitable at

FIGURE 9
The Responsiveness of Planned-Investment Expenditure to Changes in the Rate of Interest

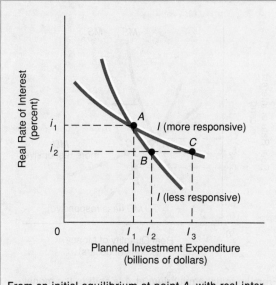

From an initial equilibrium at point *A*, with real interest rate i_1 and planned-investment expenditure of I_1 a fall in the rate of interest to i_2 results in a small increase in planned-investment expenditure (from I_1 to I_2) to point *B*. Planned-investment expenditure is relatively unresponsive ("less responsive"). But the same drop in the interest rate results in a large increase in planned-investment expenditure (from I_1 to I_3) to point *C* if the planned-investment expenditure is more responsive.

Monetary instruments are more powerful the greater the responsiveness of planned-investment expenditure to changes in the interest rate.

SHORT-RUN MONETARY POLICY

In spite of the prescriptions of Milton Friedman and other monetarist economists, monetary instruments are, in practice, used in efforts to moderate short-term fluctuations in the economy. These "activist" monetary policies are based on the proposition that monetary policy does influence real interest rates, at least temporarily, and can be used to stabilize the economy. In these applications, policymakers must consider changes in money velocity and must decide whether to counteract or accommodate short-run fluctuations in economic activity.

Changes in Money Velocity

The long-run velocity of money is determined by the basic institutional structures of the economy, such as how frequently people receive paychecks. When pay is received frequently, a given stock of money works harder and circulates faster, so velocity goes up. If people are paid less frequently, velocity is lower. However, changes in these institutional patterns take place slowly and are not critical for short-run monetary policy.

Short-run changes in the velocity of money also occur and are important for short-run monetary policy. When velocity increases, a given stock of money works harder, and the result is like an increase in the quantity of money. Similarly, a decrease in money velocity has the same effect as decreasing the quantity of money. If the goal is to have a steady rate of change in the product of M and V, increases in V must be offset by decreases in M, and vice versa. Therefore, monetary policymakers must recognize and respond to short-run changes in velocity.

this lower interest rate, and the quantity of planned investment will increase from I_1 to I_3, as indicated by point *C*. But the less responsive demand curve shows a smaller increase in planned investment, from I_1 only to I_2, as indicated by point *B*.

The actual degrees of responsiveness of planned-investment expenditure depends on conditions in the economy. If interest costs are only a small part of the total costs of investment projects or if only a small backlog of such projects exists, the quantity demanded will be relatively unresponsive to interest rate changes. This may be true in the short term. A longer-term point of view usually sees a larger backlog of investment projects and finds interest costs to be a significant part of their costs. This view expects a more responsive demand for planned-investment expenditure.

What variables influence short-run velocity?
One important variable is the optimism or pessimism of the public about their economic future.
When people are optimistic, they tend to spend
money freely and velocity rises. When they are pessimistic, they tend to hold money longer and velocity falls. These attitudinal changes tend to average
out over longer time periods, but short-run monetary policy attempts to compensate for them. For
example, fear of impending recession typically reduces money velocity and reduces the effective
money combination of M times V. In effect, this is
equivalent to a restrictive monetary policy and increases the danger of recession. Therefore, short-
run monetary policymakers attempt to counteract
such short-run reductions in velocity by increasing,
temporarily, the rate of money growth.

The opposite situation arises when velocity
increases because of public optimism or perhaps
because of fear of impending inflation. Rising velocity, other things unchanged, parallels an expansionary monetary policy and can increase the likelihood of inflation. Again, short-run monetary
policymakers attempt to compensate by lowering
the rate of growth in the money supply.

Changes in the operating procedures of the
economy's financial institutions affect velocity and
are especially troublesome for monetary policy. For
example, computers and telecommunications technology dramatically increase the speed with which
balances can be transferred from one account to
another. Speedier handling of financial transactions increases velocity. But, more critical for monetary policy, rapid transfers of balances from one

type of account to another cause changes in *measured* velocity even if no change in *actual* velocity is
taking place. If interest rates increase and balances
counted as part of M2 experience larger interest-
rate increases than balances counted only in M1,
account owners respond by transferring funds out
of M1 and into M2 balances. Measured M1 velocity rises and measured M2 velocity decreases, *ceteris
paribus*. Moreover, if balances are shifted to wealth
forms not in any of the various money supply measures, all measured velocities increase. In the
1980s, computer and telecommunications innovations, along with deregulation of financial institutions, greatly complicated the practical application
of monetary policy. Money managers, trying to adjust the money supply for changes in velocity,
could not be sure that they had accurate measures
of velocity.

Figure 10 shows the velocity of money in the
United States from 1960 through 1988 as measured by dividing nominal GNP by the M1 and the
M2 quantities of money for each year. M1 velocity
increased substantially over this period, and M2
velocity, although reasonably stable in the long
run, showed important fluctuations from year to
year.

A Policy of Accommodation

The monetary policy of **accommodation** attempts to shift the money-supply curve back and
forth in order to offset shifts in the demand for
money, thereby stabilizing the rate of interest. Accommodation is illustrated in Figure 11, which
shows the money market. In this figure, the demand-for-money curve shifts to the right from MD_1
to MD_2 (arrow 1) due, for example, to an expansion in the volume of economic activity in the
economy. Without an increase in the money supply, the equilibrium rate of interest rises from i_1 at
point A to i_2 at point B and moderates the economic

FIGURE 10
Velocity of Money in the United States, 1960–1988

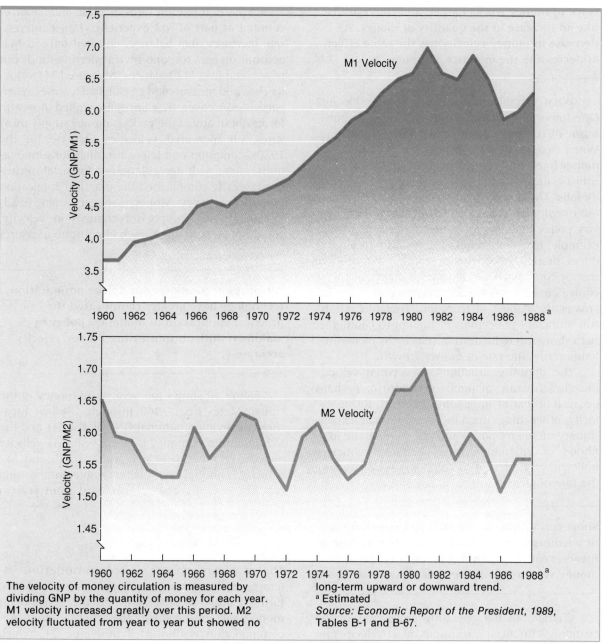

The velocity of money circulation is measured by dividing GNP by the quantity of money for each year. M1 velocity increased greatly over this period. M2 velocity fluctuated from year to year but showed no long-term upward or downward trend.

a Estimated

Source: Economic Report of the President, 1989, Tables B-1 and B-67.

expansion, since higher interest rates reduce the volume of planned business investment and household purchases. The policy of accommodation is represented by the shift of the money-supply curve from MS_1 to MS_2 (arrow 2). With this accommodating increase in the money supply, the new equilibrium is at point C and the interest rate is prevented from rising and exerting its moderating pressure on the economic expansion. In other words, the monetary policy of accommodation stabilizes interest rates rather than the volume of economic activity in the economy.

An important aspect of the policy of accommodation involves the government's sales of securities to finance its budget deficit. Other things being equal, these sales drive up interest rates and crowd out private investment. By purchasing government securities in the open market, the Federal Reserve System can reduce this upward pressure on interest rates. In this way, monetary policy accommodates not only economic expansion but also the sale of government securities.

The policy of accommodation attempts to shift the money-supply curve back and forth to offset shifts in the demand for money.

Accommodation stabilizes interest rates rather than the volume of economic activity in the economy. Accommodation may be used to help the government's sales of securities to finance its budget deficit.

The question of whether or not to follow a policy of accommodation can lead to conflict between the monetary authorities of the Federal Reserve System and the fiscal authorities of the White House and Congress, where budget decisions are made. Expansionary fiscal policy can be defeated or greatly weakened if the monetary authorities refuse to accommodate it by increasing the money supply. In the same way, restrictive fiscal policies can be defeated or weakened if the monetary authorities refuse to accommodate by reducing the growth rate of the money supply. Heated discussions arise about whether the Board of Governors, whose members are appointed rather than elected and who are or have been closely connected with banking, should have such great power. On the other hand, the tension between fiscal and monetary authorities can be viewed as another of the checks and balances that are part of the U.S. government system. Each side holds something of a veto power over the other.

Judgment-Based Monetary Policy

William McChesney Martin, Jr., who served as chairman of the Board of Governors from 1951 to 1970 (the longest tenure in the history of the Board), once characterized Federal Reserve policy during his term as "leaning against the wind," meaning that monetary policy occupied a middle ground between a steady-money-growth policy and a policy of accommodation. When the economy was in the expansion phase of an economic fluctuation, the expansion would be only partially accommodated. Interest rates would be allowed to rise some, but partial accommodation would moderate the increase in an effort to extend the expansion of the economy. On the other hand, in the contraction phase of a fluctuation, the growth of the money supply would be accelerated, pushing interest rates downward in order to stimulate the economy and moderate the contraction of economic activity.

FIGURE 11
Accommodation

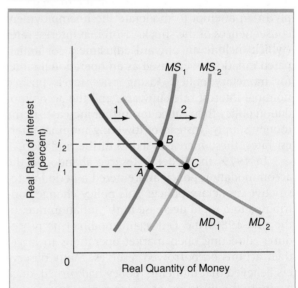

Accommodation means shifting the money-supply curve so that shifts in the demand-for-money curve do not cause changes in the rate of interest. In this diagram, we assume that the demand-for-money curve has shifted to the right, from MD_1 to MD_2 (arrow 1), perhaps because of an increase in national income and product. Without accommodation, equilibrium would move from point A to point B, and the rate of interest would rise from i_1 to i_2. However, accommodation, accomplished by shifting the money-supply curve to the right, from MS_1 to MS_2 (arrow 2), moves equilibrium to point C and prevents a rise in the rate of interest.

During the 1950s and 1960s, the Federal Reserve System followed a middle ground between a steady-money-growth policy and a policy of accommodation.

When Chairman Martin assumed his post the Federal Reserve System had freed itself of the obligation to follow the strict policy of accommodation adopted in the emergency period of World War II. He left the Board in 1970 after it had pursued severely restrictive policies attempting to limit inflationary pressures unleashed by the combination of war in Vietnam and domestic government spending under the Great Society program of President Johnson's administration.

During the 1970s, contractionary supply shocks caused both inflationary pressures and high levels of unemployment. Monetary policy partially accommodated ("validated") the higher price level by increasing the rate of growth in the money supply in an attempt to moderate the unemployment consequences of the shocks. Nominal interest rates (which include an upward adjustment for anticipated inflation) were used as an operational target for monetary policy. Rising price levels pushed nominal interest rates upward, and the accommodation policy then called for further increases in the money supply. Instead of lowering nominal interest rates, these increases led to further inflation.

In 1979, the Federal Reserve abandoned the accommodation policy and entered a period of restrictive monetary policy. This policy change contributed to a rapid decrease in the inflation rate. In the mid-1980s the Fed again modified its procedures, directing open market operations to target their actions on borrowed reserves. Many observers believed that monetary policy had turned, once again, in the direction of accommodation, because increases in borrowing through the discount procedure usually go along with higher nominal interest rates. Both borrowed-reserve targeting and interest-rate targeting lend themselves to a policy of accommodation, since stabilizing borrowed reserves tends also to stabilize interest rates.

In 1979, the Federal Reserve abandoned the accommodation policy, but to some extent turned toward it once again in the mid-1980s.

MONETARY POLICY AND INFLATIONARY EXPECTATIONS

Economic models of **inflationary expectations** attempt to explain how anticipated changes in the price level affect decisions. Such expectations are especially important for transactions that involve commitments that extend over a period of time. For example, when higher prices are anticipated, consumers tend to make planned durable goods purchases sooner than they otherwise would in order to obtain desired goods before their prices go up. Similarly, business firms acquire capital equipment sooner, other things equal, in an atmosphere of anticipated price increases than in a stable price atmosphere.

Anticipated changes in the price level affect economic decisions, especially those involving commitments that extend over a period of time.

To explain how inflationary expectations are related to monetary policy, we begin by assuming that the Federal Reserve System has carried out an expansion of the money supply in an effort to lower real interest rates and thereby increase planned-investment expenditure and the equilibrium level of national income and product. (This procedure was illustrated in Figures 6 and 7). We also assume, however, that this expansionary monetary policy triggers inflationary expectations, that is, people conclude that the money supply increase will drive the price level upward. What effect will these expectations have on nominal and real interest rates, on the volume of planned-investment expenditure, and on the equilibrium level of national income and product?

Inflationary Expectations and the Loanable-Funds Market

Figure 12 illustrates a loanable-funds market. In order to illustrate inflationary expectations, the vertical axis shows *nominal* interest rates, that is, the interest rates actually written into borrowing and lending contracts. In the absence of inflationary expectations, there is no difference between the

FIGURE 12
Inflationary Expectations in the Loanable-Funds Market

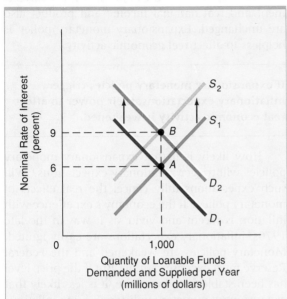

The quantities of loanable funds supplied and demanded are recorded on the horizontal axis, and the nominal (not the real) interest rate appears on the vertical axis. Point *A* represents the equilibrium before inflationary expectations arise. The nominal rate of interest is 6 percent and, since there is no inflation expected, the real interest rate also is 6 percent. Inflationary expectations cause the supply curve to shift to the left, from S_1 to S_2, as lenders require a higher nominal interest rate in order to be compensated for the loss in real value of their funds during the term of the loans. Inflationary expectations also cause the demand curve to shift to the right, from D_1 to D_2, because lenders expect to repay loans in dollars with less purchasing power than those originally borrowed. Thus, with inflationary expectations, equilibrium is at point *B*, the nominal rate of interest has risen by the appropriate percentage point rate of the expected price level increase (from 6 percent to slightly more than 9 percent if the expected rate of inflation is 3 percent), and the real interest rate has remained unchanged.

nominal and the real interest rate, and Figure 12 would be equivalent to Figure 4, which used real interest rates on its vertical axis. But, as we shall see, when inflationary expectations arise, nominal interest rates are no longer equal to real interest rates. Let us see why.

We begin with equilibrium at point *A*, with a nominal interest rate of 6 percent and $1,000 million of loanable funds demanded and supplied. We now inject an expectation that the price level is going to increase at the rate of 3 percent a year. Consider first a lender deciding whether or not to loan $100 at the nominal interest rate of 6 percent. At this interest rate, at the end of the first year of the loan, this lender would have $106. However, if the price level rises by 3 percent, this $106 will have a *real* value of only $102.91, calculated by dividing $106 by the price index number of 1.03, which reflects the 3 percent increase in the price level. Therefore, in *real* terms, the lender will have earned slightly less than 3 percent interest, rather than the 6 percent indicated by the nominal interest rate. The *real* rate of interest has turned out to be lower than the *nominal* rate by approximately 3 percentage points, which is the anticipated rate of inflation.

If the lender desires to obtain a *real* rate of return of 6 percent—the rate obtainable before inflationary expectations arose—he or she must insist on a higher *nominal* rate of interest. How much higher must this rate be? In order to have a *real* $106 at the end of one year, the lender must, at that time, have a *nominal* $109.18, determined by multiplying $106 times 1.03, reflecting the increase in the price level. Therefore, in order to receive a *real* return of 6 percent, the lender must obtain a *nominal* rate of interest of slightly over 9 percent. In other words, from the viewpoint of the lender, inflationary expectations drive the required *nominal* interest rate upward by a number of percentage points approximately equal to the expected rate of inflation. In Figure 12, the expectation of inflation causes the supply curve of loanable funds to shift to the left, from S_1 to S_2, to adjust for the expected rate of inflation.

The logic of inflationary expectations applies similarly to the borrowers of loanable funds and to the demand curve in Figure 12. Since the borrower expects to repay the loan with dollars whose real purchasing power will be smaller by 3 percent due to the higher price level, he or she is willing to pay the higher nominal interest rate in order to obtain the desired funds. Other things being equal, an investment project that appeared profitable at a *real* interest rate of 6 percent will, in the presence of an anticipated 3 percent increase in the price level, appear equivalently profitable at a *nominal* interest rate of slightly over 9 percent. Therefore, with a 3 percent anticipated rate of inflation, the demand curve in Figure 12 shifts to the right, from D_1 to D_2, and the new equilibrium is at point B, with a *nominal* interest rate of approximately 9 percent. The *nominal* interest rate has increased by approximately the amount of the expected rate of inflation, but the *real* interest rate is unchanged.

Inflationary expectations drive nominal interest rates upward by a number of percentage points approximately equal to the expected rate of inflation.

Inflationary Expectations and Monetary Policy

If expansionary monetary policies trigger inflationary expectations, the power of these policies to lower real interest rates, increase planned investment, and bring about a larger real national income and product is weakened. If a 3 percent increase in the money supply triggers the expectation of a 3 percent increase in the price level, expansionary monetary policy merely increases nominal interest rates by approximately 3 percentage points and leaves real interest rates unchanged. In turn, if real interest rates are unchanged, planned investment and real national income and product also are unchanged. Expansionary monetary policy is helpless to affect real economic activity.

If expansionary monetary policies trigger inflationary expectations, their power to affect real economic activity is weakened.

How likely is it that expansionary monetary policies will trigger inflationary expectations? Will such expectations fully cancel the real effects of monetary policy? If the economy's experience with inflation is recent and vivid, as it was in the late 1970s, inflationary expectations are easily ignited. Monetary policies are weakened and the Federal Reserve must exercise caution. But if the price level has been stable for a long time, it is less likely that expansionary monetary policy will bring inflationary expectations. In such times, monetary policy may succeed, temporarily at least, in lowering real interest rates and promoting economic expansion.

Economics in Focus

Money Supply and the Crash of 1987

For a dramatic example of the Federal Reserve's manipulation of the money supply, we can look back to the days following October 19, 1987, the date the stock market suffered a record-breaking crash. On that Monday the Dow Jones industrial average lost 508 points, or 22.6 percent of its value—the worst such plunge in history. Overall, the market value of U.S. securities declined by an astounding $500 billion. Although the stock market recovered slightly in the following week, the next Monday brought another drop of 8 percent.

Stock-market experts and ordinary citizens alike feared that the crash would bring on a recession and subsequently reduce spending and money velocity throughout the economy. More immediately, brokerage houses might fail, possibly followed by important investment banks. To prevent these occurrences, a massive increase of credit was needed.

Into the breach stepped the Federal Reserve, led by its new chairman, Alan Greenspan. Until then, Greenspan had made his mark as an inflation fighter. In fact, in the inevitable analysis after the crash, his anti-inflation policies were blamed for helping to trigger the stock market's decline. In early September the Fed had raised the discount rate for the first time in over three years. In the ten weeks between the date Greenspan took office and the morning of the crash, the yield on 30-year Treasury bonds had risen from 8.8 percent to 10.5 percent, and the federal funds rate had jumped from 6.5 percent to 7.6 percent. The critics declared that these moves had been made at exactly the wrong time, when the stock market was already showing signs of shakiness.

But on the morning of October 20, the day after the market's disaster, Greenspan began to redeem himself. He issued a one-sentence statement to reassure brokerage houses, banks, and investors: "The Federal Reserve, consistent with its responsibilities as the nation's central bank, affirmed today its readiness to serve as a source of liquidity to support the economic and financial system." Under Greenspan's guidance the Fed then reversed its restrictive policy, pumping money into the economy by buying up Treasury securities on the open market. As a result, the M1 measure of the money supply increased $8.9 billion in one week. The prime rate correspondingly fell a quarter of a percentage point. The federal funds rate dropped by over 2 percent and the yield on 30-year Treasury bonds by over 1 percent.

Nearly everyone applauded the Fed's quick reaction. Credit crises were averted; and when no recession loomed around the corner, many believed that the Fed's short-term increase in the money supply had helped the economy escape a serious danger.

Sources: Larry Martz et al., "After the Meltdown of '87," *Newsweek,* November 2, 1987, pp. 14–20; George J. Church, "Panic Grips the Globe," *Time,* November 2, 1987, pp. 22–33; Jeffrey M. Laderman, "How the Bull Crashed into Reality," *Business Week,* November 2, 1987, pp. 48–50; Jeffrey M. Laderman with David Zigas and Michael E. Kreca, "Better Keep Those Seat Belts Fastened," *Business Week,* November 9, 1987, pp. 38–39; Ann Reilly Dowd, "Where Does the U.S. Go from Here?" *Fortune,* November 23, 1987, pp. 50–58; Gene Koretz, "Is the Fed Playing It Too Close to the Vest?" *Business Week,* December 14, 1987, p. 24; Seymour Zucker, "Is Alan Greenspan Really Such a Hero?" *Business Week,* December 14, 1987, p. 35; Vince Valvano, "The Morning After: Can the Fed Save the Economy?" *Dollars & Sense,* December 1987, pp. 6–8, 22.

SUMMARY

1. The quantity-of-money theory is based on the equation of exchange, $MV = PQ$. Assuming that the velocity of money circulation is constant, the theory states that changes in the quantity of money (M) will result in an equal proportional change in nominal gross national product, PQ. An aggregate-demand and aggregate-supply interpretation of the quantity-of-money theory postulates a vertical aggregate-supply curve. (See pages 298–299.)

2. A monetary policy prescription based on the quantity-of-money theory calls for a steady growth of the money supply at a rate approximately equal to the expected growth in the economy's capacity to produce goods and services. A goal of this policy is a stable price level. The policy does not propose changes in the money supply aimed at responding to short-run economic fluctuations. (See pages 300–301.)

3. Real interest rates are determined in markets for loanable funds. In these markets, the money supply and preferences of lenders between present and future uses of funds are represented by the supply curve. The demand curve represents the willingness and ability to borrow funds of households, governments, and business firms. The expected profitability of investments is reflected in this curve. (See pages 303–304.)

4. Monetary policy seeks to influence the supply of money in the money market, which illustrates the demand and supply of money held as an asset. In this market, the demand for money arises from transactions, precautionary, and speculative motivations for holding cash balances. The equilibrium interest rate balances the quantity of money supplied with the quantity demanded. (See pages 304–309.)

5. If inflation is not anticipated, increases in the money supply lower real interest rates, and decreases in the money supply raise real interest rates. In a noninflationary atmosphere, monetary policy can influence real interest rates, which, in turn, change the volume of planned investment and the equilibrium level of real national income and product. (See pages 309–310.)

6. In the indirect transmission mechanism, the strength of monetary policy depends on the responsiveness of the quantity of money demanded in the money market and on the responsiveness of the quantity of investment expenditure demanded to changes in the rate of interest. According to the direct transmission view, money-supply changes operate directly on household spending and do not rely on interest-rate changes to have their effect. (See pages 310–312.)

7. Short-run monetary policy must adjust for changes in the velocity of money circulation in order to regulate the effective money supply, measured as M times V. Changes in financial institution technology and deregulation of these institutions have speeded the transfer of balances among different types of accounts. Velocity changes according to one money-supply concept may then differ from velocity changes according to other money-supply concepts, increasing the difficulty of short-run monetary policy. (See pages 314–315.)

8. A monetary policy of accommodation calls for changes in the money supply to match changes in the demand for money. The result is stabilization of nominal interest rates. Under this approach, monetary policy does not exert an independent force for moderating economic fluctuations or limiting inflation. Accommodation also assists Treasury sales of national debt securities by preventing such sales from increasing nominal rates of interest. Accommodation is associated with policy operations guided by interest-rate targeting or borrowed-reserve targeting. (See pages 315–317.)

9. Except for emergency periods, the Federal Reserve generally has taken a flexible approach in the direction of short-run monetary policy. This judgment-based approach authorizes only partial accommodation to changes in the demand for money. It permits some stabilizing changes in interest rates and attempts to moderate fluctuations in the volume of economic activity. (See pages 317–318.)

10. Inflationary expectations push nominal interest rates upward to levels higher than real interest rates. In loanable-funds markets, both demanders and suppliers respond to these expectations. To the extent that money-supply increases trigger inflationary expectations, monetary policy is weakened because it is not able to affect real interest rates. (See pages 318–320.)

KEY TERMS

accommodation: a monetary policy that attempts to shift the money-supply curve back and forth in order to offset shifts in the demand for money, thereby stabilizing the rate of interest (page 315).

direct transmission mechanism: the process whereby real national income and product changes, in response to money-supply changes, without going through the step of an interest-rate change (page 312).

equation of exchange: an identity that states that the quantity of money in the economy multiplied by the number of times the average dollar is used each year to purchase newly produced final products must be equal to the quantity of these final products multiplied by their average price: $MV = PQ$ (page 298).

indirect transmission mechanism: a process whereby the effects of a shift of the real money-supply curve are transmitted to the equilibrium level of real national income and product by affecting interest rates and the volume of planned investment (page 311).

inflationary expectations: expectations that the price level will rise (page 318).

interest rate: the annual payment for the use of funds, expressed as a percentage of the funds used (page 301).

liquidity: the ease with which an asset can be used in exchange or converted into a form that can be used in exchange (page 306).

liquidity trap: when people hold large amounts of money waiting for high asset prices to fall and for low interest rates to rise (page 313).

loanable-funds market: the market that brings together those who wish to lend and those who wish to borrow funds (page 303).

monetarism: a school of economic thought that proposes that monetary policy make no attempt to deal with short-term fluctuations in economic activity but should instead establish a fixed rate of increase for the money supply and stay with this rate year in and year out (page 300).

money market: the market in which money itself is treated as a commodity subject to the concepts of supply and demand (page 304).

nominal values: values that are stated or measured in terms of some monetary unit; they are not adjusted for price-level changes (page 302).

precautionary demand for money: the demand that arises because people want to be prepared for unexpected changes in the pattern of their receipts and expenditures (page 307).

quantity-of-money theory: a theory that states that the velocity of money circulation is constant in the long run, so changes in the quantity of money provide a good way to predict changes in GNP (page 298).

real interest rates: interest rates that reflect actual purchasing-power values (page 303).

real values: values that are stated or measured in terms of goods and services; they are adjusted for price-level changes (page 302).

speculation: taking actions based on expectations of future changes in the market values of assets (page 305).

speculative demand for money: the demand that arises when people seek to gain from declines in the market value of nonmoney assets (page 306).

time preferences: the relative attractiveness of consumption at the present time compared to consumption at some future time (page 303).

transactions demand for money: the demand that arises because people want to hold some of their wealth in a form that is convenient for day-to-day buying and selling of goods and services (page 307).

velocity of circulation: the average number of times each dollar is used per year to buy newly produced goods and services (page 298).

DISCUSSION QUESTIONS

1. Write down the equation of exchange and define each of its terms. Which side of the equation is actually GNP as usually measured in the national accounting system? Explain the reasoning contained in the equation, noting why this is properly an identity rather than an equation that can be used for predictions.

2. Assume that the current GNP is $1,000 billion and the stock of money averages $250 billion during the year. What is the velocity of money circulation? If this velocity is unchanged, how many dollars of added money would be needed to support a 2 percent growth in output if the price level is to remain unchanged? If the actual increase in the money supply is twice as great as your answer to the preceding question, what will be the nominal GNP after one year? If the price level in the first year was 100, what will it be in the second year?

3. Suppose that a machine costs $1,000 and, for simplicity, that it never wears out or requires any operating cost. Suppose also that using this machine will increase returns to the firm by $60 a year. Would it be profitable to purchase and use this machine if the interest rate were 5 percent? How about 10 percent? Discuss how the real rate of interest influences the amount of planned investment. Explain how a change in the productivity of machines would affect the real rate of interest if lenders kept their preferences unchanged between present and future consumption.

4. Write down, from memory, the definition of speculation, and then check in the chapter (or the Key Terms) to be sure it is correct. Under what expectations about future asset prices would a speculator decide to hold cash? When would this speculator decide to hold nonmoney assets instead of cash? Carefully explain how this reasoning suggests that a demand-for-money curve, drawn with the real interest rate on the vertical axis, would have a negative slope.

5. Explain the transactions demand for money. Suppose that there is an economic boom in your hometown, perhaps because the price of its main product has risen on the national market. The incomes of many local people have gone up. Since your hometown is a small part of the total economy, its prosperity has not influenced the interest rate. What will happen to the quantity of money demanded for transactions in the town? Explain why this is a shift and not a movement along the demand-for-money curve.

6. Assume that the monetary authorities increase the amount of M1 money in the economy

and that no one expects this to cause any increase in the price level. What will happen to the demand for stocks and bonds and other nonmoney assets? How will this affect the prices of these assets? How will this, in turn, affect the equilibrium rate of interest as determined in the market for money? Trace this same sequence for a reduction in the amount of money in the economy.

7. Without looking at Figure 7, construct the set of three graphs that illustrate the transmission of a change in the money supply to a change in equilibrium real national income and product. Trace through the transmission system, starting with an increase in the money supply. Check to be sure you have it right, and then write a brief description of the system. Include a discussion of the feedback effect.

8. If the nominal GNP is $1,200 billion and the quantity of M1 money averaged $300 billion during the year, what is the implicit velocity of money circulation? In Germany during the inflation after World War I, people wanted to be paid every day instead of only once each week. What would a change like that do to the velocity of circulation of money? Discuss the effect of electronic banking machines on the velocity of circulation of money in the United States since they were introduced in the 1970s.

9. In some circumstances, an increase in the money supply may bring a rise in nominal interest rates but no change in real interest rates. Describe the circumstances and the viewpoints of lenders and borrowers that can bring about this situation.

10. If the money-supply curve is drawn on a graph with real values on both axes, a change in the price level could cause a shift in this curve. Which way will the money-supply curve shift if the price level increases? Why? Which way will it shift if the price level decreases? Why?

11. Suppose you sign an agreement to borrow money and to pay a nominal interest rate of 10 percent. If you expect the price level to rise by 6 percent a year, what real interest rate do you expect to pay? If the lender expects the price level to rise by 5 percent a year, what real interest rate does he or she expect to receive? If the price level actually rises by only 4 percent a year, is the lender pleased with the outcome of the transaction? Are you pleased with the outcome? Explain.

Economics of Inflation

People dislike inflation—a general rise in the prices they pay. The faster the inflation, the more they dislike it. The German hyperinflation of the early 1920s is blamed for the rise of Nazism, the decline of the Weimar Republic, and the elevation of Hitler to power. Although people dislike inflation, a general rise in their incomes—which are part of the *costs* of the things they buy—looks like something quite different. It is "belated recognition of merit" or "catching up with inflation already under way." Both of these are highly popular. Failure on the part of the general public to recognize the connection between their incomes and the prices they must pay makes inflation a difficult problem for the policymaker.

Another problem is that inflation is almost entirely a redistribution of real incomes and real assets, whereas the alternatives to inflation either risk or require recession and unemployment. Inflationary redistributions are (1) from receivers of incomes that are largely fixed in monetary terms to receivers of incomes that are more flexible in those terms (from pensioners to farmers, for example), and (2) from people who hold monetary assets or are creditors on monetary contracts to holders of nonmonetary assets or debtors on monetary contracts (from savings-bank depositors to real estate speculators, or from holders of domestic government bonds to the domestic government that issued them). The redistribution need not, and usually does not, reduce either the flow of current *real* income or the total value of *real* assets. The problem is that the standard preventives and cures for inflation (restrictive monetary or fiscal policies) involve at least the risk of recession, depression, and bankruptcy. Thus, inflation and its acceleration may be considered a "least worst" alternative.

"Inflation," Milton Friedman has said, "is always and everywhere a monetary phenomenon." This sentence is the greatest half-truth in inflationary theory. Its correct implication is that inflation requires some sort of monetary fuel if it is not to be stalled or reversed. Its misleading implication is that the monetary expansion must come first in time and the price-level rise only thereafter. We shall discuss the relations between money and inflation, but an initial warning is in order: the key question of the division of a monetary stimulus between changes in the price level and changes in the volume of output has, as yet, been solved only for the polar cases of full employment on the one hand and the ultra-Keynesian "liquidity trap" on the other.

We shall now discuss nine secondary problems of inflationary theory:

1. When is inflation? (supply shocks and their monetary aftermaths)

2. When is inflation? (rationing, controls, and suppressed inflation)

3. Do budget deficits cause inflation?

4. Does inflation keep interest rates down?

5. Does inflation break the "death grip" of debt?

6. Would a restored gold standard cure inflation?

7. "Cost-pushes": should they be validated?

8. Inflation, democracy, and the separation of powers.

9. Is inflation inevitable?

WHEN IS INFLATION? (SUPPLY SHOCKS AND MONETARY AFTERMATHS)

We know from the history of supply shocks, notably the two OPEC oil shocks of the 1970s, that supply shocks run up the prices of a few key commodities, that monetary systems "accommodate" by increased money supplies, and that inflation spreads to the entire economy. But should we date the inflation from the supply shock or from the monetary accommodation? Did OPEC cause inflation in oil-importing countries or did these countries bring it on themselves?

This is more than a terminological quibble. To see this, imagine a monetary system that did not (or could not) increase the money supply to accommodate to an oil shock. What would happen? In the short run, the result would surely be recession and inflation. The prices of crude oil and oil-intensive commodities like petrochemicals would rise. No other price would fall. The measured price level would rise. There would be a money shortage with tight credit and high interest rates. There would surely be political-economic pressure to change the monetary system and accommodate the new and higher price level.

But if the authorities could resist this pressure, the non-oil commodity prices (and wages) would eventually fall. The price level would return to approximately its preshock level.[1] The permanent change would be confined to *relative* prices—those of oil and oil-intensive commodities would rise relative to the general price level, and the prices of non-oil commodities would fall.

This counterfactual scenario is not a policy prescription. (In America, the slowness and reluctance of monetary accommodation to the first oil shock is blamed for a recession in 1974–75 and the failure of President Gerald Ford's bid for re-election in 1976.) It indicates only why many, if not most, economists date supply-shock inflations not from the shocks themselves but from the monetary accommodations to them.

WHEN IS INFLATION? (RATIONING, CONTROLS, AND SUPPRESSED INFLATION)

Imagine now a popular war, either a resistance to foreign aggression (as in World War II) or a "War on Poverty" at home, financed by monetary expansion. There are popular and well-enforced systems of price controls, wage and profit-margin controls, rationing and allocations, "incomes policies," or whatever one chooses to call them.[2] The measured price

level does not rise. There is no measured inflation. People merely accumulate "undesired" hoards of cash, bank deposits, or government securities. These situations are called "suppressed" or "repressed" inflation, in contrast to the "open" inflation reflected in published price statistics.

The scenario continues. The war is won, or at any rate ended. The controls are lifted, or enforcement is curtailed. The price level rises. The suppressed inflation comes out of the closet and there is open inflation. Many economists (although not the general public) would include "suppressed inflation" as a form of inflation and date the inflation from the original resort to controls.

In a famous pamphlet called *How to Pay for the War,* Lord Keynes, the most famous economist of the twentieth century, anticipated in 1939 that the wartime expansion might be followed by a resumption of the Great Depression of the 1930s, which could itself be relieved (without inflation) by postwar spending of the balances accumulated in wartime. Had he been right, we might speak of suppressed inflation being followed by suppressed deflation or disinflation. But he was wrong, and no appropriate terminology ever developed.

DO BUDGET DEFICITS CAUSE INFLATION?

A budget deficit must be financed, but the financing need not be inflationary. Whether it is inflationary or not is a matter of political-economic decision.

The inflationary case is simple. The deficit is financed by monetary expansion, either openly or covertly.[3] The inflation will originate not with the deficit, but with its financing method.

But a deficit need not be inflationary. There are at least two alternative financing methods that do not have inflationary consequences, either singly or in combination. The more common of these, and the more consistent with the market economy, is the sale of securities to the general public without the accompaniment of expanded bank reserves. The problems here are high interest rates, both real and nominal, and the "crowding out" of some private

1. If some international "monetary base" like the world gold supply were redistributed in favor of the OPEC countries, the price level of the non-oil countries would have to fall, and OPEC policies would have *deflated* the rest of the world!

2. These controls also could be enforced harshly by an authoritarian government, perhaps with death penalties for "economic crimes" like large-scale black-marketing.

3. In a typical covert monetary expansion, a central bank buys government securities and creates new government deposits against them. When the government deposits are spent for the goods and services supplied by customers of depository institutions, deposits and reserves of these institutions are increased by equal amounts. These increased reserves form the basis for loan expansion in a fractional-reserve banking system.

investment (or consumer credit). These effects may be exported by attracting capital from abroad and keeping at home domestic capital that might otherwise go abroad. In this case, foreign interest rates come under upward pressure and overseas investors are crowded out.

A less common form of noninflationary finance is the official or unofficial requirement that financial institutions—depository institutions, savings and loan associations, insurance companies, investment houses—purchase the government's debt at below-market interest rates. This method, in (Japanese) practice,[4] produces a credit squeeze on small business and agriculture, which are forced to save more, and in some cases to borrow at unrecorded and usurious interest rates from the criminal underworld.

DOES INFLATION KEEP INTEREST RATES DOWN?

We have mentioned that noninflationary financing methods raise interest rates. By the same token, the "easy money" of inflationary finance might be expected to lower them—whether the expansion is directed at financing a government deficit, business investment, or consumer credit. Yet we also know that in rapid inflation, long-term credit (if available at all!) commands astronomical interest rates. (The American prime rate reached over 20 percent in the Carter inflation of the late 1970s, and home mortgage rates went to about 17 percent.) How can we explain this paradox?

Economists' explanations involve the distinction between real and nominal interest rates, and also a "snapback" theory of the nominal rate.

The nominal rate of interest (i) is the rate directly observed in the marketplace. Let it be the sum of two elements: the real annual rate (r) that would prevail in a regime of long-term price-level stability and an added compensation (j) to the lender for the inflation rate expected during the year. (The money that is lent has higher purchasing power than that which is received in return.) In the simplest algebraic terms, we have

$$i = r + j$$

where j is zero in a stable-price regime and negative in a deflationary one.[5]

The snapback theory says that, at least in the early stage of an accelerating inflation, the expected inflation rate (j) lags behind the actual rate and is "too low." Monetary expansion can temporarily lower both (r) and (j), only to have them rise again, usually above their initial values, when "the market" (borrowers along with lenders) realizes what is going on.

DOES INFLATION BREAK THE "DEATH GRIP" OF DEBT?

A dollar invested at 6 percent compounded interest will grow according to the following table, with the end-value depending on the time period and the frequency of compounding.

---

4. The method is more effective in Japan than elsewhere because a principal Japanese savings institution is a postal savings system whose investments are limited to public securities.

5. More precisely, we compute the total real return $(1 + r)$ as follows:

$$(1 + r) = (1 + i)(1 - j) = 1 + i - j - ij$$

so that, solving for (i):

$$i = \frac{r + j}{1 - j}$$

The $(1 - j)$ term may be important when (j) is large.

Time Period	Annual Compounding	Semi-annual Compounding	Continuous Compounding
10 years	1.791	1.806	1.822
20 years	3.207	3.262	3.320
50 years	18.420	19.219	20.086
2000 years	4.090×10^{50}	2.233×10^{51}	1.304×10^{52}

According to this table, a dollar invested at the time of the Prophet Mohammed (let alone Jesus, Moses, the Buddha, or Adam and Eve) could now buy the entire real and personal wealth of "Spaceship Earth"! This is an extreme case of what has been called the dead hand of the creditor, rentier, or coupon-clipping class. Why do not people take more advantage of the vast economic bonanzas indicated by our little table? (A pocket calculator would suffice to flesh it out much further.) An obvious reason is the length of human life. The Biblical patriarch Methuselah of the Book of Genesis and the immortal Struldbruggs of *Gulliver's Travels* would surely have been more impressed than ourselves by such a table. In addition, preferences that various interest theorists have called time preference, agio, impatience, etc., have kept saving rates down.

One cannot help feeling, however, that fear of and experience with inflation are important factors that have kept the creditor class small—and the dead hand of its power normally weak. The early Soviet economist Yevgeny Preobrazhensky compared the printing press of "War Communism" (1917–18) to machine guns mowing down the coupon-clippers of the leisure or rentier class, by expropriating their wealth and incomes and forcing them to go to work. Nearly seventy years later, Northwestern University economist Robert Eisner suggested that in thinking about American budget deficits one should also consider the effect of inflationary financing on the real value of the national debt (and the economic power of individual and institutional bondholders).

WOULD A RESTORED GOLD STANDARD CURE INFLATION?

The standard yardstick or meterstick itself has length. The standard pound weight or kilogram weight itself has weight. But what about the unit of monetary value? Should it not itself have value apart from its monetary use—as a dollar bill, for example, does not?

Such analogical thinking has been strong throughout the ages. The monetary reformer Irving Fisher warned in his *Purchasing Power of Money* that experiments with no-value "fiat" money always ended in runaway inflation. (The same argument also applied to paper money based on land values or tobacco or coonskins. As prices rose the prices of land or tobacco or coonskins rose too, offering bases for further monetary issues, and so proceeded *ad infinitum*.)

Because of its durability, uniformity, portability, and the limitation of its supply, "commodity" or "full-bodied" money has come to mean gold, or paper fully convertible with gold at some fixed price. The main thing wrong with the wampum of the American Indians was the ease with which enterprising British and Dutch colonists could augment its supply by counterfeiting. All over the world, the major defect of cattle, goats, and other livestock—our words *pecuniary, impecunious,* and *peculation* derive from the Latin word for cattle—was the lack of uniformity. Smart tradesmen try to palm off inferior specimens as standard "money," while retaining superior ones for food, hides, wool, breeding, etc.

In major inflations, a popular sport is to compute prices in terms of gold (or some foreign money convertible into gold). The arithmetic is simple. For example:

$$\text{"gold" price of a pound of fish} = \frac{\text{paper price of a pound of fish}}{\text{paper price of an ounce of gold}}$$

During the period 1864–1879, during and after the American Civil War, such computation was unnecessary, as prices were quoted in both gold and "greenbacks." Much of the painful deflation of the 1870s was confined to greenback prices. As the probability of "resumption" (convertibility) increased, gold prices were largely immune to this deflation. During inflationary times, it is not unusual to find that the gold prices of many commodities have not risen above their preinflationary values. In many cases they will have fallen, as gold is a favorite inflation hedge. This naturally adds to the nostalgia or mystique of the gold standard.

It is sometimes inferred that a system that uses gold as money would not have inflation. In actual history, however, inflation has by no means been eliminated under gold standards (or other metallic standards). Counterfeiting, usually involving adulteration with heavy base metals (most often lead), was one inflation cause. It was engaged in by chancellors of the exchequer as well as by ordinary citizens and by alchemists professing to transmute lead into gold. (Had transmutation been successful, it could have been the end of the gold standard.) More common devices were "clipping" and "sweating"; the first involved shaving the edge off a coin's circumference, the second, shaking coins together vigorously to reduce their weight and give off gold dust, which constituted the revenue of the operation. If you look at contemporary American coins, you will see that the quarter and dime have milled edges (defenses against clipping) while the nickel and penny do not. Presumably it was decided at some past time that it was worth protecting the first two against clipping, but that nobody would bother to clip nickels or pennies. As defenses against sweating, pure gold and silver were replaced by alloys that were harder and more resistant to sweating. The two main sources of "gold inflation" have been:

1. Increases in the gold stocks of the Western world, either through conquest, as in Mexico and Peru, or through discovery, as in California, Australia, the Yukon, and the Transvaal.

2. Economies in the use of gold, through technological improvements in financing and banking. These permitted gold reserves to be reduced and increased the rapidity with which money could circulate. The use of bank checks and credit cards are examples.

The world's most massive gold inflation followed the conquest of Mexico and Peru by Spain in the sixteenth and seventeenth centuries. It was slow by contemporary standards—2 or 3 percent per year on average—but long-continued. It might have been much greater than it was but for (a) the European recovery after the Black Death and (b) the European taste for such luxuries as tea, coffee, sugar, spices, silk, porcelain, and cotton textiles. The Black Death (a succession of epidemics of bubonic plague during the fourteenth century) reduced the population of Western Europe by a quarter or a third, raising

real wages as a result. Subsequent increases in the population and labor force seem to have kept wages down and thus reduced the inflation rate during the period of the gold inflow. At the same time, the European taste for Oriental luxuries, probably traceable to the earlier Crusades, caused a movement of monetary gold to India and China, where much of it was hoarded in nonmonetary forms like jewelry and ornamentation, thus disappearing from the money supply.

COST-PUSHES: SHOULD THEY BE VALIDATED?

In the first section of this essay, supply shocks were mentioned as possible causes of inflation. Such shocks were treated as *exogenous* to the domestic economy, having been brought on by foreign forces (OPEC) or natural events (drought, earthquake). The term *cost-push* refers to *endogenous* supply shocks—usually rises in money wages, profit margins, or interest rates. The successive rounds of wage and price increases following World War II in the United States were centered around "key bargains" in autos, steel, and other major industries. In these bargains, money wage gains were sandwiched between previous and subsequent profit-margin increases in a wage-price spiral that defied objective disentangling in terms of cause and effect, stimulus and response, or any similar formula.

Economists try to distinguish cost-push inflation (sometimes called "new inflation" or "administered inflation") from the "demand-pull inflation" of early Keynesian theory. In terms of aggregate supply and demand, cost-push inflation results from a leftward shift in the aggregate-supply curve, while demand-pull inflation results from a rightward shift in the aggregate-demand curve. Both shifts not only can but often do occur together.

When we discussed supply shocks, we said that the macroeconomic policy problem they present is one of accommodation versus resistance (refusal to accommodate). Accommodation, especially increases in the money-supply growth rate was, we said, the true cause of domestic inflation—not the supply shock itself. Resistance would balance the supply shock with downward demand pressures in the unshocked sectors of the economy and eliminate overall inflation in the long run at the cost, or at least the risk, of depression, stagflation, or recession, with no guarantee that it would end before the next election.

Let us imagine an epidemic of money-wage increases and/or higher profit margins over and above rises in productivity.[6] The wage increases are overtly inflationary. Profit-margin increases are disguisable as "new and improved models" or in the quiet discontinuance of standard, budget, or economy items. (As Henry Ford said, "Small cars mean small profits.") Prices rise, but will the increases stick? Our contention is that they will not, unless they are *validated* by macroeconomic accommodation—primarily an acceleration of monetary growth. In that case, the general inflation should be blamed on the macroeconomic validation and accommodation of the cost-pushes rather than on the cost-pushes themselves.

We should not forget that resistance (refusal to accommodate) has its costs in the risks of recession and social unrest, especially if organized pressure groups counterattack to force a policy reversal. For a slogan sparking such a counterattack, we quote Lane Kirkland of the United Auto Workers in the early 1970s: "We will not let Mr. Nixon's depression rob us of our wage increases!"

INFLATION, DEMOCRACY, AND THE SEPARATION OF POWERS

The political economy of inflation can be separated from the pure economics of the subject. Its basic questions are: Why do governments insist, despite the advice of financial experts, both on large-scale deficit financing and on financing their deficits increasingly by monetary expansion? If they know what to do, why don't they—why can't they—do it?

Historically, much of the blame has been put on democratic institutions, particularly on the extension of the suffrage to the propertyless, the debtors, and the recipients of public largesse. Mark Twain's recipe for political success in America was never voting for a tax or against an appropriation. (He might have added, never voting for tight money or against low interest rates.) This is supposedly an aspect of what some pessimistic political scientists have called "the increasing ungovernability" of populations under democratic regimes. It is supported by the success of armies of occupation in checking postwar inflations in the late 1940s, either by imposing financial stringency themselves (as in Japan) or

6. The case of increased interest rates is more complex. The higher rates induce their own offsets or remedies by decreasing the growth rates of money and credit.

by shielding disinflationary politicians from political reprisals (as in West Germany).

At first glance, of course, such pessimism makes little historical sense. The rise of parliamentary democracy in Western Europe and North America may be said to cover the century and a quarter between the French Revolution and World War I. But the great inflation of the recent past began a generation later, with the persistence of the "wartime" inflation of World War II into the peacetime generation that has followed it. (Mark Twain's denunciations of American congressmen and state legislators actually came from a *deflationary* period.)

There is, however, a pessimistic explanation of the delay. The rise of democracy was accompanied by what has been called a religion, or perhaps a superstition, of "sound money" backed primarily by gold and secondarily by silver. Inflationist movements—in America, the Greenbackers and the Populists—were reactions to deflations allegedly engineered on Wall Street. They faded as the deflation was reversed. As late as 1932, Franklin D. Roosevelt devoted an entire radio address to denying vile rumors that he was an enemy of the gold standard or that his election would endanger sound money. But within a year both Roosevelt and the American people had changed their minds. (The British, possibly influenced by Keynes, had already changed theirs!) The "religion of money" was no more. Inflation followed from the resulting iconoclasm, godlessness, or agnosticism of the continued populist democracy of America and Europe.

Another political economy argument, leading to similar conclusions, is about the separation of governmental powers into the executive (and administrative), the legislative, and the judicial branches. This application of eighteenth-century liberal political thought—Locke in England, Montesquieu in France, the American *Federalist* papers—allocated "the power of the purse" (increasing basic fiscal and financial control) to the legislative branch, Parliament or Congress. This was a natural reaction to the expensive dynastic warfare and courtly luxuries of such absolute monarchs as Louis XIV of France and Frederick the Great of Prussia. But after "one man (or woman), one vote" and the passing of the gold standard, a mixed bag of compassion, the pork barrel, log-rolling, and the welfare state supplemented (but did not replace) warfare and bureaucratic perquisites as sources of public deficits and inflationary financing. It now has led to calls for the curtailment of legislative fiscal and financial powers.

Specimen proposals are easy to find: increased independence and de-politicizing of central banks;

the "monetary rule" proposals of Milton Friedman and other monetarist economists to forestall excessive money creation; an "item veto" for the executive on appropriation bills—already in force in many American states; authorization of "impoundment powers" for the executive to interpret some or all appropriations as *permissions* rather than *requirements* to spend money.[7] In 1985 the U.S. Congress enacted the Gramm-Rudman Act to force automatic cuts in certain expenditure categories when budgetary deficits threatened, while exempting other categories. All these can be looked on as anti-inflationary measures or proposals.

IS INFLATION INEVITABLE?

The secular trend of the price level has undoubtedly been upward. The imaginary dollar invested (in our little table) two thousand years ago would actually be worth not 1.304×10^{52} or 4.090×10^{50} or even $1 today. Inflation (and war), like "drink and the devil" in *Treasure Island,* would have "done for the rest," meaning the whole thing. (The value today would almost certainly be zero anywhere in the world!)

7. Impoundment powers seem to have been exercised freely if infrequently by early American presidents, but fell into disuse during the nineteenth century. President Nixon attempted to revive them in 1973–74. This action was ruled unconstitutional by the Supreme Court, unless congressional consent could be obtained.

This historical record has convinced many economists that inflation control is a lost cause, or at least, that any effective cure is necessarily worse than the disease. In this view it is enough to prevent runaway inflation.

But let us take a closer look at this strange, eventful history of inflation. A long series of price indices for southern England from 1300 to the 1980s has been compiled by Ivor Pearce of the University of Southampton. He concluded that for the first five hundred years and more the level of prices showed no upward trend.[8] There were ups and downs, sometimes quite violent, but the recent U.S. experience of the doubling of prices in four to six years has only one precedent. This was a single great orgy toward the end of Henry VIII's reign. (Henry's experiments in monetary economics seem to have been no more successful than his better-known experiments in serial polygamy and domestic discipline.)

From this section and the last section of this essay, it is hard to avoid the conclusion that some combination of political democracy (including frequent elections), the current model of the separation of powers, and the abandonment of the old-time "religion of money" for the contemporary religion of the welfare-warfare state has made inflation endemic, with occasional epidemics checked but never reversed.

8. Similarly, Sherman Maisel of the University of California at Berkeley has estimated that the 1939 level of wholesale prices in the United States was approximately the same as that at the close of the American Revolution in 1780.

PART V

INFLATION, EXPECTATIONS, AND CONTEMPORARY MACROECONOMIC THOUGHT

15
Aggregate Demand, Aggregate Supply, and Potential GNP

Preview This chapter brings together almost everything that you have learned so far about macroeconomics and focuses this knowledge on two important matters: the price level and the volume of real GNP that the economy can provide in its long-run equilibrium situation.

We start with an expanded explanation of the concepts of aggregate demand and aggregate supply, which were first examined in Chapter 6. Now that you have studied the Keynesian and monetarist theories, it is possible to give a much more complete explanation of the slope of the aggregate-demand curve and of ways in which this curve may be shifted in response to public policy decisions. We are also able to give a more complete explanation of the aggregate-supply curve. The aggregate-supply curve reflects production decisions of firms and the availability of resources that can be used in production. We show how wage-cost lags and money illusion explain both the slope and shifts of the aggregate-supply curve.

To help you understand the effects of shifts of aggregate-demand and aggregate-supply curves, we use them first to describe an expansionary and then a contractionary situation in the economy. In each case, we show how a shift of the aggregate-supply curve returns the economy to its long-run equilibrium position. This long-run equilibrium position is sometimes called the economy's potential GNP.

AGGREGATE DEMAND

You were introduced to the concepts of aggregate demand and aggregate supply in Chapter 6. To refresh your memory, the graph illustrating the aggregate-demand and aggregate-supply model is reproduced here in Figure 1. This is the same graph as in Figure 8 of Chapter 6, except that the label on the horizontal axis now is Real GNP instead of the more cumbersome phrase "Aggregate Quantity of Goods and Services Demanded and Supplied."

In Chapter 6 the explanations of aggregate demand and aggregate supply were elementary and nonanalytical because at that point you had not studied the Keynesian model of planned expenditure or the monetarist model of interest rate determination. Now that you have studied these theories, a more complete explanation of aggregate demand can be given. In this chapter our intent is to show how fiscal and monetary instruments can be used together to implement macroeconomic policies.

Keynesian and monetarist theories help explain the slope and shifts of the aggregate-demand curve.

The aggregate-demand curve in Figure 1 shows an inverse relationship between changes in the price level and the resulting changes in real GNP demanded—that is, the *AD* curve has a negative slope. The theory behind this negative slope was not explained in Chapter 6 because, at that stage in your study of macroeconomics, you had not learned about interest rates or the price level or about how these can be changed by increases or decreases in the money supply. We now can explain the slope of this curve.

In explaining the slope of any curve in economics, the only variables that are allowed to change are the ones shown on the axes of the graph. In this case, these are the price level (on the vertical axis) and real GNP (on the horizontal axis). Our reasoning is that the quantity of real GNP demanded depends on the price level, other things being equal. Thus, the price level is our independent variable, and the real GNP is our dependent variable. We do not reason in the opposite direc-

FIGURE 1
Aggregate Demand and Aggregate Supply

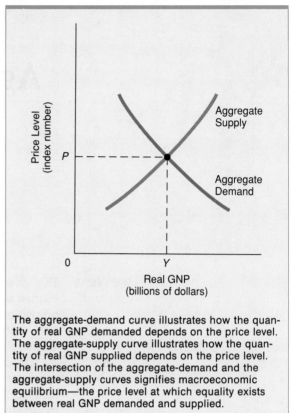

The aggregate-demand curve illustrates how the quantity of real GNP demanded depends on the price level. The aggregate-supply curve illustrates how the quantity of real GNP supplied depends on the price level. The intersection of the aggregate-demand and the aggregate-supply curves signifies macroeconomic equilibrium—the price level at which equality exists between real GNP demanded and supplied.

tion, that the price level depends on the quantity of real GNP demanded, because our theory is that the price level depends on the combination of both aggregate demand and aggregate supply, and not on either one individually. This is the same type of reasoning that is used in demand-and-supply models for particular products.[1] We present two theories that offer explanations for the slope of this curve. One is the interest rate theory and the other is the real cash balances theory.

In explaining the slope of any curve in economics, the only variables that are allowed to change are those shown on the axes of the graph.

---

1. See Chapter 5.

In aggregate-demand and aggregate-supply analysis, the price level is determined by the interaction of aggregate demand and aggregate supply and not by either of them by itself.

The Interest Rate Theory

The **interest rate theory** is based on the fact that a rise in the price level shrinks the *real* quantity of money in the economy, if other things remain unchanged. This was explained in Chapter 14. In real terms, each dollar has less purchasing power than before the rise in prices. The way this theory explains the slope of the aggregate-demand curve is shown in Figure 2, which repeats the transmission mechanism illustrated in Figure 7 in Chapter 14, but with the steps represented by the arrows running in the opposite direction. Panel (a) shows what happens to the real money supply when the price level increases. The money-supply curve shifts to the left, from MS_1 to MS_2 (step 1). This leads to a rise in the real interest rate from i_1 to i_2 (step 2). Panel (b) shows how this rise in the real interest rate reduces the volume of planned-investment expenditure from I_1 to I_2 (step 3). This reduction in planned-investment expenditure lowers the total-planned-expenditure curve in panel (c) from $C + I_1 + G + X - Im$ to $C + I_2 + G + X - Im$ (step 4). According to this demand-side reasoning, the equilibrium level of real GNP falls from Y_1 to Y_2 (step 5), as indicated by the movement of the intersection with the 45-degree line from E_1 to E_2. Panel (d) shows how all these responses are summarized in the slope of the aggregate-demand curve. At the initial price level of P_1, the real GNP demanded was Y_1, as shown by point A on the aggregate-demand curve. At the new price level of P_2, the real GNP demanded is Y_2, as shown by point B on the aggregate-demand curve. Therefore, working through the demand side of the economy, the rise in the price level has brought a reduction in real GNP. Our aggregate-demand curve therefore has a negative slope. Because this theory uses the basic Keynesian technique of linking interest rates to planned investment and real GNP, it sometimes is called the Keynes effect.

A step-by-step summary of how the interest rate theory explains the negative slope of the aggregate-demand curve is as follows:

1. A rise in the price level (P) leads to

2. an increase in the quantity of money demanded to carry on any given level of buying and selling activity in the economy. Since the *ceteris paribus* assumption specifies that the quantity of money in existence in the economy is not changed, it follows that

3. interest rates (the cost of credit which is the price for the use of money over time) will be driven upward as households and firms compete for the limited amount of money available. Because of higher interest rates

4. firms find capital goods more costly and less profitable and households find the financing of durable goods purchases more expensive. As a result

5. quantities demanded of capital goods and consumer durable goods are reduced, which means a smaller aggregate quantity demanded (QD).

There are some qualifications to this model. A lot may depend on how steep or how flat the demand-for-money curve and the planned-investment-demand curve are. There also is debate about whether the demand-for-money curve, in real terms, would shift as a result of a change in the price level. Even in view of these qualifications, however, it still seems reasonable to draw the aggregate-demand curve with a negative slope.

The interest rate theory states that the aggregate-demand curve has a negative slope because increases in the price level, *ceteris paribus*, lead to higher real interest rates and less planned investment expenditure (and vice versa).

The Real Balances Theory

The **real balances theory**[2] reasons that a rise in the price level will mean reductions in real wealth for the people who hold money or certain assets

2. This theory is sometimes called the Pigou effect, after the British economist A. C. Pigou, who analyzed how changes in wealth influence spending and saving.

whose value is given in monetary terms, such as government bonds. The real goods and services equivalent of these assets is reduced by the increase in prices. This is a familiar result of inflation. As you learned in Chapters 10 and 11, reductions in wealth can cause a downward shift in the consumption function, which is part of the $C + I + G + X - Im$ curve in the Keynesian-cross diagram, just as lower investment shifted the curve in panel (c) of Figure 2 (step 4). This shift will lower the equilibrium level of real GNP (step 5). In this way, the real balances theory also concludes that a rise in the price level will bring a drop in real GNP and that the aggregate-demand curve has a negative slope.

The net strength of the real balances effect may be quite small. Often one person's loss from inflation is another person's gain. Only a small part of the total wealth in the economy, such as cash itself, is free of this counterbalancing effect.

A step-by-step summary of how the real balances theory explains the negative slope of the aggregate-demand curve is as follows:

1. An increase in the price level (P) leads to

2. a reduction in the buying power (real value) of assets held in cash or government bonds.

Therefore,

FIGURE 2
How Changes in the Price Level Can Change Real GNP

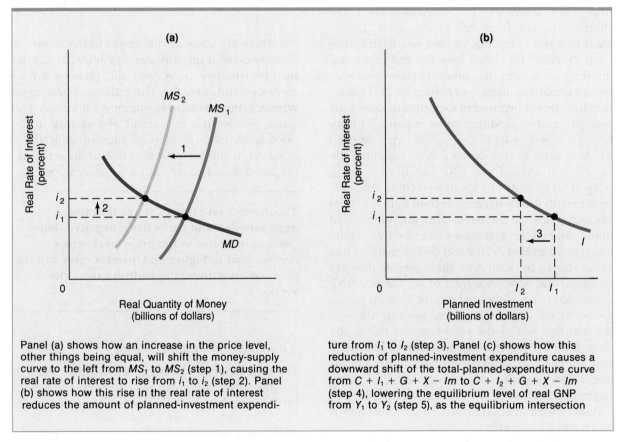

Panel (a) shows how an increase in the price level, other things being equal, will shift the money-supply curve to the left from MS_1 to MS_2 (step 1), causing the real rate of interest to rise from i_1 to i_2 (step 2). Panel (b) shows how this rise in the real rate of interest reduces the amount of planned-investment expendi-

ture from I_1 to I_2 (step 3). Panel (c) shows how this reduction of planned-investment expenditure causes a downward shift of the total-planned-expenditure curve from $C + I_1 + G + X - Im$ to $C + I_2 + G + X - Im$ (step 4), lowering the equilibrium level of real GNP from Y_1 to Y_2 (step 5), as the equilibrium intersection

Figure 2 (continued)

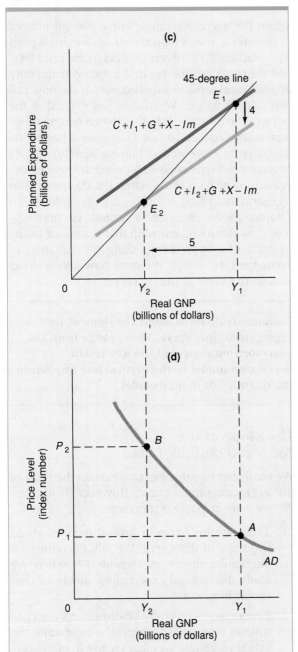

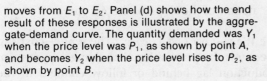

moves from E_1 to E_2. Panel (d) shows how the end result of these responses is illustrated by the aggregate-demand curve. The quantity demanded was Y_1 when the price level was P_1, as shown by point A, and becomes Y_2 when the price level rises to P_2, as shown by point B.

3. the real wealth of the holders of these assets is reduced. This reduction in real wealth leads to

4. reduced consumption expenditure and lower total planned expenditure ($C + I + G + X - Im$), which leads to

5. a reduction in the quantity of real GNP demanded.

Both the interest rate theory and the real balances theory suggest that it is reasonable to draw the aggregate-demand curve with a negative slope. We cannot say whether the aggregate-demand curve should be relatively steep or relatively flat but, for convenience, our graphs show a substantial negative slope for this curve.

The real balances theory states that the aggregate-demand curve has a negative slope because increases in the price level reduce the real wealth of those holding money-denominated assets, leading to reduced planned expenditure (and vice versa).

Shifting the Aggregate-Demand Curve

In order for the aggregate-demand curve to shift, there must be a change in some variable other than the ones shown on the axes of the graph. Since the price level *does* appear on the graph showing the *AD* curve, shifts of this curve must come from a change in some variable *other than* the price level. Now that you have studied the Keynesian and the monetarist theories, you know that many variables can alter total-planned expenditure ($C + I + G + X - Im$).

For example, when you studied the Keynesian theory, you learned (in Chapter 11) that government fiscal policy can change government purchases (G) and—by changing net taxes—change consumption expenditure (C). Fiscal policies that increase total-planned expenditure shift the *AD* curve to the right—that is, at any given price level the quantity of real GNP demanded will be greater than before the expansionary fiscal action, other things unchanged. Contractionary fiscal policies—like reductions in government purchases or increases in net taxes—shift the *AD* curve to the left, *ceteris paribus*.

Monetary policy also can shift the *AD* curve. You learned in Chapter 14 that increases in the money supply can, at least temporarily, lower real interest rates. These lower real interest rates, in turn, can increase total planned expenditure by increasing investment (*I*). With more planned investment, the quantity of real GNP demanded will be greater, at any given price level, than before the expansionary monetary policy. In other words, expansionary monetary policy shifts the *AD* curve to the right. On the other hand, if the money supply is reduced, the resulting higher interest rates will reduce planned investment, lower total planned expenditure, and lead to a smaller quantity of real GNP demanded at any given price level. Contractionary monetary policy shifts the *AD* curve to the left.

Fiscal and monetary policies that increase total-planned expenditure (*C* + *I* + *G* + *X* − *Im*) shift the aggregate-demand curve to the right, *ceteris paribus*. Fiscal and monetary policies that reduce total planned expenditure shift the aggregate-demand curve to the left.

It is important for you to recognize that in describing shifts of the *AD* curve, we have stated that the real GNP demanded would be greater or smaller *at any given price level*. Most students of economics realize that increased government purchases or increases in the money supply may, in fact, lead to increases in the price level. However, whether or not that is true, or the extent to which it is true, depends on aggregate supply as well as on aggregate demand. Therefore, we must examine aggregate supply before we can determine whether shifts of the *AD* curve will lead to changes in the price level.

AGGREGATE SUPPLY

When the aggregate-supply curve was introduced in Chapter 6, it was represented as showing a positive relationship between changes in the price level and the resulting changes in the aggregate quantity of goods and services supplied, which we now call real GNP supplied. We noted, however, that the slope of the *AS* curve is hotly debated among economists. In Chapter 10, we illustrated a horizontal *AS* curve as representing (approximately) the *AS* relationship envisioned in Keynesian theories devised to deal with times when the economy is in recession and many resources are unemployed. In Chapter 14, we illustrated a vertical *AS* curve representing the *AS* relationship that is implicit in the quantity-of-money theory using the equation of exchange ($MV = PQ$). We must now take a closer look at the slope of the *AS* curve.

Economists disagree about the slope of the aggregate-supply curve. Views range from the near-horizontal view of the Keynesian depression model to the vertical line implicit in the quantity-of-money model.

The Slope of the Aggregate-Supply Curve

We shall offer two theories that explain the slope of the aggregate-supply curve. However, before we do, we must make two statements:

1. These are only two of several theories about the slope of this curve. We will encounter an alternative theory in Chapter 17, when we study the rational expectations theory of economic behavior.

2. Economists who study labor markets are continuing their research aimed at estimating the actual wage-rate lags that we use in our explanation of the slope of the AS curve.

The Wage–Cost Lag Theory The **wage–cost lag theory** is the proposition that changes in costs of production lag behind or follow changes in the general price level. Consider labor costs, for example. Many workers in the economy are employed under contracts that run for one or more years into the future. When the prices of finished goods change, it may be some time before the wages of these workers catch up with the new cost of living. Even for workers not under contract, wage-rate adjustments usually are not made as frequently as are adjustments in the prices of final goods and services. Therefore, if a stable condition in the economy is upset by a change in the price level, it is likely that the prices of products sold by firms will change more than wage rates and labor costs of production. When the price level increases, the lag of labor costs increases profit margins and encourages firms to expand output, in order to get as much profit as possible while the favorable conditions last. When the price level falls, the lag will squeeze profit margins and firms will cut back on production so as not to suffer too much. Applying these ideas to the *AS* curve suggests that a rise in the price level will lead to an increase in the quantity of real GNP supplied and that a fall in the price level will lead to a reduction in real GNP supplied. Thus, the aggregate-supply curve will have a positive slope.

It is not only labor costs that may lag behind finished product prices when the price level changes. It is not unusual for firms to have contracts or understandings that govern the prices they pay for raw materials and intermediate products used in production. Just as for labor costs, there may be some time lag after a change in the price level before these costs of production are fully adjusted. When the price level rises, the lag will cause profit margins to increase and encourage greater output, and when the price level falls, the lag will shrink profit margins and encourage firms to reduce output. Thus, these cost lags also suggest a positive slope for the aggregate-supply curve.

When the price level starts to rise, increases in wage rates and other costs of production lag behind so that profit margins are temporarily increased. When the price level starts to fall, the lag in wage rates and other costs makes profit margins smaller. Firms react to these changes in profit margins by increasing or decreasing their levels of output.

The wage–cost lag theory is not difficult to understand, but a cautionary note is necessary at this point. As we shall see, there are circumstances when changes in wages and other costs of production can be the *cause* rather than the *effect* of changes in the general price level. We will have more to say about wage-push and cost-push theories of inflation. Those theories involve *shifts* of the *AS* curve rather than *movements along* this curve. Those theories do not concern us now because we are limiting our explanation to the slope as distinguished from the location of the *AS* curve.

A summary of the wage–cost lag explanation of the slope of the aggregate-supply curve is as follows:

1. An increase in the price level means that there has been an increase, on average, in the prices of goods and services sold in the economy. However,

2. labor and raw materials often are purchased by firms under contracts that set prices for a period of time, with the result that changes in costs of production lag behind changes in the prices firms receive from sales of final products. Therefore,

3. profit margins tend to expand when the price level starts to rise and tend to fall when the price level starts to fall. In response to these changing profit margins,

4. firms increase the quantity of goods and services supplied when the price level starts to rise and reduce the quantity of goods and services supplied when the price level starts to fall.

The wage–cost lag theory suggests that changes in real GNP supplied are positively related to changes in price level.

The Money-Illusion Theory **Money illusion** is the belief that changes in nominal values are the same as changes in real values. This belief can have an important influence on the economy when the price level is changing. For example, if all prices were to increase by 10 percent, there would be no change in relative prices among different goods and services and their real values would not have changed from what they were before the price-level increase. Of course, the real value (purchasing power) of money would have changed. A person under money illusion would believe, however, that the purchasing power of money had stayed the same and that the real value of goods and services had changed.

Money illusion is the mistaken belief that a change in a nominal value is a change in a real value.

Here is how the money-illusion theory explains the positive slope of the aggregate-supply curve. Suppose that there is an increase in the price level and that everyone in the economy operates under complete money illusion. Since wages, interest, rent, and profit are rewards for production-related (supply-side) activities, everyone who now receives greater money-rewards from these supply-side activities is apt to believe that the real tradeoff between work and leisure has changed in favor of more work. So everyone works harder, and real GNP increases. In this way, behavior based on money illusion suggests a positive slope for the aggregate-supply curve.

The money-illusion theory and the wage–cost lag theory work together to suggest a positive slope for the *AS* curve. This is because, when the general price level starts to increase, nominal wage, rent, interest, and profit rates also may increase to some extent, even though other prices are rising faster. In this situation, a worker under money illusion may believe that his or her *real* wage rate has risen, even though in fact it has fallen. Under the mistaken belief that the real wage rate has risen, the worker may be quite willing to work more hours per week, as may be requested by firms as they expand output.

Money illusion can operate also if the general price level starts to fall. If nominal wage, rent, interest, and profit rates also fall—but fall less than the prices of final goods—workers and other resource owners may mistakenly believe that their *real* rates of compensation have fallen, even though, in fact, they have risen. Under money illusion, resource owners may refuse to accept reductions in nominal rates of compensation so that strikes, layoffs, and business failures result.

A step-by-step summary of the money illusion explanation for a positively-sloped aggregate-supply curve is as follows:

1. Nominal wage rates may increase when the general price level starts to increase, even though their increases are smaller than the increases in the prices of final goods. In this situation,

2. workers under money illusion mistakenly believe that their real wage rate has increased, even though it actually has decreased. Under the illusion that their real wage rate has increased,

3. workers are willing to work more hours per week as requested by firms which, in these circumstances, are increasing their level of output.

Wage–cost lag and money illusion can work together to support the view that the aggregate-supply curve is positively sloped.

Shifting the Aggregate-Supply Curve

Any particular aggregate-supply curve is drawn on the assumption that all variables other than the price level and the real GNP are held constant. When there is a change in any other variable, a shift (change in location) of the aggregate-supply curve may occur.

In examining shifts of the aggregate-supply curve, we are interested in the two phenomena that we have already discussed in connection with the slope of this curve, that is, the wage–cost lag and the money illusion. According to our theory, with the passage of time, changes can take place in each of these variables. Specifically, both wage–cost lag and money illusion are expected to melt away with the passage of time. Such time-related changes in these variables will shift (relocate) the *AS* curve.

With the passage of time, changes can take place in the degree of wage–cost lag and money illusion. These changes can shift the aggregate-supply curve.

Wage Rates and Costs "Catch Up" The lag in wage rates and other costs of production after a price-level change will not continue indefinitely. As time passes, wage rates and other costs will start to catch up with the prices of final goods and the lag will disappear. For example, after a price-level increase, labor will demand extra wage increases as soon as possible. As these adjustments are made, the profit margins of firms shrink. Firms respond by reducing the quantity of output that will be supplied at any given price level, shifting the *AS* curve to the left.

If the price level has recently fallen, the initiative to eliminate the wage–cost lag will come from firms, which then will want to lower wage rates and other costs. As their efforts bear fruit, profit margins become larger, the quantity of output that will be supplied at any given price level is increased, and the *AS* curve shifts to the right.

When wage rates start to catch up with changes in the prices of final goods, profit margins change and the aggregate-supply curve shifts.

It is worth noting, in addition, that after the shift the *AS* curve may have a steeper slope than it had before the shift. The reason for this is that the strength of the wage–cost lag depends on the laws and customary patterns of behavior in relations between firms and workers and between firms and their suppliers. Consider, for example, the average length or time period of a labor–management contract governing wage rates and working conditions. If price levels have been stable for some time, it may have been convenient for both labor and management to have relatively long-term contracts. But

changing price levels will prompt one side or the other to want to shorten contracts in order to reduce the wage-rate lag from future price-level changes. For example, after an experience with inflation, labor will want shorter contracts and "reopener" provisions to shorten future wage-rate lags. Automatic cost-of-living adjustment (COLA) provisions may be added to contracts. On the other hand, if the recent experience has been with price-level declines, it is likely that firms, rather than their workers or their suppliers, will want to shorten contracts and to include reopener provisions. This also will make the new *AS* curve steeper than the old one. We will return to this matter when we consider theories of rational expectations in Chapter 17.

The aggregate-supply curve tends to be steeper if there has been recent experience with price-level changes.

Changes in Money Illusion The passage of time after a price-level change will also cause money illusion to melt away. Consider what happens when people finally come to realize that *all* prices, including the prices of consumption goods that they buy, have gone up? Now they begin to realize that the changes in nominal wage rates, which had led them to work harder, were not actually changes in real wage rates. Their real wage, interest, rent, or profit had not gone up but actually had gone down. When this realization dawns on them, money illusion starts to evaporate, and the tradeoff between work and leisure is re-examined. In the light of their now clearer understanding of real wage, interest, rent, and profit rates, people move back toward their old work habits. As this happens, the aggregate-supply curve shifts to the left.

How long does it take for people to recognize that changes in nominal values are not also changes in real values? The answer depends on many things. How long was the price level stable before the inflation or deflation occurred? How large is the change in the price level? How rapidly is the price level changing? In actual policy making, these questions are very important, and economists spend much time discussing and researching them. For our purposes, however, it is the concept of money illusion and the concept of shifting the aggregate-supply curve that are important.

The aggregate-supply curve shifts as the degree of money illusion changes with the passage of time, after a price-level increase.

Now that we have examined the forces that determine the slope and the location of the aggregate-supply curve, we can offer the following definition: *the aggregate-supply curve represents the relationship between changes in the price level and changes in real GNP supplied when wage-rate and cost changes lag behind changes in the price level and while money illusion due to that price-level change distorts choices between work and leisure.*

Macroeconomic Equilibrium

The intersection of the aggregate-demand and the aggregate-supply curves shows the price level at which the quantities of real GNP demanded and supplied are equal to one another. This is **macroeconomic equilibrium.** At any price level above equilibrium, there will be excess supply in the economy. Production will be reduced and prices will be lowered as firms attempt to dispose of excess inventories. Conversely, at any price level lower than equilibrium, there will be excess demand in the economy. Firms find that inventories have been reduced to below desired levels and will increase production and prices in order to regain their desired position.

Macroeconomic equilibrium exists when the price level is such as to secure an equality between real GNP demanded and supplied.

Is macroeconomic equilibrium a desirable situation for the economy? Does it represent full employment? Economists disagree on the answers to these important questions. We will explore their differing views in Chapters 16 and 17. However, to prepare for those chapters, we shall review how contractions (recessions) and expansions take place in the macroeconomy.[3] The aggregate-

demand and aggregate-supply model provides a useful framework for understanding the causes and alternative policies for dealing with changes in macroeconomic equilibrium.

RECESSION

Our first illustration is a model of recession. In Figure 3 we start at point *A*—an equilibrium condition at the intersection of aggregate-demand curve AD_1 and aggregate-supply curve AS_1. We assume that this equilibrium has lasted for a long enough time that people have become well adjusted to it. This assumption is important because it means that wage rates and other costs are in step with product prices and that people have adjusted their economic behavior to the price level, P_1.

In this illustration the recession begins with a shift of the aggregate-demand curve to the left from AD_1 to AD_2 (arrow 1 in Figure 3). Such a shift may have brought about the Great Depression of the 1930s. Keynesians find that it was caused by falling planned investment due to poor business prospects after the stock market crash. Monetarists believe that the cause was a reduced money stock due to widespread bank failures. In each view, however, there was a demand-side shock to the economy, which tended to reduce the equilibrium level of real GNP. Unplanned inventories accumulate because of the fall in aggregate demand and, in order to rid themselves of this unwanted inventory, firms lay off workers and cut production and prices. As the aggregate-demand curve shifts to the left, the equilibrium point moves down and to the left along the AS_1 curve from point *A* to point *B*. Unemployment rises and both output and prices decline to Y_2 and P_2, respectively.

The seriousness of the move from *A* to *B* depends on the slope of the aggregate-supply curve and on how far the aggregate-demand curve shifts to the left. If the aggregate-supply curve is steep, few people will lose their jobs. If it is flat, many jobs will be lost. If the recession is severe enough, the pessimism caused by rising unemployment and

---

3. See Chapter 9 for an introduction to this subject.

falling prices may bring further leftward shifts in the aggregate-demand curve. In other words, the recession may feed on itself in a pattern called **hyperdeflation**. Probably this really did happen in the Great Depression of the 1930s. For simplicity, we do not illustrate this extra shift of the aggregate-demand curve in Figure 3.

Starting from an equilibrium situation, a shift to the left of the aggregate-demand curve will cause recession, with falling real GNP and increasing unemployment.

Recovery by Deflation

Point B in Figure 3 is not a stable or long-run equilibrium position because the changes in economic conditions have set in motion forces that will shift the aggregate-supply curve. The shift comes as the wage–cost lag disappears and as the money illusion breaks down, causing the AS curve to shift to the right, from AS_1 to AS_2 (arrow 2). Wage rates and prices of other input are reduced as resource owners realize that *real* rates of compensation have not fallen. Moreover, the hard facts of the recession have sapped the financial reserves of many people. Therefore, they decide not to hold out any longer for higher wages for labor, higher interest on bonds, higher rent on natural resources, or higher profits.

The rightward shift of the aggregate-supply curve illustrates a **"deflationist"** solution for the problem of economic recession. The squeeze on profits, which motivated firms to reduce output and employment in the recession, is to be relieved by lowering wage rates and the prices of other inputs. According to the deflationist prescription, the fading money illusion will make these reductions acceptable to workers and other resource owners. As the AS curve shifts to the right, the equilibrium condition slides down the AD_2 curve, bringing lower prices and greater output. Our model shows real GNP at the new equilibrium (point C) to be exactly the same as at point A before the initial shift in aggregate demand. However, some economists doubt that the AS curve will shift far enough to bring the economy all the way back to its original level.

FIGURE 3
Recession Caused by a Decrease in Aggregate Demand

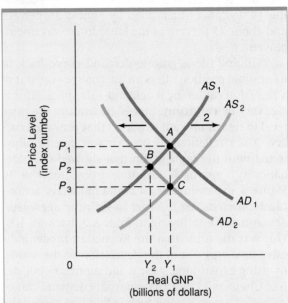

The initial macroeconomic equilibrium is at A. In this illustration, recession is caused by a reduction in aggregate demand, shifting AD_1 to the left to AD_2 (arrow 1). Macroeconomic equilibrium moves from point A to point B, the price level falls from P_1 to P_2, and real GNP falls from Y_1 to Y_2.

The "deflationist" remedy for the recession is to allow the AS curve to shift to the right (arrow 2) as the wage–cost lag and money illusion disappear. In this way, equilibrium moves from point B to point C, real GNP increases from Y_2 to Y_1 in the recovery, and the price level falls to P_3.

The "reflationist" remedy for the recession is to use expansionary monetary and fiscal policies to return aggregate demand to its original level, shifting the aggregate-demand curve from AD_2 to AD_1. Real GNP returns to Y_1 and the price level returns to P_1.

Recovery from a recession may come through reductions in wage rates and prices of other inputs. These reductions enlarge profit margins and invite increases in output.

Recovery by Reflation

In the situation that existed in the Great Depression, many people felt that solving the problem with the "deflation" solution would take too long, cause too much suffering, and endanger the political stability of the country. Over the early years of the 1930s, prices had fallen by almost 25 percent and about 25 percent of the labor force was unemployed.

Shifting the aggregate-demand curve back to its original position offers an alternative way out of a recession caused by a demand-side shock. This is recovery by **reflation,** that is, by causing the price level to return upward to a level that prevailed earlier. The "reflationist" prescription can be illustrated with the same graph that showed the "'deflationist" approach. Starting from point B in Figure 3, expansionary fiscal and monetary actions can be undertaken in order to shift the aggregate-demand curve to the right, from AD_2 back to AD_1. This was the route that the Keynesian model indicated as a way out of the depression of the 1930s. By using expansionary fiscal and monetary policies (see Chapters 11 and 14), aggregate demand can be increased, reversing the decline that had caused the recession. Both employment and prices return to their earlier levels as the equilibrium condition moves upward and to the right along the original aggregate-supply curve, AS_1.

Shifting the aggregate-demand curve to the right by monetary and fiscal policies is a reflationist proposal to obtain recovery from recession.

In retrospect, the reflationist prescription for the problems of the Great Depression appears clearly preferable to the deflationist prescription. At the time, however, the prospect of large and intentional government deficits was upsetting to many people and especially to business and financial leaders. They feared unrestrained government spending and the taxes that they believed would eventually be required. The expansionary moves undertaken by the New Deal administration were timid by later standards and produced disappointing results.[4]

4. See "John Meynard Keynes and the Great Depression" following p. 246.

EXPANSION

Our second illustration of aggregate demand–aggregate supply analysis is something like the one just studied, except that it pictures the process of **expansion.** As in the recession model, the initiating event comes from the demand side. However, this time the aggregate-demand curve shifts to the right rather than to the left. This occurred in the 1960s when fiscal and monetary instruments of government generally worked in an expansionary direction to stimulate the economy and to carry on a "War on Poverty" at home and a war in Vietnam without large rises in taxes. Another example was in the first half of the 1980s when expansion was fueled by reductions in taxes and increases in defense purchases. These expansionary policies shifted the aggregate-demand curve to the right.

Figure 4 illustrates the model of economic expansion. We begin at point A, the intersection of the initial aggregate-demand curve, AD_1, and the initial aggregate-supply curve, AS_1. Again we assume that this situation has lasted long enough for people to have adjusted their behavior to this price level and to this level of real GNP.

After the shift to the right of the aggregate-demand curve, the new equilibrium is at B, where the new aggregate-demand curve, AD_2, intersects aggregate-supply curve, AS_1. The rise in demand causes inventories to fall below planned levels, and companies respond with higher prices (to keep inventory from being used up too quickly and to make higher profits) and with increased production to restore inventories to desired levels.

Expansion may be started by monetary and fiscal policies that shift the aggregate-demand curve to the right.

Higher Output and Prices

Along the path from A to B, the economy is experiencing good times. Wages and other costs of production are lagging behind increases in prices of finished goods so profit margins are attractive. Employment is increasing. Even though wage rates are lagging behind increases in the general price level,

FIGURE 4
Expansion Caused by an Increase in Aggregate Demand

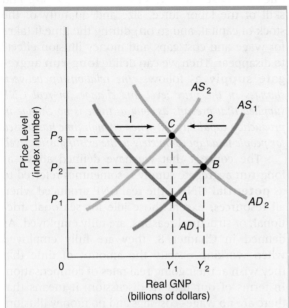

The initial macroeconomic equilibrium is at *A*. In this illustration, expansion is caused by an increase in aggregate demand, shifting AD_1 to AD_2 (arrow 1). Macroeconomic equilibrium moves from point *A* to point *B*, the price level rises to P_2, and real GNP increases to Y_2.

The expansion of real GNP ceases at point *B* when the wage–cost lag and money illusion fade away, causing AS_1 to shift to the left to AS_2 (arrow 2). While this shift is taking place—during the move from *B* to *C*—the economy suffers stagflation. At the new equilibrium, point *C*, real GNP has returned to Y_1 and the price level has risen to P_3.

workers are working longer hours and taking home larger paychecks. Because of money illusion, they overestimate their increase in real income and the attractiveness of work compared with leisure.

The mixture between price increases and output increases depends on the slope of the *AS* curve. If the curve is quite flat, prices will rise little and output will expand significantly. But if the *AS* curve is steep, as may be the case if there has been recent experience with inflation, prices may rise rapidly with only modest increases in output. In extreme situations, called **hyperinflation,** the rising prices induce further shifts of the aggregate-demand curve as people hurry to spend their income before it loses its buying power. Prices rise

faster until money becomes virtually worthless and economic collapse is threatened.[5]

In an expansion, the mixture between output increases and price-level increases depends on the slope of the aggregate-supply curve.

In hyperinflation situations, the rising price level causes people to speed up purchasing, shifting the aggregate-demand curve to the right and causing more inflation.

Stagflation

Point *B* does not represent a stable or long-run equilibrium for reasons that are parallel to those in the recession case. In the movement from *A* to *B* along the AS_1 curve in Figure 4, some people mistakenly believe that the increases in nominal wage (and profit, interest, and rent) rates represent equivalent increases in real rates. They believe that these increases in nominal wage (and profit, interest, and rent) rates have changed the real tradeoff between work and leisure in favor of working more. Because of the supposedly higher rewards, more jobs and overtime are accepted and more business ventures undertaken. However, as time passes, these people realize that some of the increases in nominal wage (and profit, interest, and rent) rates have been lost to increases in the general price level and the rising cost of living. Real wages have not increased as they thought they had.

As people gain a more accurate understanding of the relative prices of work and leisure, the money illusion evaporates. Workers start to play "catch-up" in wage negotiations, asking for wage-rate increases in excess of productivity increases so that they can make up for the purchasing power losses they have suffered from inflation. Strikes are more frequent as wages and other costs catch up from the wage–cost lag and close the gap that had existed during the expansion. Profit margins become smaller. Through these actions, reflecting the closing of the wage–cost lag and the fading of

---

5. See the discussion of inflation in Germany, pp. 152–153.

money illusion, the AS curve in Figure 4 shifts to the left, from AS_1 to AS_2 and the equilibrium condition moves along the AD_2 curve from point B to point C.

The move from B to C involves falling output, rising unemployment, and continuing increases in the price level—a combination that economists have labeled **stagflation.** Stagflation offers the "worst of both worlds" in macroeconomics. The U.S. economy and many others in the world suffered from stagflation during the 1970s, partly as a result of earlier aggregate-demand increases and partly from supply-side shocks, which we will discuss shortly. Our illustration in Figure 4 suggests that equilibrium will be established at point C, when profit margins have returned to normal and people have adapted to the new price level of P_3, so that money illusion and "catching up" no longer influence behavior.

As wage rates and other input prices catch up with earlier increases in the prices of final goods and as money illusion fades, the aggregate-supply curve shifts to the left and the economy experiences stagflation.

Monetary and fiscal policy alternatives for dealing with stagflation are unattractive. Shifting the aggregate-demand curve to the right promises still more inflation, whereas shifting it to the left threatens still greater unemployment.

LONG-RUN AGGREGATE SUPPLY AND POTENTIAL GNP

In each of the exercises just completed, the consequences of a shift of the aggregate-demand curve were, first, a movement along the aggregate-supply curve, while money illusion and wage–cost lags operated, and then a shift of the AS curve as money illusion faded and as wage rates and costs caught up with other prices. Now we must ask about the relation between the price level and real GNP supplied in the long run, after the shift of the AS curve has been completed.

To keep our discussion conceptually clear, suppose that no change takes place in physical production capabilities (level of technology, size and skill of the labor force, size and quantity of the stock of capital, and so on) during the time it takes for wage and cost gaps and money illusion effects to disappear. Then we can define **long-run aggregate supply** as follows: *the relationship between changes in the price level and changes in real GNP supplied that prevails as long as there is no change in production capability but when enough time has passed for people to adapt completely to the existing price level.*

The concept that we have defined above as long-run aggregate supply is sometimes referred to as **potential GNP**—the real GNP produced when all resources, except those idle for seasonal, frictional, or structural reasons, are fully employed. As defined in Chapter 8, they are fully employed when working exactly the amount of time that they wish at their going real rates of compensation. In terms of our present discussion, it means that there are no wage–cost lags and no money illusion.

Long-run aggregate supply (also called potential GNP) is equal to the level of real GNP that the economy will produce when wage–cost lags and money illusion are not distorting choices. All resources (except those seasonally, frictionally, or structurally out of work) are working for exactly the number of hours per week that they wish to work at the going real wage rates.

Does the Price Level Affect Long-Run Aggregate Supply and Potential GNP?

Figure 5 shows long-run aggregate supply and the potential GNP suggested in the recession and expansion models studied earlier. Let the intersection of AD_1 and AS_1 (point A) show the beginning equilibrium point for both of these models. The recession process is shown by the shift of the aggregate-demand curve from AD_1 to AD_2, followed by the shift of the aggregate-supply curve from AS_1 to AS_2 as wage–cost lags and the money illusion wear off. Equilibrium is finally restored at the intersection of AD_2 and AS_2 (point B). The expansion process is

FIGURE 5
Long-Run Aggregate Supply and Potential GNP

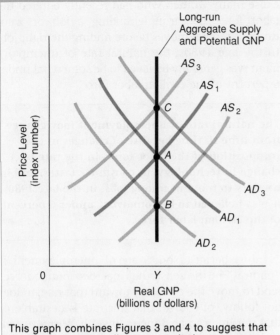

This graph combines Figures 3 and 4 to suggest that the economy eventually returns to its long-run aggregate supply or potential GNP after disturbances caused by changes in aggregate demand. The recession model starts at point A and eventually returns the economy to point B. The expansion model also starts at point A, but eventually returns the economy to point C. Long-run aggregate supply and potential GNP are represented by real GNP of Y and by the vertical line passing through points A, B, and C.

slope—that in the long-run, real GNP is greater at high price levels than at low price levels, other things being equal. These economists say that, even without wage–cost lags and money illusion, the price level can influence production behavior. It is the choice between work and leisure that is involved. Their argument parallels the real balances theory, which we explained earlier in connection with the aggregate-demand curve. It goes like this. At high price levels, assets whose values are given in fixed nominal amounts (such as money and government bonds) have low real purchasing power value. The low real wealth of people holding these assets persuades them to work harder and longer than they would at a lower price level. At low price levels, however, these assets have high real purchasing power, and their holders have greater real wealth, so they consume more leisure and do less work than at high price levels. These economists conclude, therefore, that the long-run aggregate-supply curve is not a vertical line but has some positive slope.

Although some argue that long-run aggregate supply or potential GNP is positively related to the price level, most believe that the price level has no effect on its value.

shown by the shift of the aggregate-demand curve from AD_1 to AD_3, followed by the shift of the aggregate-supply curve from AS_1 to AS_3, again as wage–cost lags and the money illusion wear off. Here, equilibrium is finally restored at the intersection of AD_3 and AS_3 (point C). In each case, we have assumed that the final equilibrium is at exactly the same real GNP as the starting equilibrium, so that the long-run aggregate-supply curve is a vertical line. In other words, we suppose that, in each case, the aggregate-supply curve shifts far enough to return the economy to its potential GNP.

Some economists believe that the vertical long-run aggregate-supply curve is a special case and that more often the curve has a positive

The Natural Rate of Unemployment

In Chapter 8 when we introduced the concept of the **natural rate of unemployment**—it was defined in the context of official government statistics—the rate that is limited to seasonal, frictional, and structural unemployment. It is also the rate of unemployment that corresponds with long-run aggregate supply and potential GNP. If the *microeconomy* were functioning perfectly, each person would be on his or her own labor-supply curve. As explained in Chapter 8, this means that each person would be working exactly the number of hours per week or per month or per year that he or she wished to work at the prevailing real wage rate. The balance between work and leisure would exactly match his or her preferences at this wage rate.

> The natural rate of unemployment is the measured rate of unemployment that exists when the economy is operating at its potential GNP.

In both the recession and the expansion exercises in this chapter, we assumed that the initial price level had existed long enough so that everyone had fully adjusted to it. Thus, there were no distortions due to wage–cost lags or money illusion. In other words, the natural rate of unemployment existed at the start of each exercise (at points A in Figures 3 and 4). Similarly, the natural rate of unemployment existed at the close of each of these exercises (at points C in these figures), since wage–cost gaps and money illusion faded out as the aggregate-supply curve shifted. What happened during these exercises was that *actual* unemployment rose above the natural rate during the recession exercise and fell below the natural rate during the expansion exercise.

> During recessions, the actual rate of unemployment is greater than the natural rate of unemployment.

What will the official or "measured" rate of unemployment be when the economy is at potential GNP? There will be some structural, some frictional, and some seasonal unemployment. The structural unemployment exists because some industries are growing and others are contracting, so that workers must retrain and move around to qualify for different job openings. Frictional unemployment exists as people seek jobs that pay better or are more satisfying. In addition, measurement problems arise because people falsely claim to be unemployed in order to collect unemployment compensation payments. There is no macroeconomic or cyclical unemployment when the economy is at potential GNP.

The natural rate of unemployment itself may change from time to time because of changes in the composition of the labor force, in consumer tastes, in the rate of change of technology, and in barriers to moving from one job to another. For example, it is likely that the natural rate of unemployment rose during the 1970s because of the great changes in relative prices caused by oil-price increases and because many women who had recently entered the labor force had trouble finding a job or went through several moves before finding the right job. In the late 1980s, the natural rate of unemployment was generally believed to be somewhat under 6 percent of the civilian labor force.

> The natural rate of unemployment may change from time to time because of changes in the composition of the labor force, in the rate of change in technology, in consumer tastes, and in barriers to moving among jobs. In the late 1980s, it was believed to be somewhat under 6 percent of the civilian labor force.

Just because some rate of unemployment is "natural" in the sense that macroeconomic forces tend to move the economy toward that rate, it does not follow, of course, that this rate is desirable or that nothing can be done to lower it. *Microeconomic* tools may be able to lower the natural rate of unemployment and so raise the real living standard of the society. Among these microeconomic tools are measures to improve mobility and reduce discrimination in job markets, ways to make more information available to workers, and so on.

Changes in Long-Run Aggregate Supply and Potential GNP

In our definition of long-run aggregate supply, we assume that there is no change in physical production capabilities, such as might come from changes in the level of technology, the size and skill of the labor force, and the size and quality of the stock of capital equipment. Now we ask what will happen if a change in physical production capability does take place.

The answer is that long-run aggregate supply and potential GNP change along with the size and productivity of the economy's labor force, the size and quality of its stock of capital goods, and its level of technology. It is ordinarily presumed that these determinants increase from year to year and nourish economic growth.

Cultural and institutional matters are important in determining long-run aggregate supply and potential GNP. Cultural factors may influence the way in which people divide their time between work and leisure, say, between enjoying a new car and watching the sunset. Institutional factors, such as whether the economy is organized through free markets or through central planning, may also be important.

SUPPLY SHOCKS

The recession and the expansion models in this chapter both began with a shift in the aggregate-demand curve. That is, they originated in demand-side events or shocks. Expansions and contractions can also be caused by shifts in the aggregate-supply curve, that is, by **supply shocks.** An expansionary

shock might be an important technological breakthrough, the discovery of a great new natural resource, or a rise in labor force participation. Such shocks would shift the aggregate-supply curve to the right and increase long-run aggregate supply and potential GNP. Contractionary supply shocks can result from the destruction of productive capacity through wars or other disasters. They can also be artificially created, as when the Organization of Petroleum Exporting Countries (OPEC) cut the output of oil in the 1970s. These shocks can shift the aggregate-supply curve to the left.

Supply shocks are events that shift an economy's aggregate-supply curve.

Figure 6 shows the two forms of supply shocks. In the contractionary supply-shock case in

FIGURE 6
Supply Shocks

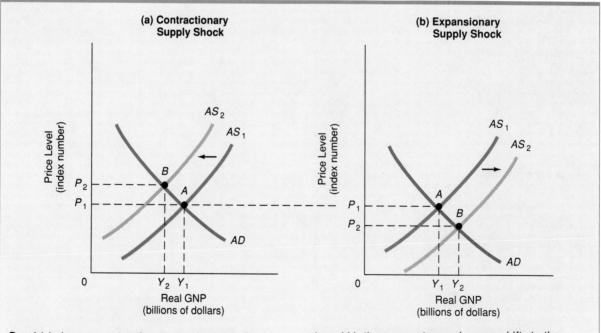

(a) Contractionary Supply Shock

(b) Expansionary Supply Shock

Panel (a) shows a contractionary supply shock. The aggregate-supply curve, AS_1, shifts to the left because of a reduction in production capability. If the aggregate-demand curve does not shift, the new equilibrium will be at B, with a higher price level and lower real GNP. In the expansionary supply shock

(panel b), the aggregate-supply curve shifts to the right because of some increase in production capability. If the aggregate-demand curve does not shift, the new equilibrium will be at B, with a lower price level and larger real GNP.

panel (a), the initial equilibrium is at *A*. A shift to the left in the aggregate-supply curve leads to a new equilibrium at *B*, a higher price level, P_2, and a lower level of real GNP, Y_2. These changes follow as long as the aggregate-demand curve does not shift, because a given money supply (implied in the aggregate-demand curve) is being used to purchase a smaller amount of output.

In the expansionary supply-shock case in panel (b), the initial equilibrium is at *A*, and the aggregate-supply curve shifts to the right. If the aggregate-demand curve does not shift, the new equilibrium will be at *B*, with a lower price level, P_2, and greater real GNP, Y_2. The given money supply (implied in the aggregate-demand curve) is being used to buy more goods and services.

An important assumption in each of these cases is that there is no shift in the aggregate-demand curve. But you know that the aggregate-demand curve can be shifted by means of the mon-

etary and fiscal instruments of government policy. So it is quite possible that the government will decide that shifts in the aggregate-supply curve should be met with shifts in the aggregate-demand curve. The aggregate-demand policy choice in the face of an expansionary supply shock undoubtedly would be to increase aggregate demand. However, aggregate-demand policy faces a dilemma in the contractionary supply-shock case. Increasing aggregate demand will push the price level further upward while decreasing aggregate demand will reduce real GNP and increase unemployment.

Monetary and fiscal policy poses a dilemma in the face of contractionary supply shocks, since expansionary policy will increase inflation while contractionary policy will increase unemployment.

Economics in Focus

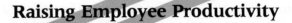

Raising Employee Productivity

Productivity is an important force causing changes in aggregate supply from year to year. Faced with increasingly stiff international competition, U.S. executives have tried various ways to raise productivity: computerizing, automating, restructuring, merging, and so on. Quite naturally, one major trend involves a focus on the largest component of the total production—the workers. Through profit sharing and employee stock-ownership plans (ESOPs), more and more firms are boosting their employees' stake in the business.

In a profit-sharing system, employees' compensation varies according to the firm's profits. In good times the employees earn more, in bad times less. The rewards can be distributed as extra cash in the paychecks or (more often) as contributions to a retirement package. In ESOPs (frequently considered a variant of profit sharing), employees receive company stock, generally as part of the pension arrangement.

Both of these methods have a number of short-term benefits for the company and may shorten lags between price-level changes and changes in wage costs. Profit sharing offers a financial cushion during hard times, and it also helps the company avoid automatic annual salary increases. ESOPs bring tax breaks, discourage corporate raiders, and often reduce the cash the company must lay out for retirement benefits. But in both cases the principal benefit may be the effect on productivity.

The A&P supermarket chain was foundering in the early 1980s when it negotiated a profit-sharing agreement with the workers at some of its stores. In exchange for a 25 percent cut in base pay, the company agreed to pay bonuses linked to productivity at each participating market. When the employees kept a store's labor costs at 10 percent of the sales total (below the industry average), A&P paid a cash bonus of 1 percent of sales. As a result, per-store sales climbed by 24 percent in two years.

An example of success with ESOPs is the Brunswick Corporation, which introduced an employee stock plan in 1983. In the next five years, sales per employee rose by almost 50 percent. Other major companies with ESOPs include Procter & Gamble, Polaroid, Texaco, and US West. In 1987 Avis became 100 percent employee-owned and was quick to proclaim that fact in advertising. By 1989 *Business Week* was able to declare that American businesses were "rushing headlong" into ESOPs.

But giving employees a stake in the company seems to work best when they also have a strong voice in operations, and this is a power many managers are reluctant to yield. Some critics say it is unfair to base compensation on profits, since poor profits may not be the workers' fault; others worry that ESOPs leave retiring employees at the mercy of stock market fluctuations. Nevertheless, profit sharing and ESOPs may well offer at least a partial remedy for ailing American productivity.

Sources: David R. Altany, "Profit-Sharing Plans Work," *Industry Week,* May 2, 1988, p. 19f.; Christopher Farrell and John Hoerr, "ESOPs: Are They Good for You?" *Business Week,* May 15, 1989, pp. 116–123 (quotation at p. 116); Christopher S. Eklund, "How A&P Fattens Profits by Sharing Them," *Business Week,* December 22, 1986, p. 44; Karen Pennar, "The Productivity Paradox," *Business Week,* June 6, 1988, pp. 100–102.

SUMMARY

1. Aggregate-demand curves and aggregate-supply curves show relationships between changes in the price level, as measured by some index number, and changes in real GNP. These concepts are helpful in understanding the economics of inflation and unemployment. (See page 326.)

2. Two theories help to explain the negative slope of the aggregate-demand curve. The interest rate theory is that higher price levels, if other things are equal, reduce the *real* money supply and cause higher real rates of interest, which reduce planned investment spending and thereby lower real GNP demanded. The real balances theory is that higher price levels lower the real value of wealth held as money or assets denominated in terms of money. These wealth reductions may reduce planned consumption spending, thus lowering the level of real GNP demanded. (See pages 327–329.)

3. A shift in the aggregate-demand curve means a change in the quantity of real GNP demanded at any given price level. Many variables may shift this curve. Monetary and fiscal policies are important because they permit governments to influence variables that change the location of this curve. (See pages 329–330.)

4. The aggregate-supply curve shows how changes in the price level affect the quantity of real GNP supplied in the economy. It has a positive slope because wage rates and other costs of production tend to lag behind changes in the price level and because, when the price level changes, the behavior of many people in the economy is affected by money illusion—the belief that changes in nominal values are the same as changes in real values. (See pages 330–331.)

5. Money illusion and lags of wage rates and costs do not continue indefinitely after a change in the price level. As wage rates and costs catch up to the change in the prices of final goods, and as money illusion fades away, the aggregate-supply curve shifts in such a way as to move the quantity supplied in the direction of the initial volume of real GNP. (See pages 331–334.)

6. In macroeconomic equilibrium, the price level exactly balances the quantity of real GNP demanded with the quantity supplied. This condition exists at the intersection of the aggregate-demand curve and the aggregate-supply curve. (See page 334.)

7. The recession model describes how an economy may experience a period of high unemployment and declining price levels due to a leftward shift in aggregate demand. But as the *AS* curve shifts to the right, the economy expands toward its original level of real GNP. (See pages 334–336.)

8. The expansion model describes how an economy may experience a period of low unemployment and rising price levels due to a rightward shift in aggregate demand. But as the *AS* curve shifts to the left, the economy contracts toward its original level of real GNP. (See pages 336–338.)

9. A situation with sluggish growth, inflation, and increasing unemployment is called stagflation. This combination of problems arises as a result of a leftward shift of the aggregate-supply curve. Demand-side remedies are unattractive in this situation. (See page 338.)

10. Long-run macroeconomic equilibrium—the economy's potential GNP—is achieved when a given price level has existed long enough so that neither wage–cost lag nor money illusion is distorting decisions in the economy. The long-run relationship between the price level and the quantity of real GNP supplied may appear as a vertical line on an aggregate-demand and aggregate-supply graph, although some economists believe that it has a positive slope. (See pages 338–339.)

11. Long-run aggregate supply and potential GNP can be changed by changes in production capabilities. Expansions in production capability increase long-run aggregate supply and potential GNP. Reductions in production capability reduce long-run aggregate supply and potential GNP. Cultural and institutional variables also are important. (See pages 338–340.)

12. The natural rate of unemployment is the rate of measured unemployment that corresponds with potential GNP. It includes seasonal, frictional, and structural unemployment, but not macroeconomic (or cylical) unemployment. This natural rate may change over time if changes take place in the labor force or in the pace of other changes in the economy. (See pages 339–340.)

13. Economic disturbances can arise from supply-side shocks, which shift the aggregate-supply curve. Shocks that reduce production shift the curve to the left, and shocks that increase production shift the curve to the right. (See pages 341–342.)

KEY TERMS

aggregate demand: the relationship between a change in the price level and the resulting change in the quantity of real GNP demanded (page 326).

aggregate supply: the relationship between a change in the price level and the resulting change in the quantity of real GNP supplied (page 326).

aggregate-supply curve: the graphic representation of the relationship between changes in the price level and changes in real GNP supplied (page 330).

cost of living adjustment (COLA): an agreement under which wage rates are changed automatically on the basis of specified changes in the price level (page 333).

deflationist policy: the plan to recover from a recession by allowing wage rates and other input prices to fall so that profit margins will expand and invite increases in output (page 335).

expansion: a situation in the economy when real GNP is increasing and unemployment is falling (page 336).

hyperdeflation: a situation in which the pessimism engendered by recession induces shifts to the left of the aggregate-demand curve, increasing the severity of the recession (page 335).

hyperinflation: a situation in which a rising price level induces shifts to the right of the aggregate-demand curve, increasing the rate of inflation (page 337).

interest-rate theory: the proposition that an increase in the price level, *ceteris paribus*, reduces the real money supply, increases the real rate of interest, and thereby reduces planned investment and the quantity of real GNP demanded. The theory works in the opposite direction for decreases in the price level; also called Keynes effect (page 327).

long-run aggregate supply: the relationship between changes in the price level and changes in

real GNP supplied that prevails as long as there is no change in production capability but when enough time has passed for people to adapt completely to the existing price level; also called, potential GNP (page 338).

macroeconomic equilibrium: the situation in which the price level is such as to secure an equality between real GNP demanded and supplied (page 334).

money illusion: the mistaken belief that changes in nominal values are changes in real values. The theory suggests a positive slope for the aggregate-supply curve (page 332).

natural rate of unemployment: the measured rate of unemployment when the economy is operating at its potential GNP. (Only seasonal, frictional, and structural unemployment exists) (page 339).

potential GNP: the quantity of real GNP indicated by an economy's long-run aggregate supply curve (page 338).

rate of economic growth: the percentage change per year in an economy's potential GNP (page 338).

real balances theory: the proposition that an increase in the price level, *ceteris paribus*, reduces the real wealth of those holding assets denominated in money terms and that this reduction in wealth leads to reduced planned expenditure and a smaller quantity of real GNP demanded. The theory works in the opposite direction for decreases in the price level; also called Pigou effect (page 327).

recession: a situation in the economy when real GNP is falling and unemployment is increasing (page 334).

reflation: an increase in the price level that returns it to a level that had existed previously (page 336).

stagflation: a situation in the economy when the price-level is rising while unemployment is increasing (page 338).

supply shock: an event which causes a shift in an economy's aggregate-supply curve (page 341).

wage–cost lag theory: the proposition that changes in wage rates and the prices of other inputs to production lag behind changes in the prices of final goods (page 330).

wage-rate and cost "catch up": the process through which wage rates and other input prices cease to lag behind the prices of final goods (page 333).

DISCUSSION QUESTIONS

1. Draw an aggregate-demand and aggregate-supply graph, being careful to label correctly each axis. Then compare your curve with Figure 1. Why is it *not* correct to refer to the $C + I + G + X - Im$ curve as a demand curve?

2. The interest rate theory (or Keynes effect) about the slope of the aggregate-demand curve uses the transmission system that you learned in Chapter 14. Without looking at Figure 2, draw the four graphs in this transmission system and then check to be sure you are right. If the investment-demand curve is steep, will the aggregate-demand curve be steep or flat? Explain.

3. What will happen to the real value of your life insurance policies when the price level rises? Will this change cause you to divide your current disposable income between consumption and saving in a different way? Explain how your answers to these questions can lead to an understanding of the real balances theory about the slope of the aggregate-demand curve.

4. Average gross hourly earnings in private nonagricultural employment were $4.53 in 1975, and $9.32 in 1988. Assuming a complete money illusion, explain how this change would affect worker behavior according to an aggregate-supply curve. After adjustment for price-level change, real wages in 1988 were almost the same as in 1975. Explain how elimination of money illusion places the economy at its long-run aggregate-supply or potential GNP level of output.

5. Without looking at Figure 3, construct the graph illustrating a recession process. Then check to be sure you have it right. Using the concepts of wage–cost lag and money illusion, explain why the first phase of the process involves rising unemployment while the second phase involves falling unemployment.

6. Hyperdeflation involves a leftward shift of the aggregate-demand curve, which is induced by the hard times resulting from some ongoing contraction of the economy. Explain hyperdeflation in terms of the graph that you drew for Question 5.

7. Thinking now about the expansion process, illustrate on a graph how a rightward shift of the aggregate-demand curve brings a higher price level and a temporary increase in real GNP. Check with Figure 4 to be sure you are correct. Explain the process in words, again stressing the role of wage–cost lag and money illusion.

8. Construct a pair of aggregate demand–aggregate supply graphs, one to illustrate a contractionary supply shock and the other to illustrate an expansionary supply shock. Compare your graphs with Figure 6. How did the drought in 1988 in U.S. agricultural areas affect the aggregate-supply curve?

9. Write down from memory our definition of long-run aggregate supply and potential GNP. Check to be sure you have it right. Explain how the wage–cost lag and money-illusion concepts relate to these values. Discuss two forces (one of them social and the other environmental) that could change long-run aggregate supply and potential GNP.

10. Explain the reasoning that concludes that macroeconomic equilibrium tends to establish the natural rate of unemployment. Why can this rate also be called full employment? How does racial discrimination or sex discrimination in labor markets affect the natural rate of unemployment? How would elimination of such discrimination change the real level of potential GNP? Explain.

16

The Phillips Curve, Adaptive Expectations, and Inflation Economics

Preview For more than half a century—ever since the Great Depression—the U.S. economy has experienced continuous increases in its price level. From the late 1960s through the early 1980s, the U.S. economy experienced almost continuous significant rates of increase in its price level. Some of the pressures for inflation during that time came from war expenditures for the Vietnam conflict, some were thrust upon the economy by supply shocks coming from increased world petroleum prices, and some arose from domestic policies such as the War on Poverty and Great Society programs. Whatever the causes, inflation became a focus of attention in economic analysis. This chapter examines several important aspects of the economic analysis of inflation.

The first section of the chapter examines the Phillips curve, which achieved wide acceptance in the early 1960s as a guide for macroeconomic policy. Although the Phillips-curve model appeared to work in the early and middle 1960s, it failed as a policy guide in the late 1960s and throughout the 1970s. We proceed, therefore, by exploring theories that contend that the Phillips-curve model failed because it requires that inflation be unanticipated when, in fact, the extended experience with inflation nourished inflationary expectation.

The second part of the chapter looks at the phenomenon of stagflation—simultaneous increases in both the unemployment rate and the inflation rate. We examine several alternative macroeconomic policies that may be adopted in the face of stagflation driven by inflationary expectations. Choosing among these alternatives was the focus of macroeconomic policy during the 1970s and early 1980s.

The last part of the chapter deals with wage and price controls, such as typically are imposed in emergency times, when large increases in aggregate demand are expected to bring inflationary pressures. We examine not only the theoretical basis for believing that controls can help fight inflation, but also the real-world difficulties in effectively sustaining these controls.

THE PHILLIPS CURVE AND ADAPTIVE EXPECTATIONS

Toward the close of the 1950s, a number of events set the stage for active macroeconomic policy. In 1957, the Soviet Union beat the United States into space by launching *Sputnik,* an orbiting space vehicle the size of a basketball. In 1958, the U.S. economy experienced its worst recession (up to that point) since World War II. The recession and the Soviet success in space contributed to the success of John F. Kennedy's 1960 campaign slogan, "Let's Get This Country Moving Again." When President Kennedy took office in 1961, Keynesian economics, which had been taught in classrooms for a generation, became the vehicle for active macroeconomic policy. Also, in 1958 an article written by A.W.H. Phillips appeared in *Economica.*[1] It described a relationship between unemployment and wage rates in Great Britain from 1861 to 1957. This relationship provided the basis for what became known as the Phillips curve, which played an important part in macroeconomic policy during the 1960s and 1970s.

A **Phillips curve** is illustrated in Figure 1. The horizontal axis shows the unemployment rate, and the vertical axis shows the inflation rate, that is, the annual percentage change in the price level. The curve is derived by plotting the actual experience of the economy for a number of years. For example, in Figure 1, in year 1 the inflation rate was 1 percent and the unemployment rate was 5 percent. In year 2, the inflation rate was 3 percent and the unemployment rate was also 3 percent. In year 3,

1. A.W.H. Phillips, "The Relationship Between Unemployment and the Rate of Change of Money Wage Rates in the United Kingdom, 1861–1957," *Economica,* November 1958.

1. A.W.H. Phillips, "The Relationship Between Unemployment and the Rate of Change of Money Wage Rates in the United Kingdom, 1861–1957," *Economica,* November 1958.

**FIGURE 1
A Phillips Curve**

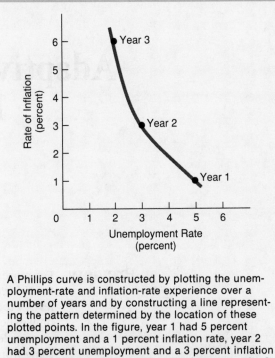

A Phillips curve is constructed by plotting the unemployment-rate and inflation-rate experience over a number of years and by constructing a line representing the pattern determined by the location of these plotted points. In the figure, year 1 had 5 percent unemployment and a 1 percent inflation rate, year 2 had 3 percent unemployment and a 3 percent inflation rate, and year 3 had 2 percent unemployment and a 6 percent inflation rate. As applied in the 1960s, the Phillips curve suggested that policymakers could choose their preferred combination of unemployment and inflation from among those located on the curve.

the inflation rate was 6 percent and the unemployment rate was 2 percent. The curve itself is generated by connecting the plotted points with a smooth line. In actual practice, points are plotted for many years, and a curve is fitted by statistical procedures.

The Phillips curve displays the relationship between the unemployment rate and the inflation rate over a number of years.

The Phillips Curve and Macroeconomic Policy

As a guide for macroeconomic policy, the Phillips curve suggests not a cause-and-effect relationship but a tradeoff between inflation and unemployment. It implies that a reduction in the unemployment rate can be "bought" by accepting an increase in the rate of inflation. On the other hand, a reduction in the rate of inflation can be "bought" by accepting a rise in the rate of unemployment. In the context of policy formulation, the curve suggests that political parties and candidates can key their economic policy platforms to particular points along the Phillips curve. Parties looking for votes from workers who feel threatened by unemployment will most likely choose points toward the upper end of the curve, accepting inflation in order to save jobs. On the other hand, parties seeking votes from people who see inflation as their more serious problem will choose points toward the lower end of the curve, accepting higher unemployment (for others) in exchange for less inflation. Election results would, in a democracy, establish the general outline for macroeconomic policy according to the Phillips-curve model.

The Phillips curve implies that a reduction in the unemployment rate can be achieved by accepting a higher rate of inflation, and a reduction in the rate of inflation can be achieved by accepting a rise in the rate of unemployment.

Aside from determining its precise location, the economist's concern with the Phillips curve is to discover ways to shift the curve in order to improve the combinations available to decision makers. A shift of the Phillips curve downward and to the left offers an improved set of choices, since the economy could then have less unemployment, or less inflation, or some combination involving less of both, compared with any point on the original curve. On the other hand, a shift of the Phillips curve upward and to the right clearly worsens the choices available, since decision makers then would have to accept either more inflation, or more unemployment, or some combination involving more of both, compared with any point on the original curve.

The economist's concern with the Phillips curve is to discover ways to shift the curve in order to

improve the combinations available to decision makers.

Phillips-Curve Experience

Figure 2 shows the inflation-unemployment combinations that actually developed from 1961 through 1969. Most of the time during these years, fiscal and monetary actions were expansionary. The economy responded with higher and higher rates of inflation (from less than 2 percent a year in the early 1960s to almost 6 percent a year by 1969) and with reduced rates of unemployment (from almost 7 percent in 1961 to around 3½ percent in 1968). The Phillips curve appeared to work as a guide for economic policy.

FIGURE 2
Unemployment and Inflation in the United States, 1961 through 1969

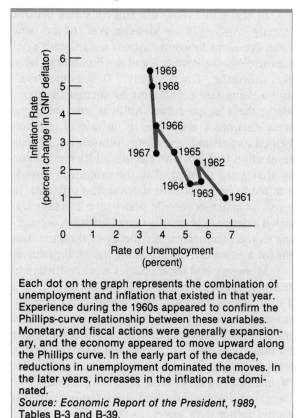

Each dot on the graph represents the combination of unemployment and inflation that existed in that year. Experience during the 1960s appeared to confirm the Phillips-curve relationship between these variables. Monetary and fiscal actions were generally expansionary, and the economy appeared to move upward along the Phillips curve. In the early part of the decade, reductions in unemployment dominated the moves. In the later years, increases in the inflation rate dominated.
Source: Economic Report of the President, 1989, Tables B-3 and B-39.

The Phillips-curve relationship was extremely favorable to expansionary macroeconomic policy in the early 1960s. The unemployment rate fell and the inflation rate remained at what today would be seen as very low levels. In a policy initiative inspired by the Keynesian model, President Kennedy's economic advisers recommended tax reduction as a means of increasing total planned expenditure and raising the equilibrium level of real GNP. Under President Johnson, individual income taxes were reduced substantially. True to the Keynesian model, economic expansion followed, and true to the Phillips-curve model, the rate of inflation increased as the unemployment rate fell.

In the 1960s, the Phillips curve appeared to work as a guide for economic policy. Under an expansionary macroeconomic policy, the rate of inflation increased as the unemployment rate fell.

In the mid-1960s, the United States became heavily involved in the Vietnam War. At the same time, President Johnson pushed forward with a domestic "War on Poverty" and the building of what was called the "Great Society." Deficits increased, and a rising rate of inflation dominated the move along the Phillips curve. Antiwar protests along with discontent about the rising rate of inflation helped to persuade President Johnson not to seek re-election in 1968. The election of Richard Nixon in that year showed that the American people wanted to be rid of both the war and inflation. In terms of macroeconomic policy, the election signaled a desire to lower the rate of inflation. According to the macroeconomic theory of the time, this meant a move downward along the Phillips curve.

Monetary and fiscal policies were restrictive in the first part of the Nixon administration (1969 and 1970). According to the Phillips-curve model, these restrictive policies should have produced a movement downward and to the right along the Phillips curve, that is, they should have resulted in a lower inflation rate and a somewhat higher rate of unemployment. Instead, the unemployment rate increased dramatically, and the inflation rate was higher rather than lower. In short, the results did *not* follow the Phillips-curve model.

In the late 1960s, Americans grew discontented with the rising rate of inflation. President Nixon's attempt to lower inflation by using restrictive monetary and fiscal policies failed, however, and both unemployment and inflation rose.

Figure 3 shows Phillips-curve plots for the years 1961 through 1988, with the years connected in chronological order. Clearly, the pattern is not as simple as it appeared in the 1960s. Some intervals show northwestward movement such as prevailed in the 1960s. These periods of falling unemployment and increasing inflation occurred for 1973, 1977, 1978, 1979, 1984, 1987, and 1988. There also were periods of rising unemployment and falling inflation rates, that is, when the movement was southeastward. These occurred for 1971, 1975, 1981, and 1982—the latter being part of the **Great Disinflation,** which eventually brought the inflation rate to below 2 percent. Both northwesterly and southeasterly moves are consistent with the Phillips-curve model.

There were, however, several years when the moves were different from the tradeoff relationship of the Phillips-curve model. The "worst of both worlds" situation appears in Phillips-curve graphs as a northeastward move. This shows stagflation, the combination of a rising unemployment rate along with a rising inflation rate. In Figure 3, the symptoms of stagflation appear in 1970, 1974, and 1980. The second and third of these bouts with stagflation were caused, in large measure, by supply shocks originating with increases in the price of crude petroleum imposed by the Organization of Petroleum Exporting Countries (OPEC) in 1973 and 1978. But oil shocks cannot explain the stagflation move for 1970, when the Phillips-curve relationship did not work for President Nixon.

Southwesterly moves identify the "best of both worlds" situations, with reductions in both the inflation rate and the unemployment rate. These good times appeared in 1972, 1976, 1985, and 1986. The 1972 record is artificial because wage and price controls were in effect. But such controls were not in effect in the other years showing a southwesterly move on the chart. Thus, the record

FIGURE 3
Phillips-Curve Experience in the United States, 1961 through 1988

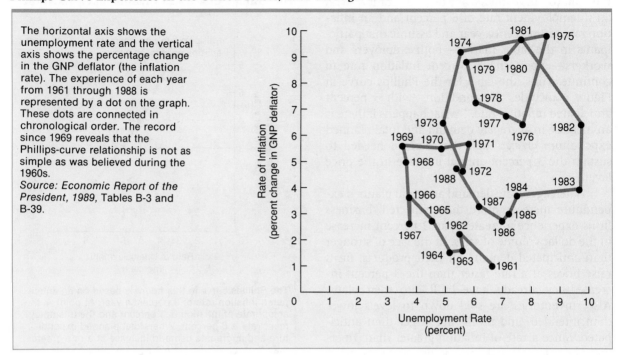

The horizontal axis shows the unemployment rate and the vertical axis shows the percentage change in the GNP deflator (the inflation rate). The experience of each year from 1961 through 1988 is represented by a dot on the graph. These dots are connected in chronological order. The record since 1969 reveals that the Phillips-curve relationship is not as simple as was believed during the 1960s.
Source: Economic Report of the President, 1989, Tables B-3 and B-39.

makes it clear that the relation between unemployment rates and inflation rates is more complex than suggested by the original Phillips-curve model.

The economy did not follow the Phillips-curve model in the 1970s and 1980s. The relationship between unemployment rates and inflation rates is more complex than suggested by the original Phillips curve.

Because experience failed to confirm predictions based on the Phillips curve, economists set to work to re-examine that model and to search for other factors affecting the inflation-unemployment relation. As explained in Chapter 15, supply shocks offered one explanation. Drastic increases in the price of a basic resource, such as petroleum, could easily force simultaneous increases in the unemployment rate and the inflation rate. But supply shocks were not the only force at work during the 1970s and 1980s. In studying the Phillips-curve model, economists concluded that expectations about coming price-level changes significantly in-

fluence the relationship between the unemployment rate and the inflation rate.

One of the factors affecting the inflation-unemployment relation is expectations about coming price-level changes.

Unanticipated Inflation

In examining the theoretical foundations of the Phillips curve, economists Milton Friedman and Edmund Phelps concluded that it contains the implicit assumption that people do not anticipate changes in the rate of inflation.[2] Friedman and Phelps reasoned that the negative relationship between the unemployment rate and the inflation rate arises because the change in the inflation rate is *not anticipated*.

2. Milton Friedman, "The Role of Monetary Policy," *American Economic Review*, March 1968, pp. 1–17; Edmund S. Phelps, "Money Wage Dynamics and Labor Market Equilibrium," *Journal of Political Economy*, July-August 1967, pp. 678–711.

Figure 4 illustrates the role of anticipation in the Phillips-curve model. We begin at point *A*, with an unemployment rate of 6 percent and an inflation rate of 3 percent a year and assume that participants in the labor market—both employers and workers—expect the 3 percent inflation rate to continue. Thus, the label for the Phillips curve in Figure 4 includes the condition "with 3 percent anticipated inflation rate." What happens if there is an increase in aggregate demand and total planned expenditure *greater* than the increase needed to sustain the 3 percent annual increase in the price level?

When aggregate demand and total planned expenditure increase more than expected, business firms experience a greater than 3 percent increase in the dollar volume of sales. In the face of stronger than anticipated demand for their products, firms raise prices at a rate faster than the 3 percent increase they already have built into their plans. Also, inventories are sold down to levels lower than intended, and profits are larger than anticipated. Since a rate of inflation greater than 3 percent is not anticipated, money illusion exists, firms believe that their *real* profit rates have increased, and, therefore, set about to expand production to earn maximum profits during the good times. To do this, they enter the resource markets to employ more labor and other production inputs.

In the labor and other resource markets, both demanders and suppliers, by assumption, expect a 3 percent increase in the price level and have built this increase into their demands and offers. If both the demand curves and the supply curves in these markets shift upward by 3 percent in nominal values, no change takes place in the equilibrium quantities demanded and supplied. However, since firms have experienced depleted inventories and profitability has increased, the demand curves for resources increase by *more* than the 3 percent built into the anticipated 3 percent inflation rate.

According to Friedman and Phelps, the negative relationship between the unemployment rate and the inflation rate arises because the change in the inflation rate is not anticipated.

FIGURE 4
The Phillips Curve and Unanticipated Inflation

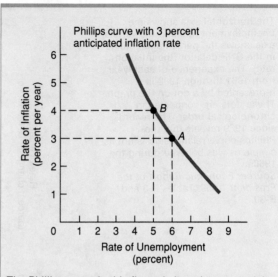

Phillips curve with 3 percent anticipated inflation rate

Rate of Inflation (percent per year)

Rate of Unemployment (percent)

The Phillips curve in this figure is based on an anticipated inflation rate of 3 percent a year. At point *A*, the actual rate of inflation is 3 percent and the unemployment rate is 6 percent. When total planned expenditure and aggregate demand increase at a rate *greater* than that required for the 3 percent inflation rate, the unemployment rate decreases because unemployed workers receive acceptable wage offers sooner than under the previous rate of increase in aggregate demand. Therefore, as the actual rate of inflation rises above the anticipated rate, the unemployment rate decreases. Point *B* illustrates the relationship between the unemployment rate and an actual 4 percent inflation rate when the anticipated rate of inflation is 3 percent.

How does this increase in demand affect the potential workers who make up the 6 percent of the labor force that is unemployed when the economy is at point *A* in Figure 4? Labor-market theory suggests that these people are engaged in a search for jobs and that each of them has in mind a **reservation wage rate**—a desired wage rate that must be found before a contract of employment is agreed to. According to this theory, at the start of a spell of unemployment, each unemployed worker's reservation wage rate is optimistically high. After all, why not aim high and hope for the best job? Job offers at wage rates below the reservation wage are rejected. Some workers find work soon at acceptable wage rates, but others, as time passes and the job search lengthens, revise their reservation wage rates downward toward what they conclude are more realistic levels.

A reservation wage rate is a wage rate that a worker desires to find before he or she will agree to a contract of employment.

In the environment of greater than anticipated increases in aggregate demand and planned expenditure, the quantities of resources demanded increase as firms increase production to restore inventories to desired levels. Workers also suffer money illusion. Job offers at or above the unemployed worker's reservation wage rate are received after a shorter than normal period of job search. Both the average duration of unemployment and the unemployment rate in the economy fall. In Figure 4, this new situation is illustrated at point B. The unemployment rate has fallen to 5 percent and the inflation rate has risen to 4 percent a year, driven mainly by increases in the price charged by firms for their products. The Phillips-curve relation prevails, but only because the actual rate of inflation (4 percent) is greater than the anticipated rate of inflation (3 percent).

Adaptive Expectations

Will employers, workers, and other resource owners continue to anticipate inflation at the rate of 3 percent when the actual inflation rate is 4 percent? Of course not. Money illusion will eventually fade away. Before very long, workers and job seekers are sure to recognize that the actual inflation rate is 4 percent, not 3 percent. They will then re-examine their expectations about future rates of inflation. What change will be made in expectations about inflation? According to the **adaptive expectations** model, the inflation rate that is being experienced during the present time period becomes the inflation rate that is anticipated for the future. In our illustration, after the economy has operated at point B for a while, business firms, workers, and other resource owners will anticipate inflation at 4 percent a year rather than at 3 percent a year.

According to the adaptive-expectations model, the inflation rate being experienced during the present time period becomes the inflation rate that is anticipated for the future.

In labor markets, the change to a 4 percent anticipated inflation rate means that reservation wage rates are boosted to reflect a 4 percent annual rate of increase. Job offers that would have been accepted under the old 3 percent inflation expectation are declined under the revised 4 percent expectation. Also, workers already on the job at pay rates negotiated under the old set of expectations demand higher pay rates as soon as their contracts permit adjustments. They demand pay boosts to compensate them for the reduced *real* pay rate under the 3 percent contract. From the point of view of employers, the revised expectation not only forces higher resource costs but also forces them to revise downward their forecasts about their profitability. Production and employment are scaled back.

Figure 5 illustrates how expectations adapted to actual experience show a new aspect of the Phillips-curve model. Points A and B and the "Phillips curve with 3 percent anticipated inflation" are the same as in Figure 4. But Figure 5 includes a new Phillips curve reflecting a 4 percent anticipated inflation rate. Point C illustrates the equilibrium suggested by the Friedman-Phelps analysis. Unemployment has returned to the 6 percent rate. According to Friedman and Phelps, when the rate of inflation is correctly anticipated, the economy operates at its natural rate of unemployment—the 6 percent rate in this illustration. The negative slope of the Phillips curve arises, according to their analysis, from the failure to anticipate correctly the rate of inflation. The unemployment rate is less than the natural rate when the actual inflation rate is greater than the anticipated inflation rate and, conversely, the unemployment rate rises above the natural rate when the actual inflation rate is less than anticipated.

In Figure 5, a line connecting points A and C would be vertical and would represent a "long-run" Phillips curve, the relationship between the rate of inflation and the rate of unemployment when the actual rate of inflation is equal to the anticipated rate of inflation, that is, when inflation is correctly anticipated.

According to Friedman and Phelps, when the rate of inflation is correctly anticipated, the economy operates at its natural rate of unemployment. The negative slope of the Phillips curve arises from the failure to anticipate correctly the rate of inflation.

The Phillips Curve and the Aggregate-Supply Curve

There is a strong parallel between the theory of the shifting Phillips curve, as illustrated in Figure 5, and the theory of the shifting aggregate-supply curve explained in Chapter 15. Since modern macroeconomics most often uses the aggregate-demand and aggregate-supply format rather than the Phillips-curve format, let us transfer what we have learned about the shifting Phillips curve into the aggregate-demand and aggregate-supply framework.

Figure 6 shows aggregate demand and aggregate supply. It essentially reproduces Figure 4 in Chapter 15 (page 337). Note first the label on the horizontal axis of the *AD-AS* graph. Real GNP increases as we move to the right on this axis. The Phillips-curve graph, in contrast, shows the rate of unemployment increasing as we move to the right on this axis. Clearly, the two axes report approximately the same information, but a move to the right on the horizontal axis of the Phillips-curve graph (increasing the unemployment rate) appears as a move to the left on the *AD-AS* graph (decreasing real GNP).

Now look at the vertical axes of these graphs. The *AD-AS* graph shows the price level on this axis, expressed as an index number. Inflation is shown as a movement upward on this axis and deflation by a movement downward. On the Phillips-curve graph, the vertical axis shows the *rate* of inflation,

FIGURE 5
The Phillips Curve Shifted by Adaptive Expectations

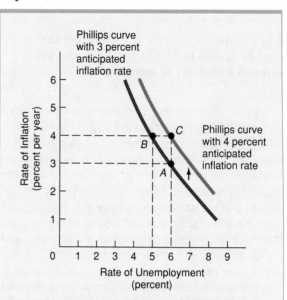

This graph continues the analysis started in Figure 4. At point *B*, actual inflation is at a rate of 4 percent a year, but the anticipated rate of inflation is only 3 percent a year. According to the theory of adaptive expectations, expectations will soon be adjusted to match the inflation rate currently being experienced. When the anticipated inflation rate becomes 4 percent a year, the Phillips curve will have shifted upward and unemployment will have risen to 6 percent. The natural rate of unemployment prevails, other things being equal, when the anticipated rate of inflation is the same as the actual rate of inflation.

that is, the annual percentage change in the price level. Again, the vertical axes of the graphs present similar information but in different ways. A given point on the vertical axis of the Phillips curve graph, such as a 3 percent inflation rate, must be represented on the *AD-AS* graph as a series of successively higher price levels if the price level rises by 3 percent each year.

Let us now examine the logic of the Phillips curve to see how it parallels the logic of the *AS* curve in the *AD-AS* framework. According to the Friedman-Phelps analysis, the negative slope of the Phillips curve arises because higher rates of inflation are not anticipated, particularly by participants in labor and resource markets. Increases in total planned expenditure and aggregate demand cause inventories of final goods and services to be reduced below intended levels and cause the prices of these goods and services to rise. But wage rates lag behind the increases in final good and service prices because workers anticipate no change in the rate of inflation. Therefore, the rate of unemployment falls as workers quickly find jobs at wage rates equal to or greater than their reservation wage rates set according to out-of-date expectations. In the *AD-AS* framework, the increase in total planned expenditure and aggregate demand ap-

pears explicitly on the graph as a shift to the right of the aggregate-demand curve, from AD_1 to AD_2 in Figure 6 (arrow 1). Because of the lag in the prices of labor inputs behind the rise in the general price level, profit rates rise and firms increase production. At the same time, the prices of final goods and services rise. Thus macroeconomic equilibrium moves from point *A* to point *B*. This parallels the movement that appears from *A* to *B* in the Phillips curve in Figure 5. There is some difference, however. The Phillips-curve graph suggests that the full inflationary effect of the expanded aggregate demand has already been realized at point *B*. The *AD-AS* format reserves some of this inflationary effect for the second stage of the process.

The second stage in the Friedman-Phelps analysis of the Phillips curve is based on the theory of adaptive expectations, that is, that workers and other resource suppliers adapt their expectations to the new, higher, inflation rate and that the Phillips curve shifts upward when this happens. In the *AD-AS* framework, this step takes place as contracts expire and other institutional barriers are overcome so that wage rates and other input prices catch up with the higher price level. As wage rates and other resource prices catch up, the aggregate-supply curve shifts to the left, from AS_1 to AS_2 in Figure 6 (arrow 2). In the *AD-AS* framework, equilibrium moves from point *B* to point *C*, with output returning to potential GNP and unemployment returning to its natural rate. This parallels the movement from *B* to *C* on the Phillips curve graph in Figure 5. In the *AD-AS* framework, this move has an upward slope because the vertical axis of the graph shows the price *level* rather than the inflation *rate*. The price level of 104—equivalent to the 4 percent inflation rate of the Phillips-curve model—is reached at point *C* in the *AD-AS* system. Thus, in the *AD-AS* framework, the second, or "catch-up," phase of the process displays the characteristic stagflation combination of both increasing unemployment and a rising price level.

FIGURE 6
Shifts of the Aggregate-Supply Curve

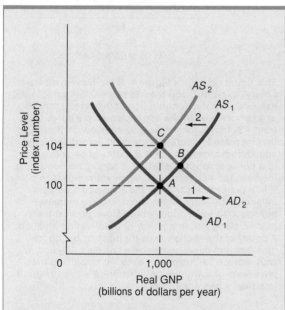

The logic of the positive slope of the AS curve parallels the logic of the negative slope of the Phillips curve. Starting at point A, an increase in aggregate demand, from AD_1 to AD_2 (arrow 1), leads to equilibrium at point B, with lower unemployment and a higher price level. Wage costs lag behind increases in the prices of final goods because the higher price level was not anticipated. When expectations adapt to anticipate a continuation of the existing inflation rate, the aggregate-supply curve shifts from AS_1 to AS_2 (arrow 2) and equilibrium moves to point C. At point C, real GNP and unemployment with it have returned to the same rate that prevailed at point A.

The Phillips-curve model can be transferred into an aggregate-demand and aggregate-supply framework.

STAGFLATION AND POLICY ALTERNATIVES

Are the inflation and output consequences of a boost in total planned expenditure and aggregate demand really completed when the economy has returned to potential GNP and when unemployment has returned to its natural rate? In the context of the adaptive expectations theory, the answer is "no." In Figure 6, when the economy has moved from point A to point B and then to point C, the society has experienced a 4 percent rise in the price level. If this has taken place over the period of one year, the rate of inflation has been 4 percent. According to the theory of adaptive expectations, both firms and suppliers of labor and other resources build this experience into their expectations about *forthcoming* changes in the price level. In bargaining for new contracts, workers add an *extra* 4 percent to their wage demands to reflect their expectation that the prices of final goods and services and the cost of living will rise by 4 percent per year during the term of the contract being negotiated. Employers, who share the same inflationary expectation, build the anticipated 4 percent increase in the price level into their sales forecasts and, other things being equal, grant the increases demanded by labor and other resource suppliers. They anticipate that the price level one year in the future will be 4 percent higher than the current price level.

Expectations of a continuing 4 percent increase in the price level are incorporated into the *AD-AS* model by shifting the aggregate-supply curve still farther to the left. Figure 7 reproduces Figure 6 and adds a new aggregate-supply curve, AS_3, with prices 4 percent higher than curve AS_2 (arrow 3). This curve incorporates the inflationary expectations adapted from the earlier experience of the price level having risen at a 4 percent rate. Business firms and workers expect the price level to be 108.16 a year in the future (104 times 1.04 equals 108.16).

The *AD-AS* model makes it clear that macroeconomic policymakers must face up to the implications of the AS_3 curve. What alternatives are available to them?

FIGURE 7

Adaptive Expectations and the Aggregate-Supply Curve

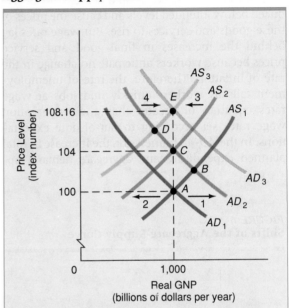

This figure continues Figure 6. If the movement from point A to point B and then to point C has established expectations of a continuation of the rate of inflation at 4 percent a year, the aggregate-supply curve shifts from AS_2 to AS_3 for the next year (arrow 3). If no further increase in aggregate demand is forthcoming, equilibrium moves to point D, but falls back to point C in a policy involving deflation. If aggregate demand is increased to AD_3 (arrow 4), equilibrium moves to point E in a policy that confirms the expected 4 percent inflation rate. If aggregate demand were increased beyond AD_3, equilibrium would move upward from point E along AS_3 in a policy of accelerating inflation. A policy of disinflation calls for locating the aggregate-demand curve somewhere between AD_2 and AD_3 with repeated adjustments aimed at stabilizing the price level or lowering the inflation rate to something less than 4 percent a year.

Deflation as a Policy Option

If macroeconomic policymakers make no adjustment in aggregate demand, that is, if they take no action to increase the money supply and initiate no expansionary fiscal policies, the aggregate-demand curve will, other things being equal, remain as shown by AD_2 in Figure 7. According to the *AD-AS* model, if no demand change is made, equilibrium moves first to point D. The movement to point D is accompanied by increasing unemployment, higher prices, and reductions in real GNP—a combination sure to be unpopular. But point D is only a temporary equilibrium. The price level will not have risen by the 4 percent anticipated by firms, workers, and other resource owners. With expectations not confirmed, with unemployment higher than the natural rate, and with output below potential GNP, employers and workers are forced to re-examine their expectations. If policymakers hold firm in their refusal to increase aggregate demand, wage rates and other prices eventually must fall, *deflation* will take place, and the economy will return to equilibrium at point C. The price level will stabilize at the 104 index number.

Is a deflation policy reasonable? The deflation policy forces the society to endure unemployment and reduced output in exchange for a lower price level. Since the economy, economists believe, can function as well at one price level as at another, there is little support for a deflation policy.

A policy of deflation—causing a reduction in the price level—forces the society to endure unemployment and reduced output in exchange for a lower price level.

Confirming Inflationary Expectations

The easiest policy to follow when the economy is at point C in Figure 7 is to increase total planned expenditure and aggregate demand, shifting the aggregate-demand curve to the right, to AD_3 (arrow 4). Under this policy, equilibrium moves upward from point C to point E. Output remains at potential GNP, unemployment is at its natural rate, and the anticipations of firms and resource suppliers that the price level will rise by 4 percent are confirmed.

Are there problems associated with a policy of confirming inflationary expectations and maintaining a constant rate of inflation, such as the 4 percent rate in the illustration? Some difficulties would undoubtedly arise in the early stages of such a policy, before all participants in the economy become aware of it and learn how to adjust their economic affairs to meet the constantly increasing price level. But if all buyers and sellers correctly anticipate price-level changes, appropriate adjustments can be built into contracts so that neither of the parties need gain or lose from the changing price level. Even anticipated inflation, however, is a burden on activities that must hold cash balances or must publish price lists.

If policymakers choose to confirm the expected price level of 108.16 for the time period during which the economy operates at point E, they must understand that the aggregate-supply curve will continue shifting, anticipating inflation at the rate of 4 percent a year. For the following year, buyers and sellers in both product and resource markets will anticipate a price level of 112.49 (that is, 108.16 times 1.04), and policymakers will have to increase aggregate demand appropriately to confirm this expectation. If the 4 percent inflation-rate policy is successfully implemented for an extended period of time, the shifts of the AS curve and the AD curve adjustments could occur smoothly and automatically with virtually no fluctuations in real GNP either above or below potential GNP.

Another approach to dealing with inflationary expectations is simply to confirm them by maintaining a constant rate of inflation. This is the easiest policy to follow, but it is a burden on those enterprises that must hold cash balances or publish price lists.

A Policy of Accelerating Inflation

Still another policy option is available to an economy at point C in Figure 7. If expansionary monetary and fiscal measures are implemented that shift the aggregate-demand curve *beyond* the level of AD_3, macroeconomic equilibrium is pushed upward and to the right of point E, that is, the price level rises *more* than expected, wage rates and other input prices again lag behind the prices of final goods and services, profits are greater than anticipated, output exceeds potential GNP, and unemployment is below its natural rate. In short, the situation parallels that at point B, when the economy experienced expansion from the initial shift of aggregate demand.

Can the economy continue for long with unemployment below the natural rate and output exceeding potential GNP? That depends on future macroeconomic policy and on how the society reacts to the now higher rate of inflation. The adaptive-expectations model suggests that the higher inflation rate soon will be built into labor and input contracts so that the aggregate-supply curve will shift to the left from the AS_3 location. Then policymakers must again decide how far to shift the aggregate-demand curve. It is conceivable that they might, once again, choose to increase aggregate demand by more than the amount needed to confirm inflationary expectations. The economy could have another period of unemployment below the natural rate and output above potential GNP.

How long could this process of accelerating inflation be sustained? According to the adaptive-expectations model, in order for the accelerating inflation policy to be effective, each year's inflation rate must be greater than the rate in the preceding year, thereby always being greater than the anticipated rate of inflation. Can policymakers deceive the economy year after year? Or will people sooner or later anticipate the higher and higher inflation rate and thus cause the accelerating inflation policy to become ineffective? It appears inevitable that a sustained policy of accelerating inflation would end with runaway inflation and an eventual breakdown of the economy in hyperinflation.[3]

Still another policy option in dealing with inflationary expectations is to accelerate the rate of inflation. This approach can lead to runaway inflation and the eventual breakdown of the economy in hyperinflation.

---

3. In hyperinflation, the rising price level persuades people to spend their incomes more quickly, increasing the velocity of money circulation and inducing a shift to the right of the aggregate-demand curve.

A Policy of Disinflation

There remains another policy alternative for an economy that has arrived at point C in Figure 7, where there has been established the anticipation of a 4 percent annual rise in the price level. This is the policy of **disinflation,** that is, the policy of gradually lowering the rate of inflation to a more acceptable level, perhaps to a zero rate (price stability). The disinflation policy calls for some increase in aggregate demand, but not enough of an increase to confirm fully the expectation that the price level will rise by 4 percent (to 108.16). Imagine, for example, an aggregate-demand curve roughly halfway between AD_2 and AD_3 in Figure 7. The new macroeconomic equilibrium occurs along the AS_3 curve, upward and to the right of point D. Output will fall from the level enjoyed at point C, and unemployment will increase. However, the expectation of a 4 percent inflation rate will *not* be confirmed and, in due time, the AS_3 curve will shift to the right, as inflationary expectations are scaled back to less than the 4 percent rate. With successive replays of this "less than full confirmation" policy, inflationary expectations can gradually be squeezed out of the economy, and equilibrium at potential GNP and the natural rate of unemployment can be achieved at whatever price level or rate of inflation is considered appropriate.

Viewed graphically, as in Figure 7, the disinflation procedure appears in a cold and analytical light. In the real world of economic policy, such a policy is anything but cold. How long can the government force the economy to operate below its potential GNP and how long can it permit unemployment to continue above its natural rate? Since disinflation requires sacrifices from the public, the ability of a government to carry out a policy of disinflation depends on the strength and determination of that government. Can the disinflation be accomplished quickly, with a sharp but short-lived period of high unemployment and depressed output? Will expectations change (shifting the AS curve) quickly enough so that the suffering will have subsided and been forgotten before the next election? Or is it better strategy to pursue the disinflation policy gradually, imposing unemployment rates only moderately higher than the natural rate but sustaining the pressure for an extended period of time?

Another policy alternative is disinflation, that is, gradually lowering the rate of inflation to a more acceptable level. This policy requires the society to endure high employment and depressed output for some period of time.

The most successful recent disinflation experience in the United States occurred in the early to middle 1980s during the administrations of President Reagan. Although fiscal policy was expansionary, the Federal Reserve maintained a restrictive monetary policy. Hardships were severe, and the Reagan administration was accused of causing, or at least increasing the severity of, the recession in the early 1980s. But the Reagan administration enjoyed a strong anti-inflation mandate carried over from the record-setting inflations of the late 1970s. Also, the disinflation policy was greatly aided by significant decreases in energy prices, as the Organization of Petroleum Exporting Countries (OPEC) failed in its efforts to restrict world petroleum production. The result was that the disinflation process advanced much farther and much faster than planned. The U.S. dollar reached new highs in international currency markets, favoring foreign travel by Americans but causing great difficulty for American exporters. Farmers were hit from all sides, with high interest rates, depressed sales, and huge indebtedness carried over from debt incurred in the 1970s.

The United States experienced a period of disinflation in the early to middle 1980s under President Reagan. Hardships were severe, especially for American exporters and farmers.

Indexing

Indexing is a procedure that automatically adjusts wage rates, savings accounts, taxes, interest rates, bond values, and all other contracts for changes in the price level. It has important applications in an economy beset by fears of inflation, by actual inflation, or by inflation arising from macroeconomic policy. The appeal of indexing is evidenced by the fact that it often is included in labor-management contracts as an **escalator clause** or a **cost-of-living adjustment (COLA)** provision. In these contracts, the parties agree to use some generally accepted measure of inflation, such as the consumer price index, as a basis for automatic changes in wage rates. For example, it might be agreed that wage rates would be increased by, say, 3 percent, whenever the consumer price index for the preceding six-month period increased by 4 percent. Automatic adjustments in wage rates need not exactly match changes in the chosen price-index number. The precise relationship is a matter for negotiation. The appeal of the escalator, or cost-of-living adjustment, is that it eases the problem of forecasting future inflation rates. Workers do not need to press for wage increases to cover anticipated increases in the cost of living, since the escalator, or COLA clause, will provide the needed adjustment should inflation actually occur.

Indexing is a procedure for automatically adjusting wage rates, savings account balances, taxes, interest rates, bond values, and all other contracts for changes in the price level. It is often included in labor-management contracts.

Indexing *as a public policy* would not be negotiated on a contract-by-contract basis but would be incorporated in rules and regulations governing all contracts and agreements in the economy. To see how indexing would work for savings accounts, suppose you have an account balance of $1,000 at the start of a year and that the interest rate on the account is specified as 6 percent per year. In the absence of inflation, your account balance at the end of the year would be $1,060, assuming you made no deposits or withdrawals. What would happen to this account if inflation, as measured by the index number specified in the indexing regulations, took place at the rate of 10 percent? In order to protect the depositor from any loss in real purchasing power, the balance in the account would be adjusted, automatically, to $1,166, which is equal to $1,060 times an inflation adjustment of 1.1. In effect, this indexing procedure increases both your initial balance and the contracted rate of interest by 10 percent—the rate of inflation indicated by the approved index number.

If indexing were established by law for all agreements, arrangements similar to the one described above would be required for all wage and salary contracts, savings accounts, checking accounts, stocks, bonds, mortgages, tuition, room and board, and so on throughout the entire economy. As it stands, however, indexing is not required by law but can be written into contracts if desired by those involved. Indexing is in effect for the U.S. Individual Income Tax. During the 1970s and early 1980s, before the tax was indexed and when inflation rates were high, taxpayers justly complained of **bracket push** because, as their incomes rose along with the price level, the unindexed tax system forced them into higher tax-rate brackets. Average tax rates paid went up even when real incomes and real standards of living did not. The government was accused of profiting from inflation and of increasing actual tax rates without passing tax legislation. Starting with the 1986 tax year, the size of personal exemptions, tax-rate brackets, and certain other features of the tax were indexed. As a result, increases in the price level no longer force taxpayers into higher rate brackets and require them to pay a higher average rate of tax on their income.

Indexing is not required by law but can be written into contracts by those involved. It is used for the U.S. Individual Income Tax.

What does indexing have to do with inflation economics and inflationary expectations? Probably the greatest appeal of indexing is the protection it offers to important groups, such as retirees, savings-account owners, and persons on fixed pension or annuity incomes. Since these groups are often committed to long-term agreements, they can easily be hurt by unanticipated inflation. But indexing also has appeal at theoretical and policy levels for an economy driven by inflationary expectations, as illustrated at point C of Figure 7. If indexing were in place, people would no longer need to build inflation expectations into their wage and other negotiated agreements. Negotiators could put inflation expectations out of their minds because each side could be sure that it would receive an appropriate adjustment for any inflation that actually arose. Overestimates of coming inflation would not drive the economy to higher inflation rates or cause hardship if such overestimates proved unfounded. So *expectations* of inflation would no longer drive the economy to higher price levels by shifting the aggregate-supply curve. In this sense, those who favor indexing claim that it would help fight inflation.

The appeal of indexing is that if it were used as a policy tool, people would no longer need to build inflation expectations into their contract agreements.

If indexing is such a great idea, why don't we have it? The basic problem is that many doubt that indexing could, in practice, be done fairly and effectively. It is hard to image a truly general and complete indexing system that would not leave out some people. Moreover, there are serious problems in finding index numbers that are unbiased and have broad applicability throughout the economy. Since inflation usually involves relative price changes as well as changes in the average of all prices, any given index number will favor some groups and disfavor other groups. For example, when food prices change, the cost-of-living impact differs between urban dwellers and rural dwellers, between large families and small families, and between high-income families and low-income families. When energy prices change, the cost-of-living impact depends on heating and cooling requirements in different parts of the country and on whether energy is provided from coal, electricity, fuel oil, or natural gas. In effect, indexing proposals are easily bogged down in disagreements over which index numbers should be used.

The drawback to using indexing as a government policy is that it would be very difficult to administer fairly and effectively.

Indexing also encounters opposition of a more general nature. Many say that indexing amounts to giving up the fight to stop inflation. If all were protected from it, who would step forward to try to stop it? Interest in indexing was great during the 1970s, when the inflation rate was high. This interest proved strong enough to achieve the indexing for social security benefits and the individual income tax. However, interest in indexing subsided with success on the income-tax and social security fronts and with the Great Disinflation of the early and middle 1980s. Even interest in escalator and cost-of-living adjustment clauses lost appeal when inflation rates fell.

WAGE AND PRICE CONTROLS

Wage and price controls are limits imposed by law on increases in wage rates and prices. Sometimes the controls are very precise and rigid, as when all prices and wage rates are "frozen"—that is, when they are not allowed to change at all. At other times they are more flexible, as when an official agency is given the power to approve or disapprove proposed changes in wage rates and prices. Sometimes the controls are mandatory, meaning that persons who violate the laws may be fined or put in prison or both. When violators cannot be officially punished, the controls are said to be voluntary (sometimes called **wage and price guidelines**). When controls are used throughout the whole economy and attempts are made to coordinate wages and prices to reach a certain set of goals, the controls are part of an **incomes policy.** Incomes policies are related to government planning for the economy. Political decisions replace market decisions in determining what, how, and for whom to produce.

Wage and price controls are limits imposed by law on increases in wage rates and prices. When controls are used throughout the whole economy and attempts are made to coordinate wages and prices to reach a certain set of goals, the controls are part of an incomes policy.

Wage and price controls have been used at one time or another in most organized economies of the world. They are a standard feature of planned economies, where the major sectors of the economy normally operate under controls. In market economies, direct controls over wage rates, prices, profits, and outputs are usually used in times of war, when massive increases in government spending are expected. The United States imposed a full set of controls during World War II and less-comprehensive controls during the Korean War. Wage and price guidelines were used during the 1960s and 1970s, by both Republican and Democratic administrations. In 1971, President Nixon, faced with inflationary pressures and serious international payments problems, placed a ninety-day freeze on all wages and prices. This was followed by a comprehensive system of controls that were applied to the economy with varying degrees of stringency until they were removed in April 1974. After these controls were removed, the price level leaped upward, leading most observers to conclude that the controls had only suppressed inflation but had not prevented it. In fact, many believed that the controls disrupted the economy so much that production was lower and the price level higher than they would have been had the controls never been used.

In market economies, direct controls over wage rates, prices, profits, and outputs are usually used only in times of war or other national emergency.

Changing the Aggregate-Supply Curve

Wage and price controls aim to change the shape of the aggregate-supply curve. This is illustrated in Figure 8. Suppose that equilibrium exists at point A, with price level P_1 and real GNP of Y_1. Now let the aggregate-demand curve shift to the right, from AD_1 to AD_2, perhaps from wartime spending or perhaps as a policy initiative to reduce unemployment. In this situation, the theories that you have studied lead economists to predict that macroeconomic equilibrium will move to point B, with a larger real GNP (Y_2) and a higher price level (P_2). These theories also suggest that the inflation will set the stage for a leftward shift of the AS curve and a period of stagflation when wage–cost lags fade away. Moreover, inflationary expectations that could lead to still further leftward shifts of the aggregate-supply curve may be built up.

If a national emergency is felt to exist, as is likely in these circumstances, strong sentiment may arise in favor of wage and price controls to hold prices at the original level (P_1). In terms of Figure 8, the aim of these controls is to make the AS curve horizontal at this price level. If the controls are effective and if patriotic enthusiasm encourages people to work hard, macroeconomic equilibrium might be reached at point C on the horizontal part of the AS curve, with price level P_1 and real GNP at Y_3. Under these ideal assumptions about the effectiveness of wage and price controls, aggregate demand could be increased with no increase in the price level. Having prevented inflation, the controls might also prevent subsequent leftward shifts of the AS curve and the stagflation that would result.

Wage and price controls attempt to change the shape of the aggregate-supply curve.

Problems with Wage and Price Controls

Experience indicates that wage and price controls do not in practice achieve the ideal results illustrated in Figure 8. Part of the problem is that controls inevitably lead to rationing and other enforcement problems. In addition, the social, political, and economic compromises built into the control program sooner or later break down.

Rationing Rationing of goods and services is likely to be used along with wage and price controls, especially if these controls are expected to remain in effect for very long. The reason for ra-

FIGURE 8
Wage and Price Controls and the Aggregate-Supply Curve

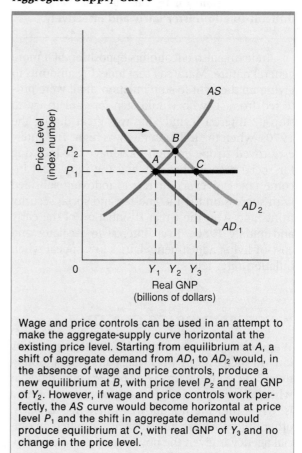

Wage and price controls can be used in an attempt to make the aggregate-supply curve horizontal at the existing price level. Starting from equilibrium at A, a shift of aggregate demand from AD_1 to AD_2 would, in the absence of wage and price controls, produce a new equilibrium at B, with price level P_2 and real GNP of Y_2. However, if wage and price controls work perfectly, the AS curve would become horizontal at price level P_1 and the shift in aggregate demand would produce equilibrium at C, with real GNP of Y_3 and no change in the price level.

tioning is easily understood from the supply and demand curves shown in Figure 9. These curves represent market demand and supply for a good or a service and *include* the inflationary pressures that price and wage controls are trying to combat. For this reason, the equilibrium price P_1 shown by the intersection of these curves is above the price set by the controls, which is shown as P_2. At the controlled price, the quantity demanded (Q_d) is greater than the quantity supplied (Q_s), and there is a shortage.

Rationing systems are intended to divide up the limited quantities of goods and services actually supplied under wage and price controls and thereby to relieve some of the upward pressure on prices. Ration coupons are issued to each individual or household for each of the various goods or services subject to rationing. Then, when a purchase is made, the buyer must give the merchant the required number of ration coupons along with the money price of the item bought.

Aside from the complexity of the system itself, a major problem is that illegal ("black") markets arise that do not require coupons and that sell rationed items at illegally high prices. Moreover, since rationing cannot cover all the goods and services that people want to buy, spending power not usable for rationed items may spill over and increase demand for nonrationed items, putting extra upward pressure on their prices. During wartime emergencies, patriotic appeals encourage cooperation with price controls and rationing, but problems increase the longer the system is in operation. Shortages become more severe and black markets more widespread. Only totalitarian systems can make rationing work over extended periods.

FIGURE 9
Rationing and Price Controls

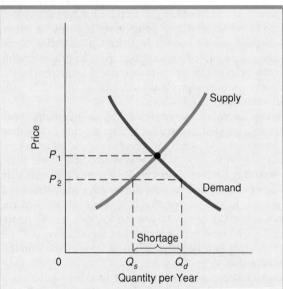

The supply curve and the demand curve include inflationary pressures that wage and price controls are designed to combat. Without controls, the equilibrium price is P_1. The controlled price for this good or service is illustrated by P_2. At this price, the quantity demanded is Q_d, where this controlled price meets the demand curve. The quantity supplied is Q_s, where the controlled price meets the supply curve. A shortage is shown by the distance between Q_d and Q_s. Rationing is used to divide up the available supply (Q_s) and to hold down pressures for prices to rise above P_2.

> **Rationing systems are intended to divide up the limited quantities of goods and services actually supplied under wage and price controls. Rationing tends to lead to black markets, which sell rationed items at illegally high prices.**

Changes in Relative Prices The second type of problem encountered by wage and price controls involves changes in relative prices and the complicated set of compromises and assurances needed to gain the political support needed to adopt and maintain controls. Besides rationing, the plan is likely to call for subsidies to industries that are asked to operate at a loss under the controlled prices and deficits for government operations that buy or import food or other goods for the public. In countries where public payrolls are a large part of total labor income, civil service wage rates are often frozen, leading to corruption, absenteeism, and poor performance on the job.

Ultimately the major problems with wage and price controls spring from hard facts of both life and arithmetic. The arithmetic fact is that it is impossible to fix the prices of two goods without automatically fixing the ratio between them. But flexibility of relative prices is essential in any economy as conditions change. The relative prices of some goods must rise, and the relative prices of other goods must fall. If these changes do not occur, shortages will appear in some markets and surpluses in others.

The facts of life are that no set of price or wage ratios can satisfy all the parties concerned even after their leaders have accepted it. For this reason, after the controls have been in place for a few months or years and the original "emergency" has somewhat subsided, they may begin to break down. Sometimes black markets expand into second economies, militants appear among the pressure groups, and there are wildcat strikes, slowdowns, and shutdowns in protest against one or another part of the system. There may be a breakdown of the controls, as in the United States after World War II and after the Nixon controls of 1971–1973 and in Britain from 1976 to 1979. At other times the country may resort to martial law or similar dictatorial methods to reinforce the system, as in Poland in 1956, 1970, and 1980–1982.

Economics in Focus

Inflationary Expectations: Actions and Reactions in Europe

Like the United States, European economies experienced some very good years in the late 1980s. Fueled by high consumer spending and solid investment, national income and product grew impressively. By the end of the decade, however, there were signs—as in the United States—that inflation would once again be a problem. Across Europe the overall inflation rate reached 5 percent by early 1989, up two points from the year before. German industrialists, worried that inflation would bring rising costs, began to push up their prices. BMW, for instance, raised its car prices an average of 2.5 percent in one jump.

In Britain the most unsettling reactions came from labor unions, which began to demand large wage increases to compensate for the anticipated rise in the cost of living. Some of these demands amounted to double-digit raises, and by early 1989 wage costs were climbing at an average annual rate of 9 percent. Analysts feared that Britain was entering an upward wage-price spiral that might damage the economy for years to come.

Among the Common Market countries, Britain and West Germany took particularly strong steps to counter the trend. British policymakers expected inflation to be severe, and their policies were equally so. When the inflation rate headed over 7 percent in Britain, Chancellor of the Exchequer Nigel Lawson prompted nine separate rises in prime-lending rates in the course of a year, so that prime rates reached 13 percent by the end of 1988. This was an uncompromising attempt to slow down the economy and cool inflationary expectations.

In West Germany the policies were similar. The Bundesbank, West Germany's central bank, boosted its discount rate three times in less than a year, and the government also raised consumer taxes and added a new withholding tax on interest income. What was remarkable about these strong measures was that German prices had risen *only 1.2 percent* in 1988. There were other reasons besides inflation for the stern policies (for example, excess growth in the money supply and a "softness" of the German mark), but some U.S. analysts complained that the Germans were overreacting. Since a slowdown in European economies would hurt efforts to curb the U.S. trade deficit, *Forbes* magazine accused the Bundesbank of "inflation paranoia."

These examples illustrate some of the ways in which inflation is linked to attitudes and expectations. A particular inflation rate—whether it be 2.5 percent of 6.9 percent—is often less important than the way people perceive it and react to it.

Sources: Bianca Riemer with Mark Maremont and John Templeman, "In Europe, Inflation Is No Longer Distant Thunder," *Business Week,* March 20, 1989, pp. 54–55; Peter Fuhrman with William Heuslein, "The Bundesbank Brakes," *Forbes,* January 9, 1989, pp. 56–58; "Other G-7 Nations Optimistic About Their Economies," *Wall Street Journal,* April 7, 1989, p. A2f.; Mike McNamee, "The Group of Seven is Acting More Like the Seven Dwarfs," *Business Week,* June 5, 1989, p. 90; "Inflation Rises in Europe," *New York Times,* April 18, 1989, p. D19; "Inflationary Flap" (editorial), *Christian Science Monitor,* April 25, 1989, p. 20.

SUMMARY

1. A Phillips curve displays a relationship between the rate of unemployment during a given year and the percentage increase in the price level that took place during that year. Rather than a cause-and-effect relationship, the curve is interpreted as identifying combinations of inflation and unemployment that can be selected as goals for macroeconomic policy. (See pages 348–349 and Figure 1, page 348.)

2. The economy appeared to follow the Phillips curve during the 1960s. However, President Nixon's attempt, at the end of the decade, to move back down the curve failed. Instead, the economy experienced a higher inflation rate and a higher unemployment rate simultaneously. A great variety of inflation-rate and unemployment-rate combinations appeared during the 1970s and 1980s. The apparent breakdown of the Phillips-curve model prompted economists to search for other variables affecting unemployment and inflation. (See pages 349–351 and Figures 2 and 3, pages 349 and 351.)

3. Economists Milton Friedman and Edmund Phelps concluded that the negative (Phillips-curve) relationship between the unemployment rate and the inflation rate arises when changes in the inflation rate are not anticipated by workers and firms in the economy. When inflation is not anticipated, increases in total planned expenditure and aggregate demand lead to depleted inventories and increased hiring by firms. When inflation is not anticipated, money illusion exists, the reservation wage rates of unemployed workers are not adjusted upward, and increased demand for labor results in shorter job searches and a lower unemployment rate. (See pages 351–353 and Figure 4, page 352.)

4. The theory of adaptive expectations states that the rate of inflation experienced by workers and employers during the present time period becomes the rate of inflation anticipated for the next time period. Changes in the anticipated rate of inflation cause the Phillips curve to shift. According to the adaptive-expectations model, unemployment is at its natural rate when the inflation rate is correctly anticipated. Unemployment is less than the natural rate when inflation is greater than anticipated and higher than the natural rate when

inflation is less than anticipated. (See pages 353–354.)

5. The logic of the slope and shifts of the Phillips curve parallels the logic of the slope and shifts of the aggregate-supply curve. The *AD-AS* format shows how shifts of the aggregate-demand curve can initiate expansion or contraction processes and how leftward shifts of the *AS* curve result in stagflation—the combination of inflation along with increasing unemployment. (See pages 354–355 and Figure 6, page 355.)

6. Once inflationary expectations are built into the plans of workers and employers, policymakers may choose among several alternative policies: a deflation policy, a policy of confirming inflationary expectations, a policy of accelerating inflation, or a policy of disinflation. (See pages 356–359.)

7. Indexing automatically adjusts wage rates, savings account balances, taxes, interest rates, bond values, and all other contracts for changes in the price level. It frequently is negotiated into labor-management contracts as cost-of-living or escalator clauses. If required of all contracts, it could weaken the power of inflationary expectations to shift the *AS* curve. (See pages 359–361.)

8. Wage and price controls are limits imposed by law on increases in wage rates and prices. These controls attempt to change the shape of the *AS* curve so that expansionary increases in aggregate demand will not lead to price-level increases and ultimately to inflationary expectations becoming built into the economy. (See pages 361–362 and Figure 8, page 362.)

9. Rationing usually is needed to go along with wage and price controls. This is because shortages arise when the legal price is below the free-market equilibrium price for a good or service. Rationing tries to divide up the available quantity of the product and to reduce pressures for price increases. Illegal ("black") markets tend to arise and erode the effectiveness of rationing and wage and price controls. (See pages 362–363.)

10. Price controls have often been used, but they typically postpone, rather than prevent, inflation when pressures for inflation persist in the economy. The main problem with controls is that they are not able to respond to needed changes in relative prices. (See pages 362–363.)

KEY TERMS

adaptive expectations: a proposition that states that the inflation rate that is being experienced during the present time period becomes the inflation rate that is anticipated for the future (page 353).

bracket push: a term that describes what happens to taxpayers during times of high inflation rates if a progressive income tax is not indexed; taxpayers are pushed into higher tax-rate brackets as their incomes rise along with the price level (page 360).

cost-of-living adjustment (COLA) (escalator clause): a provision in a labor-management contract that grants workers automatic increases in wage rates as the price level increases (page 359).

disinflation: a lowering of the rate of inflation (page 358).

escalator clause: *see* **cost-of-living adjustment.**

Great Disinflation: the period of time in the early and middle 1980s when the rate of inflation was greatly reduced (page 350).

incomes policy: a coordinated program of wage and price controls designed to implement government planning of the economy (page 361).

indexing: a process that automatically adjusts wage rates, savings accounts, taxes, interest rates, bond values, and all other contracts for changes in the price level (page 359).

Phillips curve: a graphic representation of the relationship between the unemployment rate and the inflation rate (page 348).

reservation wage rate: the wage rate that a worker feels he or she must be offered before signing a contract of employment (page 352).

wage and price controls: limits imposed by law on increases in wage rates and prices of goods and/or services (page 361).

wage and price guidelines: officially recommended limits on increases in wage rates and prices of goods and/or services (page 361).

DISCUSSION QUESTIONS

1. Construct a graph of the Phillips curve as it appeared according to U.S. data for the 1960s. How might political parties use the Phillips-curve relationship in developing their campaign platforms? Discuss how the election of Richard Nixon in 1968 involved issues related to the Phillips curve.

2. Assume that unemployed workers expect no change in the price level and that the average spell of unemployment lasts four weeks. If an inflationary increase in aggregate demand takes place, will the length of the average spell of unemployment increase, decrease, or remain unchanged? Explain your answer using the concepts of reservation wage rates and job search.

3. Assume that one of the unemployed workers from the previous question had a reservation wage rate of $12.00 an hour when he or she expected no inflation. According to the theory of adaptive expectations, what will this reservation wage become if an actual inflation rate of 3 percent is experienced? What if the actual inflation rate in the next time period turns out to be 4 percent? How do adaptive expectations affect the Phillips curve?

4. In terms of the relation between the anticipated inflation rate and the actual inflation rate, when is the natural rate of unemployment realized? When will the unemployment rate be above the natural rate? When will it be below the natural rate? How will the Phillips curve shift in these situations? Discuss what you believe the relationship is at the present time.

5. Compare the adaptive-expectations explanation for a shifting Phillips curve with the wages catch-up explanation for the shifting aggregate-supply curve. If the two curves reflect similar models of labor-market behavior, why does one have a positive slope and the other a negative slope?

6. What is the difference between a shift of the aggregate-supply curve that comes from the elimination of wage lags from past inflation and a shift of that curve that comes from inflationary expectations? List four policy alternatives available when inflationary expectations have been established in the economy. Which of these alternatives do you recommend? Why?

7. Assume that inflation is led by increases in food prices. Identify two consumer groups that would favor indexing based on the consumer price index and two groups that would oppose indexing on that basis. Do the same for an inflation led by increases in energy prices. Do you believe that indexing would be popular if the price level were to fall?

8. Draw an *AD-AS* graph, shift the aggregate-demand curve to the right, and then change the shape of the aggregate-supply curve to illustrate how wage and price controls try to prevent inflation in emergency spending periods. Do you believe wage and price controls are justified in wartime? Are they justified in peacetime? Explain. If you answer "yes" in one case and "no" in the other, explain the basis for the difference.

9. Why do wage and price controls invariably require rationing as well? If price controls and rationing are effective, discuss alternative uses for consumer spending power that cannot be utilized in purchasing controlled goods and services. Where does saving rank among these alternatives?

17

Rational Expectations and Contemporary Schools of Macroeconomic Thought

Preview The stagflation and supply shocks of the 1970s sent a good many economists halfway back to their drawing boards in efforts to refine old models and devise new ones. In microeconomics the response was a certain amount of deregulation. In macroeconomics, the response was a broad array of new models and revisions of old ones. In this chapter we look at the macroeconomist's arsenal of theories to be used and tested in the 1990s. We begin by explaining an important new theory called rational expectations, which is sometimes called the "new classical" economics. It replaces or expands the theory of adaptive expectations explained in the preceding chapter.

Keynesian economists did not sit idle while their models were under attack. The second part of the chapter describes two dimensions of the Keynesian response to the problems of the 1970s. First, traditional Keynesian models were broadened to include the money supply and monetary variables. Secondly, Keynesian economists counterattacked, criticizing the assumptions of the new classical model and, at the same time, revising their own model to utilize the aggregate-demand and aggregate-supply technique of analysis. What emerged is called the "neo-Keynesian" school of macroeconomic thought. There arose also a so-called "post-Keynesian" economics, contending that the competing models fail to penetrate to the basic problems facing capitalist economic systems. Post-Keynesian models propose basic institutional changes in the capitalist system, mainly in a Marxian direction.

The last portion of the chapter outlines supply-side economics, which achieved prominence in the first Reagan administration and still influences macroeconomic policy. Supply-side economists focus on the production side of the economy and offer their own formula for economic expansion.

RATIONAL EXPECTATIONS

As explained in Chapter 16, economists Milton Friedman and Edmund Phelps used adaptive expectations in their explanation of the Phillips curve and its shifts. Their theory—that deviations from the natural rate of unemployment and potential GNP arise because firms and resource owners are surprised by changes in the price level—raised the question of how people actually arrive at their forecasts of future price levels. The **theory of rational expectations** is an alternative to the theory of adaptive expectations. Instead of forecasts being projections of recent experience, the rational-expectations theory proposes that people learn from their mistakes and use conventional economic principles to make their forecasts, following a rational reasoning process about how one thing leads to another in economics.

An analogy will clarify the distinction between adaptive and rational expectations. Suppose that a television weather forecaster always forecasts that the weather tomorrow is going to be the same as the weather today. This would be an adaptive expectation, since it anticipates continuation of the current situation. The forecast would be accurate much of the time, but would fail to forecast *changes* in the weather. Now consider a meteorologist, with his or her carefully plotted data and maps of the jet stream and storm systems moving around the world. This meteorologist's forecast of tomorrow's weather is based on scientific principles. It is "rational," rather than "adaptive." Although the adaptive forecaster may have a high average accuracy in forecasting, the rational forecaster should do a better (but still imperfect) job of predicting changes in the weather. In our analogy, changes in the weather correspond with changes in an economic variable, such as an unemployment rate or an inflation rate. If changes in the inflation rate

cause deviations from potential GNP and the natural rate of unemployment, then forecasting such changes becomes crucial. Forecasters using rational expectations and people who follow their forecasts should fare better economically.

The theory of rational expectations proposes that people learn from their mistakes and use economic principles to make their forecasts.

Rational Expectations in the *AD-AS* Framework

How does the aggregate-demand and aggregate-supply model of macroeconomic equilibrium change when expectations are assumed to be formed rationally rather than by adaptation to current and recent past price-level experience? Figure 1 reproduces Figure 6 in Chapter 16. Starting from equilibrium at point A, suppose that expansionary fiscal and monetary policies shift the aggregate-demand curve from AD_1 to AD_2 (arrow 1). In the adaptive-expectations model, equilibrium moves from point A to point B because wage rates and other input prices lag behind the increase in the general price level. But in the rational-expectations model, no lag can be counted on. Workers, other resource owners, and business firms (or their economic forecasters) have studied the principles of economics and recognize that the increase in aggregate demand will lead to an increase in the price level. Assuming that prices adjust quickly, workers and resource owners do not permit production costs to lag behind increases in the price of final goods and services. Also, business firms do not expect or experience increases in their rates of profit and, consequently, do not expand production. Therefore, *at the same time* that the aggregate-demand curve shifts to the right, from AD_1 to AD_2, the aggregate-supply curve shifts upward and to the left, from AS_1 to AS_2 (arrow 2). Macroeconomic equilibrium moves directly from point A to point C (as illustrated by the vertical black arrow in Figure 1), with no systematic change in real GNP. In effect, to the extent that wages and prices adjust quickly, the rational-expectations model says that the aggregate-supply curve is vertical. In Figure 1,

FIGURE 1
The Rational-Expectations Model of Response to a Policy-Induced Increase in Aggregate Demand

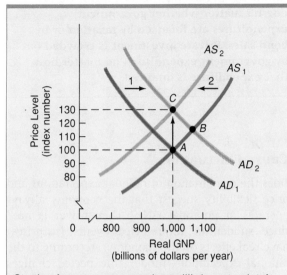

Starting from macroeconomic equilibrium at point A, the aggregate-demand curve shifts from AD_1 to AD_2 (arrow 1) as a result of government policy initiatives. However, because price-level expectations are assumed to be formed rationally, the price-level consequences of this initiative are recognized immediately and, if prices adjust quickly, the aggregate-supply curve shifts quickly from AS_1 to AS_2 (arrow 2). Macroeconomic equilibrium does not occur at point B, as in adaptive-expectations models. Instead, equilibrium moves directly from A to C as shown by the vertical black arrow. There is no systematic fluctuation in real GNP and the only effect of the policy is an increase in the price level.

we show the new equilibrium level of real GNP (at point C) as exactly the same as the original equilibrium level (at point A). This is an extreme case. According to the rational-expectations theory, point C is equally likely to be either to the left or to the right of point A.

The theory of rational expectations changes the AD-AS model of macroeconomic equilibrium by predicting that no systematic change in real GNP arises in response to fiscal and monetary policies.

Discretionary Fiscal and Monetary Policies Are Useless

What are the policy implications of the rational-expectations theory? The most striking is that, with rapidly adjusting wages and prices, it is useless for discretionary fiscal and monetary policies to try to push unemployment below its natural rate, that is, to try to raise real GNP above potential GNP. According to the rational-expectations model, workers, other resource owners, and business firms use the same economic models as government policy-makers and are as well informed about conditions in the economy. They quickly predict outcomes of policy changes. If prices and wage rates can be adjusted, the aggregate-supply curve shifts so quickly in response to policy-induced changes in aggregate demand that no changes in "real" variables—output and employment—take place. As long as policy actions do not surprise firms and resource owners, government monetary and fiscal initiatives cause changes in the price level, but they do not change real GNP.

The conclusion that demand-side macroeconomic policy is useless is a stunning implication of the combination of flexible prices and rational expectations. It wipes away the theoretical foundation for Keynesian and monetarist policy initiatives. The only demand-side policy initiatives that are systematically or predictably effective are those that come as surprises. In order to be effective, policymakers must engage in deception and concealment. Since such procedures are not compatible with democratic processes in a free society, the model suggests that democratic governments cannot take effective aggregate-demand initiatives in macroeconomic policy. Moreover, deception and concealment increase the risks involved in doing business, thus increasing costs.

The key policy implication of the rational-expectations theory is that it is useless to use discretionary fiscal and monetary policies to try to raise real GNP above potential GNP. Their only effect is to cause changes in the price level.

Deficits Don't Matter

According to some economists another implication of the rational-expectations theory is that government deficits don't matter. Those who hold this view are called **neo-Ricardians** in recognition of the early nineteenth century British economist, David Ricardo, who first pointed out the possibility. This is in sharp contrast to the traditional Keynesian view that budget deficits, if financed by money creation, increase total planned expenditure and raise the equilibrium level of real GNP. It also contradicts the view that if the central bank does not accommodate deficits by increasing the money supply, deficits are financed from private saving and crowd out private investment, cutting back the increase in total planned expenditure and dampening economic growth. According to neo-Ricardians, the rational-expectations theory suggests that the method used to finance government expenditure does not matter. It doesn't matter, they say, whether government expenditures are financed by taxation or by bond sales. In the neo-Ricardian view, taxpayers believe that budget deficits require higher taxes in the future and that they set aside (save) funds in order to prepare for the higher taxes they believe are coming. These added savings are channeled into financial markets, where they become available to purchase the new securities issued by the government to finance the deficit. Therefore, real rates of interest do not change and deficits do not crowd out private investment any more than would taxes of the same amount. Private investment is crowded out by government expenditure, regardless of how the expenditure is financed.

The theory of rational expectations can also be applied to challenge the traditional view that voters are less resistant to expenditures financed by debt than to expenditures financed by taxes. The traditional public finance view is that tax increases are unpopular with voters, so the opportunity to finance by debt biases the political process in favor of deficit finance. But, if voters behave according to the neo-Ricardian application of rational expectations, this proposition may be questioned. Voters are not biased in favor of debt finance. Government expenditure is not greater because of debt finance, and there is little need for a constitutional amendment prohibiting deficits in government budgets.

Neo-Ricardian applications of the rational-expectations theory suggest that it doesn't matter whether government expenditures are financed by taxation or by bond sales. Private investment is crowded out by government expenditure, no matter how that expenditure is financed.

Surprises Cause Fluctuations

Does the combination of rational expectations and price flexibility suggest that the economy always operates at potential GNP? The answer is no," since sudden or unpredicted events (surprises) have real effects on the economy. According to the rational-expectations model, unexpected changes in aggregate demand lead to fluctuations in employment and real GNP because firms do not correctly interpret information about these unexpected changes. Suppose, for example, that aggregate demand increases due to an increase in exports caused by unexpected events abroad, a sudden rise in consumer optimism, investor reactions to stock market gains or new technologies, or emergency government purchases. If the demand-changing events are unexpected, their price effects appear to firms to be increases in the *relative* prices of their products rather than increases in the *general* price level. They respond by increasing production. Conversely, if the price level declines unexpectedly, firms believe they are experiencing declines in the relative prices of their products and reduce output. Therefore, when unexpected changes take place in aggregate demand, the economy rises above or falls below potential GNP.

According to the rational-expectations model, unexpected changes in aggregate demand lead to fluctuations in employment and real GNP because firms do not correctly interpret information about these unexpected changes. When unexpected changes take place in aggregate demand, the economy rises above or falls below potential GNP.

The view that unexpected changes in the price level (price-level surprises) lead to changes in the quantity of real GNP supplied is illustrated graphically in Figure 2. The curve on this graph is called a **Lucas supply curve,** after Professor Robert Lucas of the University of Chicago, one of the pioneers in developing the theory of rational expectations. Note that the vertical axis on this graph shows *unexpected* changes in the price level—price "surprises." Point *A* on the curve identifies the quantity supplied when there is no unexpected change in the price level. This corresponds with the value of zero (0) on the vertical axis. The curve has a positive slope, indicating that unexpected price-level increases (the independent variable in this model) result in increases in the quantity of real GNP supplied (the dependent variable) and vice versa. The quantity supplied changes because firms misinterpret unexpected price-level changes, believing them to be changes in the relative prices of their products rather than changes in the general price level. The profit-maximizing position that the firms expect because of their misinterpretation of price changes moves up and to the right from point *A* along the Lucas supply curve when there are unexpected increases in the price level and downward to the left from point *A* along the curve when there are unexpected decreases in the price level. When the surprise wears off and firms realize that their products have not actually experienced changes in relative prices, firms retrace their route along the curve back to point *A*, and production returns to its initial (normal) volume. The prevailing price no longer is a surprise.

The Lucas supply curve illustrates graphically that price-level surprises lead to changes in the quantity of real GNP supplied. The quantity supplied changes because firms misinterpret unexpected price-level changes, believing them to be changes in the relative prices of their products rather than changes in the general price level.

The Lucas supply curve expresses much the same reaction process as the aggregate-supply curve in an aggregate-supply and aggregate-demand graph, except that the Lucas curve relates

FIGURE 2
The Lucas Supply Curve

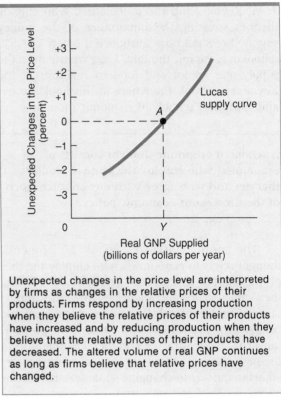

Unexpected changes in the price level are interpreted by firms as changes in the relative prices of their products. Firms respond by increasing production when they believe the relative prices of their products have increased and by reducing production when they believe that the relative prices of their products have decreased. The altered volume of real GNP continues as long as firms believe that relative prices have changed.

only to "surprises" and not to price-level changes in general. As surprises wear off, movements *along* the Lucas supply curve back to point *A* are represented by *shifts* of the aggregate-supply curve. For the Lucas supply curve itself, shifts arise from changes in the production capacity of the economy. This is the concept represented by changes in long-run aggregate-supply and potential GNP.

THE NEW CLASSICAL SCHOOL OF ECONOMIC THOUGHT

A **school of economic thought** is made up of economists who employ the same or similar theories and who agree with one another much of the time about economic policy. We have already met several such schools—the neoclassicals, who dominated economic thinking before the Great Depression and who employed concepts such as Say's Identity; the Keynesians, who accept the models of J. M. Keynes; and the monetarists, who employ theories stressing the importance of the money supply. We shall now introduce the new classical school of economic thought. Later we will meet the supply-side school and modern revisions of the Keynesian school. Elsewhere in this book we examine Marxist schools of economic thought.

A school of economic thought consists of economists who employ the same or similar theories and who agree with one another much of the time about economic policy.

The **new classical** school of economic thought refers to economists who employ the theory of rational expectations and who, in building their macroeconomic models, stress the importance of **microfoundations**—the microeconomic behavior of individuals and firms. Two propositions that have attracted considerable attention to the new classical school are that (a) market prices adjust so quickly to changing situations that fluctuations are brief and mild and (b) markets operate so effectively to equate quantities demanded with quantities supplied that high levels of welfare are achieved.

The new classical school of economic thought refers to economists who use the theory of rational expectations and who stress the importance of microfoundations—the microeconomic behavior of individuals and firms. Two propositions associated with the new classical school are that prices are very flexible and that markets are very effective in equating quantities demanded and supplied.

Price Flexibility

The price-flexibility assumption is that prices adjust so quickly to changes in supply and/or demand that very little time is required for markets to move from one equilibrium to another. In the new classi-

cal model, a shift of a demand curve or a supply curve is recognized immediately by all traders in a market. Since traders the world over are linked by computer technology and satellite communications, prices move promptly to each new equilibrium. Also, and very importantly, it is suggested that institutional barriers, such as long-term contracts or legal requirements for advance notice of proposed actions, do not interfere significantly with price adjustments.[1]

According to the new classical school, prices adjust so quickly to changes in supply and demand that very little time is required for markets to move from one equilibrium to another.

Combining the propositions that (1) only demand or supply shifts that come as surprises affect the equilibrium level of real GNP, and (2) prices adjust quickly to changes in demand and supply, new classical economists conclude that fluctuations in employment and output from sudden or surprise changes in an economic variable are both moderate and of short duration. When surprises occur, firms and resource owners mistake price-level changes for changes in relative prices so that output and employment change. But surprise evaporates quickly, shifting the *AS* curve and returning equilibrium quickly to potential GNP. In the view of new classical economists, most economic fluctuations will be brief and moderate unless government intervenes or unless there is a deliberate attempt to force government to change its macroeconomic policies. In their view, government intervention is likely to do more harm than good, since political uncertainties inherent in government intervention delay needed adjustments in the economy itself.[2]

---

1. This assumption in particular is challenged by Keynesians.

2. The argument that shocks trigger economic fluctuations and that these fluctuations will be moderate and brief does not explain business cycles—the sequence of fluctuations in which each fluctuation has its origins in the previous fluctuation. The assumptions of rational expectations and price flexibility cast doubt on traditional explanations for cycles. To fill this gap, new classical economists have developed **real business cycle theories**, built upon patterns of changing labor productivity or labor supply.

New classical economists believe that fluctuations in employment and output from surprise changes in an economic variable are both moderate and brief unless government intervenes.

Market Clearing

A second proposition of the new classical school is that, at equilibrium, markets are "cleared." **Market clearing** means that, at the equilibrium price, no potential sellers who are willing and able to sell at that price are unable to carry out their desired transaction, and no buyers who are willing and able to buy at that price are unable to carry out their desired transaction. For example, in a labor market for some specified skill level and occupation, market clearing means that if the equilibrium wage rate is $12.85 per hour, every worker willing and able to work for this wage will be employed. There will be no excess supply or demand at equilibrium. At equilibrium, unemployment does not exist and neither does any labor shortage.[3]

Market clearing means that, at the equilibrium price, no potential sellers or buyers are unable to carry out their desired transactions. There will be no excess supply or demand at equilibrium; neither unemployment nor labor shortages exist.

Market clearing has powerful welfare implications. It means that, given existing demand and supply curves, the equilibrium price maximizes the quantity of the good or service demanded and supplied. At any above-equilibrium price, less would be exchanged because demanders are unwilling or unable to buy as much as they would at the equilibrium price. Similarly, a smaller quantity would be exchanged at any below-equilibrium price, because, in this case, suppliers are unwilling or unable to supply as much as they would at the equilibrium price. These conclusions follow because, in a free market, each party—the buyer as well as the

seller—has the power to veto the transaction. With the market-clearing assumption, when equilibrium exists, buyers are "on their demand curves" and sellers are "on their supply curves," meaning that the plans of each group are being fulfilled. Potential GNP is the best that can be achieved, given the microeconomic properties (competition, monopoly, etc.) of the individual markets that make up the economy. Lower volumes of real GNP are inferior because resources are wasted through unemployment. Higher volumes of real GNP are also inferior, because the extra employment is not worth its cost in forgone leisure activities. New classical economists conclude that, at equilibrium, resources are fully employed and welfare is maximized.

New classical economists conclude that, at equilibrium, resources are fully employed and welfare is maximized.

The two propositions—that prices adjust quickly to their equilibrium levels and that markets clear at equilibrium—combine to generate very powerful conclusions from the new classical model. The price-flexibility proposition suggests that deviations from potential GNP will be moderate and brief and that government intervention is not needed to achieve and maintain that level of economic activity. The market-clearing proposition suggests that potential GNP is a very satisfactory condition in terms of economic welfare. The policy implications of the new classical school are similar to those of the neoclassical school dominant prior to the Great Depression of the 1930s—that the economy tends normally to full employment and that there is no need of government intervention. All that is needed is to follow fixed rules that everyone understands.

The policy implications of the new classical model are similar to those of the neoclassical model dominant prior to the Great Depression—that the economy tends normally to full employment and that there is no need of government intervention.

Would new classical economists refuse to make use of monetary and fiscal instruments

---

3. We assume that supply and demand curves do not appear as horizontal lines on a graph.

should an emergency arise? This question has not, as yet, been put to the test. After the stock market crash of 1929, the economy actually suffered a severe and lengthy departure from potential GNP. But the stock market crash of 1987 was not followed by such problems. The question of emergencies to one side, the basic thrust of the new classical argument is simply that, in normal times, the economy can right itself quickly from minor disturbances and that government need not preside over day-to-day operation of the economy.

NEO-KEYNESIAN ECONOMICS

Chapters 10 and 11 presented certain basic features of Keynesian economics—the consumption function, the investment function, total planned expenditure, the Keynesian cross, and so on. That model dominated macroeconomic policymaking from 1945 into the 1960s, although it was persistently criticized by monetarist economists for its failure to recognize the importance of monetary variables in determining the equilibrium level of real GNP. Extended debates took place between Keynesian and monetarist economists during the 1960s. From these debates came more sophisticated Keynesian models, preserving the basic approach but giving greater importance to monetary variables. This expanded and more sophisticated model is call **neo-Keynesian economics.** Its primary difference from the original Keynesian model is that the "monetary" dimensions of the economy—the money supply and financial variables—are added to the original consumption, investment, government, and net export variables. In the macroeconomic turmoil of the 1970s and 1980s, it was not the original Keynesian model that contested with the new classical model of the macroeconomy. Instead it was the more powerful and sophisticated neo-Keynesian model.[4]

Neo-Keynesian economics preserves the basic approach of Keynesian economics but gives greater importance to monetary variables.

---

4. Many of Keynes's direct disciples call this sort of thing "bastard" Keynesianism.

The *IS-LM* System

Modern Keynesian economics is built around the **IS-LM system,** in which *I* stands for investment, *S* stands for saving, *L* stands for liquidity (the demand for money), and *M* stands for the money supply, that is, the quantity of money existing in the economy. The hyphen in *IS-LM* signifies the division of the model into two components, the *IS* component and the *LM* component. The *IS* portion incorporates the requirement that saving must equal investment at macroeconomic equilibrium. This is the "real goods" aspect of the economy. The *LM* portion brings in the demand and supply of money and the financial aspect of the economy. We shall first explain the *IS* component, then the *LM* component, and then bring the two together to show how the modern Keynesian model explains macroeconomic equilibrium in the economy.

Modern Keynesian economics is built around the *IS-LM* model. The *IS* portion of the model incorporates saving and investment as determinants of equilibrium GNP; the *LM* component incorporates the financial aspect of the economy.

The IS Curve The investment-saving, or real goods and services component of the economy is represented by the *IS* curve in panel (b) of Figure 3. The horizontal axis of this graph shows real GNP. The vertical axis shows the real rate of interest. The *IS* curve is not a cause-and-effect relationship between these variables but shows, instead, combinations that are mutually consistent and necessary for equilibrium to exist. In other words, *ceteris paribus*, for any specified level of real GNP, there is one and only one real interest rate that is consistent with equilibrium in the real goods and services ($C + I + G + X - Im$) component of the economy. The statement can also be made in reverse. *Ceteris paribus*, for any specified real rate of interest, there is one and only one level of real GNP that is consistent with equilibrium in the real goods and services component ($C + I + G + X - Im$) of the economy.

The two panels of Figure 3 illustrate how the *IS* curve is derived from the basic Keynesian-cross model presented in Chapter 10. The illustration begins at point *A* in panel (a), which represents mac-

FIGURE 3
Derivation of the *IS* Curve

In panel (a), point *A* represents equilibrium in the real component of the economy because total planned expenditure ($C + I + G + X - Im$)$_1$ and the value of real GNP are equal at $1,000 billion. Assuming that the real interest rate is 6 percent, this equilibrium is represented in panel (b) by point *A'*. At an interest rate lower than 6 percent, total planned expenditure would be greater, *ceteris paribus*, mainly because planned investment would be greater. Therefore, in panel (a), total planned expenditure with a 4 percent real rate of interest is represented by the ($C + I + G + X - Im$)$_2$ curve. Equilibrium in the real component now is at point *B* in panel (a), with real GNP of $1,200 billion. In panel (b), this new equilibrium is represented by point *B'*. Points *A'* and *B'* lie on the *IS* curve.

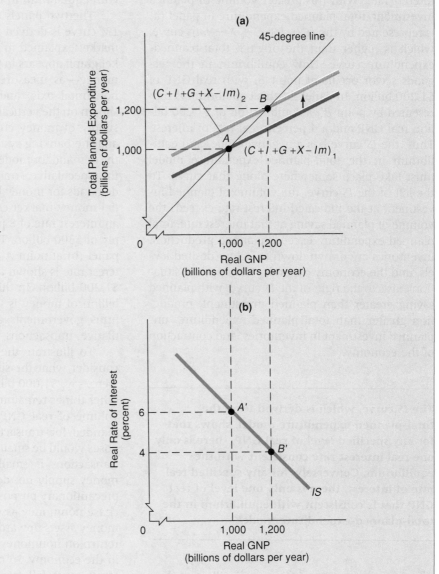

roeconomic equilibrium, according to the total-planned-expenditure model, at $1,000 billion of real GNP. At point *A*, total planned expenditure— ($C + I + G + X - Im$)$_1$—equals $1,000 billion, as shown on the vertical axis of the Keynesian-cross graph. With real GNP also at $1,000 billion, inventories are exactly at the levels planned by firms so, *ceteris paribus*, there is no reason for firms to change planned production in the next time period. In

panel (b), this equilibrium is represented at point *A'*. Point *A'* states that when real GNP is in equilibrium at $1,000 billion, there is some real rate of interest—6 percent in Figure 3—that prevails in the economy and balances planned saving and planned investment.

To identify a second point on the *IS* curve, consider what the situation would be if the interest rate were lower, say at 4 percent instead of 6 percent.

Other things being unchanged, the volume of planned investment would be greater at the lower interest rate. With this greater volume of planned investment, total planned expenditure in panel (a) is represented by the $(C + I + G + X - Im)_2$ curve, which is higher than the original total-planned-expenditure curve. Now equilibrium in the real goods sector occurs at point B, with real GNP of $1,200 billion. In panel (b) this equilibrium is represented by point B', a combination of $1,200 billion real GNP and a 4 percent real rate of interest. Thus, the IS curve has a negative slope, and equilibrium in the total-planned-expenditure model must take place somewhere along that curve. To the left of the IS curve, the volume of planned investment at the indicated interest rate exceeds the volume of planned saving at that interest rate, total planned expenditure exceeds planned production, inventories are drawn down to below-desired levels, and the economy expands. The opposite situation exists to the right of the IS curve, with planned saving greater than planned investment, production greater than total planned expenditure, unplanned investment in inventories, and contraction of the economy.

The IS curve, which is derived from the total-planned-expenditure model, shows that for any specified level of real GNP, there is only one real interest rate consistent with the equilibrium. Conversely, for any specified real rate of interest, there is only one level of real GNP that is consistent with equilibrium in the total-planned-expenditure model.

The LM Curve The LM curve is illustrated in panel (b) of Figure 4. As with the IS curve, the LM curve does not represent a cause-and-effect relationship between the real interest rate and the level of real GNP. Instead, it shows the combinations of the two variables that are consistent or necessary for equality between the quantity of money demanded and the quantity of money supplied. *Ceteris paribus*, for any given level of real GNP, there is one and only one real interest rate that is consistent with equilibrium in the money market. Con-

versely, for any given real interest rate, there is one and only one level of real GNP that is consistent with equilibrium in this market, *ceteris paribus*.

The two panels of Figure 4 illustrate how the LM curve is derived from the graph of the money market explained in Chapter 14. The money-market graph appears in panel (a). The real quantity of money—as measured by M1—is shown on the horizontal axis, and the real rate of interest is shown on the vertical axis. The MS curve shows the supply of money created by the Federal Reserve and the banking system, and the MD curve shows the demand for money as an asset as determined by the speculative, transactions, and precautionary demands for money balances. In panel (a) the initial money-market equilibrium is at point A, with an interest rate of 8 percent and a real money supply of $300 billion. This situation is represented in panel (b) at point A', where the 8 percent real interest rate is shown as consistent with real GNP of $1,200 billion. In this illustration, all of the $300 billion of money is willingly held by households, firms, governments, and foreigners for either speculative, transactions, or precautionary purposes.

To illustrate the derivation of the LM curve, consider what the situation would be if real GNP were, say, $1,000 billion instead of $1,200 billion, other things remaining unchanged. With a smaller volume of real GNP, the quantity of money demanded for transactions and precautionary purposes would be smaller as well, since the volume of transactions is smaller. The part of the existing money supply not demanded for transactions and precautionary purposes will be used instead to purchase nonmoney assets, driving the prices of nonmoney assets upward and lowering both the rate of return on nonmoney assets and the rate of interest in the economy. In our illustration, the rate of interest must fall from 8 percent to 6 percent to achieve equilibrium, *ceteris paribus*, when real GNP is $1,000 billion. This is illustrated by point B' in panel (b). What has happened is that the lower volume of real GNP has shifted the MD curve in panel (a) to the left (as shown by the arrow) enough to lower the real rate of interest to 6 percent. Otherwise, equilibrium would not have been achieved in the money market. The lower interest rate is necessary in order for the demand for money to match the $290 billion quantity of money now

FIGURE 4
Derivation of the LM Curve

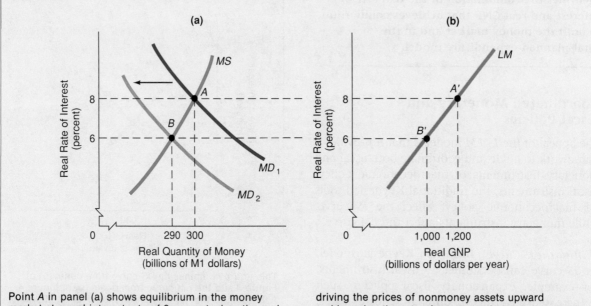

Point A in panel (a) shows equilibrium in the money market at a real interest rate of 8 percent when the real quantity of M1 money is $300 billion and real GNP is $1,200 billion. The equivalent situation is shown as point A' in panel (b). At a lower level of real GNP, less money is demanded for transactions and precautionary purposes and a greater portion of the available quantity of M1 money is used to purchase nonmoney assets,

driving the prices of nonmoney assets upward and lowering the rate of return on these assets and the real interest rate in the economy to 6 percent. This is illustrated by point B' in panel (b). The new situation is represented in panel (a) at point B. As shown by the arrow in panel (a), the lower real GNP has shifted the MD curve to the left enough to bring equilibrium in the money market at a real interest rate of 6 percent.

available in the economy. In this way, the *LM* curve displays all equilibrium combinations of the real rate of interest and real GNP. To the left of the *LM* curve, the real GNP is so low that, at the indicated rate of interest, the quantity of money demanded (L) is less than the quantity supplied (M), forcing real interest rates downward. To the right of the curve, real GNP is so large that the demand for money exceeds its supply, forcing real interest rates upward.

The *LM* curve shows the combinations of the real rate of interest and real GNP that equate the demand for money with the supply of money. For any given level of real GNP, there is only one real interest rate that will equate the demand and the supply of money. Conversely,

for any given real interest rate, there is only one level of real GNP that will provide this equality.

IS and LM Combined   Figure 5 brings together the *IS* and the *LM* curves developed in the preceding illustrations. The two curves intersect with real GNP of $1,000 billion and a real interest rate of 6 percent. According to the *IS-LM* system, this represents "full" equilibrium in the macroeconomy. The "real" economy (represented by the total-planned-expenditure model) is in equilibrium according to the *IS* curve, and the "financial" economy (represented by the money market) is in equilibrium according to the *LM* curve. No other rate of interest is consistent with equilibrium simultaneously in both dimensions of the economy.

The intersection of the *IS* and *LM* curves identifies the combination of the real rate of interest and real GNP that achieves equilibrium in both the money market and in the total-planned-expenditure model.

Coordinated Monetary and Fiscal Policies

The appeal of the *IS-LM* model is that it provides a framework to guide and coordinate both fiscal and monetary instruments of macroeconomic policy. Fiscal instruments, the traditional Keynesian tools for macroeconomic policy, affect the *IS* curve, while monetary instruments affect the *LM* curve.[5]

Shifting the IS Curve   In the neo-Keynesian model, the *IS* curve can be shifted by fiscal instruments. For example, expansionary fiscal policies, such as increased government purchases, lower taxes, or changes in tax laws that improve the after-tax profitability of investments, shift the *IS* curve to the right. With expansionary fiscal policies, at any given real rate of interest, the equilibrium level of real GNP is greater. If there is no accompanying ("accommodating") expansionary monetary policy, the *LM* curve remains stationary, and an expansionary fiscal policy results in macro-economic equilibrium moving upward and to the right along the *LM* curve. The result is higher real rates of interest and some increase in real GNP. The precise mixture of these two consequences depends on the slopes of the curves. Thus, the *IS-LM* system recognizes that the financial dimension of the economy can limit the real effects of expansionary fiscal policy.

Fiscal instruments shift the *IS* curve. The real effects of fiscal policy actions depend upon the slopes of the *IS* and *LM* curves.

Shifting the LM Curve   The *LM* curve can be shifted by monetary instruments, that is, by central

5. More advanced courses take up the questions of whether changes in *IS* can avoid also changing *LM,* and vice versa.

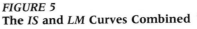

FIGURE 5
The *IS* and *LM* Curves Combined

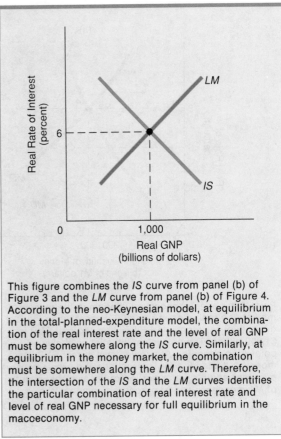

This figure combines the *IS* curve from panel (b) of Figure 3 and the *LM* curve from panel (b) of Figure 4. According to the neo-Keynesian model, at equilibrium in the total-planned-expenditure model, the combination of the real interest rate and the level of real GNP must be somewhere along the *IS* curve. Similarly, at equilibrium in the money market, the combination must be somewhere along the *LM* curve. Therefore, the intersection of the *IS* and the *LM* curves identifies the particular combination of real interest rate and level of real GNP necessary for full equilibrium in the macoeconomy.

bank policies affecting the real money supply. If the real money supply is increased, as the neo-Keynesians claim is possible through open market purchases, lower reserve requirements, and lower discount rates, the *LM* curve shifts to the right. A greater amount of money will be available, at any given real interest rate, for speculative, transactions, and precautionary purposes in the economy. If such an expansionary monetary policy is undertaken without any accompanying change in fiscal policy, macroeconomic equilibrium moves downward and to the right along the *IS* curve, resulting in lower real rates of interest and an expansion of real GNP. The precise mixture between these two outcomes depends on the slope of the *IS* and *LM* curves, that is, on the sensitivity of the economy to changes in real interest rates.

Monetary instruments shift the *LM* curve. The real effects of monetary policy actions depend upon the slopes of the *IS* and *LM* curves.

Shifting Both IS and LM   The most powerful implication of the *IS-LM* model points to simultaneous expansionary applications of *both* fiscal and monetary policies. If both curves are shifted to the right, the *IS-LM* model suggests that real GNP can be increased without an accompanying increase in real interest rates. In other words, the effectiveness of fiscal instruments would not be limited by the financial elements in the economy, nor would the effectiveness of monetary instruments be limited by unsupportive fiscal policies.

If the *IS* and *LM* curves can be shifted separately, the neo-Keynesian model suggests that it is possible to adjust the locations of the two curves to achieve some ideal combination of the real rate of interest and the real GNP. For example, real GNP could be tuned to achieve potential GNP as determined by macroeconomic policymakers. At the same time, the real rate of interest could be made consistent with the profitability of investments and the preferences of suppliers in loanable-funds markets.

If the *IS* and *LM* curves can be shifted independently, macroeconomic policy can pursue both output and interest-rate goals.

Neo-Keynesian Economics and the Price Level

Our explanation of the *IS-LM* model was carried out under the assumption of a constant price level. This enabled us to use "real" interest rates on the vertical axes of *IS-LM* graphs and "real" GNP on their horizontal axes. But the price level cannot be ignored in macroeconomics, just as individual prices cannot be ignored in microeconomics.

As you remember, the price level is an important variable in the aggregate-demand and aggregate-supply approach to macroeconomic equilibrium. But the *IS-LM* model does not use the price

level as an independent variable. Instead, price levels usually are policy variables in the neo-Keynesian system. If the goal is a stable price level, the *IS-LM* model must adapt the target GNP to match the economy's potential real GNP. Target levels of *nominal* GNP may be selected by policymakers. Such nominal targets incorporate inflation-rate considerations as well as real employment and output considerations and must consider the slope of the economy's aggregate-supply curve.

NEO-KEYNESIAN VERSUS NEW CLASSICAL ECONOMICS

During the 1970s and 1980s, both neo-Keynesian and new classical economists focused attention on the supply side of the economy. Both made use of aggregate-demand and aggregate-supply formulations. The basic differences between these two schools of modern macroeconomic thought revolve around three propositions: (1) how important are rational expectations? (2) how flexible are prices? and (3) do markets always clear?

How Important Are Rational Expectations?

Neo-Keynesian economists contend that rational expectations cannot completely eliminate the systematic effectiveness of government demand-side intervention in the economy. They grant that the society may be more knowledgeable about the price-level consequences of demand-side initiatives than it was in earlier times. They also grant that large corporations and labor unions employ competent economists who forecast the effects of economic events and government policy actions. Nevertheless, neo-Keynesian economists argue that economics is not an exact science and that these forecasts are subject to large variations. Therefore, neo-Keynesians conclude that expectations are significantly less "rational" than supposed by new classical economists. Furthermore, they conclude that the aggregate-supply curve does have a significant positive slope, and that shifts of this curve do *not* take place as quickly as supposed by the new classicals.

Because the *AS* curve has significant positive slope and does not shift quickly, neo-Keynesian economists contend that systematic government demand-side initiatives are effective and are not immediately counteracted by shifts of the aggregate-supply curve. In the neo-Keynesian view, policy-induced shifts of the aggregate-demand curve result in changes in real GNP and the volume of employment.

Neo-Keynesian economists contend that actual economic behavior is not as "rational" as the new classical economists claim and that systematic government demand-side policy initiatives are effective.

How Flexible are Prices?

Neo-Keynesian economists are emphatic in their criticism of the new classical view that markets adjust quickly to changes in demand and/or supply, that is, to the proposition that prices are flexible. They believe that rigidities and barriers to rapid price changes are significant in many parts of the economy. Rigidities and barriers are especially important, they say, in resource markets, where firms have long-term contracts and understandings for labor services and where established practices, or institutions, delay price adjustments. They argue that employers postpone layoffs and wage-rate reductions in recessions because of a sense of obligation to their employees, with whom they wish to maintain good relations, and because of concern for public opinion. Also, since firms do not want the expense of recruiting and training new employees when the recession ends, they hold on to their employees even when current sales are low. In good times, overtime work is done and wage-rate increases or expansions in employment are delayed until firms are sure that the expansion will continue long enough to justify long-term commitments to higher wage rates and additional employees. Retirement programs, unemployment insurance, and fringe benefit packages add to the costs of hiring and firing and are additional discouragements to layoffs and hirings.[6]

Keynesian economists criticize the new classical belief in price flexibility. They believe that rigidities and barriers to rapid price changes are significant in many parts of the economy.

From your study of aggregate demand and aggregate supply, you know that price flexibility is an important determinant of both the slope and the shifts of the aggregate-supply curve. The less flexible the prices, especially in resource markets, the flatter the aggregate-supply curve, since lags in resource prices contribute to large changes in profit margins and encourage increases or decreases in production. Thus, in the neo-Keynesian view, aggregate-demand shifts cause large fluctuations in employment and real GNP. Also, price inflexibility causes fluctuations to last longer. More time elapses before the aggregate-supply curve completes its "catch-up" shift. Neo-Keynesians argue that price inflexibility means that serious fluctuations take place and that large amounts of GNP are lost if government does not intervene to moderate the consequences of shocks to the economy. Moreover, since Keynesians discount the impact of rational expectations, they believe that such intervention is effective.

Neo-Keynesians argue that price inflexibility means that serious fluctuations take place and that large amounts of GNP are lost if government does not intervene to moderate the consequences of shocks to the economy.

Do Markets Always Clear?

Neo-Keynesians believe that markets do not clear as completely as claimed by the new classicals, Their doubt about market clearing is based on bar-

---

6. Price inflexibility may also arise from the expectation that government policy will bail out depressed sectors of the economy or that political pressure can force government to do so.

riers and restrictions to mobility which, they say, exist in most markets. All economists recognize that excess demand or excess supply exist when markets are in disequilibrium and prices are on the move toward their equilibrium levels. In these situations, some willing and able buyers or sellers are unable to complete transactions at the going price. All agree also that frequent shifts of demand and supply take place so that equilibrium is a "moving target." Barriers and restrictions on resource mobility slow the approach to equilibrium and cause losses in potential GNP. Neo-Keynesians believe that new classicals underestimate the seriousness of barriers and restrictions to mobility and expect equilibrium to be approached more quickly and with less lost output than in fact is the case.

A slow approach to equilibrium is not the only problem that arises from barriers and institutional arrangements, including monopoly and monopsony, that limit resource mobility. Discrimination, lack of information, and immobility contribute to serious market failures. Restrictions that deny resources access to markets that would best utilize their capabilities force these resources into other markets, where their presence creates further distortion.

Neo-Keynesians believe that because of barriers and restrictions to mobility, markets do not clear as completely as the new classical economists claim.

The notion that markets do an imperfect job even at equilibrium is not seriously open to doubt. Perfect knowledge and perfect mobility are difficult to envision. The real questions, therefore, cannot be answered simply "yes" or "no," and one cannot find a yes-or-no dividing line between new classicals and neo-Keynesians on this point. Instead, the issues are "How serious are imperfections in the market system?" "To what extent should market processes be supplemented by government intervention?" "How can markets be made to work better?" "To what extent should the market system be altered by planning?" Neo-Keynesians differ from new classicals on the answers to these questions. They tend to favor more government intervention

than do members of the new classical school. But economists working in the Keynesian tradition also disagree among themselves on the seriousness of market imperfections and on the desirability of government intervention. Intervention through traditional fiscal and monetary policy is needed, according to neo-Keynesians, but most do not argue that large increases of government involvement in specific markets or major extensions of central economic planning are also needed. Most neo-Keynesians agree that excessive government intervention can do more harm than good.

According to neo-Keynesians, intervention through traditional fiscal and monetary policy is needed, but not large increases of government involvement in specific markets or major extensions of central economic planning.

POST-KEYNESIAN ECONOMICS

Among modern Keynesians, a small but occasionally vocal group of economists called **post-Keynesians** are strongly in favor of permanent government direction of both the macro- and the microeconomy, taking positions close to Marxian socialism. They believe that market failures are frequent and serious and that government intervention is therefore desirable. Post-Keynesians believe that the basic message of J. M. Keynes in the 1930s should not have been the model that he offered to resolve the short-run crisis of the Great Depression, but rather his diagnosis of the structural problems that cause crises in market economies. These include the monopolization of product and labor markets, which brings price rigidities, as well as the highly concentrated and panic-prone collection of financial institutions that collapse in hard times and turn recessions into deep and long depressions. Post-Keynesians contend that monetary and fiscal policies deal only with the symptoms of a sick economic system and fail to attack the underlying causes of the sickness. They claim that Keynes himself "did not understand the *General Theory*"—by which they mean that he did not understand its longer-term implications. Prominent post-Keynesians include Joan Robinson (1901–1983) in England and John Kenneth Galbraith (1908-   ) in the United States.

Post-Keynesians propose greatly expanded government intervention in the economy, including detailed regulation of major industries, comprehensive systems of incentives and penalties imposed through tax laws and government expenditure programs, **incomes policies** (comprehensive wage, price, and profit controls), and a substantial amount of economic planning by the government. Post-Keynesians operate within the context of a capitalist-market economic system substantially modified by government regulations, income redistribution, and welfare-state measures.

Post-Keynesian economists take positions close to Marxian socialism in that they favor permanent government direction of both the macro- and the microeconomy.

SUPPLY-SIDE ECONOMICS

So far in this chapter, government intervention (supported in varying degrees by neo-Keynesian economists and generally disapproved of by new classical economists) has been limited to the demand side of economic activity. Now we examine **supply-side economics,** which argues that government actions affecting the aggregate-supply curve are at least as important as government actions affecting the aggregate-demand curve—and probably more. Supply-side economists were prominent in the first Reagan administration (1981–1985), when they actively promoted reductions in tax rates intended to stimulate investment and work incentives. On that basis they claimed substantial credit for the strong performance of the economy during the second Reagan administration (1985–1989).

FIGURE 6
Supply-Side Economics

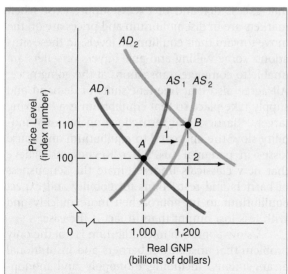

At point A, the economy is in macroeconomic equilibrium, producing its potential GNP of $1,000 billion a year at a price level of 100. Supply-side policies increase production capabilities and shift the aggregate-supply curve from AS_1 to AS_2 (shown by arrow 1). A policy of low interest rates requires some increase in the price level in order to increase potential GNP. Tax cuts and low interest rates shift the aggregate-demand curve from AD_1 to AD_2 (shown by arrow 2), bringing macroeconomic equilibrium at point B, with real output of $1,200 billion and a price level of 110.

Supply-side economists argue that government actions affecting the aggregate-supply curve are at least as important as government actions affecting the aggregate-demand curve.

Figure 6 illustrates the basic propositions of supply-side economics. Point A represents an equilibrium situation for an economy producing its potential GNP but operating without the advantages of supply-side economic policies. The price-level index number is 100, and $1,000 billion of real GNP is produced per year. Supply-side economists contend that the economy can do better than $1,000 billion of real GNP. They argue that properly conceived and executed government policies can shift both the aggregate-demand curve and the aggregate-supply curve to the right, moving macroeconomic equilibrium from point A to point B.

How are these results to be obtained? First, they say that government regulations and taxes on business have, for years, restricted the free exercise of entrepreneurship and profit seeking. To correct for this, supply-siders advocate deregulation, freeing producers from the red tape of government bureaucracy, and reductions in tax rates under the corporation income tax. These moves would give a green light to business investment and innovations. Second, supply-side economists advocate lower tax rates under the individual income tax to increase the after-tax returns to both working and saving. They especially favor lowering *marginal* tax rates—the rates payable on the *next* dollar that a person might earn. By lowering marginal tax rates on the returns on savings—and by going even further and offering tax shelters for saving—supply-siders expect to increase the amount of saving, thus providing funds to finance increased investment by firms. Some would exempt saving altogether by allowing it full deductibility in calculating income taxes. By lowering marginal tax rates on income from work, they expect to increase work incentives. Third, supply-side economists favor monetary policies that keep interest rates low in order to encourage investment and modern production facilities.

Supply-siders advocate deregulation, reductions in corporate and individual income-tax rates, and low interest rates.

The combination of these programs, they say, will increase potential GNP and shift the aggregate-supply curve to the right, as illustrated in Figure 6 by the shift from AS_1 to AS_2 (arrow 1). They grant that the easy-money policies used to keep interest rates low may cause an increase in the price level, but this, they say, is a fair price to pay for greater output.

Although supply-side economists emphasize shifts of aggregate-supply curves, they do not ignore aggregate demand. In their models, the aggregate-demand curve shifts to the right at the same time that the aggregate-supply curve shifts in that direction. They expect tax cuts and low interest rates to increase aggregate demand. In Figure 6, arrow 2 shows aggregate demand shifting from AD_1 to AD_2—just enough to produce macroeconomic equilibrium at the new potential GNP of $1,200 billion.

This "best-case" scenario usually is not achieved in the real world, of course. The tax reductions of the early Reagan years were implemented piecemeal rather than all at once, and supply-siders contend that this weakened their impact on incentives. Furthermore, supply-siders complain that restrictive monetary policies, carried out in the early 1980s to fight inflationary pressures in the economy, denied demand-side support for their programs aimed at shifting aggregate supply. The economy suffered a severe recession in the early 1980s, and supply-siders argued that their programs were not given a fair test. When the economy recovered, starting in 1982, it was not clear whether credit should go to delayed reactions from the earlier supply-side initiatives, to the stimulative effects of large government deficits arising from the combination of tax cuts and increases in military spending, or to both.

Say's Identity Again?

Doubters of the supply-side approach say that by shifting aggregate demand just enough to hit their target, supply-siders come close to reasserting **Say's Identity,** that supply creates its own demand. These critics say that there is no reason to expect that the expansion of production and the fiscal measures that brought it about will necessarily lead to just the right amount of aggregate demand.

The supply-siders' answer is much like that of physicians about "normal" body temperatures or the normal values of any other life sign. That is, they say that any failure to hit the target is a symptom of something that is wrong with the working of the economy—such as overly high tax rates or excessive regulation. So if aggregate demand doesn't shift to the proper level, it is not the policy but "something else" in the economy that must be corrected. When that "something else" is corrected, then Say's Identity will return, just as body temperature returns to 98.6 degrees when measles or pneumonia has been cured.

The Laffer Curve

A second problem for supply-side economics has to do with the possibility that tax cuts will cause large government deficits and that financing these deficits will raise interest rates, crowding out the private investment that supply-siders hope to increase through their tax cuts.

The supply-side counterargument is based on the **Laffer curve,** pictured in Figure 7. The vertical axis shows the net tax revenues of government, and the horizontal axis shows the average net tax rate. The curve itself displays Arthur Laffer's idea of how net tax revenues respond to changes in average tax rates.[7] No revenue would be collected if the tax rate were zero. But neither would any be collected at a tax rate of 100 percent, since no one would find it worthwhile to work if government took all the earnings. In between, the Laffer curve suggests that tax revenues will rise as average tax rates rise, but only up to a point. If tax rates rise above a certain level, the level corresponding to the peak of the curve, the work-discouraging effects of rate increases more than offset their revenue-raising effects, and total revenue falls.

The Laffer curve shows how net tax revenues respond to changes in average tax rates. The curve suggests that if tax rates rise above a certain level, the work-discouraging effects of rate increases more than offset their revenue-raising effects.

Many supply-side economists, among them Arthur Laffer himself, claim that the United States

7. Arthur Laffer, formerly professor of economics at the University of Southern California, is at this writing an economic consultant.

FIGURE 7
The Laffer Curve

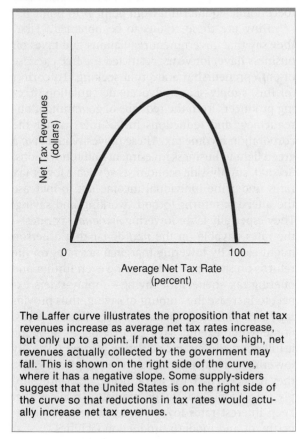

The Laffer curve illustrates the proposition that net tax revenues increase as average net tax rates increase, but only up to a point. If net tax rates go too high, net revenues actually collected by the government may fall. This is shown on the right side of the curve, where it has a negative slope. Some supply-siders suggest that the United States is on the right side of the curve so that reductions in tax rates would actually increase net tax revenues.

and many other countries are on the right-hand side of the curve. If this is true, supply-side policies can avoid large deficits, and there need be no crowding out of private investment. Lower tax rates could in fact increase tax revenues. Many economists, however, are not persuaded that the United States really is on the right-hand side of the curve.

Economics in Focus

Reagan and the Supply Side: Success or Failure?

Although the policies of Ronald Reagan's two administrations were not a pure exercise in supply-side economics, they were the closest the United States has come to direct application of supply-side principles. For that reason the successes and failures of "Reaganomics" sparked an economic debate that has continued to simmer since Reagan left office.

Supporters of Reagan and his supply-side advisers have pointed, first of all, to the long expansionary period beginning in late 1982—the longest such period in U.S. history. They note that 19 million new jobs were created between 1982 and 1989; that domestic investment increased remarkably; that, in the words of the 1989 *Economic Report of the President*, there was "an explosion of small business growth"; and that manufacturing productivity rose at an average annual rate of 4.4 percent, compared to 2.3 percent in the 1970s. Just as important, inflation was kept under control despite the expansion. And, it was flattering to Reagan when all of the major industrial nations known as the Group of Seven followed his lead in reducing tax rates.

But critics have been quick to point out the downside of Reaganomics. There was a sharp recession in 1982. The nation continued to borrow heavily from foreigners, though less so than during the Carter years. There were large, continuing budget deficits, which failed to disappear despite the administration's rosy projections. Ultimately the national debt reached astounding proportions—over two and a half trillion dollars by the time Reagan left office. Many analysts claim that the United States is now the largest debtor nation in the world, although the validity of that label is hotly disputed by the supply-siders. Perhaps most important, President Reagan's economic theories were partly responsible for his decision to slash social and educational programs. The number of homeless swelled across the country; cities increasingly struggled to maintain basic services with reduced federal support; and educators painted a picture of school systems in grave danger because of federal funding cuts and government indifference. Some of Reagan's most intense critics charged him simply with befriending the rich and abandoning the poor.

A few analysts have tried to reach a balanced assessment of Reagan's policies. They note that the national debt, huge as it may be, does not seem so threatening when it is seen as a percentage of GNP; in those terms, in fact, it is no worse than during the Kennedy administration, and far better than during World War II. Of course, there was no world war during the Reagan years. His war was against the stagflation of the 1970s—and he clearly emerged the winner. Whether he paid too high a price is the issue that still confronts us.

Sources: Paul Craig Roberts, "It's Time to Face Facts: Supply-Side Was a Smash," *Business Week,* February 6, 1989, p. 14; Paul Craig Roberts, "While Critics Carp, the Supply-Side Revolution Sweeps On," *Business Week,* April 25, 1988, p. 15; Peter Brimelow with Lisa Scheer, "Is the Reagan Prosperity for Real?" *Forbes,* October 31, 1988, pp. 85–90.

SUMMARY

1. The assumption of rational expectations is that people form their expectations about future price levels through the use of economic analysis. When applied to an aggregate-demand and aggregate-supply model, the rational-expectations assumption suggests that the aggregate-supply curve shifts as a direct result of policy-initiated shifts of the aggregate-demand curve. An alternative statement of this result is that the aggregate-supply curve is vertical. (See pages 370–371 and Figure 1, page 371.)

2. When combined with assumptions that prices and wage rates are flexible, the theory of rational expectations suggests that discretionary fiscal and monetary policies of government do not change real variables, such as output and employment, but result only in changes in the price level. (See page 371.)

3. The neo-Ricardian application of the rational-expectations theory suggests that taxpayers interpret government budget deficits as promising higher taxes in the future and respond by increasing current saving and reducing current consumption. Therefore, tax finance and deficit finance have equivalent macroeconomic effects. Crowding out comes from government expenditure, no matter how financed. The theory also suggests that the availability of deficit finance does not bias government-expenditure decisions. (See page 372.)

4. The Lucas supply curve illustrates a positive relationship between unexpected changes in the price level and the quantity of real GNP supplied per year. This relationship is based on the proposition that firms interpret unexpected changes in the price level as changes in the relative prices of their products and expand or contract output accordingly. (See page 373 and Figure 2, page 373.)

5. A school of economic thought consists of economists who employ the same or similar theories and who agree with one another much of the time about economic policy. New classical economists make extensive use of the theory of rational expectations and stress the microeconomic foundations of their macroeconomic models. They contend that prices are flexible and that markets clear so that markets operate effectively in equating quantities demanded and quantities supplied. At

equilibrium, unemployment does not exist. (See pages 373–374.)

6. The assumption of price flexibility suggests that fluctuations in output and employment are moderate and brief, provided that no deliberate attempt is made to force government to change its policies, thereby increasing uncertainty and delaying needed adjustments. (See page 374.)

7. The assumption of market clearing leads to the conclusion that, at equilibrium, the quantities exchanged in markets maximize economic welfare, given the degrees of monopoly or competition present in individual markets. Market clearing suggests that full employment is achieved at potential GNP. (See page 375.)

8. Neo-Keynesian economics extends the traditional Keynesian analysis of total-planned-expenditure to include, as well, the monetary dimension of the economy. In the IS-LM model, the IS component deals with total-planned-expenditure ($C + I + G + X - Im$) and the LM portion deals with the money market. (See page 376.)

9. The intersection of the IS and the LM curves identifies the real rate of interest and the level of real GNP that provide simultaneous equilibrium in both the real and the financial components of the economy. (See pages 376–380 and Figures 3, 4, and 5, pages 377, 379, and 380.)

10. Neo-Keynesian economists contend that the theory of rational expectations overstates the extent to which the consequences of government initiatives are counteracted by shifts of the aggregate-supply curve. They also reject the new classical assumptions of price flexibility and market clearing. Price inflexibility increases the severity of economic fluctuations. Because markets fail to clear, equilibrium does not employ all resources. (See pages 381–383.)

11. There are varying views among modern Keynesians about the seriousness of price inflexibilities and failures of markets to clear and on the extent to which government intervention is desirable. Generally, neo-Keynesians are more favorable to government intervention than new classical economists. (Sees page 382–383.)

12. Post-Keynesian economists believe that fundamental problems in market economies cause fluctuations and magnify recessions into severe depressions. They advocate substantial government

intervention in the economy. (See pages 383–384.)

13. Supply-side economics focuses on shifting the aggregate-supply curve to the right, offering greater real GNP at any given price level. Deregulation and lower marginal tax rates on both corporations and individuals are advocated in order to provide greater incentives for innovation, entrepreneurship, and work. Supply-side economists were prominent in the first Reagan administration and claim that their policies were effective even though not fully implemented. (See pages 384–385 and Figure 6, page 385.)

14. Critics contend that supply-side economics comes close to reasserting Say's Identity. The Laffer curve suggests that tax-rate reductions need not reduce government tax collections. (See pages 385–386 and Figure 7, page 386.)

KEY TERMS

incomes policies: comprehensive wage, price, and profit controls that implement economic planning (page 384).

IS-LM system: a model used in modern Keynesian economics; the *IS* curve incorporates the equilibrium requirements of the Keynesian total-planned-expenditure model, and the *LM* curve incorporates the requirements for equilibrium in the money market (page 376).

Laffer curve: a curve that shows how net tax revenues respond to changes in average tax rates (page 386).

Lucas supply curve: a curve that shows that unexpected changes in the price level lead to changes in the quantity of real GNP supplied (page 373).

market clearing: the proposition that at the equilibrium price, no potential sellers who are willing and able to sell at that price are unable to carry out their desired transaction, and no buyers who are willing and able to buy at that price are unable to carry out their desired transaction (page 375).

microfoundations: the microeconomic behavior of individuals and firms that lie behind macroeconomic models (page 374).

neo-Keynesian economics: a school of economic thought that preserves the basic Keynesian approach but includes monetary variables as well (page 376).

neo-Ricardian: an application of the rational-expectations theory that says that the method used to finance government expenditure does not matter (page 372).

new classical: a school of economic thought that employs the theory of rational expectations and accepts the propositions that prices adjust quickly and that markets clear at equilibrium (page 374).

post-Keynesian: economists who are in favor of permanent government direction of both the macro- and the microeconomy; they take positions close to Marxian socialism (page 383).

real business cycle theories: explanations of economic fluctuations based on patterns of changing labor productivity or labor supply (page 374).

Say's Identity: the view that supply creates its own demand (page 385).

school of economic thought: a group of economists who employ the same or similar theories and who agree with one another much of the time about economic policy (page 373).

supply-side economics: a school of economic thought that states that government actions affecting the aggregate-supply curve are at least as important as government actions affecting the aggregate-demand curve (page 384).

theory of rational expectations: a theory that proposes that people learn from their mistakes and use conventional economic principles to make their forecasts, following a rational reasoning process about how one thing leads to another in economics (page 370).

DISCUSSION QUESTIONS

1. List three forecasts that you might want to make. Examples: the weather for a picnic next Saturday, the score of your next home football game, the grade you will earn on the next exam. Make two forecasts for each subject, one on an adaptive-expectations basis and the other on a rational-expectations basis. What arguments appear in the rational-expectations forecast that do not appear in the adaptive-expectations forecast?

2. Construct an aggregate-demand and aggregate-supply graph, labeling the axes and the curves carefully. Assuming that your indicated equilibrium has prevailed for a long time, discuss and illustrate on the graph what would happen if an election put in office a political party that everyone expects will pursue expansionary macroeconomic policies.

3. Discuss whether a government deficit incurred today will lead to higher taxes on the next generation of taxpayers. Then consider whether that coming generation will actually pay high taxes or whether their government will sell new securities and use the money to pay off the bonds issued today. What does the neo-Ricardian application of rational-expectations theory suggest that taxpayers in each generation do?

4. Construct a Lucas supply curve, carefully labeling the axes. Suppose that prices increase and that you are an entrepreneur and, as such, correctly judge that it is an increase in the general price level. Assuming perfect price flexibility and no lags in resource prices, what change, if any, will you make in the volume of output of your firm? Are you better off or worse off than entrepreneurs who mistake the rise in the price level for a rise in the relative price of their products?

5. Discuss the similarities between the new classical school of economic thought of the 1980s and the neoclassical school of the 1920s. If a contractionary demand shock were to occur today, do you believe that the new classical prescriptions would be the same as those of the neoclassicals early in the Great Depression of the 1930s? Explain.

6. Without looking at Figure 3, construct a Keynesian-cross graph and a companion graph for the *IS* curve. Explain and illustrate what happens if government purchases are increased. Why is it important to consider possible effects of this action on the price level?

7. Without looking at Figure 4, construct a money-market graph and a companion graph for the *LM* curve. Explain and illustrate what happens if there occurs an autonomous shift to the right of the demand-for-money curve. What might cause such a shift of the *MD* curve?

8. List three contemporary schools of macroeconomic thought. Arrange these groups in order of the degree of intervention that they believe appropriate for government in modern market economies. How does this listing relate to the question of market clearing?

9. Consider leftward shifts of the aggregate-supply curve due to (a) external shocks, (b) catch-up from lags in wage rates and resource prices, (c) anticipated results of government policy actions to increase aggregate demand, and (d) realization that what was thought to be a change in relative prices was actually a change in the price level. For each of these, note the theories and/or schools of thought that recognize and deal with that shift.

18

Macroeconomics as a Branch of Knowledge

Preview This chapter concludes our explanation of basic macroeconomics. We try to show that macroeconomics is neither cut and dried nor in shambles but a developing science somewhere between these extremes. The chapter is built around several questions that, we believe, provide useful food for thought about macroeconomics.

We begin by asking if macroeconomics is practical. We suggest that a practical application of macroeconomics lies in the area of public policy and citizenship. Next we discuss what it means for a discipline to be "scientific" and note that disciplines differ in their degrees of maturity in this regard—macroeconomics being neither the least nor the most mature. Since science deals with what "is" rather than with what "ought to be," we proceed to an elementary explanation of how macroeconomists forecast the volume of economic activity for a coming time period.

If macroeconomics is practical and scientific, perhaps it can offer insights about matters that may be important in the 1990s, such as the national debt. Is the debt primarily a burden on the generation that contracted it, or does the debt constitute a burden that one generation of citizens is able to pass on to later generations of citizens? What about deficits? Should the Constitution be amended to prohibit deficits in the federal government budget?

Finally, we offer some thoughts and forecasts about macroeconomic problems that may face President George Bush. What sorts of macroeconomic crises may arise during his term or terms of office? Which would be most difficult to resolve? How would concerted efforts at deficit reduction affect these potential problems? In the world of political reality, how may the president and the Congress deal with the deficit?

IS MACROECONOMICS PRACTICAL?

Over and above idle curiosity, people have two sets of reasons for interest in their economy. One set arises from *direct* participation in the system—as suppliers and consumers of its outputs and as suppliers and demanders of inputs. The other set arises from *indirect* participation in the political economy, as voters in elections both national and local and perhaps as officeholders or civil servants.

The balance between these interests is usually different in macroeconomics than in microeconomics. As a direct participant, one's interest tends to be concentrated on immediately practical issues related to the particular goods and services one principally buys and sells—one's wage or salary, the prices of food and clothing, the sale or rental value of one's house or apartment. These are primarily microeconomic matters. But as an indirect participant in the economy—as a voter, civil servant, or legislator—the macroeconomic side enters more strongly, at least at the national level of policy formulation and administration. Perhaps, by reason of the primacy of our direct interests over our indirect ones, macroeconomics appears less "practical" than microeconomics. "Supply and demand," for example, means more to more people than "saving and investment" or even "unemployment and inflation."

As a direct participant in the economy, one's interest is usually concentrated on microeconomic issues related to the particular goods and services one buys and sells. As an indirect participant, macroeconomic issues assume more importance.

IS MACROECONOMICS SCIENTIFIC?

In this age of science, it is believed important to claim for any subject of study that it is, at least partially, scientific. By this we mean that it has an objective, factual, and systematic basis. Any admission that one's specialty is less than scientific equates it with hocus-pocus and mumbo-jumbo.

What Does It Mean to Be Scientific?

Science is about what *is* rather than what *ought* to be.[1] Also, most sciences, or most branches of science, make major use of the method of controlled experiment, although astronomy can rarely do this, nor can mathematics.

Some sciences are **pure** or theoretical, and others **applied.** One characteristic of applied sciences like medicine—despite its groundwork of chemistry and biology—is that their practices extend well beyond their theoretical bases in pure science. Medical practitioners use devices they cannot yet justify scientifically, under the rubric of "It works, but we don't yet know why." Sometimes later advances justify such practices, and sometimes they repudiate them. Few features of medicine seem less scientific than the doctor's "bedside manner," which nevertheless seems to accelerate (or retard) recovery. Few medical practices, however, seem more ludicrous than the use of leeches—a standard procedure for centuries.

The several branches of science have developed in different places and at different rates of progress. It seems obvious, for example, that physics and astronomy are further advanced in their scientific aspects than are psychology and sociology. (This is not to deny the importance of scientific elements in either of the last two disciplines as currently studied and practiced.) One irritating sign of a science's immaturity is the unsatisfactory nature of any "unified field" theory interrelating its several branches. The division between micro- and macroeconomics is an example of this defect; perhaps your generation can remedy it. But even physics has a similar difficulty; the great Albert Einstein spent much of his later years in a (futile) attempt to unify nuclear physics with the "ordinary" physics of mechanics, electricity, sound, heat and light.

---

1. Life would be easier for many engineers, for example, if all numbers were perfect squares, or if *pi* were 3 instead of 3.14159, or if Planet Earth completed its annual circuit round the sun in precisely 365 days.

But a science need not develop fully to become scientific. An embryonic science following false leads is as scientific as an adult one with all its problems solved and no loose ends for the next generation of scientists. The Ptolemaic cosmology, placing the earth at the center of the universe, was a scientific system—and an impressive one. For centuries, it was useful as a basis for forecasting such phenomena as the phases of the moon, eclipses of the sun, and the positions of stars and planets in the sky as seen from different points on the surface of the earth. The Newtonian (or Copernican) cosmology that displaced it is a *better* scientific system that does a better job of forecasting a wider range of phenomena with a somewhat simpler kit of tools. Quite generally, a theory, *T*, retains its scientific status even after displacement by superior theory *T'*. The fact of displacement does not deprive either a theory (such as Keynesian) or its field (macroeconomics) of scientific status. A more developed science may perhaps expect fewer displacements than a less developed one, but we should not forget the modifications of classical Newtonian physics in the twentieth century.

A scientific theory retains its scientific status even after displacement by a superior theory.

Nonscientific Aspects of Macroeconomics

If, to become a full-fledged science, a discipline must shed all its nonscientific aspects, the scientific status of macroeconomics is less than fully established. Let us see why this may be so by considering the macroeconomic effects of unanticipated demand and supply shocks—a major earthquake (Japan, 1923), a major drought (United States, 1988), the emergence of OPEC (1973), "black Thursday" and "black Monday" on Wall Street (1929 and 1987).

Analysis of the macroeconomic effects of such shocks cannot be confined within the limits of impersonal and automatic economic systems moving along growth paths. That is, analysis cannot be confined to scientific models. It must add estimates of the nature, size, and efficiency of highly personal and individual policy responses of agencies and people all over the world—presidents, kings, dictators, Lords and Commons and Congresses, finance ministers and central bankers and "gray eminences." Who are the authorities, worldwide? Are they wise, mad, or something in between? How much authority can they or will they exercise? Will they act in unison or at cross-purposes? Answering such questions involves us in "economic psychiatry," which (if a science at all) is less developed than macroeconomics. Such are the limitations of macroeconomics as a pure science.

Analysis of the macroeconomic effects of unanticipated supply and demand shocks cannot be confined to scientific models; it must also take into account the highly personal policy responses of agencies and people all over the world.

WHAT ABOUT FORECASTING?

We can look at **quantitative economic forecasting**—predicting the values of economic variables through systematic analysis of empirically estimated relationships—as a rough-and-ready test of the scientific validity of macroeconomics. Astronomy is an advanced and reputable science because astronomers' forecasts of tides, solar eclipses, and the appearance of certain key comets are so accurate. Meteorology has advanced by leaps and bounds in the computer age, because weather forecasts can take more variables into account, becoming more accurate for longer time periods and for smaller areas. Macroeconomic forecasts, however, have lagged in public esteem and may continue to do so indefinitely. Nonetheless, the same private citizens, public agencies, and business firms who make fun of economic forecasts also feel called upon to make them, or even to purchase forecasts made by specialized forecasting companies.

A note of caution is in order when dealing with forecasting. Economic forecasts are useful only insofar as they are known and acted upon, yet reactions to forecasts may either confirm or falsify the forecasts themselves. In the nineteenth century, for example, 1837, 1847, and 1857 were all years of recession or depression, whose ten-year periodicity gave rise to "sunspot" theories of economic fluctuations. Another depression was accordingly forecast for 1867. People appear to have responded to this forecast by cutting investment and perhaps also purchases of durable consumption goods in 1866. The result was that the recession came a year early, in 1866.[2] (One wonders how good our weather forecasts would be if some Weather Demon could adjust the jet stream in response to Weather Bureau forecasts.)

Reactions to economic forecasts may either confirm or falsify the forecasts.

A Primer on Forecasting

Nobody learns **macroeconomic forecasting** in an elementary economics class, but students can get some idea of how macroeconomics is used by some forecasters. Because forecasting is quantitative, mathematics cannot be avoided entirely, but in practice most of the math is done by computer programs. We can pose as forecasters, kindergarten-level ones perhaps, by using a simplified Keynesian model.[3] In this model neither the government nor the international sectors are separated from the private domestic economy, all functions are linear, there are no time lags, and neither taxes nor interest rates affect decisions about either saving or investment. Also, we assume no change in the price level so that the symbol for national income, Y, is the same as real GNP. Our clients are (like most such clients) interested primarily in *changes* from this year's or last year's values of the

principal variables rather than in the absolute values of aggregates like GNP.

Our simplified illustrative model is:

$$Y = C + I$$

$$C = C_o + MPC(Y)$$

$$I = I_o$$

C_o is autonomous planned consumption expenditure, MPC is the marginal propensity to consume based on national income, and I_o is autonomous planned investment expenditure. But since we are interested primarily in changes over time, for forecasting purposes we transform (differentiate) these equations with respect to time. If ΔY represents the change in Y over one time period, and similarly for ΔC and ΔI, the model becomes:

$$\Delta Y = \Delta C + \Delta I$$

$$\Delta C = \Delta C_o + MPC(\Delta Y)$$

$$\Delta I = \Delta I_o$$

Just as the original model can be solved for Y, the transformed one can be solved for ΔY.[4]

$$Y = \frac{C_o + I_o}{1 - MPC} \qquad \Delta Y = \frac{\Delta C_o + \Delta I_o}{1 - MPC}$$

Suppose that we believe, perhaps from surveying the intentions of a sample of potential consumers and investors, that our best estimates of ΔC_o and ΔI_o, respectively, are $+10$ and -5, and that the marginal propensity to consume will remain constant at, say, 0.75. Then, using the preceding equations, we can forecast

$$\Delta Y = \frac{10 - 5}{1 - 0.75} = 20$$

In other words, we can forecast that the national income, Y, will be 20 units higher this period than it was in the preceding one.

If our model is larger (contains more equations and more variables), the process becomes more difficult. Also, we or our clients may desire forecasts of ΔC and ΔI—not to mention many other

---

2. This is, of course, an oversimplification of the 1866 downturn. To mention just one other factor, the American Civil War had ended in 1865, and demobilization was under way in the following year.

3. Most commercial forecasters do in fact use Keynesian models in their work. People distrustful of Keynesian macroeconomics sometimes feel an added reason to seek out a non-Keynesian (usually monetarist) forecasting company or to do it themselves.

4. The solution for Y would have been more complex if the consumption function had been nonlinear, or if we had included a possible change in the marginal propensity to consume.

changes, along with ΔY. In such an event, the usual trick is to rewrite the "transformed" model in the following way:

$$\Delta Y - \Delta C - \Delta I = 0$$

$$-MPC(\Delta Y) + \Delta C + O = \Delta C_o$$

$$O + O + \Delta I = \Delta I_o$$

Such groups of equations can be solved readily by computer programs. In the numerical case we have just used, the solutions are:

$$\Delta Y = 20 \text{ (as before)}$$

$$\Delta C = 25$$

$$\Delta I = -5$$

These results are consistent with each other; the total change, ΔY, is the sum of its parts, ΔC and ΔI.

Problems in Forecasting

There remain many problems in forecasting, some purely technical and others with broader implications. One's entire model may be wrong or incomplete, with irrelevant variables included and relevant ones omitted. A supply-sider would reject our demand-side Keynesian model at once. Time lags between causes and their effects must often be explored if one is to understand what is going on. But in our model, all figures relate to the same time interval. Functional relations in the real world may be nonlinear, and such important coefficients as the marginal propensity to consume may change without much warning. Supply shocks—we have mentioned the Tokyo earthquake, the rise of OPEC, and the American drought—can invalidate forecasts. So, of course, can changes in public policy. Examples of policy changes include tax reforms, monetary reforms, the socialization or privatization of economic sectors, and changes in tariffs, quotas, and similar regulations of international trade and investment. Moreover, a peacetime model may not work in wartime, and a wartime model may not work if peace breaks out.

Economists of the Austrian school, most notably the late Ludwig von Mises and his disciples, oppose forecasting on philosophical grounds. When we deal with the decisions of free people,

presumably possessed of free wills, the results of their decisions cannot, they claim, be forecast either individually or in the aggregate. If a forecast is reasonably correct, this particular forecaster has merely been lucky—nothing more.

Forecasts can be incorrect because of inaccurate or incomplete models, time lags, supply shocks, and policy changes. Some economists oppose forecasting in general, believing that the results of decisions of free people cannot be forecast with any accuracy at all.

It is often argued that macroeconomic forecasting has passed the market test. Forecasting firms, some affiliated with major universities, have profited by selling their services to clients who have, presumably, profited by using them. Other concerns, mainly financial institutions, have set up their own in-house forecasting ventures, some of which pay for themselves. But the costs of subscribing to forecasting services, or of operating one's own service in-house, are tax-deductible as business expenses and therefore subsidized indirectly by the government. Without this implicit subsidy, the forecasting industry's scale of operations might be smaller. There is, accordingly, some doubt as to whether the whole forecasting enterprise is worthwhile. The same is true, however, of the operations of other for-profit professional services to business—some of the services of attorneys, accountants, consultants, etc.

WHAT ABOUT THE NATIONAL DEBT?

Macroeconomics is mainly about *flows* of economic activity over periods of definite length—this year's GNP, for example, or the level of measured unemployment during that year. Macroeconomists are therefore accused at times of insufficient concern with **stock phenomena,** which are the sums, or cumulatives, of the flows. In particular, Keynesian macroeconomics, in concentrating on annual excesses of government purchases over net taxes (budget deficits)—which are flows—is accused of being entirely too cavalier about **public debt,** which is the accumulation over time of public deficits.

Recall our discussion of deficits and the national debt in the appendix to Chapter 11. At that point in your study of macroeconomics you had only been introduced to Keynesian economics. Now you have a wider perspective from which to view some debt issues. A balanced treatment of macroeconomics should include two issues concerning the public debt. Is it in any sense a burden on the economy, comparable to the burden of an individual's private debt upon his or her private economy? If so, is it a burden primarily on the generation that contracted it or primarily upon future generations of taxpayers, who must pay the interest and other service charges on the debt, including partial or total repayment? Great Britain, we are told, has never paid for the Napoleonic Wars, while Germany and Japan were permitted to inflate away their debts from World War II. Does this help explain why West Germany and Japan have on balance outperformed the United Kingdom economically during the latter third of the twentieth century?

The "We Owe It to Ourselves" View

We can surely agree that a private individual or firm cannot spend his, her, or its way into prosperity by **deficit financing** (going into debt). Were you a plumber with expensive tastes, no significant portion of your expenditures for living beyond your means could be expected to recycle back to you as increased demand for your services as a plumber. The same is almost equally true for a small public body like Gopher Prairie (the locale of Sinclair Lewis's *Main Street*) or even for such real-world sovereign states as Vanuatu and Kiribati in the South Pacific.

The case is, however, quite different for a large country like the United States. Here a popular view has been that "we owe it to ourselves," where "it" is the **national debt** with only a small (but increasing!) portion owed to foreign bondholders. When the national debt is increased, as by continued **deficit spending,** there may be an immediate

loss to the private sector of the American economy by the surrender to public use of resources that would otherwise be used privately, although even this loss does not occur in the case of resources otherwise unemployed. But the private sector's loss is the public sector's gain. Advocates of this position make additional points:

1. With deficit financing there is no net loss to the bond purchasers because their giving up of resources for public use is in exchange for an increase in their wealth position, in the form of interest received from public securities.

2. With gains and losses to bondholders balanced out, there remains a net gain to the beneficiaries of the public expenditure. These may be public pensioners, relief clients, defense industries, users of an enlarged highway system—the list is endless.

3. As far as future generations are concerned: debt service is a redistributive matter. The new generation of taxpayers loses; the next generation of bondholders gains.[5]

According to the "we owe it to ourselves" view, public debt is not a burden to the economy, and future generations will not be burdened by it.

"We owe it to ourselves" and the arguments listed above were never convincing to all observers even before foreign capitalists and central bankers began large-scale investments in American public debt securities. Two groups of economists have carried the argument about public debt further. These are often called "neo-Ricardian" (see Chapter 17) and "public-choice" writers. We shall examine their views in that order.

The Neo-Ricardian View

Neo-Ricardians contend that the public debt *is*, in fact, a burden on future generations. First they argue that public debt instruments (government

5. A digression into formal logic. Among the fallacies catalogued by Aristotle and his followers, centuries before the birth of Christ, is the *fallacy of composition,* which is the application to the whole of an argument valid only for a part (or vice versa). Economics abounds in examples, of which this is one. (What is true of an individual's debt may not be true of a society's debt, and vice versa.)

bonds) do *not* add to a society's net wealth. Bond-holders may indeed gain net wealth as compensation for surrendering to the government command over real resources here and now, but their gains are canceled by losses to the rest of society. These gains and losses arise because rational taxpayers, including the bondholders themselves, realize that debt service requires future taxation, either in the overt form of more and higher taxes or in the covert forms of inflation or reduced future public services. Such future liabilities, say the neo-Ricardians, are largely taken into account in the planning of the present generation, and result in slower economic growth. As a result, future generations incur a burden primarily in the form of lower incomes.

The second neo-Ricardian argument is harsher and focuses more directly on the burden on future generations. From the strictly economic point of view, they say, governments do not invest as wisely as the private sector. Public debts represent potential assets dissipated in warfare, much of it misguided and useless. Or they represent potential assets dissipated in raising or maintaining the living standards of people who should have been forced to work in the private sector or left to the mercies of private voluntary charity—which supposedly distinguishes more carefully the "deserving" from the "undeserving" poor. Dissipation of resources on warfare, relief, and public-sector "make work" lowers an economy's real growth rate and therefore the level of living of future generations.[6] This argument writes off as quantitatively unimportant the public-sector contribution to the public works and public services necessary to the social infrastructure of economic growth—except for those which taxpayers are willing to support on a "pay as you go" basis.

Neo-Ricardians contend that public debt *is* a burden on future generations, primarily in the form of lower income after taxes. They also argue that governments do not invest as wisely as the private sector.

---

6. Misguided policies of *panem et circenses*—free bread and free entertainments—for the urban poor allegedly wrecked the great Roman Empire.

The Public-Choice View

Public-choice economists view suppliers and consumers of the public services as collections of special-interest groups and electorates as systematically biased in favor of the present as against the future. So these economists favor constitutional limitations on budget deficits (debt increases) or constitutional requirements of peacetime budgetary balance.

Most voters, and economists, see the public service bureaucracy as, among other functions, an impartial umpire between conflicting special interests—workers versus employers, the city versus the country, etc. Public-choice economists, however, see bureaucrats themselves as a formidable interest group. In their view, each branch of the bureaucracy is trying to maximize its own budgetary appropriation in much the same way that consumers maximize utility or satisfaction, or business firms maximize profits or the market value of their enterprises. When the several bureaucracies—the military services, the diplomatic service, the judicial services, the police and fire departments, the public-agency social workers, the public-school and public-university teachers, and so on—are added together, say public-choice economists, the full-time producer pressures for public spending threaten to overbalance the part-time consumer pressures from taxpayers and bondholders. This is especially true when parallel pressures from private industry, from the military-industrial complex to the highway lobbies, are factored in.

At the level of local government, balance is often provided by constitutional limitations, by concern for a city's credit rating, and especially by prohibitions against the issue of local-government legal-tender money. At the national level in the United States, the basic restraints have been the gold standard and the annual budgetary balance. Public-choice economists claim that these have been weakened by macroeconomic heresies, based primarily on doctrines propounded by—or blamed on—John Maynard Keynes. Public choices, it is alleged, are further biased against future generations by the voters' own time preference for the present.

Economists of all persuasions see public appropriations as providing two streams extending into the future—one a stream of benefits from public services, the other a stream of costs in the form of taxes that pay for these services. Even if the present value of the benefits exceeds the present value of the costs, public-choice theory has it that the stream of benefits tends in practice to be front-loaded and the stream of costs back-loaded so that they concentrate net benefit on the present generation and net cost on the future. To put this matter less abstractly, today's weapons systems and today's highways will generally wear out, become obsolete, or otherwise require replacement before they have been paid for. Our children and grand-children will be left to deal with the unpaid balances of the bills we contract for ourselves. Nobody believes this must be true, and everyone agrees that under ideal conditions it would not be true. But public-choice economists insist that in this imperfect world it generally *is* true.

The public-choice school has become a major intellectual force behind proposals for one or another balanced-budget amendment to the United States Constitution, although many supporters of such amendments do not associate themselves with this school.[7] In three less extreme forms, public-choice economists have backed (1) the Gramm-Rudman-Hollings plan for phased deficit reduction,[8] (2) the item veto for the president on appropriation bills, and (3) presidential authority, on behalf of taxpayers, to impound appropriated funds rather than being required to spend them.

Public-choice economists favor constitutional limits on budget deficits or constitutional requirements for a balanced budget.

From One Generation to the Next

Your generation is to past generations as future generations are to yours. So public debts surviving

---

7. Public-choice economists believe that it can be made feasible to outlaw, or at least regulate, such fancy fiscal footwork as evasion of budgetary balance by falsified forecasts, juggling of cash and accrual accounting bases, contingent public liabilities, off-budget expenditures, and similar devices often considered in advanced courses in public finance.

8. Before embarking on a political career, Senator Phil Gramm (R-Tex.) was a prominent public-choice economist as a professor at Texas A&M University.

from the past may in some sense be a burden upon you. But in what sense, precisely?

If the neo-Ricardians and public-choice economists are right, there has been slower economic growth since 1815 (or 1944), and your present living standard is lower than it would have been if the Battle of Waterloo (or the Normandy invasion) had been financed by Great Britain (or the United States) on a more nearly pay-as-you-go basis. You might be paying lower taxes; the price level might be lower; the real interest rate might be lower as well. But since your generation is, even with these burdens, more affluent than that of 1815 (or 1944), it may be thought only fair that you should share with your comparatively poor ancestors the cost of repelling Napoleon Bonaparte (or Adolf Hitler).

WHERE DO WE GO FROM HERE?

As these pages are written (1989), the administration of President George Bush has taken over from that headed for eight years by President Ronald Reagan. Americans, and not only Americans, are asking such deficit-and-debt policy questions as: To what extent was the Reagan Administration responsible for the federal deficits and the national debt? How serious are the country's current deficit and debt positions? How important is it to reduce the deficit and slow down the growth of the debt? What are the probable costs of deficit reduction? Do these benefits and costs depend significantly on the speed of deficit reduction or on the particular devices (revenue enhancement, cost containment) used to bring that reduction about?

Macroeconomics, in its present stage of development, is in a poor position to answer such questions with confidence or to forecast what the administration and Congress will finally decide to do. There is no accepted formula or rule of thumb to govern such decisions. What formula or rule of thumb should be used to tell us what proportion of public expenditure (or what proportion of a *change* in public expenditure) should be financed by taxes (or by a corresponding change in taxes)? Surely the answer, if there is one, depends on many other variables, such as the inflation, unemployment, and growth rates, and on the most desirable relation among them. Accurately predicting these matters is difficult. Most mainstream macroeconomists over thirty years of age will probably admit in their more honest and less pretentious moments that they would have predicted, from the fiscal and debt policies of the Reagan years, substantially higher rates of both interest and price inflation than actually occurred in the 1980s.

The Reagan Experience

Some consider continuous deficits and rising debt to have been Reagan innovations. But we should not forget that when President Reagan took office in 1981, the federal budget had been in deficit for twelve successive years, and the national debt was estimated at the astronomical sum of $1 trillion. On taking office, President Reagan hoped to attain budgetary balance and debt stability by 1984, despite his proposals for tax cuts and increased military expenditures. In fact, deficits increased sharply, and the debt approximately tripled (to $3 trillion) during his two presidential terms. Even so, the debt remained not much more than half of the annual GNP—the equivalent of about seven months' income. By international standards, this is not dangerously large. The debt and deficit records since 1975 are illustrated in Figures 1 and 2.

The federal debt as a percent of GNP (Figure 1) fluctuated during the 1975 to 1982 period and increased significantly during the 1983 to 1990 (estimated) period. Federal deficits as percentages of federal outlays (Figure 2) provide an indication of the federal government's success or failure in bal-

FIGURE 1
Gross U.S. Federal Debt as Percent of GNP

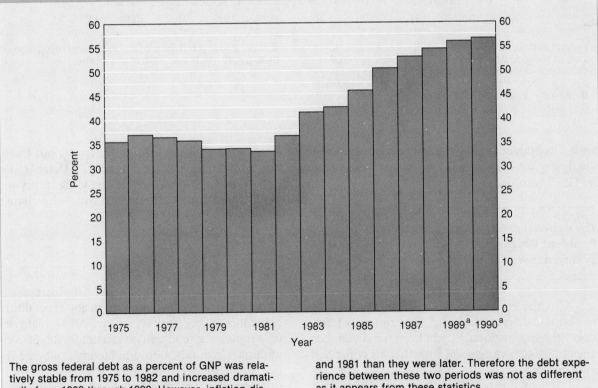

The gross federal debt as a percent of GNP was relatively stable from 1975 to 1982 and increased dramatically from 1983 through 1990. However, inflation distorts this measure of the debt because it pushes nominal GNP upward while leaving nominal debt unchanged. Inflation rates were higher between 1975 and 1981 than they were later. Therefore the debt experience between these two periods was not as different as it appears from these statistics.
Source: Economic Report of the President, 1989, Table B-76, p. 397. (1989 and 1990 are estimates.)

FIGURE 2
Federal Government Deficits as Percent of Federal Government Outlays

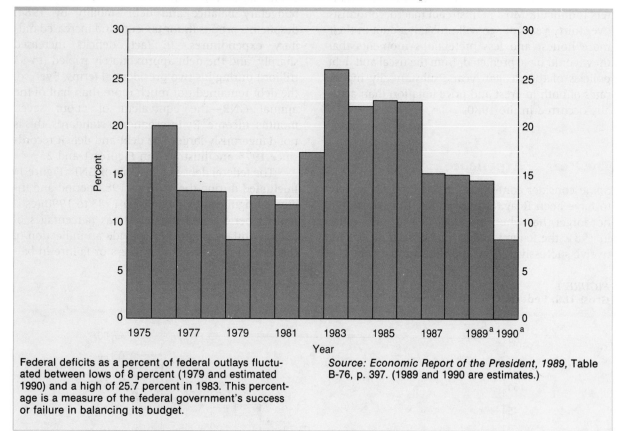

Federal deficits as a percent of federal outlays fluctuated between lows of 8 percent (1979 and estimated 1990) and a high of 25.7 percent in 1983. This percentage is a measure of the federal government's success or failure in balancing its budget.

Source: Economic Report of the President, 1989, Table B-76, p. 397. (1989 and 1990 are estimates.)

---

ancing its budget. During the time period shown in the figure, the highest deficit-to-outlay percentage was 25.7 recorded in 1983.

The national debt tripled (to $3 trillion) under President Reagan, but it is not dangerously large by international standards.

Also, the Reagan deficits and debt increases did not bring the "credit crunch," the "runaway inflation," the international "flight from the dollar," or any of the other varieties of crisis that his critics had anticipated with both apprehension and glee. Instead, general prosperity—at least in the upper and middle classes—continued for a surprisingly long period. One short, sharp downturn in 1981–82 was overcome by monetary expansion and moderating disinflationary pressure. Seven years after

Reagan was first elected president, a serious financial downturn—"Black Monday," October 19, 1987—was absorbed without spreading far beyond Wall Street. In the absence of crisis, why change policy?

Living with Deficits

A rapid move against deficits and debt increases—either a major tax increase or a major expenditure reduction (either military or civilian)—might set off a significant recession on essentially Keynesian-multiplier grounds. Could monetary policy be relied upon to overcome such a recession, while stopping short of accelerated inflation? It seems dangerous and unnecessary to risk the results of such contractionary fiscal policy. The path of least resistance is rather to do little about the deficit or the debt, while taking the politician's customary refuge in rhetoric and oratory. We have learned, it seems, to live with a deficit and a rising-debt economy—perhaps even to manage such an economy. Why not continue? Why take chances of upsetting apple carts? Such, as we see it, is the path of least resistance.

Such is also our tentative guess at the compromise the Republican administration of President Bush and the Democratic Congress may be forced into by the exigencies of the political process and the disinterest of the electorate in economic technicalities. It is a policy of living with, and perhaps even managing, the deficit and the debt, and blaming the other party for failure to do more. Until a crisis develops, macroeconomic thinking will be on hold. Moreover, the American body politic may well consent to continuing deficits and rising debt—not, we repeat, for their own sakes but as paths of least risk and least resistance.

A major policy initiative against deficits and debt increases, such as a tax increase or expenditure reduction, might set off a significant recession. Unless a crisis develops, the best policy may be simply to live with the deficit and rising debt.

Possible Crises

If an economic crisis develops, such as a credit crunch, an accelerating inflation, or a capital flight from dollar assets, the policy response may include cuts in the deficit by tax increases and cuts in public spending. In other countries, it may also include partial or complete debt repudiation or renegotiation, which would free public expenditures for immediately useful purposes and away from debt servicing. We shall encounter this alternative in connection with the problems of developing-country debt, but it is extremely unlikely for the United States.

If the crisis is an underconsumption, underinvestment, or debt-deflation one like the Great Depression of the 1930s, both deficits and the national debt may deliberately be increased again, paralleling the Roosevelt New Deal experience.

Most difficult would be a stagflationary crisis—prices, interest rates, and unemployment all rising, while real consumption, investment, and GNP are stagnant or falling. In such an **inflationary depression,** deficit and debt policy would indeed require rethinking, if we do not yield instead to the Man on Horseback (or in a plane or tank, or at the head of a mindless mob) to impose order by dictatorial methods.

Economics in Focus

Budget Arithmetic

Most detailed discussions of the national debt and budget deficits rely on numerical estimates and projections—numbers that by their very specificity take on the guise of hard-edged facts. But in reality the numbers are often in dispute. Expert fiscal analysts disagree with Congress, which in turn disagrees with the president. For instance, Ronald Reagan's last budget proposal, presented to Congress just as he was leaving office, projected a 1990 deficit of $27 billion above the target set by the Gramm-Rudman-Hollings Act. Congress, however, estimated that the 1990 deficit would run $41 billion above the target. That is quite a difference, and it obviously had great implications for policy decisions.

Budget projections often suffer from two questionable assumptions. One is that the economy will continue to grow at a reasonable rate. Even if the rate chosen is close to the historical average, the assumption leaves no room for a downturn or recession. Historically, of course, recessions do occur. Second, projections often assume that spending for many or most established government programs can be held in check, with little or no growth in real terms. Because of the vast number of programs the U.S. government maintains—as well as the constant pressures for better health care, improved education, drug-abuse prevention, and so on—this assumption frequently proves unrealistic.

A further problem is that politicians and policymakers do not like to be the bearers of bad news. No one wants to cut a popular program or demand an unpopular tax increase, especially if this would involve fudging on a campaign promise. As President Bush tried to reduce the deficit and simultaneously live up to his 1988 promise of no new taxes, *The Economist* put his predicament succinctly: "The political loser in the budget game is the first player to be caught using the word tax."

Squeezed between political pressures on the one hand and the demands of the Gramm-Rudman-Hollings Act on the other, the budget-makers have resorted to complicated fixes. Some expenses are shifted from one fiscal year to another to meet deficit-reduction goals. In other cases, spending can be declared "off-budget" despite the fact that the money will actually be spent. For example, in the 1989 bailout for savings and loan institutions, some of the funds were not counted in the national budget because they would technically be spent by a new quasi-governmental agency rather than by the government itself.

Critics charge that such inventive maneuvers, especially when combined with rosy projections, obscure the problem and make deficits more difficult to overcome. Others counter that the Gramm-Rudman-Hollings Act invited this kind of budget manipulation. Economists, whether they agree or disagree with current policies, must constantly be aware of the quirky nature of budget arithmetic.

Sources: "Curtain Up on the Budget Ballet," *The Economist,* January 14, 1989, pp. 25–28 (quotation at p. 27); Rudolph G. Penner, "What Worries Me Now About Federal Deficits," *Across the Board,* July/August 1989, pp. 50–54; Joseph J. Minarik, "Fiscal Reality and Exploding Myths," *Challenge,* July–August 1988, pp. 4–13.

SUMMARY

1. The practicality of microeconomics arises mainly from its usefulness in guiding direct participation in supplying and demanding inputs and outputs. The practicality of macroeconomics arises from its usefulness in guiding indirect participation in the economy, as voter, legislator, or civil servant. (See page 392.)

2. Science deals with what is. Among the several branches of science, some are more mature than others, but a branch of science can be scientific even if not fully developed. As a less than fully established science, macroeconomics can expect its theories to be displaced as better theories are devised. (See pages 392–393.)

3. One of the problems of macroeconomic forecasting is that outcomes often depend in part on highly individualized responses by agencies and people all over the world. These responses cannot be confined to scientific models. In addition, the forecasts themselves may bring responses that may, in turn, confirm or invalidate the forecasts. (See pages 393–394.)

4. Elementary forecasting can be illustrated using the Keynesian model, in which a change in income (ΔY) equals the sum of a change in planned consumption spending (ΔC) and a change in planned investment spending (ΔI), with $\Delta C = \Delta C_o + MPC(\Delta Y)$. (See pages 394–395.)

5. Although there are many ways in which forecasts can go wrong, it appears that forecasting has passed the market test, testifying to some usefulness in practical affairs. The Austrian school of economic thought, however, argues that the actions of people with free will cannot be forecast reliably. (See page 395.)

6. Among economists, views differ on whether the public debt is a burden on the economy and, if so, whether this burden falls upon the present or a future generation. The "we owe it to ourselves" view concludes that public debt is not a burden on the economy and that future generations are not involved. (See pages 395–396.)

7. The neo-Ricardian view is that taxpayers recognize that public debt requires future taxation and that these future taxes are taken into account by the present generation. As a result, debt falls as a burden on future generations, primarily in the form of lower incomes after taxes. Neo-Ricardians also argue that government uses resources unwisely, thus reducing the economic inheritance of future generations. (See pages 396–397.)

8. The public-choice view is that public debt reflects the present-generation bias of voters, bureaucrats, and legislators who, as interest groups, place their own interests above those of future generations. This view supports constitutional amendments limiting budget deficits. It also supports the item veto and presidential impoundment of appropriated funds. (See pages 397–398.)

9. The national debt was about $1 trillion when President Reagan took office and grew to about $3 trillion over his two terms. At somewhat over one-half of GNP, the U.S. public debt is not dangerously large by international standards. Nor did the Reagan policies result in any of the serious crises that many economists feared would arise. (See page 399.)

10. The U.S. economy appears to have learned how to live with public deficits. Deficit finance, consequently, is likely to be the practice under President Bush, barring serious economic crisis. Among several crises that could arise, a stagflation crisis would call for the most serious reconsideration of national debt policy. (See pages 400–401.)

KEY TERMS

applied science: an objective, factual, and systematic search for knowledge that includes practical utilizations along with theoretical inquiries (page 392).

deficit financing: funding those expenditures that are in excess of current receipts through borrowing, that is, through incurring debt (page 396).

deficit spending: expenditures that are in excess of current receipts (page 396).

inflationary depression: a situation in which an economy experiences a decrease in real GNP and also an increase in its general price level (page 401). See also **stagflation**.

macroeconomic forecasting: predicting the values of economic variables through systematic analysis of empirically estimated relationships (page 394).

national debt: the total value of outstanding securities issued by a nation's government (page 396).

public-choice economists: economists who specialize in the study of the decision making procedures and outcomes of governments (page 397).

public debt: see **national debt**.

pure science: an objective, factual, and systematic search for knowledge utilizing assumptions, principles and rules, but not engaging in practical applications (page 392).

quantitative economic forecasting: the practice of using observed and/or estimated values for the variables in a macroeconomic model in order to predict future values for those variables (page 393).

stock phenomena: the sums or quantities of economic variables as they exist at a specified time, as distinguished from flows of such quantities over a specified period of time (page 395).

DISCUSSION QUESTIONS

1. Many colleges and universities recommend microeconomics in one semester and macroeconomics in another—some in one sequence and some in the other. To what extent is the sequencing choice based on a view that one or the other course is more practical? What other considerations may influence the sequencing choice?

2. Discuss the maturity of macroeconomics as a science, organizing your discussion around the concepts of (a) displacements of one theory by another and (b) a "unified field" for economics. What, if any, displacements have taken place? Is there any progress toward a unified field?

3. As a review of your understanding of forecasting using the Keynesian system, make up a set of values (different from those in the chapter) for the marginal propensity to consume (*MPC*), the

change in autonomous consumption spending (ΔC_O), and the change in investment (ΔI). Calculate the change in income (ΔY). Now retain the ΔY value, remove one of the independent variables, and ask a classmate to solve the equation for the missing variable. The process may continue to other classmates. You may want to continue the exercise by changing one of the independent variables—such as the marginal propensity to consume—and observing the effect on the calculated value of ΔY.

4. Business publications and bank newsletters frequently publish macroeconomic forecasts. Your reference librarian can help you locate one of these. Examine it for forecasts and then discuss how actual GNP might be affected by (a) war in the Middle East that cuts off supplies of crude petroleum, (b) a threat of war and shortages that do not actually happen, and (c) some other event of your own choosing. Is there any sense to the statement "My forecast was good, but reality was wrong?"

5. Suppose the U.S. Treasury offers to sell you a security that would pay you $100 a year but that carries no maturity date, that is, the Treasury promises to pay $100 interest per year forever but makes no promise ever to repay the initial sum borrowed. Would you buy the security? What is the amount of the national debt based on this security? Will this debt burden future generations?

6. Discuss how the U.S. economy "lives with" a deficit in the budget of the federal government. When new issues of Treasury securities are sold, does it matter who buys them? What effect does the sale have on interest rates, *ceteris paribus?* Do Federal Reserve open market operations make any difference? Does the growth rate of the U.S. economy matter?

7. Review the three types of crises noted in the chapter as possibilities during the administration of President Bush. Have any of them actually arisen? Have the consequences been as anticipated in this chapter?

The New Frontier
and After

BACKGROUND

The two Eisenhower administrations (1953–1961) in the United States are known as years of the "American celebration" and of general prosperity—interrupted only briefly by three mild recessions. At the close of the 1950s, however, critics noted that in these recessions the measured unemployment rate rose to increasingly higher points and that in the revivals it fell by increasingly smaller amounts.[1] This small sample of statistical measurements gave rise to worry about economic stagnation and demands to get the economy moving again. These concerns played a considerable part in the presidential election of 1960, in which John F. Kennedy narrowly defeated the sitting vice president, Richard Nixon.

Because of his youth and personal charm, his rhetorical gifts both oral and written, his openness to new ideas, his war record, and his great wealth, President Kennedy (1917–1963) was already a uniquely attractive figure to activist reformers of his generation. The Washington, D.C., of his term and the first years of the Lyndon Johnson administration that followed his death[2] was called the "New Frontier."

Kennedy's main intellectual interests were politics and history, but he had developed a collateral interest in economics as a student at Harvard. Among the activist reformers of his age group—"the best and the brightest" of their generation—were a number of Keynesian economists, interested in putting Lord Keynes's idea into posthumous practice. (Keynes had died in 1946.)

POLICIES OF THE NEW FRONTIER

As things worked out, Keynesian stabilization policy reached its zenith in the United States during a brief five-year period of the Kennedy-Johnson administration (1961–1966). The major economic aspects of their "practical Keynesianism on the New Frontier" can be summarized in a half-dozen propositions.

1. The importance of the maintenance and growth of aggregate demand was emphasized, while aggregate supply was relatively neglected. Some critics have devised a short statement they call *Keynes's Law:* "Aggregate demand creates its own supply in the presence of significant unemployment." This statement, which stands Say's Identity on its head, would surely have been disowned by Keynes himself. Also, the growth path of high-employment GNP was taken as technically given, or at least as independent of changes in macroeconomic policy.

2. Fiscal policy—the management of public receipts, expenditures, surpluses, and deficits—was to bear primary responsibility for maintaining income and employment, with monetary policy relegated to inflation and interest-rate control. However, New Frontier economics did not include any legal obligation for the government to act as employer of last resort in providing jobs for all.[3]

---

1. Many economists now discount these figures as "statistical artifacts." That is, they resulted chiefly from the entry of more married women into the labor force and from the movement of black workers from subsistence-level self-employment in rural southern agriculture to better-paid industrial jobs in urban areas.

2. Johnson was Kennedy's vice president. Many of the Kennedy policies passed into law only under Johnson's leadership. It is doubtful how many could have been enacted at all without Johnson's political skills—he had been majority leader in the Senate—and without the wave of sympathy for Kennedy's ideas after his assassination.

3. This extreme extension of Keynesian employment theory was proposed later in the Humphrey-Hawkins Bill of the 1970s. It was not, however, included in the Humphrey-Hawkins Act as passed in 1978.

To the disappointment of many veterans of the New Deal of the Franklin Roosevelt administrations in the 1930s, the expansive fiscal policy of the New Frontier meant cuts in tax rates rather than expansions of public expenditure. In the atmosphere of the early 1960s, however, these cuts raised federal receipts rather than lowering them. Also, President Kennedy read Michael Harrington's *The Other America*, an intellectual inspiration for the War on Poverty. Before Kennedy's assassination, Walter Heller, chairman of the Council of Economic Advisers, was preparing the groundwork for a bold new expenditure program without waiting for either a recession or a balanced budget.

3. Okun's Law was another basic proposition of New Frontier Keynesian economics, with which Keynes had no connection. This law is a statistical generalization from actual U.S. experience—when a growth rate of 3.75 percent a year had seemed to keep the unemployment rate stable while the labor force grew. Okun's Law stated that the measured unemployment rate would fall by one percentage point for every three percentage points by which the GNP growth rate exceeded 3.75 and rise by one percentage point for every three percentage points of shortfall in this growth target.

4. The Phillips curve was another extension of Keynesian doctrine the New Frontiersmen accepted. The Phillips curve maintains that to lower the unemployment rate, one must also accept some acceleration of wage inflation, which might in turn lead to acceleration of price inflation. Price stability in the United States was estimated by Paul Samuelson and Robert Solow to require a 6 or 7 percent unemployment rate—an unacceptable bargain.

5. New Frontier economists accepted the bland proposition that "money matters"—that Federal Reserve action to increase or decrease the supply of money makes a difference—but only for regulating the inflation rate and the (nominal) interest rate. When these rates could not be held down simultaneously, New Frontier doctrine considered it at least as important to restrain interest rates by easy money (increasing the supply of money) as to restrain inflation by tight money (decreasing the supply of money).

6. The practical Keynesians of the New Frontier cared about income distribution. They sought to increase the worker's share of the national income (which meant reducing the property owner's share) and also to reduce the measured degree of inequality in the personal distribution of income. Accord-ingly, they favored low interest rates over high ones and progressive direct taxation (of incomes and estates) over indirect sales and excise taxes.

CLOSING THE NEW FRONTIER

New Frontier policies are credited today by many economists with keeping the American growth rate high and the American unemployment and inflation rates low during the first half of the 1960s. These policies also gave economics, and especially Keynesian macroeconomics, a prestige and self-confidence that economics had seldom, if ever, possessed previously and that it has not yet regained. At their height—in fact, somewhat thereafter—their success led President Nixon (President Johnson's successor in office) to assure the public that "we are all Keynesians now."

What closed the New Frontier? Not so much the gestation and development of anti-Keynesian economics as a series of external shocks to which the system was prevented from adjusting by political considerations. The first shock was the explosion of the American involvement in Vietnam into a full-scale intervention and undeclared war, which America eventually lost. The second was President Johnson's refusal to finance the war either by raising taxes or by postponing the War on Poverty. The third shock—perhaps an aftershock—was the sudden quadrupling of the world price of oil by OPEC in 1973–74, followed by a further rise after the Iranian revolution of 1979.

SOME NEW FRONTIERSMEN

From among the eminent economists who assisted Lord Keynes (and his ghost) in framing New Frontier economic ideas, we choose a half-dozen for special mention: Walter Heller, Lawrence Klein, Arthur Okun, Paul Samuelson, Robert Solow, and James Tobin. None was over forty-five years old when President Kennedy was inaugurated. All but one were old enough to have lived through the Great Depression in a state of social consciousness. All were partisans of both Keynes and the New Deal. Most came from, and returned to, prestigious academic posts. Four eventually received Nobel Prizes in economics. Most remained active in policy formulation into the 1980s.

Walter Heller (1915–1987, University of Minnesota) was chairman of Kennedy's Council of Economic Advisers (CEA). A specialist in public finance,

Heller was a principal architect of the Kennedy fiscal policies. A superb communicator, he retained a common touch that belied both expertise and eminence.

Lawrence Klein (1920–   , University of Pennsylvania), Nobel laureate and author of *The Keynesian Revolution,* became the country's macroeconomic model-builder *par excellence.* An obvious CEA possibility, Klein remained in the background, lest his youthful radicalism embarrass the administration, but the fundamental "numbers" of New Frontier policies were worked out by methods of his devising.

Arthur Okun (1928–1980, Yale University and Brookings Institution) devised Okun's Law during his service with the Kennedy administration. He later served as chairman of President Johnson's CEA. His interest in income distribution is reflected in his book *Equality and Efficiency,* while his interest in labor problems is apparent in *Prices and Quantities,* which presents a theory of implied contracts in labor relations that keep wages impervious to monetary

and fiscal policy until substantial unemployment develops.

Paul Samuelson (1915–   , MIT) is a Nobel laureate and leader of his generation of American Keynesians. Samuelson writes at every level, from letters to the editor and columns in weekly magazines to mathematical and philosophical contributions to abstract scholarly journals. He has contributed to almost every branch of economics. As a student, he fitted the first statistical consumption function. Rather than seeking power in the Washington bureaucracy, Samuelson prefers the role of "grey eminence" behind the throne.

Robert Solow (1924–   , MIT) is also a Nobel laureate. Solow's principal scholarly contributions have been in the economics of growth, capital, and production functions. We have mentioned his application (with Samuelson) of the Phillips curve to American data. Like Heller, Solow is a celebrated communicator outside as well as within the classroom.

James Tobin (1918–   , Yale University) is another Nobel laureate and a specialist on monetary and investment theory, including portfolio balance. Tobin served with Heller on Kennedy's CEA. In the fields we have mentioned, as an econometrician, and in studies of income distribution, the quiet, unpretentious Tobin has retained his Keynesianism through thick and thin, including a preference for inflation, even accelerating inflation, over tolerance of continued unemployment.

POTENTIAL SUCCESSORS

As we shall soon see, the New Frontier has survived. However, as it seemed to close, interest tended to shift to two groups of successors, almost as hostile to each other as each was to the Keynesian "heresy." Some of these potential successors to the New Frontiersmen may be called *monetarists* and others *supply-siders*.[4] Despite their disagreements, they are often confused in the press. Both were important in the Reagan administrations, where Reaganomics represented less a settled body of doctrine than a series of compromises in their competition for the economic "soul" of the president.

The basic tenets of monetarism, as expounded by "Chicago School" economist, Milton Friedman, are as follows:

1. The money supply, defined in any consistent manner, is the principal determinant of aggregate demand and the level of economic activity in nominal terms. In particular, it is more important than the autonomous expenditures I, G, and X in the Keynesian model. This is a generalized restatement of the classical quantity theory of money.

2. The money supply exercises its influence not immediately, but with a long and variable lag that economists do not yet understand well. In general, monetary influences on real income and product appear before their influences on the price level, and the price-level effects often counteract and nullify the real-income ones.

3. The historical record suggests that discretionary monetary policy, or monetary "fine-tuning," has not been successful. Whether exercised by politicians, bureaucrats, bankers, or academic experts, monetary policy has been unable to wait for the lags to work themselves out. Instead, it has accentuated economic fluctuations and increased their amplitude. In short, it has been destabilizing. It would be better to replace such discretion with a monetary rule, requiring some monetary aggregate to grow steadily at a rate approximating the long-term growth rate of real GNP, regardless of resulting fluctuations in interest rates.

Monetarists do not agree among themselves about what the monetary rule should be—whether the indicator should be the monetary base, M1, or M2, whether account should be taken of shifts in *liquidity preference* (the demand for money as an asset), and how, if at all, the demand variables should be factored in.

As a monetarist subgroup, we should mention the rational-expectations school headed by Robert Lucas (University of Chicago) and Thomas Sargent (Stanford University). These economists believe that the responses of commodity, security, and labor markets to policy and policy changes are rational—that they do not include the confusion between nominal and real changes called *money illusion.* They also believe that all markets are therefore in the neighborhood of equilibrium, with Phillips curves nearly vertical at the natural rate of unemployment and with search unemployment treated as voluntary.[5] In such a world, policy exercises important influence only on the price level. It systematically influences output or employment only when the markets have been deceived as to what the policy is or how it will soon change. The best the policymaker can hope to do—purely random fluctuations apart—is to reduce risk (an element in production costs) by announcing and following policy rules, particularly about the money supply and its growth rate.

Monetarists are not Keynesians but, like them, they view macroeconomic policy as largely a matter of influencing aggregate demand. Supply-siders, on the other hand, propose to shift the emphasis back to aggregate supply, where it was before the "repeal" of Say's Identity. Indeed, the supply-siders can be interpreted as implying that Say's Identity holds in a well-run economy. In such an economy, aggregate supply creates its own demand.

4. Public-choice economists, whose chief spokesman has been the Nobel laureate James Buchanan (George Mason University) are of somewhat less importance. They insist that budgetary balance be required as a corollary of fiscal policy and blame Keynesian doctrine for the several "great inflations" of World War II and thereafter.

5. Search unemployment is interpreted as a preference for spending time looking for "good" jobs over spending it at work in "bad" jobs—whether or not the good ones in fact exist.

Robert Lucas

Thomas Sargent

What is a well-run economy? How does it differ from the existing one, if indeed it does? Supply-siders see two weaknesses in the existing American economy: excessive taxation and excessive regulation. They are not libertarians or anarchists. They do not propose to dispense with either taxation or public regulation completely. They believe only that excessive taxation and excessive regulation should be cut back sharply. The cuts can be made together, since some of the costs of regulation are borne by taxpayers. Supply-siders believe that income-tax progressivity should not go too far and that corporate income tax rates should not be too high. As for regulation, favorite targets include antimonopoly legislation, delays in technical progress in the name of safety, health, or the environment, and increases in the cost of employing labor. The latter includes minimum wages, encouragements to trade unionism, and high relief standards—which reduce the labor supply.

The Laffer curve, a supply-side artifact, caught the public eye in the early 1980s. Arthur Laffer, then an economist at the University of Southern California, argued that not only GNP but government reve-nues as well could be increased by tax cuts and the deficit reduced. In addition to the well-known Laffer curve, Laffer presented evidence from several episodes in American history—including the New Frontier tax cuts of twenty years before—and from the effects of lowered high-bracket income tax rates on the taxes received from high-bracket taxpayers weaned from tax shelters to more productive investments. The record, however, has not borne out Laffer's optimistic anticipations.[6] *Revolution,* Martin Anderson's account of the Reagan years, denies that short-run "Lafferism" ever dominated the administration's fiscal policy.

---

6. This apparent failure is explained away by Lafferite supply-siders on two grounds: Federal Reserve disinflationary policy and the timing of the tax cuts. In lowering the inflation rate, the Federal Reserve permitted interest rates to remain high. The high cost of credit, supply-siders believe, offset the effect of lower taxes on economic activity and thus on government receipts. Also, the tax cuts themselves were staggered over three years instead of being made all at once in 1981. Anticipation of further cuts in later years may have reduced the effectiveness of the 1981–82 tax reductions.

KEYNESIAN REVIVAL

During a fifteen- or twenty-year period beginning in the late 1960s, essays and lectures entitled "Is Keynes Dead?" were featured in economists' professional journals and conventions on three important Keynesian anniversaries—Lord Keynes's birth (1883), the publication of the *General Theory* (1936), and his death (1946). While a great many economists argued that Keynesian macroeconomics was dead, others not only defended its worth but by their research and theorizing laid the groundwork for a genuine Keynesian revival. The surviving New Frontiersmen have played important parts in this revival, aided and abetted by such younger disciples as Alan Blinder (Princeton University) and Lester Thurow (MIT).

Survivals and revivals are more common in the social than in the natural sciences and strengthen doubts about the "scientific" character of the "softer" social studies. Seventeenth-century mercantilism never really died in the business community, in contrast to the phlogiston theory, its approximate contemporary in chemistry. Karl Marx, who died the year Keynes was born, survives numerous "autopsies" and remains very much alive, perhaps less so in the capitalist countries than in socialist ones.

In the case of Keynes, the shortcomings of monetarism and the supply side have favored Keynesian revival. The monetarists never solved their difficulties with the definition of money, the specification of the monetary rule, and the ingenuity of the financial community in devising evasions in near-money and money-substitute forms.[7] In addition, monetarists seem to have underestimated the consequences of high nominal interest rates, such as result from the disinflationary tightening of money during the interval before inflation rates actually collapse. Hope, however, springs eternal in the human breast—including hope for the superior acumen of the next generation of monetary experts, now aided by computers and international cooperation.

Supply-side economics was largely an American phenomenon and was blamed in the United States, rightly or wrongly, for both the apparent fiasco of Lafferism and the burgeoning deficits of the Reagan administrations. More important to economists, however, was the anatomy of the accompanying Reagan prosperity. Supply-siders had expected the tax cuts and deregulation of the Reagan years to fuel an expansion primarily of private investment, supported by increased private saving more than proportionate to the rise in GNP. In Keynesian terms, this would have been a rise in both saving and returns on investment. Keynesians expected, instead, a movement along existing functions and a consumption boom with no significant change in either saving or investment as proportions of GNP. The Keynesian anticipations were in fact correct, and influentially so. Private saving ratios actually *fell*,[8] and investment was maintained largely by tapping the savings of foreigners, both European and Japanese, with a smattering of Canadians as well.

---

7. To Sir Charles Goodhart (Bank of England) we owe "Goodhart's Law" that empirical regularities break down when policy is based on them. Sir Charles surely had in mind the thwarting of British monetarism by the superior ingenuity of the London financial community.

8. Harvard University's Martin Feldstein ascribes this decline in the private saving ratio largely to the expanded Social Security and Medicare systems, which reduce the need to save for old age and its medical accompaniments. Though he was chairman of the CEA during most of the Reagan period, Feldstein became increasingly "out of sync" with the remainder of the administration.

Exchange Rates, International Balances, and
International Finance

Free Trade versus Protection

Economic Growth

Economic Development

PART VI

INTERNATIONAL TRADE, ECONOMIC GROWTH, AND ECONOMIC DEVELOPMENT

19
Exchange Rates, International Balances, and International Finance

Preview   When people in one country trade with people in another country, the price levels in the two countries must somehow be related to one another. When people in one country make investments in another country, the interest rates in the two countries must somehow be related to one another. So far, in our economic analysis, we have not explored these relationships. In this chapter, we examine those portions of international economics which do explore them.

It is quite unrealistic to presume that international economic relations do not affect economic behavior. After making this point, we start our analysis by examining how foreign exchange markets determine the value of a country's money in terms of the monies of other countries. From here, we go on to explain how governments sometimes intervene in the operation of these markets and try to control the exchange value of different monies. We discuss the question of whether foreign exchange rates should be fixed or free to find their own relationships, and we briefly review the history of exchange rate fixing schemes, from the gold standard to the present-day "dirty float" arrangement.

The second part of the chapter explains the balance of payments accounting system and what is meant by "favorable" or "unfavorable" balances of trade and payments. We trace the evolution of a country from immature debtor to mature creditor and examine balance-of-payments problems and possible solutions.

The appendix to this chapter explores international macroeconomics. Specifically, it examines (a) exchange rate systems that are consistent with macroeconomic policy autonomy, (b) simultaneous equilibrium for both the domestic economy and the balance of payments, and (c) a set of macroeconomic identities that specify interrelationships between the domestic and the international aspects of a nation's macroeconomy. This appendix is best understood by students who have already studied the principles of macroeconomics.

THE WORLD IS ALWAYS WITH US

Before we plunge into the details of international trade and finance, let us note how important these topics are. In the United States, it is estimated that one out of every six workers owes his or her job to exports, two out of every five acres of farmland produce for export, and about 20 percent of industrial output is exported.

The world's financial markets are more closely interconnected than ever before, thanks to instantaneous international transmission not only of voices but also of documents, statistical data, and computer output. Since time zones remain different, people wonder "When can the Chief Financial Officer sleep?" This question is not always funny. The decisions of a few large Tokyo and Hong Kong companies in 1985 to withdraw their very large (and therefore uninsured) deposits from the Continental Illinois Bank in Chicago were made during East Asian business hours—in the middle of the night, Chicago time. Chicago bankers who had gone to bed under normal conditions were awakened in the small hours of the morning with the news that Continental Illinois, the eighth-largest bank in the United States and the largest in the entire Midwest, was threatened with bankruptcy.

International trade and finance also play large roles in world politics. Early in the Great Depression, both the United States and the British Empire raised their **tariffs** (taxes on imported goods), trying to "export unemployment" to other countries by producing at home goods previously imported. The United States passed the high Hawley-Smoot tariff in 1930 to keep foreign goods out. At about the same time, Britain set up a system of Imperial Preference, or tariffs against non-Empire countries. Later other tariffs were added to protect the British Isles themselves. A major victim of these tariffs was Japan, a resource-poor country that depended upon its exports to pay for its imports of both food and industrial raw materials. Largely in order to

avoid the serious economic effects expected from the Anglo-American blockage of their exports, the Japanese sought for themselves a "co-prosperity" sphere of influence in China and East Asia from which they could import the goods that they needed, and in which they could sell their exports, free from Anglo-American competition. In 1931 they set up a puppet government in Manchuria, as a source of iron ore, coal, soybeans, and salt for fertilizer. They also built up mines and factories in Manchuria. This aggression started Japan on the slippery slope toward Pearl Harbor.

We cannot say how the course of history would have been different if the United States or Great Britain or Japan had behaved differently in their international economic relations. Knowledge about how these international relationships operate will not guarantee the peaceful resolution of problems. But to understand them and search for solutions, we must learn the basics of international trade and finance.

International trade and finance play key roles in world politics.

FOREIGN EXCHANGE MARKETS

Let us start the study of international trade and finance with **foreign exchange markets,** which are markets in which the monies of different countries are exchanged (traded) for one another. In fact, **foreign exchange** simply means the money of other countries. The reason these markets are needed is that the people who produce and sell things want to be paid in the money of their own country. Therefore, if the buyer has only the money of another country, some exchange of monies must take place. It is a convenient simplification to suppose that a German who wishes to buy something from the United States must first buy American dollars and then buy the American good or service, or that an American who wishes to buy something from Japan must first buy Japanese yen and then buy the Japanese product.

Foreign exchange is the money of other countries. Foreign exchange markets are markets in which the monies of different countries are traded for one another.

Foreign exchange markets are needed because the people who produce and sell things want to be paid in the money of their own country.

Two-Country Model

Figure 1 illustrates a foreign exchange market as it might exist between the U.S. dollar and the Japanese yen, assuming for the moment that these are the only monies in the world.[1] The quantity of dollars demanded and supplied in international transactions is shown on the horizontal axis, and the price of these dollars is shown on the vertical axis. The price of the dollar is expressed in terms of foreign exchange, which, in this case, is Japanese yen. In this illustration, the equilibrium value of the dollar is 200 yen, balancing the quantity demanded with the quantity supplied at $5 billion a year. At a higher exchange value, say, 300 yen per dollar, a greater number of dollars would be supplied, but fewer would be demanded, so that the exchange value of the dollar would tend to fall. At a lower exchange value, more dollars would be demanded but fewer supplied, pushing the exchange rate upward.

The foreign exchange value of a country's money tells how much of a foreign country's money can be exchanged for one unit of the domestic money.

In this simple two-country illustration, part of the demand for dollars comes from Japanese who want to buy American goods and services. Some of these buyers are Japanese tourists in the United States. Others are residents of Japan who want to import American goods, such as coal or lumber, or

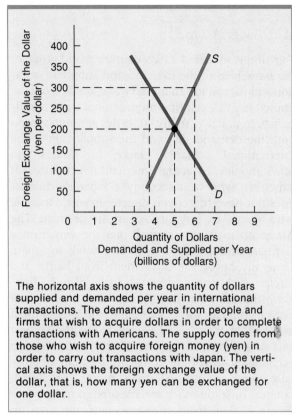

FIGURE 1
Two-Country Foreign Exchange Market

The horizontal axis shows the quantity of dollars supplied and demanded per year in international transactions. The demand comes from people and firms that wish to acquire dollars in order to complete transactions with Americans. The supply comes from those who wish to acquire foreign money (yen) in order to carry out transactions with Japan. The vertical axis shows the foreign exchange value of the dollar, that is, how many yen can be exchanged for one dollar.

Japanese companies that want to import American machines for their factories. Some of the demand for dollars comes from Japanese investors who want to purchase bonds or shares of stock in U.S. stock and bond markets, and some comes from Japanese who send money to relatives in the United States. A portion of the demand may also come from the Japanese government itself, if it wishes to acquire American dollars to hold as part of Japan's official reserves.[2]

The supply of dollars, on the other hand, comes from Americans who wish to buy Japanese goods or travel in Japan, who want to invest through the Japanese bond and stock markets, or who want to send money to Japanese friends or relatives. The U.S. government may even supply

1. In practice, most foreign exchange transactions involve short-term government securities rather than money. But the explanation is clearer if we assume that money is exchanged.

2. Official reserves will be described later in this chapter in connection with balance of payments accounting.

dollars in order to acquire yen to hold as part of its official reserves.

Multilateral Trade

Our simple model of a two-country world provides the basic idea of the demand and supply of a nation's money in international trade, but it is only of limited use in exploring international trade and finance. In practice, many countries are involved on both the demand side and the supply side of the international exchange market for dollars and other monies. In actual international finance, an American who wants to buy a Japanese product does not have to get yen directly from a Japanese who wants to buy an American product. The American may, just as well, get the yen from a German who got them by selling goods to Japan. Generally he or she buys them from banks and foreign exchange dealers who specialize in handling monies from many countries. We can still draw a graph for the U.S. dollar in the international exchange market, as in Figure 1, but the vertical axis now should be labeled simply as the foreign exchange value of the dollar, rather than as Japanese yen, or West German marks, or British pounds, or some other specific foreign money (see Figure 2). For actual measurements, the units on the vertical axis are an average value of all foreign monies, "trade-weighted" by their importance in trade with the United States, without reference to capital movements involving the dollar. In practice, the units on the vertical axis are index numbers, with the exchange value of the dollar on some chosen date or base year set equal to 100. We shall simply refer to the dollar's exchange value as P so that we can say that the foreign exchange value of the dollar rises or falls, without measuring the rise or fall in any specific money. It is important to do so because the American dollar may possibly rise in its foreign exchange value even while it is falling in its exchange relation with some specific money, if that other money is rising even faster in its foreign exchange value.[3]

3. Of course, it is still possible and useful in many cases to express the international exchange value of the dollar in terms of some specific money. If you plan to travel to Canada, for example, you want to know the exchange rate between the American dollar and the Canadian dollar.

FIGURE 2
Foreign Exchange Market for the Dollar

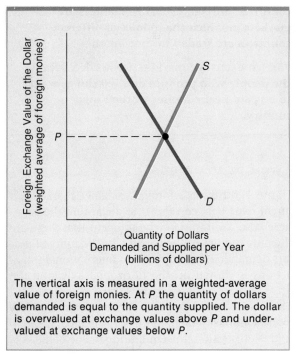

The vertical axis is measured in a weighted-average value of foreign monies. At P the quantity of dollars demanded is equal to the quantity supplied. The dollar is overvalued at exchange values above P and undervalued at exchange values below P.

The Slopes of Demand and Supply Curves

In Figure 2, the demand and supply curves for the American dollar look much the same as demand and supply curves for actual goods and services. But there is an important difference that must be cleared up before we go on to talk about equilibrium in foreign exchange rates. Let us concentrate on the supply curve and suppose that the dollar's exchange value goes up for some reason. Does this mean that the quantity of dollars supplied to the international exchange market will increase? The answer depends on how the change in exchange value affects the behavior of the people and firms that are supplying dollars. Americans who buy foreign goods are one of these supplier groups. The increased exchange value of the dollar means that the dollar price of foreign goods has fallen. As a result, we expect that these Americans will buy more foreign goods, but we do not know how much more they will buy. Suppose that the exchange value of the dollar rises by 10 percent and that, as a result, Americans purchase 10 percent more foreign goods. Is there any change in the number of dollars supplied to the international exchange market? The answer is no, because the effective cut in the unit price of foreign goods exactly cancels the increase in the number of these goods bought. In this situation, the supply curve of dollars in the international exchange market would be a vertical line.

This exercise tells you that when we draw a positively sloping supply curve for dollars, we are assuming that Americans (and others who supply dollars) are quite sensitive to changes in the dollar's exchange value—so sensitive in fact that their response in actual buying and investment and so on is more than proportional to the change in the dollar's exchange value. This is a reasonable assumption that is borne out by experience in normal times. It often does not hold for short time periods or in abnormal times.

The responsiveness conditions that we have just outlined for the supply curve also apply to the demand curve for the dollar. In this case, the reasoning process asks you to put yourself in the place of those who demand dollars and consider how you would respond to changes in its exchange value. More than proportionate responses to exchange value changes give this curve the negative slope shown in Figure 2.[4]

Equilibrium Foreign Exchange Rates

Movements toward equilibrium in foreign exchange markets operate in essentially the same way as in markets for goods and services (see Chapter 5). At any exchange rate above P in Figure 2, the dollar is said to be "overvalued," which means that a dollar will buy more in foreign countries than it will buy at home. An overvalued dollar also means that American goods are overpriced in international trade. In this case, more dollars will be supplied than are demanded, and pressure is exerted for a decrease in the exchange value of the dollar. The exchange value of the dollar will decline if it is free to move in response to market

conditions. In the language of foreign exchange, the dollar will **depreciate**. At any exchange rate below P, on the other hand, the dollar is said to be "undervalued" in the sense that it will buy less in international trade than it will buy at home. An undervalued dollar also means that American goods are underpriced in international trade. Now more dollars will be demanded than supplied, and pressure will be exerted for a rise in its exchange value. If exchange rates are free to move in response to market conditions, the dollar will **appreciate** as its exchange value rises. When equilibrium exists in a free international exchange market, the dollar is neither overvalued nor undervalued.

An overvalued dollar means that American goods are overpriced in international trade. If exchange rates are free to move in response to market conditions, the dollar will depreciate as its exchange value falls.

An undervalued dollar means that American goods are underpriced in international trade. If exchange rates are free to move in response to market conditions, the dollar will appreciate as its exchange value rise.

To extend our understanding of foreign exchange rates and markets, let us think of a foreign exchange market as divided into two separate submarkets. One submarket (which will be called the "capital account" when we study the balance of payments accounting system) is limited to transactions involving stocks, bonds, bank accounts, and other financial assets. In this "capital account" submarket, equilibrium would mean that the dollar rate of return on $1,000 would be the same as the foreign-money rate of return on $1,000 worth of foreign money after conversion to U.S. dollars. This condition is called **rate-of-return parity**.

Rate-of-return parity means that the rate of return on a dollar invested at home is the same as it would be if that dollar were exchanged for foreign money and invested in a foreign country.

---

4. If you have already studied microeconomics, you will recognize that the slopes of foreign exchange market demand and supply curves involve the well-known concept of elasticity.

The other submarket (which will be called the "current account" when we study the balance of payments accounting system) is limited to transactions in goods and services. In the current account submarket, equilibrium involves a condition known as **purchasing power parity.** This means that, as far as traded goods and services are concerned, a country's money will buy as much in traded goods abroad as it will at home. (Nontraded goods and services, like homes and haircuts, are not really in the picture.)

Purchasing power parity exists when the buying power of a country's money for traded goods and services is the same at home as abroad.

In practice, these two submarkets cannot be separated. The actual common or overall exchange rate is usually somewhere between the purchasing power and the rate-of-return parity values, so that neither parity condition is satisfied. A rate that over- or undervalues a currency in terms of either purchasing power or rate of return may nevertheless be a persistent equilibrium condition. How, for example, are we to explain the steady rise of the dollar against the yen over a six-year period (1979–1985) when the Japanese export balance in bilateral trade was generally rising and the American export balance accordingly falling? There are two major reasons. First, on the U.S. side, increasing public deficits had to be financed by the sale of securities to the public. If the inflation rate was simultaneously to be brought down, high interest rates had to be offered to sell these securities. Second, on the Japanese side, financial internationalization removed the legal and extralegal limitations on investment abroad and increased the demand for the higher-interest-bearing American securities.

FIXED VERSUS FLEXIBLE EXCHANGE RATES

Foreign exchange rates are called **free,** or **floating,** or **flexible,** when they are free to move up or down in response to shifts in demand and supply curves arising from the ordinary operations of international trade and finance. But many countries have been and remain unwilling to allow the international values of their monies to move freely. Politically persuasive arguments have generally led to **fixed exchange rates**—rates maintained through government intervention. We shall first describe how the exchange values may be fixed. Then we shall present both sides of the debate about fixed versus flexible rates.

Foreign exchange rates are called flexible (or floating) when they are free to move up or down in response to shifts in demand and supply curves arising from the ordinary operations of international trade and finance. Fixed exchange rates are rates maintained through government intervention.

Fixing Exchange Rates

Governments generally hold reserves of gold and monies (both their own and those of other countries). The governments of the major trading countries are therefore able to influence exchange rates if they choose to do so. They may be able to raise (or lower) the prices of foreign monies by buying (or selling) them. (Recall that a rise, or fall, in the price of foreign exchange constitutes depreciation, or appreciation, of the domestic money.) A government may choose not to recognize the exchange value set by the market. It may instead choose to set an official value for its money. Changing such an official exchange value is called **revaluation.** Lowering its official value is called **devaluation.**

During the 1960s, the United States held the foreign exchange value of the dollar above its free-market equilibrium rate as it tried to maintain a fixed rate in spite of a decline in the dollar's free-market value. The essentials of how this influence may be applied are easy to see by looking at Figure 3, which shows the international market for dollars. To maintain the dollar's value at, say, P_1, the United States dipped into its reserves of gold and foreign exchange and sold them for dollars. As long as the United States had enough reserves to purchase quantity *AB* of dollars per year, it could support the exchange value of the dollar at P_1. In effect, the demand curve became horizontal at the fixed rate, as shown by D_2, and the equilibrium moved to point *B*. On the other hand, if the United States wants to push the exchange value of the dollar below the free-market equilibrium level, say, to P_2, it can take dollars from its reserves or create more dollars and sell them in the foreign exchange market. If it sells quantity *EF* per year, it will succeed in depreciating the exchange value of the dollar to P_2. In this case, the supply curve becomes horizontal (as shown by S_2) at the fixed exchange rate, and equilibrium moves to *F*. A depreciated dollar would lower the cost of U.S. goods to foreign buyers and promote U.S. exports.[5]

Governments may try to influence exchange rates by buying or selling foreign monies. A rise (or fall) in the price of foreign exchange constitutes depreciation (or appreciation) of the domestic money. Governments may also set official values for their monies. Lowering an official value is called devaluation.

The Case for Flexible Rates

Those who favor flexible rates argue that they are prices like any others. They say that flexible exchange rates are better than fixed or government-controlled rates simply because free markets generally do a better job of setting prices and allocating resources than governments do. They also say that fixed rates are not really as safe and sure and stable as their advocates claim or hope. Governments, they say, often try to fix rates that they cannot maintain with the gold and foreign exchange re-

5. Some countries, such as Nazi Germany, developed very complex multiple exchange rates. Such systems are usually combined with **exchange controls,** which require licenses to buy foreign money or forbid its use to buy luxury imports, to travel abroad, or to buy foreign securities or other assets abroad. Generally, multiple rate systems involve the central bank selling foreign exchange to importers cheaply for essential imports and selling it dearly for less important uses. An **inconvertible currency** can exist under such control systems. For example, the Soviet ruble is inconvertible because Soviet citizens must have special licenses in order to buy foreign currency legally.

FIGURE 3
Fixing Foreign Exchange Rates

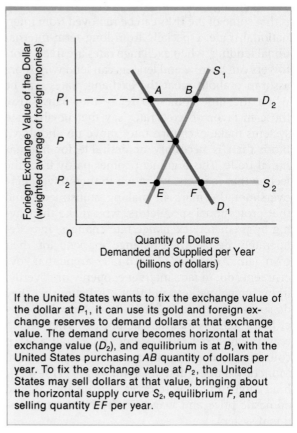

If the United States wants to fix the exchange value of the dollar at P_1, it can use its gold and foreign exchange reserves to demand dollars at that exchange value. The demand curve becomes horizontal at that exchange value (D_2), and equilibrium is at *B*, with the United States purchasing *AB* quantity of dollars per year. To fix the exchange value at P_2, the United States may sell dollars at that value, bringing about the horizontal supply curve S_2, equilibrium *F*, and selling quantity *EF* per year.

serves at their command.[6] When the reserves run out, drastic exchange rate changes can do more harm than the steady and moderate movements that would have come under a free-rate system. Worse yet, governments often resort to tariffs, quotas, and direct controls when their reserves start to fall too low. These direct controls reduce freedom and seriously distort world trade.

Adherents of flexible rates believe that free markets do a better job of setting prices and allocating resources than governments do.

---

6. This is often a matter of prestige. A falling value of a country's money—rising prices of foreign monies—can, rightly or wrongly, be taken to signifiy weakness or failure of the government's economic policies.

The Case for Fixed Rates

The main argument of those who favor fixed rates is that some of the risks can be removed from international trade, especially from long-term international lending, when exchange rates are fixed. Borrowers can borrow and lenders can lend with more assurance about what the exchange rates will be when the time comes to repay the loans. Also, those in favor of fixed rates say that flexible-rate systems make exchange rates move up and down more than is necessary or desirable for international trade. This argument comes partly from the feeling that markets, when left to themselves, may overshoot the mark in making adjustments and that professional speculators, who make their living by predicting exchange rate changes, may deliberately destabilize exchange markets for their own gain. Adherents of fixed rates argue that governments do, in fact, intervene, openly or covertly, in exchange markets and that it is better that they do so overtly, under a fixed-rate system, than covertly for reasons that may be unclear. They see no reason why fixed-rate systems should not work if countries, with the assistance of the International Monetary Fund (described on pages 413–414), hold large sufficient reserves and do not impose domestic price and wage rigidity on the international system.

Adherents of fixed rates believe that some of the risks can be removed from international trade, especially from long-term international lending, when exchange rates are fixed. Since governments intervene in exchange markets anyway, it is better that they do so openly, under a fixed-rate system.

A Brief History of Exchange-Rate Systems

Historically, fixed-rate systems have been more common than floating-rate systems. Probably the best-known system for fixing exchange rates is the gold standard, which was used by most major trading countries from the 1870s to the 1930s, except for the World War I period. After World War II, a new rate-fixing system was set up under the Bret-

ton Woods plan and carried out through the International Monetary Fund. We shall take a look at these systems and at why the most recent system broke down in the 1970s. We shall also see how Eurocurrencies fit into this picture.

The best-known system for fixing exchange rates is the gold standard.

The Gold Standard   Under the **gold standard,** countries promised to back their own money with a fixed amount of gold. That is, they promised to buy their own money and pay a stated amount of gold for it. Among the countries that followed this system, exchange rates were fixed, because a money that can be exchanged for twice as much gold as another money could also be exchanged for twice as much of that other money. For this reason, the price levels in gold-standard countries were linked to one another. Except for goods and services not traded and the costs of shipping goods and gold, the price levels in the trading countries would match (inversely) the fixed exchange ratios of their monies. A country whose money had a low gold equivalent would have a high price level, and a country whose money had a high gold equivalent would have a low price level. The price-level change would tend to bring purchasing power parity into international trade.

Under the gold standard, countries promise to back their own money with a fixed amount of gold. Under this system, the price levels of trading countries tend to match inversely the fixed exchange ratios of their monies.

The major problems with the gold standard came in times of rapidly changing economic conditions. For example, if a recession caused prices to fall in one country, its goods would become attractive in international trade compared with the goods of countries whose prices had not fallen. In the country suffering from the recession, exports would grow, helping it to recover. In order to carry out these purchases, foreigners would buy the exporting country's money partially with gold or convertible monies. Under the gold standard, such "gold inflows" or increases in reserves, would expand the exporting country's money supply, causing its price level to rise back toward its original level. But its trading partners would have falling exports and rising imports. They would lose international reserves, including gold, and they might suffer recession. Of course, if price levels and wage rates could change quickly enough, the linkage would not bring much hardship and unemployment, but if wage rates and prices were slow to change, unemployment would grow. The gold-standard linkage could be uncomfortable as economies not suffering recession found themselves vulnerable to the effects of recessions elsewhere in the world. Recession and unemployment afflicting one country could spread to its trading partners.

The major problems with the gold standard come in times of rapidly changing economic conditions. Recession and unemployment affecting one country could spread to its trading partners.

For smooth working of the gold standard, at least one of the major trading countries must be willing to permit its price and employment levels to be affected by events and/or policies originating in other countries. Also, at least one major trading country in the system must "make a market" for "distress goods" exported by countries in recession, despite the resulting damage to its domestic import-competing industries and work forces.

Great Britain satisfied these conditions in the Victorian and Edwardian generations before 1914. It maintained world confidence in the pound sterling, and reduced deflationary and contractionary pressures on its trading partners during depressions, at considerable sacrifice to Great Britain itself.

After World War I, the United States and (after 1925) France, both protectionist countries, took over Great Britain's leading role in the gold-standard system, but did not follow the policies required for smooth working of the gold standard. Therefore, the gold standard took on, for countries suffering recession, a pronounced deflationary bias, while concentrating the burdens of economic ad-

justment on these same countries. Small wonder that, in the first major test of the postwar gold standard—the Great Depression of the 1930—it failed miserably. Country after country, including Great Britain itself in 1931 and the United States in 1933, went "off gold" in the sense that they no longer provided gold to holders of their domestic currencies, even though the price of gold remained fixed.

The mid-Depression abandonment of gold led to a six-year period (1933–1939) of **competitive depreciation** and **exporting unemployment** that lasted until the outbreak of World War II. Countries anxious to increase exports, reduce imports, and reflate their domestic price levels bid up the prices of foreign monies and thereby cheapened their own. The process was accompanied by increased protection all around and, in many countries, by exchange controls as well. The volume of world trade contracted. Resource-poor countries like Japan, and to some extent Germany and Italy, doubting their ability to prosper by trade, turned eagerly to military imperialism as a replacement, with disastrous consequences.

The gold standard was abandoned in the 1930s, leading to a six-year period of competitive depreciation and exporting unemployment.

The International Monetary Fund   The **International Monetary Fund (IMF)** was set up shortly before the end of World War II at a meeting of central bankers and finance ministers at Bretton Woods, New Hampshire, and is sometimes called the **Bretton Woods system.** Its major goal was to maintain stable exchange rates and to avoid competitive depreciations and devaluations. Gold and the U.S. dollar were established as joint monetary standards, tied to each other at the ratio of $35 per ounce of gold, and the exchange values of other monies were fixed ("pegged") in relation to the dollar. Thus, a new set of fixed exchange rates was set up. Next, a fund (the IMF) was established from contributions of gold and monies from the major trading countries, roughly in proportion to their trading activity. The IMF directors then could make loans from the fund to help individual countries maintain these fixed exchange rates.

The International Monetary Fund (IMF), or Bretton Woods system, was established at the end of World War II to maintain stable exchange rates and avoid competitive depreciations and devaluations.

To understand how the fund was expected to operate, look again at Figure 3. Suppose that the fixed, or pegged, exchange value of the country's money is P_1, where the IMF believes the demand and supply curves will intersect in normal times. In other words, the IMF directors believe that the demand and supply curves, as shown in Figure 3, represent temporary circumstances and that they eventually will shift to bring equilibrium back to the P_1 exchange value. To maintain the fixed value, gold or foreign exchange in the amount of AB per time period would have to be used to support the demand for the nation's money. If the country did not have enough reserves of gold or foreign exchange to continue to pay out this quantity, an IMF loan could tide it over until demand and supply curves shifted back to "normal" positions and made the equilibrium value match the fixed value. If these shifts were not expected to take place, the IMF could deny the loan and require the country to devalue its money. Or it could set conditions for its assistance, generally in the form of lowered inflation rates and lowered budget deficits. The idea of the fund was that such devaluations would be limited and would not be permitted to lead to competitive devaluations as they had before World War II.

The Breakdown of Fixed Rates   How did the Bretton Woods system actually work out? The U.S.S.R. and the Soviet bloc never joined the IMF, and that body itself could impose its wishes mainly on the weaker developing countries, which came to resent IMF-imposed "austerity." Nevertheless, the Bretton Woods system worked reasonably well until the Vietnam War and the War on Poverty combined to put increasing downward pressure on the dollar itself, and fears arose that the United States would not have enough gold or other reserves to maintain the $35 per ounce relationship with gold. The resulting European preference for gold rather than dollars in their reserve holdings added further

to this pressure. After the failure of various compromise solutions, President Nixon "pulled the plug" on the Bretton Woods system in August 1971 by refusing any longer to exchange gold for dollars even with foreign governments and central banks.

Since then, foreign exchange markets have operated under what has become known as a **dirty float.** Many developing countries have pegged their money to the dollar, in practice at least. But individual governments often try to influence the exchange value of their own money by buying or selling large amounts of foreign exchange. The result is a weak imitation of a fixed-rate system.

The Bretton Woods system collapsed in 1971 when the United States refused to continue exchanging gold for dollars. Since then, foreign exchange markets have operated under a dirty float, in which individual governments try to influence the exchange value of their money by buying or or selling large amounts of foreign exchange.

Eurocurrencies

We hear a great deal about Eurodollars today. Why are there no Eurodollar bills? Is a Eurodollar different from a U.S. dollar?. Is a Euromark or Eurofranc different from an ordinary Deutschmark or Swiss franc?

To answer these questions, we turn to history. The **Eurocurrency** system began in the 1950s with the Eurodollar, which in turn seems to have begun with the Soviet Union. The Soviet authorities needed dollar reserves for purchases in the West, but they did not want to hold dollars in the United States, where the government might freeze or confiscate them if the Cold War heated up. It was tempting for them to buy pounds or francs and earn the higher interest rates that then prevailed in western Europe, but the instability of European monies was a problem. The dollar was the world's most stable money and was widely used in contracts between and among citizens of European countries. So the Soviets deposited their dollar funds in special dollar accounts in European banks.

For the European banks, these dollar accounts could serve as reserves for dollar loans at high European interest rates—the best of both worlds, so to speak. The dollar accounts in European banks became known as Eurodollars.

The system spread. Financiers from all countries, the United States included, took advantage of it to increase their interest earnings when U.S. interest rates were low. The dollars that European banks were lending came to include not only their depositors' dollar funds in Europe but other dollar funds purchased or borrowed and then deposited. From an original base in London, the market spread all over Western Europe and beyond. When the dollar weakened in the wake of the Vietnam War, the market expanded from Eurodollars to include the other Eurocurrencies.

The Eurocurrency's main attraction is freedom. A dollar deposit in a London bank, which may be a London branch of a New York or San Francisco bank, is not subject to U.S. laws and regulations about reserve ratios, interest rates, and the quality or its loans, because it is located physically in Britain. But neither is it subject to British law, since the status of the British money and the ordinary British depositor are not involved. (If the British should try to regulate the Eurodollar market too much, it would soon leave London!)[7] So it has grown into a major oasis of freedom in an overregulated world (according to its friends) or a major unguided missile on the world financial scene (according to its enemies).

Eurodollars are dollar accounts in European banks. Eurocurrencies are deposits of a country's money in banks in a foreign country, which are free of the issuing government's laws and regulations about reserve ratios, interest rates, and the quality of loans.

The Eurocurency market has expanded greatly over the years. The principal expansion has been a *Eurobond* market in dollar bonds issued and marketed outside the United States, to avoid U.S. regulations on matters that may include taxes, interest rates, insurance, trading practices, credit rationing, and so on. Similarly, a *Euroyen*, or "Samurai" bond, is a yen bond issued outside Japan to avoid Japanese regulations and "administrative guidance." In addition to markets in Europe itself, there are also offshore markets physically close to a country's financial centers yet still unregulated. These may even be located within the country's territorial waters, like the Isle of Wight in the English Channel. The Bahamas, the Cayman Islands, and the Republic of Panama have been offshore financial markets of the United States.

When regulation increases in severity, and when real interest rates diverge between countries, Eurocurrency, Eurobonds, and similar instruments gain in importance. On the other hand, when deregulation and financial internationalization proceed, and when the world moves closer to uniformity of real interest rates, markets using these instruments decline.[8]

The Eurodollar should not be confused with the **European Currency Unit (ECU),** which is the monetary unit of the European Currency Union. There is no physical distinction between an ordinary dollar and a Eurodollar, but the ECU is a money of account, which does not exist in any physical sense. It is a weighted average of the values of a number of European Community (EC) monies. Although ECUs cannot be circulated, bank accounts may be held in them. The value of the ECU is not fixed relative to the dollar, the yen, or any other "outside" money, but it is hoped that it will fluctuate less violently than the Deutschmark, the Dutch guilder, or other member-country monies.

BALANCE OF PAYMENTS ACCOUNTS

Our next task is to explain the accounting system that countries use to keep track of the international transactions that give rise to the demands for and supplies of their money. The record of transactions affecting the international demand and supply for a

---

7. Much of the Eurodollar "market" is now international, with centers in such places as Tangier, Hong Kong, and Singapore.

8. An excellent brief treatment of this subject is "Euromarkets," *The Economist* (London), May 16, 1987.

nation's money is that nation's **balance of payments account.** In order to introduce you to the idea of international transactions, we first present two hypothetical cases. Then we outline the U.S. balance of payments accounts.

A balance of payments account is the record of transactions affecting the international demand and supply for a nation's money.

We start by limiting our attention to a single pair of international transactions. The two are, we shall suppose, of equal size. Herr Braun, of Hamburg, West Germany, has instructed his broker to buy for him $15,000 worth of International Business Machines (IBM) stock on the New York Stock Exchange on Wall Street. Payment must be made in dollars, but we suppose that Herr Braun and his broker have only German marks. At the same time, Mr. Brown, of Chicago, buys from a local dealer a $15,000 sports car made by the Toyota Company in Nagoya, Japan. Eventually Toyota wants payment in Japanese yen, but both Mr. Brown and the Toyota dealer in Chicago have only American dollars.

What do these two transactions mean in terms of U.S. international balances? Herr Braun's purchase of IBM stock is part of both the demand for American dollars and the supply of German marks in foreign exchange markets. From the American point of view, transactions such as this are usually called positive, active, credit, or favorable because they build up American-owned reserves of foreign currency. On the other hand, Mr. Brown's purchase of the Toyota automobile is part of both the American demand for foreign exchange (in this case the Japanese yen) and the supply of American dollars as seen by foreigners. From the American point of view, transactions such as this are usually called negative, passive, debit, or unfavorable because they draw down American reserves of foreign exchange. Later we shall see how important this distinction is and whether a positive item, leading to the accumulation of foreign exchange, is really any more favorable than a negative item, which draws down such reserves. For the moment, we shall look at the accounting system that keeps track of international transactions.

U.S. International Accounts

Actual international data cover thousands, even millions, of transactions taking place among more than 150 countries. Few of these transactions cancel out quite as neatly as in our hypothetical cases. Also, the number of different types of transactions is much greater.

Table 1 presents the U.S. international account balances at five-year intervals from 1967 to 1987. It summarizes the millions of transactions that took place between Americans and foreigners during those years. Each transaction recorded in the international accounts system must be entered as either a credit (+) or a debit (−) to show its effect on the exchange value of the dollar.

What determines whether any particular transaction is recorded as a credit (positive item) or a debit (negative item) in the account? The general rule is as follows. If a certain kind of transaction normally leads to a demand for domestic (in this case, U.S.) money or a supply of foreign money, it is a positive transaction. If it generally leads to a demand for foreign money or a supply of domestic money, it is a negative transaction. This is clearly shown by the entries in the current account part of Table 1, where exports are positive and imports are negative. Exports of U.S. goods generally mean that foreigners demand dollars and supply their own money in international exchange markets to pay for goods purchased from U.S. citizens. On the other hand, when Americans buy goods from foreigners, they must supply dollars and demand foreign money in order to pay for these imports. It is a bit harder to understand the positive and negative entries in other sections of the accounts, but the general rule holds there as well.

If a certain kind of transaction generally leads to a demand for domestic money or a supply of foreign money, it is a positive transaction (a credit). If it generally leads to a demand for foreign money or a supply of domestic money, it is a negative transaction (a debt).

The next step in understanding the international accounts in Table 1 is to note that the differ-

TABLE 1
U.S. International Account Balances, Five-Year Intervals, 1967–1987 (billions of dollars)

	1967	1972	1977	1982	1987
Current Account					
1. Merchandise Exports	30.7	49.4	120.8	211.2	249.6
2. Merchandise Imports	−26.9	−55.8	−151.9	−247.6	−409.9
3. BALANCE OF TRADE	3.8	−6.4	−31.1	−36.4	−160.3
4. Investment Income Receipts	8.0	14.8	32.2	83.5	103.8
5. Investment Income Payments	−2.7	−6.6	−14.2	−54.9	−83.4
6. BALANCE ON INVESTMENT INCOME	5.3	8.2	18.0	28.7	20.4
7. Balance on Remittances and other Services	−6.5	−7.6	−1.4	−1.0	−14.1
8. CURRENT ACCOUNT BALANCE	2.6	−5.8	−14.5	−8.7	−154.0
Capital Account					
9. Capital Inflow	7.4	21.5	51.3	93.7	211.5
10. Capital Outflow	−9.8	−14.5	−34.4	−116.2	−85.1
11. CAPITAL ACCOUNT BALANCE	−2.4	7.0	16.9	−22.5	126.4
12. Statistical Discrepancy	−0.2	−1.9	−2.0	36.1	18.5
13. U.S. OFFICIAL RESERVES[1]	0.0	0.7	−0.4	−5.0	9.1

[1] Includes allocations of Special Drawing Rights by the International Monetary Fund. This is one concept of the overall balance of payments.

Note: Detail may not add to total because of rounding.

Source: Economic Report of the President, 1989, Table B-102, p. 424f.

ent types of transactions that take place during the year are listed (and numbered) down the left side of the table. To explain how the accounting system works, we will work through the accounts from one concept of balance to the next.

Balance of Trade   The **balance of trade** (line 3 in Table 1) is the most familiar and therefore the easiest to understand. It is the amount by which the value of a country's exports of goods (line 1) exceeds or falls short of the value of its imports of goods (line 2). The U.S. balance of trade has been negative since the mid-1970s, after two generations of positive values. Mr. Brown's purchase of the Toyota automobile would be recorded as an import in this part of the account.

The balance of trade is the amount by which the value of a country's exports of goods exceeds or falls short of the value of its imports of goods

---

Balance on Investment Income   In Table 1, line 4 shows investment income (dividends, interest, and rent) received by Americans from foreigners. This item is a credit in the U.S. international accounts because it represents a demand for dollars and a supply of foreign monies. Line 5 shows the flow of investment income from Americans to foreigners. It is a debit item in the U.S. international accounts. Line 6 shows the balance on investment income. The balance was positive throughout the period shown in Table 1, but the positive balance declined between 1982 and 1987. If the U.S. national debt continues to rise, this balance threatens to turn negative because of interest payments to foreign holders of U.S. government securities.

Current Account Balance   The **balance on current account,** sometimes called simply the **current balance,** is also easy to derive. It adds transactions in services and unilateral transfers such as individual gifts and foreign aid (line 7 in Table 1) to the balance of trade and the balance on investment income. The current account balance is shown on line 8 of Table 1. It became negative between 1967 and 1972. Its negative balance increased enormously between 1982 and 1987 mainly due to the larger negative entry for the trade balance.

The balance on current account, or current balance, adds such items as transactions in services and unilateral transfers to the balance of trade and the balance on investment income.

Capital Account Balance   The figures on lines 9 to 11 of Table 1 show the U.S. capital inflow (line 9), the U.S. capital outflow (line 10), and the *balance on capital account,* or *capital balance,* (line 11) as the difference between them. Both private and public capital movements are included in all of these accounts. We need go into detail only with regard to the capital outflow, or export figures.

The balance on capital account, or capital balance, is the difference between capital inflow (imports) and capital outflow (exports).

Capital exports, or outflows, are purchases of foreign assets and should not be confused with exports of capital goods. The foreign sellers of foreign securities, foreign real estate, or the control of a foreign firm ordinarily demand foreign money in payment; the exporters of trucks or oil-well rigs ordinarily demand domestic money. So a capital export is a debit item, whereas a capital-goods export is a credit item.

Capital outflows (line 10) include private purchases of foreign assets and similar purchases by the government. Capital imports, or inflows (line 9), are presented in the same way. Changes in the government's official reserves of gold, convertible foreign monies, and credits with the International Monetary Fund are treated separately (line 13).

Statistical Discrepancy   When we add a country's balance on current and capital account (Table, 1, lines 8 and 11), including also the change in government official reserves (line 13), the theoretical result is zero, by the principles of double-entry bookkeeping. The sum is, in practice, never zero, and a special account called ''statistical discrepancy'' or ''errors and omissions'' is added to force a balance—*not* an approved accounting practice!

With the rise of illegal traffic in drugs and weapons (on current account) and of illegal capital flight (on capital account), the ''statistical discrepancy'' account has risen disconcertingly even though there was a significant decrease between 1982 and 1987 (see line 12 of Table 1). In fact, imports of all reporting countries taken together amount to $800 billion more than their exports—a ''black hole'' of international economics. Since trade with the moon and with outer space remains physically impossible, we ascribe the great bulk of this current-account discrepancy to crime, smuggling, and fraudulent evaluation.

Theoretically, a country's current account balance plus its capital account balance, and the changes in official reserves, should equal zero. In practice, it never does—a balance is forced by using a special ''statistical discrepancy'' account.

Balances of Payments   After the insertion of the artificial ''statistical discrepancy'' entry, each country's international accounts for each period are apparently in balance. So what is this thing called the balance of payments? Do not the payments always balance?

In practice, most attention focuses on the balance concepts already described—the trade balance, the investment-income balance, the current account balance, and the capital account balance. Is there any concept that gives an overall view and that could be called *the* balance of payments? One popular approach is to define a country's balance of payments is as the sum of its balance on current account and its balance on whatever capital-account transactions may have been undertaken for their own sakes, rather than merely in settlement for other transactions. Economists, however, are not mind readers, so how can they know the motivations of each and every capital movement?

They do not know, but use various rules of thumb to divide the capital accounts into autonomous items and settlement items.

Another concept of *the* balance of payments is the entry called "U.S. Official Reserves" on line 13 of Table 1. This line indicates small buildups or draw-downs of U.S. government holdings of "official reserve assets" each year. In the special vocabulary of balance-of-payments specialists, this means that the American "official settlements" balance was slightly in surplus or slightly in deficit. But the American government refuses to attach any precise meaning to these figures. It does not take sides among the several varieties of balance-of-payments concepts and does not publish balance-of-payments figures of its own.

A country's balance of payments is sometimes defined as the sum of its balance on current account and its balance on whatever capital-account transactions may have been under taken for their own sakes, rather than merely in settlement for other transactions. The entry for changes in U.S. official reserves also is sometimes used as an indication of the payments situation.

Balance of Payments Stages

A country's balances of trade and capital movements generally go through several stages of balance and imbalance in the course of economic growth and development. Table 2 illustrates one theory about how this happens. Plus signs (+) indicate credit balances, and minus signs (−) indicate debit balances. (Two pluses or two minuses indicate greater magnitude.) According to this view, a country such as the United States moves from the stage of an "immature debtor" to that of a "mature creditor" in the following way.

1. An **immature debtor,** such as the North American colonies in the seventeenth century, imports goods and especially capital goods. The result is a deficit in the goods and services entries of the balance of payments accounts. Payment is through capital inflow from abroad, which is a positive item in the capital account. There is some return flow as loans are repaid, but the net flow still is positive.

2. A **mature debtor,** such as the American colonies in the eighteenth century and the United States through much of the nineteenth century, has developed agricultural exports (wheat, cotton, and tobacco), which turn its trade balance positive. It continues to import capital, but its return flow of dividends, interest, and loan repayments has become much larger over the years and the net flow is now negative.

An immature debtor imports goods, especially capital goods, resulting in a deficit in the goods and services entries of the balance of payments accounts. A mature debtor has developed agricultural exports, which turn its trade balance positive.

---

3. There is often an intermediate stage, which was cut short in the United States by World War I. The trade balance remains normally positive, but the country begins a net export of capital, mainly to less developed countries like Canada and Mexico. The return flow of dividends, interest, and loan repayments due to previous European loans and investments in America continues so that the combined return-flow account may go either way. The net flow is generally negative.

4. An **immature creditor,** like the United States from the end of World War I through World War II and until about 1960, exports enough capital to balance both return flows and continuing trade surpluses.

5. From the point of view of the payments balance, a **mature creditor,** like the United States today, tends to live off its income from investments abroad. Repayments from past capital exports exceed its present capital exports. The country's trade balance also turns negative, because some of its natural resources have been depleted and it has become a high-living, high-cost country. It is not unusual for a rich mature creditor country's receipts from repayment of past loans from any particular poor country to exceed its new exports of

TABLE 2
Balance of Payments Stages

Stage No.	Stage Description	Trade in Goods and Services	Capital-related Transactions		
			New Investments	Interest, Dividends, and Loan Repayments	Net Flow
1	Immature debtor	−	+ +	−	+
2	Mature debtor	+	+	− −	−
3	Intermediate	+	−	?	−
4	Immature creditor	+	− −	+	−
5	Mature creditor	−	−	+ +	+

This table lists five international payments stage through which a country may pass in the course of its economic development. Plus signs (+) indicate net credit balances, and minus signs (−) indicate net debit balances. Two pluses (+ +) or two minuses (− −) indicate greater magnitude.

capital to that country, so that money appears to be flowing from the poor country to the rich one. The capital flow between Latin America and the United States is following this pattern insofar as the Latin American countries are servicing their large debts to the United States. This pattern is therefore causing great resentment in Latin America. In the United States itself, the rise of the national debt has reduced the net new investments abroad and the receipts of "interest, dividends, and loan repayments'" entries in Table 2. Therefore, the net flow of capital-related transactions, which combines current and capital account items, is probably less positive than the typical case.

An immature creditor exports enough capital to balance both return flows and continuing trade surpluses. A mature creditor tends to live off its income from investment abroad.

Favorable or Unfavorable Balance?

An active, positive, or surplus balance of trade or payments is often called a **favorable balance.** It is thought to be a good thing. On the other hand, a passive or negative balance is often called a deficit, or **unfavorable balance**—a bad thing. These terms were developed by the mercantilist school of political economy, which dominated Western economic thought for 250 years ending in about 1750 and which is now being revived under the banner of protectionism. According to mercantile theory, which has never died, gaining and keeping positive international balances and accumulating treasure should be among the major goals of a country's trade policy.

A positive, or surplus, balance of trade or payments is called a favorable balance. A negative, or deficit, balance of trade or payments is called an unfavorable balance.

The mercantilist policy makes a good deal of sense when the macroeconomy's main problem is achieving or maintaining high employment, since exports add to aggregate demand and imports often have a negative effect. But when the main problem is inflation, or too little domestic aggregate supply, the reverse of the mercantilist policy makes sense. In order to control inflation, a negative balance is a good thing and a positive balance is a bad thing. Countries may restrict exports to hold down prices at home. For example, in the 1970s the United

States put restrictions on the export of Alaskan oil, building materials such as lumber, and animal feed such as soybeans. When a country is experiencing stagflation, with *both* unemployment and inflation, there is no general answer to the question of whether a positive or a negative balance is better.

A positive balance of trade is good if the economy is trying to achieve high employment, but when the main problem is inflation, a negative balance is good.

Readers may notice that the "favorable-unfavorable" terminology, like the mercantilist and protectionist viewpoints from which it developed, recognizes people's interests as producers but ignores their interests as consumers, which may be radically different. This point is emphasized further in the chapter which deals with free trade versus protection.

BALANCE OF PAYMENTS PROBLEMS

When one speaks of a country as suffering balance-of-payments problems, this usually means that the country is losing international reserves so persistently and rapidly at the current exchange rate that these reserves will soon be exhausted. This is a primary payments problem. An example of a primary balance-of-payments problem is Brazil, which, in the same decade, seemed condemned (in the absence of debt relief) to two large negative capital-related balances, a negative investment balance on debt service and a negative capital balance on the debt itself. These threatened to swallow up so large a portion of Brazil's positive export balance as to leave little for economic growth. To preserve its international reserves, Brazil claims to have sacrificed a decade of development. In ordinary times, primary balance-of-payments problems are now largely limited to developing countries. (This was decidedly untrue during periods of large-scale warfare and postwar reconstruction like 1914–1925 and 1939–1955.)

A balance-of-payments problem means that a country is losing international reserves of gold and convertible foreign monies so persistently and rapidly that these reserves will soon be exhausted.

Secondary payments difficulties arise when either a country's current or capital balance turns sharply negative, even without affecting its international reserve position. A large negative capital balance, however, is usually *not* a payments problem when it represents the accumulation of assets overseas. In the 1980s, the Japanese case is the obvious example. For the first two-thirds of the twentieth century, the obvious example was the United States. Continued *accumulation* of reserve assets may, however, be unwise. Why not buy more foreign goods or other foreign assets instead? Why emulate King Midas, the legendary hoarder of gold?

SOLUTIONS FOR PAYMENTS PROBLEMS

The treatment of payments problems, whether primary or secondary, presents a maze of unsolved problems in both theory and policy. Economists want not only to remedy the difficulties but to do so at minimum cost in terms of income, employment, development, and economic freedom. Although we must leave full analysis to more advanced students in international trade and finance, our introductory discussion in terms of domestic policy can be helpful as a first step.

Consider, for example, what is called the "classical medicine" of **laissez faire**. This policy permits prices and wage rates to fall until the trade and current accounts rise sufficiently not only for their own balance but also to compensate for any negative capital accounts. In macroeconomics this translates into a disinflationary monetary policy with passive fiscal policy.

A laissez-faire policy permits prices and wage rates to fall until the trade and current accounts

---

rise sufficiently to compensate for any negative capital accounts.

Many suggested remedies for balance-of-payments problems, however, go well beyond ordinary macroeconomic policy and introduce additional variables. We shall comment on a half-dozen of these.

Among the most popular, although perhaps less so than formerly, has been currency depreciation, or **devaluation**. It is usually intended to raise current balances by raising the prices of imports at home and lowering the prices of exports overseas. In the practice of the 1980s, it appears to have raised capital account balances instead. For example, in the American and Japanese cases, as the dollar fell and the yen rose, U.S. assets became better bargains than U.S. goods.

International loans—bilateral or multilateral, conditional or unconditional—are additional capital movements. They raise either the present capital balance or the present international reserve position of the receiving country, at the expense of future balances when the loans are serviced or repaid.

International aid is a pure transfer, increasing the receiving country's current account and international reserves. It need not be repaid and makes negative payments balances easier to live with, pending growth or technical change to permit receiving countries to restore their economic health. The Marshall Plan from the United States to western Europe in the late 1940s and early 1950s is the classic example of success here.

Protection of domestic industries that face competition from imports and *subsidy* of export industries increases trade and current balances, at the expense of consumers and taxpayers. They may also attract foreign capital to locate inside the country and thereby avoid the tariff and other trade restrictions. If so, they increase the country's capital balance as well.

Exchange controls can increase a country's current account by disallowing entire classes of foreign-exchange purchases—for foreign travel, for transmission of investment income, etc. Controls can also increase the capital balance by disallowing

both capital export and debt repayment. They are in practice difficult to enforce without major restrictions on fundamental personal liberties.

Countertrade is a modernized version of primitive barter. It is the direct exchange of contracted amounts of goods (or occasionally services) between two or more countries, with (almost) no pressure on the international reserves of any of the trading partners. When one trading partner is a large country like Nazi Germany, on whom a number of economic or political satellites are economically dependent for goods, for markets, or both, the satellites often lose from such arrangements. They may lose by accepting lower terms of trade for their goods than they might have obtained on the world market, by accepting imports they do not want and must re-export, or by exporting goods they need for home consumption.

Countertrade is the dominant trading system of the Comecon (Soviet bloc) countries,[9] many of which would apparently prefer to reduce their dependence on countertrade with the Soviet Union in favor of ordinary trade with the hard-currency countries of the West. Their particular grievance is that they must export goods they need for home consumption.

Much countertrade is not reported to international authorities. Some suggest that as much as a third of all world trade is carried on in this way, but these estimates include "in-house" trading between branches of affiliated multinationals, partners in joint ventures, etc.

Suggested remedies for balance-of-payments problems include currency depreciation, international loans, international aid, protection of income-competing industries and subsidy of export industries, exchange controls, and countertrade.

---

9. The Comecon system is not pure countertrade. Accounts are kept in world prices and, at year's end, outstanding balances are in principle settled in Soviet rubles.

Economics in Focus

Buying and Selling America

Who owns America? Not long ago, such a question would have prompted debate about the roles of big business, government, the average worker and homeowner, and other traditional segments of American society. Now, however, the answer is likely to be a shouted chorus: America is owned by the British! By the Japanese! By all of the foreign investors who are buying up not only American stocks and bonds but also entire corporations and large chunks of real estate.

By 1988 the value of U.S. assets owned by foreigners was estimated at $1.5 trillion. The largest landlord in Manhattan was Canadian, and major portions of other American cities were owned by the Japanese. Firestone Tire was purchased by Bridgestone, a Japanese company. RCA Records went to Bertelsmann, a giant media firm from West Germany. Such familiar American brand names as Endicott Johnson shoes, Ball Park franks, and Inglenook wines belonged to the British. Foreign investment in the United States was setting new records each year—$40.6 billion in 1987 alone—and increasingly it was directed toward "hard" assets, such as land and manufacturing, rather than bonds or stocks.

The reasons for this trend were clear. The continued U.S. trade deficits left foreigners with large quantities of dollars to invest, and the best buy for a dollar was in America. Moreover, because of the stock market crash of 1987, as well as fluctuations in the bond market and in currency exchange rates, foreign investors were wary of paper assets; they preferred tangible property whose value would grow over the long term.

The general public's reaction to the trend has been overwhelmingly negative. In a survey conducted by Smick Medley & Associates, 78 percent of the respondents said they would like to see limits placed on foreign purchases. But many economists have argued that the wave of foreign investment has much to recommend it. First, the foreign money has financed American economic growth. Foreign owners have created jobs for American workers, and they are paying $80 billion in wages each year, not to mention $8 billion in corporate taxes. In addition, they have brought in new technology and production techniques that will benefit American industry for years to come.

As of the late 1980s, U.S. holdings abroad still exceeded the total value of foreign investment in America. Besides, the much-feared foreign assets accounted for only 2 percent of U.S. corporate profits. Thus most economists have seen no immediate reason to panic. On the other hand, they do believe the rapid pace of foreign acquisition should not go on indefinitely. In the long run, if the current trends persist, the U.S. standard of living will decline and foreign investors will control large segments of the American economy. The solution, in the view of many observers, is not to penalize or exclude foreign buyers but to increase the U.S. saving rate and improve the trade deficit.

Sources: Jaclyn Fierman, "The Selling of America (Cont'd)," *Fortune,* May 23, 1988, pp. 54–64; Gene Koretz, "The Buying of America: Should We Be Worried?" *Business Week,* May 9, 1988, p. 36; Peter Brimelow with Lisa Scheer, "Is the Reagan Prosperity for Real?" *Forbes,* October 31, 1988, pp. 85–90.

SUMMARY

1. Open economies cannot conduct economic policies as though they were closed to international trade and capital movements. What the rest of the world does affects the economy of a country. (See page 405.)

2. The money of one country is exchanged for the money of another country in foreign exchange markets. These markets are needed in international trade because people wish to be paid in the money of their own country. (See page 406.)

3. The intersection of the demand curve and the supply curve in the foreign exchange market indicates the equilibrium foreign exchange value of a nation's money. Purchasing power parity exists when the buying power of a country's money for traded goods and services is the same at home as abroad. Transactions on the capital account involve the concept of rate-of-return parity, where the rate of return on a dollar invested at home is the same as it would be if that dollar were exchanged for the foreign money and invested there. (See pages 409–410.)

4. Countries may try to raise the exchange value of their money by using their gold and foreign exchange reserves to supplement the demand for their money. They may lower its exchange value by selling their own money in the foreign exchange market. (See page 410.)

5. The argument for flexible exchange rates is that they do a more efficient job of pricing goods and allocating resources than do government-controlled rates. Moreover, government attempts to control rates often break down and cause serious problems. (See page 411.)

6. The argument for fixed exchange rates is that they reduce uncertainty and thus help international trade and investment. Moreover, since governments usually influence exchange rates anyway, it is better that it be done openly. (See page 412.)

7. Under the gold standard, monies are linked to each other because each is guaranteed to be exchangeable for a stated amount of gold. Under this system, gold and trade flows tend to force the price levels in gold-standard countries into fixed relationships, corresponding inversely to the gold backing of their monies. The gold-standard system collapsed in the unstable economic conditions following World War I. (See pages 412–413.)

8. The International Monetary Fund was set up near the end of World War II to make loans to countries to help them hold the exchange value of their monies in line with fixed exchange rates approved by the IMF directors. This fixed-exchange-rate system broke down in 1971 when the United States refused to continue to exchange gold for dollars, thus letting the reserve money itself float in foreign exchange value. (See page 413.)

9. Eurocurrencies are deposits of a country's money in banks in a foreign country. These deposits are free from their issuing government's controls over reserve ratios, interest rates, and the quality of loans. The advantages of this freedom from control have led to a great expansion of Eurocurrency accounts. (See pages 414–415.)

10. Balance of payments accounts record transactions that involve demands (credit entries) and supplies (debit entries) for a nation's money in international payments. Widely recognized concepts of balance are (a) the balance of trade, (b) the balance on investment income, (c) the balance on current account, (d) the balance on capital account, and (e) the official settlements balance of payments. (See pages 415–416 and Table 1, page 417.)

11. If the sum of a country's current and capital accounts is positive, the country's balance of payments is in surplus. If the sum is negative, its balance of payments is in deficit. (See pages 418–419.)

12. It is sometimes suggested that countries move through several balance of payments stages in the course of economic development. They start as immature debtors and end as mature creditors, living off dividends and interest from previous investments abroad. (See pages 419–420 and Table 2, page 420.)

13. Following mercantilist views, a positive payments balance usually is considered favorable and a negative balance is unfavorable. However, in terms of macroeconomic policy, these judgments depend on whether the goal is to expand the economy or to fight inflation. (See page 420.)

14. A country has a primary payments problem if its international reserves of gold and convertible foreign monies are low and its balance of pay-

ments is usually negative. (See page 420).

15. A country has a secondary payments problem (1) if its current account is in deficit but its payments are balanced by undesired capital imports, or (2) if its capital account deficit, or *capital flight*, is absorbing a large portion of the export surplus the country had hoped to use for other purposes. (See page 420).

16. Remedies for payments problems, either primary or secondary, include price deflation—the so-called "classical medicine" of laissez faire—currency devaluation or depreciation, international aid or lending, trade protection, exchange controls, and countertrade. (See pages 421–422.)

KEY TERMS

appreciation: an increase in the exchange value of a country's money in the foreign exchange market (page 409).

balance of payments account: the record of transactions affecting the international demand and supply for a nation's money (page 416).

balance of trade: the amount by which the value of a country's exports of goods exceeds or falls short of the value of its imports of goods (page 417).

balance on current account (current balance): the balance of trade plus the balance on investment income plus such items as transactions in services and unilateral transfers (page 417).

Bretton Woods system: international financial arrangements that fixed exchange rates and were built around the International Monetary Fund. It was set up just before the end of World War II (page 413).

competitive depreciation: the practice of causing a depreciation of a nation's money for the purpose of achieving an exchange value lower than that of the monies of competing countries (page 413).

current balance: see **balance on current account.**

depreciation: a decrease in the exchange value of a country's money in the foreign exchange market (page 409).

devaluation: lowering the official exchange value of a country's money (page 422).

dirty float: when individual governments try to influence the exchange value of their money by buying or selling large amounts of foreign exchange (page 414).

Eurocurrency: a deposit of a country's money in a foreign bank which is, therefore, free of the issuing government's regulations about reserve ratios, interest rates, and the quality of loans (page 414).

European Currency Unit (ECU): the monetary unit of the European Economic Community (page 415).

exchange controls: a set of regulations governing licenses required to buy foreign money and permission to buy luxury imports, to travel abroad, or to buy foreign securities or other assets (page 422).

exporting unemployment: causing unemployment to decrease at home and increase abroad by restricting the import of foreign-made goods (page 413).

favorable balance: an active, positive, or surplus balance of trade or payments; the value of exports exceeding the value of imports (page 420).

fixed exchange rates: foreign exchange rates maintained through government or international monetary agency intervention (page 410).

foreign exchange: the money of other countries (page 406).

foreign exchange markets: markets in which the monies of different countries are exchanged (traded) for one another (page 406).

free (floating, flexible) exchange rates: foreign exchange rates that are free to move up or down in response to shifts in demand and supply curves arising from the ordinary operations of international trade and finance (page 410).

gold standard: a system for fixing exchange rates through a country's promise to exchange its money for a fixed amount of gold (page 412).

immature creditor: a creditor country that exports enough capital to balance both return flows and continuing trade surpluses (page 419).

immature debtor: a debtor country that imports goods, especially real capital goods (page 419).

inconvertible currency: the money of a country that does not allow it to be freely exchanged for money of other countries (page 411).

International Monetary Fund (IMF): an agency established just before the end of World War II by the major trading countries to maintain stable exchange rates and to avoid competitive depreciations and devaluations (page 413).

laissez faire: a policy of government noninvolvement in economic affairs (page 421).

mature creditor: a creditor country that tends to live off its income from investments abroad (page 419).

mature debtor: a debtor country that has developed agricultural exports, which turn its trade balance positive (page 419).

purchasing power parity: when a country's money will buy as much in traded goods abroad as it will at home (page 410).

rate-of-return parity: when the rate of return on a unit of money invested at home is the same as it would be if that money were converted into the money of a foreign country and invested there (page 409).

revaluation: changing the official exchange value of a country's money (page 422).

tariffs: taxes on imported goods (page 406).

unfavorable balance: a passive or negative balance of trade or payments; an excess of the value of imports over the value of exports (page 420).

DISCUSSION QUESTIONS

1. Construct a graph showing the demand and supply for U.S. dollars in the foreign exchange market. Describe an action that the U.S. government might take or a development in the U.S. economy that would cause the dollar to depreciate in exchange value. Use your graph to illustrate why this would happen.

2. What interests in the American economy benefit when the dollar rises on the international exchange markets? What interests benefit when the dollar falls?

3. What is the difference between fixed and flexible exchange rates? What are the advantages and disadvantages of each for the United States?

4. It is often proposed in conservative circles that the United States return to the gold standard, but not to the pre-1971 gold price of $35 an ounce. How do you think an appropriate gold price might be estimated? What would happen if the estimate were seriously wrong in either direction?

5. What are Eurodollars? Why are they important to an entrepreneur?

6. Explain how it can happen that a country can have a positive balance of trade at the same time that it has a negative balance of payments, or vice versa.

7. Explain why an export of a country's capital and an export of capital goods (such as machinery) have opposite effects on a country's international balances.

8. Analyze the effects of a currency devaluation on a country's balances on current and capital account if both its domestic demand for imported goods and services and foreign demand for its own goods and services are completely unresponsive to price changes.

9. Does the United States have either a primary or a secondary payments problem?

Appendix:
International Macroeconomics*

THE POLICY AUTONOMY ISSUE

Most countries and their governments believe that it is important to protect their freedom to choose and carry out internal fiscal and monetary policies with little thought about the rest of the world. But whether this policy autonomy favors fixed or flexible exchange rates depends on whether fiscal or monetary tools are most important to the country's policy. On the one hand, freedom to use fiscal policy for lowering the measured unemployment level is protected more fully under fixed rates. On the other hand, freedom to use monetary policy for the same purpose is protected more fully under flexible rates. Let us see why this is so.

Expansionary fiscal policy, aimed at reducing measured unemployment, usually raises government budget deficits. These deficits must be financed. If inflation is to be avoided, financing a deficit requires an increase in the supply of government securities. This increase lowers security prices and raises interest rates. In the foreign exchange market, the higher rates shift the demand curve for the country's money to the right, because the opportunity of earning higher returns makes the country a more attractive place for foreigners to invest—and makes foreign countries less attractive places for the country's own citizens to invest. Under floating rates, the resulting inflow of capital causes an appreciation of the country's money. With this higher value of the country's money, its exports may fall and its imports may rise, making the expansionary fiscal policy less effective. Under fixed rates, higher net capital inflows promote the expansionary policy without interfering with international trade. Instead of currency appreciation, there is an accumulation of foreign currency re-

serves, sometimes called a *positive balance of payments*.

Expansionary monetary policy, on the other hand, favors flexible exchange rates. Expanding the money supply would normally lead to lower real interest rates in the short run (see Chapter 14). Fixed exchange rates would increase the flow of capital out of the country and would mean less investment at home. Under floating rates, however, there would be a lower exchange value for the country's money, reducing the capital outflow, encouraging exports, and discouraging imports.

Freedom to use fiscal policy to lower measured unemployment is more fully protected under fixed rates. Freedom to use monetary policy to lower measured unemployment is more fully protected under flexible rates.

For countries wishing to disinflate—reduce their inflation rates—these arguments work in the opposite direction. As witnessed in the early 1980s in the United States, disinflationary *monetary* policy raises interest rates at home and brings capital inflows. Disinflationary *fiscal* policy, by lowering interest rates at home, raises capital outflows. So a country that is trying to lower its inflation rate by monetary means would favor fixed exchange rates to avoid a loss of exports. If such a country stresses fiscal disinflation, it would favor flexible rates to help its exporters. Table 3 sums up each of these cases.

A country that is trying to lower its inflation rate by monetary means would favor fixed exchange rates. A country that stresses fiscal disinflation would favor flexible rates.

---

* The material in this appendix presumes that students have already studied macroeconomics.

TABLE 3
Which Exchange-Rate Regime Maximizes Internal Macroeconomic Policy Autonomy?

Primary Policy Instrument	Policy Goal	
	Reducing Unemployment	Disinflation
Fiscal policy	Fixed rates	Flexible rates
Monetary policy	Flexible rates	Fixed rates

PAYMENTS EQUILIBRIA AND DISEQUILIBRIA

In our study of the domestic economy, we have learned that it tends at any time to an equilibrium real income and an equilibrium real interest rate. But these domestic-equilibrium values will not necessarily equilibrate the country's international payments as well. On the contrary, they may leave the country accumulating reserve assets it does not particularly want or facing the prospect of exhausting its reserves altogether.

Changes in a country's income level and interest rates affect its current and capital account balances in the following principal ways:

1. Changes in *income* affect primarily the *current* balance. A rise in income tends to decrease this balance because it brings about a rise in imports of goods and services. A fall in income tends to increase the current balance because it brings about a fall in imports of goods and services.

2. Changes in *interest rates* affect primarily the *capital* balance. A rise in the interest rate tends to increase this balance because it attracts capital from abroad and also reduces capital export by the country's own residents. A fall in the interest rate tends to decrease the capital balance because it repels capital from abroad and increases capital export by the country's own residents.

Changes in a country's income level affect primarily the current balance. Changes in interest rates affect primarily the capital balance.

We also know that in an isolated economy:

1. An easy *fiscal* policy aimed at reducing unemployment tends to raise both income levels and interest rates. A tight fiscal policy aimed at disinflation tends to lower both income levels and interest rates.

2. An easy *monetary* policy aimed at reducing unemployment tends to raise income levels and lower interest rates. A tight monetary policy aimed at disinflation tends to lower income levels and raise interest rates.

An easy fiscal policy tends to raise both income levels and interest rates; an easy monetary policy tends to raise income levels and lower interest rates. A tight fiscal policy tends to lower both income levels and interest rates, while a tight monetary policy tends to lower income levels and raise interest rates.

It follows that an easy *fiscal* policy, taken by itself with monetary policy passive, will tend to reduce the country's *current* account balance and increase its *capital* account balance. An easy *monetary* policy, however, taken by itself with fiscal policy passive, will tend to reduce *both* the current and capital account balances. A tight fiscal policy, with monetary policy passive, will tend to increase the country's current account balance and decrease its capital account balance. A tight monetary policy, with fiscal policy passive, will tend to increase both the current and capital account balances.

For the more interesting cases where fiscal and monetary policy operate together, we combine all the preceding information and derive Table 4. This table summarizes the effects of different policy combinations on both the current and capital accounts of the country concerned. (A zero entry in the table indicates only that the policies counteract each other to some extent, not that they must offset each other completely.)

TABLE 4
Effects of Fiscal-Policy and Monetary-Policy Combinations on Current and Capital Account Balances

			Aim of Fiscal Policy	
			Reduced Unemployment	Disinflation
Aim of Monetary Policy	Reduced Unemployment	Current Account	−	o
		Capital Account	o	−
	Disinflation	Current Account	o	+
		Capital Account	+	o

The primary international effect of fiscal policy acts through changes in income and is on the country's current account. The primary international effect of monetary policy acts through changes in its real interest rate and is on the country's capital account.

(+) and (−) denote increases and decreases, while (o) denotes minimal or offsetting effects.

INTERNATIONAL MACROECONOMIC IDENTITIES

There are many important connections between the macroeconomics of the domestic and the international economies. A great deal of political and journalistic discussion of international trade and finance is flawed by violation of one or more of three fundamental macroeconomic identities that arise from these connections—or by reading particular causal patterns into them.

There are three basic macroeconomic identities that arise from the connections between the macroeconomics of the domestic and the international economies.

The first identity comes from our study of total planned expenditure and the circular flow. It is

$$Y = C + I + G + X - Im$$

where Y represents real GNP, C is consumption expenditure, I is investment expenditure, G is government purchases, X is exports, and Im is imports. Mercantilists read a special pattern of causation into this identity. They say that net exports $(X - Im)$ *determine* real GNP (Y).

Mercantilists say that net exports determine real GNP.

To derive our second identity, we examine the uses of income in the macroeconomics of a closed economy, that is, in an economy with neither exports nor imports. You can recognize these uses of income from the left side of the circular-flow diagram. With no imports, household uses of funds consist of consumption expenditure (C), saving (S), and net tax payments (T_n). Therefore, we have $Y = C + S + T_n$. To derive our second international macroeconomic identity, we subtract this equation from our first identity and get

$$(C + I + G + X - Im) - (C + S + T_n) = 0$$

The consumption terms cancel and the remaining terms can be rearranged into the form that we wish to use for the second identity. This is

$$(I - S) + (G - T_n) + (X - Im) = 0$$

This identity says that the sum of the three balances must be zero so that they cannot all be either positive or negative. The three balances are between private domestic investment and private domestic saving $(I - S)$, between government purchases and net taxes $(G - T_n)$, which is the public deficit,[10] and between exports and imports of goods and services $(X - Im)$, which is the current-account balance.[11]

The sum of three balances, $I - S$, $G - T_n$, and $X - Im$, must be zero.

The third international macroeconomic identity arises from the fact that international economic transactions are not limited to goods and services currently produced. Assets and titles to assets can also be transferred internationally. Therefore, payments for goods and services may take the form of either the creation or the transfer of assets—whether these are government securities or private IOUs. Conversely, payments for foreign assets may take the form of exports of goods and services currently produced.

To develop the third international macroeconomic identity, we will write X_k for capital exports and Im_k for capital imports. From the balance, $X_k - Im_k$, we exclude the change in monetary assets held as official reserves, which we label BP for balance of payments. We must then have, as accounting identities:

$$(X - Im) = (X_k - Im_k) + BP$$

which may be restated as

$$(X - Im) + (Im_k - X_k) - BP = 0$$

These identities state that a *positive* balance on current account $(X - Im)$ is also an acquisition of foreign assets, either in the form of a *negative* balance on capital account $(X_k - Im_k)$ or of a *positive* balance of payments (BP). Similarly, a *negative* balance on current account $(X - Im)$ is a diminution of foreign assets, either in the form of a *positive* balance on capital account $(X_k - Im_k)$ or a *negative* balance of payments (BP).

10. Confusion is easy at this point, because the deficit enters the identity as a *positive* item and a public surplus as a *negative* one.
11. *Not* the balance of trade. Strictly speaking, $(X - Im)$ is the current-account balance abstracting from international transfer payments, which do not enter into Y.

A negative balance on current account is a diminution of foreign assets.

Before we proceed to consider applications of these identities, let us review them and note that they can be expressed in terms of *changes*. The three identities are

$$Y = C + I + G + X - Im$$

$$(I - S) + (G - T_n) + (X - Im) = 0$$

$$(X - Im) + (Im_k - X_k) - BP = 0$$

In applying these identities to actual situations, we will be interested in year-to-year changes in values more than in absolute values. Therefore, it will be helpful to restate the identities in differentiated form, that is, in the form of changes. We use the symbol Δ (*delta*) to mean *change in*. In this form, the identities are

$$\Delta Y = \Delta C + \Delta I + \Delta G + \Delta X - \Delta Im$$

$$(\Delta I - \Delta S) + (\Delta G - \Delta T_n) + (\Delta X - \Delta Im) = 0$$

$$(\Delta X - \Delta Im) + (\Delta Im_k - \Delta X_k) - \Delta BP = 0$$

Illustration: The Trade Act

The omnibus trade act passed by the United States in 1988 provided protection against "unfair" imports and retaliation against "market closing" by America's trading partners to American exports. Debates leading to this legislation indicated that it was expected to raise the American current account balance (ΔX positive and ΔIm negative). These effects, in turn, were expected to raise income and employment (ΔY positive)—all without changes in American habits as reflected in other macroeconomic variables. Thus, the debates leading up to this act stressed the first identity in its differentiated form:

$$\Delta Y = (\Delta C + \Delta I + \Delta G) + (\Delta X - \Delta Im)$$

But when we consider our second identity in differentiated form,

$$(\Delta I - \Delta S) + (\Delta G - \Delta T_n) + (\Delta X - \Delta Im) = 0$$

it becomes clear that all the anticipated benefits of the trade act could occur only to the extent that income and employment increases were shunted into saving net of investment ($\Delta I - \Delta S$) and net tax payments net of government purchases ($\Delta G - \Delta T_n$). Did Congress and the media miss this point in the debate? Or did they ignore it as "too technical" for the average voter to understand? Probably both, but especially the first.

The trade act sought an increase in real GNP, but its supporters often failed to see that this result would also require changes in the other components of the second identity.

Illustration: Trade Shifting

Americans are sometimes urged to shift imports from country A (often East Asian) to country B (often Latin American) because the United States has a large negative bilateral trade balance with country A but not with country B. It should be clear immediately that such a shift would not raise the U.S. current account balance at all. Its effects would only be a cosmetic reduction of the bilateral balance with A, an injury to A's export industries, and perhaps some injury to American consumers.

Shifting trade from one trading partner to another will not raise the total U.S. current account balance.

Illustration: "Twin Towers"

The Reagan administration fiscal policies (such as tax cuts) combined with congressional qualms about cutting social spending and the ever-present local pork barrels, raised American budget deficits and the national debt in the mid-1980s both absolutely and as percentages of the GNP. At the same time, the American current account deficit rose to record levels, again both absolutely and relative to GNP. The budgetary and current-account deficits were called "twin towers" by the president's critics, on the theory that the current-account deficit was a *necessary* consequence of the budgetary one. This criticism involves our second identity which, in differential form and related to income growth

(ΔY) is

$$\left(\frac{\Delta I}{\Delta Y} - \frac{\Delta S}{\Delta Y}\right) + \left(\frac{\Delta G}{\Delta Y} - \frac{\Delta T_n}{\Delta Y}\right) + \left(\frac{\Delta X}{\Delta Y} - \frac{\Delta Im}{\Delta Y}\right) = 0$$

From this, it becomes clear that the rising budget deficit relative to GNP

$$\frac{\Delta G}{\Delta Y} - \frac{\Delta T_n}{\Delta Y}$$

might have been balanced by a fall in the private investment–private saving balance relative to GNP

$$\frac{\Delta I}{\Delta Y} - \frac{\Delta S}{\Delta Y}$$

that is, a rise in the ratio of private saving to GNP greater than the rise in the ratio of private domestic investment to GNP. But the saving ratio fell, and its fall was quantitatively more important than the rise in the deficit. Thus, the trade deficit, in fact, increased relative to GNP. The administration had hoped for and anticipated a higher saving ratio but also a higher investment ratio!

The "twin towers" viewpoint suggested that the trade deficit was an inevitable consequence of the budget deficit—but the identities show that this was not necessarily true.

Illustration: Predatory Foreigner or Prodigal American?

In attempts to explain the difficulties of the international economic position of the United States after approximately 1960, we encounter two rival scenarios, each a causal interpretation of our third international macroeconomic identity: ($\Delta X - \Delta Im$) + ($\Delta Im_k - \Delta X_k$) − $\Delta BP = 0$. One is the "predatory foreigner" thesis and the other is the "prodigal American" thesis.

The "predatory foreigner" thesis is as follows: by dumping and subsidizing their exports to the United States, by closing their domestic markets to U.S. exports, and by shifting to the United States the burdens of defense against aggression, foreigners have achieved positive current balances with the United States. These have cheapened the dollar in the world's exchange markets. Next, foreigners use their current surpluses to buy up American assets "on the cheap" (ΔIm_k). They have displaced the United States from its dominant position as the world's creditor and their holdings of both debt and equity securities permit them to influence American political and economic decision making in their own interests. If nothing is done, the United States will become their economic colony, with its workers limited to menial jobs and its government at the mercy of foreign bondholders' threats to refuse or to dump its securities. Thus, the "predatory foreigner" thesis traces causation from the current account balance ($\Delta X - \Delta Im$) to the capital account balance ($\Delta Im_k - \Delta X_k$).

The "prodigal American" thesis accuses America of three economic misdemeanors: (1) unrealistic expectations that its high wages and incomes (relative to foreign ones) were part of the natural order of things and should survive the rest of the world's recovery after World War II; (2) a penchant for fighting undeclared wars and overextending its commitments beyond its borders; and (3) living beyond its means domestically. Americans, it was said, financed their prodigalities by selling securities and other assets, including an increasing fraction of the rising American debt. To make American assets attractive to foreigners, in large amounts, their prices had to fall. So the value of the dollar has fallen, and American interest rates have stayed high. To finance such purchases of American assets, foreigners chose to reduce purchases of U.S. goods below what they would otherwise have been and also to sell aggressively their own goods in U.S. markets. Thus, the "prodigal American" thesis traces causation from the capital account to the current account.

The predatory foreigner thesis traces causation from the current account to the capital account, while the prodigal American thesis traces causation from the capital account to the current account.

The point is that these self-serving causal interpretations are at best half-truths that ignore many other things going on at the same time (such as the demographics of population and its distribution and the development and exhaustion of such resources as fossil fuel and agricultural land). The advantage of an algebraic identity, on the other hand, is that it expresses the result of *all* the forces acting on it—not just the one or two chosen with an eye to propaganda. At the same time, the maintenance of the identity may restrain the variability of each force taken individually, after the fashion of Newton's Third Law about forces generating their own counterforces. Our exercises in macroeconomic identities illustrate, we believe, the usefulness of economic analysis in understanding the complex world of international exchanges.

The advantage of an algebraic identity is that it expresses the result of all the forces acting on it—not just the one or two chosen with an eye to propaganda.

SUMMARY

1. Many countries wish to maintain their freedom to carry out domestic macroeconomic policy without adverse effects from international trade and capital flows. Whether this suggests flexible exchange rates or fixed exchange rates depends on whether the policies are aimed at reducing unemployment or at reducing inflation and on whether they are carried out with fiscal or monetary instruments.

2. An apparent equilibrium in a single country's macroeconomy may actually involve deficits and surpluses in the country's various international accounts.

3. These surpluses or deficits may be in either the country's current or its capital accounts and may be remedied in principle by changes in the country's macroeconomic policies.

4. Changes in a country's real national income and product affect primarily its trade and current account balances. The effects are inverse. Increases in real national income operate primarily to reduce the current-account balance by increasing imports, and vice versa.

5. Changes in a country's real interest rates affect primarily its capital-account balance. The effects are direct. Increases in real interest rates operate primarily to attract foreign capital and discourage capital exports.

6. A looser (tighter) fiscal policy tends to lower (raise) a country's current-account balance and raise (lower) its capital-account balance.

7. A looser (tighter) monetary policy tends to lower (raise) a country's current-account balance and also to lower (raise) its capital-account balance.

8. Three international macroeconomic identities assist in understanding relationships between the international and the domestic dimensions of the economy. These identities are

$$Y = C + I + G + X - Im$$

$$(I - S) + (G - T_n) + (X - Im) = 0$$

$$(X - Im) + (Im_k - X_k) - BP = 0$$

9. Negative U.S. balances on current account have been balanced by positive balances on capital account—the purchase of U.S. assets by foreigners. It has been feared that this may impair U.S. control of its resources and also the autonomy of its macroeconomic policy.

10. Applications of international macroeconomic identities reveal that the effects of legislation, such as trade shifting and the omnibus trade act, depend on accompanying actions taken in the domestic economy.

11. The U.S. budget deficit is associated with its current account deficit only because the U.S. private sector is investing more than it saves.

DISCUSSION QUESTIONS

1. Analyze the effects of a disinflationary monetary policy with fixed exchange rates on a country's balances on current account and capital account.

2. If the U.S. private saving rate rises to 10 percent of disposable personal income, what would happen to the country's international accounts?

3. Explain why a country's balances of private saving and investment, of public expenditures and receipts, and of exports and imports of goods and services, cannot all have the same sign.

4. If the U.S. public sector were to balance its combined budget, the so-called "twin towers" theory implies that the U.S. current-account deficit would also be eliminated. Is this correct?

5. Since the U.S. negative balance on current account is approximately balanced by a positive balance on capital account, why has it caused so much concern?

20
Free Trade versus Protection

Preview The choice of free trade versus protection has been a key policy issue for generations and centuries. In the past, it was a conflict between market and planning principles. Those who favored free trade believed that competition among trading countries would lead to greater economic efficiency. Those favoring protection felt that a certain amount of protection of domestic industries from the effects of trade with other countries was necessary.

We begin with a simple case of a freely traded standardized product in a freely competitive world. We discuss gains and losses in both importing and exporting countries from trade in such a product. Then we turn to a second question: Which goods will a country export when free trade is opened up, and which goods will it import? This leads to the classical idea of "comparative advantage," and the various reasons or explanations for its existence. One explanation is based on differences in productive efficiency, and another on differences in "endowments" of resources or factors of production.

Next we examine the gains from trade between two or among several countries and the effects of trade on wage and interest rates in the trading countries. You will see that free trade has much the same effect as free immigration or free movement of capital in equalizing wage and interest rates between countries. This is called "factor price equalization."

So much for free trade. Next we define *protection* and consider some of protection's many forms: tariffs, quotas, antidumping duties, and administrative protection, including an important distinction between *nominal* and *effective* rates of protection. We present a number of arguments for protection. Some of these are economic, relating to such questions as "cheap foreign labor" and helping "infant industries." Others are noneconomic, such as those related

435

to national defense and the dangers of boycott or blockade. These formal defenses of protection, however, may have little to do with its wide popularity. Many economists believe that its popularity is due largely to the activities of "intense minorities," otherwise known as "special interests."

The last major subjects that we cover are international negotiation and the shifting U.S. trade position. Trade treaties are discussed and then customs unions and free trade areas, which can be viewed as attempted compromises between free trade and protection. Finally we present the reasons why the United States experienced negative trade balances during the 1980s.

GAINS AND LOSSES FROM TRADE

The basic principles of international trade are among the best established in the whole field of economics. Economic arguments for free trade were prominent in the writings of the classical economists of England in the eighteenth and nineteenth centuries and fit in well with the trading interests of an island nation.

The basic case for free international trade is an extension of the case for free trade among individuals. For individuals, the freedom to engage in trade makes it feasible for each person to specialize in the tasks for which he or she is relatively well suited. As each person specializes, production goes up and the fruits of the greater output can be traded with others who, likewise, have specialized in the things they do relatively well. In other words, trading opens the door to specialization, specialization increases productivity, and higher productivity raises real living standards.

International free trade arguments simply observe that these same principles hold when the two parties to an exchange are of different nationalities. Even though most actual international trade is carried on between individuals or firms in one country and individuals or firms in another, it is usual to speak of countries trading with one another. Then it is noted that, just as individuals differ from one another in talent and endowments, countries differ in climate, soil conditions, the size and skill of their labor forces, the availability of capital, and so on.

Thus, the theory readily shows that free international trade can raise the per capita real income in all trading countries.[1] Once the advantages of free international trade have been demonstrated, debate then usually centers on the following two questions. First, given the level of aggregate input and output, which goods should a country produce for itself and which ones should it produce for export? And second, what other goods, if any, would it be cheaper to import?

Trading opens the door to specialization, specialization increases productivity, and higher productivity raises real living standards. Thus, free international trade can raise the per capita income in all trading countries.

Just as individuals differ from one another in talent and endowments, so do countries differ in resources, size and skill of labor forces, availability of capital, etc.

Unfortunately, for those who favor internationalism, even though free trade may raise the measured real production and income per capita in all trading countries, it is not true that all persons who are affected gain from such trade. For example, when a country increases its exports, domestic consumers of the exported goods face higher prices for those goods, and their living standards may go down. In the same way, when a country increases its imports, domestic producers of goods that compete against these imports may lose. These facts of life must be recognized in understanding the conflict between free trade and protection.

When a country increases its exports, domestic consumers of the exported goods face higher prices for those goods. Likewise, when a country increases its imports, domestic producers of goods that compete against these imports may lose.

---

1. The principles governing trade and payments between American states are the same as those between countries. If U.S. prosperity is attributed largely to its being the world's most important free trade area, why not extend the same principle to whole continents, to the capitalist world, or to the world as a whole?

FIGURE 1
Trade in a Single Commodity

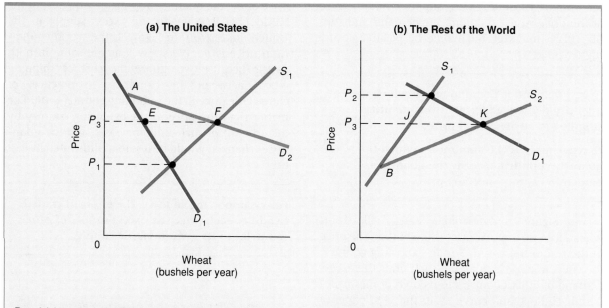

(a) The United States

(b) The Rest of the World

Panel (a) represents the wheat market in the United States and panel (b) represents the wheat market in the rest of the world, treated as one country. In each panel, D_1 and S_1 represent demand and supply before there is any international trading in wheat. Excess supply exists in the United States at prices above P_1. In panel (b), the U.S. excess supply at each price is added to the domestic supply in the rest of the world to generate the supply curve S_2 for the rest of the world.

In the rest of the world, excess demand exists at any price below P_2. In panel (a), this excess demand at each price is added to domestic demand in the United States, generating the demand curve D_2. Equilibrium international trading occurs (ignoring shipping costs) at price P_3, with quantity EF exported by the United States and quantity JK (which is equal to EF) imported by the rest of the world. At equilibrium, there remains neither excess demand nor excess supply in either country.

Trade in a Single Commodity

We begin by describing the effects of trade in one commodity, such as wheat, which is produced in two countries. To keep our analysis simple, we shall consider trade between the United States and "the rest of the world," as if the rest of the world were all one country. Actually, the United States trades with many separate countries, involving many different situations.

Figure 1 shows the market for wheat in each of these two "countries." We use the same scale on the vertical (price) axis of both graphs. This means either that the two countries use the same money or that their monies exchange in a fixed ratio to each other.[2] In each graph, the demand curve D_1 shows only demand from domestic purchasers, and

2. The determination of exchange rates between monies is explained in Chapter 19.

the supply curve S_1 shows only the supply from domestic suppliers. In the absence of trade, wheat sells for P_1 per bushel in the United States and for P_2 in the rest of the world. These prices differ from each other because the two countries differ in their demands for wheat and in their endowments of resources used in producing it. Without trade, wheat would be more expensive in the rest of the world than in the United States.

We can illustrate the results of opening up trade between these countries by using the concepts of excess demand and excess supply. **Excess demand** is the amount by which the quantity demanded exceeds the quantity supplied at any specified price. In the absence of trade, excess demand would be zero in each country at the price at which domestic demand, D_1, intersects domestic supply, S_1. But a positive amount of excess demand would exist at any lower price. **Excess supply** is the amount by which the quantity supplied exceeds the quantity demanded at any specified price. In the absence of trade, excess supply would be zero at the price where the domestic demand and supply curves intersect, but would be positive at any higher price.

Excess demand is the amount by which the quantity demanded exceeds the quantity supplied at any specified price.

Excess supply is the amount by which the quantity supplied exceeds the quantity demanded at any specified price.

In Figure 1, the United States will export wheat because the U.S. price is lower than the price in the rest of the world. For an exporting country, the effect of trade is to add at each price the excess demand of other countries to its own domestic demand. The demand curve D_2 in the U.S. panel of Figure 1 shows the result of adding, at each price, excess demand from the rest of the world to the domestic demand, D_1, in the United States. Point A corresponds to the pretrade price for wheat in the rest of the world, so that excess demand in those countries is zero. In the United States, the horizontal distance between the demand curve (D_1) and the demand curve (D_2) is the same as the horizontal distance between S_1 and D_1 in the rest of the world at prices below P_2. At the world equilibrium price of P_3, the quantity exported by the United States (distance EF) is the same as the quantity imported by the rest of the world (JK).

For an exporting country, the effect of trade is to add at each price the excess demand of other countries to its own domestic demand.

The parallel situation for the rest of the world is illustrated by the supply curve S_2 in panel (b) of Figure 1. Point B corresponds to the price at which there is no excess supply in the United States. But at higher prices, excess supply exists in the United States, measured by the horizontal distance between its domestic demand and supply curves. The supply curve S_2 for the rest of the world is drawn by adding, at each price, excess supply from the

United States to the domestic supply curve (S_1) of the rest of the world. At the world equilibrium price of P_3, the quantity imported by the rest of the world (JK) is equal to the excess supply in the United States (EF). In Figure 1, the world equilibrium price is P_3. We show it as the same in both panels because we ignore the cost of shipping wheat between the countries. In practice, of course, the price in the importing country would be higher than the price in the exporting country by the amount of such shipping costs, and the quantity exchanged would be less than illustrated in Figure 1.

For an importing country, the effect of trade is to add at each price the excess supply of other countries to its own domestic supply.

Gains and Losses to Producers and Consumers

To analyze the gains and losses from trade to producers and consumers, we shall use Figure 2, which reproduces Figure 1, but adds further information. Let us first examine what happens in the exporting country (the United States). Before international trade, Q_1 bushels of wheat were sold at price P_1. After equilibrium is reached in international trade, Q_2 bushels of wheat per year were sold at price P_3. Total gain to wheat producers in the United States is shown by the gold (both light and dark) area in panel (a). For all outputs up to Q_2, their prices have risen more than their costs, which are represented by the supply curve. U.S. consumers of wheat lose, however. Before international trade, they consumed Q_1 bushels and paid price P_1, but after equilibrium is reached in international trade, they consume only Q_3 bushels per year and pay price P_3. The higher price, P_3, that they pay for the quantity that they purchase, Q_3, is clearly a loss to consumers. They also lose the **consumers' surplus** (the benefit to consumers from being able to buy at a uniform price rather than the sum of the amounts they might have been willing to pay for each unit separately) on the quantity of wheat between Q_1 and Q_3. Thus, the wheat consumers' loss is represented by the dark gold area that lies to the

FIGURE 2
Gains and Losses from Trade in a Single Commodity

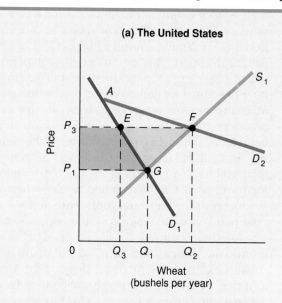

(a) The United States

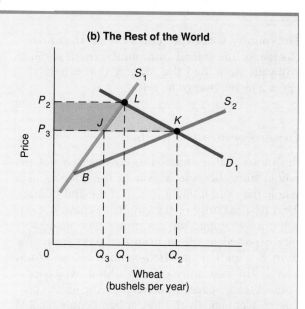

(b) The Rest of the World

The demand and supply curves on these graphs are the same as those on the graphs in Figure 1. In the United States, export of wheat causes the price to rise to P_3 and the quantity supplied to increase to Q_2. Producers' gain is represented by the gold (both light and dark) area in this panel. But U.S. wheat consumers pay a higher price (P_3) and consume fewer bushels (Q_3). The consumer loss is the dark gold area to the left of the demand curve (D_1). The net gain in the United States is the light gold triangular area *EFG*.

In the rest of the world, importing causes the price to fall to P_3 and consumers increase their purchases to Q_2 bushels per year. Their gain is shown by the gold (both light and dark) area in panel (b). Wheat suppliers in the importing country lose because they sell less wheat at a lower price. Their losses are represented by the dark gold area to the left of the supply curve (S_1). The net gain from trading for the importing country is the light gold triangular area *JKL*.

left of the demand curve (D_1). The total of producers' gain is greater than the total consumers' loss in the exporting country by the area of the light gold triangle *EFG* in the U.S. panel of Figure 2. This shows the presumed net gain from export trade in wheat.

Panel (b) traces a similar argument for the rest of the world. Before international trade, consumers purchased Q_1 bushels of wheat per year and paid price P_2. After equilibrium is reached in international trade, these consumers purchase Q_2 bushels per year at price P_3. The combination of more wheat and the lower price expands their consumers' surplus by the amount represented by the gold (both light and dark) area in the rest-of-the-world panel. But wheat producers in the importing country lose from international trade. Before such trade, they sold Q_1 bushels at price P_2, but interna-

tional trade causes both the price and the quantity that they sell to fall. Their loss is the dark gold area to the left of the supply curve S_1. But the gain to consumers in the importing country is greater than the loss to producers by the light gold triangular area *JKL* in panel (b).

Our analysis has demonstrated that both the exporting country and the importing country gain from free international trade. It does not necessarily follow, however, that the gains are evenly divided. The country that experiences the greatest price change for the traded commodity will gain more than the country that experiences a lesser change in price, other things unchanged. From this fact, we can reason that small countries may gain more from international trade than do large countries, which tend to dominate world trade and whose domestic prices may not change as much as a result of trade. This view is contrary to a popular one that the economic giants gain most from trade.

The country that experiences the greatest price change for the traded commodity, *ceteris paribus*, will gain more than the country that experiences a lesser change in price.

Other Economic Effects

Per capita real income gain, however, is not the whole story, because a gain to the country as a whole may still imply a loss to some and perhaps even to a majority of the country's citizens. Consider, for example, the cheap machine-made textiles exported to China from the West (primarily from England) in the half-century before World War I. The consumer gain to China, which economic theory suggests outweighed the loss to producers, went chiefly to those urban people (skilled workers, middle and upper classes) who bought them. The producers' loss was borne chiefly by poor peasants who had in the past spun and woven textiles to earn second incomes in the agricultural slack season. China was then an 80 percent peasant economy. So more individual Chinese lost than gained from the textile imports, and the distributional effects were in the direction of greater inequality. Moreover, the loss of a dollar of income probably meant more (in terms of utility, or anticipated satisfaction) to a rural peasant than to an urban white-collar worker. From this point of view, China may well have lost by the textile trade. As you can see, the presumption of net gains from trade is not a conclusive argument that trade is desirable.

The presumption of net gains from trade is not a conclusive argument that trade is desirable.

Another point is that not all products are traded between countries. Some, like real estate, are physically tied to one place. The more common problem, however, is that transportation costs are so high in relation to the prices of some goods that they are not exported or imported. Can producers and consumers of nontraded goods be left out when we try to assess the gains and losses from trade? The answer is "no" if these nontraded goods are complementary to or substitutes for either imports or exports in either production or consumption.[3] For example, consider the case of a Latin American country that exports a cash crop (such as coffee, sugar, or bananas) raised on land that might have been used for domestic food production (such as beans, rice, or other vegetables). In this case, producers of domestic food will lose from trade, because of the higher prices and rents they must pay for land and labor. The consumers of domestic food will also lose, because the price of domestic food will rise. Antitrade feeling results when the producers and/or consumers of domestic food are "the poor" and the majority of the population.

Another example is the importing of rice cookers into the United States. Invented in Japan, these cookers increased the American demand for American rice, by making it easier to cook and reducing the risk of cooking failures. (In this example, American rice plays the role of a nontraded good, though in fact much of it is exported.) Rice is complementary to rice cookers in consumption. The import of rice cookers, by raising the demand for rice, might be expected to raise its price—a good thing for rice producers but not for rice consumers.[4]

Producers and consumers of nontraded goods that are complementary to or substitutes for traded goods may gain or lose from trade.

COMPARATIVE ADVANTAGE

India and western Europe were almost completely cut off from each other for more than 500 years after the decline of the western Roman Empire.

---

3. Two goods are substitutes in production if they both use the same specialized inputs. Examples are corn and soybeans, which require the same type of land and climate. Two goods are complementary in production when they are joint products of a single production process, such as beef and hides, or when one is a raw material or an intermediate product in the making of another, as fish and fishing boats. Substitution and complementarity in consumption have been discussed in Chapter 23.

4. In fact, however, American agricultural policy both supported the domestic price of American rice above the world level and prevented the rice cooker from raising it further.

This period was the so-called Dark Ages. But despite high transportation costs and high risks, a trickle and then a stream of trade developed during and after the Crusades. What determined which goods would move in each direction? Similarly, what goods did Japan export and import when she was forced to open her doors to trade after 250 years of semi-isolation under the Tokugawa Shoguns?

Economists try to answer such questions by using the theories of comparative advantage. Here is the argument. When there is no trade or when it is restricted, a country will normally have a set of relative prices that is different from the set that exists in the rest of the world. For example, the price of apples may be twice the price of potatoes in one country, but may be three times the price of potatoes in the rest of the world. This is so because countries normally will have different combinations of resource endowments or will have developed special skills in different things. A good whose pretrade price or restricted-trade price is relatively lower in a country than in the rest of the world is likely to be exported by that country. On the other hand, a commodity whose pretrade or restricted-trade price is relatively higher in a country than in the rest of the world will likely be imported by that country. This is the well-known principle of **comparative advantage**.

According to the principle of comparative advantage, a good whose pretrade price or restricted-trade price is relatively lower in a country than in the rest of the world is likely to be exported by that country. A commodity whose pretrade or restricted-trade price is relatively higher in a country than in the rest of the world will likely be imported.

The following illustration, which comes from the English economist David Ricardo (1772–1823), is the classic demonstration of the principle of comparative advantage. Assume that one unit of English cloth requires 100 hours of English labor and that one unit of Portuguese wine requires 80 hours of Portuguese labor. Assume also that 120 hours of English labor would have been needed to produce a unit of wine in England. If, at equilib-

rium, one unit of cloth is exchanged for one unit of wine in international trade, England gains the product of 20 hours of labor by importing wine from Portugal in exchange for cloth. Ricardo does not tell us how many hours of Portuguese labor would be required to produce a unit of cloth. But any figure above 80 would give Portugal a gain from trade. If we suppose the figure to be 90, we would have the following costs for the two countries.

Country	Labor Cost per Unit Traded (in hours)	
	Cloth	Wine
England	100	120
Portugal	90	80

In terms of labor cost, Portugal has an **absolute advantage** in both cloth and wine since she can produce either one with less labor than would be required in England. Relative prices, however, would be 5:6 (100:120) in England and 9:8 (90:80) in Portugal. Cloth is relatively cheaper in England and wine is relatively cheaper in Portugal, giving England a *comparative* advantage in cloth and Portugal in wine. England would gain the product of 20 hours of English labor through trade and Portugal would gain the product of 10 hours of Portuguese labor. One partner's gain does not mean a loss to the other. However, one partner's gain may be larger than the other's. For example, were a unit of cloth in Portugal to cost 81 hours of Portuguese labor, the Portuguese gain would have been very small. Were a unit of wine in England to cost 101 hours of English labor, the major gain from trade would have gone to Portugal.

Another way to look at Ricardo's case is that Portugal is one-third better than England in wine production (40/120 = 1/3), but only one-tenth better in cloth production (10/100 = 1/10). Therefore, once we grant the existence of gains from trade, it is rational for England to export cloth and Portugal to export wine.

A later explanation of comparative advantage came from two Swedish economists, Eli Heckscher (1879–1952) and Bertil Ohlin (1899–1979). They explained comparative advantage as being due to differences between countries in their "endowments" of productive inputs, which affect the pretrade prices of goods traded. The United States, for example, has accumulated a great deal of capital equipment, but its labor has remained relatively scarce. This means that American real interest rates have been generally low, but American real wage rates generally high. For this reason, according to this theory, the United States should export capital-intensive goods and import labor-intensive ones, while the trade of Mexico or Guatemala should follow the opposite course.

Of course, there are complications and modifications. Countries produce many goods that can be traded. Comparative advantage cannot tell us exactly where the lines will be drawn between the potential exports, nontraded goods, and potential imports. Demand or supply may be so price inelastic that relative prices may change (and comparative advantage with them) when trade is freed. And trade may itself affect tastes and techniques so much and so permanently that the pretrade relative prices become entirely obsolete. But even with these and other qualifications, comparative advantage remains important in explaining trade patterns.

Comparative Advantage and Choosing a Career

A simple example of comparative advantage, outside the realm of international economics, is in students' choices of college majors and careers. Most economics teachers have had "star" students ask them about possible careers as economists. It is clear from their classroom performances that they have *absolute* advantages in economics. Absolute advantage simply means being more proficient than others in doing a given thing. However, *comparative* advantage is another matter. For all the economics teacher knows, the star student may be even more outstanding in history or mathematics, or even better suited to a career in law or medicine or engineering or journalism. So all the teacher can do for students is to estimate the size and the meaning of their *absolute* advantages in economics,

while advising them to estimate for themselves their *comparative* advantages in various fields before making up their minds.[5]

It is equally rational for a mediocre student to choose a major or a career in some field where his or her performance, while below average, is still better than in any other subject in terms of class ranking. Such a student's absolute disadvantage might be the least in economics, giving him or her a comparative advantage in that field as large or larger than that of the class's star student.

The Dynamics of Comparative Advantage

So far, we have presented comparative advantage as something static. That is, we might say, "A country *has* a comparative advantage in agriculture." To do so, however, is misleading in the light of economic history. As a country develops, its comparative advantages generally shift away from farming and handicrafts, first toward light industry and then toward heavy industry and later to service industries. These changes take place because land becomes more scarce, industrial capital accumulates, and labor increases in skill. In some cases, the process is only partial, as in Denmark or Iowa, which are developed areas that remain largely agricultural. In other cases, the process is nearly complete, as in the Ruhr Valley of West Germany or the "silicon valley" of California.

As a country develops, its comparative advantages generally shift away from farming and handicrafts, first toward light industry and then toward heavy industry and later toward service industries.

An especially interesting aspect of changes in comparative advantage over time is called the **product cycle**. At first, the comparative advan-

5. Of course, the relative incomes to be expected in different fields of endeavor are important too. One might hesitate to advise a student to become a tramp, a bum, or a hobo, however great that student's comparative advantage might be in such occupations.

tage in producing steel or automobiles is in developed high-wage countries that export to lower-wage developing ones. As the developing countries learn the manufacturing processes, and as these processes themselves become less skill-intensive, the less developed countries can first reduce their imports and then take up exporting on their own. After a time, the comparative advantage has shifted to newly industrialized developing countries, which come to dominate the world market. If the older developed country's import-competing industries survive, they do so largely because they are protected. The following "cycle" takes place in the developed country's industry. At first it is purely domestic. Next it becomes more and more of an export industry. Then, as lower-wage countries take over, it becomes more and more an import-competing industry.

In the product cycle, an industry that develops a product first produces for the domestic market, then adds production for export, but eventually becomes an import-competing industry as foreign producers, with lower input prices, learn how to produce the product.

Some high-wage countries and their labor movements fear that comparative-advantage dynamics will eliminate first their exports and then their domestic production of one manufactured good after another and thus "hollow out" their industrial sectors—first lower and then higher technology. Such countries could pay for imports in many ways—exports of farm products and of services, earnings on investments abroad, selling domestic assets (capital imports), or drawing down international reserves. Few or none of these are pleasant prospects, especially to the highest-paid elements of the industrial labor force. However, no country's industrial sector has actually become "hollowed out" and perhaps none ever will because, as one group of industries is lost, another may replace it. But the United States is a potential candidate for this sort of "hollowing out" under free trade and in the absence of factor price equalization—a feature of free trade to which we now turn.

FACTOR PRICE EQUALIZATION

Up to this point, we have explained that, except for transportation costs, freedom of trade equalizes the prices of traded goods and services across frontiers. However, what about the prices of nontraded inputs, such as wage rates for labor and interest rates for capital? The **factor price equalization theorem** states that free trade of goods and services across countries not only equalizes output prices but also input (or resource or factor of production) prices.

The factor price equalization theorem states that free trade of goods and services across countries not only equalizes output prices but also input prices, even when these inputs are not traded.

To illustrate this theorem, let us consider two countries (Mexico and the United States), two commodities (tractors and textiles), and two inputs (labor and machinery). Tractors and textiles are freely traded between the two countries. However, there is no migration of labor or trade in machinery between them, and in the short run neither the stock of labor nor the stock of machines in either country changes. We further assume that the quality of labor and of machines is identical between the two countries.

Suppose that, before trade, the price of textiles in relation to the price of tractors is higher in the United States than in Mexico and that the price of tractors in relation to the price of textiles is higher in Mexico than in the United States. Comparative advantage predicts that the United States will export tractors and that Mexico will export textiles. If the textile industry is labor intensive, its expansion in Mexico will cause Mexican wage rates to rise in real terms and also in relation to interest rates in Mexico. In the United States, where the capital-intensive tractor industry is expanding because of the export of tractors, the realignment of industry causes the return to machines (interest rates) to rise both in real terms and in relation to wage rates. So the real wage rate of Mexican workers should come closer to the real wage rate of American workers and would ultimately equal the American real wage rate if the volume of trade in textiles were large enough. Similarly, interest rates (the return to investments in machinery) in the United States should rise both in real terms and in relation to the U.S. wage rate as the American tractor industry expands. These interest rates will come closer to real interest rates in Mexico and would ultimately equal the Mexican real interest rates if the volume of trade were large enough. Thus, trade tends to equalize input prices, even when these inputs themselves were not traded.

In the real world, this theorem operates only as a general tendency. Free trade does tend to draw input prices closer together, but without leading to full factor price equality.[6] In practice, wage rates differ more than interest rates between countries, since capital moves more freely than labor migrates. However, even in its weakened real-world form, the factor price equalization theorem helps to explain why opposition often arises to free trade between countries with widely differing real wage and interest rates.

The factor price equalization theorem helps to explain why opposition often arises to free trade between countries with widely differing real wage and interest rates.

---

6. Why doesn't the equalizing process go all the way to bring about complete uniformity? Or to put the matter differently, what further conditions beyond freedom of trade are needed for our theorem to hold literally? Here are seven such conditions.
1. Conditions are stationary, with fixed amounts of each input in each country.
2. Transportation costs can be ignored.
3. Specialization is incomplete. Each country continues to produce some of each traded good under free trade.
4. Knowledge is uniform. Each country has access to the same set of production techniques, the same ''book of blueprints.''
5. Production takes place in both countries under purely competitive and increasing-cost conditions.
6. There are no factor-intensity ''crossovers.'' If farming, let us say, is more labor-intensive than manufacturing when wage rates are low and interest rates are high, it will remain so even when wage rates are high and interest rates are low.
7. The number of separate outputs equals the number of inputs.

PROTECTION

The term **protection** makes most people think at once of **tariffs** (taxes on imports) and **quotas** (limitations on the quantity of imports) used to protect domestic import-competing industries. These are the most important forms of the old, or traditional, protection, but many other forms have arisen.

Tariffs are taxes on imports, and quotas are limitations on the quantities of imports. Tariffs and quotas are used to protect domestic industries from competition with imports.

The most important form of the so-called ''new'' protection is the wide variety of practices lumped together as **administrative protection**, perhaps developed most fully by the Japanese government's Ministry of International Trade and Industry (MITI). Under administrative protection, the right to import may be withdrawn, limited to public agencies, or awarded to the import-competing industries themselves. A more common method is to subject competitive imports to burdensome, idiosyncratic, costly, and time-consuming specifications or inspection procedures—ostensibly for reasons of safety and health. Germany has long banned beer with any preservatives whatever—or, more accurately, such beer can be imported but not sold as beer. Belgium has required that butter be packed in containers of different shapes from those used by the neighboring countries of France, Germany, and the Netherlands. The long-standing American ban on fresh beef from Argentina was imposed at a time when many Argentine cattle suffered from contagious hoof-and-mouth disease.

A more recent form of protection, called administrative protection, involves subjecting competitive imports to burdensome, idiosyncratic, costly, and time-consuming specifications or inspection procedures.

An export industry may be protected by an export bounty or a subsidy.[7] Or an import-competing industry may receive its own protection in bounty or subsidy form, in an effort to meet world prices. An American example has been shipbuilding.

Of more complex examples of protection, we need note only two. During the nineteenth and twentieth centuries, British duties on *exporting* wool were protective—for the rising British textile industry, to which the duties ensured cheap wool as raw material.[8] The OPEC countries collected large export duties on crude oil, which were intended to raise money and also to gain time for these countries to develop their agricultural and industrial economies before their oil resources were used up. (These policies became progressively less effective as non-OPEC countries increased their production and as oil-importing countries developed substitutes for petroleum products and otherwise economized on their use.) This is a form of protection for an economy as a whole rather than for any *specific* industry.

Nominal versus Effective Protection

The **nominal protection** given for an industry is simply the rate of the tariff imposed on the importation of foreign supplies of the industry's product. **Effective protection** involves two further variables. The first is whether protection also is given to goods that are raw materials or intermediate goods used in producing the protected good. Suppose that we want to estimate effective protection for the textile industry. If cotton is a raw material or intermediate good for the textile industry, and if cotton also is protected from foreign competition by a tariff, the effective protection for the textile industry is reduced. The reason is that the protection for cotton raises its price and so also raises the cost of producing the textiles. Foreign textile producers, who can buy cotton at lower (world) prices may be able to move into the "protected" market in spite of the tariff on imported textiles.

The second variable in estimating effective protection centers on the value added (mainly the profits earned and wages paid) by the protected industry. Owners and workers in protected industries are interested in how much protection they get as a percentage of their own earnings, that is, of the value added. Suppose that for every $100 of textiles produced, $50 is paid out for raw materials and other intermediate goods and that $50 goes for wages and profits. If there is no tariff on raw materials or intermediate goods but the tariff on textiles allows the price of textiles to rise to $110, the tariff has raised wages and profits by 20 percent, that is, by $10 from the original $50. Effective protection will almost always be greater than nominal protection, unless raw materials and intermediate goods are given substantial protection at the same time.[9]

Nominal protection is the rate of the tariff imposed on the importation of foreign supplies of an industry's product. Effective protection takes into account tariffs on the raw materials or intermediate goods used in producing the protected good and the value added by the protected industry.

---

7. If an industry that produces only for the domestic market is subsidized, bountied, or tax-relieved, it is not being protected in the international economic sense. But what of an industry that sells part of its output at home and part as exports? This is an important question in U.S.–Japanese economic relations because Japan uses general or production subsidies, without special favors for exports. The United States feels free to impose countervailing duties on goods benefiting from *specific* export subsidies, but what is the status of *production* subsidies, such as the Japanese, that extend also to domestic sales?

8. The U.S. Constitution (Article I, Section 9) bans export duties. This provision was a concession to southern agricultural interests. It is not clear whether this provision can also be extended to cover export bounties (negative export duties).

9. An equation for estimating effective protection is as follows: Let t_x be the tariff rate on imports that compete with an industry's output (such as textiles). Let t_y be the tariff rate on raw materials and intermediate goods (such as cotton), and let q be the share that raw materials and intermediate goods contribute to the value of final output. Then we have

$$T = \frac{t_x - qt_y}{1 - q}$$

where T is the rate of effective protection.

> **Effective protection will almost always be greater than nominal protection, unless raw materials and intermediate goods are given substantial protection at the same time.**

Disguised Forms of Protection

Besides these forms of more or less open protection, there are also three forms of hidden, or disguised, protection: (1) voluntary export restrictions, (2) orderly marketing agreements, and (3) the trigger price mechanism. Since World War II they have gained in popularity as substitutes for open protection in countries that, like the United States, have pressed other countries for greater freedom of trade.

Voluntary export restrictions are usually bilateral (between just two countries)[10] and seldom completely voluntary. Usually, an exporting country agrees to lower its exports to an importing country to a certain level or in accordance with a certain formula. For example, the United States has put pressure on Japan first to reduce and then not to increase too rapidly her exports of cars and trucks to the United States. **Orderly marketing agreements** are another form of disguised protection. They try to prevent "disorderly" price cutting in importing countries and are generally multilateral. That is to say, several exporting countries and/or several importing countries are usually involved. In most cases, the agreement is carried out under the threat of protective duties or quotas by one or more of the importing countries. A **trigger-price mechanism** need involve no agreement at all. An importing country, like the United States in the case of steel products, acting alone, may announce one or more "trigger prices" for different types of steel. Any imports below these prices are considered to be **dumping** (a sale below what authorities consider average total cost plus a fair markup) and subject to special "antidumping" duties.[11]

> **Under voluntary export restrictions, an exporting country agrees to lower its exports to an importing country to a certain level or in accordance with a certain formula. Orderly marketing agreements try to prevent price cutting in importing countries.**

> **Imports below certain trigger prices are considered to be dumping—offering a good for sale at a price below average total cost plus a fair markup.**

Protection Against Protection

In a number of trade acts since 1974, the United States established and strengthened the Office of the U.S. Trade Representative (USTR). The USTR, which now has a seat in the president's cabinet, was deliberately made independent of the old-line State, Treasury, and Commerce departments, whose economic viewpoints were allegedly diluted by political considerations and by the interests of consumers and importers. In its capacity as spokesperson for labor, business, and agricultural interests in export and import-competing branches of the American economy, the USTR has developed novel trade strategies.

USTR and its Advisory Committee for Trade Negotiations (ACTN) now proposes a **market-opening strategy** as protection against foreign protectionism. This strategy is directed especially against the new protectionism practiced by countries with positive bilateral balances in their trade with the United States and also against inbred foreign mercantilist prejudices against competitive imports. Market opening discriminates against a specific group of countries that reject competitive American exports at the same time that they run positive trade balances with the United States.

What is this strategy of market opening? It is a system of guaranteed minimum quotas for American goods in foreign markets—a quota system in

10. We usually treat the European Community (EC) as a single country.
11. The traditional international economic meaning of *dumping* has been the sale of some product abroad at a price lower than its domestic price (plus transportation costs). Dumping was regarded as a predatory tactic, designed to drive competitors out of business and then to exploit consumers. For this reason, countries impose antidumping duties, which are not usually considered strictly protective.

However, as goods have become less standardized and marketing tactics more complex, the term *dumping* has been redefined in the United States to mean any sale below what American authorities consider "average total cost plus a fair markup," regardless of price in the exporting country.

reverse. In periodic bilateral negotiations with "Country X," the USTR insists that a certain amount or percentage of the X market in one or another group of goods be reserved for U.S. exports—the percentage being based on U.S. market penetration in other countries somewhat similar to Country X. Country X is left with the responsibility of selecting U.S. products of adequate quality and reasonable (world) prices. If Country X refuses to open its markets adequately or with sufficient speed (in USTR's opinion), USTR is to initiate retaliatory measures of penalty tariffs or quota restrictions against Country X's exports to the United States. For example, to increase its share of the internal Japanese semiconductor market, the United States has imposed restrictions on Japanese exports of electronic products to the United States—which indeed include semiconductor components.

Market-opening strategy, a system of guaranteed minimum quotas for American goods in foreign markets, is targeted toward countries that reject competitive American exports at the same time that they run positive trade balances with the United States.

USTR and its clients in business, labor, and agriculture claim that market opening, unlike standard protectionism, aims at increasing trade rather than decreasing it. In this strategy, trade contraction is a second-best alternative. How this will work in practice, we cannot yet say with confidence. Much depends on the reasonableness of rival negotiating positions and on the willingness of negotiating partners to compromise. The trade negotiations involving market-opening strategies have so far tended to be quite bitter in tone and have not increased international good will.

Unlike standard protectionism, market opening aims at increasing trade rather than decreasing trade.

Economic Arguments for Protection

"Free trade wins all the arguments, but protection wins all the votes." There is a great deal of truth in this statement. The historical record reveals the political effectiveness of "intense minorities" and "special interests."

Steel companies, their workers, and whole "steel communities" like Pittsburgh, Gary, and Birmingham *care* about that import-competing industry's prosperity, because steel is their livelihood. Steel consumers all over the United States may well lose more, in total, from steel protection than the steel industry gains. But each individual consumer's loss is minor, and consumers are spread over a wide area.

But over and above these political arguments, there are sound economic ones, which we should not forget. We shall briefly describe several of these arguments.

The Infant Industry Argument   Perhaps the most important of the economic cases that favor protection is the **infant industry argument,** sometimes referred to as "learning-by-doing." We have already pointed out that comparative advantage is generally not a static but a changing concept. Why not speed up the changes if they seem desirable, or slow them down if they seem harmful?

The desire to speed up a change and the willingness to accept a loss in the present for the sake of the future were the base of the infant industry argument for protection, which Alexander Hamilton outlined in his *Report on Manufactures* during the late eighteenth century. The reason why American manufacturers were less efficient than their British or European counterparts, Hamilton believed, was that they lacked experience and on-the-job training. For this reason, Hamilton urged the country to protect American manufacturers temporarily while they were gaining experience. Then the next generation would be better off, particularly if manufacturing demanded higher skills and paid better wages than agriculture did.

The infant-industry argument is that an industry should be protected while it develops the skills and industrial techniques needed to compete effectively against foreign producers.

Sometimes we hear this argument in exaggerated form, to the effect that the latecomer's disadvantage simply *cannot* be overcome at all without some measure of protection. To see that this argument is often wrong, we might look at Japan in the last third of the nineteenth century. Manufacturing developed very rapidly, even though Japan had been forbidden, by "unequal treaties" with Western powers, from imposing tariffs on foreign goods at rates higher than 5 percent. Or consider a case of free trade within the United States—the southward migration of the cotton textile industry. Under free trade, the South eventually developed comparative advantage in textiles. However, trade might have shifted earlier had the Confederacy won the Civil War and imposed tariffs on the New England textiles. One can compare the infant industry argument to a request for a loan at zero interest from today's consumers, who pay higher prices, to tomorrow's workers and consumers, who may, as a result, have higher incomes.

Since there are senile as well as infant industries, there is also a "senile industry" argument for protection. It is quite different from the infant industry argument, however. Consumers are asked to pay more for certain goods to keep specialized workers in dying industries employed and off the relief rolls. This is an act of charity—which also saves taxes.

The High Wage Rate Argument The *high wage rate* or "cheap foreign labor" argument for protection is very popular in high-wage-rate countries. A high-wage-rate country tries to limit imports of a low-wage-rate country's goods to check or slow down the working of the factor price equalization theorem, to raise real wage rates even higher, or, perhaps also to make income distribution in the high-wage-rate country more nearly equal. Most workers in a high-wage-rate country feel that it is "unfair" that they should have to compete with goods from low-wage-rate countries. American textile workers, for example, complain about competition from Taiwan and South Korea. Workers in Taiwan or South Korea might complain about unfair competition between people and the "cheap American machinery," which replaces labor in America. Essentially, the cheap foreign labor argument is an outright rejection of the theory of comparative advantage. Less developed countries rightfully complain that this form of protection impedes their development.

The high-wage-rate argument for protection is a rejection of the basic comparative-advantage theory of international trade.

The Terms of Trade Argument A country's **terms of trade** are measured by an average of its export prices divided by an average of its import prices. The terms of trade improve when the average price of the country's exports rises or the average price of its imports falls, both being computed net of tariffs. Higher terms of trade with a given trade volume are considered beneficial. However, a rise in the terms of trade may not be favorable if the trade volume decreases. Lower terms of trade, similarly, are considered disadvantageous unless the trade volume rises.

Terms of trade arguments for protection make use of any monopoly or monopsony (buyers' monopoly) power that a country may have to drive up its own terms of trade ratio and to drive down the terms of trade ratio of its trading partners. If a country has monopsony power, it can impose a tariff that would raise the price of an imported good to consumers and lead them to reduce the quantity demanded. The foreign producers then face the uncomfortable choice of either (a) lowering their prices to cancel the effect of the tariff or (b) accepting a lower volume of sales, which may mean unemployment and hardship. Countries that depend on the monopsonist's market often will lower their price, and part of the tariff is actually shifted to the resource owners in the producing country. A country with monopoly power can accomplish the same result by imposing export duties, as OPEC tried to do. These duties are borne mostly by customers in consuming countries.

The terms of trade argument for protection makes use of a country's monopoly or monopsony power to force up the price of its exports or force down the price of its imports.

The Home Market Argument In the nineteenth century, the protectionist "American System of Political Economy" had two major parts. One was the Hamilton infant industry argument, stated previously, which was addressed mainly to urban people. The other part, addressed to farmers, was the "home market" argument associated with Henry Clay, the "great compromiser" who would "rather be right than be president."[12] Clay's view was that some farm income should be sacrificed in favor of greater stability and certainty. The more U.S. agriculture remained dependent on the European market for its exported staples (cotton, corn, tobacco, and wheat), the more subject it would remain to disruption from European warfare, revolution, and depression—and also from European protection. Tariffs on European manufactured goods would reduce farm sales to Europe, but these tariffs would bring prosperity to American manufacturing and expand the home market for U.S. farm products. Farm prices would remain high and uncertainty would be reduced. The general idea involved is *risk aversion*, or at least a preference for one bundle of risks over another. It remains important even though Henry Clay's "American system" has been largely forgotten.

The home-market argument for protection asked American farmers to accept tariffs on manufactured goods in order to face less instability in the demand for their farm products.

The Capital-Attraction or Tariff Factory Argument The capital-attraction, or **tariff factory**, argument states that, if a country's market is important, tariffs and quotas set to keep out foreign goods will induce foreign capitalists to invest in that country and employ that country's labor in order to avoid the tariff. Canada has applied this approach effectively against the United States. American visitors to Canada may be surprised at the number of "American" brand names attached to products of "XYZ Company, Canada," with headquarters in Toronto, as distinguished from "XYZ Company" itself, with headquarters in New York. During the 1950s and the early 1960s, the European Community (EC) caused many Ameri-

can firms to establish European branches not only by setting up high Community-wide tariffs against U.S. goods but also by eliminating tariffs between member countries. This last change meant that a single American tariff factory in, say, Belgium, could service the whole EC. Thus there would no longer be any need to set up separate factories in each member country, a costly and often uneconomical procedure.

The tariff factory argument for protection says that tariffs will persuade foreigners to build factories in the tariff-imposing economy and hire workers there.

The Retaliation or Bargaining Argument The *retaliation* or *bargaining* argument for protection, like the infant industry one, involves "time preference." A retaliatory tariff or quota has the same harmful short-run welfare effects as any other tariff or quota. But, according to this argument for protection, in the long run it may cause foreigners to lower their duties or ease their quotas against one's exports. The historical record, however, suggests that retaliatory tariffs seem rather to lead to further retaliation and feed on themselves, growing more and more restrictive over time. Interest groups that gain from the retaliatory tariff gain strength the longer it remains effective. As time passes, it becomes increasingly difficult to oppose the political strength of these groups.

The bargaining argument for protection claims that foreigners will give up their tariffs in order to obtain the removal of the tariffs erected for bargaining purposes.

Macroeconomic Arguments We may lump together a number of economic arguments for protection that aim at relieving macroeconomic ills. For example, if a country has widespread unemployment, a tariff may be used to keep foreign goods out in order to open up more jobs for that country's own people. Or if the government's budget is in deficit, an argument can be made that tariffs should be used to raise revenue, rather than

---

12. It is quite a feat in any field to be at once a great compromiser and always right!

lowering public spending or taxing the people directly. Or if a country's total value of imports is exceeding the total value of its exports so that it is running a balance of payments deficit, tariffs may be used to reduce these imports and the deficit.[13]

Political Arguments for Protection

The political arguments for protection have been even more effective than the economic ones. Some of these are described below.

The National Defense Argument The national defense argument was persuasive for Adam Smith himself. In a famous passage from *The Wealth of Nations,* defending the Navigation Acts[14] against which the Thirteen Colonies were then protesting, Smith admitted that "defense is of much more importance than opulence." So he joined the chorus in favor of protecting potential defense industries.

The aim of the British Navigation Acts was to maintain ships and sailors for the Royal Navy. In the same way, Imperial German tariffs on grain were justified by the argument that country boys from the farm made better soldiers than city boys from the factory. However, the most common national defense arguments today are based on the need for tariffs and quotas on the importation of such "defense goods" as steel and ships. The country, it is said, should not become dependent on unreliable foreign sources for important defense needs.

The "Critical Minimum" Argument Allied to the national defense argument is protection aimed at supporting a *critical minimum* of production in some basic industry. An example today is from Ja-

pan, which imports a larger proportion of its staple foods (rice and wheat) than any other country in recorded history—larger even than Great Britain, which suffered under German submarine blockades in two world wars. It is therefore necessary for Japan—so runs the argument—with its dense population and its small post-1945 "maritime self-defense force," to protect its agriculture from low-price American and other import competition. At the very least, it must keep its dependence on foreign food from increasing any further.

The Predatory Foreigner Argument The *predatory foreigner* argument assumes that foreign suppliers have hostile intentions. According to this argument, it is especially dangerous to let one's country become dependent on unfriendly countries, which may cut off one's supplies of some critical commodity for political reasons or form cartels and raise prices. Even previously friendly countries can become hostile. If the United States had listened to free traders and become completely dependent on imported oil, the Arab boycott of 1973–74 would have caused even more harm than it did. The United States is fortunate, or so runs the argument, to have protected its high-cost domestic oil industry during the years before the boycott.

Special Interests The most effective way of getting protection, year in and year out, has been *intense minority* or *special interest* pressure. The beneficiaries of protection, however few they may be, put their hearts and their money into their cause. They also tend to be concentrated in particular areas. On the other hand, the injuries from protection are spread too thinly, both geographically and economically, for the victims to be mobilized year after year for commodity after commodity.

---

13. Macroeconomic arguments for tariffs and quotas are discussed more fully in Chapter 19.

14. During the seventeenth and eighteenth centuries these acts limited British and colonial coastwise trade, as well as trade between Britain and its colonies, to British and colonial ships with British and colonial crews. They also prohibited import trade in ships other than those of Britain, its colonies, and the exporting country—a move aimed at French and Dutch competition in the "carrying trade" between third countries. Present American law bans only coastwise trade to foreign shipping, but requires that the bulk of American aid goods be carried in American ships.

Political arguments for protection include: (1) protection of national defense industries, (2) support of a critical minimum of production in certain basic industries, and (3) protection against hostile foreign suppliers. The political influence of special interest groups is very effective in obtaining protective legislation.

COMMERCIAL TREATIES, FREE TRADE AREAS, AND CUSTOMS UNIONS

Trade between countries is governed by commercial treaties and other forms of international negotiation. We shall outline some of the important principles of these treaties, including those that involve customs unions and free trade areas.

Commercial Treaties

A **commercial treaty** is an agreement between countries dealing with economic and trade relations. Since World War II, most such treaties have been reasonably reciprocal. For example, under a treaty, the rights and duties of American citizens in Yugoslavia would be much the same as those of Yugoslav citizens in America, with certain allowances for such facts as America being a capitalist and Yugoslavia a socialist country.

However, many, if not most, nineteenth-century commercial treaties between more developed countries (MDCs) and less developed countries (LDCs) were very unequal. Some gave westerners in LDCs what was called "extraterritorial" rights to civil and criminal trial under MDC law in MDC courts attached to MDC embassies or consulates, without giving the same rights to Turks (or Persians or Chinese) living in the West. One reason for such laws was the practice of some LDC legal systems of getting evidence from people by torture and imposing "cruel and unusual punishment" for minor offenses. Other provisions of unequal treaties gave westerners rights to seize LDC customs receipts for payment of debts owed to MDC governments, restricted LDC rights to put tariffs on MDC goods, set aside areas in LDC cities where only MDC citizens could live, and so on. In all these cases, there were no reciprocal rights for LDCs. None of these unequal treaties survived World War II.

Commercial treaties are generally in force for a term of years, after which either party may reject the treaty and perhaps propose a new one more favorable to its interests. But even while the treaty is in force, the legal standing of its provisions varies between countries. No U.S. Congress can bind those that follow it. In fact, many Congresses have felt free to amend or to make laws in violation of commercial treaties that earlier Congresses had approved. For this reason, many countries feel that the United States is not a very reliable partner for a commercial treaty.

A commercial treaty is an agreement between countries dealing with economic and trade relations.

Free Trade Areas and Customs Unions

Commercial treaties may raise the degree of economic integration among the contracting parties, rather than simply legalizing and regulating the existing situation. Recent economic integrations have taken the forms of free trade areas and customs unions. In both cases, trade between the members is made free, either immediately or after periods of adjustment, by one or more commercial treaties. Differences exist, however, in how they deal with outsiders.

In a **free trade area,**[15] there are no tariffs or other trade restrictions for member countries, but each member country has its own set of tariffs, quotas, and so forth, for nonmember countries. In a **customs union**, there is also free trade for members, but a common tariff, generally based on an average of the member countries' previous tariffs, which nonmembers must face. (Each country, however, may keep its separate quota arrangements.) So an American exporter faces different tariffs in Norway and Sweden, both members of the European Free Trade Association (EFTA), but the same tariff in France and West Germany, both members of the European Community (a customs union).

---

15. A free trade area should be distinguished from a *free port*. In a free port like Hong Kong or Singapore, there is a special restricted area where raw materials or goods in process are landed duty free, processed further by local labor and materials, and then re-exported without entering the general Hong Kong or Singapore market.

In a free trade area, there are no tariffs or other trade restrictions for member countries, but each member country has its own set of tariffs for nonmember countries. In a customs union, there is free trade for members and a common tariff for nonmembers.

Today the most important experiment in economic integration is the European Community (EC). It developed in the 1950s from a number of multilateral agreements about (a) the division of Marshall Plan aid from the United States for rebuilding after World War II and (b) the reorganization of European production of such commodities as coal, steel, and atomic energy. Its founders and supporters, including many Americans, hoped that it might become a strong economic and financial community with a common circulating currency, and a political community as well. Another early hope, especially in the United States, was that the EC would be satisfied with a low common tariff, and that countries like the United States, Canada, and several former British dominions would join with it economically. In this way, the EC would not be simply a Western European power but would become a non-Communist world economic power as well.

These things have not happened. The British, who favored low tariffs, refused to join unless allowed to continue to import cheap food from the dominions. Representatives of high-cost European agriculture would not make this concession. Without the British, the EC became a high-tariff organization, especially after the strongly nationalist General Charles de Gaulle took power in France and a "farm bloc" of French and German agricultural interests gained political power. It has remained a high-tariff organization even after Great Britain, Ireland, and several other countries later joined.

Today the most important experiment in economic integration is the European Community.

Because the free trade area and customs union appear to be movements away from economic nationalism and protectionism, they seem to be steps toward freedom of trade. We might expect many internationalists and free-trade economists to welcome them wholeheartedly as steps in what they believe to be the right direction. In fact, their enthusiasm has been lukewarm at best. How can this be?

The problem is that a free trade area, a customs union, or any other experiment in partial economic integration has a dual effect on trade. Within the free trade area or the customs union itself, it *creates* trade between the individual member countries, which might not have developed if each country had kept its own tariff wall. At the same time, the free trade area or customs union *diverts* trade from nonmember to member countries, and in this case is usually a step away from freedom of trade.

If a highly isolationist self-sufficient country like North Korea today were to join a free trade area or customs union, the trade-creation effect would dominate the trade-diversion effect. If a free trade country like pre-1914 Britain were to join the same free trade area or customs union, the trade-diversion effect would dominate.

An example of trade diversion might be American automobiles in Denmark. Before Denmark joined the EC, U.S. automobiles competed there on equal terms with automobiles from Britain, France, Germany, and Italy. (Denmark itself has no automobile industry.) After Denmark joined the EC, competition for the Danish automobile market shifted favorably to Denmark's new EC partners, and away from outsiders like the United States and Japan. This move was against freedom of trade, even though Ford and General Motors continued to sell in Denmark the products of their European subsidiaries.

Free trade areas and customs unions create trade between member countries but divert trade from nonmember to member countries.

The EC in 1992 and Thereafter Trade-creation and trade-diversion issues will take on greater significance if the EC carries out its plans to achieve full economic unification by the end of 1992. Will the resulting New Europe be a trade-diverting "Fortress Europe" from which American and Japanese products, in particular, are effectively excluded by tariff walls, quotas, and the myriad "dirty tricks" of administrative protection?[16] Or will such outside producers be able to profit by expanded trade created by the integration of what is already the world's largest economic bloc—25 percent of total world trade?

ITO and GATT

After World War II, the "free world" members of the United Nations proposed that the world economy return to freer and less-discriminatory trade than had prevailed in the 1930s and that a new international code of conduct be set up to regulate quotas and other forms of nontariff protection. Their representatives drew up a charter for an **International Trade Organization (ITO).** The proposed charter, however, included a number of safeguards and escape clauses, which the U.S. Senate considered discriminatory against the United States. The Senate refused to ratify the proposed charter, and the ITO never came into being.

To replace the aborted ITO, a number of countries, mainly the industrial countries of North America and Western Europe, framed a less-formal **General Agreement on Tariffs and Trade (GATT).** GATT established its own bureaucracy, and representatives of GATT countries have held several "rounds" of meetings. It seeks to carry out gradually and by stages what ITO hoped to accomplish more quickly. GATT, however, has become something of an exclusive club for the wealthier nations, in the view of many LDCs. These countries, preferring a New International Economic Order (NIEO) to trade liberalization, have hesitated to cooperate with GATT. But within the so-called First World, GATT remains an active and often successful organization.

The General Agreement on Tariffs and Trade (GATT) seeks to reduce the general level of tariff and nontariff protection among its members, who are mostly First World nations.

---

16. American and Japanese *companies* will be able to compete in Europe through European subsidiaries or through joint ventures with European firms. Such subsidiaries, however, must be more than "screwdriver" assembly plants, and their outputs can only qualify as "European" if a sufficiently large percentage of its value is added in Europe.

THE SHIFTING U.S. TRADE POSITION

The U.S. balance of merchandise trade (as distinguished from services), which had been in surplus since the 1890s, went into deficit about 1970. In 1987, the trade deficit was about $160 billion—8 percent with Canada and 35 percent with Japan, America's most important trading partners in recent years. Preliminary statistics for 1988 show a 12 percent drop in the trade deficit and forecasts for 1989 are for another decline of at least that magnitude.[17]

Table 1 suggests the wide range of products involved. For nonfarm products—especially in those industries employing skilled and high-paid labor—the deficits reflect mainly rises in imports. In agriculture, which remains in surplus, exports have risen only slowly. The change also involves the great majority of U.S. trading partners, as can be seen from the data in Table 2.

The combined effect of these changes has been consternation in the United States, where a positive balance of trade had come to be regarded as part of the natural order of events. The present deficit situation has been called the "export of good jobs" and is blamed for making the nation "an economy of hamburger stands." It has been blamed on unfair tactics overseas—low wage rates, export subsidies, administrative protection, market closing, and "dirty tricks" in general. While most of these are practiced by the United States as well, the shift to a trade deficit has given rise in the United States to demands for increased trade restrictions more rigorously enforced, for negotiated opening of trading partners' "closed markets," and for an industrial policy of government planning and subsidies for industry and the management of trade relations.

The shift to a trade deficit in the United States has given rise to demands for increased trade restrictions more rigorously enforced, for opening of closed markets, and for an industrial policy.

---

17. The last previous decline was in 1980, as compared with 1979. It did not last.

TABLE 1
U.S. Trade Balances by Commodity Groups, 1970 and 1987 (billions of dollars)

	Agricultural Products	Petroleum	Industrial Materials	Capital Goods[a]	Automotive Goods	All Others[b]	Total
1970							
Exports	7.4	n.a.	12.3	14.7	3.9	4.2	42.5
Imports	5.8	2.9	12.3	4.0	5.7	9.2	39.9
Balance	1.6	−2.9	0.0	10.7	−1.8	−5.0	2.6
1987							
Exports	29.5	n.a.	62.8	88.1	26.3	42.9	249.6
Imports	20.4	42.9	71.2	84.8	85.2	105.4	409.9
Balance	9.1	−42.9	−8.4	3.3	−58.9	−62.5	−160.3
Net Change							
Exports	22.1	n.a.	50.5	73.4	22.4	38.7	207.1
Imports	14.6	40.0	58.9	80.8	79.5	96.2	370.0
Balance	7.5	−40.0	−8.4	−7.4	−57.1	−57.5	−162.9

a. Except automotive.
b. Mainly consumer goods other than automotive.
Source: Economic Report of the President, 1989, Tables B-100 and B-103, pp. 422 and 426.

In the early 1980s, the shift in the U.S. trade balance was blamed largely on an allegedly overvalued dollar. The overvaluation itself had been brought on by the combination of budget deficits and disinflationary monetary policies, which raised interest rates and increased the foreign demand for dollars. This is clearly wrong. The depreciation of the dollar relative to the Japanese yen—from ¥260 in 1985 to less than ¥130 in 1988–89—has not reduced either the overall American trade deficit or the bilateral American deficit with Japan. Nor should the American deficit be blamed on the OPEC cartel and the oil shocks of the 1970s. Both of these macroeconomic factors—the dear dollar and the shocks to aggregate supply—played significant roles in the history of the American trade balances. However, as Table 3 shows, the decline in this balance was already under way at the time of the first oil shock (1973–74), and it continued through the period of the falling and allegedly *un*dervalued dollar of the Carter administration (1977–1981). A significant macroeconomic factor—discussed in Chapter 19—has been the long declines in the saving rates of both the private and the public sectors of the U.S. economy.

The shift toward deficit in U.S. international trade began well before the OPEC oil embargos of the 1970s and the high value of the dollar in the early 1980s.

The Passing of the "Dollar-Shortage" Era

A full history of the U.S. trade balance must go back to the end of World War II and to the half-generation (1945 to 1966 approximately) that followed. During that period, North America (the United States and Canada) was the paramount source of both agricultural and manufactured goods for the entire world outside the Soviet bloc,[18] which, after 1949, included China. Because of America's dominant position, these twenty-one

18. Under the Marshall Plan in 1947, the United States offered to extend economic assistance to Soviet bloc countries. But the Soviet Union rejected the American offer and required its allies to do likewise—even after Czechoslovakia and Poland had already accepted. This rejection was due to Stalin's fear that economic dependency on the United States would lead to economic and political subordination.

years, particularly the first ten, were times of "dollar shortage"—since foreign countries had little to exchange for American goods. The leading American firms in a number of industries and American growers of a number of farm products found themselves in a position to obtain higher profits from their monopoly control. In turn, these high returns were reflected in the wages of specialized labor in those industries, the prices of agricultural land, and even in the sizes of welfare programs in the public sector.

Roughly midway in what was described as America's "soaring sixties," foreign recovery, accelerated by American aid, gradually brought this euphoric period to a close.

TABLE 2
U.S. Trade Balances by Area, 1979 and 1987
(billions of dollars)

	1979	1987	Change
Total Exports	184.5	249.6	65.1
Industrial Countries	115.9	164.9	49.0
Canada	38.7	61.1	22.4
Japan	17.6	27.6	10.0
Western Europe	54.2	68.8	14.6
Other Countries[a]	68.5	84.7	16.2
OPEC	14.6	10.7	−3.9
Eastern Europe	5.9	2.2	−3.7
Total Imports	212.0	409.8	197.8
Industrial Countries	112.8	259.8	147.0
Canada	39.2	73.6	34.4
Japan	26.3	84.5	58.2
Western Europe	41.8	96.2	54.4
Other Countries[a]	99.2	150.1	50.9
OPEC	45.0	24.4	−20.6
Eastern Europe	1.9	1.9	0.0
Overall Balances	−27.5	−160.3	−132.8
Industrial Countries	3.1	−94.9	−98.0
Canada	−0.5	−12.6	−12.1
Japan	−8.6	−56.9	−48.3
Western Europe	12.4	−27.5	−39.9
Other Countries[a]	−30.7	−65.4	−34.7
OPEC	−30.5	−13.7	16.8
Eastern Europe	4.0	0.3	−3.7

a. Includes transactions with international organizations and "unallocated." (Figures may not add to total because of rounding.)

Source: Economic Report of the President, 1989, Table B-104, p. 427.

TABLE 3
The Falling U.S. Trade Balance Since World War II, Five-Year Intervals, 1947–1987
(billions of dollars)

Year	Exports	Imports	Balance
1947	16.1	6.0	10.1
1952	13.4	10.8	2.6
1957	19.6	13.3	6.3
1962	20.8	16.3	4.5
1967	30.7	26.9	3.8
1972	49.4	55.8	−6.4
1977	120.8	151.9	−31.1
1982	211.2	247.6	−36.4
1987	249.6	409.8	−160.3

Source: Economic Report of the President, 1989, Table B-102, p. 424.

The special demands and inflationary financing of the Vietnam War postponed public awareness of this development, which emerged as something of a shock when hostilities died down in the early 1970s. Hindsight makes it clear that many segments of the American economy have been unwilling or politically unable to adapt to the new situation by appropriate or sufficient combinations of lower real wage rates, lower profit margins, lower tax burdens, higher productivity growth rates, and improved product quality. The net result of this refusal or inability is called declining American international "competitiveness." It is blamed on labor (by business), on management (by labor), on government waste (by taxpayers), and so on. No group has been willing to accept any substantial share of the blame. The universal path of least resistance has been to blame the foreigner—particularly the Asian foreigner—and to push for bigger and better protection, while leaving unquestioned the comfortable, if outmoded, relics of the dollar-shortage period.

Many segments of the U.S. economy have been unwilling or politically unable to adapt to the country's reduced international competitiveness by appropriate or sufficient combinations of lower real wage rates, lower profit margins, lower tax burdens, higher productivity growth rates, and improved product quality.

Changing Factor Endowments

An additional element in the new U.S. trade position has arisen from changes in rival countries' factor endowments, especially their endowments of human capital. The American view of Oriental labor remained, for entirely too long, that of illiterate coolies producing, with little mechanical aid, bottom-quality merchandise for the bottom fourth of the world's income distribution, while subsisting on "a fishhead and a handful of rice a day." However incorrect this picture might already have become before World War II, it became much more inaccurate thereafter. Oriental labor acquired training and skills, and Oriental wage rates became a larger fraction of American wage rates. It paid Oriental employers to increase labor productivity with better and newer machines of various kinds. In short, Asian labor could enter advanced industries formerly thought to be reserved for the West in general and for America in particular.

An Accelerated Product Cycle

Another element in the changing U.S. trade position has been an acceleration of the product cycle. We have already mentioned this cycle by which an economic innovation in a high-wage-rate country moves by stages from a domestic industry in that country to an export industry and then to an export industry in some lower-wage-rate country with the product imported into the country where the innovation originally took place. The automobile, radio, television, and computer industries in the United States are examples of this. We did not inquire then how long such a product cycle might take.

For the mass-produced automobile, forty years seem to have been required for the Ford Model T and its American successors (Chevrolet, Plymouth, and later Ford models) to be threatened seriously in their home market. When the threat came, it was initially from relatively high-wage-rate European companies—Volkswagen of Germany, Renault of France, Fiat of Italy, and Austin and Morris of Great Britain. An additional ten to fifteen years were required for Japanese competitors to enter the American domestic market to any serious extent. But the product cycle took much less time (only five or ten years) for the television set (first black and white and then color), the computer (whether hand-held, mainframe, or personal), the videocassette recorder, the air conditioner and heat pump, or the recreational vehicle and motorcycle developments of the automobile itself. Pity the American television set or computer manufacturer counting on a full generation's profits on its technological lead before foreign competitors would invade not only its export market but even its domestic market!

The acceleration of the product cycle by the up-market moves of competitors in lower-wage-rate countries is an economic aspect of the more general phenomenon popularized by the sociologist Alvin Toffler as *Future Shock*—except that the shocks are not future ones, but present and recent-past ones. The moral is that one cannot safely rest on one's laurels as many traditional American export industries have sought to do. Together, the passing of the "dollar-shortage" era, changing factor endowments, and the accelerated product cycle surely have been more important causes of the change in America's international trade position than the popular "dirty tricks," "subsidies," or "market closure" explanations so often given.

The changes in the U.S. trade position have resulted, in part, from changes in rival countries' factor endowments, an acceleration of the product cycle and the unwillingness or potential inability of many segments of the U.S. economy to adapt to the new situation.

Economics in Focus

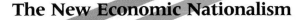

The New Economic Nationalism

To many Americans, it seems unfair that Japanese companies can reap huge revenues by selling cars to the United States but Americans cannot sell rice to Japan. Furloughed autoworkers are especially indignant, and situations of this sort—combined with concern about bulging U.S. trade deficits—have led to the rise of a new economic nationalism, a general demand that the United States stop being mild-mannered toward foreign competitors and begin a more aggressive pursuit of America's "own interests." Political leaders, especially those from areas hard-hit by foreign competition, have spoken out for a new toughness in foreign trade. The 1988 Trade Act, which gave the federal government increased powers to combat unfair trading policies, was actually a compromise; Congress considered other measures that were even more protectionist.

By 1988 U.S. trade restrictions had already been expanding for some time. Although President Reagan was philosophically committed to free trade, his two terms in office witnessed the greatest rise in protectionism since before the Great Depression. According to one estimate, about 25 percent of U.S. imports were subject to protectionist policies by the end of Reagan's tenure. A change has also occurred within the economics profession: more and more economists are speaking out for economic nationalism. Questioning the time-honored principle of comparative advantage, they advocate one or another form of "managed trade." Some even argue that nationalistic principles, if pursued correctly, can benefit not only the country that adopts them but other countries as well.

In this climate public sentiment can easily swing too far. We can start thinking of foreign industries as enemies of the American worker, guilty of undermining our way of life. We can convince ourselves that an autoworker's job in Detroit is more deeply significant than the fate of a Japanese worker. Doing so, we can build up a great deal of moral fervor, but this may ultimately obscure our vision.

Analyzed objectively, some of the recent forays into protectionism seem dubious. The "voluntary" restrictions on Japan's auto exports to the United States probably hurt Americans more than Japanese. Japan's automakers, forced to ship fewer cars, raised their prices and moved toward the upscale end of the market; as a result they may have become stronger competitors. When domestic automakers boosted their prices too, American consumers paid royally for the jobs that had been saved.

On the other hand, many experts believe the government missed early opportunities to protect U.S. interests in semiconductors and high-definition television, two key technological fields. Economic nationalism needs to rely on reason more than on indignation or the desire to retaliate. Policymakers need a better understanding of the likely gains and losses from particular protectionist actions. Perhaps help will come from the economists who are casting a fresh glance at the question.

Sources: Rahul Jacob, "Export Barriers the U.S. Hates Most," *Fortune,* February 27, 1989, pp. 88–89; Robert Kuttner, "Economic Nationalism," *The New Republic,* November 21, 1988, pp. 19–22; David R. Henderson, "The Ugly Truth About Trade," *Fortune,* June 5, 1989, p. 330; Karen Pennar, "The Gospel of Free Trade Is Losing Apostles," *Business Week,* February 27, 1989, p. 89; "Talking Loudly and Carrying a Crowbar," *The Economist,* April 29, 1989, pp. 23–24; Samuel Bowles, "Economic Justice—For Us and Them," *Harper's Magazine,* December 1988, pp. 29–32 (reprinted from *Tikkun,* September/October 1988).

SUMMARY

1. Trade makes it feasible for people to specialize in jobs for which they have special talents. Specialization increases productivity. Therefore trade can play a role in raising real production and income. (See page 436.)

2. Because countries differ from one another in resources and special talents, trade between countries can be shown, under competitive conditions, to benefit both the exporting country and the importing country. (See pages 437–438.)

3. Nevertheless, particular groups lose from trade. Consumers of exportable goods lose from export trade under competitive conditions. Producers of importable or import-competing goods lose from import trade under the same conditions. Producers and/or consumers of nontraded goods may also lose from trade if the particular nontraded goods they produce or consume are complementary to or competitive with imports or exports in consumption or in production. (See pages 438–440.)

4. A country is said to have a comparative advantage in the production of one good and a comparative disadvantage in the production of another good if its pretrade or restricted-trade relative price of the first good is lower, and its relative price of the second good is higher, than those of its actual or potential trading partners or in the rest of the world. (See pages 440–441.)

5. Comparative advantages and disadvantages, when they exist, may be due to a number of different causes. The classical (Ricardian) theory stresses differences in productivity for different goods and services. The later Heckscher-Ohlin theory puts the most stress on differences in "factor endowments," meaning supplies of the several productive inputs. (See pages 441–442.)

6. Comparative advantage is not a static concept, but varies over time. The so-called product cycle is a case in point, as applied to advanced industrial products. (See page 442.)

7. Fears that free trade and an accelerated product cycle could wipe out the industrial sector of an economy ("hollow out" the economy) may be unfounded because new industries typically develop to replace those lost to foreign producers. (See page 443.)

8. Free trade also tends to equalize input re-

source prices between trading countries in the same manner as migration. (See pages 443–444.)

9. We cannot define protection rigorously. However, it includes a wide variety of aids to a country's import-competing goods and to its exports. It extends well beyond the traditional import tariffs and quotas to a wide range of bounties, tax preferences, and types of administrative protection. Administrative protection subjects competitive imports to burdensome, idiosyncratic, costly, and time-consuming specifications or inspection procedures. (See pages 444–445.)

10. The effective rate of protection is usually different from the nominal rate. The effective rate takes account of the protection given to the raw materials and components that go into a product in addition to the nominal rate on the product itself. Protection given to raw materials lessens the effect on that given to final products. (See page 445.)

11. To counteract administrative protection and mercantilistic public attitudes abroad, the Office of the U.S. Trade Representative (USTR) has adopted a strategy of market opening in countries with large positive trade balances with the U.S. According to this strategy, such countries must either guarantee U.S. exporters a reasonable share of their markets or face discriminatory penalties against their own exports to the U.S. (See pages 446–447.)

12. Among economic arguments for protection, the most effective have been the infant industry (learning-by-doing) and the high-wage-rate (cheap foreign labor) arguments. Others have been: the terms of trade argument; avoidance of risks by developing the home market; the attraction of foreign capital, and sometimes also of skilled labor, to "tariff factories"; the response or bargaining reaction to foreign protection; and the solution of problems connected with the country's employment level, payments balance, or government budget. (See pages 447–450.)

13. Among the political (and social) arguments for protection are: the national defense argument; the critical minimum of basic goods argument; resistance to possible predatory activities by foreign interests; and, most important, the political influence of "intense minorities," otherwise known as "special interests." (See page 450.)

14. Commercial treaties regulate trade and commerce among nations. Multinational treaties can be used to form free trade areas and customs

unions, which are important means of economic integration. They differ mainly in that the members of a free trade area retain their separate tariffs against nonmember countries, while a customs union has a common tariff structure. (See page 451.)

15. The European Community is the most important move toward economic integration today. It is a customs union. There is also a European Free Trade Association. (See pages 451–452.)

16. Free trade areas and customs unions both create and divert trade. The trade-creation effects are welcomed by internationalists as moves toward greater freedom of trade; the trade-diversion effects work in the opposite direction. (See page 452.)

17. After World War II, a proposed International Trade Organization (ITO), affiliated with the United Nations, never came into being because of United States opposition. The various First World countries, however, are seeking to reduce the general level of tariff and nontariff protection among themselves, using for this purpose a General Agreement on Tariffs and Trade (GATT). (See page 453.)

18. After a long period of positive balances, the U.S. balance of trade has been increasingly negative since about 1970. America's reduced international competitiveness is attributed to an inability or unwillingness to adjust to increased productivity in the rest of the world. Factor endowments in foreign countries have improved, and the product cycle has accelerated. (See pages 453–456.)

KEY TERMS

absolute advantage: being more proficient than others in doing a given thing (page 441).

administrative protection: a form of protection that subjects competitive imports to burdensome, idiosyncratic, costly, and time-consuming specifications or inspection procedures (page 444).

commercial treaty: an agreement between countries dealing with economic and trade relations (page 451).

comparative advantage: the principle that states that a product whose pretrade or restricted-trade price is relatively higher in a country than in the rest of the world will likely be imported by that country and that a product whose pretrade or restricted-trade price is relatively lower will likely be exported (page 441).

consumers' surplus: the benefit to consumers from being able to buy at a uniform price rather than at the sum of the amounts they would have been willing to pay for each unit separately (page 438).

customs union: a form of economic integration in which there is free trade among members and a common tariff for nonmembers (page 451).

dumping: the sale of a product below what authorities consider average total cost plus a fair markup (page 446).

effective protection: the net tariff advantage to a producer taking account not only of the tariff on the final product but also any tariffs on inputs used in producing the product (page 445).

excess demand: the amount by which the quantity demanded exceeds the quantity supplied at a specified price (page 436).

excess supply: the amount by which the quantity supplied exceeds the quantity demanded at a specified price (page 436).

factor price equalization theorem: a theorem that states that free trade of goods and services across countries not only tends to equalize output prices but also input prices (page 443).

free trade area: a form of economic integration in which there are no tariffs or other trade restrictions among member countries but each member country has its own set of tariffs, quotas, etc. for nonmember countries (page 451).

General Agreement on Tariffs and Trade (GATT): an organization of First World nations that attempts to regulate tariffs, quotas, and other forms of nontariff protection (page 453).

infant industry argument: an argument for protection based on the proposition that an industry should be sheltered from foreign competition while it develops needed skills and production techniques (page 447).

International Trade Organization (ITO): a proposed organization to regulate quotas and other forms of nontariff protection; the forerunner of GATT (page 453).

market-opening strategies: a system of guaranteed minimum quotas for American goods in foreign markets, intended to counteract foreign protectionism (page 446).

nominal protection: the rate of the tariff imposed on the importation of foreign supplies of an industry's product (page 445).

orderly marketing agreements: multilateral agreements that try to prevent price cutting in importing countries (page 446).

product cycle: the sequence of situations beginning with production for the domestic market and then for the export market, but ultimately becoming an import-competing industry (page 442).

protection: the general term applied to efforts to shelter domestic producers from foreign competition (page 444).

quotas: limitations on the quantity of imports (page 444).

tariff factory: an argument for protection that states that, if a country's market is important, tariffs and quotas set to keep out foreign goods will induce foreign capitalists to invest in that country and employ that country's labor to avoid the tariff (page 449).

tariffs: taxes on imports (page 444).

terms of trade: an average of a country's export prices divided by an average of its import prices (page 448).

trigger-price mechanism: a price assigned to a given import below which the product is considered to be dumped (page 446).

voluntary export restrictions: bilateral arrangements under which an exporting country agrees to lower its exports to an importing country to a certain level or in accordance with a certain formula (page 446).

DISCUSSION QUESTIONS

1. To remedy famine and malnutrition in poor countries, it has been suggested that they raise "food first" and consume it locally, rather than raising cash crops for export (tobacco, coffee, cotton, rubber, etc.). Can such suggestions be reconciled with the theory of comparative advantage?

2. Students often complain that many good teachers prefer to do their own research, leaving the teaching to ineffective teachers. To meet this complaint, one college president suggested that students grade their teachers, and that teachers

graded lowest by the students be assigned exclusively to research. Would this suggestion make "comparative advantage" sense?

3. The theory of factor price equalization has not been borne out by historical experience. Why do you think this is so, and does the experience invalidate the theory?

4. What do you think is meant by the term *dumping?* Do you think antidumping duties are justified? What about duties against goods whose production has been subsidized? What about duties against goods whose export has been subsidized?

5. Should high-wage-rate domestic industries be protected from the products of lower-wage-rate foreign labor? Should labor-intensive industries be protected from the products of automated or robotized foreign plants, which use less labor or none at all?

6. Do you think most American industries enjoy higher or lower effective protection than is suggested by nominal tariff rates? Explain.

7. Why has protection shifted away from tariffs to quotas, voluntary export agreements, orderly marketing arrangements, and other forms of administrative protection?

8. What is the difference between a customs union and a free trade area? How would you characterize the arrangements between the fifty American states?

9. It is generally agreed that American prosperity has been enhanced by the regional specialization permitted by the absence of interstate tariffs and other forms of protection. Should this result be applied to the world as a whole?

10. Can you find examples of product cycles in the histories of such American industries as shoes, steel, or automobiles? Explain.

11. Why has the American "industrial crisis of the 1980s" developed? Is it a real crisis? What, if anything, should be done about it?

12. Country X exports goods to the U.S. in exchange for U.S. assets (securities and real estate). The Xians are not interested in buying U.S. exports, which they consider both overpriced and of inferior workmanship. The USTR proposes to negotiate agreements with Country X to open its markets. This would force Xians to accept U.S. goods instead of U.S. assets, on penalty of reducing Country X's own exports to the U.S. Is this sound microeconomics?

21
Economic Growth

Preview How have we progressed and whither are we drifting? The key questions of economic change, economic evolution, economic progress, or economic drift are usually treated by economists under two heads. One of these is the economic *growth* of those countries that have apparently progressed sooner and faster than the rest of the world. The other is the economic *development*, or underdevelopment, of the much larger group of countries, with a much larger population, that have developed later and more slowly. These are the so-called *less-developed countries* (LDCs). The two sets of problems are by no means independent of each other. A persistent question is: "Has growth of the rich countries advanced or retarded the development of the poor countries?"

This chapter is about the economic growth of the advanced countries, sometimes called DCs or MDCs (developed countries, more developed countries) in contrast to LDCs. These advanced countries include those in North America, Western Europe, and Australasia, as well as Japan, South Africa, and Israel, with a number of "newly industrializing countries" (NICs) knocking at the gates. Almost all the advanced countries are industrial, and some are postindustrial. This means that their nonagricultural sectors produce large and growing parts of their GNPs and national incomes. The manufacturing, mining, construction, and transport sectors dominate in the industrial countries, and the various service sectors (trade, finance, education, government, etc.) dominate in the postindustrial ones.

Are advanced countries rich because they are industrial, or industrial because they are rich? Or does some third factor (technical progress, perhaps, or human capital) account for both their greater wealth and their greater emancipation from agricultural

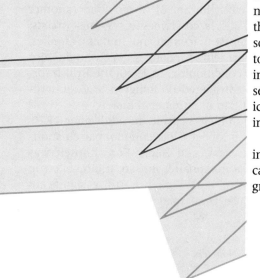

461

stoop labor? Many hold strong views on these questions, but we do not know the answers.

The advanced countries might be thought of as the swanky suburbs of a largely underdeveloped world. We shall first consider why they have developed as they have. This is the relatively upbeat part of the chapter. We then discuss their prospects for future growth, assuming that it will take place at approximately the same rates as in the recent past. Here the picture is mixed, partly because of environmental problems and partly because of a mathematical problem. An economy growing at a constant percentage rate, or by constant amounts, must eventually "explode." That is to say, its GNP must eventually exceed any preassigned limit. It will approach infinity, as the mathematicians say. Since this is economically impossible, growth rates and growth amounts must eventually decrease. GNP must approach some upper limit. One international group of distinguished economists, engineers, environmentalists, and other social scientists, called the Club of Rome, expects demographic and environmental limits to growth to begin operating early in the next (twenty-first) century. Most economists, however, are less alarmist.

The general public assumes without question that economic growth is a good thing. This assumption, however, is not necessarily correct. We end the chapter by taking up the dissenting views in regard to the further growth of advanced industrial countries.

WHAT DOES GROWTH MEAN?

In a statistical sense **economic growth** is an increase in the real GNP of a country. Since some notion of improved material welfare is usually intended, an increase in per capita GNP is the most common measure. To put life into the abstraction of economic growth, think of a person born during or soon after the First World War (1914–1918) being asked by a grandchild; "Grandpa, what did people eat when you were a boy?" or "Grandma, when you were a girl, how could you have fun without TV?" The answers to questions like these are what growth "means." If the human life span were longer, answers to the questions of great-great-grandchildren would tell us even more about the meaning of economic growth.

Economic growth is an increase in real GNP, usually measured on a per capita basis.

Let us take for an example the period since World War I. Let us focus on the United States, which may have seen either more or less change than other advanced countries in the period we are considering. What are the principal advantages of "modern" life that the American youngster of, say, 1920, would have known nothing about except perhaps as amazing science fiction? (There was, of course, amazing science fiction well before 1920. Jules Verne in France and H.G. Wells in England were two great names in that field.)

To the grandchild, perhaps most immediately impressive would be electronic news and entertainment—radio, television, VCRs, and all that. The first American radio broadcast transmitted 1920 election returns from station KDKA in Pittsburgh. Boys and girls with technically gifted parents and older brothers or sisters could, soon thereafter, hear the squawks and squeals of stations in Chicago, New York, Montreal, or even Havana, often in the middle of the night. There were (silent) movies. Records could be played on (wind-up) phonographs.

Next came electric appliances—the refrigerator, home laundry, and vacuum cleaner. Some were completely unknown in 1920, while others were highly experimental, not to say temperamental. These, with the aid of frozen food (another newcomer), displaced domestic servants (maids, cooks, laundresses), icemen and, in many families, unmarried or retired relatives. We should also mention air conditioning. In 1920, the British foreign service considered Washington, D.C., a hardship post, due to its summer climate!

The automobile became an adult after 1920. True, the Ford Model T was commonplace nationwide in that year, and Henry Ford himself was many times a millionaire. But an automobile trip from Boston to New York was still a significant adventure. The rural road system alternated between choking dust and impassable mud. The shopping center was unknown. The horse and wagon dominated home deliveries, and the trolley car dominated urban transit as well as short-distance intercity transit—Boston to Worcester, Long Beach to Los Angeles, Chicago to Milwaukee, Hartford to New Haven.

As for the airplane, one was called outside to crane one's neck for a glimpse of a two-seater biplane when it appeared. Air travel was unknown. Intercontinental travel was by sea—a week across the Atlantic by the ''monarchs of the seas,'' and ten days to two weeks across the Pacific in less pretentious vessels. Only the rich and adventurous went. The ordinary John or Joan Q. Public lived his or her entire life in one state, with perhaps a graduation, honeymoon, or retirement trip to one or two neighboring ones.

This listing leaves to the end the developments of nuclear power and electronic computation. To the grandchild, these may mean little more than computer games and shortcuts in homework, but they have revolutionized energy generation and business practice. Neither existed in 1920.

In numerical terms, the U.S. GNP was $482 billion in 1920, compared to $4,030 billion in 1988, both measured in 1982 dollars. The later figure was 8.4 times the earlier one—a rise of 3.2 percent per year on the average over that 68-year period.[1]

THE ECONOMIC GROWTH RECORD

After the Goths sacked Rome (A.D. 476), the various ''barbarian'' sovereignties of western Europe that succeeded the western Roman Empire had neither

hope nor ambition for what we call economic growth. ''The glory that was Greece and the grandeur that was Rome'' were apparently gone for good, relics of a vanished paradise of living standards, culture, and civilization. Survival sufficed for the ''Dark Ages.'' The eastern Roman Empire, centered in Byzantium, of Constantinople, was more hopeful, and struggled on for nearly a thousand years before the fall of Constantinople to the Turks in 1453.

We can only guess when and why economic growth became an objective of various western European city-states—initially Venice and Genoa in northern Italy—and of emerging national states like Spain, Portugal, France, and England. Chiefly through the seven medieval Crusades, western Europeans became acquainted quite early with the wealth and power of the Arab and Turkish caliphates and sultanates of the Middle East and with the fading glories of the eastern Roman Empire. Later travels by Marco Polo, Christopher Columbus, Vasco da Gama, and their followers acquainted Europe with the wealth of India and China in the Far East and of the Aztecs and Incas of the New World. Europeans recognized the gains to be made from trade or conquest in these areas. Also, as gunpower replaced the armored knight, and the castle proved susceptible to artillery, the religious, dynastic, and other wars of Europe came to be fought largely with mercenary armies. Mercenaries had to be recruited and paid, not merely dragooned. They had the bad habits of going home, or deserting to the enemy, when the money ran out. Two centuries before Adam Smith's discourse in *The Nature and Causes of the Wealth of the Nations* (1776), monarchs, princes, barons, and republics alike had come to see wealth and income as routes to power as well as to luxury and also as attainable even beyond the levels they associated with the ancient world of Greece and Rome.

The West subsequently surpassed classical antiquity in economic matters and continued to grow. Important changes of economic structure occurred. Economic historians disagree as to what the most important of these changes were. They also disagree on whether change was gradual or ''revolutionary.'' For example, was there any industrial ''revolution'' in Britain during the long reign of George III (1760–1820), or have we simply gener-

---

1. If a number, Y_o, grows r percent per period over n periods, its value at the end of the growth process, Y_n, is given by the formula:

$$Y_n = Y_o(1 + r)^n \qquad \text{or} \qquad \log Y_n = \log Y_o + n \log (1 + r)$$

By this formula, a number growing at 1 percent per year will double at the end of 69.7 years (not 100!). To check this result, solve for n when $Y_o = 1$, $Y_n = 2$, and $r = .01$. And if the growth rate is 2 percent, or .02, the number will double in 35.0 years (not 50!).

alized from the experience of a few industries, particularly the cotton textile industry?[2]

Economic growth gradually became an objective of western European countries during the course of the Middle Ages.

Changes in the economies of the West involved more than the development of the modern corporation and mass production. They also involved more than the shift in emphasis from **primary production** (agriculture, forestry, and fisheries) to **secondary production** (manufacturing, mining, construction, and transport) and eventually to **tertiary production** (the service industries of trade, finance, government, education, etc.). These changes are themselves among the things the economic historian needs to explain.

Some of the structural changes in the economies of the West are listed and discussed in the opening chapter of *How the West Grew Rich* by Nathan Rosenberg and L.E. Birdzell, Jr.[3] A slightly modified Rosenberg-Birdzell list of fundamental causes for the economic performance of the West since about 1500 includes:

1. The rise of an autonomous economic sphere and a merchant class with substantial and secure property rights, independent of royal courts, the military, and the established churches.

2. Innovation (invention made practical), plus other changes not usually considered invention at all. Rosenberg and Birdzell list extension of trade, discovery of new resources, introduction of new products, and lowering costs of production.

3. Development of sources of innovative ideas, including educational systems, patent systems, etc.

4. Diversity, uncertainty, and experimentation, as opposed to centralized, continent-wide patterns of doing things sanctioned by governments, by religious bodies, or by economic organizations like guilds and trade associations.

Fundamental causes for the economic performance of the West since 1500 include the rise of a merchant class, innovations and inventions, development of sources of innovative ideas, and diversity, uncertainty, and experimentation.

Equally important is the Rosenberg-Birdzell list of factors often claimed, by detractors of the West, to have largely explained Western economic growth but that Rosenberg and Birdzell downgrade. This list includes:

1. Natural resources
2. "Economistic" psychology
3. Inequalities of wealth and income
4. Slavery
5. Exploitation of less developed countries, including countries with higher degrees of civilization but less developed military arts and sciences
6. Miscellaneous misconduct by modern standards (looting, piracy, etc.)
7. Pure blind luck

Certainly these factors existed or occurred. The unsettled question, however, is just how important were they in the five-hundred-year sweep of modern Western economic history, or in the West as a whole? We shall see some of the more derogatory items on this list again, as explanations for the poverty of the LDCs. Look for them in the next chapter, under the heading "Dependencia Theories of Underdevelopment."

A SUPPLY-SIDE ECONOMIC GROWTH MODEL

We now turn from economic history to economic analysis to explain economic growth after its desir-

---

2. For the skeptical "new view" that change was evolutionary, and also the view that western European development did not follow the British model, see Rondo Cameron, "A New View of European Industrialization," *Economic History Review* (February 1985).

3. Nathan Rosenberg and L.E. Birdzell, *How the West Grew Rich: The Economic Transformation of the Industrial World* (New York: Basic Books, 1986).

ability and attainability became recognized by those in power.

To explain growth from the supply side (that is, based on inputs to production), it is natural for an economist to turn to one of his standard tools, a *production function,* such as

$$Y = f(K, N)$$

in which the symbols are defined as follows:

  Y an estimate of the annual real GNP of a country.

  K an estimate of the **rental value**—roughly, the sale value times the interest rate—of the country's capital (machinery and equipment) and natural resources.

  N an estimate of the country's employed labor force—measured in years of labor (person-years), including self-employed and family labor at one end of a scale of liberty and slave labor at the other end.

Production functions such as this one explain economic growth quite well for periods of a generation or so.[4]

A production function shows the relationship between inputs and outputs for short periods—about a generation—but is unsatisfactory for long-term growth estimates.

Expanding their production-function analysis, many economists now break down the supply-side causes of economic growth into five broad groups of factors, with many individual items under each head. Edward F. Denison of the Brookings Institution and the United States Department of Commerce has been an international leader in this sort of work, devising both time series and comparisons between countries. The principal groups of causative factors in economic growth can be classified as:

1. The *quantity of labor* employed.

2. The *quality of labor* employed. This is seen as dependent on such subfactors as the education and age of the labor force and the length of the working week. Education is a plus and the decline of the work week is a minus. Also, a labor force should neither be too young nor too old.

3. The *quantity of capital* (machinery and equipment) and *natural resources* employed, with adjustments for depreciation and obsolescence. Land and natural resources are generally treated separately. Capital and natural resources that are available but not in use are a serious statistical problem, especially in recession or depression years.

4. The *quality of capital* employed, which includes technical change. For example a new-model computer or word processor is of higher quality than one of less recent vintage, because it embodies the most recent improvements, even when the older model is still usable.

5. **Disembodied technical change,** that is, technological change reflected incompletely or not at all in the quality of specific types of labor or machinery. Examples might be an improved road network or long-distance communications system.[5]

According to the supply-side model, the main factors of economic growth are the quantity of labor, the quality of labor, the quantity of capital, the quality of capital, and disembodied technical change.

---

4. But when short-run production functions are extended over longer periods, they significantly underestimate *Y*. The longer the period covered, the greater the underestimate. There is an unexplained residual, sometimes called the Abramovitz residual for the Stanford University economist who focused professional attention on it. Clearly, the ordinary production function is an unsatisfactory long-term growth estimator.

5. Disembodied technical change can be explained this way. Suppose an improved highway system lowers transport costs for both inputs and outputs and therefore shifts supply curves to the right for a wide range of industries in the neighborhood of the improved highway system. Some of these industries are agricultural, some are manufacturers of various kinds, and some may be service industries. The cost reductions and supply increases occur whether or not the highway-construction industry uses modernized equipment or whether any of the beneficiary industries do so. In technical terms, there is no embodied technological change anywhere in the economy.

Some Results from the Supply-Side Model

Let us compare U.S. GNP in 1983 with U.S. GNP fifty years earlier, at the inauguration of Franklin Roosevelt and the beginning of the New Deal in 1933. Both GNPs are expressed in 1982 dollars. The fifty-year growth rate was 3.97 percent per year (see footnote 1), almost precisely 4 percent.[6] Using this elementary and optimistic result for the United States alone as representing the world's advanced industrial countries generally, we can, perhaps, use 4 percent growth for such countries. This does not in the least deny the possibility of much higher growth rates over shorter periods of "miraculous" growth for Japan or Korea or Hong Kong, which were reconstructing after warfare or introducing foreign technology at abnormal speed. Japan, for example, grew at rates of 10.9, 8.7, 9.7, and 12.2 percent in four successive five-year periods, from 1951–1970.[7] For a really long-term trend, however, estimates of 4 percent growth (3 percent per capita if population rises 1 percent a year) are more likely to err on the high side than on the low.

Four percent growth per year, or 3 percent per capita growth, are hardly exciting numbers in themselves, but they accumulate rapidly over the generations, as illustrated in Table 1. The income figures are impressive, although too high to be credible, at least for the third and fourth generations. We offer, also, several other observations on the growth experience of the past half-century.

1. The rate of employment has been falling in the wake of the population growth rate (after adjustments for such shorter-period phenomena as the 1946–1958 baby boom that followed World War II).

2. Labor quality has been rising because of increased education and improved on-the-job training (OJT). This has more than offset a downward drift in the length of the working week, which affects labor productivity statistics in the same way as a quality decline.

6. Our comparison has some upward bias because 1933 was the bottom of the Great Depression and 1983 was a year of high prosperity. Short-term business fluctuations therefore raise the apparent long-term trend.

7. Yutaka Kosai, *The Era of High-Speed Growth*, Table 9-1, p. 4.

3. There is as yet no evidence of a declining growth rate of the quality-adjusted labor force.

4. The growth rate of the capital stock has been greater than that of the labor force, both before and after adjustments for changes in quality.

5. The capital-labor ratio has grown, and at an increasing rate.

6. Measured average productivity per unit of labor and per unit of capital services, both unadjusted for quality change, have risen, especially for labor.

7. General, or multifactor, productivity has risen at an intermediate rate, lower than labor productivity but higher than capital productivity. **Multifactor productivity** is a weighted average of labor and capital productivity. The weights are the labor and property shares in the national income—between two-thirds and three-fourths for labor and between one-third and one-fourth for capital.

8. Productivity growth rates and growth rates of the national income fell below their long-term trends during the 1970s. These slow growth rates were largely caused by environmental concerns, energy supply shocks, and inadequate responses to them. There has been partial but not complete recovery in the 1980s.

Over the past fifty years, the rate of employment has been falling in the wake of the population growth rate, labor quality has been rising, the growth rate of the capital stock has been greater than that of the labor force, the capital-labor ratio has grown, and measured average productivity per unit of labor has risen, as has multifactor productivity.

The Neoclassical Growth Model

Observations and results such as those just cited yield a simple supply-side explanation of economic growth, sometimes called the **neoclassical growth model.** Its main idea is that a country's growth rate is the weighted sum of the changes in the productivities of its productive inputs (such as

TABLE 1
The Power of Sustained Growth in Income

	4% Growth per Capita per Year	3% Growth per Capita per Year
Initial Per Capita Income (index number)	1.00	1.00
One generation later (after 25 years)	2.67	2.09
Two generations later (after 50 years)	7.11	4.38
Three generations later (after 75 years)	18.95	9.18
Four generations later (after 100 years)	50.51	19.22

Because growth in one year becomes part of the base for growth in the next year, sustained rates of growth result in large increases in income from one generation to the next. For example, with a sustained 4% a year per capita growth rate, grandchildren can be more than seven times as affluent as their grandparents.

changes in the output per hour of labor), changes in their qualities, and an additional term reflecting disembodied technical progress. The model involves major statistical problems of practical numerical estimations, some of which have caused professional controversy among statisticians.

According to the neoclassical growth model, a country's growth rate is the weighted sum of the changes in the productivities of its productive inputs plus an additional term reflecting disembodied technical progress.

A sample of the data used in neoclassical growth models for the United States is presented in Table 2. Note the important distinction between the *levels* of productivity in part A of this table and the *rates* of productivity growth in part B. In making sense of the figures, we should recall that "units of capital services" are overestimated in recession periods by the inclusion of machinery and equipment that is available but not actually in use. Also, automation and robotization raise "labor" rather than "capital" productivity because the equipment itself is expensive and because it makes possible increases in output with minimal increases in employment.

Table 3, estimated by John W. Kendrick of George Washington University, deals with the slowing of U.S. private sector growth rates from 1948 to the year 2000. Kendrick estimated that the growth rate of real gross product in the United States was 3.7 percent a year over the quarter century from 1948 to 1973, then fell to 2.1 percent a year from 1973 to 1981, but would recover to 4.0 percent in the decade from 1981 to 1990 and to 3.2 percent in the last decade of the century. Advances in knowledge and changes in labor quality made important contributions to productivity and growth in all periods studied. Other forces estimated by Kendrick seem to be neutral or negative.

The neoclassical growth model is often said to assume continuous full employment. In fact, it merely assumes that microeconomic market adjustments and macroeconomic fiscal and monetary policies work together to keep employment rates fairly steady. When unemployment rates are in fact rising, neoclassical growth projections tend to be overly optimistic. When unemployment rates are falling, neoclassical projections tend to err on the side of pessimism.

A DEMAND-SIDE ECONOMIC GROWTH MODEL

Assuming that a 4 percent real annual growth rate (3 percent per capita) is attainable on the supply side, is there any guarantee of its absorption on the demand side? To deal with this question, the rele-

TABLE 2
Levels and Rates of Change of U.S. Productivity, Selected Years, 1960–1987

A. Levels (index numbers, 1977 = 100)					
	1960	1970	1979	1983	1987
All private business					
Output per hour of all persons	67.3	88.4	99.5	103.0	111.2
Output per unit of capital services	103.7	102.7	99.7	88.3	93.7
Multifactor productivity	78.5	93.1	99.6	97.6	104.7
Manufacturing only					
Output per hour of all persons	66.2	80.8	101.4	112.0	131.9
Output per unit of capital services	103.0	99.1	99.5	86.7	102.0
Multifactor productivity	72.0	85.3	100.9	105.0	123.6

B. Annual Percentage Rates of Growth						
	1982	1983	1984	1985	1986	1987
All private business						
Output per hour of all persons	−0.2	2.7	2.5	2.2	2.2	0.8
Output per unit of capital services	−6.2	2.0	5.0	0.2	0.1	0.7
Multifactor productivity	−2.4	4.3	3.4	1.5	1.5	0.8
Manufacturing only						
Output per hour of all persons	2.0	5.8	5.4	4.6	3.3	3.3
Output per unit of capital services	−8.3	6.3	10.1	1.9	1.1	3.3
Multifactor productivity	−6.1	6.4	6.8	3.8	2.7	3.4

Source: Monthly Labor Review (December 1988), Table 43, p. 98.

vant apparatus comes from macroeconomics. We explore a growth identity devised by a Keynesian economist, Sir Roy Harrod, Keynes's official biographer.[8]

Harrod utilized a **capital coefficient** or **capital-output ratio** representing the amount of additional capital required, under current technology, for a unit increase in the net national product. His

8. Sir Roy argued as early as 1939 that the growth rate of the economy, $(\Delta Y/\Delta t)/Y$, where Y is GNP, t is a time period, and Δ stands for a small incremental change in the value of a variable, should be written, to the first approximation, as:

$$\frac{\Delta Y/\Delta t}{Y} = \frac{\Delta Y/\Delta t}{I} \cdot \frac{S}{Y} = \frac{\Delta Y/\Delta t S}{\Delta K/\Delta t Y}$$

using the saving-investment identity in an economy with balanced public budgets and balanced current accounts in international trade. The second step in the derivation equates investment with an incremental change in the capital stock, which is true if investment is *net* of depreciation and obsolescence, in which case Y is no longer GNP but NNP.

incremental capital output ratio is written as $(\Delta K/\Delta t)/(\Delta Y/\Delta t)$, or simply as $\Delta K/\Delta Y$. If we use the symbol K for capital, t for a time period, Y for NNP, v for the incremental capital-output ratio, G for the growth rate, and s for the saving ratio (saving, net of depreciation, as a percentage of NNP), we have the Harrod equation (or identity):

$$Gv = s \quad \text{or} \quad G = s/v$$

The capital coefficient, or incremental capital-output ratio, represents the amount of additional capital required for a unit increase in the net national product. According to Sir Roy Harrod, an economy's growth rate (*G*) equals its saving ratio (*s*) divided by its incremental capital-output ratio (*v*), that is *G* = *s*/*v*.

TABLE 3
Sources of Growth in Real Gross Product for the U.S. Domestic Economy, 1948–1981, with Projections to 2000

Source of Changes in Real Gross Product	1948–73	1973–81	1981–90	1991–2000
Changes in variables influencing productivity				
1. Advances in knowledge	1.4	0.7	1.2	1.0
2. Changes in labor quality[a]	0.5	0.6	0.9	0.9
3. Changes in quality of land	—	−0.2	−0.3	−0.3
4. Resource reallocations	0.4	0.1	—	—
5. Volume changes[b]	0.3	−0.3	0.6	0.4
6. Net government impact[c]	—	−0.2	−0.1	−0.1
7. Other productivity variables[d]	−0.6	−0.6	−0.5	−0.5
Subtotal (total factor productivity)	2.0	0.1	1.8	1.4
Changes in quantity of productive resources	1.7	2.0	2.2	1.8
Total change in real gross product	3.7	2.1	4.0	3.2

Note: Figures are averages of annual percentage rates of change.

a. Includes changes arising from education and training, health, and age-sex composition of labor force.

b. Includes effects of economies of scale and intensity of demand.

c. Includes services to business and the effects of government regulations.

d. Includes the ratio of actual efficiency to potential efficiency and items not elsewhere classified.

Source: John W. Kendrick, "Long-Term Economic Projections: Stronger U.S. Growth Ahead," *Southern Economic Journal* (April 1984), Table 1, p. 953. Used by permission.

The Harrod model can be illustrated with U.S. data. In 1985 the U.S. net national product was $3,192.0 billion, and net domestic private investment was $210.3 billion, both in 1982 dollars. In 1986 net national product (still in 1982 prices) rose to $3,278.5 billion, an increase of $86.5 billion.[9] If we ignore statistical discrepancies in these estimates, the Harrod equation gives us the following figures for 1986:

a growth rate (*G*) of 2.71%, that is, 86.5/ 3,192.0

an incremental capital-output ratio (*v*) of 2.43, that is, 210.3/86.5

a saving rate (*s*) of 6.59%, that is, 210.3/ 3,192.0

The year 1986 was prosperous, but not a high-growth year. All the above numbers, which are of course mutually consistent, are somewhat low by long-period standards. For a 4 percent growth rate

9. *Economic Report of the President, 1989*, Tables B-2 and B-17.

with an incremental capital-output ratio of 3, the United States would require a saving rate (combining private saving, any budget surpluses of government, and any international surplus on current account) adding up to 12 percent of the net national product.[10] This was not attained in 1986, and in fact the budget surplus and international current account numbers were negative. Thus, it appears that the check to American growth in the mid-1980s was neither oversaving nor a shortage of demand.

An equilibrium path of economic growth should satisfy both an expanded production function on the supply side and the Harrod equation on the demand side. But what happens if the paths diverge? To deal with this question, let us suppose an advanced economy cruising along at 4 percent

10. The Harrod equation can be adjusted to an international economy with current-account and budgetary imbalances by redefining saving (*S*) to include surpluses, as follows: $S = S' + [(T_n - G) + (X - Im)]$, where S' is private domestic saving, T_n is net taxes, G is government purchases, X is exports, and Im is imports.

real annual growth and at high employment equilibrium. There is a sudden shock either to the supply side or to the demand side. What is likely to happen? Even if the initial shock comes only from one side, we must consider consequences on both supply and demand.

An equilibrium path of economic growth should satisfy both an expanded production function on the supply side and the Harrod equation on the demand side.

Supply-shock cases are the easier ones to analyze, if not to deal with in practical politics. For example, should energy become scarce, the aggregate-supply curve shifts to the left and upward. In the Harrod equation, the capital-output ratio rises because, to compensate for the increased energy cost, more capital is required per unit of income increase. The growth rate falls. On the other hand, if a technical advance—safer nuclear power or cheaper solar energy—solves our recurrent energy crisis, the aggregate-supply curve shifts to the right. The capital-output ratio falls, and the growth rate rises. In each of these cases, workers may have to move to different jobs as the economy adjusts to different supply conditions, but, once the moves have been made, there is no reason, in economic theory, for total employment to fall.

Analysis of demand-side shocks is more difficult. For our first example, let us suppose a successful thrift campaign that increases the saving ratio with no change in the inducement to invest at any given interest rate.[11] The Harrod equation suggests that the higher saving ratio requires a higher growth rate. But what is there about a higher saving rate that *causes* income to grow faster? If a higher saving ratio means a drop in consumption purchases, a likely short-run effect of a thrift campaign would be a fall in employment. Then with less labor employed, there would be a *decline* in the growth rate. In the Harrod equation, less salable output would be obtained from the same capital

stock. In fact the capital-output ratio may rise by more than the saving ratio, if a lower interest rate encourages capital formation. However, in the absence of offsetting changes, a decline in the income growth rate is an expected outcome.

Now suppose a demand shock of the opposite sort—a successful campaign to increase domestic spending on current output. The saving ratio tends to fall, and interest rates tend to rise. If there is already high employment, and if the incentive to invest is presumed unchanged, the real income growth rate has little if any room to increase. Therefore, there must be a fall in the capital-output ratio approximately parallel to that in the saving ratio. Where does it come from? Primarily, one supposes, from the rise in the interest rate. The higher interest rate is the villain of the piece on the supply side as well, where it restrains the growth of both the quantity and the quality of capital equipment so that the growth rate moves little if at all.

LOOKING AHEAD

Thus far, our analysis of economic growth has been based mainly on economic history and its extrapolation. Its tone has been optimistic, although less so than it would have been at the beginning of this century. At that time, informed opinion was not only optimistic about economic growth but also held that long wars between the world's great powers were economically unprofitable and therefore obsolete. A sad mistake!

As the century draws to its close, following two enormously destructive world wars, it is difficult to remain optimistic about economic growth in advanced countries. In addition to the threat of renewed military spasms and to the difficulties of relationships between the advanced countries and less-developed countries, it is worthwhile to call attention to three problems related to continued economic growth in the advanced countries. These problems are:

1. Resource exhaustion and environmental pollution.

2. Aging of advanced-country populations and the prospect of intergenerational conflict.

---

11. In the loanable-funds market, we are supposing that the supply curve shifts to the right while the demand curve remains in its initial position.

3. Possible contradiction between distributional equity and the encouragement of growth through public finances.

Three principal problems that hinder continued economic growth in advanced countries are: resource exhaustion and environmental pollution, aging of advanced-country populations and the prospect of intergenerational conflict, and the dilemma of growth versus distributional equity.

Resource Exhaustion and Environmental Pollution

Ever since the dawn of civilization, and quite possibly before, mankind has been in the process of running out of exhaustible resources like wood, coal, oil, and metals. In the 1870s, the eminent British economist William Stanley Jevons wrote *The Coal Question*. His thesis was that Britain's industrial empire would fall because of exhaustion of its high-grade coal resources. Jevons was wrong, or at least premature, because non-British coal supplies came to the rescue and because other fuels replaced coal. Thus, technical "fixes," including cheap transport of foreign supplies, intervened to save the day. But can we be sure that technical fixes will always be available? Do we have replacements in the offing for petroleum? For uranium?

Environmental pollution, a great by-product of economic growth, raises two important economic issues that are, and may always remain, unsolved. The first is, whether (and by whom) the basic rules of the market game should be changed to ban "excessive" pollution—treating it like murder, robbery, and fraud. A less drastic action would recognize pollution as a cost of production and would internalize this cost by making producers pay for a "license to pollute."[12] Would such less drastic action suffice?

The second economic issue is how any worldwide scheme of regulating or reducing pollution can, simultaneously, (a) meet the concerns of environmentalists like the several Green parties of Europe, (b) maintain employment in "dirty" industries in advanced countries, and (c) permit industrial development in the LDCs. This is a tradeoff problem, and tradeoffs are conceivable, but how are the terms of the tradeoff to be determined and enforced?

Two questions about pollution are: (1) should the rules of market economies be changed to reduce pollution and (2) how can pollution reduction balance the concerns of environmentalists, workers in "dirty" industries, and the development hopes of LDCs?

As we enter the 1990s, the principal large-scale pollution problems include the following:

1. The gradual heating of the earth's atmosphere under the influence of increased carbon dioxide (CO_2) production. This is the so-called greenhouse effect. It threatens to melt both polar ice caps and to flood important coastal areas.

2. The destruction of the atmosphere's ozone (O_3) layer by hydrofluorocarbons and other emissions. This threatens to admit more carcinogenic ultraviolet rays from outer space.

3. The destruction of forests—in advanced countries by acid rain (sulfur dioxide, or SO_2, and other sulfur compounds)—and in other countries by rapid clearing of tropical rainforests.[13]

4. The killing of rivers, lakes, and even ocean areas with assorted chemical wastes, causing red tides and fish kills and threatening important parts of the food chain.

5. The threats of catastrophic disasters from nuclear-plant accidents —especially in areas sub-

---

12. A variant, which is more complex but which many economists find preferable, would be to subsidize low-pollution methods of production where they exist.

13. Many of the areas affected are in the LDCs. The motivation for the destruction in the LDCs is the export of lumber to the developed countries or the clearing of land for ranching and cash-crop agriculture, also primarily for export.

ject to earthquakes—and the accumulation of radioactive waste products.[14]

These pollution processes may be reversible. Some have already been reversed to some extent. For example, "dead" areas like Lake Erie, the Hudson River, and parts of Japan's Inland Sea have been restored to life. But reversing past pollution is expensive and directly competitive with provision for future growth as well as with various forms of private consumption, private investment, and public service.

Reducing pollution and using resources to undo previous pollution damage is directly competitive with economic growth.

Aging of Advanced-Country Populations

In economic demography, the immediate and direct issue for the world's advanced countries is the aging of their populations. Part of this problem— perhaps only the smaller part—is the anticipated decline of the quantity and quality of their labor forces. Aging enables an increasing proportion of advanced-country populations to leave the labor force to live in retirement. Meanwhile, there has been a tendency for retirement ages to fall while post-retirement second careers have not become popular. Labor-force participation rates for male workers over sixty have fallen. To make matters still worse, an increasing proportion of the active labor force will be rising into what are sometimes unkindly called the "dead wood" years shortly preceding retirement. In these years a worker's attention is supposedly fixed on the prospects for the good life ahead, with neither hope nor ambition for further advancement or recognition on the job. Of at least equal importance is the prospect of intergenerational conflict. It is symbolized by disquieting forecasts of the falling number of prime-age workers available, however unwillingly, to support each member of the elderly population in the style

14. Nor should we forget that the breakdown of uranium, in nature and without human intervention, has among its by-products a carcinogenic gas called radon.

to which the elderly feel entitled. The next step is doubt about the willingness of the young to bear the increasing burden of supporting the old. In the United States, at least, the elderly seem somewhat more inclined than are younger voters to exercise their rights to vote and have become conscious of their power to vote themselves expensive pensions, health care, and other entitlements at public expense.

Such trends need not, of course, lead to intergenerational conflict. A retired parent or grandparent can help a young man or woman begin his or her career in the same way as an employed parent or grandparent, given the same income. The retired parent or grandparent might even afford greater generosity than an employed one, if his or her future income and health-care are insured. But a real intergenerational problem may arise if the falling size of the nuclear family is reflected in a rising proportion of senior citizens with few close relatives who need their aid, or a rising proportion living isolated and alienated from younger family members. The reluctance of retirement communities to support bond issues for public schools may be an indication of a diversion of funds away from provision for growth toward support of the elderly. In his *Constitution of Liberty,* the philosophical economist Friederich Hayek wondered whether disenfranchising the elderly might not be desirable so as to limit the diversion of public funds to the elderly and away from, among other things, financing future growth.

The aging of the populations of advanced countries reduces the labor force and poses the prospect of intergenerational conflict.

Growth versus Equity

Providing for economic growth requires the saving and investment of resources in both the private and the public sector. We have mentioned the possibility, in an aging society, of such resources being drained away to support senior citizens. The poor and the near-poor of preretirement age are another large class of advanced-country populations with claims competing with those of economic growth.

Their claims to guaranteed useful employment, to self respect, and to guaranteed incomes above the conventional poverty line have been forcibly espoused for Americans in a pastoral letter by a group of Roman Catholic bishops (as well as others) under the leadership of Archbishop Rembert Weakland of Milwaukee. Do the costs of eliminating poverty, guaranteeing employment, and assuring distributional equity (in conformity with the moral law as interpreted by the bishops and others) include the slowing down of economic growth? Should we include, in the costs of economic growth, the toleration of "immoral" distributions of income and wealth and "immoral" rates of unemployment, longer than might be necessary in a static society? Economic policies, like economic goods, have their opportunity costs.

Answers to these questions are related to answers to another question that we avoided earlier in this chapter. Has the principal check to long-term growth come from the supply side (production functions) or the demand side (the Harrod equation)? Redistribution of income and wealth toward greater equality aims, after all, at increasing the consumption of necessities at the expense not only of luxuries but also of saving and investment as well. Insofar as the ceiling on growth is a supply-side matter of inadequate capital formation, there is a conflict between growth and distributional equity. But insofar as the ceiling reflects high capital-output ratios (capital coefficients) due to capital used below capacity by reason of inadequate demand, there may be no conflict at all. Rather, the reverse may be true.

Conflict may exist between the promotion of economic growth and the provision of guaranteed employment and distributional equity.

IS GROWTH A GOOD THING?

Most of us would rather be rich than poor, or at least we would like to have some of the comforts of life. Only a few of us really seek plain living, with or without high thinking. Those few become hermits, join communes, vow allegiance to Lady Poverty, and remember the sad emperor of China. (His psychiatrist proposed to cure his depression by having him sleep in the shirt of a happy man. When the happy man was found, he had no shirt!)

Advantages of Growth

The consumption advantages of higher income, and thus of growth, are clear despite the tendencies of MDC people to "'dig their graves with their teeth" and bang each other with automobiles. There are also security advantages if crime and environmental pollution can be controlled and if basic welfare can be assured without too great a cost in individual freedom or the right to privacy. There seems no doubt that the average MDC worker lives better than the medieval lord and lady did in their unheated castle, covered with "ermine and vermin," and expecting death or major illness before the age of fifty.

For society, growth yields a dividend, which can be used to raise the standard of living for those at the lowest levels and even redistribute income and wealth above these lowest levels without absolute loss to the "haves" or the community. The moral of Lester Thurow's *Zero-Sum Society* is that "doing something about poverty" is more costly to the rich and the middle class when the country's per capita income is stagnant than when it is growing.

The same principles hold between countries. MDCs can be expected to offer more aid to LDCs when MDC income per capita is growing than when it is not. And the more that world income growth slows down, the greater the likelihood that the LDCs must give up all ambition for catching up with today's MDCs.

There are personal consumption and security advantages to economic growth, and there are societal advantages as well in that growth yields a dividend that can be used to raise the standard of living for those at the lowest levels.

Antigrowth Arguments

Antigrowth literature is not quite as old (among economists) as progrowth literature, but it too dates back at least to the English classical school. David Ricardo (1772–1823), the greatest economist of his time, feared that growth would end in a "stationary state" as capital accumulated. Since capital was subject to diminishing returns, profits would fall to a low point, and net saving and investment would then fall to zero. This prediction, though less extreme than Marx's, helped to give economics the name of "dismal science."

John Stuart Mill   John Stuart Mill (1806–1873) did not agree. His *Principles of Political Economy* (1848) included a *defense* of the stationary state and an attack on what we now call **growthmanship** (an overemphasis on measured economic growth). Here is a quotation:

> I cannot regard the stationary state with . . . unaffected aversion. . . . [It] would be a very considerable improvement on our present condition. I am not charmed with the ideal of life held out by those who think that the normal state of human beings is that of struggling to get on: that the trampling, crushing, elbowing, and treading on each other's heels, which form the existing type of social life, are the most desirable lot of human kind, or anything but the disagreeable symptoms of one of the phases of industrial progress.[15] . . . [The] best state of human nature is that in which, while no one is poor, no one desires to be richer, or has any reason to fear being thrust back by the efforts of others to push themselves forward. It is only in the backward countries of the world that increased production is still an important object; in those most advanced, what is economically needed is a better distribution. . . .
>
> . . . Nor is there much satisfaction in contemplating the world with nothing left to the spontaneous activity of nature; with every rood [unit of measure] of land brought into cultivation, which is capable of growing food; every flowery waste ploughed up, all quadrupeds or birds which are not domesticated for man's use exterminated as his rivals for food, and scarcely a place left where a wild shrub or flower could grow without being eradicated as a weed. If the earth must lose that great portion of its pleasantness which it owes to things that the unlimited increase of wealth and population would extirpate from it, I sincerely hope, for the sake of posterity, that they will be content to be stationary, long before necessity compels them to it.
>
> A stationary condition of capital and population implies no stationary state of human improvement. There would be as much scope as ever for mental culture, and moral and social progress; as much room for improving the Art of Living, and much more likelihood of its being improved, when minds cease to be engrossed by the art of getting on.

Ezra Mishan   The twentieth-century equivalent of Mill (in his antigrowth opinions) has been Ezra Mishan, author of *The Costs of Economic Growth* and *The Economic Growth Debate*. Mishan puts Mill's points in today's context. He sees industry, urban sprawl, the automobile, and tourism as great dangers to the environment. And he fears the effects on human life of radio, television, air travel, the computer, herbicides, pesticides, the civilian and military applications of nuclear technology, and other recent inventions.

Erich Schumacher   Erich Schumacher wrote *Small Is Beautiful*, subtitled *Economics as if People Mattered*. Economists, incidentally, agree that they do! Schumacher is not against growth but against *growthmanship*. He wants a world in which people live in greater harmony with their natural environment than they do in large cities. In such a world, people will have interesting jobs, which they need not fear losing to machines or to robots. He wants people to know where their work fits into some useful finished product, and to be regarded as something more than faceless numbers on time cards or stations on assembly lines. He believes that excessive concern for higher measured growth has

---

15. At this point Mill's first edition paid its respects to the United States. "The northern and middle states of America are a specimen of this stage of civilization in very favourable circumstances; the proportion of capital to land is such as to ensure abundance to every able-bodied member of the community who does not forfeit it by misconduct. All that these advantages seem to have done for them is that the life of the whole of one sex is devoted to dollar-hunting, and of the other to breeding dollar-hunters." This passage was later dropped.

pushed the division of labor, the substitution of machinery for human skills, the alienation of the worker, and the pollution of the environment too far. These trends not only should be prevented from spreading to the LDCs but should be reversed in the MDCs. The key to this better world is "appropriate technology," an undefined term in Schumacher's book. It may not always exist. A major task is to develop it when it does not, as well as to apply it when it does exist despite any sacrifice in growth.

Limits to Growth Another strain of antigrowth literature tells us that growth will end in catastrophe. Technical fixes for one problem will give rise to other problems—or make other problems worse. The best-known "model of doom" is *Limits to Growth*, published by the Club of Rome.

The Club-of-Rome analysis of growth begins with an undeniable mathematical fact. Growth of any quantity at any constant rate "explodes," going beyond any finite upper limit. For this reason, it is impossible, in the long run, unless the upper limit is itself growing at the same rate (or at a higher one). But given a finite limit set by the earth's resources growing only slowly or not at all (and they may be falling!), the growth rate must eventually fall toward zero.

The Club-of-Rome pessimism, however, is more immediate than we have suggested so far. If population, especially in the LDCs, continues to explode, and if per capita real income and product levels as a consequence decline, some terrible combination of fatal maladies lies ahead in the short-term future (twenty-first century). There will be starvation, war, and disease if the food supply runs out. If countries return to agricultural production, living standards will fall sharply. There will be a sharp rise in environmental pollution if technical fixes are used to keep total output rising on a limited resource base. *Limits to Growth* spells out these alternatives in the language of computer simulation. However, the underlying statistical proofs for the equations fed into the computers are not always made clear. The Club of Rome sees "hope" only in drastically limiting population in the short-term future.

Arguments against growth include John Stuart Mill and Erich Schumacher's attacks on growthmanship, Ezra Mishan's concerns about the environment and the quality of human life, and fears about the ultimate outcome of continued growth.

Economics in Focus

South Korea: Two Sides of a Miracle

The startling growth in the South Korean economy has been called a miracle, and the statistics look miraculous indeed. Between 1953 and 1988 the real national income in South Korea rose 1,200 percent. Back in 1961 the per capita GNP was less than $100 a year; by 1988 it was nearly $3,000. In some years the economy's growth rate has reached 14 percent, propelled by a population that seems to thrive on a 54-hour work week. As a result, South Korea has become one of the young powerhouses of world trade—the "next Japan," many observers have said.

The spectacular growth began after the coup that installed Park Chung Hee as president in 1961. Park's government borrowed large sums of money, mainly from the United States, to build Korean industry. The concentration was on export industries: steel, autos, ships, and so on. government policies encouraged the rise of the *chaebol*, a handful of huge corporations that have come to dominate the Korean economy. The success of the *chaebol* has been built on broad diversification: Hyundai, for example, makes not only cars and trucks but also ships and computers; Samsung manufactures textiles, ships, military planes, and computers and also sells insurance.

The growth has helped create a solid and prosperous middle class. Education is now excellent: the literacy rate is well over 95 percent, and more than a third of Korean students reach the university level. The material trappings of middle-class life are also prevalent: in 1970 only 2 percent of the households had refrigerators, but now that figure has risen to about 75 percent. Furthermore, South Koreans live almost twenty years longer than they did two generations ago. To round out the miracle, South Korea has been struggling toward a more genuine democracy.

But is the miracle as great as it looks at first glance? Many critics say it is not. They say that the *chaebol* hold too dominant a position and that smaller businesses have been discouraged. They say that housing, welfare, and care of the elderly have been left on the back burner. Many Koreans themselves see an intolerable gap between the rich and the poor. Moreover, there are strong regional disparities. While Seoul has built office towers and expressways, major cities such as Kwangju, a provincial capital in the south, are still dominated by peasants with their handcarts. Finally, in the political arena, the long march toward democracy has been punctuated with student riots, thousands of labor union strikes, and scandals surrounding political leaders.

Seen as a whole, the South Korean economy demonstrates the differences between growth and development. Growth may help to provide the opportunity for development, but it does not automatically resolve problems of income distribution, health and welfare, and the overall quality of life.

Sources: "South Korea," *The Economist*, May 21, 1988, p. 3ff.; Laxmi Nakarmi, Larry Armstrong, and William J. Holstein, "Korea," *Business Week*, September 5, 1988, pp. 44–50; Louis Kraar, "Korea: Tomorrow's Powerhouse," *Fortune*, August 15, 1988, pp. 75–81; Pico Iyer, "The Yin and Yang of Paradoxical, Prosperous Korea," *Smithsonian*, August 1988, pp. 47–58; Peter C. Du Bois, "Olympian View: A Skeptical Look at South Korea," *Barron's*, September 26, 1988, p. 75.

SUMMARY

1. The meaning of economic growth can be illustrated by the impressive changes that have taken place in the United States since World War I. (See pages 462–463.)

2. Economic historians do not agree on the causes of the economic growth of Western countries during the past five hundred years. Rosenberg and Birdzell offer a number of fundamental causes as well as a number of less important explanations. (See pages 463–464.)

3. Production function analysis is helpful in explaining short-period economic growth but significantly underestimates GNP for periods much longer than a single generation. (See page 464.)

4. Supply-side causes of economic growth may be grouped into those involving (1) the quantity of labor, (2) the quality of labor, (3) the quantity of capital, (4) the quality of capital, and (5) disembodied technical change. (See page 465.)

5. Advanced-country growth experience over the past 50 years has been impressive, although the rate of 4 percent per year (3 percent per capita per year) probably cannot be sustained. (See page 466.)

6. When examining the past fifty years of advanced-country growth experience, one should recognize that the rate of employment has been falling, the growth rate of the quality-adjusted labor force has not declined, the capital-labor ratio has grown at an increasing rate, and average productivity per unit of labor and per unit of capital have risen, with the former rising more than the latter. (See page 466.)

7. Neoclassical (supply-side) growth theory focuses on the quantities and qualities of the major inputs to production and also on disembodied technical progress. Its projections are overly optimistic when unemployment rates are rising and overly pessimistic when unemployment rates are falling. (See pages 466–467 and Tables 2 and 3, pages 468 and 469.)

8. Keynesian (demand-side) growth theory is represented by a Harrod model. It shows the growth rate to be the quotient of two ratios: the saving ratio (saving, net of depreciation, as a percent of income) is the numerator, and the capital-output ratio (the net amount of additional capital required to increase output by one unit) is the denominator. (See pages 468–469.)

9. Demand-side and supply-side shocks can affect both the production function and the Harrod equation. (See page 470.)

10. Resource exhaustion and environmental pollution problems loom before us. We cannot be sure that technical fixes will bail us out, nor can we be sure that we will choose the best methods of protecting ourselves from destructive pollution. Should we change the basic rules of the market mechanism? (See pages 471–472.)

11. Another problem for economic growth in advanced countries stems from the aging of their populations, which may lead to serious intergenerational conflicts. (See page 472.)

12. Economic growth in advanced countries may also be threatened by the diversion of savings and investment from such growth-stimulating functions as research and development and education to equity uses, such as supporting the aged, the poor, and the homeless. (See page 473.)

13. The advantages of economic growth include both material comforts and greater opportunities for society to devote resources to matters of social concern. (See page 473.)

14. Antigrowth arguments range widely over matters related to the welfare of individuals swept along in the dynamics of growth and concerns about environmental damage resulting from it. (See pages 474–475.)

KEY TERMS

capital coefficient (capital-output ratio): the amount of additional capital required for a unit increase in the net national product (page 468).

disembodied technical change: technical change reflected incompletely or not at all in the quality of specific types of labor or machinery (page 465).

economic growth: an increase in the real GNP of an economy, usually stated on a per capita basis (page 462).

growthmanship: an overemphasis on measured economic growth (page 474).

multifactor productivity: a weighted average of labor and capital productivity (page 466).

neoclassical growth model: a model that describes a country's growth rate as the weighted sum of the changes in productivities of its productive inputs plus an additional term reflecting disembodied technical progress (page 466).

primary production: agriculture, forestry, and fisheries (page 464).

rental value: in a production function such as $Y = f(K, N)$, it is the K or roughly the sale value times the interest rate of a nation's capital and natural resources (page 465).

secondary production: manufacturing, mining, construction, and transport (page 464).

tertiary production: trade, finance, government, education—the service industries (page 464).

DISCUSSION QUESTIONS

1. How should we distinguish between economic *growth* and economic *development?*

2. What is the difference between *embodied* and *disembodied* technical change? Between *labor* and *multifactor* productivity?

3. Would the economic development of present-day Central America be easier or more difficult if the United States had not recovered from the Great Depression?

4. What is the difference between neoclassical and Keynesian growth theories?

5. What is the Club of Rome? Is its pessimistic "model of doom" valid?

6. Would you expect the antigrowth arguments of Mill, Schumacher, Mishan, and others to have their greatest appeal in MDCs or in LDCs? Explain your opinion.

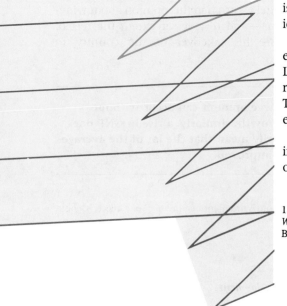

22

Economic Development

Preview Poverty has always been the norm of the human economic condition. Economic history and economic geography are stories of
almost unrelieved wretchedness. The typical human society permits a humane existence to only a small number, while the great
majority lives in abysmal squalor. In part by the grace of poetry,
romance, and legend—which celebrate those who live well and
forget those who live in the silence of poverty—we forget the
misery. Eras and areas of misery have been mythologized and may
even be remembered as golden ages of pastoral simplicity. They
were not, and are not.[1]

This chapter is about the efforts of the great majority of the
world's countries and population to lift themselves out of the mo-
rass of poverty. We begin by pointing out that the less-developed
countries (LDCs) are not all alike. They differ among themselves in
many ways. Also, they are neither jungles nor deserts nor coral
islands. Like the more-developed countries (MDCs), they are rapidly becoming urbanized.

Our next topic is development theory. Does standard (MDC)
economic analysis apply? Has MDC growth helped or hindered
LDC development? Why have some countries developed more
rapidly than others? What hope is there for the present-day LDCs?
There are as yet no agreed-upon answers to these questions. We
examine a number of contrasting views.

Next we introduce the subject of income distribution, comparing the "growth first, distribution later" implications of the work
of Simon Kuznets with the "redistribution with growth" stand of

1. Condensed and adapted from Nathan Rosenberg and L.E. Birdzell, Jr., *How the
West Grew Rich: The Economic Transformation of the Industrial World* (New York: Basic
Books, 1986), p. 3.

the Institute of Development Studies in Britain and with the "basic human needs" approach, which sacrifices measured growth to development.

During the present generation, political-economic relations between the so-called First World of advanced industrial countries ("the North") and the Third World ("the South") have tended to deteriorate. Many LDCs feel that the MDCs have prospered because of cheap raw materials and labor from the LDCs. "The South" has accordingly voiced a set of demands through the United Nations Conference on Trade and Development (UNCTAD) and other UN agencies. These demands call for a New International Economic Order (NIEO). We list a number of NIEO demands but concentrate on the most acute one, namely, the renegotiation of the debt burdens of Third World countries to First World governments and commercial banks.

WHAT IS ECONOMIC DEVELOPMENT?

Economic development means that progress is taking place in some sense that brings gains in welfare, making life better for the masses. We may look at the process through the eyes of the **basic human needs (BHN)** approach. To its partisans, a country is developing if and only if a steadily increasing percentage of its people has an adequate diet, clean water, decent shelter, basic health care, elementary education, and a means of expressing individual views through petitions, demonstrations, and genuine elections. When attention shifts to BHN, it makes no difference whether economic growth, as measured by changes in per capita GNP, slows down or even turns negative. There can be development without growth, just as (they claim) too much growth is unrelated to development.

According to the basic human needs approach, a country is developing if and only if more and

---

more of its people are gaining adequate diets, clean water, decent shelter, basic health care and education, and a peaceful means of making their views known to the government.

Clearly, economic development means different things to different people. To many Americans, it means progress toward a goal not very different from an idealized version of the present American economy. To many Russians, one supposes, the developmental goal is an idealized form of the Soviet economy, possibly after a certain measure of reform (*perestroika*). To members of certain countercultures, the development goal is a world of idealized Israeli *kibbutzim*, communes, labor-managed cooperatives, or similar groups, sharing such ideas as "plain living and high thinking" or "respect for nature and the environment."

Many development economists and LDC politicians emphasize more sharply than we the distinction between economic growth and economic development. Situations in which "the numbers prosper while the people suffer"[2] may be growth, but they are not development. What Premier Papandreou, the author of this statement, wanted to avoid was situations of rising GNP, total and per capita, that left the person on the street or behind the plow worse off than before, if not in absolute terms at least by comparison with the rich. Also, a rise in measured GNP may reflect largely the growth of goods and services that critics call "decadent" rather than "civilized"—"bads" rather than "goods." Fidel Castro had this opinion about wide-open Havana—and to a lesser extent the rest of Cuba—before his takeover of the country in 1959.

Economic development can occur without economic growth; similarly, a rise in GNP does not necessarily mean that the lot of the average person has improved.

---

2. The quotation is from former premier of Greece, George Papandreou.

TABLE 1
Population, Income, and Growth Rate of Countries, 1987

Country or Countries	Population (millions) Mid-1987	GNP per Capita 1987 (U.S. dollars)	Annual Average Growth Rate of GNP per Capita 1965–1987 (%)
42 Low-Income Countries	2,822.9	290	3.1
(China and India)	(1,866.1)	(300)	(3.9)
53 Middle-Income Countries	1,038.5	1,810	2.5
(35 Lower-Middle Income Countries)	(609.6)	(1,200)	(2.2)
(18 Upper-Middle Income Countries)	(432.5)	(2,710)	(2.9)
25 High-Income Countries	777.2	14,430	2.3
(United States)	(243.8)	(18,530)	(1.5)
(Japan)	(122.2)	(15,760)	(4.2)
(Canada)	(25.9)	(15,160)	(2.7)
(United Kingdom)	(56.9)	(10,420)	(1.7)

Note: The U.S.S.R. is among countries not reporting to the World Bank.

Source: The World Bank, *World Development Report*, 1989, Table 1, pp. 164–165. New York: Oxford University Press, 1989. Used with permission.

The Vast and Variegated Majority

Statistics cannot bleed. However, despite their emotional unconcern and their technical flaws, much can be gained by examining them. Table 1 shows per capita incomes (GNPs), measured growth rates, and populations, for somewhat more than two-thirds of the world's 170-odd countries. The omitted countries are nearly all small, poor, and underdeveloped. Although the table is neither accurate nor complete, it does show how the **First World** of industrial-market economies (most of the 25 high-income countries in the table) differs from the **Third World** of 100 or so LDC countries scattered among the low- and middle-income countries.[3] Note the wide range of per capita income among countries. Per capita income in the 42 low-income countries was less than 2 percent of the per capita income in the United States. In the lower and upper middle-income countries, per capita incomes were, respectively, 6.5 percent and 14.6 percent of the U.S. per capita income. Even granting the difficulties of statistical comparison (see Chapter 7), the differences are almost beyond comprehension.

The figures in Table 1 do not confirm the common claim that the gap between the richer and the poorer countries is increasing over time in percentage terms. From 1965 to 1987, for example, the 25 high-income countries of the First World grew at a 2.3 percent rate, compared to 2.5 percent for the middle-income countries and 3.9 percent for the 42 low-income countries of the Third World. The lowest-income LDCs, sometimes called the Fourth World, grew still faster at 3.1 percent. At the same time, the *absolute* gap between rich and poor countries is indeed increasing for the same reason that 2 percent of 100 is less than 1 percent of 500.

3. The **Second World** comprises the centrally planned economies, regardless of their degrees of development or industrialization. Most of them, including the Soviet Union, are "nonreporting nonmembers" of the World Bank.

The First World consists of advanced industrial countries, the Second World of centrally planned economies, and the Third World of developing countries. The lowest-income countries are sometimes called the Fourth World.

Table 2 presents basic data (for the LDCs only) on a geographical basis. It uses **gross domestic product (GDP)**—the production and income generated within a country—rather than gross national product (GNP) figures which counts all income of the citizens of a country, even when that income is generated in a foreign country. The most important difference between GDP and GNP figures is their treatment of international payments of property income. For example, rent, interest, and other service charges on the international indebtedness of Mexico and its residents are part of Mexico's GDP because the capital services were presumably carried on in Mexico. But they are counted as part of the U.S. GNP because they were received by residents of the United States. It follows that an international creditor country's GNP may rank somewhat higher than its GDP, and vice versa for an international debtor.

An international creditor country's GNP may be somewhat higher than its GDP, while an international debtor country may have a higher GDP than GNP.

The figures in Table 2 point out the differences between and among the Third World countries more clearly than do the figures in Table 1. East Asia is apparently doing quite well, despite downward drag from the Philippines and the three Indochinese countries. Sub-Saharan Africa is apparently doing very badly, although Kenya is a special case.

We put primary stress on per capita income estimates because the individual welfare of a person or family is connected more closely with per capita than with total income. But if one of the social goals of a nation, a race, or a religious body is to achieve a large population—for reasons ranging from cannon fodder to propagation of the faith—

the total income becomes more important. Nor do these figures give the full picture about population and income. There are rich people in the poorest countries, just as there are poor people in the richest ones. Foreign aid, in fact, is sometimes criticized as a process for transferring income from poor people in rich countries to rich people in poor countries. Moreover, a country's position can change both drastically and rapidly. In the mid-1950s Libya was an economic "basket case"—like Bangladesh a generation later. But then oil was discovered in Libya. (Will Bangladesh be equally fortunate?) Finally, the Third World differs from such poverty pockets as the Scottish Highlands or Appalachia because of the number of Third World cities with populations in the millions. Mexico City is a contender for the dubious distinction of being the world's largest city. Bangkok (Thailand), Buenos Aires (Argentina), Cairo (Egypt), Calcutta (India), Ibadan and Lagos (Nigeria), Jakarta (Indonesia), Nairobi (Kenya), São Paulo (Brazil), Seoul (Korea), and Taipei (Taiwan) are not far behind.

Differences in Living Standards

Personal and family income statistics surely exaggerate differences between MDCs and LDCs. Activities like baking bread, making clothes, and building homes commonly involve the market in the First World, and account is therefore taken of them in income statistics. In the Third World, these activities are commonly performed within households and are excluded from the statistics. Even recognizing these statistical problems, however, the difference between First World and Third World per capita income is huge. Here, from Robert Heilbroner's *The Great Ascent*, is a comparison between life in the United States and life in an urban area of some low-income LDC. We have adjusted Heilbroner's numbers for the inflation that has occurred since his book was published (1963). The facts, unfortunately, need no adjustment.

> [Let us imagine] how a typical American family could be transformed into an equally typical family of the under-developed world.
> We begin by invading the house of our American family to strip it of its furniture. Everything goes: beds, chairs, tables, TV set. . . . Each member of the family may keep his oldest suit or

TABLE 2
GDP Annual Growth Rates of Developing Countries by Geographical Area, 1980–1987

Geographical Area	GDP (percent)			GDP per Capita (percent)		
	1980–1987	1986	1987	1980–1987	1986	1987
All Developing Countries	3.3	4.9	4.5	1.2	2.8	2.3
Sub-Saharan Africa	−0.5	2.0	−1.5	−3.6	−0.5	−5.1
East Asia	7.7	7.3	8.6	6.2	5.7	7.0
South Asia	5.4	4.7	2.7	3.1	2.4	0.5
Europe, Middle East, and North Africa	2.9	4.2	3.1	0.6	2.0	1.1
Latin America and the Caribbean	0.2	3.8	2.5	−2.0	1.6	0.4

Source: Reuters Information Services, Inc., New York. Reprinted with permission.

dress, a shirt or blouse. We permit a pair of shoes to the head of the family, but none for the wife or children.

We move into the kitchen. . . . The box of matches may stay, a small bag of flour, some sugar and salt. A few moldy potatoes, already in the garbage can, must be rescued, for they will provide much of tonight's meal. We leave a handful of onions and a dish of dried beans. We take away: the meat, the fresh vegetables, the canned goods. . . .

. . . Next we take away the house. The family can move to the toolshed. It is crowded, but "it is not uncommon for a family of four or more to live in a bedspace, that is, on a bunk bed and the space it occupies—sometimes in two or three tiers—their only privacy provided by curtains."

All the other houses in the neighborhood have also been removed; our suburb has become a shantytown. Our family is fortunate to have a shelter. . . . [In] Cali, Colombia, "on one hillside alone, the slum population is estimated at 40,000—without water, sanitation, or electric light. And not all the poor of Cali are [so] fortunate. Others have built their shacks on land which lies beneath the flood mark. To these people the immediate environment is the open sewer of the city, which flows through their huts when the river rises."

Communication must go next. No more newspapers, magazines, books—not that they are missed, since we take away our family's literacy

as well. Instead, in our shantytown we will allow one radio.

Now government services must go. No more postman, no more fireman. There is a school, but it is three miles away. . . . There are no hospitals or doctors nearby. The nearest clinic is 10 miles away and tended by a midwife. It can be reached by bicycle, provided the family has a bicycle, which is unlikely. Or one can go by bus—not always inside. . . .

. . . We will allow our family a cash hoard of $20. Meanwhile the head of the family must earn his keep. As a peasant cultivator with three acres, he may raise the equivalent of $500 to $1,500 worth of crops a year. If he is a tenant farmer, a third or so will go to his landlord, and probably another 10% to the local moneylender. But there will be enough to eat. Or almost enough. The human body requires an input of 2,000 calories [a day] to replenish the energy consumed by its cells. If our displaced American fares no better than an Indian peasant, he will average no more than 1,700–1,900. His body, like any insufficiently fueled machine, will run down. . . .

This is only an impression of life in the underdeveloped lands. It is not life itself. There are lacking the things that underdevelopment gives as well as those it takes away: the urinals smell of poverty, the disease, the flies, the open sewers. And there is lacking a softening sense of familiarity. A [scene], shocking to American eyes, is less shocking to eyes that have never known any other. . . . When we are told that half the world's population enjoys a standard of living "less than $400 a year," this is what the figures mean.[4]

The difference between First World and Third World per capita income and living conditions is huge.

THEORIES OF DEVELOPMENT AND UNDERDEVELOPMENT

There is as yet no generally accepted theory to explain why some countries have developed while others have not. Historically speaking, of course, there have been a number of different theories. We shall sample a few of the more important ones.

A number of different theories have attempted to explain why some countries have developed and others have not.

The development economist Albert Hirschman, now at the Institute of Advanced Studies at Princeton, suggests classifying these theories in the following ways:

1. According to whether or not the theories assume what Hirschman calls **monoeconomics,** that is, whether they assume that economic analysis methods devised in MDCs to deal with MDC problems work equally well in LDCs, despite differences in religion, culture, and history. For example, suppose we are studying the demand for automobiles in three countries (A, B, and C). In A and B, the quantity demanded depends exclusively on price and income, although price is more important than income in A but less important than income in B. In country C, demand for automo-

4. Robert L. Heilbroner, *The Great Ascent* (New York: Harper, 1963), pp. 23–27. Abridged and adapted from "The Tableau of Under-Development" in *The Great Ascent* by Robert L. Heilbroner. Copyright © 1963 by Robert L. Heilbroner. Reprinted by permission of Harper & Row, Publishers, Inc.; and by permission of William Morris Agency on behalf of the author.

biles depends, in addition, on astrological forecasts about the weather and the crops. Monoeconomics holds between A and B. It does not hold between C and either of the other countries.

Monoeconomic theories assume that methods of economic analysis devised to deal with MDCs work equally well in LDCs.

---

2. According to whether or not the theories claim community of interest between MDCs and LDCs, that is, whether or not the theories claim that a set of policies that helps (or injures) one group of countries will also help (or injure) the others.

We shall soon see that Adam Smith's development theory, for example, is strongly monoeconomic, while *dependencia* theory denies community of interest.

Some theories of economic development claim community of interest between MDCs and LDCs—that a set of policies that help (or injure) one country will help (or injure) the others.

Adam Smith's Development Theory

Oldest in time is the sunny optimism of Adam Smith (1723–1790), as seen in the following words quoted from an essay on development, written in 1755, twenty-one years before his *Wealth of Nations:*

> Little else is requisite to carry a state to the highest degree of opulence, from the lowest barbarism, but peace, easy taxes, and a tolerable administration of justice; all the rest being brought about by the natural course of things.

This is less simple-minded than it sounds, for Smith goes on:

> All governments which thwart this natural course, which force things into another channel or which endeavor to arrest the progress of society at a particular point, are unnatural, and to support themselves are obliged to be oppressive and tyrannical.

How many of today's LDCs, either as colonies or as independent countries, have enjoyed "peace, easy taxes, and a tolerable administration of justice" under governments not "oppressive and tyrannical?" The Chinese case is instructive. For 109 years (1840–1949), the country had one civil or international war after another, from the Opium War to the conquest of power by Mao Zedong's Communists. With peace came development, for which communism claims the credit.

In Book III of *The Wealth of Nations*, Adam Smith spelled out "the natural course of things" mentioned in the quotation. It leads from agriculture to manufacturing, and finally to (foreign) trade. But even so, "Smith on Development" seems to a present-day reader to underestimate the problems and the roadblocks. At the very least, he might have noted the danger of population explosion. It may well be, as suggested in Julian Simon's *Ultimate Resource,* that the world would be better off with a higher population level, which might include the additional inventors and innovators necessary to overcome static diminishing returns to population. But the population-explosion argument is about the *rate* at which the population grows. The growth rate can be "too high" even when the population level is "too low."

Smith might also have noted the need to obtain natural resources that the developing country may not have within its own borders. However, many LDCs have been too quick to claim they have "nothing to export" in exchange for imports. Under free trade, a poor country can become what is called a *processing economy* and export its imports plus the value added by its cheap labor. For example, it can import cotton and export cloth, import leather and export footwear, and so on. Japan, Korea, Hong Kong, and other East Asian countries have done just this in their LDC histories.

Adam Smith optimistically believed that little else was necessary for economic development than peace, low taxes, and just administration of laws. He overlooked, however, the difficulties caused by an ever-increasing population growth rate and the importance of access to natural resources.

Malthusian Pessimism

The name of Thomas Robert Malthus (1766–1834) has come to symbolize pessimism about long-term growth in any economic system whatever. According to Malthus, populations increase faster than the food supply, thus leading ultimately to poverty and hunger. "Products rise by one, two, three, four but people rise by one, two, four, eight," or, as another poet put it:

> Come, Malthus, and with Ciceronian prose
> Show how a rutting population grows,
> Till all the produce of the earth is spent,
> And brats expire from lack of aliment.

Malthus did not envisage invention and innovation as benefits of population growth. Moreover, his limited evidence was drawn largely from what is today the Atlantic seaboard of the United States, where population seemed to be doubling every generation in the eighteenth century—assisted, however, by immigration, including the slave trade. Modern Malthusianism has a certain racist tinge when, after it has proved quite wrong for themselves, it is applied by MDC pessimists to "those people" in the LDCs.

Thomas Malthus pessimistically believed that ever-growing populations meant that no economy could avoid poverty and hunger in the long run.

Marxian Theories

It is no surprise to find Karl Marx (1818–1883) and his followers less cheerful than Adam Smith about development under capitalism. Their conclusions, however, are based on more than the intuitive emotionalism of much Marxist political activism. Let us see how the Marxist answer is derived.

Exploitation and the Falling Rate of Profit   The key proposition in Marxian economics is that all value comes from labor and, for that reason, the profits of capitalists arise from the exploitation of labor—that is, by taking from workers some of the fruits of their labor. In Marxian reasoning, capitalist profits are plowed back into production through ever-rising investments in machines. But this increasingly capital-intensive method of production lowers the proportion of new labor input, in this way allowing the capitalist fewer chances for further exploitation. The result is a falling rate of profit, for each dollar invested. The capitalist's responses to this falling rate of profit are the keys to Marxist forecasts of economic suffering, the collapse of capitalism, the rise and fall of imperialism, and the problems of the Third World. Rather than raising their consumption as the classical economists expected, Marxists contend that capitalists will keep on accumulating and simply hoard money or cash balances. The results of this hoarding, as Keynes would agree, are stagnation, unemployment, and misery, ending, Marxists say, in revolution and capitalist downfall.

According to Karl Marx, the profits of capitalists arise from the exploitation of labor. He predicted that when profit rates decreased, capitalists would hoard money, leading to stagnation, unemployment, and—ultimately—revolution and capitalist downfall.

Impact on the Third World After Marx's death, the writings of his followers spelled out what the falling rate of profit would mean for imperialism and the Third World. In the view of Lenin (1870–1924), the great theorist of imperialism, Third World countries will be brought into the capitalist system. As capital accumulates, it will be exported there, and native people will be put to work at lower (more exploitative) wages than are paid in the more developed countries. In this way, stagnation in the MDCs can be slowed down or even reversed, and the capitalist system can continue onward and upward for a while. But the LDCs themselves will neither grow nor develop. The profits from their businesses go mainly to MDC residents.

Other Marxists, especially Rosa Luxemburg (1871–1919), saw imperialism somewhat differently. In "Red Rosa's" view, to keep up employment and get rid of goods that its own consumers could not buy at profitable prices, each capitalist country would take over LDC areas as happy dumping grounds. The poor LDCs would pay for these goods mainly by selling their assets, meaning the control of their land and mineral resources. The final results of "Luxemburg" imperialism were to be no different from those of "Lenin" imperialism.

Both Lenin and Luxemburg predicted that the end will come because the Third World too is limited in size. The rival imperialist powers will clash over colonization or control of the most promising LDCs. Within its LDCs, each imperialist power will face "liberation movements" that are pitted against the mother country and against its allies in the native capitalist class. The United States fought Spain over Cuba, the Philippines, and Puerto Rico. Later the U.S. fighting in Vietnam gave rise to civil disobedience and rioting in the United States itself. The end result of all this warfare and revolution, the Marxists say, will be the downfall of capitalism, for the wars will spread beyond the Third World. As Lenin put it during World War I, "The road to London and Paris leads through Peking and Calcutta."

Dependencia Theories of Underdevelopment

Dependencia (dependency) theories of LDC underdevelopment spring from the Third World, particularly from Latin America. This is why they are known by their Spanish name. They are forms of neo-Marxism, in which MDC protectionists and labor unions play "bad guy" roles alongside MDC capitalists. They go beyond standard Marxism to argue that the prosperity of the First World is *dependent upon* the poverty of the Third—"They are rich because we are poor." And similarly, the poverty of the Third World is *dependent upon* the prosperity of the First.

According to *dependencia* theory, the prosperity of the First World is dependent upon the poverty of the Third World; similarly, the poverty of the Third World is dependent upon the prosperity of the First World.

To understand *dependencia* theory, let us go back in time to Europe of the sixteenth, seventeenth, and eighteenth centuries. The dominant economic thinking of the time was *mercantilism.* In England, France, the Netherlands, Spain, and elsewhere, the mercantile system took different forms, but all agreed that the goal of a state's economic activity was to strengthen its political (military) power in Europe. This is the key to mercantilist doctrine. The aim was to win colonies in faraway lands, first as sources of precious metals and industrial raw materials for the mother country, and second to keep such riches away from that country's rivals. It was believed to be dangerous for colonies, especially for their non-European natives, to develop any kinds of modern industry that would compete with mother-country producers or provide economic bases for revolt and independent political existence.

According to a number of writers, both the present MDCs and the present LDCs were undeveloped at the start of the mercantilist age, but the MDCs had the edge in military technology. This they used to gain control over the rest of the world, profiting from the world's resources and confining "the natives" to low-paid unskilled work. And the gains that resulted from such exploitation financed the subsequent Industrial Revolution and prosperity. To quote the late Premier Jawaharlal Nehru of India, Britain's Industrial Revolution was "financed by the loot of Bengal."

The mercantilist system of the sixteenth, seventeenth, and eighteenth centuries encouraged the acquisition of colonies as sources of raw materials. According to *dependencia* theory, the countries that had the edge in military technology were able to gain colonies and thus develop themselves at the expense of the colonies.

Mercantilism never died. After their American colonies won their freedom, the mother countries and other powers kept on using colonies as raw material sources by putting high tariffs (import taxes) on their manufactures and other finished goods while admitting their food and raw materials tax-free, even though they competed with the mother country's own farmers and landlords. Still mainly for military reasons, MDCs tried for some time to control the "trade secrets" of the Industrial Revolution against all others, even their old colonies. Students of U.S. economic history may remember Samuel Slater, who memorized the blueprints of advanced British textile machinery whose export was against the law, brought his secret to Rhode Island, and started the New England textile-manufacturing business.

Later in the nineteenth century, as labor movements developed in western Europe and the United States, skilled workers came more and more to support what is called *neomercantilism.* Modern industry offered more skilled jobs than farming had, and these jobs were more highly paid than unskilled ones. Workers and their unions demanded protection against low-wage LDC competition, with the same results for the LDCs as they had known under the older military mercantilism.

Mercantilism survived as neomercantilism—a demand by MDC workers and their unions for protection against low-wage LDC competition, with the same results for the LDCs as under the old brand of mercantilism.

Also, technical progress has had different effects on manufacturers in MDCs and on farm products and raw materials in LDCs. In the LDCs, progress led to higher outputs and lower prices on competitive export markets. But in the MDCs, progress appeared to be used mainly to raise profits and wages while holding prices steady or raising them. In the LDCs, the prices of exports generally seemed to fall as compared to the prices of imports. The opposite seemed to be true for the MDCs. These tendencies have been stressed by *dependencia* writers.

Dependencia thinking is an important basis for LDC pressure for bigger and better OPECs, price supports for their countries' exports of goods, and for what is called "redeployment," or transfer, of a higher percentage of world manufacturing capacity into LDC countries from the MDCs. (Because of the lower wage scales in the LDCs, some redeployment is occurring in textiles, clothing, and shoes, to the great concern and dismay of the U.S. labor movement.)

Rostow's Non-Communist Manifesto

W. W. Rostow's *Stages of Economic Growth* is subtitled *A Non-Communist Manifesto*. It may be regarded as an argument not only against Marxism but also against *dependencia* theory, which was not well known when Rostow was writing (1960). Rostow's work is an example of an institutional stage theory.

The Rostow stages of growth are five in number: (1) traditional society, (2) preconditions for takeoff, (3) takeoff itself (the kernel of the theory), (4) drive to maturity, and (5) high mass consumption.

W. W. Rostow offered a five-part institutional stage theory. His five stages of growth are traditional society, preconditions for takeoff, takeoff, drive to maturity, and high mass consumption.

We need say little about stage 1. Even though economic activity is limited largely to farming and handicrafts and per capita income is low and stationary, life is not always as miserable as that portrayed by Heilbroner earlier in this chapter.

In stage 2, which may last a long time and in which many LDCs now find themselves, there may develop Adam Smith's combination of "peace, easy taxes, and a tolerable administration of justice." In this stage countries often have some accumulation of **social overhead capital** (roads and harbors, schools and public health facilities), and also one or more leading industries (textiles and transportation in Britain and the United States, oil extraction and refining in the OPEC countries).

The takeoff (stage 3) is quite sudden when it comes. It covers just about one generation. Rostow's estimates are 1783–1802 for Britain, 1843–1860 for the United States, 1850–1873 for Germany, 1878–1900 for Japan, 1890–1914 for (czarist) Russia. It is marked by two features. One is the spread of modern methods from the leading sectors to the rest of the economy, which supplies their raw materials and purchases most of their products. The second feature is a sudden sharp rise in saving and investment, often aided by an influx of foreign capital.

The takeoff stage is marked by the spread of modern methods from the leading sector to the rest of the economy and by a sudden sharp rise in saving and investment, often aided by an influx of foreign capital.

After the takeoff, Rostow believes the drive to maturity (stage 4) is a much easier matter because it is aided by reinvestment of the gains from takeoff—or the force of compound interest. However, takeoffs may be followed by crashes, as in Mexico under Porfirio Díaz (due to revolution) and Russia under Nicholas II (due to World War I). Maturity itself is described by Rostow in terms of higher average labor skills, a shift in economic leadership from self-made "robber barons" to professionally trained managers, and a certain "boredom with the miracle of industrialization," leading to moves in other directions. It was supposedly reached in Britain about 1850, in the United States about 1910, in Japan about 1940, and in (Soviet) Russia in about 1950.

Once maturity (stage 5) is achieved, Rostow says, it can be used in some combination of three ways: militarism and imperialism, the welfare state, and high mass consumption. Rostow favors some judicious combination of the last two. He criticizes Germany and Japan for concentrating on the first for as long as they did, and believes that the Soviet Union still has its choice to make. He believes that the United States used too much of the gains from growth to pay for a postwar "baby boom." His advice to the LDCs is to speed up their takeoffs, and he pays little attention to whether MDC policy speeds up or slows down LDC growth. You should also remember that Rostow sees nothing inevitable in this whole evolution.

"Vicious-Circle" Theory

Decidedly less optimistic than Rostow's theory are the "vicious-circle" theories popular in the West during the 1950s. They were developed primarily by the Baltic refugee economist Ragnar Nurkse. Their moral is that, under contemporary conditions, a poor country cannot develop without external aid, simply because it is poor.

Vicious circles are set up on both supply and

demand sides. The supply-side argument is that, because a country is poor, it cannot save. Because it cannot save, it cannot increase its capital stock unless it receives foreign assistance. Without an adequate stock of physical capital, its labor productivity and income level will both remain low. Demand-side arguments are usually put in Keynesian terms to fit more easily into the Harrod-model analysis of the last chapter. Because a country is poor, its consumption level is low. Therefore, investment to supply its home market is not a commercially attractive proposition. Without investment on concessionary terms, productivity and incomes will remain low.

According to the vicious-circle theory, a poor country cannot save and therefore cannot increase its capital stock unless it receives foreign assistance, nor can it attract investment to its home market.

The vicious-circle theory has some drawbacks. For example, it has difficulty explaining Japan, especially Meiji Japan (1868–1912), when that country raised itself from the ranks of the LDCs without significant foreign financial aid. Also, as human-capital theorists point out, the theory ignores both the quantity and the quality of the labor force.

Cultural-Development Theories

The theories we have treated thus far have been essentially economic—even monoeconomic in Hirschman's sense. Cultural-development theories, on the other hand, are espoused widely—mainly by others than economists. These theories emphasize the importance of religion, custom, tradition, and other cultural factors, even in the very long run (over centuries).

The father of such theories may be the great German sociologist and social historian Max Weber, the author of *The Protestant Ethic and the Spirit of Capitalism* (1904). Weber concentrated his attention on the Protestant Reformation, on the breakdown of the authority of the church and canon law in economic matters, and on the probusiness applications of Calvinism in particular. More recently, Japanese economist Michio Morishima's *Why Has Japan Succeeded?* (1982) ascribes his country's economic performance largely to Confucian doctrine in its specifically Japanese variant. The American social psychologist David McClelland's *Achieving Society* (1961) traces economic development largely to a society's "need for achievement," which is implanted by its methods of child rearing and manifested in the stories children read and listen to. American area specialist Lawrence Harrison, in an attack on *dependencia* theories in *Underdevelopment Is a State of Mind* (1985), claims that Latin American culture, influenced by that of the Spanish and Portuguese *conquistadores*, is "anti-progress, anti-intellectual, and, among the affluent, anti-work." In Harrison's view, this culture, reinforced in some countries by various African-based religious traditions known as voodoo, has been the main obstacle to development south of the Rio Grande.

Cultural-development theories emphasize the importance of religion, custom, and tradition in economic matters.

DEVELOPMENT AND INCOME DISTRIBUTION

How is economic development related to equality and inequality in income distribution? We shall give three different views on this question.

The Kuznets Hypothesis

Analyzing historical development and income distribution statistics for the present MDCs, the Nobel Prize-winning economist Simon Kuznets has noted a pattern of inequality over time. As development progresses, measured inequality has first risen and then fallen in most countries. At the same time, labor's share of income first fell and then rose.[5]

---

5. The "macroeconomic history" of *American Inequality*, by Jeffrey Williamson and Peter Lindert (1981), uses more data than was available to Kuznets himself.

Kuznets notes incidentally that the mid-nineteenth century, when Karl Marx was writing, marks the period of the greatest inequality in Great Britain, where Marx was living in exile. Could Marx have assumed, from what was happening in his lifetime, that the trend toward inequality would continue unchanged?

In the Kuznets model, three factors are interwoven to explain the pattern of rising and falling inequality. Part of the explanation is that capital accumulation first comes from profits and inequality, but later declines as the rate of return on capital falls because of its greater abundance relative to other inputs. Population and labor force growth also play a role. Population growth rates go up at first, increasing inequality, but go down later, raising wages and reducing inequality. Third, as time passes, highly paid skills are learned by a larger part of the work force, raising the proportion of high-paying jobs.

According to the Kuznets model, measured inequality first rises and then falls in most countries as development progresses.

What this theory means for the LDCs is presented in the following quote from the Canadian economist Harry G. Johnson:

> There is a conflict between economic efficiency and social justice. The importance of this conflict is likely to vary according to the state of economic development. The more advanced a country is, the more likely are its citizens to have consciences about the distribution of income, and the higher the level of income reached, the less serious will be any slowing down of the rate of growth brought about by redistribution policies. An advanced country can afford to sacrifice some growth for the sake of social justice. But the cost of greater equality may be great to any economy at a low level of economic development. It would therefore seem unwise for a country anxious to enjoy rapid growth to insist too strongly on policies aimed at ensuring economic equality.[6]

Development and Redistribution

Johnson's advice has not sat well with LDC political leaders, who either represent the political left in their countries or fear leftist revolution in the short run if they wait for the Kuznets turning point. They want *Redistribution with Growth,* which is the title of a joint study by economists at the World Bank and

6. Harry G. Johnson, *Money, Trade, and Economic Growth,* 2nd ed. (London: Unwin, 1964), p. 159.

the Institute of Development Studies in England. According to this study, redistribution can come about by "appropriate technology" and an "appropriate product mix," which substitutes labor, especially semiskilled labor, for capital goods and the more highly skilled specialties of the labor aristocracy. It can also come about by pouring capital into the LDCs either free of interest charges or on special terms from MDC governments or from international bodies. In either case, MDC taxpayers would eventually foot the bill.

Advocates of redistribution with growth say economic development can be achieved by substituting semiskilled labor for capital goods and by pouring MDC capital into LDCs.

Basic Human Needs

More extreme than "redistribution with growth" is the basic human needs strategy, already described. It aims directly at economic development, meaning by "development" first the reduction and finally the end of poverty and alienation. It is not concerned with measured rates of economic growth or with overall statistics in general. It is less popular in most LDC government circles than in MDC universities and in international organizations. (The LDC civil service is an important part of the country's urban labor aristocracy.)

Basic human needs strategy aims to achieve economic development by ending poverty. It is not concerned with measured rates of economic growth or with overall statistics.

DUALISM AND ENCLAVES

Imagine an MDC visitor returning to a Third World country after a lapse of five or ten years. The visitor will generally land at a major city airport, and spend the first few days in and around that city. Before leaving, the visitor will usually travel for some distance into the surrounding countryside.

What differences is he or she likely to find? Probably much of the capital or any other major city (aside from the slums) will seem more "modern" than it was during the earlier visit. There will be more pavement, more automobiles, more Western-style buildings, more neon signs, more billboards, and so on. But on a trip fifteen to twenty miles out into the farming areas, the banana trees or rice paddies will seem largely unchanged unless the traveler visits a model farm or commune.

This is the visual aspect of **economic dualism.** Dualism may be looked on as another distribution problem, a regional one, between the large cities and the rural areas. The cities, and particularly the areas where foreigners live and work, can easily become islands, or enclaves, of modernization and prosperity in otherwise stagnant and miserable LDCs.

To spread development from its original urban enclaves to the rural hinterland is the LDCs' great "second-generation" development problem. Some even call it a dilemma. It is in any case much more difficult than the spread of development from, say, Chicago to rural Illinois or from Montreal to rural Quebec.

Unless an export market suddenly opens up for a specialized item like cocoa in Ghana or cocaine in Colombia, the obvious path to rural development is by way of increasing farm prices. These prices may rise as a natural result of urban growth and development or from active agricultural policy. But the danger is the reaction of the urban poor, including former farmworkers who have migrated to the cities. A riot against increases in staple-food prices could topple most democratic, well-intentioned, pro-Western governments—especially, it seems, in Africa on either side of the Sahara.

But if no new crops emerge and farm prices remain stagnant, *rural* revolt may result, involving peasants and farmworkers and directed initially against landowners. Three examples are Mao Zedong's agrarian revolution within the communist revolution, Pancho Villa's career in Mexico, and more recently the Shining Path (*Sendero Luminoso*) in Peru.

Another distribution problem manifests itself as economic dualism, wherein Third World cities

---

become enclaves of prosperity in otherwise stagnant LDCs.

THE NORTH-SOUTH CONFRONTATION

We turn now to a fuller examination of the mutual-benefit issue in development theory, or rather, to the widespread rejection of this theory in the LDCs. The question can be phrased as follows: To what extent, if at all, do the interests of MDCs and LDCs—the "North" and "South," respectively—converge?[7] The neo-Marxian and *dependencia* theories imply that their interests do not converge at all, at least under capitalism. They say that there is a basic hostility between the MDCs and LDCs. From these theoretical bases, plus doses of MDC racism and condescension, LDC resentment and envy, and unconcern on each side with the other group's problems, has sprung today's North-South confrontation and conflict, culminating in the demand of the South for a New International Economic Order (NIEO).

From the ongoing hostility between the MDCs and LDCs has sprung the demand of the South for a New International Economic Order (NIEO).

A New International Economic Order?

Spokespersons and sloganeers for the South are more united in denouncing the existing international economic order (which they tend to equate with the freedom of trade) than in specifying what their proposed replacements might be. However, the following set of demands is fairly common:

---

7. The "North-South" geographic split should not be taken literally. The "North" includes MDCs from the Southern Hemisphere—Australia, New Zealand, and South Africa are examples. The "South" includes most of the tropical countries, whether in North America, South America, Africa, or Asia.

On LDC Trade

1. Preferential access of LDC-manufactured exports to MDC markets by general statutes of preference (GSPs), without reciprocal opening of LDC markets to MDC producers.

2. More remunerative and more stable world prices for LDC agricultural and mineral exports, with stockpiling financed by international agencies. These agencies are to be financed mainly by MDC taxpayers.

3. MDC acceptance of LDC cartels, modeled on OPEC, to raise the prices of LDC exports.

4. Eventual redeployment of industrial capacity to the LDCs, particularly light, labor-intensive industries like textiles. New capacity in such industries is to go mainly to LDCs.

On Debts, Aid, and Capital Movement

1. Renegotiation of LDC debts to MDC governments and banks including longer terms, lower interest rates, and new loans to finance the servicing of existing debts. This is the most pressing of the South's existing demands. It sometimes extends further, to outright cancellation of these debts. We shall soon deal separately with the debt problem.

2. Increased Official Development Assistance (ODA) from MDCs to LDCs, extending to 1 percent of MDC GNPs by the year 2000.[8] Such assistance, they say, is not charity but reparation payments for past sins of colonization and exploitation.

3. LDC access to international lending on concessional (preferential and below market) terms.

4. Use of International Monetary Fund (IMF) special drawing rights (SDRs or "paper gold") as a form of additional aid to LDCs.

On LDC Internal Economies

1. Low-cost transfer of technology to LDCs and, where such technologies do not yet exist or are not operational, development of appropriate technologies for LDCs by international bodies.

2. Acceptance by MDCs of full LDC control of the activities of multinational corporations (MNCs) within their borders.[9]

3. Eliminating conditionality in international lending to LDCs. IMF lending, in particular, has often been made conditional on highly unpopular austerity programs in the domestic LDC economy. When such programs are not carried out, the loans are discontinued.

On Essentially Political Issues

1. A larger share of LDC control of international financial institutions, especially the IMF and the World Bank.

2. Respect for LDC sovereignty. For example, LDCs want limitations on appeals to international tribunals of LDC domestic decisions on such matters as nationalization and confiscation of MNC property.

3. International control of natural resources in the open sea and its seabed to provide additional funding for LDC development.

4. MDC disarmament to free MDC resources for the purchase of LDC exports and for the provision of Official Development Assistance.

The South wants solutions for the problems of LDC trade, debts, aid, capital movement, internal economics, and various political issues.

What Can the South Do?

Among the countries of the North, Sweden and the Netherlands have gone farthest in making concessions to the South's demands, but these are relatively small countries. The largest industrial countries have made only token concessions,

8. This figure is suggested as a target or goal by the Brandt Report, *North-South: Program for Survival* (1980).

9. Both the political and economic activities of multinational corporations have been at times highly controversial, especially in situations where the economic resources of an MNC rival those of the governments that attempt to regulate it. MNC problems are taken up in advanced courses in both international and development economics. The best-known indictment of MNC activities in Third World countries is R. J. Barnet and R. E. Mueller, *Global Reach* (1974). For a more neutral view, see Raymond Vernon, *Sovereignty at Bay* (1971) and *Storm Over the Multinationals* (1977). Considerably more advanced and technical is Richard Caves, *Multinational Enterprise and Economic Analysis* (1982).

concessions only to their former colonies, concessions "subject to approval of Congress," or no concessions at all. Along the line of Stalin's "How many divisions does the pope have?" some have wondered, "Why should we pay any attention at all?"

It does appear that the South can do little to press its claims without injuring itself more than it hurts the North. Its most obvious weapon is repudiation or default on interest and/or principal payments on debts, which amounted to $1.2 trillion as of 1988. With that total, each 1 percent rise (fall) in the interest rate increases (decreases) the annual interest burden of the LDCs as a group by about $6 billion. Repudiation or default, advocated most stridently by Fidel Castro, might set off a financial crisis in the North and risk cutting the South off from future financial aid.

Some LDCs (Albania, Burma, Ethiopia, and North Korea) advocate (but do not always practice) "self-reliance." This more drastic tactic amounts to an economic boycott of the First World, while counting on other Third World countries plus the communist bloc for imports, for markets, for loans, and for aid in case of emergency. A historical precedent is the one ship a year that Japan allowed the Dutch, representing the entire Western world, to bring to Nagasaki, Japan's only open port, over a 250-year period ending in the mid-nineteenth century. There is no doubt that such a move would hurt the South, but some LDC politicians and ideologues claim that it would be the North that could not stand the strain. They argue that northern postindustrial growth has weakened its agricultural and industrial bases, while accustoming its people to affluent lifestyles. Perhaps neither capitalism nor the market economy could survive, if both require (as per *dependencia* theory) the exploitation of "peripheral" Third World countries. The more general Third World view, however, now seems to admit that it may be better to be "exploited" (even by MNCs) than not to be "exploited" at all, as would be the case if North-South economic relations were broken off completely.

There is little the South can do to force the North to accede to its demands. Strategies such

as repudiation of debt and economic boycott would most likely end up hurting the South as well as the North.

THIRD WORLD DEBT

Third World debt is the most acute aspect of North-South confrontation and conflict. Table 3 indicates the size of the capital sums involved and also identifies the seventeen countries called by the World Bank "heavily indebted" relative to their GNPs and their export volumes.[10]

The table shows that "the poorest of the poor"—such low-income countries as the African Sahel—do *not* have heavy debts (Nigeria is an exception). Their creditworthiness is very small by anyone's standards. Twelve of the seventeen heavy debtors are in Latin America, including the Caribbean. The others are the Ivory Coast, Morocco, and Nigeria in Africa, the Philippines in Southeast Asia, and Yugoslavia in Europe. Thirteen of the seventeen are heavy oil importers, but four (Ecuador, Mexico, Nigeria, and Venezuela) are important oil exporters. Of these, all but Mexico are OPEC members.

Debt History

The great bulk of Third World debt dates from the initial oil shock of 1973–74. The Middle Eastern members of OPEC (Iran, Iraq, Kuwait, Qatar, Saudi Arabia, and the United Arab Emirates) rapidly accumulated large surpluses in convertible currency—more than they felt they needed for their own development. The funds were mainly held in American banks. In varying degrees, these countries were anti-American—alienated by what they considered a pro-Israel tilt in American Middle Eastern policy. The more radical of their leaders proposed withdrawing their balances from America, preferably in the form of gold. Such action might have produced a short-term financial panic

---

10. The World Bank apparently believes that private indebtedness is underreported by $200–$250 billion, since the total in the table is that much less than its own debt estimate.

TABLE 3
Debt in Developing Countries, 1987 (in billions of dollars)

Country or Countries	Long-Term Debt Public or Publicly Guaranteed	Total External Debt
Low-Income Countries (38)	216.1	263.3
(Nigeria)	(25.7)	(28.7)
Lower-Middle-Income Countries (34)	376.1	456.7
(Bolivia)	(4.6)	(5.5)
(Chile)	(15.5)	(21.2)
(Colombia)	(13.8)	(17.0)
(Costa Rica)	(3.6)	(4.7)
(Ecuador)	(9.0)	(10.4)
(Ivory Coast)	(8.5)	(13.6)
(Jamaica)	(3.5)	(4.4)
(Morocco)	(18.5)	(20.7)
(Mexico)	(82.8)	(107.9)
(Peru)	(12.5)	(18.1)
(Philippines)	(22.3)	(30.0)
Upper-Middle-Income Countries (15)	288.8	387.4
(Argentina)	(47.5)	(56.8)
(Brazil)	(91.7)	(123.9)
(Uruguay)	(3.0)	(4.2)
(Venezuela)	(25.2)	(36.5)
(Yugoslavia)	(14.4)	(23.5)
All Developing Countries	881.0	1,107.4
(17 Heavily Indebted Countries)	(402.1)	(527.1)

Note: Parentheses identify "heavily indebted" countries.
Source: The World Bank, *World Development Report 1989*, Table 21, pp. 204–205. New York: Oxford University Press, 1989. Used with permission.

on Wall Street—a bank run comparable to that of 1933. We can only guess how the Nixon administration in Washington, already embroiled in the Watergate crisis, might have reacted.

Third World debt is the most acute aspect of North-South confrontation. The great bulk of this debt dates from the oil shock of 1973–74.

The American financial community, anxious to avoid such a panic, proposed to offer the OPEC countries high interest rates for "recycling" their oil revenues, which meant keeping these revenues in the larger American banks. But how could they afford the interest rates that might be necessary to

retain those mainly Moslem-owned "petrodollars?"[11] In the short run, this turned out to be no problem. Oil-importing countries, mainly in Latin America, had already embarked on ambitious development plans that depended on uninterrupted oil supplies. To secure these oil supplies at the high OPEC prices, the oil-importing countries needed dollars, and for the dollars, they were willing to pay the high interest rates requested by American banks. In many cases, it was the American lenders

11. An interesting sidelight is that, under the *Sharia* (Moslem religious law)—as under medieval Christian canon law—receipt of interest is strictly illegal! A lender must participate in the borrower's risk and uncertainty so that his income can pass as a profit, or he must prove "opportunities forgone" by the loan, which, under the law, do not include alternative opportunities to earn interest.

who took the initiative in negotiating the loan agreements. Large loans also were made to some non-Moslem oil-exporting LDCs, such as Mexico, avid to obtain funds to expand non-oil industries in advance of future oil revenues.

American lenders negotiated high-interest loans to oil-importing countries, mainly in Latin America, which these countries were subsequently unable to repay.

The loan agreements were drawn up and signed at high speed, without sufficient scrutiny by either side.[12] The oil importers were going to repay the dollar loans mainly from the proceeds of their new industries. Brazilian steel was an important example, and Brazil was the largest borrower. The oil exporters, most notably Mexico, had similar hopes, along with their plans for expanded oil outputs.[13] Both sides apparently assumed that the oil price would not fall or if it did, that Uncle Sam and the World Bank would between them bail out the banks if their loans soured. In these circumstances, ''bailout'' means paying off the banks' loans and themselves assuming the thankless creditor positions.

Sour the loans did, beginning with an unexpected Mexican default in the summer of 1982. OPEC could not enforce its quota limitations on oil production and exports. In addition, non-OPEC oil production increased—mainly from Mexico, the North Sea in Europe, and the North Slope in Alaska. The world demand for oil turned out to be more sensitive to price changes in the long run than in the short run. A Saudi attempt to use price cuts to force cooperation of non-OPEC members with OPEC rules was a failure. The trend of oil prices turned downward, although remaining above the pre-1973 level even in real terms. At the same time, borrowing countries and their rulers squandered much of the borrowed funds in corruption, capital flight, military budgets, and poorly planned projects.

Much of the borrowed money was squandered, even as oil prices turned downward.

The flamboyant Philippine president, Ferdinand Marcos, and his shoe-loving wife Imelda, became symbols of what went on, although they apparently concentrated their gains in American real estate and securities in preference to the Swiss bank accounts favored by LDC ''malefactors of great wealth.'' Marcos was overthrown in 1986. Why should his successors, or the Filipino people as a whole, repay the bankers for the Marcos family's securities, real estate, and shoe collection—not to mention its mistakes and its corruption?[14] To protect new governments and their peoples, should there be some international equivalents of bankruptcy?[15]

Another part of the debt problem involves import restrictions set up by MDCs. We have mentioned Brazil's steel industry, which has indeed become one of the world's lowest-cost producers. Its expansion, however, has been crippled by a variety of barriers which limit its access to its potential output markets, which include the United States, western Europe, and Japan. And what is true for Brazilian steel is perhaps even more true for agricultural exports like sugar, coffee, and meat. U.S. bans on Argentine beef, except in cans, date back to the 1920s.

Would the suffering of the innocent be avoided by debt forgiveness all around, as suggested by Fidel Castro? When bank capital is so badly impaired that banks are required to close, or when large de-

---

12. Conventional ''hard-nosed'' commercial and investment banking practice refuses loans unless the borrower presents evidence of ability to earn more than the interest rate on the sum borrowed, over and above meeting the schedule of principal repayment.

13. Not being an OPEC member, Mexico was not contractually subject to that organization's restrictions and quotas on its members' oil production and exports. Although many OPEC members violated their obligations, Mexico refrained in practice from attempts to undermine OPEC.

14. The Aquino government of the Philippines sought to recycle the burden back to the American taxpayer by raising the rent for American military and naval bases there.

15. *Extra*legal equivalents are nothing new, as will be attested to by any holder of Confederate or czarist bonds! On the other hand, to quote President Coolidge on the 1917–1920 interallied war debts: ''They borrowed the money, didn't they?'' In 1931, Coolidge's successor, President Hoover, proposed a oneyear moratorium on these debts and also on German reparations. The one-year moratorium then became permanent in practice.

positors withdraw their funds, the financial system comes under substantial strain.

If it is a government institution (rather than a privately owned bank) in a creditor country, or if it is the World Bank itself whose assets are impaired by debt cancellation, the result is an increase in national debts.[16] Directly or indirectly, the residents of creditor countries must pay assessed taxes or inflation taxes when what were to be loans to LDCs actually become grants-in-aid. In development economics as elsewhere, there is no such thing as a free lunch.

The Debt Impasse

The first Mexican debt crisis (1982) was followed by one or more debt crises a year, as one or another country got in trouble or as an earlier solution unraveled. The result looks like Ponzi finance—the carrying charges on debts are being paid, but the total volume of debt rises despite the repayments.[17] This is because new money has been lent to finance new programs as well as to finance old debts. The new loans are often conditional on "austerity"—higher taxes, lower public expenditures, reduced credit expansion and monetary growth, lower inflation rates, scrapping of price and wage controls, etc. When LDC legislatures, military, or trade-union movements reject or overturn some of these conditions, we call the result an unraveling of the previous solution and the outbreak of a new crisis.

The Mexican debt crisis of 1982 was followed by at least one LDC debt crisis a year for several years. The total volume of LDC debt keeps rising as new money is lent to finance both new programs and old debts.

Other provisions of debt renegotiations have been longer repayment periods, lower interest rates, and moratoria on principal repayments.[18] On the LDC side, there have been frequent attempts to form united fronts of debtor countries to demand still easier terms. None of these has as yet had great success. However, several plans for longer-term settlement have been suggested and to some extent put into effect. We mention four of these: the Baker plan, debt-equity swaps, the Camdessus plan, and the Miyazawa plan.

The Baker Plan   James Baker was secretary of the United States Treasury in the second Reagan administration. His plan included generous renegotiations on a case-by-case basis, LDC austerity undertakings, and a substantial supply of new money by private banks on their own responsibilities (not involving American taxpayers). Many smaller lending banks, with little or no interest in the LDCs, refused to "send good money after bad" and did not cooperate. The Treasury Department made no serious attempt at administrative guidance or other forms of indirect pressure on the banks.

Debt-Equity Swaps   Debt-equity swaps have become quite common, although on a relatively small scale. In a debt-equity swap, an LDC debt is written down by its creditor bank, which sells some part of that debt at a discount to a business firm. The firm then uses these (dollar) funds to buy LDC currency at a discount below the official rate and to erect facilities there, or it may choose to buy equity interests in existing LDC companies, either public or private. A serious problem arises when this device is used on a large scale or with regard to strategic companies. This is because MDC firms are not interested in minority stock ownership without effective control, while LDC governments and politicians worry about ceding too much control to foreigners, especially in public utilities and defense industries.

The Camdessus Plan   Michel Camdessus, from the French Central Bank (Banque de France) and director-general of the International Monetary Fund, proposes new issues of Special Drawing Rights (SDRs, alias "paper gold"). His expectation

---

16. As for the World Bank, it raises most of its loan funds by the sale of its own securities on the open market, but its capital is subscribed by member governments. An impairment of its capital would therefore be a debt increase for all these member governments, even those of the LDCs.

17. Ponzi finance is a process of servicing old debts by disbursing "profits" out of the proceeds of new loans or contributions. It surely antedates Ponzi himself, an international swindler of 1919–20.

18. Many loan agreements call for interest rates a certain percentage above the London Inter-Bank Offered Rate (LIBOR). The LDCs prefer low rates independent of LIBOR.

is that LDC SDR allocations will be used to reduce their outstanding debts. The United States is skeptical about this approach, claiming that such increases in world liquidity are unnecessary and probably inflationary. For the same reason, the United States has opposed the large increases in IMF capital that would be required to put the plan into effect.

The Miyazawa Plan   Kiichi Miyazawa, minister of finance in the first Takeshita cabinet in Japan, has suggested that his country lend money to LDC governments that are willing to cooperate. Japan would lend only to countries willing to carry out austerity and privatization programs under Japanese supervision, and the cooperating LDCs could repay part or all of their debts with the loan proceeds. The new Japanese loans would be guaranteed by the World Bank. Japan also looks with favor on the Camdessus (IMF) plan. The United States opposes the Japanese proposal as indirectly requiring taxpayers to guarantee loan repayments and as reducing the responsibilities of the lending banks.

Several plans for longer repayment periods have been suggested: the Baker plan (generous renegotiations, LDC austerity, loans by private banks), debt-equity swaps, the Camdessus plan (new issues of SDRs), and the Miyazawa plan (Japanese loans based on promises of austerity).

Effect on North-South Relations

Since 1982, the protest of the South has shifted at least temporarily from the grandiose NIEO package to the more prosaic matter of easing its own debt burden and considering a united front to present the North with a common set of debt-lightening demands. In the autumn of 1988, the IMF held an international conference in West Berlin. Radical partisans of the South picketed this meeting and conducted a four-day "people's tribunal" of the IMF and World Bank on the ground that the conditions they attach to financial aid to Third World countries amount to economic war against them.

Susan George, an American sociologist, attacked the North's position. She alleged that the debt obligations have become a means through which First World countries gain control over Third World countries. By insisting on austerity in the debtor countries, the IMF and World Bank assure that raw materials can be purchased at low prices, thereby maintaining the vitality of First World economies and keeping the debtor countries in dependency. In arrangements that swap debt for equity, creditors gain control of the infrastructures of these debtor countries, thereby gaining even greater control.[19]

---

19. Associated Press dispatch from Berlin (*Japan Times*, September 28, 1988). To George's remarks, George Wald, 1967 Nobel-laureate biologist, added: "The Third World debt is a marvelous instrument of control. And its advantage is, it's so large that it can never be paid back."

Economics in Focus

Debt-for-Nature Swaps

While economists worry about Third World debt, environmentalists have become alarmed about the destruction of tropical forests, the extinction of wildlife species, and other ecological damage in developing countries—damage that affects the entire globe, not just the nation in question. But Third World countries with huge debts have no extra funds for the environment, and they resent the suggestion that they should slow their development by setting aside critical lands and resources for conservation. Often they believe they must exploit every available resource to service their loans.

Recently some groups have tried to resolve the impasse with arrangements called debt-for-nature swaps. The details may vary, and they tend to be complex, but consider this hypothetical illustration. A U.S. environmental organization purchases $1 million of Costa Rica's debt from an American bank. Because the prospects of complete repayment are slim, the bank sells the debt for only $300,000. Next, the environmental group trades the debt (still worth $1 million at face value) to Costa Rica for new government bonds, also valued at $1 million but issued in Costa Rica's own currency. The U.S. organization then donates these bonds to a private Costa Rican environmental group that will use the proceeds for important conservation projects. Ideally, everyone benefits. Costa Rica has traded debt in hard-to-raise dollars, owed to foreigners, for debt in local currency that will be used for the nation's good. The environmental group has made a $1 million donation by spending less than a third of that amount. And the bank gets a tax deduction for its $700,000 paper loss, now dubbed a charitable contribution.

Debt-for-nature swaps have already taken place in Costa Rica, Bolivia, and Ecuador. In Costa Rica some of the funds have aided a massive effort to restore a dryland forest. In Ecuador the funds are being used to protect national parks. As of early 1989, further swaps were being negotiated for Peru, Mexico, the Philippines, and Jamaica, and environmental groups were trying to arrange similar deals for yet other nations that owed large sums to Western governments or international banks.

There are some drawbacks, however. These swaps can account for only a small portion of Third World debt. Thus, as larger-scale plans for handling the debt take hold, the swaps may seem less attractive to banks or to governments. Some analysts also worry that the exchanges aggravate inflation in the developing country by raising domestic spending.

Nevertheless, supporters believe the idea is worth pursuing. According to Alvaro Umaña, Costa Rica's minister of natural resources, "If you just do debt relief, you may be supporting an overvalued currency or faulty industrial policies. We would like to see debt relief support conservation instead—a policy that everybody agrees is good."

Sources: Clemens P. Work and Geri Smith, "Using Red Ink to Keep Tropical Forests Green," *U.S. News & World Report,* March 6, 1989, pp. 48–49; Thomas A. Lewis, "Nature Reaps a Cash Bonanza," *International Wildlife,* January-February 1989, p. 37; Thomas A. Sancton, "Hands Across the Sea," *Time,* January 2, 1989, pp. 62–63; "Banking on African Conservation," *Science News,* January 28, 1989, p. 62; Umaña quotation from Jason Zweig, "Capital Conservation," *Forbes,* April 17, 1989, p. 208.

SUMMARY

1. Economic development is different from economic growth. Economic development includes structural change, as progress is made toward some specific goal or set of goals that improve the welfare of the masses. (See page 480.)

2. Of the 129 countries reporting to the World Bank, close to 100 are regarded as LDCs belonging to the Third World. The First World comprises the essentially capitalist industrialized MDCs. (See page 481 and Table 1, page 481.)

3. There is no generally accepted theory of economic development. Hirschman classifies theories according to whether they assume that MDC analysis works well with LDCs (monoeconomics) and whether the theories assume that there is community of interest. (See page 484.)

4. Adam Smith was a development optimist. He believed that growth required little beyond "peace, easy taxes, and a tolerable administration of justice." (See page 484.)

5. Thomas Malthus was a development pessimist. He foresaw population increases overtaking food supplies and holding incomes to subsistence levels. (See page 485.)

6. Karl Marx and his followers—among them Lenin and Rosa Luxemburg—were pessimists about capitalist development. They saw development as leading to stagnation, imperialism, and war by a number of alternative routes. (See pages 485–486.)

7. Dependencia theory, pessimistic and influenced by Marxism, bases much of its argument on neomercantilism as well as capitalism generally. The division of labor between LDCs and MDCs, or between the mother country and her colonies, plays an important part in this theory. (See pages 486–487.)

8. The most striking feature of W. W. Rostow's "Non-Communist Manifesto" theory of economic development is its stress on a single-generation "takeoff" in which saving rates rise and "leading industries" increase sharply in both number and importance. (See page 488.)

9. The "vicious-cycle" theory states that unless helped from the outside, poor countries will remain poor because they cannot save and build the capital stock required to raise productivity, nor are they able to attract investment funds due to their low demand for most goods and services. (See pages 488–489.)

10. Cultural-development theories by social scientists outside of economics emphasize cultural factors such as religion, custom, and tradition. (See page 489.)

11. The development process in the present MDCs has been marked, according to the Kuznets hypothesis, by rising income inequality in its early stages—a trend that is later reversed. (See page 490.)

12. The World Bank seeks to correct the pattern of inequality in the present LDCs. The bank's efforts have stressed the basic human needs strategy and "appropriate technology" that keeps up the demand for semiskilled labor in meaningful jobs. (See page 490.)

13. Another distributive problem is the dualism between urban (industrial) and rural (agricultural) areas, as well as between modern and traditional industries, which usually accompanies growth. (See page 490–491.)

14. There is considerable hostility between the industrialized MDCs of the First World (the North) and the LDCs of the Third World (the South). LDC resentment and envy have brought about the South's demand for a New International Economic Order (NIEO) to replace the present system. Many LDCs consider the present system exploitative and blame it for their underdevelopment. (See page 491.)

15. LDCs' demands cover the areas of trade; debt, aid, and capital movements; internal economic policies; and political issues. (See pages 491–493.)

16. Third World debt is currently the greatest source of North-South confrontation and conflict. The World Bank has identified seventeen "heavy debtor" countries that have a combined external debt of about $527 billion. (See pages 493–494 and Table 3, page 494.)

17. Much of the outstanding Third World debt can be traced back to the desire of American banks to hold large sums of OPEC "petrodollars," for which high interest rates had to be paid, and the subsequent lending of these funds to oil-importing LDCs. (See pages 494–495.)

18. Debt crises have become commonplace as one LDC or another gets into financial difficulty or an earlier plan unravels. New loans, often to finance old debts, are frequently conditional on certain austerity behavior of the LDCs. (See page 495.)

19. We discuss four plans for longer-term Third World debt settlement that have been suggested and at least partially put into effect. These are the Baker plan, debt-equity swaps, the Camdessus plan, and the Miyazawa plan. (See pages 496–497.)

KEY TERMS

basic human needs (BHN): an approach to economic development that says a country is developing if and only if more and more of its people are gaining adequate diets, clean water, decent shelter, basic health care and education, and a peaceful means of making their views known to the government (page 480).

dependencia: neo-Marxist theories of underdevelopment that argue that the prosperity of the First World is dependent upon the poverty of the Third World, and the poverty of the Third World is dependent upon the prosperity of the First World (page 486).

economic development: economic progress that brings gains in welfare, making life better for the masses (page 480).

economic dualism: a regional distribution problem wherein LDC cities become enclaves of modernization and prosperity in otherwise stagnant countries (page 491).

First World: the advanced industrialized countries (page 481).

gross domestic product (GDP): the total value of production that takes place per year in a country (page 482).

monoeconomics: economic theories that assume that methods devised in MDCs to deal with MDC problems also work well in LDCs (page 484).

Second World: countries with centrally planned economies (page 481).

social overhead capital: roads, harbors, schools, and public health facilities (page 488).

Third World: the developing countries (page 481).

DISCUSSION QUESTIONS

1. Describe two patterns of economic change in Faroffistan: (a) a process of growth without development, and (b) a process of development without growth.

2. To expand Adam Smith's prescription for development, what factors would you add to his "peace, easy taxes, and a tolerable administration of justice"?

3. Compare the Marxist-Leninist and the *dependencia* development theories.

4. Is there, in your opinion, a monoeconomics equally applicable to MDCs and LDCs?

5. Are the growth and development processes in the MDCs helpful or harmful to LDC aspirations?

6. What is the basic human needs approach to development theory?

7. Summarize the existing international economic order that the South is attacking. Are its free-trade or its protectionist features most under attack?

8. Do you agree that direct aid and concessional loans are owed by MDCs to LDCs as reparations for colonialism, imperialism, and/or MNC exploitation?

9. Some LDCs are oil exporters; most are oil importers. Nevertheless, the solidarity of the South was not broken after the rise of OPEC. How can this be explained?

10. Many Latin American countries consider the 1980s a "lost decade" or "dead decade" in economic development. Can you explain this?

Japanese-American Economic Warfare?

Japanese-American relations have taken a paradoxical turn in the last third of the twentieth century, as World War II (1941–1945, in the Pacific Theater) and the Allied Occupation of Japan (1945–1952) have faded into the mists of "ancient" history. The political and economic aspects of the two countries' relations have gone "out of sync" with each other. On the political front, a Japanese-American alliance has become a keystone of each country's diplomatic and defense policy in the entire Pacific basin. On the economic front, rivalry, hostility, and mutual recrimination have taken center stage, perhaps more in America than in Japan.[1] Doctrinaire economic "interpretationists" of political history assure us that in such cases economics will eventually dominate and politics will follow along. Most of the rest of us—Japanese, Americans, and citizens of other countries—hope that this will not occur. There is considerable historical support for our hopes.[2]

MACROECONOMIC ASPECTS—BEHIND THE HEADLINES

Let us review what has happened. The traditional surplus position of the peacetime American bilateral trade and current-account balances with Japan be-gan to fall in the 1950s as a result of Japan's postwar recovery—the so-called "second economic miracle"—which raised production of both potential exports and import-competing goods. The American surplus fell to zero during the Vietnam War period of the mid-1960s. By the early 1980s, the bilateral balance—now negative for America and positive for Japan—had become the largest such balance between any two countries in the entire history of international trade. Amounting to approximately one-third of the total (multilateral) American trade deficit, this negative bilateral balance with Japan became, not surprisingly, the focus of American producer-interests' resentment. The erosion of America's trade position—both the relative decline of its exports and the absolute increase in its imports—presented a very threatening situation. The American trade problem became, in the public media, a "Japan" problem.

The changes in the American trade and current-account positions were, however, *multilateral,* not merely bilateral with Japan or any other single country. In fact, by the mid-1980s, the United States had negative bilateral balances with almost all of its principal First World trading partners.

The opposite was true for Japan. The Japanese bilateral trade and current-account balances turned positive, not only with the United States but also with nearly all of Japan's trading partners, capitalist and socialist, advanced and developing. Australia became the only large country combining bilateral trade surpluses with Japan and bilateral trade deficits with the United States.

---

1. Japanese pollsters periodically survey public opinion, including questions on which foreign countries the Japanese like best (or dislike least). The United States has continued to rank quite high in this popularity contest, especially as compared with the Soviet Union.

2. Anglo-American relations were similarly "out of sync" in the last third of the nineteenth century. Political friendship coexisted with economic hostility, at least on the American side. Britain, secure in her position as "workshop of the world," was a free-trade country "too proud to fight" and waited complacently for America's dominant Republican party to repent the errors of its anti-British protectionism. The rise of Hohenzollern Germany, culminating in World War I, brought on a triumph of political friendship over economic rivalry. More recently, American relations with the European Community (EC) have also come to follow the same out of sync path as American relations with Japan.

The multilateral character of the changes in both American and Japanese international balances suggests that they reflect economic phenomena affecting their entire economies rather than relations between the two countries themselves. To examine such macroeconomic matters, we can employ macroeconomic identities. For each country, as we have seen,[3]

$$(I - S) + (G - T_n) + (X - I_m) = 0$$

and also

$$(\Delta I - \Delta S) + (\Delta G - \Delta T_n) + (\Delta X - \Delta I_m) = 0$$

In the American case, $(I - S)$ has trended upward because of a declining trend of private saving as a fraction of GNP.[4] At the same time, $(G - T_n)$ has also trended upward as a consequence of tax cuts, military-budget increases, congressional attachment to social spending, and home-district "pork barrels." The combination of positive $(I - S)$ and $(G - T_n)$ requires negative $(X - I_m)$, the multilateral current-account deficit.[5]

The international macroeconomic identities, precisely because they are identities, do not by themselves imply that the decline in the U.S. saving rate and the increase in government purchases caused the current account deficit. This sequence simply appears more realistic than other sequences, which might, for example, interpret the falling American saving rate as the result of deficits in the current account and the public finances.

The Japanese case is slightly, but only slightly, more complex. In Japan, private saving has traditionally been a high percentage of the national income. Its absolute amount has therefore risen with income more rapidly than has private domestic investment, so that $(I - S)$ has turned negative. While retreating from the Occupation's disinflationary insistence on budgetary balance, Japanese macroeconomic policy has in most years remained restrictive, so that the deficit $(G - T_n)$, while positive, has been close enough to zero for the subtotal $[(I - S) + (G - T_n)]$ to remain negative. Japan's positive multilateral current-account balance $(X - I_m)$ could therefore be regarded as a result of domestic saving and fiscal policies.[6]

THE EXCHANGE RATE

Let us grant that American macroeconomic practice and policy have led to a negative multilateral balance of the American current account, while Japanese macroeconomic practice and policy have led to a positive balance. The question remains, to what extent are these multilateral divergences reflected in the bilateral balances between these countries themselves? Any full answer to this question in real terms must include the sizes of the two economies, and the dependence of each country on its imports from and exports to the other. We shall not attempt to answer these questions here. We concentrate instead on a monetary factor, namely the exchange rate between their two monies. The yen-dollar exchange rate was fixed at ¥360 to the dollar in 1949, by the Allied Occupation under the command of General Douglas MacArthur. It remained at that level until 1971. Since that date it has fluctuated sharply. For example, the dollar rose fairly steadily from ¥170 to ¥260 between 1980 and 1985, then fell steadily to ¥120 in 1988. What difference have these fluctuations made? Has the cheaper dollar banked or fed the flames of Japanese-American economic cold warfare? Neither the one nor the other, from the American side at least. The principal effect of the cheaper dollar has been some shift of hostilities from the *trade* to the *capital*

---

3. Recall that:

I	is investment	T_n	is net taxes
S	is savings	*X*	is exports
G	is government purchases	*Im*	is imports

4. There is as yet no agreement among economists regarding the responsibility for this decline. Among the candidates are Madison Avenue and its advertising industry, the rise of "plastic money" as an engine of easy credit, the expansion of welfare-state institutions—particularly Social Security and private pensions—and a tax system allegedly biased in favor of consumption, not saving.

5. The "twin towers" explanation of the trade deficit as the result of the towering budgetary deficit is at best a half-truth because it ignores the $(I - S)$ balance of the private sector.

6. A more devious, not to say conspiratorial, causation pattern is occasionally alleged by Japan-bashers. Hungry to build up their foreign assets (by capital exports), the Japanese have required current-account surpluses to pay for them. Maintenance of current-account surpluses, combined with Japan's large private saving $(I - S)$ deficit, prevents the Japanese government from stimulating domestic demand by increasing spending (or cutting taxes) as much as foreign critics would like. There seems to be no historical evidence for this pattern.

front. In the following paragraphs, we examine the effects of the so-called "bargain-basement dollar" on the bilateral current and capital accounts.

Current-Account Effects An increasing American complaint against Japan, in the last dozen years of the ¥360 rate, was Japan's unwillingness to recognize and remedy the alleged undervaluation of the yen. As Japanese productivity rose, the ¥360 rate—fixed by the Occupation, not by the Japanese—made Japanese products "unfairly" cheap in America and American products "unfairly" expensive in Japan. A "level playing field," as surveyed in America, apparently required a stronger yen to avoid wage cuts and "speedups" for American workers. The converse of a stronger yen was, of course, a weaker dollar—a phrase taboo outside of economics classes!

After 1973 the yen floated—usually not quite freely. The subsequent record seemed to show the American trade and current-account balances with Japan becoming more negative as the dollar rose and less negative as the dollar fell, but only after a time lag of eighteen to twenty-four months, and only in smaller degree than the Americans had hoped.[7]

Capital-Account Effects The fluctuating dollar has capital-account effects as well, and in the opposite

7. The so-called Marshall-Lerner condition for exchange markets tells us, under a number of restrictive conditions, that cheapening of a country's currency will increase its current-account balance if the sum of two price elasticities exceeds unity. These elasticities are the country's demand for imports from its trading partner and the trading partner's demand for the country's exports. (This topic is discussed more fully in advanced courses in international economics.)

direction to the current-account effects. A strong yen—or, if you prefer, a weak dollar—makes American real estate, government bonds, corporate securities, and companies themselves cheaper for the Japanese. It also makes the corresponding Japanese assets expensive for Americans. The so-called "bargain-basement dollar" accordingly fostered a significant net passage of American assets into Japanese ownership—chiefly urban real estate and public and private securities but also "directly productive facilities," meaning operating business enterprises.[8] Three features of this transfer process arouse American apprehension, sometimes approaching paranoia.

1. Concentration in particular localities, especially the Hawaiian Islands, southern California, and Alaska. These regions, the Japan-bashers claim, are in danger of becoming Japanese economic enclaves, with the American "natives" reduced to the second-class status of the Polynesians of Hawaii or the Eskimos of Alaska.

2. Holdings of Treasury securities—the national debt. In the short run, of course, Japanese demand has the effect of lowering interest rates. In the longer run, it may give Japanese interests too much control over American macroeconomic policy, including the power to destabilize the economy by "dumping the debt" and driving up U.S. interest rates. This means either perpetual depression or runaway inflation, at the will of the Japanese "malefactors of great wealth."

3. Holdings by Japanese multinationals. The great bulk of Japanese investments in American private securities seems to be passive "portfolio" investment by individuals seeking dividends and capital gains. It is criticized, however, as though it would soon become direct investment, which also strives for partial or complete control. Moreover, widespread control of American firms by large Japanese multinational conglomerates like Mitsubishi or Sumitomo may, say the critics, have frightening consequences for American national defense, for the location of research and development, for the international movement of technology, and for the advancement of American workers, both blue collar and white collar.

All three of these concerns may be less than rational, both quantitatively and qualitatively. There is too much American ownership to be bought up so easily—America is not Luxembourg or Monaco. Foreign ownership is more European and Canadian than it is Japanese. Most Japanese owners are merely portfolio investors. Foreign firms in America, including Japanese-controlled ones, are no more likely to be oppressive or predatory than American-owned firms in Canada, in Europe, or in other advanced countries (including Japan itself).[9] Finally, the checkered historical record of foreign investment in American enterprises, notably European investment in canals, railroads, and real estate before World War I, features the victimization of the gullible European investors by the American "robber barons," not the reverse.

MICROECONOMIC ASPECTS—THE HEADLINES THEMSELVES

Headlines, cover stories, and TV programs about Japanese-American economic rivalry have been about specific industries, from rice to computers. The macroeconomic storms, like cold waves from Siberia, have moved from one area to another, making headlines as they went.

In the mid-1950s, rivalry began with textiles and clothing. The Japanese "dollar blouse" was a symbol. It then moved in two directions. The first was

8. This essay does not inquire *why* the dollar fluctuated as it did. However, in the important case of the 1979–1985 run-up of the dollar in Tokyo—in the face of a negative and falling American current-account balance with Japan—the rate seems to have responded chiefly to the rise of American interest rates, which cheapened American assets for Japanese buyers, plus liberalization of Japanese rules that previously restricted the holding of such assets by Japanese. Summary: capital-account considerations were in this case more important than current-account ones in governing exchange markets.

9. In the dear dead days of the ¥360 dollar, you may well ask, why did *Americans* not buy up *Japanese* assets and gain access to all that productive, low-cost Japanese labor, not to mention that pool of low-interest Japanese saving? Because the Japanese did in fact fear infusion of American capital with as much paranoia as the Americans would later display toward Japanese capital. Any such invasion plans were therefore warded off by the Japanese Ministry of International Trade and Industry, the "notorious MITI," using the device of exchange control. MITI did not permit large-scale purchase of yen by present or potential rivals of Japanese firms in key industries.

toward heavy industry and high technology: autos, steel, electronics, semiconductors, financial services. The second direction was agricultural: beef, citrus, and rice.

There have also been two patterns of conflict. Most obvious to Americans has been the Japanese entry into the American market—the most lucrative and most nearly open fraction of the world market. Most obvious to the Japanese have been the American attempts to expand their footholds in the newly important Japanese markets for farm products and a wide range of services (banking, insurance, construction).

No single microeconomic skirmish in either country means very much in terms of the underlying macroeconomic realities. Each skirmish in its turn, however, has been where the action is.

Popular economics in both America and Japan has been conditioned by mercantilistic stress on producer as against consumer interests, and also by historical experience hardened into something close to "natural law." The American economy of mass production and high wages was fostered by a protectionist tradition dating from Alexander Hamilton and Henry Clay. "Yankee ingenuity" and relative immunity from the costs of two world wars gave twentieth-century America, it was commonly believed, a natural right to a God-given position as the world's technological leader, creditor, and economic power, with the world's most durable trade surplus and the world's highest standard of living. "All power corrupts, and absolute power corrupts absolutely," in economics as in politics. Japanese folk economics is colored by Japan's lack of natural resources. Forced to import both raw materials for their manufactured exports and (in the twentieth century) a significant fraction of their staple food, the Japanese came to regard as unpatriotic additional imports of goods that could be produced at home, either in the present or in the near future. This mercantilism was hardened by a history of periodic negative balances and import shortages causing recession or depression, or leading to malnutrition and dependence on American aid. Was the post-1965 prosperity a new order of things, or just a dreamlike interlude?

Why has Japanese-American competition become so embittered? The answer is different in each industry, which makes it difficult to avoid passing on horror stories—true and false—on both sides of each key industry. The Americans blame the Japanese. The Japanese are unfair. They play "dirty tricks." Japanese rules keep changing and are enforced selectively against foreign exporters. They dump subsidized products overseas below cost to gain market share and drive out competition. Their home market is surreptitiously but systematically closed. Their policy is to sell without buying. And the Japanese blame the Americans. The Americans engage in Japan-bashing and complain to Washington instead of adapting to the new realities of Japanese postwar recovery. The Americans cling to wage rates, labor costs, and profit margins that are now uncompetitively high, and to productivity and quality standards that are now uncompetitively low. Perhaps for racist reasons, they refuse to adjust their export offerings to foreign tastes and foreign ignorance of English. The oversized American car with its steering wheel on the "wrong" side was for many years a symbol in this regard.

The new protectionism of quotas, administrative protection, "voluntary" export restrictions, and "orderly marketing arrangements" is different from the old protectionism of tariffs. The guiding genius of the new protectionism was probably the American-born German banker Hjalmar Schacht, who became Hitler's finance minister. Japan learned the new protectionism more quickly and accepted it more wholeheartedly than America. This may be because Japan's elitist higher civil service, including MITI, recruits a larger fraction of its country's top legal and economic brains than its American equivalent and is more confident of its own knowledge of its country's best interests. Also, the bureaucracy and business interests are closely allied in Japan, whereas in America, the bureaucracy includes elements that business considers to be neutral, if not downright hostile.

GRIEVANCES AND POLITICAL REPERCUSSIONS

"Beauty," we say, "is in the eye of the beholder." Fairness, likewise, is in the ethos of the judge—especially between competitors who claim to be playing different games under different rules. When Japanese and American negotiators, public and private, cannot agree upon the rules and how they should be enforced, the best we can hope for may be an agreed-upon grievance procedure patterned after the binding arbitration provisions of collective-bargaining contracts in domestic industrial relations.

They might, but need not, proceed most smoothly and expeditiously under the auspices of GATT (the General Agreement on Tariffs and Trade). Binding arbitration has its problems too, however, even with the most knowledgeable and impartial of arbitrators.

Will increasing numbers of microeconomic Japanese-American controversies simply be allowed to fester unresolved? Each one is of supreme importance to participants on either side, and sometimes also to localities such as metropolitan Detroit with its auto plants and Akron with its tire plants. The eventual consequences of accumulating unresolved disputes may be also highly unpleasant to politicians in one or both countries.

Consider the following scenario, which may become more plausible in the future than it is now:

Another American trade bill goes into effect, with harsher provisions than the 1988 legislation.

There is now to be automatic discrimination across the board against unspecified countries with large positive bilateral trade balances with the United States who close their markets to American exports or whose own imports sell in America at prices below their average costs of production (plus 8 percent profit) as estimated by the American government. This law is enforced in practice primarily against Japan. Contemporaneously with this intensified Japan-bashing, the Soviet Union reverses its anti-Japanese stand. The Soviets offer to return to Japan the four southern-most islands of the Kurile chain, which have been in dispute between the two countries since 1945,[10] as part of a treaty of peace and friend-

10. These islands were part of Hokkaido Prefecture before 1945 and had never been under Russian rule. Their present population, however, is believed to include only Soviet citizens, all Japanese having been repatriated.

ship officially ending the Pacific War. The treaty also increases and improves investment opportunities for Japanese companies in the development of Soviet Siberia. In exchange, Japan is asked to become neutral, or "nonaligned," like Sweden, Switzerland, or India. This would require ending the Japanese-American Security Treaty of 1960 and require American evacuation of military, naval, and air bases in Japan and Okinawa. This consequence of festering trade disputes would surely be bad news for the American Department of Defense, even though it would not move Japan behind the Iron Curtain.

POSTSCRIPT

Discussions similar to this one could also be directed toward American economic relations with the European Community or with the newly industrialized economies of East Asia such as Korea, Taiwan, Hong Kong, and Singapore. They could also be written about Japanese economic relations with the European Community and with the East Asian countries just mentioned. The Japanese-American relationship differs from the others primarily because of its larger size and longer duration.

Comparative Economic Systems—
More Planning or Less?

Radical Economics

PART VII

COMPARATIVE
ECONOMIC SYSTEMS

23

Comparative Economic Systems—More Planning or Less?

Preview As you learned earlier, societies manage their scarcity problems in different ways. In today's world, the most important of these are the impersonal *market* and deliberate *planning* by the public authorities, though in some places *traditional* economies survive.

You also know that no existing economy is *pure* and that all are *mixed*. The United States is primarily, but by no means exclusively, a market economy, since about 30 percent of the American gross national product now passes through the public sector and need not "meet the test of the market." Similarly, the Soviet Union is primarily but not exclusively a planned economy, since much of its agricultural output is raised and marketed by peasants from their private plots.

The question raised in this chapter is a normative one. Should we favor using "more planning" or "less planning" by public agencies in our economy? In other words, should we shift our economic "mix" toward greater reliance on public planning, greater reliance on the market, or leave it alone?

We begin by reviewing our criteria for judging economic systems. Next we discuss the relationship of planning to freedom and power, and distinguish among planning, collectivism, and the welfare state. Even though these three kinds of institutions are often found together, a country may have any one or two without the rest. Then, turning specifically to planning, we introduce several general planning types.

At this point, we discuss first the Soviet Union as a representative of collectivist (also socialist) planning, and then Japan and Sweden as two widely different examples of economic planning under capitalism. As examples of socialist collectivism that is combined with a largely market economy, we turn to the countries of Yugoslavia and China.

To illustrate some of the problems raised by the Russian experience in particular, we return to theory for the last part of the chapter. One theory that we present is the market socialist model of Oskar Lange and A. P. Lerner. The other is the forecast of Ludwig von Mises and Friedrich von Hayek that planning is incompatible with freedom and will lead eventually to what Hayek calls "serfdom."

SOCIAL GOALS

We take as given the goals suggested in Chapter 1, but not their relative importance. These goals are as follows:

1. High *present* standards of living
2. High growth rates, leading to high *prospective* standards of living
3. Equitable distribution of income and wealth
4. Security of the standard of living against short-term downward shocks from recessions and depressions, and also against long-term shocks from resource exhaustion and technological change
5. Compatibility of economic institutions with personal liberty and civil rights
6. Compatibility of economic institutions with physical and mental health

Even with agreement on these goals, the question of "more planning or less?" arouses violent and sometimes irrational emotions. Two stories illustrate this point.

The first story is about Hassan, an Egyptian student of one of the authors, who was describing the wonders that the Aswan Dam, built in the late 1950s, would bring to his country. The teacher recalled that the British, during their period of rule over Egypt, had also built an Aswan Dam and placed high hopes on it, with disappointing results. "But, Professor," said Hassan politely, "you don't understand. This Aswan Dam is *planned!*" Hassan knew that the British dam was also planned—engineering projects always are! He meant that the Egyptian dam was part of a comprehensive national plan for Egypt, whereas the British dam had been an isolated project. Confidence like Hassan's

that a plan will work just because it *is* a plan is what we call "magic wand" planning. Much of the appeal of some of the more grandiose kinds of planning is of the magic wand sort.

The second story is about a Polish friend of one of the authors. When the Nazis invaded Poland in 1939, this man fled to the Soviet Union. The U.S.S.R., then allied with the Nazis, sent him to a remote part of Siberia. There, after the Nazis had invaded the U.S.S.R., a peasant asked him if the Nazis were as bad as he had been told. The Polish refugee assured the Siberian peasant that the Nazis were indeed bad people who committed atrocities, but the peasant was not satisfied. "Do the Nazis have collective farms in Germany?" he asked. (Collective farms are the basis for Soviet agricultural planning.)

"No, there are no collective farms in Germany."

"Well, then, the Nazis cannot be so bad as you say," concluded the peasant.

The question of the amount of deliberate planning by public agencies needed to achieve economic goals is a controversial one.

PLANNING, FREEDOM, AND POWER

When economists speak of planned economies, the planning they have in mind is done by legislators, experts, and civil servants. But in any case, every individual, to some extent, plans for himself or herself. Every family plans for itself. Every organization—be it a corporation, a university, a club, or a government bureau—plans for itself. In economics **planning** means an institutional arrangement in which some individual or organization in a public position plans for another individual or organization, who or which has little say about the plan and whose economic freedom is restricted by the planning decision.

The relation between freedom and planning is by no means a simple matter. When I plan for myself today, my freedom is restricted by whatever long-term plans I may have made earlier. For example, I cannot buy a new car or take a trip to Europe because I carried out last year's plan to buy a house, and "my mortgage payments are killing me." Families and organizations present even more problems than individuals. Students have lost their best friends because their parents decided to move from one neighborhood to another, or from the Snow Belt to the Sun Belt. Workers have lost their jobs when their employer's home office decided to close their factory or office. Retailers have gone bankrupt when major suppliers or customers closed down or moved away—or when competitors opened up shop across the street. When City Hall, the State Capitol, or "Washington" carries out some plan we dislike, and which limits our economic freedom in some way, are we hurt any less because we can still vote for legislators who promise to change or repeal the plan, or because we can "vote with our feet" by moving to some other place? One point should be clear: public planning, when carried out through laws and regulations, may be either more or less restrictive of freedom than private planning, when carried out through market forces.

In economics, planning means an institutional arrangement in which some individual or organization in a public position plans for another individual or organization, whose economic freedom is restricted by the planning decision. The relationship between freedom and planning is complex.

Public planning, when carried out through laws and regulations, may be either more or less restrictive of freedom than private planning, when carried out through market forces.

Freedom should be distinguished from *power*. You are quite free to visit the moon, or Mars for that matter, but are powerless to exercise that freedom unless you are an astronaut, a cosmonaut, or a flying-saucerite from outer space. You have the power to abuse small children or drive while drunk, but your freedom does not extend to such illegal activities. Planners, too, often do not have the power to carry out plans they are free to make. The controversial architect and city planner Frank Lloyd Wright said that one American city "needs

another fire" and that another should be "torn down and started over," but no urban planner has the power to burn or tear down any city.

Freedom-versus-power problems arise whenever the protection of someone's freedom interferes with someone else's planning power, or whenever the protection or enhancement of someone's planning power interferes with someone else's freedom. Yet a more basic freedom-power problem is this one: Can a person be said to have freedom at all, when either natural forces or the actions of others—including their economic plans—deprive him or her of the power to exercise it effectively? Is your freedom of speech worth anything if you do not own a newspaper or a television station, have no pulpit or professorship, and cannot otherwise persuade people to listen to you? What is it worth to be free to air your views if you are shunned by your customers or lose your job because of them, even when you fear neither legal prosecution nor mob violence? And if your freedom of speech cannot be translated into the power to influence others, how much better off are you than someone else who must follow the "party line," keep his or her mouth shut, or else face "re-education" in prison, labor camp, or mental hospital?

Freedom should be distinguished from power. Can a person be said to have freedom at all when either natural forces or the actions of others deprive him or her of the power to exercise it effectively?

PLANNING, COLLECTIVISM, AND THE WELFARE STATE

We have already suggested that planning is related to both freedom and power. Now we consider how it is related to collectivism and to the so-called welfare state.

In **collectivist economies**, land and physical capital such as buildings and machinery are largely or completely owned by collective agencies, not by private individuals or business firms. Most planned economies are in fact collectivist, and most of them are socialistic. In **socialistic economies** these col-

FIGURE 1
Types of Economic Systems

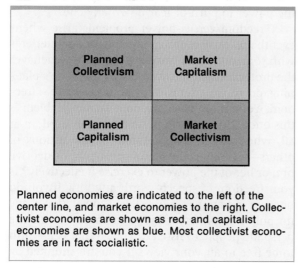

| Planned Collectivism | Market Capitalism |
| Planned Capitalism | Market Collectivism |

Planned economies are indicated to the left of the center line, and market economies to the right. Collectivist economies are shown as red, and capitalist economies are shown as blue. Most collectivist economies are in fact socialistic.

lective agencies are governmental.[1] On the other hand, most but not all market economies are **capitalistic.** In these economies, land and physical capital are owned largely by private individuals or business firms. Aside from traditional economies, there are four distinct types of economic systems, as pictured in Figure 1. In this figure, planned economies are shown to the left of the center line and market economies to the right. Collectivist (usually socialist) economies are colored red, and the capitalist ones colored blue.

Just as many people confuse planning with socialism or communism, and the market with capitalism, they also associate planning with the welfare state, and the market with something less compassionate.

In collectivist economies, land and physical capital are largely or completely owned by collective agencies, not by individuals or business firms. In socialist economies, these collective agencies are governmental.

---

1. A **communist** is a socialist who believes that socialism on a world scale will lead to an economy of abundance, and who accepts violence, revolution, and dictatorship as a means to that end.

Most market economies are capitalistic—land and physical capital are owned largely by private individuals or business firms.

A **welfare state** is an economy that places an especially high value on our goals 3 and 4 among the objectives of the economy. The "equity" of its income and wealth distributions is a matter of first importance. "Equity," moreover, is treated as including a relatively high poverty line or "safety net," below which no person or family need remain for long, along with a high degree of distributional equality above this poverty line. Either a capitalist or a socialist economy, and likewise either a planned or a market economy, may be a welfare state. Any of these may also be something other than a welfare state.

Any economic system, whether capitalist, socialist, planned, or market, that places great value on a high poverty line and a high degree of distributional equality above this line may be called a welfare state.

TYPES OF PLANNING

You have learned that not all markets are alike. Monopoly, for example, is different from competition. In the same way, planning systems are not all alike. In the next few paragraphs we outline several of the major types of planning.

Imperative Planning

The most rigorous form of planning is **imperative planning.** It is imperative in that, to quote Josef Stalin, "A plan is a command." Failure to reach an important plan target is a criminal offense. In extreme cases those who fail may be punished by imprisonment or even death, as sometimes happened in Stalin's Russia. Imperative planning goes beyond the aggregate economy to include the "fine structure" of the economy as a whole and also of a country's regions.

Indicative Planning

A milder form of planning is **indicative planning.** It operates mainly by convincing plan participants that following the plan will help them economically, though in some cases they are threatened with the denial of privileges (or even with penalties) for not following "administrative guidance." Most peacetime capitalist planning is of this kind. Indicative planning is generally also *consensual*, meaning that the planning authority includes representatives of various interest groups as well as civil servants and planning technicians. Among the groups represented may be some or all of the following: the financial community, the military, organized business, organized labor, organized agriculture, organized taxpayers, organized consumers, and spokespersons from the different regions of the country.

Most peacetime capitalist planning is indicative: it operates mainly by convincing participants that following the plan will help them economically. Indicative planning is generally consensual.

Public Sector Planning

Public sector planning covers only the public sector. The many different organs of central and local government, while producing a small percentage of the total national income and product, often dominate the economy's "commanding heights," or key industries, in mixed systems. To treat them as a single enterprise, therefore, goes a long way toward controlling the whole economy. However, it is also hard to do so, because of jealousy between different branches of the government—between "national defense" and "social services," between the central and local governments, and between the more and less advanced parts of the country. The private sector is also affected by public sector planning because private companies sell to or buy from public agencies, and because the plan gives the public sector priority over strategic and especially over imported resources. This kind of planning has been used most widely in India.

Macroeconomic Planning

Macroeconomic planning is less ambitious than any of the three kinds of planning covered so far. Planned or target quantities generally include standard aggregate measures such as gross national product, the division between consumption, investment, and government sectors, the supplies of money and credit, the government surplus or deficit, international balances, and interest rates. The fine structure of the aggregates is left to the market.

Macroeconomic planning generally includes the simple forecasting or projection of present policies or the results of certain changes that have been proposed. This is technically not planning at all. Indeed, it is sometimes done entirely by computer simulation, with little aid from human hands or brains. It often precedes real planning, but is treated as planning by the mass media.

Magic Wand Planning

We have already noted **"magic wand" planning.** A magic wand plan is built around a collection of projects and/or an appealing slogan. The projects or the slogan are expected to produce all kinds of good things by some unspecified processes, including the mystical power of the word *planning*. One example is the "fourth national plan" proposed for Japan in Herman Kahn's *Japanese Challenge*. This plan proposed to produce an industrialized environmentalist utopia, called "the machine in the garden." Another is the Humphrey-Hawkins bill in the United States. In its original form, it called for targets of low inflation and low unemployment that were to have been reached in 1983, but indicated only in the vaguest language how this was to have been done.

In the next few parts of this chapter, we shall present case studies of actual economies illustrating planned collectivism, planned capitalism, and market socialism. (Most of this book has assumed a market-capitalist economy, and so we see no need to illustrate such an economy again here.)

The several major types of planning include imperative planning, indicative planning, public

---

sector planning, macroeconomic planning, and magic wand planning.

A PLANNED COLLECTIVIST ECONOMY: THE SOVIET UNION

We begin with the Soviet model of imperative planning. Its vision of the economy is a huge factory, producing not only the country's final products, or consumer goods, but also its own intermediate products. As his model for Russia, Vladimir Lenin (1870–1924) may have used the Ford works in and around Detroit, which were the industrial marvels of his time. Ford produced not only automobiles, trucks, and tractors, but also many of their parts, and raw materials like coal and steel. Another vision was one that the Soviets shared with many other hostile critics of capitalism: that business administration can be reduced to the clerical routine of "office management," if the firm only had the information that a plan could provide and if it need not be concerned with competition. In this way, Lenin hoped that a national plan, maximizing welfare for the whole society much as a business firm plans to maximize profits, could be made simple and clear enough so that the average worker, without formal training in economics or statistics, could understand it and criticize it intelligently.

The Soviet model of imperative planning views the economy as a huge factory, producing not only the country's consumer goods but also its intermediate products.

Stalin and the Growth of Gosplan

The Russian revolutions of 1917 were followed by civil war, foreign intervention, and famine. With all these troubles, the planning process floundered over the years from 1917 to 1928. After Lenin died in 1924, the "Soviet" planning model developed under the leadership of Josef Stalin (1880–1953). This model was both imperative and highly centralized in a single agency, called **Gosplan,** which has since grown to huge proportions. Gosplan is subdivided along both industrial and regional lines, with consultation extending down to and up from the individual factory. That is, the manager of a factory or a collective farm is informed of his or her role in the plan: what outputs should be produced, and what inputs should be used to produce them. The manager may suggest changes, but final authority rests with Gosplan in Moscow.

The plans are usually but not necessarily for five-year periods. The actual length of time is a practical compromise. Shorter periods may not allow completion of many planned projects, and could overtax Gosplan facilities. Longer periods might result in many plants being out of date by the time they were built.

Every part of the plan must be coordinated with other parts, since in economics nearly everything depends on nearly everything else. Every output has to be expanded as fast as its inputs, and no faster than its own demand. To coordinate the parts of the plan, the Soviets have used two specialized techniques—materials balancing and input-output analysis.

Materials Balancing The simpler of the two seems to be **materials balancing.** For every one of the thousands of final and intermediate products, potential supplies and demands are estimated for each year of the plan, allowing for both domestic production and international trade. The problem with this method is the difficulty of tracing the results of changes from the last plan, of technological progress, or of economic growth. For example, how much will a rise in the output of heavy trucks, including their engines and tires and fuel, eventually increase the demand for coal? And by how much will these trucks increase the supply of coal?

Input-Output Analysis To solve problems of this last sort, **input-output analysis** was developed (outside the U.S.S.R.) by the Russian-born Nobel Prize–winning economist Wassily Leontief (1906–   ).

TABLE 1
An Input-Output Table (in dollars)

Supplying Industry	Using Industry				
	Agriculture and Fisheries (1)	Food and Kindred Products (2)	Tobacco Manufactures (3)	Textile Mill Products (4)	Apparel (5)
(1) Agriculture and Fisheries	.2609	.4041	.2941	.2139	.0015
(2) Food and Kindred Products	.0572	.1319	.0055	.0062	.0007
(3) Tobacco Manufactures	0	0	.3110	0	0
(4) Textile Mill Products	.0015	0	0	.1341	.2955
(5) Apparel	.0011	.0055	0	0	.1494

This is a portion of the American input-output table for 1947, published by the Bureau of Labor Statistics and condensed in Robert Dorfman's book, *The Price System* (Englewood Cliffs, N.J.: Prentice-Hall, 1964); used with permission.

We focus our attention on the highlighted number .2955. It says that to produce a dollar's worth of its own output, a using industry (apparel) bought $.2955 worth of products from a supplying industry (textiles).

For a complete input-output table, each column and each row would add up to 1.00 (one dollar), since "industries" can be included for "households," "foreign trade," or any other source or use of output.

Input-output analysis is based on matrix algebra, which is studied in more advanced economics as well as mathematics courses. We can illustrate the basic features of the process with the help of Table 1, which is part of an input-output table. The first step in setting up the system is to divide the economy into separate industries for which data can be collected. The table illustrates five such industries—agriculture and fisheries, food and kindred products, tobacco manufactures, textile mill products, and apparel. Each of these industries is listed twice in the table, once as a supplying industry at the left end of a row, and again as a using industry at the head of a column in the table. In the body of the table, each number shows the value of goods from a supplying industry that is used to produce a dollar's worth of goods from a using industry.

For example, the highlighted number in the table tells us that $.2955 worth (or 29.55 cents' worth) of supplies from the textile mill products industry is used by the apparel industry for each dollar's worth of apparel produced. In the complete system, the whole column for the apparel industry would add up to 1.00 (one dollar). Similarly, the whole row of values for the textile mill products industry would add up to 1.00, since all of its output supplied will be used somewhere in the economy. One of the "industries" is "households," so that consumption is recognized. Another "industry" can be foreign trade, to account for exports and imports, and so on.

For the planning specialists at Gosplan, the problem is to estimate accurately what the actual input-output relationships are for the economy. If their estimates do not correspond to what happens in the actual execution of the plan, shortages and surpluses will develop, and the goals of the plan will not be met. As you can easily imagine, the method becomes unwieldy when the classification of the outputs and inputs approaches the fineness of materials balancing. One needs not only to have enough steel for rails but also to have it in the form of rails as distinguished from girders, stainless steel, or armor plate. Nevertheless, progress in planning has been marked by a rise in the relative importance of input-output techniques.

Under Stalin, the imperative planning process was highly centralized in a single agency, called Gosplan, which uses the techniques of materials balancing and input-output analysis.

Problems of Soviet Planning

Far from being clear enough for Lenin's "ordinary worker" to understand, Soviet planning is a highly complex system that has not worked very well. Before the day of the computer, Soviet writers feared "drowning in an ocean of paper" by the year 1980, in the effort to record, digest, and apply the information needed in forming and revising plans. Even though the computer provided a breathing space, the danger of "drowning in computer output" remains for the planners.

In practice, the key problems of Soviet planning can be reduced to three. The first is disappointingly low productivity, particularly for labor on collective farms. (Peasants do much better, it appears, on their private plots.) Second, since planning is done in terms of physical quantities or weights of goods, quality is often skimped or products are too heavy for use, particularly toward the ends of planning periods. Third, the plans are too rigid. They do not allow for unavoidable shortfalls, so that they have seldom, if ever, been carried out in full. For this reason, the plans include a **leading links** system. This means that when the whole plan cannot be carried out, certain leading links are completed in full, and the rest of the plan is postponed in part until the next planning period. The leading links are generally military hardware and capital goods; the postponements are generally in consumption goods. This is why each successive plan promised Western European living standards to the Soviet citizen, and why the promises have remained unfulfilled. However, the conditions of the Russian economy and the Russian consumer were so poor under the Czarist regime[2] that to the Soviet citizen these deficiencies of Soviet planning seemed minor when compared with the advances made over prerevolutionary Russia, and with the conditions of most LDCs of the present world.

The key problems of Soviet planning are: (1) disappointingly low productivity, (2) poor quality of goods, and (3) inflexibility.

---

2. Some economic historians, notably Alexander Gerschenkron, have argued that Czarist Russia was making rapid progress during the 1890–1913 generation, so that continuation of the 1890–1913 trend would have equaled actual Soviet performance had Czar Nicholas II and his ministers avoided the disastrous World War I. But this is conjecture.

Under the leading links system, when the whole plan cannot be carried out, certain parts (leading links—generally military hardware and capital goods) are completed in full, and the rest of the plan is postponed until the next planning period.

From Stalin to Gorbachev

Stalin died in 1953. Under his first few successors, Soviet planning became on balance somewhat less severe in the U.S.S.R., despite occasional Stalinist revivals under the leadership of Leonid Brezhnev. Change was actually more marked in the socialist countries of Eastern Europe and in China (after the death of Mao Zedong in 1976) than in the Soviet Union itself. After partial successes in Hungary and China, the pace of reform accelerated in the Soviet Union under General Secretary Mikhail Gorbachev, who came to power in 1985. The reforms are lumped together under the Russian title, **perestroika** (restructuring)—a term applied by Gorbachev and his economic adviser, Abel Agenbegyan.[3]

The principal components of *perestroika* appear to be as follows.

1. A much wider scope for an unplanned and private (but noncapitalist) "dual economy" alongside the planned socialist economy.[4] This aspect of *perestoika* is resisted strongly by Soviet conservatives in the Communist party, in the Gosplan, and in the other ministries charged with centralized planning of such sectors of the economy as agricul-

---

3. An earlier reform attempt, supported hesitantly and intermittently by General Secretary Nikita Khrushchev in the late 1950s and early 1960s, was called **Libermanism,** from the name of an early academic advocate, Yevsei Liberman. Libermanism did not long survive Khrushchev's fall from power in 1964.

4. How can a private economy be noncapitalist? In the first place, private firms do not own land or capital instruments. They hold land and capital only under lease from the state, which retains the legal title. In the second place, the private enterprises are family firms or producers' cooperatives (in Russian, *artels*). They do not employ more than a limited number of people in "commodity production," and their growth outside the service industries is strictly limited. Employment of workers for wages or fees as servants, doctors, lawyers, etc., is quite legal under socialist regimes because no salable goods are produced for private profit.

ture, construction, and heavy industries in general. These bureaucrats fear not only for their own power and prestige but consider themselves orthodox Marxist-Leninists ideologically opposed to "taking the capitalist road."

2. Much more slack in the plans themselves so that a bad harvest or a drought or a power failure can be absorbed without extensive plan revisions.

3. More leeway for plant managers to run their plants without the continuous supervision of functionaries from either the Soviet state or the Communist party bureaucracies. Indeed, if planned targets are met at planned prices, and if the state receives its planned rents from the land and capital goods the (socialist) firm uses, the firm may make a "profit." If it does, some or all of the profit may be kept within the firm and spent at the manager's discretion as bonuses for the work force, for improvements in housing and other facilities, or even for the manager's own use. For obvious reasons, this reform is viewed with alarm by state and party conservatives and bureaucrats.

The principal components of *perestroika* (restructuring) include: (1) a much wider scope for an unplanned private economy alongside the planned economy, (2) more flexible plans, and (3) more leeway for plant managers to run their plants.

To illustrate the three components of *perestroika,* let us consider a Hungarian bakery, run by a large family with many relatives or by a producers' cooperative. Hungary has moved further away from Stalinism than have other Eastern European countries. The bakery receives each week a planned amount of flour, from which it must produce planned amounts of bread, to be sold at planned prices. But the plan is incomplete, or "slack," so that the bakery is free to buy additional flour at higher prices on the open market and to sell cake and pastry to private customers for whatever prices the market will bear.

At the current stage of *perestroika,* Soviet managers are not free to change output prices, wage rates, or employment levels. It appears that existing Soviet outputs are priced too low and that existing

Soviet payroll costs and rents are too high to encourage enough additional production to remedy widespread consumer shortages under existing production methods. At the same time, prices cannot be raised, wages cut, or excess workers fired without endangering (in the short run) the living standards of Soviet citizens, which are already low by comparison with the West and with Japan. Indeed, the representative Soviet firm appears to run at a loss under present prices, with the loss made up by grants or "loans" from the state, financed by monetary expansion. This, in turn, raises the money supply, which adds to aggregate demand and to the suppressed inflation, shortages, and outages that plague the Soviet economy.[5] It is not clear what the reallocation of administrative power within the firm—more to the manager, less to the regulators—would do about this situation. Some outside specialists, notably Marshall Goldman of Harvard and Wellesley, doubt that the malaise can be cured at all within the Soviet system. In this view, *perestroika* is little more than another slogan. What needs to be done is to get the prices right.

A more sanguine view makes the key factor not prices but productivity. Since payrolls are so largely fixed in the representative firm, Soviet marginal costs are extremely low. Expanded production, even at existing prices, could be profitable if some combination of carrots and sticks could increase productivity and reduce waste of materials. *Perestroika* apparently expects managers to use more carrots. Stalinist conservatives prefer bigger and better sticks. If neither carrots nor sticks work, the Soviet firm may be like the legendary businessperson who "takes a loss on every item but makes it up on volume."

It appears that existing Soviet output prices are too low and existing Soviet payroll costs and rents are too high to encourage enough additional production to remedy widespread consumer shortages under existing production methods.

---

5. The Soviet housewife's shopping bag is called an *avoska,* which translates as "perhaps." "Perhaps" something in short supply will be available today and she can snap it up.

The Chinese Variant

Under the Chinese variant of Stalinist economic planning, as propounded by Mao Zedong (Mao Tse-tung, 1892–1976), rural people lived and worked in large collective farms called *communes*. Many of them went far beyond Soviet models in drawing up their own plans to produce and consume not only farm products but also a wide variety of manufactured goods (including parts).[6]

Each commune presented to the authorities in its provincial capital—and indirectly to the capital in Beijing (Peking)—a list of its expected surpluses and deficits (production minus consumption). The planning authorities acted as a clearinghouse for the communal plans, trying to match the surpluses and deficits of the communes with the less thoroughly organized outputs of the cities and with planned imports and exports—always with minimal changes in prices.

When economic reform came to China after Chairman Mao's death, peasants were permitted to lease land for private plots, as indeed they could again do in the Soviet Union. On both private plots and on communal land, peasants could (within broad limits) grow or manufacture whatever they wished. Only the prices of basic foods remained fixed, and communes were required to make deliveries of specified minimum amounts at these prices. A result, which seems not to have been anticipated, was that peasants shifted production to high-priced luxuries—including rabbits, raised for meat and fur—and away from basic foodstuffs like wheat and rice. This side effect led to food shortages, black markets, and inflation in urban China.

Under the Chinese variant of imperative economic planning, rural people lived and worked in large collective farms called communes. After Chairman Mao's death, economic reforms were instituted that

---

6. In Russia, this system is called *argogorod,* or agricultural city. It was never tried on a large scale in the U.S.S.R. Even after its failure in China, President Nicolae Ceausescu attempted to implement it in Rumania, demolishing farm villages in the process and forcing peasants into urban-style apartment blocks. This large-scale forced movement of the rural population had seldom if ever been done in China.

---

permitted peasants to lease land for private plots on which they could grow whatever they wished.

PLANNING UNDER CAPITALISM: JAPAN AND SWEDEN

Business people and procapitalists desire planning chiefly under one or more of four sets of conditions: (1) a serious or prolonged depression; (2) a major war, including both its preparation and its aftermath; (3) a widespread desire to speed up economic growth beyond what the market has provided; (4) a desire to ensure that political power will be held by moderates more dedicated to planning than to socialization. (By going along with a limited amount of planning, one perhaps can avoid the socialization of one's business and have a voice in the planning process.)

The United States has not been immune to the desire for planning. A planning "boom," led by business people along with academics, was a feature of the Great Depression of the 1930s. One of the most widely discussed plans was outlined by Gerard Swope, then president of General Electric. The National Recovery Administration was a 1933 New Deal experiment that reflected the planning philosophy but accomplished little and was finally ruled unconstitutional by the Supreme Court. During the Great Stagflation of the 1970s, the desire for planning revived in the form of the Humphrey-Hawkins bill, which we have already mentioned. Calling for the reduction of both unemployment and inflation, it made the government the employer of last resort. (It was passed by Congress only in weakened form after Senator Hubert Humphrey's death as a tribute to his memory. In its weakened form, as we have said, it mandated nothing even though it expressed fond hopes.)

Because large-scale "capitalist planning" has had little success in the United States, we draw our examples from overseas. The Japanese plan, our first example, was inspired by the desire to move beyond mere recovery to rapid growth after the disaster of World War II. Carried out under conservative governments, it featured the doubling of the GNP in less than a decade. The Swedish plan, our next example, arose under the long rule of the Social Democratic party, partly as a defense against nationalization of the private sector. Because the two systems turned out so differently, we describe both. Other countries that we might have cited are France, the Netherlands, Norway, and India.

Proposals for more comprehensive planning in the United States were made during the Great Depression of the 1930s and the Great Stagflation of the 1970s. The two best examples of large-scale planning under capitalism, however, are Japan and Sweden.

Japan, Inc.?

In *Taking Japan Seriously,* the British sociologist and Japanologist Ronald Dore views Japan as a modernized version of a **corporate society**.[7] A corporate society is organized in accordance with principles advocated by nineteenth-century reformists—mainly ethicists and theologians—and formulated most influentially in papal encyclicals of Roman Catholicism. It preserves capitalist private ownership of the means of production but reserves large regulatory powers for the state. The state is expected to delegate these powers largely to such corporate bodies as trade associations, farm cooperatives, and trade unions, whose negotiations would determine "fair" prices, wages, and income distributions in accordance with the public interest, as itself determined by the state and its ruling party.

Japan, according to Ronald Dore, is a modern version of a corporate society; it preserves capitalist private ownership of the means of production but reserves large regulatory powers for the state, which delegates these powers to trade associations, farm cooperatives, and trade unions.

---

7. Ronald P. Dore, *Taking Japan Seriously: A Confucian Perspective on Leading Economic Issues* (Stanford: Stanford University Press, 1987).

Corporatism fell into disrepute in the mid-twentieth century. Its doctrines, taken over and distorted by nationalistic, militaristic, fascist movements in Italy and Germany, came to be associated with dictatorship, concentration camps, aggressive warfare, mass murder, and genocide. However, the contemporary Japanese variant of corporatism has none of these outgrowths. If it is fascist at all—which the Japanese vigorously deny—the Japanese corporate society is "Fascism with a Human Face."

The Japanese economy has been called "Japan, Inc." by critics who claim that it subordinates all other interests to those of big business. Other critics say it is run by its bureaucracy and by graduates of the Tokyo University Faculty of Law, with its chief power center in Japan's notorious MITI.[8]

Clearly, these charges cannot both be true. If there is an economic power elite in Japan, it must include both big business and the big bureaucracy. But it must also include, as guardians of the public interest, the Liberal Democratic party, which has ruled the country since 1948. And, many Japanologists add, one must include Big Agriculture, since the rural vote is disproportionately powerful in Japan's political structure and therefore also in its political economy. Workers and consumers, however, are "on the outside looking in," although they would be equal partners in the idealized corporatism of the papal encyclicals.

Planning—capitalist planning—there is. Perhaps for this reason, Japan is sometimes described as "in the neighborhood of capitalism" rather than as a capitalist economy. Japan's plans are drawn up not in MITI but in a small Economic Planning Agency (EPA) connected with the Finance Ministry (MOF). In drawing up its plans, EPA receives information and suggestions from other departments, including MITI and MOA, from business and agricultural organizations, and from anyone desirous of feeding his or her ideas into the hopper.

Japan's plans, both long-term and short-term, are purely indicative. In fact, Japan's plans are often imperfectly consistent with one another and

8. MITI is the acronym for the Ministry of International Trade and Industry in the Japanese government. Similarly, MOF is the Ministry of Finance, and MOA is the Ministry of Agriculture, Forestry, and Fisheries—two other important bureaucratic players in the political-economic game.

are often ignored. Nevertheless, the government is more likely to approve and assist projects consistent with these plans. As long as they operate within the plans and thus in accord with the public interest, the plans protect the larger Japanese companies against failure, forced cutbacks, or "excessive competition," especially competition from foreign companies and their Japanese affiliates.[9]

For companies planning overambitious expansion programs to increase their shares of Japanese and world markets, there may be "administrative guidance" against such rashness. If, on the other hand, supply shocks or world market conditions force a Japanese industry to cut back production, administrative guidance suggests the timing and allocation of the cuts with an eye to minimizing the pain and suffering involved and to preserving the competitive status quo among the leading firms of the industry. Administrative guidance has no legal force, but carries with it the veiled threat of unspecified government displeasure—selective enforcement of tax and antimonopoly laws, unfavorable consideration in government purchases, etc.—if it is violated too frequently or too brazenly. In some firms and on some issues, administrative guidance has the force of (unwritten) law. In other firms and other industries, it is a matter of little concern.

Japan's planning system is indicative. The plans serve mostly to protect the larger Japanese companies against failure, forced cutbacks, or excessive competition.

Productivity Another feature of the Japanese economy is its high and rising labor productivity. Even though the government plan allows for this high productivity, the planning for it is done only by individual companies, with the cooperation of the educational system, both public and private. Many male workers (but fewer females) are hired with the expectation that they will never be fired or laid off, but will be kept on until retirement or until the company goes out of business. For this reason, it pays the employer to invest heavily and continu-

ously in their on-the-job training and retraining. Neither workers nor their unions[10] object to technological progress. At the same time, "dead wood"—defined as people hard to train or to promote—is reduced by careful selection and training programs. The most successful companies limit their search to high-level graduates of "good" high schools and universities.[11] They investigate and interview even the brightest and most promising applicants in order to weed out troublemakers, deviants, militants, or even simple nonconformists. The successful candidates are then subjected to a period of "basic training," observation, and "socialization" by the company before they are accepted as permanent employees. Young men and women who do not make the grade may find work in less good firms, in a succession of temporary jobs, or in family businesses. As a result, unemployment has been a serious problem only for young people who have "dropped out" for a while, or for older workers whose employers have gone out of business.

Even though the government plan allows for Japan's high and rising labor productivity, the planning for it is done only by individual companies, with the cooperation of the educational system.

Reaction to Japan's Success The outstanding success of the Japanese economy and the high rate of measured Japanese growth since the end of the Korean War (1953) have inspired great interest in the West. At the same time, they have caused great envy and resentment, expressed in the form of restrictions on the export trade that Japan needs in order to buy both its food and nearly all of its industrial raw materials. Such restrictions have been strongest in the countries of the European Community. As anti-Japanese protectionism has spread to the United States and the Third World, Japan's

---

9. "Excessive competition" is an elastic term that appears to include any degree of competition that forces leading Japanese firms to cut their domestic prices, profit margins, scales of operation, or employment.

10. Japanese unions are enterprise and not craft unions. This means that a worker can be retrained in a different craft—a welder as a machinist, for example—without jurisdictional disputes between separate union locals.

11. Entrance examinations are required for Japanese high schools and universities, both public and private. A "good" high school or university is one whose entrance examinations are difficult, and which can reject a high percentage of applicants on academic grounds.

economy, its capitalism, and its indicative planning are all being severely tested. Japan remains a fragile economy, dependent on the good will of its suppliers and its customers.

The outstanding success of the Japanese economy since the end of the Korean War has inspired both interest and resentment in the West, and anti-Japanese protectionism has spread from the European Community to the United States and the Third World.

Sweden's Welfare State

Sweden is famous for its welfare-state institutions. The Social Democratic party has dominated Swedish politics since the Great Depression, and Sweden has had a flourishing consumer cooperative movement for many years. For these reasons, many non-Swedes believe Sweden to be a socialist country. It is not. The Swedish mixed economy remains largely capitalist, with certain features that are called "laboristic." That is, even though capital and land are privately owned, employees as well as stockholders must be represented on the boards of directors of large Swedish corporations, and corporate decisions are "co-determined" by labor and capital.[12] Swedish companies must share their profits with workers and are allowed to establish foreign branches or export capital to existing branches only with the consent of their workers in Sweden.

Elements of Swedish Planning   Most of Sweden's plans are indicative and short term. In a changing world, and particularly in a small country like Sweden, dependent on both foreign imports and foreign markets, it seems impractical to draw up comprehensive five-year plans. One-year plans are the standard practice. However, there are some long-term public works and housing projects as well.

A Swedish corporation does not have to pay corporate income tax on the part of its profits that it places in a special investment reserve. As a rule,

---

12. This co-determination system is not peculiar to Sweden. It is most highly developed in West Germany, and is common in Northern Europe.

---

funds in this reserve cannot be invested free of tax during boom periods when labor is in short supply, but can be invested tax free whenever unemployment exists or is threatened. Moreover, these investment reserves can be invested tax free only in those parts of Sweden where there is underemployment and surplus labor—often in the cold northern half of the country. If the United States were to follow this Swedish policy, the government would be guiding capital to the Snow Belt by offering tax privileges, rather than letting Snow Belt workers find their own way to the Sun Belt, where investment has been concentrated in recent years.

Swedish planning is also *consensual*. That is to say, the indicative plan targets must be acceptable to representatives of large and small business, labor, agriculture, finance, the public sector, and so on. Such major macroeconomic variables as the growth rates of money, credit, employment, labor productivity, and wage and price levels must also be agreed on. The same is true of changes in taxes and spending, as well as the means of financing deficits and surpluses. Even changes in imports, exports, capital movements, and the balance of payments position must be approved by consensus.

Sweden has a largely capitalist mixed economy characterized by many welfare-state institutions. Most Swedish plans are indicative and short term, and labor plays a large role in corporate decisions.

Problems of Swedish Planning   Two basic problems have developed in connection with Swedish planning and have given the economy an inflationary twist. The first has to do with forecasts. It is nearly always easier to reach a planning consensus under optimistic "first-best" assumptions, which let every interest group have most of what it wants, than under more cautious assumptions, whose results would disappoint some or all of the bargainers. For example, the forecast of a sharp rise in labor productivity plus ideal weather on the farms will permit larger wage increases, smaller price rises, and a more positive trade balance than will more realistic forecasts. In fact, "first-best" assumptions are very seldom justified. There may be droughts and floods, strikes and absenteeism,[13] oil shocks and foreign wars, tax evasions and welfare frauds. The public deficit, the volume of credit, and the money supply are the variables with most "give" when the first-best combination of circumstances does not come about, so that the inflation is generally greater than expected.

In mentioning strikes, we have already hinted at the second problem. Suppose that a general 5 percent rise in wage rates is accepted by the representative of the national labor federation. Further suppose that this rise keeps all wage differentials in place, in percentage terms. The problem is that no representative of any pressure group can speak for all the subgroups within it, particularly in the case of labor. It has happened that the workers with less skill or education or the workers in jobs hiring mainly the young, the elderly, or the female worker may demand that the traditional differentials be ended or reduced. However, if these demands are met and the differentials are reduced, the skilled workers and male family heads may press for the return of their advantage on grounds of custom, usage, and equity. This kind of whipsaw movement raises wage rates all around. The next step is a price rise. If consumers are not willing to pay higher prices, the government meets the resulting unemployment with unplanned transfer payments or unplanned public-service jobs financed by unplanned money and credit expansion along with higher-than-planned inflation rates, and so on.

Swedish planning has two basic flaws that lead to inflationary pressures: a bias in favor of "first-best" forecasts and a tendency toward inflation to deal with demands for higher wages.

The Meidner Plan The planned Swedish economy has remained largely capitalistic, but some elements of the socialist-dominated trade union movement and the Social Democratic party pro-

pose to turn it sharply in a collectivist direction. The labor economist Rudolf Meidner is author of a nonviolent but revolutionary proposal for bringing this change about.

The basic Meidner plan is simple. Corporate income taxation of large companies is increased. The revenues from the increased tax rates go to the trade unions.[14] The unions use these revenues to buy shares in Swedish corporations on the stock exchange. With this process repeated every year, the unions eventually own enough stock to control all the larger corporations of Sweden.[15] This result would be technically **syndicalist**, with the economy controlled by trade unions rather than by the government as under socialism. It is ordinarily called socialism, however.

The main arguments against the Meidner plan are the power it gives the trade-union leadership and the fear that union-controlled firms would try to maximize wage rates and employment, which might lead to featherbedding and low productivity. Such union-controlled companies may eventually need subsidies to keep going, may oppose labor-saving technological changes, and may fail in international competition with capitalist business. In addition, private saving is likely to fall, in which case investment would presumably be financed by still higher taxes, or by inflation.

To forestall such problems, the Meidner plan, at least the mild version adopted in 1984, shares control over the "workingman's funds" between union leaders and civil servants, the latter representing the interests of the nonunion public. Also, control is decentralized regionally, rather than being centralized in Stockholm.

The Meidner plan has brought some collectivist elements to Sweden's largely capitalist economy. The plan proposes gradually to bring the economy under the control of trade unions.

---

13. Swedish companies and unions have led the way in devising ingenious systems of job sharing and job rotation, aimed at motivating workers and reducing high absenteeism rates on Mondays and Fridays particularly. So far, these systems have not been notably successful.

14. *Not* to individual workers! Socialists fear that profit-sharing will turn workers into petty capitalists, and oppose it.

15. Were American unions to control pension funds, invest these funds in corporate stock, and vote that stock at stockholders' meetings, the United States too might become a country of "pension-fund socialism" (actually syndicalism).

MARKETS UNDER SOCIALISM: YUGOSLAVIA AND CHINA

The Yugoslav Case

Karl Marx's attempt to control the International Workingmen's Association (First International) was opposed by **anarchists**. Anarchists propose to abolish all forms of government compulsion. For example, they believe that compulsory collection of taxes is a form of robbery. Instead, they would like to have people join and contribute to small voluntary associations, which they could leave at any time, either to join some other group or to form new ones. These associations could themselves combine voluntarily to manage larger projects. The anarchists accused Marx and his followers of planning to substitute bureaucratic control for capitalistic ownership of the means of production. Such a change, they thought, was likely to make matters worse rather than to help the people.

Marshal Josip Broz Tito of Yugoslavia (1892–1980) was a Marxist and a communist, not an anarchist. Even while rebelling in 1948 against the spread of Soviet Stalinism to his own country, he kept his strong government under Yugoslav Communist party control. For the Yugoslav economy, however, Tito and his advisers downgraded central planning, substituting a system of *workers' self-management* that attracted a great deal of attention during Tito's lifetime but that has largely broken down since his death.

The Role of Workers' Collectives Yugoslavia is a socialist state where land and capital goods are publicly owned. However, many of these resources are leased to and operated by groups of workers at rentals set by the state. These workers' collectives or cooperatives decide their own inputs and outputs as well as their own membership of workers with various skills. They elect their own managers and set their own prices for the goods they produce. If they make any profits after taxes are paid, they may distribute them among their members as they wish (subject to the requirement that minimum "wages" be paid), or they may use them for such purposes as housing or environmental improvements. To a certain extent, they may even act as a bank and lend surplus funds to other groups.

Yugoslavia is a socialist state, but many of its resources are leased to and operated by groups of workers.

The Role of the Central Authorities Plenty is left for the central economic authorities of Yugoslavia to do, as well as for the authorities of the six republics that make up the country. They must enforce minimum income levels for participants in the cooperative firms. The authorities also make sure that new or younger people in these firms have equal shares in management and are not simply disguised employees of the older workers. They must judge the creditworthiness of the firms' requests for continued and expanded rentals of land and capital, and keep them from wasting these resources. When a new firm is either being set up "from scratch" or separating from an old one, the authorities must judge whether it should receive land and capital at all.

Failure of the Yugoslav System More than many other economic systems, the Yugoslav system developed disappointing weaknesses in practice, particularly after the death of Marshal Tito. It is now regarded as less a helpful model than a horrible example. We list seven of its principal weaknesses, many of which are more peculiar to Yugoslavia itself than to the Yugoslav economic experiment.

1. Yugoslavia is by no means the only socialist country beset by regional, linguistic, or religious conflicts. It is, however, one of the least successful in controlling them, especially after the passing of Marshal Tito's unifying influence. The Yugoslav (Southern Slav) state is a federation of six republics. Two of them, Croatia and Slovenia, were relatively developed under somewhat enlightened Austro-Hungarian rule well before World War I. The other four (Serbia, Montenegro, Macedonia, and Bosnia-Herzegovina) had suffered under Turkish rule during the long decay of the Ottoman Empire and had been involved in both civil and international warfare after Turkish rule ended. They were economically far behind the two leaders. Political power, however, was concentrated in Serbia, the most important of the economically backward republics. The Serbian-dominated central government, including its planning bureaucracy, concentrated resources on the backward areas even though these resources could have been used more productively in Croatia and Slovenia. The central government practiced regional redistribution in preference to economic growth, and achieved neither.

2. Marxian doctrine treats paper money as "fictitious capital." Consequently, many socialist governments pay little attention to its management. In Yugoslavia, the collectives managing the banks included representatives of the banks' debtors—collectives that had borrowed from the banks and that wanted more loans on easier terms in the future.[16] The banks' creditors—the depositors—did not have equal representation. Although Yugoslavia did not use inflation deliberately to ruin the rentier class, it soon had one of the highest inflation rates in Europe and has not been able to get it under control. In this respect, Yugoslavia is a claimant for the unenviable title of Europe's Brazil.

3. Labor-managed firms are sometimes run by a small minority of "labor aristocrats," usually skilled or white-collar workers, while the other members remain passive most of the time.

4. The Yugoslav Communist party has feared the creation, within the labor-managed firms, of an economic base for opposition political movements like the Polish Solidarity movement. The party has therefore encouraged its individual-enterprise "cells" to interfere in in-plant elections so as to win managements supportive of government policies. In such attempts, it has allegedly had the strong-arm support of the local and national police forces.

5. Once in place and flourishing, the more established Yugoslav firms have been able to use a good deal of political influence and monopolistic power to delay and limit the progress of rival firms and the opening up of Yugoslavia to foreign competition.

6. The labor-managed firm of the Yugoslav sort can be looked on as maximizing net income *per worker* rather than its total net income or profit. This puts the Yugoslav firm under pressure to use more capital and less labor than would a private company in a similar case. This is unfortunate in a country like Yugoslavia, which is capital-poor and labor-rich.[17]

7. Partly for the same reason—too much capital per worker—Yugoslavia seldom attains high employment in practice. To find jobs, Yugoslav workers have left the country in large numbers and become "guest workers" in other European countries.

The Yugoslav economic system developed several major weaknesses that have caused it largely to break down.

The Chinese Case

Mao Zedong, "Great Helmsman" of Chinese communism and author of a *Little Red Book* containing cryptic answers to all social problems, died in 1976. Chairman Mao's death set off a struggle between the so-called "Gang of Four," who were headed by his widow and faithful to his doctrines, and the so-called "Capitalist Roaders," headed by Deng Xiaoping (Deng-Hsiao-ping, 1904–   ), who proposed various "revisionist" reforms.

With almost no bloodshed, the capitalist roaders won, and Premier Deng proceeded with "four modernizations" of China's agriculture, economy, technology, and national defense. Progress since 1977 has been marked in the countryside—less so in the cities. To the foreign observer, the most interesting points include these four.

1. Drastic modification—which some call abolition—of Mao's communes. The state still owns all agricultural land, but now leases plots to indi-

---

16. The justification for such loan extensions is the **productive credit theory**—that if more credit to a firm (whether socialist or capitalist) is matched by a corresponding increase in the firm's output, the loan is not inflationary. This argument is fallacious, as is the theory on which it is based. If, after receiving more credit, the firm increases its output by bidding resources away from other firms, there is an output increase for the community only if the borrowing firm is more efficient than the other users of the resources. And even if the community output increases, the new money circulates more rapidly than the new goods, so that the net effect of the credit will be inflationary.

17. Maximizing company income per worker also leads to "wrong" reactions to product price changes—raising output when prices fall, and vice versa.

vidual families, which are no longer compelled to join collective farms or communes (although a great majority have chosen to remain members).

2. Breaking Mao's "iron rice bowl." Under Mao, full employment meant, in practice, the assignment of workers by batches of 50,000 or more to organizations that might or might not have any use for them. Also, managers and supervisors could not dismiss individual workers, so that laziness and absenteeism were prevalent. The worker's "rice bowl" (his or her income) was "iron," meaning it could not be broken or the worker dismissed. Workers are still assigned in batches and wages remain fixed, to the great disgust of foreign concerns used to "cherry-picking" individual workers by paying wages above the market level.

While full employment is still officially enforced, many young high school graduates spend months or even years waiting for their "work assignments." (Nobody is expected to look for a job in China.) To keep these people busy and out of trouble, they may be herded into "collectives," given some machinery and a little training, and let loose on society without wages or benefit guarantees. Some of the collectives, and their members, have been highly successful. Most, however, have not.

3. The one-child family. To reduce both present consumption and future "assignment problems," the Deng regime has imposed a stringent one-child policy on Chinese families. (Minority races are exempted, and pressure to conform seems to be looser in rural areas.) Families with two or more children are discriminated against in various ways, such as access to education and medical care. The program is allegedly voluntary, but there are many reports of compulsory abortion. Also, in a society that has traditionally undervalued its female members, the one-child family has led to neglect and even infanticides of sickly, defective, and girl babies to give the family another chance for a "good" (i.e., healthy male) child. The rigor of this policy is expected to be relaxed. It was adopted as a short-run expedient when the population of China ran to over a billion people.

4. Special economic zones. In a number of areas, many of them close to Hong Kong, foreign companies have been invited to set up shop and earn profits much as they would in a capitalist country. (Legal details are difficult to specify, however, since Communist China has neither a commercial code nor a governing body of case law.) The areas are expected to do two things: offer Chinese workers training in high technology and process both imported and Chinese raw materials for export. Initial reports indicate that production is mostly low-tech, that it is aimed at the Chinese internal market, and that the zones themselves threaten to become foci of "dangerous thoughts," "capitalist decadence," and other forms of sacrilege to the memory of the Great Helmsman.

"Special economic zones" have, at various times, been established in many Third World countries as aids to the country's international trade and financial position. A special financial zone has even been proposed for the United States, where participants might enjoy the protection of American law without the handicaps of American taxes and financial regulations. But nowhere else were "special economic zones" to play so large a part in the twentieth-century economic development of their host country.

Under Deng Xiaoping, China has made further reforms in its planned economy. Families are no longer compelled to join communes, changes are being made in the system of guaranteed full employment, a one-child policy has been adopted for the short term, and special economic zones for foreign industry have been established.

Aside from these special features, Chinese socialism appears to be evolving in ways less different from post-Stalin Soviet and European socialisms than is generally supposed. Like the U.S.S.R., but unlike Yugoslavia, China concentrates development in certain key areas—the Pacific Coast, the Yangtze Valley, and the Northeast (Manchuria)—leaving the rest of the country to catch up later. At the same time, the Chinese have achieved their first and greatest successes in agriculture, while the agricultural sector has remained thus far a weak spot in Gorbachev's *perestroika*. Like their European counterparts, the Chinese encountered serious inflation problems, which delayed the pace not only of price reform but of the entire reform process in the later 1980s. China's central bank, called the People's Bank of China, is assigned responsibility for the money supply and the price level, but its authority has not extended to the lavish credits granted by local governments and exports industries. The theory of *productive credit*, noted in our discussion of Yugoslavia, is popular in China, too. Were the People's Republic of China (P.R.C.) a small country instead of including nearly a quarter of the world's population—or were it still a Soviet dependency or satellite—Premier Deng's experiments would receive less attention than economists now accord them.

In mid-1989 there is much uncertainty concerning China's path or at least the speed with which she will continue to pursue economic reform. The 1989 student demonstrations for greater freedom and democracy, that ended in bloodshed and purges, have left questions concerning the ease with which past reforms can be carried out, new reforms instituted, and, possibly most important, the degree of willingness by foreign governments and firms (including U.S. firms) to do business with China.

THE THEORY OF MARKET SOCIALISM

Market socialism is an adaptation of the microeconomics of pure competition to a socialist system. Oskar Lange (1904–1965), born and educated in Poland, and Abba Lerner (1904–1982), born in Bessarabia and educated in Britain, were both socialists. After meeting in Britain in the 1930s, the two men continued their friendship in the United States.[18] Their views are not in complete agreement, but the term *market socialism* applies equally well to the work of either man.

Market socialism is an adaptation of the microeconomics of pure competition to a socialist system.

---

18. Lange, then a political refugee, later became Polish ambassador to the United States, Polish delegate to the United Nations, and finally vice president of Communist Poland after World War II—after disavowing many of the views that will concern us here.

How the System Works

The Lange-Lerner theory of market socialism reacts strongly against both the weakened capitalism of the Great Depression and the tough Stalinist planning methods of arbitrary pricing, imperative production quotas, and consumer rationing. Under the Lange-Lerner system, prices would be set by public authorities, but they would be changed when necessary to maintain approximate equilibrium between supply and demand for most products. Managers of firms would be civil servants, who need not depend on capitalists or on workers or on consumers. They would be required to operate industrial plants or large farms so as to keep the marginal cost of output about equal to output price at all times. Similarly, they would be required to keep the marginal revenue product of each input equal to the input price at all times. In the short run, profits would go to the state, with losses subsidized by the state (unless it was decided to shut the business down). In the long run, it was hoped that changes in the number and/or size of firms would reduce both profits and losses almost to zero.

Under the Lange-Lerner model of market socialism, prices would be set by public authorities, but they would be changed when necessary to maintain approximate equilibrium between supply and demand for most products. Managers of firms would be required to operate industrial plants and farms so as to keep the marginal cost of output about equal to output price at all times and to keep the marginal revenue product of each input equal to the input price at all times.

So far, this theory is just like that of pure competition, but with fuller and more reliable information available to both buyers and sellers of all goods and services. However, since the economy would be a socialist one, there would be no landlords and capitalists to claim the returns from land and capital, which would go instead to the state. The state would accept these returns in place of taxes and carry on the usual government activities including subsidies to businesses suffering losses. Whenever possible, the state would distribute what would otherwise be property income equally to all the people as a social dividend—so much for each person or for each family. If socialism could also sharply lower military spending, the social dividend would be far greater than transfer payments in any capitalist welfare state!

Of course, if the socialization process were undertaken within the rule of law, the socialist state would have a huge debt for buying the capitalists' properties. This burden might be expected to keep the social dividend very low over its first few generations.

Planning for the proportion of national income to be saved and invested would be left in the hands of a central planning agency. The agency could raise the investment rate, and most likely the rate of growth as well, by imposing higher taxes or lowering social dividend distributions, and using the extra funds for investment. Private saving and dissaving would be entirely legal, but at zero or very low rates of interest to keep a capitalist class from springing up.[19] Private investment in single-family housing would also be legal, with gains from resale or speculation taxed at high rates for the same reason: to keep capitalism from returning.

Criticisms of the Theory

Many questions about technique and procedure have been raised in criticism of the Lange-Lerner scheme of market socialism. How, in real life, would managers be chosen and assigned? What if they followed the rules but were lacking in "human relations" skills? How could one decide after the fact whether the rules had been followed without turning half the population into accountants, statisticians, or computer technologists?

Suppose, however, that it was determined that a manager had failed to equate marginal cost to output price, or marginal revenue product to input price. The problems would not be over. Was the differential avoidable, or had there been unforeseeable problems like machine breakdowns, worker illness, or delays in delivery of raw materials or parts? If the differential appeared both large and avoidable, was it a misdemeanor or a crime? Was it

just an honest mistake, or was it unlawful speculation that prices might change in the course of production? Was it an attempt to influence future prices by creating shortages or surpluses, after the fashion of a monopolistic firm or the members of a cartel?

Let us consider a hypothetical case from Lange-Lernerland. Sourpuss Smith and Jovial Jones are plant managers in Podunk. They are also rival candidates for promotion to a larger and more important plant in Megalopolis. Sourpuss Smith, a lightning calculator, has followed all the rules to the letter and the last decimal place. In doing so, he has come to be regarded as a holy terror by his subordinates. Morale and productivity in the Smith plant are low, and it is plagued by high labor turnover. Jovial Jones, on the other hand, plays fast and loose with the rules, some of which he is not smart enough to apply accurately. He hires "too many" workers, puts them into wage brackets that are "too high," turns out "too much" product, and fails to maximize returns. But productivity in the Jones plant is the pride of Podunk, so that costs are correspondingly low. Which manager should get the Megalopolis promotion?

This answer is easy by business standards under the rules of the capitalist game: Jones goes onward and upward to Megalopolis, and Smith goes back to Podunk or perhaps to a cost accountant's job. But it is not clear that this will happen under the Lange-Lerner rules.

From a socialist point of view, a more important social or philosophical question is raised by the whole process of market socialism, and by the Lange-Lerner variety in particular. Among other things, socialism aims at fostering the new socialist men and women, who subordinate their personal interests to the interests of the society as they have been taught to see them. Such persons demand fewer economic rewards, especially consumer goods and leisure time, than they would have demanded as individualists, and also supply more and better labor services. The Lange-Lerner men and women, however, remain essentially individualists in socialist clothing. To maximize their own utility, they demand what they want when they want it. They supply labor according to their own labor-leisure choices and are subject to dismissal if the value of their marginal revenue product falls below their wage rate. Such "selfish" individual-

19. At minimal interest rates, the demand for personal consumption loans (dissaving) might well exceed the supply (saving), creating a black market in consumer credit. As a control on such a market, loan contracts between private individuals could be made unenforceable at interest rates above the legal limit.

ism, relying on "economic" as against "moral" incentives, makes market socialism suspect in socialist eyes, particularly in the eyes of the advocates of socialist central planning.

Socialists distrust market socialism because it does not try to create men and women who subordinate their personal interests to the interests of society.

AUSTRIAN THEORY: PLANNING AS THE ROAD TO SERFDOM

Many writers take strong stands against planning, whether the planning is socialist or capitalist. They claim that pricing and resource allocation in a planned economy must be arbitrary and dictatorial, unless the planners adopt the international prices of the remaining market-economy countries. These writers argue that the processes of setting and enforcing arbitrary prices and wage rates lead to an increasingly serious loss of individual freedoms.

Many economists take strong stands against planning, whether socialist or capitalist. They argue that the processes of setting and enforcing arbitrary prices and wage rates lead to an increasingly serious loss of individual freedoms.

Three economists are well known for their views on this question—Friedrich von Hayek (1899–   ), Ludwig von Mises (1881–1973), and Joseph Schumpeter (1883–1950).[20] All three were born and educated in Austria, and their views are called "Austrian." None of the three ever lived under communist rule. However, it is interesting to note that many refugees from socialist or communist countries share the Austrian view of planning.

20. Schumpeter, unlike both Mises and Hayek, saw socialism and planning as inevitable consequences, like death and taxes, of capitalism and of the "treason" of intellectuals who have lost social status to business people. Schumpeter's vision of the socialist planned economy was also less grim than Hayek's serfdom or Mises' "planned chaos."

The Growth of Controls Under Planning

Four points, all made by Hayek, explain why he thinks planning leads to "serfdom." The first is that partial planning or control tends to grow in its extent and rigor, in order to keep people from dodging its rules. For example, one might ask: Why not simply control prices and wages in "essential" industries and jobs in order to check inflation and leave the rest of the economy free? The answer is that if the uncontrolled sectors are free to pay higher wages and make higher profits, labor and capital will move, unless restricted, away from essential to nonessential activities—from making work shirts to making sports shirts. One might also ask how civil liberties could be preserved while preventing capital from being taken out of a country where most of "the rich" distrust the economic plan. Hayek believes that people are clever about arranging "capital flights" by mail, by telephone, and by foreign travel, in underpriced exports, overpriced imports, and other fictitious deals. For this reason, mail and telephone censorship, as well as passport controls over people on "watch lists," would be essential to the enforcement of capital controls.

Arbitrary or Corrupt Bureaucracy

The second point that Hayek stresses is that, however detailed and comprehensive a plan may be, it cannot cover all the special cases that later arise under it. So a great deal of leeway must be left to administrative (bureaucratic) judgment. For example, if a Soviet citizen wants to repair or enlarge his or her house in a city where building materials are in short supply, the citizen must obtain two permits if the work is to be legally done. The person must convince one government official that his or her needs are great enough to obtain certain building materials. Once the materials are received, another official (possibly located at the other end of the city) must be convinced that he or she *has* these materials, and that they are adequate for the project. Such procedures allow plenty of opportunity for arbitrariness, which is our problem here, and also for corruption.

Propaganda and Suppression

According to Hayek's third point, morale is so important to the success of the plan that critics are often silenced. Official propaganda will of course sing the plan's praises and advertise its successes. The temptation is very great to suppress and punish any who spread pessimistic rumors about the plan and its feasibility, who forecast its failure in whole or in part, or who want the present plan scrapped in favor of another one—or in favor of the market. Under Soviet and Eastern European conditions, critics blame the plan's concentration on the "leading links" of heavy industry and military hardware for shortages of consumer goods and civilian housing. Prior to Gorbachev, at least, it was rare for such critics to be allowed open expression of their views, let alone access to the public, since the plan regulates the supply of paper, the programs of the schools, and the broadcast media, as well as the economy. Nevertheless, the misdeeds of particular incompetent, tyrannical, or corrupt bureaucrats or administrators are often exposed in official publications, and punished in official courts.

The Power Seekers

Finally, "the worst get on top," Hayek claims. This fourth and last point means that the would-be dictator, the corrupt grafter, and the envious or vindictive person is most likely to seek work in carrying out the daily and minor details of running and enforcing the plan. Such people are also very likely to call for extending the plan's authority over the remaining unplanned sectors of the economy.

The Austrian economist Friedrich von Hayek believes that partial planning tends to grow in extent and rigor in order to keep people from dodging its rules, that the system is prone to arbitrariness and corruption, that criticism is stifled, and that the system tends to be run by corrupt, power-hungry, vindictive people. In short, planning leads to "serfdom."

Criticism of the Theory

Many criticisms of the Austrian theory have been voiced. The simplest is the claim that the benefits of planning are worth its costs, and that the critics of planning are reactionaries who are destined for "the dust-bin of history." This approach is most effective where the market economy is associated with recent-past colonialism, backwardness, or dependency, and where there has been no experience with successful liberal democracy. In more advanced countries, however, it is argued that existing liberal or democratic traditions will be strong enough to keep the citizens from traveling the road to serfdom despite the problems Hayek sees. Furthermore, as in Sweden, dependence on foreign trade with countries that have market economies will limit the spread and the impact of arbitrary planning. One can even rely on institutions based on merit, such as schools, colleges, and civil service examinations, to lower the likelihood that the worst will get on top.

Perhaps the most effective anti-Austrian argument is that serfdom does not have to be the end of the road. One can gain comfort from the experience of the U.S.S.R., Poland, Hungary, and Yugoslavia in backing away from the extremes of Stalinism after Stalin's death in 1953; and from the experience of the Chinese People's Republic in reversing the Maoist "cultural revolution" after Mao Zedong's death in 1976. But optimism must be tempered by experience. Gorbachev's liberalization efforts face stiff opposition. The Chinese government's bloody suppression of the prodemocracy movement may stifle criticism for a long time.

Economics in Focus

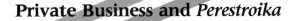

Private Business and *Perestroika*

Perestroika, Mikhail Gorbachev's program of economic restructuring, has permitted more private business in the Soviet Union. Known as "cooperatives," the new private companies are intended to improve consumer products and services, bring the underground economy above ground, and give budding entrepreneurs a chance to exercise their creativity. The Wheel cooperative in Michurinsk, for example, makes auto parts in a factory that was formerly notorious for its organized crime ring. After the plant was leased to the *kooperativshchiki,* output tripled and theft declined. Long-time observers of the Soviet economy considered this a minor miracle.

Between 1987 and June 1989, more than 100,000 cooperatives were founded, and their employment mushroomed to 2.7 million workers, over 2 percent of the Soviet labor pool. If the trend continues, the cooperatives will become a major force in the Soviet economy. Their areas of business include manufacturing, engineering, management consulting, and tourism. Not content with the domestic trade, some are pursuing foreign markets as avidly as Western capitalists.

Nevertheless, the Soviet Union's black market—which the cooperatives should supposedly replace—continues to flourish. Well over three-quarters of Soviet citizens use the black market when they cannot find the goods they need in state-run stores. For years Gorbachev's predecessors allowed the underground economy to prosper, and observers believe that hundreds of illegal factories dot the countryside. According to one estimate, as many as 20 million people worked in black-market activities in 1989, a number that dwarfed the infant cooperative movement. As consumers, Soviet citizens complain about high prices charged by cooperatives, but they freely buy at even higher prices from underground merchants.

In competing with the black market, cooperatives face a certain distrust simply because they bear the government's stamp of approval. Furthermore, rumors circulate about racketeering in the cooperatives: extortion, robbery, money laundering, and the like. In fact, since many cooperatives depend on the willingness of central planners to allocate raw materials and equipment, the potential for corruption is obvious. Some Soviets assert that in spite of Gorbachev's stern anticorruption campaign, the black marketers have bribed bureaucrats to keep goods away from the cooperatives. In such a climate of suspicion, many would rather deal with the old evil they know than the new evil they suspect.

In a country where blue jeans can sell for the equivalent of three weeks' pay, the free market's potential seems golden. Yet the change to free-market practices requires a revolution in industrial methods, in bureaucratic operations, and in the entire society's way of thinking. As the Soviets are well aware, revolutions do not come easily.

Sources: Peter Galuszka, "The Paradox of *Perestroika:* A Raging Black Market," *Business Week,* June 5, 1989, pp. 66, 70; Richard I. Kirkland, Jr., "Why Russia Is Still in the Red," *Fortune,* January 30, 1989, pp. 173–175; John Kohan and Yuri Shchekochikhin, "Tambov: *Perestroika* in the Provinces," *Time,* April 10, 1989, pp. 86–92.

SUMMARY

1. The controversy between advocates of market and planned economic systems is a heated one, even though all existing economies are mixed systems. The distinction between the two types of systems is a useful one. (See pages 501–502.)

2. Every person or organization plans for itself. However, we speak of an economy as being planned only when a central planning body (public, private, or mixed) makes plans that dominate those of the individual persons, firms, or industries that make up the economy. (See page 502.)

3. A market economy is more likely to be capitalist than is a planned one. A planned economy is more likely to be collectivist than an unplanned one. (See pages 502–503.)

4. Planning and collectivism are not the same thing, any more than capitalism and a market system are the same. Furthermore, neither planning nor collectivism should be confused with the welfare state. Any economic system that places high value on a high poverty line and on lowering inequality in the distribution of income and wealth may be called a welfare state. (See pages 503–504.)

5. Planning is of different sorts. We distinguish imperative, indicative, public sector, macroeconomic, and magic wand planning. We do not consider statistical projections of past trends to be plans at all, unless they are combined with measures to see that these trends continue. (See pages 504–505.)

6. The Soviet Union under Stalinist rule has been the most important example of imperative planning under socialist collectivism. Planning was highly centralized in a single agency called Gosplan, using the techniques of materials balancing and input-output analysis. Since 1985, General Secretary Mikhail Gorbachev has been engaged in a process called *perestroika*, aimed at decentralizing the planning process and increasing the scope of economic incentives in individual decision-making. (See pages 506–510.)

7. The United States has a large public sector and so has more public-sector planning than is generally realized. Proposals for more comprehensive planning in the United States were made during the years of the Great Depression (for example,

the National Recovery Administration), during both world wars, and more recently in the original Humphrey-Hawkins bill. (See page 510.)

8. Japan and Sweden are widely differing examples of economic planning within a capitalist framework. In the Japanese case, sometimes called "Japan, Inc.," the principal planners come from big business, agriculture, and the public bureaucracy. In Sweden, labor also participates in the planning, and the government is dominated by the Social Democratic party. (See pages 511–514.)

9. Yugoslavia is a socialist country with a substantial degree of workers' management supplementing or even replacing its central plan. (See pages 515–516.)

10. China, under the leadership of Deng Xiaoping, has moved ever further from the Soviet planning model. Agricultural collectivization is now voluntary. The "iron rice bowl" variety of full employment is in the process of being eliminated. Foreign techniques and management methods are permitted to foreign firms in special economic zones. Prices and wages, however, remain fixed, and the government continues to own land and capital goods. (See pages 517–518.)

11. The Lange-Lerner scheme of market socialism attempts to combine the advantages of market and planned economies in a somewhat utopian socialist model. (See pages 518–520.)

12. A number of writers, chiefly Austrian, hold that planning, once undertaken under either capitalism or socialism, tends to increase in both importance and arbitrariness over time. They expect planning to end in a servile state, which Hayek has called "serfdom," with few individual freedoms and civil rights remaining. Some writers of the "Austrian school" believe that there is little hope of preserving the market economy and avoiding "serfdom," but others are more optimistic. (See pages 520–521.)

KEY TERMS

anarchist: one who proposes to abolish all forms of government compulsion (page 515).

capitalistic economies: economies in which land and physical capital are owned largely by private individuals or business firms (page 504).

collectivist economies: economies in which land and physical capital such as buildings and machinery are largely or completely owned by collective agencies (page 503).

communist: a socialist who believes that socialism on a world scale will lead to an economy of abundance and who accepts violence, revolution, and dictatorship as a means to that end (page 504).

corporate society: a society organized to preserve capitalist private ownership of the means of production but that reserves large regulatory powers for the state (page 511).

Gosplan: the Soviet agency in charge of planning the economy in the U.S.S.R. (page 506).

imperative planning: a form of economic planning that must be followed; failure to reach an important plan target is considered a criminal offense (page 504).

indicative planning: a form of economic planning that operates mainly by convincing plan participants that following the plan will help them economically (page 505).

input-output analysis: an integrated analysis for an entire economy focusing on organizing information about the relationships between resources used in production and the goods and services produced (page 506).

leading links: a feature of the Soviet planning system whereby, when the whole plan cannot be carried out, certain leading links (usually military hardware and capital goods) are completed in full, and the rest of the plan is postponed in part until the next planning period (page 508).

Libermanism: an early attempt to reform Soviet planning (page 508).

macroeconomic planning: a form of economic planning that covers gross national product, the division between consumption, investment, and government sectors, the supplies of money and credit, the government surplus or deficit, international balances, and interest rates (page 505).

"magic wand" planning: a form of economic planning built around a collection of projects and/or an appealing slogan (page 505).

market socialism: a theoretical adaptation of the microeconomics of pure competition to a socialist system (page 518).

materials balancing: a technique used to coordinate the Soviet planning system; for every one of the thousands of final and intermediate products, potential supplies and demands are estimated for each year of the plan, allowing for both domestic production and international trade (page 506).

perestroika: restructuring; reforms of the Soviet planning system that include a wider scope for an unplanned economy, more flexible plans, and more leeway for plant managers (page 506).

planning: an institutional arrangement in which some individual or organization in a public position plans for another individual or organization, who or which has little say about the plan and whose economic freedom is restricted by the planning decision (page 502).

productive credit theory: a theory that states that if more credit to a firm is matched by a corresponding increase in the firm's output, the loan is not inflationary (page 516).

public sector planning: economic planning that covers only the public sector (page 505).

socialist economies: economies in which government agencies own the land and physical capital (page 503).

syndicalist: an economy controlled by trade unions (page 514).

welfare state: an economy that places an especially high value on equitable distribution of income and wealth and security of living standards (page 504).

DISCUSSION QUESTIONS

1. Jonathan Swift (1667–1745) is best known as the author of *Gulliver's Travels* and is considered the greatest satirist in the English language. His works include a *Modest Proposal for Preventing the Children of Poor People from Being a Burden to Their Parents or the Country.* (They are to be fattened, and then sold for food to the rich.)

Suppose that one were to believe seriously—as Swift did not—in exporting fattened babies from overpopulated poor countries for food in rich countries as part of a development plan for the poor countries. Should such a person be allowed to propagate his or her "outrageous" opinions? Suppose that this person were an organic chemist; should he or she be permitted to teach organic chemistry? If his or her specialty were development economics, what would your answer be? Suppose that this person were already teaching development economics before being converted to cannibalism, should he or she be forbidden to continue teaching in this field? Finally, are your answers to the four preceding parts of this question logically consistent with one another?

2. The Swedish economist Knut Wicksell was prosecuted and imprisoned, at the turn of the century, for propagating certain radical ideas, including contraception and the disestablishment of the state church. (One of his major works, *Interest and Prices*, was finished in prison.) When his jail term was over, Wicksell returned to his teaching at the University of Lund. Some years later, the American economist Scott Nearing, a socialist and pacifist, advocated strict neutrality in World War I and opposed "preparedness." He was not prosecuted, but his contract (at the University of Pennsylvania) was not renewed, and he could obtain no other teaching post. Did the Swedish or American system impinge more harshly on freedom of expression?

3. Distinguish among collectivism, socialism, and communism.

4. Can a market-capitalist economy also be a welfare state? Explain.

5. Briefly distinguish among imperative planning, indicative planning, public sector planning, and macroeconomic planning. Which, if any, of these are used in the United States?

6. Distinguish between materials balancing and input-output analysis as tools for economic planning.

7. What is *perestroika?* Assess the chances of its success in raising the living standards of the Soviet people.

8. Describe the important features of the Japanese economic system that have contributed to Japanese economic growth. Do you believe that similar arrangements would be workable and desirable for the United States?

9. Briefly summarize the Meidner plan. Do you believe that it is a feasible alternative to socialist revolution? Explain.

10. Market-socialism proposals, such as those of Lange and Lerner, are usually proposed for societies in which all production processes are already known. How would an innovation (a new product or process) be introduced under market socialism? (In your answer, assume that there are no other economies from which to copy.)

24
Radical Economics

Preview

This chapter goes beyond economics as usually conceived. It deals with questions that political scientists, sociologists, or psychologists handle more fully and expertly than economists do. We begin by discussing the dissatisfactions that many people (not only radicals) feel with market-capitalist institutions as they exist in North America. Rather than arguing about the justice of this indictment, we go on to outline the social theory that is used by the radical Left in advocating the overthrow of capitalism. Marxian economics is a very important part of this theory. As further "background," we note certain characteristics that distinguish the radical from the reformist critic of market-capitalism.

In the second half of the chapter, we look at contemporary radical movements, primarily but not only on the political Left. First we take up the so-called New Left, which has itself become divided into a number of groups—some socialist, some anarchist, and some syndicalist. Then we consider the radical Right, which may be descended from what is called Social Darwinism—the doctrine of "survival of the fittest" among social groups and institutions.

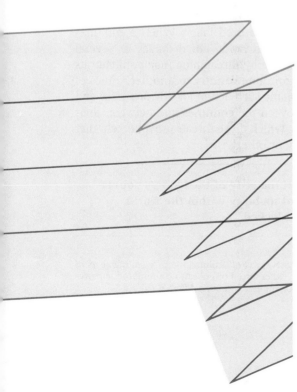

INDICTMENTS OF CAPITALISM

In the eyes of its critics, capitalism is "the root of all (social) evil." To many people, some of the indictments seem far-fetched, or related to industrialization under any economic system. Nevertheless, we offer a sweeping picture of the indictment, to show the scope and intensity of radical views. At the beginning of the book, we singled out six criteria for judging economic systems and for preferring one system to another.[1] In none of these does market-capitalism represent any utopian ideal.

With discontent about every point, we single out three criteria among our six, since they seem to have caused the greatest amount and intensity of discontent. These are:

1. The alleged maldistribution of income and wealth, both within and between individual countries.

2. The alleged insecurity of the standard of living already achieved against downward pressure, both short run and long run.

3. The alleged incompatibility of the system with full physical and mental health.

Criticism of capitalism centers around three points: (1) inequality of the distribution of income and wealth, (2) insecurity of the standard of living against downward pressure, and (3) incompatibility of the system with physical and mental health.

Maldistribution

It is no secret that the distribution of income is unequal both within and between individual countries, that people at the bottom of the income and wealth distributions are living in poverty, that "it takes money to make money," and that in many fields of economic activity "nice guys finish last." For the great majority of the world's population, upward mobility within the world economy is blocked, except by rules and on terms set by those already at the top. A low-wage country's rise to affluence may be blocked if it can no longer use the cheapness of its labor as a competitive advantage because the access of its goods to affluent markets is blocked by protectionism. When its workers cannot migrate to high-wage areas, the country's rise is limited to methods more acceptable to those who are already affluent. One route may be receiving aid on terms set by the givers. Others may include a more restrictive population policy, or more reliance than the low-wage country desires on unskilled hand labor in agriculture and mining.

Within a country like the United States, the question is the *terms* on which blacks or other minorities can rise. When black people's chances of becoming wealthy depend largely, as is alleged, on following white people's rules, the economically successful blacks are not, to put it mildly, objects of admiration within the black community itself. For this reason, their chances of advancement are much less in fact than they are in the statistics.[2]

To some extent, inequality is based on prejudice—race, gender, religion, language, and so forth. Capitalism and the capitalists are blamed for fostering such prejudices to keep workers or farmers disunited, reducing both their economic and their political power. When blacks came north or were brought north during and after World War I to break strikes or to forestall them, one result was an outbreak of race riots, and another was a weakening of organized labor. When a multinational corporation holds down wages in several countries at once by threatening major shifts of its operations from one country to another, critics of capitalism blame such action for any prejudice and hostility between the countries and between their populations, which those threats provoke, whether intentionally or otherwise.

For the great majority of the world's population, upward mobility within the world economy is blocked.

---

1. See Chapter 1.

2. Anthropologists speak of "cultural rape" when members of one culture are either forced or bribed to conform to the mores and standards of another and quite different culture.

Insecurity

Under capitalism, mass living standards are supposedly under constant pressure, both from the short-term shocks associated with business-cycle declines and from the long-run shocks associated with chronic inflation, technological change, pollution, resource exhaustion, warfare, and so on. "Hoovervilles," which were shantytowns for the unemployed in flood plains and city dumps, are among the best-remembered pictures of the Great American Depression of the 1930s.

On the individual level, there are different kinds of threats to the living standards of certain people, especially the aged or otherwise immobile. One such threat is inflation, a device to which capitalism has often turned for recovery from recessions and depressions. Capitalism is also blamed for technical change, symbolized by automation and robotization, which throws some people out of work at the same time that it provides opportunities for others. Pollution is a third living standard threat blamed on capitalism and population growth. Pollution has turned fields and forests into lunar landscapes, and rivers and streams into open sewers. Also, its health effects may become apparent only after many years, often in the form of cancer. A fourth threat is resource exhaustion, which turns prosperous lumbering, mining, and oil-well communities into ghost towns, and fertile farmland into desert. And finally, there is war, the supreme pollutant, now associated with genocide, nuclear holocaust, and the possible extermination of humanity.

In all of these cases, capitalism is blamed for failure either to prevent the catastrophes or to provide adequate "safety nets" to those who are injured. In every case, market capitalism and the urge for short-term profits are blamed for causing or at least accelerating the catastrophe and for allowing too little time for adjustments to be made.

Capitalism is indicted on the grounds that mass living standards are under constant pressure, both from the short-term shocks associated with business-cycle declines and from the long-run shocks associated with chronic inflation, techno-

---

logical change, pollution, resource exhaustion, and warfare.

Alienation

The characteristic psychological ailment of capitalism—and also of any other social system in which one or another social class or group dominates or exploits the rest of the society—is called **alienation**. This ailment is most serious among the victimized classes, races, or other social groups. However, a "guilty conscience" can also lead to alienation in the upper classes.

When one feels always hostile or indifferent to someone or something that people in one's society generally consider attractive, one is said to be "alienated" from that person or thing. Alienation may appear in many different forms. The victim may actively hate himself or herself, or be bored to the point of disgust, not with "the real me," but with the self as "processed" by advertising, propaganda, television, or the school system. Or one's feelings of alienation may focus on a "dull" or "commonplace" family, a "meaningless" or "dehumanizing" job, a "hopeless" future, a "drab" community, a society "rotten to the core."

The sufferer from alienation may just become sleepy, lazy, and vaguely depressed. In more acute cases, he or she may take refuge in overeating or starving, in overconsumption or oversaving, in drink or drugs or sex, in "dropping out" of mainstream society, or even in suicide. Alienation may also lead to violent or criminal behavior, even to terrorism and mass murder.[3]

While admitting or even insisting that criminal behavior be punished, critics of capitalism believe that an exploitative society is, in the last analysis, responsible for the actions of those whom it alienates. They protest against "blaming the victim," meaning the criminal, whom they see as being hurt by the society.

3. The Jonestown colony of Guyana had both an alienated leader and an alienated population when it exploded in 1978. Many leaders and members of the Nazi party were alienated both by the Germany of the Weimar Republic, which followed World War I, and the whole "Jazz Age" civilization of the 1920s.

Here is a single extreme case:

CAMBRIDGE—A former Polaroid Corp. engineer who attacked his wife and child with an ice pick won a $1.9 million out-of-court settlement from Polaroid, claiming that the company was negligent in treating the depression that led to his assault.

Lawrence L. Okerblom, Jr., his wife and son, will receive the money in monthly payments for at least 25 years. Most of the money will go to the son, who was brain-damaged and lost much of his vision in the attack.

After attacking his family, Mr. Okerblom tried to kill himself. The family split up after the incident.

In the suit filed in 1974, Mr. Okerblom said that a Polaroid doctor and counselor were negligent in treating his anxiety. Mr. Okerblom was in a "psychotic state" because he feared Polaroid was about to fire him, his lawyer said. The Polaroid doctor and counselor didn't take Mr. Okerblom's symptoms seriously and didn't prescribe the proper treatment, the attorney said. Polaroid officials weren't available for comment.[4]

Both the "insecurity" and the "alienation" aspects of this case are obvious and interrelated. There is, of course, also a "maldistribution" aspect. Do you think the settlement was unreasonably high or low, given the circumstances? Was Polaroid exploiting Mr. Okerblom, or was Mr. Okerblom exploiting Polaroid? If similar cases had arisen among lower-ranking blue-collar workers, do you think they would have been handled in the same way?

Alienation—a feeling of continual hostility or indifference toward something or someone that people in one's society generally consider attractive—is the characteristic psychological ailment of capitalism.

---

4. Abridged from *The Wall Street Journal*, March 10, 1983. Reprinted by permission of *The Wall Street Journal*, © Dow Jones & Company, Inc. 1983. All rights reserved worldwide.

SOME MARXIAN PROPOSITIONS

In North America leftist critics of market capitalism may not think of themselves as Marxists, and have never read much of Marx's writings. Nevertheless, they have almost certainly been influenced indirectly by some of Marx's ideas.

Karl Marx (1818–1883), a German philosopher and economist of Jewish descent, lived the last thirty-five years of his life as a refugee in London. He was both capitalism's greatest critic and socialism's greatest prophet. He may also have been the greatest overall secular (nonreligious) social scientist who has yet lived. He made important contributions not only to economics but to the other social sciences as well, including history and philosophy.

It is an injustice to Marx, and likewise to his great coworker Friedrich Engels (1820–1895), to compress their whole system into a small set of propositions, which is all we can do here. These propositions are eight in number. Although we have tried to ensure that they are distilled accurately from the writings of Marx and Engels, none is a direct quotation.

1. Natural science and technology have advanced to the point where, in a well-run world, all basic goods and services can be made free to all, the economy of abundance can be realized, and the profession of economist can become obsolete.[5]

2. The history of past societies has shown that nearly all surplus production, above some minimal subsistence level, has been appropriated by the social class that owns strategic inputs or factors of production. At successive stages of history, these strategic inputs have been raw physical labor (in slave societies), farmland and mines (in feudal societies), and industrial plant and equipment (in capitalist societies). At every stage, membership in the ruling class has been largely hereditary.

5. In the late twentieth century this seems an extravagant conclusion to have drawn a century earlier. But Marx and Engels were both greatly impressed by the technical achievements of the Industrial Revolution in England, then in full swing—as well as with its seamy side, which inspired much of their anticapitalism.

3. The exclusion of the main body of a society from the bulk of that society's economic surplus is called **exploitation**. Because of their exploitation and their resentment of it, members of exploited classes often become alienated from the society, from their work, from each other, and even from themselves. That alienation leads to crime and other ills, which societies blame on the victims of alienation rather than on the exploiting institutions that have brought about the alienation.

4. The governmental, educational, religious, and other noneconomic institutions of society generally support and legalize the interests of its ruling class. At the same time, they seek to suppress the hostilities of the exploited and the alienated. Examples are "pie in the sky when you die" religion, relief systems that "regulate the poor," judicial systems too costly for the average person, representative governments with voters' choices limited to candidates who supply or attract large-scale campaign financing, and so on. The list is long and scandals under each head are, to the Marxist, more than just scandals. Rather, they are the way the system works.

5. What is important in history is the record of conflict between one exploiting class and its successor, or between the exploiters and the exploited. This is the meaning of the Marxist statement that "history is the record of class struggles." As in proposition 4, certain excesses and outrages on both sides are more than scandals. They are the way the system has worked, with war and violent revolution as integral parts of the whole process.

6. Whereas Adam Smith called the market-capitalist economy "the obvious and simple system of natural liberty," Marxists think of it as just another exploitative regime. True, it has accomplished great things—which Marx and Engels took great pains to recognize in their *Communist Manifesto* of 1848—but it harbors within itself class conflicts and "contradictions," which will lead ultimately to its collapse. The *economic* aspects of Marxism enter into the demonstration of this proposition. We shall outline them in the next part of this chapter.

7. The revolution that overthrows capitalism will involve the whole exploited underclass, the workers or **proletariat**. When the proletariat comes to power, it will own the means of production through a government that it controls. This is the regime of socialism, in which there will be no class left to be exploited because all the means of production will be owned by society as a whole.[6]

8. In a relatively few years after the firm establishment of socialism in the major countries of the world, there will emerge **New Socialist Man and Woman**. Such persons will willingly work harder and more skillfully than anyone in the past. As Leon Trotsky (1879–1940) put it, the average man or woman will rise to the level of "an Aristotle, a Hegel, or a Marx." At the same time, the New Socialist Man or Woman will demand less from society in terms of wealth or the consumption of luxuries. A few generations will be enough to bring on the economy of abundance and to overcome scarcity. With no scarcity or class conflict, the repressive political state can and will wither away.

The main tenets of Marxian thought include the propositions that members of exploited classes often become alienated, that this alienation leads to crime and other social ills, that the governmental, educational, and religious institutions of society generally support and legalize the interests of its ruling class, that a proletariat revolution will eventually overthrow capitalism, that all the means of production will then be owned by society as a whole, and that under socialism a new socialist man and woman will appear.

Marxian Economics: The Statics

Marxian economics is most easily explained in macroeconomic terms, though Marx himself set it out microeconomically. We shall begin with the statics of how the capitalist economy operates and

---

6. But *ownership* need not be *control*, and anti-Marxists see Marxian socialism as a regime controlled by a "new class" of military and civilian bureaucrats and administrators, with the rest of society exploited much as the proletariat is exploited under capitalism.

then go to the dynamics of how it changes through time. Remember that Marx was analyzing market capitalism as he saw it. (Marxian economic analysis deals with capitalism and not with socialism.)

The macroeconomic formulation of Marx's theory uses W to represent the national income, evaluated in hours of labor. This W is divided into three parts, also expressed in labor hours. These are constant capital (C), variable capital (V), and surplus value (S). Therefore,

$$W = C + V + S$$

Constant Capital Of total labor input (W per period), **constant capital** (C) is the number of labor hours embodied in (used to produce) raw materials and in the depreciation of machinery and other long-lived capital goods. Marxian constant capital is not the same as the "fixed capital" of conventional accounting.

Variable Capital Nor is V the "variable capital" of conventional accounting. **Variable capital** represents hours of direct labor—mainly blue-collar labor, but also the "productive" portions of white-collar labor[7]—but not all those hours! Suppose that you work a 40-hour week on an assembly line but that your week's wages will buy only 30 hours of others' labor as embodied in food, clothing, and other consumption goods. In that case, your 40 hours of labor will represent only 30 hours of variable capital, the Marxian V.

Surplus Value But what of the other 10 hours of your labor? Marx does not forget them, but calls them "surplus" labor. The value of the surplus labor is retained by the employer. Out of it is paid all kinds of property income—interest, rent, and profits—and also the "unproductive" portion of white-collar labor (including, for example, doctors, lawyers, soldiers, bureaucrats, and teachers as pre-

dominantly dependents, or hangers-on of the capitalist class). Surplus labor is, in the case of your work on the assembly line, your personal contribution to total **surplus value** or S.

How large is this surplus value, in relation to the total of variable capital? In this microeconomic case, it is $10/30$ or $1/3$. In an aggregate economy with $C = 5,000$, $V = 3,000$, $S = 1,000$, W would equal their sum, or 9,000, and the ratio S/V would again equal $1/3$. In many of the numerical illustrations in his *Capital*, Marx himself sets this ratio equal to one. However, Marxists believe that in the United States today it is actually above one and tending to rise over time, at least in periods of prosperity.

The ratio S/V or S' is called the **rate of surplus value**, or sometimes the **exploitation rate**. It represents the contribution of each hour of variable capital to the total of surplus value. It is important in Marxian economic analysis, as you will see.

S/V, the rate of surplus value (the exploitation rate), is the amount of labor-produced value retained by the employer divided by the amount of labor-produced value received by the worker. All value is labor-produced.

Profit The Marxian concept of profit comprises all surplus value, including the wages and salaries of unproductive labor. This concept of profit is clearly more inclusive than the "net income" of either conventional economics or conventional accounting.

The Marxian concept of profit comprises all surplus value, including the wages and salaries of unproductive labor.

To compute a rate of profit, which Marx calls P', we divide total surplus value S by total capital, defined as $C + V$. The result is: $P' = S/(C+V)$.

If we divide both numerator and denominator of this expression by variable capital V, the numerator becomes, by definition, the exploitation rate S/V, which Marx called S'. In the denominator, dividing by V gives us $C/V + V/V$ or $C/V + 1$. Marx used the term **organic composition of capital** for the

---

7. The distinction between "productive" and "unproductive" labor is very difficult in all economic theories that, like the Marxian, make such a distinction. For an elaborate explanation of the issues from a Marxian viewpoint and with careful attention to Marx's own statements, see David Laibman, "Unproductive Labor: Critique of a Concept," in William L. Rowe, editor, *Studies in Labor Theory and Practice* (Minneapolis: Marxist International Press, 1982).

ratio between constant capital (raw materials plus depreciation) and variable capital (direct labor, as described above). Calling this ratio k, Marx's formula for profit becomes

$$P' = \frac{S'}{1 + k}$$

In terms of our figures for an aggregate economy if $C = 5,000$, $V = 3,000$, and $S = 1,000$, the organic composition of capital k becomes $5,000/3,000$ or $5/3$, and the exploitation rate S' is $1/3$. This makes the profit rate equal to

$$P' = \frac{1/3}{1 + 5/3} = \frac{1/3}{3/3 + 5/3} = \frac{1}{8}$$

The organic composition of capital is the ratio between constant capital (raw materials plus depreciation) and variable capital (direct labor).

Marxian Economics: The Dynamics

Then Marx goes on to investigate "the laws of motion of capitalism." The main purpose of all his apparatus was dynamic. As he moves from economic statics to economic dynamics, Marx uses the last equation. He argues that the organic composition of capital k (like the static capital-labor ratio) tends to rise over time. It rises because, in the absence of war or of natural catastrophe, the capital stock generally grows at a faster rate than does the labor force or employment, and also because innovations tend to be motivated to save direct labor costs more than to save capital costs. That is, they are more likely to be labor-saving than capital-saving.[8] As capitalism progresses and capital is accumulated, the rising trend of k means that the profit

rate P' must fall, that the exploitation rate S' must rise, or most commonly both.

Marx argued that the organic composition of capital tends to rise over time because the capital stock generally grows at a faster rate than does the labor force or employment and also because innovations tend to save direct labor costs more than capital costs.

Falling Rate of Profit At some point, however, either of the above developments will be disastrous for capitalism. If the rate of profit falls below a certain level, capitalists will no longer find it worthwhile to invest much more than the amount needed to replace fixed capital as it wears out. Marx thought that capitalists would not raise their consumption very much but would try to hoard money, real estate, "collectibles," or other goods not currently being produced. In this way, they would in turn lower the equilibrium level of national output and raise the unemployment rate. Increasing unemployment is one form of what Marxists call the "increasing misery" of the working class, which they see as the consequence of capitalism as it matures.

Marx predicted long-term stagnation for capitalism, with short business-cycle booms and long business-cycle depressions and with a rising rate of measured unemployment. In Marxian literature this is called a **liquidity crisis**. If wages were raised in relation to prices to maintain mass purchasing power, the liquidity crisis would only be intensified, since the rate of profit would fall even lower. Falling-rate-of-profit arguments are used by Marxists against liberal reformers and trade unionists who propose to save capitalism by income-redistribution measures.

Marx foresaw increasing unemployment as the consequence of maturing capitalism. He predicted a liquidity crisis—long-term stagnation, with short business-cycle booms and long business-cycle depressions, along with rising unemployment.

---

8. Notions of class warfare are not required to explain the tendency of innovations to be labor-saving rather than capital-saving. A sufficient explanation is that labor costs (primarily payrolls) are a larger part of production costs than are capital charges, so that a 1 percent saving of labor costs is worth more than a 1 percent saving of capital charges. In contemporary North America, a 1 percent saving of labor cost is worth approximately as much as a 2.5 percent saving of capital charges.

Tendency to Overproduction Suppose that capitalists form cartels to keep profit rates up or even raise them, in spite of the rising organic composition of the capital. Marxists answer that such moves cause prices to rise in relation to wages and cause the exploitation rate S' to rise, and that the capitalists will not find buyers for the goods produced. As the exploitation rate rises, a falling proportion of the labor force is needed to produce the output that the masses can still buy. Again there is rising unemployment and increasing misery, even though the profit rate remains high. Such a development is called a **realization crisis**. This argument is used by Marxists to answer the conservatives who would call for "self-government in business," as well as for wage cutting, union busting, and similar cures for business recessions and depressions.

As the exploitation rate rises, a falling proportion of the labor force is needed to produce the output the masses can still buy. This is called a realization crisis.

In closing this section, we make three final points. First, Marx's *Capital* is about capitalism, and it has little to say about how a socialist system would manage the problems that capitalism allegedly mismanages. Second, Marx's labor theory of value builds on the classical theories of Smith and Ricardo and does not deal with demand and utility as determinants of value. Finally, the Marxian analysis leaves no major role for government fiscal or monetary policy. In Marx's day, these instruments most likely played too small a part for them to make much difference. Could they today offer a way out of the Marxian dynamic-economic dilemma?

Marxian analysis is about capitalism; it has little to say about how a socialist system would manage these same problems. Also, Marx's labor theory does not deal with demand and utility as determinants of value, nor does it grant an important role to governmental fiscal or monetary policy.

ARE YOU A RADICAL?

In the dictionary, the term **radical** is defined as extreme, sweeping, or revolutionary. However, yesterday's radical ideas may be today's moderate, conservative, or reactionary ones, and today's radical ideas may be tomorrow's moderate, conservative, or reactionary ones. And what is true over time is equally true over space. The Soviet "conservative" is a Stalinist.

The conventional connotation of *radical* is unfavorable, at least in the United States. Its associations are with mob violence, terrorism, bomb-throwing, and assassination. What is overlooked is that radical ideas have sometimes been correct in the past and may be so again. Within the radical movement itself, on the other hand, the connotation of the term is favorable. Anything less than radicalism is cowardly, pussyfooting, compromise with "the Establishment" or with "the Great Satan." What the movement overlooks is that radical ideas can be and have been wrong. Neither radicalism nor its alternatives can insure anyone against making stupid mistakes.

Radicalism, including radical economics, may be of the political Left or the political Right. In the context of planning versus the market, the radical Left generally, but not always, calls for giant steps toward a purely planned economy, and the New Right proposes equally giant steps toward a purely market one.

The radical Left generally calls for a purely planned economy, while the radical Right favors a purely market economy.

It is a long way from Karl Marx developing "the laws of motion of capitalism" in the British Museum to the campus radical howling down some visiting speaker who he or she has been told is "reactionary." Marx himself, by the way, warned his audience that he was not a Marxist!

Here is a set of seven questions. If you answer "Yes" to most or all of them, you probably qualify as a true believer "under the radical sign."

1. Are you sure that piecemeal reforms (monetarism or fiscalism, demand side or supply side, more deregulation or less, freer trade or more protection) are like "rearranging of deck chairs on the *Titanic*"—too marginal to carry out the "radical restructuring" that society needs?

2. If some combination of such reforms (as in the last paragraph) were indeed massive enough and well enough thought out to do much good, would you oppose the reforms all the more? Do you want to see "the system" overthrown *rather than* improved, even when improvement is possible?

3. Do you believe "the Revolution" must take place very soon—in your own generation—if world war or world pollution or some similar catastrophe is to be avoided?

4. Do you favor mass demonstrations and "direct action,"[9] distrusting the electoral process and representative government because the electoral process is too slow, too heedless of intense-minority opinion, too easily thwarted by judges or bureaucrats, or "all of the above"?

5. Is the present system so bad that there is no real danger that its overthrow would lead to something worse? Is there no danger of jumping from the frying pan into the fire?

6. Do you have no clear idea of what the new system that would succeed the present one might look like, beyond such general ideas as "a planned society" or "public ownership of the means of production" or "more equality"? Are you willing to leave the everyday details to be worked out "in the course of the struggle"?

7. Do you believe the intellectual support for your position has already been worked out well enough by one or more great intellectual leaders to allow you to accept it as given, so that you can depend on nonrational ways of knowing—such as faith, intuition, song lyrics, or the authority of the leadership group of your particular movement?

Most radicals believe that society needs large-scale restructuring, which can be accomplished only by overthrowing the current system.

---

9. "Direct action" may range from individual kidnappings and assassinations to mass revolts and revolutions, which turn violent if resisted.

THE NEW LEFT

In most countries the main body of radical economists has been affiliated with the so-called **New Left**. However, most supporters of the New Left are neither economists nor radicals as we have described radicalism. A question then arises: If Marx and Engels may be taken to represent the Old Left at its best, why do we need a New Left?

In the first place, Marx's theories were not accepted by all the political Left of Marx's own day. Marxists struggled continually both with reformists and with anarchists for control of the First International—the International Workingmen's Association of which Marx was a founder and which was the center of his political activism for the last dozen years of his life. Today we would call the reformists liberals or social democrats.[10] We shall discuss the anarchists later in this chapter.

In the second place, within fifteen years after Marx's death, Marxists began to differ among themselves with increasing vehemence.[11]

In the third place, and most importantly, the victories of European fascism in the period between the two world wars were blamed on disagreement and disunity among members of the political Left. The story was especially tragic in Germany, where the Social Democratic party had been both strong and well organized, but had been unable to form any common front with the Communist party to check the rise of Hitler and his National Socialists (Nazis). The Social Democratic party collapsed after Hitler came to power in 1933.

The New Left hopes to avoid a similar fate by playing down intellectual hair-splitting and by maintaining a united front. The American New Left grew out of the conviction of both liberals and radicals that the "McCarthyism" of the 1950s was a

---

10. In most of the nineteenth century the term *liberal* meant a doctrinaire disciple of free enterprise and *laissez-faire*. Now it means an advocate of various economic and social reforms attached to a framework that includes private ownership of most of society's capital goods. A *social democrat* differs from a liberal in advocating public ownership of the means of production. But, like a liberal, the social democrat proposes to achieve change entirely by nonviolent means centering on free elections.

11. We discuss the evolution of Marxian ideas "from Karl Marx to the New Left" in the essay that concludes this part of the book.

real fascist threat, which the country had been lucky to avoid. Next came the formation of a university-based (not labor-based) organization called Students for a Democratic Society (SDS) at Port Huron, Michigan, in 1962. In the SDS "Port Huron Statement," doctrinal differences, both economic and political, were papered over with evangelical language. However, the SDS was overcome by some of these same differences—in particular, the role of violence—and broke up in 1968–69.

The American New Left grew out of the conviction that the McCarthyism of the 1950s was a real fascist threat that the country had been lucky to avoid. The main organization of the New Left, the Students for a Democratic Society (SDS), was prominent during the 1960s but broke up at the end of the decade.

SDS was founded before the upsurge of the civil rights movement and any extensive military involvement in Indochina. These issues became the focal points for agitation against the entire capitalist civilization, including the capitalist economy. As the civil rights movement and the Vietnam War retired from the front page, student interest shifted from reform or revolution to qualifying for good jobs in the world much as it was. The SDS, the New Left, and the racial and campus riots all retreated into ancient history, sometimes tinged with nostalgia. (Something similar happened in other countries, where direct involvement with American civil rights and Vietnam problems had been minimal but where pervasive anti-Americanism had become part and parcel of the political Left.)

Since 1970, there have been a number of efforts to revive the New Left coalition of the late 1960s, but around other issues. Some candidates for a unifying issue have been ecology and environmentalism, nuclear war, feminism, South African *apartheid*, and American policy in Central America. As of 1989, none of these issues had succeeded. Nevertheless, the "ancient history" label is premature for the New Left.

Branches of the New Left

The New Left is not and never has been an exclusively radical movement. It has always had and

continues to have a liberal and reformist following. Its radical vanguard, however, has been divided among anarchists, socialists, and syndicalists, who get along together well at some times, badly at others. All three are **collectivist,** since they all oppose individual or private ownership of the means of production. All of them want capital goods—including consumers' goods held in inventories—to be owned "collectively." But they mean quite different things by collective ownership. It may be helpful to classify the New Left radicals further into five groups. There seem to be two quite distinct anarchist groups, two different socialist (or communist) groups, and a single embryonic syndicalist group.

The subgroups of the New Left—two anarchist groups, two socialist groups, and a syndicalist group—are all collectivist, since they oppose private ownership of the means of production.

Anarchism I **Anarchists,** who fear the state as much as they fear the capitalist class, want control of capital goods to be by purely voluntary associations, which people may enter by negotiation and leave more or less as they please. These groups would have no power to levy taxes or to impose compulsory penalties on members except to suspend or expel them from membership.

What we shall call *Anarchism I* includes a great number of variations on a theme that calls itself "the counterculture." Their common feature is withdrawal from organized society into independent communes, whose members now and then go forth with food, medical aid, and political propaganda for people in the slums. These groups attempt to show the larger society the error of its ways. They hope that such demonstrations will lead to the reorganization of society as a network of larger communes.

Some communes are rural, with strong back-to-the-land, ecological, or primitivistic flavors, like the *kibbutzim* in Israel. Others are urban, sometimes using violent guerrilla tactics. They may center on economic, sexual, or psychedelic experimentation, religious revivalism, occultism, or simply "living cheap." More than any other radicals, these people often feel that economic issues are irrelevant. So, while most radicals call for massive redistribution of income and wealth, these folks would most likely accept the following view:

> Distribution is irrelevant because income is irrelevant. There is already too much consumption of the wrong kind: soul-less, artificial "satisfaction" encouraged by advertising, which robs people of their freedom, makes them empty and unhappy. Property is theft, and 'income distribution' fits in with it. We ought to abandon the whole rotten production and consumption structure of industrialism. We ought to live in communes, be directly supplied with simple, natural goods, and arrange distribution in direct consultation with one another.[12]

Terrorism and parasitism are among the charges that have been made against this radical group. However, those who believe in violence as a way of life are a rather small fraction. Most prefer to provoke the Establishment, by ridicule or violence, into dropping its liberal front and showing its true colors, which they consider repressive. Neither should they be considered parasites. Many traffic and barter with "straight" society, selling farm products and handicrafts to earn money for what they need to buy. Parasitism is dependence on handouts from parents, friends, passers-by, and the government relief system. This aspect of communal living also obviously exists, but only as an offshoot.

Counterculture anarchists withdraw from society into independent communes and would like to see society as a whole organized into a network of communes.

Anarchism II This group works within society but only to destroy it, either by violence (terror) or by ridicule.

In the United States of the late 1960s, the favorite weapon was ridicule, in the grand tradition of Till Eulenspiegel, Voltaire, and Bernard Shaw. Their "revolution" would be a day or week of merry pranks—fraternity initiations on a grand scale. It is hard to believe that their manifestos were meant to do more than shock people into serious thought about social issues—people such as:

And there's doctors and lawyers,
And business executives,
And they're all made out of ticky tacky,
And they all look just the same.[13]

Their high priest, Abbie Hoffman, produced the best known of these manifestos for the 1968 Democratic Party convention held in Chicago. Planks 7 and 8 dealt with economic matters:

7. The abolition of money, the abolition of pay housing, pay medicine, pay transportation, pay food, pay education, pay clothing, pay medical help, and pay toilets.

8. A society which works for and actively promotes the concept of full unemployment. A society in which people are free from the drudgery of work. Adoption of the concept "Let the machines do it."

"Machines" were to produce everything we need, and repair each other in their spare time, whatever damages they may have suffered in the Revolution. The people, meanwhile, would dance and sing, write poetry, make love, and heighten their awareness through "body chemistry."[14]

New Left anarchists have subsequently stopped playing games and turned to terroristic violence. The Baeder-Meinhof gang in West Germany and the Red Brigades in Italy seem to be examples of terrorism with an anarchist accent. (The American Weathermen, the violent offshoot of the SDS, were, however, Trotskyist rather than anarchist.)

The Anarchism II group of the New Left turned to terroristic violence in its attempt to restructure society.

It is in general a great, though common, mistake to associate terrorism exclusively with anarchism, socialism, or any other form of radicalism, Old or New, Left or Right. Terrorism is a set of violent tactics that, when used by others than the uniformed armed forces and the police, is aimed at some sort of social change and is denounced by

---

12. Jan Pen, *Income Distribution: Facts, Theories, Policies* (London: Allen Lane, 1971), p. 293.

13. Extract from the song "Little Boxes." Words and music by Malvina Reynolds. © 1962 Schroder Music Company. Reprinted with permission.

14. "Free" [Abbie Hoffman], *Revolution for the Hell of It* (New York: Dial Press, 1968).

worldwide public opinion. But the American Ku Klux Klan, the Nazi Gestapo, the Irish Republican Army (IRA), the extremist factions of the Palestine Liberation Organization, and the shadowy overseas agencies of the Khadafy government of Libya are none of them either anarchist or primarily leftist in orientation. They aim at such diverse goals as white supremacy, anticommunism, a united Ireland, and the elimination of Israel from the Middle East. Some profess leftist sympathies and others profess antileftist ones, but the particular cause seems unrelated to the tactics. Terrorism, in short, is not an economic category.

Terrorism is a set of violent tactics aimed at social change. It should not be associated exclusively with radicalism of the Left or Right.

Socialism I **Socialists** are both more numerous and more important than the anarchists within the New Left. Their tradition is also more rational and less emotional, as indicated by the importance attached to Marxian analysis. Socialists (and communists)[15] see ownership of land and capital by the political state and its agencies (themselves controlled by a political party representing the working class) as the only feasible short-run alternative to capitalism. When the world turns socialist, it may be sensible to speak of the eventual "withering away" of political states. At the present time, say the socialists, such talk is a harmful diversion.

Socialists see ownership of the land and capital by the political state and its agencies as the only feasible short-run alternative to capitalism.

What we shall call *Socialism I* embodies a neo-Stalinist approach, which its enemies call "Red Fascism." The economy is to be planned on scientific principles, and planning is to be largely imperative—the Plan plus a machine gun or a firing squad. Dissent, including economic dissent, is tolerated only "repressively," if at all, meaning that the dissenters may let off steam harmlessly, short of action. Monopoly of the formal means of propaganda is imposed and reinforced if necessary by compulsory study and by criticism and self-criticism sessions. In such group therapy, orthodoxy is drummed into the members, who are expected to apply it to current practical problems. No one is allowed to remain silent, or to hide dissent behind a mask of ignorance. "I don't know" is not an escape hatch.

"Liberty," Lenin is supposed to have said, "is a commodity so precious that it must be rationed." Under the neo-Stalinists, civil rights are subordinated to the dictates of planning. The rule of law normally remains in effect, but the content of the law is shifted in favor of the state and against defendants in such "details" as the presumption of innocence, protection against self-incrimination, free choice of defense lawyer, double jeopardy, and the statutes of limitation.

One branch of socialism embodies a neo-Stalinist approach and advocates imperative planning coupled with monopoly of the formal means of propaganda and education, little toleration of dissent, and subordination of civil rights.

Socialism II The camp we call *Socialism II* is often referred to as "Marxist humanism." Its inspiration comes from the younger Marx of the 1830s and 1840s, who was more concerned with "human values" and less with "class struggles" than he would become later on. Socialism II is less authori-

---

15. Communists go beyond socialists in three main ways, more political than economic.

First, they believe more firmly than other socialists that an economy of abundance would shortly follow the establishment of socialism on a world scale. In this way, they are closer to the teachings of Marx.

Second, orthodox communists (or Marxist-Leninists) accept violence as a necessary aspect of revolution, especially in less developed countries. They propose not only to use it in self-defense, but also to take the offensive when the time is right. As

a result, they want their political party to be limited to activists, and to be disciplined tightly like a military organization.

Third, orthodox communists also see a need for a dictatorship of the proletariat (and its "vanguard party") for a long period after the socialist revolution—again, especially in less developed countries.

They do not believe that any existing economy has actually gone beyond socialism to communism, though Mao Zedong hoped to attain communism for China in a "Great Leap Forward," which ended in failure in 1958–1962.

tarian than Socialism I, and seems less concerned with orthodoxy. However, the government monopoly of formal education and propaganda is as strong as under Socialism I. In practice, Socialism II may lead to the substitution of mob rule for bureaucracy, as in the Chinese Cultural Revolution of Mao Zedong's last decade (1966–1975).

Among the leading economic doctrines of Socialism II are the following: (1) there should be equality of income and wealth; (2) a wider range of goods and services should be made available completely free of charge; (3) "material incentives" should be replaced by "moral incentives" for economic activity; (4) there should be an end to the hierarchy and alienation of modern industrial society.

Marxist humanist socialists are less authoritarian and less concerned with orthodoxy than the neo-Stalinists, although government monopoly of formal education and propaganda remain strong. Marxist humanists advocate equality of wealth and income, a wide range of free goods and services, moral incentives for economic activity, and an end to the alienation of modern industrial society.

Isn't it likely that Socialism II would degenerate in practice to Socialism I? Without doubting the sincerity of Marxist humanists, one may indeed wonder if a society can go from the status quo to Marxist humanism without a longer or shorter period of "proletarian dictatorship." There is also the danger that a ruling bureaucracy under Socialism I would not permit the peaceful transition to Socialism II. One may also wonder if the degree of ideological control needed to make the New Socialist Man and Woman out of ordinary people can be combined with the Bill of Rights quite as easily as Socialist II followers expect or hope.

Syndicalism **Syndicalists** favor the separate ownership of each productive facility (which may be a single workshop, a factory, or a large industrial complex) by its own workers, who would elect representatives to a weak state, which would referee disputes between groups of workers and coordinate their economic plans. *Syndicalism* is an almost-forgotten word today. But California's "anti-Red" laws of World War I were anti-*syndicalist* rather than anti-*communist*, and a well-known economist chose the title "Reflections on Syndicalism" for his attack on the New Deal for strengthening the organized labor movement.[16]

Syndicalism is a system of economic and political rule by syndicates—a *syndicate* being another name for a guild or trade union. The syndicates are themselves above the law. Thus syndicalism could mean replacing Congress by a national assembly made up of trade unions. At one time, the Industrial Workers of the World (IWW) embodied the syndicalist threat in the United States.

An interesting feature of syndicalism is its strategy of the general strike rather than political revolution as the weapon of social change. Syndicalists hope not only to win strikes but also to prevent the workers' gains from being passed on to consumers in price rises. Starting with individual companies, syndicalism would spread to the whole economy as local strikes grew into general strikes, and as the issues turned from the purely economic to the openly political. The process of winning strikes, repeated over and over again, would both bring the value of the owners' equity down to zero and paralyze the economy. The unions could then buy out their employers for little or nothing.

It goes without saying that unions would be free to break all contracts and would not be subject to any lawsuits. Also, laws against striking or using the strike weapon for political ends would be ignored.

Many proposals and activities, not necessarily radical, have syndicalist implications. For example, in support for public employees' and welfare recipients' rights to strike and bargain collectively, the "syndicalist" feature is that their bargains are considered sacred. Elected legislatures may not refuse funding to carry them out. A case on the local level is a teachers' union (not consciously syndicalist) bargaining for higher pay and smaller classes, and in this way using the strike weapon to force hikes in property tax rates, which the people through their elected representatives may have refused. In other words, the elective machinery of government

---

16. Henry C. Simons, *Economic Policy for a Free Society* (Chicago: University of Chicago Press, 1948), Chapter 6.

is downgraded in relation to bargaining by employee unions, in terms of control of the taxpayer's dollar. If the legislature is limited to backing up the results of collective bargaining, the government's "power of the purse" is weakened.

Earlier versions of syndicalism were built around economic *blitzkrieg*, or lightning warfare. All workers were to lay down their tools at the same time, and that would be enough to paralyze the economy immediately. It was hoped that such a general strike might be spontaneous, so that the capitalists would be taken by surprise. There have in fact been general strikes. Some of them have succeeded, but the successful ones have been a part of or a trigger for political revolution, not substitutes for it.

Syndicalism is a system of economic and political rule by trade unions, which are free to break contracts and are not subject to lawsuits. Syndicalists favor the separate ownership of each productive facility by its own workers. They also advocate the general strike, rather than the political revolution, as the weapon of social change.

THE NEW RIGHT

From the New Left, we turn to the **New Right.** More than the New Left, it changes in character from one country to another. Moreover, it lacks any towering figure who corresponds to Karl Marx. The New Right is composed of people disgusted with things as they have become, but should not be confused with conservatism. Neither should it be confused with fascism, for its majority is composed of people bitterly opposed to authoritarian regimes. In the United States at least, the incidence of radicalism as we have defined it is less in the New Right than in the New Left. However, the truly radical New Right is a collection of paramilitary cells, which stage shoot-outs and bust-ups with people they call "commies" or racially inferior or which plot guerrilla warfare to follow nuclear attacks or communist takeovers. The Ku Klux Klan and the

Survivalists, respectively, exemplify these two strains.

Three intertwined branches compose the American New Right. Only one of these, the market-economy New Right, is primarily economic. The other two branches are ethical-religious and political. The ethical-religious branch wants the recognition of absolute ethics and morality. The political branch is strongly anti-Soviet, fearing Soviet plots for world domination and empire.

The Market-Economy New Right

The market-economy New Right glories in being reactionary, and proposes a return to the old-time religion of *laissez-faire*. On the macroeconomic side, it also calls for restoring the gold standard, the annually balanced budget, and sometimes Say's Identity (aided by downward wage rate flexibility) to ensure high employment. The New Right's god is Adam Smith, whose faith in free enterprise was much less fervent than their own.

The market-economy New Right can be subdivided into those for and those against trust-busting and similar controls. The **trust-busters** see a "decline of competition," which they would like to reverse. They fear that control by a big-business oligarchy will restrict output and employment, raise prices, and stifle the opportunity for new businesses to enter the prosperous mainstream of the American economy. Another of their fears is that a growing proportion of the people are being pushed into a relatively poor competitive segment of the economy.

The **laissez-faire** New Right is less impressed by the threat of economic segmentation into tightly knit oligopoly and competitive sectors. It depends not on antitrust laws or other controls but on technological change, which Joseph Schumpeter called "creative destruction," to overcome any tendencies toward segmentation. This group points, for example, to the displacement of the railroad "octopus" of the late nineteenth century by trucks, buses, planes, and automobiles less than fifty years later. It also points to a "product cycle" in international trade that leads to more foreign competition for companies like General Motors and Ford in automobiles, or like USX and Bethlehem Steel in the steel industry. To these people, monopoly and tightly knit oligopoly may indeed be diseases, uncomfortable where they strike and while they last, but more like the common cold than cancer. They believe that the struggle to gain and hold on to market positions in oligopolistic industries spurs both invention and innovation.

The market-economy New Right proposes a return to laissez-faire economic policies and calls for restoring the gold standard and the balanced budget. The "trust-buster" segment of the New Right wants to restore competition, which they feel is threatened by big business; the "laissez-faire" segment believes that technological change will overcome any tendencies toward long-term monopoly control.

The two groups within the market-economy New Right agree in general that the economy would do better with less regulation and greater reliance on law and equity. But how much less regulation? Less in what fields of economic activity? Which regulations should be lightened or scrapped first? We find disagreement on the specifics.

Similar disagreement on specifics plagues the New Right case against progressive taxation of income and wealth. But there is nearly unanimous New Right support for the view that such taxes be cut, that they should be simplified, and that their degree of progression should be reduced—possibly to zero.

Both groups within the New Right agree that the economy would do better with less regulation and greater reliance on law and equity.

The Libertarian Movement

The most radical branch of the economic New Right in its thinking, although decidedly not in its political tactics—is the **Libertarian** movement. There is no gospel common to all libertarians. Radical libertarians are like anarchists in their fear of the state as an engine of tyranny. However, they depart from collectivist anarchism by supporting private ownership of the means of production. Libertarians offer many proposals for changes in the rules of the economic game, intended to allow the market to govern and reduce the state (and therefore social planning) to zero. Money, defense, protection, streets, sewers, and the framing and administration of law would all be left to private firms and associations. Any person or voluntary group could found a new firm, or buy an existing one in any field (including the practice of law or medicine) without any formal certification of training or competence. All taxes would be replaced by payments for services and by voluntary dues to cooperative associations. People could move freely from place to place and from association to association, but no association would be forced to accept any particular new member or partner.

Libertarians believe the market should govern and the state should cease to exist.

Objectivism and Social Darwinism

Objectivism is the belief that each person's most objective view of "the good" is his or her knowledge of what is in his or her own (subjective) best interest. Another objectivist argument is that "altruism," "the general good," and "social equity" in practice are often self-interest arguments of various other people, who usually do not turn out to be in any way admirable. In the words of objectivist leader Ayn Rand (1905–1982), objectivism is "rational selfishness."[17]

To those who call themselves objectivists, the world and the economy are so interrelated that the Darwinian principle of "survival of the fittest"

---

17. Ayn Rand was Russian-born, and was (like Karl Marx) a philosopher by training. Disgusted with Soviet Russia after the Revolution, she emigrated to America in 1926. She became a Hollywood screenwriter, and later wrote a series of novels or "tracts for the times." Her ideas are expressed most clearly in the novel *Atlas Shrugged*, which deals with the disastrous things that would happen to society if the few superior individuals should all decide, like ordinary workers, to go on strike. Of her nonfiction works, a collection called *Capitalism: The Unknown Ideal* is the most explicitly economic. In it there is much that could pass as libertarian doctrine, but never a hint of anarchism.

should include survival of those who perform the best in the free market.

Objectivism is the belief that each person's most objective view of "the good" is his or her knowledge of what is in his or her own best interest.

The ideas of Rand and her followers are a revival of a philosophy called **Social Darwinism,** associated particularly with the English sociologist and philosopher Herbert Spencer (1820–1903). Social Darwinists believe that the survival and prosperity of individuals, families, nations, and races are determined, like those of animal species, by their biological and psychological fitness in perpetual struggle against each other and against the environment. It is dangerous in the long run for any family, nation, or race to thwart this struggle for survival, either by placing restrictions on its fittest members or by giving special aid to the least fit. It is not that "the fittest" are above the law, but if enforcement of the laws must be bent in any direction, it is better for society's future if the favored party is the superior person.

Social Darwinists believe that the survival and prosperity of individuals, families, nations, and races are determined by their biological and psychological fitness.

THE FUTURE OF RADICAL ECONOMICS

This final section of this final chapter returns to the radicalism of the Left, especially of the New Left. This is the only form of radical economics that can currently be regarded as a threat or menace to the established order, although it is now clearly in decline. Attempts to revive it—searches for moral equivalents of the Vietnam War in Central America, South Africa, the antinuclear movement, or saving the whales—have had little response or none at all. We observe four principal reasons for the decline.

1. For all of its bombastic manifestoes and its hopes for "the greening of America," the movement—or at least its rank and file—has been satisfied easily with minor victories. The most important of these, in the United States, were the phasing out of military conscription and the abandonment of the South Vietnamese regime to its fate.

2. During the Vietnam period, the domestic market for white-collar labor was unusually tight. The risk of long-term career damage from a police record, from draft-dodging in Canada, or from a year or two of "dropping out" in a counterculture commune seemed negligible. As American participation in Indochina wound down, and as Vietnam veterans rejoined the domestic labor market, this ceased to be true. At the same time, obvious and lucrative opportunity remained at hand for the conformist who "kept his nose clean and avoided dangerous thoughts." This middle way between labor shortage and mass unemployment provided the Establishment an optimal opportunity to discriminate against the unconventional, including of course the radical and the ex-radical. There seems to be no evidence, however, that the Establishment "planned it" that way.

3. The New Left, like the Old, helped dig its own grave by splitting into feuding factions, particularly over the desirability of violence and guerrilla warfare, and over the likelihood of race riots coalescing into a "black revolt." Such organizations as the Weathermen, the Black Panthers, and the Symbionese Liberation Army lost not only their skirmishes but their potential friends and allies as well. Lost them, moreover, for radicalism as a whole as well as for themselves.

4. As we saw in the last chapter, most socialist countries are apparently adopting reform programs that outside observers see as converging with reformist capitalism—however much the socialist leaders denounce any "convergence hypothesis" as backsliding from Marxian fundamentals. This means that radical splinter groups like the Revolutionary Communist party and the Communist Workers party in America, the Red Brigades in Italy, or the Shining Path guerrillas in Peru can no longer model themselves on idealized versions of

Soviet or Chinese reality. The unrealized or repudiated visions of a Leon Trotsky, or the "cultural revolution" of a superannuated Mao Zedong, seem to be inadequate substitutes.

But while radicalism may be hibernating, it is by no means dead. A serious depression or an exceptionally tight labor market would revive it in America, if the foregoing analysis is correct. A return to large-scale military conscription would be another path to radical revival. A third path might be intervention in foreign countries to support pro-American dictatorships or oligarchies. Fear of re-igniting the New Left was probably one reason for governmental reluctance to oppose Leftist revolts and revolutions in Nicaragua and El Salvador or even to arm or support openly such movements as the Contras against the Nicaraguan Sandinista government. Closing the book on radical economics is, in other words, a more difficult task than ending this chapter about it.

The New Left is currently in decline, partly because it split into feuding factions and partly because of current economic realities, but radicalism could easily be revived by a serious depression, a return to large-scale military conscription, or U.S. intervention in foreign countries to support pro-American dictatorships.

Economics in Focus

Toward a New Socialism

Even though socialism fell into eclipse in the 1980s as the New Left's energies dwindled, a number of theorists have tried to revive the movement by reexamining its goals and values. This is particularly true among the ranks of democratic socialists—those who insist on a firm commitment to democracy. Many of them believe that capitalism is approaching a crisis (probably a "slow" crisis) that will bring a new opportunity for socialism. Although the democratic socialists often disagree among themselves, they tend to unite on a few key proposals.

In the first place, they want to transform the nature of work through a radical type of economic democracy. Workers would be given a large degree of control over their factories and offices, either through ownership (as in worker cooperatives) or through democratic forms of self-management. Government tax policies and financial support would encourage such developments. Furthermore, the work week would be shortened, perhaps with government wage subsidies so that people could earn the same income for fewer hours of work without harming the company balance sheet. The shorter working hours would make jobs available for those who are currently unemployed, and workers would enjoy the higher quality of life that comes from greater leisure time. Both self-management and enhanced leisure would raise the creativity of the typical worker, the socialists argue, resulting in a rise in productivity.

There would also be direct measures to reduce inequality by redistributing income. The income tax would be revised in a progressive direction, and inheritance taxes may be changed to discourage the transmission of huge fortunes to single individuals. Government would guarantee a decent income and essential services to every member of society.

In most of their proposals the democratic socialists stress grass-roots participation. Planning, instead of being rigidly centralized, would begin at the local level: the community, the neighborhood, the shop floor. Since planning decisions in a technological society often require technical expertise, the government would support better education programs to make this kind of knowledge more widely available.

In this version of socialism, nationalization of industry is not necessarily a dominant feature. Some industries may be state-owned—health and education services, for example, as well as natural monopolies such as utilities—but others would not. The democratic socialists tend to distinguish "social" ownership and control from state ownership.

Finally, unlike orthodox Marxists, most of these theorists do not say that socialism is inevitable—only preferable. They envision the transition to socialism as a long, gradual process. But they insist that only socialism can bring a genuine realization of freedom and justice.

Sources: Michael Harrington, *Socialism: Past and Future* (New York: Arcade, 1989) and *The Next Left: The History of a Future* (New York: Henry Holt, 1987); "Voices from the Left: A Conversation Between Michael Harrington and Irving Howe," *New York Times Magazine,* June 17, 1984, p. 24ff.; Irving Howe, *Socialism and America* (San Diego: Harcourt Brace Jovanovich, 1985); Andrew Levine, *Arguing for Socialism: Theoretical Considerations* (Boston: Routledge & Kegan Paul, 1984); Stanley Aronowitz, "Are We Afraid to Be Radical?" *The Progressive,* September 1985, pp. 14–15; Peter Kellner, "When Democratic Socialists Must Come Off the Fence," *New Statesman,* November 28, 1986, p. 5; "New Ideas for the Left: Preserve the Goals, Rethink the Means," *The Economist,* September 26, 1987, pp. 25–28.

SUMMARY

1. Opposition to the capitalist-market economy centers on three problems: (a) inequality of the distributions of income and wealth; (b) insecurity of the standard of living against downward shocks, both cyclical and long term; and (c) incompatibility with physical and mental health. The major problem is psychological alienation. Alienation takes many forms and explains many forms of social pathology, ranging from boredom to violent crime. (See pages 528–529.)

2. Marxism is an integrated, unified system of social philosophy, including both economic statics and economic dynamics, and culminating in certain "laws of motion of capitalism." (See pages 530–531).

3. While admitting the accomplishments of the Industrial Revolution, Marxian economics uses a strict labor theory of value to develop certain "contradictions of capitalism." In its Marxian form this theory develops ideas about the exploitation of the worker and the receipt of surplus value by the capitalist class. (See pages 531–532.)

4. In the economic dynamics of Marx's theories, the contradictions of capitalism lead to "increasing misery" and to the eventual downfall of capitalism, either because a falling rate of profit leads to a *liquidity* crisis or because a tendency toward overproduction leads to a *realization* crisis. (See pages 533–534.)

5. Marxian analysis leaves no important role for monetary and fiscal policy. Also, the labor theory of value does not deal with demand and utility as determinants of value. (See page 534.)

6. Radicalism may be radical either because of what it proposes to accomplish, as in "a radical restructuring of society," or because of the tactics that it considers legitimate to accomplish these ends, which sometimes include illegality, violence, dictatorship, and the disregard of public opinion by a tightly organized political party. (See pages 534–535.)

7. The American New Left arose in the early 1960s as a search for unity on the political Left. Disunity of the Old Left was blamed for the rise of fascism in the period between World War I and World War II and McCarthyism in the 1950s. It is not an exclusively radical movement, but its leadership is for the most part radical. It has lost impor-

tance since 1970, but keeps trying for revival using new issues in domestic and foreign policy. (See pages 535–536.)

8. The radical groups within the New Left are all *collectivist*. They favor collective ownership of the means of production. Subdivisions are *anarchist, socialist,* and *syndicalist.* (See page 536.)

9. The anarchist wing of the New Left can be subdivided into the "counterculture," which withdraws from the mainstream of society into communes, and the revolutionary wing, which proposes tearing down institutions and then possibly starting over. (See pages 536–537.)

10. Terrorism is a set of violent tactics, which can be used by partisans of a great variety of political, religious, racial, economic, or social positions, but it is not itself a category of economic thought. It is a great mistake to associate terrorism exclusively with any economic philosophy—radical or conservative, old or new, Right or Left. (See pages 537–538.)

11. Socialists favor state ownership of the means of production. The socialist wing of the New Left can be subdivided into neo-Stalinist imperative planners and "Marxist humanists," who emphasize equality, mass participation in decision making, and moral (rather than material) incentives. (See pages 538–539.)

12. Syndicalists favor ownership by trade unions of the workers. They believe that unions can bring down capitalism by winning strikes. Unions would be immune from lawsuits and could break all contracts. (See page 539–540.)

13. The economic New Right concentrates on achieving *laissez-faire*; the ethical-religious New Right, on re-establishing the old-time religion and morality, and the political New Right on thwarting alleged communist conspiracies to dominate the world. These three groups overlap to some extent, and only the first is relevant to our study of economics. It includes both libertarians and objectivists. (See pages 540–541.)

14. Libertarians are, ideologically speaking, the most radical branch of the economic New Right. They favor complete reliance on the free capitalist market and hope for the demise of the political state. They are distinguished from collectivist anarchists by their beliefs in private enterprise and private property. (See page 541.)

15. Objectivists believe that our most nearly

objective knowledge of the "good" and the "just" is our knowledge of what is good for ourselves. We should follow this knowledge rather than the urgings of ethical altruism, which is often a cover for dishonesty. (See page 541–542.)

16. Objectivists are impressed with the contribution to society of the few superior individuals. They fear that human evolution toward some ideal will be sidetracked if such people are restricted or if inferiors are helped to survive and reproduce. To this extent objectivists are Social Darwinists, applying the principle of "survival of the fittest" to social as well as biological relations. (See page 542.)

KEY TERMS

alienation: the characteristic psychological ailment of capitalism; hostility or indifference to something or someone generally considered attractive in society (page 529).

anarchists: people who believe that government should be abolished (page 536).

collectivist: a philosophy characterized by opposition to individual or private ownership of the means of production (page 536).

constant capital: in Marxian economics, the labor hours embodied in (used to produce) raw materials and in the depreciation of machinery and other long-lived capital goods (page 530).

exploitation: in the Marxist perspective, the exclusion of the main body of a society from the bulk of that society's economic surplus (page 531).

exploitation rate: *see* **rate of surplus value.**

laissez-faire: a branch of the market-economy New Right that believes that technological change will overcome any tendencies toward long-run monopoly in the economy (page 540).

Libertarian: a branch of the economic New Right that believes there should be private ownership of the means of production and that the market should govern and the state cease to exist (page 541).

liquidity crisis: according to Marxian thought, a long-term stagnation in a capitalist economy, with short business-cycle booms and long business-cycle depressions and a rising rate of unemployment brought on by a falling rate of profit (page 533).

New Left: contemporary groups that generally call for major changes away from the market economy (page 535).

New Right: contemporary groups that generally call for major steps toward a purely market economy (page 540).

New Socialist Man and Woman: people who will emerge after the establishment of socialism; they will work harder and more skillfully than workers in the past and will demand less from society in terms of wealth and material goods (page 531).

objectivism: the belief that each person's most objective view of "the good" is his or her knowledge of what is in his or her own best interest (page 541).

organic composition of capital: in Marxian economics, the ratio between constant capital (raw material plus depreciation) and variable capital (direct labor) (page 532).

proletariat: the workers (page 531).

radical: extreme, sweeping, revolutionary (page 534).

rate of surplus value: in Marxian economics, the ratio between the amount of labor-produced value taken from the worker and the amount that the worker is allowed to retain (page 530).

realization crisis: in Marxian thought, a crisis caused by a rising exploitation rate; as the exploitation rate rises, a falling proportion of the labor force is needed to produce the output that the masses can still buy (page 534).

Social Darwinism: a belief that the survival and prosperity of individuals, families, nations, and races are determined by their biological and psychological fitness in perpetual struggle against each other and the environment (page 542).

socialists: those who see ownership of land and capital by the political state and its agencies as the only feasible short-run alternative to capitalism (page 538).

surplus value: in Marxian economics, labor-produced value in excess of the amount that the worker is allowed to retain (page 532).

syndicalists: those who favor the separate ownership of each productive facility by its own workers (page 539).

trust-busters: a branch of the market-economy New Right that fears that control by a big-business oligarchy will restrict output and employment, raise prices, and stifle the opportunity for new businesses to enter the mainstream of the American economy (page 540).

variable capital: in Marxian economics, the purchasing power of the wage paid to labor, measured in labor hours embodied in consumption goods (page 532).

DISCUSSION QUESTIONS

1. Do you believe that the inequalities in the American distributions of income and wealth constitute "maldistribution"? Explain why or why not.

2. Does the market capitalist economy make adequate provision for a future in which the relative prices of natural resources and energy are both high and rising steadily? Would a socialist economy do better? Explain.

3. Is alienation the root cause of social pathology, as Karl Marx believed, or are those who engage in pathological behavior responsible for their own actions? Explain your answers.

4. What is meant by the Marxist "economic interpretation of history," "contradictions of capitalism," and "principle of increasing misery"?

5. Karl Marx states in the first chapter of *Capital* what he considers the chief theoretical problem of competitive capitalism. A capitalist buys labor power, raw materials, and intermediate goods at their values. He also sells his final product at its value, and still makes a profit. But where does this profit come from, and why has not competition eliminated it?

Marx then goes on to answer his own questions at some length. What, do you think, is the nature of Marx's solution?

6. Do you think that Marx would be satisfied with the economic performance of the contemporary United States? The contemporary Soviet Union? Contemporary Cuba or China? Explain why or why not in each case.

7. Distinguish between: (a) the Marxist and conventional concepts of profit and (b) the breakdowns of capital into "fixed and variable" (conventional) or "constant and variable" (Marxian).

8. To what extent is it reasonable to associate terrorism with the New Left or with any particular wing of the New Left, or with the New Left in general?

9. Distinguish libertarianism from both anarchism and objectivism.

10. What is Social Darwinism? How does it differ from ordinary (biological) Darwinism? Is it a racist doctrine? Explain why or why not.

11. Do you have an economic explanation for the relative decline of the American New Left after the end of the Vietnam War? Explain what economic circumstances, if any, might cause its revival.

From Karl Marx to the New Left

A prominent slogan of the New Left in the 1960s and early 1970s was "Marx, Mao, and Marcuse!" To this trio we add Lenin, whose importance is reflected in the fact that today Communist parties call themselves Marxist-*Leninist,* and not merely Marxist. Here we shall give a thumbnail sketch of the contributions of Lenin, Mao, Marcuse, and several other left-wing economists and social philosophers during the period between the deaths of Marx and Engels (late nineteenth century) and the rise of the American New Left, which we date from the SDS "Port Huron Statement" of 1962. Our account does not pretend to be a connected history of socialist thought.

Marx died in 1883. Engels, who lived until 1895, edited the last two volumes of Marx's *Capital.* At the same time, however, Engels's revolutionary zeal seemed to wane both with the passing of Marx and the failure of the Revolution to arrive "on schedule"[1] in any of the advanced countries of Europe and North America, where the evolution of capitalism had gone the furthest toward its expected downfall. In spite of several serious economic depressions in the 1870s and 1890s, the socialist revolution seemed much more remote when Engels died than it had seemed in the 1848 "year of revolution," when he and Marx had written their *Communist Manifesto.*

MARX'S FOLLOWERS

The first split in the Marxist ranks came in 1899, sixteen years after Marx's death and only four years

Karl Marx

after that of Engels. It came within the German Social Democratic party, then mainly Marxist and also the world's leading socialist party. The arch-heretic was Eduard Bernstein (1850–1932), who had been Engels's secretary. Bernstein wrote a book best known under its English title of *Evolutionary Socialism.* Bernstein's main points were the following:

1. Capitalism was *not* collapsing from internal contradictions. The middle class was *not* dying out, workers' living standards were *not* falling, and large-

---

1. Marx and Engels never drew up a timetable for the Revolution. They apparently expected it for 1848 or shortly thereafter. When it failed to occur, they wisely refrained from "rescheduling" it. But surely they would be disappointed to find capitalism still controlling major industrial countries in the late twentieth century.

scale agriculture was *not* replacing either the American family farm or its European equivalents.

2. Capitalism would not collapse, and therefore socialism must prove its own superiority and "fitness" in free competition in the marketplace of ideas.

3. Accordingly, socialists should stress reformist electoral and parliamentary paths, and give up the idea of violent revolution in the republics and constitutional monarchies of Europe and America.

Bernstein was answered by Karl Kautsky (1854–1938), "the Socialist Pope" and Engels's successor as editor of Marx's unpublished manuscripts. The German party, and other European Social Democratic parties,[2] officially accepted Kautsky's "orthodox" answer to Bernstein's economic heresies, but then quietly began to follow Bernstein's recommendations on political tactics.[3] For this reason, social democracy is regarded today as reformist rather than revolutionary.

The then much weaker and less important Russian Social Democratic party, operating largely underground and in exile, faced the same conflict. Its Menshevik (minority) faction favored positions close to Bernstein's. Its Bolshevik (majority) faction, which would later be led by Vladimir Ilich Lenin (1870–1924), also known as Nikolai Lenin, went beyond Kautsky in the vigor of its denunciations. In view of the later world leadership of the Russian party and of Lenin's remarkable success in combining theoretical and practical leadership, we move on to discuss the "Leninist" component of Marxism-Leninism.

Vladimir Ilich Lenin

LENIN

Lenin's major contributions to world socialism—as distinguished from his contributions to specifically Russian problems—are three in number, two of them ideological and the third tactical.

1. Lenin more than any other single Marxist writer is responsible for the "internationalization" of

the argument in Marx's *Capital*.[4] Lenin's explanation of capitalist survival was imperialism, the export of capital and capitalist domination to the less developed countries of the world. This extension kept the organic composition of capital—the k term in Marxian equations—low, thereby avoiding both the falling rate of profit and the "increasing misery" of at least the organized labor aristocracy of the capitalist countries. Lenin called such workers the "pampered palace slaves" of capitalism. But imperialism, with or without colonial rule, was not a permanent cure for capitalism's contradictions. On the one hand, it led to imperialist war between rival capitalist powers, for example, World War I. On the other hand, it led to warfare with the natives of the countries being "imperialized." In either form of warfare, the masses in

2. The American Socialist party was never a Marxist party, though many of its individual leaders were Marxists.

3. The test came with the outbreak of World War I in 1914. The Social Democratic party, demonstrating its patriotism, voted to support war credits (war loans). Kautsky went along with this decision. Social Democratic parties in other countries on both sides also expressed patriotic solidarity with their capitalist governments, though the pre-1914 party line had been to resist and sabotage international warfare and transform it into socialist revolution.

4. A number of Marxist writers made important contributions to this "internationalization" process, summarized in Anthony Brewer, *Marxist Theories of Imperialism* (London: Routledge and Kegan Paul, 1980). Chapter 2 deals explicitly with Lenin's *Imperialism, the Highest Stage of Capitalism*.

the capitalist countries must be armed and could be turned against their capitalist exploiters. "The road to London and Paris," Lenin once said, "runs through Peking and Calcutta."

2. It followed for Lenin that the worldwide socialist revolution against capitalist rule need not begin in those lands where capitalism had gone the furthest. It might just as well begin with a war of liberation in some colonial backwater, and spread from there. In fact, it might just as well begin in Czarist Russia, where misery and oppression were particularly bad, even though Russia was, economically speaking; only a backward outpost of European capitalism, and even though Russian capitalism was not well developed.

3. In a backward country like Russia, the workers were not ready for revolutionary activity "on their own." Marxists believed that trade unions could easily be sidetracked into "economism"—that is, concentrating on economic demands for small groups of labor aristocrats "within the system" and ignoring the need to overthrow the system as a whole. What was needed was a revolutionary "vanguard party" to represent the workers' true interests. Such a vanguard party must, Lenin felt, be revolutionary. It must not only be an elite group, unfettered by bourgeois law and morals, but must include an underground core organized in military fashion. This underground party must be prepared to seize full power in the revolutionary struggle, with no need for alliances with liberals and other reformists. Membership in the vanguard party should be limited to loyal activists who make the Revolution the main object of their lives. Also, once the vanguard party has seized power, it should hold on to its "proletarian dictatorship" until socialism is firmly established once and for all, ignoring the forms and machinery of electoral democracy. Of course, for Russia today, the vanguard party is the Communist party.[5]

LUXEMBURG

A middle position in these conflicts, both in Germany and Russia, was held by Rosa Luxemburg (1870–1919). Born in Poland, "Red Rosa" spoke German and Russian as well as Polish, and was active in the revolutionary Marxist politics of all three countries.[6] Her views have come to be respected since her death even more than during her rather short life.

Luxemburg too had a theory of imperialism. But whereas Lenin stressed the export of capital to prop up the domestic rate of profit and prevent *liquidity* crises, Luxemburg stressed the dumping of consumer goods in the less developed countries, when they could not be sold domestically at profitable prices. In terms of Marxist theory, the Luxemburg approach concentrates on avoiding *realization* crises by imperialist expansion.

Luxemburg was no Bernstein disciple or Menshevik reformist. Neither was she an "orthodox" follower of "Pope" Kautsky. She broke with him over the "war credits" issue in 1914, just as Lenin broke with the "patriotic" Mensheviks in Russia. Also, like Lenin, Luxemburg favored an activist, paramilitary vanguard party, ready to seize power in revolutionary struggles without waiting for the election returns. Unlike Lenin, however, she was always suspicious of party dictatorship. She took the "democracy" of the Social Democratic party label seriously in its conventional sense, which calls for the rule "of" and "by" the people as well as "for" them. Though welcoming the Bolshevik seizure of power in Russia in November 1917, she opposed the reign of terror by which the Bolsheviks held on to their power in the following years, beginning when they dissolved a constitutional convention in January 1918. These aspects of her thinking are highly respected by the "Marxist humanist" wing of the New Left.

FROM LENIN TO STALIN

Lenin died in 1924. In the Soviet Union his death signaled a long struggle for power among the subordinate Bolshevik leaders, ending in the dictatorship of Josef Stalin (1880–1953) and the execution of most of Stalin's rivals. This struggle too had important economic implications.

Faced with domestic economic disorganization and a major famine after the end of the Russian Civil

---

5. After the two Russian Revolutions of 1917, the Bolshevik wing of the former Social Democratic party called itself the Communist party. The Menshevik wing continued to call itself the Social Democratic party, but was largely liquidated in the Red Terror and Russian Civil War of 1918–1920.

6. She was assassinated in Berlin while under arrest as a leader of the "Spartacist" revolt. This was an attempt to duplicate in Germany the success of the Bolsheviks in Russia, in the chaos that followed the German defeat in World War I and the abdication of the last Hohenzollern Kaiser, Wilhelm II.

War, Lenin had modified his extremism[7] and accepted a "New Economic Policy" for the Soviet Union. Under this policy, private enterprise was allowed in small-scale industry, light industry, and agriculture, while heavy industry and finance remained in state hands. In the midst of economic revival, an agricultural crisis developed. Russia had lost perhaps 20 million people during World War I, the 1917 revolutions, and the Civil War. Because of the rapid industrialization of the New Economic Policy, many workers left the farms for jobs in the cities.[8] Farm prices began to rise, lowering workers' real wages and hampering industrialization by lowering the urban-rural income differential. But the pace of industrialization had to be maintained, both to prevent any future capitalist "encirclement" or economic "squeeze" and to provide an industrial working class that would support continued socialization. To the Marxist, the peasant was essentially a small capitalist, interested mainly in owning land and profiting by its produce. What was to be done?

In this crisis, the Communist Right Wing (later called *Right Deviation*) was led by an economist, Nikolai Bukharin (1888–1938).[9] Bukharin considered the rising trend of agricultural prices to be only temporary, since he expected that the higher farm prices would lead to more farm production. He saw no need to abandon the New Economic Policy or to put direct pressure on the peasants. The Left Wing (later called *Left Deviation*) was led by Leon Trotsky (1879–1940), whose lieutenant in economic matters was Yevgeny Preobrazhensky (1886–1937). Trotsky's position is not easy to understand. On the one hand, he favored the use of "persuasion" on the peasants to squeeze out more production at controlled prices while making them consume less and save more. But he also favored bringing the peasants into collective farms, along with their private holdings of land, machinery, farm animals, stored grain, and so on.

In the power struggle, Stalin at first sided with Bukharin against Trotsky and Preobrazhensky. Since that time, "Trotskyism" has remained a label attached in the Soviet Union to almost any Left deviation from the current party line. At the same time, Trotskyism became a flag under which dissidents from Stalinism rallied outside the Soviet sphere of influence.[10] Trotsky himself was sent to Siberia, exiled, and later murdered in Mexico. With Trotsky out of the way, Stalin adopted and intensified what had been the Left Wing economic platform. The New Economic Policy was followed by the Five Year Plans. The peasants were collectivized on harsher terms than had been recommended by the Left Wing. A quarter-century of Stalin's dictatorship ended only with his death in 1953.

MAO ZEDONG AND COMMUNIST CHINA

Our scene now shifts to China. To the historian of economic thought, the most important innovation of Mao Zedong (1894–1976) was his basing of the Chinese Communist revolution on discontented peasant farmers (for the most part tenants of richer farmers or absentee landlords), rather than on urban workers (the Marxian proletariat). In the late 1920s and early 1930s, urban-based attempts at revolution in China had failed despite Soviet support and advice, and the Soviets had been lukewarm in their backing of Chairman Mao's successful leadership in the late 1940s.[11]

Then, ten years after expelling the previous Chinese government to the island of Taiwan, Mao first led a "Great Leap Forward" (1958–1962) and then a "Great Cultural Revolution" (1966–1976). The Great Leap was intended to achieve the Communist goal of an economy of abundance through largely decentralized communes, combining agricultural and industrial production in "rural cities." The Cultural Revolution aimed at substituting moral incentives

---

7. Lenin's "extremism," shared by other Bolshevik economists at the time of the Bolshevik Revolution, had been based on an oversimplified planning system modeled after a concept of the country as "one big factory" and intuitively understandable to the average worker. Such a plan would, it was hoped, permit the Soviet Union to operate on a barter system, dispensing with the "bourgeois" social contrivance of money.

8. Technically, this drain of workers from the farms was largely a return flow. Urban workers and demobilized soldiers had gone to the country (where the food was) during the Civil War and the famine that followed it. With greater availability of food in the cities by the middle 1920s, many of these people were simply returning there.

9. Bukharin was the model for the hero Rubashov in Arthur Koestler's *Darkness at Noon*.

10. Trotsky lives on in literature as Emmanuel Goldstein in George Orwell's *Nineteen Eighty-Four*.

11. The Soviets have generally looked with disfavor on Communist party leaders in other countries who have assumed leadership positions without receiving their training in Russia and without the blessings of the Soviet leadership when other leaders having these advantages were available. Mao Zedong is the most important example.

for material ones, at equalizing income and wealth, and at preventing the rise of any bureaucratic "New Class" of white-collar elite workers within the Communist party, the government, or the People's Liberation Army.

Both of these innovations are now judged as failures. The Great Leap Forward, which planned to take over from the Soviet Union the world leadership of the communist movement, led instead to a near-famine in China and to a breakdown in the shaky alliance between the two leading Marxist countries. Such breakdowns were not dreamed of in Marx's philosophy. The Cultural Revolution degenerated into chaos and mob rule, which required military intervention to restore order and revive the economy. Before its failure, however, the Cultural Revolution had attracted worldwide New Left support for its "participatory democracy," its attacks on the Chinese bureaucracy, and its status as an egalitarian alternative to the Soviet system.[12]

12. Strangely enough, Mao Zedong found Stalinism less reprehensible than the somewhat milder regimes that were in power between Stalin's passing and his own death twenty-three years later.

MARCUSE AND THE NEW LEFT

Our account continues with Herbert Marcuse, the final member of the trio "Marx, Mao, and Marcuse." Marcuse (1898–1981) was a German sociologist of the so-called Frankfurt school. For much of his early life he was an academic, respected for his scholarship, but quite unknown to the general public. And before his death he had already been almost forgotten. But after fleeing to America to escape Hitler, he enjoyed more than a decade of fame, both in his native Europe and his adopted America, as a darling of the New Left. The slogan "Marx, Mao, and Marcuse" meant what it said. Marcuse was, for the time being, classed with Marx and Mao, despite the handicap of a difficult literary style.

Marcuse's main contributions were four in number. They ranged from his treatment of demand in economics to theories in the fields of sociology, psychology, and philosophy, with which Marcuse was more at home.

1. There has always been a libertine "free love" tradition in the political Left, which has had to exist along with the rival puritanical tradition, which equates sexual experimentation with "capitalist decadence." In *Eros and Civilization,* Marcuse combined ideas of Karl Marx and Sigmund Freud, and argued that true socialism means freedom for the human spirit. Such freedom, he said, must include sexual freedom—the liberation from "middle-class morality." This was what some members of the Left wanted to hear, and they welcomed it with enthusiasm.

2. "Work is a four-letter word," according to the hippies, and Marcuse "proved" it was quite unnecessary. In *One-Dimensional Man,* Marcuse argued that if we could only restrain our demands, we should easily be able to produce all we want by voluntary work, and could have the economy of abundance the minute after the Revolution. Also, we would be just as well off as we are now. Consumption—more goods, newer goods, new models, more *de luxe* frills—is simply narcotic and does *not* give more satisfaction. Marcuse argued that we are alienated from our society, as Marx had said, but we still expect fancier and more numerous consumer goods to cure our alienation, even though they have never done so in the past. So we become one-dimensional people—consumers of goods. It is better to forget about consumption and standards of living and to give up the rat race in favor of the natural life of play and song and love, all "on the cheap."

3. Marcuse said that the working class is hopelessly narcotized by consumerism and by advertising. It cannot be trusted to overthrow the system. Who then can overthrow it? Marcuse's answer is the student youth, not yet quite overcome by the pressure to consume, and possibly still able to resist the lure of one-dimensional "consumer fascism." As for allies, there are the underclasses at home and abroad—racial minorities, Third World peoples, domestic drifters, dropouts, junkies, hippies, migrants, even criminals—whom Marx himself had scored as *lumpenproletariat* (bums). The youth and the students, not the blue-collar working stiffs, will be the vanguard of the new society.

4. Nor did Marcuse believe in the need to tolerate the opposition. After all, he argued, Mussolini's Fascists and Hitler's Nazis got their start because of misplaced tolerance. They should not have been tolerated at all, but put down at once. Furthermore, today's Establishment uses toleration mainly to allow opponents to "let off steam" ineffectually. This tolerance simply conceals the repressive nature of society, which becomes apparent whenever the opposition becomes a real danger to "things as they are" or to the interests of the capitalist class. Such is the message of Marcuse's *Critique of Pure Tolerance.*

All this was heady stuff for student radicals, who were used to being patted on the head or told to go home and grow up. It went over big in the 1960s and the early 1970s. In fact, Marcuse's message was never refuted. Instead, the job market tightened after the Vietnam War, placing a greater value on "a smile and a shoeshine" and making potential troublemakers "think twice."[13] So the New Left and its heroes fell from fashion into nostalgia, with Marcuse a principal victim. Will New Left ideas and New Left tactics return to favor in the next period of high employment and labor shortage? We do not know, and we dare not forecast.

13. Unlike the situation of the Great Depression, unemployment was not a severe problem for the white students with the proper credentials and "nothing against them." Employers could and did engage in political discrimination. If the situation had deteriorated further, with no jobs for anyone, discrimination would have again been meaningless.

Glossary

ability-to-pay principle a guide for taxation that advocates that tax liability should be a larger fraction of income (or wealth) for high-income (or high-wealth) receivers than for low-income (or low-wealth) receivers.

absolute advantage being more proficient than others in some branch of production.

absolute amount of cost difference (entry barrier) an entry barrier based upon the difference in average total costs existing between established firms in an industry and potential entrants.

accelerating inflation a situation in which the rate of inflation is increasing; if the acceleration is unexpected, money illusion and wage-cost lags continue to affect employment decisions, and unemployment remains below its natural rate.

accelerator effect the effect that a change in the rate of expansion or contraction in the economy has on the absolute volume of production and income in capital goods industries.

accommodation an action by monetary authorities shifting the money-supply curve so that shifts in the demand-for-money curve do not cause changes in the rate of interest; sometimes called *validation*.

accord, the an agreement reached in 1951 between the Federal Reserve System and the U.S. Treasury under which the Fed was freed from a wartime commitment to support the price of government securities.

acquisition See *merger*.

actual monopoly a real-world form of monopoly; a market in which there is a single seller, sellers in other markets may offer fairly good substitutes, potential competition cannot be ruled out, and the government protection that an actual monopoly may enjoy is not secure, as it may be taken away or altered.

adaptive expectations a proposition that states that the inflation rate that is being experienced during the present time period becomes the inflation rate that is anticipated for the future.

administrative protection a form of protection that subjects competitive imports to burdensome, idiosyncratic, costly, and time-consuming specifications or inspection procedures.

aggregate demand the total value of goods and services demanded in an economy, measured at some specified price level; the relationship between a change in the price level and the resulting change in the quantity of real GNP demanded.

aggregate-demand curve a graphic illustration of the relationship between a change in the price level and the quantity of real national income and product demanded.

aggregate economic concentration a measure of the share of economic activity undertaken by the largest firms in a region of the world, in an economy, or in some major sector beyond traditional industry lines.

aggregate quantity demanded the sum of total purchases, $C + I + G + X - Im$, of an economy during a specified time period at a certain price level.

aggregate quantity supplied the sum of all the goods and services that firms will produce and offer for sale in an economy during a specified time period at a certain price level.

aggregate supply the total value of all goods and services supplied in an economy, measured at some specified price level; the relationship between a change in the price level and the resulting change in the quantity of real GNP supplied.

aggregate-supply curve a graphic illustration of the relationship between the price level and the quantity of real national income and product supplied.

agricultural fundamentalism the doctrine or argument that since food is a necessity and since the countryside is the main market for the manufactured products of the city, farm revenue cannot fall below a certain percentage of national income or GNP without bringing on a depression; the doctrine that, since food is necessary to life, farmers should be at least as well off as any other group.

alienation a psychological ailment expressed in the feeling of hostility or indifference to someone or something in one's society that is generally considered attractive to others in that society.

allocation function the function or role of government involving influence upon the kinds and quantities of different goods and services produced in the economy.

American Federation of Labor (AF of L) a federation of national unions established in 1886 to practice business unionism and merged with the CIO in 1955 to form the AF of L–CIO.

anarchist one who opposes all forms of government compulsion and favors a society organized on the basis of voluntary associations, which individuals can leave at any time.

antitrust policy the course of action (by the government) aimed at maintaining or restoring competition in markets.

applied science an objective, factual, and systematic search for knowledge that includes practical utilizations along with theoretical inquires.

appreciation (in foreign exchange rates) an increase in the foreign exchange value of a nation's money.

arbitrage the purchase of a product in one market for the purpose of immediately reselling it in another market in order to take advantage of a price difference.

arbitration a procedure for settling union-management disputes by having a neutral outside party make a decision that is binding on both sides.

area of inequality the space between a Lorenz curve and the diagonal line of perfect equality on a Lorenz curve diagram.

assets valuable items that are owned; balance sheet entries recording the values of items that are owned.

assumption a statement that is accepted as being true in order to set forth the limits of the variables in a theory.

automatic (or built-in) stabilizers provisions of tax and spending laws that work automatically to moderate expansions and contractions of the economy.

automatic transfer service (ATS) a procedure through which balances can be changed automatically from one account to another in a financial institution.

autonomous consumption expenditure the amount of planned consumption expenditure that is independent of the level of disposable personal income.

average fixed cost (AFC) the total fixed cost of a firm divided by the quantity level of its output in that period. It is also the difference between a firm's average total cost and its average variable cost.

average product the total product that a firm produces in a given period divided by the quantity of a variable input that it uses to produce it.

average propensity to consume (APC) the amount of planned consumption expenditure (C) divided by the amount of disposable personal income (DPI).

average propensity to save (APS) the amount of planned saving (S) divided by the amount of disposable personal income (DPI).

average revenue the total revenue of a firm in a given period divided by the quantity level of output that it sells in that period.

average total cost (ATC) the total cost of a firm in a given period divided by the quantity level of its output in that period.

average variable cost (AVC) the total variable cost of a firm in a given period divided by the quantity level of its output in that period. A firm's average variable cost plus its average fixed cost equals its average total cost.

B

balanced-budget multiplier a change in the equilibrium level of national income and product divided by the size of the (equal) changes in government purchases and net taxes that brought it about.

balance of payments account a record of transactions affecting the international demand and supply for a nation's money.

balance of trade the amount by which the value of a country's exports of goods exceeds the value of its imports of goods. It may be negative.

balance on current account (current balance) the balance of payments account entry showing the extent to which credit items exceed debit items in a country's international transactions in goods, services, investment income, and unilateral transfers.

balance sheet an accounting report on the condition of a business firm or other organization as of the close of business on a particular date.

bank charter a document issued by a state or the federal government granting permission to engage in banking and specifying the terms and conditions of such permission.

bank examiner a government agent who investigates the condition and operation of a bank.

banking the business of accepting deposits and making loans including commercial loans.

bank note a certificate issued by a bank which promises to pay a specified sum to the bearer of the certificate.

bankruptcy a legal concept indicating a state of insolvency—of being unable to repay creditors.

bargaining unit the workers for whom a particular union is bargaining and to whom a particular labor contract applies.

barometric firm price leadership a condition in an oligopolistic industry in which one firm's price changes are followed by other firms in that industry because they respect the price leader and see its changes as being "correct" responses to market conditions.

barter the exchange of one good or service for another without the use of money as a medium of exchange.

base period the time period chosen as the reference period in constructing an index number.

basic balance of payments the international balance of payments concept that adds a country's long-term private capital imports and subtracts that country's long-term private capital exports from its balance on current account.

basic human needs amounts of food, clothing, shelter, education, health care, and access to public decision making considered to be necessary as a minimum before attention should be directed to conventional economic growth; a point of view that development is taking place only when a steadily falling percentage of the people of a country lacks good food, clean water, decent shelter, basic health care, elementary education, and a means of presenting their views to their government.

basing-point system an industry agreement calling for each firm, no matter where it is located, to charge a delivered price that includes transportation charges based on the presumption that the product was shipped from a common origin. It is a form of price discrimination.

beneficial externalities See *externalities*.

benefit-cost analysis a procedure for the systematic evaluation of the economic merits of a proposed undertaking.

benefit-received principle (of taxation) a guide for taxation that advocates that the tax payment made by an individual or a firm should be related to the value of goods and services provided by the government to the taxpayer.

bilateral monopoly a market situation in which a monopolist seller faces a monopsonist buyer.

black market an illegal market in which goods or services are sold above a legally set maximum price. See also *ceiling price*.

Board of Governors (of the Federal Reserve System) seven people, appointed by the President of the United States to establish policy for and supervise the operation of the Federal Reserve System.

bond a certificate of indebtedness promising to repay a principal sum and interest on specified dates.

borrowed reserves reserves borrowed by depository institutions at the discount window from district Federal Reserve Banks.

boycott refusal to engage in trade with another country or firm in specific goods of that country or firm; in labor-management relations, an attempt by employees (or a union) to block the distribution and sale of an employer's product.

bracket push (creep) the effect that inflation has of pushing taxpayers into higher tax rate brackets and increasing the proportion of income payable under progressive income tax systems that are not indexed.

break-even point in macroeconomics, the level of disposable personal income at which planned consumption expenditure equals disposable personal income and planned saving is zero; in microeconomics, a level of output at which a firm's total revenue is equal to its total cost.

Bretton Woods system the rules and institutions established at Bretton Woods, New Hampshire, in 1944, to regulate the international economic system. The principal Bretton Woods institutions are the World Bank and the International Monetary Fund.

budget deficit See *deficit*.

budget line in the indifference analysis theory of consumer behavior, a line showing the combinations of goods and/or services measured on the axes of a graph that can be purchased by an individual who has a particular income and who faces particular prices for these goods and/or services.

buffer stocks government holdings of farm products kept as reserves against periods of bad weather or other disasters to ensure an adequate supply. An "ever-normal granary" is a buffer stock of a basic grain such as wheat or rice.

building cycle   See *Kuznets cycle*.

built-in stabilizers   See *automatic stabilizers*.

bullionism   a seventeenth- and eighteenth-century school of economic thought that emphasized the accumulation of treasure.

burden (of a tax)   a reduction in real income resulting from a tax.

business cycles   expansions and contractions in the volume of aggregate economic activity that alternate with some regularity in an economy. Referred to as business "fluctuations" by those who wish to imply less regularity.

business unionism   a union philosophy that relies on economic power to achieve goals of higher real wages and better working conditions.

C

capital (or capital resources)   a factor of production or resource that is composed of goods and skills that are used as inputs for production. Unlike the other resources, it must first be produced itself before it is available for use in further production. See also *human capital*.

capital account   in balance of payments accounts, the record of international transactions in securities, long- and short-term loans, and deposits in financial institutions.

capital coefficient   the amount of additional capital required for a unit increase in the net national product.

capital consumption allowance   the national income accounting estimate of the value of capital goods (production equipment) used up in producing other goods. It is subtracted from gross national product to obtain net national product.

capital gain (or loss)   the gain (or loss) from a change in the market value of an asset that takes place while it is owned by a given individual.

capital goods   See *physical capital*.

capital resources   See *capital*.

capitalist system   an economic system in which most physical instruments of production are owned by private individuals and business firms.

capital/output ratio   the value of capital used in production divided by the value of output produced per time period.

capital requirement (entry barrier)   an entry barrier based upon the minimum amount of money needed to acquire the capital goods necessary for a new firm to compete adequately with the established firms in an industry.

capital resources   See *capital; physical capital*.

capital skills   See *human capital*.

cartel   an organization (a collusive arrangement) that coordinates and limits the outputs of producers for the purpose of raising the price of the product and the profits of the producers.

ceiling price   a maximum price at which a product can legally be sold. A meaningful ceiling price is set below the equilibrium price that would otherwise be established in that market.

Celler-Kefauver Antimerger Amendment   a 1950 amendment to the Clayton Act, which added coverage of asset acquisitions and eliminated the wording that made the Act applicable only to horizontal mergers.

ceteris paribus   a Latin phrase meaning "other things being equal," used in economic theorizing to hold constant all variables but those being considered.

checkable accounts   See *transactions accounts*.

checkoff   a form of union security that calls for the employer to deduct union dues from workers' paychecks and to pay those dues directly to the union.

circular flow equilibrium   when the sum of consumption purchases, investment purchases, government purchases, and net exports equals the amount paid out by firms for resources used in production plus expected profits: $C + I + G + X - Im = Y$.

circular flow model   a diagram illustrating the macroeconomic functioning of an economy as a system in which funds that flow from business firms to households constitute the national income and flows from households to business firms through various channels make up the national product.

Civil Rights Act   a law passed by the U.S. Congress in 1964. Title VII prohibits discrimination in hiring, firing, or promotions based on race, color, religion, sex, or national origin.

civilian employment rate   the number of civilians employed as a percent of the total civilian noninstitutional population age 16 years and over.

civilian labor force   the noninstitutional civilian population age 16 and over who are willing and able to work and who are either employed or actively seeking employment.

civilian labor force participation rate   the percentage of the civilian noninstitutional population age 16 or older that is working or looking for work.

civilian unemployment rate   the percentage of the civilian labor force that is unemployed according to official statistics.

classical economics   the school of economic thought, based on the ideas of Adam Smith (1723–1790), David Ricardo (1771–1823), and their successors, which was prominent in the first half of the nineteenth century.

Clayton Act   a law passed by the U.S. Congress in

1914 to control anticompetitive price discrimination, mergers, exclusive dealing and tying arrangements, and interlocking directorates. It also excluded trade union activities from the scope of the antitrust laws.

closed economy a country that severely restricts trade across its borders.

closed shop a form of union security arrangement requiring that a person must be a member of a certain union before he or she can be hired. It is illegal under the Taft-Hartley Act of 1947.

coincident indicators index numbers that move along with the total economy; they should be used to measure fluctuations.

collective bargaining the approach used by labor unions to negotiate with employers or their representatives.

collective goods and services goods and services which, by their nature, must be consumed in common by all people in an area.

collectivist a philosophy characterized by opposition to individual or private ownership of the means of production.

collectivist system an economic system in which land and physical instruments of production are owned by collective agencies, such as the government or labor organizations, not by private individuals or business firms.

collusion (or collusive agreement) an agreement among buyers, sellers, and/or outsiders upon a particular course of action. Firms may collude to gain monopoly control in order to achieve high economic profit. See also *price fixing*.

commercial bank a financial institution that provides a wide range of services including checking accounts.

commercial treaty an agreement between countries dealing with economic and trade relations.

commission a charge made by a stockbroker for services rendered in carrying out a transaction.

Common Market a term generally used in reference to the European Community, which is a customs union of nations in Europe.

common property a legal arrangement that gives everyone equal rights to particular resources.

commune a cooperative farm or other collectively organized unit.

communist a socialist who believes that after a few generations of near-worldwide socialism, socialist economies will reach a stage of communism where most or all important goods will be free and scarcity will have been eliminated. Violence, revolution, and dictatorship are accepted means to that end.

comparable worth basing pay in different occupa-
tions on scores or point systems weighing, for example, the arduousness of the work, education requirements, and so on.

comparative advantage a principle of international trade that explains which commodities a given country is likely to import and export.

comparative statics the technique of studying variations in equilibrium positions that result from changes in the underlying variables.

competition used in two different senses in economics: (1) rivalry among sellers or buyers; striving among a number of rivals in a contest aimed at purchasing or selling a particular product; (2) the market structure resulting from pure competition.

competitive depreciation a situation in which countries contest with each other in trying to increase exports and reduce imports by lowering the foreign exchange value of their monies.

complements (or complementary goods) products that are used in conjunction with each other such as automobiles and gasoline or cameras and film.

concentration ratio a measure that expresses the percentage share of some key variable such as sales or assets accounted for by the largest firms. See also *economic concentration*.

concessional loan credit extended on terms that are more favorable to the borrower than are available in loanable funds markets; typically, long-term development loans to LDCs at interest rates well below international market rates.

condition of entry the "extent to which established sellers can persistently raise their prices above a competitive level without attracting new firms to enter the industry" (Bain, *Barriers to New Competition*).

conglomerate merger the acquisition by a firm of another firm engaged in a different industry.

Congress of Industrial Organizations (CIO) a federation of national industrial unions established in 1938 and merged with the AF of L in 1955.

conspicuous consumption the use of certain goods and services to display the owner's wealth and to gain prestige and the envy of others.

constant capital a Marxian concept describing the labor hours embodied in raw materials and in the depreciation of machinery and other long-lived capital goods.

constant dollars dollars adjusted by an index number to base year purchasing power.

constant returns to scale long-run returns when an increase in the level of output of a firm is exactly proportionate to the increase in that firm's inputs.

consumer equilibrium the condition existing when an individual has made all purchases and finds that the marginal utility per dollar spent for each good or service is the same. Maximum possible utility and satisfaction are realized. *Consumer equilibrium* (or *consumer equilibrium rule* in the theory of indifference analysis): the condition achieved when an individual consumes the combination of goods and services indicated at the point where his or her budget line is tangent to one of his or her indifference curves.

consumer price index (CPI) an index number representing a weighted average of the prices of all goods and services purchased by representative families in an economy; often called the cost-of-living index, used to measure changes in the cost of purchasing a group of basic consumer goods and services.

consumer rationality See *rational consumer.*

consumer sovereignty the theory that the consumer is free to determine the mix of goods and services that he or she will purchase, subject only to income limitations and prices to be paid.

consumers' surplus the difference between the amount that a consumer pays for purchases of a product and the total utility obtained from these products by that consumer; the benefit that consumers gain from being able to buy many units of a good or service at the price they are willing to pay for the last unit consumed.

consumption purchases (C) expenditure by households and individuals on goods and services; household use of goods and services.

consumption function the relationship between the level of disposable personal income and the amount of planned expenditures by households on currently produced consumer goods and services.

contestable markets markets that are very easy to enter and leave. Such markets may be actual monopolies, but the ease of potential entry makes them poor candidates for government regulation.

contractionary gap a gap between the equilibrium level and the target level of the national income and product that exists when the equilibrium level is less than the target level.

contraction phase the portion of a business cycle or fluctuation in which the volume of economic activity in an economy is steadily falling.

contractionary disequilibrium when the aggregate quantity supplied is greater than the aggregate quantity demanded so that output will be reduced and prices lowered.

controls See *price controls.*

corporate society a society organized to preserve capitalist private ownership of the means of production but that reserves large regulatory powers for the state.

corporation a business firm chartered by the government and established as a legal person separate from its owners and managers; common features are unlimited life for the corporation and limited liability for individual shareholders.

corporation income tax a tax based on the net income of corporations.

corrective tax a tax on a particular good or service imposed for the purpose of correcting for resource misallocations due to harmful externalities.

cost See *opportunity cost.*

cost of living adjustment (COLA) a provision in a labor contract specifying automatic changes in wage rates based on changes in an index number of prices.

cost of living index See *consumer price index.*

cost-plus pricing principle a rule of thumb practiced in some industries in which firms determine their selling price by adding a uniform percentage to certain elements of average total cost.

cost-push inflation a rise in the price level due to a leftward shift in the aggregate-supply curve.

Council of Economic Advisers three persons appointed by the President under the authority of the Employment Act of 1946, whose job is to conduct research and to advise the President on economic policy.

countertrade a fancy name for barter.

craft union a union representing a particular type of skilled worker such as carpenters, typographers, or plumbers.

credit an amount of money loaned; also, a positive accounting entry.

cross demand the relationship between the price of one product and the quantity demanded of another product.

cross elasticity of demand the percentage change in the quantity demanded of a product divided by the percentage change in the price of a different product that caused it.

crowding out the reduction in planned investment that takes place when real interest rates rise because of government borrowing to finance budget deficits; when some of the saving flowing through the financial markets is used to pay for government purchases rather than to finance investment purchases.

currency paper money usually issued by a government or central bank and given legal tender status.

current balance see balance on current account.

current dollars dollars with purchasing power based on the price level prevailing at the time when a purchase is made or income is received.

customs union a form of economic integration

among a group of countries that establishes a common tariff against nonmembers.

cycle theories theories that imply that a regular, predictable pattern exists to explain changes in the economy.

cycles See *business cycles.*

cyclical deficit the amount of government budget deficit that arises because the economy is operating below its target level of national income and product.

cyclical unemployment joblessness that arises because there are not enough job openings at current wage rates for all those qualified to fill them. See also *macroeconomic unemployment.*

D

debit a negative entry in an accounting system.

debt renegotiation changing the terms of existing loans, usually by extending or "stretching out" repayment dates without increases in nominal interest rates.

decelerating inflation a situation in which the rate of inflation is falling. See *disinflation.*

decision-making lag the time required to debate alternative remedies for economic problems and to choose among them.

deficiency payment In U.S. farm programs, a payment to a farmer from the government equal to the difference between the target price and the support price for quantities sold by the farmer.

deficit a state of budget imbalance in which expenditures exceed receipts; in balance of payments accounting, a condition in which negative or debit entries exceed positive or credit entries; government purchases greater than net taxes.

deficit financing funding those expenditures that are in excess of current receipts through borrowing, that is, through incurring debt.

deficit spending expenditures that are in excess of current receipts.

deflation a sustained decrease in the general level of prices, usually measured by the rate of change in some index number.

deflationist policy the plan to recover from a recession by allowing wage rates and other input prices to fall so that profit margins will expand and invite increases in output.

demand the willingness and ability to buy at certain prices. See also *individual consumer demand, market demand, quantity demanded.*

demand curve graph of a demand schedule; a curve illustrating the quantities of a good or service that are demanded at various possible prices.

demand deposits funds placed with a financial institution under terms that require the institution to pay out upon the demand of the depositor. A type of checkable account or transaction account.

demand for money the quantity of the monetary unit desired to be held as cash balances. See *precautionary, speculative,* and *transactions demands for money.*

demand-for-money curve the relationship between the rate of interest and the quantity of money demanded.

demand schedule a table showing the relationship between different prices of a good or service and the quantity demanded of that good or service at each of these prices.

demand-side economics an approach to macroeconomic analysis that emphasizes the aggregate-demand curve and includes both Keynesian and monetarist positions.

dependencia (theory of underdevelopment) the theory that countries with an early advantage in military technology used this power to impose domination over other countries and to prevent them from developing by taking their resources, denying them technological knowledge, and shifting the terms of trade against them.

dependent variable a variable that depends upon some other variable or variables in a functional relationship.

depletion allowance a provision of income taxation permitting resource owners to deduct from taxable income part of the value of resources that are extracted from the earth.

deposit-contraction process the sequence of events through which a withdrawal of funds from depository institutions leads to a contraction of the total amount of checkable account balances.

deposit-expansion factor the ratio between the amount of a change in total checkable account balances and the amount of a new deposit that caused that change. The factor is estimated to be approximately equal to the reciprocal of the reserve ratio.

deposit-expansion process the sequence of events through which a new deposit in the system of depository institutions leads to an increase in the amount of checkable account balances.

deposit insurance insurance issued by the Federal Deposit Insurance Corporation or other agencies to protect depositors from loss in the event of the failure of a financial institution.

depository institution an organization such as a bank, a savings and loan association, or a credit union that accepts deposits of funds and offers checking services.

Depository Institutions Deregulation and Monetary Control Act of 1980 legislation that, among other things, required the elimination, over a six-year-period, of upper limits on interest rates payable on deposits in depository institutions. See also *Monetary Control Act of 1980.*

depreciation the decline in the market value of a capital good as it wears out or becomes old-fashioned and out-of-date. In foreign exchange theory, a decline in the foreign exchange value of a nation's money.

depression severe contraction phase of a business cycle involving high rates of unemployment and a decline in national income.

deregulation the repeal of monopoly regulation.

derived demand a demand for a resource or factor of production that arises because of the demand for a product that it helps to produce.

desired excess reserves reserves held by depository institutions that are over and above those required by law so that they can avoid problems from unexpected withdrawals or be ready to accommodate customers who ask for loans.

devaluation the lowering of the foreign exchange value of a currency by reducing its official value, i.e., by lowering the amount of gold that will be exchanged for it.

diminishing marginal utility an assumption in the theory of utility analysis that during some specified time period an individual's added satisfaction grows less and less as he or she consumes more and more units of the same good or service.

diminishing returns decreases in marginal product that eventually set in when a variable input is successively added to one or more fixed inputs.

direct relationship (or positive relationship) a relationship in which the dependent and independent variables change in the same direction.

direct transmission mechanism the means whereby changes in the money supply affect the equilibrium level of national income and product through planned consumption expenditure with no necessary change in interest rates.

dirty float a situation in which official exchange rates among monies are not fixed but governments intervene in exchange markets from time to time to influence foreign exchange rates.

discounting the practice of purchasing securities or promissory notes for less than their maturity values; a procedure through which a Federal Reserve Bank makes loans to member institutions; also, the process of calculating the present value of payments to be received in the future.

discount rate the rate of interest that Federal Reserve Banks charge on loans to depository institutions.

discouraged workers people who have stopped searching for work because they believe there is little chance of finding a job; they are not counted in official measurements of the labor force.

discrimination the practice of treating persons differently on the basis of their personal characteristics, as in offering different economic opportunities on the basis of gender, race, or ethnic origin. See also *price discrimination.*

diseconomies of scale long-run decreasing returns resulting when an increase in the output level of a firm is less than proportionate to the increase in that firm's inputs; also called decreasing returns to scale or increasing long-run average total cost.

disembodied technical change technical change reflected incompletely or not at all in the quality of specific types of labor or machinery.

disequilibrium a state in which opposing forces are not in balance, so that there is a tendency for change to take place.

disinflation a reduction in the rate of increase in the price level; a lowering of the rate of inflation.

disintermediation the widespread withdrawal of funds from financial institutions that may occur when the limits on interest rates payable by these institutions are lower than rates of return that can be obtained elsewhere.

disinvestment a reduction in the stock of capital goods or inventories.

dismal science the label attached to economics in the nineteenth century because of forecasts of subsistence wages and diminishing returns.

displacement effect a change in one component of planned expenditure that arises because of and offsets an opposite change in some other component.

disposable personal income (DPI) the amount of personal income that remains after personal taxes and certain nontax items are subtracted. It is the amount available to households for either saving or consumption spending.

dissaving negative saving; financing current consumption by borrowing or by drawing from past savings.

distribution function the function or role of government involving changes in the amount of income or wealth inequality among people in the society.

dividends distributions of money or additional stock from a corporation to its shareholders.

division of labor labor specialization; the assignment of tasks among workers.

do-it-yourself production production without exchange, such as growing food in a family garden plot; often not included in official measures of national income and product.

dominant firm price leadership a condition in an oligopolistic industry where one firm is so powerful that small and relatively weak firms follow the price that it sets.

dumping the sale of some product abroad at an unfairly low price, as measured against its domestic price; the sale of a product below what authorities consider average total cost plus a fair markup.

duopoly an oligopoly made up of two firms.

dynamic analysis the description of the process of adjustment between equilibrium positions.

E

easy entry the absence of entry barriers in an industry.

econometrics an aspect of economics that combines theory, mathematics, and statistics to analyze economic questions.

economic concentration a measure of the control of a particular economic activity in an industry, in a sector of the economy, in an entire economy, or in a region of the world.

economic concentration ratio See *concentration ratio*.

economic development economic growth plus other changes that are judged to constitute progress or to make life better; progress in some sense that makes life better in an economy or society and brings gains in welfare for the people.

economic dualism a situation that arises in developing countries in which a relatively modern and prosperous economy, often urban, exists while most of the country, especially the rural areas, continues in age-old patterns of poverty.

economic earnings (also economic rent) the part of the earnings of a resource that is not required to keep that resource at its present use.

economic efficiency the lowest dollar cost of inputs that a firm requires to produce a certain amount of output.

economic growth increasing per capita real output in an economy.

economic loss an amount of accounting profit or loss that is less than normal profit.

economic maldistribution a division of income and wealth among individuals and groups that has an undesirable effect on the operation of the economic system.

economic profit an amount of accounting profit that is greater than normal profit.

economic rationality an assumption made in many economic theories that people can and will take actions that will make them better off or will prevent them from becoming worse off.

economic rent See *economic earnings*.

economics the social science concerned with using or administering scarce resources so as to attain the greatest or maximum fulfillment of society's wants; a method rather than a doctrine, an apparatus of the mind, a technique of thinking that helps its possessor to draw correct conclusions.

economic systems the combinations of institutions that different societies have developed to deal with economic problems.

economic theory See *model, theory*.

economies of scale long-run increasing returns occurring when an increase in the output level of a firm is more than proportionate to the increase in that firm's inputs; also called increasing returns to scale or decreasing long-run average total cost.

effective protection the tariff rate on a product, reduced by the tariffs on raw materials and intermediate products that go into it, with the result expressed as a percentage of the value added by the producers of that product.

efficiency See *economic efficiency, technical efficiency*.

effluent charge a price that is charged for depositing waste in the earth or its atmosphere.

elastic demand a condition existing whenever the percentage response in the quantity demanded is greater than the percentage change in the price that caused it.

elasticity a measure that relates the percentage change in quantity to the percentage change in price or income that caused it.

elasticity coefficient the numerical value of elasticity.

elasticity of demand See *cross elasticity of demand, income elasticity of demand, price elasticity of demand*.

elastic supply a condition existing whenever the percentage response in the quantity supplied is greater than the percentage change in the price that caused it.

elasticity of supply See *price elasticity of supply*.

employment labor engaged in regular work for pay.

Employment Act of 1946 landmark legislation through which the U.S. government announced its goals and established procedures to promote maximum employment, price stability, and economic growth.

employment rate See *civilian employment rate*.

Engels' Law the tendency for the percentage of a family's budget spent for food to decline as its income rises.

enterpriser (or entrepreneur) one of the factors of production or resources employed in production; a person who visualizes needs and takes the necessary action to initiate or change the process by which they will be met or the products used to meet them.

entitlements certificates used in the United States during the 1970s authorizing the purchase of oil from domestic producers at controlled prices, which were lower than the prices of oil from other sources; government transfer payments, the amount of which has been connected to events or circumstances in such a way that the recipients understand that the payment is assured once these conditions are met.

entrepreneur See *enterpriser*.

entry the act of coming into an industry by a new firm which adds capacity to that industry.

entry barriers See *absolute amount of cost difference entry barrier, capital requirement entry barrier, minimum optimal scale effect entry barrier, product differentiation entry barrier.*

equation of exchange the statement that the quantity of money in the economy multiplied by the number of times the average dollar is used each year to purchase newly produced final products must be equal to the quantity of these final products multiplied by their average price. The equation is $MV = PQ$.

equilibrium a state of balance in which the forces for change within a system offset each other so that there is no net tendency for change.

equilibrium price a price that equates the quantity demanded with the quantity supplied in a market.

equilibrium quantity a quantity of a good, service, or resource that equates the quantity supplied and the quantity demanded at a particular price in a market. The quantity supplied and demanded in a market when the equilibrium price prevails.

equity fairness and justice in the distribution of consumption, income, and wealth; also, ownership share in a corporation.

escalator clause See *cost-of-living adjustment.*

ethical maldistribution lack of correspondence between the actual income or wealth distribution and some standard of what is considered just or fair. See also *maldistribution.*

Eurocurrency deposits of one nation's money in banks of a different nation, which provide reserves for loans and which are free from regulations.

European Community (EC) a customs union among a number of nations in Europe.

European Currency Unit (ECU) the monetary unit of the European Currency Union; a money of account that does not exist in a physical sense; a weighted average of the value of the monies of member countries.

ever-normal granary See *buffer stocks.*

ex ante identifying a viewpoint of planned or anticipated activity as distinguished from an *ex post* viewpoint, relating to past activity.

excess burden (of a tax) the amount by which the burden or economic loss caused by a tax exceeds the amount of money received by the government from the tax.

excess demand the amount by which the quantity demanded of a good, service, or resource exceeds the quantity supplied at any specified price.

excess reserves official reserves held by depository institutions over and above the reserve requirement.

excess supply the amount by which the quantity supplied of a good, service, or resource exceeds the quantity demanded at any specified price.

exchange controls restrictions on the purchase or sale of foreign exchange, such as requiring licenses to engage in this trade and/or applying different exchange rates to different transactions.

exchange value (of a currency) See *foreign exchange value.*

excise tax a tax imposed on the manufacture or sale of a product.

exclusive dealing arrangement an agreement that gives a firm the exclusive opportunity to obtain a product from a supplier within a specified geographic area, usually on the condition that it will not buy the products of competing suppliers.

exhaustible natural resources gifts of nature usable in production, the supply of which could be eliminated by human use.

exit a firm leaving an industry as a result of its inability to earn at least normal profit in the long run. See also *normal profit.*

expansion a situation in the economy when real GNP is increasing and unemployment falling.

expansionary disequilibrium when the aggregate quantity demanded is greater than the aggregate quantity supplied so that output will be increased and/or prices raised.

expansionary gap a gap between the equilibrium and the target level of national income and product that exists when the equilibrium level is higher than the target level.

expansion phase the portion of a business cycle or fluctuation in which the volume of business activity in an economy is steadily increasing.

experience variables   variables that oligopolists take into account in addition to consumer demand and cost variables. Examples include the previous reactions by rival firms to price changes in the industry, personality traits of key managers of rival firms, and the political consequences of the rivals' reactions.

explicit costs   money payments by firms for the use of inputs to production.

exploitation   restriction of some members of a society to an inferior income or welfare position; a wage rate that is less than the marginal revenue product; in the Marxist perspective, the exclusion of the main body of a society from the bulk of that society's economic surplus.

exploitation rate (or rate of surplus value)   a ratio representing the proportion of each hour of labor contributed to surplus value in Marxian economics.

exporting unemployment   efforts to create jobs in the domestic economy by expanding exports and reducing imports, usually by trade restrictions and manipulation of foreign exchange rates.

exports   goods and services sold to foreigners.

ex post   identifying past actions, as distinguished from an *ex ante* viewpoint, which deals with planned or anticipated events.

external benefit   a benefit experienced by someone not a party to a transaction; a benefit experienced by one receiving a beneficial or positive externality.

external cost   a cost experienced by someone not a party to a transaction; a cost experienced by one suffering a negative externality.

external growth   See *merger*.

externalities   costs or benefits from the consumption or production of a good or service affecting people other than the buyer and seller of the good or service; a source of market failure that may lead to government intervention.

F

factor price equilization theorem   a proposition stating that free trade tends to equalize input prices among trading countries.

factors of production (or resources)   inputs to production that are used to create goods and services (labor, entrepreneurship, capital, natural resources).

fallacy of composition   the false notion that what is true for one part is necessarily true for the whole, or vice versa.

farm parity   the relationship between the purchasing power or real income of farmers compared with the purchasing power or real income of others in the economy.

favorable balance (of trade)   a positive, credit, or surplus balance in a country's international transactions in merchandise.

featherbedding   the practice of forcing an employer to pay for services that workers do not actually perform.

Federal Deposit Insurance Corporation (FDIC)   a U.S. government agency that insures deposits in certain financial institutions.

federal funds   official reserve deposits of depository institutions with a Federal Reserve Bank.

federal funds rate   the rate of interest charged when federal funds (reserve deposits at the Federal Reserve Bank) are loaned by one depository institution to another.

Federal Open Market Committee (FOMC)   twelve people, including the seven members of the Board of Governors of the Federal Reserve System, who are responsible for directing the buying and selling of securities for the system.

Federal Reserve Banks   the twelve district banks that together constitute the Federal Reserve System.

Federal Reserve Note   currency issued by Federal Reserve Banks.

Federal Reserve System   twelve district Federal Reserve Banks under the direction of policies set by its Board of Governors, appointed by the President of the United States, and fulfilling the functions of a central bank; the central bank of the United States.

federal system   a system of government consisting of several distinct levels of government such as the national, state, and local governments in the United States.

Federal Trade Commission (FTC)   a federal agency established in 1914 which enforces legislation aimed at deterring unfair methods of competition and restraint of trade.

Federal Trade Commission Act   a law passed by the U.S. Congress in 1914 to prohibit unfair methods of competition among firms and establish the Federal Trade Commission.

financial intermediaries   banks, credit unions, saving and loan associations, stock and bond brokers and other institutions that accept deposits of income saved and offer to loan these funds, in return for interest payments, to those who wish to borrow.

financial markets   the organized interaction of buyers and sellers of financial assets.

fine tuning   an approach to macroeconomic policy that calls for frequent adjustments in government spending, taxing, open market operations, and so forth, aimed at holding the economy near some target level of national income and product, employment, price level, foreign exchange rates, and interest rates.

firm a business that combines factors of production or resources—natural resources, capital, labor, and entrepreneurship—to produce certain goods or services.

First World the more-developed countries of Western Europe and North America plus Australia, Japan, and New Zealand.

fiscal related to the taxing and spending operations of a government.

fiscal federalism a system under which financing responsibilities are shared among different levels of government; the study of ways to allocate financial responsibilities among different levels of government.

fiscal instruments taxing and spending devices used to influence the performance of the economy. Examples are tax rates and government purchases.

fiscal policy a government's attempt to influence macroeconomic variables by changing the amount that it taxes or spends.

fixed cost See *total fixed cost.*

fixed exchange rate the exchange value at which a nation's money is held through government or international monetary agency buying and/or selling of official reserves in the foreign exchange market, or through the operation of a metallic standard.

flat tax a tax without any graduation of rates; a tax with a single rate applicable to all amounts of the tax base.

flexible exchange rates See *free exchange rates.*

floating exchange rates See *free exchange rates.*

floor price (or support price) a minimum price that is legally set for a product. A meaningful floor price is set above the equilibrium price that would otherwise be established in that market.

fluctuations See *business cycles.*

foreign aid a unilateral transfer from one nation to another, usually as an encouragement to economic development.

foreign exchange the money of other countries.

foreign exchange markets markets in which the monies of different countries are bought and sold.

foreign exchange value the price of one nation's monetary unit in terms of the monetary units of another country or group of countries, or a weighted average of such monetary units.

45-degree line a straight line drawn at a 45-degree angle from the origin of a diagram, such as the Keynesian cross.

Fourth World those Third World countries that are the "poorest of the poor."

fractional reserves See *partial reserves.*

free enterprise freedom of opportunity to pursue any business venture; no legal restrictions to entry.

free (or floating or flexible) exchange rates foreign exchange rates that can move up or down in response to shifts in demand and supply arising from international trading and finance and that are not purposefully influenced by governmental action.

free market a market in which the economic forces of demand and supply have the full opportunity to alter the price.

free rider problem the fact that people usually will not voluntarily pay for a good or service if they believe that they can consume it without paying.

free trade area a form of economic integration among a group of countries that allows each member to maintain its own set of tariffs, quotas, etc., against nonmembers.

frictional unemployment joblessness that arises because time is required to change from one job to another.

fringe benefit a form of worker compensation other than wages, such as a pension, life insurance, health plan, vacation, and holidays.

full employment a situation in which the volume of employment in an economy meets certain criteria of desirability. See *natural rate of unemployment* and *potential GNP.*

Full Employment and Balanced Growth Act (1978) See *Humphrey-Hawkins Act.*

full-employment balanced-budget (rule) a policy guideline under which Congress would decide on the amount of government purchases that voters would want at full employment, and would set tax rates and transfer payment systems so that net taxes would balance government purchases at full employment. Neither the tax rates nor programs would be changed because of business cycle conditions. Automatic stabilizers would moderate economic fluctuations.

function the way in which one variable depends on some other variable or variables.

functional distribution of income the division of income between different types of production inputs, such as labor and property.

G

game theory an approach to analyzing competition in an oligopoly market that likens economic behavior to a game of cards (like poker) or chess, and even to war.

Garn–St. Germaine Depository Institutions Act (1982) provided aid for depository institutions in distress and expanded the lending authority of thrift institutions.

General Agreement on Tariffs and Trade (GATT) an agreement, mainly between the industrial countries of North America, Western Europe, and Japan for the gradual liberalization of world trade.

general equilibrium analysis a method of analysis that takes into account all the different effects related to the specific variables that are being studied.

general fund a budget category denoting a source of financing available for a variety of expenditures.

generalized (macroeconomic) protection attempts by a country to deal with its international balance of payments problems by imposing a flat overall tax on all imports or by imposing restrictions on the export of capital.

general price level an average of all prices in the economy.

geographic market extension conglomerate merger the acquisition by a firm of another firm engaged in the same activity, existing on the same level, but serving a different geographic market.

Gini ratio a measure of income inequality computed by dividing the area between a Lorenz curve and the line of equality by the entire area under the line of equality on a Lorenz curve diagram. See also *Lorenz curve*.

Glass-Steagall Act (1932) legislation affecting the banking industry and permitting Federal Reserve Banks to use government securities as backing for Federal Reserve Notes.

GNP implicit price deflator an index number that shows the ratio between GNP measured at current prices and the amount that would have been required to purchase the same goods and services in a base year.

gold standard a monetary system featuring a constant price of gold in units of a country's money; for example, a system in which the monetary authorities of a country promise to exchange a specified amount of gold per unit of the country's money.

good a tangible product that is considered desirable or "good" by those who own it or could acquire it.

Gosplan the central planning agency of the Soviet Union.

government purchases currently produced goods and services bought by government.

Gramm-Rudman-Hollings Act legislation passed by the U.S. Congress in 1985 establishing deficit reduction targets and procedures to reach these targets.

grants-in-aid money given by a superior government, such as the federal or a state government, to a subordinate government, such as a state or local government.

Great Depression the period of severe unemployment, falling price level, and economic stagnation extending through the decade following the stock market crash of 1929.

Great Disinflation the period of time in the early and middle 1980s when the rate of inflation was greatly reduced.

greenbacks originally, inconvertible currency issued by the U.S. Treasury during the Civil War; sometimes used in reference to any U.S. currency.

greenhouse effect an acceleration of a long-term heating of the earth's atmosphere caused primarily by the burning of fossil fuels and the wholesale cutting of the world's forests.

Green Revolution the development and propagation of high-yielding dwarf and hybrid varieties of wheat and rice.

Gresham's Law the statement that the base (less valuable) money will always drive the dear (more valuable) money out of circulation and into hoards.

gross domestic product (GDP) the total value of production that takes place per year in a country.

gross national product (GNP) the total of all spending—by consumers, business firms, governments, and (net) foreigners—to purchase currently produced goods and services; the total market value of all currently produced goods and services.

growthmanship an overemphasis on measured economic growth.

guilds predecessors of modern unions; charitable and mutual-aid societies made up of workers in certain crafts who after a time took on certain activities that we now associate with unions, but including master craftsmen who employed journeymen and apprentices.

H

Herfindahl-Hirschman Index (HHI) a measure of market economic concentration derived by summing the squares of the individual market shares of all the firms in a market.

horizontal merger the acquisition by a firm of another firm engaged in the same activity, existing on the same level, and serving the same geographic market.

household a group living together and pooling major expenses in the same dwelling unit. Usually, members are related by blood, marriage, or adoption.

human capital (or capital skills) the portion of the productive power of individuals that has been developed through expenditures for education, job training, and health care.

Humphrey-Hawkins Act legislation, passed by the U.S. Congress in 1978, establishing goals in terms of price stability and low unemployment, but providing no enforcement mechanism.

hyperdeflation a situation in which the pessimism generated by unemployment and falling prices induces a leftward shift in the aggregate-demand curve, so that a recession feeds on itself, becomes worse, and is not alleviated by falling prices.

hyperinflation a situation in which the price level is rising rapidly, causing an increase in the velocity of circulation of money, and usually culminating in the breakdown of the monetary system.

I

identity an equation whose two sides are equal by definition.

immature creditor the international trade and finance situation of a country in the stage of its economic development in which its current balance is positive and its capital balance negative. Its exports of capital exceed return flows to it from investments abroad.

immature debtor the international trade and finance situation of a country in an early stage of its economic development in which its current balance is negative and its capital balance is positive.

imperative planning a rigorous form of planning under which failure to reach an important plan target may be treated as a criminal offense.

implementation lag the time required for programs to take effect, after they have been decided upon.

implicit costs costs incurred by firms for inputs for which no money payment is made and no transaction takes place; usually because the firms are using resources which they own themselves.

implicit price deflator for GNP an index number used to compare GNP measured in current dollars with the amount that would have been needed to purchase the same goods at the prices existing in some base year.

imports goods and services and resources purchased from foreign suppliers.

income the amount of money or its equivalent received in exchange for services rendered, or as net receipts over costs of a firm.

income and product budgets budgets that treat government transfer payments as negative taxes rather than as expenditures.

income effect the effect that a change in a person's real income (resulting from a change in the price of a good or service that the person buys) has on the quantity that this person demands of that good or service.

income demand the relationship between the quantity demanded for a product and the income level of consumers or potential consumers of that product.

income elasticity of demand the percentage change in the quantity demanded for a product divided by the percentage change in the income level of the consumers or potential consumers of that product.

income redistribution an attempt to alter the amount of income or wealth inequality among people in a society.

incomes policy an application of wage and price controls in a coordinated attempt to reach a set of macroeconomic goals.

income statement (or profit and loss statement) an accounting report of the operations of a business firm over some specified period of time.

inconvertible currency the money of a country that does not allow it to be freely exchanged for money of other countries.

increasing returns short run gains in marginal product that often occur over low levels of output when a variable input is successively added to one or more fixed inputs.

increasing returns to scale See *economies of scale.*

increasing total utility an assumption in utility analysis theory that during some specified time period an individual's total satisfaction increases as he or she consumes additional units of the same good or service.

independent variable the variable on which another variable depends in a functional relationship.

indexing a system that automatically builds an inflation or deflation adjustment into agreements for wage rates, savings accounts, taxes, interest rates, bond values, and other contracts in an economy.

index number a number that expresses a particular value in relation to some other value that has been specified as a base or reference value.

indicative planning a form of planning that operates primarily by convincing participants of a plan's economic benefits to them.

indifference curve analysis a theory of consumer behavior that expresses consumers' tastes in curves based on the ranking of combinations of goods and/or services in order of preference, but avoids the notion of measurable utility.

indifference curve a curve representing all of the combinations of goods and/or services measured on the axes that satisfy a consumer equally well.

indifference map   a graph displaying some of the infinite number of indifference curves representing an individual's preferences.

indirect business taxes and subsidies   an entry in the national product section that removes the tax and subsidy components of market prices; taxes imposed on and subsidies given to the production or sale of goods and services.

indirect transmission mechanism   a process whereby the effects of a shift of the real money-supply curve are transmitted to the equilibrium level of real national income and product by affecting interest rates and the volume of planned investment.

individual consumer demand   the amount of a good or service that an individual consumer wants and is able to purchase at a particular moment at each possible price that might be charged for that good or service.

individual firm supply   the amount of a good or service that an individual business firm is willing and able to sell at a particular moment at each possible price that it might receive for that good or service.

individual maldistribution   an unsatisfactory situation in respect to the particular people at the upper and lower ends of the income or wealth distribution.

induced expenditure   in Keynesian analysis, a change in the volume of planned consumption, investment, government purchases, exports, or imports caused by a change in level of national income and illustrated as a movement along the $C + I + G + X - Im$ curve.

industrial union   a union representing all the workers in an industry, such as auto workers, mine workers, or clothing workers.

industry   a group of competing firms.

inelastic demand   a condition existing whenever the percentage response in quantity demanded is less than the percentage change in the price that caused it.

inelastic supply   a condition existing whenever the percentage response in the quantity supplied is less than the percentage change in the price that caused it.

infant industry (argument for protection)   a proposal for temporarily protecting a country's new industries to give them time to develop skills comparable with more efficient foreign industries.

inferior good or service   a good or service for which there is a negative relationship between quantity demanded and income level.

infinitely elastic   See *perfectly elastic*.

infinitely elastic demand   a condition existing when a price change causes an infinite response in the quantity demanded.

infinitely elastic supply   a condition existing when a price change causes an infinite response in the quantity supplied.

inflation   a significant and sustained increase in the general level of prices, usually measured by the rate of change in some price index number.

inflationary depression   a situation in which an economy experiences a decrease in real GNP and also an increase in its general price level. See also *stagflation*.

inflationary expectations   anticipations that the price level will rise in the near future.

inflation rate   the rate of change in the index number that has been selected for measuring the general price level; a measurement of the change in the price level calculated by dividing the GNP deflator value for each year by the GNP deflator value for the previous year, subtracting 1.0, and multiplying the result by 100.

information costs   the costs of acquiring information that decreases the uncertainty of making transactions.

infrastructure   See *social overhead capital*.

injections   planned expenditures other than consumption purchases, that is, planned investment (I), government purchases (G), and exports (X).

injunction   a court order enjoining or prohibiting a person or firm from following a specific course of action.

innovation   the development of an invention from the original discovery to a practical use.

innovator   one who brings an invention out of the laboratory, makes it practical, and applies it to actual production.

input-output analysis   a technique, developed by Wassily Leontief, that uses matrix algebra to solve production planning problems, including the relation between economic sectors.

inputs (or factors of production or resources)   the labor, entrepreneurship, natural resources, and capital that are used in production.

interdependence   a small enough number of firms in an industry to require that each considers its rivals' reactions to any action that it is thinking of taking; the most important characteristic of an oligopoly industry.

interest (or interest payment)   the return or payment to capital in production.

interest rate   the annual payment for the use of funds, expressed as a percentage of the funds used.

interest rate parity   a condition in international capital account transactions when the domestic-money rate of return would be the same as the foreign-money rate of return after conversion to domestic money.

interest-rate theory   the proposition that an increase in the price level, *ceteris paribus*, reduces the real money supply, increases the real rate of interest, and thereby reduces planned investment and the quantity of real GNP demanded. The theory works in the opposite direction for decreases in the price level; also called the *Keynes effect*.

interlocking directorates the potentially anticompetitive practice of having the same person serve on the boards of directors of two or more competing firms.

intermediate product an output which itself becomes an input in further production.

internal growth the growth of a firm through building from within as contrasted to acquiring other firms.

international fundamentalism an explanation for the Great Depression asserting that the U.S. economy was not able to support prosperity throughout the world and that recession elsewhere spread to the United States.

International Monetary Fund (IMF) an organization established in 1944 for the purpose of stabilizing exchange rates in international trade; a pool of gold and foreign exchange from which loans can be made to help countries stabilize foreign exchange rates. See also *Bretton Woods system*.

International Trade Organization (ITO) an organization proposed by "free world" members of the United Nations aimed at making world trade freer and less discriminatory. Never went into operation.

interstate banking when bank holding companies own banks in more than one state.

invention discovery of a new product or a new technical tool or process.

inventor one who discovers or devises a new or improved process or product.

inventory stocks of unsold goods and resources.

inventory cycle See *Kitchin cycle*.

inverse relationship (or negative relationship) a relationship in which the dependent and independent variables change in opposite directions.

investment (or investment purchases, I) the creation of capital; in national income accounting, the purchase of currently produced capital goods and additions to inventories.

investment decision a decision made by a firm as to whether to provide for the creation of new capital and, if so, how much.

investment income receipts from capital goods or from securities, usually in the form of dividends or interest.

iron law of wages the doctrine that population growth will push wages down to the subsistence level.

IS-LM system a model used in modern Keynesian economics; the *IS* curve incorporates the equilibrium requirements of the Keynesian total-planned-expenditure model, and the *LM* curve incorporates the requirements for equilibrium in the money market.

isocost line a line showing the alternative combinations of inputs that a firm can buy for a given cost outlay.

isoquant same quantity; a curve (derived from a firm's production function) that shows all of the technically efficient combinations of inputs for producing a particular quantity of output.

isoquant map a graph showing several out of an infinite number of isoquants, one for every quantity of output that a firm could possibly produce.

J

job security in collective bargaining agreements, conditions for hiring, job continuance, and the handling of grievances.

Joint Economic Committee a committee of the Congress established under the Employment Act of 1946 to conduct research and advise the Congress on economic policy.

Juglar cycle a business fluctuation that has a period of some seven to ten years and that has been a prominent feature in economic history.

jurisdictional strike a strike concerning which union shall represent a given group of workers.

K

Keynes effect the relationship between the price level and the quantity of real national income and product demanded that arises because of an induced change in real rates of interest.

Keynesian a person who accepts the teachings of John Maynard Keynes. One who believes that government purchases and tax collections are key instruments of macroeconomic policy.

Keynesian cross graphic representation of a relationship between the flow of planned expenditure and the level of national income and product.

Keynesian economics the school of economic thought based on the work of John Maynard Keynes (1883–1946), particularly *The General Theory of Employment, Interest and Money* (1936).

Keynesian-monetarist debate an extended discussion among macroeconomists concerning the best demand-side instruments to use in carrying out macroeconomic policy.

Keynesian theory the systematic body of knowledge associated with the work of the British economist John Maynard Keynes.

Keynesian transmission mechanism the means whereby changes in the real money supply affect the equilibrium level of national income and product through changes in interest rates and planned investment expenditure; an "indirect" transmission mechanism.

kinked demand curve a curve (characteristic of some oligopolistic industries) made up of two demand segments divided at the industrywide price that has been established with the segment related to lower prices less elastic than the segment related to higher prices.

Kitchin (inventory) cycle a business cycle that has a length of some three to five years and that is believed to be connected with the alternate buildup and depletion of business inventories; sometimes called the *inventory cycle.*

Kondratieff cycle a long wave or cycle of economic activity that has a length of 30 to 50 years and is sometimes thought to be associated with major technological innovations.

Knights of Labor, Noble Order of one of the first national federations of unions in the United States. Established in 1869, it was the forerunner of the AF of L.

Kuznets (building) cycle a business cycle that lasts between 15 and 25 years and appears based on the construction and replacement of buildings and transportation facilities; also called the *building cycle.*

L

L (money supply) M3 money supply plus near money (U.S. Savings Bonds, certain kinds of U.S. government securities, payment promises by large corporations, and other items that are potentially convertible into spendable money).

labor the resource or factor of production that includes most forms of human work effort directed toward production.

labor force See *civilian labor force.*

Labor-Management Relations Act See *Taft-Hartley Act.*

Labor-Management Reporting and Disclosure Act See *Landrum-Griffin Act.*

labor mobility the degree to which workers will move to available jobs or more attractive jobs.

labor resources See *labor.*

labor union (or trade union) a labor organization whose immediate objective is to improve the wage rates and the working conditions of its members.

Laffer curve a curve representing a relationship between average tax rates and the amount of govern-

ment net tax revenue collected, and suggesting that tax revenues will rise as average tax rates rise, but only up to a point. Beyond that point, higher tax rates will result in lower tax revenues.

lagging indicators index numbers that tend to change direction after changes in the volume of total economic activity.

laissez-faire a policy position favoring the market economy and opposing interference in the economy by the government; a branch of the market-economy New Right that believes that technological change will overcome any long run tendencies toward monopoly in the economy.

land the ground or the earth that makes up a large portion of the factor of production or resource called natural resources.

Landrum-Griffin Act (or Labor-Management Reporting and Disclosure Act) an act passed by the U.S. Congress in 1959 that set forth rules governing the relationship between union governments and their members.

Lange-Lerner theory a socialist plan that attempts to retain the advantages of competitive market economies.

leading indicators index numbers that tend to anticipate changes in the total economy.

leading links (system) a policy followed in Soviet planning that calls for the fulfillment of production plans for goods that the government considers most important even at the expense of other parts of the plan.

leakages uses of funds that take them out of the consumption path of the circular flow, such as net taxes, savings, or imports.

legal reserves See *official reserves.*

legal tender currency that, when offered in payment of an obligation, precludes the creditor from denying that payment was offered and from collecting further interest on the debt.

lender of last resort a responsibility of Federal Reserve Banks to make loans to member banks facing crisis situations.

less developed countries (LDCs) nations with levels of per capita income far below those in the industrialized or modern countries.

leveraged buy-out (LBO) a form of speculation through acquisition in which investors rely almost entirely on debt financing to acquire a company.

liabilities claims that outsiders have for payments from a business firm—usually the value of such claims as reported on a balance sheet.

Libermanism a policy position favoring a number of reforms aimed at introducing market-style decisions into Soviet-style planning; an early attempt at reform in the Soviet Union.

libertarian one who fears government control of the economy, supports private ownership of the means of production and, in extreme cases, private control of money, defense, police protection, streets, sewers, and law-making and administration; a branch of the economic New Right that believes there should be private ownership of the means of production and that the market should govern and the state cease to exist.

limited liability a characteristic of the corporate form of business that limits the responsibility of stockholders for losses suffered by the business.

limited life a condition in which a business firm does not continue to exist after the death or withdrawal of a proprietor or a partner.

linear relationship a relationship which, when plotted on a graph, will appear as a straight-line curve.

liquidity the ease with which an asset can be used in exchange or converted into a form that can be used in exchange.

liquidity crisis in Marxian terms, the long-term stagnation that results as capitalism matures. It is caused by the fall of the profit rate to a level that discourages investment and encourages hoarding.

liquidity trap a situation in which increases in the supply of money are absorbed into cash balances and do not lower the rate of interest or increase investment.

loanable funds money demanded and supplied for loans.

loanable funds market the arrangements and procedures for carrying out transactions between people who want to borrow money and people who want to lend money.

lockout a work stoppage in which the employer closes the plant to its workers.

locomotive theory the view that a large country, by expanding its economy and letting its inflation rate rise, can and should stimulate economic expansion in other countries.

long run in microeconomics, a period of time long enough to permit all changes that a firm wants to make within the limits of its existing production function; in macroeconomics, a period of time long enough to eliminate money illusion and wage-cost lags from price level changes.

long-run aggregate-supply the relationship between changes in the price level and changes in the quantity of real national income and product supplied that prevails as long as there is no change in physical production capability but when enough time has passed for people to eliminate wage-cost lag and money illusion; also called potential GNP.

long-run average total cost (*LRAC*) the long-run total cost of a firm divided by the quantity level of its output.

long-run consumption function the relationship between disposable personal income and planned consumption expenditure when the level of disposable personal income has existed for a long enough period of time for consumers to adjust to it.

long-run marginal cost (*LRMC*) the addition to a firm's long-run total cost when it produces one more unit of output.

long-run total cost (*LRTC*) the total cost of producing a certain level of output when a firm is able to vary all of its inputs.

Lorenz curve a curve that illustrates income inequality by plotting the cumulative percentage of total income received by successive percentages of the population, starting from the lowest-income persons and proceeding cumulatively upward. See also *Gini ratio*.

lower turning point the point in a business cycle when a contraction phase ends and an expansion phase begins; also called the *trough*.

Lucas supply curve a curve that shows that unexpected changes in the price level lead to changes in the quantity of real GNP supplied.

M

M1 money supply concept coins, currency, and checkable account balances.

M2 money supply concept M1 plus such less liquid assets as small time deposits, money market mutual fund balances, noncheckable savings balances, repurchase agreements, and Eurodollars.

M3 money supply concept M1 and M2 plus large time deposit balances, long-term repurchase agreements, and certain other assets that are somewhat harder to convert into spendable money.

macro-dot a combination of the real rate of interest and the volume of real national income and product such that the flow of planned expenditure exactly matches real production in an economy and the demand for the country's stock of money is equal to its supply.

macroeconomic equilibrium the situation in which the real national income and product demanded at a given price level is equal to the real national income and product supplied at that price level; the condition existing at the intersection of an aggregate-demand curve and an aggregate-supply curve.

macroeconomic forecasting predicting the values of

economic variables through systematic analysis of empirically estimated relationships.

macroeconomic planning planning that includes target quantities only for macroeconomic measures (national income and product; the division between consumption, investment, and government sectors; the supplies of money and credit; the government surplus or deficit; international balances; and interest rates) but not the composition of the aggregates.

macroeconomic protection See *generalized protection*.

macroeconomics the branch of economics that focuses on aggregate or grand total economic activity. Unemployment and inflation are major problems considered in macroeconomics.

macroeconomic unemployment unemployment that exists throughout the whole economy or affects many parts of the economy at the same time and is not related to particular decisions about what or how to produce. See also *cyclical unemployment*.

"magic wand" planning a plan built around a collection of projects and/or an attractive slogan, which promises good things but does not specify adequately any processes for achieving them.

maldistribution excessive inequality or equality of personal income or wealth. See also *economic maldistribution, ethical maldistribution,* and *individual maldistribution*.

Malthusian theory of population the proposition that population increases according to a geometric progression until stabilized by death rates, which rise because of inadequate food supplies.

margin requirement the percentage of the value of a stock which the purchaser must finance from his or her own resources.

marginal additional or incremental.

marginal analysis a method used by economists for predicting or evaluating outcomes that is based on the last unit added or the next unit to be added.

marginal benefit the additional advantage gained when one more unit of a good or service is consumed.

marginal cost (MC) the addition to total cost when one more unit of output is produced.

marginal factor cost (MFC) the extra cost that a firm incurs for an additional unit of a resource or factor of production.

marginal physical product (MPP) the additional output that a firm can produce by using one more unit of a resource or factor of production.

marginal product, short run the amount of extra output that results from the addition of one more unit of a variable input to one or more fixed inputs.

marginal propensity to consume (MPC) the frac-tion or percentage of a change in disposable personal income that appears as a change in planned consumption expenditure.

marginal propensity to save (MPS) the fraction or percentage of a change in disposable personal income that appears as a change in planned saving.

marginal revenue (MR) the extra revenue that a firm receives when it sells one more unit of output.

marginal revenue product (MRP) change in the total revenue of a firm resulting from the sale of the additional quantity of output that one more unit of a resource allows it to produce.

marginal tax rate the rate of income tax that applies to additional income received by an individual; the percentage of an additional dollar of income that would be payable in income tax.

marginal utility the additional utility gained from one more unit of a good or service.

margin requirements rules set down by the Federal Reserve Board specifying the minimum portion of the price of stock purchased that must be paid by the purchaser (not borrowed from the stockbroker).

market the organized action between potential buyers (market demand) and potential sellers (market supply) that permits trade.

market clearing the proposition that at the equilibrium price, no potential sellers who are willing and able to sell at that price are unable to carry out their desired transaction, and no buyers who are willing and able to buy at that price are unable to carry out their desired transaction.

market demand the sum of all the individual consumers' quantities demanded at particular prices for a particular product in a particular geographic area over some period of time.

market economic concentration the number and size distribution of firms in a specific market or industry. See also *Herfindahl-Hirschman Index*.

market economy an economic system in which the interaction of buyers and sellers is the main mechanism for making economic choices.

market failure a market outcome judged to be inadequate or unacceptable in relation to some goal of the society.

market-opening strategies a system of guaranteed minimum quotas for American goods in foreign markets, intended to counteract foreign protectionism.

market price the equilibrium price that tends to be established by the interaction of demand and supply for a specified product.

market socialism an adaptation of the microeconomics of pure competition to a socialist system.

market supply the sum of all of the individual firms'

quantities supplied at particular prices of a particular good or service in a particular geographic area over some period of time.

materials balancing a planning technique that requires estimating potential supplies of and demands for each of a number of final and intermediate products taken separately.

mature creditor the international economic situation of a country in an advanced stage of its economic development, in which its current balance is negative and its capital balance is positive. Returns from previous investment abroad are greater than current capital exports (net of repayments).

mature debtor the international trade and finance situation of a country in an intermediate stage of economic development, in which its current balance is positive and its capital balance is negative. The return flow of capital to foreigners (repayment of past debts) exceeds net capital inflows from them.

mechanism (basis for classifying economic systems) procedures used for making economic decisions—for example, markets, planning, and tradition.

medium of exchange a function of money that enables people to trade with one another more easily, since they do not need to match their specific wants with those of other people.

member bank a commercial bank that is a member of the Federal Reserve System.

menu costs costs entailed during a period of inflation by the need for frequent updating of price lists.

mercantilism an eighteenth-century school of economic thought that emphasized the achievement of economic power as a basis for military power. It emphasized high population and employment, low interest rates, accumulation of money, and strict regulation of trade, particularly international trade.

merger (or external growth or acquisition) the acquisition of one firm by another firm which adds to the acquiring firm's productive capacity.

microeconomics the branch of economics that focuses on the behavior of individual decision makers such as consumers, workers, business firms, and governments, assuming the major macroeconomic variables to be given. It focuses on how their behaviors affect the types of goods and services produced, the methods of production, and the distribution of income in the economy.

microeconomic unemployment unemployment that can be traced to decisions about what to produce or how to produce. It includes seasonal, frictional, and structural unemployment.

microfoundations the microeconomic behavior of individuals and firms that lie behind macroeconomic models.

millage the rate of tax applied under a property tax, with one mil equal to one-tenth of one percent.

minimum optimal scale effect (entry barrier) an entry barrier based upon the effect on the price of the product of an industry that results from adding the volume of output that a new firm of minimum optimal scale would supply if it enters that industry.

minimum wage a wage rate set by government as the lowest that firms are allowed to pay.

mixed economy an economic system combining significant elements of both planning and market modes of organization.

mobility See *labor mobility.*

model a formal statement of a theory.

monetarism the belief that the nominal money supply is usually more closely related to nominal national income and product than are nominal government expenditures and nominal investment expenditures; a school of economic thought that proposes that monetary policy make no attempt to deal with short-term fluctuations in economic activity but should instead establish a fixed rate of increase for the money supply and stay with this rate year in and year out.

monetarist a person who believes that control of the money supply is an important element in macroeconomic policy.

monetary base the total of official reserves and coins and currency in circulation in the economy.

Monetary Control Act of 1980 legislation that broadened the authority of the Board of Governors of the Federal Reserve System, including the authority to set required reserve ratios for all institutions offering checking account services. The full name of the legislation is the Depository Institutions Deregulation and Monetary Control Act of 1980.

monetary growth rule a policy guideline under which the money supply is increased at a constant rate without regard to cyclical fluctuations in the economy. The rate of money supply increase is to be approximately equal to the long-term growth trend in real productive capacity of the economy.

monetary instruments controls over financial markets and intermediaries used to influence the performance of the economy. The principal monetary instruments are reserve requirements, open market operations, and discount rates.

monetary policy a plan or a course of action governing the use of monetary instruments in an economy; a government's attempt to influence macroeconomic variables by changing the economy's money supply.

monetary-policy-target variable a variable used by the Federal Reserve System as a guide in implementing monetary policy.

monetized debt financial obligations that provide reserves to support money, as when loans provide a step in the expansion of bank deposits.

monetizing a public debt supporting the price of public debt instruments by monetary expansion if necessary.

money anything that is generally accepted in an economy as a medium of exchange, a unit of account, a store of purchasing power, and a standard for deferred payment.

money illusion the belief that nominal values are the same as real values; a belief that changes in nominal values brought on by a price-level change are also changes in real values; a theory implying that the aggregate-supply curve has a positive slope.

money income receipts measured in terms of the monetary unit and not adjusted for changes in the price level.

money market the interaction of the demand-for-money and the supply-of-money for use as a financial asset.

money multiplier the ratio between the amount of money (such as M1) in the economy and the size of the monetary base.

money supply (stock of money) the total quantity of money existing in an economy at a particular time (See *L, M1, M2,* and *M3* money supply concepts).

money supply curve the graphic representation of the relationship between the real rate of interest and the total quantity of money existing in an economy.

M1 (money supply concept) a money supply concept widely used by economists, consisting of coins and currency, demand deposits, and other checkable account balances.

M2 (money supply concept) the M1 money supply plus savings accounts, small time deposits, short-term repurchase agreements, money market mutual funds, and Eurodollars.

M3 (money supply concept) the M2 money supply plus fairly long-term repurchase agreements, large time deposits, and certain other assets.

monoeconomics economic theories that assume that methods devised in MDCs to deal with MDC problems also work well in LDCs.

monopolistic competition a market structure with a large number of sellers, some product differentiation, and fairly easy entry and exit.

monopoly a market in which there is only a single seller. See also *actual monopoly, pure monopoly.*

monopoly control (or monopoly power) the degree of control or power that a firm has over the price of the product it sells. Varying degrees are possessed by all but purely competitive firms.

monopoly regulation rules and laws that apply to firms granted monopoly status by the government and that involve the firm's level of output, its prices, and the scope of its production.

monopsonistic resource market (monopsony, oligopsony, monopsonistic competition) a market in which individual firms have some control over the quantity demanded of a resource and thus can influence the resource price.

monopsony a market in which there is only a single buyer.

moral suasion attempts by government and Federal Reserve System officials to persuade depository institutions and others in the economy to cooperate with their policy views or actions.

movement along a demand (supply) curve a change from one point on a demand (supply) curve to another point on the same curve due to a change in the price of the product.

multifactor productivity a weighted average of labor and capital productivity.

multinational (or transnational) corporation a corporation that has its headquarters in one country and carries on important business operations in several countries, including the home country.

multiplier the ratio of the change in the equilibrium level of national income and product to the change in planned expenditure that caused equilibrium to change. It is estimated to be equal to $1/(1 - MPC)$ when no changes are induced in net taxes or in expenditure streams other than consumption.

N

national banks banks whose charters are issued by the federal government.

national debt the total value of outstanding securities issued by a nation's government.

national income (NI) in national income accounting, the total amount earned by owners of resources used in producing goods and services during the accounting period.

national income and product accounts a set of reports on the volume and composition of economic activity in the United States over a specified time period; it consists of three major parts: the national product section, the national income section, and the personal income section.

national income gap the difference between the target level of national income and the level that is predicted to prevail if the government undertakes no new action to change that level.

National Industrial Recovery Act (NIRA) legislation enacted in 1933 containing a variety of emergency programs designed to help the economy recover from the Great Depression. Major portions of the act were ruled unconstitutional.

National Labor Relations Act See *Wagner-Connery Act*.

national product in national income accounting, the value of all goods and services produced in the economy during a given year, measured in terms of the prices prevailing at the time of production. See also *gross national product* and *net national product*.

natural monopoly an industry in which only a single seller is required for efficient production.

natural rate of unemployment the rate of unemployment that combines seasonal, frictional, and structural unemployment; believed by many economists to approximate full employment; the rate consistent with potential GNP.

natural resource one of the factors of production or resources; a ''gift of nature'' that can be used in production, such as unimproved land or minerals in the ground.

near money forms of wealth such as U.S. Savings Bonds, relatively liquid U.S. government securities, payment promises by large corporations, and so on, which can, with some delay, be converted into more liquid wealth forms, which would be counted as money.

negative income tax a tax under which persons receiving less than a specified amount of income would also receive payments from the government.

negative relationship See *inverse relationship*.

negative returns, short run a decrease in total product (negative marginal product) that may occur after a great deal of a variable input has successively been added to one or more fixed inputs.

negative slope an inverse relationship between variables, as shown on a graph.

negative taxes transfer payments from the government.

negotiable order of withdrawal account (NOW) a type of checkable account provided by savings and loan associations.

neoclassical economics the school of economic thought based on the work of Alfred Marshall (1842–1924) and others, which dominated non-Marxian economic thought in the late nineteenth and early twentieth centuries.

neoclassical growth model a model that describes a country's growth rate as the weighted sum of the changes in productivities of its productive inputs plus an additional term reflecting disembodied technical progress.

neocolonialism domination by a more developed country over a less developed country, carried out without a military presence of the more developed country, and without any formal colonial relationship.

neo-Keynesian economics a school of economic thought that preserves the basic Keynesian approach but includes monetary variables as well.

neo-Ricardian an application of the rational-expectations theory that says that the method used to finance government expenditure does not matter.

net exports the entry in the U.S. national income and product accounts showing the excess of exports over imports of currently produced goods and services. It may be negative.

net national product (NNP) in national income accounting, the value of all currently produced goods and services (GNP) minus an estimated capital consumption (depreciation) allowance.

net taxes the total amount of taxes paid minus transfer payments from the government.

net worth the difference between the amount of total assets and the amount of total liabilities as reported on a balance sheet.

new classical a school of economic thought that employs the theory of rational expectations and accepts the propositions that prices adjust quickly and that markets clear at equilibrium.

New Deal a name used to refer to the economic programs of the first two administrations of President Franklin Roosevelt (1933–1941).

New International Economic Order (NIEO) a pattern of international economic relations proposed by less developed countries as a replacement for the existing arrangements of international trade and aid; a set of demands from less developed countries for a restructuring of economic relations between developed and less developed countries.

New Left contemporary radical groups that generally call for major steps away from a market economy.

New Right contemporary radical groups that generally call for major steps toward a purely market economy.

New Socialist Man or Woman a person, expected to emerge after socialism is firmly established, who will work harder than anyone in the past and will demand less in terms of wealth and luxurious consumption.

nominal protection the statutory rate of a tariff on a product.

nominal value value that is stated or measured in terms of some monetary unit and that has not been adjusted for changes in the general price level.

nominal wage rate the amount of money a worker receives per hour (or other time unit) of work.

nonborrowed reserves total reserves in depository institutions minus amounts borrowed through discounting from Federal Reserve Banks.

nonexcludability the characteristic of public goods and services that makes it impossible or prohibitively expensive to prevent someone from consuming them, once they have been provided for others.

nonexhaustible natural resources gifts of nature usable in production, the supply of which cannot be eliminated by human use.

nonlinear relationship a relationship in which equal changes in the independent variable do not bring about the same responses in the dependent variable. When plotted on a graph, it will not appear as a straight line.

nonprice competition competition among firms by such nonprice means as advertising and product changes.

nonrenewable resources inputs for production that, once used, cannot be regenerated by natural processes within a time span that is relevant from the point of view of humans.

nonrival consumption consumption of a good or service by one person that does not prevent another person from consuming it.

no-recourse loan a government loan that a farmer may obtain on a crop at some percentage of its support price, and on which the government has no recourse against the debtor except the crop itself.

normal good or service a good or service for which there is a positive relationship between the income level and the quantity demanded.

normal profit the return to enterprise that is necessary for a firm to receive in order for it to be willing to continue its present business in the long run.

normative economics an approach to economics that is subjective and expresses an opinion or preference.

Norris-LaGuardia Act a U.S. law passed in 1932 granting workers full freedom of association and self-organization; it also limited the courts' power to issue injunctions and made the yellow-dog contract unenforceable.

O

objectivism the belief that each person's most objective view of the "good" is knowledge of what is in his or her own best interest.

obsolescence the process of becoming less or no longer useful or economically feasible for some intended purpose in production.

official reserves vault cash and deposits in Federal Reserve and other banks that are approved by the Federal Reserve System as meeting requirements.

official settlements balance the international balance of payments concept that combines all the entries in the capital account with all the entries in the current account and shows the net effect of all transactions except those in official government reserves.

oligopolistic coordination practices in oligopoly industries by which firms coordinate their output levels and pricing decisions. Practices include collusive agreement, price leadership, and rules of thumb.

oligopoly a sellers' market structure made up of a few interdependent firms.

oligopsony a market in which there are few buyers so that individual buyers can influence the price.

OPEC (Organization of Petroleum Exporting Countries) international petroleum cartel.

open economy a country that allows relatively unrestricted trade across its borders.

open market operations the buying and selling of government securities in the open market by the Federal Reserve System.

opportunity cost the true cost of choosing one alternative over another; that which is given up when a choice is made.

orderly marketing agreement an agreement among countries aimed at preventing price cutting in importing countries.

organic composition of capital the ratio between Marxian constant capital (raw materials plus depreciation) and variable capital (direct labor).

origin the point of intersection of the horizontal and vertical axes of a graph.

other things being equal See *ceteris paribus*.

outputs the economic goods and services that business firms produce for sale to consumers, other business firms, and governments.

overemployment working more hours than desired at a given wage rate.

owners' equity See *net worth*.

ownership (basis for classifying economic systems) the entities such as individuals, firms, collectives, or governments that are permitted to hold legal title to natural resources and capital goods.

P

paper gold See *special drawing rights*.

paradox of value the observation that consumers sometimes pay lower prices for goods and services that they consider essential than for goods and services that they consider relatively unimportant.

parity price (of a farm product) a price of an agricultural product that gives it a purchasing power, with respect to prices farmers pay, equivalent to what its price provided in some past period.

partial equilibrium analysis a method of analysis that deals with the effects of some disturbance on one set of economic variables, assuming that all other variables are unaffected.

partial (or fractional) reserves the situation in which cash or immediately available funds kept on hand by depository institutions are less than the total of the obligations to the people who have deposited money in the institutions.

participation rate See *civilian labor force participation rate.*

partnership a business firm created through an agreement in which two or more people share financial and managerial responsibilities as well as profits and losses.

patent a right of temporary limited monopoly over a new product or process granted to its inventor or to a firm that purchases the right from the inventor.

payments equilibrium in a balance of payments account, any situation in which a country's balance on current account is matched by an equal but opposite balance on its capital account.

PCE deflator an index number of prices for goods and services included in the personal consumption expenditures component of gross national product.

perestroika restructuring; reforms of the Soviet planning system that include a wider scope for an unplanned economy, more flexible plans, and more leeway for plant managers.

perfect competition a purely competitive market with the added feature that buyers and sellers have complete and continuous knowledge of all bids and offers in the market and the mobility to take immediate action on the basis of that knowledge.

perfectly elastic a condition existing when a price change causes an unlimited change in quantity.

perfectly elastic demand See *infinitely elastic demand.*

perfectly inelastic demand a condition existing when a price change causes no response in the quantity demanded.

perfectly inelastic supply a condition existing when a price change causes no change in the quantity supplied.

permanent income hypothesis the proposition that the level of a household's planned consumption expenditure is based on what it believes to be its long-run or ''permanent'' level of income.

perpendicular a straight line drawn from a point on a graph to form a right angle with the horizontal axis or the vertical axis on a graph.

personal deduction in individual income taxation, an allowance for certain expenditures that may be subtracted from income in determining the tax base.

personal exemption the amount that can be deducted for the taxpayer(s) and each dependent in calculating income subject to tax.

personal income (PI) the national income accounting concept equal to national income plus receipts not earned and minus earnings not received.

personal income distribution the division of income among individuals classified according to income size.

Phillips curve a relationship between an economy's unemployment rate and its inflation rate suggesting that trade-offs exist between these two rates such that policy makers can choose a preferred combination from among those that constitute the curve.

physical capital (or capital goods) resources or factors of production such as factory buildings, tools, and equipment that enable business firms to produce more efficiently.

physiocrats an eighteenth-century school of economic thought contending that economies operate according to certain natural laws and that government interference was useless and wasteful.

picketing the parading of striking workers before the entrance to their work place in the hope of convincing other workers, customers, or supplies not to enter.

Pigou effect the relationship between the price level and the quantity of real national income and product demanded that arises because of the effect of price-level change on the value of wealth holdings.

planned consumption in Keynesian analysis, the amount of expenditure on currently produced consumption goods and services that households intend to carry out in the time period under study.

planned economy an economic system in which the government coordinates decisions about what, how, and for whom to produce.

planned investment in Keynesian analysis, the amount of expenditure on currently produced capital goods and inventories that firms intend to carry out in the time period under study.

planned saving in Keynesian analysis, the amount of current disposable personal income that households intend to withhold from expenditure on consumption.

planning the directing of economic activity through prearranged priorities, and procedures, sometimes enforced by sanctions.

Planning-Programming Budget System (PPBS) a budgeting procedure that requires agencies to specify the programs they wish to carry out and to plan expenditure needs several years in advance.

plant a factory or other production facility in a particular geographic location that belongs to a firm, which may operate only this one plant or a number of different plants.

political economy the economic analysis of public policy questions.

populism a protest movement in the United States during the last decades of the nineteenth century that expressed farm dissatisfaction with the prices farmers paid and the prices they received, with interest and repayment requirements on farm loans, and with deflationary monetary policies.

positive economics the aspect of the discipline dealing with objective facts (what is) rather than value judgments and opinions (what ought to be).

positive relationship See *direct relationship.*

positive slope a direct relationship between variables, as shown in a graph.

post-Keynesians economists who use Keynesian and neo-Keynesian models, but emphasize institutional features of the economy, such as monopoly power and price rigidity, and often advocate incomes policy.

potential entry the likelihood that one or more firms will enter an industry or market.

potential GNP the quantity of real GNP when the economy is operating at its natural rate of unemployment; the economy's long-run aggregate supply.

poverty living at a standard or level below that considered adequate by the society.

poverty line an income level below which poverty is said to exist.

Prebisch thesis that the international economy has developed in a way that is unfair to agricultural and raw material producers because the producers of these goods are not able to restrict output and raise prices, as can be done by producers of manufactured goods.

precautionary demand for money a desire to hold money in order to be prepared for unexpected changes in the pattern of receipts or expenditures.

predatory price cutting reduction in price aimed at forcing competitors out of business.

preference revelation the indication or pronouncement of an individual's desire for public goods and services.

present value the discounted value at the present time of a sum of money to be received in the future. See also *discounting.*

present value formula the equation that illustrates the determination of the present value of an asset by the relation between the expected income flow and the rate of interest: PV = expected annual income flow/the rate of interest.

price the exchange value of a product or resource.

price controls the setting of maximum or minimum prices by the government. See also *ceiling price, floor price.*

price differential a difference between the prices charged to different buyers by a firm for the same product at the same time.

price discrimination the practice of charging a price differential that is not justified by a difference in cost to the seller.

price-earnings ratio the ratio between the price of a share of a firm's stock and the firm's earnings per share.

price elasticity of demand the degree of responsiveness of the quantity demanded of a good, service, or resource to a change in its price.

price elasticity of resource demand the degree of responsiveness of the quantity demanded of a resource to a change in its price.

price elasticity of supply the degree of responsiveness of the quantity supplied of a good, service, or resource to a change in its price.

price fixing agreement among the firms in an industry to establish specific prices. See also *collusion.*

price leadership a practice by firms in some oligopoly industries that coordinates their pricing behavior, where one or more firms announce a price change and other firms in the industry quickly follow it.

price leadership to avoid competition a practice in an oligopolistic industry based on voluntarily following the price changes of significant firms in that industry in order to avoid price competition harmful to industry profits; it is an alternative to collusion.

price level an average of all prices prevailing in an economy expressed as an index number based on the average prices that prevailed in a selected base year.

price maker a firm with sufficient monopoly power or control to be able to affect the price it can charge (or pay) by the level of output it chooses to produce (or the level of input it chooses to buy). See also *price searcher.*

price rigidity a tendency for prices to be sticky or rigid in oligopoly industries because of the interdependence among firms and their fear of being misinterpreted by rivals.

price searcher a firm that is able to choose the price for its product, but because it lacks full information, it must search for its profit-maximizing price.

price-specie flow the process of adjustment that the gold standard offered for countries with international balance of payments problems; the flow of gold to settle international payments imbalances and the resulting change in the price levels of trading partners.

price supports (in agriculture) government-operated programs that make sure the prices farmers receive for certain crops do not fall below specified levels. See also *floor price, parity (price)*.

price taker a firm that accepts prices set by the market as given and cannot influence them by changing its own sales or purchases. Characteristic of pure competition.

primary production agriculture, forestry, and fisheries.

primitive economy an economic system, usually traditional, that uses technologies significantly less advanced than those used elsewhere.

private benefit benefits that accrue to individuals and firms as distinguished from benefits that accrue to the society as a whole.

private cost the value of opportunities forgone by individuals and firms directly involved in the production and consumption of a good or service. It does not include external cost.

private returns benefits that accrue to certain individuals or firms as contrasted to society as a whole.

private sector the part of an economy directed by the decisions of individuals and firms.

producer price index a measure of the level of prices paid for inputs, expressed in terms of base year prices. See also *consumer price index*.

product the output of a firm; either goods or services or both.

product cycle a principle that explains changes over time among countries in their comparative advantage in producing a given product.

product differentiation changes in basically similar products in order to create some differences among them in the eyes of consumers.

product differentiation (entry barrier) an entry barrier determined by the extent to which established firms can differentiate their relatively well-known products from those of a newcomer.

product extension conglomerate merger the acquisition of a firm in an allied industry—one whose product is functionally associated with that of the acquirer.

production the transformation of inputs into outputs by firms.

production controls, agricultural legislation requiring farmers to limit their output of a supported crop.

production function a relationship that shows the maximum output that can be obtained from given amounts of inputs as of a specified point in time.

production possibilities boundary a curve that represents all of the alternative maximum combinations that can be produced during a given period of time with a given stock of resources and technological knowledge.

production possibility a concept describing the maximum quantity of goods and services that can be produced with a given stock of resources and technological knowledge during any given period of time.

productive credit theory a theory that states that if more credit to a firm is matched by a corresponding increase in the firm's output, the loan is not inflationary.

productivity the amount of output produced by a unit of resource input during a given span of time.

profit the return to the entrepreneurial resource or factor of production; also the difference between a firm's total revenue and total cost.

profit and loss statement See *income statement*.

profit maximization an assumption made in the theory of the firm that a firm will seek to produce a level of output and charge a price so that its total revenue exceeds its total cost by the greatest possible amount. A consequence is that its marginal cost equals its marginal revenue.

progressive tax a tax under which the percentage of income paid in tax increases as the amount of the taxpayer's total income increases.

proletariat a term used by Karl Marx to refer to the working class, which would come to power after the socialist revolution.

propensity to consume the inclination of households to spend a predicted portion of disposable personal income on goods and services for current consumption.

propensity to save the inclination of households to desist from spending a predicted portion of disposable personal income for consumption goods and services.

property rights the rights enjoyed by a property owner by reason of his or her ownership.

property tax a tax imposed on the estimated value of specified types of property, typically land and buildings.

proportional tax a tax under which the percentage of income paid in tax is the same without regard to the size of the taxpayer's income.

proprietorship a business firm owned and managed by one person.

prosperity a condition of an economy existing when living standards are relatively high and unemployment is relatively low; also, the expansion phase of a business cycle.

protection a system of tariffs and other measures aimed at defending a country's industries from foreign competition in its home market.

protectionism a policy position favoring aid to import-competing industries by tariffs, subsidies, quotas, other restrictions on imports, and sometimes also aid to export industries by direct or hidden subsidies.

proven reserves estimates of the amount of a natural resource that remains available for economically feasible extraction.

psychic returns nonmonetary returns such as prestige, excitement, and other personal feelings of satisfaction and enjoyment; may be earned from investing in human capital.

public choice an area of study that combines economics and political science ideas to gain a better understanding of how governments actually operate.

public-choice economists economists who specialize in the study of the decision making procedures and outcomes of governments.

public debt See *national debt.*

public enterprise a government commercial undertaking such as the U.S. Postal Service or Amtrak on the federal level; state lotteries or parks; local sewage disposal or libraries; often an actual monopoly.

public goods and services goods and services supplied either wholly or in large part through government because externality, nonrivalry, and nonexcludability features are so important that provision through market processes is seriously deficient.

public sector the part of an economy directed by government.

public sector planning planning that covers only the public sector of the economy.

public utility a private firm that is granted a monopoly position by the government and is regulated by the government.

pump-priming temporary injections of government money in an effort to build up business confidence and to raise planned investment; an economic policy model of the mid-1930s.

purchasing power of the dollar the reciprocal of the index number for the consumer price index, or the goods and services that a dollar will buy in a given year compared to what it would buy in the base year.

purchasing power parity a condition prevailing when the quantity of internationally traded goods and services that can be bought with a unit of a nation's money is the same in international trade as at home.

pure competition a type of market structure with a large number of sellers, a standardized product, no artificial restrictions on price or quantity, and easy entry and exit into and out of the industry, so that each firm is a price taker.

pure monopoly a market structure in which there is only a single seller, no acceptable substitutes are available for the product offered for sale, and no entry into the market is possible.

pure science an objective, factual, and systematic search for knowledge utilizing assumptions, principles and rules, but not engaging in practical applications.

pyramiding of reserves the arrangement in effect before the Federal Reserve System was established in 1913, under which reserves of country banks were held as deposits in city banks, which held their reserves in still larger banks in major cities (reserve cities).

Q

quadrant one of four sections of a graph formed by the intersection of horizontal and vertical axes. Each axis usually represents a variable with both positive and negative values.

quality bias the effect on a price index number of the failure to recognize that the quality of goods and services changes over time.

quantile ratio the percentage or fraction determined by dividing the percentage of total income received by the highest k percentage of the population with the percentage of the total received by the lowest k percentage. (k is a fraction. Commonly chosen values are .05, .10, and .20.)

quantitative economic forecasting the practice of using observed and/or estimated values for the variables in a macroeconomic model in order to predict future values for these variables.

quantity demanded the amount demanded per time period of a good, service, or resource at a certain price. See also *demand, individual consumer demand, market demand.*

quantity supplied the amount supplied per time period of a good, service, or resource at a certain price. See also *individual firm supply, market supply, supply.*

quantity theory of money the proposition, based on the equation of exchange, that changes in the quantity of money provide a useful way of predicting changes in nominal GNP; a theory that states that the velocity of money circulation is constant in the long run, so changes in the quantity of money provide a good way to predict changes in GNP.

quota a limitation on the quantity of imports.

R

radical extreme, sweeping, or revolutionary; a person whose beliefs are radical.

rate of economic growth the percentage change per year in an economy's potential GNP.

rate of return   the proceeds or receipts from an undertaking expressed as a percentage of the amount put into it.

rate-of-return parity   when the rate of return on a unit of money invested at home is the same as it would be if that money were converted into the money of a foreign country and invested there.

rate of surplus value   See *exploitation rate*.

rate structure (for a public utility)   pattern of prices charged according to such criteria as customer classification, quantity purchased, and time of delivery.

rational consumer   an assumption that consumers seek to maximize their satisfaction—to get the most out of their income by selecting the mix of goods and services that promises to offer the greatest amount of personal satisfaction.

rational entrepreneur (business firm decision maker)   a person who seeks to maximize profit and minimize loss over a certain period.

rational expectations   the theory that, after sufficient experience with inflationary consequences of increases in aggregate demand, people will adjust their price-level expectations quickly when expansionary monetary or fiscal actions are taken, so that such actions have little effect on real output in the economy.

rationality   See *economic rationality*.

rationing   any method of restricting the demand for a good or a service. Government may formally invoke a system of rationing in order to deal "fairly" with what would otherwise be an excess demand situation.

Reaganomics   the package of economic policy positions arising from the groups backing the Reagan administrations: anti-inflationists, anti-high-taxers, anti-high-interest-rate advocates, and those who favored more defense spending.

real balances   wealth holdings adjusted for changes in the price level.

real balances theory   the proposition that changes in the price level affect aggregate demand through changes in the real value of assets; called the Pigou effect.

real business cycle theories   explanations of economic fluctuations based on patterns of changing labor productivity or labor supply.

real income   the quantity of goods and services that can be purchased with the money received by a household; receipts adjusted for changes in the price level.

real interest rates   interest rates that reflect actual purchasing-power values.

realization crisis   in Marxian terms, the stage of capitalism where the profit rate remains high but less than full-employment output can be bought by workers and other consumers.

real values   values stated or measured in terms of goods and services; numerical values that have been adjusted for price-level changes by applying an index number or deflator.

real wage rates   wage rates adjusted for changes in the price level.

recession   the contraction phase of a business cycle; a period of a relatively low volume of production and income in an economy.

recognition lag   the time required for economists to recognize that there is trouble in the economy, to diagnose the trouble, and to prescribe remedies.

recovery   the early part of the expansion phase of a business cycle; the phase immediately following the lower turning point of a business cycle.

reflation   a rise in the price level toward a level that prevailed earlier.

regressive tax   a tax under which the percentage of income paid in tax decreases as the amount of a taxpayer's total income increases.

regulated industries (or regulated firms)   industries or firms whose prices (and sometimes other operations) are subject to monopoly regulation.

regulation   See *monopoly regulation, social regulation*.

regulatory commissions   federal and state agencies that regulate firms that have been given public utility status.

regulatory lag   the length of time that it takes for a regulated firm's changes in costs to be reflected in rate changes.

relative price   the market value of a good or service compared to the market value of certain other goods and services.

relatively pure conglomerate merger   the acquisition by a firm of a firm whose activities have only remote relationships to those of the acquirer.

renewable resources   inputs to production that, under normal conditions, can be replaced through natural processes.

rent   the return or payment for the use of natural resources in production.

replacement cost   the value of a firm's capital estimated by what it would cost to replace it.

required reserves   See *reserve requirement*.

reservation price   a price below which a resource will be held for future use or sale by its owner.

reservation wage rate   the wage rate that a worker feels he or she must be offered before signing a contract of employment.

reserve ratio   the total official (government-approved) reserves held by a depository institution divided by the amount of checking account liabilities of that institution.

reserve requirement   the amount of official reserves that a depository institution must, by law, maintain in order to avoid legal penalities.

reserves   vault cash and deposits with the Federal Reserve Bank, which may be used by a depository institution to fulfill official reserve requirements.

resource allocation   the division of resources among alternative uses.

resource package   a combination of two or more of the factors of production or resources necessary for production.

resources   See *factors of production.*

revaluation   changing the official exchange value of a country's money.

revenue   See *total revenue.*

revenue sharing   a system under which revenues collected by a superior government are transferred to subordinate governments in a federal system.

risk   the probability that a harm or loss will be suffered.

rivalry   competition among sellers or among buyers.

Robinson-Patman Act   a 1936 amendment to the Clayton Act, which strengthened the government's control with respect to price discrimination.

roundabout production   the diversion of resources from the direct production of consumer goods to the production of capital goods, which are then used in further production.

rule of reason   a guiding principle adopted by the Supreme Court in 1911 that focused on intent and conduct rather than the presence or absence of substantial monopoly control.

rules of thumb   conventions developed as a means of coordinating decisions among firms in an oligopoly industry.

run on a bank   a situation in which many of a bank's depositors want to withdraw their deposits at the same time, and immediately.

S

sales tax   a tax imposed on the sale of a product.

satisfice   to seek satisfactory profit rather than maximum profit.

saving   setting aside current income in order to increase wealth.

saving function   the statement of a relationship between the level of disposable personal income and the volume of planned saving.

Say's Identity   a proposition that states that the sum of all the wages, salaries, rents, interest, and profits in the economy must provide enough purchasing power to allow households to pay for all the goods and services produced at whatever price level was in effect when they were produced.

scaling   the marks and numbers that indicate units of measure of the variables on the horizontal and vertical axes of a graph.

scarcity   the circumstance in which the supply of something would not be sufficient to satisfy the demand for it if it were provided "free of charge."

school of economic thought   a group of economists who employ the same or similar theories and who agree with one another much of the time about economic policy.

seasonal unemployment   joblessness that arises because some occupations require workers during only part of each year.

SDRs   See *special drawing rights.*

secondary boycott (or strike)   a boycott (or strike) by a union against an employer other than the one with which the union has a dispute.

Second World   countries with centrally planned economies.

secondary production   manufacturing, mining, construction, and transport.

self-liquidating loans   extensions of credit that are to be repaid from charges collected for goods or services financed by the credit.

seniority rule   the requirement that the worker who has been on the job the longest shall receive preferential treatment in respect to layoff, rehiring, and other conditions of employment.

services   intangible products.

share-draft account   a checkable account in a credit union that permits the payment of interest.

shares of stock   securities that represent ownership rights in a corporation.

Sherman Antitrust Act   a law passed by the U.S. Congress in 1890 prohibiting the restriction of competition, monopolization, and attempts to monopolize.

shift of a demand (supply) curve   a displacement of an entire demand (supply) curve to the right or left showing a change in demand (supply).

shoe-leather costs   costs entailed during a period of inflation by the switching of assets from one form to another.

shop steward   a worker elected to represent the union on the job.

shortage   a disequilibrium market situation that results in excess demand; the extent to which the quantity demanded exceeds the quantity supplied at some specific price.

short run   the period of time during which at least one of a firm's inputs cannot be varied; a period of time not long enough for entry into an industry or exit from an industry to take place.

short-run consumption function the relationship between disposable personal income and planned consumption expenditure during a limited time period after changes in disposable personal income.

shutdown decision the prediction in the theory of the firm that in the short run a firm will cease producing if its revenue is insufficient to at least cover its variable cost.

skill See *technological know-how.*

slope the change in the variable read on the vertical axis of a graph divided by the associated change in the variable read on the horizontal axis of that graph.

social cost the total value of opportunities forgone because of the production and consumption of a product. It includes both private cost and external cost.

Social Darwinism the belief that the survival and prosperity of individuals, families, nations, and races are determined, like those of animal species, by their biological and psychological fitness in the struggle not only against each other but also against the environment.

socialist system an economic system in which land and physical instruments of production are largely or completely owned by the state.

social overhead capital facilities such as roads, harbors, schools, and public health installations that provide public sector services needed by a society; also known as infrastructure.

social regulation rules and laws that protect the public against potentially harmful practices by business firms. Examples are environmental protection, food and drug, truth-in-packaging, and occupational health and safety rules.

social returns benefits that accrue to society as a whole as contrasted to individuals or firms.

Social Security Act (1935) legislation establishing a compulsory system of retirement and survivors' benefits financed by taxes from employers and employees. The system has since expanded to include certain disability, hospital, and medical care benefits.

special drawing rights (SDRs) or paper gold credit entries on the books of the International Monetary Fund given to particular countries, which can, in turn, uses them to meet their international obligations.

speculation taking action based on expectations of future changes in market values.

speculative demand for money a desire to hold money arising because of an expectation that the market values of nonmoney assets are going to fall in the future, or that interest rates will rise in the future.

stabilization function the function or role of government involving the direction of the aggregate economy in order to prevent serious depressions or inflations and to maintain high levels of employment and a reasonable rate of economic growth.

stable equilibrium a state of balance that tends to restore itself after disturbances.

stages of production (short-run theory of the firm) the division of a firm's input-output relationships into three categories when a firm adds successive units of a variable input to one or more fixed inputs. In Stage I average product increases. In Stage II average product decreases, but marginal product remains positive. In Stage III total product also decreases, and marginal product is negative.

stagflation a prolonged combination of inflation, substantial unemployment, and sluggish growth.

standard deduction in individual income taxation, an amount that can be subtracted from income provided that the taxpayer does not itemize personal deductions.

Standard Industrial Classification (SIC) system a classification system, used by the U.S. Bureau of the Census, that divides the outputs of firms into industry and product groupings.

standard for deferred payment a function of money used to specify amounts to be exchanged at some future date.

standardized product the product of different firms that is so much alike that customers do not prefer one seller's product over another's. Sometimes called a homogeneous product.

standard of living the well-being of people, usually expressed in terms of current income or consumption per person of real goods and services.

standards and controls rules governing such characteristics of goods as methods of production or methods of waste disposal.

static analysis the description of an equilibrium state.

statistical discrepancy in national income and product accounting, the difference between the estimate of national income and the estimate of net national product after allowing for indirect business taxes and subsidies.

stock a fixed quantity, such as the stock of money; also, a certificate denoting an ownership share in a corporation.

stockbroker an individual or firm which carries out transactions in corporate securities (stocks and bonds) on behalf of their buyers and sellers.

stock exchange an organization through which transactions in corporate stocks may be carried out.

stock phenomena the sums or quantities of economic variables as they exist at a specified time, as distinguished from flows of such quantities over a specified period of time.

store of purchasing power a function of money that enables people who have money to save some of it for use at a later time.

strike a work stoppage in which employees refuse to work until certain conditions are met.

structural deficit the total government budget deficit minus that portion arising because the economy is operating below its target level of national income and product.

structural unemployment unemployment that occurs when there is a mismatch between worker qualifications and job requirements; it often arises when changes occur in production methods and in the types of goods and services produced.

subsidy a grant or gift, often from a government, designed to give aid to and provide incentives for the recipient.

substitutes (substitute goods or services) goods or services that may be used instead of one another, such as beer and ale or pastel blue shirts and pastel green shirts.

substitution effect the effect that a change in relative prices of substitute goods or services (resulting from a change in the price of a good or service) has on the quantity that a person demands of that good or service.

supply the willingness and ability to offer for sale at certain prices. See also *individual firm supply, market supply, quantity supplied.*

supply curve graph of a supply schedule.

supply schedule a table showing different prices of a good or service and the quantity supplied of that good or service at each price.

supply shock an independent or exogenous event that shifts the aggregate-supply curve for an economy.

supply-side economics the approach to economics that is concerned with the forces that can shift the aggregate-supply curve of an economy.

support price See *floor price.*

surplus the excess supply that stems from a disequilibrium situation; in budgets, the excess of receipts over expenditures for the budget period.

surplus value a Marxian concept describing the value of labor that the employer retains to pay interest, rent, dividends, profits, and the unproductive portion of white-collar labor.

sustainable annual yield the quantity of a renewable natural resource that can be harvested each year consistent with maintaining a stable population of that resource.

syndicalism the ownership of individual capital facilities (such as workshops, factories, or industrial complexes) by their own workers, who would elect representatives to a weak government, which would act as a referee in disputes and as an economic plan coordinator.

T

Taft-Hartley Act (or Labor-Management Relations Act) a U.S. law passed in 1947 that forbade unions to interfere with the organization of employers, to refuse to bargain with employer representatives, or to enter into closed shop agreements.

target level of national income and product the level of national income and product that policy makers believe to be most desirable in terms of its effects on employment, prices, economic growth, and other goals of the economy.

target price a price for an American-grown farm product set by the U.S. Secretary of Agriculture under the Agriculture and Consumer Protection Act of 1973. Farmers who qualify under the terms of the legislation receive payments from the government if they sell their crop for less than the target price.

tariff a tax on imports.

tariff factory a plant set up by a foreign firm in order to avoid a tariff imposed by the country in which the plant is located.

tax a payment to government required by law.

tax base the amount of income or value on which tax liability is calculated.

tax brackets in individual income taxation, the layers or portions of income subject to different tax rates.

tax-change multiplier the ratio between a change in the level of equilibrium national income and product and the change in net tax collections that brought it about.

tax shifting transferring the burden of a tax to some person or group other than the one making the actual payment to government.

technical efficiency the least amount of inputs, measured in physical terms, required to produce a certain amount of output; a method of production that does not waste resources.

technological know-how the ability to combine resources in producing goods and services.

technological progress an advance in knowledge of the industrial arts and/or improved techniques of organizing production.

terms of trade the ratio of an index number of the prices of the goods and services that a country exports to an index number of the prices of the goods and services that it imports.

tertiary production trade, finance, government, education—the service industries.

theory a systematically organized body of knowledge that can be applied in a fairly wide range of circumstances and that provides a set of rules or assumptions for analyzing information and studying relationships.

Third World all countries not classified as in the First World or the Second World; characteristically, the less developed countries.

thrift institutions depository institutions such as savings and loan associations, mutual savings banks, and credit unions that accept deposits and make primarily consumer and mortgage loans.

Thrift Institutions Advisory Council a council set up in 1983 to provide a channel through which savings and loan associations, mutual savings banks, and credit unions can present their views to the Federal Reserve Board of Governors.

time deposit funds placed in a financial institution under terms that allow the institution to delay repayment for some period.

time lag the amount of time it takes for a change in an economic variable to have an effect.

total cost (*TC*) the entire cost incurred by a firm producing a certain level of output. In the short run it is the sum of total fixed costs and total variable costs; explicit and implicit costs that a firm incurs in production.

total fixed cost (*TFC*) short-run costs of a firm that do not vary with the quantity level of output that the firm produces.

total planned expenditure the sum of planned consumption expenditure, planned investment expenditure, government purchases, and exports minus imports.

total product the total quantity of output produced by a firm during a period of time.

total revenue the total income or receipts during a period of time that a business firm receives from selling what it produces.

total utility the sum of all the marginal utilities a person gains from successive units consumed of any good or service over a particular period of time.

total variable cost (*TVC*) the sum of those costs of a firm that vary with the quantity level of output that the firm produces. (In the long run, all costs are variable.)

tradeoff an exchange of one thing for another; especially, the quantity of one good or service that must be given up to gain a certain quantity of another good or service.

traditional economy an economic system in which decisions are made primarily on the basis of past practice.

transaction costs the costs associated with facilitating the workings of a market by enabling potential buyers and sellers to interact.

transactions accounts deposits in financial institutions that provide the depositor with checking-account privileges; also called *checkable accounts*.

transactions demand for money the desire to hold some wealth in the form of money because money is convenient for day-to-day buying and selling of goods and services.

transfer earnings the part of the earnings of a resource that is equal to the earnings that this resource could command in the next-best use to which it could be put.

transfer payments payments, such as Social Security benefits, unemployment compensation, or welfare, that are not compensation for any service rendered or product sold during the current accounting period; considered to be negative taxes.

transmission mechanism the means whereby changes in the money supply affect the level of national income and product. See *Keynesian transmission mechanism* and *direct transmission mechanism*.

transnational corporation See *multinational corporation*.

Treasury Bills a short-term debt instrument issued by the U.S. Treasury.

trend line of economic activity a pattern of growth taking place in the economy because of increases in the size and quality of labor, the quantity of capital, and better technology.

trigger-price mechanism a method of protection whereby an importing country unilaterally announces one or more prices, below which all sales are considered to be below cost and subject to antidumping duties.

trust a legal device through which supposedly competing firms allow a central board of trustees to vote all of their stock.

trust-buster an advocate of the market economy who fears control by big-business oligarchy and believes that the decline in competition should be reversed; a branch of the market-economy New Right.

turning point in business cycle measurement, the change from expansion to contraction or from contraction to expansion in the volume of economic activity.

tying arrangement a practice that forces a firm to buy certain products along with certain other products.

U

uncertainty the condition of not knowing the probability of the outcome of an event.

underemployment working fewer hours than desired at a given wage rate; working at a job that does not utilize all of the skill and training that the worker possesses.

underground economy income and production, both criminal and otherwise, that are not reported in official statistics, often because people want to evade regulations, union rules, or taxes.

undistributed profits tax a tax on the portion of corporation net income not distributed as dividend payments to stockholders.

unemployment in official statistics, a condition in which a person who desires and is able to work at the going wage rate is not able to find a job; in economic theory, a condition in which a person is spending more time for leisure than desired and less time for wage earning than desired at the going wage rate.

unemployment rate See *civilian unemployment rate.*

unfair labor practices practices by employers and by unions made illegal in the Wagner-Connery Act and the Taft-Hartley Act.

unfavorable balance (of trade) a negative, debit, or deficit balance in a country's international transactions in merchandise.

unilateral transfer in balance of payments accounting, a current account entry recording amounts of funds transmitted not in exchange for goods and services, such as gifts, donations, or foreign aid.

union (labor union/trade union) an organization of workers for the purpose of collective bargaining.

union shop a form of union security arrangement that allows employers to hire nonunion employees but requires that they join the union soon after employment.

unitary elasticity a condition existing where the percentage response in quantity is exactly equal to the percentage change in the price that caused it.

unitary elastic demand a condition existing when the percentage response in quantity demanded is exactly equal to the percentage change in the price that caused it.

unit of account a function of money that enables people to measure the values of different items.

unlimited liability an obligation that is not restricted or confined to a specified amount. For example, a proprietor's or a partner's responsibility for the obligations of a firm is not restricted to the amount of his or her financial investment in the firm.

unlimited life a condition in which the continued existence of a business firm is not restricted to the period of participation of any owner or manager; a characteristic of the corporate form of business organization.

unstable equilibrium a state of balance that has no tendency to restore itself if upset.

upper turning point the point in a business cycle when an expansion phase ends and a contraction phase begins; also called a *peak.*

user charge a price that government charges for services that it renders.

util a unit of anticipated satisfaction used to express an individual consumer's degree of pleasure derived from a unit of a product.

utility a measure or expression of an individual consumer's anticipated satisfaction to be derived from goods and services.

utility analysis a theory of consumer behavior based on assumptions of consumer rationality, the measurability of utility, decreasing marginal utility, increasing total utility, limited income, and knowledge of prices.

V

validation See *accommodation.*

value added the increase in the value of a good in each stage of its production; the difference between the value of materials that a firm buys and the value of what it sells.

value in exchange the transaction price of a good, service, or resource; the value of a good or service as determined by what people are willing to pay for the last unit that they buy.

value in use the value of a good or service as determined by the total satisfaction received from it; the total utility that is gained from a product.

value of output a method of measuring national income and product that makes no attempt to avoid double counting.

variable a quantity that can assume any of a set of values.

variable capital a Marxian concept of direct labor hours—not hours actually spent at work, but hours used to produce goods consumed by workers.

variable cost See *total variable cost.*

velocity (of circulation of money) the number of times a year, on the average, that a dollar of the money supply is spent in the purchase of currently produced goods and services. Velocity is usually measured by dividing the GNP by some measure of the money supply, such as M1.

vertical merger the acquisition by a firm of a firm that operates on a different level of a particular business activity, such as one that is a supplier or a customer of the acquirer.

very long run the period of time long enough so that a new technology can be introduced and the production function itself can be altered.

voluntary export restriction reduction of exports to a certain level or in accordance with a certain formula, undertaken by an exporting country.

W

wage and price controls restrictions imposed by law on wage rates and prices of goods and services.

wage and price guidelines suggested and voluntary constraints on changes in wage rates and prices of goods and services.

wage-cost lag theory the proposition that changes in costs of production and wage rates lag behind changes in the general price level.

wage differentials differences in wage rates usually due to different qualifications of workers, desirability of the job, and the institutions of the labor market.

wage rate the payment to labor per unit of time worked.

wage-rate and cost "catch up" the process through which wage rates and other input prices cease to lag behind the prices of final goods.

wages the return or payment to labor in production.

Wagner-Connery Act (or National Labor Relations Act) a pro-union act passed by the U.S. Congress in 1935. It proposed to guarantee rights of collective bargaining, outlawed various employer labor practices as unfair, and set up a National Labor Relations Board as its enforcement mechanism.

wealth an accumulation of assets.

weighting bias the failure of the CPI to recognize that consumer buying patterns tend to change when the price level changes.

welfare the state of well-being or the quality of life; also, a term applied to government transfer payments designed to alleviate poverty.

welfare loss triangle a graphic representation of the amount of economic well-being that is lost to consumers because a product is produced and sold by a monopolist instead of by purely competitive firms.

welfare state an economic regime that places an especially high value on the equity of income and wealth distributions and on the provision of a floor or "safety net" below which income should not fall.

Wheeler-Lea Amendment a 1938 amendment to the Federal Trade Commission Act that outlaws unfair or deceptive acts or practices aimed at the consumer.

wildcat banking banking practices in which depositors were persuaded to entrust their savings to institutions that then made loans and issued bank notes until their obligations far exceeded their readily available assets.

worker's self-management a system of production, most notably in Yugoslavia, in which workers' collectives operate and manage firms with capital leased from the state.

work standards criteria determining the amount of work to be performed, such as the size of a work crew for a job or the number of units to be handled on an assembly line during a certain period of time.

X

X-inefficiency waste of inputs due to a lack of motivation by management, which results in high-cost internal practices; often displayed by monopolists.

Y

yellow-dog contract an agreement that a worker will not join a union, which was often made a condition of employment before the Norris-LaGuardia Act of 1932.

Index

Macroeconomics (*cont.*)
  as scientific, 392–393
  unemployment and, 154–164
  see also Circular flow; International macroeconomics; National debt
Madigan, Kathleen, 165, 211
Magic wand planning, 505
Main, Jeremy, 137
Malthus, Thomas Robert, 485
Manager(s), goals of, 91
Manipulation, of market, 94–97
Mao Zedong, 13, 485, 491, 508, 510, 516, 521, 543
  planned economy under, 510
Marcos, Ferdinand and Imelda, 495
Maremont, Mark, 364
Marginal, 51
Marginal amount, 51–52
Marginal analysis, 51–53
  criticism of, 53
  in functional relationships, 51
  marginal, average, and total amount and, 51–52
  marginal cost and benefit and, 52–53
Marginal benefit, marginal cost and, 52–53
Marginal cost (MC), marginal benefit and, 52–53
Marginal opportunity costs, increasing, 72–73
Marginal propensity to consume (MPC), 196–197, 196 (table), 202 (table)
  multiplier calculation and, 228–229
Marginal propensity to save (MPS), 197, 196 (table), 202 (table)
  multiplier calculation and, 228–229
Margin requirements, 282
Market(s), 91
  black, 363
  free, 94
  loanable funds, 303, 645
  manipulation of, 94–97
  see also specific markets
"Market basket," of consumer goods, 143
Market-capitalist economy, 9
Market clearing, 375–376, 382–383
Market demand, 91–97
  equilibrium price and quantity and, 92–94
  market manipulation and, 94–97
Market economy, 9–10
Market failure, 33. *See also* Externalities
Marketing agreements, 446
Market manipulation, 94–97
Market-opening strategy, 446–447
Market socialism, 518–520
  criticisms of, 519–520
Market supply, 91–97
  equilibrium price and quantity and, 92–94
  market manipulation and, 94–97
  see also Supply; Supply curve
Marshall, Alfred, 197n
Marshallian cross, 197n

Marshall Plan, 422, 454n
Martin, William McChesney, Jr., 317, 318
Martz, Larry, 321
Marx, Karl, 10, 67, 489n, 515, 530, 531, 534, 535, 538
  on capital, 67
  on cycles, 177
  on economic development, 485–486
Marxian economics, on capitalism, 530–534
Marxian socialism, post-Keynesians and, 383
"Marxist humanism," 538
MasterCard, 211
Materials balancing, 506
Mature creditor, 419
Mature debtor, 419
MC, *see* Marginal cost
MDCs, *see* More developed countries
Measure of economic welfare (MEW), 136
Mechanism basis, of economic systems, 9–11
Medicaid, rationing health care and, 77
Medium of exchange function of money, 248–249
Meidner, Rudolf, 514
Meidner plan, 514
Mental health, as criterion for evaluating economic systems, 13
Menu costs, of inflation, 152
Mercantilism
  balance of payments and, 420–421
  net exports and real GNP and, 429
  underdevelopment and, 487
Merrick, Thomas W., 37
Merrill Lynch, 268
MEW, *see* Measure of economic welfare
Mexico, 491
  economic growth, 488
  loans to, 495, 496
Michael, Robert T., 146n
"Microbanks," 137
Microeconomic unemployment, 3
Microeconomics, 3, 104
Microfoundations, 374
Mill, John Stuart, on economic growth, 474
Miller, Frederic A., 268
Minarik, Joseph J., 402
Minorities
  income distribution among, 12
  unemployment rates of, 162–163
Mises, Ludwig von, 520
Mishan, Ezra, on economic growth, 474
Mistaken causation, 55–56
Miyazawa, Kiichi, 497
Miyazawa plan, 497
Model, 42
  econometric, 120
  forecasting and, 395
"Mommy track," 37

Monetarism, 300
  of Friedman, 300
  see also Quantity-of-money theory
Monetary base, 285
Monetary Control Act of 1980. *See* Depository Institutions Deregulation and Monetary Control Act of 1980
Monetary instruments, 273, 278–282
  discount rate as, 281
  effects on real national income and product, 311–312
  expansionary, 294
  feedback to demand-for-money curve and, 312
  historical record of use of, 291–295
  with inflation, 318–320
  without inflation, 309–314
  inflationary expectations and, 318–320
  interest rate changes and, 318–320
  margin requirements as, 282
  monetary base and, 285
  money multiplier and, 285–286
  moral suasion and, 282
  open market operations as, 279–281
  reserve requirements as, 278–279
  strength of, 312–314
  transmission mechanisms and, 310–312
  see also Federal Reserve System
Monetary policy, 282–286
  accommodation as, 283–284, 315–317, 318
  aggregate demand and, 119
  expansionary, 427
  Federal Reserve System and, 282–287
  foreign exchange rates and, 427
  goals, 282–283
  income levels and interest rates and, 428–429
  inflationary expectations and, 318–321
  judgment-based, 317–318
  neo-Keynesian economics and, 380–381
  operating targets for, 283–286
  quantity-of-money theory and, 300–301
  rational-expectations theory and, 371
  short-run, 314–318
  unemployment and inflation and, 427–429
  see also Depository institutions; Money
Monetary-policy-target variable, 283
"Monetized" debt, 252. *See also* Glass-Steagall Act
Money, 248–254
  checkable account balances as, 252
  coins as, 250–251
  currency as, 251–252
  defined, 250–252
  demand for, 305–308, 312–313
  M1 measure of, 252–253, 285–286
  M2, M3, and L measures of, 253–254, 285–286
  medium of exchange function of, 248–249

Selected Data for 120 Countries (in ascending order of 1987 per capita GNP)

| | Population (millions) | | | Crude birth rate per thousand population 1987 | Life expectancy at birth (years) 1987 | Urban population as percentage of total population 1987 | GNP per capita[a] | | |
	1987	2000[a]	2025[a]				Dollars 1987	Average annual growth rate (percent) 1965–87	Average annual rate of inflation[a] (percent) 1980–87
Low-income economies	**2,824 t**	**3,625 t**	**5,161 t**	**31 w**	**61 w**	**30 w**	**290 w**	**3.1 w**	**8.6 w**
Ethiopia	44	66	122	48	47	12	130	0.1	2.6
Bhutan	1	2	3	39	48	5	150	..	..
Chad	5	7	13	44	46	30	150	−2.0	5.3
Zaire	33	49	97	45	52	38	150	−2.4	53.5
Bangladesh	106	144	217	41	51	13	160	0.3	11.1
Malawi	8	12	29	53	46	13	160	1.4	12.4
Nepal	18	24	37	41	51	9	160	0.5	8.8
Lao PDR	4	5	8	42	48	17	170	..	46.5
Mozambique	15	22	42	45	48	23	170	..	26.9
Tanzania	24	37	75	50	53	29	180	−0.4	24.9
Burkina Faso	8	12	23	47	47	8	190	1.6	4.4
Madagascar	11	16	28	46	54	23	210	−1.8	17.4
Mali	8	11	24	51	47	19	210	..	4.2
Burundi	5	7	14	49	49	7	250	1.6	7.5
Zambia	7	11	23	50	53	53	250	−2.1	28.7
Niger	7	10	22	51	45	18	260	−2.2	4.1
Uganda	16	24	46	50	48	10	260	−2.7	95.2
China	1,069	1,269	1,528	21	69	38	290	5.2	4.2
Somalia	6	8	16	49	47	36	290	0.3	37.8
Togo	3	5	9	49	53	24	290	0.0	6.6
India	798	1,010	1,365	32	58	27	300	1.8	7.7
Rwanda	6	10	23	52	49	7	300	1.6	4.5
Sierra Leone	4	5	10	48	41	26	300	0.2	50.0
Benin	4	6	11	48	50	39	310	0.2	8.2
Central African Rep.	3	4	6	43	50	45	330	−0.3	7.9
Kenya	22	37	83	52	58	22	330	1.9	10.3
Sudan	23	33	56	44	50	21	330	−0.5	31.7
Pakistan	102	156	286	47	55	31	350	2.5	7.3
Haiti	6	8	11	34	55	29	360	0.5	7.9
Lesotho	2	2	4	41	56	19	370	4.7	12.3
Nigeria	107	157	286	47	51	33	370	1.1	10.1
Ghana	14	20	35	46	54	32	390	−1.6	48.3
Sri Lanka	16	19	23	23	70	21	400	3.0	11.8
Yemen, PDR	2	3	6	48	51	42	420	..	5.0
Mauritania	2	3	5	48	46	38	440	−0.4	9.8
Indonesia	171	214	279	29	60	27	450	4.5	8.5
Liberia	2	3	6	45	54	42	450	−1.6	1.5
Afghanistan	..	..	..	..	..	..	..	..	..
Burma	39	52	72	32	60	24	..	..	..
Guinea	6	9	16	47	42	24	..	..	..
Kampuchea, Dem.	..	..	..	..	..	..	..	..	..
Viet Nam	65	88	127	34	66	21	..	..	..
Middle-income economies	**1,038 t**	**1,329 t**	**1,862 t**	**30 w**	**65 w**	**57 w**	**1,810 w**	**2.5 w**	**62.3 w**
Senegal	7	10	20	46	48	37	520	−0.6	9.1
Bolivia	7	10	16	43	53	50	580	−0.5	601.8
Zimbabwe	9	13	22	44	58	26	580	0.9	12.4
Philippines	58	74	101	30	63	41	590	1.7	16.7
Yemen Arab Rep.	8	13	23	48	51	23	590	..	11.4
Morocco	23	32	47	35	61	47	610	1.8	7.3
Egypt, Arab Rep.	50	67	99	36	61	48	680	3.5	9.2
Papua New Guinea	4	5	8	39	54	15	700	0.8	4.4
Dominican Rep.	7	9	11	31	66	58	730	2.3	16.3
Côte d'Ivoire	11	18	36	51	52	44	740	1.0	4.4
Honduras	5	7	11	40	64	42	810	0.7	4.9
Nicaragua	4	5	9	41	63	58	830	−2.5	86.6
Thailand	54	65	82	25	64	21	850	3.9	2.8
El Salvador	5	6	10	36	62	44	860	−0.4	16.5
Congo, People's Rep.	2	3	7	47	59	41	870	4.2	1.8
Jamaica	2	3	3	26	74	51	940	−1.5	19.4
Guatemala	8	12	20	41	62	33	950	1.2	12.7
Cameroon	11	16	33	45	56	46	970	3.8	8.1
Paraguay	4	6	9	35	67	46	990	3.4	21.0
Ecuador	10	13	19	33	65	55	1,040	3.2	29.5
Botswana	1	2	2	35	59	21	1,050	8.9	8.4
Tunisia	8	10	14	30	65	54	1,180	3.6	8.2
Turkey	53	67	90	30	64	47	1,210	2.6	37.4
Colombia	29	36	48	26	66	69	1,240	2.7	23.7
Chile	13	15	19	24	72	85	1,310	0.2	20.6